STREET ON TORTS

STREET ON TORTS

Fifteenth Edition

CHRISTIAN WITTING

*Professor of Private Law, Queen Mary University of London
Co-Chair of the University of London LLM Exam Board
Barrister and Solicitor, High Court of Australia and
Supreme Court of Victoria*

OXFORD
UNIVERSITY PRESS

OXFORD
UNIVERSITY PRESS

Great Clarendon Street, Oxford, OX2 6DP,
United Kingdom

Oxford University Press is a department of the University of Oxford.
It furthers the University's objective of excellence in research, scholarship,
and education by publishing worldwide. Oxford is a registered trade mark of
Oxford University Press in the UK and in certain other countries

© Oxford University Press 2018

The moral rights of the author have been asserted

Twelfth edition 2007
Thirteenth edition 2012
Fourteenth edition 2015

Impression: 2

Public sector information reproduced under Open Government Licence v3.0
(http://www.nationalarchives.gov.uk/doc/open-government-licence/open-government-licence.htm)

Published in the United States of America by Oxford University Press
198 Madison Avenue, New York, NY 10016, United States of America

British Library Cataloguing in Publication Data
Data available

Library of Congress Control Number: 2017964395

ISBN 978–0–19–881116–9

Printed in Great Britain by
Bell & Bain Ltd., Glasgow

PREFACE

Textbooks have a tendency to grow like a coral reefs. They are added to here and there over successive editions and there is always the danger that they will lose their shape and their focus. Over the three editions of my authorship or co-authorship of *Street on Torts*, I have endeavoured continually to shape and re-shape this book in order to provide a proper format for exposition of the law and to ensure a focussed discussion.

The re-shaping of this edition has been more extensive than originally envisaged. This is due to two things. The first is the careful market research that has been conducted by Oxford University Press into who uses this book and what their needs are. The second is the decision to re-orient the book more closely to the needs of students and their teachers. We hope that the result is a more user-friendly and helpful book.

I owe a particular debt of gratitude to Natasha Ellis-Knight at Oxford University Press, who oversaw the market research and helped plan the new edition, and to those teachers who took part in the exercise.

I have attempted to state the law as it stood and was available to me on 15 August 2017, though it was possible to add some material that post-dates this.

CW
London
19 November 2017

NEW TO THIS EDITION

The fifteenth edition of *Street on Torts* has been revised to reflect all important developments in the law and academic literature since publication of the fourteenth edition, including:

- Coverage of the Consumer Rights Act 2015
- Coverage of key cases, including: *Hughes-Holland v BPE Solicitors* (on scope of duty of care); *Dunnage v Randall* (on responsibility/standard of care while under a mental impairment); *OPO v Rhodes* (on intentional infliction of harm); *Patel v Mirza* (on the illegality defence); *Campbell v Peter Gordon Joiners Ltd* (on breach of statutory duty); *Lawrence v Fen Tigers (No 2)* (on nuisance); *Emerald Supplies Ltd v British Airways plc (Nos 1 & 2)* (on conspiracy); *Lachaux v Independent Print Ltd* (on serious harm in defamation); *PJS v News Group Newspapers Ltd* (on intrusion into private life); *Willers v Joyce* (on malicious commencement of civil proceedings); *Armes v Nottinghamshire CC, Cox v Ministry of Justice, and Mohamud v Wm Morrison Supermarkets plc* (on vicarious liability); *Fish & Fish Ltd v Sea Shepherd UK* (on accessory liability); and *Knauer v Ministry of Justice* (on fatal accidents damages)
- References to a wide range of authoritative texts at the end of each chapter have been updated to ensure further reading is well directed.

In addition, the book has been re-shaped in the following ways:

- Introduction of new duty of care chapters centred on bodily injury/psychiatric illness and property damages/purely financial loss.
- Extensive restructuring and re-writing of chapters on causation, breach of statutory duty, privacy, and remedies
- Move to gender inclusivity with alternating 'his' and 'her' language in the chapters
- New conclusions to each chapter
- Problem questions for all chapters except the first.

CONTENTS

PART III INTENTIONAL INVASIONS OF INTERESTS IN THE PERSON AND PROPERTY

PART IV MISREPRESENTATION-BASED AND 'ECONOMIC' TORTS

PART V TORTS INVOLVING STRICT OR STRICTER LIABILITY

PART VI INTERESTS IN REPUTATION: DEFAMATION

TABLE OF CASES

TABLE OF LEGISLATION

References to 'W' relate to the additional chapter 'Animals' which can be found on the online resources.

Statutory Instruments

Treaties and Conventions

European Secondary Legislation

National Legislation

Australia—NSW

United States

PART I
Introduction

1

Overview of tort law

KEY ISSUES

(1) The place of tort law

Tort law is a branch of the law of obligations, which also includes contract, and the law of unjust enrichment. This branch of the law is concerned with the obligations that individuals owe each other during the course of their interactions.

(2) Definition

Tort obligations are owed by one person to another and embody norms of conduct that arise outside (or in addition to) contract and unjust enrichment. Tort enables the person to whom the obligation is owed to pursue a remedy where breach of a relevant norm results in a substantial infringement of his personal interests.

(3) Bases of liability

Tort law imposes liability for the breach of norms of conduct by reference to two main factors: the type of interest at stake, and the degree of fault present in the actor. Generally speaking, these factors are inversely related: where the interest at stake is an important one (such as bodily integrity or property), a lesser degree of infringement will suffice for liability than where the interest at stake is less important (such as with purely financial interests).

(4) Theories of tort

Theories of tort are designed to distil the nature of tort actions. The basic contrast is between theories which are concerned purely with achieving justice between the parties before the court, and those which would use tort law in order to advance wider, social interests as well.

Section 1 What is a tort?

Definition The very word 'tort' might pose a conundrum for the novice law student. Crime and contract will be terms with which he is already familiar, but what does 'tort' mean? What is tort law about? Much ink has been spilt in attempts to define this concept. Although a satisfactory definition remains somewhat elusive, the following working explanation might be offered:

> Tort is that branch of the civil law relating to obligations imposed by operation of law on all natural and artificial persons. These obligations, owed by one person to another, embody

norms (or standards) of conduct that arise outside (or in addition to) contract and unjust enrichment.[1] Tort enables the person to whom the obligation is owed to pursue a remedy on his own behalf where breach of a relevant norm of conduct results in a substantial infringement of his personal interests.

Although these matters are the subject of debate among torts scholars, pertinent aspects of this working definition (and of the practices that lie behind it) are as follows. First, *persons* commence tort actions because they have suffered an infringement of their own interests—usually resulting in a measurable loss of some kind. The claimant seeks compensation in order to ameliorate the impact of the loss—and, perhaps, for subsidiary reasons involving the vindication of his dignity and sense of rectitude, as well as the desire to deter future wrongdoing. (Indeed, we might note here that courts frequently assert the idea that tort law has the twin goals of compensating the claimant and deterring future wrongdoing.)[2] Second, *the state* facilitates tort actions for several reasons. One reason relates to the need to maintain order amongst its citizenry—to prevent persons engaging in their own vendettas with the potential that this might have for blood to be spilt.[3] Another reason relates to the state's instrumentalist desire to create appropriate standards of conduct among persons. Tort law is a non-contractual means of ensuring that persons, who might well be strangers to each other, are able to interact in the knowledge that certain minimum standards of conduct will be respected—thus solving the 'co-ordination problems' that are characteristic of communal societies.[4] A third reason is that the tort system permits the state to create and uphold these standards without having to accept complete responsibility for studying co-ordination problems in advance and being proactive in the provision of solutions[5]—the system is one of private enforcement, which is a cost-effective way of achieving the state's instrumentalist aims. This is not to deny that, in more pressing cases, the state will step in and pass legislation that directly addresses problems—which it does occasionally in tort law when it has 'become disenchanted with an outdated [or inappropriate] social norm that has become entrenched as a matter of tort doctrine'.[6]

Protected interests   We can see already that torts are designed also to protect fundamental human interests. Certainly, no claim in tort can succeed, however morally reprehensible the defendant's conduct, unless the court first recognises some form of damage suffered by the claimant that involves a violation of an interest sufficient to

---

[1] On norms, see S Smith (2011) 31 OJLS 1.

[2] See, eg, analysis in *Michael v CC of South Wales Police* [2015] AC 1732, at [127]; *Crawford Adjusters Ltd v Sagicor Insurance Ltd* [2014] AC 366, at [87].

[3] See Goldberg and Zipursky (2013) 88 Indiana LJ 569, esp. 572–3 (government has a duty to provide alternatives to self-help in disputes).

[4] P Cane, *Responsibility in Law and Morality* (2002), 184; CC Tilley (2017) 126 Yale LJ 1320, 1347, 1364, and 1376. In her instructive article, Tilley describes tort law as being a favoured means by which the state, through the courts, can mould norms of interaction so that they facilitate the construction of community.

[5] CC Tilley (2017) 126 Yale LJ 1320, 1349–50, and 1392.   [6] CC Tilley (2017) 126 Yale LJ 1320, 1356.

confer on the claimant a legal right to protection of that interest.[7] Here, 'interests' can be defined as the kinds of natural and other attributes and goods[8] that people need to lead satisfying lives, and which a civilised society ought to recognise as worthy of (some degree of) protection. Tort, therefore, serves to determine which of the many human (and related) interests are so fundamental that the law should impose obligations upon all persons that are designed primarily to protect those interests and, secondarily, to provide a remedy when those interests are wrongfully violated by others. It will be useful, therefore, to consider the various rights and interests which tort law protects. First, however, further preliminary remarks are in order about the notion of 'wrongfulness' in tort law, the history and development of tort law, the forms of action, and matters of pleading.

Wrongfulness It is not enough merely to identify the kinds of interest that tort law protects. The kinds of wrongful conduct considered sufficient to violate those interests must be identified also.[9] Often, wrongful conduct provides a crucial reason for court intervention in a dispute between private parties. The two general kinds of wrongdoing are based on deliberate or intentional action and on failures in care (or negligence).

The *deliberate* invasion of a protected interest often demonstrates a level of wrongdoing sufficient to compel judicial intervention requiring the defendant to compensate for the harm he has caused the claimant. An act is deliberate when the defendant 'meant to do' that act. This is the type of 'intention' required in trespass torts, and to be distinguished from the type of intention required in the economic torts (especially) which requires greater culpability. The law more readily imposes liability with respect to protected financial interests when this more serious type of intention characterises the defendant's conduct.[10]

Certain interests are so crucial to persons, and so vulnerable to 'accidental' harm, that *negligence* on the part of the defendant suffices to engage his liability in tort. Negligence, as a type of fault, subsists in failures by the defendant actor to reach the standard of care set by the law. In this sense, negligence subsists in the failure *to act* as the law requires rather than in mental states of inadvertence.

The law does not always impose liability in tort based on wrongfulness in the defendant's conduct. In some cases, the relationship of the claimant and the defendant, or the nature of the defendant's conduct, is such as to give rise to *strict* liability. Strict liability is liability regardless of fault. This means that the law does not inquire into whether the

---

[7] See, eg, *Rogers v Rajendro Dutt* (1860) 25 JP 3; *Bradford Corpn v Pickles* [1895] AC 587; *Pickering v Liverpool Daily Post and Echo Newspapers plc* [1991] 2 AC 370. For academic explanations, see J Goldberg and B Zipursky (2002) 88 Virg LR 1625; S Perry, 'Risk, Harm and Responsibility' in DG Owen (ed), *Philosophical Foundations of Tort Law* (1995), ch 14; A Ripstein, *Equality, Responsibility, and the Law* (1999), 75.

[8] For consideration of what these might be, see: JM Finnis, *Natural Law and Natural Rights* (2nd edn, 2011); NJ McBride, 'Tort Law and Human Flourishing' in SGA Pitel, JW Neyers, and E Chamberlain (eds), *Tort Law: Challenging Orthodoxy* (2013), ch 2.

[9] See P Cane, *The Anatomy of Tort Law* (1997); W Lucy, *Philosophy of Private Law* (2007), ch 6.

[10] See, esp. P Cane (200) 20 OJLS 533.

defendant was at fault or not. (It cannot be equated with the absence of fault.) In such instances, the law requires the defendant to bear a greater (but not absolute) responsibility for protecting the claimant's interests. Liability arises, not on the basis of wrongfulness, but simply because an unwanted outcome occurs. Strict liability has been said to assist in controlling injurious activity levels in a way that is more effective than under fault-based torts.[11]

It is important to note that the above bases of liability in tort (intention, negligence, and strict liability) are not mutually exclusive of each other. This is because they arise in different ways. Intention is a state of mind. Negligence is concerned with external acts falling short of standards of care set by law. And strict liability is neither; it is not concerned with either mental states or with whether a standard of conduct has been reached. Strict liability is concerned with whether unwanted outcomes (losses) have occurred. In this way, each of these liability bases can overlap on particular facts.[12]

Section 2 Brief history of tort law

(A) Trespass and case

The history of tort law,[13] especially as regards its earliest stages of development, is subject to a surprising level of conjecture and debate.[14] However, some broad points can be made: by the thirteenth century, the Royal Courts had asserted jurisdiction to hear certain kinds of dispute involving 'trespasses' (direct infringements of others' bodily and property interests). Jurisdiction was based upon the claim that the defendant's wrongful conduct was in 'breach of the King's Peace'.[15] Various kinds of action were recognised, including trespass torts protective of the body—what we now know as battery, assault, and false imprisonment.[16] Over the centuries, the basic level of protection offered evolved into a more comprehensive system, allowing personal actions with respect (especially) to wrongs to the person, goods, land,[17] and the conduct of legal actions.[18]

---

[11] Eg, S Shavell (1980) 9 JLS 1.   [12] Eg, P Handford (2010) 32 Syd LR 29.

[13] The best introductory work is D Ibbetson, *A Historical Introduction to the Law of Obligations* (1999).

[14] Eg, TFT Plucknett, *A Concise History of the Common Law* (5th edn, 1956), 369–70 (setting out several possible origins of trespass).

[15] D Ibbetson, *A Historical Introduction to the Law of Obligations* (1999), 39; SCF Milsom, *Historical Foundations of the Common Law* (2nd edn, 1981), 287.

[16] SCF Milsom, *Historical Foundations of the Common Law* (2nd edn, 1981), 303. In early times, when crime and tort were not distinguishable, 'breach of the King's Peace' primarily covered 'deeds of violence done to persons': F Pollock and FW Maitland, *The History of English Law* (2nd edn, 1968), 452. A 'Christian reluctance to shed blood' meant that the law moved from bodily punishment to payments of fines: ibid, 460. Strictly, the Royal Courts had power only to *imprison*, but this was avoided by *bargaining* as to the appropriate fine to be paid: ibid, 517—the fine being the predecessor of 'damages' awards. The point about damages, properly so-called, was that they were not prescribed but assessed 'having regard to the facts of the particular case': ibid, 523.

[17] D Ibbetson, *A Historical Introduction to the Law of Obligations* (1999), 15 and 64; SCF Milsom, *Historical Foundations of the Common Law* (2nd edn, 1981), 283 and 303.

[18] F Pollock and FW Maitland, *The History of English Law* (2nd edn, 1968), 519.

Actions were commenced by way of writ.[19] The writs were formulaic documents, but over the course of the late fourteenth century the requirement that actions be characterised by use of 'force and arms' in breach of the King's Peace became a mere incantation which eventually was abandoned.[20] By this stage, many actions that had been restricted to the local courts migrated to the Royal Courts, which became the most important mechanism for the resolution of disputes between persons.[21] The level of protection that the courts offered for fundamental personal interests was expanded, especially from the fifteenth century, through the development of the 'action on the case'. This was an exceptional kind of action (special action for trespass on the case) which permitted a claimant to provide the reasons in justice why he should be able to bring an action despite *not* satisfying one or more of the requirements of the subsisting trespass writs.[22] It was through the action on the case that the courts developed many torts permitting recovery for indirectly caused harms[23]—actions such as nuisance, conversion, and defamation were established by the early sixteenth century,[24] and the development of negligence was on the horizon.[25] The first English textbook on the subject was Addison's *Wrongs and their Remedies, being the Law of Torts* published in 1860.[26]

(B) Forms of action

Abolition of forms Until the passage of the Common Law Procedure Act 1852 and the Judicature Act 1875, a claimant could sue in tort only if he brought his cause of action within a recognised form of action—that is, one for which a suitable writ was available.[27] Although the forms of action have been abolished, many old cases cannot be understood without some knowledge of what they were. Moreover, classifications of torts derive from the various writs grounding suit, so that rules worked out under them necessarily have been the starting point for any growth in tort law which has taken place since. Many seemingly arbitrary divisions between one tort and another are explained today by reference only to the forms of action. As observed already, the writ of trespass lay only for direct infringements of interest, while the 'action on the case' developed

---

[19] D Ibbetson, *A Historical Introduction to the Law of Obligations* (1999), 14, 40, and 49–50. See also section 2(B).

[20] D Ibbetson, *A Historical Introduction to the Law of Obligations* (1999), 41 and 52–4; SCF Milsom, *Historical Foundations of the Common Law* (2nd edn, 1981), 289–91.

[21] SCF Milsom, *Historical Foundations of the Common Law* (2nd edn, 1981), 300ff.

[22] D Ibbetson, *A Historical Introduction to the Law of Obligations* (1999), 55–61; SCF Milsom, *Historical Foundations of the Common Law* (2nd edn, 1981), 304.

[23] See *Reynolds v Clarke* (1725) 1 Str 634, at 636; *Day v Edwards* (1794) 5 TR 648.

[24] D Ibbetson, *A Historical Introduction to the Law of Obligations* (1999), ch 6.

[25] D Ibbetson, *A Historical Introduction to the Law of Obligations* (1999), 164ff.

[26] SCF Milsom, *Historical Foundations of the Common Law* (2nd edn, 1981), 308. It might be noted also that, although tort law has a long pedigree, it was not a very large feature of life until the advent of mechanisation, large businesses, and insurance: TFT Plucknett, *A Concise History of the Common Law* (5th edn, 1956), 459–60.

[27] For a list of writs (from 'Aiel, Besaiel, Coinage' to Wardships), see F Pollock and FW Maitland, *The History of English Law* (2nd edn, 1968), 565–7. See also FW Maitland, *The Forms of Action at Common Law* (1909); TFT Plucknett, *A Concise History of the Common Law* (1956), 360ff; D Ibbetson, *A Historical Introduction to the Law of Obligations* (1999), ch 3; J Gordley, *Foundations of Private Law: Property, Tort, Contract and Unjust Enrichment* (2006), ch 9.

separately for indirect injuries. And it will be seen in due course that, even now, trespass is not committed where the interference is indirect.[28]

Pleading in tort In theory, a claimant today does *not* have to plead the tort of negligence, trespass or whatever; he needs simply to set out the relevant facts said to demand redress.[29] A judge could find for the claimant merely by holding that, on the facts proved, there was a tort. But, given the complexity of modern tort law, pleading the commission of a specific tort or torts is important for a number of practical reasons: so that the defendant knows the case to be made against him; so that evidence related to the particular tort(s) can be gathered; so that the costs of bringing legal action can be kept down; and so that the court can be 'guided' to the result desired (the making of a particular award). The utility of a textbook such as the one that you are now reading lies in its explanation of the 'elements' that must be proved in order to succeed in each kind of tort action. With regard to any particular decided case, the student of tort law will be concerned to know not only that the claimant has succeeded on certain facts (and obtained the desired award or some variation thereof), but also which tort has been committed. In short, it is important to know both the elements of each tort and the general principles of tortious liability.[30]

Section 3 Protected rights and interests

(A) Introduction

We return now to the issue of what rights and interests tort law protects. Here we observe that the terminology of 'rights' and 'interests' has become contentious in modern tort scholarship (but less so in the courts). A breed of torts scholar has emerged who believes that tort law has as its main goal the protection of 'rights' that the claimant enjoyed prior to the injurious interaction between the parties, and which resulted in the bringing of a tort action.[31] In the view of the present author, such theories of tort law tend to be overly rigid and do not reflect what happens in tort cases.[32] They fail to acknowledge that courts do not explicitly concern themselves with identification of pre-existing rights (unless this is necessary for title to sue, as to which see, eg, chapters 10 and 17, below)

---

[28] See chs 10–12.   [29] *Letang v Cooper* [1965] 1 QB 232, at 242–3.

[30] See P Cane, 'General and Special Tort Law: Uses and Abuses of Theory' in J Neyers et al (eds), *Emerging Issues in Tort Law* (2007), ch 1.

[31] See, eg, A Beever, *Rediscovering the Law of Negligence* (2007); R Stevens, *Torts and Rights* (2007).

[32] For criticism, see A Robertson and HW Tang (eds), *The Goals of Private Law* (2009), chs 8 and 10. Descheemaeker explains eloquently reasons for preferring the term 'interests' over that of 'rights': '[T]he use of the term "right" in respect of [matters] like reputation, physical integrity or the enjoyment of one's land is misleading. It is for instance not true that we have a "right to reputation" if by this is meant that we have an entitlement, good against the world, not to have our reputation violated by someone else's conduct. What we do have [which is not the same thing] is a right that it should not be violated in a wrongful manner. Our reputation is protected [in the same way that other interests are] against a range of infringements (wherever the law provides a remedy) but not against others': (2009) 29 OJLS 603, 605 fn 2.

and fail to explain such things as: how supposed pre-existing rights are established; how clashes of rights ought to be resolved; why, in many cases, tort law permits redress only when the defendant was *at fault*; and so on. This last point reflects the fact that tort law is concerned not merely with the position of the claimant, but with the position of the defendant also—who should not have to provide redress unless this can be justified.[33] Rights theories downplay the importance of judicial norm-making, and fail to give due regard to the sophisticated nature of the adjudicatory process. In this book, this kind of rights dogma is avoided. Instead, we distinguish between 'rights' and 'interests' on a more empirical basis: 'rights' are those interests which are strongly protected by courts, while 'interests' are those other attributes and goods for which persons frequently seek legal protection.

(B) Human rights

Tort law and rights Tort law has always protected certain 'human rights', such as the right to bodily integrity. The enactment of the Human Rights Act 1998 was intended to enhance this protection, especially as regards governmental activities affecting individuals by formalising recognition of rights and systemising remedies for their breach. To understand the ways in which the Act is significant *for tort law*, it is necessary to say a little about its workings.

Convention rights The Human Rights Act does not 'incorporate' the European Convention on Human Rights into English law. Rather, it provides that, wherever possible, legislation should be interpreted in a way that is compatible with 'Convention rights'[34] and that it is unlawful for any public authority (including a court of law,[35] but not the legislature[36]) to act in a way that is incompatible with a 'Convention right'.[37] 'Convention rights' are the fundamental rights and freedoms set out in Articles 2 to 12 and Article 14 of the Convention, as well as Articles 1 to 3 of the First Protocol (concerning rights to property, education, and free elections) and Articles 1 and 2 of the Sixth Protocol (abolishing the death penalty).[38] The Human Rights Act 1998, section 11, makes it clear that 'Convention rights' exist in addition to, not in substitution for, rights and freedoms already endorsed at common law.

Compatibility At first glance, it might seem odd that no express provision of the Act appears to require that judges *develop the common law* in a manner consistent with 'Convention rights'. What is required is that English courts 'take into account any… judgment, decision, declaration or advisory opinion of the European Court of Human

---

[33] See P Cane, *Responsibility in Law and Morality* (2002), 97–100.

[34] Human Rights Act 1998, s 3. For an introductory account of the Act, see K Ewing (1999) 62 MLR 79.

[35] Human Rights Act 1998, sub-s 6(3)(a).   [36] Human Rights Act 1998, sub-s 6(3)(b).

[37] Human Rights Act 1998, sub-s 6(1). For these purposes, 'acts' include 'failures to act'—eg, failures to fulfil positive obligations under the Convention. See, eg, *Z v UK* (2002) 34 EHRR 97, where local authorities failed to take all reasonable steps to avoid a real and imminent risk of ill-treatment of children of whom they had actual or imputed knowledge.   [38] Human Rights Act 1998, s 1.

Rights...'.[39] Two factors explain this approach. First, in recent decades English courts have sought to ensure, wherever possible, that the common law *is* consistent with such rights.[40] Second, and more importantly, section 6 of the Act makes it unlawful for any public authority, including a court, to act in a way that is incompatible with 'Convention rights'. That being so, a judge adjudicating on a claim in tort might believe himself compelled compelled to develop the common law so as to be compatible with 'Convention rights'.[41]

Enforceability The Human Rights Act makes 'Convention rights' directly enforceable against public authorities, thus permitting an individual who considers his rights to have been violated to sue for damages.[42] However, recourse to such damages under the Act might not be the only option available. This is because the self-same rights conferred by the Convention *might* be protected by tort law already. For example, Article 5 provides for a right to liberty and security, and protects citizens against arbitrary detention.[43] But the ancient tort of false imprisonment does likewise. Equally, a person alleging unlawful arrest by the police will not need to claim a breach of Article 5. This is because he can sue in false imprisonment and, indeed, might prefer to do so.[44] Even so, in determining whether that arrest was lawful, the court will be mindful of the provisions of Article 5 and of the jurisprudence of the European Court of Human Rights.[45]

Developing areas of tort But what if a 'Convention right' is not so well established in domestic law? Privacy is such a case.[46] The claimant might elect, then, to bring his claim under the Act alleging breach of Article 8 (which requires respect for private and family life). If he elects for a Convention remedy, the claimant can sue under the Act *so long as* the defendant is a public authority.[47] But what of the case where the wrongdoer is a private individual—let us say, a neighbour who invades my privacy by persistently peering through my window and monitoring my private correspondence? Some common law remedy might be found in such circumstances. The 'snooper' who peers through windows and opens mail could be liable for harassment[48] or trespass to goods.[49] But, if the facts of the case do not lend themselves to the invocation of an existing common law action, the position is not entirely clear. This is important because, despite a move in the

---

[39] Human Rights Act 1998, sub-s 2(1)(a).
[40] See, eg, *Rantzen v Mirror Group Newspapers* [1993] 4 All ER 975; *Olotu v Home Office* [1997] 1 WLR 329; *R v CC of North Wales Police, ex p AB* [1998] 3 WLR 7.
[41] Otherwise the court itself acts unlawfully under the Human Rights Act 1998, s 6. But note that s 6 does not require the courts to create brand-new rights that mirror those in the Convention.
[42] Human Rights Act 1998, ss 7–8.   [43] See, eg, *Austin v Comr of Police* [2009] 1 AC 564 for discussion.
[44] Generally, tort damages are intended to put the claimant (C) in the position he would have occupied but for commission of the tort, but in respect of this tort, exemplary damages might be available. Not only would exemplary damages not be available under the Act, but also it is by no means clear that C would be put in the position he would have occupied since under the Act, 'in considering whether to award compensation and, if so, how much, there is a balance to be drawn between the interests of the victim and those of the public': *Anufrijeva v Southwark LBC* [2004] QB 1124, at [56].
[45] As is already the case, illustrated in *Olotu v Home Office* [1997] 1 WLR 328.
[46] For the limited extent to which tort law protects privacy, see ch 22.   [47] For discussion, see ch 5.
[48] See ch 10.   [49] See ch 11.

direction of allowing an invasion of privacy to be treated as a full-blown tort, English tort law has gone no further than to allow a claimant to sue in respect of the misuse of private personal information[50] and certain intrusions into private life.[51] While English courts do seem to be moving towards a convergence of common law and Convention rights in this area, the obligation to develop the common law in a manner consistent with the Convention does not empower them to engage in free-and-easy judicial legislation, especially in an area so politically charged as privacy rights.[52]

The judicial view of the impact of the European Convention on Human Rights on the development of the common law is still unfolding. However, as we shall see in chapter 5, the position of the Supreme Court appears (at the moment) to be that, where there is a Convention right, the need for protection of that right *in tort law* is diminished.[53] This is to say that the existence of an enforceable Convention right reduces the need for an action to be available in tort. If this is the case, it would appear that certain parts of tort law might become 'frozen in time'—a rather ironic outcome. As Steele notes: 'The emerging separation of tort from HRA actions contradicts a generally held view at the time of enactment that tort, being closely akin to the new action, was sure to adapt and expand in order to protect Convention rights more fully.'[54]

(C) Interests protected by tort law

The Human Rights Act aside, we look now at the kinds of interest that *tort law* specifically protects.[55] These interests are arranged, below, according to the degree of protection that they are offered in tort law, starting with the most strongly protected interests (or 'rights') and ending with the least (or most speculatively) protected interests. Naturally, we can expect some evolution in the way that protection of these interests develops over time.

(1) Personal and proprietary interests

The protection of the person from physical harm, restrictions on freedom of movement, and the protection of interests in tangible property—especially the right to non-interference with land and goods—were originally the most important concerns of tort law. The relevant modern torts which provide this protection include interference with goods and trespass in its various forms. (It is these torts which provide the foundation

---

[50] See *Campbell v MGN* [2004] 2 AC 457; *Douglas v Hello! Ltd (No 6)* [2006] QB 125.

[51] *PJS v News Group Newspapers Ltd* [2016] AC 1081.

[52] In *Wainwright v Home Office* [2004] 2 AC 406, Lord Hoffmann expressed the view (at [31]–[33]) that the matter was one that would require an Act of Parliament.

[53] See *Smith v CC of Sussex Police* [2009] 1 AC 225.

[54] J Steele [2008] CLJ 606, at 606. For arguments about how the Human Rights Act 1998 might influence the development of torts 'horizontally' as between private persons, see G Phillipson and A Williams (2011) 74 MLR 878.

[55] Cane has supplied a simpler list than the one provided here. It covers broadly the same ground, but differs in emphasis. He suggests that tort law protects (1) interests in the person; (2) property interests; (3) contractual interests; (4) non-contractual expectancies; (5) trade values; and (6) wealth: P Cane, *The Anatomy of Tort Law* (1997), 66–89.

of the protection of 'Convention rights' to life (Article 2),[56] freedom from torture or degrading treatment (Article 3), freedom from slavery (Article 4), liberty (Article 5), and peaceful possession of property (First Protocol, Article 1).) Whereas the law of trespass is concerned with deliberately inflicted injury, since the landmark decision in *Donoghue v Stevenson*[57] the courts have developed the tort of negligence to provide further protection to personal safety (including, within limits, mental integrity) and property interests. Indeed, personal and proprietary interests have come to rank so highly that further torts have emerged offering protection for those interests against conduct which is not necessarily, or cannot be proved to be, either intentional or negligent. For example, there are torts of ancient origin—such as nuisance—as well as others of more recent vintage—such as the rule in *Rylands v Fletcher* (developed during the height of the industrial revolution when a new range of threats to private property arose almost overnight)[58]—which protect these interests. The former highlights the degree of importance vested by the common law in the landowner's interest in his property. In addition, action has been taken by the legislature to protect tort law's core interests. The action for breach of statutory duty represents the common law's response to welfarist legislation, usually designed to improve standards of public health and personal safety.[59] Parliament has introduced, also, a regime of strict liability for injuries caused by defective products.[60]

(2) Reputation

Tort law has long protected an individual's interest in his reputation via the torts of libel and slander (collectively known as 'defamation'). But these torts, subject to recent legislative reform, have suffered from a newfound enthusiasm for 'free speech'. They are of limited scope and subject to a wide range of partial and complete defences, which circumscribe their operation.[61] In addition, these torts are expensive to litigate.

(3) Interests in intellectual property

Interests in tangible property, land, and goods are, as we shall see, well protected by the common law. By contrast, intellectual property in confidential information, copyright, and patents presents greater problems. Much of the law in this field is statutory; and interests in intellectual property generally overlap with interests in economic relations. But this is not invariably so. For example, the tort based on private information eventually might embrace both a patient's right to confidentiality from his doctor and a multinational company's right to protection of its trade secrets.

(4) Due process

A right to protection from malicious abuse of the judicial process is recognised in the tort of malicious prosecution and its ancillary tort of abuse of process. Now it seems

---

[56] The focus of protection offered under the Convention and under the common law is different, although their areas of operation overlap. With respect to Article 2, see, eg, *Savage v South Essex Partnership NHS Trust* [2009] 1 AC 681, at [91].   [57] [1932] AC 562.
[58] See J Murphy (2004) 24 OJLS 643.   [59] See N Foster (2011) 33 Syd LR 67.   [60] See ch 16.
[61] See, eg, the defences available in defamation discussed in ch 21.

that a tort to prevent abuse of the administrative process also is in its early infancy; and the European Convention on Human Rights, Article 6 might well contribute to its development.[62]

(5) Interests in economic relations, business, and trade interests

For a variety of reasons, including the absence of any requirement that harm be inflicted 'directly' in the tort of negligence, courts have adopted a cautious approach to protecting purely financial interests from negligently inflicted harm. There is a group of economic torts,[63] which are founded upon intentional action, which do offer a level of protection of financial and business interests but these torts are somewhat unclear in their scope.[64] In addition to the classic economic torts of interference with contractual relations, conspiracy, and intimidation, other torts of significance in this context are passing off and deceit.

(6) Privacy

The most obvious example of a possible lacuna in tort law has already been noted: the protection of privacy which is to be guaranteed under the European Convention on Human Rights by Article 8. However, tort is slowly developing some degree of protection in this area. This development started with rights to protect confidential information[65] and has grown to protection of information about which there is a proper expectation of privacy.[66] In other jurisdictions, rights to privacy also extend to rights to seclusion and one would expect some further development of the United Kingdom law in these areas.

Section 4 Theoretical perspectives on tort law

In recent decades, there has been much theorising about the appropriate parameters of tort law,[67] about the bases of tortious liability,[68] and about whether tort law should serve individual or collective goals.[69] This section briefly considers some different perspectives on tort law in order to give readers a sense of the debate (and as a counterpoint to the present author's views, summarised in section 1). Scholars theorise about the law in order to understand it better. This is done by removing from consideration those aspects of the law which are peripheral and by focusing on its core features. Many 'theories of tort' are ex post rationalisations of the rules, which are oblivious to the way in which tort actions have evolved historically. The strength of a particular theory is determined by how well it explains the subsisting law. Theories that seem to explain the

---

[62] It has been raised in connection with the striking out of negligence claims: see, eg, *Z v UK* (2002) 34 EHRR 97 and *TP and KM v UK* (2002) 34 EHRR 42.

[63] See H Carty, *An Analysis of the Economic Torts* (2nd edn, 2010) and chs 14–15 below.

[64] See further ch 15.   [65] *Attorney General v Guardian Newspapers Ltd (No 2)* [1990] AC 109.

[66] *Campbell v MGN* [2004] 2 AC 457.

[67] See, eg, E Descheemaeker, *The Division of Wrongs* (2009); J Gordley, *Foundations of Private Law: Property, Tort, Contract, Restitution* (2006).

[68] See, eg, J Coleman, *Risks and Wrongs* (1992); E Weinrib, *The Idea of Private Law* (1995).

[69] See, eg, A Robertson and HW Tang (eds), *The Goals of Private Law* (2009).

law well, and that can be used to predict the ways in which it will apply to new facts, are better than those that have limited 'fit' and predictive value.

(A) Corrective justice

In this short introduction to tort theory, two contrasting types of approach will be highlighted. The first, to be discussed in this section, is that of corrective justice. The second is the instrumentalist approach, our discussion encompassing related notions of efficiency, internalising losses, and deterrence, to be considered in the next section.

Corrective justice is concerned with the circumstances in which a wronged party is able to obtain reparation (usually damages) from a wrongdoer.[70] Theories of corrective justice aim to demonstrate 'that the basic features of tort law are not a mere historical byproduct, . . . but instead [reflect] a system designed for the goal of correcting private injustices . . .'.[71] The focus is upon the parties to the allegedly wrongful interaction. The concerns of the state (when not a party) and of other parties external to the wrongful interaction are ignored.

The most well-known exponent of corrective justice is Ernest Weinrib, whose major works encompass *The Idea of Private Law* (1995), *Corrective Justice* (2012), and many articles which explain his position.[72] According to Weinrib, the tort action is brought after the claimant suffers an injustice involving an infringement of his rights. He brings the action against the person said to have caused the injustice. In this way, two parties are joined together in a 'bipolar' relationship. Corrective justice theory illuminates the conditions under which the injustice arising within this relationship is corrected. In Weinrib's view, the two most important conditions for correction are correlativity and personality. Correlativity entails that the reasons for which the defendant is made liable for a wrong are the mirror image, or reflect, the reasons for which the claimant is entitled to reparation. Weinrib explains:

> Since the defendant, if liable, has committed the same injustice that the [claimant] has suffered, the reason the [claimant] wins ought to be the same as the reason the defendant loses. In specifying the nature of the injustice, the only normative factors to be considered significant are those that apply equally to both parties—for example, the defendant's having a deep pocket or being in a position to distribute losses broadly—is an inappropriate justification for liability because it is inconsistent with liability's correlative nature.
>
> In holding the defendant liable to the [claimant], the court is making not two separate judgments (one that awards something to the [claimant] and the other that coincidentally takes the same from the defendant), but a single judgment that embraces both parties in their interrelationship.[73]

Second, 'personality' grounds the defendant's duties and the claimant's rights in the fact that they are purposive human beings. Each person has a capacity for purposiveness,

---

[70] M Stone (1996) 9 CJLJ 235, 253.   [71] JCP Goldberg (2003) 91 Geo LJ 513, 571.
[72] A good summary is available in EJ Weinrib (2001) 2 Theoretical Inquiries in Law 107.
[73] EJ Weinrib (2001) 2 Theoretical Inquiries in Law 107, 116–17.

this being an ability to develop a life that is meaningful to that person. Tort law embodies a system of negative duties of non-interference with the rights of others. These rights protect the individual's capacity for purposiveness. How does one determine what rights there are? Weinrib says that 'the law regards a right as the power to treat something as subject to one's will as a consequence of an antecedent connection that one's will has established with the thing in question'.[74] He continues:

> Among these rights are the right to the integrity of one's body as the organ of purposive activity, the right to property in things appropriately connected to the external manifestations of the proprietor's volition, and the right to contractual performance in accordance with the mutually consensual exercises of the parties' purposiveness. The existence of these rights gives rise to correlative duties of non-interference whose content and application depend upon the nature of the right.[75]

Where there is no recognised right, there is no recognised duty of non-interference.

Connecting correlativity and personality, Weinrib emphasises the importance of tort law's inner coherence:

> The juridical conception of corrective justice regards injustice as consisting in the defendant's doing or having something that is incompatible with a right of the [claimant]. Right and duty are correlated when the [claimant]'s right is the basis of the defendant's duty and, conversely, when the scope of the duty includes the kind of right-infringement that the [claimant] suffered. Under those circumstances the reasons that justify the protection of the [claimant]'s right are the same as the reasons that justify the existence of the defendant's duty.[76]

Weinrib does not seek to justify and explain all existing tort actions. In fact, he believes that there is no room for strict liability in tort because it 'one-sidedly refers to the [claimant]'s injuries' and does not depend on any fault in the defendant. Weinrib rejects also the idea that the purposes of tort law are derived from outside the bipolar relationship. For him, resolution of a tort dispute is not to be influenced by external purposes; it is not an instrument for achieving wider social goals.

Certain criticisms can be levelled at Weinrib's theory. In many cases it is not possible to state that a court will provide a remedy for wrongdoing simply on the basis of interference with pre-defined rights. Yet Weinrib presents no theory of wrongdoing, no substantial account of why it is that courts might decide to shift a loss from the claimant to the defendant. We find those reasons in such things as the description of prohibited conduct and sophisticated notions of fault. Moreover, Weinrib's theory does not have great explanatory power. It is inconsistent with strict liability, and recovery for purely financial loss. Finally, Barbara Fried has observed that theories such as Weinrib's focus almost wholly upon the study of tort law as a subsisting phenomenon. However:

> . . . it is easy to lose sight of the fact that what *is* is entitled at most to a presumption that it is right. It might be wrong. At some point, the presumption of rightness has to be defended

---

[74] EJ Weinrib (2001) 2 Theoretical Inquiries in Law 107, 121.
[75] EJ Weinrib (2001) 2 Theoretical Inquiries in Law 107, 122–3.
[76] EJ Weinrib (2001) 2 Theoretical Inquiries in Law 107, 118.

in light of articulated norms. In my view, most of the [duty-based] literature on tort law never gets to that last step. As a result, it often confuses convention for some external notion of morality and institutional designs adopted for pragmatic reasons for ones that reflect a deeper normative commitment.[77]

(B) Instrumentalism

Whereas corrective justice has a relatively confined focus, 'instrumentalist' views of tort law are predicated upon the idea that tort law exists for reasons which include, but which go beyond, the resolution of disputes between the parties before the court. This is to say that tort law might be used in order to achieve wider, social goals. Here we consider a small selection of related instrumentalist theories, these being: the efficient use of resources; making the wrongdoer who profits from injuring others pay (enterprise liability); and deterring future wrongdoing (economic deterrence theory).

Efficiency The 'economic analysis of law' (EAL) involves evaluating law by reference to efficiency criteria.[78] Here we consider a particular type of EAL, which is concerned to ensure that aggregate wealth is maximised—essentially by putting resources to their best use.[79] The analysis can be conducted at a number of levels—for example, at the system level, or at the level of specific rules.

At the system level, EAL entails paying attention to the costs of tort actions which arise in such things as the use of court buildings, employment of judges, use of legal counsel, finding of facts, etc.[80] Costs are determined by prices charged for these inputs and the efficiency with which the inputs are used. Prices are set in the market according to the forces of supply and demand. They reflect the combined preferences of those who constitute the market. Where those persons who constitute the market have a high demand for goods which are in limited supply, the price is driven up. The price mechanism helps to allocate society's scarce resources to those who are willing to pay the most for them—presumably because they can obtain the greatest economic return from their use. In the present context, the crucial issue is whether tort law permits the avoidance, or redress, of wrongs in a cost-justified way. If it does not, then tort law should be replaced by a more efficient alternative. Frequently it has been noted that the tort system is a very expensive means of obtaining redress for wrongdoing, which is available to relatively few injured persons. A high proportion of the total costs of the system are expended, not upon compensation for victims, but upon obtaining evidence and retaining lawyers.[81] (However, it must be borne in mind, also, that many accident victims need not obtain redress through the legal system because, where applicable rules

---

[77] B Fried (2012) 18 *Legal Theory* 231.

[78] For an overview of the development of EAL, see N Duxbury, *Patterns of American Jurisprudence* (1995), ch 5.

[79] N Duxbury, *Patterns of American Jurisprudence* (1995), 394ff.

[80] Eg, WM Landes and RA Posner, *The Economic Structure of Tort Law* (1987), 65.

[81] P Cane, Atiyah's *Accidents, Compensation and the Law* (8th edn, 2013), ch 7.

are relatively clear, they can 'bargain in the shadow of the law' and reach out-of-court settlements at a greatly reduced cost.[82])

EAL can be used, also, in order to shape specific legal rules so as to encourage the best use of resources by individuals. For example, Richard Posner has argued that the negligence standard of liability in tort law and 'a number of related doctrines (contributory negligence, . . . assumption of risk, and others) were methods of bringing about an efficient allocation of resources to safety and care'.[83] The judge in an accident case tries to 'ascertain whether the injurer and the victim were behaving carefully in the sense of trying to minimize the sum of expected-accident and accident-avoidance costs'.[84] This statement contains the insight that courts in negligence cases do *not* attempt completely to eradicate all accidents; to do so would require very large precaution costs and slow down commerce and industry. What negligence law tries to do is to ensure that the costs of accidents are no greater than the costs of taking precautions to avoid them.[85] This is the optimal rule for expenditure on precaution-taking for most kinds of activity. However, in cases of highly dangerous activities, EAL proponents such as Posner believe that tort law operates by controlling overall activity levels. This is done by the imposition of strict liability rules,[86] which make it easier for claimants to succeed because they do not require proof of fault.

EAL is not an all-embracing explanation of tort law; it fails to account for broader considerations of justice—as EAL proponents themselves admit.[87] Courts must consider other values in various kinds of case. More problematically, EAL has been criticised on several grounds that include both the unrealistic assumptions about human behaviour upon which it rests (for example, that all persons act in full knowledge of alternatives and pursue maximisation strategies), and also in its failure definitively to prove that tort law, by and large, leads to efficient outcomes.[88] Not surprisingly, English judges are wary of relying on academic expositions of economic analysis when deciding cases.[89]

Enterprise liability Moving away from the core body of EAL, we see that economic insights have had some success in trying to explain discrete areas of tort law. 'Enterprise liability' is a theory which has grown, in part, out of Ronald Coase's theories about how 'firms' grow by internalising within them transactions that otherwise would take place in the market, thereby increasing the firms' own opportunities to profit.[90] Enterprise liability

---

[82] PH Rubin (1977) 6 J of Legal Studies 51. See also P Cane, *Atiyah's Accidents, Compensation and the Law* (8th edn, 2013), ch 10.

[83] WM Landes and RA Posner, *The Economic Structure of Tort Law* (1987), 8, referring to RA Posner (1972) 1 J of Legal Studies 29.

[84] WM Landes and RA Posner, *The Economic Structure of Tort Law* (1987), 23.

[85] WM Landes and RA Posner, *The Economic Structure of Tort Law* (1987), 60. See also G Calabresi, *The Costs of Accidents* (student edn, 1970), 17–18.

[86] WM Landes and RA Posner, *The Economic Structure of Tort Law* (1987), 107ff.

[87] WM Landes and RA Posner, *The Economic Structure of Tort Law* (1987), 23–4.

[88] N Duxbury, *Patterns of American Jurisprudence* (1995), 411.

[89] Although they do take economic efficiency into account in determining the limits of liability for negligence on occasion: see, eg, *Stovin v Wise* [1996] AC 923.

[90] R Coase (1937) 4 Economica NS 386 (available at http://www3.nccu.edu.tw/~jsfeng/CPEC11.pdf).

is a theory about how the law should encourage businesses (enterprises) to internalise the full costs of their activities—including the injuries that they cause. Initially, it was thought that industrialisation created *unavoidable* risks of injury. Worker injuries were viewed as an unfortunate 'cost' of large-scale business operations, which employers were in a position either to absorb through reductions in profits, or to spread through insurance or marginal increases in product prices.[91] This idea encouraged movement in United States' courts towards strict liability doctrines in the common law of tort.[92] In time, scholars and courts began to question the *inevitability* of industrial accidents. Industrialisation was understood to have created a world of long-run production and recurrent risks, which were not discrete and random, but the result of planned processes. This fostered incentives to take precautions against 'characteristic' risks in those who controlled production.[93] 'Characteristic' risks are those that inhere in an enterprise's long-run business activities (despite the taking of reasonable precautions),[94] although compensation is required only in cases of risks which are 'different from those attendant on the activities of the community in general'.[95] Enterprises are viewed as having the ability to anticipate those accidents that issue from their characteristic risks, take steps in advance to minimise their incidence, and disperse their costs after accidents occur.[96] The imposition of liability upon the enterprise without the need to prove which individual employee was causally responsible is to the obvious advantage of injured persons.[97] The theory of the business, and actors connected to it, as 'enterprise' has been used to explain several types of liability rule. These include the stricter aspects of products liability law (which extend liability beyond the supplier to other parties in the chain of manufacture and distribution)[98] and the law of vicarious liability (by making the employer liable for torts committed by workers either in the course of employment or where there is a sufficient connection between the tort and the employment relationship).[99]

Economic deterrence Under economic deterrence theory (which, to repeat, is related to enterprise liability), the purpose of tort law is to promote social welfare by deterring accidents in the future.[100] Indeed, along with compensation of losses caused by tortious conduct, this is a purpose which courts state frequently that they are pursuing.[101] The starting point of economic deterrence theory is the assumption that 'an individual (or entity) makes the decision about whether or how to engage in a given activity by weighing its costs and benefits' as they will fall on him (or it).[102] Tort law can modify the actor's behaviour by increasing the costs of risky activities that he undertakes—ensuring that

---

[91] Eg, JCP Goldberg (2003) 91 Geo LJ 513, 542; GL Priest (1985) 14 J of Legal Studies 461, 466; F James Jr (1952) 27 NYULR 537, 538. The apparent conflict between goals of internalisation, and loss distribution, has been noted: eg, R Flannigan (1987) 37 UTLJ 25, 28.

[92] GC Keating (2001) 54 Vand LR 1285, 1287 and 1290.   [93] GC Keating (1997) 95 Mich LR 1266.

[94] GC Keating (1997) 95 Mich LR 1266, 1279.   [95] GC Keating (1997) 95 Mich LR 1266, 1290.

[96] GC Keating (1997) 95 Mich LR 1266, 1354.

[97] LA Kornhauser (1982) 70 Calif LR 1345, 1370. See also K Graham (2014) 98 Marquette LR 555, 568–9.

[98] Consumer Protection Act 1987.

[99] Eg, *Mohamud v Wm Morrison Supermarkets plc* [2016] AC 677, at [40]; D Tan (2015) 27 Singapore Academy of Law J 822.   [100] JCP Goldberg (2003) 91 Geo LJ 513, 544.

[101] Eg, *Gravil v Carroll* [2008] ICR 1222, at [28]. Contrast *E v English Province of Our Lady of Charity* [2013] QB 722, at [52]–[53].   [102] JCP Goldberg (2003) 91 Geo LJ 513, 545.

costs which otherwise would be borne by tort victims are internalised by the actor. As Goldberg observes: 'By providing successful [claimants] with injunctions and monetary damages, tort law generates penalties—sanctions that give future actors a material incentive either to take precautions while acting or to avoid the activity altogether.'[103] Like the other theories surveyed already, economic deterrence theory has its shortcomings. One is that the information required to calculate the optimal standard of deterrence is not easy to obtain. Moreover, the usual questions about the assumptions that underlie economic analyses (considered above) arise as well. In this context, it must be acknowledged that people do not always respond to the general threat of liability awards because they do not behave in ways that deterrence proponents believe to be rational. By contrast, judges sometimes might be cautious about invoking principles of deterrence with respect to some defendants, fearful that tort liability will lead to over cautious, defensive conduct. This concern is evident particularly in connection with medical litigation.

(C) Pluralism

The approaches to tort law discussed so far in this section of the chapter have one thing in common: they are 'monistic' because they each seek to describe tort law largely in terms of only one value. However, there can be little doubt that the true nature of tort law is more complex. Several scholars have attempted to recognise this complexity by presenting 'pluralistic' views of tort law. This they have done, in the main, by selecting what they consider to be the strongest two of the monistic approaches and 'bolting' them together. The most frequently encountered mixed theories are those seeking to combine into a model of tort law corrective justice and deterrence theories. An example lies in the work of Gary Schwartz, who proposed that 'we take seriously a mixed theory of tort law, which can attend to both deterrence and corrective justice.'[104] Schwartz saw these theories of tort law as being complementary with each other. Thus, tort law does a better job of enhancing the security of persons when it has a deterrent effect than when it simply offers compensation to those who have been injured already. He wrote that: affording the claimant 'a compensation right indeed gives him an incentive to bring the suit that serves the purpose of deterring injurers . . . . While the tort suit for damages is structurally imperfect as a device for achieving optimal deterrence [because only those who have caused injury are subject to censure], it can still function reasonably well.'[105] It functions reasonably well, perhaps, because it provides ex ante signals to all those who might be in a similar position to the defendant in the future. Examining particular tort doctrines in light of his pluralistic theory, Schwartz opined that:

> The reasonable care standard in various tort doctrines is justified by the aim of correction of wrongs—indeed, it provides a standard of wrongdoing—and also by deterrence because

---

[103] JCP Goldberg (2003) 91 Geo LJ 513, 544. In partial confirmation of this theory, we see, eg, in *Michael v Chief Constable of South Wales Police* [2015] AC 1732, at [121], that where a court doubts its ability to deter future wrongdoing, it is less likely to impose an obligation upon an ostensible wrongdoer (here police who were alleged to have failed to prevent a murder).   [104] GT Schwartz (1997) 75 Texas LR 1801, 1801.
[105] GT Schwartz (1997) 75 Texas LR 1801, 1817–18.

> its dictates require defendants to implement 'cost-effective safeguards' against injuries occurring; Strict liability for abnormally dangerous activities is justified by both corrective justice and deterrence. There is justice in imposing strict liability upon the defendant who conducted the activity because the dangerous activity is under his/her control. The defendant is the cheapest cost-avoider of injury also—'the party most capable of reducing risk by either adopting precautions, reducing the level of its activity, or abstaining from the activity altogether'.[106]

Perhaps it is surprising that tort scholars who have an interest in theory have not more readily embraced the idea that tort law might have several different aims. However, this idea does seem to attract a greater number of proponents than it once did.[107] A challenge facing such scholars is to set out a fuller theory that explains the priorities attached to each theory in different areas of tort law—for, as the reader will have gathered already, different tort problems require different emphases.

(D) Limits on the effectiveness of tort law

Though there is much theorising about what should and should not be actionable in tort,[108] many are of the view that tort law remains essentially practical. This manifests itself in such things as recent judicial intolerance for 'trivial' claims. For example, judges might deny a remedy by way of trespass to the person for mere touching in a social setting, even if this is unwanted.[109] They recognise the limits of the wrongs that the law is capable of redressing, however morally reprehensible those wrongs might be. For example, avarice, brutal words, and ingratitude cannot form the basis of an action in tort law. Along with this is a judicial dread of a flood of actions. Often, it is for this reason that the courts have been reluctant to allow claims for negligently inflicted purely financial loss where the range of claims resulting from a single incident might be large.[110] The courts display a marked caution also in the context of awarding damages for non-material harms.

Another reality is that damages in many torts cases cannot be fixed with mathematical precision. For example, the calculation of damages in, say, the tort of false imprisonment, cannot be conducted in the same way as damages for breach of a contract based on failure to fulfil a sale of goods agreement. For this reason, the courts have been on their guard to restrain 'gold-digging' actions. Nonetheless, it is apparent that sometimes they have been excessively wary; and later courts have had to overrule earlier decisions. The cases on the negligent infliction of psychiatric harm illustrate this point.[111]

---

[106] GT Schwartz (1997) 75 Texas LR 1801, 1812.

[107] Eg, A Robertson, 'Rights, Pluralism and the Duty of Care' in D Nolan and A Robertson (eds), *Rights and Private Law* (2012), ch 15.

[108] And, indeed, what might properly be taken to constitute tort law: see N McBride and R Bagshaw, *Tort Law* (2005), 30–5 and 727–88.

[109] See *Collins v Wilcock* [1984] 1 WLR 1172. See also *White v Withers LLP* [2010] 1 FLR 859, at [72] (insusceptibility of courts to actions brought to 'prove a point').

[110] See ch 4. See also K Barker, 'Economic Loss and the Duty of Care: A Study in the Exercise of Legal Justification' in C Rickett (ed), *Justifying Private Law Remedies* (2008), ch 8.

[111] As in *White v CC of South Yorkshire Police* [1999] 1 All ER 1.

Conclusions

This chapter has attempted to provide some guideposts to the study of the complex area of law that we know as 'tort law'. But explanation has been given in general terms, with much of the context still missing. Perhaps the most important points for the student to remember are that tort law is made up of a number of different causes of action, and that these causes of action have their own distinctive mixes of 'elements'. Typically, a tort cause of action has a conduct requirement—the conduct in question having been wrongful in some way; has a fault requirement; and is protective of certain definable interests. However, not all torts include a fault element; some are strict in nature, which means that the courts do not inquire into the presence or absence of fault. Typically, tort law is more protective of certain interests (the body, reputation, and property) than it is of other interests (such as intangible wealth and privacy). Where protection is highest, the relevant tort is more likely to be either strict liability or based on negligence (that is, sub-standard conduct); conversely, in cases where less protection is offered, the courts are more accepting of claims that stem from blatant forms of fault (such as an intention to injure). Although there is debate about what the goals of tort law are, the courts themselves most frequently attribute to it the goals of compensating the injured and deterring wrongful conduct in the future.

Further reading

BALGANESH AND PARCHOMOVSKY, 'Structure and Value in the Common Law' (2015) 163 *University of Pennsylvania Law Review* 1241

CANE, *Responsibility in Law and Morality* (2002)

GOLDBERG, 'Twentieth-Century Tort Theory' (2003) 91 *Georgetown Law Journal* 514

GOLDBERG, 'Introduction: Pragmatism and Private Law' (2012) 125 *Harvard Law Review* 1640

GORDLEY, *Foundations of Private Law: Property, Tort, Contract and Unjust Enrichment* (2006), chs 9–12

IBBETSON, *A Historical Introduction to the Law of Obligations* (1999)

LUCY, *Philosophy of Private Law* (2007)

OBERDIEK (ed) *Philosophical Foundations of the Law of Torts* (2014)

OWEN (ed) *Philosophical Foundations of Tort Law* (1995)

SCHWARTZ, 'Mixed Theories of Tort Law: Affirming both Deterrence and Corrective Justice' (1997) 75 *Texas Law Review* 1801

STEVENS, *Torts and Rights* (2007)

TILLEY, 'Tort Law Inside Out' (2017) 126 *Yale Law Journal* 1320

WEINRIB, *The Idea of Private Law* (1995)

WEINRIB, *Corrective Justice* (2012)

PART II
Negligent invasions of personal, property, and financial interests

2

Duty of care I: foundational principles

KEY ISSUES

(1) Tort of negligence

The tort of negligence is composed of several elements. The claimant must prove the existence of a duty of care owed to her at the time of the alleged injurious interaction, breach of the duty, and factual causation of damage. The onus then shifts to the defendant to prove either remoteness of damage or the presence of a valid defence in order to escape liability. This chapter is concerned with the first of these elements.

(2) Existing duty categories

In most negligence cases, the claimant will invoke an existing duty of care category in bringing her claim—such as the duty of care owed by motorists to pedestrians. The duty of care signifies the presence of a legally recognised relationship between the parties, which grounds an obligation of care.

(3) Duty of care elements

Only in novel or contentious cases is it necessary to apply first principles in order to determine whether a duty of care arises. In such cases, the test for duty of care comprises three stages: reasonable foreseeability of injury to a class of person including the claimant; a sufficient relationship of proximity between the claimant and defendant; and inquiry into whether it would be fair, just, and reasonable to recognise a duty.

(4) Reasonable foreseeability

Reasonable foreseeability involves an objective test of capacity. The court is concerned with whether a reasonable person in the position of the claimant could reasonably have foreseen that carelessness might lead to injury of the kind suffered (whether bodily, psychiatric, property damage, or purely financial) to a class of person including the claimant.

(5) Proximity

This test is concerned with whether there existed, prior to the defendant's failure to take care, sufficient factual links between the parties so as to establish proximity (in the sense of 'neighbourhood' or 'closeness') such as would support the imposition of a duty of care. Proximity indicates the presence of pathways to harm, the existence of such pathways providing a reason for imposing a legal obligation upon the defendant to take care.

(6) Fair, just, and reasonable limb

Where foreseeability and proximity are found to have existed at the time of the injurious interaction in question, the pre-conditions are present for the court to recognise a duty of care. In determining whether to do so, it might assess various mid-level 'policy' issues that argue in favour of and/or against the imposition of a duty of care.

Section 1 Introduction

Emergence of negligence Many more people suffer damage from the negligent (or 'sub-standard') acts of others than from intentional wrongdoing. Accordingly, tort law has a special concern about negligently inflicted harm, and has long recognised that, in appropriate circumstances, persons responsible for negligent conduct should be liable to those whom they injure. Indeed, the liability of those engaged in certain common callings—such as smiths and innkeepers—goes back to the fourteenth century. But not until around 1825 did negligence begin to emerge as a separate tort. Up to that point, there existed merely a list of situations in which the victims of sub-standard conduct might recover damages. Thereafter, actions on the case (explained in chapter 1) for negligence became common, spurred on by the increase in negligently inflicted injuries through the use of new technologies such as the railways, and later by the abolition of the forms of action.[1] The concrete emergence of negligence as a separate tort with a distinct set of principles became irresistible, and, in practical terms, it is now the most commonly pleaded (and most important) tort of all. It must be realised, however, that negligently inflicted harm does not always sound in the tort of negligence alone; negligent conduct relating to the use of land may well, for example, give rise to nuisance liability[2] and there are many other examples of overlap.

Legally recognised obligation It is not the case that anyone who suffers harm as a result of another's sub-standard conduct can sue. The tort of negligence requires more than 'heedless or careless conduct'.[3] The injured party must establish that the defendant owed her a duty to take reasonable care to protect her from the kind of harm suffered,[4] that she was in breach of that duty by falling below the legally required standard of care, and that it was the defendant's breach of duty that caused the claimant's injury. Duty, breach, and injury must be established in every claim in negligence.[5]

This chapter begins by seeking to identify the essential principles concerning the duty of care. The concept of duty is fundamental, for without it no legal obligation arises on the part of the defendant class of persons to take care with respect to the claimant class. This is to say that the courts recognise actions in negligence only in cases where a legally recognised relationship arises as between persons such as to impose obligations to take care (the content of which are specified at the standard-breach stage according to the particular facts). Although there is debate about the role of the duty of care in negligence,[6] it seems that it is a 'quasi-jurisdictional' concept. The duty of care signifies that a legal

---

[1] The main milestones were *Vaughan v Menlove* (1837) 3 Bing NC 468; *Winterbottom v Wright* (1842) 10 M & W 109; *Heaven v Pender* (1883) 11 QBD 503.   [2] But for criticism see C Gearty [1989] CLJ 214.

[3] *Lochgelly Iron and Coal Co v M'Mullan* [1934] AC 1, at 25.

[4] In *Caparo Industries plc v Dickman* [1990] 605, at 627, Lord Bridge said: 'It is never sufficient to ask simply whether A owes B a duty of care. It is always necessary to determine the scope of the duty by reference to the kind of damage from which A must take care to save B harmless.' Accordingly, where X is instrumental in injuring Y in circumstances where no duty was owed to Y to take care not to injure Y *in that way*, X will not be liable for want of duty: *Sam v Atkins* [2006] RTR 14.

[5] However, judges do not clearly distinguish always between the three: eg, in *Roe v Minister of Health* [1954] 2 QB 66, at 85.   [6] Eg, D Nolan (2013) 129 LQR 559.

obligation exists as between persons who might otherwise be strangers to each other, that care must be taken by one class of person in their interactions with the other class, and that *a court will hear an allegation that there has been a failure in care*.[7] In most cases, it will be sufficient for the claimant to invoke the existence of a *recognised* duty category.[8] It is only when doubt arises as to the existence of such a duty category that a court will be required to apply a *test* for duty. This chapter seeks to explain the general test for a duty of care.

Section 2 The emergence of a duty framework

Seminal cases The concept of duty of care in negligence[9] emerged towards the end of the eighteenth century, and is so firmly rooted now that there can be no doubt that actions in negligence must fail where no duty is recognised.[10] The first recognised attempt to rationalise the situations in which a duty can be imposed was made in *Heaven v Pender* by Brett MR. He said:

> [W]henever one person is by circumstances placed in such a position with regard to another that everyone of ordinary sense who did think would at once recognise that if he did not use ordinary care and skill in his own conduct with regard to those circumstances he would cause danger or injury to the person or property of the other, a duty arises to use ordinary care and skill to avoid such danger.[11]

That statement recognised the importance of 'recognition', or foreseeability of risks of injury to others. Building upon this attempt to generalise the circumstances in which duties of care arise, Lord Atkin in *Donoghue v Stevenson* (decided in 1932) enunciated the seminal 'neighbour principle':

> The rule that you are to love your neighbour becomes in law, you must not injure your neighbour; and the lawyer's question, Who is my neighbour? receives a restricted reply. You must take reasonable care to avoid acts or omissions which you can reasonably foresee would be likely to injure your neighbour. Who, then, in law is my neighbour? The answer seems to be persons who are so closely and directly affected by my act that I ought reasonably to have them in contemplation as being so affected when I am directing my mind to the acts or omissions which are called in question.[12]

This 'neighbour principle' is not the *ratio decidendi* of the case and it is probable that Lord Atkin never intended it to be a comprehensive statement of law.[13] However, the importance of *Donoghue v Stevenson* was twofold: first, it established a new category of

---

[7] See T Lipton (2015) 46 Ottawa LR 275 (one meaning of jurisdiction concerns choices made about which cases to hear). [8] See, eg, *Michael v Chief Constable of South Wales Police* [2015] AC 1732, at [102].

[9] Duties similar to those discussed here under common law negligence might also arise under statutes or contracts. See, eg, the 'common duty of care' under the Occupiers' Liability Act 1957, sub-s 2(2).

[10] *Heaven v Pender* (1883) 11 QBD 503, at 507; *Thomas v Quartermaine* (1887) 18 QBD 685, at 694; *Le Lievre v Gould* [1893] 1 QB 491, at 497; *Grant v Australian Knitting Mills Ltd* [1936] AC 85, at 101; *Bourhill v Young* [1943] AC 92. [11] (1883) 11 QBD 503, at 509.

[12] [1932] AC 562, at 580. [13] Cf *Haseldine v CA Daw & Son Ltd* [1941] 2 KB 343, at 362.

duty, namely that of a manufacturer of goods owed to the eventual users of those goods (a category that has since widened much further);[14] second, it set at rest any possible doubts about whether the tort of negligence was capable of further expansion and provided a framework for consideration of new duty of care categories.

Established categories Although Lord Atkin's neighbour principle was established as a broad guide to the circumstances in which a duty of care might be imposed, it must not be forgotten that the question of duty is one of law, not fact. The question whether a duty exists often is straightforward, for there are numerous examples of relationships between persons which are treated by the courts as imposing duties of care. Examples include doctors owing a duty to their patients, employers owing a duty to their employees, and makers of goods owing a duty to those who use them. Accordingly, before one falls back on any duty framework (to be explained later), one must ascertain whether on similar facts the courts have recognised a duty already. This was made clear in the negligence case of *Michael v Chief Constable of South Wales Police*, where Lord Toulson stated:

> The established method of the court involves examining the decided cases to see how far the law has gone and where it has refrained from going. From that analysis it looks to see whether there is an argument by analogy for extending liability to a new situation, or whether an earlier limitation is no longer logically or socially justifiable. In doing so it pays regard to the need for overall coherence. Often there will be a mixture of policy considerations to take into account.[15]

It is implicit in the statement from the *Michael* case that there are cases in which the law unequivocally denies the existence of duties of care. A landowner, for example, may abstract percolating water from below the surface of her land with impunity, even though this results in the subsidence of a claimant's adjoining buildings. She is not liable because she owes no duty of care in respect of percolating water.[16] Similarly, there is no duty in respect of loss caused by damage to the property of an individual other than a person with a current proprietary or proprietary interest in the damaged property.[17]

Section 3 The rise and fall of *Anns*

Categories not closed Were courts to hold that no duty of care exists unless an earlier precedent established it, tort law would remain frozen and static for all time. Yet Lord Macmillan stated in *Donoghue v Stevenson* that the 'categories of negligence are never closed'.[18] This

---

[14] This was an instance of the courts taking account of the new conditions of mass production and complex marketing of goods (wherein there are many intermediaries between manufacturer and consumer), and imposing on manufacturers certain minimum standards of care in favour of the consumer. The clearest exposition of this function of *Donoghue v Stevenson* is the speech of Lord Devlin in *Hedley Byrne & Co Ltd v Heller & Partners Ltd* [1964] AC 465.

[15] *Michael v Chief Constable of South Wales Police* [2015] AC 1732, at [102]. See also *Kennedy v Cordia (Services) LLP* [2016] 1 WLR 597, at [114] (*Caparo* test not relevant in employer liability case).

[16] Eg, *Langbrook Properties Ltd v Surrey CC* [1969] 3 All ER 1424.

[17] Eg, *Leigh & Sillivan Ltd v Aliakmon Shipping Co Ltd* [1986] AC 785.

means at the very least, as Asquith LJ said in *Candler v Crane Christmas & Co*, 'that in accordance with changing social needs and standards new classes of persons legally bound or entitled to the exercise of care may from time to time emerge'.[19] So, over several decades beginning with Lord Atkin's formulation of the 'neighbour principle', new duty-situations were readily recognised by the courts. For example, it was held that an electricity authority that had high-voltage wires near a climbable tree owed a duty of care to a child who trespassed off a nearby footpath, climbed the tree, and was killed.[20] And an education authority owed a duty to the driver of a vehicle to exercise reasonable supervision over children in its nursery adjoining the highway so as to prevent them from endangering her safety on the road.[21]

Development of duty framework What each of the above examples has in common is that the defendant failed to take care with respect to her 'neighbour'. She could have foreseen, and should have taken steps to prevent, the injury suffered by the claimant. So was the 'neighbour test' the sole criterion determining whether a duty arose? In a series of judgments from 1970 to 1982 the courts came close to accepting as much. First, in *Home Office v Dorset Yacht Co Ltd*, Lord Reid declared that 'the time has come when we can and should say that' Lord Atkin's neighbour principle 'ought to apply unless there is some justification or valid explanation for its exclusion'.[22] Then, in *Anns v Merton LBC*, Lord Wilberforce proposed a two-stage test for duty:

> the position has now been reached that in order to establish that a duty of care arises in a particular situation, it is not necessary to bring the facts of that situation within those of previous situations in which a duty of care has been held to exist. Rather the question has to be approached in two stages. First, one has to ask whether, as between the alleged wrongdoer and the person who suffered damage there is a sufficient relationship of proximity or neighbourhood such that, in the reasonable contemplation of the former, carelessness on his part may be likely to cause damage to the latter, in which case a *prima facie* duty of care arises. Secondly, if the first question is answered affirmatively, it is necessary to consider whether there are any considerations which ought to negative, or to reduce or limit the scope of the duty of the class of person to whom it is owed or the damages to which a breach of it may give rise.[23]

The two-stage test looked deceptively simple. Applied fairly literally, a judge ruling on a novel duty situation might reason thus: was the harm to the claimant foreseeable, so bringing her within the 'neighbour principle'? If yes, was there any valid policy reason to deny the existence of a duty to the claimant?[24] In effect, the claimant having established foreseeability raised a presumption of the existence of a duty which the defendant had to rebut on policy grounds. However, Lord Wilberforce himself recognised in

---

[18] [1932] AC 562, at 619.   [19] [1951] 2 KB 164, at 192.

[20] *Buckland v Guildford Gas Light and Coke Co* [1949] 1 KB 410.

[21] *Carmarthenshire CC v Lewis* [1955] AC 549; *Barnes v Hampshire CC* [1969] 3 All ER 746.

[22] [1970] AC 1004, at 1027.   [23] [1978] AC 728, at 751–2.

[24] For example, to refuse a remedy to C, a criminal, who is injured by the negligence of his drunken companion while driving their getaway car. Injury to C was readily foreseeable but as a matter of policy no duty was recognised as owed by one participant in crime to another: *Ashton v Turner* [1981] QB 137.

McLoughlin v O'Brian that policy factors have a central role to play in determining the scope of a duty: 'at the margin, the boundaries of a man's responsibilities for acts of negligence have to be fixed as a matter of policy'.[25] But in the very same case, Lord Scarman, who was fearful that judicial conservatism would lead to unjust rigidity in the common law, came close to declaring foreseeability to be the *sole* test of the existence of a duty. Rejecting any policy-oriented limitations on liability for psychiatric harm, he argued:

> if principle inexorably requires a decision which entails a degree of policy risk, the court's function is to adjudicate according to principle, leaving policy curtailment to the judgment of Parliament.[26]

During the period from 1970 to 1984, the categories of negligence looked infinitely expandable. The boundaries of liability expanded in respect of both psychiatric harm[27] and financial loss.[28] The tort of negligence looked set to undermine the very boundaries of contract and tort, and, more particularly, the doctrines of consideration and privity of contract.[29] However, from 1984 judicial caution resurfaced and the House of Lords led a retreat from *Anns*, bringing the tort of negligence back to a much more category-based approach. Their Lordships' determination to restrict the unchecked expansion of the tort and to prevent the emergence of any presumption that all kinds of damage were the responsibility of someone other than the claimant, was summed up by Lord Hoffmann in *Stovin v Wise*:

> The trend of authorities [since 1984] has been to discourage the assumption that anyone who suffers loss is *prima facie* entitled to compensation from a person (preferably insured or a public authority) whose act or omission can be said to have caused it. The default position is that he is not.[30]

The retreat from *Anns* began in *Governors of the Peabody Donation Fund v Sir Lindsay Parkinson & Co Ltd*[31] The House of Lords denied a remedy to a development company suing a local authority for the financial loss occasioned by an inadequate drainage system, the plans for which they alleged the authority had negligently approved. Lord Keith said of the *Anns* test:

> There has been a tendency in some recent cases to treat these passages as being themselves of a definitive character. This is a temptation to be resisted in determining whether or not a duty of care of a particular scope was incumbent on the defendant. It is material to take into consideration whether it is just and reasonable that it should be so.[32]

In effect Lord Keith demanded that the *claimant* identify the policy grounds upon which a duty should arise and the defendant should be made responsible, in part, for her welfare.

---

[25] [1983] 1 AC 410, at 421.   [26] *McLoughlin v O'Brian* [1983] 1 AC 410, at 430.

[27] See, eg, *McLoughlin v O'Brian* [1983] 1 AC 410, at 430; *Attia v British Gas plc* [1988] QB 304.

[28] See, eg, *Ross v Caunters* [1980] Ch 297; *Junior Books Ltd v Veitchi Co Ltd* [1983] 1 AC 520 (the high-water mark of foreseeability sufficing to impose a duty).

[29] Since then, much of the doctrine of privity has been unpicked by the Contracts (Rights of Third Parties) Act 1999.

[30] [1996] AC 923, at 949.   [31] [1985] AC 210.   [32] [1985] AC 210, at 240.

Foreseeability and proximity Judicial disapproval of the *Anns* test continued apace thereafter.[33] It became clear beyond doubt that foreseeability of harm to persons alone is not enough to create a duty of care:

> It has been said almost too frequently to require repetition that foreseeability of likely harm is not in itself a sufficient test of liability in negligence. Some further ingredient is invariably needed to establish the requisite proximity of relationship between the [claimant] and defendant, and all the circumstances of the case must be carefully considered and analysed in order to ascertain whether such an ingredient is present.[34]

Foreseeability of harm to persons remains a necessary pre-condition of liability. But there must be proximity of relationship also between the actual claimant and the defendant; the 'neighbourhood' or closeness and directness of which Lord Atkin originally spoke in *Donoghue v Stevenson*. In *Sutradhar v NERC*,[35] the House of Lords insisted that proximity must be proved even in cases where physical injury results from careless certification. Crucial to the non-liability of the National Environment Research Council (NERC) (which failed to identify the presence of arsenic in a potential Bangladeshi water supply after testing it) was the fact that there was 'nothing like the directness and immediacy between the defendant's role in events and the claimant's injuries ... the essential touchstones of proximity are missing'.[36] In other words, given that the testing had been commissioned by a third party, the claimant who suffered arsenical poisoning in consequence of drinking the water was unable to establish a sufficiently close relationship between himself and the NERC, and it was not enough that it was foreseeable that someone would suffer such poisoning if the water was certified to be reasonably pure by the NERC.

Although proximity would appear a rather intuitive concept, the courts have had some difficulty in further defining it, especially in cases involving indirectly caused harms—a matter to which we shall return. For now, however, the important point that we have established is that, where foreseeability of harm and proximity between the parties before the court have been established, this creates the factual basis upon which a duty of care might be imposed (and governs the obligations of other similarly situated parties in the future).

Fair, just, and reasonable In addition to the fact-based foreseeability and proximity requirements, it was reasserted after *Anns v Merton LBC* that the courts would require, also, that there be normative grounds on which to impose on the defendant class of persons responsibility for the harm in question; reasons, in other words, why it would be fair, just, and reasonable to expect the defendant class to safeguard the claimant's interests rather than to expect the claimant to keep herself safe from harm. How difficult a task the claimant faces in this respect will vary depending on both the kind of harm suffered and whether or not third parties are involved. The courts are more ready to impose responsibility to safeguard others from physical injury and damage to their

---

[33] *Yuen Kun-yeu v A-G of Hong Kong* [1988] AC 175, at 190–4; *Rowling v Takaro Properties Ltd* [1988] AC 473, at 501. [34] *Hill v CC of West Yorkshire* [1988] 2 All ER 238, at 241. [35] [2006] 4 All ER 490. [36] [2006] 4 All ER 490, at [47]–[48]. See also at [38].

property than from merely financial (or 'economic') losses (those not consequent upon initial injury to physical interests, mental integrity, or damage to property). Lord Bridge said in *Caparo Industries plc v Dickman*:

> One of the most important distinctions always to be observed lies in the law's essentially different approach to the different kinds of damage which one party may have suffered in consequence of the acts or omissions of another. It is one thing to owe a duty to avoid causing injury to the person or property of others. It is quite another to avoid causing others to suffer purely economic loss.[37]

Where physical harm is caused to a person (or her property) by another's carelessness, establishing that the claimant is proximate and that it is fair, just, and reasonable that the defendant *ought* to be responsible for the harm thus inflicted is often unproblematic. As Lord Oliver put it in *Caparo*: 'the nexus between the defendant and the injured claimant can rarely give rise to any difficulty [in such cases]'.[38] And in *Murphy v Brentwood District Council*[39] he further implied the presumption of a duty in such cases, stating that '[t]he infliction of physical injury to the person or property of another universally requires to be justified'.

Nonetheless, the House of Lords made it clear in *Marc Rich & Co AG v Bishop Rock Marine Co Ltd*[40] that, even with respect to claims of physical damage, foreseeability alone is insufficient to create a duty of care. Lord Steyn confirmed[41] that, *whatever the nature of the relevant harm*, the court must consider not only the foreseeability of such harm to persons, but also the relationship between the actual parties and, in every case, be 'satisfied that in all the circumstances it is fair, just, and reasonable to impose a duty of care'. The facts of the *Marc Rich* case were as follows:

> Cs' cargo had been loaded on D1's vessel under contracts incorporating the usual terms and conditions of international shipping. Mid-voyage, the ship put into port with a crack in her hull. A surveyor employed by D3, a classification society responsible for checking the safety of ships at sea, inspected the vessel and certified that after some temporary repairs it should proceed on its voyage. A few days later the ship sank and the cargo worth £6m was lost. Cs recovered some of that sum from D1, but D1's liability was limited by statute. Cs then attempted to recover the balance of the loss from D3. Cs had suffered readily foreseeable physical damage to property as a result of the society's negligent inspection of the ship and the subsequent 'green light' the society's surveyor had given for the ship to carry on with the voyage.

Giving the majority speech in the House of Lords, and finding no duty to the cargo owners, Lord Steyn acknowledged that, where one person's carelessness *directly* causes physical damage to another, the law readily recognises a duty of care. However, the infliction of loss to the claimants in this case was indirect. There was no contract between the claimant and the society, and no direct reliance by the claimants on the expertise of the society. Imposing a duty would undermine the framework established by the

---

[37] [1990] 1 All ER 568, at 574.   [38] [1990] 1 All ER 568, at 585.   [39] [1990] 2 All ER 908, at 935.
[40] [1996] AC 211.   [41] [1996] AC 211, at 235.
[42] For analogous reasoning, see *Raja v Austin Gray* [2003] 1 EGLR 91.

Hague-Visby Rules (an international maritime convention), which allocated responsibility for losses to various parties.[42] Equally, it was considered relevant that classification societies are independent, non-profit-making bodies that act in the public interest to promote the collective welfare of people and property on the seas. Faced with litigation of this sort, such societies might act defensively, refusing to carry out urgent or problematic inspections with a high risk of liability. Furthermore, limited resources would be diverted from the societies' fundamental work and directed to the conduct of complex litigation. Thus, it would be unfair and unjust to impose a duty in respect of the claimants' lost cargo. The societies' responsibility was primarily for the collective welfare of those at sea, and individual cargo owners should be left to their contractual remedies.

Lord Lloyd dissented. He perceived the facts as little more than a straightforward application of principles derived from *Donoghue v Stevenson*. The surveyor certifying the ship as fit to sail de facto controlled its fate. Had he refused a certificate, the ship-owners would not have continued the voyage. Therefore, Lord Lloyd argued that in instances of physical harm it would require an exceptional case to refuse to impose a duty on the grounds that it would not be fair, just, and reasonable. In other words, Lord Lloyd felt that in a case of physical harm to persons or property, once foreseeability of harm and proximity are proven there should be a strong presumption of liability. He concluded that: '[o]therwise there is a risk that the law of negligence will disintegrate into a series of isolated decisions without any coherent principles at all, and the retreat from *Anns* will turn into a rout.'[43]

Incremental approach Notwithstanding the universal support in *Caparo Industries plc v Dickman*[44] for the three-stage test based on foreseeability, proximity, and it being fair, just, and reasonable to impose a duty, it was asserted simultaneously in that case that the elements of the test are inherently vague. Concepts such as 'proximity' and 'fairness', for instance, were thought by Lord Bridge to be 'not susceptible of any precise definition as would be necessary to give them utility as practical tests'.[45] And the need to introduce some element of predictability into the development of duty-situations perhaps underscores the comment he made immediately afterwards:

> Whilst recognising ... the importance of the underlying general principles common to the whole field of negligence, ... the law has now moved in the direction of attaching greater significance to the more traditional categorisation of distinct and recognisable situations as guides to the existence, the scope and the limits of the varied duties of care which the law imposes. We must now ... recognise the wisdom of the words of Brennan J in the High Court of Australia in *Sutherland Shire Council v Heyman*,[46] where he said:
>
> It is preferable ... that the law should develop novel categories of negligence incrementally and by analogy with established categories, rather than by a massive extension of a *prima facie* duty of care restrained only by indefinable 'considerations, which ought to negative, or to reduce or limit the scope of the duty or the class of person to whom it is owed'.[47]

---

[43] [1996] AC 211, at 230.   [44] [1990] 2 AC 605.

[45] *Caparo Industries plc v Dickman* [1990] 1 All ER 568, at 574. See also the speech of Lord Oliver (at 585): 'to search for any single formula which will serve as a general test of liability is to pursue a will-o-the wisp'.

[46] (1985) 60 ALR 1, at 43–4.

[47] [1990] 1 All ER 568, at 574. See also *Murphy v Brentwood DC* [1990] 2 All ER 908, at 915.

Lord Bridge was not arguing for a return to a pre-*Donoghue v Stevenson* approach. A claimant in an action for negligence will not fail simply because the duty-situation she relies on never has been recognised previously. The House of Lords did not close the categories of negligence.[48] Rather, a claimant seeking recognition of a duty of care in a new fact situation must argue her case in the context of existing authority, and persuade the court that to extend liability into this new situation is a sound development of the law. Moreover, as was implicit in the earlier quote from Lord Toulson's judgment in *Michael v Chief Constable of South Wales Police*,[49] a finding of no duty in analogous cases will tell against the claimant without completely binding a superior court. So, in *X v Bedfordshire County Council*,[50] it was sought to establish that local authorities owe a duty of care in relation to their powers to protect children from abuse and neglect. There was no precedent in relation to a public authority's administration of a social welfare scheme. However, Lord Browne-Wilkinson[51] looked at analogous powers vested in the police to protect society from crime and in the financial regulatory bodies to protect investors from fraud. Finding no duty in either of those contexts, he suggested that establishing a duty in relation to child protection would be incongruous.

Similar reasoning has been applied also in relation to financial losses arising out of property damage. In *Leigh & Sillivan Ltd v Aliakmon Shipping Co Ltd*,[52] Lord Brandon[53] denied the existence of a duty of care in respect of financial loss to X arising out of damage to Y's property. He noted authorities dating back prior to 1980[54] insisting that a duty of care would be owed only to those with the requisite proprietary or possessory interest in the property concerned.[55] Lord Brandon was adamant that well-established authority had settled the matter,[56] and thus, regardless of how foreseeable financial loss to others might be, that loss was irrecoverable. There could be no question of 'a duty of care in a factual situation in which the existence of such a duty had been repeatedly held not to exist'.[57]

A preference for certainty　　Judicial refusal to review the existence of categories of negligence previously denied does ossify the tort of negligence to some extent. But consider some of the reasons justifying such an approach. Principles in tort need to be reasonably predictable, otherwise litigation can proliferate fruitlessly; and tort law helps to define those obligations imposed on us by law. Whereas we know what our contractual obligations entail because we choose to enter into them, justice demands that we have some means of knowing what other obligations we must honour. There is the question of insurance also. In many tort cases, the dispute is not really between the claimant and defendant but between their insurers.[58] The decision as to when a person should insure

---

[48] See, eg, *Spring v Guardian Assurance plc* [1995] 2 AC 296.
[49] [2015] AC 1732, at [102]. See text above.　　[50] [1995] 2 AC 633.
[51] [1995] 2 AC 633, at 751.　　[52] [1986] AC 785.　　[53] [1986] AC 785, at 815.
[54] See *Margarine Union v Cambay Prince Steamship Co Ltd* [1969] 1 QB 219; *The Mineral Transporter* [1986] AC 1.
[55] Cf *Shell UK Ltd v Total UK Ltd* [2011] QB 86.
[56] See also *Stephens v Anglian Water Authority* [1987] 1 WLR 1381.　　[57] [1986] AC 785, at 815.
[58] R Merkin and J Steele, *Insurance and the Law of Obligations* (2013).

against loss to herself, and when she should insure against liability to others, depends on an understanding of the circumstances in which a duty of care will arise. If you know it is highly likely that a certain kind of loss will be left to lie where it falls, as a prudent person you will insure yourself against that loss. Similarly, if you know that a particular sort of careless conduct probably will give rise to liability towards another person, you will insure against that liability.

Insurance considerations A final factor to note in the context of the retreat from *Anns* is increased judicial willingness to address openly the issue of insurance.[59] The fact that one party might be insured formerly was said to be irrelevant to liability.[60] However, *who ought* sensibly to have insured against the relevant loss, given the social and economic realities of the parties' relationship, is a factor sometimes used now to determine whether it is fair, just, and reasonable to impose a duty on the defendant.[61] Merkin and Steele believe that the interaction between the law of obligations and insurance should be seen as being even more pervasive than this approach suggests:

> Tort duties are best seen as relational; and in this respect, their interaction with insurance relationships and with duties to insure is frequent and significant. It is partly for this reason … that we do not think it appropriate to condemn insurance factors of all kinds to the realms of (extrinsic) 'policy factors'. Insurance is part of the relational fabric of the law of obligations.[62]

In essence, their suggestion is that insurance is of *systemic* importance to the development of tort law, given that the majority of parties appearing before the courts in tort cases are insured, that the cases frequently are 'run' by the insurers, and that, in personal injury cases, damages are very likely to be funded by insurance. The debate on this issue continues.

Section 4 Modern approaches to the duty of care

Although the expressed preference for incrementalism in decision-making about the duty of care has not resulted in a finite set of duty categories, it does constrain the growth of the tort. First, it becomes more difficult to establish a new category of negligence that is significantly different from, or wider in scope than, any of its predecessors.[63] Second, when a duty-situation is not entirely novel, but analogous to a category in which courts in

---

[59] An early example can be seen in *Spartan Steel and Alloys Ltd v Martin & Co (Contractors) Ltd* [1973] QB 27, at 38.   [60] *Capital and Counties plc v Hampshire CC* [1997] 2 All ER 865, at 891.

[61] See *Murphy v Brentwood DC* [1990] 2 All ER 908, at 923; *Marc Rich & Co AG v Bishop Rock Marine Co Ltd* [1996] AC 211, at 241; *Stovin v Wise* [1996] AC 923, at 954. This is to say that courts pay attention to the intended allocation of duties to insure and of risks more generally, especially in commercial relationships: R Merkin and J Steele, *Insurance and the Law of Obligations* (2013), 20.

[62] R Merkin and J Steele, *Insurance and the Law of Obligations* (2013), 31.

[63] See now *Robinson v CC of West Yorkshire Police* [2018] 2 WLR 595, which approves of this approach.

earlier decisions refused to recognise a duty, the assumption must be that a new duty category will not be permitted. Yet it must not be overlooked that it is the three-stage *Caparo*
framework that provides the primary framework according to which new duties of care
are to be recognised; so the frontiers of negligence are capable of gradual expansion.

(A) The *Caparo* duty framework

According to their Lordships in *Caparo Industries v Dickman*,[64] a duty of care may be
recognised if three requirements are satisfied: (1) the claimant must be reasonably foreseeable (bearing in mind the kind of harm involved); (2) there must be a relationship of
proximity between the claimant and the defendant; (3) it must be fair, just, and reasonable in the circumstances for a duty of care to be imposed on the defendant. Each limb
of this test requires closer consideration.

(1) The reasonably foreseeable claimant

The test for reasonable foreseeability is objective in nature; it is concerned with what the
reasonable person in the position of the defendant reasonably could have foreseen prior
to the injurious interaction between the parties. The threshold of foreseeability is not
particularly high, envisaging real possibilities rather than probabilities. But the concept
is somewhat malleable in nature. Thus, in *Grieves v FT Everard & Sons*, Lord Hoffmann
stated that the 'answers to a test of foreseeability will vary according to, first, the precise
description of what should have been foreseen and, secondly, the degree of probability
which makes it foreseeable'.[65]

Foreseeability of injury to class of persons What must be reasonably foreseen is the
possibility that, if care is not taken, injury might be caused to a member (or members)
within a certain class of persons.[66] However, in some cases, it will suffice for the court to
focus upon foreseeability of injury to the particular claimant—especially when the facts
are not likely to recur, so that there is no need to generalise about obligations between
classes of person. These propositions follow from the fact that the duty of care is about
legal relations *between persons*. Another point to keep in mind is that foreseeability of
harm to persons, being about future possible consequences of failures in care, is affected
by both the kind of injury in question and by the number of parties involved.[67] Thus,
while foreseeability of directly caused injury often is easy to establish, foreseeability of
indirectly caused injury might be more difficult to establish. To take an example: it is
easily foreseeable that a person's failure to take care in driving a vehicle will cause bodily injury to persons in the immediate vicinity, such as pedestrians. But is it reasonably
foreseeable that a psychiatric illness might be caused to another driver after a minor
prang? Is it reasonably foreseeable that the stricken driver's children will no longer be
able to attend private schools, and that their future earning power will be diminished?

---

[64] [1990] 2 AC 605.   [65] [2008] 1 AC 281, at [29].
[66] See JCP Goldberg and BC Zipursky (1998) 146 U Penn LR 1733, 1838.
[67] See also J Goldberg and BC Zipursky, *The Oxford Introductions to US Law: Torts* (2010), 81.

These are questions the answers to which are less intuitive, and with respect to which judgments about what is reasonably foreseeable become more important.

Illustration The operation of the reasonable foreseeability requirement is neatly illustrated by *Haley v London Electricity Board*.[68] The defendants, acting under statutory authority, dug a trench in the street. They took some measures to help ensure the safety of passers-by, but these precautions catered only to those with decent eyesight. The claimant, who was blind and walking alone, suffered serious injury when he tripped over a long hammer left lying on the ground by the defendants. The House of Lords held that it was incumbent on the defendants to take reasonable care for the safety of all persons using the streets, including the blind and the infirm. The fact that blind persons constitute a small percentage of the population does not make them unforeseeable. As Lord Reid asserted:

> We are all accustomed to meeting blind people walking alone with their white sticks on city pavements ... . I find it quite impossible to say that it is not reasonably foreseeable that a blind person may pass along a particular pavement on a particular day.[69]

As will become apparent in the chapters on breach and remoteness of damage, foreseeability is a component of a number of elements in negligence. The focus is slightly different at each stage. At the duty stage, the *Haley* case assists in underlining that foreseeability is important as an objective test of minimal capacity to comprehend risk of injury *to persons* and in its absence there is no need to go further because no duty of care will be owed.

(2) Proximity

In many instances, the concepts of reasonable foreseeability and proximity might be thought of as informing each other. In the case of road users, for example, the duty of care that is owed is founded, in part, on the fact that one can readily foresee that careless driving by X might result in adverse consequences for innocent driver Y, who was unfortunate enough to be in X's vicinity. But the thing that makes Y a reasonably foreseeable claimant is the fact that she is on the same stretch of road as X at the time of X's careless driving. In other words, Y's proximity (relational and spatial) is a determinant of her reasonable foreseeability.[70]

A distinct requirement However, it is clear that the requirement of proximity is a distinctive limb of the *Caparo* test.[71] The Court of Appeal's decision in *Goodwill v British Pregnancy Advisory Service*[72] illustrates this nicely:

---

[68] [1965] AC 778.   [69] [1965] AC 778, at 791.

[70] It might also be thought that the fact that C was both foreseeable and proximate is what makes it fair, just, and reasonable to impose a duty of care on D. In other words, it could be argued that the three elements are really only 'three facets of the same thing' and 'not to be treated as wholly separate and distinct requirements': see *Marc Rich & Co AG v Bishop Rock Marine Co Ltd* [1996] AC 211, at 235.

[71] This proposition has been denied in Australian cases: eg, *Sullivan v Moody* (2001) 207 CLR 562; *Miller v Miller* [2011] HCA 9, at [59] (the demise in Australian law of proximity 'is now complete'). Instead, the court will examine the 'relations, juxtapositions, situations or conduct or activities' in question!: *Miller v Miller*, at [64].

[72] [1996] 1 WLR 1397. See also *Roe v Minister of Health* [1954] 2 QB 66.

D performed a vasectomy on a man who became C's lover three years later. Knowing that he had had a vasectomy, the couple did not use contraception. But C became pregnant and gave birth to a child. The vasectomy had reversed spontaneously as a very small number of such procedures do. C claimed that D owed her a duty and was negligent in failing to warn her lover of the possibility that he might regain his fertility. Her claim was struck out.

Peter Gibson LJ suggested, *obiter*, that, if the claimant's lover had been her husband or partner, and if the doctor had known that the vasectomy was intended to be as much for her benefit as the patient's, a duty might have been owed to the claimant. But without such a connection between the doctor and the claimant—who was merely one of an indeterminate class of persons with whom the man in question might have had sexual intercourse during his lifetime—the relationship with the defendant was insufficiently proximate for a duty to be imposed on the doctor in her favour.

Definition of proximity As we have seen, the House of Lords in *Caparo Industries plc v Dickman* had concerns about the 'vagueness' of the proximity concept.[73] How to define what constitutes 'proximity'? This issue has been the subject of significant academic debate. One debate has been about whether the proximity limb of the test for duty encompasses both the positive—that is, factual features of the relationship between claimant and defendant—as well as the normative—that is, elements of policy reasoning. This issue has not been authoritatively resolved and is thus a matter for argument. In the present author's view, the position should be viewed in this way: policy factors have influenced the development of the proximity concept; they 'underpin' (in Cane's terminology)[74] the use of the concept in the three-stage test for duty. The main policy behind the use of the concept is the simple one that parties who are proximate to each other usually ought to be careful because of the capacity to harm that such closeness brings with it. This policy is reflective of the internal logic of the structure of the tort of negligence.[75] But policy factors need not be invoked upon the application of the proximity test itself, even if (as is obvious) what constitutes proximity is a matter of judgment. The proximity test is applied simply according to a judgment of the evidence of the facts surrounding the injurious interaction between the parties. If proximity is present between the parties, this will support the recognition of a duty of care; the prerequisite of proximity is fulfilled.

But we still have not answered the question—what *is* proximity? Clearly, proximity, 'neighbourhood', and 'closeness' were intended by Lord Atkin in *Donoghue v Stevenson* to be synonymous concepts. Proximity, we might surmise, is concerned with the factual relationship between the actual parties before the court. Logically, it is concerned with the existence of that relationship *prior to* the alleged failure in care—it is *because of* the proximity between the parties that a duty is recognisable and, where recognised, gives rise to an obligation of care. Proximity is concerned, thus, with the factual relations

---

[73] *Caparo Industries plc v Dickman* [1990] 1 All ER 568, at 574.

[74] P Cane (2004) 120 LQR 189, 192. See also N MacCormick, *Legal Reasoning and Legal Theory* (1978), 263.

[75] C Witting (2007) 71 MLR 621; id (2007) 31 MULR 569.

between the parties which, prior to the injurious interaction between them, signified the real potential for the defendant to cause harm to the claimant. In this way, 'proximity' is the word that we use to indicate the presence of pathways to harm between the parties. These pathways are not restricted to those which signify the potential for physical injury. They might include pathways to other recognised forms of harm.

The judges have not expressly referred to the concept of proximity in this way—and in some instances they have used it in ways which are inconsistent with this view (such as when they mix positive and normative issues).[76] Even so, it is hoped that the conceptualisation of proximity just provided will assist the student in analysing the cases and in thinking through legal problems. But it is important to remember that the mere fact that proximity is present does not automatically entail the recognition of a duty of care. Indeed, below we will look at a class of case (involving omissions) where proximity between the parties frequently is not sufficient to ground a duty. Something more is required.

(3) Fair, just, and reasonable

While in *Anns v Merton London Borough Council* the House of Lords made explicit reference to the role of 'policy', it is apparent in the wake of the *Caparo* case that the same kinds of concern as are embraced by the term 'policy' are now to be considered under the banner of what is 'fair, just, and reasonable'.

Normative reasoning   There is a continuing scholarly debate about this limb of the *Caparo* test for duty of care. On the one hand, Allan Beever believes that there is no need for it.[77] He believes that the duty inquiry is purely a matter of fact-finding: '[t]he duty of care is concerned to link the parties by tracing the defendant's negligence to the claimant'.[78] On the other hand, Jane Stapleton believes that most choices about the imposition of the duty of care are policy choices.[79] Undoubtedly, the 'truth' lies somewhere in the middle of these claims. This is to say that a finding of both foreseeability and proximity does not automatically imply the existence of a duty of care. The judicial function has a *normative* aspect to it; it is concerned with the imposition of desirable norms for the solution of co-ordination problems amongst persons in society,[80] and so the court must make a determination that, in its view, the imposition of a duty would assist in resolving these problems. But this is not to say that the discretion inherent in the application of this element should overwhelm the process of determining the duty

---

[76]   Eg, *Robinson v CC Constable of West Yorkshire Police* [2014] PIQR P14, at [56] (Hallett LJ stating that the term proximity 'has a particular meaning … far beyond mere presence'; it could not be assumed to be established on the basis of physical closeness alone); *Taylor v A Novo (UK) Ltd* [2013] 3 WLR 989, at [28] (Lord Dyson MR saying that 'the concept of proximity depends more on the court's perception of what is the reasonable area for the imposition of liability than any process of logic'—a somewhat circular conception of proximity).

[77]   A Beever, *Rediscovering the Law of Negligence* (2007), 29–30.

[78]   A Beever, *Rediscovering the Law of Negligence* (2007), 129.

[79]   J Stapleton, 'Duty of Care Factors: A Selection from the Judicial Menus' in P Cane and J Stapleton (eds), *The Law of Obligations: Essays in Honour of John Fleming* (1998), ch 4; J Stapleton (2003) 24 Aust Bar Rev 135, at 136. See also WVH Rogers, *Winfield and Jolowicz on Tort* (18th edn, 2010), 181 and 189.

[80]   See C Witting (2007) 71 MLR 621, 630; S Smith (2011) 31 OJLS 215.

of care.[81] As the incremental approach would suggest, the fair, just, and reasonable issue is determined against the background of a *gradual* development of the duty concept—taking it into new areas, or withdrawing it from its current area of operation. Policy should not be used continually to re-make the law on duty.[82]

Impact upon future parties In a thought-provoking paper, Andrew Robertson has argued that policy considerations grouped together under the fair, just, and reasonable limb of the *Caparo* test logically fall into two categories—one that relates to 'justice between the parties'[83] and one that relates to wider, systemic concerns which he terms 'justiciability, community welfare and other non-justice considerations'.[84] Robertson argues that clarity of thought is aided by separating these two kinds of policy. The crucial point concerns the second part of the policy inquiry, which:

> is concerned only with issues going beyond the interests of the parties themselves, such as concerns about the adverse effects that recognition of the duty may have on the legal system or on people's behaviour.[85]

Robertson's framework undoubtedly captures some important ideas about the duty cases, although one *might* object that the distinction between types of 'policy' argument is more apparent than real. To the extent that the court's concern is about the likely consequences of the imposition of a duty of care for future parties, the dispute before it (surely) will be a test case and the issue a live one. This is in accordance with the common law doctrine of precedent. To the extent that the court seeks to determine negligence cases by reference to the potential impact of a decision upon others of whom the parties are *not* representative (but only to this extent), this is a contestable practice. Although United Kingdom courts occasionally have indicated their amenability to prospective rulings (applicable not to the parties before them, but to future parties only),[86] this is not a practice that has been widely accepted.

Typical policy concerns Most of the problematic duty cases that have come before the appellate courts in recent years have been dominated by two broad kinds of policy

---

[81] There is a debate about whether the term 'discretion' is proper. The Master of the Rolls would argue that the matter is one of judgement—'Even though one can qualify it as being a "value" judgment or describe it as a balancing exercise, it raises a question of law, to which, as a matter of principle, and however difficult it may be to resolve, there is only one right answer': *Flood v Times Newspapers Ltd* [2011] 1 WLR 153, at [46] (discussing the role of an appeal court in a case of qualified privilege to defamation). See also ibid at [49] and [107].

[82] The present author's own views on duty are even more particular than those set out in the text. He has argued that 'the presence of substantial pathways to harm between persons ought, ordinarily, to ground a duty of care … . Courts should be wary about using the tort of negligence to achieve policy aims in conflict with negligence law's standards-setting/compensatory rationale, C Witting (2007) 31 MULR 569, 576. See now *Robinson v CC of West Yorkshire Police* 2 WLR 595, which used such reasoning in a case of police negligence.

[83] See, eg, inconsistency with the contractual matrix and unreasonableness of the burden upon the defendant: A Robertson (2011) 127 LQR 370, 380.

[84] (2011) 127 LQR 370, 372. Eg, 'justiciability' and the 'effect on class of potential defendant': ibid at 385–6.

[85] (2011) 127 LQR 370, 371.

[86] *R v Panel on Takeovers and Mergers; ex parte Datafin plc* [1987] QB 815.

issue: whether certain areas of activity (eg, the work of public authorities, or certain professionals) warrant the imposition of a duty of care; and whether the risk of certain kinds of harm (eg, financial loss and psychiatric harm) can be encompassed by the law of negligence. It is in such contexts that arguments about whether it is fair, just, and reasonable to impose duties of care are most likely to surface. And in relation to certain areas of activity, it is mid-level economic and political arguments that come to the fore. Ordinarily, these arguments are concerned with the consequences of the imposition of particular rules on future parties (of whom the parties before the court are representative), relationships, and activities. Policy-based reasoning usually has a predictive element in it—the court tries to determine what the effect of a holding of duty or no duty would be upon these future parties, relations, and activities. This inevitably involves what the courts would term 'experience' and 'judgement'; but what critics might call 'guesswork'.

Frequently encountered policy arguments are derived from various sources. Thus, the courts might be assisted by reference to the: policy evident in relevant statutes,[87] including the Human Rights Act 1998;[88] policy inherent in surrounding case law; and legal 'values' such as individual autonomy (freedom from unwarranted burdens).[89] Typical policy concerns[90] have included such matters as:

(1) the preference for protection of physical interests over the purely psychiatric or purely financial interests;[91]

(2) the preference for protection of vulnerable parties, for example the blind;[92]

(3) the idea that persons generally should take responsibility for their own actions;[93]

(4) the general desire to impose liability upon primarily responsible and not secondarily responsible parties, such as regulatory authorities;[94]

(5) the idea that persons should, where possible, act to protect themselves from loss either by taking appropriate precautions or by self-insuring;[95] and

(6) the need to avoid conflicts between areas of law, for example, that between negligence and defamation law.[96]

Often enough, these policies will pull in different directions and so the question will be on which side of the line the weight of the argument lies.

Illustrations So much for theory. The use of the fair, just, and reasonable test can be illustrated by reference to both its negative use (in denying or limiting the scope of a duty

---

[87] Eg, *Green v Royal Bank of Scotland* [2014] PNLR 6, esp at [30].

[88] Eg, *Campbell v MGN Ltd* [2004] AC 457 (privacy case).

[89] Eg, *Tomlinson v Congleton BC* [2004] 1 AC 46; *Rabone v Pennine Care NHS Trust* [2012] 2 AC 72, at [100] (human rights case).

[90] In addition to the following list, see A Robertson (2012) 32 LS 1 for substantive consideration of various legal policies. [91] *Murphy v Brentwood DC* [1990] 2 All ER 908, 935.

[92] *Haley v London Electricity Board* [1965] AC 778.

[93] *Tomlinson v Congleton BC* [2004] 1 AC 46; *Reeves v Commissioner of Police for the Metropolis* [2000] 1 AC 360, 368. [94] D Nolan (2013) 4 JETL 190; J Stapleton (1995) 111 LQR 301.

[95] Eg, PS Atiyah, *The Damages Lottery* (1997). [96] *Spring v Guardian Assurance plc* [1995] 2 AC 296.

of care) and its positive use (in recognising a duty of care). Cases falling within the former category include *Marc Rich & Co AG v Bishop Rock Marine Co Ltd*,[97] the facts of which have been noted already. The House of Lords held that no duty was owed by the defendant classification society to a cargo owner whose claim in damages had been limited to an amount fixed according to an international maritime convention. Their Lordships conceded that the requirements of foreseeability and proximity were satisfied, yet held ultimately that it was not fair, just, and reasonable to impose a duty of care. Their Lordships noted that a delicate balance of risks was established by the convention in question, and that the recognition of a duty of care would subvert that balance with severe potential consequences for both marine insurance and freight costs. It was pointed out, also, that the imposition of a duty of care might lead to classification societies refusing to survey high-risk vessels in the future with potentially harmful consequences for public safety at sea.[98]

As mentioned earlier, considerations of fairness, justice, and reasonableness can be employed also to ground the *imposition* of a duty of care; either in circumstances in which no such duty has existed previously, or in circumstances where a duty has been denied.[99] In *White v Jones*,[100] for example, the facts were as follows:

> D, a solicitor, was instructed by a testator to draw up a new will to replace an earlier one. Due to D's negligence, the new will had not been drafted by the time the testator died. Under the new will, unlike the old one, the testator's daughters would have been named as beneficiaries. The testator's daughters therefore mounted an action in negligence against D alleging that his negligence had cost them their inheritance.

By a majority of three to two, the House of Lords held that the daughters were owed a duty of care. The foreseeability of the daughters' loss was not doubted. Equally, in recognising the solicitor's assumption of a responsibility to draft a replacement will, their Lordships were satisfied that the requirement of a relationship of proximity between the defendant and the claimants existed.[101] But their Lordships ran up (among other things)[102] against the problem that the case involved an omission to act on the part of the solicitor. As we are about to see, the courts generally are loath to impose liability in cases of nonfeasance. However, Lord Goff noted several practical reasons why a duty should be imposed, each clearly rooted in considerations of fairness and justice. These encompassed the law's recognition of the importance of legacies, the role played by solicitors in ensuring that testamentary intentions are fulfilled, and the need to ensure that a remedy is available to the most appropriate parties.[103]

While *White v Jones* constitutes an example of the courts invoking the fair, just, and reasonable test in order to justify the creation of a *new duty-situation*,[104] the decision of the House of Lords in *Arthur JS Hall & Co v Simons* goes one step further by employing it to justify the imposition of a duty of care on advocates who, formerly, had enjoyed

---

[97] [1996] AC 211. See also *White v Jones* [1995] 2 AC 207.
[98] Cf *Perrett v Collins* [1998] 2 Lloyd's Rep 255.   [99] See *Stovin v Wise* [1996] AC 923, at 949.
[100] [1995] 2 AC 207.   [101] This is questionable: see J Murphy [1996] CLJ 43.
[102] See P Benson, 'Should *White v Jones* Represent Canadian Law? A Return to First Principles' in JW Neyers et al (eds), *Emerging Issues in Tort Law* (2007), ch 6.   [103] [1995] 2 AC 207, at 259–60.
[104] To like effect, see also *Spring v Guardian Assurance plc* [1995] 2 AC 296.

a well-established immunity in respect of their conduct of (at least civil) litigation on a client's behalf. In removing that immunity, Lord Hobhouse declared that, in the civil justice system, 'the legitimate interest of the client, the appropriateness of the tort remedy and the absence of clear or sufficient justification all militate against the recognition of an advocate immunity'.[105]

(4) Omissions example

In order to give further substance to the preceding discussion (and before moving on to chapters dealing with various other duty categories), it might pay to consider a duty category in which matters of both proximity and policy have been important—that concerning omissions. The significance of the omissions example lies, in part, in demonstrating that, where a duty of care is recognised, it bridges a conceptual gap between persons involved in an injurious interaction, who are just as likely to be strangers as acquaintances, and creates a basis for legal intervention by the courts in circumstances where there was no prior relationship. It grounds the courts' jurisdiction to intervene.

Categorisation A first point to note is that it is not always easy to classify the defendant's 'contribution' to an injurious interaction as an omission ('nonfeasance') rather than positive conduct ('misfeasance'). Although omissions involve an absence of conduct somewhere in the events leading up to the injurious interaction, accuracy in categorisation requires the court to look at matters in their full factual and relational context. For example, the question might arise whether failing to apply the brakes of a car at a red traffic light is an omission to act, or the positive act of sub-standard driving?[106] Almost certainly it is the latter. Yet a failure to repair expeditiously a breached sea wall such that subsequent flooding to a claimant occurred was not misfeasance. The threat posed by the breach in the sea wall had arisen naturally and the defendants' duty did not stretch to the prevention of future damage for which they were not responsible. Nor were they under a duty to shorten the period in which such damage could occur.[107]

Proximity not decisive In *Stovin v Wise* Lord Nicholls declared it to be 'one matter to require a person to take care if he embarks on a course of conduct which may harm others. It is another matter to require a person, who is doing nothing[,] to take positive action to protect others from harm for which he is not responsible.'[108] An omission to act generally will not give rise to the tort of negligence, however readily foreseeable the harm to the claimant.[109] Indeed, a mere fortuitous physical proximity between the

---

[105] [2002] 1 AC 615, at 749–50.

[106] In *Johnson v Rea Ltd* [1962] 1 QB 373, Ds (who were stevedores), without lack of care, dropped soda ash on a surface over which they subsequently invited C to pass. It was held that D had a duty to take care that the surface was safe, and the failure to remove the ash was actionable. But was this an omission or merely negligence in a chain of positive conduct beginning with the unloading of the bags of soda ash? See also *Kane v New Forest DC* [2001] 3 All ER 914.   [107] *East Suffolk Rivers Catchment Board v Kent* [1941] AC 74, at 105.

[108] [1996] AC 923, at 930.

[109] *Sutradhar v NERC* [2006] 4 All ER 490; *Glaister v Appelby-in-Westmorland Town Council* [2010] PIQR P6.

parties is insufficient to create a positive duty, as is mere knowledge of a source of danger created by someone else.[110]

In a two-party scenario, a passer-by who stands and watches a child drown in a shallow pool of water is under a negative obligation not to harm the child through her actions. But this is not the relevant issue in an omissions case. The issue is whether there is a positive duty to act, and save the child from drowning, and here the law is clear that the passer-by is not liable for *failing to intervene* to save the child, even though she could do so at minimal risk to herself. A 'Bad Samaritan', who neglects even to summon aid to the victims of a road accident and prioritises getting to work on time, is not liable for her omission.[111]

The same rule applies, a fortiori, in three-party scenarios. Thus, an omission to warn a next-door neighbour that she has left a door open, or a failure to telephone the police when you see a suspicious person in her garden, results in no liability on your part for the burglary committed by that person. Mere ability to prevent injury does not entail responsibility for it. Consider *Perl (P) (Exporters) Ltd v Camden LBC*:[112]

> The local authority owned a block of flats, the basement flat of which was unoccupied. Cs were tenants of an adjoining flat. The empty flat was left unsecured and there had been several burglaries in the area. Burglars entered the empty flat, knocked a hole through the 18-inch common wall and stole Cs' property.

The Court of Appeal found that the authority owed the claimants no duty of care in respect of the loss inflicted by the burglary. The relationship of neighbouring property owners of itself was not sufficiently 'special' to justify the imposition of a duty of care to guard the claimants against the foreseeable risk of burglary by way of an unsecured property.[113] Similarly, in *Smith v Littlewoods Organisation Ltd*[114] the House of Lords rejected a claim for damage caused by a fire started by vandals in a disused cinema owned by the defendants that spread to the claimants' property.[115]

Policy For good or ill, English law, which favours individual autonomy over the bonds of community,[116] imposes no duty to rescue others from harm.[117] In *Stovin v Wise*, Lord Hoffmann justified the rule against liability for pure omissions according to an array of political, moral, and economic arguments:

---

[110] See *Stovin v Wise* [1996] AC 923.

[111] Although this seems like a harsh—not to say immoral—rule, it can be said safely that few children have drowned on account of it. Indeed, this aspect of the omissions rule is famous for both its academic interest and its practical irrelevance.   [112] [1984] QB 342.

[113] In *Stansbie v Troman* [1948] 2 KB 48, by contrast, a decorator engaged by the claimant left the door of the claimant's house open while he went to get wallpaper. In his absence, a thief entered the house and stole a diamond bracelet and some clothes. The Court of Appeal held that a duty existed in this case, and that the decorator was liable for the claimant's loss.   [114] [1987] 1 All ER 710.

[115] However, the situation might be different when the defendant with control also had a greatly superior ability to identify the particular risks of harm in question.

[116] *Reeves v Commissioner of Police of the Metropolis* [2000] 1 AC 360, 368.

[117] Such a duty is imposed in a number of civil law systems: see *Smith v Littlewoods Organisation Ltd* [1987] 1 All ER 710, at 729.

In political terms it is less of an invasion of an individual's freedom for the law to require him to consider the safety of others in his actions than to impose upon him a duty to rescue or protect. A moral version of this point may be called the 'Why pick on me?' argument. A duty to prevent harm to others or to render assistance to a person in danger or distress may apply to a large and indeterminate class of people who happen to be able to do something. Why should one be held liable rather than another? In economic terms, the efficient allocation of resources usually requires [that] an activity should bear its own costs. If it benefits from being able to impose some of its costs on other people (what economists call 'externalities') the market is distorted because the activity appears cheaper than it really is. So liability to pay compensation for loss caused by negligent conduct acts as a deterrent against increasing the cost of the activity to the community and reduces externalities. But there is no similar justification for requiring a person who is not doing anything to spend money on behalf of someone else.[118]

Individuals are not subject to any general duty to protect their 'neighbours' from others' tortious conduct. And, as we have seen, this is so even where the loss or injury in question is readily foreseeable and preventable.[119] Thus, the Court of Appeal in *Glaister v Appelby-in-Westmorland Town Council*, referring to three-party omissions cases, stated that:

A defendant, D, is not ordinarily liable to a claimant, C, for personal injuries or physical damage caused by the negligence of a third person, T, merely because D could have foreseen and prevented it. Something more is required to place on D a duty to protect C from the consequences of foreseeable negligence on the part of T.[120]

In *Michael v Chief Constable of South Wales Police*, the Supreme Court held that there are two general exceptions to this position:

The first is where D was in a position of control over [a third party] T and should have foreseen the likelihood of T causing damage to somebody in close proximity if D failed to take reasonable care in the exercise of that control … . The second general exception applies where D assumes a positive responsibility to safeguard C … . It embraces the relationships in which a duty to take positive action typically arises: contract, fiduciary relationships, employer and employee, school and pupil, health professional and patient.[121]

Although there will be cases of overlap, most of the cases in which duties of care have been recognised can be categorised in either one or the other of these exceptions to the default rule of no-liability. Let us examine some examples.

Exercise of control The cases demonstrate that, when the defendant has the right to control the conduct of the third party, a failure of control resulting in the very kind of

---

[118] [1996] AC 923, at 943–4. Cf E Weinrib (1981) 90 Yale LJ 247; T Honoré, 'Are Omissions Less Culpable?' in P Cane and J Stapleton (eds), *Essays for Patrick Atiyah* (1991), 31ff; A Simester (1995) 1 Legal Theory 311; A Beever, *Rediscovering the Law of Negligence* (2007), 205–10.

[119] *Weld-Blundell v Stephens* [1920] AC 956, at 986; *Smith v Leurs* (1945) 70 CLR 256, at 261–2; *Glaister v Appelby-in-Westmorland Town Council* [2010] PIQR P6, at [45].

[120] *Glaister v Appelby-in-Westmorland Town Council* [2010] PIQR P6, at [45].

[121] [2015] AC 1732, at [99]–[100].

damage likely to result from lack of control might be actionable by the claimant. Thus, when parents or teachers fail to supervise young children adequately, they might be in breach of a duty not only to the child if she injures herself, but also to any other person injured by intentional or negligent wrongdoing by that child.[122]

In *Home Office v Dorset Yacht Co Ltd*,[123] the Home Office's contention that no duty of care could arise in the case of a wrong committed by a person of full age and capacity who was not the servant of, or acting on behalf of, the defendant, failed. The statutory duty to control the detainees was the source of a duty of care to those at immediate risk of loss or damage from any negligent failure to exercise carefully that control. The duty placed the borstal officers in a 'special relationship' with the detainees which, coupled with the existence of an identifiable and determinate class of potential victims (the yacht owners) gave rise to the duty owed to the latter.[124] This was because, in the words of Lord Pearson, 'control imports responsibility'.[125] And in this context, the 'responsibility' was that of the officers towards those members of the public whose property borstal boys attempting an escape foreseeably would affect adversely.[126] In other words, 'responsibility' was synonymous with the required relationship of proximity. Similarly, Lord Diplock was of the view that the critical factor was the relationship of proximity between the officers and the yacht owners. He said:

> To give rise to a duty on the part of the custodian owed to a member of the public to take reasonable care to prevent a borstal trainee from escaping from his custody before completion of the trainee's sentence there should be some special relationship between the custodian and the person to whom the duty is owed which exposes that person to a particular risk of damage in consequence of that escape which is different in its incidence from the general risk of damage from criminal acts of others which he shares with all members of the public.[127]

Assumption of responsibility Again, there are clear examples falling in the second exceptional category of omissions case mentioned in *Michael v Chief Constable of South Wales Police*. If a hospital admits a patient, a duty to provide care then arises. Similarly,

---

[122] Eg, when lack of supervision allows a child to stray on to a road where a driver is injured swerving to avoid him: *Carmarthenshire CC v Lewis* [1955] AC 549.   [123] [1970] AC 1004.

[124] Note that it was not the statutory duty alone that gave rise to the common law duty. This is because, as Lord Hoffmann explained in general terms in *Commissioners of Customs and Excise v Barclays Bank plc* [2007] 1 AC 181, at [39]: '[a] statute either creates a statutory duty or it does not … . But you cannot derive a common law duty of care directly from a statute.'   [125] [1970] AC 1004, at 1055.

[126] Proximity was absent where the mother of a serial killer's last victim sought on behalf of her daughter's estate to sue the police for negligence in failing to apprehend the killer earlier: *Hill v CC of West Yorkshire* [1989] AC 53. Unlike the Home Office in Dorset Yacht, there was, before his arrest, no right vested in the police to control the killer's conduct; nor was there anything to distinguish Miss Hill from any other member of the public. Moreover, the courts are reluctant to recognise a duty of care which would require protection of individuals from identifiable persons: eg, *Smith v CC of Sussex Police* [2009] 1 AC 225. In *Michael v Chief Constable of South Wales Police* [2015] AC 1732, [120], Lord Toulson explained that this was because the relationship between the police and the eventual victim invariably would not be close enough (or sufficiently proximate) for the imposition of a private law duty of care. Given these shortcomings in negligence, claimants are beginning to bring claims under the Human Rights Act 1998: eg, *Sarjantson v CC of Humberside Police* [2014] 1 All ER 960.   [127] [1970] AC 1004, at 1070.

a general practitioner who has accepted a patient on to her NHS list might be liable if, later, she omits negligently to treat the patient, refusing to visit him, or turning him away from the surgery. Accepting responsibility for the patient's NHS care imposes a positive duty to act. (But if a doctor simply 'happened to witness a road accident' there would be no duty since the doctor, in the absence of a previous relationship with the accident victim 'is not under any legal obligation to [provide assistance]'.[128]) And, similarly, as *Kent v Griffiths*[129] illustrates, if an ambulance service accepts an emergency call, this is viewed as an undertaking of responsibility, and a duty of care arises between the ambulance service and the person in need of attention. As Stuart-Smith LJ explained in *Capital and Counties plc v Hampshire County Council*:

> As a general rule a sufficient relationship of proximity will exist when someone possessed of a special skill undertakes to apply that skill for the assistance of another person who relies upon such skill and there is direct and substantial reliance by the plaintiff on the defendant's skill.[130]

It is notable that undertakings other than those associated with persons of special skill seem now also to suffice. Consider *Barrett v Ministry of Defence*.[131] A sailor drank himself insensible and later asphyxiated on his own vomit after being put in his bunk at a remote base. The Court of Appeal held that the Navy owed no general duty to prevent him abusing alcohol. But, when colleagues put him in his bunk, the Navy had undertaken responsibility (vicariously) for his welfare once he could no longer care for himself. Similarly, a duty arose to supervise a drunken soldier after an army commander organised an evening's drinking and transportation home.[132]

(B) Incrementalism

So far in this section, dealing with modern approaches to duty of care, we have considered the duty framework set out in *Caparo plc v Dickman*. But, as mentioned earlier, superior courts have endorsed other approaches as well. Indeed, we have already noted that, in the *Caparo* case, the House of Lords approved Brennan J's dictum in *Sutherland Shire Council v Heyman* suggesting that '[i]t is preferable ... that the law should develop novel categories of negligence incrementally and by analogy with established categories'.[133] But we have yet to explore the nature of this incremental approach, and its relationship with the three-stage test that emerged from the *Caparo* decision. In *Perrett v Collins*, a case in which a certificate of airworthiness was negligently issued in respect of a light aircraft, with the consequence that a passenger in it was subsequently injured, Hobhouse LJ said:

---

[128] *Capital and Counties plc v Hampshire CC* [1997] QB 1004, at 1060 (*obiter*).
[129] *Kent v Griffiths* [2001] QB 36. See also *Reeves v MPC* [2001] 1 AC 360.
[130] *Capital and Counties plc v Hampshire CC* [1997] QB 1004, at 1060. See also *White v Jones* [1995] 2 AC 207.
[131] [1995] 3 All ER 87.
[132] *Jebson v Ministry of Defence* [2000] 1 WLR 2055. In *Reeves v MPC* [2000] 1 AC 360 it was held that the police might owe a duty to even a sane person placed in their cells where it is foreseeable that the prisoner may attempt suicide. But the risk of suicide must be foreseeable: see *Orange v CC of West Yorkshire* [2002] QB 347.
[133] (1985) 60 ALR 1, at 43–4.

> It is a truism to say that any case must be decided taking into account the circumstances ...,
> but where those circumstances comply with established categories of liability, a defendant
> should not be allowed to seek to escape from liability by appealing to some vaguer con-
> cept of justice or fairness; the law cannot be re-made for every case. Indeed, the previous
> authorities have by necessary implication held that it is fair, just and reasonable that the
> [claimant] should recover in the situations falling within the principles they have applied.
> Accordingly, if the present case is covered by the decisions in, or the principles recognised
> by, previous authorities—and it is ... we remain bound to follow them.[134]

It is clear from this passage that his Lordship envisaged that the three-stage test could be
ousted in circumstances where an incremental step beyond existing authorities could
be taken. Such an approach seeks to guarantee a measure of consistency in the ever-
growing body of case law by adherence to the doctrine of precedent. But it is questionable whether this approach is a rival to the three-limbed *Caparo* test. For while it is
consonant with the technique of analogical reasoning so central to the common law,
it does not tell us how far any given incremental step may take us beyond the decided
cases. Ultimately, therefore, the courts will have recourse to concepts such as justice and
reasonableness in order to set the limits to what amounts to legitimate incrementalism.
In doing so, they are applying effectively (the third stage of) the *Caparo* test to which
incrementalism is said to be an alternative. Where the instant case is closely analogous
to a previously decided case in which a duty has been imposed, all the court is doing is
assuming that the foreseeability and proximity requirements probably are satisfied in
the case before it, and simply asking whether it is fair, just, and reasonable to extend the
duty of care by the marginal amount required in order to cover the particular facts of
the case.[135]

(C) Assumption of responsibility

There is another approach to duty of care which is said to be a rival to the *Caparo* three-
stage test. This involves use of 'assumption of responsibility' reasoning.

Recent origins In *Hedley Byrne & Co Ltd v Heller & Partners Ltd*,[136] the House of Lords
recognised the possibility of negligence liability in respect of negligent misstatements
when a defendant 'voluntarily assumes' responsibility for the accuracy of a statement
made to a claimant in circumstances where a special relationship exists between them
and the claimant places reasonable reliance on the accuracy of the statement. While this
approach can be explained upon the basis of concern in that case about the potential
for negligence liability to undermine the sanctity of contractual relations, the phrase
'assumption of responsibility' would appear to make sense only in those cases where

---

[134] [1998] 2 Lloyd's Rep 255, at 263.
[135] See now *Robinson v CC of West Yorkshire Police* [2018] 2 WLR 595. And for an explicit confirmation that
the two tests may be used together (with recourse also to the 'assumption of responsibility' test), see *Commissioners of Customs and Excise v Barclays Bank plc* [2007] 1 AC 181. [136] [1964] AC 465.

there is a voluntary, subjective acceptance of legal obligations towards the claimant. The problem is that the courts have sought to apply the test in an objective, all-things-considered, way.

Relationship to *Caparo* test The relationship between the *Caparo* three-stage test for duty and that of 'assumption of responsibility' was the subject of discussion by the House of Lords in *Commissioners of Customs and Excise v Barclays Bank plc*,[137] the purport of which was that the former encompasses the latter. It was observed that the 'test' for an assumption of responsibility is now seen as objective in nature, not depending upon the subjective attitude of the defendant.[138] Rather, in conformity with the approach of Lord Steyn in *Williams v Natural Life Health Foods Ltd*, the court will examine the exchanges that 'cross the line' between the parties.[139] This is very similar to the exercise of determining whether there is proximity between them. *Ipso facto* it makes sense to view 'assumption of responsibility' as a type of proximity,[140] ordinarily of importance in misstatement and negligent provision of service cases. Where an 'assumption of responsibility' is apparent, there is no need to look for any further indication of proximity between the parties.[141] But it is important to acknowledge, the House of Lords indicated, that both of these are organising concepts, which direct consideration to the more detailed factors that link the parties one to the other.[142] Furthermore, in most cases it is likely to be unnecessary to consider the third stage of the *Caparo* test where the assumption of responsibility test is satisfied; such a finding will itself speak of the fairness of imposing a duty of care.[143]

Continued usage Despite concern about the defensibility of the assumption of responsibility test, it has continued to be invoked—even in cases where the loss in question was personal injury.[144] This was the position in *Chandler v Cape plc*,[145] where the issue was whether a parent company owed a duty of care to an employee of its subsidiary company, who had been exposed to asbestos in the workplace and suffered the lung disease asbestosis. The claimant employee could not sue the subsidiary because it had been dissolved. Although the *Caparo* three-stage test was the logical test to be applied in this case, it appears that the assumption of responsibility test was invoked by analogy with *Williams v Natural Life Health Foods Ltd*[146] because of judicial concerns about making shareholders (in this case, the parent company) liable for the debts of the company in which they invest. Even so, Arden LJ recognised that the term 'assumption of responsibility' is a misnomer and that the law is, more accurately, concerned with the 'attachment' of responsibility by the courts.[147] This is on the basis, no doubt correct,

---

[137] [2007] 1 AC 181.   [138] [2007] 1 AC 181, at [5], [35], and [86].   [139] [1998] 1 WLR 829, at 835.

[140] *Customs & Excise* [2007] 1 AC 181, at [5], [35], and [73].

[141] *Customs & Excise* [2007] 1 AC 181, at [4]. By contrast, where there is no assumption of responsibility, the court will apply a more general test of proximity: ibid at [87].

[142] *Customs & Excise* [2007] 1 AC 181, at [83].   [143] *Customs & Excise* [2007] 1 AC 181, at [35] and [93].

[144] See A Robertson and J Wang, 'The Assumption of Responsibility' in K Barker, R Grantham, and W Swain (eds), *The Law of Misstatements* (2015), ch 3.   [145] [2011] 1 WLR 3011.

[146] [1998] 1 WLR 829.   [147] *Chandler v Cape plc* [2011] 1 WLR 3011, at [64].

that '[w]hether a party has assumed responsibility is a question of law'.[148] The Court of Appeal found a duty of care to be owed on the basis of what were, in reality, proximity factors, especially those of control over operations and superior expertise in matters of health and safety.[149]

Suggested role It is submitted that the assumption of responsibility test is of real relevance in those few cases in which the evidence suggests that the defendant has voluntarily, subjectively assumed a responsibility for certain legal obligations owed to the claimant. In such a case, a court is able to recognise the existence of a duty of care consistent with the defendant's intentions. In all other cases, the law should focus upon application of the *Caparo* three-stage test—and this goes for financial losses just as much as for other types of loss. To retain an 'objective' version of the assumption of responsibility test alongside *Caparo* is simply unnecessary and productive of confusion.[150]

(D) Scope of duty

Where a duty of care between certain classes of person is established, it will be subject inevitably to limits on its scope. This is to say that the duty will not be imposed for the general benefit of the claimant: in some cases it will be imposed in respect of a certain type of activity or a certain type of loss. The reason why this concept is treated as a matter of duty, rather than of standard and breach or remoteness, is that it is expressed with reference to classes of person—and is not fact-dependent in the way that the issues of the appropriate standard of care and remoteness are.[151]

Activities The duty of care recognised in a particular case will apply to some (the relevant) activities, but not to all of them. *Mitchell v Glasgow City Council*[152] illustrates that a landlord owes a duty of restricted scope to his tenant. The duty will include, inter alia, an obligation to let premises which are habitable and safe for occupation.[153] The question was whether the landlord, the defendant council, was required to warn a tenant, the claimant, of the fact that it had arranged a meeting with the claimant's neighbour, who was violent and abusive and whom the defendant was seeking to relocate after numerous nasty disputes between the neighbours. Consistent with *Smith v Littlewoods*, discussed earlier, it was held that the duty of care which was owed by the defendant to the claimant, as its tenant, did not extend to protecting him from the acts of a third-party criminal.[154] It was noted that the defendant had provided no undertaking to warn;[155] and a host of policy reasons were invoked, which need not be rehearsed here.

---

[148] [2011] 1 WLR 3011, at [64].   [149] [2011] 1 WLR 3011, at [80].
[150] See, further, C Witting, 'What are We Doing Here? The Relationship between Negligence in General and Misstatements in English Law' in K Barker, R Grantham, and W Swain (eds), *The Law of Misstatements* (2015), ch 9.   [151] This point was made clear in *Hughes-Holland v BPE Solicitors* [2017] 2 WLR 1029, at [53].
[152] [2009] 1 AC 874.   [153] Landlord and Tenant Act 1985, ss 8 and 10; Housing Act 2004.
[154] [2009] 1 AC 874, at [26]–[28], [41], [62], [77], and [82].
[155] [2009] 1 AC 874, at [29], [63], and [83].

Further cases illustrate the proposition that any duty of care will be restricted to certain kinds of activity. In *Hughes-Holland v BPE Solicitors*,[156] it was held that a firm of solicitors retained to draw up a facility agreement and charge for a loan transaction, and to confirm one point about it among a host of other considerations, had no obligation to provide additional advice about the commercial merits of the transaction. Lord Sumption stated that, in a case such as this, 'a professional adviser contributes a limited part of the material on which his client will rely in deciding whether to enter into a prospective transaction, but the process of identifying the other relevant considerations and the overall assessment of the commercial merits of the transaction are exclusively matters for the client (or possibly other advisers)'.[157] Although closer to the borderline, it was held in *Swain Mason v Mills & Reeve (a firm)*[158] that a firm of solicitors retained to advise a businessman about the sale of shares in a company had no obligation to provide additional advice about the inheritance tax consequences of the transaction in circumstances where the firm was informed that the businessman was to undergo heart surgery. The latter case illustrates the importance of the terms of any relevant contractual retainer in determining the scope of a duty of care in negligence, especially given the fact that a client will ordinarily pay for a restricted number of professional services only (as to which, see also chapter 4).

Kinds of loss Again, the scope of a duty might be limited to certain kinds of loss and not others. The concept is most obviously suited to discussion of obligations with respect to kinds of *primary* loss, rather than with respect to *consequential* losses, given that all kinds of consequential loss are recoverable pursuant to the suffering of primary loss to a recognised interest. (Despite this, there are instances of courts using the scope of duty concept to discuss recovery of consequential losses.[159]) While a defendant might be under a duty to protect the claimant from personal injury, she might not be under a similar duty in respect of merely financial loss.[160] A general practitioner advising her patient on treatment for his heart condition and high blood pressure owes a duty to safeguard that patient's health, but will not be liable for the financial loss caused to the patient if she also gives him an unsuccessful tip for the Grand National and the horse comes in last!

Conclusions

The aim of this chapter has been to indicate something of the history of the duty of care in negligence, and to outline the frameworks by which courts determine novel duty of care cases. As we have seen, the main framework involves application of the three-stages from *Caparo Industries v Dickman*, involving foreseeability of harm to classes of person, proximity (or pathways to harm between the actual claimant and

---

[156] [2017] 2 WLR 1029.   [157] [2017] 2 WLR 1029, at [41].   [158] [2012] EWCA Civ 498.
[159] Eg, *Network Rail Infrastructure Ltd v Conarken Group Ltd* [2011] 135 Con LR 1.
[160] *Desmond v CC of Nottinghamshire Police* [2011] EWCA Civ 2, at [35].

defendant), and a forward-looking policy assessment. As we saw in *Michael v Chief Constable of South Wales Police*, courts prefer to reason by analogy and to build on existing duty categories—this being known as the 'incremental' approach. Rarely will they make conceptual leaps from an existing duty category into the unknown. Moreover, in some types of case—especially involving purely financial loss, as we shall see—courts will look for a strong kind of proximity linking the claimant and defendant through the latter's 'assumption of responsibility' to the former. But, as the *Michael* case makes clear, it is necessary to utilise the duty of care framework only when there is no existing authority on the matter. In the next chapters, we examine the duty of care authorities in various established categories of case.

Problem question

June lives next door to Amanda. June knows that Amanda, who is the parent of a two-year-old infant, frequently drinks to excess. In the past, June had to call the police when she found Amanda drunk in her front garden. Last week, June heard continual screams coming from the room in Amanda's house in which her infant son, Gregory, slept. June also observed that Amanda's front door had been left open for two days. But June did nothing about these things. Eventually, Amanda's parents discovered that Amanda had abandoned her home. They found Gregory in his room filthy and malnourished. As a result, Gregory suffered from a bowel condition and impaired vision.

Explain whether or not June owed a duty of care to Gregory.

 Visit **http://www.oup.com/uk/street15e/** for answer guidance.

Further reading

Beever, *Rediscovering the Law of Negligence* (2007)

Honoré, 'Are Omissions Less Culpable?' in Cane and Stapleton (eds), *Essays for Patrick Atiyah* (1991)

Merkin and Steele, *Insurance and the Law of Obligations* (2013)

Nolan, 'Deconstructing the Duty of Care' (2013) 129 *Law Quarterly Review* 559

Perry, 'The Role of Duty of Care in a Rights-Based Theory of Negligence Law' in Robertson and Tang (eds), *The Goals of Private Law* (2009), ch 4

Plunkett, *The Duty of Care in Negligence* (2018)

Robertson, 'Justice, Community Welfare and the Duty of Care' (2011) 127 *Law Quarterly Review* 370

Robertson, 'On the Function of the Law of Negligence' (2013) 33 *Oxford Journal of Legal Studies* 31

Stapleton, 'Duty of Care Factors: A Selection from the Judicial Menus' in Cane and Stapleton (eds), *The Law of Obligations: Essays in Honour of John Fleming* (1998)

Witting, 'Duty of Care: An Analytical Approach' (2005) 25 *Oxford Journal of Legal Studies* 33

3

Duty of care II: bodily injury and psychiatric illness

KEY ISSUES

(1) Primary and consequential losses
This chapter commences our discussion of the kinds of interest which tort law protects through the recognition of duties of care in negligence. The focus at the duty stage is upon primary losses—that is, upon the initial kind of injury sustained as a result of a failure to take care. The concern is not with those injuries that flow as a consequence of the primary loss sustained.

(2) Bodily injury
The law offers a high degree of protection to interests in bodily integrity, and the law of negligence is no exception. Given that cases of negligence giving rise to bodily injury typically involve external impacts or the introduction of a mechanism of physical change, the imposition of a duty of care ordinarily turns on the foreseeability of physical injury.

(3) Pregnancy and birth
Lawmakers have had to contend with difficult cases involving negligence claims: by the parents having to support 'unwanted' children;

and by children suffering from disabilities inflicted while in utero. While statute permits actions by the child (when born alive) in the latter kind of case, in the former kind of case the courts have denied damages to the parents for the costs of bringing up 'unwanted' children; the parents simply are awarded a fixed sum signifying that a wrong has been done to them by doctors or prescribers of contraceptives who have failed to prevent conception.

(4) Psychiatric illness
Psychiatric illness cases have been divided into those concerning persons within the area of physical harm, termed 'primary victims', and those who have suffered illness, known as 'secondary victims', as a result of witnessing the death, injury, or imperilment of intermediate parties,. The courts have been amenable to primary victim claims, but have insisted upon the presence of several proximity links between the parties in secondary victim cases.

Section 1 Introduction

Categories of duty Having set out, in chapter 2, the framework for determining how new duties of care are recognised in English law,[1] we move now to consider some initial duty of care 'categories' in the tort of negligence. Categorisation of types of problem permits us to bring together cases with similar factual situations (including proximity factors), and to analyse them against the background of policy issues that attend such situations. Our treatment of the duty categories in this and subsequent chapters indicates how far the courts have gone in recognising duties of care in those types of fact situation considered. In some cases, courts have established liberal rules that reflect the importance of the interests protected in those fact situations. In other cases, courts offer little or no protection. This reflects the existence of a 'hierarchy' of protected interests in tort law (considered in chapter 2). As a general proposition, a duty of care will be recognised more readily with respect to threats to physical integrity, whether of person or property, than with respect to either mental or financial interests.[2]

Primary losses In categorising duty cases, we must be careful to distinguish between 'primary losses' and 'consequential losses'. The focus is upon 'primary losses'—that is, upon the *initial* kinds of injury sustained as a result of failures to take care. In a road accident, for example, the initial kind of injury is likely to be physical in nature (broken legs, perhaps). It is the initial, physical injuries that determine the duty category to be applied, and this is so whether or not there are further losses which flow because of those physical injuries—such as psychiatric illness and/or financial losses. The concern at the duty stage is not with those injuries that flow merely as a consequence of primary losses, these consequential losses being limited not by duty rules but by the rules of causation and remoteness (considered in chapter 7). However, at this stage we might note that the law is quite accepting of claims for both psychiatric illness and financial losses that are consequential upon physical losses. The latter are recoverable (as are all consequential losses) insofar as they are reasonably foreseeable.[3]

New primary loss categories Lawyers are always attempting to test the limits of actionability by extending duties of care to cover new forms of primary loss. The advent of the Human Rights Act 1998 and protection under the European Convention on Human Rights have been catalysts for such arguments. These have extended beyond development of public authority liability (considered in chapter 5) to claims about the

---

[1] For some alternative approaches, see, eg, *Cooper v Hobart* [2001] 3 SCR 537 (Canada); *Sullivan v Moody* (2001) 207 CLR 562 (Australia); *Spandeck Engineering (S) Pte Ltd v Defence Science and Technology Agency* [2007] 4 SLR(R) 100 (Singapore).

[2] See, eg, *Murphy v Brentwood DC* [1991] 1 AC 398, at 487; *An Informer v A Chief Constable* [2013] QB 579, at [76].

[3] This is to say that the English law appears to be that both the initial loss and the consequential loss must be foreseeable: *Robinson v Post Office* [1974] 2 All ER 737. However, there is much to be said for the New Zealand rule, which is that no such foreseeability test applies to consequential losses: *Stephenson v Waite Tileman Ltd* [1973] 1 NZLR 152. The latter rule prevents over-analysis of cases involving cascading consequences.

appropriate 'horizontal' development of the common law; that is, the law as it is applicable between private parties. In recent times, for example, claims for extended protection in negligence have been made with respect to such interests as personal 'autonomy' and educational development.[4] One issue is whether such claims are best addressed as new protected interests, or by reference to pre-existing categories of loss.[5] Claims for negligent failure to promote the educational development of children, for example, might be best analysed in terms of diminished earning capacity, or expenditure on remedial lessons (both purely financial losses). The argument against this approach is that existing categories of damage are too limited and in need of expansion. The argument might be, for example, that the failure of a public authority or school to promote the educational development of the child results in more than just financial loss—that is, in literary, artistic, and social deprivation.[6] While this might be true, we need to keep in mind that neither tort law, nor the law of negligence, is a solution for all social ills. The law of negligence might not be extended to cover these kinds of loss because of its essentially modest aims and prosaic nature.[7] In such circumstances, protection will have to be found elsewhere in the law.

Section 2 Harm to persons

In this chapter, we will be concerned principally to examine categories of duty of care concerned with the bodily integrity of persons and interests closely allied to the integrity of persons. The primary losses considered are various kinds of bodily injury and psychiatric illness. In this particular section, we will consider the following issues: what constitutes bodily injury, the duty rules in cases of positive infliction of harm, and rescue cases.

(A) Bodily injury

Context Bodily integrity has long been a highly protected legal interest. It is the subject of a range of protections by the criminal law, and lies at the heart of the trespass to the person torts (considered in chapter 10). Whereas the trespass torts are concerned with interferences with bodily integrity that arise from 'deliberate' actions resulting in 'direct' infringements of the claimant's body, autonomy and/or dignity, actions in negligence are available for primary losses that arise on the basis of 'failures in care'. In this way, negligence law offers an especially wide protection for interferences with bodily integrity.

---

[4] See the survey of novel claims in D Nolan (2007) 70 MLR 59.

[5] D Nolan (2007) 70 MLR 59, 85–6.

[6] There is no injury as such in ignorance: *Donoghue v Copiague Union Free School District* 407 NYS 2d 874, 880 (1978); D Nolan (2007) 70 MLR 59, 84–5.

[7] See, eg, *White v CC of South Yorkshire Police* [1999] 2 AC 455, at [98].

Reduced functionality Ordinarily, cases of bodily injury entail interaction between the claimant and defendant involving external impact upon the body of the claimant, and/or the introduction of some mechanism of physical change.[8] The physical change need not be brought about 'directly' (in the way required in trespass); however, 'direct-ness' is a factor that a court might consider in determining whether the requisite 'prox-imity' exists between the parties[9] (as to which, see below). In order to have a claim, the claimant must suffer a bodily change which the law recognises as an *injury*. In the usual case, this means a *deleterious* physical change, being substantial in nature, which reduces functionality—even if the sufferer is not immediately aware of this.[10] An exam-ple of a case that illustrates this point, and that we will come back to later in this chapter, is *Rothwell v Chemical & Insulating Co Ltd*:[11]

> Cs were exposed negligently to asbestos by their employers. They developed pleural plaques, which are 'areas of fibrous thickening of the pleural membrane which surrounds the lungs'.[12] The plaques caused no symptoms. However, because they indicated the pres-ence of asbestos fibres in the lungs, Cs developed anxiety about their conditions, fear-ing that eventually they would suffer from life-threatening diseases, such as asbestosis or mesothelioma.

The House of Lords held that the claimants had not suffered any form of compen-sable bodily injury.[13] This was because the fibrous thickening of the pleura had made no difference to the claimants' lung capacity, or general physical health. Moreover, the mere risk of physical injury (in the form of disease) arising in the future was not a form of compensable harm.[14] Another illustration of the principle arose in *Greenaway v Johnson Matthey plc*, where the Court of Appeal held that workers negligently exposed to platinum salts who developed a sensitisation to this substance could not claim dam-ages for physical injury because this condition had no impact upon their everyday lives (except that they had to be removed from work involving further potential exposure).[15] By contrast, if the workers had developed an allergy to platinum salts, which could result in bronchial problems, skin irritation, and/or watery eyes, recovery was likely to be available.[16] In the usual case, we find that claimants are able to claim redress for death and for bodily injuries such as disablement (eg, broken arms and legs, organ failures), disease, and other palpable illnesses.

***Caparo* test for duty** Given the accumulated list of duty cases covering causation of bodily injury, rarely will a claimant be required to prove a new duty of care category in order to prove the existence of an obligation of care, but it remains a possibility. The test

---

[8] Eg, *George v Skivington* (1869) LR Ex 1 (defective hair shampoo).

[9] *Perrett v Collins* [1999] PNLR 77, at 108–10.

[10] *Cartledge v E Jopling & Sons Ltd* [1963] AC 758, 778–9; *Greenaway v Johnson Matthey plc* [2016] 1 WLR 4487, at [21].   [11] [2008] 1 AC 281.

[12] [2008] 1 AC 281, at [1].   [13] [2008] 1 AC 281, at [2], [50], [63], and [88].

[14] [2008] 1 AC 281, at [67] and [88]. See also *Gregg v Scott* [2005] 2 AC 176.

[15] [2016] 1 WLR 4487, at [5], [10], [27], and [30].   [16] [2016] 1 WLR 4487, at [6].

for duty of care in *Caparo Industries plc v Dickman*[17] applies in this context, as it does in novel duty of care cases more generally. When there is a need to consider duty of care, proof of reasonable foreseeability and proximity might be uncontentious. The simple fact of the defendant's causation of bodily injury via application of external physical force, or the introduction of a mechanism of physical change, is sufficient for proof of proximity between the parties because these things create pathways to harm. However, as we saw in chapter 2, there are cases in which foreseeability of bodily injury can be established but in which claims fail, nevertheless, for lack of proximity. This was the case in *Sutradhar v NERC*,[18] where the House of Lords held that there was 'nothing like the directness and immediacy' required in order to establish the requisite proximity[19] between the defendant NERC, which had been engaged by a third party to report on water samples and failed to identify the presence of arsenic in a potential Bangladeshi water supply, and the claimants, who suffered arsenical poisoning in the consumption of that water.

Policy Where the defendant's failures cause bodily injury to the claimant and he can prove the requisite foreseeability of harm to persons and proximity of relationship, establishing that it is fair, just, and reasonable that the defendant ought to have taken care frequently is unproblematic. As Lord Oliver put it in *Murphy v Brentwood District Council*:[20] '[t]he infliction of physical injury to the person … universally requires to be justified'. This statement implies that the law *presumes* the existence of a duty of care as between classes of person in physical proximity, where pathways to bodily injury arise. However, examples do exist of prima facie duties being negated on policy grounds, such as in a case involving active military engagement, in which the Court of Appeal held that the Ministry of Defence owes no duty of care to its own soldiers injured by friendly fire.[21]

Under the parameters of the present discussion, the defendant is assumed to cause bodily injury either by external impact upon the claimant, or by the introduction of some mechanism of physical change. The policy reasons in favour of duties of care in such cases are different from those that arise in cases of 'pure omission', considered with the discussion of proximity in chapter 2. In cases of pure omission, the primary defendant causes infringement of the claimant's bodily integrity, but suit is brought against a secondary defendant (typically with 'deeper pockets') such as the ambulance service, the fire brigade, or the police. We have seen that, as a general proposition, ambulance services owe a duty of care where they undertake to attend a person in need,[22] but otherwise the emergency services owe no duty of care to endangered persons for the policy reasons discussed in chapter 2.

---

[17] [1990] 2 AC 605.   [18] [2006] 4 All ER 490.
[19] [2006] 4 All ER 490, at [47]–[48]. See also at [38].   [20] [1990] 2 All ER 908, at 935.
[21] *Mulcahy v Ministry of Defence* [1996] QB 732. Cf *Smith v Ministry of Defence* [2014] AC 52.
[22] *Kent v Griffiths* [1999] PIQR P192.

(B) Rescue

The duty issue has arisen as well in cases where 'rescuers' have claimed that a person creating a peril, and giving rise to the need for assistance (either by that person or by a third-party victim), owes them a duty of care. Such claims have arisen with respect to both bodily and psychiatric injury, raising two important questions. First, does the claimant rescuer fall within a foreseeable class of affected person? Second, if he does, and given that he 'elects' to undertake the rescue, can he claim that the originator of the danger owes him any obligation in respect of his safety given that he has 'chosen' to imperil himself in undertaking the rescue? In *Haynes v Harwood*, the Court of Appeal held that a defendant, who owed a duty of care to pedestrians at risk of physical injury from the escape of some horses, also owed a duty to those who foreseeably might attempt to rescue the pedestrians from the peril in which the defendant's negligence had placed him.[23] Subsequent case law consistently has affirmed the notion that rescuers are foreseeable claimants, since it is well understood that '[d]anger invites rescue' and that '[t]he cry of distress is a summons to relief'.[24] Whether the rescuer is a member of the emergency services, whose public duty it is to embark on the rescue mission, or a well-meaning member of the public,[25] a duty is owed to him personally.[26] On the other hand, the obligation owed to rescuers is not especially favourable. It suffices to note here that the usual rules apply[27] and that the controversial question of whether it is appropriate to compensate professional service personnel in circumstances where ordinary citizens would recover nothing for psychiatric harm arising from the witnessing of a tragic event is considered fully later in this chapter.

As mentioned earlier, the duty to rescuers is imposed not only on those who endanger other people or their property so as to invite rescue, but also on anyone endangering themselves or their own property so as to make rescue likely. Thus, a householder who negligently set his own roof alight was held liable to the fireman who was later burnt when fighting the blaze.[28]

Section 3 Pregnancy and birth

Having considered the basic duty of care rules applicable in cases involving the causation of bodily injury, we now move on to consider several related issues. As we will see first, difficult questions have arisen about what duties of care are owed by medical

---

[23] [1935] 1 KB 146.   [24] *Wagner v International Rly Co* 232 NY Rep 176 (1921).

[25] *Baker v T E Hopkins & Son Ltd* [1959] 3 All ER 225; *Chadwick v British Transport Commission* [1967] 2 All ER 945.

[26] In *Videan v British Transport Commission* [1963] 2 QB 650 it was held that a duty was owed to a stationmaster rescuing his small son who had been trespassing on the lines. At that time, no duty was owed to the child trespasser. But the duty owed to the stationmaster was not derived from, or dependent upon, any duty owed to the son. An emergency requiring a rescue was foreseeable, thus creating a direct, personal duty towards the stationmaster.   [27] *White v CC of South Yorkshire Police* [1999] 1 All ER 1.

[28] *Ogwo v Taylor* [1988] AC 431.

professionals and prescribers of medicines and appliances in cases involving contraception, delivery of children, and birth defects.

(A) Duty to the unborn

Born alive rule Whether a duty of care was owed to a child injured by another's negligence *before* his birth remained unresolved until 1992. In *Burton v Islington Health Authority*[29] the Court of Appeal held, finally, that a duty is owed to the unborn child, but that it does not crystallise until the live birth of the child. Prior to that decision, however, Parliament had intervened with the Congenital Disabilities (Civil Liability) Act 1976, which provides that a child who is born alive, but disabled as a result of an occurrence before his birth, has a cause of action in certain circumstances against the person responsible for that occurrence.[30] The significance of the child being 'born alive' is that this is when the law recognises legal personhood in the human, and when rights and obligations in law begin to be acquired.

Disability The 1976 Act applies only in respect of children born with a 'disability', and 'disability' is defined in terms of 'any deformity, disease or abnormality including predisposition (whether or not susceptible of immediate prognosis) to physical or mental defect in the future'.[31] It is arguable, therefore, that any injury falling short of a disability remains governed by the common law rule established in *Burton*.[32] There are other limits to the scope of the Act, also, that leave untouched a still wider residual role for the common law. Therefore, it is necessary to provide some account of the Act.

Occurrence The duty imposed under the Act relates to any 'occurrence', whether it affects the reproductive capacity of either parent before conception, or affects the mother during pregnancy. The peculiarity of the obligation to the child is that it is derivative in nature. The relevant occurrence must have been capable of giving rise to liability in tort to the affected parent. But it is no answer that the parent suffered no actionable injury so long as 'there was a breach of legal duty which, [had it been] accompanied by injury, would have given rise to ... liability'.[33]

Mothers' liability Not surprisingly, mothers are granted an immunity from general liability under the Act.[34] How could a mother damaging her baby by smoking or drinking too much be in breach of a duty to herself? Would she be in breach of a duty to the father in injuring his child? Section 2 provides expressly for the only direct obligation owed to her unborn child under the 1976 Act. A woman may be liable for damage to her

---

[29] [1993] QB 204; and see *De Martell v Merton and Sutton HA* [1992] 3 All ER 820.

[30] Congenital Disabilities (Civil Liability) Act 1976, sub-s 1(1). Note that the Human Fertilisation and Embryology Act 1990, s 44 extends the 1976 Act to cover negligently inflicted disability in the course of licensed fertility treatment.   [31] Congenital Disabilities (Civil Liability) Act 1976, sub-s 4(1).

[32] See J Murphy (1994) 10 PN 94.   [33] Congenital Disabilities (Civil Liability) Act 1976, sub-s 1(3).

[34] See Congenital Disabilities (Civil Liability) Act 1976, s 1. Fathers are not immune. But what sorts of circumstance could create paternal liability—infecting the mother and baby with AIDS?

child inflicted by her negligent driving of a motor vehicle when she knows or ought to know herself to be pregnant. The justification for this exceptional instance of maternal liability probably is that, in such circumstances, her insurers will meet the cost of the child's claim.

Wrongful life A crucial question in the context of pre-natal injuries is the extent to which negligence law recognises 'wrongful life' claims, where the claimant argues that he should not have been born because of the prospect that he would lead a life of disability and suffering. In *McKay v Essex Area Health Authority*,[35] it was held that English common law recognises no such claims:

> C was born before the 1976 Act with terrible disabilities resulting from her mother having contracted rubella during pregnancy. The mother had undergone pregnancy tests when she realised that she had been in contact with the disease and had been negligently told that the tests were negative. She would have opted for an abortion had tests proved positive. Subsequently, the child sued in respect of the harm caused to her by being born disabled.

The Court of Appeal held that it was impossible to measure the harm resulting from entry into a life afflicted by disability where the only alternative was no life at all. It was unprepared, therefore, to impose on doctors a duty of care that was in essence a duty to bring about an abortion. In relation to births subsequent to the 1976 Act, Ackner LJ said in the *McKay* case[36] that the Act provides a cause of action only in respect of occurrences causing disabilities that otherwise would not have afflicted the child. It does not afford a remedy *to a child* whose birth was caused by the defendant's alleged negligence (even though the child born was afflicted by a disability). The Act is unsupportive of a claim for 'wrongful life'.[37]

(B) Wrongful conception

A related category of case is concerned with whether damages are recoverable in respect of the birth of an unplanned baby subsequent to a negligently performed sterilisation. In *Udale v Bloomsbury Area Health Authority*,[38] Jupp J refused the mother compensation towards the upkeep of the child despite the defendant's admission of negligence. Limiting her damages to compensation for the discomfort of her pregnancy, he said that, in the eyes of the law, the child's birth was a 'blessing' and that the financial cost associated with such a 'blessing'[39] was irrecoverable. It offended both society's notion of what is right and the value afforded to human life. Jupp J also thought that the knowledge that his parents had claimed damages in respect of his birth might later distress and damage the child emotionally as he grew to maturity.

---

[35] [1982] QB 1166.   [36] [1982] QB 1166, at 1187.
[37] See likewise *Harriton v Stephens* (2006) 226 CLR 52; C Symmons (1987) 50 MLR 269. Cf C Witting (2007) 31 MULR 569.   [38] [1983] 2 All ER 522.
[39] [1983] 2 All ER 522, at 531.

A year later, the Court of Appeal in *Emeh v Kensington Area Health Authority*[40] over-ruled Jupp J on the policy issue. The court was not convinced that policy objections should prevent recovery of damages. Subsequently, in *McFarlane v Tayside Health Board*[41]—another case involving an unplanned child—the House of Lords suggest-ed that damages were payable in respect of the pain and suffering associated with an unwanted pregnancy and confinement, but that the costs of bringing up the child were irrecoverable. Largely attempting to side-step the policy issues, their Lordships took the view that child-rearing costs were a form of purely financial loss and thus irrecover-able.[42] Furthermore, it would seem to make no difference if the woman who undergoes a negligently performed sterilisation operation and gives birth is herself disabled: the costs of rearing a healthy child remain irrecoverable.[43] On the other hand, the woman will be able expressly to recover a fixed sum for the loss of autonomy associated with having the child;[44] and if the child is born with a disability, the special costs associated with bringing up that disabled child following a negligently performed sterilisation will be recoverable.[45] Even so, the courts continue to take the view that the birth of any child is an unquantifiable benefit at least equivalent to the costs associated with raising a healthy child.[46]

Goodwill v British Pregnancy Advisory Service[47] is also worthy of mention in this context:

> C sued the clinic which she alleged had failed to warn her lover of the potential failure rate of a vasectomy. Their relationship had begun some time after his surgery. But C argued nonethe-less that, had her partner been adequately advised by D, he would have communicated the rel-evant information to her so that she would then have taken appropriate contraceptive precau-tions. She argued that the birth of her child was a consequence of the defendants' negligence.

It was held that the defendants owed no duty of care to the claimant because the claim-ant was not a person whom they could have been expected to identify as immediately affected by the services they rendered to her lover. The man's future sexual partners were not persons for whose benefit the vasectomy was performed.

Classifying failed sterilisation as financial loss to the parent(s)—whether or not that claim succeeds—has a certain logic to it. The main purpose of compensation will be to meet the costs of raising the child. Yet classifying the loss in this way does not simplify

---

[40] [1985] QB 1012.   [41] [2000] 2 AC 59.

[42] On the other hand, Lord Steyn ([2000] AC 59, at 82) did recognise the cogency of the policy arguments against the imposition of liability based on the sanctity and value of human life, and Lord Hope (at 97) ac-knowledged the benefits associated with having a child that (were they calculable) would have to be set off against the costs of bringing up a child (were they recoverable, which they were not).

[43] *Rees v Darlington Memorial Hospital NHS Trust* [2004] 1 AC 309, at [9] and [18].

[44] [2004] 1 AC 309, at [123]. A subsequent endorsement of compensation for loss of autonomy can be found in *Chester v Afshar* [2005] 1 AC 134, at [18].

[45] *Parkinson v St James and Seacroft University Hospital NHS Trust* [2002] QB 266. This is so regardless of whether it is a matter of pure bad luck that the child comes to be born with a disability, or whether it manifests within a few weeks of birth: *Groom v Selby* (2001) 64 BMLR 47.

[46] *Rees v Darlington Memorial Hospital NHS Trust* [2004] 1 AC 309.   [47] [1996] 2 All ER 161.

the issue of recoverability. The special costs of raising a disabled child, or the special costs of a disabled woman raising any child, are equally forms of purely financial loss, yet, according to the Court of Appeal, these are recoverable. It is submitted that these decisions were reached only by somewhat clumsy judicial manipulation of the three-stage test for duty and the extended *Hedley Byrne* assumption of responsibility test.[48] But it is worth setting out in full the compound reasoning of Brooke LJ in *Parkinson v St James and Seacroft University Hospital NHS Trust*:

> (i) … the birth of a child with congenital abnormalities was a foreseeable consequence of the surgeon's careless failure to clip a fallopian tube effectively; (ii) there was a very limited group of people who might be affected by this negligence, viz Mrs Parkinson and her husband (and, in theory, any other man with whom she had sexual intercourse before she realised that she had not been effectively sterilised); (iii) there is no difficulty in principle in accepting the proposition that the surgeon should be deemed to have assumed responsibility for the foreseeable and disastrous economic consequences of performing his services negligently; (iv) the purpose of the operation was to prevent Mrs Parkinson from conceiving any more children, including children with congenital abnormalities, and the surgeon's duty of care is strictly related to the proper fulfilment of that purpose; (v) parents in Mrs Parkinson's position were entitled to recover damages in these circumstances for 15 years between the decisions in *Emeh*'s case and *McFarlane*'s case, so that this is not a radical step forward into the unknown; (vi) for the reasons set out in (i) and (ii) above, Lord Bridge of Harwich's tests of foreseeability and proximity are satisfied, and for the reasons given by the Supreme Court of Florida in *Fassoulas v Ramey*[49] an award of compensation which is limited to the special upbringing costs associated with rearing a child with a serious disability would be fair, just and reasonable; (vii) if principles of distributive justice are called in aid, I believe that ordinary people would consider that it would be fair for the law to make an award in such a case, provided that it is limited to the extra expenses associated with the child's disability.[50]

Section 4 Liability for psychiatric illness

Another important category of duty of care concerning the person is that which is protective of mental integrity. Here we find that, for several related reasons, the courts have been cautious in recognising duties. Taking a pragmatic approach, they have permitted recovery only for the more extreme, and deserving, cases of negligence causing recognised psychiatric illnesses. In this section, we will consider the following issues: what constitutes psychiatric illness; categories of claimant; and the rules that apply to each category.

(A) Psychiatric illness

Non-compensable harm In *Rothwell v Chemical & Insulating Co Ltd*[51] (the facts of which appear above), the House of Lords affirmed two important propositions about

---

[48] These tests were considered in ch 2 and we will return to their applications in the context of purely financial loss in due course. [49] 450 So 2d 822 (1984).

[50] [2002] QB 266, at [50].   [51] [2008] 1 AC 281.

what counts as compensable psychiatric illness within the law of negligence. First, there could be no recovery for mere grief or anxiety.[52] These are temporary emotional states, which the law expects persons to endure without compensation. Second, the court rejected the idea that it is permissible to aggregate the various hurts that the claimants had suffered—the pleural plaques *and* the anxiety derived from fear for the future—on the ostensible basis that the sum was greater than its individual parts.[53] Lord Scott put it bluntly in stating that 'nought plus nought equals nought'.[54]

Compensable harm By contrast to temporary emotional states, for the purposes of the law of negligence a psychiatric illness is a *medically recognised*[55] condition of a sustained nature that disturbs the normal functioning of the mind. It might or might not be accompanied by overt physical symptoms.[56] As a broad category, the term 'psychiatric illness' encompasses many more specific illnesses. For the most part, the relevant case law has concerned physical events (or 'stressors') leading to the onset of post-traumatic stress disorder (PTSD). However, the courts have recognised that this is not the only kind of compensable psychiatric harm and have begun to explore others. Thus, in *Vernon v Bosley*, Thorpe LJ stated that, while PTSD is a useful classification, it could not 'be adopted in personal injury litigation as the yardstick by which the [claimant's] success or failure is to be measured'.[57] Indeed, in recent times, courts have considered the argument for redress in cases of negligence not based upon any external 'event' giving rise to psychiatric illness, but in cases in which the claimant has been overladen with work by his employer or exposed to a substance (such as asbestos) which causes him to 'fear for the future'.[58] We will explore this type of case momentarily.

(B) Types of claim

Categories of claim Much of the early case law in this area concerned allegations of negligence involving external events that caused 'shock' to the claimant followed

---

[52] [2008] 1 AC 281, at [2], [66], and [89]. See also, eg, *McLoughlin v O'Brian* [1983] AC 410, at 431; *White v CC of South Yorkshire Police* [1999] 2 AC 455, at 465 and 491; *W v Essex CC* [2001] 2 AC 592, at 600.

[53] [2008] 1 AC 281, at [17] and [73].   [54] [2008] 1 AC 281, at [73].

[55] *White v Chief Constable of South Yorkshire Police* [1999] 2 AC 455, 491. The Supreme Court of Canada has held that this is not a requirement of Canadian law; however, there is still a need to prove 'serious and prolonged injury': *Saadati v Moorhead* 2017 SCC 28, at [9].

[56] See American Psychological Association, *Diagnostic and Statistical Manual of Mental Disorder* (5th revised edn, 2013) ('DSM 5') (available at http://www.dsm5.org/Pages/Default.aspx); P Handford, *Mullany and Handford's Tort Liability for Psychiatric Damage* (2nd edn, 2006), chs 2–3. The latter work indicates that the term preferred in psychiatry is 'psychiatric disorder': ibid at 30. Note that there is scepticism in some quarters about the scientific credibility of the diagnostic criteria: 'Only 3 per cent of DSM disorders have any known biological causes. The causes of the remaining 97 per cent … are not known … . Billions of research dollars have been spent on trying to establish a link between neurotransmitters and mental disorder, and the attempts have failed. For all the scientific terminology, psychiatric diagnoses are based on subjective judgments': T Stevenson, 'Mind field' *Financial Times*, Life and Arts Supplement (London, 25–26 May 2013), 8. There is, moreover, criticism of the legal usages of diagnostic manuals such as DSM 5: see R Mulheron (2012) 32 OJLS 77.

[57] [1997] 1 All ER 577, at 610. See also ibid at 607.

[58] The full breadth of such claims in considered in P Handford, *Mullany and Handford's Tort Liability for Psychiatric Damage* (2nd edn, 2006), ch 27.

thereafter by physical consequences, such as claimant death or miscarriage.[59] It was in such cases that courts began to recognise limited duties of care.[60] Later claims typically involved allegations that the external stressor caused PTSD, which can arise in a number of ways. First, a claimant who suffers severe physical injury, for example in a road accident, might succumb, also, to mental illness triggered by the terror of the accident and his consequent pain and suffering.[61] Second, a person might be so badly treated following a traumatic event that psychiatric harm ensues.[62] Both of these categories of claim will be assessed as cases of 'bodily injury' by reference to principles considered earlier in this chapter.[63] Third, an accident might occur in which the claimant falls within the physical 'zone of danger', but in which he suffers no bodily injury, only immediate shock and fear (or some such emotions) and eventual psychiatric illness. Such a claimant, who seeks compensation for his injury, is described in the law as a 'primary victim'. Fourth, the claimant might not be involved directly in the original accident, or be at risk of physical injury, but nonetheless witness injury to others and suffer psychiatric harm as a result. A good example would be a mother who witnesses an horrific injury to her children.[64] In such cases, the claimant is classified as a 'secondary victim' of the defendant's negligence.[65] Much of the law on liability for psychiatric illness has concentrated upon primary and secondary victim-type cases. However, new categories of claim have arisen that do not involve physical event stressors, and something will be said about them later in this section.

Recognition of claims   As a general proposition, the courts have been wary of permitting a wide ambit of liability for psychiatric illness, whether in cases involving an external event stressor or not. The policy reasons expressed for adopting a cautious approach include: the intangible nature of many psychiatric illnesses, and the risk of fictitious claims and excessive litigation; the indirect nature of their causation and consequent problems of proving the causal link between the defendant's negligence and injury to the claimant; the potential for liabilities which are large and disproportionate

---

[59] 'Shock' has been defined formally as involving 'the sudden appreciation by sight or sound of a horrifying event, which violently agitates the mind': *Alcock v CC of South Yorkshire Police* [1992] 2 AC 310, at 401.

[60] Eg, *Dulieu v White & Sons* [1901] 2 KB 669; *Hambrook v Stokes Bros* [1925] 1 KB 141. Again, the focus here is upon the *initial* injury caused. Unless the law recognises a duty of care with respect to the causation of the initial psychiatric illness, there can be no compensation for any consequential physical losses (which might be quite severe, such as was evident in the many miscarriages that accompanied early cases in this area).

[61] See discussion in *White v CC of South Yorkshire Police* [1999] 2 AC 455, at 491.

[62] See, eg, *Brooks v MPC* [2005] 1 WLR 1495 (although on the facts, there was no duty owed by the police to C, a murder witness). Consider, too, *McLoughlin v Grovers* [2002] QB 1312, where the traumatic occurrence was C's wrongful conviction due to the negligence of his solicitors; it was held that C had an arguable case that he might be entitled to recover in negligence for the psychiatric illness he developed as a consequence of that wrongful conviction.

[63] Where the primary victim suffers physically and psychologically, the psychological harm need not be a recognised psychiatric condition. Thus, in *Gregg v Scott* [2005] 2 AC 176, it was held that C could claim for the anxiety caused by a physical condition for which D was answerable in negligence: the anxiety merely falls within the recognised head of 'pain and suffering' that has long been recoverable in conjunction with physical injuries.   [64] Eg, *Hambrook v Stokes Bros* [1925] 1 KB 141.

[65] Again, the Supreme Court of Canada has refused to adopt such classifications: *Saadati v Moorhead* 2017 SCC 28; *Mustapha v Culligan of Canada Ltd* [2008] 2 SCR 114.

to the defendant's fault (often a simple failure to take care); and the difficulties of putting monetary values on successful claims.[66] As mentioned earlier, the courts have taken a cautious and pragmatic approach to claims in this area—especially those beyond primary victim cases. They have engaged in a process of working out a set of rules which permit recovery in the most extreme and deserving circumstances.

Despite the policy concerns which continue to affect the law in this area, gradual judicial recognition of the genuine nature of psychiatric illness led to the abandonment of the nineteenth-century attitude that non-physical harms to the person are irrecoverable.[67] The courts began to award damages for what was, for many years, called 'nervous shock'.[68] A claimant who became mentally ill because of the shock to his nervous system caused by a physical event that either threatened his own safety (the primary victim case),[69] or involved witnessing exceptionally distressing injuries to others (the secondary victim case),[70] could potentially recover compensation for psychiatric illness.

(1) Foreseeability

Let us now consider the modern rules of liability. In every novel case involving a claim of the negligent causation of psychiatric illness, the claimant will succeed on the duty of care issue, in accordance with the test in *Caparo Industries plc v Dickman*,[71] only when able to prove foreseeability of 'harm' to persons.[72] However, the cases differ on the kind of harms that must be foreseen. The rules relating to physical event stressors are more liberal in 'primary victim' cases than they are in 'secondary victim' cases. Basically, the primary victim, who falls within the zone of danger created by an external physical event, need prove only foreseeability of *either* bodily injury or psychiatric illness in a person of normal mental fortitude (collectively, cases of 'personal injury');[73] while the secondary victim must prove the foreseeability of psychiatric illness in a class of persons of reasonable fortitude (which includes him) arising from an external event involving an intermediate party who is killed or injured.[74] In cases which do not involve physical event stressors, the rules are slightly different—reflecting the different manner of causation. In cases involving stress at work, as mentioned earlier, *Hatton v Sutherland* requires that the defendant employer be able to foresee the development of psychiatric illness in an employee of ordinary phlegm—*unless* something in the employee's work history sufficiently alerts the employer to a particular susceptibility of which the employer should take note. In the following 'fear for the future' case, the claim was denied on the basis of a lack of foreseeability. In *Grieves v FT Everard & Sons Ltd*:

[66] Eg, *McLoughlin v O'Brian* [1983] 1 AC 410, at 421; *White v CC of South Yorkshire Police* [1999] 2 AC 455, at 493–4.

[67] For the nineteenth-century view, see *Victorian Railways Comrs v Coultas* (1888) 13 App Cas 222.

[68] The phrase can be misleading and should be regarded as no more than a customary means of grouping together cases where C becomes mentally ill as a consequence of an assault upon his nervous system: see *Alcock v CC of South Yorkshire* [1991] 4 All ER 907, at 923. See also *McLoughlin v O'Brian* [1982] 2 All ER 298, at 301.

[69] *Dulieu v White & Sons* [1901] 2 KB 669.   [70] *Hambrook v Stokes Bros* [1925] 1 KB 141.

[71] [1990] 2 AC 605.

[72] The specific need for foreseeability of harm in this category of case was established in *Bourhill v Young* [1943] AC 92.   [73] *Page v Smith* [1996] AC 155.

[74] *Bourhill v Young* [1943] AC 92; *Alcock v CC of South Yorkshire* [1992] 1 AC 310.

> C was exposed negligently to asbestos dust by his former employers. Following an x-ray examination, he developed clinical depression as a result of his fears that eventually he would develop a life-threatening asbestos-related illness.

Absent some special knowledge about the claimant's susceptibility to psychiatric illness, it had to be assumed that the claimant was of ordinary mental fortitude.[75] The problem was that it was not reasonably foreseeable to an employer that the claimant would suffer illness in this manner.[76] There was no relevant external event, such as occurs in the more usual psychiatric illness case, with respect to which it had been foreseeable that he might suffer a psychiatric reaction.[77] The *Grieves* case cannot be taken to rule out the possibility that an employer (or other defendant) might be liable in negligence for an employee's exposure to asbestos or some other substance which causes a psychiatric illness because of the employee's fears of developing a fatal or other disease.[78] However, it does emphasise the importance in such cases of the defendant employer's knowledge of the claimant's susceptibility to psychiatric illness.[79] Unless there was some reason for the defendant to know or have reason to suspect, prior to a failure in care, such vulnerability, claims of this nature appear to be unavailable.

(2) Primary victims

Let us now examine the physical event duty categories in turn, starting with the primary victim case.

Page v Smith *Page v Smith*[80] is the leading case on the duty of care rules applicable to primary victim cases:

> C was involved in a collision with a car negligently driven by D. He suffered no physical injury. However, almost immediately, he succumbed to a revival in an acute form of the chronic fatigue syndrome (ME) from which he had suffered periodically in the past. He became so ill that he was unable to work. D argued that, as C had suffered no physical injury, he was not liable for injury through shock. A normal person with no previous history of psychiatric illness would not be expected to become ill as a result of a minor collision.

The House of Lords found for the claimant. In cases involving external physical events causing psychiatric illness, they held, the accepted distinction between primary and secondary victims becomes apposite. In claims by the latter (as we shall see), certain 'control mechanisms' limit the defendant's potential liability for psychiatric harm. Moreover, shock in a person of normal fortitude must be foreseeable. But Mr Page was a primary victim of the defendant's negligence. It was held to be readily foreseeable that he would be exposed to personal injury, and (for present purposes) physical and psychiatric harm were not to be regarded as different kinds of damage. Once physical

---

[75] [2008] 1 AC 281, at [26] and [99].   [76] [2008] 1 AC 281, at [57], [75], and [99]–[100].
[77] [2008] 1 AC 281, at [30].   [78] Cf *Grieves v FT Everard & Sons Ltd* [2008] 1 AC 281, at [2].
[79] See the test laid out in *Hatton v Sutherland* [2002] ICR 613 (applied in *Barber v Somerset CC* [2004] 1 WLR 1089).   [80] [1996] AC 155, neatly dissected in S Bailey and D Nolan (2010) 69 CLJ 495.

injury to a primary victim is foreseeable, the primary victim can recover both for any actual physical harm that he suffers and/or for any recognised psychiatric illness ensuing from the defendant's breach of duty.[81] In cases where the claimant is outside the zone of physical danger, but reasonably believes himself to be imperilled by some physical event, he can recover for psychiatric illness where the risk of developing this kind of illness is foreseeable.[82] Indeed, it appears that, even if distress is the only thing foreseeable, the claimant can sue in respect of any recognised form of psychiatric illness that goes beyond such distress (even though that specific illness was not foreseeable).[83]

Critique The decision in *Page v Smith* has been subject to criticism,[84] in part because tests for foreseeability in negligence ordinarily encompass specific kinds of damage (as discussed in chapter 2). The test in *Page* conflates the foreseeability of two kinds of damage, typically caused in different ways. Usually, personal injuries arise from external impacts (or the introduction of some mechanism of physical change), whereas psychiatric illnesses develop indirectly through involuntary reactions to events. The limitations of the *Page* test have become obvious in subsequent cases. In *Grieves v FT Everard & Sons Ltd*, considered already, it was held to be confined to the kind of factual situation that it involved—that is, an external physical event. It would not apply in cases of negligent exposure to asbestos, radiation, or contamination of food which had caused no proven physical harm, but which led to anxiety and subsequent psychiatric illness.[85]

(3) Secondary victims

Control mechanisms A series of decisions have set limits (beyond foreseeability), often referred to as 'control mechanisms', on those persons who can claim as secondary victims of psychiatric illness.[86] As a first matter, courts largely have confined recovery to cases involving external physical events which are 'shocking' or capable of giving rise to 'shock' in those who witness them. In *Liverpool Women's Hospital NHS Foundation Trust v Ronayne*, the Court of Appeal summarised the requirement as being that (at least in the typical case) the external physical event must be 'horrifying' in an objective sense—that is, as judged 'by reference to persons of ordinary susceptibility'.[87] It is not sufficient that the claimant was a witness to 'a series of events over a period of time' leading to a 'gradual realisation' of serious risks of death or injury to the

---

[81] A variation of the primary victim case in which the claimant occasionally succeeds involves the introduction by social services, through their negligence, of a violent or abusive minor into an adoptive family or foster home, that minor then committing disturbing acts affecting other persons present: see, eg, *A v Essex CC* [2004] 1 WLR 1881, at [71].

[82] *McFarlane v EE Caledonia* [1994] 2 All ER 1 (discussed later; no liability in this case).

[83] *Essa v Laing* [2004] ICR 746.

[84] See M Jones, 'Liability for Psychiatric Damage: Searching for a Path between Pragmatism and Principle' in JW Neyers et al (eds), *Emerging Issues in Tort Law* (2007), ch 5; S Bailey and D Nolan (2010) 69 CLJ 495.

[85] [2008] 1 AC 281, at [31]–[34], [53]–[54], [77], [95], and [97]. This ruling has been argued to be arbitrary, adding 'further complexity and uncertainty to the law': S Bailey and D Nolan (2010) 69 CLJ 495, 524.

[86] *Bourhill v Young* [1943] AC 92; *McLoughlin v O'Brian* [1983] 1 AC 410. The leading case is now *Alcock v CC of South Yorkshire Police* [1992] 1 AC 310.   [87] [2015] EWCA Civ 588, at [13].

intermediate party.[88] Second, there is a need for proof of several proximity-based 'control mechanisms' which link the parties, which are important in identifying the cases most deserving of compensation and keeping litigation within acceptable limits. Two House of Lords decisions were important in establishing the relevant rules.

McLoughlin v O'Brian   The conditions for liability to a secondary victim established by the case law up to 1982 generally required that the claimant should be present at the scene of the accident, or very close by, so that he perceived what happened with his unaided senses. But then *McLoughlin v O'Brian*[89] was decided:

> C's husband and three children were involved in a car accident caused by D's negligence. All four of her family members were injured, one so seriously that she died almost immediately. An hour later, a friend told her of the accident at her home two miles away. They went to the hospital where C was told of the death and then saw the three remaining family members before they had been properly cleaned up. Though a woman of reasonable fortitude, C suffered severe shock, organic depression, and a change of personality.

The House of Lords insisted that the claimant should demonstrate her proximity in time and space to the traumatic events. But it held that, in coming upon the 'immediate aftermath' of the accident in which her family had been so grievously injured, the claimant was within the scope of the duty to avoid causation of psychiatric illness. Witnessing the aftermath was equivalent to witnessing the incident itself since nothing about the horrendous state in which her family members appeared at the hospital had been altered by that stage.

***Alcock*'s case**   The leading case on liability to secondary victims for psychiatric harm is now *Alcock v Chief Constable of South Yorkshire Police:*[90]

> In April 1989, 95 people died and over 400 were injured when South Yorkshire police allowed an excessive number of spectators to crowd into Hillsborough football ground. People were literally crushed to death. Cs' actions were for psychiatric illness ensuing from the horror of what had happened to their relatives (or in one case, a fiancé).

In the House of Lords, two issues were pre-eminent: first, could relatives other than parents or spouses bring actions for psychiatric illness as secondary victims? Second, could those who witnessed coverage of the disaster on television recover? Their Lordships refused to prescribe rigid categories of potential secondary victim claimant in psychiatric illness cases. They held that, generally, there must be a close tie of love and affection between the claimant and the primary victim of the sort normally enjoyed by spouses and by parents and children.[91] In the absence of special factors, siblings

---

[88] [2015] EWCA Civ 588, at [36].

[89] [1983] 1 AC 410. For more recent insistence on first-hand experience of traumatic sights, see *Palmer v Tees HA* [1999] Lloyd's Rep Med 351.   [90] [1991] 4 All ER 907.

[91] [1991] 4 All ER 907, at 914, 919–20, 930, and 935.

and other more remote relatives would fall outside such a relationship. Consequently, claims by brothers, sisters, and brothers-in-law failed in *Alcock*, while a fiancé's claim was allowed. However, claims by more distant relatives were not precluded completely. So, for instance, a grandmother who had brought up a grandchild since infancy might qualify upon proof of the required bond of love and affection.[92]

A degree of proximity in time and space between the claimant and the accident is required. Normally, the claimant either must witness the accident himself or come upon the aftermath within a very short period of time.[93] Identifying a relative several hours after death usually will not suffice; nor will witnessing the accident on television.[94] Parents who watched the Hillsborough disaster unfold on television had their claims rejected. Normally, television images cannot be equated with actual sight or hearing of the event or its aftermath, especially since the broadcasting code of ethics prohibits graphic coverage of individual suffering.[95] Once again, there *might* be exceptional cases in which simultaneous broadcasts of a disaster that cannot be edited will equate to personal presence at the accident.[96] Indeed, in the Court of Appeal in the *Alcock* case, Nolan LJ gave the example of a balloon carrying children at some live broadcast event suddenly bursting into flames.[97] But this type of scenario is yet to be litigated successfully.

The relevant psychiatric illness must be shown to result from the trauma of the event or its immediate aftermath.[98] There is no recovery in circumstances where a person is injured at work and dies three weeks later, her daughter being a witness not of the former but only of the latter, ultimate consequence of the accident.[99] And psychiatric illness resulting from being informed of a loved one's death, however gruesome the circumstances, is not recoverable in English law.[100] So, if a young child is crushed by falling masonry at school and, within an hour, her mother comes to her deathbed at the hospital, the mother may recover for the trauma of coming upon the immediate aftermath of the accident. But, if the child's father has a heart attack when told over the phone of the girl's fate, his loss remains irrecoverable.[101]

Police The decision in *Alcock* provoked many questions. Several important cases have explored further the boundaries of liability in secondary victim cases. *White v Chief Constable of South Yorkshire Police*[102] was concerned with the position of police claimants:

---

[92] Lord Ackner suggested that, in cases of exceptional horror, where a reasonably strong-nerved individual would suffer shock-induced psychiatric injury, even a bystander unrelated to the victim should be able to recover: [1991] 4 All ER 907, at 919. See also at 930.

[93] [1991] 4 All ER 907, at 914–15, 920–1, 930–2, and 936. See also *Hunter v British Coal* [1998] 2 All ER 97.

[94] [1991] 4 All ER 907, at 937.   [95] [1991] 4 All ER 907, at 921.

[96] [1991] 4 All ER 907, at 921 and 931.   [97] [1991] 3 All ER 88, at 122.

[98] After *Vernon v Bosley* [1997] 1 All ER 577 it is no longer necessary that it be exclusively shock that triggers C's illness.   [99] *Taylor v A Novo (UK) Ltd* [2013] 3 WLR 989.

[100] [1991] 4 All ER 907, at 914–15. Cf *Tame v NSW* [2002] HCA 35 and *Gifford v Strang Patrick Stevedoring Pty Ltd* [2003] HCA 33.

[101] As it would be if his illness were precipitated by identifying his daughter at the mortuary the next day.

[102] [1999] 1 All ER 1, overturning the decision of the Court of Appeal.

> Cs were police officers who claimed damages for psychiatric illness resulting from their professional involvement in events at the Hillsborough disaster in which many died or were seriously injured in the crush at the football ground. Five of the six claimants assisted the injured and sought to ensure that, subsequent to the peak of the disaster, no further danger faced those leaving the ground. The sixth claimant was on duty at the mortuary. None of the officers were exposed to any personal risk of physical injury.

The Court of Appeal held that a duty of care was owed to the officers actually present at the ground (but not to the one at the mortuary).[103] The decision provoked outrage from relatives of those killed and injured at Hillsborough who had been refused compensation in the *Alcock* case. The House of Lords reversed the Court of Appeal decision, acknowledging that it would be unacceptable to compensate police officers at the ground in the course of their jobs while denying recovery to brothers and sisters who saw their relatives die in horrific circumstances.[104] Their Lordships ruled that the claimants were not to be classified as primary victims of the defendants' negligence because they were never in physical danger themselves.[105] As secondary victims, they were in no better position than normal bystanders. The Hillsborough police officers witnessed the disaster at close quarters, but lacked the requisite close ties of love or affection with the victims in order to be able to sue. Although an employment relationship had existed between the defendant and the claimants, this did not change matters. This is because an employer's duty to safeguard employees from personal injury is simply part of the ordinary law of negligence. The claimants' alternative argument in the *White* case was that they were owed a duty of care in their capacity as rescuers. Yet here, too, the House of Lords insisted that, in relation to psychiatric illness, rescuers must meet the same conditions as any other witnesses of injury to third parties. They either must have exposed themselves to actual danger, or have reasonably believed themselves to have done so.[106] They must meet, also, the other conditions limiting recovery by secondary victims, which they could not do.

Emergency services personnel and primary victims A nice point was left open following *Alcock v Chief Constable of South Yorkshire Police*.[107] Could a primary victim be liable for harm to another person, in particular emergency services personnel, caused by the shock arising from witnessing a physical accident where the primary victim was the author of his own injury? In *Ogwo v Taylor*,[108] a negligent householder was made liable to a fire-fighter injured in a fire caused by his carelessness. But, in *Greatorex v Greatorex*,[109] it was held that a drunk driver who caused an accident did not owe a duty of care to his father (who happened to be the fire officer called to the scene of the accident) in respect of his father's psychiatric harm. To impose such a duty would be, the court said, too much of an imposition on the drunken man's 'right' to conduct himself broadly as he pleased.

---

[103] *White v CC of South Yorkshire Police* [1997] 1 All ER 540.   [104] [1999] 1 All ER 1, at 48.

[105] Where claimant rescuers were in physical danger, their claims can be determined according to principles applicable to other primary victims: see *Chadwick v British Transport Commission* [1967] 1 WLR 912.

[106] See also *Cullin v London Fire and Civil Defence Authority* [1999] PIQR P314.

[107] [1992] 1 AC 310.   [108] [1988] AC 431.   [109] [2000] 1 WLR 1970.

Self-determination involves the ability to injure ourselves without owing others a duty when they witness our injury. Perhaps one distinction between the two cases is that, in *Ogwo*, the claimant suffered physical harm (burns), whereas the fireman in *Greatorex* suffered only psychiatric illness. But as the House of Lords, relying on the formulations contained in the Limitation Acts pointed out in *Page v Smith*,[110] psychiatric illness is merely part of the broader category of harm known as 'personal injury'. A second possible distinction is that, in *Ogwo*, the fire officer would have satisfied the test for a primary victim set out in *White v Chief Constable of South Yorkshire Police*,[111] whereas the claimant in *Greatorex* was in no personal danger (nor in a position to claim reasonably that he thought he was in personal danger). But this, too, is unconvincing, for the primary/secondary victim distinction operates to differentiate between two types of claimant, both of whom are suing for psychiatric illness. A third explanation might be that a person attempting to save property (as in *Ogwo*) will be owed a duty more readily than a person rescuing fellow human beings (as in *Greatorex*). But such a distinction—if we accept that the law seeks to treat rescuers kindly—runs counter to the usual hierarchy of protected interests in tort law. Perhaps the simplest explanation of the decision in *Greatorex* is the one implicit in the fact that not a single mention of *Ogwo* was made in that case!

Bystanders   Questions have remained about the liability to *bystanders* of those who cause accidents involving the death of, or bodily injury to, intermediate parties. In the *Alcock* case, Lord Ackner suggested that a truly horrific disaster might entitle even unrelated bystanders to recover damages for psychiatric illness. Yet consider *McFarlane v EE Caledonia Ltd*:[112]

> C witnessed the destruction of an oil rig from aboard a support vessel involved in attempts to rescue survivors of the explosion which tore apart the rig. C was not himself involved in the rescue effort and was far enough away from the burning rig to be in no personal danger. However, a more horrifying spectacle is difficult to imagine.

The Court of Appeal refused his claim. A rescuer personally at risk in such circumstances would have been entitled to compensation as a participant in the terrifying event. But, crucially, the claimant was neither a rescuer nor otherwise a participant (that is, at no objective risk nor in a position reasonably to believe himself to be at risk).[113] As a bystander only, it was not foreseeable that he would suffer such shock. Stuart-Smith LJ effectively sought to close the door, left ajar in *Alcock*, on liability to bystanders. Practical and policy reasons, he said, militated against such liability: reactions to horrific events were 'entirely subjective'.[114]

Future claims   It appears that, to some extent, *White v Chief Constable of South Yorkshire Police*[115] has closed the door on further expansion of liability for psychiatric

---

[110] [1996] AC 155.   [111] [1999] 1 All ER 1.
[112] [1994] 2 All ER 1. For critique, see J Murphy (1995) 15 LS 415. See also *Hegarty v EE Caledonia Ltd* [1996] 1 Lloyd's Rep 413.   [113] [1994] 2 All ER 1, at 13.
[114] [1994] 2 All ER 1, at 14.   [115] [1999] 1 All ER 1.

harm. Yet the courts' repeated insistence upon shock-induced injury has enjoyed a liberal interpretation in some cases, even embracing a reaction to a protracted event that
lasted some 36 hours.[116] Equally, a further important issue in this context that has never
much troubled the judiciary is that of the application of the 'egg-shell skull' rule. It may
be invoked with respect to psychiatric illness just as it may in relation to bodily injury.[117]
Thus, if psychiatric illness would have been foreseeable in respect of a reasonably mentally tough individual, the extended degree to which the claimant actually suffers psychiatric illness is irrelevant.[118] And even if psychiatric illness per se is not foreseeable,
so long as the physical injury which triggers, or otherwise leads to, psychiatric harm is
foreseeable, the claimant may recover for the psychiatric illness nonetheless.[119]

As mentioned earlier, until the decision in *Vernon v Bosley*,[120] the courts had insisted
that a secondary victim of psychiatric harm must show PTSD. In that case, the facts
were as follows:

> C's two young children were passengers in a car driven by D, their nanny, when it veered
> off the road and crashed into a river. C did not witness the original accident, but was called
> to the scene immediately afterwards and watched unsuccessful attempts to salvage the car
> and rescue his children. These efforts failed and the children drowned. C became mentally
> ill and his business and marriage both failed. D accepted that C's illness resulted from the
> tragic deaths of his children, but argued that his illness was caused not by the shock of what
> he experienced at the riverside, but by pathological grief at his loss in an illness, distinct
> from PTSD, called pathological grief disorder.

The Court of Appeal held that, although damages for ordinary grief and bereavement
remain irrecoverable,[121] a secondary victim can recover damages for psychiatric illness
where he establishes the general pre-conditions for such a claim (set out above), and
that the negligence of the defendant caused or contributed to his mental illness. The
claimant in this case was able to do so and could recover compensation regardless of the
fact that his illness consisted partly of an abnormal grief reaction.[122] On the other hand,
the decision in *Vernon v Bosley* does not imply that every person who loses a loved one
and becomes ill through grief can sue the negligent individual responsible for the death
of the primary victim. For example, the grandmother in Newcastle who is told of the

---

[116] In *North Glamorgan NHS Trust v Walters* [2003] PIQR P232, the Court of Appeal allowed a claim in respect of a woman who 'reeled under successive blows [to her psyche]' as the condition of her child visibly wors-
ened before her eyes when medics failed to diagnose that the child was suffering from acute hepatitis. However,
this case is of doubtful authority: see, eg, *Liverpool Women's Hospital NHS Foundation Trust v Ronayne* [2015]
EWCA Civ 588.   [117] *Brice v Brown* [1984] 1 All ER 997; *Vernon v Bosley* [1997] 1 All ER 577.

[118] *Brice v Brown* [1984] 1 All ER 997.

[119] *Simmons v British Steel plc* [2004] ICR 565, at [55]. For the argument that the egg-shell skull principle
is inappropriately applied in the context of psychiatric harm, see M Jones, 'Liability for Psychiatric Damage:
Walking a Path between Pragmatism and Principle' in JW Neyers et al (eds), *Emerging Issues in Tort Law*
(2007), ch 5.   [120] [1997] 1 All ER 577.

[121] See also *Alcock v CC of South Yorkshire Police* [1991] 4 All ER 907, at 917.

[122] Note that the courts are prepared to make a discount in the award of damages where C's grief merges with
a recognisable psychiatric disorder: see, eg, *Rahman v Arearose Ltd* [2001] QB 351. Furthermore, D will only
be liable for that part of C's psychiatric harm that he actually caused: *Hatton v Sutherland* [2002] 2 All ER 1.

death in a car crash of her grandson in Norwich has no claim in negligence. She cannot establish the requisite conditions limiting any claim by secondary victims.

(4) Stress at work

Many cases involving claims of the negligent causation of psychiatric illness have arisen in the workplace context. From *White v Chief Constable of South Yorkshire Police*,[123] we know that, where claims arise from witnessing the death of, or injury to, intermediate parties, claimants are to be treated in exactly the same way as other secondary victims.[124] However, a separate category of case has emerged involving claims that have nothing to do with external, physical events. These are cases in which the claimant has been employed by the defendant and has been unable to cope with the volume of work that he has been expected to complete—the stress of his workload leading to the causation of psychiatric illness. Stress-at-work cases generally have been unsuccessful—despite the fact that employers owe their employees non-delegable duties of care to provide a physically safe workplace. Although recovery was allowed in *Walker v Northumberland County Council*[125] (which concerned a social services officer who, after suffering a nervous breakdown, took leave from his employment managing very difficult child care cases and returned to work later only to find a large backlog of new cases that he was expected to process), subsequent authorities have limited the ambit of claims. This is not for the wont of proximity between the parties—but on the basis of both problems in establishing foreseeability (considered already) and policy reasons, including those relating to the importance of the contract of employment in determining what the employer has the right to demand of the employee. In *Barber v Somerset County Council*,[126] the House of Lords approved the approach to these cases taken in the court below by Hale LJ. Her Ladyship had said that, usually, after suffering a nervous breakdown the question would be whether psychiatric illness was reasonably foreseeable by the employer, not in the person of ordinary fortitude, but in the individual employee. This was because of the existence of an actual, working relationship between the parties (which would establish the requisite proximity of relationship). In determining whether or not injury was foreseeable in the particular employee, relevant factors would include the nature and extent of work being done by the employee, signs of ill health from the employee, and frequent or prolonged absences from work.[127] In the view of one set of commentators, the present judicial approach 'effectively insulates the employer from liability in the quite typical case where the employee will not admit to experiencing stress for fear of being unable to cope'.[128]

---

[123] [1999] 1 All ER 1.

[124] In *Farley v Skinner* [2002] AC 732 it was held that C would have a contractual claim in respect of distress arising out of a breach *where the contract was specifically designed to protect C from distress*. Extrapolating from this, there seems no reason in principle why a tort claim could not be brought in respect of distress if a *tortious duty* to protect C from distress could be found.　　　　　[125] [1995] 1 All ER 737.

[126] [2004] 1 WLR 1089.　　　　[127] [2002] ICR 613, at [25]–[30]. At the breach stage, it might be material whether, in a job known to be stressful, the employer failed to provide counselling services: *Hartman v South Essex Mental Health and Community Care NHS Trust* [2005] ICR 782.

[128] M Lunney and K Oliphant, *Tort Law: Text and Materials* (5th edn, 2013), 367.

(5) Reform

As Lord Steyn admitted in *White v Chief Constable of South Yorkshire*, 'the law on the recovery of compensation for pure psychiatric harm is a patchwork quilt of distinctions which are difficult to justify'.[129] Even after judicial attempts to clarify the principles governing liability for psychiatric harm and to package claims neatly according to a scheme of primary and secondary victims, loose ends remain. To see this, we might reflect on the following examples:

(1) A final-year student arrives home to witness her hall of residence burning to the ground. In her room are all her revision notes and the only copy of her dissertation. Unsurprisingly, she succumbs to clinical depression. Can she recover damages? If the fire was caused by faulty wiring and the university can be shown to have been negligent in its maintenance of the residence, could she argue that she is a primary victim because her psychiatric illness is consequent on the damage to her property? Might she assert, if a secondary victim, 'a close tie of love and affection to her work'? In *Attia v British Gas plc*,[130] decided before *Alcock*, a woman was permitted to pursue damages after suffering a nervous breakdown caused by witnessing her home burn down.[131]

(2) A second, equally unlucky, student is working in a university laboratory when an explosion rocks the building. He feels the shockwaves and hears the blast, but only minimal damage ensues in the laboratory where he is at the time. Even so, it is immediately clear that the neighbouring laboratory has been completely destroyed and his four closest friends were working there. His fears are justified.[132] All four were killed in the blast. The surviving student succumbs to psychiatric illness. If he shows that his illness resulted from reasonable fear for himself, does he recover as a primary victim? If he admits that it was the shock of his friends' fate which triggered his illness, does he fail because of the absence of the requisite 'close tie of love and affection'?

There have been frequent calls for reform of the law in this area. Three very different solutions have been advanced. Jane Stapleton advocates the abolition of recovery in tort for pure psychiatric harm.[133] She argues the case for a return to the harsh, but clear rules of the Victorian judges contending that 'no reasonable boundaries for the cause of action [can] be found and this [is] an embarrassment to the law'. Peter Handford contends that no special rules should limit claims for psychiatric illness.[134] Foreseeability

---

[129] [1999] 1 All ER 1, at 38.   [130] [1988] QB 304.

[131] This being a case involving a strike-out motion, it is of limited precedent value. Cf *Boumedien v Delta Display Ltd* [2008] EWCA Civ 368.

[132] For a case on broadly analogous facts, where C succeeded, see *Dooley v Cammell Laird & Co Ltd* [1951] 1 Lloyd's Rep 271. In *White v Chief Constable of South Yorkshire* [1999] 1 All ER 1, Lord Hoffmann suggested that this case might have to be treated as falling outside the general rules and control mechanisms for secondary victims.

[133] J Stapleton, 'In Restraint of Tort' in P Birks (ed), *Frontiers of Liability* (1994), 83.

[134] P Handford, *Mullany and Handford's Tort Liability for Psychiatric Damage: The Law of Nervous Shock* (2nd edn, 2006). See also H Teff [1998] CLJ 91.

of psychiatric injury should be the only condition of recovery of compensation. Finally, the Law Commission recommends a 'middle way'.[135] The condition that secondary victims enjoy a close tie of love or affection with the individual who suffers physical harm would stay. All other 'control mechanisms' would be abolished.[136] Perhaps the present author is one of the very few who is content with the pragmatic rules which have been shaped (and continue to be shaped) in this area of negligence, which reflect a gradual working out of appropriate limits to recovery—and which is an example of the common law in action.

Conclusions

In this chapter, we have examined duty of care categories concerning the body and mind. We have seen that courts offer a high degree of protection in cases of negligence involving bodily injury, although there are circumstances in which duties of care have been denied on policy grounds. Issues of charaterisation of damage, and of policy, have been prominent in cases of negligence concerning conception, pregnancy, and birth. This reflects the desire of the courts both to uphold professional standards, whilst discouraging claims the purported effect of which would be to devalue human life. Finally, we examined cases involving the negligent infliction of psychiatric illness, in which the duty of care rules are complex and represent (again) a desire to balance competing interests—here involving mental integrity and the desire to avoid crushing liabilities. While primary victims of negligence, who suffer psychiatric illness, are afforded a wide duty of care, recovery by secondary victims is restricted to those whom the courts believe most worthy of compensation because of the horror of the events in which they have been caught up.

Problem question

Jeff is a firefighter. His firefighting unit was called to fight a fire at Myra's home, which was caused by Myra's failure to turn off a faulty electric cooker. Jeff drove quickly to the scene because he had been told that there might be a small child in Myra's burning house. Just as he was driving the fire truck into the property, Myra's dog jumped in front of it and was killed—leaving a gruesome scene. Myra watched this with her own eyes and would have broken down immediately but was preoccupied by overwhelming concerns for her child. Jeff was able to break through a wooden wall and rescue the child. He was temporarily overcome by fumes but recuperated physically. Unfortunately, Jeff's experiences that night caused him great stress—and added to the growing feeling of helplessness that he has been experiencing in his work life.

---

[135] *Liability for Psychiatric Illness*, Law Com No 249 (1998).

[136] For the argument that most of the extant control mechanisms can be rationalised in terms of the general test for the imposition of a duty of care, see J Murphy (1995) 15 LS 415.

Explain whether either Myra or Jeff have a cause of action for the psychiatric illnesses that they have developed.

 Visit http://www.oup.com/uk/street15e/ for answer guidance.

Further reading

BAILEY AND NOLAN, 'The *Page v Smith* Saga: A Tale of Inauspicious Origins and Unintended Consequences' (2010) 69 *Cambridge Law Journal* 495

HANDFORD, *Mullany and Handford's Tort Liability for Psychiatric Damage* (2nd edn, 2006)

MULHERON, 'Rewriting the Requirement for a "Recognised Psychiatric Injury" in Negligence Claims' (2012) 32 *Oxford Journal of Legal Studies* 77

NOLAN, 'New Forms of Damage in Negligence' (2007) 70 *Modern Law Review* 59

NOLAN, 'Damage in the English Law of Negligence' (2013) 4 *Journal of European Tort Law* 259

TEFF, *Causing Psychiatric and Emotional Harm: Reshaping the Boundaries of Legal Liability* (2008)

WITTING, 'Physical Damage in Negligence' (2002) 61 *Cambridge Law Journal* 189

4

Duty of care III: property damage and purely financial loss

KEY ISSUES

(1) Property damage

Courts offer a high degree of protection to those who have recognised interests in property that is physically damaged by the negligence of another. This reflects the traditional importance of tangible property in enabling people to live their lives as they see fit.

(2) Purely financial loss

Purely financial loss cases are different. They involve no external impacts upon the claimant's tangible property. However, they can arise from the construction of buildings or assembly of structures that are defective from the beginning. They arise also from relational economic losses, from the making of misstatements, and

the poor execution of services. Duties of care rarely feature in the former two categories of case. In the latter two categories, courts utilise the concept of 'assumption of responsibility' in order to determine whether or not to recognise duties of care.

(3) Concurrent obligations in contract and tort

Obligations arising in tort and contract can overlap, especially in the kinds of case considered in this chapter. Courts have taken the view that the terms of contracts entered into between disputant parties are very important in determining the scope of duties of care in negligence.

Section 1 Introduction

This chapter continues our discussion of recognised categories of duty of care in negligence, moving beyond protection of personal interests (considered in chapter 3) to the protection of property and financial interests. Here we find that the law more readily recognises duties of care in the former case than the latter. A question arises as to why this is so. A theory that appeals to the present author is that historically the law has, and continues to place emphasis upon tangible rather than intangible manifestations of wealth because these are (in the majority of cases) more basic to immediate human needs. Moreover, many items of property can be closely identified with their owners (under the personhood theory of property), whereas bank credits and money as currency do not play an important role in constructing the self.[1]

Section 2 Damage to property

General Recognition of a duty of care to avoid physical damage to another's property raises no unique problem of principle. In conformity to the duty of care framework set out in *Caparo Industries plc v Dickman*,[2] it is necessary in novel cases for the claimant to demonstrate that the risk of physical damage to the property of a class of person was reasonably foreseeable, and that there was the necessary proximity between the parties and/or their property. As in cases of bodily injury, proximity usually arises from the fact that the parties and/or their property were in physical propinquity, a failure in care resulting in some external impact or introduction of a mechanism of physical change.[3] Should a negligent driver, by the narrowest of margins, avoid injuring me in my person, I can recover the cost of the designer suit that is ripped open by her vehicle. Should the careless driver, swerving to avoid me, crash into another's front wall, she can recover the cost of repairing the wall. Whether the damaged property is a chattel or real property, a duty to take reasonable care not to inflict that kind of harm arises.[4] Having said as much, we need to examine important issues: first, that the claimant is the right person to sue; and second, the judicial treatment of various kinds of claim involving allegations of property damage.

Title to sue The House of Lords in *Leigh & Sillivan Ltd v Aliakmon Shipping Co Ltd* confirmed the rule that a duty of care in respect of loss or damage to property is owed only to persons having 'legal ownership of, or a possessory title to, the property concerned at the time when the loss or damage occurred'.[5] Should an old house in the process of conversion to flats be destroyed by a fire caused by negligence, only the owner of the house, or a tenant, may recover compensation. The builders, the plumbers, the decorators, all of whom lose out on valuable contracts to convert the property, are left remediless. Contractual rights in relation to property might well be adversely affected by loss or damage to that property, but, in the absence of a 'special relationship', they are insufficient to give rise to a duty of care.

Property damage In its core conception, property damage involves some deleterious change in the physical state or structure of property.[6] These changes impair the

---

[1] See M Radin (1982) 34 Stanford LR 957.   [2] [1990] 2 AC 605.

[3] Clearly, foreseeability alone is insufficient. Moreover, there are occasional cases in which policy issues intrude: *Marc Rich & Co AG v Bishop Rock Marine Co Ltd* [1996] AC 211.

[4] *Leigh & Sillivan Ltd v Aliakmon Shipping Co Ltd* [1986] 2 All ER 145. See also *The Mineral Transporter* [1986] AC 1; *Tate & Lyle Industries Ltd v Greater London Council* [1983] 2 AC 509. Where, however, the parties are neighbouring property owners, the action might lie in nuisance rather than negligence.

[5] [1986] 2 All ER 145, at 149. See also *Simaan General Contracting Co v Pilkington Glass Ltd (No 2)* [1988] QB 758.   [6] C Witting (2002) 61 CLJ 189.

functional characteristics of the thing in question. Whether the law will regard the physical change as damage depends, at the borderline, on 'the evidence and the circumstances'.[7] There are some rather difficult borderline cases. For example, the need to decontaminate a ship after it has been doused in acid, which causes no tangible damage to the ship, has been characterised as physical damage.[8] A similar interpretation has been placed on the ingress of water into a gas supply line such that householders become deprived of a gas supply for several days.[9] But, in order to be able to recover for property damage, the claimant must suffer more than merely trivial harm.[10] As with bodily injury (considered in chapter 3), the claimant is able to succeed, ordinarily, where the interference with a property interest is such as to seriously impair the functionality or use value of the property.[11]

Often, property damage results from the operation of some external force, but this need not be so. Cases like *Spartan Steel & Alloys Ltd v Martin & Co (Contractors) Ltd*[12] indicate that the positive acts of the defendant might make it foreseeable that the claimant will react in a certain way causative of damage, perhaps in order to avoid worse consequences occurring. Alternatively, the very failure of the defendant to do something that should have been done might cause damage to property.

Negligent certification In negligent 'certification' cases, typically the defendant is a governmental or semi-governmental agency which has responsibility for certifying that property is fit for use. A certificate (or licence to operate) is negligently granted when the property is not fit for use and the claimant suffers physical damage to property as a result. The difference between this type of case and the category of 'negligent misstatement' cases, considered below, is that having a proprietary or possessory interest in physical property makes the difference and the claimant ordinarily can claim in negligence. Assuming the foreseeability of property damage should care not be taken in the issue of the certificate, the defendant's position in issuing the certificate indicates control over an activity and pathways to harm between it and the claimant's property, and justifies recognition of a duty of care.[13] In a small number of certification cases, courts have denied duties of care on policy grounds. The most well-known example of such denial of a duty of care arose in *Marc Rich & Co AG v Bishop Rock Marine Co Ltd* (considered in chapter 2).[14] The defendant ship classification society had been negligent in issuing a certificate which permitted a ship to sail despite the need for significant repairs. The defendant failed to take care in doing this, and the ship subsequently sank, leading to claims of property damage for losses not covered under applicable international conventions for carriage of goods by sea. In refusing the claims of the cargo owners, the House of Lords provided several policy reasons. These included the fact that the international carriage of goods regime and insurance provisions were predicated upon

---

[7] *Hunter v Canary Wharf Ltd* [1997] AC 655, at 676.   [8] *The Orjula* [1995] 2 Lloyd's Rep 395.
[9] *Anglian Water Services Ltd v Crawshaw Robbins Co Ltd* [2001] BLR 173.
[10] Reaffirmed in *Rothwell v Chemical & Insulating Co Ltd* [2008] 1 AC 281, a case concerned with personal injury.   [11] Eg, *Hunter v Canary Wharf Ltd* [1997] AC 655, at 676.
[12] [1973] 1 QB 27.   [13] *Perrett v Collins* [1998] PNLR 77, at 88.   [14] [1996] 1 AC 211.

particular allocations of responsibility for losses, and the potential for overly defensive conduct on the part of ship classification societies.

Section 3 Purely financial loss

We turn now to cases of purely financial (or 'economic') loss, typically arising from business-oriented transactions and industrial accidents affecting third parties. This is another area of negligence law in which courts have taken a restrictive approach. We begin with a definition and some preliminary observations about purely financial loss cases before moving on to examine the main categories of purely financial loss.

Definition Purely financial loss can be defined in the negative as a loss which is not physical damage or injury to intellectual property rights or reputation. It is, furthermore, not merely consequential upon these kinds of injury. The concern is with losses not immediately bound up in one of the primary interests of person, property (including intellectual property), or reputation. In positive terms, purely financial loss involves such things as money expended and opportunities to profit forgone as a result of the defendant's failure to take care.[15] In accordance with the hierarchy of protected interests discussed in chapter 2, the law of negligence offers a higher degree of protection to physical interests (and mental integrity) than to purely financial interests.[16]

Categories of case Purely financial loss cases fall into a number of (to some extent overlapping) categories. In English law, recovery is permitted most frequently in cases involving the negligent provision of advice or information ('*Hedley Byrne*' cases). This category of case merges into a more amorphous category concerning the negligent provision of professional services ('extended *Hedley Byrne*' cases). Other recognised categories, which feature less frequently successful claims, include those of defective property/products and relational financial losses (arising when damage is done to the property of intermediate parties upon which the claimant relies in some way). Each of these categories is explained and explored in the remainder of this chapter.[17]

Concerns about recovery Generally, the courts have been cautious about recognising duties of care in cases of purely financial loss.[18] There are various reasons for this, some more convincing than others, including: the abstract nature of financial interests; the indirect ways in which financial losses arise (often in circumstances where persons act on advice or rely upon the expertise of another); the potential for a 'ripple effect' among

---

[15] M Bussani and VV Palmer (eds), *Pure Economic Loss in Europe* (2003), 14.

[16] Reputation is protected through the tort of defamation, as to which see ch 20. Intellectual property rights are protected in torts such as passing off, as to which see ch 14.

[17] For more detailed analyses of the various kinds of claim which can arise, see, eg, M Bussani and VV Palmer (eds), *Pure Economic Loss in Europe* (2003).

[18] See J Stapleton (1991) 107 LQR 249; id (1995) 111 LQR 301; C Witting (2001) 21 LS 481.

successive groups of persons; the potential for indeterminate liability; the potential for disproportionate liability; and the difficulty of proving such losses.[19]

Limits to recovery According to Lord Fraser in *The Mineral Transporter*, 'some limit or control mechanism has to be imposed on the liability of a wrongdoer towards those who have suffered economic damage as a consequence of his negligence'.[20] The restrictive approach to purely financial loss means that, in practice, it is recoverable only where *either* the loss is consequential upon physical damage also suffered by the claimant *or* the claimant can establish a 'special relationship' between herself and the defendant.[21] It is as well to note at the outset that 'special relationships' exist not just where the defendant has made a statement or proffered advice upon which the claimant relies, but also where she has undertaken to perform various forms of service. However, historical development of the law in this area makes it simpler to begin by examining purely financial loss resulting from inaccurate statements and advice.

(A) Misstatements

Problematic features Two difficulties beset the imposition of any duty to avoid making careless statements. First, there is a difference in the potential effects of careless words and careless acts. For, while negligent acts inevitably have a limited range of impact, negligent words might be widely broadcast without the consent or foresight of the speaker so as to cause successive waves of damage. Second, misstatements often inflict only financial loss and must be treated with caution because of the limited ability of tort law to protect financial interests.[22]

Development of doctrine The development of the duty of care regarding the making of statements with the potential for causing financial losses is linked inextricably to the troubled history of liability for purely financial loss in general. The original difficulty was that a person suffering financial loss through reliance on a misstatement was expected to sue in the tort of deceit. In *Derry v Peek*,[23] the House of Lords held that to establish deceit the claimant must prove fraud—that is, broadly, that the defendant knew that her statement was untrue, or was reckless as to its untruth. Mere negligence would be insufficient.[24] In *Hedley Byrne & Co Ltd v Heller & Partners Ltd*,[25] the House of Lords exposed the fallacy in this early case law:

---

[19] The reasons are reviewed in C Witting (2001) 21 LS 481.

[20] [1985] 2 All ER 935, at 945. See also *White v CC of South Yorkshire Police* [1999] 1 All ER 1, at 31.

[21] *Williams v Natural Life Health Foods Ltd* [1998] 2 All ER 577; *Henderson v Merrett Syndicates Ltd* [1995] 2 AC 145.

[22] But it should not be overlooked that careless words, whether written or spoken, do have the potential to cause harm to the person. See, eg, *De Freville v Dill* (1927) 96 LJKB 1056; *Sharp v Avery* [1938] 4 All ER 85; *Clayton v Woodman & Son (Builders) Ltd* [1961] 3 All ER 249 (revd on other grounds [1962] 2 All ER 33) and certification cases discussed in text above.   [23] (1889) 14 App Cas 337.

[24] *Candler v Crane, Christmas & Co* [1951] 2 KB 164.   [25] [1964] AC 465.

> Cs asked their bankers to inquire into the financial stability of a company with which they were having business dealings. Cs' bankers made inquiries of Ds, the company's bankers, who carelessly gave favourable references about the company. Reliance on these references caused Cs £17,000 in wasted expenditure. Cs sued Ds for their misstatements.

The action failed only because Ds had expressly disclaimed any responsibility. However, the House of Lords established the principle that liability could arise for negligence in the making of misstatements. In doing so, their Lordships limited the rule in *Derry v Peek* to its proper function of defining the limits of the tort of deceit, and thus held it to be irrelevant to the issue whether a duty of care arose in negligence. The absence of a contract was irrelevant also. As Lord Devlin said:

> A promise given without consideration to perform a service cannot be enforced as a contract by the promisee, but if the service is in fact performed and done negligently the promisee can recover in an action in tort.[26]

However, their Lordships were not prepared to recognise a duty of care in respect of negligent misstatements on the basis of the *Donoghue v Stevenson*[27] neighbour principle alone. For liability to be imposed with respect to misstatements resulting in financial loss, some narrower test than that of foreseeability of the loss had to be satisfied.[28] The House was careful not to formulate rules in a way that might expose a statement maker to liability to a large, indeterminate class of claimants. For instance, newspapers were not to be accountable to everybody who read negligently written advice columns and suffered loss in reliance on them.[29] Instead, their Lordships said that the claimant seeking to recover for a negligent misstatement must establish that the statement was made within a relationship where the claimant reasonably could rely on the skill and care of the defendant. She must show some 'special relationship' with the defendant, in which the defendant could be seen to have undertaken responsibility for the accuracy of the statement made.[30] Reasons for taking this approach were inherent in Lord Reid's statement that:

> Quite careful people often express definite opinions on social or informal occasions, even when they see that others are likely to be influenced by them; and they often do that without taking that care which they would take if asked for their opinion professionally, or in a business.[31]

Special relationship Subsequent case law has elucidated the meaning of the phrase 'special relationship' and the circumstances in which duties of care are to be recognised.

---

[26] [1964] AC 465, at 526.   [27] [1932] AC 562.   [28] [1964] AC 465, at 483 and 537.

[29] [1971] AC 793. A trade association making available certain information about its members' products does not owe a duty of care to those who use that information to contact a member and with whom a contract is subsequently entered into, given that the website itself 'urges independent inquiry': *Patchett v Swimming Pools & Allied Trades Association Ltd* [2010] 2 All ER (Comm) 138.

[30] This is not to say that the House of Lords limited liability for negligent misstatements to cases involving undertakings: see C Witting, 'What Are We Doing Here? The Relationship between Negligence in General and Misstatements in English Law' in K Barker, R Granthamm and W Swain, *Law of Misstatements: 50 Years on From Hedley Byrne v Heller* (2015), ch 9.   [31] [1964] AC 465, at 487.

In *Mutual Life and Citizens' Assurance Co Ltd v Evatt*,[32] Lord Diplock suggested that liability for misstatements would arise in the context of certain professional relationships only, where giving advice is the primary purpose of the relationship. So, in general terms, solicitors would be responsible for legal advice offered to clients, and stockbrokers for financial guidance, but an insurance company volunteering financial advice to a policyholder would not be liable.

However, the Court of Appeal largely ignored the *Evatt* case. In *Chaudhry v Prabhakar*[33] the defendant, who considered himself something of an expert on motor cars, was held liable to his friend, whom he agreed to assist with the purchase of a car, when his advice proved to be negligent. Indeed, the trend up until 1989 appeared to be to allow a liberal interpretation of what constituted a special relationship.

But two subsequent decisions of the House of Lords—*Caparo Industries plc v Dickman*[34] and *Smith v Eric S Bush*[35]—outlined more authoritatively the parameters of liability for financial loss arising from negligent advice. Although the *Caparo* case was decided subsequently to *Smith v Bush*, it helps to consider it first:

> Ds were auditors who acted for Fidelity plc. They had prepared annual accounts on the strength of which Cs bought shares in Fidelity and then mounted a successful takeover bid. Cs alleged that the accounts were inaccurate and misleading, showing a large pre-tax profit when they should have recorded a sizeable loss. Had Cs been aware of this, they would never have bid for Fidelity.

The House of Lords held that four conditions must be met for a defendant to be liable for financial loss resulting from negligent advice or information: (1) The defendant must be *fully* aware of the nature of the transaction which the claimant has in contemplation as a result of receipt of the information. (2) She must either communicate that information to the claimant directly, or know that it will be communicated to him (or a restricted class of persons of which the claimant is an identifiable member).[36] (3) She must specifically anticipate that the claimant *properly* and *reasonably* will rely on that information when deciding whether to engage in the transaction in question. (4) The purpose for which the claimant does rely on that information must be connected with interests that it is reasonable to require the defendants to protect.

On the facts of the *Caparo* case, the auditors were found to owe no duty of care in respect of the accuracy of the accounts, either to members of the public who relied on them to invest in the company, or to existing individual shareholders who relied on them to increase their shareholdings.[37] If auditors were liable to *any* investor who relied on the published accounts to deal with the company simply because such conduct is foreseeable, they would be liable to anyone else who dealt with the company to her or its

---

[32] [1971] AC 793.   [33] [1988] 3 All ER 718. See also *Esso Petroleum Co Ltd v Mardon* [1976] QB 801.
[34] [1990] 2 AC 605.   [35] [1990] 1 AC 831.
[36] The absence of this element was problematic in the three-party reference case of *Playboy Club London Ltd v Banca Nazionale del Lavoro SpA* [2016] 1 WLR 3169.
[37] The Court of Appeal had held that existing shareholders were owed such a duty, distinguishing the shareholder investors from other members of the public: [1989] 1 All ER 798.

detriment, for example, banks lending the company money, or tradespersons extending credit terms.[38] Yet auditors prepared company accounts under the companies legislation, not to promote the interests of potential investors, but in order to assist the shareholders collectively to exercise their right of control over the company.[39]

Caparo sought to argue that the vulnerability of Fidelity to takeover should have alerted the auditors to the likelihood of a company, such as Caparo, mounting a takeover bid, and that they were not just *any* potential investor, but existing shareholders. Their Lordships held that the defendants were under no duty to safeguard the financial interests of corporate predators,[40] and that the statutory duty imposed on them by Parliament was to protect the existing interests of the shareholders in the client company,[41] not to facilitate investment decisions whether by existing shareholders or others.[42]

Illustrative cases A positive avalanche of cases on the limits of *Hedley Byrne* liability followed. Just a few examples are given here to illustrate the application of the *Caparo* principles in action. In one case, it was held that directors of a company who issued a prospectus to invite shareholders to take up a rights issue were not under a duty to those shareholders who relied on the prospectus to make further investments.[43] Nor were accountants advising a creditor company on the appointment of a receiver liable to that company's debtors.[44] In both cases, the relationship between the parties lacked the necessary proximity. The defendants had done nothing to assume responsibility for the financial welfare of the claimants.

But, what if some express representation has been made directly to the claimant, on the basis of which she argues that she decided to go ahead with a particular transaction? Much will turn on the facts of the case. In *James McNaughton Paper Group v Hicks Anderson & Co*,[45] the defendant accountants became aware that the claimants were considering a takeover of their clients. At a meeting between the two companies, the defendants were asked to confirm the accuracy of draft accounts, and they did this in very general terms. The Court of Appeal found that no duty was owed to the claimants. The draft accounts were not prepared for their benefit, and the defendants reasonably would expect a party to a takeover bid to take independent advice and not rely exclusively on draft accounts. However, in another case where it was pleaded that the defendants had prepared profit forecasts expressly in order to induce the claimants to increase their bid for a company at risk of takeover, the Court of Appeal refused to strike out the claim.[46]

---

[38] See *Al Saudi Banque v Clark Pixley* [1990] Ch 313.   [39] [1990] 1 All ER 568, at 580–1 and 600–1.

[40] Why should auditors be responsible for the success of those actively seeking to destroy their client?

[41] As to whether an existing shareholder might sue if her existing proprietary interest was damaged by negligence on the part of the auditors (ie, sold at an undervalue) see [1990] 1 All ER 568, at 580–1 (Lord Bridge—probably yes) and 601 (Lord Oliver, leaving the question open).

[42] See also *MAN Nutzfahrzeuge AG v Freightliner Ltd* [2008] PNLR 6.

[43] *Al-Nakib Investments (Jersey) Ltd v Longcroft* [1990] 3 All ER 321.

[44] *Huxford v Stoy Hayward & Co* (1989) 5 BCC 421.   [45] [1991] 2 QB 113.

[46] *Morgan Crucible v Hill Samuel Bank Ltd* [1991] 1 All ER 148.

Perhaps the key question in this sort of case is whether the defendant's advice has been given in a context in which the assumption that claimants generally should look after their own financial interests can be displaced. Have the defendants, in effect, induced the claimants to place faith in their judgement? In *Henderson v Merrett Syndicates Ltd*,[47] managing agents at Lloyds, who placed monies entrusted to them by Names at Lloyds in underwriting contracts, owed a duty of care to 'their' Names. The agents undertook responsibility for advising the claimants and finding appropriate investments for their money. They effectively 'took over' the claimants' financial affairs.

Williams v Natural Life Health Foods Ltd[48] is instructive also:

> The second defendant set up a company to franchise out health food businesses. The claimants approached the company to obtain a franchise. Having received from the company, Natural Life, a glowing brochure and prospectus which included testimonies to the second defendant's experience and success, the claimants proceeded to obtain a franchise. At no stage in the pre-contractual negotiations did they have any contact with the second defendant personally. The claimants' shop failed to make money, resulting in severe financial loss. They sued the company, Natural Life, and the second defendant personally. The company went into liquidation so the action proceeded against the second defendant alone.

The House of Lords found that there had been no special relationship between the second defendant and the claimants because there were no substantial personal dealings between them,[49] so that it could not be concluded that the second defendant had assumed personal responsibility for the claimant's affairs. Nor was there evidence that the claimants relied on his personal undertakings to safeguard their financial wellbeing as franchisers. The dealings were all with the company. Unlike the Lloyds' agents in the *Henderson* case, the second defendant took on no role as an individual in 'managing' the claimants' business interests.

We move now to look at *Smith v Eric S Bush*;[50] but we do so noting that, in the *Caparo* case,[51] Lord Oliver described that case as being at the outer limit of *Hedley Byrne* liability:

> Ds were surveyors acting for a building society, the mortgagees. They gave favourable reports on the properties to be purchased by C, the mortgagor. An express disclaimer denied any liability to C.[52] Nonetheless, the evidence was that 90% of house purchasers rely on the mortgagees' report[53] and do not engage their own surveyors. C paid the surveyor's fee and Ds were well aware that C (whose identity they knew) would rely on the report and would suffer loss if it were negligently prepared.

---

[47] [1995] 2 AC 145. As to concurrent liability in tort and contract see ch 2. See also S Whittaker (1997) 17 LS 169.   [48] [1998] 2 All ER 577.

[49] However, the Court of Appeal judgment shows this assertion by the House to have been incorrect: see [1997] BCC 605.   [50] [1990] 1 AC 831.

[51] [1998] 2 All ER 577, at 598.

[52] The disclaimer was invalid under the Unfair Contract Terms Act 1977. See also Consumer Rights Act 2015.

[53] *Smith v Eric S Bush* was a consolidated appeal concerning two separate claimants. In one case the mortgagee showed the actual report to C1. In the other, the report itself was not disclosed to C2.

The House of Lords unanimously found that, in such circumstances, a duty of care was owed to the mortgagor. Unlike in *Caparo*, the defendants were well aware of the identity of the claimant, knew that their advice would be transmitted to the claimant, and appreciated exactly how the claimant would act in reliance on that advice. There was no element of uncertainty relating to the transaction consequent on that advice. There was no question of liability other than to one identifiable claimant.[54] There was no conflict between the interests of the surveyors' client and the mortgagors.[55] If the surveyors had done the job properly and produced a proper valuation, they would have discharged their duty to both mortgagee and mortgagor. The claimants, who paid their fees, were entitled to rely on their professional skill and advice.[56]

Adoption of third-party statements *Hedley Byrne* and other cases establish that, where the defendant makes a negligent misstatement and it is passed on to an intermediate party X, who then disseminates it to the claimant, the defendant might be liable to the claimant. It has been established, also, that X herself might be liable, if the preconditions for a 'special relationship' are met—notably, when X 'adopts the information as her own' or else negligently represents that she believes the information supplied by the defendant to be correct.[57]

Scope of duty An important matter to keep in mind in misstatement cases is that duties of care inevitably are of limited scope. They are likely to be wider in cases where the defendant statement maker is being asked to advise on an ultimate decision, and narrower in cases where she is required merely to provide certain information to be taken into account by her client when the client makes the ultimate decision.[58] This means that, where negligence arises in the giving of advice or information with respect to which the defendant has no duty of care, the defendant is not responsible for subsequent losses that flow from the errant advise or information.[59]

(B) The extended *Hedley Byrne* principle

Assumption of responsibility What, then, is the basis of *Hedley Byrne* liability? In *Smith v Bush*, Lord Griffiths dismissed as unhelpful the notion that liability rests on

---

[54] The likelihood that a purchaser might emerge in the future who will suffer loss if a survey is carelessly conducted is insufficient. A particular individual who will almost inevitably place faith in the report and act to her detriment must be within D's contemplation: *The Morning Watch* [1990] 1 Lloyd's Rep 547. Contrast *Smith v Bush* with *Goodwill v British Pregnancy Advisory Service* [1996] 2 All ER 161.

[55] Cf *West Bromwich Albion FC Ltd v El Safty* [2007] PIQR P7.

[56] Lord Griffiths and Lord Jauncey both made references to the reasonableness of purchasers at the lower end of the market relying on the building society survey rather than facing the additional expense of an independent report. Yet the *Smith v Bush* approach was applied to a mid-range property in *Beaumont v Humberts* [1990] 49 EG 46. Cf *Scullion v Bank of Scotland plc* [2011] 1 WLR 3212, where the Court of Appeal rejected a claim that a surveyor providing a valuation for the mortgagee owed a duty of care to the mortgagor of a buy-to-let property.   [57] *Webster v Liddington* [2014] EWCA Civ 560, especially at [46]–[47].

[58] See, esp, *Hughes-Holland v BPE Solicitors* [2017] 2 WLR 1029, at [40]–[41] and [53]; *South Australia Asset Management Corp v York Montague Ltd* [1997] AC 191.

[59] *Hughes-Holland v BPE Solicitors* [2017] 2 WLR 1029.

an 'assumption of responsibility' by the defendant.[60] Indeed, the defendants in *Smith v Bush* manifested every intention not to accept responsibility, attempting expressly to disclaim liability. A duty, Lord Griffiths argued, can arise, not only where the defendant either expressly or implicitly undertakes responsibility to the claimant for advice or information, but also where the particular relationship between the two is such that it is just that the defendant be subject to such responsibility.[61] Lord Griffiths' criticism of any principle of assumption of responsibility was strongly supported by a number of academic commentators.[62]

However, subsequent decisions of the House of Lords have endorsed the 'assumption of responsibility' test as the basis of an 'extended *Hedley Byrne*' principle, which embraces negligent performance of services as much as negligent statements and advice;[63] and which extends now to cases characterised by *both* dependency *and* reliance on the part of the claimant.[64] In *Henderson v Merrett Syndicates Ltd*,[65] for example, Lord Goff rested his finding of liability on the part of the managing agents on their assumption of responsibility towards those who relied on their special expertise in underwriting. In *White v Jones*, Lord Browne-Wilkinson affirmed the centrality within *Hedley Byrne* liability of discovering whether the defendant had assumed responsibility for the advice or task undertaken. He was of the view, however, that what is crucial is 'a conscious assumption of responsibility for the *task* rather than a conscious assumption of legal responsibility to the claimant for its careful performance'.[66]

Wider liability In more general terms, the decisions *Henderson v Merrett Syndicates Ltd, White v Jones*, and *Williams v Natural Life Health Foods Ltd* confirm that the *Hedley Byrne* case opened the doors to much wider liability in respect of financial loss in tort than had been available previously.[67] In *Hedley Byrne* itself, Lord Devlin stated:

> Cases may arise in the future in which a new and wider proposition, quite independent of contract, will be needed. There may, for example, be cases in which a statement is not supplied for the use of any particular individual.[68]

Just such a duty of care came to pass in *So v HSBC Bank plc*,[69] although liability was not established because causation of financial loss could not be proved:

---

[60] [1998] 2 All ER 577, at 865, confirming the decision of the Court of Appeal in *Ministry of Housing and Local Government v Sharp* [1970] 2 QB 223.

[61] See *Al Saudi Banque v Clark Pixley* [1989] 3 All ER 361, at 367.

[62] See, eg, K Barker (1993) 109 LQR 461; B Hepple (1997) 50 CLP 69; C Witting (2013) 24 KLJ 343.

[63] *Williams v Natural Life Health Foods Ltd* [1998] 2 All ER 577.

[64] Even with this description of the extended *Hedley Byrne* principle problems can arise in explaining the decided cases. In some, the courts have had to alight upon tenuous notions of 'an assumption of responsibility' (see, eg, *White v Jones* [1995] 2 AC 207). Equally, there are some rather fictitious instances of reliance to be found in the cases. For some judicial recognition of this, see *Customs and Excise Commissioners v Barclays Bank plc* [2005] 1 WLR 2082 (reversed on other issues [2007] 1 AC 181).

[65] [1995] 2 AC 145, at 182.   [66] [1995] 2 AC 207, at 274.

[67] But note that 'extended *Hedley Byrne*' liability is not necessarily confined to financial loss. It has been accepted, for example, that it could in principle be invoked in relation to psychiatric illness caused by being wrongfully convicted due to the negligence of C's solicitors: *McLoughlin v Grovers* [2002] QB 1312.

[68] [1964] AC 465, at 530.   [69] [2009] 1 CLC 503.

> An employee of the defendant bank signed and stamped a document supplied by and returned to their client, 5th Avenue. The document, which purported to be a letter of instruction relating to the payment of money out of 5th Avenue's bank account for the strict purpose of investment, obviously was capable of misleading third parties. The document was used in order to defraud 5th Avenue's customers, who believed that the defendant bank would safeguard their payments.

The Court of Appeal held that a duty of care was owed to non-clients of the defendant bank on the basis that, by providing the document, HSBC had represented that it 'intended to carry out and had accepted the instructions'.[70]

Wills cases   Seeking to extend the boundaries of a duty to avoid inflicting financial loss on others, in *Ross v Caunters* Megarry V-C took a robust approach:

> D, a solicitor, drew up a will negligently and failed to fulfil his client-testator's instruction to benefit C. C then sued D in negligence.[71]

In no sense could the claimant be said to have relied on the solicitor, yet his action succeeded. The judge held that the law had so developed by 1979 that he should apply the neighbour principle in *Donoghue v Stevenson* in the absence of any policy factors negativing or limiting the scope of such a duty. There was close proximity between the claimant and the defendant. His contemplation of her was 'actual, nominate and direct', so proximity arose out of the duty he owed to the testator. It was in no way 'casual, accidental or unforeseen'. The liability arising from the duty was to one person alone.[72] Accordingly, the spectre of indeterminate liability did not arise.

In *White v Jones*,[73] the House of Lords found for the claimant on facts reminiscent of those in *Ross v Caunters*:

> After a family quarrel, the testator (aged 78) disinherited Cs (his daughters). A few months later, the family was reconciled and, on 17 July, the testator instructed Ds (his solicitors), to draw up a new will including legacies of £9,000 to each daughter. Ds failed to act on those instructions before the testator died some months later. As a result of Ds' negligent delay in acting on the testator's instructions, Cs failed to be awarded their legacies.

The claim in *White v Jones* posed a number of conceptual difficulties:[74] First, the defendant's contractual duty was owed only to his client, the now dead testator. Privity of contract rules excluded the extension of *this* duty to the disappointed beneficiaries. Second, the claimants' actions, being founded on purely financial loss, could succeed only on the basis of some form of application of *Hedley Byrne*; yet there was neither an obvious

---

[70] [2009] 1 CLC 503, at [40].
[71] [1980] Ch 297. And see *Al-Kandari v JR Brown & Co* [1988] QB 665.
[72] See *Caltex Oil (Australia) Pty Ltd v Dredge Willemstad* (1976) 136 CLR 529 (noting the importance in relation to financial loss of there being a single identifiable C rather than a diffuse class of potential Cs).
[73] [1995] 2 AC 207.   [74] Detailed in full [1995] 2 AC 207, at 260–2.

assumption of responsibility towards the claimants nor any corresponding reliance on their part. For this reason, it was straining logic to suggest that the claimants had lost anything at all.[75] Third, if liability were to be imposed, establishing clear and manageable limits to it would be hard to achieve. The House of Lords thought these difficulties could be surmounted.[76] While Lord Goff made it clear that their Lordships did not endorse Megarry V-C's simplistic approach in *Ross v Caunters*, which based liability on the neighbour principle alone,[77] the conceptual grounds on which their Lordships established liability are difficult to ascertain.[78] Lord Goff was frank in admitting that he was strongly motivated by an impulse to do 'practical justice'. He pointed out the 'extraordinary fact' that, if no duty in tort were owed to the claimants, the only persons who might have a valid claim (the testator and his estate) had suffered no loss, and the only persons who suffered any kind of loss (the disappointed beneficiaries) would have no claim.[79]

So what did *White v Jones* decide? The following propositions were at its heart: (1) The existence of a contract between the defendants and a third party (the testator) did not, by virtue of the rules on privity of contract, exclude a duty in tort to the claimant. (2) Such a duty could arise if, quite apart from the contract, the circumstances of the case gave rise to a 'special relationship' between the parties. (3) On the facts of *Hedley Byrne* itself, proof that the claimant relied on the advice given, or statements made, by the defendants, and that the defendants should have foreseen such reliance, was an 'inevitable' condition of liability. However, reliance is *not* a necessary condition for the creation of a special relationship in every case giving rise to a duty to safeguard another from financial loss (including *White v Jones* itself). (4) A special relationship will arise when the defendant assumes responsibility for providing services knowing and accepting that 'the future economic welfare of the intended beneficiary is dependent on his careful execution of the task'.[80] (5) On the facts of *White v Jones*, there were no policy reasons why such a duty should not be imposed on the defendants, and indeed good reasons in favour of it. The actual outcome of the decision in *Ross v Caunters*, imposing liability on solicitors for negligently executed wills, had worked well and had not given rise to unlimited claims. In such cases there was no conflict of interest[81] between the duty owed to the testator in contract, and the duty owed to the claimants in tort. Fulfilling the contractual obligation to the defendant at one and the same time would have discharged the duty of care owed to the claimants.

Furthermore, *White v Jones* clarifies three crucial principles: (1) A duty of care in cases of financial loss is confined to special relationships within which the defendant has assumed responsibility for protecting the claimant's financial welfare.[82] (2) Such a relationship will arise only where the claimant is readily identifiable as an individual or a member of a class of persons for whom the defendant undertakes responsibility (in the loosest sense)[83] in the performance of a particular task. (3) 'Extended *Hedley Byrne*'

---

[75] See P Benson, 'Should White v Jones Represent Canadian Law?' in JW Neyers et al (eds), *Emerging Issues in Tort Law* (2007), ch 6.   [76] Note the powerful dissent of Lord Mustill.
[77] [1995] 2 AC 207, at 268.   [78] See J Murphy (1996) 55 CLJ 43.   [79] [1995] 2 AC 207, at 259–60.
[80] [1995] 2 AC 207, at 275.   [81] Cf *White v Jones* with *Clarke v Bruce Lance & Co* [1988] 1 All ER 364.
[82] Whether all the cases supposedly decided according to this principle actually meet this requirement upon close scrutiny of their facts is questionable. See, eg, *Merrett v Babb* [2001] QB 1174.
[83] See J Murphy (1996) 55 CLJ 43.

relationships are not confined to negligent misstatements and careless advice. Provision of services, including services provided at the behest of a third party, might create a special relationship in appropriate conditions.[84] Reliance is not an essential ingredient of a special relationship,[85] though in its absence there must be dependency on the part of the claimant (in the sense that the claimant's wellbeing depends upon the care and skill of the defendant).

References A willingness to give a liberal, extended interpretation to *Hedley Byrne* liability married to an apparent impetus to provide justice for an unfortunate claimant is apparent once again in *Spring v Guardian Assurance plc*:[86]

> C sued his former employers for negligence because the reference they provided for him when he sought appointment as an agent for another insurance company was so unfavourable that the company refused to appoint him. The reference suggested that C was dishonest. The trial judge found that the reference had been prepared carelessly and found for C in negligence.

The House of Lords held that there had been an implied term in the contract of employment that any subsequent reference be supplied with due care. The Law Lords ruled in the claimant's favour in tort also. In supplying a reference—at least where references were required as a matter of regulation[87]—the defendant should be treated as having assumed the responsibility to prepare the reference with care. Of course, the *Hedley Byrne* case established that the defendants owed such a duty to the recipient of the reference. But in the instant case, the duty claimed was one owed to the person *about whom it was written*. Therefore, it represented an extension of the *Hedley Byrne* principle that could be justified on the basis that an employee relies on her employer to carry out this service with appropriate care. Her interests are 'entrusted' to the skill of the referee; her financial prospects are in the hands of that person. The law should encourage referees to act carefully with proper regard for the interests of both the recipient and the subject of the reference. A strong desire to offer the claimant redress for a perceived injustice can be seen in their Lordships' opinions.[88]

---

[84] In *West Bromwich Albion FC v El-Safty* [2005] EWHC 2866, it was held that, if the three limbs of the *Caparo* test were met, a surgeon whose treatment of a professional player that had been arranged through the club's physiotherapist would owe a duty of care to the club in respect of the financial loss it would suffer if the player were to receive negligent treatment, ending his career. On the facts, however, the *Caparo* test was not satisfied (affirmed [2006] EWCA Civ 1299). See also *Williams v Natural Life Health Foods Ltd* [1998] 2 All ER 577; *Carr-Glynn v Frearsons* [1998] 4 All ER 225.

[85] C's reliance is often the means by which causation can be established, but it has no normative significance of its own; it tells us nothing about the nature of D's conduct such that it is appropriate for D to be made liable to C.

[86] [1995] 2 AC 296. Note also the growing impetus in negligence law simply to do justice in: *Parkinson v St James and Seacroft University Hospital NHS Trust* [2002] QB 266; *Rees v Darlington Memorial Hospital NHS Trust* [2004] 1 AC 309; *Chester v Afshar* [2005] 1 AC 134.

[87] The regulatory authority (LAUTRO) which governed the conduct of insurance companies required both that the company seeking to appoint C must seek a reference and that Ds must supply such a reference.

[88] See [1994] 3 All ER 129, at 172. Cf *Kapfunde v Abbey National plc* [1999] ICR 1.

Terms of liability *Williams v Natural Life Health Foods Ltd*[89] confirmed the terms of 'extended *Hedley Byrne*' liability. Lord Steyn made three crucial points. (1) Once it is established that a case falls within the extended *Hedley Byrne* principle—that is, where there is a special relationship between the parties[90]—'there is no need to embark on any further inquiry whether it is fair, just and reasonable to impose liability for economic loss'.[91] (2) He acknowledged, and commended, the 'essential gap-filling role' of the law of tort so that, while contractual privity rules might prevent substantial justice being done in that branch of law, this should not prevent tort law from filling that gap. *Spring* illustrates that this interstitial role might operate as between different torts as well. For, there, negligence was utilised to correct what their Lordships regarded as a deficiency in defamation law. (3) Outside any special relationships blessed by the extended *Hedley Byrne* principle, claimants suffering purely financial loss will not, it seems, recover that loss in tort. Lord Steyn declared: 'The extended *Hedley Byrne* principle is the rationalisation or technique adopted by English law for the recovery of damages in respect of economic loss caused by the negligent performance of services.'[92]

(C) Proximity factors in pro-liability cases

Having examined the two categories of purely financial loss case in which claims succeed regularly, we can summarise the kinds of proximity factor that go towards establishing a "special relationship" between the parties. Proximity factors are important in demonstrating both the potential for harm doing and the justice of imposing a duty of care upon the defendant requiring that care be taken in either making a statement or giving advice, or offering a knowledge-based service. In this way, the presence of several proximity factors can help to allay fears of indeterminate or disproportionate liability also. Pertinent proximity factors include:[93]

(1) professional–client or equivalent pre-existing relationships between parties—evidencing expectations that minimum standards will be observed;

(2) special skill or competence in the defendant, greater than the claimant's;[94]

(3) in the absence of actual skill/competence, a holding out of such by the defendant;[95]

(4) an inducement by the defendant inviting the claimant to rely upon her;[96]

---

[89] [1998] 2 All ER 577.   [90] [1998] 2 All ER 577, at 581.

[91] How this is to be reconciled with the clear emphasis on the endeavour to do practical justice in both *Spring* and *White v Jones* is by no means clear. See also the approach of Brooke LJ in *Parkinson v St James and Seacroft University Hospital NHS Trust* [2002] QB 266, at [17].

[92] *Williams v Natural Life Health Foods Ltd* [1998] 2 All ER 577, at 581.

[93] C Witting, 'What are We Doing Here? The Relationship between Negligence in General and Misstatements in English Law' in K Barker, R Grantham, and W Swain (eds), *Liability for Misstatements: 50 Years on from Hedley Byrne v Heller* (2015), ch 9.

[94] *Hedley Byrne v Heller* [1964] AC 465; *Henderson v Merrett Syndicates* [1995] 2 AC 145.

[95] *Hedley Byrne v Heller* [1964] AC 465.

[96] *Morgan Crucible Co plc v Hill Samuel Bank & Co Ltd* [1991] 1 All ER 148.

(5) a request from the claimant to the defendant and supply of advice/information to the claimant for a known purpose;[97]

(6) in three-party cases where a request from the claimant to the defendant is less likely, courts focus upon supply of statements for known purposes;[98]

(7) a duty is more likely to arise where the defendant is the only real source of information about a matter or where the claimant is especially likely to rely upon the defendant;[99]

(8) a duty is more likely to arise from business meetings than from things said on social occasions.[100]

Courts will note the terms of relevant statutes/contractual provisions that are inconsistent with a duty of care;[101] but inconsistent contractual provisions might not be determinative of the situation in tort[102] (as to which, see more below).

(D) Other purely financial loss categories

General Outside the 'extended *Hedley Byrne*' principle, it might seem that courts take the view that no duty to protect others from purely financial loss arises however predictable the loss[103] and however just and reasonable that the defendant should bear the loss. Yet such a duty would be capable of recognition in cases of an actual, *subjective* assumption of responsibility by the defendant for the proper conduct of the task in question.[104] The two most relevant classes of case here concern defective property and relational financial losses.

Defective property Physical damage to, or defects in, property which renders it less than value for money but *not* dangerous is classified as financial loss. So, if one buys a central heating boiler which heats the house inefficiently and at vast expense, the loss one suffers is financial loss, which might be recoverable in contract but normally is not recoverable in tort. However, where the defective property *is* dangerous a line of authority relating to buildings suggested that, if there were an imminent danger of damage to person or *other* property, the cost of rectifying the defect and avoiding the danger could be categorised as physical damage—although no tangible physical

---

[97] *Spring v Guardian Assurance* [1995] 2 AC 296; *Law Society v KPMG Peat Marwick* [2000] 1 WLR 1921.

[98] *Caparo Industries v Dickman* [1990] 2 AC 605; *Playboy Club London Ltd v Banca Nazionale del Lavoro SpA* [2016] 1 WLR 3169, [19].

[99] *Spring v Guardian Assurance* [1995] 2 AC 296 (ex-employer providing reference); *Smith v Eric S Bush* [1990] 1 AC 831 (surveyor providing valuation of modest house). Compare *Scullion v Bank of Scotland* [2011] 1 WLR 2112); *White v Jones* [1995] 2 AC 207 (solicitor failing to execute will).

[100] *Hedley Byrne v Heller & Partners Ltd* [1964] AC 465; but see *Chaudhry v Prabhakar* [1989] 1 WLR 29.

[101] *Harris v Evans* [1998] 1 WLR 1285.   [102] *Smith v Eric S Bush* [1990] 1 AC 831.

[103] See, eg, *Simaan General Contracting Co v Pilkington Glass Ltd (No 2)* [1988] 1 All ER 791.

[104] As opposed to the objective test adopted in *Williams v Natural Life Health Foods Ltd* [1998] 1 WLR 830, considered earlier.

damage had yet materialised.[105] In *Murphy v Brentwood District Council*,[106] the House of Lords rejected that line of authority, holding that physical damage entails actual physical harm to other property (in the manner explained already). Where no such damage has materialised,[107] the loss caused by the need to repair defective property to obviate the danger to person or property is a financial loss. The facts in the *Murphy* case were as follows:

> C had purchased a house built on an infilled site over a concrete raft foundation. In 1981 he discovered cracks in the house threatening the whole fabric of the property. Had he done nothing, the house might have collapsed on top of him. He sued the local council for negligently approving the plans for the foundations. The House of Lords held that the council could not be liable unless the builder would have been so liable.[108]

Their Lordships conceded that a builder of premises is subject to the same duty of care in tort as the manufacturers of goods to 'avoid injury through defects in the premises to the person or property of those whom he should have in contemplation as likely to suffer such injury if care is not taken'.[109] So, if the ceiling had collapsed on Mr Murphy, injuring him or destroying his piano, he might have had a claim for personal injuries or property damage against the builder. However, until actual physical damage occurs, the loss associated with the cost of making the house safe (or any diminution in its value) is treated as purely financial. In the absence of a special relationship, neither manufacturers of goods nor builders of premises are subject to a duty of care in relation to the quality of their work. To impose any such general duty would introduce into the law of tort transmissible warranties of quality.[110] Such guarantees are provided only by contract. Thus, there was perceived to be no general need for tort to fulfil an interstitial role.[111]

The *Murphy* doctrine does not appear to be defensible. It provides persons whose life, limb, and property are in danger of physical harm with no incentives (other than the obvious ones) to take action to arrange for repairs. While the house owner *can* sue then to recover compensation for that physical damage,[112] it should be noted that, in a number of cases, Commonwealth jurisdictions have declined to

---

[105] *Batty v Metropolitan Property Realisations Ltd* [1978] QB 554; *Anns v Merton LBC* [1978] AC 728.

[106] [1991] 1 AC 398. See the powerful critique of the law from this case in S Green and PS Davies, '"Pure Economic Loss" and Defective Buildings' in A Robertson and M Tilbury (eds), *Divergences in Private Law* (2016), ch 4.

[107] Where C buys a house built by X with a central heating system made and installed by Y, and some months after the purchase an explosion damages the house (but injures no one), an action would lie against Y for her negligently manufactured item that has damaged separate property, the house itself: *Murphy v Brentwood DC* [1990] 2 All ER 908, at 928.

[108] For direct authority on the liability of builders see *Department of the Environment v Thomas Bates & Son Ltd* [1991] 1 AC 499.

[109] [1991] 1 AC 398, at 461. Note that the question of the liability of the council even for physical injury was left open.   [110] *D & F Estates Ltd v Church Comrs for England* [1988] 2 All ER 992, at 1010.

[111] See *Williams v Natural Life Health Foods Ltd* [1998] 2 All ER 577.

[112] See *Nitrigin Eireann Teoranta v Inco Alloys Ltd* [1992] 1 All ER 854. Would D be able to plead contributory negligence? See ch 7.

follow the *Murphy* 'doctrine' and preferred to allow claimants in analogous circumstances to succeed.[113]

Relational financial loss A second category of case in which the House of Lords has declared that financial loss is irrecoverable is more straightforward. A claimant who suffers financial loss consequent on physical injury to another person, or consequent on damage to property in which, at the time damage occurred, she had no proprietary or possessory interest, cannot recover that loss in tort.[114] These are cases of 'relational financial loss'. Loss to the claimant arises because of her dependence upon the continuing integrity of another person or of property owned by another.

In *Weller & Co v Foot and Mouth Disease Research Institute*,[115] the defendants carelessly allowed cattle to become infected by foot and mouth disease. The claimants were auctioneers, whose business suffered badly when quarantine restrictions prevented them holding auction sales of cattle. Widgery J said that no duty of care was owed to the claimants for their losses of profits. The scope of any duty owed was limited to cattle owners who suffered physical damage to their property when cattle had to be destroyed. The loss occasioned to the auctioneers was readily foreseeable, but so was financial loss to countless other enterprises: pubs, cafés, shops, and car parks that benefit from visitors on market day. Policy required that a cut-off point be set. Widgery J set it at those suffering physical harm.

A series of decisions on the damages recoverable when services such as water, gas, or electricity were negligently interrupted confirmed Widgery J's finding that financial loss not consequent on physical damage was irrecoverable. In *British Celanese Ltd v Hunt*[116] and *SCM (UK) Ltd v WJ Whittall & Son Ltd*,[117] the negligent severing of electricity supplies damaged the claimants' machines and materials, resulting in losses of production. The claimants in these cases recovered both their expenditures in replacing and repairing machinery and their loss of profits on missed production runs. The Court of Appeal in the latter case held that the financial loss (that is, loss of profits) was recoverable, as it was immediately consequent on physical damage to the claimants' property.

The Court of Appeal considered financial loss again in *Spartan Steel and Alloys Ltd v Martin & Co (Contractors) Ltd*:[118]

> The defendants' negligence caused the cable carrying electricity to the claimant's factory to be cut through, interrupting the supply for 14½ hours. To avoid molten metal solidifying in the furnaces, the claimants used oxygen to melt it and pour it out of the furnaces. This reduced the value of the metal and lost the claimants the £400 profit they would have expected to make on that melt. The claimants lost a further £1,767 on the other four melts which they would have completed in the time that the electricity was cut off.

---

[113] See, eg, *Invercargill CC v Hamlin* [1996] 1 All ER 756; *Bryan v Maloney* (1995) 182 CLR 609. Cf *Woolcock Street Investments Pty Ltd v CDG Pty Ltd* (2004) 216 CLR 515.

[114] For a statutory exception in relation to C's financial loss arising from harm to another, see the Fatal Accidents Act 1976. Note also the Latent Damage Act 1986, s 3.

[115] [1966] 1 QB 569. And see *Cattle v Stockton Waterworks Co* (1875) LR 10 QB 453.

[116] [1969] 2 All ER 1252.   [117] [1971] 1 QB 337.

[118] [1973] QB 27 and see *Electrochrome Ltd v Welsh Plastics Ltd* [1968] 2 All ER 205; *The Kapetan Georgis* [1988] 1 Lloyd's Rep 352.

The majority of the Court of Appeal held that the claimants could recover the loss in value of the metal actually in the furnaces and the loss of profit on that melt. The remaining loss was financial loss unrelated to any physical damage and irrecoverable. Edmund-Davies LJ, dissenting, considered that such foreseeable and direct financial loss should be recoverable. For him, the occurrence or non-occurrence of physical damage was a fortuitous event with no relevance in legal principle. In language similar to that later employed by Megarry V-C in *Ross v Caunters*, he argued that if that very kind of financial loss to that claimant was a reasonably foreseeable and direct consequence of want of care, a duty to avoid that kind of loss arose.

Notwithstanding the powerful dissent in the *Spartan Steel* case, the Court of Appeal firmly endorsed the majority opinion in *Muirhead v Industrial Tank Specialties Ltd*:[119]

> C, a fish merchant, devised a plan to buy lobsters in the summer when prices were low and to store them for sale at a Christmas market. The lobsters had to be stored in tanks through which seawater was pumped, filtered, and re-circulated. The pumps proved to be defective because the electric motors were not suitable for use in the United Kingdom. C sued the manufacturers of the electric motors for: (1) the loss of several lobsters that died in the tanks; (2) expenditure on attempts to correct the fault; and (3) loss of profits on the enterprise.

The Court of Appeal held that the claimant could recover only for the loss of his property (dead lobsters) and any loss of profit consequent on those dead lobsters. This is to say that only financial loss directly consequent on physical damage could be recovered in tort. In the absence of any evidence of express reliance on, or close proximity to, the defendants, the defendants owed no duty to protect the claimant against financial loss (whether that loss be wasted expenditure or loss of profit). Manufacturers owe no duty in tort to ensure products are value for money.

English law having established these very clear rules about the recovery (or lack thereof) of relational financial losses, the Court of Appeal in *Shell UK Ltd v Total UK Ltd*[120] extended the rules in a way that is problematic:

> The claimant company, with three other oil companies, was the holder of shares in certain service companies. The service companies held legal title to fuel storage and pipeline facilities that were damaged in a fire caused by the defendant's negligence. The assets were held 'on trust' for the four oil companies. The oil companies had entered into certain contractual agreements for the use of these facilities but had no possession or immediate right to possession. The claimant argued that it should be entitled to claim as beneficial owner of the damaged property for the financial losses 'consequent' upon the physical damage caused by the fire. These financial losses consisted in increased costs of supply and profits lost from the claimant's reduced ability to supply customers.

The Court of Appeal held that the claimant was the 'beneficial owner' of the damaged property and, thus, could recover its financial losses, at least where the legal owner

---

[119] [1985] 3 All ER 705.   [120] [2011] QB 86.

could be joined in the proceedings. The court explained that 'it would be a triumph of form over substance to deny a remedy to the beneficial owner of that property where the legal owner is a bare trustee for that beneficial owner'.[121] The court effectively set aside the separate legal personality of the service companies and created a new area of liability for financial loss inconsistent with cases we have examined in this section of the book. It can only be hoped that the Supreme Court overturns this development.[122]

Section 4 Tort and contract

In bringing this chapter to a close, one final topic ought to be dealt with because it arises most frequently in cases involving the negligent offer of services giving rise to either property damage or purely financial loss. This is the topic of concurrent liability in contract and tort.

Historical position Concurrent liability was judicially recognised where the defendant exercised a 'common calling', for example a blacksmith, innkeeper, or common carrier. In such cases, the law imposed an implied duty to exercise the degree of skill normally expected of a person exercising that particular 'calling'. But, in the case of many professionals, such as solicitors and architects, traditionally it was held that, where there was a contract between the parties, the claimant was confined to a remedy in contract alone.[123] In *Tai Hing Cotton Mill Ltd v Liu Chong Hing Bank Ltd*, Lord Scarman tried to maintain this rule and exclude concurrent liability in contract and tort. He said:

> [t]hough it is possible as a matter of legal semantics to conduct an analysis of the rights and duties inherent in some contractual relationships either as a matter of contract law when the question will be what, if any, terms are to be implied, or as a matter of tort law when the task will be to identify a duty arising from the proximity and character of the relationship between the parties, their Lordships believe it to be correct on principle and necessary for the avoidance of confusion in the law to adhere to the contractual analysis, on principle because it is a relationship in which the parties have, subject to a few exceptions, the right to determine their obligations to each other, and for avoidance of confusion because different consequences do follow according to whether liability arises from contract or tort, eg, in the limitation of action.[124]

A series of conflicting decisions from the Court of Appeal followed *Tai Hing*.[125] At the heart of these cases was an essentially practical question: 'When a person enters into a

---

[121] [2011] QB 86, at [143]. The problem with this is that it completely ignores the very real advantage of limited liability enjoyed by a shareholder in another company.

[122] See K Low (2010) 126 LQR 507; PG Turner [2010] CLJ 445.

[123] *Bagot v Stevens, Scanlan & Co Ltd* [1966] 1 QB 197. Cf *Esso Petroleum Co Ltd v Mardon* [1976] QB 801; *Midland Bank Trust Co Ltd v Hett, Stubbs & Kemp* [1979] Ch 384; *Batty v Metropolitan Property Realisations Ltd* [1978] QB 554.   [124] [1986] AC 80, at 107.

[125] Compare, eg, *Forsikringsaktieselskapet Vesta v Butcher* [1988] 2 All ER 43 with *Lee v Thompson* (1989) 6 PN 91. See also the disagreement within the Court of Appeal in *Johnstone v Bloomsbury Health Authority* [1992] QB 333.

contract, in circumstances where, were there no contract, there would nonetheless be a duty in tort, should she forfeit the potential advantages that suing in tort may have over contract?'[126]

Henderson v Merrett Syndicates   The House of Lords in *Henderson v Merrett Syndicates Ltd*[127] finally resolved the issue, holding that, in general, there is concurrent liability in contract and tort. Provided that a duty in tort is not contrary to the terms of the contract, a duty in tort arising out of the special relationship between the parties lies concurrently with the obligations imposed by the contract. Lord Goff declared:

> the common law is not antipathetic to concurrent liability, and there is no sound basis for a rule which automatically restricts the [claimant] to either a tortious or contractual remedy. The result may be untidy; but given that the tortious duty is imposed by the general law, and the contractual duty is attributable to the will of the parties, I do not find it objectionable that the [claimant] may be entitled to take advantage of the remedy which is most advantageous to him, subject only to ascertaining whether the tortious duty is so inconsistent with the applicable contract that, in accordance with ordinary principle the parties must be taken to have agreed that the tortious remedy is to be limited or excluded.[128]

Effect of contract   Subsequent to the *Henderson* case, it has become clear that the terms of the subsisting contract will be *very important* in considering whether or not a court should recognise obligations in tort that go beyond it. In part, this is because the terms of the contract are likely to indicate to both of the parties what to expect of each other and might well provide a natural boundary to their interaction. In *Minkin v Landsberg*,[129] for example, the Court of Appeal took into account the limited nature of the task required of the defendant solicitor in drafting a consent order for her client. Although the court held that a tortious duty to provide incidental advice about the consent order arose, it was not appropriate to impose a duty of care which would entail assessment by the solicitor of the merits of the agreement that the client had reached with her husband and which formed the basis of the consent order.[130]

Concurrency   A claimant who either expressly or implicitly has agreed to give up any remedy in tort cannot go back on her word. She cannot assert a duty in tort quite contrary to the framework of agreed contractual terms.[131] However, where a contract deals with only part of the relationship between the parties, a duty of care wider than the contractual duty might arise from the circumstances of the case. Such duties might be

---

[126] Such advantages most regularly relate to the rules of limitation of actions. That is, C will normally have longer in which to bring her action if she sues in tort. In contract the limitation period begins to run from the date of the breach of contract. In tort the start might be delayed until the date when C could reasonably have become aware of the breach of the duty. Furthermore, extensions under the Latent Damage Act 1986 apply only to tort actions: *Iron Trades Mutual Insurance Ltd v Buckingham (JK) Ltd* [1990] 1 All ER 808.

[127] [1995] 2 AC 145. See S Whittaker [1997] LS 169.   [128] [1995] 2 AC 145, at 193–4.

[129] [2016] 1 WLR 1489.   [130] [2016] 1 WLR 1489, at [38] and [42]–[43].

[131] See *Robinson v PE Jones (Contractors) Ltd* [2011] 1 WLR 1617, where it was held that entry into a NHBC contract for the construction of a house, setting out a staggered-liability regime, was inconsistent with further tortious obligations for purely financial losses.

concurrent without being co-extensive.[132] Thus, if we entrust our portfolio of shares in United States' companies to a paid financial adviser, our contract will govern her professional liability to us. If that contract excludes a duty in tort, we cannot elect to sue in tort in respect of those dealings between us. If, however, that same defendant also gives us general advice on how to reinvest our US profits elsewhere, no bar exists to a duty of care in respect of those aspects of our relationship not governed by the contract. But context is important in determining the appropriateness of extending obligations in tort. Courts might be wary of extending subsisting contractual obligations, for example in employment cases, where the loss in question is purely financial because of the highly regulated nature of agreements between the parties and the potential for upsetting expectations about insurance and other matters.[133]

Three parties The relationship between tort and contract continues to be relevant not only to questions of concurrent liability, but also to cases where a third party seeks to establish that A who owes a duty in contract to B also owes a duty in tort to her.[134] *Donoghue v Stevenson*[135] dismissed the fallacy that privity of contract per se prevents such a duty to the third party ever arising. If there is the necessary proximity between the parties, then a duty in tort may arise independently of any contract between A and B. Nonetheless, the courts will be wary of extending liability in tort to third parties where the defendant's primary duty rests on a contractual obligation to someone else. They will seek to ensure that a duty in tort to the third party does not conflict with the primary contractual duty. The decision of the House of Lords in *White v Jones*[136] (discussed above) confirms, however, that liability in tort for breach of an obligation owed in contract to another party can arise in appropriate circumstances. Furthermore, in *Williams v Natural Life Health Foods Ltd*[137] the House of Lords acknowledged that tort may play an interstitial role where contract law fails to deliver justice. Privity of contract, then, is not a bar to liability; it is simply a consideration which should not be overlooked.

Separated by contract The discussion in the previous paragraphs has concerned cases where parties are *joined* by contract; but certain parties may be *separated* by contract and the question is what effect does this have upon the operation of the tort of negligence? Where the parties have *structured relations* so that there is no contract between them and so that they deal through an intermediary, this may be an indication of an intention to preclude obligations in tort. Thus, in major projects involving interlocking (especially construction) activities, the conscious structuring of relations might be

---

[132] *Holt v Payne Skillington* [1996] PNLR 179; *Cramaso LLP v Ogilvie-Grant* [2014] 2 WLR 317.
[133] *Greenaway v Johnson Matthey plc* [2016] 1 WLR 4487, esp at [49]–[51].
[134] For a third party statutorily to acquire the benefit of terms included in a contract between two others, three conditions must be satisfied: (1) it must be clear that the contract purports to confer a benefit on that third party; (2) there must be no contrary agreement in the contract; (3) the third party must be expressly identified in the contract: Contracts (Rights of Third Parties) Act 1999: sub-ss 1(1)(b), 1(2), and 1(3).
[135] [1932] AC 562.   [136] [1995] 1 All ER 691.   [137] [1998] 2 All ER 577.

inconsistent with a duty of care.[138] However, the context will be important. Thus, in *Riyad Bank v Ahli United Bank (UK) plc*,[139] the Court of Appeal held that a Kuwaiti bank owed a duty of care in providing investment advice to a Saudi bank separated by contract in circumstances where the separation was artificially effected for purposes of reputation and marketing of products.

Conclusions

This chapter has considered the rules on duty of care insofar as they apply in cases of property damage and purely financial loss. Courts offer a wide ambit of protection to those who have suffered property damage, but have put in place restrictive rules in cases of purely financial loss. The main categories of case in which duties have been recognised involve the making of negligent misstatements and the provision of substandard services. Although courts frequently utilise 'assumption of responsibility' reasoning in these purely financial loss cases, we have seen that most of the cases conform to the three-stage test from *Caparo Industries plc v Dickman*. This is because the courts look to proximity factors in order to determine whether there has been an 'assumption of responsibility' or 'special relationship'. Finally, we have noted that obligations arising in tort and contract can overlap, especially in the kinds of case considered in this chapter. Courts have taken the view that the terms of contracts entered into between disputant parties are very important in determining the scope of relevant duties of care.

Problem question

Denise was interested in investing money in a rental property. During a dinner conversation with her sister, Kayla, she was advised to buy immediately because Kayla (who works in financial services) believed that interest rates would soon be cut and house prices would become more expensive as a result. Denise bought a rental property. But interest rates were not reduced. In fact, the government introduced new taxes on second homes and these have had a negative impact on house prices. After Denise's tenant, Jackson, moved into the rental property, there was an accident at a nearby bridge when a ship, *The Maida Vale*, collided with it while sailing up river. This was due to faulty navigation equipment manufactured by Sonar Express. As a result, Jackson had to drive the long way to work every morning for a year. After the year was up, with the bridge still not repaired, Jackson decided not to renew the tenancy agreement.

Advise on the rights to recovery for purely financial losses by Denise and Jackson.

 Visit **http://www.oup.com/uk/street15e/** for answer guidance.

---

[138] *Henderson v Merrett Syndicates Ltd* [1995] 2 AC 145, at 195; *White v Jones* [1995] 2 AC 207, at 279.
[139] [2007] PNLR 1.

Further reading

BARKER, 'Unreliable Assumptions in the Modern Law of Negligence' (1993) 109 *Law Quarterly Review* 461

BARKER, GRANTHAM, AND SWAIN (eds), *Liability for Misstatements: 50 Years on from Hedley Byrne v Heller* (2015)

VAN BOOM, KOZIOL, AND WITTING (eds), *Pure Economic Loss* (2004)

BUSSANI AND PALMER (eds), *Pure Economic Loss in Europe* (2003)

BUXTON, 'How the Common Law gets Made: *Hedley Byrne* and other Cautionary Tales' (2009) 125 *Law Quarterly Review* 60

FELDTHUSEN, *Economic Negligence: The Recovery of Pure Economic Loss* (4th edn, 2000)

GREEN AND DAVIES, ' "Pure Economic Loss" and Defective Buildings' in Robertson and Tilbury (eds) *Divergences in Private Law* (2016), ch 4

STAPLETON, 'Duty of Care and Economic Loss: A Wider Agenda' (1991) 107 *Law Quarterly Review* 249

STAPLETON, 'Duty of Care: Peripheral Parties and Alternative Opportunities for Deterrence' (1995) 111 *Law Quarterly Review* 301

WHITTAKER, 'The Application of the "Broad Principle" in *Hedley-Byrne* as between Parties to a Contract' (1997) 17 *Legal Studies* 169

WITTING, *Liability for Negligent Misstatements* (2004)

5

Duty of care IV: public authorities

KEY ISSUES

(1) Public authority
Public authorities encompass ministries of state, councils, schools, hospitals, the police, and the armed forces. Other actors might be classed as public authorities also where they fulfil functions of a public nature, this being determined according to various factors including statutory empowerment, service in the public interest, and funding by government.

(2) Special difficulties
Public authority cases give rise to special difficulties in the law of negligence because frequently they are constituted and empowered by statute, are subject to Human Rights Act 1998 provisions, have a measure of discretion in their decision-making, make decisions as to the allocation of resources, act in the public interest, and might be subject to alternative avenues of redress (especially judicial review of administrative decisions). These factors give rise to issues about the justiciability of claims and the proper application of the *Caparo* three-stage test for duty.

(3) Justiciability
The first question for a court deciding a negligence claim brought against a public authority is whether the court is able to hear and determine the matter at all. Cases on the duty of care involving public authorities are susceptible to failure at this stage, especially where duties are directed towards areas of social planning and development, which, it might be argued, are issues best addressed at the ballot box rather than in court. Courts have employed various tests in examining this issue, such as whether the decision in question involves either policy or operational matters—the latter more frequently being the subject of obligations in negligence than the former. However, Human Rights Act 1998 considerations have reduced the number of cases excluded from adjudication on this ground.

(4) Application of *Caparo* principles
In cases where an action in negligence against a public authority can be entertained, still the court will have the ability to deny recognition of a duty of care through application of the *Caparo* three-stage test for duty—especially where the view is taken that the imposition of a duty of care would not be fair, just, and reasonable. Duties have been denied on this basis, for example, because of the conflicting interests to which they might give rise.

Section 1 Introduction

Public authorities deserve separate consideration from other topics concerning the duty of care in negligence because of their special nature on the border of public law and private law. This is reflected in the need for the courts to apply the principles of negligence so as to take into account the statutes which create and empower public authorities, the operation of the Human Rights Act 1998, the alternative avenues of redress that are available (especially judicial review of administrative decisions), the measure of discretion that public authorities might have in their decision-making, and the potential consequences to the public of negligence liability (including the impact of liability upon their ability to deliver services). The chapter defines the term 'public authority' and discusses the application of the Human Rights Act 1998, the concept of justiciability, and the application of the *Caparo* three-stage test for duty.

Section 2 Background

(A) Statutory and public dimensions

History By the late Middle Ages, the centralisation of government under the King was being mirrored by centralisation of the judiciary. The Courts of Common Pleas, King's Bench, and Exchequer had been established, each emanating from the King's own administrative offices.[1] Indeed, until the reign of Edward I, the King's own attendance at King's Bench was usual.[2] Actions at common law were commenced mostly by writ, issued from the Chancery.[3] But the King's actions could not be questioned in the writs, which (after 1258) could be adapted only with the consent of his own council.[4] As far as the council (and the royal courts) were concerned, the King could do no wrong and could not be vicariously liable for the wrongs of his officials.[5] However, in *The Case of Prohibitions*[6] Sir Edward Coke famously asserted the right of the courts to provide redress against oppression and misgovernment.[7] This created a new sense of accountability by government. After the Glorious Revolution in 1688, executive power and functions gradually were transferred from the Monarch and from the Justices of the Peace to government ministers and to the departments of state. Government functions

---

[1] JH Baker, *An Introduction to English Legal History* (4th edn, 2007), 12; SFC Milsom, *Historical Foundations of the Common Law* (2nd edn, 1981), 31–2.

[2] JH Baker, *An Introduction to English Legal History* (4th edn, 2007), 39.

[3] JH Baker, *An Introduction to English Legal History* (4th edn, 2007), 53–4; SFC Milsom, *Historical Foundations of the Common Law* (2nd edn, 1981), 34–6.

[4] JH Baker, *An Introduction to English Legal History* (4th edn, 2007), 56.

[5] P Cane, 'Tort Law and Government Liability in the Administrative State' in K Barker et al (eds), *Private Law and Power* (2017), 86.

[6] *The Case de Modo Decimandi, and of Prohibitions* (1609) 13 Coke 37; 77 ER 1448.

[7] JH Baker, *An Introduction to English Legal History* (4th edn, 2007), 151.

grew over time, coming to encompass such things as health and safety at work.[8] This meant that a growing number of persons were affected by the negligence of Crown servants. There followed the idea that wrongdoing by Crown servants should be capable of action by private persons.[9] Although attempts were made to permit this through petitions of right, courts held this not to be suitable on the theory that Crown conduct could not, in fact, amount to tortious conduct.[10] While courts persisted in the idea that immunity attached to the activities of the Crown, they did permit suits in tort that were brought against public officials personally.[11] However, change came in *Mersey Docks and Harbour Board Trustees v Gibbs*,[12] where the House of Lords held that Crown immunity would not extend to all government bodies. The Crown Proceedings Act 1947 liberalised the rules in a more systematic way. Section 1 removed actions against the Crown from the fiat of the King. Section 2 provided that the Crown was to be liable in tort, essentially, on the same basis as private persons. In this way, the Crown is vicariously liable for the wrongs of its servants, although actions are brought formally against particular ministers and their departments.[13] However, an issue of *justiciability* still remains in tort actions against the Crown and its emanations. This means courts must always consider their own powers to hear cases involving these parties (as we will see).[14]

Definition It is more important to define the term 'public authority' for the purposes of the Human Rights Act 1998 than it is for the purposes of tort law, given that a court's jurisdiction under the 1998 Act depends upon the status of the defendant,[15] while the same is not necessarily true of actions in negligence. However, given that it is desirable for the purposes of exposition to identify the area of overlap between these two sources of law concerning public authorities, an attempt is made here to provide a rough definition and examples. The definition is 'rough' because, as the House of Lords acknowledged in *YL v Birmingham City Council*, there are dangers in trying to be too precise in the course of a fairly abstract discussion of the issues.[16]

The Human Rights Act 1998, section 6 divides public authorities into two categories: 'core' public authorities, every function of which falls within the Act's remit, and 'hybrid' public authorities, which are bodies (to use a neutral word) undertaking limited

---

[8] P Cane, 'Tort Law and Government Liability in the Administrative State' in K Barker et al (eds), *Private Law and Power* (2017), 85.

[9] P Cane, 'The Tort Liability of Public Authorities: A Comparative Analysis' in A Robertson and M Tilbury (eds), *The Common Law of Obligations: Divergence and Unity* (2016), 155.

[10] P Cane, 'The Tort Liability of Public Authorities: A Comparative Analysis' in A Robertson and M Tilbury (eds), *The Common Law of Obligations: Divergence and Unity* (2016), 155.

[11] P Cane, 'The Tort Liability of Public Authorities: A Comparative Analysis' in A Robertson and M Tilbury (eds), *The Common Law of Obligations: Divergence and Unity* (2016), 156.

[12] (1866) LR 1 HL 93, esp at 110–11.

[13] P Cane, 'Tort Law and Government Liability in the Administrative State' in K Barker et al (eds), *Private Law and Power* (2017), 90.

[14] Alternatively, while immunities have largely disappeared, liability might be denied in public authority cases on the basis of no duty: see, eg, *Michael v CC of South Wales Police* [2015] AC 1732, at [44]ff; *Brooks v Comr of Police* [2005] 1 WLR 1495, at [27].

[15] Human Rights Act 1998, s 6.   [16] [2008] 1 AC 95, at [5], [91], and [137].

public functions. In the latter class of case, the 1998 Act applies only to the public functions of these bodies and not to their private functions.[17] The key issue is to determine which bodies are hybrid public authorities. Ability to do this depends upon consideration of various criteria, several of which are likely to be present in this special category of defendant. The criteria are: (1) The body will be constituted under an Act of Parliament, pursuant to secondary legislation, or through the exercise of the royal prerogative. Ordinarily, it (2) will have certain powers of action, likely to be set out in legislation,[18] a royal charter,[19] letters patent, or (potentially) a government contract,[20] or else it will occupy an historically acknowledged role. (3) Ordinarily, the body will act for public[21] or governmental purposes.[22] Finally, (4) the greater part of the funding for the public function(s) in question is likely to come from government.[23]

The term 'public authority' clearly encompasses ministries of state, councils, universities, schools, hospitals, the police, and the armed forces.[24] It covers, also, those organisations tasked with the responsibility of running prisons, the National Society for the Prevention of Cruelty to Children, and various regulatory bodies.[25] *R v Panel on Takeovers and Mergers, ex parte Datafin plc*[26] decided that a public authority need not have statutory backing in order to be amenable to judicial review—the important point about the Takeover Panel (as then constituted) being that it served a public purpose in the regulation of takeovers and mergers between companies. Although the term 'public authority' encompasses courts and tribunals,[27] much of their work will be covered by judicial immunities so that liability *in negligence* (if it arises at all) will be rare.[28]

Human Rights Act 1998 As mentioned earlier, in cases against public authority defendants, ordinary negligence principles are now applied bearing in mind the statutory and public law dimensions present.[29] On the one hand, a putative duty of care in

---

[17] *YL v Birmingham CC* [2008] 1 AC 95, at [81] and [131].

[18] Eg, Local Government Act 1972, sub-s 111(1). See also *Aston Cantlow and Wilmote with Billesley Parochial Church Council v Wallbank* [2004] 1 AC 546, at [12]; *YL v Birmingham CC* [2008] 1 AC 95, at [26], [100]–[102], [154], and [166]–[167].

[19] Eg, Royal Charter on Self-Regulation of the Press (2013), establishing a Recognition Panel for the purposes of media regulation.

[20] See Deregulation and Contracting Out Act 1994; Health and Social Care Act 2008, s 145. Cf *YL v Birmingham CC* [2008] 1 AC 95.

[21] Eg, Human Rights Act 1998, sub-s 6(3)(b); *YL v Birmingham CC* [2008] 1 AC 95, at [102] and [154]; *R v Panel on Takeovers and Mergers, ex parte Datafin plc* [1987] QB 815, at 835.

[22] *Aston Cantlow and Wilmote with Billesley Parochial Church Council v Wallbank* [2004] 1 AC 546, at [10], [49], [88], and [159]–[160]; *YL v Birmingham CC* [2008] 1 AC 95, at [102].

[23] *Aston Cantlow and Wilmote with Billesley Parochial Church Council v Wallbank* [2004] 1 AC 546, at [12]; *YL v Birmingham CC* [2008] 1 AC 95, at [26]–[27], [103], [154], and [165].

[24] *Aston Cantlow and Wilmote with Billesley Parochial Church Council v Wallbank* [2004] 1 AC 546, at [7].

[25] *Aston Cantlow and Wilmote with Billesley Parochial Church Council v Wallbank* [2004] 1 AC 546, at [9].

[26] [1987] QB 815. See also *R v Code of Practice Committee of the British Pharmaceutical Industry, ex parte Professional Counselling Aids Ltd* (1990) 3 Admin LR 697. Compare *R (on the Application of West) v Lloyd's of London* [2004] Lloyd's Rep IR 755 (Lloyd's of London not amenable to judicial review).

[27] Human Rights Act 1998, sub-s 6(3)(a).   [28] See ch 25.

[29] Sometimes these public law and statutory features are irrelevant (eg, when an action is brought against a public authority qua employer—in respect of, say, an unsafe workplace. The duty in such a case would be the ordinary duty of care owed by any employer to an employee). Sometimes, also, the question of negligence liability is irrelevant (eg, if the statute itself creates a civil law action for breach of statutory duty: see ch 19).

negligence must not fall foul of relevant legislation on account of inconsistency. The imposition of a duty of care must not prevent the public authority from achieving its statutory purposes. On the other hand, courts will need to consider any negligence claim in accordance with the provisions of the Human Rights Act 1998. As explained in chapter 1, when developing and applying the law, public authorities must act in a way that is compatible with Convention rights.

ECtHR decisions The 1998 Act requires,[30] moreover, that English courts take into account European Court of Human Rights (ECtHR) decisions in determining the actionability of claims which have a rights basis and the extent of redress available. The (potential) negligence liability of public authorities in English law had to be reappraised in the light of ECtHR decisions in *Z v United Kingdom*[31] and *TP and KM v United Kingdom*.[32] These cases found the reception of English courts to claims against public authorities in negligence to be unsatisfactory in a number of ways. Further, since it became independently possible to hold public authorities liable in respect of breaches of the European Convention on Human Rights,[33] it has been necessary for the courts to show a new-found tolerance in hearing the claims of those seeking to sue public authorities on the basis of common law negligence.[34]

Developing the law of negligence The result of a court's deliberations might be the development or extension, in the tort of in negligence, of a duty of care owed by the public authority towards the claimant and fellow members of his class, although this is not inevitable. Courts are *not* required to develop the law of negligence so as to give effect to ECtHR decisions.[35] The courts (often as a result of the pleadings) might eschew tort law altogether, and provide a remedy under the Human Rights Act 1998 itself. In *Rabone v Pennine Care NHS Trust*, for example, the claimant parents brought an action against a health trust under the 1998 Act for breach of Article 2 of the European Convention. They alleged failures in care regarding their suicidal daughter, in circumstances where there was no existing remedy in English tort law for the anguish that they suffered.[36] The Supreme Court awarded modest damages for breach of their Convention rights.[37] Having said as much, it *is clear* that English courts have developed the law of negligence regarding public authorities with certain ECtHR values in mind—as the following discussion will demonstrate[38]—even if this has not yet occurred in any consistent way.

---

[30] Human Rights Act 1998, sub-s 2(1).   [31] (2002) 34 EHRR 97.   [32] (2002) 34 EHRR 42.

[33] Human Rights Act 1998, s 7.   [34] *D v East Berkshire Community NHS Trust* [2005] 2 AC 373.

[35] Eg, *Van Colle v Chief Constable of Hertfordshire Police* [2009] 1 AC 225. See also comment in *Smith v Ministry of Defence* [2014] AC 52, at [67] (priority in securing Article 2 right to life is 'putting in place effective criminal law offences').

[36] [2012] 2 AC 72, esp. at [92]. See, likewise, *Sarjantson v CC of Humberside Police* [2014] 1 All ER 961.

[37] This decision has been criticised (rightly, it is submitted) for devaluing the fundamental protections of the 1998 Act while, at the same time, undermining limits to actionability under the Fatal Accidents Act 1976 (as to which, see ch 26): A Tettenborn (2012) 128 LQR 327. The effect is also to undermine the rule against compensation for mere grief in negligence.

[38] See also F Du Bois (2011) 127 LQR 598, esp. 590–1 (ways in which human rights law might impact on tort).

The extent to which the courts *should* develop the English law of negligence in conformity with ECtHR decisions is the subject of controversy. Contemporary English courts appear to be of the view that the advent of Human Rights Act remedies make it *unnecessary* to expand liability in negligence; if redress is available under the Convention, the domestic law of negligence has no more work to do.[39] This was the view of Lord Brown in *Smith v Chief Constable of Sussex Police*:

> [C]onvention claims have very different objectives from civil law actions. Where civil actions are designed essentially to compensate claimants for their losses, convention claims are intended rather to uphold minimum human rights standards and to vindicate those rights.[40]

In *Michael v Chief Constable of South Wales Police*, Lord Toulson confirmed this view and noted that the difference between the purposes underlying the Convention, on one hand, and the tort of negligence, on the other, 'has led to different time limits and different approaches to damages and causation'.[41] The contrary view of what the proper relationship between these two areas of law should be, now on the wane, is that they should develop in harmony with each other[42]—that domestic courts should be wary of allowing large disparities in protected interests to develop. The tort of negligence has an inherent flexibility that makes it an especially useful vehicle for giving effect to Convention rights. Development of the tort might be called for at times, given that a failure to provide an adequate domestic remedy to a breach of Convention rights itself is a breach of Article 13 of the Convention.[43] To the extent that the tort of negligence is appropriate for development, a good argument exists that this should happen in an incremental fashion.[44]

(B) Negligence liability: reasons for caution

Starting point Having explained the interaction between human rights law and the law of negligence in a general way, we must now focus upon the manner in which the principles of negligence apply in the public authority context. An important point is that, although there are exceptions,[45] there is, to repeat, no longer any *general* rule granting public authorities immunity from liability in negligence just because they are public (or performing public functions) and not purely private bodies.[46] In *Michael v Chief Constable of South Wales Police*, Lord Toulson noted that, in some areas of activity:

---

[39] *Jain v Trent Strategic HA* [2009] 1 AC 853, at [39]; *Smith v CC of South Sussex Police* [2009] 1 AC 225, at [136] and [138].

[40] *Smith v CC of South Sussex Police* [2009] 1 AC 225, at [138].

[41] [2015] AC 1732, at [127]. See also analyses in F Du Bois (2011) 127 LQR 598 and D Nolan (2013) 76 MLR 286.   [42] *Smith v CC of South Sussex Police* [2009] 1 AC 225, at [58].

[43] *MAK and RK v UK* [2010] ECHR 363, criticised in K Greasley (2010) 73 MLR 1026. See also C McIvor (2010) 69 CLJ 133, 149–50.

[44] By analogy with G Phillipson and A Williams (2011) 74 MLR 878 (discussing development of negligence as between private parties).   [45] See ch 25.

[46] *Mersey Docks and Harbour Board Trustees v Gibbs* (1866) LR 1 HL 93; *Allen v Gulf Oil Refining Ltd* [1981] AC 1001; *Desmond v CC of Nottinghamshire Police* [2011] 1 FLR 1361, at [32].

such as health care and education, public authorities provide services which involve relationships with individual members of the public giving rise to a recognised duty of care no different from that which would be owed by any other entity providing the same service. A hospital and its medical staff owe the same duty to a patient whether they are operating within the National Health Service or the private sector. A school and its teaching staff owe the same duty to a pupil whether it is a state maintained school or a private school.[47]

Difficulties Difficulties in establishing a duty of care can arise, nevertheless, where the alleged negligence of a public body derives from its exercise of, or failure to exercise, statutory powers designed to ensure the provision of some public function or other.[48] These difficulties, some of which have been mentioned, include the following: (1) Many statutory powers enabling public authorities to provide public services confer on the authority a measure of discretion as to how, or even *whether*, the relevant power should be exercised. This discretion has been described as involving 'power delegated within a system of authority to an official or set of officials, where they have some significant scope for settling the reasons and standards according to which that power is to be exercised, and for applying them in the making of specific decisions'.[49] The award of such discretion is seen as necessary in making the exercise of governmental power efficient and effective.[50] In such cases, courts must be wary of imposing obligations that undermine this discretion (the exercise of which ordinarily will reflect priorities for which the public body is accountable either to Parliament or a government department), especially where it is provided by legislation. (2) This reluctance to interfere will be compounded where alternative remedies are available (especially judicial review of administrative decisions). (3) Decisions made by public authorities might have a significant policy element, for example with respect to the allocation of resources across large groups of people, for the pursuit of which (once again) it is accountable to a superior body.[51] (4) Very often, what the claimant alleges is not that the authority itself negligently created the danger which befell him, but that it failed to protect him from that danger. This gives rise to a problem of negligent omissions (discussed in chapter 2). (5) Arguments might arise as to the (presumed) effect of frequent litigation on limited public funds, and the manner in which statutory functions would be performed in the face of possible negligence actions. These factors impact upon both issues of justiciability and whether it is fair, just, and reasonable to impose liability on a public authority.[52]

---

[47] [2015] AC 1732, at [112]. Duties of care can also arise, even where losses are purely financial, when the public authority enters into a 'special relationship' with the claimant: eg, *Sebry v Companies House* [2016] 1 WLR 2499.

[48] See, eg, S Bailey and M Bowman (2000) 59 CLJ 85.

[49] D Galligan, *Discretionary Powers: A Legal Study of Official Discretion* (1986), 21. This is a somewhat simplistic definition, and various shades of meaning have been identified: see K Barker, 'Public Power, Discretion, and the Duty of Care' in K Barker et al (eds), *Private Law and Power* (2017), 210–18.

[50] K Barker, 'Public Power, Discretion, and the Duty of Care' in K Barker et al (eds), *Private Law and Power* (2017), 208.

[51] Eg, *Smith v Ministry of Defence* [2014] AC 52, at 65 (Lord Hope stating that the 'allocation of resources to the armed services and as between the different branches of the services, is . . . a question which is more appropriate for political resolution than it is by a court').

[52] See also B Markesinis et al, *Tortious Liability of Statutory Bodies: A Comparative and Economic Analysis of Five English Cases* (1999), ch 3; K Barker, 'Public Power, Discretion, and the Duty of Care' in K Barker et al (eds), *Private Law and Power* (2017), 219–21.

Section 3 Justiciability

Where the statutory powers of a public authority are in issue, the initial question for the court (which generally is subject to the will of Parliament) is whether the alleged negligent act or omission on the part of that public authority is justiciable. This is to say that the court considers whether it is able to adjudicate on the matter at all. Ordinarily, public bodies are held to account in respect of the specific exercise of their statutory functions by one or more of the following: judicial review, ombudsmen, complaints procedures set out in the enabling legislation,[53] actions based on a breach of the Human Rights Act 1998, and, occasionally, default powers afforded to the relevant Secretary of State.[54] In short, public law (in one form or another) ordinarily provides the means of redress in respect of public law wrongs. Allowing private law remedies in such cases might be seen as undermining the public law system.[55] However, the argument that damages for negligence ought to be available where a claimant suffers loss or injury is a powerful one and might be difficult to resist. That being so, the courts have struggled to identify the touchstones of justiciability.

(A) General principles

Bedfordshire case In *X v Bedfordshire County Council*,[56] Lord Browne-Wilkinson sought to rationalise the principles relating to the justiciability of public bodies' negligent acts and omissions.[57] The case dealt with two groups of appeals relating to failures in public services. The first group of cases, the 'child care' appeals, comprised allegations that local authorities had acted negligently in relation to statutory powers to protect children from abuse. The second group of cases, the 'education' cases, involved claims that education authorities had acted negligently in the exercise of their powers in relation to the provision of education. Lord Browne-Wilkinson acknowledged the factual diversity of the claims, but recognised that each raised the question of the extent to which public authorities charged with statutory duties can be held liable in negligence for the negligent (non-)performance of those duties.

Lord Browne-Wilkinson made three essential points. First, wherever a claim relates purely to the exercise of a statutory discretion, 'nothing which an authority does within the ambit of that discretion can be actionable at common law'.[58] But if the decision complained of falls outside the statutory discretion, 'it *can* (but not necessarily will) give rise to common law liability'.[59] This, expressed in the language of public lawyers, means that any *intra vires* exercise of statutory discretion cannot give rise to a duty of care for the purposes of negligence law, but that a *Wednesbury* unreasonable decision *might* be justiciable.

---

[53] That is, the legislation that confers upon the public body the relevant powers and duties.
[54] For examples of each of these in relation to local authorities' duties towards children in need, see J Murphy (2003) 23 LS 103.
[55] Eg, *Desmond v CC of Nottinghamshire Police* [2011] 1 FLR 1361, at [48]–[49] and [51].
[56] [1995] 2 AC 633, at 736.   [57] See D Brodie (1998) 18 LS 1.   [58] [1995] 2 AC 633, at 738.
[59] [1995] 2 AC 633, at 738.

Second, Lord Browne-Wilkinson sought to place even *Wednesbury* unreasonable decision-making beyond the reach of negligence law where the statutory discretion that is alleged to have been abused relates to matters of policy that are unfit for consideration by the courts. In such cases, no action would lie because the courts simply would have no jurisdiction to examine (let alone determine) whether there has been an excess of the discretion afforded. Finally, his Lordship distinguished between (1) *decision-making* cases, where it is contended that the defendant owes a duty of care in respect of the manner in which it exercises a statutory discretion; and (2) *implementation* cases, concerning the manner in which a previously formulated policy is put into practice. Although this distinction has been shown to be an imperfect one,[60] decisions about how to ensure pupil safety, for example, would fall into the first category, while the practical measures actually implemented in order to achieve that policy objective would fall into the second.[61] In relation to the implementation of a policy, the *Caparo* three-stage test for duty could be applied in determining whether or not to recognise a duty of care owed by the public authority to affected claimants.

***East Berkshire* case**   The foregoing three principles must be read subject to the reasoning of the House of Lords in *D v East Berkshire Community NHS Trust*:[62]

> There were three conjoined appeals. In the first, health professionals wrongly accused C of having harmed her own daughter. She sued in negligence on the basis of the resultant anxiety and stress that she suffered. In the second case, a father and daughter brought an action against social workers who removed the daughter into local authority care on the incorrect basis that the father had sexually abused her. In the third case, Cs were a mother and father who, again, brought an action on the ground of false accusations that led to a compulsory separation from their daughter. In all three cases, the social services applied to have the negligence actions struck out on grounds of non-justiciability.

The House of Lords rejected the suggestion that a duty of care might be owed to any of the parents in these cases because of the *perceived* conflict of interests entailed,[63] but conceded that, arguably, a duty was owed to the daughter in the second case. Accordingly,

---

[60] For criticism, see *Stovin v Wise* [1996] AC 923, at 951; S Bailey and M Bowman (1986) 55 CLJ 430, and id (2000) 59 CLJ 85.

[61] The fact that the service is provided pursuant to statute is not necessarily incompatible with a normal relationship of proximity between the school and pupils: [1995] 2 AC 633, at 735.

[62] [2005] 2 AC 373.

[63] It was said to be contrary to public policy to hold, in a case where a child was suspected of being abused, that the relevant public authority investigating the case would owe the parents a duty of care in the conduct of its investigation. The thinking was as follows: while the authority would be statutorily bound to do what it could to ensure the child's welfare—by, eg, removing the child into care in spite of parental opposition—there necessarily would be a conflict of interests if the authority was liable to be sued in negligence by the parents if it should transpire that the child was not in need of protection. Yet, as Lord Bingham observed in his dissenting speech ([2005] 2 AC 373, at [37]), the prospect of liability towards the parents might galvanise the authority into doing its job with care and sensitivity.

their Lordships permitted only the second claim, brought by the daughter, to proceed. It struck out all the remaining actions.

For present purposes, it is important to note, also, the way in which the Court of Appeal circumscribed the principles established in the *Bedfordshire* case, where it had been held that no duty would be owed in respect of a child wrongfully removed into local authority care. According to the Court of Appeal in *East Berkshire*[64]—and the House of Lords did not disturb this finding—what materially had changed was the enactment of the Human Rights Act 1998. For since its enactment, it had become possible to bring an action directly under that Act in two important circumstances: first, where a child's Article 8 right to respect for privacy and family life would be infringed by taking a child into care where there was no proper basis for so doing, and second, for infringement of the child's Article 3 right to be free from inhuman and degrading treatment where he should have been removed into care but was left at home with abusive parents.[65] In short, the Human Rights Act 1998 had undermined the immunity established in the *Bedfordshire* case, so it was supposed that there was no longer any point in trying to preserve one at common law.[66]

(B) Policy and discretion

In *X v Bedfordshire County Council*, although Lord Browne-Wilkinson gave examples of 'social policy, the allocation of finite public resources [and] . . . the balance between pursuing desirable social aims as against the risk to the public inherent in so doing',[67] he failed to provide an exact definition of what he meant by a statutory discretion so imbued with considerations of policy as to render it non-justiciable for the purposes of the law of negligence.[68] This lingering uncertainty simply added to that associated with the somewhat difficult policy/implementation dichotomy[69] upon which he also placed great emphasis. So, when should a statutory discretion be regarded as so bound up with policy considerations as to be non-justiciable? This is by no means an easy question to answer, but Lord Slynn provided some guidance in *Phelps v Hillingdon LBC* when he observed:

> The fact that acts which are claimed to be negligent are carried out within a statutory discretion is not in itself a reason why it should be held that no claim in negligence can be brought in respect of them. It is only where what is done has involved the weighing of competing public interests or has been dictated by considerations on which Parliament could

---

[64] [2004] QB 558.

[65] That these actions would lie was made clear in *TP and KM v UK* [2001] 2 FLR 549 and *Z v UK* [2001] 2 FLR 612, which arose from appeals in the *Bedfordshire* case.

[66] Arguably, the Human Rights Act 1998 had undermined it only partially, since actions under it are subject to a shorter limitation period of one year (sub-s 7(5)) and since damages under the Act will not be as generous as those under the law of tort, being assessed on quite separate, narrower bases.

[67] [1995] 2 AC 633, at 736.

[68] Any such decisions will remain open to the public law supervision of the courts by way of judicial review: see *A v Essex CC* [2004] 1 FLR 749, at [33].

[69] For details of the problems associated with this dichotomy, see S Bailey and M Bowman (1986) 55 CLJ 430.

> not have intended that the courts would substitute their views for the views of ministers or officials that the courts will hold that the issue is not justiciable.[70]

This dictum would appear to explain Lord Browne-Wilkinson's example of competing public interests in the case of decisions concerning the allocation of scarce resources. Take, for example, a local authority that decides to devote certain limited resources to making provision X for children in need rather than provision Y. Its decision so to do (even if negligent) would be non-justiciable because the court is not entitled to substitute its view for that of the public authority on the thorny question of how best to allocate such resources in the furtherance of competing public interests. Applying this approach, it has been held since that the courts are not in a position to second-guess discretionary decisions made by adoption agencies concerning the level of information that is revealed to prospective adopters prior to an adoption.[71] On the one hand, the parents have an interest in knowing a good deal about the child they are proposing to adopt, but, on the other hand, there is the child's interest in keeping certain information confidential (at least so long as the interested parties are merely *prospective* adopters). Parliament has invested adoption agencies with the discretion to decide just how much information to release and it is not for the courts to second-guess such decisions.

Apart from these illustrations, it is difficult to provide 'hard-and-fast' guidance on when a statutory discretion will be regarded as too intricately bound up with matters of policy as to be non-justiciable. The reality seems to be that the negligent exercise of a statutory discretion must always be addressed on a case-by-case basis in order to decide whether policy (or human rights considerations, bearing in mind the *East Berkshire* decision) will render the negligent exercise of that discretion justiciable or not.

(C) Ambit of the discretion principle

While it is easy to state that a decision that falls beyond the discretion conferred upon a public authority is justiciable, it is more difficult to justify this statement. In the *Bedfordshire* case Lord Browne-Wilkinson invoked the test of *Wednesbury* unreasonableness,[72] so that a decision purportedly taken according to a statutory discretion should be treated as justiciable within the law of negligence if it was 'so unreasonable that no reasonable authority could have made it'.[73] However, it is difficult to comprehend why a public law test should be used to determine the existence of a private law cause of action and it seems that the real issue in most of the cases goes to statutory intention.[74] Yet, despite a notable attempt in *Carty v Croydon London Borough Council* to relocate the unreasonableness issue to the court's decision on whether there has been a breach of an already established duty of care,[75] it is difficult to square that approach with Lord

---

[70] [2001] 2 AC 619, at 653. To similar effect see *Barrett v Enfield LBC* [2001] 2 AC 550.

[71] *A v Essex CC* [2004] 1 FLR 749.

[72] See *Associated Provincial Picture Houses Ltd v Wednesbury Corp* [1948] 1 KB 223.

[73] [1995] 2 AC 633, at 740.

[74] K Barker, 'Public Power, Discretion, and the Duty of Care' in K Barker et al (eds), *Private Law and Power* (2017), 227.   [75] [2005] 1 WLR 2312, at [26] and [32].

Browne-Wilkinson's dictum and with Hale LJ's judgment in *A v Essex County Council*, where she spoke of 'an area of discretion which can only be challenged if it falls outside the realms of reasonableness'.[76] Thus, although the public law principle of *Wednesbury* unreasonableness looks odd in this context, it appears fairly well entrenched as a relevant principle.

Section 4 Application of *Caparo*

(A) General

Once it has been decided that an action in negligence brought against a public authority is justiciable, it remains for the claimant to establish that a duty of care was owed to him. The existence of duties of care appears well established in one set of cases, where a public authority has committed a positive act and adversely affected the claimant's interests. Thus, in *East Suffolk Rivers Catchment Board v Kent*,[77] Lord Romer accepted as a basic proposition that a public authority would be liable where it added to damage already suffered. Beyond such straightforward cases, and the established categories of case in which duties of care have been held to apply previously, the duty issue is to be decided (according to Lord Browne-Wilkinson in the *Bedfordshire* case) by applying the three-stage test established in *Caparo Industries plc v Dickman*.[78] And, in applying this test, the greatest difficulty that arises against public authority defendants typically comes at the third stage: showing that it would be fair, just, and reasonable to impose a duty of care.

(B) Policy arguments

In the *Bedfordshire* case, Lord Browne-Wilkinson adverted to a number of factors that might impinge on the issue whether to recognise a duty of care owed by a public authority. The first was whether Parliament had created specific remedies within the statute conferring the discretion, for it would be inappropriate for the court to superimpose a duty of care on the remedies that had been created by Parliament.[79] (At the same time, the *absence* of a specific statutory remedy might tell against the existence of a common law duty of care: '[i]f the statute does not create a private right of action, it would be . . . unusual if the mere existence of a statutory duty could generate a common law duty of care'.)[80] Second, the fact that the statutory framework in the *Bedfordshire* case required co-operation between many individuals and agencies might mean (1) that it would be unfair to single out any individual or agency for potential liability; and (2) that the imposition of a duty of care on the local authority could lead to a disruption in the operation of that partnership. Third, Lord Browne-Wilkinson was troubled by the fact that no analogous case in relation to a statutory social welfare scheme had been identified where a common law duty had been imposed. This concern has the capacity—since

---

[76] [2004] 1 FLR 749, at [48].   [77] [1941] 1 AC 74, 102.   [78] [1990] 2 AC 605.
[79] [1995] 2 AC 633, at 748–51. The point was endorsed in *Gorringe v Calderdale MBC* [2004] 1 WLR 1057, at [70].   [80] *Gorringe v Calderdale MBC* [2004] 1 WLR 1057, at [23] and [90].

it was expressed in very general terms—to apply more widely than simply to the facts of the *Bedfordshire* case.

Since the decision in that case, appellate courts have stressed a number of other factors relevant to the question whether it would be *fair, just, and reasonable* to impose a duty of care on a public authority. These include the potential for conflict in the exercise of a power between two classes of person, whose interests are (to a greater or lesser extent) opposed. Thus, in *Jain v Trent Strategic Health Authority*,[81] Lord Scott examined a number of cases where the potential for conflict arose and concluded that there was a general principle underlying them:

> [W]here action is taken by a state authority under statutory powers designed for the benefit or protection of a particular class of persons, a tortious duty of care will not be held to be owed by the state authority to others whose interests may be adversely affected by an exercise of a statutory power. The reason is that the imposition of such a duty would or might inhibit the exercise of the statutory powers and be potentially adverse to the interests of the class of persons the powers were designed to benefit or protect, thereby putting at risk the achievement of their statutory purpose.[82]

For this reason, there was no duty to take care imposed upon the defendant authority in making an *ex parte* application to a magistrate under the Registered Homes Act 1984, section 30 for cancellation of the claimants' registration to operate a nursing home. The effect of the cancellation was the immediate removal of elderly residents from the home and dissipation of the fee income which their residence provided. Although the claimants had their business destroyed as a result of negligence in the exercise of the power, the main object of the power was the protection of elderly care home residents.[83]

Other factors of relevance in determining what is fair, just, and reasonable include the risk that potential liability might lead to defensive practices on the part of the public authority and the wastefulness of a public authority having to devote sizeable amounts of its limited financial resources to defending negligence actions.[84]

(C) Proximity

(1) Child cases

The decided cases have highlighted also problems in establishing a sufficient relationship of *proximity* between public authorities and claimants; especially where the claimants have been children asserting negligence on the part of social services departments or education authorities. To an extent, such problems might have been predicted since not every single child suffering from some form of familial or educational problem is likely to be known personally to the relevant public authorities. It is not surprising, therefore, that the courts have more readily found there to be a sufficient relationship of

---

[81] [2009] 1 AC 853.   [82] [2009] 1 AC 853, at [28].   [83] [2009] 1 AC 853, at [20].
[84] *Stovin v Wise* [1996] AC 923; *Gorringe v Calderdale MBC* [2004] 1 WLR 1057; *A v Essex CC* [2004] 1 FLR 749. For a growing judicial scepticism, see *Gregg v Scott* [2005] 2 AC 176; and for critique, see B Markesinis et al, *Tortious Liability of Statutory Bodies: A Comparative and Economic Analysis of Five English Cases* (1999).

proximity once the authority has undertaken to provide a particular assessment (in the case of children with educational problems) or welfare service (in the case of children who have been formally admitted to local authority care). In *Barrett v Enfield London Borough Council*, where a child in care complained of a series of negligent acts and omissions on the part of the local authority during his time in local authority care, Lord Hutton observed:

> [I]n the present case the [claimant] was not a member of a wide class of society which the defendant was obliged to seek to protect, but was an individual person who had been placed in the care of the defendant by statute, and . . . it would not constitute a novel category of negligence to hold that the defendant owed him a common law duty of care.[85]

In a similar vein, in *Phelps v Hillingdon London Borough Council*, where an educational psychologist engaged by the local education authority failed to diagnose the claimant's dyslexia and thence organise special educational provision, Lord Slynn recognised the connection that existed between them which 'created the necessary nexus and duty'.[86]

(2) Omissions cases

A second difficulty associated with the proximity requirement has arisen when it is alleged that a public authority has *failed to perform* a statutory function. *Stovin v Wise*[87] is illustrative:

> C suffered serious injuries when his motorcycle collided with a car driven by D1 who came out of a junction. The junction was dangerous because a bank on adjoining land obscured road users' views. Accidents had occurred at the junction on at least three earlier occasions. The local council, which was the authority responsible for the highway, was joined as a second defendant. It was alleged that the council owed a common law duty of care to road users. The council was aware of the danger posed by the junction. At a meeting prior to the accident in which C was injured, the council had acknowledged the visibility problems and recommended removal of part of the bank so long as the owners of the land, British Rail, agreed. The owners did not respond to the council's proposal. The council did, however, possess statutory powers to issue a notice compelling British Rail to act to eliminate the danger to the highway.

The question arose whether the council could be liable for its failure to exercise its statutory power to issue a notice to British Rail. Public law demands that councils exercise their power responsibly, but it does not follow that an authority 'necessarily owes a duty of care which may require that the power should actually be exercised'.[88] Thus, while a public authority exercising its statutory powers so as to cause independent or additional damage might be liable in negligence, it would be quite exceptional for a court to

---

[85] *Barrett v Enfield LBC* [2001] 2 AC 550, at 589. Note that this reasoning was followed in *Kent v Griffiths* [2000] 2 WLR 1158, where it was held (at 1170) that the statutory power granted to the ambulance service to answer an emergency call crystallised into a specific duty to respond to a particular 999 call which was owed to C as a particular individual.

[86] [2001] 2 AC 619, at 656.   [87] [1996] AC 923.

[88] [1996] AC 923, at 950. See also *Gorringe v Calderdale MBC* [2004] 1 WLR 1057, at [39]–[40] and [73].

subvert a discretionary statutory 'power' by imposing a common law 'duty' that effectively removed that discretion, and forced the authority to act.[89] Notwithstanding the rejection of a common law action in that case, *Stovin v Wise* did not rule out negligence actions completely in respect of failures to exercise statutory powers. The minimum pre-conditions for any such duty were said to be (1) that it would be irrational not to have exercised the power so that there would be a public law duty to act; and (2) that there were 'exceptional grounds for holding that the policy of the statute requires compensation to be paid to persons who suffer loss because the power was not exercised'.[90]

Since then, Lord Hoffmann attempted in *Gorringe v Calderdale Metropolitan Borough Council* to clarify this proposition, explaining that an 'assumption of responsibility' of the extended *Hedley Byrne* variety (considered in chapter 4) is required in order to transform a statutory *power* into a common law *duty*, and that it was just such assumptions of responsibility that underpinned the decisions in the *Barrett* and *Phelps* cases.[91] In such cases, claimants will be required to show evidence of *general reliance* within the community on the provision of the service in question. It should be established that patterns of behaviour depend on a near-universal and reasonable expectation that the public authority will deliver protection from particular kinds of harm almost as a matter of routine, and that the service would be one which was much the same whomever it was provided for. Indeed, Lord Hoffmann suggested that routine building inspections by local authorities might fall within the test as being something upon which there would be universal reliance. By contrast, not all motorists are foolish enough to treat the occasional absence of warning signs along the road as a licence to disregard the obvious risks associated with driving too fast at the crest of a hill. That being so, there will be no liability on the part of a highway authority in respect of a failure to signpost each and every potential hazard on the road.

An interesting variation upon the theme of failure to exercise a statutory power arose in *Connor v Surrey County Council*,[92] in which the defendant council as employer owed a duty of care to the claimant, an employee head teacher of a primary school. The question was whether the council was negligent for failing to protect the claimant from the machinations of a dysfunctional school governing body. The council had a power under statute to replace the governing board with an interim executive board but did not do so, despite numerous warning signs of disruption in school life and of stress and risks to the claimant's health. As a result of continuous fighting with the governing body, the claimant had to retire early from her post with clinical depression. Although the case was primarily concerned with the question of breach, it demonstrates that the law might require that a pre-existing private law duty of care (here in both contract and tort) be fulfilled by the exercise of a public law power. The proviso is that this can be done 'consistently with the duty-ower's full performance of his public law obligations'.[93] Laws LJ explained:

---

[89] Cf *Kane v New Forest DC (No 1)* [2001] 3 All ER 914, where the authority had entered into a formal undertaking to improve (but had failed to improve by the time of the accident) visibility where a footpath met the inside of a bend on a main road. It was held that there was a strong possibility of the action succeeding.

[90] [1996] AC 923, at 953.   [91] [2004] 1 WLR 1057, at [39]–[40].

[92] [2011] QB 429.   [93] [2011] QB 429, at [106].

> The demands of a private law duty of care cannot justify, far less require, action (or inaction) by a public authority which would be unlawful in public law terms. The standard tests of legality, rationality and fairness must be met as they apply to the use of the public law power in the particular case. If the case is one where the action's severity has to be measured against its effectiveness, it must also be proportionate to whatever is the statutory purpose.[94]

Section 5   Vicarious liability

One further issue that arose in *X v Bedfordshire County Council* concerned the possibility of vicarious liability on the part of public bodies in respect of the acts of their employees.[95] The House of Lords said of such vicarious liability for public service employees generally[96] that the employee would owe a duty of care to the individual member of the public only where (1) the existence of such a duty is 'consistent with the proper performance of his duties to the . . . authority'; and (2) it is appropriate to impose such a duty on the employee. In both the *Bedfordshire* case[97] and *Phelps v Hillingdon London Borough Council*[98] it was recognised that a duty of care was incumbent on the individual professionals for which the council could be vicariously liable.[99] The perceived advantage of pursuing an action on the basis of vicarious liability is that it becomes much easier to demonstrate the requisite elements of foreseeability and proximity.

Section 6   Proposed reform

In 2008, the Law Commission proposed significant modification of the private law consequences of 'substandard administrative action'.[100] This was on the basis that '[t]he uncertain and unprincipled nature of negligence in relation to public bodies, coupled with the unpredictable expansion of liability over recent years, has led to a situation that serves neither claimants nor public bodies'.[101] Redress in the case of 'truly public' activities would have been restricted to situations where the statutory regime under which the public authority acted was designed to 'confer a benefit on the relevant class

---

[94] [2011] QB 429, at [107].

[95] As to the distinction between direct and vicarious liability in this context see *X v Bedfordshire CC* [1995] 2 AC 633, at 739–40.

[96] [1995] 2 AC 633, at 739–40.   [97] [1995] 2 AC 633, at 763, 766, and 770.

[98] [2000] 3 WLR 776 (negligence of an educational psychologist in failing to diagnose C's dyslexia causing C's future education to suffer could result in the employer-council being held vicariously liable).

[99] See also *Carty v Croydon LBC* [2005] 2 All ER 51.

[100] Law Commission, *Administrative Redress: Public Bodies and the Citizen* (Law Com Consultation Paper No 187, 2008).

[101] Law Commission, *Administrative Redress: Public Bodies and the Citizen* (Law Com No 322, 2010), at [1.18]. Note that a study of claim rates has found no evidence to support the assertion that claims against local authorities and schools have been rising, although there is evidence to suggest an increase in claims against the NHS from the 1970s to 2000: A Morris (2007) 70 MLR 349, 359–61.

of persons' and to failures evidencing 'serious fault'.[102] However, these proposals were dropped after considerable resistance, including resistance by the Government. Law Commission consultees were of the view that the rules of negligence as applied to public authorities are 'appropriate'.[103] Indeed, the law of negligence performs an important role in ensuring proper standards of conduct; it provides a means of accountability for the actions of public officials and assists in improved delivery of their services.[104]

Thus, the law of negligence will continue to play a role as the main means of private law redress for the failure of public bodies. Indeed, in light of developments following the commencement of the Human Rights Act 1998,[105] it is more difficult than in earlier times for a public authority to have a negligence action against it struck out.[106] But this does not mean that public authorities are more likely to be held liable in negligence. Instead, the cases suggest that future decisions will continue to be characterised by three particular difficulties which might constitute high hurdles for claimants. These are: (1) showing that in all the circumstances of the case it will be fair, just, and reasonable to impose a duty of care;[107] (2) showing that the claimant was in a sufficient relationship of proximity with the public authority;[108] and (3) showing that, even if a duty of care existed, the local authority was in breach of that duty of care (given the ongoing resource limitations under which all such authorities operate).

Conclusions

This chapter has considered the approach to the duty of care issue adopted by courts in cases involving allegations of negligence against public authority defendants. Public authority defendants require special treatment for a number of reasons, which include the measure of statutory discretion that they are given, the fact that they act (or should act) in the wider public interest, and their accountability to Parliament and/or to departments of state. Given their position, courts might need to consider an issue of justiciability before proceeding to apply the *Caparo Industries plc v Dickman* framework for duty of care. Justiciability concerns the fundamental ability of the court to hear the issue. If the court is able to determine the case against the public authority, then it is likely to require consideration of policy issues at the third stage of the *Caparo* framework.

---

[102] Law Commission, *Administrative Redress: Public Bodies and the Citizen* (Law Com No 322, 2010), at [1.20]–[1.21].

[103] Law Commission, *Administrative Redress: Public Bodies and the Citizen* (Law Com No 322, 2010), at [3.7].   [104] See R Mullender (2009) 72 MLR 961, esp. 974–5.

[105] Eg, *Osman v UK* (1998) 29 EHRR 245; *TP and KM v United Kingdom* [2001] 2 FLR 549; and *Z v UK* [2001] 2 FLR 612.

[106] But not impossible: see *Brooks v MPC* [2005] 1 WLR 1495.

[107] Thus, there was no departure from the '*Hill* principle' in *Smith v CC of Sussex Police* [2009] 1 AC 225.

[108] See, eg, *Cowan v CC of Avon and Somerset* [2002] HLR 44; *Desmond v CC of Nottinghamshire Police* [2011] 1 FLR 1361.

Problem question

The Farms Inspectorate is a government body established under the Farms Act 2000 and funded by levies imposed upon milk and other farm products. It is accountable to the Minister for Agriculture, to whom an annual report is addressed each year. Charlotte phoned the Inspectorate to complain that her neighbour, Joseph, who owns the 'Happy Valley Farm', has been under cutting her produce prices by the use of illegal workers. The call-handler at the Inspectorate said that she thought this would be a matter for the Ministry of Labour to investigate, but that she would find out and call Charlotte back. However, the call-handler made no inquiry and did not phone Charlotte back. Charlotte lost further contracts for the sale of produce—which were awarded to Happy Valley—and brought action against the Farms Inspectorate. The evidence is that the Farms Inspectorate does have statutory responsibility for prosecuting farmers who employ workers illegally.

Advise Charlotte as to any action in negligence that she might have.

 Visit **http://www.oup.com/uk/street15e/** for answer guidance.

Further reading

BAILEY, 'Public Authority Liability in Negligence: The Continued Search for Coherence' (2006) 26 *Legal Studies* 155

BARKER, 'Public Power, Discretion, and the Duty of Care' in K Barker et al (eds), *Private Law and Power* (2017) , ch 9

BOOTH AND SQUIRES, *The Negligence Liability of Public Authorities* (2006)

CANE, 'The Tort Liability of Public Authorities: A Comparative Analysis' in Robertson and Tilbury (eds), *The Common Law of Obligations: Divergence and Unity* (2016), ch 8

CRAIG and FAIRGRIEVE, 'Barrett, Negligence and Discretionary Powers' [1999] Public Law 626

DU BOIS, 'Human Rights and the Tort Liability of Public Authorities' (2011) 127 *Law Quarterly Review* 598

FAIRGRIEVE, *State Liability in Tort: A Comparative Law Study* (2003)

NOLAN, 'Negligence and Human Rights Law: The Case for Separate Development' (2013) 76 *Modern Law Review* 286

OLIPHANT(ed), *The Liability of Public Authorities in Comparative Perspective* (2016)

OLIVER, 'Functions of a Public Nature under the Human Rights Act' [2004] *Public Law* 329

STEELE, 'Damages in Tort and under the Human Rights Act: Remedial or Functional Separation?' (2008) 67 *Cambridge Law Journal* 606

VARUHAS, 'A Tort-Based Approach to Damages under the Human Rights Act 1998' (2009) 72 *Modern Law Review* 750

6

Breach of duty

KEY ISSUES

(1) Three steps to breach
In determining whether the defendant was in breach of her duty of care to the claimant, the court will examine (i) the foreseeability of harm should care not be taken; (ii) and the appropriate standard of care owed by the defendant to the claimant, which depends upon a number of factual matters concerning the risk of harm which arose. The court will then (iii) compare the conduct of the defendant with the expected standard of care, to see whether the defendant met the standard or fell below it.

(2) Setting the standard involves considering the circumstances of the case
Ordinarily, in setting the standard of care, the court will be concerned with what the hypothetical reasonable person would have done in the circumstances. This involves considering factors such as the likelihood of harm, the seriousness of harm, and the social utility of the defendant's activity.

(3) In some cases, the court will consider attributes of the defendant
This will be so where the defendant is a child. Everyone knows of the lesser ability of the child to take care and the law must take this into account. The court might take into account also any physical affliction that overcame the defendant and about which she was not aware at the time of the failure in question.

(4) The claimant might be assisted by the use of the res ipsa loquitur doctrine in concluding that a breach has occurred
Res ipsa loquitur is a method of reasoning in the absence of direct evidence that signifies a likelihood of the defendant having failed to take care in circumstances where the claimant is involved in an accident which ordinarily does not occur without negligence.

Section 1 The standard of care

General So far in our consideration of the tort of negligence, only the persons to whom the defendant owes a duty of care and the types of harm to which the duty extends have been considered. In chapter 2, we saw that the duty of care is concerned with whether a legal obligation to take care arises between classes of person. This chapter is concerned with an examination of what this entails—with what the law requires of the actual defendant in order to take care and avoid potential liability in negligence. There are a number of components to this exercise:

(1) There is a threshold issue of whether risk of harm to the claimant was reasonably foreseeable by the hypothetical person in the position of the defendant.[1]

(2) If this threshold of reasonable foreseeability is met, the court must determine the appropriate standard of conduct that was applicable to the interaction between the claimant and the defendant.[2] An objective test is applied.[3] The test is objective in the sense that it is a *generalised* standard, made to suit the hypothetical reasonable person rather than the actual defendant; and it is an *external* standard, in that it focuses mostly upon external acts and omissions (rather than upon any state of mind).[4] The setting of the appropriate standard entails consideration of a number of factors concerned with the nature of the risk that arose in that interaction and the defendant's ability to respond.[5]

(3) The result will be a *normative* statement of what the law expected of the reasonable person faced with a risk of the type that arose on the facts of the case. This statement is normative in that it retrospectively creates a norm—or standard—of conduct for application to the facts.

(4) Lastly there is the question of breach—of whether the defendant fell below the standard of conduct expected by the law. The question whether the defendant has breached a duty of care is a mixed one of law and fact;[6] but the standard of care required of the defendant is an exclusively legal construct and based on the standard of a hypothetical reasonable person. If the defendant causes loss or injury to the claimant, but is able to show that she acted in a way that a reasonable person would have acted, no liability will attach.[7]

---

[1] *Bourhill v Young* [1943] AC 92, at 98; *Glasgow Corpn v Muir* [1943] AC 448, at 454 and 460; *Bolton v Stone* [1951] AC 850, at 858 and 861. Foreseeability indicates a minimal ability to take steps to avoid harm: S Perry, 'The Distributive Turn: Mischief, Misfortune and Tort Law' in B Bix (ed), *Analyzing Law: New Essays in Legal Theory* (1998), ch 7.

[2] *Orchard v Lee* [2009] PIQR P16, at [7] and [9].

[3] *Glasgow Corpn v Muir* [1943] AC 448.

[4] J Goldberg and B Zipursky, *The Oxford Introductions to US Law: Torts* (2010), 85–8.

[5] *Morris v West Hartlepool Steam Navigation Co Ltd* [1956] AC 552, at 574; *Baker v Quantum Clothing Group Ltd* [2011] 1 WLR 1003, at [82]. Although the Social Action, Responsibility and Heroism Act 2015, s 3, requires that the court, when 'determining the steps that [D] was required to take to meet a standard of care' should consider whether she 'demonstrated a predominantly responsible approach', this makes *no sense*—the standard of care and D's actual conduct are considered at *different* stages of the breach inquiry. The other provisions of the Act are considered in the text, below.

[6] See, eg, *Barber v Somerset CC* [2004] 1 WLR 1089: the appeal to the House of Lords turned on the question whether the Court of Appeal had been entitled to disturb the trial judge's finding of fact that D had failed to meet the standard of reasonable care.

[7] See, eg, *Al-Sam v Atkins* [2005] EWCA Civ 1452. Note that it is not always easy to specify what is reasonable. Take, as an example, the near-100-page split decision of the Supreme Court concerning whether employers should have supplied protection from noise at work in *Baker v Quantum Clothing Group Ltd* [2011] 1 WLR 1003.

Logical progression The logical progression from the duty of care issue to the breach issue in cases of negligence was established in a series of seminal cases. For example, after deciding that the appellants owed a duty to take reasonable care for the safety of children on the premises, Lord Thankerton explained in *Glasgow Corporation v Muir* that a further question had to be addressed, namely, 'the test by which . . . the standard of care is to be judged'.[8] Here, the issue changes from being one about obligations between classes of person to one about particular risks of harm.

Foreseeability In *Bolton v Stone*,[9] the House of Lords held that the law is not concerned with bare risk—with the theoretical possibility of a risk of harm manifesting itself in injury. The law is concerned only with the creation of substantial risks of harm[10]— although this should *not* be taken to entail that a relevant risk need be 'probable' insofar as the latter phrase means 'more likely than not'. The requisite level of foreseeability is encapsulated in the idea that the law takes account of those risks which are 'reasonably foreseeable'. A failure in care by a motorist might manifest itself in the risk of collision with a vehicle or other object, or in the running down of a person. Normally, such risks are reasonably foreseeable. However, it is not reasonably foreseeable that a failure to drive within the speed limit might give rise to a risk of space junk falling from the sky and hitting the vehicle, thereby injuring a passenger. Therefore, there is no need for the motorist to consider taking precautions with respect to the latter risk.

Reasonable care Risk cannot be eliminated entirely from human behaviour;[11] '[s]ome risk of . . . injury is the price of activity'.[12] Given this reality, the law does not require that those to whom a duty of care is owed should be safeguarded against every conceivable risk. The modest aspiration of tort law is to provide a certain degree of physical safety and to attempt to ensure that interactions between persons can be undertaken according to minimal standards of conduct. If the defendant owes the claimant a duty of care in negligence, she must attain the standard of a 'reasonable person' in order to fulfil her obligation under the tort of negligence. The obligation is one to take what amounts to reasonable care *in the circumstances* of the case.[13] Needless to say, if reasonable care was taken by the defendant there is no liability simply on the basis that the defendant caused harm nevertheless to the claimant.

Factors to consider In some cases, strong guidance as to the appropriate standard of conduct expected by the law will be given by statute, custom, or professional standards.[14] The more problematic cases are those 'unbounded' cases in which there are no clear pre-existing norms.[15] The courts might have recourse to a range of factors in determining what the standard of reasonableness requires. Some of these factors relate to

---

[8] [1943] AC 448, at 454.   [9] [1951] AC 850.   [10] [1951] AC 850, at 864 and 867.
[11] *Bolton v Stone* [1951] AC 850, at 860–1; JCP Goldberg (2003) 91 Geo LJ 513, 545.
[12] G Keating (2003) 56 Vand LR 573, 701.   [13] *Paris v Stepney BC* [1951] AC 367.
[14] Mere failure to conform is not determinative of breach: see *Baker v Quantum Clothing Group Ltd* [2011] 1 WLR 1003; *Ryan v Victoria (City)* [1999] 1 SCR 201, at 222 (statute); and *Ward v The Ritz Hotel (London) Ltd* [1992] PIQR 315 (professional standards).   [15] KS Abraham (2001) 53 Vand LR 1187, 1203.

matters extraneous to the defendant—such as whether she acted in an emergency situation created by no fault of her own—while others refer to attributes of the defendant, not as an individual, but as a member of a class, such as her standing as a professional person possessing (or professing to possess) certain skills. The factors considered in section 2 reflect those commonly referred to by the courts, but they are not presented on the basis that they constitute an absolutely comprehensive list. Indeed, there is no closed list of factors relevant to determining what a reasonable person would do by way of response to a risk.

Section 2 Factors relevant to establishing the required standard

Risks should be reduced where it is practicable to do so, or where otherwise required in the interests of justice. We now consider the factors that assist courts in assessing risks and in determining the required standard of care.[16] Although our concern is with how courts set the standard of care after injurious interactions have occurred, it seems clear that in some contexts responsible bodies (such as employers) must conduct 'risk assessments' involving largely the same factors prior to action in order to fulfil their obligations to at-risk persons.[17]

(A) Factors extraneous to the defendant

(1) The likelihood of harm

Rule The more likely that a risk of harm will manifest itself, the greater is the need for precaution to be taken. Thus, in *Northwestern Utilities Ltd v London Guarantee and Accident Co Ltd*, Lord Wright said that the degree of care which the law requires 'must be proportioned to the degree of risk involved if the duty of care should not be fulfilled'.[18] The likelihood of harm occurring is a factual matter to be determined according to the evidence about the injurious interaction that occurred and circumstances surrounding it. *Bolton v Stone*[19] provides an illustration:

> C was hit by a cricket ball struck from a cricket ground surrounded by a fence 17 feet above the level of the square. The batsman was 80 yards away. The ball was only the sixth in about 30 years to be hit out of the ground. The House of Lords held that there had been no breach of duty by the club in allowing cricket to be played without taking further precautions.

Lord Radcliffe stressed two points: first, the fact that the ball had to clear the fence, which itself was a remote possibility, and, second, that it would then have to strike a

---

[16] See also R Kidner (1991) 11 LS 1.

[17] *Kennedy v Cordia (Services) LLP* [2016] 1 WLR 597, at [110]–[111].

[18] [1936] AC 108, at 126 (appd by Lord Normand in *Paris v Stepney BC* [1951] AC 367, at 381). Cf *Palsgraf v Long Island RR Co* 284 NY 339 (1928): 'The risk reasonably to be perceived defines the duty to be obeyed' (Cardozo CJ); and *Glasgow Corpn v Muir* [1943] AC 448, at 456: 'the degree of care required varies directly with the risk involved'.   [19] [1951] AC 850.

passer-by (an even more remote possibility). Lord Oaksey said that 'an ordinarily careful man does not take precautions against every foreseeable risk . . . life would be almost impossible if he were to attempt to take precautions against every risk'.[20] On the facts, the chance of harm occurring was so small that a reasonable person in the position of the cricket club would not be expected to take additional precautions. By contrast, where the risk of injury to a road user from a football being kicked from a patch of open land was much greater, the defendant responsible for the land was held to be in breach of a duty of care.[21]

Vulnerable parties Particular vulnerability on the part of the claimant will be taken to increase the likelihood of harm if the defendant knew, or ought to have known, of that vulnerability. This should not be seen as subjectivising the standard of care: it is just that the standard of care is determined according to what the reasonable, prudent defendant would do given actual or constructive knowledge of the claimant's vulnerability.[22] In *Barber v Somerset County Council*,[23] for example, the Court of Appeal held that an overworked teacher known to his employers to be suffering from stress was entitled to be treated according to the standard of a reasonable and prudent employer taking positive steps for the safety of its workers in the light of what it knew or ought to have known about their susceptibilities.

(2) The seriousness of harm

Just as the likelihood of harm affects the standard of care demanded, so too does the seriousness of the potential harm. In *Paris v Stepney Borough Council*,[24] the House of Lords held that the court should assess the gravity of the consequences of an accident befalling an already disabled man when fixing the level of care required of the defendant.[25] Thus, the potential for injury to the claimant's only good eye was a material consideration. For a normally sighted individual, there would have been 'merely' the risk of being struck and blinded in one eye. For the actual claimant, however, the risk of being struck in his remaining good eye meant the catastrophic risk of total blindness, so that greater precautions were required.

(3) The social utility of the defendant's act

Rule In setting the standard of care, the court will take into account any relevant social utility associated with the defendant's conduct. This involves a determination of the general public interest so that matters other than those in dispute between the

---

[20] [1951] AC 850, at 863.

[21] *Hilder v Associated Portland Cement Manufacturers Ltd* [1961] 1 WLR 1434. See also *Miller v Jackson* [1977] QB 966 (breach of duty where cricket balls were struck out of a ground about eight or nine times every season). [22] See D Nolan (2013) 72 CLJ 651.

[23] [2004] 1 WLR 1089. See also *Haley v LEB* [1965] AC 778: D's standard of care was set according to the fact that D ought to have foreseen the possibility of blind persons coming into the vicinity of the hole dug by D in the pavement. [24] [1950] 1 KB 320.

[25] [1951] AC 367. Cf *Withers v Perry Chain Co Ltd* [1961] 3 All ER 676 (health risk to C had to be balanced against her interest in keeping her job).

claimant and defendant can be taken into account in assessing the standard of care required of the defendant. *Daborn v Bath Tramways Motor Co Ltd*[26] provides a useful illustration. The issue was whether, during wartime, the driver of a left-hand-drive ambulance had been negligent in turning into a lane on the offside of the road without giving a signal. Holding that she had not breached the relevant standard, Asquith LJ said:

> In determining whether a party is negligent, the standard of reasonable care is that which is reasonably to be demanded in the circumstances. A relevant circumstance to take into account may be the importance of the end to be served by behaving in this way or that. As has often been pointed out, if all the trains in this country were restricted to a speed of five miles an hour, there would be fewer accidents, but our national life would be intolerably slowed down. The purpose to be served, if sufficiently important, justified the assumption of abnormal risk. The relevance of this applied to the present case is this: during the war which was, at the material time, in progress, it was necessary for many highly important operations to be carried out by means of motor vehicles with left-hand drives, no others being available. So far as this was the case, it was impossible for the drivers of such cars to give the warning signals which could otherwise be properly demanded of them. Meanwhile, it was essential that the ambulance service should be maintained. It seems to me, in those circumstances, it would be demanding too high and an unreasonable standard of care from the drivers of such cars to say to them: 'Either you must give signals which the structure of your vehicle renders impossible or you must not drive at all.'[27]

It has been held that what might be want of care towards an employee in a commercial enterprise will not necessarily be want of care towards a fire officer, for 'one must balance the risk against the end to be achieved', and 'the commercial end to make profit is very different from the human end to save life or limb'.[28] Indeed, the courts have demonstrated an increased interest in the importance of community-minded activity, not simply in emergency situations, but also in more recreational settings.[29]

Statute By the Compensation Act 2006, section 1 it is now provided that, where a court is considering a claim in negligence, it may, in setting the required standard of care, 'have regard to whether a requirement to take those steps [necessary to meet that standard] might (a) prevent a desirable activity from being undertaken at all, to a particular extent or in a particular way, or (b) discourage persons from undertaking functions in connection with a desirable activity'. Since it reflects the pre-existing law, this provision cannot be seen to have altered the way in which courts are to approach the question of breach of duty.

---

[26] [1946] 2 All ER 333.   [27] [1946] 2 All ER 333, at 336. Cf *Quinn v Scott* [1965] 2 All ER 588, at 593.
[28] *Watt v Hertfordshire CC* [1954] 2 All ER 368, at 371. On the other hand, where D can reasonably expect that others will take care for their own safety, and where the cost of eliminating a danger would involve the removal of a social amenity, the social amenity's benefit might well outweigh the obvious risks that exist: see *Tomlinson v Congleton BC* [2004] 1 AC 46 (case regarding Occupiers' Liability Act 1984).
[29] Eg, *Cole v Davis-Gilbert* (2007) *Times*, 6 April.

(4) Emergencies

A defendant might act in an emergency, with little time for reflective decision-making, in a manner that falls below the standard of care normally expected.[30] The court will fix the appropriate standard of care mindful of these circumstances. *Watt v Hertfordshire County Council*[31] provides a good illustration:

> The fire service was called upon to save a woman trapped under an overturned lorry. In order to do so, they needed to use a heavy jack that stood on wheels. They could not transport the jack in the usual vehicle because that vehicle was otherwise engaged. Instead, they tried to get the jack to the required destination in a substitute vehicle. While en route, the driver of the vehicle made an emergency stop, causing the jack to shoot forwards whereupon it injured C, one of the fire officers.

It was held that there was no breach of duty, given the short amount of time that the fire service had to act, and in view of the endeavour to save the woman trapped underneath a lorry. On the other hand, it is important to appreciate that an emergency does not exonerate the defendant from taking any care at all; it merely reduces the standard demanded. Thus, if a fire engine goes recklessly through a red light on the way to a fire, there might still be a breach.[32]

(5) The relative cost of avoiding the harm

Balancing exercise The court must balance the expected cost of averting a risk against the potential cost of the risk manifesting itself.[33] In *Latimer v AEC Ltd*,[34] an exceptional storm had caused a factory floor to become flooded. When the water receded, the floor was left covered with a slimy mixture of oil and water so that its surface was slippery. The issue was whether the factory owners were in breach of their obligation towards a worker who, some hours later, was injured by slipping on the floor. In holding there to have been no breach, Lord Tucker said:

> The only question was: Has it been proved the floor was so slippery that, remedial steps not being possible, a reasonably prudent employer would have closed down the factory rather than allow his employees to run the risks involved in continuing work?[35]

---

[30] Many of the cases on the standard of care in emergencies deal with contributory negligence: see, eg, *Jones v Boyce* (1816) 1 Stark 493. On primary liability and emergency, see *Parkinson v Liverpool Corpn* [1950] 1 All ER 367; *Ng Chun Pui v Lee Chuen Tat* [1988] RTR 298; *Marshall v Osmond* [1983] QB 1034.

[31] [1954] 2 All ER 368. See also *S (A Child) v Keyse* [2001] All ER (D) 236.

[32] *Ward v London CC* [1938] 2 All ER 341. See also *Craggy v CC of Cleveland Police* [2009] EWCA Civ 1128.

[33] The idea is that if great expense is required to reduce only slightly an existing risk, then it will be acceptable to do nothing. In *US v Carroll Towing Co* 159 F 2d 169 (1947), at 173 Learned Hand J expressed the matter in terms of a formula: 'if the probability be called P; the injury, L; and the burden, B; liability depends upon whether B is less than L multiplied by P; ie, whether B<PL'. See S Gilles (2001) 54 Vand LR 813; C Witting (2009) Torts LJ 242.

[34] [1952] 2 QB 701, at 711. Cf *Watt v Hertfordshire CC* [1954] 2 All ER 368 (duty of fire authority to firemen in respect of equipment), where the dictum of Asquith LJ, in *Daborn v Bath Tramways Motor Co Ltd* [1946] 2 All ER 333 was also approved.   [35] [1953] AC 643, at 659.

In *The Wagon Mound (No 2)*, the Privy Council stated the rule to be that a reasonable person would neglect a risk of a small magnitude only 'if he had some valid reason for doing so, eg, that it would involve considerable expense to eliminate the risk'.[36]

Private actors The courts will require those who act to do what is reasonable, which might entail the defendant incurring expense in order to eliminate risk. In the case of a private individual or enterprise, there comes a point where, if the defendant lacks the resources to minimise a significant risk of injury to others, she must cease to engage in the relevant activity. Put otherwise, if the defendant does not possess sufficient resources to undertake an activity with reasonable care, then she should not engage in it at all.[37] For example, if a sports club cannot afford to replace a wooden spectator stand constituting a fire risk, it should not allow spectators to use it.[38]

Public authorities By contrast, where the defendant is a public authority, the position might be different. This is because certain services provided by the public authority are mandated by statute or are essential to communal life, and yet inadequately resourced. In *Knight v Home Office*[39] the claimant's husband committed suicide while detained in a prison hospital wing. The judge accepted that the standard of care and supervision for suicidal prisoners might well have fallen below that to be expected in an NHS psychiatric facility. Yet he dismissed her claim saying:

> In making the decision as to the standard demanded the court must . . . bear in mind as one factor that resources available for the public service are limited and that the allocation of resources is a matter for Parliament.[40]

Arguably, cases such as this demonstrate that negligence does not necessarily lie in the final link in a chain of decision-making, where a prior policy decision is being implemented by the defendant at the most basic, practical level. In some cases, decisions made at a high political level inevitably entail difficulty in meeting 'service targets', or in underservicing, and must be expected to result in failures in care. The failures in care that result are systemic in nature. Their 'acceptability' is politically pre-determined and courts might have little authority to redress them.[41] The systemic bias in the National Health Service towards undertreatment might be an example of this.[42]

Contrasting approach Whereas the focus in the English cases usually is upon the cost of *the* untaken precaution that would have prevented harm to *the particular* claimant, the focus has been widened in Australian public authority cases. The High Court of

---

[36] [1967] 1 AC 617, at 642. See also *Goldman v Hargrave* [1967] 1 AC 645, at 663; *Baker v Quantum Clothing Group Ltd* [2011] 1 WLR 1003, at [82].   [37] *Bolton v Stone* [1951] AC 850, at 867.

[38] See *Latimer v AEC* [1953] AC 643, at 659.   [39] [1990] 3 All ER 237.

[40] [1990] 3 All ER 237, at 243. See the similar reasoning in *Walker v Northumberland CC* [1995] 1 All ER 737.

[41] C Witting (2001) 21 OJLS 443.

[42] R Klein, P Day, and S Redmayne, *Managing Scarcity: Priority Setting and Rationing in the National Health Service* (1996), 90. See Law Commission, *Administrative Redress: Public Bodies and the Citizen* (Law Com No 322, May 2010), [3.12]–[3.13]; *Savage v South Essex Partnership NHS Foundation Trust* [2009] AC 681, at [100].

Australia took the lead,[43] but the matter now finds a place in statute.[44] The effect of the law is that, in all breach cases determined under the statute, the court is required to assess the whole range of risks to which the defendant's activity foreseeably might have given rise, and the whole range of potential responses, including their cost. Although this does seem to focus minds on the practicability of taking precautions, it creates an evidential burden upon claimants also and a complex assessment task for the courts. Inevitably, the effect will be to reduce the chances of claims success in public authority and other cases involving mass production or service provision.

(6) Common practice

Commonly, a defendant will support her claim to have exercised due care by showing that she conformed to the common practice of those engaged in the activity in question. Obviously, such evidence is relevant.[45] Indeed, conforming to the practice of a trade or profession often (but not always) will be conclusive in claims against trades persons[46] or professionals. So, a specialist who failed to diagnose the claimant's ailment was held not to have been negligent when he used the normal methods of British medical specialists, although the use of an instrument usually employed in the United States might have resulted in a correct diagnosis.[47] By contrast, consider *Cavanagh v Ulster Weaving Co Ltd*:

> C slipped while coming down a roof ladder. Despite unchallenged evidence that the 'set-up' accorded perfectly well with established practice, the House of Lords restored the jury's verdict that D was negligent.[48]

Failure to conform to a standard imposed by a statute, although it might constitute a breach of statutory duty, is not conclusive evidence of negligence in itself.[49] However, it might constitute prima facie evidence of a failure in care.[50]

(7) The exigencies of life

While common practice is of importance in setting relevant standards of care, the reasonable person test rests largely upon matters of common sense and the exigencies of everyday life. A good example of the allowance made by the law for the 'hurly burly of life' can be seen in cases relating to parental and quasi-parental duties.

---

[43] *Vairy v Wyong SC* (2005) 223 CLR 422.   [44] See, eg, Civil Liability Act 2002 (NSW), s 5B.
[45] See, eg, *Baker v Quantum Clothing Group Ltd* [2011] 1 WLR 1003.
[46] *Gray v Stead* [1999] 2 Lloyd's Rep 559. See also *Baker v Quantum Clothing Group Ltd* [2011] 1 WLR 1003.
[47] *Whiteford v Hunter* (1950) 94 Sol Jo 758. Cf *Vancouver General Hospital v McDaniel* (1934) 152 LT 56; *Wright v Cheshire CC* [1952] 2 All ER 789.   [48] [1960] AC 145.
[49] In *Powell v Phillips* [1972] 3 All ER 864, it was held that breach of the Highway Code, despite the Road Traffic Act 1972, sub-s 37(5), creates no presumption of negligence calling for an explanation. It is just one relevant circumstance. In *Trotman v British Railways Board* [1975] ICR 95, it was held that breach of a regulation in the British Railways' Rule Book created a rebuttable inference of negligence. A breach of a navigational bye-law is particularly cogent evidence of negligence: *Cayzer, Irvine & Co v Cannon Co* (1884) 9 App Cas 873, at 880–1.
[50] *Blamires v Lancashire and Yorkshire Rly Co* (1873) LR 8 Exch 283; *Phillips v Britannia Hygienic Laundry Co* [1923] 1 KB 539, at 548 (affirmed [1923] 2 KB 832); *Anglo-Newfoundland Development Co Ltd v Pacific Steam Navigation Co* [1924] AC 406, at 413. See also *Harrison v National Coal Board* [1951] AC 639; *National Coal Board v England* [1954] AC 403. And compliance with a statutory requirement does not exclude liability in negligence: *Bux v Slough Metals Ltd* [1974] 1 All ER 262. See also *Budden v BP Oil Ltd* (1980) 124 Sol Jo 376.

In *Carmarthenshire County Council v Lewis*,[51] the defendant council was held liable when an infant wandered out of his nursery school and on to a nearby road, causing an accident in which the claimant's husband died. The council was negligent because premises accommodating small children should be designed to ensure that they cannot wander off, endangering themselves and others. But Lord Reid said that the teacher who had not noticed the boy leave her classroom while she attended to an infant with a cut knee was not negligent.[52] The gist of his reasoning was that those in charge of small children cannot have eyes in the backs of their heads.

In *Surtees v Kingston-upon-Thames Borough Council*[53] a child was injured when her mother left her momentarily by a wash basin and she somehow managed to turn on the hot water tap, thereby scalding her foot. The Court of Appeal held that the mother's apparent oversight was not negligence. Courts should be slow to characterise incidents in family life as negligence 'given the rough and tumble of home life'. Beldam LJ dissented. He argued that it would have required only momentary thought to remove the child from the vicinity of the tap.

(B) Factors pertaining to the defendant

Before considering various attributes associated with the defendant that might affect the standard of care demanded by the law, it is useful to consider a fundamental background principle concerning negligence. It was held in *Blyth v Birmingham Waterworks Co* that:

> Negligence is the omission to do something that a reasonable man, guided upon those considerations which ordinarily regulate the conduct of human affairs, would do, or doing something which a prudent and reasonable man would not do.[54]

It follows from this definition that the standard of care is not the standard of the defendant herself, but of a person of 'ordinary prudence',[55] a person using 'ordinary care and skill',[56] in fact a 'hypothetical' person.[57] In *Glasgow Corporation v Muir*, Lord Macmillan said that the standard of foresight of the reasonable person 'eliminates the personal equation and is independent of the idiosyncrasies of the particular person whose conduct is in question'.[58] In short, the standard of care is set objectively. But even so, it is erroneous to think that no reference can be made to the attributes of the particular defendant. The definition of the reasonable person is not complete unless the words 'in the circumstances' are appended. These words import the need to take some account of the particular defendant. But the overwhelming majority of the cases that explicitly recognise the relevance of who the defendant is do so in terms that eliminate considerations pertaining to the defendant's idiosyncrasies. Instead, they consider those of her attributes that are characteristic of a class to which the defendant belongs.

---

[51] [1955] AC 549.   [52] [1955] AC 549, at 564. See also *Kearn-Price v Kent CC* [2003] PIQR P11.
[53] [1991] 2 FLR 559.   [54] (1856) 11 Exch 781, at 784.
[55] *Vaughan v Menlove* (1837) 3 Bing NC 468, at 475.   [56] *Heaven v Pender* (1883) 11 QBD 503, at 507.
[57] *King v Phillips* [1953] 1 QB 429, at 441.
[58] [1943] AC 448, at 457. See also the earlier dictum of Holmes J in *The Germanic* 196 US 589 (1904): 'The standard of conduct . . . is an external standard, and takes no account of the personal equation of the man concerned.'

(1) Motives

Under the Social Action, Responsibility and Heroism Act 2015, when a court is 'determining the steps' that a defendant to a claim of negligence ought to have taken in response to risks of harm to others, it must take into account two potential motives: first, whether she was 'acting heroically by intervening in an emergency to assist an individual in danger' (section 4), and, second, whether she was 'acting for the benefit of society or any of its members' (section 2). The first requirement is a reflection of the fact that courts naturally ought to consider whether the defendant was acting in a high-pressure situation, so that time was short and decisions needed to be made in haste. In such situations, as we saw from discussion of *Watt v Hertfordshire County Council*,[59] the court is likely to demand less of the defendant. In this way, the 2015 Act does not change the substantive law, but simply mandates that the court consider the issue in a systematic way. The second requirement is more amorphous, but again becomes a required matter to be considered in the course of setting the relevant standard of care.

(2) Intelligence and knowledge

Intelligence The defendant's actions must conform to certain criteria expected of a person of normal intelligence in a given situation. It is no defence that someone acted 'to the best of her own judgement' if her 'best' is below that of the reasonable person.[60] A person, whose intellect is lower than average, is not excused thereby. And likewise, a woman whose intelligence is superior is not liable for failing to use those above-average qualities, unless she has professed to have some special skill or expertise, in which case the law demands that she must manifest that skill or expertise to a reasonable degree.[61]

Memory and experience Two branches of knowledge must be considered separately. The first is that of memory and experience. If X had been on a certain highway several times, and a reasonable person who had been there as often would know that it was busy, then X is expected to know it to be busy also, even though her memory is so poor that she does not actually remember it. Similarly, people are deemed to know those things which adults from their experience are expected to know: that some things easily explode, that others burn, that gravity exists, etc.[62] There is one refinement of this rule. Where, in the circumstances, the status of the defendant is relevant, the standard is set according to that status. Thus, in *Caminer v Northern and London Investment Trust* the knowledge required of a landowner with regard to elm trees on his estate, their proneness to disease, lack of wind resistance, and the like, was of a standard between that of an urban observer and a scientific arboriculturist.[63] Taking a similar approach, the

---

[59] [1954] 2 All ER 368. See also *S (A Child) v Keyse* [2001] All ER (D) 236.
[60] *Vaughan v Menlove* (1837) 3 Bing NC 468, at 474.   [61] See *Wooldridge v Sumner* [1963] 2 QB 43.
[62] *Caminer v Northern and London Investment Trust* [1951] AC 88. Cf *Haynes v Harwood* [1935] 1 KB 146, at 153.
[63] [1951] AC 88, at 100. See also *Clarke v Holmes* (1862) 7 H & N 937 (employer required to know more about the dangers of unfenced machinery than worker); *Quinn v Scott* [1965] 2 All ER 588.

Privy Council in *The Wagon Mound* (*No 2*)[64] held that the ship-owner was liable for a fire caused by discharging oil into Sydney Harbour because the chief engineer should have known that the discharge created a real risk of the oil on the water catching fire. Again, if someone elects to take on a particular task, although she is not an expert or professional in the field, she will be expected to have the necessary degree of knowledge to complete the task competently.[65]

Knowledge   Second, we must consider what knowledge of the facts and circumstances the defendant must have. She will not be excused for failing to observe what a reasonable person would have observed. Thus, a dock authority that does not know, but ought to know, that the dock is unsafe might be held negligent.[66] Furthermore, even if a reasonable person could not be expected to know something personally, she might be required to obtain expert advice. Thus, the landlord of flats must consult a specialist engineer about the safety of her lift if she lacks the relevant expertise herself.[67]

Of course knowledge—in particular expert knowledge—does not remain static over time. Scientific and technological advances lead to constant revisions of, and improvements in, safety standards.[68] In a negligence action, therefore, the defendant must be judged in the light of the state of scientific, technological, or other expert knowledge available at the time of the alleged breach. This means, for example, that evidence that a drug damaged a foetus is not conclusive that either the doctor prescribing the drug, or the pharmaceutical company marketing it, was negligent.[69] The test is: 'At the time when the drug was prescribed or marketed, should the risk of injury to the foetus have been foreseen?' As Lord Denning put it when a claimant sought damages in respect of a medical accident which had never occurred before: 'We must not look at the 1947 accident with 1954 spectacles.'[70]

Commercial enterprises must take steps to keep abreast of scientific developments. Often, this can be done by conforming to 'best practice' within an industry, where this embodies the results of the scientific evidence and collectively agreed responses to risk. But industry best practice might not always be determinative.[71]

Where an advance occurs in knowledge, so that new measures must be taken, the courts accept that often there will be an unavoidable time lag between innovation and implementation.[72]

---

[64] [1967] 1 AC 617.   [65] See *Chaudhry v Prabhakar* [1989] 1 WLR 29.

[66] *Mersey Docks and Harbour Board Trustees v Gibbs* (1866) LR 1 HL 93.

[67] *Haseldine v Daw & Son Ltd* [1941] 2 KB 343, at 356.

[68] See, eg, *Baker v Quantum Clothing Group Ltd* [2011] 1 WLR 1003.

[69] The drug thalidomide undoubtedly caused serious deformities in babies whose mothers took the drug in early pregnancy. One of the major obstacles confronting claims for compensation by the damaged children was doubt whether, at the time the drug was first available, as opposed to after the births of several deformed babies, doctors, and embryologists appreciated that drugs could cross the placental barrier and injure the foetus.

[70] *Roe v Minister of Health* [1954] 2 QB 66, at 84.

[71] *Baker v Quantum Clothing Group Ltd* [2011] 1 WLR 1003, at [23], [101], and [126].

[72] *Baker v Quantum Clothing Group Ltd* [2011] 1 WLR 1003, at [42] and [105].

Reasonableness The issue is always one of reasonableness. Less is expected within the realm of the family than in commercial and public service settings. Thus, although a parent hiring a bouncy castle for a children's birthday party might have the ability to obtain technical guidance on the safety of such paraphernalia and form views as to its appropriate use in its light, this is not customarily done and is not expected of the parent by a court.[73] Moreover, courts will need to distinguish between defendants undertaking superficially similar activities, to ensure that it adopts the relevant standard of care. Thus, if a general practitioner were to be consulted by a patient complaining of stomach trouble, she would not be expected to have the same level of knowledge as a consultant gastroenterologist. However, she must recognise her own limitations and know when the patient needs to be referred to a specialist. The same general rule has been applied in contrasting cases involving auction houses. In *Luxmoore-May v Messenger May-Baverstock*,[74] the claimant took a painting to a local auctioneer for valuation and sale. The defendants were held not liable for failing to discover that it was a painting by a well-known artist of the eighteenth century. By contrast, the Chancery Division held in *Thwaytes v Sotheby's*[75] that a higher standard of care was expected from the world-famous auction house, including employment of 'highly qualified people' and the devotion of sufficient time to attributions.

(3) Skill

Holding out When a person holds herself out to the public as being capable of attaining particular standards of skill—for example, by driving a car—she is required to display the skill normally possessed by persons doing that thing.[76] A doctor failing to diagnose a disease cannot excuse herself by showing that she acted to the best of her skill if a reasonable doctor would have diagnosed it.[77] Nor can a young hospital doctor escape liability simply by pleading that she is inexperienced or overworked. She must attain the level of competence expected from a person holding her 'post' and entrusted with her responsibilities.[78] The same principle applies to newly qualified solicitors.[79] But in such cases, one must be careful to ascertain exactly what skill the defendant did hold herself out to possess.

Different views Where a skilled person conforms to practices accepted as proper by *some* responsible members of her profession or trade, she will not be held liable in negligence merely because other members would take a different view. This principle

---

[73] *Harris v Perry* [2009] WLR 19.   [74] [1990] 1 All ER 1067.

[75] [2016] 1 WLR 2143, esp at [76]–[77].

[76] It is immaterial if D does not in fact have that skill; if she engages in conduct usually associated with persons having that skill, the standard demanded is that of those who actually do possess that skill: *Adams v Rhymney Valley DC* [2000] Lloyd's Rep PN 777. In *Nettleship v Weston* [1971] 2 QB 691, although the standard of a qualified driver was expected of a learner driver, the point was made that if a uniform standard were not applied, the courts would face insuperable difficulties in assessing the skills and competencies of every individual defendant. See also *Imbree v McNeilly* [2008] HCA 40 (bringing Australian law into line with *Nettleship*).

[77] *Bolam v Friern Hospital Management Committee* [1957] 2 All ER 118.

[78] *Wilsher v Essex Area HA* [1987] QB 730 (reversed on a different point [1988] AC 1074).

[79] *Newcastle International Airport v Eversheds LLP* [2013] EWCA Civ 1514.

is applied most frequently in the context of medical negligence where differences of opinion often arise as to the best way to address any given medical problem. In such circumstances, the courts will not choose between rival schools of professional thought.[80] Nor, in other circumstances where two non-negligent courses of action were possible, will the courts hold a defendant liable for failing to take that course which has been revealed, with the benefit of hindsight, to have been preferable.[81]

Relevant standard In *Philips v William Whiteley Ltd*, where the claimant had her ears pierced by a jeweller and subsequently contracted a disease that might have been avoided had the work been done with normal medical skill, the jeweller was required only to show the skill of a jeweller doing such work, not that of a doctor.[82] A similar approach was taken in *Wells v Cooper*, where a householder fitted a new door handle insecurely. When the claimant pulled on it, he lost his balance and was injured. The defendant householder was required to show only the standard of care of a normal DIY enthusiast, not that of a qualified carpenter.[83] On the other hand, while someone who practises alternative medicine is only liable if she fails to meet the standard applicable to her art, it will be relevant nonetheless to take into account findings within conventional medicine which reveal dangers associated with aspects of her art.[84]

Where someone has not held herself out as having special skill, she is not liable when she shows merely average skill in the circumstances, although she does in fact have special skill.[85] Skill, just like every other aspect of the standard of care, has to be assessed in the light of all the circumstances surrounding the alleged breach of duty, and the degree to which the defendant represents that she holds a particular skill is merely one among several considerations.

Sports Where negligence is alleged in the course of playing a sport, the fact that the object of competitive sport is to win, and the fact that spectators attend sporting occasions to see competitors exhibit their skill at the game, will be relevant. So, in *Wooldridge v Sumner*[86] Diplock LJ held that, where a show-jumper was concentrating his attention and exerting his skill to complete his round of the show-jumping circuit, this had to be taken into account in determining whether a momentary misjudgement constituted negligence.[87] By contrast, in *Condon v Basi*[88] a footballer managed successfully to sue in negligence when he suffered a broken leg as a result of a tackle by the defendant which was found by the referee to be serious foul play. The Court of Appeal held that a clear breach of the rules of the game would be a relevant (though not conclusive) consideration in deciding whether there had been actionable negligence. The overall test, since confirmed by the Court of Appeal,[89] is whether the defendant's disregard for the claimant's safety can be characterised as deliberate or reckless (bearing in mind the level of

---

[80] *Bolam v Friern Hospital Management Committee* [1957] 2 All ER 118.
[81] *Adams v Rhymney Valley DC* [2000] Lloyd's Rep PN 777.   [82] [1938] 1 All ER 566.
[83] [1958] 2 QB 265.   [84] *Shakoor v Situ* [2001] 1 WLR 410.
[85] *Wooldridge v Sumner* [1962] 2 All ER 978, at 989.   [86] [1963] 2 QB 43.
[87] See, in similar vein, *Caldwell v Maguire and Fitzgerald* [2002] PIQR P45.   [88] [1985] 2 All ER 453.
[89] *Caldwell v Maguire* [2002] PIQR P6; *Blake v Galloway* [2004] 1 WLR 2844.

competency to be expected from players of the defendant's class), in which case the defendant will be held to be in breach.

(4) Special knowledge concerning the claimant

The defendant's actual knowledge of the claimant's frailties and susceptibilities will affect the required standard of care. Thus, the level of care owed to a woman known to be pregnant,[90] to a worker with one eye,[91] or to employees especially susceptible to stress[92] will take account of these conditions *so long as* the defendant knows of them. If the defendant neither knows, nor ought to know, of these circumstances, however, the standard of care is unaffected by the claimant's susceptibility. As Lord Sumner explained:

> a measure of care appropriate to the inability or disability of those who are immature or feeble in mind or body is due from others, who know of or ought to anticipate the presence of such persons within the scope and hazard of their own operations.[93]

In *Haley v London Electricity Board*[94] the House of Lords applied Lord Sumner's dictum in holding that a body conducting operations on a city road should foresee that blind persons would walk along the pavement, and that it owes an obligation to take those precautions reasonably necessary to protect them from harm. On the facts, it was held liable, although a person with normal vision would not have been injured in consequence of its operations. Similarly, in *Johnstone v Bloomsbury Health Authority*,[95] in which the level of care owed by an employer to junior doctors who were required to work excessive hours was in issue, Stuart Smith LJ said:

> [I]t must be remembered that the duty of care is owed to an individual employee and different employees may have a different stamina. If the authority in this case knew or ought to have known that by requiring him to work the hours they did, they exposed him to risk of injury to his health, then they should not have required him to work in excess of the hours that he safely could have done.

It is no answer to a claim in negligence to respond that you did not appreciate the risk that your conduct would injure the claimant, if the reasonable defendant with your knowledge of the claimant and the circumstances would have recognised that risk. Human frailty must be taken into account and defendants cannot shift their obligations to such claimants by arguing that all claimants must always look out for themselves. So, in *Pape v Cumbria County Council*[96] it was insufficient for employers to supply their workers with rubber gloves. They had to warn them, also, of the risk of dermatitis unless the gloves were worn, since the prudent employer would take all reasonable steps to ensure that safety equipment is understood properly and used by employees. Again,

---

[90] *Bourhill v Young* [1943] AC 92, at 109.   [91] *Paris v Stepney BC* [1951] AC 367, at 385 and 386.
[92] *Sutherland v Hatton* [2002] PIQR P241.
[93] *Glasgow Corpn v Taylor* [1922] 1 AC 44, at 67. Of course, there are numerous cases where Ds have not been held in breach of a duty to infants (eg, *Donovan v Union Cartage Co Ltd* [1933] 2 KB 71) or to blind persons (eg, *Pritchard v Post Office* (1950) 114 JP 370).   [94] [1965] AC 778.
[95] [1992] QB 333.   [96] [1992] 3 All ER 211.

in *Newcastle International Airport v Eversheds LLP*,[97] it was held to be necessary for a law firm to supply a schedule of alterations when returning detailed service contracts to a client company. This was to ensure, so far as possible, that the company's directors, who were not legally trained, could understand the contracts and their very significant financial implications. By contrast, in *Eastman v South West Thames Regional Health Authority*[98] the defendants were held not liable when the claimant was thrown out of her seat in an ambulance and injured when the driver braked hard. She claimed that the driver had been negligent in not expressly instructing her to wear her seat belt. But a notice in the ambulance carried just that instruction. The claimant was not herself a patient. She was accompanying her mother-in-law to hospital. The court held that the ambulance staff had done all that was reasonably required in the circumstances. Had the claimant herself been a sick and confused elderly person, the outcome might have been different.

(5) Defendant's ability to foresee acts of third parties

Sometimes harm-doing occurs in a sequence, beginning with the failure—not of the defendant, but—of a third party. The question will be whether the defendant's actions were reasonable given the risks which arose. Whether the defendant has shown a proper standard of care frequently will depend on what acts or omissions of another she reasonably could have anticipated. If the claimant is injured because a third party has done something that the defendant could not reasonably foresee she would do, the defendant is not liable.[99] Yet, in *London Passenger Transport Board v Upson*,[100] Lord Uthwatt said:

> It is common experience that many do not [assume a fellow road user will act with reasonable care]. A driver is not, of course, bound to anticipate folly in all its forms, but he is not, in my opinion, entitled to put out of consideration the teachings of experience as to the form those follies commonly take.[101]

Nor is one excused by relying on another to take action unless that reliance was reasonable. *Manchester Corpn v Markland*[102] illustrates the point:

> The appellant was the statutory authority for the supply of water to the borough of Eccles. One of the appellant's service pipes in a road in Eccles burst. Three days later, the resulting pool of water froze, and a car skidded on the ice knocking down and killing a man.

In a negligence action brought by the dependants of the deceased against the appellants, it was held to be no defence that the appellants chose to rely on Eccles Corporation to notify them of bursts: they themselves should have taken proper precautions.

---

[97] [2013] EWCA Civ 1514, at [71] and [83].   [98] [1991] 2 Med LR 297.
[99] *Donaldson v McNiven* [1952] 2 All ER 691.   [100] [1949] AC 155.
[101] [1949] AC 155, at 173. Cf *Grant v Sun Shipping Co Ltd* [1948] AC 549, at 567.   [102] [1936] AC 360.

(6) Child defendants

In *Mullin v Richards*,[103] the Court of Appeal confirmed that, in relation to a child, the standard of care is determined by what degree of care and foresight reasonably can be expected of a child of the defendant's age. Two 15-year-old girls were fooling about during a mathematics lesson, fencing with plastic rulers. One of the rulers snapped and a fragment of plastic entered the claimant's eye ultimately causing her to lose any effective sight in that eye. Adopting the approach of the High Court of Australia in *McHale v Watson*,[104] the court held that the claimant had failed to establish that her schoolfriend was negligent. A 15-year-old, unlike an adult, might not foresee the risk of her behaviour, particularly as this kind of tomfoolery had never been banned at school, nor had any similar accident occurred previously. Some degree of irresponsibility can be expected of children playing together.[105] Indeed, the courts appear to look for a clear deviation from the norms of children's behaviour in order to find a breach of the obligation of care.[106]

An unresolved question, in relation to the standard of care demanded of children, is whether the test is entirely objective or will take into account the child's *actual* mental ability, maturity, and experience.[107]

(7) Disability and infirmity

Issue A question arises as to the extent to which the standard of the reasonable person will be adjusted to allow for the disabilities and infirmities of individual adults.

Wholly beyond control In *Roberts v Ramsbottom*,[108] the defendant suffered a slight stroke just before getting into his car. He was completely unaware that he had had a stroke, although he admitted that he felt somewhat dizzy. A few minutes after starting his journey, he was involved in a collision, injuring the claimant. It was held that, even though his carelessness resulted from impaired consciousness of which he was unaware at the time of the collision, he was liable in negligence. Neill J suggested two grounds to support the finding of negligence. He said that the defendant was liable, first, because he 'continued to drive when he was unfit to do so and when he should have been aware of his unfitness' and, second, because any disability affecting a defendant's ability to drive could exempt him only from the normal, objective standard of care where the disability placed his actions 'wholly beyond his control'.

In *Mansfield v Weetabix Ltd*,[109] a lorry driver was involved in a collision when he lost partial consciousness as a result of a hypoglycaemic state induced by a malignancy of which he was unaware. Overruling the trial judge's finding of breach, the Court of

---

[103] [1998] 1 All ER 920. See also, in relation to contributory negligence, *Yachuk v Oliver Blais Co Ltd* [1949] AC 386; *Gough v Thorne* [1966] 3 All ER 398; *Morales v Eccleston* [1991] RTR 151.
[104] (1964) 111 CLR 384.   [105] *Mullin v Richards* [1998] 1 All ER 920, at 928.
[106] *Orchard v Lee* [2009] PIQR P16, at [12].
[107] Compare *Yachuk v Oliver Blais Co Ltd* [1949] AC 386, at 396 with *McHale v Watson* (1964) 111 CLR 384, where Owen J's yardstick was a 'child of the same age, intelligence and experience'.
[108] [1980] 1 All ER 7.   [109] [1998] 1 WLR 1263.

Appeal held that, where a disability or infirmity prevented the defendant from meeting the objective standard of care, and the defendant was not, and could not reasonably have been, aware of his condition, that condition must be taken into account in determining whether or not the defendant was negligent. The court opined that Neill J's 'loss of control' test from the *Ramsbottom* case came close to equating liability in negligence with strict liability. (With respect, however, this is to lose sight of the fact that the 'fault' in negligence simply is the failure to live up to the standards of the ordinary, reasonable person.)

In more recent times, the Court of Appeal appears to have reverted to the approach in the *Ramsbottom* case. In *Dunnage v Randall*,[110] a person named Vince brought a can of petrol into the claimant's home and, eventually, poured it over himself and set himself alight. The claimant was injured in this event. Vince suffered from a florid psychotic state that overwhelmed his ability to exercise self-control without depriving him of his ability to understand the nature and quality of his acts.[111] In a case involving the construction of an insurance policy, the court held that Vince had to be treated as legally responsible for his acts. Rafferty LJ said that '[u]nless a defendant can establish that his condition entirely eliminates responsibility, . . . he remains vulnerable to liability if he does not meet the objective standard of care'.[112] Vos LJ agreed with this statement, and characterised the issue as one concerning volition: 'It is only if the defendant can properly be said to have done nothing himself to cause injury that he escapes liability.'[113] This approach appears to be the correct one.

Section 3 Professional negligence[114]

(A) The background

Ordinary principles applicable In terms of fundamental principle, there is no distinction between the approach to ascertaining the standard of care of professionals from that applicable to any other person. Whether the defendant is a plumber or an architect or a consultant surgeon, the primary question is whether the defendant acted with the skill and competence to be expected from a person undertaking her particular activity in all the circumstances and professing her specific skill.

Particular concerns But problems do arise in actions against professionals, including the following: (1) There might be disputes within the profession as to what constitutes proper practice. (2) The implications of professional negligence might be far reaching. When a carpenter makes an error fixing a new door, the householder might suffer personal injury if the door falls off, but the range of potential harm is limited. Should an

---

[110] [2016] QB 639.   [111] [2016] QB 639, at [27]–[29].   [112] [2016] QB 639, at [114].
[113] [2016] QB 639, at [131] and [133].
[114] For full treatment of this topic, see J Powell, R Stewart, and R Jackson, *Jackson and Powell on Professional Negligence* (7th edn, 2013).

architect make a design error in her plans for a tower block of flats, however, hundreds of people are at risk, and the financial cost of correcting the error in several blocks of flats might be astronomical. (3) The potentially high cost of professional negligence has resulted in massive increases in insurance premiums for architects, solicitors, account-ants, etc. Many professions are now calling for statutory limits on damages awards made against the relevant professionals, even though limited liability partnerships might assist in limiting exposure to personal liability. (4) Particularly acute difficulties affect medical practitioners. Limited NHS funding means that doctors might be overworked and hospitals under-resourced, yet patients increasingly wish to play a greater part in decision-making. (5) Finally, a professional defendant normally will be worth suing. The rules of the profession are likely to oblige her to take out professional indemnity cover. On the other hand, professional negligence actions are apt to be defended vigor-ously by the professional backed by her insurers.

Some further guidelines are given here, therefore, on the current state of the law in England and Wales relating to professional negligence.

(B) Concurrent obligations

Very often, obligations of care will arise concurrently in tort and pursuant to the contract between the professional and her client. Save where an NHS professional is treating a patient, most professional–client relationships are founded on a contract for services. The client, for example, pays the solicitor or the accountant for advice. An obligation of care will be implied into that contract,[115] but will obligations arise concur-rently in tort allowing the client to opt whether to sue in contract or tort? After years of conflicting decisions, the House of Lords in *Henderson v Merrett Syndicates Ltd*[116] ruled in favour of concurrent liability, provided that imposing a duty in tort does not conflict with the contractual terms agreed between the parties.[117] When obligations of care do arise concurrently, the question whether there has been a breach of duty generally will be determined by the same principles, whether the action is framed in tort or contract. However, contract might impose obligations beyond those covered by the tortious duty of care[118]—a point to be kept in mind in the discussion that follows.

(C) The reasonable professional

Rule The standard of care imposed will reflect the level of skill and expertise that the professional holds herself out as having, *or* which it is otherwise reasonable to expect in the circumstances.[119] In the latter case, the defendant must exhibit the degree of skill which a member of the public would expect from a person in her position. Ordinarily,

---

[115] See the Consumer Rights Act 2016, s 49; Supply of Goods and Services Act 1982, s 13.

[116] [1995] 2 AC 145.

[117] Note, also, *Bellefield Computer Services Ltd v E Turner & Sons Ltd* [2002] EWCA Civ 1823, in which the limit of the contractual duty was relevant to construing the limit of the tortious duty.

[118] Cf *Thake v Maurice* [1986] QB 644; *Eyre v Measday* [1986] 1 All ER 488.

[119] *Chaudhry v Prabhakar* [1989] 1 WLR 29, at 34.

the law presumes that the professional person has sufficient time and resources properly to provide the service requested. This includes the time necessary to conduct any research required to reach an informed opinion about a matter.[120] Pressures on her—even pressures for which she is in no way responsible—will not excuse an error on her part. Negligence is not to be equated with moral culpability or general incompetence. In *Wilsher v Essex Area Health Authority*,[121] for example, a premature baby was admitted to a specialist neo-natal unit. An error was made in that the medical staff failed to notice that the baby was receiving too much oxygen and the baby became blind. The Court of Appeal held that the doctors were negligent and, by a majority, that they must be judged by reference to their 'posts' in the unit. It would be irrelevant that they were inexperienced, doing a job that a consultant should have done, or just grossly overworked.

Evidence of practice In determining the standard demanded in a particular type of position, or 'post', expert evidence of proper practice must be called so that the court has a basis for setting the appropriate standard of care. Where practice is disputed, however, conformity with a responsible body of opinion within the profession generally will suffice.[122] Nonetheless, the court remains the ultimate arbiter of what constitutes reasonable and responsible professional practice. In *Edward Wong Finance Co Ltd v Johnson*,[123] the defendant solicitors followed a uniform practice regarding transfers of land among the profession in Hong Kong. The solicitors paid the purchase price to the vendors in return for the promise to ensure that a property was free of encumbrances. The vendors fraudulently failed to do so, and the claimant thus failed to obtain an unencumbered title to the property. The Privy Council held that, while evidence of the practice of the profession went a long way towards showing that the defendant was not negligent, it was not conclusive. The risk of fraud should have been foreseen and precautions taken to avoid that risk.

Logical basis Until recently, judges in claims against doctors seemed rather unwilling to challenge expert professional opinion. Indeed, Lord Scarman castigated a trial judge for presuming to prefer one body of distinguished professional opinion to another.[124] However, in *Bolitho v City and Hackney Health Authority*,[125] Lord Browne-Wilkinson stressed that to constitute evidence of proper, non-negligent practice, expert opinion must be shown to be reasonable and responsible: 'the court has to be satisfied that the exponents of the body of opinion relied on can demonstrate that such opinion has a logical basis'.[126] If 'in a rare case' it can be shown that professional opinion cannot withstand logical analysis, then in a claim against a doctor, as much as in a claim against any other professional,[127] a judge is entitled to find that expert opinion is not reasonable or responsible.[128]

---

[120] *Independent Broadcasting Authority v EMI Electronics Ltd* (1980) 14 BLR 1.
[121] [1987] QB 730 (reversed on the issue of causation [1988] AC 1074).
[122] *Bolam v Friern Hospital Management Committee* [1957] 2 All ER 118.   [123] [1984] AC 296.
[124] *Maynard v West Midlands Regional HA* [1984] 1 WLR 634, at 639.
[125] [1998] AC 232. See also *Hucks v Cole* [1993] 4 Med LR 393.   [126] [1998] AC 232, at 241–2.
[127] Eg, *Carribbean Steel Co Ltd v Price Waterhouse* [2013] PNLR 27, at [46] (firm of accountants).
[128] An analysis of when this occurs is provided in R Mulheron (2010) 69 CLJ 609.

Errors of judgement Errors of judgement *simpliciter* are not indicative of negligence. The issue in all cases is whether the error in question evidenced a failure of professional competence. The virtual immunity offered to doctors for errors of clinical judgement was firmly condemned by the House of Lords in *Whitehouse v Jordan*. As Lord Edmund Davies put it:

> The test [of negligence] is the standard of the ordinary skilled man exercising or professing to have that special skill. If a surgeon fails to measure up to that standard in any respect (clinical judgement or otherwise) he has been negligent.[129]

Medical advice In cases where medical practitioners must advise their patients about the risks of medical treatment, the law of England and Wales modifies their ordinary obligations to act as reasonable professionals in order to take account of the patient's right to know. This is the effect of the Supreme Court decision in *Montgomery v Lanarkshire Health Board*:[130]

> C had endured a high-risk pregnancy. Her doctor had failed to set out risks of 'mechanical problems' involved in a vaginal birth because the doctor believed that a caesarean delivery was not appropriate. C's child was born severely injured as a result of complications during birth; these injuries would have been avoided had a caesarean been undertaken.

The court departed from *Sidaway v Board of Governors of the Bethlem Hospital*[131] in its approach to the obligations of medical practitioners in providing advice, because in that case the House of Lords had not placed sufficient emphasis upon the patient's right to know about risks with respect to which she had not asked specific questions. The issue of what risks to disclose should not depend upon prevailing medical opinion because the patient might have valid personal considerations to take into account. Rather, the patient is entitled to be able to make an informed decision:

> An adult of sound mind is entitled to decide which, if any, of the available forms of treatment to undergo, and her consent must be obtained before treatment interfering with her bodily integrity is undertaken. The doctor is therefore under a duty to take reasonable care to ensure that the patient is aware of any material risks involved in any recommended treatment, and of any alternative or variant treatments. The test of materiality is whether, in the circumstances . . . , a reasonable person in the patient's position would be likely to attach significance to the risk, or the doctor is or should reasonably be aware that the particular patient would be likely to attach significance to it.[132]

On the facts, it was held that there had been a failure to advise of a material risk of injury to the baby, and that if the claimant had been properly advised, she probably would have elected to undergo a caesarean. However, the material risk principle can be departed from in exceptional cases, where the doctor reasonably considers that disclosure of the risk 'would be seriously detrimental to the patient's health' and in cases of necessity to treat where the patient is either unconscious or unable to make a decision as to treatment.[133]

---

[129] [1981] 1 WLR 246, at 258.   [130] [2015] 2 WLR 768.   [131] [1985] AC 871.
[132] [2015] 2 WLR 768, at [87].   [133] [2015] 2 WLR 768, at [88].

Section 4   The standard of care and precedent

Issue Accepting, then, that the standard of care is fixed as a matter of law in the light of *factual* considerations outlined in sections 2 and 3, one must ask the further question whether the standard of care has to be particularised in detail in terms of its obligations. A motorist fails to sound her horn at a crossing and is held liable in negligence to another motorist, with whom she collides. The court holds that she should have sounded her horn. Would such a decision thenceforth be authority for the proposition that a motorist has an obligation to sound her horn when approaching an intersection?

Factual differences Although superficially attractive, we must be cautious of adopting this approach. Ordinarily, the circumstances of each case are sufficiently different in at least one material respect to make it inapt to formulate a catalogue of obligations based on each individual decision. In 'running down' cases, for example, it will be relevant, usually, to consider the speed of the vehicles, the degree of visibility, the state of the road, the distance within which the vehicles could have pulled up, etc.

No precedent Given this backdrop, it is unsurprising that, in terms of judicial practice, the higher courts generally[134] have rejected attempts to particularise obligations in negligence. In *Baker v E Longhurst & Sons Ltd*,[135] for example, Scrutton LJ appeared to formulate a principle that a person driving in the dark must be able to pull up within the limits of her vision. Shortly afterwards, in another road traffic case, Lord Wright said that:

> no one case is exactly like another, and no principle of law can . . . be extracted from those cases. It is unfortunate that questions which are questions of fact alone should be confused by importing into them as principles of law a course of reasoning which has no doubt properly been applied in deciding other cases on other sets of facts.[136]

Most important of all is *Qualcast (Wolverhampton) Ltd v Haynes*,[137] in which the House of Lords went out of its way to stress that a judge's reasons for finding want of reasonable care are matters of fact, not law, for otherwise 'the precedent system will die from a surfeit of authorities'.[138] That judges now give reasons for conclusions formerly arrived at by juries without reasons must not be allowed to elevate these decisions of fact into propositions of law.

Guidance only Naturally, in certain common kinds of claim—notably those arising out of road traffic accidents—factual situations do repeat themselves. Judges properly

---

[134] Though, for the contrary approach see, eg, *Caminer v Northern and London Investment Trust Ltd* [1951] AC 88.   [135] [1933] 2 KB 461, at 468.
[136] *Tidy v Battman* [1934] 1 KB 319, at 322. Cf *SS Heranger (Owners) v SS Diamond (Owners)* [1939] AC 94, at 101.   [137] [1959] AC 743.
[138] [1959] AC 734, at 758.

can refer to earlier decisions for guidance as to what constitutes reasonableness in the circumstances. The infinite variability of human conduct, however, makes it undesirable to express such a standard in terms of an inflexible legal duty. *Worsfold v Howe*[139] illustrates the point:

> D, a car driver, edged blind from a side road across stationary tankers and collided with a motorcyclist approaching on the main road past the tankers. Because the Court of Appeal had held in a previous case that a driver so edging out was not negligent, the trial judge felt bound to absolve D from liability.

The Court of Appeal held that the previous decision laid down no legal principle, that such decisions were to be treated as ones of fact, and, in the instant circumstances, held the defendant negligent. In *Foskett v Mistry*,[140] the Court of Appeal reinforced that approach, ruling that, in 'running down' claims, the question whether reasonable care had been taken must be judged in the light of all the facts of the particular incident.

Section 5 Proving breach

(A) Burden of proof

Whether what is in issue is the veracity of primary facts alleged or the validity of the inferences to be drawn from those facts, the claimant shoulders the burden of establishing (1) that the defendant was in breach; and (2) that her negligence resulted in the claimant's loss or injury. Should the evidence be evenly balanced so that the accident might have been the result of lack of care or competence, but might just as easily have occurred without carelessness, the claimant fails for she will not have established negligence to the required standard of proof.[141] In *Ashcroft v Mersey Regional Health Authority*,[142] for example, the claimant suffered a partial paralysis in her face when in the course of surgery on her left ear the surgeon cut into a facial nerve. Some expert evidence showed this to be an inherent risk of such surgery, even when performed with the greatest skill, while other experts acknowledged that it also occurred sometimes because of a failure in skill. The claimant's action failed.

At least Mrs Ashcroft knew what had happened even though her counsel failed, ultimately, to establish negligence on the defendant's part. In many cases of alleged negligence, the claimant knows only that she has been injured. How she came to be hit on the head by a falling object or a collapsing wall, or why a swab remained in her abdomen after surgery, is a mystery. In a number of such cases, however, the claimant might be able to plead res ipsa loquitur. In others, section 11 of the Civil Evidence Act 1968 might be of use.

---

[139] [1980] 1 All ER 1028.   [140] [1984] RTR 1.

[141] As to why, see A Porat and A Stein, *Tort Liability Under Uncertainty* (2001), ch 1.

[142] [1983] 2 All ER 245 (affirmed [1985] 2 All ER 96n).

(B) Res ipsa loquitur

In some cases, claimants can invoke res ipsa loquitur when direct evidence about what caused an accident is not available. By arguing it, the claimant might be able to establish an inference of defendant negligence.[143]

(1) Leading case

In *Scott v London and St Katherine's Docks Co*[144] the facts were as follows:

> While near the door of D's warehouse, C was injured by some sugar bags falling on him. The judge directed the jury to find a verdict for D on the ground of lack of evidence of negligence by D, who called no evidence. On appeal a new trial was directed.

The court justified this direction of a new trial in the following terms, which have since become known as the res ipsa loquitur principle:[145]

> There must be reasonable evidence of negligence. But where the thing is shown to be under the management of the defendant or his servants, and the accident is such as in the ordinary course of things does not happen if those who have the management use proper care, it affords reasonable evidence, in the absence of explanation by the defendant, that the accident arose from want of care.

(2) Method of reasoning

In the past there has been a tendency to elevate res ipsa loquitur to the status of a principle of substantive law, or at least a doctrine. In the 1970s, however, the Court of Appeal decisively swung away from that approach. In *Lloyde v West Midlands Gas Board*, Megaw LJ stated that res ipsa loquitur simply describes a method of reasoning:

> I doubt whether it is right to describe *res ipsa loquitur* as a 'doctrine'. I think that it is no more than an exotic, although convenient, phrase to describe what is in essence no more than a common-sense approach, not limited by technical rules, to the assessment of the effect of evidence in certain circumstances. It means that a [claimant] *prima facie* establishes negligence where (i) it is not possible for him to prove precisely what was the relevant act or omission which set in train the events leading to the accident, but (ii) on the evidence as it stands at the relevant time it is more likely than not that the effective cause of the accident was *some* act or omission of the defendant or of someone for whom the defendant is responsible, which act or omission constitutes a failure to take proper care for the [claimant's] safety.[146]

It is necessary still to examine the content of the res ipsa loquitur principle, but always with that warning in mind. Three separate requirements must be satisfied.

---

[143] *David T Morrison & Co Ltd v ICL Plastics* [2014] SC 222, at [98].   [144] (1865) 3 H & C 596.

[145] (1865) 3 H & C 596, at 601. It is not necessary to plead the doctrine; it is enough to prove facts which make it applicable: *Bennett v Chemical Construction (GB) Ltd* [1971] 3 All ER 822.

[146] [1971] 2 All ER 1240, at 1246, affirmed by the Court of Appeal in *Turner v Mansfield Corpn* (1975) 119 Sol Jo 629. See also *Ng Chun Pui v Lee Chuen Tat* [1988] RTR 298.

(a) The absence of explanation[147]

This limb merely means that, if the court finds on the evidence adduced how and why the occurrence took place, then there is no room for inference. So, in *Barkway v South Wales Transport Co Ltd*[148]—where the tyre of a bus burst and the bus mounted the pavement and fell down an embankment—res ipsa loquitur did not apply because the court had evidence of the circumstances of the accident and was satisfied that the system of tyre inspection in the defendants' garage was negligent.

The word 'explanation' must be qualified in this context by the adjective 'exact'.[149] This is to make it clear that a claimant who is able to present a partial account of how an accident happened is not precluded from relying on res ipsa loquitur for further inferences essential to winning her case. The partial explanation might make it more obvious that an inference of negligence can be drawn. But of course, as in the *Barkway* case, even if res ipsa loquitur is inapplicable because all the material facts are proved, those facts might still be found to constitute negligence.[150]

(b) The harm must be of such a kind that it does not ordinarily happen if proper care is being taken

The courts have applied res ipsa loquitur to things falling from buildings,[151] and to accidents resulting from defective machines, apparatus, or vehicles.[152] It applies also where motor cars mount the pavement,[153] or where aircraft crash on attempting to take off.[154] On the other hand, it was held inapplicable when neighbouring rooms were damaged by fire spreading from a lodger's room in which a fire had been left alight in the grate.[155]

It will be recalled that the classic definition of Erle CJ referred to accidents happening 'in the ordinary course of things'. *Mahon v Osborne*[156] raised the question whether this means that it must be a matter of common experience, so that the experience of the expert is irrelevant. Goddard LJ held that the principle applied where swabs had been left in the body of a patient after an abdominal operation.[157] But Scott LJ thought

---

[147] *Barkway v South Wales Transport Co Ltd* [1950] 1 All ER 392, at 394.

[148] [1950] 1 All ER 392. And see *Swan v Salisbury Construction Co Ltd* [1966] 2 All ER 138. In *Richley v Faull* [1965] 3 All ER 109, D's car hit C's car when D's car was on the wrong side of the road. D proved that he skidded. Without mentioning res ipsa loquitur, the court reached the solution supported by common sense that D was liable unless he showed that the skid occurred through no fault on his part. Similarly in *Henderson v Henry E Jenkins & Sons* [1970] AC 282, the sudden failure of brakes on a lorry owing to a corroded pipe in the hydraulic braking system was held to impute negligence to the owners.

[149] *Ballard v North British Rly Co* 1923 SC (HL) 43, at 54.

[150] Conversely, D is not liable for an unexplained accident, to which res ipsa loquitur might otherwise apply, if he establishes that he himself was not negligent: *Barkway v South Wales Transport Co Ltd* [1948] 2 All ER 460, at 463.

[151] *Byrne v Boadle* (1863) 2 H & C 722 (flour barrel falling from upper window on to C walking on the street below); *Kearney v London and Brighton Rly Co* (1870) LR 5 QB 411.

[152] *Ballard v North British Rly Co* 1923 SC (HL) 43; *Kealey v Heard* [1983] 1 All ER 973.

[153] *McGowan v Stott* (1930) 143 LT 219n; *Ellor v Selfridge & Co Ltd* (1930) 46 TLR 236; *Laurie v Raglan Building Co Ltd* [1942] 1 KB 152.

[154] *Fosbroke-Hobbes v Airwork Ltd and British-American Air Services Ltd* [1937] 1 All ER 108.

[155] *Sochacki v Sas* [1947] 1 All ER 344.   [156] [1939] 2 KB 14.   [157] [1939] 2 KB 14, at 50.

that the principle did not apply where the judge could not, as she could with surgical operations, have enough knowledge of the circumstances to draw an inference of negligence.[158] Since then, the Court of Appeal has held it to be prima facie evidence of negligence that a man leaving hospital after a course of radiography treatment on his hand and arm should suffer four stiff fingers and a useless hand.[159] Equally, a court was influenced by expert evidence in rejecting the application of res ipsa loquitur to a case where a patient sustained a fractured jaw as a result of a dental extraction.[160] Yet where an unexplained accident occurs from a thing under the control of the defendant, and medical or other expert evidence shows that such accidents would not happen if proper care were used, there is strong evidence of negligence.[161]

(c) The instrumentality causing the accident must be within the exclusive control of the defendant

The meaning of 'control'   Res ipsa loquitur applies only when the defendant is in control. *Turner v Mansfield Corporation*[162] is illustrative:

> C, a driver of D's dust-cart, was injured when its back raised itself up as C drove it under a bridge. It was held that, since C was in control, it was for him to explain the accident. As he was unable to furnish any evidence from which negligence could be inferred, he failed.

McGowan v Stott[163] is an important case also in that it called a halt to previous attempts to insist on complete control of all the circumstances before the rule could apply. A court had previously indicated[164] that the scope of res ipsa loquitur was severely limited in highway accidents because all the essential surrounding circumstances were seldom under the defendant's control. Yet, the court in *McGowan v Stott* refused to follow this approach, declaring the doctrine to be applicable to accidents on the highway where the defendant was in control of the vehicle causing the damage. Two actions brought against railway companies by claimants who had fallen out of trains illustrate the degree of control essential for the doctrine to apply:

> In *Gee v Metropolitan Railway Co*,[165] a few minutes after a local train had started its journey, C leaned against the offside door, which flew open. This was held to be evidence of negligence on the part of the railway company.

---

[158] [1939] 2 KB 14, at 23. It is impossible to be certain of the view of MacKinnon LJ, in view of the conflicting reports perhaps the fullest of which is at (1939) 108 LJKB 567.

[159] *Cassidy v Ministry of Health* [1951] 2 KB 343. *Saunders v Leeds Western HA* [1993] 4 Med LR 355.

[160] *Fish v Kapur* [1948] 2 All ER 176. Cf the patient who swallows a throat pack: *Garner v Morrell* (1953) *Times*, 31 October.   [161] *Lillywhite v UCL Hospitals NHS Trust* [2006] Lloyd's Rep Med 268.

[162] The case is briefly reported at (1975) 119 Sol Jo 629, but the text here is based on a full Court of Appeal transcript.

[163] (1930) 143 LT 219n. Where the apparatus is in C's house—eg, gas apparatus—the onus is on C to show that it was improbable that persons other than D could have interfered with it. Only then can he invoke res ipsa loquitur: *Lloyde v West Midlands Gas Board* [1971] 2 All ER 1240. In *Ward v Tesco Stores Ltd* [1976] 1 All ER 219, C slipped on yoghurt that had been spilt on the floor of D's supermarket. Even though there was no evidence as to how long the yoghurt had been on the floor, it was held to be a case of prima facie negligence.

[164] *Wing v London General Omnibus Co* [1909] 2 KB 652, at 663–4.

[165] (1873) LR 8 QB 161.

In *Easson v London and North Eastern Railway Co*,[166] C's claim failed, Goddard LJ holding that 'it is impossible to say that the doors of an express corridor train travelling from Edinburgh to London are continuously under the sole control of the railway company'.

Where one of two or more persons is in control If the instrumentality is in the control of one of several employees of the same employer, and the claimant cannot point to the particular employee who is in control, res ipsa loquitur can be invoked still so as to make the employer vicariously liable. Thus, a hospital authority has been held answerable for negligent treatment where the claimant could not show which of several members of the staff was responsible.[167] Furthermore, if a surgeon is shown to be in general control of an operation, and the patient cannot establish whether it was the malpractice of the surgeon or one of the theatre staff which inflicted injury on her in the course of that operation, it seems that res ipsa loquitur applies in an action for negligence against the surgeon.[168] If, on the other hand, the surgeon is not in control of all the relevant stages of the treatment, and if the claimant cannot prove that the act complained of took place at a time when the defendant surgeon was in control, res ipsa loquitur cannot be invoked.[169]

Walsh v Holst & Co Ltd[170] extends the principle further. When the defendant's duty is so extensive that she is answerable for the negligence of her independent contractor, and an accident occurs while the independent contractor is performing the work delegated to him, the claimant can invoke res ipsa loquitur against both the defendant and her independent contractor.[171]

A related, though distinct, problem is the position of a claimant who establishes, without invoking res ipsa loquitur, that the damage to her was caused either by the negligence of A or by the negligence of B. If she is merely able to show that only A or B but not both must have been negligent, then she is not entitled to a judgment against both unless the defendants have refused to give evidence, in which case adverse inferences against them may be drawn.[172] It is, however, the duty of the trial court to come to a definite conclusion on the evidence. It must not dismiss the action because of uncertainty as to which party was free from blame.[173] If the inference is that one or other or both have been negligent, the claimant has made out a prima facie case against either A or B, or both.[174]

---

[166] [1944] KB 421, at 424.   [167] *Cassidy v Ministry of Health* [1951] 2 KB 343.

[168] *Mahon v Osborne* [1939] 2 KB 14.

[169] *Morris v Winsbury-White* [1937] 4 All ER 494. Perhaps Somervell LJ disagreed with this statement of law in *Roe v Minister of Health* [1954] 2 QB 66, at 80.

[170] [1958] 3 All ER 33; *Kealey v Heard* [1983] 1 All ER 973.

[171] Apparently, the employer conceded that he was liable even though C had not established that the act did not occur within that area of the independent contractor's operations for which the employer is not answerable: viz, acts of collateral negligence.

[172] *Baker v Market Harborough Industrial Co-operative Society Ltd* [1953] 1 WLR 1472; *Cook v Lewis* [1952] 1 DLR 1 decided that where either X or Y has committed a tort against C and it is the careless act of both of them that prevents C from knowing which caused the harm, both are liable (X and Y were hunters, one or other of whom fired the shot which hit C).   [173] *Bray v Palmer* [1953] 2 All ER 1449.

[174] *Roe v Minister of Health* [1954] 2 QB 66; *France v Parkinson* [1954] 1 All ER 739. Where vehicles collide either at crossroads or on the brow of a hill, and both drivers are dead, a passenger has a prima facie case, in the absence of other evidence, against both drivers or either of them: *Davison v Leggett* (1969) 133 JP 552.

Of course, if the circumstances do not warrant the inference that one or other has been negligent, the claimant fails.[175]

Beyond setting out the above guidance, one cannot define the circumstances where res ipsa loquitur applies. The Court of Appeal has held, in any case, that the cases do not lay down any principles of law; they are merely guides to the kinds of circumstances in which the res ipsa loquitur principle might successfully be invoked.[176]

(d) The effect of res ipsa loquitur[177]

Two uses In some cases the inference to be drawn by resorting to the principle is two-fold: that the defendant caused the accident, and that she was in breach. In others, the cause is known, and only the inference of breach arises.[178]

Inference of breach As we have seen, on any given facts it might be just as likely that the event happened without breach as that it happened in consequence of breach, in which case there is no hint of negligence. However, if in such circumstances res ipsa loquitur applies, its effect is to make it 'relevant to infer negligence'[179] from the fact of the accident. This means that there is in law evidence on which the judge can find for the claimant.[180] The distinctive function of res ipsa loquitur is to permit an inference of breach from proof of the injury and the physical instrumentality causing it, even though there is no proof of the facts identifying the human agency responsible. Looked at in this way, its affinity to the ordinary rule of evidence that circumstantial evidence is admissible to prove negligence is clear. As Atkin LJ put it:

> all that one wants to know is whether the facts of the occurrence do as a matter of fact make it more probable that a jury may reasonably infer that the damage was caused by want of care on the part of the defendants than the contrary.[181]

The effect of res ipsa loquitur is to afford prima facie evidence of breach. It does not shift the burden of proof to the defendant[182] in the sense that, in the absence of the defendant rebutting the inference on the balance of probabilities, the courts must find for the claimant. But once res ipsa loquitur has been successfully invoked to raise an inference of breach against the defendant, if the defendant fails to adduce any countervailing evidence, the judge will be entitled to find for the claimant. Thus, a successful plea has the effect of shifting the evidential burden onto the defendant to establish facts that would negative that inference.[183]

---

[175] *Knight v Fellick* [1977] RTR 316.

[176] *Easson v London and NE Rly Co* [1944] KB 421, at 423.

[177] For the clearest judicial statement, see the eight rules laid down by Evatt J in *Davis v Bunn* (1936) 56 CLR 246, at 267–8.

[178] *Barkway v South Wales Transport Co Ltd* [1950] 1 All ER 392, at 399–400.

[179] *Ballard v North British Rly Co* 1923 SC (HL) 43, at 54. See also *David T Morrison & Co Ltd v ICL Plastics* [2014] SC 222, at [98].   [180] *Cole v De Trafford (No 2)* [1918] 2 KB 523, at 528.

[181] *McGowan v Stott* (1923), in (1930) 143 LT 219n. Cf *Langham v Governors of Wellingborough School and Fryer* (1932) 101 LJKB 513, at 518.

[182] On burden of proof generally see *Wilsher v Essex AHA* [1988] AC 1074.

[183] *David T Morrison & Co Ltd v ICL Plastics* [2014] SC 222, at [98].

Historically, the judge could not have withdrawn the case from the jury. But it might now be that certain facts are so clear that the inference of breach is sufficiently cogent that the judge must rule in favour of the claimant. On the other hand, this will by no means always be the case. As Du Parcq LJ said:

> The words *res ipsa loquitur* . . . are a figure of speech, by which sometimes is meant that certain facts are so inconsistent with any view except that the defendant has been negligent that any jury [or judge] which, on proof of these facts, found that negligence was not proved would be giving a perverse verdict. Sometimes, the proposition does not go as far as that, but is merely that on proof of certain facts an inference of negligence may be drawn by a reasonable jury [or judge].[184]

Defendant's evidence and onus The effect of res ipsa loquitur where the defendant gives evidence must be considered also. Plainly, the effect of the doctrine is to shift the onus to the defendant in the sense that the principle continues to operate unless the defendant calls credible evidence which explains how the accident might have occurred without breach; and it seems that the operation of the rule is not displaced merely by expert evidence showing theoretically possible ways in which the accident might have happened without the defendant's negligence. But beyond this, the courts describe its effect in two different ways. Sometimes they state that once the defendant has furnished evidence of the cause of the accident consistent with her having exercised due care it becomes a question whether, upon the whole of the evidence, the defendant was in breach or not; and the defendant will succeed unless the court is satisfied that she was in breach.[185] On other occasions they state that the defendant loses unless she proves that the accident resulted from a specific cause which does not connote breach on her part but, on the contrary, points to its absence as more probable.[186] There is possibly no inconsistency in these judicial utterances; all may depend on the context of the cases and the cogency of the rebutting evidence in the particular case.[187]

A useful example of how a defendant can rebut an inference of res ipsa loquitur can be seen in *Ng Chun Pui v Lee Chuen Tat*.[188]

> A coach veered across the road, colliding with a bus coming in the opposite direction. C called no evidence and the Privy Council held that the facts per se raised an inference of negligence. But Ds testified that an unidentified car cut across their coach, causing the driver to brake suddenly and skid across the road. Ds were found to have rebutted any inference of breach since the driver's reaction to an emergency beyond his control did not constitute any breach of duty.

(C) Civil Evidence Act 1968, section 11

Whereas res ipsa loquitur can be a seen as a partial exception to the general rule that the claimant must prove the defendant's breach in that it raises a rebuttable

---

[184] *Easson v London and NE Rly Co* [1944] KB 421, at 425.

[185] Eg, *Ballard v North British Rly Co* 1923 SC (HL) 43, at 54; *The Kite* [1933] P 154; *Colvilles Ltd v Devine* [1969] 2 All ER 53. [186] Eg, *Moore v R Fox & Sons Ltd* [1956] 1 QB 596.

[187] See, eg, *Lillywhite v University College London Hospitals NHS Trust* [2005] EWCA Civ 1466.

[188] [1988] RTR 298.

presumption of that breach, the Civil Evidence Act 1968, section 11 goes slightly further. It reverses the burden of proof in certain circumstances. Where a defendant previously has been convicted of a criminal offence against the claimant, and the claimant subsequently brings civil proceedings on the basis of the same facts that led to the defendant's conviction, section 11 makes that conviction prima facie evidence of the defendant's civil liability. It then falls to the defendant to demonstrate to the judge (on the balance of probabilities) in civil proceedings that she should not be held liable in damages.[189] This she is entitled to attempt to do,[190] although the court must be mindful of a potential abuse of process whereby the defendant is effectively attempting to re-litigate her criminal conviction.[191] Thus, in *Grealis v Opuni*[192] the fact that the defendant had been in breach of road traffic legislation (by driving at 38mph in a 30mph zone) did not detract from his ability to show that the claimant was contributorily negligent (80% to blame, in fact).

Conclusions

In this chapter, we have considered the second element that needs to be proved in order to have an action in negligence. The standard of care is determined according to a full assessment of relevant aspects of the risks incurred, and the types of precautions available to reduce the prospects of injury. The court determines this standard by reference to what reasonably could be expected of the ordinary, reasonable person faced with a similar set of circumstances. The test is objective, so that the idiosyncrasies of the defendant are excluded from consideration. However, the law recognises that age is not an idiosyncrasy, and adjusts the standard of care expected of actors by reference to it—especially when they are children. By contrast, in the usual case no account is taken of a defendant's disability or infirmity. In cases of professional defendants, they must adhere to the higher standards expected of those holding themselves out as experts with certain special skills and experience. After setting the relevant standard of care, the court will compare this with the actions of the defendant in order to determine whether she fell below that standard, and should be adjudged to have breached it.

Problem question

Oliver required emergency treatment for appendicitis and he was brought to the Royal Wallingsworth Hospital for treatment. Oliver was in great pain and the medical team determined that there was no time to test for allergies to anaesthetic. The operation was a success in dealing with the immediate problem of the appendicitis, but Oliver suffered a mild reaction to the use of the anaesthetic. For two weeks his vision was fuzzy and he suffered from headaches. Another issue became evident later. The medical team did

---

[189] See *Wauchope v Mordecai* [1970] 1 WLR 317.   [190] *J v Oyston* [1999] 1 WLR 694.
[191] *McCauley v Hope* [1999] PIQR P185.   [192] [2003] 12 LS Gaz R 32.

not notice a small, cancerous polyp near the site of Oliver's appendix. In normal circumstances, such a polyp could be investigated while a patient is under anaesthetic and after the intended operation is completed. However, the medical team was hampered in the conduct of the surgery by a flickering light in the operating theatre. The hospital had installed a light globe of insufficient wattage—although the wattage conformed to the minimum specified in the Hospital Operating Theatres Standard of 1978 published by the British Hospitals Association (which was the Standard relevant at the time of construction of the building).

Advise Oliver as to any potential breaches of the standard of care in negligence.

 Visit **http://www.oup.com/uk/street15e/** for answer guidance.

Further reading

AMIRTHALINGAM, 'Medical Negligence and Patient Autonomy' (2015) 27 *Singapore Academy of Law Journal* 666

BRAZIER AND MIOLA, 'Bye-Bye *Bolam*: A Medical Litigation Revolution?' (2000) 8 *Medical Law Review* 85

KIDNER, 'The Variable Standard of Care, Contributory Negligence and *Volenti*' (1991) 11 *Legal Studies* 1

MULHERON, 'Trumping *Bolam*: A Critical Legal Analysis of *Bolitho*'s Gloss' (2010) 69 *Cambridge Law Journal* 609

NOLAN, 'Varying the Standard of Care in Negligence' (2013) 72 *Cambridge Law Journal* 651

RAZ, 'Responsibility and the Negligence Standard' (2010) 30 *Oxford Journal of Legal Studies* 1

WITTING, 'National Health Service Rationing: Implications for the Standard of Care in Negligence' (2001) 21 *Oxford Journal of Legal Studies* 443

WITTING, 'The Hand and *Shirt* Tests for Breach and the Civil Liability Acts' (2009) 17 *Torts Law Journal* 242

7

Causation and remoteness

KEY ISSUES

(1) Causation in fact

The primary question in the law on causation is whether the defendant can be said to have been a factual cause of the claimant's loss or harm. In most cases, this question can be answered by applying the 'but for' test. According to this test, the defendant generally can be said to have been a factual cause of the claimant's damage if, but for the defendant's breach of a duty owed to the claimant, the claimant would not have suffered in the way that he did. However, there are a number of exceptional types of case in which the application of the basic 'but for' approach will not be practicable. Since the courts cannot shy away from such hard cases, they have been forced to develop alternative tests to resolve them. As a result, there is no universal test for causation in fact.

(2) Causation in law

There is a second aspect to causation in cases where the defendant commits a tort earlier in time and, later in time, a second event occurs which gives rise to further damage. The question is whether the defendant is liable for the further damage. In such instances, the task for the courts is to identify the legally significant cause: it is reducible to asking whether the subsequent event can be regarded as a *novus actus interveniens* (or new intervening cause) so as to sever the chain of causation flowing from the tort.

(3) Remoteness of damage

The law does not allow recovery for all damage that can be linked—no matter how tenuously—to a prior tort. Limits are placed on the losses for which any given defendant will be held responsible and required to pay compensation. In other words, some forms of loss will be regarded as too remote from the defendant's tort for the defendant to be held liable in respect of those losses. The general test of remoteness in tort law is whether the harm in question was reasonably foreseeable.

Section 1 Introduction

Causation and responsibility Readers will by now be aware that a claimant in the law of tort, generally speaking, is able to claim for his losses only when he can prove a causal relationship between the defendant's wrong, or breach of duty, and losses suffered. The basic reason for this lies in the importance of notions of personal responsibility for losses in the assignment of liability.[1]

Three issues Causation is a topic relevant to all torts since, across the board, problems arise concerning whether the defendant's wrongful conduct did in fact cause the claimant's damage and whether the defendant ought to be held responsible for the full extent of that damage. Causation will be dealt with in this chapter in three stages. First, we will consider causation in fact—the matter of how (and to what standard of proof) the claimant must establish that the damage of which he complains resulted from the defendant's negligent conduct. Second, we will consider causation in law: that is, whether a subsequent intervening event—a *novus actus interveniens*—can be said to sever the chain of causation such that the subsequent event is treated in law as the only relevant cause of the claimant's damage. Finally, we shall consider the principles governing remoteness of damage.

Notes While causation is relevant throughout tort law, it is dealt with in this part of the book for two reasons. First, very many, though not all, of the more complex causation cases concern negligence. Second, negligence is actionable only when the claimant suffers a recognised form of damage. In the usual case of negligence, the claimant must be able to prove a causal connection between the defendant's failure to take care, and the ensuing damage.[2] Many of the rules on factual causation have been developed in claims involving this tort. It should be noted, however, that the principles governing remoteness of damage can vary in the remainder of tort law. The rules discussed here, pertaining to negligence, are the ones most widely applied. Where the rules are different in relation to certain other torts, the relevant principles are explained in the appropriate chapters.

Section 2 Causation in fact

(A) Context

Complex of conditions Establishing cause and effect might be far from easy. Every occurrence is the result of a combination of multiple different events. Any incident resulting in injury to a claimant is the product not simply of the defendant's tortious acts and omissions, but also of the conditions in which those events took place. These can include incidents both prior to and subsequent to the allegedly tortious conduct of the defendant. Consider the facts of *Wright v Lodge*.[3]

> D2 was driving her car at night along a dual carriageway in the fog. The road was unlit. Her car's engine failed and the vehicle came to a stop in the near-side lane. A few minutes later, as D2 was trying to restart her vehicle, an articulated lorry being driven by D1 at 60 mph crashed into her car virtually destroying it and seriously injuring a passenger in the

---

[1] S Steel, *Proof of Causation in Tort Law* (2015), 104. See also J Stapleton (2015) 35 OJLS 1, 22.

[2] For detailed discussion, see, eg, S Steel, *Proof of Causation in Tort Law* (2015).

[3] [1993] 4 All ER 299.

back seat. After hitting the car, the lorry careered across the central reservation and fell on to its side, blocking the road. Four vehicles collided with it. One driver died of his injuries and another was seriously injured.

What or who caused those additional injuries? Had the second defendant not chosen to go out that evening, or had it not been foggy, or had the road been lit, the accident might never have happened. In one sense, then, each of those factors is a cause without which the accident would not have occurred. But the law looks primarily to the impact of human actors. The unlit road and the fog are merely part of the complex of conditions which produced the accident, but they are not regarded as causes in law. On the other hand, not all human acts constitute the cause in law of an event. No one would suggest that by driving out that night, the driver of the car (or lorry) was responsible for the three claimants' injuries. What must be identified is the relevant factual cause or causes (and in this case it was the lorry driver alone who was held liable in respect of the second set of crashes even though his lorry would not have been blocking the carriageway had it not been for the car driver negligently failing to move her car out of the way).

Identifying relevant causes As the foregoing illustration demonstrates, frequently the identification of the relevant cause(s) from a complex of factors is far from simple. One reason for this is that the underlying issue involves comparison of what actually happened in the case brought by the claimant, which might itself be a matter of speculation and reconstruction, with what would have happened had the defendant not been in breach. That is, it involves the application of a counter-factual to determine whether the defendant's breach 'made a difference' through the causation of damage[4]—an exercise which, in many cases, can be undertaken only on the basis of a 'best guess'. Another reason for difficulty is that, in some cases, the application of the counter-factual is futile, given the state of scientific or medical evidence about the way in which relevant causal mechanisms work. An alternative mode of reasoning must be adopted. In still other cases, there is no relevant physical process initiated by the defendant's breach because the relevant breach is a failure to act (an omission). The result of these difficulties is that the courts must shape rules as best they can to come to defensible decisions about tortious responsibility for damage. In choosing the relevant causes of damage, a court will wish to inform itself of the policy basis of a particular rule of law.[5] In *Environment Agency v Empress Car Co (Abertillery) Ltd*,[6] Lord Hoffmann explained that:

> Questions of causation often arise for the purpose of attributing responsibility to someone, for example, so as to blame him for something which has happened or to make him . . . liable in damages. In such cases, the answer will depend upon the rule by which responsibility is being attributed.

---

[4] See T Honoré, 'Necessary and Sufficient Conditions in Tort Law' in DG Owen (ed), *Philosophical Foundations of Tort Law* (1995), ch 16; D Hamer (2014) 77 MLR 155, 163–4.

[5] In *Gregg v Scott* [2005] 2 AC 176, at 197, Lord Hoffmann admitted openly that 'an apparently arbitrary distinction [in the law] obviously rests on grounds of policy'. See also *Fairchild v Glenhaven Funeral Services Ltd* [2002] 3 All ER 305; *Barker v Corus UK Ltd* [2006] 2 AC 572; D Hamer (2014) 77 MLR 155, 158ff; D Nolan, 'Causation and the Goals of Tort Law' in A Robertson and HW Tang (eds), *The Goals of Private Law* (2009), ch 7.   [6] [1999] 2 AC 22, at 29.

In most cases of causal uncertainty, the court will want to consider in advance also the desirability of finding factual causation in a particular actor—that is, to ensure that it will reach an acceptable result. But this is not to say that the law of factual causation is not governed by any rules at all. Such rules are there, even if (in the end) they are no more than rules of thumb which are accompanied by various exceptions.[7]

(B) The 'but for' test

Basic test The basic test for factual causation is the 'but for' test, the question being whether, but for the defendant's breach of duty, the loss would have occurred.[8] If the answer is 'no', and there is no complication in the case,[9] the court will hold the defendant liable (subject to whether the harm in question is too remote to permit recovery). If the answer is 'yes', the court will hold that the defendant is not liable—because he made no difference to the claimant's fortunes. Thus, in *Barnett v Chelsea and Kensington Hospital Management Committee,* where a man who later died of arsenical poisoning was sent home from a casualty department without treatment after complaining of acute stomach pains, his widow's claim against the hospital failed even though it admitted breach.[10] Even if he had been given prompt and competent medical treatment, it was too late to administer an antidote and he would have died in either case.

(C) Evidence of causation

In cases of uncertainty about causal processes, either or both of the burden and the standard of proof can become very important in reaching a result. In terms of the burden of proof, the usual rule is that he who asserts must prove. In terms of the standard of proof, it must be shown that it is *more likely than not* that the wrongful conduct of the defendant caused the claimant's loss or injury.[11] Where there is *some evidence* that the defendant's conduct might have contributed to the claimant's injury, the burden rests with the claimant. It does not fall to the defendant to rebut the possibility that his conduct *might* have caused the claimant's loss. It follows that, when the damage in question is a disease, the claimant's task can be formidable. Consider the example of a person claiming that he developed dermatitis because of contact with substances at work caused by his employer's failure to supply proper protective clothing. The medical

---

[7] The complexity—at a number of levels—of causation issues is evident in the number of ways in which the material is presented in textbooks on torts. One finds, for example, that any particular case on causation might be considered under various different headings in different texts.

[8] For a detailed explanation of why this test is central, see J Stapleton (2015) 35 OJLS 1.

[9] As will be explained, there might be real evidential uncertainty in the application of the 'but for' test. Another kind of complication arises from cases (most often hypothesised by scholars rather than coming before the courts) of 'causal over-determination', with respect to which more than one sufficient cause operates: eg, a case of two tortiously lit fires converging to burn down C's house (as to which, see later). In such a case, the straightforward 'but for' test cannot be applied and scholars have argued that an alternative test of causal necessity might be applied, such as the 'NESS' test: see, esp. HLA Hart and T Honoré, *Causation in the Law* (2nd edn, 1985); R Wright (1985) 75 Calif LR 1735. But note that one influential writer advocates a move away from tests based upon causal necessity: J Stapleton (2013) 129 LQR 39.   [10] [1969] 1 QB 428.

[11] *Hotson v East Berkshire Area HA* [1987] AC 750.

evidence might reveal that contact with those substances was merely one possible cause. But it might indicate also that several other possible causes can be identified. In such a case, the claimant must show that it was more likely than not that those substances caused the dermatitis;[12] and the question whether he has produced sufficient evidence to do this is one of law, not fact.

(D) Cases of evidential uncertainty

(1) Cases involving the 'loss of a chance'

Hotson **case** A number of cases involving 'the loss of a chance' have come before the English courts and illustrate the importance of the standard of proof in this context.

> In *Hotson v East Berkshire Area Health Authority*,[13] C fell several feet from a tree, injuring his hip. He was rushed to hospital but his injury, thanks to D's breach of duty, was not diagnosed until five days later. The hospital admitted breach and responsibility for the pain C suffered during the five days that treatment was delayed but denied liability for the avascular necrosis that C developed as a result of a failure in the blood supply to his injured hip. The trial judge found that there was a 75% chance that avascular necrosis would have developed as a result of the injury even if promptly treated, and a 25% chance that it was due to the delay. He held the hospital liable for the loss of the 25% chance that the condition could have been avoided (that is, 25% of the compensation which would have been payable had D been entirely responsible for C's condition).

In the House of Lords, it was held fatal to the claimant's case that the accident alone was more than likely the cause of his condition.[14] If the claimant had been able to show that the delay was the more probable cause of the necrosis, he would have been able to recover in full. But, since it was the less likely cause, he could recover nothing.[15] Though a contentious decision,[16] it was accepted by a majority of the House of Lords in *Gregg v Scott*,[17] where the claimant sought to claim on the basis of a reduced prospect of surviving cancer based on a doctor's misdiagnosis of his condition and consequent failure to refer him to a specialist for confirmation (or otherwise) of that diagnosis. In fact, the claimant had a malignant lymphoma, but this was not discovered until over one year later. Medical evidence showed, on the balance of probabilities, that, even had there been an immediate referral, the claimant would not have secured any greater life expectancy.

Importantly, from a legal perspective the *Hotson* case did not involve the loss of a chance (for which loss a claim of proportionate damages could be made). Either the boy's hip was sufficiently damaged at the time of his fall that he would be permanently disabled or it was not. Unfortunately, the evidence available was inadequate to show beyond doubt that it was so damaged. All that could be said was that it was more likely

---

[12] Cf the exceptional case of mesothelioma: see *Sienkiewicz v Grief* [2011] 2 WLR 523 (discussed later).
[13] [1987] AC 750.   [14] [1985] 3 All ER 167, at 240 and 248.
[15] See also *Kay v Ayrshire and Arran Health Board* [1987] 2 All ER 417 (C unable to prove on the balance of probabilities that D, who supplied C with an overdose of penicillin, had caused C's deafness).
[16] See J Stapleton (1988) 104 LQR 389; M Lunney (1995) 15 LS 1.   [17] [2005] 2 AC 176.

than not that, at the time of his fall, the boy's hip was so severely damaged that even prompt treatment could not have prevented his future disability. The decision might appear unpalatable insofar as there was a small chance that immediate treatment might have made a difference. But, from the legal point of view, the fact that it was more probable than not that even prompt treatment would have made no difference meant that the boy could not be regarded as having lost a chance of being cured. The law treated the onset of avascular necrosis as inevitable.

Perhaps one of the reasons why the House of Lords in the *Hotson* case adopted this approach was that allowing claims generally for lost chances (by way of proportionate damages) would radically change the shape of tort law. It would open the way for many more claimants to litigate their cases and might have serious repercussions for insurance companies and the National Health Service, given that the deleterious effects of medical mishaps frequently are uncertain. Presumably, it would mean also a reduction in the damages for those (currently able to recover in full) who are able to show a greater-than-even probability that the defendant's negligence caused them to lose the chance of being cured or the chance of avoiding a particular condition. Weighing up the pros and cons of each approach is by no means easy, since speculation is required in either case. Recognising these difficulties, Lord Phillips confined himself to deciding no more than he had to in *Gregg v Scott*. He left open the question whether he would have been prepared to develop the law along the lines of loss of chance in misfeasance cases. That being so, it might well be that, notwithstanding the decisions in *Hotson* and *Gregg*, the Supreme Court will be required at some future time to address this difficult issue once again.[18]

Three-party cases   Leaving misfeasance cases to one side, a loss of chance *is* recoverable where the claimant's loss is attributable to a negligent omission and the question of causation turns on the hypothetical actions of a third party. In *Allied Maples Group Ltd v Simmons & Simmons*[19] the facts were as follows:

> Cs had been advised by Ds (their solicitors) in relation to the purchase of certain businesses from another company. At one stage, the proposed contract included an undertaking by the vendor company that there were no outstanding liabilities in respect of their properties. In the course of negotiations, however, that undertaking was deleted. After purchasing the business, Cs found themselves liable for substantial sums arising from leases previously held by the vendor. The original undertaking would have protected them from such liabilities. Cs argued that Ds were negligent in not advising them that its removal exposed them to liabilities that would not have arisen if the clause had been retained. The issues were whether Cs would have tried to insist on its retention had they been properly advised, and whether the vendors, in turn, would have agreed to its retention.

---

[18] *Gregg v Scott* leaves unanswered the question why the loss of a chance is recoverable in professional negligence cases resulting in financial loss (see, eg, *Allied Maples Group Ltd v Simmons & Simmons* [1995] 1 WLR 1602), but not where the professional negligence is that of a doctor. One might say that it is (in light of the general hierarchy of protected interests in tort law) objectionable to permit claims in respect of the loss of a chance of a financial gain but not the loss of a chance of physical cure. Cf *Gouldsmith v Mid-Staffordshire General Hospitals NHS Trust* [2007] EWCA Civ 397.   [19] [1995] 1 WLR 1602.

The Court of Appeal held that the claimants had to prove on the balance of probabilities that it was more likely than not that, properly advised, they would have approached the vendors. This would establish the loss of a chance to renegotiate the contract. Having done so, they did not need to go on and show that it was also more likely than not that the vendors would have consented to the clause being reinserted. It was enough merely to show a substantial (as opposed to a speculative) chance that they would have agreed.[20] This was enough to make meaningful the claim that the claimants had lost a chance to renegotiate the agreement. That said, the probability of the vendors agreeing would need to be determined in order to assess the proper quantum of damages.

Another case in which a claim for a lost chance succeeded was *Spring v Guardian Assurance plc*.[21] An employer was found liable for negligently giving a bad reference about the claimant to a prospective employer. The claimant recovered for his loss of a chance of new employment. While he could not prove that he definitely would have been given the job, he could prove that with a properly written reference he would have had a decent chance of getting it.

Analysis These two cases, as well as others in which *Allied Maples* has been applied,[22] can be distinguished from the *Hotson* case. In *Hotson*, it was argued that the boy had lost a 25% chance of recovering had he been treated. But the probability was calculated according to expert evidence grounded on statistical analysis of outcomes in previous cases. Such evidence was of the kind: in 25 out of 100 falls, prompt treatment might save the hip. But this means merely that, when the boy came to hospital, most probably he was one of the 75 unfortunate ones for whom prompt treatment would make no difference. As such, he could not be heard to argue along the lines that he might 'possibly have avoided the condition' in the same way that, for example, the claimant might 'possibly have got the job' in *Spring*. After the event—that is, after the necrosis had set in—it was not possible to say whether he had ever had a chance of recovery (assuming the provision of proper treatment). Therefore, the uncertainty in *Hotson* was of a qualitatively different kind.

In the cases just considered, the courts did not perceive the need to depart from the usual 'but for' test that must be proved on the balance of probabilities. It is true that they were affected by a certain amount of evidential uncertainty, but there were sufficient facts to retain the usual rules. In *Allied Maples*, it was certain that the claimant lost the chance to renegotiate the terms of the purchase agreement; in *Spring*, it was certain that the claimant had lost the chance of employment. Furthermore, in both cases there was only one possible cause of the loss of the respective chances: the breach of duty of the defendant.

(2) Cases involving hypothetical conduct by the claimant

Certainty Where what the claimant would have done had the defendant not been in breach is certain or virtually certain, there are no especial problems for the law of

---

[20] A not entirely groundless claim would suffice: *Dixon v Clement Jones Solicitors* [2005] PNLR 6.

[21] [1995] 2 AC 296.

[22] See, eg, *Dixon v Clement Jones Solicitors* [2005] PNLR 6 and *Batty v Danaher* [2005] EWHC 2763.

causation. Take, for example, *Cummings (or McWilliams) v Sir William Arrol & Co Ltd.*[23]
An employer failed to comply with a statutory duty to provide a safety harness to an
employee who ended up falling from a great height to his death. It was established that,
even when harnesses had been supplied in the past, the deceased employee had seldom,
if ever, worn one. That being so, it was virtually certain that, even if the employer had supplied one on the occasion in question, the employee would not have worn it. Accordingly,
the defendant's negligent non-provision of the harness could not be regarded as the 'but
for' cause of the employee's death. (Importantly, the employer's duty was limited merely
to providing, but not ensuring or supervising the wearing of, the harness.)[24]

Uncertainty[25]   Where, by contrast, there is lingering uncertainty about what the claimant would have done had the defendant not been in breach, matters become much more
difficult. The House of Lords in *Chester v Afshar* considered the kinds of problem that
arise in depth:[26]

> C had a long history of back pain and was advised by D, her surgeon, that she required
> spinal surgery. But the surgeon failed to tell her that the operation, which she underwent
> three days later, carried with it a risk of neurological damage calculated at 1–2%. Even
> though the surgery was not performed negligently, the injury materialised and C brought
> an action based on the surgeon's negligent failure to disclose the risk of injury.

Difficulty arose in the fact that, had the patient been advised of the risk, she would have
sought further medical advice before deciding what to do, and, following that advice,
she might or might not have had the operation at a later date. Now, if she merely had
delayed treatment until after she had received further advice, the overwhelming probability is that the injury would not have materialised. The operation at that later date
still would have carried only a 1–2% chance of the neurological damage occurring.
Alternatively, had she decided not to have the surgery, it would have been impossible
to succumb to the neurological damage. So either way, it would have been extremely
unlikely that she would have suffered the injury that she ultimately suffered. That being
so, on the usual 'but for' principles, the defendant *could* be held to have caused the
claimant's injury. But a bare majority of the House of Lords held that the defendant
had caused the claimant's injury—on grounds of *policy* rather than conventional 'but
for' principles.[27] What then was the complicating factor? Put briefly, it was that all that

---

[23] [1962] 1 All ER 623.

[24] On the relationship between scope of duty and causation, see J Stapleton (2003) 119 LQR 388.

[25] At the commencement of this section, it should be noted that A Porat and A Stein have identified five
(sometimes overlapping) kinds of evidential uncertainty: (1) cases of wrongful damage where the wrongdoer
is unidentifiable; (2) cases of wrongful damage where the precise injured party is unidentifiable (eg, cases in
which, say, D has emitted radiation affecting many citizens but it is not certain whether C was among their
number); (3) cases of wrongful conduct that might or might not have resulted in damage; (4) cases of damage
wrongfully inflicted by separate wrongdoers; and (5) cases of damage arising from both a wrongful and a non-
wrongful cause: *Tort Liability Under Uncertainty* (2001), ch 2. The approach to the cases taken in this chapter
does not map on to this typology directly.   [26] [2005] 1 AC 134.

[27] The majority *did* accept that the 'but for' test was satisfied: [2005] 1 AC 134, at [19], [61], and [94]; but
the analysis did not stop there.

the defendant's failure to warn had caused was the patient to undergo the operation on the day that she did. The failure to warn did not, they thought, increase the risk inherent in the surgery: which remained a constant 1–2%.[28] On this analysis, the majority seemed to be hinting (but not saying explicitly) that the surgery, rather than the failure to warn, was the overwhelming cause of the claimant's injury. However, if one accepted that the failure to warn was legally eclipsed by the subsequent surgery, this would lead to the conclusion that the duty to warn counted for nothing. As Lord Hope put it, the duty would be 'a hollow one, stripped of all practical force and devoid of all content'.[29] Therefore, he went on to say, the claimant's loss '*can be regarded as having been caused, in the legal sense*, by the breach of that duty'.[30] In order to make the decision more palatable still, their Lordships identified the loss to the claimant as a loss of autonomy (that is, the loss of her right to choose whether to have her operation or delay it until after getting further advice).[31] This approach makes the gist of the action patient autonomy rather than neurological damage; yet it seems that it was for the neurological damage that compensation was awarded. This is by no means explicable in logical terms.[32]

In the light of its controversial nature, the Court of Appeal has been keen to emphasise since that the result in *Chester v Afshar* was an extraordinary one reached on policy grounds, and to confine it to its own limited context: that is, cases involving a negligent failure to warn a patient of the dangers associated with a particular medical procedure.[33]

(3) The material contribution to harm principle

Principle English law allows negligence claims to be brought by a claimant able to show (1) that the defendant was in breach of a duty of care; and (2) that the breach of duty materially contributed to his injury. The fact that the claimant cannot identify precisely the degree to which the defendant's wrongdoing caused his injury is not regarded as a

---

[28] See, eg, [2005] 1 AC 134, at [7], [31], and [61]. This assumption is questionable, however, since there might have been something about the patient *or* the surgeon on the particular day that made the risk of injury more likely to occur. All that the 1–2% statistic represents is the fact that either one or two persons out of one hundred undergoing such surgery would succumb to the syndrome that afflicted the claimant. We might therefore assert (quite reasonably) in the case of any individual patient, that there is a 1–2% risk of injury. This can be described as 'epistemic probability'. But it does not reflect the actual, subjective probability (which might well vary for any given patient), which is unknown due to an information deficit (about, for instance, the particular susceptibilities of the claimant, or the relative skills of different surgeons). For further explanation of the difference between epistemic and subjective probability and of their application to causation problems, see S Perry, 'Risk, Harm and Responsibility' in DG Owen (ed), *Philosophical Foundations of Tort Law* (1995), ch 14.

[29] This too is questionable. If the patient would not have delayed the operation while she sought further advice, but would have declined the operation outright, then the duty to warn would have counted for something. Perhaps this is why Lord Walker did not entirely agree, but preferred to state that the duty would be 'empty in many [but not all] cases': [2005] 1 AC 134, at [101]. [30] [2005] 1 AC 134, at [87] (emphasis added).

[31] Lord Bingham noted that the rationale of the duty to warn was 'to enable adult patients of sound mind to make for themselves decisions intimately affecting their own lives and bodies': [2005] 1 AC 134, at [5]. See also ibid at [33] and [56].

[32] Recognising this, Lord Hoffmann suggested that, in respect of the infringement of the patient's right to choose, 'there might be a case for a modest solatium': [2005] 1 AC 134, at [34].

[33] See, eg, *White v Paul Davidson & Taylor* [2005] PNLR 15 (*Chester* inapplicable to solicitor's negligent advice); *Beary v Pall Mall Investments* [2005] PNLR 35 (*Chester* inapplicable to negligent advice regarding financial matters).

sufficient basis on which to refuse the claimant a remedy. In such cases, according to the Court of Appeal in *Bailey v Ministry of Defence*, so long as he can 'establish that the contribution of the negligent cause was more than negligible . . . the claimant will succeed'.[34]

Seminal case In *Bonnington Castings Ltd v Wardlaw*[35] the facts were as follows:

> C, who was D's employee, contracted pneumoconiosis after inhaling silicon dust at work. The dust came from two sources—swing grinders and pneumatic hammers. Only the dust thrown out by the swing grinders was avoidable by use of a proper extraction mechanism. In the absence of such a mechanism, C's exposure to this dust was regarded as tortious. However, the dust generated by the hammers was not produced tortiously. The question was whether it was the 'innocent' or the 'tortious' dust that had caused C's condition. There was no evidence as to the proportions of 'innocent' and 'tortious' dust that C had inhaled. Therefore, it was impossible to apply the usual 'but for' test, since C could not show on the balance of probabilities that, had a proper extraction mechanism been used, he would not have contracted the disease.

Yet the House of Lords found for the claimant. Lord Reid held that the source of the claimant's 'disease was the dust from both sources, and the real question is whether the dust from the swing grinders materially contributed to the disease'.[36] Importantly, the claimant recovered damages in full despite the fact that the tortious dust only made a contribution to his illness. However, where successive employers expose the claimant to the same harmful agent and the disease the claimant contracts is divisible (ie, it gets progressively worse with more exposure), each defendant will be held liable for only that proportion of the claimant's disease for which he is responsible (assuming the respective shares can be calculated).[37]

It has been held that the material contribution to harm principle is applicable in cases involving more than a single agent of harm.[38] For example, in *John v Central Manchester NHS Foundation Trust*, Picken J noted that 'nowhere in the *Bonnington* case itself is there a suggestion that the "material contribution" approach is confined to "single agency" cases. On the contrary, . . . Lord Reid appeared to view the "material contribution" approach as being of general application'.[39] On the facts, the approach was applied to a case where the claimant's brain injuries were caused by hospital negligence leading to undue intracranial pressure in addition to the claimant's prior fall (presumably his own responsibility) and the onset of post-operative infection (a naturally occurring event).[40] In circumstances where the evidence did not permit a finding of the relative

---

[34] [2009] 1 WLR 1052, at [46]. See also *Dickins v O2 plc* [2009] IRLR 58 (failure to refer an already stressed employee to the works' occupational health department a material contribution to stress-related psychiatric harm).

[35] [1956] AC 613. [36] [1956] AC 613, at 621.

[37] *Holtby v Brigham & Cowan (Hull) Ltd* [2000] PIQR Q293. Stuart-Smith LJ (at Q298) was content that there had been no reduction of damages in the *Bonnington* case simply because this had not been argued. It has been confirmed that the material contribution to harm principle applies in cases of successive events: *Williams v Bermuda Hospitals Board* [2016] 2 WLR 774, at [39].

[38] *Ellis v Environment Agency* [2008] EWCA Civ 1117, at [39]. Indeed, this coheres with the idea, noted below, that this principle is the equivalent of the application of the 'but for' test to a part of the damage in divisible cause cases. [39] [2016] 4 WLR 54, at [95]. See also ibid at [97].

[40] [2016] 4 WLR 54, at [102].

contribution of each factor, the claimant was able to recover all of his losses from the defendant hospital.

(4) The material contribution to the risk of harm principle

Extension of principle The principle in *Bonnington Castings v Wardlaw* was extended in *McGhee v National Coal Board*:[41]

> D failed to provide adequate washing facilities so that, at the end of the working day, employees could not remove from their bodies the brick dust to which they were non-tortiously exposed. The brick dust to which C's skin was exposed caused him to contract dermatitis. But it was unclear whether C would have contracted it if he had not been exposed to the dust for the prolonged period attributable to D's failure to provide proper washing facilities. In other words, C could not invoke the usual 'but for' test.

The House of Lords found for the claimant nonetheless. Crucial to the decision in *McGhee* was the tortious quality of the prolonged exposure to the brick dust and the claimant's ability to show a real increase in the *risk* of harm. A failure to show any material increase in the risk of harm will yield nothing.[42]

Because the claimant in *Bonnington* suffered the onset of pneumoconiosis—a divisible disease—the House of Lords was able to say, at least, that the tortious dust had made his illness worse,[43] even if it could not specify the precise extent to which this was the case. Furthermore, in *McGhee* there was no doubt that it was silicon dust that had caused the dermatitis. However, there was no evidence that the claimant's disease had been caused by any negligent exposure to brick dust.[44] The expert evidence had gone no further than to establish that unnecessary exposure to brick dust after work, caused by the non-provision of showering facilities, materially increased *the risk* of the claimant contracting dermatitis. There was, then, even greater evidential uncertainty in *McGhee* than in *Bonnington*. But the House of Lords, while acknowledging the difference, was prepared to treat the two types of evidential uncertainty *as though* they were the same. However, it is manifest that these are very different tests for causal responsibility.

Principle endorsed The *McGhee* principle was endorsed in *Sienkiewicz v Greif*,[45] where the Supreme Court was required to determine what constitutes a material contribution for these purposes:

> Karen Sienkiewicz was the daughter of a woman who had died of mesothelioma, which she had contracted by inhaling asbestos fibres during her working life. The fibres that she inhaled came from two sources: her employer's workplace (which was a tortious exposure),

---

[41] [1972] 3 All ER 1008.   [42] *Wootton v J Docter Ltd* [2009] EWCA Civ 1361.

[43] In this way, the argument exists that 'but for' causation could be demonstrated, at least with respect to some part of the damage suffered: S Steel (2015) 131 LQR 363, 364. Steel described the *Bonnington* case, therefore, as involving 'the but-for test in disguise'. See also S Bailey (2010) 30 LS 167.

[44] As is made clear in S Steel, *Proof of Causation in Tort Law* (2015), 228: 'Analytically, … increasing the risk of an outcome is simply not itself a kind of causation, no matter the context; the fact that x has increased the risk of y leaves it an open question whether x was a cause of y.'   [45] [2011] 2 WLR 523.

and the general atmosphere around where she lived (which was non-tortious). Of the two, the latter was much more significant. Indeed, the tortious exposure increased the risk of her contracting mesothelioma by a mere 18%.

That being the case, the defendants sought to argue that no liability should be imposed given that, on the balance of probabilities, it was fibres from the non-tortious source that caused her mesothelioma. In essence, the claim was that the defendants would be liable only if they had more than doubled the risk of the victim contracting the disease. The Supreme Court rejected this argument.[46] It applied the material contribution to risk of harm test, holding that a material contribution constituted a more than minimal increase in the risk. Lord Brown put it this way: 'any person who negligently or in breach of duty exposes another more than minimally to the inhalation of asbestos fibres will be liable'.[47] An 18% increase in the risk being more than minimal, the defendants' appeal was dismissed.

(5) Material contribution to the risk of harm among several wrongdoers principle

Fairchild case In the *McGhee* case, the medical evidence confirmed that the claimant's dermatitis could have begun with a single abrasion, acting while he was working (non-tortiously), or after work, while he was cycling home with brick dust still on his body (tortiously). It was conceivable, too, that the disease might have had a non-occupational origin. What was clear, however, was that there was only one wrongdoer. But in *Fairchild v Glenhaven Funeral Services Ltd*[48] there had been several negligent employers and other evidential uncertainties:[49]

C contracted mesothelioma—an invariably fatal form of cancer—by exposure to asbestos during his earlier working life. One complication was that C had worked for several employers, all of whom negligently had exposed him to asbestos. A second complication arose from the fact that medical science does not fully understand the aetiology of mesothelioma, so that it was impossible to say when he had contracted the condition first. This meant that the responsible employer could not be identified. Third, because mesothelioma is not a divisible disease, the material contribution to harm principle could not be applied. Finally, some of C's former employers had ceased to trade, so C was limited in the number of former employers he could sue.

The House of Lords reasserted the principle espoused in *McGhee* and found for the claimant.[50] But the case is distinguishable from *McGhee*, for if the condition already had been triggered by a period of prior employment, it is entirely feasible

---

[46] For analysis, see J Stapleton (2012) 128 LQR 221 (arguing that the rejection of the 'doubles the risk' approach was correct, but for reasons different from those given by the Court).

[47] [2011] 2 WLR 523, at [175].   [48] [2003] 1 AC 32.

[49] For analysis, see J Stapleton (2002) 10 Torts LJ 276.

[50] Lords Hoffmann, Hutton, and Rodger saw the case as an application of the principle in *McGhee* notwithstanding the additional evidential uncertainty associated with the fact that there were multiple wrongdoers in *Fairchild*: [2003] 1 AC 32, at [74], [116], and [153].

that the defendants did not contribute in any meaningful way to the risk of harm.[51] Similarly, if some of the relevant employers had not been in breach of a duty in exposing the claimant to asbestos, and the condition had been triggered while in the employment of one such employer, the defendant again would find himself liable despite the entirely innocent way in which the disease was contracted. He would have contributed to neither the harm itself, nor even to the risk of the harm.

Principle The principle that has evolved from *Fairchild v Glenhaven Funeral Services Ltd*[52] applies in cases involving exposure of the claimant to more than one source of asbestos fibre, the claimant suffering eventually from the indivisible disease mesothelioma. Cases have considered situations in which the sources have included a negligent employer, and either: another negligent employer,[53] the claimant himself,[54] or the background environment[55] (which, in urban settings, is likely to contain significant quantities of asbestos fibre).[56] The problem for the claimant in such cases remains that medical science does not comprehend fully the ways in which mesothelioma can be caused. Although additional exposure increases the chances that the victim will suffer from it,[57] small doses might be sufficient to cause the disease too. Moreover, it was believed at the time of the *Fairchild* case that a single fibre might be sufficient.[58] This means that there can be no certainty about the source of the fibres that have caused the claimant's mesothelioma.

The current position in English law is that the claimant can recover from any negligent employer that has exposed him to asbestos (and, thus, to a material *risk* of harm),[59] so long as the claimant subsequently contracted mesothelioma. This is despite the existence of other sources of asbestos fibres to which the claimant was exposed. The negligent employer will be fully liable for the loss,[60] unless able to obtain contribution from another liable party, or able to reduce damages by pleading contributory negligence successfully. In this way, the risk of an incorrect finding about causation is borne by the negligent employer, rather than the claimant.[61] In the mesothelioma cases to which it applies, the Compensation Act 2006 imposes a presumptive rule of apportionment between joint wrongdoers based on 'the relative lengths of the periods of exposure for

---

[51] For the view that each employer can be treated as having, in law, contributed to the risk of harm and that he can be liable for that risk creation (assuming mesothelioma has transpired in the claimant), see *Barker v Corus UK Ltd* [2006] 2 AC 572. [52] [2003] 1 AC 32.

[53] *Fairchild v Glenhaven Funeral Services Ltd* [2003] 1 AC 32.

[54] *Barker v Corus UK Ltd* [2006] 2 AC 572. [55] *Sienkiewicz v Greif (UK) Ltd* [2011] 2 AC 229.

[56] J Stapleton (2002) 10 Torts LJ 276, 277.

[57] J Sanders, 'Risky Business: Causation in Asbestos Cancer Cases (and Beyond?)' in R Goldberg (ed), *Perspectives on Causation* (2011), 18 ('the more asbestos fibres in one's lungs, the greater the probability some fibre or set of fibres will cause the genetic damage that generates the disease').

[58] This possibility was rejected by the High Court of Australia in *Amaca Pty Ltd v Booth* (2011) 283 ALR 461, at [79], which held that, on the basis of evidence available to it, the causation of mesothelioma from a single asbestos fibre is not physically possible. See also *Sienkiewicz v Greif (UK) Ltd* [2011] 2 AC 229, at [101]–[102]; G Turton, *Evidential Uncertainty in Causation in Negligence* (2016), 169; S Green, *Causation in Negligence* (2015), 130.

[59] *Barker v Corus UK Ltd* [2006] 2 AC 572, at [109] and [126]; *International Energy Group Ltd v Zurich Insurance plc UK Branch* [2016] AC 509, at [135]. [60] Compensation Act 2006, s 3.

[61] *Fairchild v Glenhaven Funeral Services Ltd* [2003] 1 AC 32, at [33].

which each [tortfeasor] was responsible'.[62] The presumption *can* be overturned, either when some agreement as to responsibility among wrongdoers is reached, or when 'the court thinks that another basis for determining contribution is more appropriate in the circumstances of a particular case'.[63]

Juristic basis of *Fairchild* The juristic basis for the *Fairchild* principle is uncertain. On one approach, it rests on a combination of justice-based arguments for recovery (especially by 'innocent' sufferers of mesothelioma) in combination with the facts of exposure, and subsequent contraction of the disease.[64] Although this might be considered an exception to the but for test of causation, another way of describing the result is to say that it involves an *exception to the need for proof of causation*,[65] because it is not expressed to apply via a reversed onus of proof. Indeed, at this point in time, reversing the onus of proof is futile because there is a 'rock of uncertainty' about the way in which mesothelioma is caused.[66]

Extensions of principle The *Fairchild* principle is a narrow exception to the ordinary but for test of causation applicable in mesothelioma cases. But there has been debate about whether the underlying principle might be applicable in analogous cases of evidential uncertainty and indivisible disease. Use of the principle might be restricted to cases involving exposures to the same causal agent,[67] or to exposures to different agents that act in the same way so as to cause disease.[68] Alternatively, the principle might be extended to all cases of evidential uncertainty involving agents that have the potential to cause the same indivisible disease.[69] In *Heneghan v Manchester Dry Docks*,[70] the Court of Appeal effectively opted for the last alternative. It decided that the *Fairchild* principle *is* applicable to cases of negligent exposure by multiple employers to asbestos resulting in lung cancer (an indivisible disease) because a finding had been made that 'the carcinogens were caused by exposure to asbestos fibres' and the Court saw no relevant difference from the eponymous case.[71] However, while the *Fairchild* case was concerned with exposure to asbestos only (a 'single agent'), the *Heneghan* case *was different*

---

[62] Compensation Act 2006, sub-s 3(4). The position at common law, where it applies, is that which was set out in *Barker v Corus UK Ltd* [2006] 2 AC 572. That is to say that the liability of each responsible party is proportionate. See confirmation of this in *International Energy Group Ltd v Zurich Insurance plc UK Branch* [2016] AC 509, esp. at [100].

[63] Compensation Act 2006, sub-ss 3(4)(a) and (b).

[64] See, eg, *Fairchild v Glenhaven Funeral Services Ltd* [2003] 1 AC 32, at [2]; *Durham v BAI (Run Off) Ltd (in scheme of arrangement)* [2012] 1 WLR 867, at [58]; A Ripstein and BC Zipursky, 'Corrective Justice in an Age of Mass Torts' in GJ Postema (ed), *Philosophy and the Law of Torts* (2001), ch 6 (justice argument).

[65] *Barker v Corus UK Ltd* [2006] 2 AC 572, at [126] ('persons are made liable for damage even though they may not have caused it at all') and [127]; see AC Hutchinson (2016) 39 Dalhousie LJ 651, 656.

[66] *Sienkiewicz v Greif (UK) Ltd* [2011] 2 AC 229, at [160]; C Miller (2012) 32 LS 396, 410.

[67] *Fairchild v Glenhaven Funeral Services Ltd* [2003] 1 AC 32, at [170]. See also S Green, *Causation in Negligence* (2015), 149.

[68] *Barker v Corus (UK) plc* [2006] 2 AC 572, at [24]. See S Steel, *Proof of Causation in Tort Law* (2015), 237.

[69] See J Morgan, 'Causation, Politics, and Law' in R Goldberg (ed), *Perspectives on Causation* (2011), 80. The fact that the claimant suffers from exposure to toxin would allow the court to distinguish the case from *Wilsher v Essex AHA* [1988] 1 All ER 871. Contra C Miller (2012) 32 LS 396, 403.   [70] [2016] 1 WLR 2036.

[71] [2016] 1 WLR 2036, at [41] and [48].

because it involved exposure to both asbestos and cigarette smoke (two agents), which operate in different ways to cause lung cancer.[72] So, the question arises whether the UK Supreme Court will accept this as a legitimate development.[73] For the moment, the extension to lung cancer cases having been made because Compensation Act 2006, section 3 does not apply to them, each defendant is liable *in proportion* to its contribution to the risk of injury.

(6) The one among several causative agents principle

Given that considerable time has elapsed since the decision in the *Fairchild* case, it seems safe to say (as mentioned earlier) that it has not given rise to any clear, new, universal principle of law. It is unclear also where the principle in *McGhee* stops, and the rule in *Wilsher v Essex Area Health Authority*[74] begins:

> In *Wilsher*, junior doctors negligently administered excess oxygen to C, a premature infant. C later developed retrolental fibroplasia (RLF), a condition that left him blind. Medical practice required careful monitoring of infants receiving oxygen because of evidence that excess oxygen might cause RLF in premature babies. But there were said to be five other possible causes of RLF in very sick, very premature babies. The trial judge ruled that C, having proved a breach of duty arising from a failure to protect him from the risk of the very sort of damage which materialised, could shift the onus of proof to the defendants to prove that some other cause actually resulted in that damage.

The House of Lords rebuked the trial judge for his endeavour to shift the onus of proof. Their Lordships did not accept, furthermore, the Court of Appeal's argument[75] that the principle in *McGhee* could extend to the facts of *Wilsher*. The claimants had not established that it was more probable than not that an excess of oxygen, rather than any of the other possible causes, had caused the claimant to succumb to RLF. Indeed, although the trial judge largely overlooked it, there was a good deal of conflicting scientific evidence in the case. Their Lordships made it clear that in no circumstances did the burden of proof shift to the defendant and they ordered a retrial on the causation issue. Lord Bridge warned against the dangers of allowing sympathy for the claimant to overrule the established principles of proof:

> the law . . . requires proof of fault causing damage as the basis of liability in tort. We should do society nothing but disservice if we made the forensic process still more unpredictable and hazardous by distorting the law to accommodate the exigencies of what may seem hard cases.[76]

Wilsher clearly endorses the point made in *Hotson* that causation must be proven on the balance of probabilities. So, where only two possible causes are in contention, the court

---

[72] S Steel (2015) 131 LQR 363, 366.

[73] S Green (2017) 133 LQR 25; S Steel (2015) 131 LQR 363 (both arguing no causation).

[74] [1988] AC 1074.   [75] [1987] QB 730.

[76] [1988] AC 1074, at 1092. Note, however, that the court might draw an inference that D's breach of duty caused C's loss even though C cannot prove the exact causal process, so long as damage of the kind that occurred was a probable consequence of such a breach: *Drake v Harbour* [2008] 21 Con LR 18.

will be entitled to treat the more likely of the two as being the cause of harm *so long as* neither is an improbable cause.[77]

(E) Concurrent tortious causes

Multiple sufficient causes If two tortious acts arising at the same time ('concurrently') result in damage, and either would have produced the same damage—as, for example, when two fires are started and merge to burn out a building—then the perpetrator of each act is responsible for the whole damage because it would be nonsensical to exculpate tortfeasor X (or Y) simply because what tortfeasor Y (or X) did would have resulted in the same harm being suffered. (If the latter approach were adopted, neither party would be held liable, even though both were in breach of a duty. Thus, this can be classed as a case of 'causal overdetermination'.) So, if two ships negligently collide, injuring a third party[78], each of those in breach of a duty of care are fully liable. Matters might be different, however, where a person's breach combines with a natural force. In such cases, it has been suggested, the fact that the natural force alone would suffice to produce the harm complained of will exculpate the defendant, on the basis that the defendant's breach would fall short of a material contribution to the harm suffered.[79]

Combined causes By contrast, if the defendant commits a tort (or an act which will become tortious if non-remote damage ensues) and, before the force of his act is expended, some later tortious act combines with it to produce a particular result which would not have been produced without the operation of the second act, the defendant will be liable only if it is found by applying the rules already stated that his act caused the damage.[80] In *Hale v Hants and Dorset Motor Services Ltd*,[81] the facts were:

> A company in breach of duty allowed tree branches to overhang a highway. C was a passenger in a bus negligently driven by D (a bus company's servant) in such a way that a branch struck the window of the bus with the result that he was blinded by broken glass.

It was held that both the first company and the bus company were liable in full to the claimant. Each was in breach in not foreseeing that their failure to care would combine with that of the other so as to produce the harm that eventuated.

---

[77] *Ide v ATB Sales Ltd* [2009] RTR 8, at [4]. But even if it were not the more likely, it would seem capable of falling within the material contribution to the risk of harm principle: see *Novartis Grimsby Ltd v Cookson* [2007] EWCA Civ 1261, at [72].

[78] *The Koursk* [1924] P 140. Should D remain liable if the other 'cause' is the non-tortious act of another person, or the act of C himself? Cf *Cummings (or McWilliams) v Sir William Arrol & Co Ltd* [1962] 1 All ER 623.

[79] *Bailey v MOD* [2009] 1 WLR 1052, at [46]. But why not liability for a material contribution to the risk of harm: because there is not sufficient evidentiary uncertainty for that principle to apply?

[80] *Rouse v Squires* [1973] QB 889, at 898, per Cairns LJ: 'If a driver so negligently manages his vehicle as to cause it to obstruct the highway and constitute a danger to other road users, including those who are driving too fast or not keeping a proper lookout, but not those who deliberately or recklessly drive into the obstruction, then the first driver's negligence may be held to have contributed to the causation of an accident of which the immediate cause was the negligent driving of the vehicle which, because of the presence of the obstruction, collides with it or with some other vehicle or some other person.'

[81] [1947] 2 All ER 628; *Robinson v Post Office* [1974] 2 All ER 737.

Contemporaneity Importantly, where an act takes place *almost contemporaneously* with the first breach of duty, it seems that the rules on concurrent causes (rather than successive causes) apply. In *Fitzgerald v Lane*,[82] the claimant was crossing a pelican crossing when a car driven by D1 hit him. The collision threw him on to the bonnet of the car and back on to the road, where a car driven by D2 struck him immediately. He suffered severe injuries, including damage to his neck resulting in partial tetraplegia. Whether it was contact with the car driven by D1 or D2 that caused the neck injury could not be established. Both were held jointly liable, and the claimant was held contributorily negligent.

(F) Successive causes

Issue In cases of successive causes, D1's breach of duty earlier in time is followed later by a separate[83] event that is either a breach (committed by D2) or a natural event. The issue is whether D1 can be held liable after the occurrence of the second event for the level of damage that he caused or whether his liability for that damage is negated upon the occurrence of the second event. Because D1's relationship to the initial level of damage after the second event is questionable, the issue is one of factual causation rather than of a new intervening act (considered later). Here we find that the House of Lords has adopted contrasting approaches—which are not easy to reconcile.[84]

Baker v Willoughby In *Baker v Willoughby*[85] the defendants admitted to breach in injuring the claimant in the leg. After that injury, the claimant was forced to take a new job. While working at the new job, but before the action came to trial, burglars shot him in the same leg, which had to be amputated. The House of Lords held that the defendants remained liable for the claimant's initial loss of amenity; the commission of the second tort did not relieve them of liability. Lord Reid explained that a claimant:

> is not compensated for the physical injury: he is compensated for the loss which he suffers as a result of the injury. His loss is not in having a stiff leg: it is his inability to lead a full life, his inability to enjoy those amenities which depend on freedom of movement ... . In this case the second injury did not diminish any of these. So why should it be regarded as having obliterated or superseded them?[86]

Though there is logic in this reasoning, it is not clear how the *approach* to the occurrence of subsequent harm can be reconciled with that taken in the next case to be examined.

Jobling v Associated Dairies Ltd In *Jobling v Associated Dairies Ltd*,[87] the claimant was incapacitated partially by an accident at work. Later, but before trial, he suffered the onset of a supervening illness of a kind causing the same type of incapacitation. The

---

[82] [1989] AC 328.

[83] While some textbooks claim that the second event is 'independent' of the first, this is doubtful with respect to the first case we discuss.

[84] The view exists that the rules considered in this section, although traditionally treated as rules of causation, in fact are not so: eg, S Steel, *Proof of Causation in Tort Law* (2015), 42.   [85] [1970] AC 467.

[86] [1970] AC 467, at 492.   [87] [1982] AC 794.

House of Lords held that the defendant was responsible only for the claimant's loss of earnings up until the time he succumbed to the illness. The court stressed that tortious damages aim to place the claimant, so far as money can do it, in the same position he would have been in 'but for' the tort. Claimants are not supposed to profit. The claimant in *Jobling* eventually would have been unable to work even if the tort had never been committed. Disease, according to the House of Lords, is a vicissitude of life and one in respect of which, on policy grounds, their Lordships were unprepared to make the defendants responsible. Indeed, when awarding damages for loss of future earnings, courts make allowances routinely for the possibility of future incapacitation. Where incapacitation—or premature death—occurs before the court hears a damages case, it must reduce the damages to reflect what was inevitable.[88] And where the claimant commits a criminal offence resulting in his imprisonment, the commission of the offence will be regarded as a vicissitude of life, and the loss of earnings due to imprisonment will be taken into account in just the same way as a supervening illness or disease.[89]

Analysis Why the onset of a natural disease should be regarded as having 'obliterated or superseded' the effects of the defendant's negligence in *Jobling v Associated Dairies Ltd*, while the gunshot in *Baker v Willoughby* should be treated as having had no such effect, is difficult to understand. The only explanation hinted at in *Jobling* is that the onset of a natural disease can be regarded as a 'vicissitude of life' severing the chain of causation, whereas a subsequent tortious act is not such a vicissitude. Of the two decisions, *Jobling* seems preferable insofar as, by 1976, the claimant would have been incapacitated in any case, and quite irrespective of the defendant's tort. That being so, it is easy to see why the defendant was held not liable for incapacitation occurring *after* 1976. Yet although *Baker* looks odd, the Court of Appeal has since stated that subsequent tortious acts are to be disregarded in assessing the damage for which the first tortfeasor will be held responsible.[90] Such an approach seems defensible where, as in one case, the third party's breach of duty does not contribute materially to the occurrence or severity of an accident.[91] Otherwise, it is difficult to justify and reconcile this approach with *Jobling*.

Section 3 New intervening causes: causation in law

(A) General principles

Issue The issue of causation *in law* arises only when the claimant has succeeded (on whatever basis) on the factual causation issue. Legal causation is a particular issue in cases where the defendant commits a tort earlier in time, and a second event occurs later in time which gives rise to further damage. The question is whether the defendant is liable for that further damage (this question being different from that arising in cases of successive causes, which are concerned mostly with liability for the *initial* level

---

[88] See, eg, *Whitehead v Searle* [2009] 1 WLR 549.   [89] *Gray v Thames Trains Ltd* [2009] 1 AC 1339.
[90] *Heil v Rankin* [2001] PIQR Q16.   [91] *Green v Sunset & Vine Productions Ltd* [2010] EWCA Civ 1441.

of damage). For example, the claimant might suffer minor injuries at the hands of the defendant (D1), but later die as a result of bungled medical treatment (committed by D2). D1 is not necessarily liable for all the damage which, as a factual matter, he has caused. In *Hughes-Holland v BPE Solicitors*,[92] Lord Sumption noted that, with respect to issues such as this, '. . . the law is concerned with assigning responsibility for the consequences of the breach, and a defendant is not necessarily responsible in law for everything that follows from his act, even if it is wrongful. A variety of legal concepts serve to limit the matters for which a wrongdoer is legally responsible.' In the present context, the relevant concept is the *novus actus interveniens*, or 'break in the chain of *legal* causation' (as the metaphorical language of the law describes it). When a break in the chain of causation occurs, D1 is relieved of further liability for the consequences of his tortious conduct. (But where there is no break in the chain and the second event was tortious, D1 and D2 will be liable concurrently for that *further* injury.)

Three categories It is well settled that a *novus actus interveniens* might take one of three forms. First, the intervening event might be an act of nature (or of God, as it is sometimes described).[93] Second, the claimant's own conduct might constitute a *novus actus interveniens*. Third, the act of a third party might break the chain of causation. In each of the latter two categories of case, the subsequent act is itself (in most, if not all cases) a *reaction* to the commission (earlier in time) by the defendant of the tort or its consequences. Given that the second act occurs by way of reaction, the defendant's factual causal responsibility is established. But the issue is one of legal causation—of whether the law will treat a factual cause as a continuing, relevant cause of damage.

Foreseeability Before considering examples of each type of *novus actus interveniens*, it is as well to notice the criteria that the courts utilise in determining whether the chain has been broken by the occurrence of the second event. First, the more foreseeable the intervening cause, the more likely that the court will *not* treat it as breaking the chain of causation. *Reeves v Metropolitan Police Commissioner*[94] illustrates the point. The claimant's husband hanged himself in his prison cell. There was no evidence that he had been diagnosed as suffering from any mental disorder, but he had been identified as a 'suicide risk'. The House of Lords held that his suicide did not constitute a *novus actus interveniens*. The evidence available to the defendants of his emotionally disturbed state and suicidal tendencies imposed on them a duty to protect the deceased, effectively from himself. Suicide was a kind of harm which they should have contemplated and guarded against. They failed to do so, and were liable when he committed suicide.

Similarly, damage incurred in rescuing a person imperilled by the defendant's act does not break the chain of causation where such rescue could have been anticipated.[95] Equally, where the injuries negligently inflicted by the defendant on a claimant's husband induced a state of acute anxiety neurosis which persisted for 18 months and caused

---

[92] [2017] 2 WLR 1029, at [20].   [93] *Nichols v Marsland* (1876) 2 Ex D 1.
[94] [2000] 1 AC 360. Note, however, that a reduction in the damages was made for contributory negligence. Cf *Corr v IBC Vehicles Ltd* [2008] 2 WLR 499.   [95] *Baker v TE Hopkins & Sons Ltd* [1959] 3 All ER 225.

him ultimately to take his own life, the defendant was held liable to the claimant.[96] In each of these cases, the ulterior harm was within the foreseeable risk.

Voluntariness Second, in respect of intervening causes in the second and third categories, generally it is the case that the smaller the extent to which the conduct in question is a voluntary act of folly, the less likely a court will be to treat that conduct as a *novus actus*. In *Scott v Shepherd*,[97] for example, it was held to be no defence to the man who first threw a firework into the crowd that the claimant would have suffered no loss had a third party not picked it up and thrown it again after the defendant had thrown it, because the third party, in throwing it, was acting predictably for his self-preservation. In another case, the claimant's ship lost its compass and charts when the defendant's ship negligently collided with it. The claimant's ship consequently ran aground while trying to make for port. The defendant was held liable for this further harm.[98] In both cases, the subsequent events were not sufficiently abnormal responses to the situation created by the defendant's negligence.

With these two general points in mind, let us now consider examples of each type of *novus actus interveniens*.

(B) Act of nature

In this class of case, the defendant's tort can be taken (as stated earlier) to be a factual cause of the claimant's damage, but the question is whether the defendant should be liable for the further damage which arises as the result of a natural event occurring after the tort. The issue was discussed by Lord Hoffmann in *obiter* comments in *Environment Agency v Empress Car Co (Abertillery) Ltd*,[99] where his Lordship stated:

> A factory owner carelessly leaves a drum containing highly inflammable vapour in a place where it could easily be accidentally ignited. If a workman, thinking it is only an empty drum, throws in a cigarette butt and causes an explosion, one would have no difficulty in saying that the negligence of the owner caused the explosion. On the other hand, if the workman, knowing exactly what the drum contains, lights a match and ignites it, one would have equally little difficulty in saying that he had caused the explosion and that the carelessness of the owner had merely provided him with an occasion for what he did. One would probably say the same if the drum was struck by lightning. In both cases one would say that although the vapour-filled drum was a necessary condition for the explosion to happen, it was not caused by the owner's negligence. One might add by way of further explanation that the presence of an arsonist workman or lightning happening to strike at that time and place was a coincidence.

Although this would appear to be perfectly good reasoning, a question arises as to whether this kind of case is best described as involving a successive sufficient cause

---

[96] *Pigney v Pointers Transport Services Ltd* [1957] 2 All ER 807. See also *Kirkham v CC of Greater Manchester Police* [1990] 2 QB 283.   [97] (1773) 2 Wm Bl 892.
[98] *The City of Lincoln* (1889) 15 PD 15.   [99] [1999] 2 AC 22, at 30–1.

or a break in the chain of causation. This is not easy to answer. Although one might liken Lord Hoffmann's lightning example to events in *Jobling v Associated Dairies Ltd*,[100] analysed earlier, a major difference is that the claimant in that case was always going to suffer from a disabling disease, whereas there was no inevitability about the vapour in the drum being ignited. However, the category of natural events (including the hypothetical) is also different from other kinds of *novus actus interveniens* case, involving *reactions* to earlier negligence. But one point seems to be clear, which is that for an act of nature to constitute a *novus actus*, it must be something overwhelming and unpredictable, so that it cannot be said that the defendant acting earlier in time had an obligation to take care to avoid it.

(C) Claimant's own conduct

Principle The claimant's own conduct might constitute a *novus actus interveniens* so that the defendant is not liable for further damage arising as a result of it. As Lord Bingham has explained: '[i]t is not fair to hold a tortfeasor liable, however gross his breach of duty may be, for damage caused to the claimant not by the tortfeasor's breach of duty but by some independent, supervening cause' and '[t]his is not the less so where the independent, supervening cause is a voluntary, informed decision taken by the victim'.[101]

Illustrations In *McKew v Holland & Hannens & Cubitts (Scotland) Ltd*,[102] the facts were as follows:

> D's negligence caused injury to C's leg. C later broke his ankle attempting, while still suffering from the effects of the first injury, to descend a steep staircase unaided. C's imprudent and unreasonable conduct constituted a fresh and separate cause of the second injury.

The defendant was only liable for the initial injury.[103] Compare this with *Wieland v Cyril Lord Carpets Ltd*,[104] where the claimant suffered neck injuries and had to wear a collar in consequence of the defendants' negligence. She later fell downstairs because, as a result of the initial injury and the neck collar, she could not use her bifocal lenses with her usual skill. Her further injury was found to be attributable to the defendants' original negligence. Unlike the rash Mr McKew, Mrs Wieland suffered a further injury triggered by her original disability. There was no unreasonable conduct on her part that could be taken to constitute a *novus actus interveniens* which broke the chain of causation. Similarly, where a defendant's negligence causes X to suffer acute depression, X's subsequent suicide cannot be said to break the chain of causation for the purposes of a fatal accidents claim by X's dependant since X's act—which is influenced by the depression—cannot be characterised as entirely volitional.[105]

---

[100] [1982] AC 794. [101] *Corr v IBC Vehicles Ltd* [2009] 2 WLR 499.
[102] [1969] 3 All ER 1621. [103] In similar vein, see *Wilson v Coulson* [2002] PIQR P300.
[104] [1969] 3 All ER 1006. [105] *Corr v IBC Vehicles Ltd* [2008] 2 WLR 499.

Unreasonable conduct Defining unreasonable conduct will not always be easy or uncontentious as *Emeh v Kensington, Chelsea and Westminster AHA*[106] illustrates:

> C conceived a child after an operation to sterilise her carried out by D. D admitted breach but denied liability for the cost of the upkeep of the child. That loss to C, he contended, resulted from her 'unreasonable' decision not to seek an abortion, and the judge at first instance agreed with him. However, the Court of Appeal held that, since by the time C realised she was pregnant she was well into the second trimester of pregnancy, it was not unreasonable for her to refuse the trauma and risk of a late abortion.

Slade LJ made it clear that, save in exceptional circumstances, he would never regard it as unreasonable to refuse an abortion, even early on in pregnancy when the procedure is relatively simple and free of risk.[107] Waller LJ, however, was far less clear about this.[108] The divergence of views simply serves to exemplify the fact that, frequently, it will be difficult to classify acts or omissions on the part of the claimant as unreasonable where a moral dimension is present.[109] And an additional complication is this: even if the claimant's act might be viewed as immoral or unreasonable, it will not constitute a *novus actus interveniens* where the defendant could foresee such an act and was under a duty to take care to prevent it occurring. Thus, in *Reeves v Metropolitan Police Commissioner*,[110] the fact that a prisoner was a known suicide risk combined with the fact that the defendants were under a duty to take care to prevent his suicide meant that the defendants were causally responsible when he did in fact commit suicide. As Lord Hoffmann explained, 'it would make nonsense of the existence of such a duty if the law were to hold that the occurrence of the very act that ought to have been prevented negatived the causal connection between the breach of duty and the loss.'[111]

Other matters There are two final points worth noting. The first is that, in just the same way as we saw in chapter 6 that professional status will cause the standard of care to be raised in relation to professional persons who cause harm to others, so too will higher expectations be placed upon them in respect of the protection of their own interests in this context. (Thus, a former solicitor's failure to take heed of limitation periods of which he was fully aware constituted a *novus actus interveniens* in an action he was attempting to bring against a firm of solicitors acting on his behalf.)[112] The second is that, even where a claimant's own unreasonable act does not break the chain of causation, it might lead to a finding of contributory negligence (and pinpointing exactly where contributory negligence stops and a *novus actus interveniens* begins can be hard to do).[113]

---

[106] [1985] QB 1012.

[107] [1985] QB 1012, at 1053. See also *McFarlane v Tayside Health Board* [1999] 3 WLR 1301.

[108] [1985] QB 1012, at 1048.

[109] On the related issue of the duty to minimise damages by accepting medical treatment, see *Selvanayagam v University of the West Indies* [1983] 1 All ER 824.   [110] [2000] 1 AC 360.

[111] [2000] 1 AC 360, at 367–8. Cf *Grieves v FT Everard & Sons* [2008] 1 AC 281, where C's anxiety about the onset of a long-term asbestos-related disease was foreseeable, but there was no duty to take reasonable care to prevent C suffering such anxiety.   [112] *Kaberry v Freethcartwright (A Firm)* [2002] EWCA Civ 1966.

[113] See *Spencer v Wincanton Holdings Ltd* [2010] PIQR P10, at [45]. However, it is submitted that where C has contributed to the causation of the damage only (as opposed to the accident itself)—eg, where a car passenger fails to wear a seat belt—C's folly can never be a *novus actus inteveniens*. See also *Corr v IBC Vehicles Ltd* [2009] 2 WLR 499.

(D) Acts of third parties

Issue The issue in these cases is whether some act of a third party breaks the chain of causation so that the defendant is not liable for the causation of further damage. Difficulties stem from the different ways in which the two general principles of foreseeability and reasonableness of response can be combined.[114] Thus, while it can be asserted with some confidence that an unforeseeable and unreasonable premeditated act by a third party almost certainly will sever the chain of causation, it is more difficult to classify unforeseeable reasonable acts, and foreseeable unreasonable acts, as new intervening causes.[115] Furthermore, it might be tricky to determine the reasonableness (or otherwise) of the third party's behaviour.

Seminal case The seminal case on acts of third parties constituting a new intervening cause was *The Oropesa*,[116] the facts of which were as follows:

> D's breach caused a collision at sea. In the ensuing circumstances, the captain of the damaged vessel ordered a lifeboat to be put to sea so that salvage arrangements could be made with D. In traversing the waters between the two ships, the lifeboat capsized and several crew members were lost, including C's son.

While the death of the claimant's son was caused, as a factual matter, by a combination of the defendant's initial breach with the captain's subsequent order to board the lifeboat in rough seas, it was held nonetheless that his order was reasonable in the circumstances. The defendant was wholly liable for the loss of life.

Subsequent medical negligence A common type of case in which third-party intervention arises involves the defendant causing an injury to the claimant that requires subsequent medical treatment, which itself is performed in breach of duty. In *Rahman v Arearose Ltd*[117] the facts were as follows:

> C had been assaulted by two youths. The assault left C needing surgery. The surgery that followed was in breach of duty by D and as a result C was left blind in one eye. Partly in response to the blindness and partly in consequence of the assault, C also suffered a psychiatric response that fell within the definition of post-traumatic stress disorder (PTSD).

It was held that the blindness was attributable exclusively to the negligent surgery even though that surgery had been necessitated by the original torts of the two youths. On the other hand, the surgical failure was only part of the cause of the psychiatric harm

---

[114] That the two principles are relevant is clear from Lord Wright's insistence in *The Oropesa* that a third party's act will break the chain of causation if it is '*either* unreasonable *or* extraneous or extrinsic': [1943] P 32, at 39 (emphasis added).

[115] If, however, the 'unreasonable act' involves deliberate or reckless wrongdoing, that act—even if foreseeable—will sever the chain of causation: *Rouse v Squires* [1973] QB 889, at 898. Certainly, for it not to do so, the subsequent act would have to be more foreseeable (and thus probable) than a mere possibility: *Chubb Fire Ltd v Vicar of Spalding* [2010] 2 CLC 277.   [116] [1943] P 32.

[117] [2001] QB 351. In similar vein, see *Knightly v Johns* [1982] 1 All ER 851.

and the youths remained partly responsible for that.[118] Similarly, where a patient's GPs failed to refer her to hospital promptly and the hospital, when she was referred a couple of days later, subsequently failed to treat her swiftly such that she suffered permanent damage to her hip, the GPs' breach was held to remain causatively significant. According to Lord Neuberger MR, 'the negligence of the defendants and the failings of the hospital had a synergistic interaction, in that each tends to make the other worse'.[119] In the usual formulation, subsequent medical negligence will not be held to be a *novus actus interveniens* unless it is gross or egregious in nature.[120]

Section 4 Remoteness of damage

There are torts—deceit is one example—with respect to which it is considered justifiable to impose liability for all the damage flowing from the relevant wrongdoing. Such extensive liability is exceptional.[121] In negligence and most other torts certain consequences of the defendant's tortious conduct will be considered too remote from his wrongdoing to impose on him responsibility for them. It is considered to be unjust to make the defendant answerable for events too far removed from his original breach of duty. We must now consider rules on remoteness of damage.

(A) *The Wagon Mound*

The decision in *The Wagon Mound (No 1)*[122] is the leading authority on the remoteness of damage in negligence:

> Ds carelessly discharged oil from their ship into Sydney Harbour. The oil was carried by wind and tide beneath Cs' wharf, 200 yards away. After being advised that they could safely do so, Cs continued welding operations on their wharf. Later, molten metal from the welding operations, when fanned by the wind, set fire to some cotton waste or rag floating in the oil beneath the wharf. The burning cloth ignited the oil and fire severely damaged the wharf. Ds neither knew nor (more contentiously) ought to have known that the oil was capable of being set alight when spread on water.

The Privy Council held that the defendants were not liable in negligence because they could not reasonably have foreseen that the claimants' wharf would be damaged by fire when they carelessly discharged the oil into the harbour. It was, in short, harm of an unforeseeable kind.

---

[118] [2001] QB 351, at [34]. Cf *Horton v Evans* [2007] PNLR 17 (chain of causation not broken between (1) a pharmacist's breach in dispensing tablets that were too strong; and (2) a doctor subsequently following the dosage on the pill bottle provided by the pharmacist).

[119] *Wright (a child) v Cambridge Medical Group* [2013] QB 312.

[120] See K Amirthalingam (2012) 128 LQR 208, 209–10.

[121] In respect of wrongful interference with goods, the test for remoteness might, depending on whether D's conduct was intentional or negligent (since both may suffice), be the one relating to the directness of the consequence (as in deceit), or the one (as in negligence) based on the foreseeability of the kind of harm: *Kuwait Airways Corp v Iraq Airways Co* [2002] 2 AC 883.

[122] *Overseas Tankship (UK) Ltd v Morts and Dock & Engineering Co Ltd* [1961] AC 388.

(B) Foreseeable type of harm

Principle *The Wagon Mound* established that, if the damage which materialises is damage by fire, then, for the defendant to be liable, he must have been able reasonably to anticipate damage by fire. It was insufficient that he could anticipate damage by fouling the wharf's slipways. An unbroken succession of subsequent cases at all levels—House of Lords,[123] Privy Council,[124] Court of Appeal,[125] and first[126]—has followed the principle that the harm suffered must be of a kind, type, or class that was reasonably foreseeable as a result of the defendant's negligence.

Illustrations *Bradford v Robinson Rentals Ltd*[127] is a typical illustration of this principle. The defendants carelessly exposed their employee, the claimant, a van driver, to extreme cold in the course of his duties. In consequence, he suffered frost-bite. The court held that the defendants had exposed the claimant to severe cold and fatigue likely to cause a common cold, pneumonia, or chilblains. It held further that, since frost-bite was of the same type and kind as these forms of harm, the defendants could be held liable for it.

Again, in *Malcolm v Broadhurst*, the claimants, who were husband and wife, were injured in a road accident. The wife sustained psychological injury, which arose in part from the effect upon her of the fact that, since being injured physically in the accident, her husband had undergone a change in personality. This did not prevent the wife from claiming damages: the harm was of a foreseeable type and 'the fact that it arises or is continued by reason of an unusual complex of events does not avail the defendant'.[128]

Kind of damage Notwithstanding the apparent simplicity of the test for remoteness of damage, there remains uncertainty in defining 'kind of damage', as *Tremain v Pike* illustrates:[129]

> C, a herdsman, while working for Ds, contracted a rare condition called Weil's disease. The disease was caused by coming into contact with rats' urine. Weil's disease, per se, was not foreseeable, even though other diseases associated with rats were foreseeable. Ds were held not liable.

Payne J stated that Weil's disease 'was entirely different in kind from the effect of a rat bite, or food poisoning by the consumption of food or drink contaminated by rats. I do not accept that all illness or infection arising from an infestation of rats should be regarded as of the same kind.'[130]

---

[123] *Hughes v Lord Advocate* [1963] AC 837; *Donaghey v Boulton and Paul Ltd* [1968] AC 1, at 26; *Banque Financière de la Cité SA v Westgate Insurance Co Ltd* [1991] 2 AC 249.

[124] *The Wagon Mound (No 2)* [1967] 1 AC 617.

[125] *Stewart v West African Terminals Ltd* [1964] 2 Lloyd's Rep 371, at 375; *Doughty v Turner Manufacturing Co Ltd* [1964] 1 QB 518, at 529.

[126] *Wieland v Cyril Lord Carpets Ltd* [1969] 3 All ER 1006, at 1009; *Tremain v Pike* [1969] 3 All ER 1303, at 1308.   [127] [1967] 1 All ER 267.

[128] [1970] 3 All ER 508, at 511. See also *Brice v Brown* [1984] 1 All ER 997 (shock foreseeable: thus D liable for C's acute mental illness; no need to foresee exact process leading to the ultimate result); cf *French v CC of Sussex* [2006] EWCA Civ 312.   [129] [1969] 3 All ER 1303.

[130] [1969] 3 All ER 1303, at 1308.

The difference between the approaches of the Court of Appeal and House of Lords in *Jolley v Sutton London Borough Council*[131] is also worth noticing. A 14-year-old boy was injured while playing with a disused boat. In the Court of Appeal, his injury (sustained while crawling underneath the boat which had been propped up) was held to be of an unforeseeable kind: the foreseeable kinds of injury when fooling around with such a boat were those that would occur while climbing upon rotten planking liable to give way. In the House of Lords, however, the foreseeable type of harm was cast much more broadly so as to include any injury occurring in consequence of messing about with a disused boat. As a result, the harm that the Court of Appeal had treated as too unforeseeable became suddenly—because of the broad conception applied—foreseeable.

A similar broad conception of the type of harm suffered was used by the House of Lords in *Corr v IBC Vehicles Ltd*, where their Lordships held that the victim's suicide was the same kind of harm as the depression that was negligently inflicted upon him (so as to justify a claim in respect of his death under the Fatal Accidents Act).[132] And, equally, in *Alexis v Newham London Borough Council* it was held that a schoolgirl's prank was all that had to be foreseen when she was allowed unsupervised access to a classroom, rather than the particular act of putting whiteboard cleaning fluid into a teacher's water bottle.[133]

(C) Means by which the harm was caused

Since *The Wagon Mound*, the courts have reiterated frequently that the defendant might be liable even though he could not envisage the precise set of circumstances which caused harm of the foreseeable kind.

> In *Hughes v Lord Advocate*,[134] C, aged eight, and another boy, aged ten, were playing on an Edinburgh highway. Near the edge of the roadway was a manhole some nine feet deep, over which a shelter tent had been erected. Post Office workers working on underground cables left the area after dark, placed red paraffin warning lamps there and took the ladder from the manhole and laid it on the ground. The boys came up and started meddling with this equipment and C, while swinging one of the lamps by a rope over the hole, stumbled over the lamp, and knocked it into the hole. An explosion followed. C was thrown into the manhole and was severely burned. The explosion occurred because paraffin from the lamp escaped, vaporised, and was ignited by the flame. D was held liable for the negligence of the workers.

The defendant was liable because the claimant was injured as a result of the type or kind of accident or occurrence that could reasonably have been foreseen, even though the workers could not have foreseen (1) the exact way in which he would play with the alluring objects that had been left lying around; or (2) the exact way in which, in so doing, he might get hurt. The workers' conduct created a risk of the relevant kind of harm—personal injury by burning—and this materialised.

---

[131] [1998] 1 WLR 1546 (CA); [2000] 1 WLR 1082 (HL).

[132] [2008] 2 WLR 499. Whether, on a strict construction of the Act, death must not be too remote is questionable since sub-s 1(1) simply provides that death must be 'caused by any wrongful act, neglect or default'.

[133] [2009] ICR 1517.   [134] [1963] AC 837.

If harm of a foreseeable kind occurs, normally it will be no defence that the precise mechanics of the way in which the negligent act results in that harm could not be foreseen.[135] Equally, the fact that an explosion much greater in magnitude than was foreseeable resulted in damage to the claimant will be no defence.[136] In general, it is only when the accident is caused by the intrusion of some new and unforeseen factor that the way in which the damage was caused is relevant. Lord Reid in *Hughes v Lord Advocate* discussed *Glasgow Corporation v Muir*,[137] where the facts were as follows:

> Two picnickers were allowed to carry a tea urn through a passage of D's tea house. For a reason never made explicit, one of the picnickers slipped, and children buying sweets at a counter in the passage were scalded. An action by the children in negligence against D failed.

Lord Reid said of this case that a person carelessly carrying a hot tea urn near children would not be liable if it were upset and caused by an extraneous event, and he gave the example of the ceiling collapsing on to those carrying the urn.

One case is particularly difficult to reconcile with the principles set out here: *Doughty v Turner Manufacturing Co Ltd*, the facts of which were as follows:[138]

> Ds placed an asbestos cement cover over a heat treatment bath containing sodium cyanide as a very hot molten liquid. Ds' employees carelessly dislodged this cover so that it slid into the bath. The molten liquid exploded. It erupted from the bath and injured C, a nearby worker. Although it was reasonably foreseeable that damage by splashing would result from dislodging the cover, it was not reasonably foreseeable that an explosion would ensue.

The defendants were held not liable, even though the relevant kind of harm—damage by burning—was foreseeable. They would have been liable for damage by splashing. But since the risk of damage by explosion was not foreseeable, and since this risk differed so substantially from the one that was foreseeable, *Hughes v Lord Advocate* was distinguished. Even so, the distinction drawn between a burn caused by a splash and a burn caused by an explosion is a fine one. This point was noted by the Privy Council in *Attorney-General v Hartwell*, where Lord Nicholls specifically questioned whether the decision in *Doughty* was correct[139] (though of course he was in no position, qua Privy Council judge, to attempt to overturn the decision in that case).

(D) Extent of the damage

Where the very kind of damage that was foreseeable has occurred, it has always been the case that the defendant cannot plead that the claimant was earning more than the average victim, or that goods were exceptionally valuable in order to reduce his liability in damages. This is because damages are not restricted to the average loss of earnings or average value of goods in the circumstances, even supposing that such a sum is

---

[135] *Draper v Hodder* [1972] 2 QB 556; *Wieland v Cyril Lord Carpets Ltd* [1969] 3 All ER 1006.
[136] *Vacwell Engineering Co Ltd v BDH Chemicals Ltd* [1971] 1 QB 88 (on appeal [1971] 1 QB 111).
[137] [1943] AC 448.   [138] [1964] 1 QB 518.   [139] [2004] PIQR P27, at [29].

calculable. So, if the facts can be proven, the shop assistant who usually earns only £350 per week will recover her full loss if she is knocked down on her way to fulfil a highly lucrative, once-in-a-lifetime television contract.

At one time, it was thought that the claimant's impecuniosity could be relevant in this context. In *Liesbosch (Dredger) v Edison*[140] the claimants' dredger was sunk owing to the negligence of the defendants. It was held that the exorbitant cost of hiring a replacement dredger needed to fulfil an existing contract (and hired because the claimant could not afford to buy a new one), was too remote a loss. Since then, however, the House of Lords has overruled *The Liesbosch*. In *Lagden v O'Connor*, their Lordships decided that losses attributable to a claimant's impecuniosity should be treated no differently from any physical weakness with which the claimant might be afflicted.[141] Thus, the impecunious claimant in that case, whose car the defendant had damaged, and who was only able to obtain a replacement at 30% above the standard rate for car hire, was nonetheless able to recover the full cost of hire.

(E) Concurrent liability cases

Established rule In chapter 4, it was explained that a claimant complaining of the defendant's failure in care might be able to establish a concurrent liability, which means that he has available to him actions in both contract and tort. Yet, the rules of remoteness are prima facie different in contract and tort. By contrast with the position described in this chapter, in contract a more restrictive 'reasonable contemplation' test is applied.[142] Given that the different rules of remoteness can result in different awards of damages, the House of Lords in *Henderson v Merrett Syndicates Ltd*[143] held that the claimant is able to elect which cause of action finally to pursue. In most cases, the claimant would want to seek final judgment on the tort action, given the more expansive recovery likely to be available.

Departure from rule? The rule on election has been undermined by the Court of Appeal in *Wellesley Partners LLP v Withers LLP*, where the view was taken that the remoteness rule in contract must prevail—even when the claimant elects for the tort remedy. Thus, Floyd LJ stated that, when parties contract, an opportunity for consensus arises as to the damages that shall be payable on breach. As such, '[i]t makes no sense at all for the existence of the concurrent duty in tort to upset this consensus'.[144]

There are several problems with the decision in the *Wellesley* case. One is that it is inconsistent with the idea, asserted in *Henderson v Merrett Syndicates Ltd*, that tort law provides the background against which the parties contract.[145] By this we might assume that the wronged party, who does not negotiate contracts on the assumption that the professional adviser *will* be negligent,[146] is able nevertheless to rely upon the standards of conduct which tort law imposes. Those standards are embodied, for example, in

---

[140] [1933] AC 449. Cf *The Daressa* [1971] 1 Lloyd's Rep 60.   [141] [2004] 1 AC 1067.

[142] *Koufos v C Czarnikow Ltd (The Heron II)* [1969] 1 AC 350, at 388 and 406. Cf *The Achilleas* [2009] AC 61.

[143] [1995] 2 AC 145, at 191.   [144] [2016] Ch 529, at [80].   [145] [1995] 2 AC 145, at 193.

[146] A point admitted in the *Wellesley* case: [2016] Ch 529, at [186] ('[t]here is, of course, no express communication and undertaking of risk in the usual solicitor and client relationship').

the law of negligence—which has attached to it a particular rule of remoteness. Why the simple fact of concurrency should mean that that rule is overridden is difficult to understand. The effect is not the availability of concurrent actions, but the availability of the contract action alone. A second problem concerns the fallacious reasoning adopted regarding the importance of assumption of responsibility in negligence cases involving purely financial losses—with respect to which the reader is referred back to discussion earlier in the book.[147] *Wellesley* is a case crying out for overruling.

(F) The 'egg-shell skull' rule

Personal injury Before *The Wagon Mound* was decided, it was well established that, in relation to personal injury, the defendant had to 'take the claimant as he found him'. This meant that the victim could claim damages for the entire harm to his person, even though, owing to some special bodily sensitivity, it was greater than would have been suffered by the ordinary individual. Thus, a haemophiliac,[148] or an extreme neurotic,[149] who sustains greater damage than the ordinary person, can recover the full extent of their loss, even though the defendant could not have foreseen such extensive harm. The courts have held that *The Wagon Mound* has not affected this principle, commonly termed the 'egg-shell skull' rule. *Smith v Leech Brain & Co Ltd*[150] is illustrative:

> A negligently inflicted burn on C's lip resulted in him dying of cancer. The tissues in his lip in which the cancer developed were in a premalignant condition at the time when the burn occurred. Ds were held liable for the damage resulting from the death.

In a similar way, in *Robinson v Post Office*,[151] the defendants carelessly lacerated the claimant's leg. A doctor's subsequent anti-tetanus injection caused encephalitis because the claimant was allergic to the injected serum. The defendants were held liable.[152]

Property damage There is no authoritative ruling on whether the same principle applies to property damage in tort. In *Parsons v Uttley Ingham*,[153] the defendants negligently failed to install proper ventilation in a device used in the feeding of the claimant's pigs. The ground nuts fed to the pigs became mouldy and the pigs died of a rare disease. Some mild 'food poisoning' might have been foreseen as a consequence of feeding pigs mouldy nuts, but death was a highly unusual consequence. The Court of Appeal held, in effect, that the defendants had to 'take the pigs as they found them', and awarded full compensation for the loss of them. The decision resulted from a claim for breach of

---

[147] See chs 2 and 4.   [148] *Bidwell v Briant* (1956) *Times*, 9 May.
[149] *Love v Port of London Authority* [1959] 2 Lloyd's Rep 541; *Malcolm v Broadhurst* [1970] 3 All ER 508; *Brice v Brown* [1984] 1 All ER 997.   [150] [1962] 2 QB 405.
[151] [1974] 2 All ER 737.
[152] See also *Environment Agency v Ellis* [2009] PIQR P5 (C had a degenerative spinal condition prior to the accident for which D was responsible: this was, according to May LJ, at [36], akin to an egg-shell skull).
[153] [1978] QB 791.

contract but the Court of Appeal acted on the erroneous basis that the rules of remoteness in contract and tort were the same.[154]

Surrounding physical circumstances Presumably, the defendant takes as he finds them, not only the physical state of the damaged person or property, but also the surrounding external physical circumstances. This is the crux of *Great Lakes Steamship Co v Maple Leaf Milling Co*:[155]

> Ds negligently failed to lighten Cs' ship at the time stipulated. When the water level fell, the ship grounded and was damaged. This damage was more extensive because the ship settled on a large submerged anchor which Ds neither knew nor could have expected to be there. Ds were liable for all the damage to the ship.

The decision is assuredly correct: the damage was of a foreseeable type; it was of a greater extent than foreseeable, not because of internal characteristics of the property, but because of special external circumstances.

Financial loss In *Network Rail Infrastructure Ltd v Conarken Group Ltd*,[156] the defendant's employee negligently damaged rail infrastructure belonging to the claimant, with the result that certain train operating companies (TOCs) could not run scheduled services along the relevant routes. Naturally enough, the defendant was liable for the relatively small costs of physical repair. The defendant was also held liable for very large compensation payments that the claimant was required to pay the TOCs pursuant to commercial contracts with them (calculated on the basis, inter alia, of expected loss of future custom). In other words, the defendant was liable for foreseeable financial loss, which was much greater in extent than might have been anticipated. But Pill LJ underlined the importance of proper limits on recovery in such cases. He stated that, under a similar contractual arrangement, payments might be made by the claimant for the consequences to passengers 'of lost business, or medical appointments, or job interviews but such consequences are likely to be too remote to charge to a third party in tort'.[157]

---

[154] This view has since been discredited. In contract, remoteness turns on what was foreseeable to *both the contracting parties*, as opposed to what was foreseeable to the reasonable person: *Jackson v Royal Bank of Scotland* [2005] 1 WLR 377. But in relation to the foreseeability of illness caused to pigs by mouldy nuts, this later decision is of no import. Such illness would be foreseeable by both contracting parties and the hypothetical reasonable person.   [155] (1924) 41 TLR 21.

[156] [2011] 135 Con LR 1. The similarity between this case and those involving relational financial loss (as to which, see ch 4) has been noticed: J O'Sullivan (2011) 70 CLJ 496. Why was this not a relational financial loss case? Because the same person claimed all of the losses. The case is thus about physical damage, consequential financial loss, and remoteness of the damage (as O'Sullivan explains). However, it does present the interesting point that, by entering into contracts with TOCs to absorb their financial losses, the loss-suffering parties were able to avoid the operation of the usual no-duty rule in relational financial loss cases. The Court of Appeal acknowledges that it has 'opened a door': [2011] 135 Con LR 1, at [84] (Pill LJ).

[157] [2011] 135 Con LR 1, at [69]. See also ibid, at [145] (Jackson LJ).

(G) Scope of duty and remoteness

Principle In chapter 2, it was explained that duties of care are not of unlimited scope in the tort of negligence. This means that the defendant can be liable only for breaches of duty which are within the scope of the duty itself. This principle has the logical consequence that the defendant should be liable only for those losses which flow from breaches of duty within the scope of the duty of care. In other words, although the defendant's negligence might be a but for cause of a wide range of foreseeable losses, he should be held liable only in relation to those that are specifically within the remit of the duty of care actually owed.[158]

SAAMCO case *South Australia Asset Management Corp v York Montague Ltd*[159] was concerned with the application of the scope of duty principle in terms of liability for loss, the ratio from the case being generally referred to as the *SAAMCO* principle. The facts were as follows:

> There were three joined appeals in which Ds had been asked by Cs to supply open market valuations of various properties in relation to which Cs were considering lending money by way of mortgages. In the light of the advice given, Cs lent the money, but in respect of each property, the borrowers defaulted. It further turned out that the properties had been negligently overvalued; while a final complication was the fact that the market for the properties had also fallen since the time of the loans. In one case, C1 had advanced £11 million on a property valued at £15 million, but the true value (at the time of the valuation) was really only £5 million. In the end, the property was sold for only £2.5 million. In a second case, C2 lent £1.75 million on a property valued at £2.5 million. The true value at the time of valuation was £1.8 million, yet after the fall in market value, the property was eventually sold for only £950,000.

It fell to the House of Lords to assess the extent to which the claimants could recover their losses from the negligent defendants. It was held that the valuer's duty of care to a lender was to supply a careful estimate of the market value of the property at the date of valuation. That being the case, the extent of a valuer's liability will be limited to the foreseeable consequences of the information being wrong. These do not include losses associated with the *unforeseeable drop* in market value since a loss of that kind is not a consequence of the valuer's negligence. When applied to the highlighted cases, then, the effects were as follows. In the first case, due to the defendant's negligence, the claimant had £10 million less security than it thought. So as things turned out, the whole of C1's loss (£8.5 million) could be attributed fairly to the defendant. In the second case, by contrast, only part of C2's total loss (£800,000) could be attributed to the defendant, because the claimant had £700,000 less security than it thought. The remaining £100,000 of C2's loss was attributable purely to the unforeseeable drop in market price.[160]

---

[158] *Caparo Industries plc v Dickman* [1990] 2 AC 605, at 627.   [159] [1997] AC 191.

[160] Cf *Rubenstein v HSBC Bank plc* [2012] EWCA Civ 1184 (liability of negligent bank extended to all losses arising from 'unusual events' surrounding the global financial crisis, given the client's overriding need for a low-risk investment of proceeds from sale of home).

The crucial point in *SAAMCO* was that the claimants had requested from the defendant a valuation *for the specific purpose of avoiding a loss when lending money.* In that circumstance, recoverable losses were confined to those amounts that were attributable to the defendants' overvaluations. Although the analysis from the case is considered to be of continuing validity, it appears that the Supreme Court would prefer that the underlying issue be considered today as a matter of scope of duty,[161] and readers are referred back to the discussion of that matter in chapter 2.

Conclusions

In this chapter, we have considered rules concerning causation in tort law. At a broad level, these rules are concerned with matters of 'factual' and 'legal' causation. Factual causation is about tracing causes and effects as they actually occur in the physical or other 'real' worlds. The main test for factual causation is the 'but for' test, which compares what has happened with what would have happened had the defendant not failed to take care. Various exceptions to this test have sprung up, concerned with cases of evidential uncertainty (where the exceptional rules bridge the gap in scientific knowledge and understanding) and cases of causal over-determination (where a surfeit of causal factors otherwise would mean that no factor is treated as a cause). The difficulties created for courts, lawyers, insurers, and others when exceptions to the but for test are widened have been acknowledged by the Supreme Court recently in *International Energy Group Ltd v Zurich Insurance plc UK Branch*.[162] By contrast with factual causation, legal causation takes as a given the fact that the defendant has caused the claimant particular damage. The question is whether the court will permit recovery with respect to that damage in the face of argument that this would not be fair. One, somewhat crude, test for limiting the defendant's exposure to liability is to look for a *novus actus interveniens.* The basic idea is that some event occurring after the defendant's failure in care has broken the chain of causation, so that any increase in the amount of damage is not regarded, legally, as having been caused by the defendant. Another limiting device is that of the test for reasonable foreseeability of the kind of damage; unforeseeable losses will be regarded as too remote from the defendant's tort for the defendant to be held liable for them.

Problem question

Diane worked as a truck driver for Speedy Deliveries Ltd. One day, she was filling the truck up with petrol when, absent-mindedly, she took out a cigarette and started to smoke it. A sudden and unusually strong gust of wind blew the cigarette out of her hand and over to a part of the petrol station forecourt where there was some residue petrol on

---

[161] *Hughes-Holland v BPE Solicitors* [2017] 2 WLR 1029, at [53].   [162] [2016] AC 509, at [128].

the ground. The petrol erupted in flames and caused damage to James's car. Diane was sacked from her job. A year later, Diane was diagnosed as having lung cancer. Medical science could not say to what extent this was caused by her years of delivering asbestos-based materials for Speedy Deliveries, by her chronic smoking, or by a combination of the two factors. After finding out that she had lung cancer, Diane took to drinking excess alcohol and was injured in a pub brawl.

Explain how the causation issues in this scenario would be determined in negligence actions brought against Diane and Speedy Deliveries, respectively.

 Visit **http://www.oup.com/uk/street15e/** for answer guidance.

Further reading

Goldberg (ed), *Perspectives on Causation* (2011)

Green, *Causation in Negligence* (2015)

Hamer, ' "Factual Causation" and "Scope of Liability": What's the Difference?' (2014) 77 *Modern Law Review* 155

Hart and Honoré, *Causation in the Law* (2nd edn, 1985)

Hutchinson, 'Out of the Black Hole: Toward a Fresh Approach to Tort Causation' (2016) 39 *Dalhousie Law Journal* 651

Lunney, 'What Price a Chance?' (1995) 15 *Legal Studies* 1

Miller, 'Causation in Personal Injury After (and Before) *Sienkiewicz*' (2012) 32 *Legal Studies* 396

Nolan, 'Causation and the Goals of Tort Law' in Robertson and Tang (eds), *The Goals of Private Law* (2009), ch 7

Porat and Stein, *Tort Liability under Uncertainty* (2001)

Stapleton, 'Cause-in-Fact and the Scope of Liability for Consequences' (2003) 119 *Law Quarterly Review* 388

Stapleton, 'Unnecessary Causes' (2013) 129 *Law Quarterly Review* 39

Stapleton, 'An 'Extended But-For' Test for the Causal Relation in the Law of Obligations' (2015) 35 *Oxford Journal of Legal Studies* 1

Stauch, 'Risk and Remoteness of Damage in Negligence' (2001) 64 *Modern Law Review* 191

Steel, *Proof of Cauation in Tort Law* (2015)

Turton, *Evidential; Uncertainty in Causation in Negligence* (2016)

Wright, 'Causation in Tort Law' (1985) 75 *California Law Review* 1735

8

Defences to negligence[1]

KEY ISSUES

(1) Contributory negligence

Contributory negligence is a failure by the claimant to take reasonable care for her own safety that contributes to the damage about which she complains. Contributory negligence results in the apportionment of responsibility for damages. Damages are reduced to such an extent as the court thinks is 'just and equitable' having regard to the parties' respective shares in responsibility for the claimant's loss.

(2) Voluntary assumption of risk

The defence of voluntary assumption of risk, or *volenti non fit injuria*, results in the denial of the claimant's action. It applies when the claimant knew of the risk of injury and freely accepted it. It is unclear whether this defence negates a duty of care or is a rule that prevents liability from arising even though all of the elements of the action in negligence are present. The defence has a very limited sphere of application, primarily because the courts prefer to avail themselves of the more flexible defence of contributory negligence.

(3) Express exclusion or limitation of liability

Liability may be expressly excluded or reduced by a contract or notice. There are important statutory restrictions on the circumstances in which this defence applies. Legislation provides that liability for personal injury or death resulting from negligence cannot be excluded or limited by a contract or notice insofar as the liability is trader liability to consumers or a 'business liability'. In other cases, liability can be modified by this defence only where the relevant term is either not unfair to consumers or is 'reasonable'.

(4) Illegality

A claimant who is injured while committing a criminal offence might have her action barred. Where the claimant was engaged jointly with the defendant in a criminal enterprise at the relevant time, liability will be denied if it is not feasible to ask how the reasonable person in the defendant's position should have acted. Where the parties are not co-offenders, the circumstances in which liability will be denied are unclear but the seriousness of the claimant's offence is a key factor. The illegality defence usually applies to actions brought in respect of sanctions imposed by the criminal law. The defence might deny actions also insofar as damages are sought for loss of income if the lost income would have been derived in contravention of the criminal law.

[1] The defences chapters were re-written by Dr James Goudkamp for the 13th edition of this book and retain much of his input.

Section 1 Introduction

If the claimant establishes that the defendant committed the tort of negligence, liability will not necessarily arise or arise in full. This is because there are various defences[2] that a defendant who has been found negligent might be able to invoke. This chapter examines four defences to negligence: contributory negligence; voluntary assumption of risk; express exclusion or limitation of liability; and illegality.[3] The plea of voluntary assumption of risk, when accepted, results in the defendant avoiding liability altogether. The defences of express exclusion of liability and illegality, when applicable, generally do too, although they might merely reduce the extent of the defendant's liability. By contrast, contributory negligence merely reduces the defendant's responsibility for the claimant's damage. It does not eliminate it. Contributory negligence is by far the most important of these defences in practical terms[4] and it has had a substantial impact on the scope of the other defences. For these reasons, it will be examined first.

Section 2 Contributory negligence

Contributory negligence[5] is a failure by the claimant to take reasonable care for her own safety that contributes to the damage about which she complains. At common law, contributory negligence, however trivial compared with the defendant's negligence, prevented liability from arising. This rule, often harsh to claimants,[6] was abolished by the Law Reform (Contributory Negligence) Act 1945 (the 'Act'), sub-section 1(1) and replaced by a system of apportionment of damages for contributory negligence.[7] Sub-section 1(1) provides:

> Where any person suffers damage[8] as the result partly of his own fault and partly of the fault of any other person or persons, a claim in respect of that damage shall not be defeated by reason of the fault of the person suffering the damage, but the damages recoverable in respect thereof shall be reduced to such extent as the court thinks just and equitable having regard to the claimant's share in the responsibility for the damage.

[2] The word 'defence' is used in different ways: see J Goudkamp, 'A Taxonomy of Tort Law Defences' in S Degeling, J Edelman, and J Goudkamp (eds), *Torts in Commercial Law* (2011), ch 19. Compare L Duarte D'Almeida, 'Defining "Defences" in A Dyson et al, *Defences in Tort* (2015), ch 3. For present purposes, 'defence' is used to mean any rule that precludes or reduces a defendant's liability.

[3] These defences are not the only defences to liability arising in the tort of negligence. Many other defences, such as limitation bars (see ch 26), are available.

[4] Empirical evidence regarding the applicability of the defence of contributory negligence is discussed in P Cane, *Atiyah's Accidents, Compensation and the Law* (7th edn, 2006), 59–60.

[5] The leading doctrinal analysis of contributory negligence is G Williams, *Joint Torts and Contributory Negligence* (1951). See also K Simons (1995) 16 Cardozo LR 1693.

[6] It was, however, mollified to some extent by various principles, the most notorious of which was the 'last opportunity rule', established in *Davies v Mann* (1842) 10 M & W 546; 152 ER 588 (Exch). See G Williams, *Joint Torts and Contributory Negligence* (1951), ch 9.

[7] The genesis of this provision is explored in J Steele, 'Law Reform (Contributory Negligence) Act 1945: Dynamics of Legal Change' in J Steele and TT Arvind (eds), *Tort Law and the Legislature* (2012), ch 8.

[8] 'Damage' is defined in s 4 to include 'loss of life and personal injury'. It extends to financial loss (see, eg, *Calvert v William Hill Credit Ltd* [2009] Ch 330) and to property damage (see, eg, *Sahib Foods Ltd v Paskin Kyriakides Sands* [2003] EWCA Civ 1832).

Section 4 defines 'fault' as 'negligence, breach of statutory duty or other act or omission which gives rise to a liability in tort or would, apart from this Act, give rise to the defence of contributory negligence'. This definition must be read in view of the fact that the word 'fault' refers to fault on the part of the claimant when it is first used in the apportionment provision, and to fault by the defendant on the second occasion that it appears.[9] Accordingly, fault, in relation to the claimant, means 'negligence, breach of statutory duty or other act or omission which ... would, apart from this Act, give rise to the defence of contributory negligence'. Insofar as the defendant is concerned, 'fault' means 'negligence, breach of statutory duty or other act or omission which gives rise to a liability in tort'.

The onus of pleading[10] contributory negligence and proving[11] that the apportionment provision applies rests on the defendant.

(A) Fault on the part of the claimant

(1) Definition and examples

As mentioned, the apportionment provision will be enlivened only if the claimant was at 'fault'. The focus of the courts has been on whether the claimant was negligent, although a breach of statutory duty can constitute fault too. A claimant will be negligent for the purposes of the apportionment provision if she failed to take as much care as the reasonable person in her position would have taken for her own safety.[12] Findings of contributory negligence, as with holdings that the defendant was negligent, have no precedential value since they are determinations of fact.[13] Nevertheless, it is worth giving some illustrations of conduct that constitutes contributory negligence. Examples include: a passenger in a car who does not wear a seat belt,[14] knows that the car's footbrake does not work,[15] or is aware that its driver is so drunk that her capacity to drive carefully is compromised;[16] a motorcycle rider who does not wear a crash helmet,[17] or fails to fasten it securely;[18] and a woman bitten by a dog having put her face in proximity to its jaws.[19]

(2) The standard of care

The principles used to ascertain whether a defendant breached a duty of care that she owed to the claimant[20] are applied for the most part to determine whether the claimant

---

[9] *Reeves v Commr of Police* [2000] 1 AC 360, at 369; *Co-Operative Group (CWS) Ltd v Pritchard* [2012] QB 320, at [29]–[30].

[10] *Fookes v Slaytor* [1978] 1 WLR 1293.

[11] *Flower v Ebbw Vale Steel, Iron and Coal Co Ltd* [1936] AC 206, at 216; *Booth v White* [2003] EWCA Civ 1708, at [7]; *Stanton v Collinson* [2009] EWHC 342 (QB), at [140].

[12] There is no need for the defendant to show that the claimant owed her or any other person a duty of care: *Nance v British Columbia Electric Railway Co Ltd* [1951] AC 601, at 611; *Jones v Livox Quarries Ltd* [1952] 2 QB 608, at 615; *Sahib Foods Ltd v Paskin Kyriakides Sands* [2003] EWCA Civ 1832, at [62]. This is one important respect in which the doctrine of contributory negligence parts company with the tort of negligence.

[13] See ch 6.   [14] *Froom v Butcher* [1976] QB 286.   [15] *Gregory v Kelly* [1978] RTR 426.

[16] *Owens v Brimmell* [1977] QB 859.   [17] *O'Connell v Jackson* [1972] 1 QB 270.

[18] *Capps v Miller* [1989] 1 WLR 839.   [19] *Neeson v Acheson* [2008] NIQB 12.   [20] See ch 6.

is guilty of contributory negligence.[21] First, just as the defendant does not have to guard against unforeseeable risks, the claimant can ignore risks of harm that the reasonable person would not have contemplated.[22] Second, both negligence and contributory negligence are objective forms of fault. The fact that the claimant or defendant was incapable of living up to the reasonable person standard is no answer in either setting. Third, just as the adequacy of the defendant's conduct must be judged by the standards of the day rather by than those prevailing at the time of the trial,[23] the quality of the claimant's behaviour is assessed by reference to how the reasonable person in her position would have conducted herself at the time the injury was sustained.[24] Fourth, as is the case when deciding whether the defendant was negligent, in asking whether the claimant failed to take reasonable care for her own safety, the risk of injury and the magnitude of the potential harm to the claimant are weighed against the cost and inconvenience of taking precautions and the utility of the impugned conduct. Thus, claimants do not have to take the utmost care to avoid getting hurt. For instance, a pedestrian does not need to keep her eyes glued to the pavement.[25] But where a claimant, who has notice of a hazard, proceeds without paying proper attention, contributory negligence might be found.[26] Similarly, a passenger in a motor vehicle is not required to interrogate her host before accepting a ride with him as to the precise amount of alcohol that he has consumed.[27] But if the passenger has reason to suspect that the driver is intoxicated, she might be contributorily negligent if she fails to make inquiries in this connection.

(3) Relevance of the claimant's characteristics

The standard of care demanded of child defendants was discussed earlier.[28] It will be recalled that, where it is the defendant's behaviour that is in issue, the fact that the defendant is a child is taken into account in determining the standard of the reasonable person. The defendant's conduct is compared with the benchmark of the reasonable child of the same age. The same rule applies in relation to contributory negligence. Thus, the adequacy of the conduct of infant claimants accused of contributory negligence is judged against the standard of the similarly aged reasonable child[29] rather than against the yardstick of the reasonable adult. As a result, ordinarily it is more difficult for the defendant to establish contributory negligence if the claimant is an infant than where she is an adult. Infants under the age of approximately five are incapable of contributory negligence.[30]

In contrast to the situation that prevails in relation to negligence, where the defendant's characteristics other than her youth typically are excluded from consideration, in

---

[21] Restatement (Third) of Torts: Apportionment of Liability at § 3.
[22] *Jones v Livox Quarries Ltd* [1952] 2 QB 608, at 615; *Cooper v Carillion plc* [2003] EWCA Civ 1811, at [16].
[23] See ch 6.   [24] *Smith v Finch* [2009] EWHC 53, at [43].
[25] *Piccolo v Larkstock Ltd* [2007] All ER (D) 251.
[26] *Ellis v Bristol CC* [2007] EWCA Civ 685, at [52]–[53] (C employee ignored the risk of slipping in a pool of urine in a home for the elderly despite signs warning that the floor might be wet).
[27] *Booth v White* [2003] EWCA Civ 1708.
[28] See ch 6.   [29] *Gough v Thorne* [1966] 1 WLR 1387; *Morales v Eccleston* [1991] RTR 151.
[30] *Beasley v Marshall* (1977) 17 SASR 456, at 459.

the context of contributory negligence the courts are more willing to adjust the standard of care that the claimant is required to achieve on account of her idiosyncrasies. In other words, while the standard that the claimant has to meet remains objective, it is less objective than that which the defendant must attain. Consider the decision in *Condon v Condon*.[31] The claimant passenger, who had been injured in a motor vehicle accident, had failed to wear a seat belt. She did not wear one because she feared that, if she wore one, she would be trapped inside the vehicle if an accident occurred. The court held that this phobia should be attributed to the reasonable person and, accordingly, that the claimant did not fail to take reasonable care for her safety.[32] It is unlikely that a similar allowance would be made for a defendant.[33] Another illustration concerns insanity. Insane defendants are held to the standard of the reasonable sane person. However, in the context of contributory negligence, the claimant's insanity is taken into account in determining how the reasonable person in her position would have acted.[34] One reason for which the courts are more lenient towards claimants by taking cognisance of their idiosyncrasies has to do with the differential impact of finding negligence as opposed to contributory negligence. Defendants rarely bear the financial cost of a finding of negligence since, normally, they are insured. Conversely, claimants usually suffer personally the monetary consequences of being held contributorily negligent.

(4) Emergencies

Claimants confronted by an emergency caused by the defendant's negligence are treated leniently. They will not be liable for contributory negligence simply because they made an error of judgement in the agony of the moment. In *Jones v Boyce*,[35] the claimant, a passenger in a horse-drawn coach, reasonably believed that the coach was about to overturn owing to the defendant's negligent driving. Therefore, the claimant jumped off, breaking a leg. As things transpired, the coach did not overturn, but the claimant was adjudged not to be contributorily negligent. A more recent decision on point is *Moore v Hotelplan Ltd.*[36] The claimant was riding a snow-mobile while on a holiday that had been organised by the defendant. She was not given proper instructions in the use of the snow-mobile by the defendant's representative, who led the claimant's ride. Mistakenly believing that the snow-mobile's brakes had failed, the claimant panicked and accidentally depressed the throttle. Her snow-mobile ran into a car park and

---

[31] [1978] RTR 483.

[32] See also *Mackay v Borthwick* 1982 SLT 265 (C found to have acted reasonably in not wearing a seat belt because using a seat belt would have been painful owing to a hernia from which she suffered).

[33] In *Leahy v Beaumont* (1981) 27 SASR 290, at 294 White J said: 'Every driver, even a … driver suffering from fear of spiders, bees and moths in the car, … must drive in as good a manner as a driver of skill, experience and care.'

[34] *Baltimore & PR Co v Cumberland* 176 US 232, 238 (1990); Restatement (Third) of Torts: Liability for Physical and Emotional Harm at § 11, cmt e. See also G Williams, *Joint Torts and Contributory Negligence* (1951), 357. Another case in which C's characteristics were taken into account is *Calvert v William Hill Credit Ltd* [2009] Ch 330, at 352 [70]. Allowance was made for the fact that C was a gambler in the grip of an addiction.

[35] (1816) 1 Stark 493; 171 ER 540. See also *Baker v TE Hopkins & Son Ltd* [1959] 1 WLR 966, at 984.

[36] [2010] EWHC 276 (QB). See also *Kotula v Edf Energy Networks (Epn) Plc* [2010] EWHC 1968 (QB), esp. at [49].

collided with a vehicle, injuring the claimant. She was found not guilty of contributory negligence. The critical question in cases involving an emergency is whether the claimant behaved reasonably in the light of the dilemma in which the defendant's negligence placed her. Due account must be taken of the alarm which such a situation would engender in the reasonable person and the fact that the claimant lacked the opportunity for calm reflection as to how she should act.

The 'agony of the moment' principle was extended in *Brandon v Osborne, Garrett & Co*[37] to encompass threats to the safety of the claimant's immediate family. The claimant and her husband were in a shop. Owing to the negligence of contractors working at the premises, a shard of glass fell from the ceiling and imperilled the claimant's husband. The claimant instinctively attempted to pull her husband to a place of safety and strained her leg in the process. Had she not done so, she would not have been injured. She was found to have acted reasonably. Whether the principle extends to instinctive acts performed in an emergency to protect strangers, or interests other than personal safety, is yet to be decided.

(5) Rescuers

Closely related to the principles regarding instinctive reactions in an emergency situation are rules concerning rescuers. Generally speaking, the common law treats rescuers sympathetically.[38] In order to ensure that altruism is not discouraged, the courts are slow to find them guilty of contributory negligence.[39] Only those rescuers who act with reckless disregard for their own safety will be penalised under the apportionment provision. The rule that rescuers must be particularly irresponsible before being found contributorily negligent frequently is engaged at the same time as the agony of the moment principle, discussed in the previous section. But these rules do not cover identical terrain. While rescues often are carried out hastily, this is not necessarily the case.

(6) Expectations that other persons will act reasonably

Claimants are entitled to expect that persons who owe them a duty of care will take reasonable precautions for their safety, although some carelessness might need to be allowed for.[40] In *Tremayne v Hill*,[41] a vehicle driven by the defendant struck the claimant pedestrian. The claimant was crossing the road at a designated crossing area while the defendant was disobeying a red light. The defendant alleged that the claimant was guilty of contributory negligence because he failed to check for oncoming traffic. This submission was rejected. It was held that the claimant acted reasonably in assuming that drivers would obey traffic signals.[42] This decision sits uncomfortably with *Purdue v Devon Fire and Rescue Services*,[43] where the claimant was injured when his vehicle entered

---

[37] [1924] 1 KB 548.   [38] See generally AM Linden (1971) 34 MLR 241.

[39] *Baker v TE Hopkins & Son Ltd* [1959] 1 WLR 966.

[40] *Jones v Livox Quarries Ltd* [1952] 2 QB 608, at 615 (C's 'reckonings ... must take into account the possibility of others being careless').

[41] [1987] RTR 131.

[42] See also *Grant v Sun Shipping Co Ltd* [1948] AC 549; *Cooper v Carillion plc* [2003] EWCA Civ 1811.

[43] [2002] EWCA Civ 1538.

an intersection and was struck by a fire engine proceeding against a red light. The fire engine's lights were illuminated but its driver negligently omitted to sound the siren. It was held that the reasonable driver in the claimant's position would have noticed the fire engine approaching. Hence, the claimant was liable for contributory negligence.

(7) Intentional conduct on the part of the claimant

Contributory negligence, like negligence, is a type of conduct, not a state of mind. It involves a failure to take as much care as the reasonable person would have taken for her own safety. Accordingly, findings of contributory negligence are not restricted to cases in which the claimant was inattentive to risks. A claimant who deliberately harms herself might be guilty of contributory negligence since the reasonable person does not do such things. Thus, in *Reeves v Commissioner of Police of the Metropolis*,[44] where a sane prisoner was able to commit suicide owing to negligence on the part of the police, it was held that the act of suicide constituted contributory negligence.

(8) Mere inattention by employees

The bare fact that the claimant employee was not paying attention at the time of suffering injury will not constitute contributory negligence, especially when performing repetitive tasks at her place of work.[45] This is because it is the employer's duty to guard against risks of injury resulting from inattention, which is readily foreseeable. As Lord Tucker stated in *Staveley Iron & Chemical Co Ltd v Jones*,[46] not every risky act by an employee 'due to familiarity with the work or some inattention resulting from noise or strain' is contributory negligence.

(9) Imputed contributory negligence

If a person is vicariously liable for another individual, the latter's contributory negligence is imputed to the former. For example, just as an employer might be answerable for the negligence of her employee, so too might the contributory negligence of an employee afford a defence to one who is sued by the employer. Suppose that A drives B's car for B and is struck by C's vehicle due to C's negligence. If A were contributorily negligent, her carelessness might count against B in proceedings against C in respect of the damage to his vehicle.[47] However, the contributory negligence of an independent contractor is not imputed to the principal save in those situations in which a principal is vicariously liable for such a contractor.[48] Nor is the contributory negligence of a driver imputed to a passenger,[49] or of a bailee to the bailor.[50] And when an adult accompanies a child, the contributory negligence of the adult is not imputed to the child.[51] Consider

---

[44] [2000] 1 AC 360.   [45] *Tafa v Matsim Properties Ltd* [2011] EWHC 1302 (QB), at 166.

[46] [1956] AC 627 (HL), at 648.   [47] *Kenfield Motors Ltd v Hayles and Rees* [1998] CLY 3919.

[48] G Williams, *Joint Torts and Contributory Negligence* (1951), 432.

[49] *Mills v Armstrong (The Bernina)* (1888) LR 13 App Cas 1 (principle held to apply in the case of ships).

[50] *France v Parkinson* [1954] 1 WLR 581.

[51] Although where a disabled child's action rests on the Congenital Disabilities (Civil Liability) Act 1976, her damages will be reduced if it is shown that her parents shared the responsibility for her being born disabled: sub-s 1(7).

Oliver v Birmingham and Midland Motor Omnibus Co Ltd.[52] The claimant, an infant in the care of his grandfather, was crossing a road when he was injured by the negligent driving of the defendant's bus by its employee. Although his grandfather was negligent also, the infant was entitled to recover in full.

The issue of imputed contributory negligence is relevant, also, to actions in respect of the death of a person and will be examined later.[53]

(B) The claimant's fault contributed to her damage

Causal relation The mere fact that the claimant failed to take reasonable care for her own safety is not enough to engage the apportionment provision. Her fault must be causally related to the damage about which she complains. As Lord Atkin put it: 'if the [claimant] were negligent but his negligence was not a cause operating to produce the damage there would be no defence.'[54] This principle was applied in *Lertora v Finzi*.[55] The defendant motorist failed in his plea of contributory negligence against the driver of another car on the basis that the latter failed to wear a seat belt, as he could not show that his injuries would have been less severe had he used a seat belt.

A case that went the other way was *Jones v Livox Quarries Ltd*.[56] The claimant employee had been riding on the rear of an excavation vehicle contrary to his employer's instructions. While he was in this position, another vehicle struck his vehicle from behind and the claimant was injured. Although the main risks to which the claimant had exposed himself related to falling off the vehicle or being trapped in some part of it, the claimant was vulnerable also to being injured in the way that he was. He would not have been injured had he been using the vehicle as instructed. Accordingly, the defence of contributory negligence succeeded. The outcome would have been different if the claimant's injury had been totally foreign to the risk to which he had negligently exposed himself.[57] Suppose, for example, that the driver of the vehicle on which the claimant was riding negligently caused it to catch on fire with the result that the claimant was burned. As the claimant would have been burned regardless of his carelessness, contributory negligence would be inapplicable.

Relevant cause Occasionally, a claimant's lack of care might be a necessary condition of the injury about which she complains but not be treated as a relevant cause. Thus, in *St George v Home Office*[58] the claimant was addicted to alcohol and illegal drugs. He had been sentenced to a term of imprisonment for theft. While in custody, he suffered seizures caused by withdrawal symptoms and fell from his bunk, suffering serious

---

[52] [1933] 1 KB 35. However, if the parent is in breach of her duty to protect the child's safety, D may seek contribution from the negligent parent. Contribution is discussed in ch 25.

[53] See ch 26.   [54] *Caswell v Powell Duffryn Associated Collieries Ltd* [1940] AC 152, at 165.

[55] [1973] RTR 161. See also *Condon v Condon* [1978] RTR 483; *Toole v Bolton MBC* [2002] EWCA Civ 588.

[56] [1952] 2 QB 608.

[57] Singleton LJ took the view that there would be no defence if C carelessly sat upon an unsafe wall, and a driver negligently ran into the wall and injured C (at 612). Similarly, Denning LJ thought that C would succeed if, while riding on the vehicle, he had been hit in the eye by a shot from a gun fired by a negligent sportsman (at 616).   [58] [2009] 1 WLR 1670.

injury. The defendant, through its employees, knew that the claimant might experience seizures but negligently allocated him a top bunk. The defendant argued that the claimant was liable for contributory negligence in becoming addicted to alcohol and drugs. This submission was rejected. The Court of Appeal held that, while the claimant would not have been injured but for this carelessness, his disregard for his own safety 'was too remote in time, place and circumstance and was not sufficiently connected with the negligence of the prison staff'.[59] It was 'no more than part of the history that led to [the claimant's condition] when he was [imprisoned]'.[60]

Loss not accident The claimant's fault must be causally related to the loss about which she complains and not merely to the accident that caused the loss. Thus, in *Froom v Butcher*[61] the claimant was a passenger in a motor vehicle who had been injured by the defendant's negligence. He did not wear a seat belt. He contended that his failure in this regard should be ignored since it did not contribute to the accident. This submission was rejected. Lord Denning MR, speaking for the Court of Appeal, held that the fact that the claimant's carelessness was causally related to his damage was sufficient to trigger the apportionment provision.

(C) Apportionment of damages

(1) General principles

If the claimant is liable for contributory negligence, it is necessary to consider how her damages should be apportioned. The claimant's carelessness cannot be disregarded;[62] some reduction must be made.[63] The apportionment provision directs the court to reduce the claimant's damages as it thinks 'just and equitable having regard to the claimant's share in responsibility for the damage'. The way that this provision is applied in practice is as follows. The judge identifies the degree to which each party is responsible for the claimant's loss as a percentage. These percentages add up to 100%. The claimant's damages are then reduced by the percentage allocated to her. For example, if the claimant and defendant are responsible for the claimant's loss in the order of 40% and 60% respectively, the claimant's damages will be cut back by 40%.

In determining the appropriate reduction, two factors must be considered. The first factor is the relative blameworthiness of the parties[64] (evidenced generally by the extent to which they deviated from the standard of the reasonable person). In considering this, it is well to notice that, while the defendant has breached her duty *to another*, frequently the claimant will have breached an obligation of care to *herself alone*.[65] The second factor

---

[59] [2009] 1 WLR 1670, at [56].   [60] [2009] 1 WLR 1670, at [56].   [61] [1976] QB 286.

[62] Although some cases suggest that damages need not be apportioned where C's contributory negligence is *de minimis*: see, eg, *Boothman v British Northrop* (1972) 13 KIR 112; *Capps v Miller* [1989] 1 WLR 839 (CA), at 848–9. However, where C's fault is slight, the question arises whether he should have been found contributorily negligent.

[63] The apportionment provision is couched in mandatory language: 'requires'.

[64] *Sahib Foods Ltd, Co-operative Insurance Society Ltd v Paskin Kyriakides Sands (a firm)* [2003] EWHC 142.

[65] *Jackson v Murray* [2015] UKSC 105, at [27].

is the causal potency[66] of the parties' respective acts. The law on this point was summarised by Lord Reid in *Stapley v Gypsum Mines Ltd*:[67]

> A court must deal broadly with the problem of apportionment and in considering what is just and equitable must have regard to the blameworthiness of each party, but 'the claimant's share in the responsibility for the damage' cannot, I think, be assessed without considering the relative importance of his acts in causing the damage apart from his blameworthiness.

Generally, decisions on apportionment will be reached on a common-sense basis.[68]

(2) Pedestrians and motorists

An important context in which to consider apportionment is actions by pedestrians against motorists. In this setting, the courts have held that both factors relevant to apportionment—blameworthiness and causal potency—support, all other things being equal, assigning the bulk of responsibility for the claimant's damage to the negligent motorist. This is because of the 'destructive disparity'[69] between a motor vehicle and a pedestrian. As Simon Brown LJ put it, a 'motorist is driving a potentially lethal piece of machinery, whereas [a] pedestrian is basically harmless'.[70] The main situation in which a pedestrian will be found to bear greater responsibility for an accident than a defendant motorist is where she moves suddenly into the defendant's path, especially where the defendant could not see her before she stepped on to the road.[71] Where the pedestrian is intoxicated, the proper approach is to look objectively at how she behaved rather than why she behaved as she did.[72]

(3) Seat belt cases: standard reductions

In seat belt cases, the reduction from *Froom v Butcher*[73] applies. Lord Denning MR suggested the norm of a 25% reduction if wearing the seat belt would have prevented the injury entirely, and a 15% reduction if it would have reduced the severity of the injury only.[74] (If wearing a seat belt would have made no difference to the claimant's injuries,

---

[66] *Davies v Swan Motor Co (Swansea) Ltd* [1949] 2 KB 291, at 326; *Pride Valley Foods Ltd v Hall & Partners (Contract Management) Ltd* [2001] EWCA Civ 1001.

[67] [1953] AC 663 (HL), at 682. See also *Corr v IBC Vehicles Ltd* [2008] 1 AC 884, at [44].

[68] *St George v Home Office* [2009] 1 WLR 1670, at 1683.

[69] *Eagle v Chambers* [2003] EWCA Civ 1107, at [15].

[70] *Wells v Trinder* [2002] EWCA Civ 1030, at [19]. See also *Henry v Thames Valley Police* [2010] RTR 14, at [39].

[71] *Eagle v Chambers* [2003] EWCA Civ 1107, at [16]. See, eg, *Belka v Prosperini* [2011] EWCA Civ 623 (C two-thirds to blame). Compare *Jackson v Murray* [2015] UKSC 5.

[72] *Liddell v Middleton* (1996) PIQR P36, at 40 and 43; *Lunt v Khelifa* [2002] EWCA Civ 801, at [16]–[19].

[73] [1976] QB 286. See also *O'Connell v Jackson* [1972] 1 QB 270 (motorcyclist's damages reduced by 15% for not wearing a crash helmet); *Capps v Miller* [1989] 1 WLR 839 (10% where C motorcyclist was wearing a helmet but had not fastened it). Conversely, in *Welsh v Messenger* [2006] CLY 2875 a passenger on a coach who failed to wear a seat belt and was injured did not have her damages reduced. There was no legal requirement to wear a belt on coaches at the time; nor was wearing a belt on coaches recommended in the Highway Code.

[74] The principles enunciated in *Froom* have survived several challenges: see, eg, *Stanton v Collinson* [2009] EWHC 342 (QB).

the apportionment provision is inapplicable.)[75] If the claimant is contributorily negligent, not just in failing to wear a seat belt but in some other respect, a greater reduction may be made. Thus, in *Gregory v Kelly*,[76] where the claimant did not wear his seat belt and knew also that the car had a faulty footbrake, damages were reduced by 40%. In *Gleeson v Court*,[77] the claimant not only failed to wear a seat belt but also travelled in the boot of a car driven by a driver whom he knew to be intoxicated. His damages were reduced by 30%.

(4) Infants

Infant claimants are treated very leniently because of their vulnerability. Even when they are found to be contributorily negligent (recall that the standard of care expected is adjusted where the claimant is a child),[78] often apportionment is made very much in their favour.[79]

(5) 100% contributory negligence?

It is unclear whether damages can be reduced by 100% on account of the claimant's contributory negligence. The issue has been considered on several occasions and the authorities are divided.[80] But the better view is clear. A finding of 100% contributory negligence would mean that the claimant is wholly responsible for the damage about which she complains. However, if the claimant's damage is entirely her own fault, the question of contributory negligence cannot arise because she will be unable to establish that the defendant's negligence caused her damage. The definitional elements of the action in negligence will be incomplete. For this reason, suggestions that claimants can be found guilty of 100% contributory negligence are incoherent.

(6) Apportionment and exemplary damages

The apportionment provision operates on compensatory damages (which include aggravated damages). Although the Law Commission has suggested that exemplary damages are susceptible to reduction for contributory negligence,[81] this makes little sense. It overlooks the primary rationale of awarding exemplary damages, which is to punish the defendant. Reducing awards of exemplary damages on account of the claimant's fault will undermine the goal of ordering the defendant to pay such damages. Awards of exemplary damages, if apportioned, will not be proportionate to the defendant's culpability.

---

[75] See ch 7 on application of causation principles. [76] [1978] RTR 426.
[77] [2007] EWHC 2397 (QB). [78] See ch 6.
[79] *Russel v Smith* [2003] EWHC 2060 (QB), at [15]–[16].
[80] Findings of 100% contributory negligence are impermissible according to *Pitts v Hunt* [1991] 1 QB 24, at 48; *Buyukardicli v Hammerson UK Properties plc* [2002] EWCA Civ 683, at [7]; *Anderson v Newham College of Further Education* [2003] ICR 212. Consider also *Reeves v Commissioner of Police of the Metropolis* [2000] 1 AC 360, at 372 and 387. The converse position is supported by *Imperial Chemical Industries Ltd v Shatwell* [1965] AC 656, at 672; *McMullen v National Coal Board* [1982] ICR 148; *Jayes v IMI (Kynoch) Ltd* [1985] ICR 155, at 159.
[81] Law Commission, *Aggravated, Restitutionary and Exemplary Damages*, Report 247 (1997), at 81 n 475.

(7) Multiple tortfeasors

Where two or more defendants cause the claimant indivisible damage (ie where the damage caused by one defendant cannot be separated from the damage caused by the other defendant), the extent of the claimant's contributory negligence is assessed against the totality of the defendants' negligence.[82] Suppose, for example, that C, a pedestrian, is injured by the negligence of D1 and D2, two motorists. C's share of the responsibility for her damage is 30%. D1 and D2 are 40 and 30% responsible, respectively. C will be able to recover 70% of her damages from either D1 or D2. Once C has recovered her damages, D1 and D2 will be able to bring proceedings against each other for contribution in an effort to ensure that their liabilities correspond to their individual responsibility for C's damage. Matters are simpler if the damage is divisible. Suppose that C suffers property damage due to D1's negligence and personal injury because of D2's breach of duty. Assume also that C was contributorily negligent and that her carelessness was causally related to both types of damage. Each defendant's negligence would be compared separately with the claimant's share in the responsibility for the damage in question.

Section 3 Voluntary assumption of risk

(A) The elements of the defence

Meaning The defendant will be able to avoid liability in the tort of negligence if she proves that the claimant voluntarily assumed the risk of injury. Often, this plea is referred to by the maxim *volenti non fit injuria* (no injury is done to one who consents), or '*volenti*' for short.[83] According to Lord Herschell in *Smith v Charles Baker & Sons*, the defence 'is founded on good sense and justice. One who has invited or assented to an act being done towards him cannot, when he suffers from it, complain of it as a wrong.'[84] In order to establish that the claimant was *volens* to the risk of injury, the defendant must prove that the claimant had full knowledge of the risk and voluntarily agreed to incur it. These requirements will be considered shortly.

Preliminary remarks It is convenient, however, to make some preliminary remarks about the defence. First, in contrast to contributory negligence, the defence of voluntary assumption of risk, when applicable, prevents liability from arising. It does not merely reduce the extent of the defendant's liability. Second, since the enactment of the apportionment provision, the circumstances in which the defence of *volenti* is available have been restricted.[85] Usually, courts prefer to award claimants injured through negligence partial damages pursuant to the apportionment provision rather than to deny liability altogether on the basis of *volenti*.[86] Consequently, the defence of voluntary

---

[82] *Fitzgerald v Lane* [1989] AC 328.
[83] See P Jaffey (1985) 44 CLJ 87; KS Simons (1987) 67 BU L Rev 213; R Kidner (1991) 11 LS 1; SD Sugarman (1997) 31 Val ULR 833.
[84] [1891] AC 325, at 360.
[85] See *ICI Ltd v Shatwell* [1965] AC 656, at 671–2; *Nettleship v Weston* [1971] 2 QB 691, at 701.
[86] The preference is made explicit in *Nettleship v Weston* [1971] 2 QB 691, at 701.

assumption of risk rarely succeeds. Third, the defence of *volenti*, when engaged, can be triggered simultaneously with the apportionment provision, as a person who assumes a risk of injury might be acting unreasonably with respect to her own safety. However, the terrain covered by the *volenti* defence and the apportionment provision is not identical. This is because voluntarily assuming certain risks might not be unreasonable. Fourth, it is unclear exactly how the voluntary assumption of risk defence operates. Some judges have said that, when applicable, it results in a duty of care being waived.[87] On this account, if the claimant is *volens* to the risk of injury, no tort is committed. On other occasions, it has been suggested that, like contributory negligence, it is a rule to which defendants who have committed a tort can appeal.[88] The difference between these views is important. As a matter of principle, the way in which the defence operates ought to affect, for example, the allocation of the onus of pleading and proof in respect of it.

Illustrations It might be helpful to provide some illustrations of cases in which the *volenti* defence succeeded. In *Morris v Murray*,[89] the claimant had spent an afternoon drinking heavily with a friend. The claimant agreed to his friend's proposal that they take a joyride in a light aircraft. At the airport, the claimant helped to prepare the plane and his friend assumed the pilot's seat. Soon after take-off, the plane crashed. The claimant's friend was killed and the claimant was injured. The claimant brought an action in negligence against his friend's estate. The Court of Appeal upheld the estate's plea of *volenti*. Their Lordships said that accepting a flight with an obviously drunken pilot was akin to confronting deliberately some dangerous physical condition brought about by the defendant.

The defence applied also in *Freeman v Higher Park Farm*,[90] which arose out of a horse-riding accident. The claimant was an experienced rider who wanted an exciting ride on a lively horse. She attended the defendant's stables and took out one of its horses. She knew that the horse in question had a propensity to buck. When breaking into a canter, the horse bucked and the claimant fell off. She sued the defendant for her injuries. The court held that the claimant had voluntarily assumed the risk of injury and that her action in negligence and under the Animals Act 1971[91] therefore failed.

(1) The claimant knew of the risk of injury

Rule The claimant must have been aware of the risk of injury that materialised,[92] for one cannot consent to a risk of injury if one does not know that it exists. The fact that the reasonable person in the claimant's position would have known about the risk is insufficient. If, for example, the claimant is too drunk to comprehend a given risk, the defence will not be available if the risk materialises (although she might be guilty of

---

[87] *Thomas v Quartermaine* (1887) LR 18 QBD 685, at 697–8; *Dann v Hamilton* [1939] 1 KB 509, at 512; *Geary v JD Wetherspoon plc* [2011] EWHC 1506 (QB), at [46].

[88] *Wooldridge v Sumner* [1963] 2 QB 43, at 69; *Ashton v Turner* [1981] QB 137, at 146.

[89] [1991] 2 QB 6.   [90] [2008] EWCA Civ 1185.

[91] This Act is discussed in the extra chapter in the Online Resources. Sub-s 5(2) provides for a defence that is essentially equivalent to the common law defence of voluntary assumption of risk: cf *Cummings v Grainger* [1977] QB 397, at 408.

[92] *Bennet v Tugwell* [1971] 2 QB 267, at 273; *Morris v Murray* [1991] 2 QB 6, at 18.

contributory negligence).[93] Of course, if the reasonable person would have been aware of the risk in issue, that fact might suggest that the claimant was conscious of it. But this pre-condition to the defence's application ultimately imposes a subjective test.

Illustrations A case in which this prerequisite to the defence's application was determinative is *Neeson v Acheson*.[94] This was an action brought by a woman who had been bitten by her neighbour's dog after she placed her face close to its jaws. As she had befriended the animal over the course of several months prior to the incident, she had no reason to expect that it would bite her. The defendant argued that the claimant had voluntarily assumed the risk of injury. This submission was rejected. The judge held that, as the claimant did not foresee any risk of injury, the defence was inapplicable.

Poppleton v Trustees of the Portsmouth Youth Activities Committee is another case in which the defence failed for want of full knowledge by the claimant of the risk of injury.[95] The claimant was a novice rock climber. At the relevant time, he was scaling the defendant's artificial climbing wall. Having ascended the wall, the claimant jumped off it and attempted to catch a metal bar running across the ceiling with a view to then dropping safely to the floor. His momentum prevented him from maintaining his grip on the bar and he fell to the ground and broke his neck. The court held that the matting on the floor gave the false impression that it was safe to jump from the wall to the ground. Therefore, the claimant did not have comprehensive knowledge of the risk of injury that materialised.

(2) The claimant voluntarily agreed to incur the risk

Rule It is not enough to enliven the defence of *volenti* that the claimant knew of the risk of injury.[96] She must have agreed also to run the risk. As Scott LJ explained in *Bowater v Rowley Regis Corp*:[97]

> For the purpose of the rule … a man cannot be said to be truly 'willing' unless he is in a position to choose freely, and freedom of choice predicates, not only full knowledge of the circumstances on which the exercise of choice is conditioned, so that he may be able to choose wisely, but the absence from his mind of any feeling of constraint so that nothing shall interfere with the freedom of his will.

Two points should be noticed about this statement. First, it sets the bar very high. If the claimant's decision to expose herself to a risk of injury is influenced by the slightest pressure, the defence will fail. Second, the knowledge requirement is, in a sense, a subelement of the voluntary agreement requirement. This is because, as Scott LJ observed, an agreement to run a risk without comprehending it is no agreement at all. However, it is convenient for expository purposes to treat the knowledge requirement and the voluntary agreement requirement as distinct.

---

[93] This proposition is implicitly supported by *Morris v Murray* [1991] 2 QB 6, at 16, 27–9, and 32.
[94] [2008] NIQB 12.   [95] [2007] EWHC 1567 (QB).
[96] *Nettleship v Weston* [1971] 2 QB 691, at 701.   [97] [1944] KB 476, at 479.

Limits As a result of the voluntary agreement requirement, the *volenti* defence does not lie against rescuers,[98] including those whose job requires them to go to a person's aid.[99] The decision of a person to assist another imperilled by an emergency is not unencumbered in the sense required to trigger the defence. This is because it is the product of a moral or legal duty to act. The voluntariness requirement excludes also the defence where the claimant engaged in acts of self-harm that the defendant, in breach of a duty owed to the claimant, failed to prevent. Thus, in *Reeves v Commissioner of Police of the Metropolis*,[100] the estate and dependants of a man who committed suicide while in police custody brought a claim in negligence. As the police were under a duty to prevent the deceased from committing acts of self-harm,[101] it was held that the defendant could not succeed on the *volenti* defence. It was held that allowing liability to be avoided by way of the defence effectively would empty the duty of its content. The outcome would have been the same had the deceased been a mental patient in the defendant's hospital.

(B) Specific contexts

(1) Actions by employees against employers

The defence of voluntary assumption of risk used to be important in actions by workers alleging negligence by their employers. In the nineteenth century, it was held that the defence generally would be enlivened if the employee knew of the risk, regardless of whether she had any real choice in running it. The House of Lords (reflecting shifting social and economic attitudes) altered this approach in *Smith v Charles Baker & Sons*.[102] The claimant, who was the defendant's employee, was required to drill holes in a rock cutting. He was aware that a crane carrying crates of stones often swung overhead. A stone fell out of a crate and injured him. He brought an action in negligence against the defendant, who pleaded voluntary assumption of risk. The House held that, notwithstanding the claimant's knowledge of the risk, the evidence justified a finding that he had not voluntarily assumed it. Hence, the defence was inapplicable. Lord Watson said:[103]

> The question which has most frequently to be considered is not whether [the employee] voluntarily and rashly exposed himself to injury, but whether he agreed that, if injury should befall him, the risk was to be his and not his master's. [Whether continuing to work knowing of the danger will enliven the voluntary assumption of the risk defence] depends ... upon the nature of the risk, and the [employee's] connection with it, as well as upon other considerations which must vary according to the circumstances of each case.

A series of employer/employee cases followed *Smith* in which the defence of *volenti* failed for want of consent. *Bowater v Rowley Regis Corp*[104] is typical. The claimant was ordered by his employers to take out a horse known by them to be unsafe. The claimant

---

[98] *Haynes v Harwood* [1935] 1 KB 146; *Baker v TE Hopkins & Son Ltd* [1959] 3 All ER 225; cf *Cutler v United Dairies (London) Ltd* [1933] 2 KB 297. See further AL Goodhart (1934) 5 CLJ 192.

[99] *Ogwo v Taylor* [1988] AC 431 (fireman); *Merrington v Ironbridge Metal Works Ltd* [1952] 2 All ER 1101 (same); *D'Urso v Sanson* [1939] 4 All ER 26 (night-watchman extinguishing fire on employer's premises).

[100] [2000] 1 AC 360.   [101] See *Orange v CC of West Yorkshire Police* [2002] QB 347.

[102] [1891] AC 325.   [103] [1891] AC 325, at 355.   [104] [1944] KB 476.

protested but eventually complied. Later, he was thrown off a cart being drawn by the horse when the horse bolted. The claimant sued his employers in negligence. The Court of Appeal rejected the defence of voluntary assumption of risk. Goddard LJ said:[105] 'it can hardly ever be applicable where the act to which the servant is said to be "*volens*" arises out of his ordinary duty, unless the work for which he is engaged is one in which danger is necessarily involved'.[106]

An important case in which the defence succeeded is *Imperial Chemical Industries Ltd v Shatwell*.[107] The House of Lords noted that the plea of *volenti* rarely will defeat a claim by an employee against his employer. However, their Lordships held that, where the claim rests on vicarious liability for joint and flagrant disobedience of a safety rule by the claimant and a co-employee (where the latter was not the claimant's superior or one whose orders she was bound to obey), the employer could succeed on the defence. Thus, the claimant in *Shatwell*, a miner who agreed with a co-worker to detonate an explosive charge in a dangerous manner contrary to safety regulations, was denied recovery for his injuries.

(2) Motor vehicle cases

In the past, the defence of *volenti* often was enlivened where the claimant accepted a ride from a driver whom she knew to be intoxicated.[108] Now the Road Traffic Act 1988, section 149, which applies to accidents involving vehicles in respect of which it is compulsory to obtain liability insurance, excludes the defence. Of course, a drunk driver who causes injury to her passenger might be able to reduce her liability on the ground that the claimant was guilty of contributory negligence in accepting a ride from an intoxicated driver.[109]

(3) Dangerous activities

Another context in which the defence of voluntary assumption of risk might be applicable is that of dangerous activities, including sport.[110] As in other settings, before the defence can arise the defendant must show that the claimant consented not only to some risk of harm intrinsic to the activity, but also to the particular risk that culminated in injury. Thus, in *Gillmore v London City Council*[111] the claimant was a member of the defendant's physical training class. During an exercise in which the members of the class lunged at each other, the claimant was injured by losing his balance on a floor which was slippery due to the defendant's negligence. Du Parcq LJ held[112] that the claimant had not consented to this specific risk (although, of course, he had consented

---

[105] [1944] KB 476, at 480–1.

[106] Although even this might not be sufficient. In *Davies v Global Strategies Group (Hong Kong) Ltd* [2009] EWHC 2342 (QB), at [86] the employee was paid 'danger money' to work as a security contractor in Iraq. He was fatally shot by insurgents. The plea of *volenti* was held to be inapplicable in an action by the deceased's dependants against the deceased's employer.

[107] [1965] AC 656.

[108] See, eg, *Dann v Hamilton* [1939] 1 KB 509; *Buckpitt v Oates* [1968] 1 All ER 1145; *Bennett v Tugwell* [1971] 2 QB 267; *Ashton v Turner* [1981] QB 137.

[109] See, eg, *Owens v Brimmell* [1977] QB 859.   [110] See S Yeo (2001) 9 Tort L Rev 114.

[111] [1938] 4 All ER 331.   [112] [1938] 4 All ER 331, at 336.

to the physical contacts which might occur in the course of the lunging exercise). Thus, the defence of voluntary assumption of risk failed.[113]

(4) Entrants and occupiers

A statutory defence analogous to that of *volenti non fit injuria* applies in relation to occupiers' liability. This defence is discussed elsewhere.[114]

Section 4 Express exclusion or limitation of liability

Preliminary Section 3 addressed the defence of voluntary assumption of risk. Liability can be expressly excluded or limited also by a contract between the parties or by way of notice. The relationship between this defence and that of *volenti* is unclear. Often it is said that *volenti* is concerned with implicit consent by the claimant to run the risk of injury that caused her damage, whereas the defence that is the subject of this section deals with express consent. This understanding might not be not entirely accurate because some cases of *volenti* might involve express acceptance of a risk. But, since it is fairly entrenched, this chapter will not deviate from it.

UCTA 1977/CRA 2015 As a general rule, persons can allocate their liabilities by a contract or by a notice. However, this principle is subject to significant exceptions. The most important exceptions are those created by the Consumer Rights Act 2015 (applicable as between traders and consumers, T2C contracts), sections 62, 63, 65, and Schedule 2, Part 1, and the Unfair Contract Terms Act 1977 (applicable as between other contracting parties), sub-section 2(1), the latter of which provides: 'A person cannot by reference to any contract term … exclude or restrict his liability for death or personal injury resulting from negligence.'[115] Any term that purports to exclude or limit liability in these circumstances is invalid.

In the case of loss other than death or personal injury: first, the 2015 Act provides that unfair terms in T2C contracts are not binding on the consumer, 'unfairness' being determined by reference to what is detrimental to the consumer's interests or contrary to good faith;[116] and, second, the 1977 Act provides that an exclusion or limitation of 'business liability' or consumer liability is invalid 'except insofar as the term or notice satisfies the requirement of reasonableness'.[117] The criterion of reasonableness in the 1977 Act was considered in *Smith v Eric S Bush*.[118] Surveyors were instructed by a mortgage provider to inspect and report on a house that the claimant wished to buy. The surveyors expressly excluded any liability to the claimant. The House of Lords found that

---

[113] See also *Cleghorn v Oldham* (1927) 43 TLR 465. C recovered damages from her golf companion, who had injured her with a golf club on the course.   [114] See ch 9.

[115] Consumer Rights Act 2015, sub-ss 2(2) and 76(2); Unfair Contract Terms Act 1977, sub-s 1(3).

[116] Consumer Rights Act 2015, s 62. Relevant contract terms and notices must also be transparent: s 68.

[117] Unfair Contract Terms Act 1977, sub-s 2(2) and s 11.

[118] For the scope of each Act, see: [1990] 1 AC 831. See also *Bank of Scotland v Fuller Peiser* 2002 SCLR 255.

in the absence of the purported disclaimer, a duty of care was owed to the claimant;[119] but that in the circumstances the disclaimer was unreasonable. In the vast majority of cases, house purchasers, as surveyors well knew, rely on the report commissioned by the mortgagee (a report for which the purchaser will pay). Lord Griffiths suggested four factors by which to assess reasonableness:[120] whether the parties were of equal bargaining power; whether it was practicable to expect the claimant to obtain independent advice; the complexity of the task which formed the subject of the disclaimer; and the practical consequences of striking down the disclaimer.[121]

Section 5 Illegality

(A) Introduction

Context As a result of the proliferation of criminal offences, it is not uncommon for victims of negligence to suffer injury while engaged in illegal conduct. For example, a driver hurt in a motor vehicle accident by the carelessness of another road user might have been driving under the influence of alcohol, without wearing a seat belt, or in excess of the speed limit. Indeed, it is thought that most personal injury actions arising out of motor vehicle usage involve the commission of an offence by the claimant.[122] The extensive regulation of many of life's ordinary activities by the criminal law thus gives considerable significance to the effect of a claimant's unlawful behaviour on her entitlement to a remedy in tort.

In certain situations, tort law grants a negligent defendant a defence[123] if the claimant whom she injured was acting in breach of the criminal law at the relevant time.[124] Reasons for having the defence were restated by the Supreme Court in *Patel v Mirza*, where Lord Toulson said that 'there are two broad discernible policy reasons for the common law doctrine of illegality as a defence to a civil claim', these being: first, 'that a person should not be allowed to profit from his own wrongdoing' and, second, that 'the law should be coherent and not self-defeating, condoning illegality by giving with the left hand what it takes with the right hand'.[125]

Often referred to by the maxim *ex turpi causa non oritur action* (from a wrongful cause no action arises),[126] the illegality defence assumes different hues depending on the context in which it is raised. There are three different types of case: first, cases in which the parties were committing a criminal offence jointly when the claimant was injured ('joint illegal enterprise cases'); second, cases involving actions in which the defendant

---

[119] [1990] 1 AC 831, at 843–5.   [120] [1990] 1 AC 831, at 858–9.

[121] Presumably, this includes any effect that holding the exclusion clause invalid might have on the cost or availability of the service provided by D.

[122] *Great NE Railway Ltd v Hart* [2003] EWHC 2450 (QB); *Vellino v CC of Greater Manchester* [2002] 1 WLR 218, at 229.

[123] The defence of illegality is not confined to the negligence context. It is of general application. It is discussed in relation to intentional torts to the person or to property: ch 13.

[124] The defence's arrival in the negligence context was belated. It was not recognised until *Ashton v Turner* [1981] QB 137.   [125] [2017] AC 467, at [99].

[126] 'No cause of action may be founded upon an immoral or illegal act' (*Revill v Newbery* [1996] QB 567, at 576).

was not implicated in the claimant's illegal conduct ('unilateral illegality cases'); and, third, cases involving proceedings that constitute an attempt by the claimant to use tort law in order to deflect the impact of a sanction imposed on her by the criminal law ('sanction-shifting cases'). The operation of the defence in each of these settings will be examined momentarily.

General rules We begin, however, with some general rules. First, the defence must be pleaded and proved by the defendant on the balance of probabilities.[127] It is not necessary for the defendant to show beyond reasonable doubt that the claimant committed an offence. Second, the defence is concerned with illegal conduct and is of potential application in cases involving criminal acts[128] and quasi-criminal acts featuring corruption or dishonesty.[129] Indeed, the defence is of potential application in cases of grossly *immoral* acts,[130] at least where these offend the public interest in aiding the enforcement of obligations.[131] (All of this is subject to the need for proportion in application of the illegality defence, discussed below). Third, if the claimant has a complete defence to criminal liability, the illegality defence is unlikely to apply.[132] Possession of a partial criminal law defence, such as diminished responsibility or loss of control, probably is insufficient to exclude the illegality defence.[133] Fourth, the offending must be contemporaneous. Thus, if the claimant withdraws from a criminal enterprise before suffering damage, the defence will be inapplicable.[134] Fifth, the mere fact that the claimant was engaged in a criminal act at the time of the defendant's tort will not enliven the defence. The claimant's offending must be related causally to her damage. For example, if the claimant's vehicle is struck by another car while she is transporting a person whom she had kidnapped, the defence would be inapplicable because her offending did not materially contribute to the loss. Finally, and perhaps most significantly, not *every* breach of the criminal law, quasi-criminal law, or immorality is sufficient to trigger the defence. In determining whether a claim of illegality ought to succeed, the court is permitted to consider the policy arguments for and against it. In *Patel* v *Mirza*, the Supreme Court held that a court:[135]

---

[127] *Lindsay v Poole* 1984 SLT 269, at 269; *Sloan v Triplett* 1985 SLT 294, at 296; *Wilson v Price* 1989 SLT 484, at 486.

[128] At least where mens rea is involved. Strict liability offences might be insufficient: see *Les Laboratoires Servier v Apotex Ltd* [2015] AC 430, at [29]. Conviction in a criminal court is not a necessary pre-requisite: *Flint v Tittensor* [2015] 1 WLR 4370, at [43].

[129] *Les Laboratoires Servier v Apotex Ltd* [2015] AC 430, at [25].

[130] In *Patel v Mirza* [2017] AC 467, at [120], the Supreme Court preserved this possibility. See also *Bilta (UK) Ltd (in liq) v Nazir (No 2)* [2015] 2 WLR 1168, at [55]; *Les Laboratoires Servier v Apotex Ltd* [2015] AC 430, at [23], [25], and [28]. The conduct must be of serious moral turpitude: eg, *Nayyar v Denton Wilde Sapte* [2009] EWHC 3218 (QB) (payment of civil law bribe); *Safeway Stores Ltd v Twigger* [2010] 3 All ER 577 (anti-competitive behaviour). [131] *Les Laboratoires Servier v Apotex Ltd* [2015] AC 430, at [28].

[132] *Miller v Miller* (2009) 54 MVR 367, at [78] (point was not dealt with on appeal: *Miller v Miller* (2011) 85 ALJR 480).

[133] *Gray v Thames Trains Ltd* [2009] 1 AC 1339. [134] *Miller v Miller* (2011) 85 ALJR 480.

[135] [2017] AC 467, at [101]. This was an unjust enrichment case, but all the indications are that the same rule would apply in tort, a number of justices emphasising the need for coherence in the common law. The Supreme Court departed from use of the 'reliance' test, which makes the defence available when the claimant must rely upon her illegal act in order to seek relief from the court (as applied in *Tinsley v Milligan* [1994] 1 AC 340): see ibid at [110]. See also *Hounga v Allen* [2014] 1 WLR 2889.

> cannot judge whether allowing a claim which is in some way tainted by illegality would be contrary to the public interest, because it would be harmful to the integrity of the legal system, without (a) considering the underlying purpose of the prohibition which has been transgressed, (b) considering conversely any other relevant public policies which may be rendered ... less effective by denial of the claim, and (c) keeping in mind the possibility of overkill [against the claimant] unless the law is applied with a due sense of proportionality.

In determining the proportionality issue, relevant factors are likely to include the seriousness of the claimant's conduct, its centrality to the tort claim, whether it was intentional, and 'whether there was a marked disparity in the parties' respective culpability'.[136] The courts have stressed the necessity of steering a course between the extreme positions of denying all claims affected by illegality and ignoring the claimant's unlawful behaviour.[137] As mentioned earlier, only fairly serious offending is sufficient.[138] Consequently, the defence is unlikely to be applied in cases involving trivial infractions of the criminal law,[139] or 'mere' private law wrongdoing by the claimant (such as where she is in breach of a patent).[140]

(B) Three types of illegality case

(1) Joint illegal enterprise cases

Joint illegal enterprise cases involve the defendant injuring the claimant while engaged in a criminal enterprise jointly with her.[141] The Court of Appeal has taken two contrasting approaches in determining these cases. The duty of care approach was adopted in *Pitts v Hunt*.[142] The claimant was hurt while a pillion passenger on a motorcycle. The motorcycle was being driven by his 16-year-old friend, who was unlicensed, uninsured, and intoxicated. When rounding a bend while travelling on the wrong side of the road, the motorcycle collided with an oncoming vehicle. The claimant brought an action against his friend's estate (his friend was killed in the accident). The Court of Appeal[143] held that no duty of care will be recognised between participants to a joint criminal enterprise if the nature of the enterprise is such that it would be infeasible to ask how much care the reasonable person in the defendant's position would have taken in the circumstances. This test was satisfied on the facts.

In two subsequent decisions, the Court of Appeal adopted an alternative approach, based on the application of causation principles. In *Joyce v O'Brien*,[144] the claimant and

---

[136] [2017] AC 467, at [107].   [137] *Saunders v Edwards* [1987] 1 WLR 1116, at 1134.

[138] *Les Laboratoires Servier v Apotex Ltd* [2015] AC 430, at [29]; *Henwood v Municipal Tramways Trust (SA)* (1938) 60 CLR 438, at 446.

[139] *Vellino v CC of Greater Manchester* [2002] 1 WLR 218, at 229; *Currie v Clamp* 2002 SLT 196, at [20]–[21].

[140] *Les Laboratoires Servier v Apotex Inc* [2015] AC 430, at [30].

[141] E Weinrib (1976) 26 UTLJ 28; J Goudkamp (2010) 34 MULR 425.

[142] [1991] 1 QB 24. See also *Ashton v Turner* [1981] QB 137.

[143] The court was heavily influenced by Australian authority, especially *Jackson v Harrison* (1978) 138 CLR 438. The High Court of Australia has now taken the jurisprudence regarding the illegality defence in a different direction: *Miller v Miller* (2011) 85 ALJR 480.   [144] [2014] 1 WLR 70.

first defendant stole some ladders from a front garden. The ladders were too long to fit inside the van they were using, so that, when fleeing the scene, the claimant had to stand at the back of the van, trying to keep the ladders from falling out of the open door with one arm while holding on to the vehicle with the opposing hand. The first defendant drove sharply around a corner and the claimant fell off and was injured. In denying recovery in negligence, the Court of Appeal followed the approach to joint illegal enterprise in its earlier *obiter* reasoning in *Delaney v Pickett*.[145] The correct approach was as follows:

> where the character of the [sufficiently serious] joint criminal enterprise is such that it is foreseeable that a party or parties may be subject to unusual or increased risks of harm as a consequence of the activities of the parties in pursuance of their criminal objectives, and the risk materialises, the injury can properly be said to be caused by the criminal act of the Claimant even if it results from the negligent or intentional act of another party to the illegal enterprise.[146]

On the facts, the making of a speedy getaway in the manner adopted from the scene of the crime was such as foreseeably would result in the kind of injuries that occurred. However, Elias LJ explained that matters would have been different 'if the [first defendant] had deliberately driven with the intention of harming the [claimant], or if he had physically attacked him as they were escaping from the scene'.[147]

(2) Unilateral illegality cases

Claimants who act unlawfully independently of the defendant at the time of the defendant's tort might also fail under the illegality defence. In *Revill v Newbery*,[148] the claimant was attempting to break into a shed owned by the defendant. The defendant was sleeping in the shed at the time in order to protect belongings that he kept inside it. Roused by the claimant's efforts to gain entry, the defendant fired a shotgun through a hole in the door to scare the claimant. The blast struck the claimant, who commenced proceedings in negligence and under the Occupiers' Liability Act 1984. He succeeded at first instance, although his damages were reduced for contributory negligence. The defendant's appeal to the Court of Appeal was dismissed. Neill LJ stated that, if the illegality defence applied, it would effectively render the claimant an outlaw yet the legislature, in enacting the Occupiers' Liability Act 1984, implicitly discountenanced such a result.[149]

Another important decision is that in *Vellino v Chief Constable of Greater Manchester*.[150] The claimant had been arrested frequently by police at his apartment. Although his apartment was situated two floors above street level, the claimant often attempted to escape from the police by jumping out of an apartment window. One evening, the police came to the apartment in response to a complaint about a noisy party. The claimant was arrested. An altercation ensued and the claimant jumped out

---

[145] [2012] 1 WLR 2149.   [146] [2014] 1 WLR 70, at [29].   [147] [2014] 1 WLR 70, at [46].
[148] [1996] QB 567.   [149] *Revill v Newbery* [1996] QB 567, at 577–8. See also at 579 and 580.
[150] [2002] 1 WLR 218.

of a window. On this occasion, he was catastrophically injured by the fall. The Court of Appeal held that the police did not owe the claimant a duty of care because the seriousness of the claimant's unlawful behaviour meant that the third stage of the *Caparo* test[151] (concerned with fairness, justice, and reasonableness) was not satisfied.

It should be noted that the reasons given for the decisions in *Revill* and *Vellino* focused on quite different considerations. In *Revill*, it was important that denying the claimant relief would have sat uncomfortably with the policy behind the Occupiers' Liability Act 1984. In *Vellino*, no such concern arose. The central factor was the seriousness of the claimant's offending. Unfortunately, therefore, it is difficult to determine what test governs unilateral illegality cases.

(3) Sanction-shifting cases

Sanction-shifting cases are actions in which the claimant sues the defendant complaining that the defendant's negligence caused her to incur a criminal sanction.[152] With few exceptions,[153] they have been unsuccessful.[154] The leading decision is that of the House of Lords in *Gray v Thames Trains Ltd*.[155] The claimant was the victim of a train crash that occurred due to the defendants' negligence. His physical injuries were relatively minor but he developed a serious psychiatric illness. Nearly two years after the train accident, the claimant stabbed to death a drunken pedestrian with whom he had had an altercation. He was convicted of manslaughter on the ground of diminished responsibility. The claimant then sued the defendant for various losses, including several stemming from his conviction such as his loss of freedom, a loss of income while imprisoned, and the damage that his conviction did to his reputation. The House held that these losses were irrecoverable, its logic being that to award damages would mean that tort law would undermine the criminal law because it would involve restoring that which the criminal law had taken away, and coherence demanded that different branches of the law should not stultify each other. However, the claimant was entitled to damages in respect of losses not associated with the criminal sanction, such as pain and suffering caused by his physical and psychiatric injuries. The non-stultification principle means that, as a general rule, sanction-shifting cases will fail on the ground of illegality. Perhaps the only such cases that might succeed are those in which the sentence of the criminal court is solely rehabilitative rather than punitive.

(C) Limiting redress under specific heads of damages

The illegality defence, when successfully invoked, usually works to completely deny actions. Alternatively, it might prevent recovery under specific heads of damages. For example, in *Gray v Thames Trains Ltd*, recovery was denied only in respect of losses

---

[151] *Vellino v CC of Greater Manchester* [2002] 1 WLR 218 at 222, 226, and 233–4.
[152] See J Goudkamp (2006) 14 TLJ 20; EK Banakas (1985) 44 CLJ 195.
[153] See, eg, *Meah v McCreamer* [1985] 1 All ER 367.
[154] See, eg, *Clunis v Camden and Islington HA* [1998] QB 978; *Worrall v British Railways Board* [1999] CLY 1413.   [155] [2009] 1 AC 1339.

that were caused by the claimant's convictions. The defence can prevent recovery of compensation, also, for a loss of earnings where the loss is tainted by unlawful conduct. For example, compensation for a loss of income has been denied where the claimant derived it from working as an illegal bookmaker,[156] without the necessary immigration permit,[157] and in contravention of planning regulations.[158] Damages for a loss of income have been refused also where the claimant had kept earnings secret in order fraudulently to claim social security benefits.[159] No definitive test exists as to when recovery under a specific head of damages will be limited on the ground of illegality. However, the Court of Appeal has indicated that it won't apply where loss is obliquely connected with, or is collateral to, a breach of the criminal law.[160]

Conclusions

This chapter has considered the main defences to actions in negligence. The plea of voluntary assumption of risk, when accepted, results in the defendant avoiding liability altogether. The defences of express exclusion of liability and illegality, when applicable, generally do too, although they might merely reduce the extent of the defendant's liability. By contrast, contributory negligence merely reduces the defendant's responsibility for the claimant's damage without eliminating it.

Problem question

Janice agreed to drive her father, Alex, to his tax accountant. As was by now his usual practice, the accountant was tasked with squirreling away Alex's earnings so that they were out of reach of the tax office. On the way to the accountant's, Janice gained the impression that her car was being followed—so she sped away. She asked her father whether he knew who was following them. It turns out that the police had noticed that Janice's car had faulty lights. Janice was trying to escape from the police car when she crashed into a fire hydrant. Alex, who suffered a badly injured knee in the accident, got out of the car in a hurry and, trying to dodge the traffic, he walked into an open drain in the street. Alex's left leg needed to be amputated thereafter.

Advise Alex on defences that might be available against him in suing either Janice or the local council responsible for maintaining the roadway.

 Visit **http://www.oup.com/uk/street15e/** for answer guidance.

---

[156] *Meadows v Ferguson* [1961] VR 594.   [157] *Lee v McClellan* (1995) 127 FLR 383.

[158] *McNichols v J R Simplot Co* 262 P 2d 1012 (1953); contra *Mills v Baitis* [1968] VR 583.

[159] *Kanu v Kashif* [2002] EWCA Civ 1620. See also *Hunter v Butler* [1996] RTR 396; cf *Newman v Folkes and Dunlop Tyres Ltd* [2002] PIQR Q2.

[160] *Hewison v Meridian Shipping Services Pte Ltd* [2003] ICR 766, at 781–2, 785–6.

Further reading

DUARTE D'ALMEIDA, *Allowing for Exceptions: A Theory of Defences and Defeasibility in Law* (2015)

DYSON, GOUDKAMP, AND WILMOT-SMITH, *Defences in Tort* (2015)

GILIKER, 'The Consumer Rights Act 2015—A Bastion of European Consumer Rights?' (2017) 37 *Legal Studies* 78

GOUDKAMP, *Tort Law Defences* (2013)

SIMONS, 'Assumption of Risk and Consent in the Law of Torts: A Theory of Full Preference' (1987) 67 *Boston University Law Review* 213

SIMONS, 'The Puzzling Doctrine of Contributory Negligence' (1995) 16 *Cardozo Law Review* 1693

SUGARMAN, 'Assumption of Risk' (1997) 31 *Valparaiso University Law Review* 833

WEINRIB, 'Illegality as a Tort Defence' (1976) 26 *University of Toronto Law Journal* 28

9

Liability for defective premises and structures

KEY ISSUES

(1) Occupiers' liability
The bulk of this chapter concerns the potential liability of occupiers to those who suffer injury and/or other forms of loss by virtue of the state of the occupier's premises.

(2) Statutory (not common law) liability
The means by which an occupier's liability is to be determined is governed almost exclusively by statute. The Occupiers' Liability Act 1957 governs the duty owed by occupiers to visitors. The Occupiers' Liability Act 1984 governs the duty owed by occupiers to non-visitors. The former offers a much greater degree of protection to the persons covered by it than does the latter.

(3) Statutory terms
Because occupiers' liability is governed almost entirely by statute, it is vital to determine li-ability in accordance with the Acts' pivotal terms—such as 'occupier', 'visitor', 'non-visitor', and 'common duty of care'. (It is a mistake to assume that the language of the common law can be used interchangeably with the language of the statutes.) The injured claimant will try always to convince the court that he was a 'visitor' to the premises where he was injured.

(4) Non-occupiers' liability
The latter part of this chapter considers the residual classes of defendant who might be held liable in tort for losses and injuries arising from the defective state of premises. These non-occupiers include landlords, builders, architects, and engineers; and the rules governing their liability also are to be found in a statute: viz, the Defective Premises Act 1972.

Section 1 Introduction

Liability for defective premises[1] to those who suffer loss or damage on those premises[2] rests generally with two main types of defendant. The first comprises those persons actually occupying the premises. Here, responsibility generally is for personal injuries,

---

[1] For the purposes of this chapter, the term 'premises' shall be used to connote not just any building owned by D, but also any land owned by him, regardless of whether there are any buildings on it.

[2] If C was elsewhere than on the D's premises when he was injured, he must frame his action in negligence, public nuisance, or the rule in *Rylands v Fletcher* (as to which, see chs 17 and 18).

such as a broken ankle sustained when a rotten floorboard gives way. Second, someone other than the occupier might be liable for defects in the premises. This latter category of potential defendants is broad in scope and includes landlords, builders, and professionals such as architects and consulting engineers. While in some cases the relevant defect might cause personal injury, in many cases it might be financial loss only that the claimant suffers (such as the discovery, after the developer has gone into liquidation, that the house one bought from it is in need of repair). An action against the original builder or architect in such circumstances is designed to recover the financial loss represented by the property's diminished value and/or the cost of repair. However, the liability of non-occupiers for financial loss associated with defective premises is significantly restricted in scope.

Section 2 Occupiers' liability

Occupiers' liability is defined predominantly by statute, but there remains (according to case law) a small, residual role for the common law in relation to certain negligently performed activities taking place on the defendant's premises.[3] For this reason, it is necessary to consider the liability of occupiers under three headings: first, the Occupiers' Liability Act 1957 (governing liability to visitors to the defendant's premises); second, the Occupiers' Liability Act 1984 (governing liability to non-visitors); and finally the residual common law rules (applicable to both visitors and non-visitors injured by particular activities on the defendant's premises).

(A) The Occupiers' Liability Act 1957

(1) Who is an occupier?

The first pre-condition of a defendant's liability under the Occupiers' Liability Act 1957 is that he must be the occupier of the premises on which the claimant's loss occurs. The 1957 Act provides no statutory definition of occupier. Instead, it provides that those who would be treated as occupiers at common law should be treated likewise for the purposes of the Act;[4] and the leading definition of 'occupier' derives from *Wheat v E Lacon & Co Ltd*:[5]

> Ds owned a public house of which Mr R was their manager. Mr R and his wife were allowed by agreement to live in the upper floor, access to which was by a door separate from the licensed premises. Mrs R was allowed to take paying guests on the upper floor. A guest suffered an accident on the staircase leading to the upper floor. It was held that, although C was injured in the private area of the premises, Ds (along with Mr and Mrs R) were liable nevertheless. They had enough residual control over that part of the premises to be occupiers.

---

[3] See, eg, *Ferguson v Welsh* [1987] 3 All ER 777; *Ogwo v Taylor* [1988] AC 431.
[4] Occupiers' Liability Act 1957, sub-s 1(2).   [5] [1966] AC 552.

The case clarifies that there might be two or more occupiers simultaneously and that exclusive occupation is not required. The test of occupation is whether a person has some degree of control associated with, and arising from, his presence in and use of, or his activities in, the premises. A good example of the scope for multiple occupancy can be seen in *AMF International Ltd v Magnet Bowling Ltd*,[6] where both a contractor and the owner were held to have sufficient control to be joint occupiers of the premises in which the claimant's equipment was damaged by rainwater entering the building via a leaking doorway.[7]

On the question of who might qualify as a sole occupier for the purposes of the Act, it is clear that the following earlier decisions remain sound. A concessionaire without a lease in a fairground is an occupier.[8] So too is a local authority that has requisitioned a house[9] (even in respect of those parts of the house in which it allows homeless persons to live);[10] as is a contractor converting a ship into a troopship in dry dock.[11] By contrast, a decorator undertaking to do no more than paint a house does not have sufficient control to be regarded as its occupier.[12]

(2) Scope of the Act

Prior law Prior to the Occupiers' Liability Act 1957, the duty owed by an occupier to entrants upon his land varied according to their common law status. The highest standard of care was owed to those, such as hotel guests, who were on his land by virtue of contract. A lesser duty was owed to his invitees,[13] and a lower duty still was owed to mere licensees (who were permitted, but not requested, to be there). In relation to trespassers, the occupier was obliged to do no more than refrain from deliberately or recklessly causing them injury.[14] A further complexity in the common law lay in the fact that the content of the duty varied according to the manner in which the claimant's injury was sustained. A distinction was drawn between injuries sustained by virtue of something done on the defendant's premises and injuries caused merely by the dangerous state of the premises.[15]

Abolition of common law The Occupiers' Liability Act 1957 was enacted to give effect to the recommendations contained in the Law Reform Committee's Third Report,[16] which were designed to eliminate the confusion surrounding the common law rules on liability to entrants. Thus, Occupiers' Liability Act 1957, sections 2 and 3 'have effect, in place of common law rules, to regulate the duty which an occupier of premises owes to his visitors in respect of dangers due to the state of the premises or to things done or omitted to be done on them'.[17]

---

[6] [1968] 2 All ER 789.

[7] The degree of care that C might expect from each occupier turns on the degree of control held by each: *Wheat v Lacon* [1966] AC 552, at 581 and 601.

[8] *Humphreys v Dreamland (Margate) Ltd* [1930] All ER Rep 327.

[9] *Hawkins v Coulsdon and Purley UDC* [1954] 1 QB 319.   [10] *Greene v Chelsea BC* [1954] 2 QB 127.

[11] *Hartwell v Grayson Rollo and Clover Docks Ltd* [1947] KB 901.   [12] *Page v Read* (1984) 134 NLJ 723.

[13] That is, those who had a mutual business interest with the occupier, such as customers in a shop.

[14] *Robert Addie & Sons (Collieries) Ltd v Dumbreck* [1929] AC 358.

[15] These were termed, respectively, the 'activity duty' and the 'occupancy duty'.   [16] Cmd 9305.

[17] Occupiers' Liability Act 1957, s 1.

(a) Visitors

Visitors and others The Occupiers' Liability Act 1957 imposes a duty in respect of 'visitors'.[18] 'Visitors' for the purposes of the Act are those persons who were invitees or licensees at common law:[19] that is, anyone to whom an occupier gave any invitation or permission to enter or use his premises. Accordingly, in terms of the level of duty owed, the common law distinction between invitees and licensees is no longer of importance.[20] However, it remains important to distinguish between visitors and other types of entrant since the later Occupiers' Liability Act of 1984 governs the duties of an occupier to those other entrants who fall within the definition of 'non-visitors'.[21]

Dual status The question arises whether, in the case of multiple occupiers, a person might be a visitor in relation to Occupier A but a trespasser in relation to Occupier B. Lord Goff answered this question in *Ferguson v Welsh*:

> If it is the case that only one such occupier authorises a third person to come onto the land, then plainly the third person is *vis-à-vis* that occupier, a lawful visitor. But he may not be a lawful visitor *vis-à-vis* the other occupier. Whether he is so or not must . . . depend on . . . whether the occupier who authorised him to enter had authority, actual (express or implied) or ostensible, from the other occupier to allow the third party onto the land . . . if he had not, then the third party will be, *vis-à-vis* that other occupier, a trespasser.[22]

Non-visitors Those entrants covered by the Occupiers' Liability Act 1984 often are called 'trespassers', but the class 'non-visitors' is not confined only to persons whose presence constitutes trespass. If they are on the premises of the defendant without his permission, then even though they have not gone there voluntarily[23]—for example, if they were chased there—they fall within this group, just as much as if they have committed the tort of trespass. Similarly, although he is not a trespasser:

> [a] person entering any premises in exercise of rights conferred by virtue of (a) section 2(1) of the Countryside and Rights of Way Act 2000,[24] or (b) an access agreement or order under the National Parks and Access to the Countryside Act 1949, is not, for the purposes of this Act, a visitor of the occupier of the premises.[25]

Private rights of way It has been held also that the same non-visitor status extends to those using a private right of way.[26] But a more complex situation exists with respect to persons who sustain injury on a public right of way. At one time it was thought that no one using a public right of way could be classed as a visitor for the purposes of the

---

[18] In doing so, it envisages not only personal injury suffered by a visitor, but also any property damage he might suffer: Occupiers' Liability Act 1957, sub-s 1(3)(b).   [19] Occupiers' Liability Act 1957, sub-s 1(2).
[20] *Campbell v Northern Ireland Housing Executive* [1996] 1 BNIL 99.
[21] See, eg, *Stone v Taffe* [1974] 3 All ER 1016.   [22] [1987] 3 All ER 777, at 785.
[23] If D's negligence causes a visitor involuntarily and unpremeditatedly to encroach slightly on land where he has no permission to go, he retains visitor's rights: *Braithwaite v Durham Steel Co Ltd* [1958] 3 All ER 161.
[24] This sub-section refers to those exercising a right of access to open land for recreational purposes.
[25] Occupiers' Liability Act 1957, sub-s 1(4).   [26] *Vodden v Gayton* [2001] PIQR P52.

Occupiers' Liability Act 1957.[27] However, the matter was shown to be less straightforward than this in *McGeown v Northern Ireland Housing Executive*:[28]

> C's husband was the tenant of a house on Ds' housing estate. The house was accessed by a path over which the public had acquired a right of way. It was upon this path that C tripped and sustained a broken leg. She argued that Ds were liable to her as a visitor under the Occupiers' Liability Act (Northern Ireland) 1957.[29] The House of Lords held that she was not a visitor and could not sue under the statute.

The complexity in this case stems from the fact that their Lordships confined their decision to persons using a public right of way qua members of the general public (for example, a hill-walker who neither knows, nor is interested in, who owns the *solum* of the right of way).[30] As Lord Keith put it: 'Once a public right of way has been established, there is no question of permission being granted by the owner of the *solum* [to] those who choose to use it.'[31] The idea of using a right of way by virtue of 'permission' is similar to that of using it qua licensee. But what, wondered Lord Browne-Wilkinson, of those who are expressly invited on to the land?

> In the case of an invitee there is no logical inconsistency between the claimant's right to be on the premises in exercise of the right of way and his actual presence there in response to the express or implied invitation of the occupier. It is the invitation which gives rise to the occupier's duty of care to an invitee.[32]

This *obiter* proposition has since been dismissed by the Court of Appeal in *Campbell v Northern Ireland Housing Executive*,[33] where a claimant who was injured on a public right of way, on the way to the shops, was held to be outside the scope of the Occupiers' Liability Act 1957. Despite this rejection of Lord Browne-Wilkinson's distinction, there is much to be said for the logic underlying his view, even though it would mean giving new life, in the limited context of persons using public rights of way, to the significance of an invitee/licensee dichotomy.[34]

Implied permissions Whether one accepts or rejects Lord Browne-Wilkinson's reasoning, the pre-Act cases on *implied* permissions and invitations to be on the occupier's premises remain relevant. This is because the Act defines visitors in terms of those who were formerly regarded as invitees and licensees at common law. In *Edwards v Railway Executive*, it was held that permission should not be implied merely because the occupier knew of the claimant's presence or because he failed to take the necessary steps to prevent his entry.

---

[27] *Greenhalgh v British Railways Board* [1969] 2 QB 286, at 292–3. On the other hand, although no action will lie for nonfeasance according to *McGeown v Northern Ireland Housing Executive* [1995] 1 AC 233, cf *Thomas v British Railways Board* [1976] QB 912, where it was said that an action can be brought in respect of any injury caused by D's misfeasance—eg, digging and leaving uncovered a hole in the right of way into which C later falls.   [28] [1995] 1 AC 233.

[29] This Act is the same, in all material respects, as the English Act of that name and year.

[30] But note that those exercising access rights under the Countryside and Rights of Way Act 2000 are now denied the status 'visitor' under the amended Occupiers' Liability Act 1957, sub-s 1(4)(a).

[31] [1995] 1 AC 233, at 246.   [32] [1995] 1 AC 233, at 248.   [33] [1996] 1 BNIL 99.

[34] See further J Murphy (1997) 61 Conv 362.

Rather, '[t]here must be evidence either of express permission or that the land-owner has so conducted himself that he cannot be heard to say that he did not give it.'[35]

In each case, it is a question of fact whether permission to enter can be implied and the burden of proving it rests with the claimant seeking to rely on it.[36] Although the rules are capable of being applied to adults,[37] in practice they are most pertinent in relation to children who, sometimes, are able to prove an implied permission on the basis of an 'allurement' that would present no temptation to an adult. In *Glasgow Corporation v Taylor*,[38] for example, shiny red berries growing in the open on the defendant's land were held to be an allurement to a child aged seven, to whom the berries looked like cherries or blackcurrants. Similarly, the House of Lords has held that a rotting boat was a sufficiently alluring plaything to constitute an implied permission.[39] The presence of an allurement in a location that is accessible to children will tend to aid the inference of permission to enter.[40] But the mere fact that the occupier has on his premises a dangerous and alluring object will not make him liable to every child who comes on to his land. For example, the child might be old enough to read a notice to the effect that the owner did not want him to be present there, in which case the child will be a trespasser, and thus forced to rely on the lower level of protection afforded by the Occupiers' Liability Act 1984. Furthermore, in some circumstances, occupiers are deemed only to permit young children on to their land subject to the condition that a responsible adult accompany them.[41]

Of course, in cases concerning adults, it is inapposite to talk of implied permission based on allurements. But even in such cases, permission might be implied still. As Lord Porter pointed out in the *Edwards* case:

> an open pathway, as in *Cooke v Midland Great Western Rly of Ireland*,[42] or a knowledge that a track is and has long been constantly used, coupled with a failure to take any steps to indicate that ingress is not permitted, as in *Lowery v Walker*,[43] may well amount to a tacit licence.[44]

Statutory and contractual rights Persons entering as of right—such as police with search warrants and a host of other officials statutorily empowered to enter premises—are deemed by the Occupiers' Liability Act 1957 to be present with the occupier's permission,[45] and are afforded the same duty of care as visitors. So, too, potentially, are contractual entrants; for

---

[35] [1952] AC 737, at 747.   [36] [1952] AC 737.
[37] See, eg, *Harvey v Plymouth CC* [2010] PIQR P18 (C not on the facts an implied visitor).
[38] [1922] 1 AC 44.   [39] *Jolley v Sutton London BC* [2000] 1 WLR 1082.
[40] *Hardy v Central London Rly Co* [1920] 3 KB 459; *Latham v R Johnson and Nephew Ltd* [1913] 1 KB 398.
[41] *Latham v R Johnson and Nephew Ltd* [1913] 1 KB 398; *Bates v Stone Parish Council* [1954] 3 All ER 38. In *Phipps v Rochester Corpn* [1955] 1 QB 450, Devlin J criticised this rule for a lack of precision: eg, what degree of incapacity on the part of the child and what qualifications on the part of his companion are called for? But the rule still stands on the authority of the Court of Appeal.   [42] [1909] AC 229.
[43] [1911] AC 10.
[44] [1952] AC 737, at 744. See also *Robert Addie & Sons (Collieries) Ltd v Dumbreck* [1929] AC 358, at 372–3; *Darby v National Trust* [2001] PIQR P 372. Cf *Gough v National Coal Board* [1954] 1 QB 191.
[45] Occupiers' Liability Act 1957, sub-s 2(6). Police officers pursuing inquiries without a warrant may take advantage of the generally implied licence to approach a front door via the garden path: *Robson v Hallett* [1967] 2 QB 939. But like other visitors they will cease to have visitor status if they fail to leave immediately the licence is expressly withdrawn: *Snook v Mannion* [1982] RTR 321.

under sub-section 5(1) there is an implied term in the contract whereby, subject to effective contrary provision, the claimant is afforded the very same duty of care.[46]

(b) Against what risks does the Occupiers' Liability Act 1957 afford protection?

State of the premises The Occupiers' Liability Act 1957 plainly governs the duty of the occupier in relation to structural defects or other dangers due to the state of the premises, or indeed 'things' on the premises such as vicious dogs roaming free in the garden.[47]

Things done or omitted The 1957 Act refers also to dangers due to 'things done or omitted to be done' on the premises. As such, the Act covers acts and omissions which have created a dangerous condition of a continuing nature which later causes harm. But a more difficult question is whether the Act extends also to acts (whether of the occupier *or others*) that cause harm directly to the visitor. Sub-section 1(2) provides that the Act 'shall regulate the nature of the duty imposed by law in consequence of a person's occupation or control of premises'. At common law, an occupier had a duty not to permit others to use his premises in such a way that foreseeably would harm other persons on those premises.[48] Regardless of whether such cases previously fell within that branch of the law of negligence imposing special duties on occupiers towards invitees or licensees, the effect of sub-sections (1) and (2) is to bring those situations within the Act—the duty of care arises in consequence of the fact that the defendant is an occupier.[49] This appears to have been confirmed by *Everett v Comojo (UK) Ltd*,[50] the Court of Appeal holding that the provisions encompass personal injuries caused on premises by guests permitted into a hotel or nightclub by its manager. On the other hand, activities not directly associated with occupation that caused harm to visitors were governed by ordinary principles of negligence, and not by the special rules relating to occupiers.[51] It has been stated judicially that the Act does not apply to such activities (regardless of whether the act in question was the occupier's, a contractor's, or a visitor's), since the duty of care is imposed on the actor by virtue of his performing an act foreseeably likely to cause harm to others present on the premises, and not because the actor occupies the land.[52]

---

[46] See sub-s 2(A)(4)(c).

[47] *Hill v Lovett* 1992 SLT 994. At common law, if the danger confronted the visitor while on the premises, although he actually suffered the harm off the premises—eg, by falling off an unfenced cliff into the sea—the rules regulating the duties of occupiers towards visitors applied: *Perkowski v Wellington Corpn* [1959] AC 53. The wording of sub-s 1(1) of the Act is also wide enough to cover this situation.

[48] *Glasgow Corpn v Muir* [1943] AC 448.

[49] See *Videan v British Transport Commission* [1963] 2 QB 650 (*obiter*).

[50] [2012] 1 WLR 150, at [36]. See also *Lear v Hickstead Ltd* [2016] 4 WLR 73, at [40]–[43] (occupiers owe a duty under the 1957 Act, where they set up a parking system which created temporary obstruction causing third parties to create a danger to the claimant).

[51] See *Ferguson v Welsh* [1987] 3 All ER 777; *Fairchild v Glenhaven Funeral Services Ltd* [2003] 1 AC 32.

[52] *Revill v Newbery* [1996] 1 All ER 291. The rationale here is that the restrictive wording of the Occupiers' Liability Act 1957, sub-s 1(2)—'The rules so enacted shall regulate the nature of the duty imposed by law *in consequence of a person's occupation or control* of premises'—excludes this class of acts. Thus, when premises were set alight by their occupier, this was a negligent act performed otherwise than *in consequence of occupation or control*, and one for which damages under the general law of negligence (rather than the Occupiers' Liability Act 1957) were available: *Ogwo v Taylor* [1988] AC 431.

Election between causes Before the Occupiers' Liability Act 1957, some cases had held that a claimant might have the choice of suing either under the general law of negligence or by virtue of the special duty owed by occupiers.[53] Since the Act seemingly displaces only the common law rules imposed in consequence of occupation, it follows that if some other duty is imposed by the common law or another statute, the claimant may rely on either the Occupiers' Liability Act 1957 *or* the other cause of action, *or* both. Thus, a worker injured on his employer's premises may rely on the 1957 Act's common duty of care, the duty of the employer to provide a safe system of work, or even some statutory duty of the employer to provide safe access or the like.[54]

(3) The common duty of care

(a) General principles

Reasonable care The common duty of care is an obligation to take such care as is reasonable in all the circumstances to see that the visitor will be reasonably safe in using the premises for the purposes for which he is invited or permitted by the occupier to be there.[55] Under this rule, a landlord was held liable for the removal by a contractor of a door handle on a heavy door, which then became dangerous to close, resulting in a tenant losing part of her finger.[56] But the obligation is not to safeguard against all harm.[57] So a school authority was not liable when it left until the school holidays the repair of a faulty door with an automatic closing mechanism, given that the door had caused trivial injury on the only prior occasion that a child was hurt and repair during term time would have created its own problems.[58] Again, in *Laverton v Kiapasha*[59] a takeaway food store's manager could not prevent the premises' floor becoming wet because, on rainy days, customers were constantly coming in with wet feet. There was no liability under the 1957 Act after a customer slipped and injured her ankle on a very wet night since the restaurant had done what was reasonable to keep the floor dry.[60]

Particular considerations Occupiers' Liability Act 1957, sub-section 2(3) provides:

> The circumstances relevant for the present purpose include the degree of care, and of want of care, which would ordinarily be looked for in such a visitor, so that (for example) in proper cases:
>
> (a) an occupier must be prepared for children to be less careful than adults; and

---

[53] See, eg, *Slade v Battersea and Putney Group HMC* [1955] 1 All ER 429.

[54] Eg, *Ward v Hertfordshire CC* [1970] 1 All ER 535 (duties of local authority both as education authority and occupier considered when child hurt by playground flint wall, though D held not liable under either head because the wall was not dangerous).

[55] Occupiers' Liability Act 1957, sub-s 2(2). See also *Baldacchino v West Wittering Estate Plc* [2008] EWHC 3386.

[56] *Alexander v Freshwater Properties Ltd* [2012] EWCA Civ 1048.

[57] *Pierce v West Sussex CC* [2013] EWCA Civ 1230, at [18].

[58] *Richards* v *Bromley LBC* [2012] EWCA Civ 1476.   [59] [2002] NPC 145.

[60] As a related matter, an occupier cannot reasonably be expected to deal with hazards with absolute immediacy: *Tedstone v Bourne Leisure Ltd (t/a Thoresby Hall Hotel & Spa)* [2008] EWCA Civ 654. See also *Richards v Bromley LBC* [2012] EWCA Civ 1476.

(b) an occupier may expect that a person, in the exercise of his calling, will appreciate and guard against any special risks ordinarily incident to it, so far as the occupier leaves him free to do so.

Bearing in mind the similarity between the gist of this provision and the ordinary law of negligence, it would seem appropriate to invoke parallel common law decisions as guides to the way in which this sub-section should be applied. In particular, the following common law principles would appear to be important. In deciding whether there was a danger, regard must be had to the limited physical and mental powers of a child visitor: for, what is not a danger to an adult might be a danger to a child.[61] In determining the standard of care owed to a child who is not accompanied by a guardian, therefore, it will be material to enquire whether, in the circumstances, the occupier reasonably could have expected the presence of the unaccompanied infant.[62] (If the occupier cannot expect the unaccompanied child, that child inevitably will be a trespasser. But since the passage of the Occupiers' Liability Act 1984, it is of much less significance that he cannot sue for his injuries qua visitor.)[63] If an adult accompanies the child, and the danger would be obvious to the latter, the occupier will have discharged his duty of care.[64]

The significance of sub-section 2(3)(b), insofar as it deals with the care to be shown to visitors possessed of a particular profession, can be illuminated by decisions at common law too. A window cleaner injured through the insecurity of some part of the exterior of the premises which he uses as a foothold or handhold for the purpose of cleaning the outside of the windows can be expected by the occupier to have guarded against this risk which is ordinarily incidental to the job of a window cleaner.[65] By contrast, there is no reason why the occupier should not be liable if the window cleaner is injured through some defect in the staircase when he is going upstairs, in the ordinary way, to reach the windows on an upper floor.[66] But a self-employed plasterer injured when scaffolding collapses beneath him may recover damages from an occupier since the risk was inherent in the defective state of the premises, and was not an expected risk of his employment as a plasterer.[67] In short, the special skills of the entrant are *relevant* in determining whether the occupier is in breach of the common duty of care, but they do not automatically absolve the occupier from responsibility (especially where the risk is not one ordinarily encountered by a person possessed of the particular entrant's skills).[68] Nor will the fact

---

[61] *Cooke v Midland Great Western Rly of Ireland* [1909] AC 229, at 238. Cf *Gough v National Coal Board* [1954] 1 QB 191.   [62] See *Phipps v Rochester Corpn* [1955] 1 QB 450.

[63] The Occupiers' Liability Act 1984 replaced the harsh rules of common law that had traditionally been applied to trespassers. The difference in the child's protection is therefore equal to the discrepancy between the duties imposed by the 1957 and 1984 Acts.

[64] *Phipps v Rochester Corpn* [1955] 1 QB 450. However, it does not follow that the adult would be liable given that an accident can befall a child at any second: *Bourne Leisure Ltd v Marsden* [2009] 29 EG 99, at [17]–[21].

[65] *Christmas v General Cleaning Contractors Ltd* [1953] AC 180.

[66] See *Moon v Garrett* [2007] PIQR P3 (deliveryman injured by virtue of falling into an unguarded trench adjacent to the path).   [67] *Kealey v Heard* [1983] 1 All ER 973.

[68] *Eden v West & Co* [2002] EWCA Civ 991.

that the entrant's employer is under a duty to safeguard the visitor exonerate the occupier (though an occupier found liable in such a case can claim for contribution from the visitor's employer).[69]

Exceeding licence Another similarity between the duty of care owed under the ordinary law of negligence and the duty owed under the 1957 Act inheres in the fact that no duty is owed under the Act to those who use the premises in excess of their permission to be there. So, someone who was a lawful visitor to the shores of a lake on a hot day became a trespasser once he entered the water in order to swim, when swimming was prohibited.[70] By way of analogy, Scrutton LJ said: 'When you invite a person into your house to use the stairs, you do not invite him to slide down the banisters.'[71] Thus, there is 'no difference between a person who comes upon land without permission and one who, having come with permission, does something which he has not been given permission to do'.[72]

Differences One apparent, if questionable, difference between the common law and the duty owed under the 1957 Act is that the defendant's failure to discharge the common duty of care need not amount to negligent misfeasance. Thus, a football club that can anticipate crowd trouble from visiting supporters, yet fails to make the game all-ticket or ban those visiting supporters, might be liable still in respect of injuries sustained by a police officer when those supporters use loose pieces of concrete as projectiles.[73] But it is difficult to see why the failure of the football club to take preventive steps would not be actionable as common law negligence. Similar events had occurred at earlier games (making the injury to the police officer foreseeable) and the contractual nexus between the parties presumably would satisfy the proximity requirement.

A second difference between the common law and the duty owed under the 1957 Act inheres, as mentioned earlier, in the fact that, under sub-section 2(6) of the Act, those entering the occupier's premises by virtue of a right conferred by law will be afforded the common duty of care also. Importantly, this sub-section *does not* extend the notion of 'visitor' to such persons; it merely broadens the circumstances in which an entrant will be owed the common duty of care by providing that such persons are to be treated as if they were permitted by the occupier to be there for the purpose of exercising the specific right conferred by law.[74] By contrast, the common law of negligence does not afford special obligations to those exercising rights conferred by law.[75]

---

[69] *Lough v Intruder Detection and Surveillance Fire & Security Ltd* [2008] EWCA Civ 1009, at [13].
[70] *Tomlinson v Congleton BC* [2004] 1 AC 46.   [71] *The Carlgarth* [1927] P 93, at 110.
[72] *Tomlinson v Congleton BC* [2004] 1 AC 46, at [13]. Applied in *Maloney v Torfaen CBC* [2005] EWCA Civ 1762.   [73] *Cunningham v Reading Football Club* [1992] PIQR P141.
[74] *Greenhalgh v British Railways Board* [1969] 2 QB 286, at 292–3.
[75] See, eg, *White v CC of South Yorkshire Police* [1999] 2 AC 455.

(b) Warning

At common law, an occupier discharged his duty to a visitor by a warning sufficient to convey to the visitor full knowledge of the nature and extent of the danger. That rule was changed by sub-section 2(4)(a) of the 1957 Act which provides that:

> where damage is caused to a visitor by a danger of which he had been warned by the occupier, the warning is not to be treated without more as absolving the occupier from liability, unless in all the circumstances it was enough to enable the visitor to be reasonably safe.

In *Roles v Nathan*[76] Lord Denning provided a helpful example of where the mere provision of a warning would not discharge the duty under the 1957 Act. He suggested that simply warning visitors of the danger of a footbridge over a stream would be insufficient to ensure a visitor's safety if there were only one footbridge and it was essential to use it to enter the defendant's land. But he added that, if there were two bridges and one of them was safe, a warning about the unsafe bridge would then fulfil his duty.[77]

In line with the requirement that the warning must be sufficient to enable the visitor to be kept safe, a warning has been held to be ineffective also where it was very small in size and posted in an insufficiently prominent position.[78] On the other hand, if a warning is given, but ignored by the visitor—for example, where a customer fails to observe a shopkeeper's warning not to go to the far end of the shop because of a slippery floor—a court probably would hold that the common duty of care had been discharged. If the defendant does not know of the danger, he cannot rely on sub-section 2(4)(a) of the 1957 Act, although he might have a defence based on exclusion of liability (discussed later).[79]

(c) Assumption of risk

The common duty of care does not impose on an occupier any obligation to a visitor in respect of risks willingly accepted as his by the visitor. Under Occupiers' Liability Act 1957, sub-section 2(5) an occupier is not in breach of his duty of care where the claimant voluntarily assumed the risk.[80] So, for example, in *Staples v West Dorset District Council*,[81] damages were refused where the claimant slipped and was injured on the defendant council's algae-covered rocks of which he had full knowledge, and in respect of which it was proven that he would have ignored any warning had one been given.[82] Equally, actions will fail where they are based on mishaps caused either by swimming

---

[76] [1963] 2 All ER 908.   [77] [1963] 2 All ER 908, at 913.   [78] *D v AMF Bowling* [2002] 12 CL 476.

[79] *White v Blackmore* [1972] 2 QB 651.

[80] But note Unfair Contract Terms Act 1977, sub-s 2(3) (where occupier occupies premises for business purposes, agreement to contract term or awareness of notice excluding liability for negligence does not automatically indicate voluntary acceptance of risk). But the provision does not apply to consumer contracts or notices: sub-s (4) (as to which, see Consumer Rights Act 2015, ss 62 and 65 explained in ch 8).

[81] (1995) 93 LGR 536.

[82] In similar vein, see *Poppleton v Portsmouth Youth Activities Committee* [2009] PIQR P1.

in deep and murky ornamental ponds that are obviously perilous *for swimmers*, or by diving into shallow water.[83]

(d) Remoteness of damage

Jolley v Sutton London Borough Council[84] confirms that the same test for the remoteness of damage found in the ordinary law of negligence applies under the 1957 Act;[85] in order to recover damages, the claimant must be able to show that he suffered loss or injury of a kind that was reasonably foreseeable (as to which see Chapter 7).

(e) Contributory negligence

The Occupiers' Liability Act 1957, sub-section 2(3) provides that, in deciding whether the occupier has discharged his common duty of care, the want of care which ordinarily would be looked for in such a visitor is a relevant circumstance. In other words, the claimant cannot by his own carelessness enlarge the duty of care owed to him by the defendant. Therefore, it is implicit in sub-section 2(3) that the apportionment provisions of the Law Reform (Contributory Negligence) Act 1945 apply to an action for breach of the common duty of care in the same way that they do to any action for ordinary negligence.[86]

(f) Liability for independent contractors

General The Occupiers' Liability Act 1957, sub-section 2(4)(b), provides that, where damage is caused to a visitor by virtue of a danger attributable to the faulty execution of any work of construction, maintenance, or repair[87] by an independent contractor employed by the occupier, the occupier is not to be treated, without more,[88] as answerable for the danger if, in all the circumstances, he had acted reasonably in entrusting the work to an independent contractor and had taken such steps (if any) as he reasonably ought in order to satisfy himself that the contractor was competent and that the work had been done properly. Notably, the instances of defective construction, maintenance, and repair mentioned in sub-section 2(4)(b) are stated to be no more than examples

---

[83] See *Darby v National Trust* [2001] PIQR P372; *Tomlinson v Congleton BC* [2004] 1 AC 46. Note, however, that it has been held that there is nothing per se dangerous about lakes *for those on land: Tomlinson v Congleton BC* [2004] 1 AC 46. But for a very young child trespasser, unsteady on his feet and unable to swim, a lake might well constitute a danger. In *Donoghue v Folkestone Properties Ltd* [2003] QB 1008 the CA held that s 1 of the 1984 Act permits the court to take account of differences between adults and children who are non-visitors in deciding whether a duty is owed under the 1984 Act.

[84] [2000] 1 WLR 1082.

[85] The Court of Appeal categorised the harm—injury caused by an 'alluring', dangerous old boat that fell on to C—as too remote since the injury was caused in an unforeseeable way. HL overturned the decision, accepting that it was foreseeable that physical injury could arise from interference.

[86] Eg, *Bunker v Charles Brand & Son Ltd* [1969] 2 QB 480.

[87] This expression covers work incidental to construction and demolition work: see *AMF International Ltd v Magnet Bowling Ltd* [1968] 2 All ER 789; *Ferguson v Welsh* [1987] 3 All ER 777.

[88] In *Coupland v Eagle Bros Ltd* (1969) 210 EG 581, C was electrocuted by a live wire which the electrical contractor had not switched off while carrying out electrical work. D knew that the wire was dangerous and had not warned anyone. The 'without more' provision did not absolve him from liability, for he was concurrently careless with the contractor.

of the kinds of danger that can be attributed to independent contractors. Thus, where independent contractors run an amusement facility on the occupier's land, and that facility causes injury to a visitor, the occupier might be liable if he does not check the contractor's competence in just the same way as he would be liable if he failed to check, say, construction work—although only the latter is referred to in sub-section 2(4)(b).[89]

Reasonable delegation In applying sub-section 2(4)(b), the court must consider whether, initially, it was reasonable for the occupier to engage an independent contractor to undertake the construction, maintenance, or repair work. It is not obvious what this entails for it is difficult to envisage a situation in which the court would expect the occupier to have performed construction work himself in preference to engaging an independent contractor.[90] That being the case, we might be tempted to presume it reasonable for an occupier to engage a contractor wherever, as in *Haseldine v C A Daw & Son Ltd*,[91] the work to be done requires special skill or equipment not possessed by the occupier. Delegation should, at the very least, be reasonable where it is normal commercial practice to engage contractors for such work (for example, in undertaking office cleaning).

Checking for competence The Occupiers' Liability Act 1957 stipulates that the occupier *might* have to check the competence of the contractor. Here, again, it would seem that if the work is of a fairly standard nature the contractor may be trusted.[92] Where, however, the work entrusted to a contractor is of a kind that necessarily involves a risk to future visitors if it has been carelessly executed,[93] the occupier *will* be under a duty to check the competence of the contractor. Moreover, the occupier will need 'to take such steps as he reasonably ought (if any) in order to satisfy himself that . . . the work had been properly done'.[94] It is unclear from the statute whether this involves a subjective test or an objective one. If the test is subjective, limited financial resources might provide a sufficient reason for not engaging, say, an architect to assess the quality of the work. If the test is objective, the only relevant factor would be the degree of risk inherent in the kind of work done.

Supervision of work Since the Occupiers' Liability Act 1957 uses the past tense in relation to work done, it is clear that sub-section 2(4)(b) does not envisage the occupier employing a suitable professional to supervise the ongoing work of an independent contractor. Instead, it provides only an example of how the common duty of care

---

[89] *Gwilliam v West Hertfordshire Hospitals NHS Trust* [2002] 3 WLR 1425. Cf *Bottomley v Todmorden Cricket Club* [2003] EWCA Civ 1575.

[90] On the other hand, where the contractor is permitted to run a fairground concession which necessarily carries a risk of injury, the occupier might be required to check whether the contractor is properly insured: *Gwilliam v West Hertfordshire Hospitals NHS Trust* [2002] 3 WLR 1425.   [91] [1941] 2 KB 343.

[92] *Cook v Broderip* (1968) 206 EG 128.

[93] Eg, the careless repair of a lift clearly poses a risk to subsequent visitors. Here, D is under a duty 'to obtain and follow good technical advice': *Haseldine v Daw & Son Ltd* [1941] 2 KB 343, at 356.

[94] Occupiers' Liability Act 1957, sub-s 2(4)(b).

might be discharged. Thus, in some circumstances, it might be expected of the occupier that he will have the contractor's work supervised. In *AMF International Ltd v Magnet Bowling Ltd*,[95] it was said that if the occupier were to invite the claimant to bring valuable timber on to the site while construction work was ongoing, then to escape liability he might have to employ a supervising architect to ensure that the contractors had made the premises sufficiently safe for that timber to be brought there. On the other hand, it was said in *Ferguson v Welsh*[96] that normally an occupier will not be liable to the contractor's employee for injuries sustained because the premises were unsafe by virtue of the dangerous system of work adopted by the independent contractors. But if, according to Lord Keith, the occupier has reason to know that the contractor is using an unsafe system of work, he might be liable for not ensuring that a safe system was employed.[97]

(4) Some special cases falling within the Occupiers' Liability Act 1957

(a) Fixed or movable structures

The Occupiers' Liability Act 1957, sub-section 1(3) provides that:

> The rules so enacted in relation to an occupier of premises and his visitors shall also apply, in like manner and to the like extent as the principles applicable at common law to an occupier of premises and his invitees or licensees would apply, to regulate:
>
> (a) the obligations of a person occupying or having control over any fixed or movable structure, including any vessel, vehicle or aircraft . . .

It is clear that the term 'premises' is not confined simply to land: it includes permanent buildings erected on the land. Apart from vessels, vehicles, and aircraft, the term 'movable structures' covers such things as gangways and ladders. The test is probably whether one might go into or upon the structure. However, it is more difficult to interpret 'fixed structure', for this term presumably encompasses things not normally included within the other two terms. Thus, 'fixed structures' might be taken to connote non-movable chattels erected on land, such as docks,[98] garden sheds, and swings in a playground.

(b) Damage to property

The Occupiers' Liability Act 1957, sub-section 1(3) also covers:

> (b) the obligations of a person occupying or having control over any premises or structure in respect of damage to property, including the property of persons who are not themselves his visitors.

This sub-section imposes a duty on the occupier to prevent damage to goods on the premises arising from the defective physical condition of the premises. For example, the

---

[95] [1968] 2 All ER 789.   [96] [1987] 3 All ER 777, at 783.
[97] [1987] 3 All ER 777. Note, however, that any such liability would not arise qua occupier but rather qua joint tortfeasor with the contractor: see ibid at 786.
[98] See *Thomson v Cremin* [1956] 1 WLR 103 (ship-owner's responsibility for falling shore).

injured visitor would be able to recover damages for his torn clothes and presumably for damage to his property, even if he himself is uninjured.[99] But the expression 'damage to property'[100] does not cover loss of property so that the section does not cover the duty of boarding-house keepers to keep safe custody of visitors' goods. Still less will it reverse the common law decision that a publican owes no duty of care to prevent a customer's motorcycle from being stolen from the yard of the public house.[101] On the other hand, it seems consistent with what was said in section 1 that, whenever the occupier would have owed a duty at common law to prevent damage to goods on his land due to the state of the premises, the common duty of care applies.[102]

(c) Liability in contract

Implied term At common law, contracts for the use of premises were deemed to contain implied terms relating to the safety of the premises.[103] In lieu of those implied terms,[104] the Occupiers' Liability Act 1957, section 5 provides that:

> (1) Where persons enter or use, or bring or send goods to, any premises in exercise of a right conferred by contract with a person occupying or having control of the premises, the duty he owes them in respect of dangers due to the state of the premises or to things done or omitted to be done on them, in so far as the duty depends on a term to be implied in the contract by reason of its conferring that right, shall be the common duty of care.
>
> (2) The foregoing subsection shall apply to fixed and movable structures as it applies to premises.

The effect of this section is that, where a person enters the occupier's premises under a contract with the occupier, the occupier is obliged to extend the common duty of care to that entrant subject to any effective contractual term to the contrary.[105] Of course, it is open to the occupier specifically to increase the level of care by express contractual provision. And any such protection might extend to third parties where the terms of the Contracts (Rights of Third Parties) Act 1999 are satisfied.[106] On the other hand, the extent to which he is free to exclude or limit his responsibilities towards contractual entrants is governed by the operation of the rules discussed in section 3.

Election between causes The Occupiers' Liability Act 1957, section 5 is not limited in its operation to personal injury caused by the defective state of the occupier's premises; it covers damage to goods also. What was less clear is whether an action by a

---

[99] *AMF International Ltd v Magnet Bowling Ltd* [1968] 2 All ER 789.

[100] See P North (1966) 30 Conv 264. [101] *Tinsley v Dudley* [1951] 2 KB 18.

[102] Supported by *AMF International Ltd v Magnet Bowling Ltd* [1968] 2 All ER 789.

[103] See especially *Francis v Cockrell* (1870) LR 5 QB 501; *Gilmore v LCC* [1938] 4 All ER 331.

[104] The expression 'the duty . . . shall be the common duty of care' shows that the duty replaces, and is not merely alternative to, the terms implied at common law. [105] See, eg, *Maguire v Sefton* [2006] EWCA Civ 316.

[106] Under this legislation, there are three such conditions. First, it must be clear that the contract purports to confer a benefit on a third party (eg, the employee or contractor who has agreed to do work for the occupier); second, there must be no contrary agreement in the contract; third, the third party must be expressly identified in the contract: Contracts (Rights of Third Parties) Act 1999: sub-ss 1(1)(b), (2), and (3).

contractual entrant must be based solely on contract—on the basis of the term implied into the agreement by virtue of section 5—or whether he has the alternative of suing in tort. The matter was resolved in *Sole v W J Hallt Ltd*.[107] There, a tradesman who had come on to the occupier's premises to perform some plastering work was injured when he fell down an unprotected stairwell. Swanick J held that contractual entrants had the option of suing either in contract (under sub-section 5(1)), or in tort (under sub-section 2(1)).[108]

Contractual silence Another question not resolved by the Act is whether sub-section 5(1) operates where the contract is silent on the issue of the occupier's liability, but it is of a kind that traditionally attracted a different implied term at common law. An example would be a passenger on a railway platform who was protected at common law by a duty owed by the railway company to make the platform reasonably safe.[109] Others present on the platform, such as relatives saying farewell, were afforded the usual duty extended to licensees. But are fare-paying passengers now protected by the traditional common law implied term which, apart from the statute, would form part of the contract of carriage, or can they invoke only the common duty of care by virtue of sub-section 5(1)? It is submitted that the implied term under the Act applies since the statutory implied term is to be included in the contract *wherever* 'the duty depends upon *a term* to be implied in the contract'.

(5) Exclusion of liability

General The Occupiers' Liability Act 1957, sub-section 2(1) provides:

> An occupier of premises owes the same duty, the 'common duty of care', to all his visitors, except in so far as he is free to and does extend, restrict, modify or exclude his duty to any visitor or visitors by agreement or otherwise.

The occupier has two options if he wishes to modify the common duty of care owed to his visitors. First, where the visitor enters by virtue of a contract—for example, a contractor who enters to carry out work on premises—an express term of the contract may be drafted to govern the situation. Second, in respect of non-contractual entrants, a clear and unequivocal notice,[110] either affixed at the point of entry to the land,[111] or included in a programme or ticket providing access to it,[112] will suffice. However, these two broad options must be read subject to section 3 of the 1957 Act, which sets out limits on the occupier's freedom to limit or exclude his liability.

---

[107] [1973] 1 All ER 1032. *Quaere* the effect of any contributory negligence.

[108] This decision is almost certainly wrong since the Act specifically limits visitors (to whom the Occupiers' Liability Act 1957, sub-s 2(1) refers) to those who were either invitees or licensees at common law. The whole purpose of s 5 is to ensure some protection to contractual entrants where no such protection is mentioned in the contract. It is a decision at first instance and there is no obligation for any future court to follow it.

[109] *Protheroe v Railway Executive* [1951] 1 KB 376.

[110] Note the difference between a notice (excluding or restricting liability) and a warning (alerting entrants to a danger present on the premises).   [111] *Ashdown v Samuel Williams & Sons Ltd* [1957] 1 QB 409.

[112] *White v Blackmore* [1972] 2 QB 651.

Limits on exclusions The Occupiers' Liability Act 1957, sub-section 3(1) provides that the duty of care owed by an occupier to those visitors whom he is bound to admit on to his premises by virtue of a contract, who are nonetheless 'strangers to the contract',[113] cannot be excluded or restricted.[114] The provision is designed to ensure the protection of employees of the person with whom the occupier has a contract. Thus, if the occupier contracts with Y for Y's employees to do work on his premises, he may not restrict or exclude any liability to them. The sub-section provides also that any term of the contract obliging him to increase the level of care offered to such entrants will be effective in determining the standard of care to be shown.

Limit on liability The Occupiers' Liability Act 1957, sub-section 3(2) further provides:

> A contract shall not by virtue of this section have the effect, unless it expressly so provides, of making an occupier who has taken all reasonable care answerable to strangers to the contract for dangers due to the faulty execution of any work of construction, maintenance or repair or other like operation by persons other than himself, his servants and persons acting under his direction and control.

Heightened responsibility On reflection, it is apparent that the responsibility of the defendant under section 3 is greater than that imposed by the common duty of care because he is unable to delegate to independent contractors any part of his duty to take care.[115] Furthermore, while section 3 places some restrictions on the ability of an occupier to limit or exclude his liability, further restrictions upon his freedom to do so are imposed under the Unfair Contract Terms Act 1977. This later Act drastically reduces the ability of a person who occupies premises for 'business purposes' to exclude or restrict his liability.[116]

UCTA 1977 The Unfair Contract Terms Act 1977 renders invalid certain contract terms or notices purporting to exclude or restrict liability for death or personal injury[117] resulting from breach of the common duty of care under the Occupiers' Liability Act 1957, that is where the premises are occupied for the occupier's business purposes[118]

---

[113] Defined as 'a person not for the time being entitled to the benefit of the contract as a party to it or as the successor by assignment or otherwise of a party to it, and accordingly includes a party to the contract who has ceased to be so entitled': sub-s 3(3).

[114] A similar effect is achieved in relation to contractors who enter premises under a contract with the landlord, where the tenant has agreed with the landlord (extra-contractually) to allow such contractors to enter the premises.

[115] The duty in respect of independent contractors now imposed by sub-ss 3(1) and (2) is not exactly the same as the common duty of care imposed by sub-s 2(4)(b). First, sub-s 3(2) limits the liability not only in respect of, as in sub-s 2(4)(b), 'the faulty execution of any work of construction, maintenance or repair', but also in respect of any 'other like operation'. Second, whereas sub-s 2(4)(b) specifies in detail what would be reasonable care by the occupier in relation to the conduct of the independent contractor, sub-s 3(2) provides that he shall take 'all reasonable care' without further particularising this standard—it cannot simply be assumed that the two standards are identical.

[116] Note that the Unfair Contract Terms Act 1977 and Occupiers' Liability Act 1957, s 3 often work in tandem since most, if not all, s 3 cases are likely to involve an occupier for 'business purposes'.

[117] Unfair Contract Terms Act 1977, sub-s 2(1).   [118] Unfair Contract Terms Act 1977, sub-s 1(1)(c).

(except where a consumer transaction is involved).[119] In the case of other loss or damage, any contract term or notice designed to restrict or exclude liability is subject to the requirement of reasonableness[120] (except where a consumer transaction is involved).[121] If the exclusion is in the form of a contract term, its reasonableness is to be determined by reference to 'the circumstances which were, or ought reasonably to have been, known to or in the contemplation of the parties when the contract was made'.[122] If the exclusion of liability is in the form of a notice, its reasonableness is to be judged in the light of 'all the circumstances obtaining when the liability arose'.[123] Of the two tests, the one relating to notices is the more claimant-friendly, for 'all the circumstances' presumably include those both within and beyond the actual or imputed contemplation of the parties. The less claimant-friendly test applied to contract terms can be justified on the basis that, at the time of contracting, the claimant had the theoretical ability to reject the inclusion of any such term.

Agreement to, or knowledge of, the term or notice is not necessarily evidence that the visitor has assumed the risk of injury giving rise to the defence of *volenti non fit injuria*.[124] Equally, oral stipulation of any such term or notice, made at the time of the entrant's visit, will fail to render the entrant necessarily *volens*; for under the Unfair Contract Terms Act 1977, any such announcement constitutes a notice.[125]

Business purposes The Unfair Contract Terms Act 1977 clearly leaves an occupier free (via a notice on a front gate) to exclude liability to some of his visitors since its operation is limited to those entering in connection with business purposes[126] (except where a consumer transaction is involved).[127] In some cases it will be clear that the occupier's business purposes are in issue. Consider, for example, *Ashdown v Samuel Williams & Sons Ltd*:[128]

> By a licence granted by D, C crossed D's land. A notice board purported to curtail the liabilities of D to licensees. The Court of Appeal held that because D had taken reasonable steps to bring the conditions of the notice to the attention of C, these conditions (designed to exclude liability for damage sustained in the way in which C's injuries were caused) were effective in excluding D's liability. But if the case had arisen after 1977, D would not have been able to exclude liability under the Occupiers' Liability Act 1957.

But what would happen if the facts of *White v Blackmore*[129] were to recur? There, notices at the entrance to the racetrack and in the programme handed to spectators and competitors excluded liability for injuries occurring in jalopy races. The races were being run to raise money for charity. In 1972 the notices sufficed to exclude the organisers'

---

[119] Unfair Contract Terms Act 1977, sub-s (4). For such cases, see the topic 'CRA 2015' below.
[120] Unfair Contract Terms Act 1977, sub-s 2(2).
[121] Unfair Contract Terms Act 1977, sub-s (4). See the topic 'CRA 2015' below.
[122] Unfair Contract Terms Act 1977, sub-s 11(1).　　　[123] Unfair Contract Terms Act 1977, sub-s 11(3).
[124] Unfair Contract Terms Act 1977, sub-s 2(3).　　　[125] Unfair Contract Terms Act 1977, sub-s 14.
[126] Section 14 of the 1977 Act defines 'business' so as to include 'a profession and the activities of any government department or public or local authority'.
[127] Unfair Contract Terms Act 1977, sub-s (4). See the topic 'CRA 2015' below.　　　[128] [1957] 1 QB 409.
[129] [1972] 2 QB 651.

and occupiers' liability. Today, a preliminary question would be whether the track was occupied for business purposes.

The only further attempt at clarification of the definition of 'business purposes' is to be found in the Occupiers' Liability Act 1984, section 2, which amends the Unfair Contract Terms Act 1977 to provide:

> but liability of an occupier of premises for breach of an obligation or duty toward a person obtaining access to the premises for recreational or educational purposes, being liability for loss or damage suffered by reason of the dangerous state of premises is not a business liability of the occupier unless granting that person such access for the purposes concerned falls within the business purposes of the occupier.[130]

The purpose of this provision appears to be to allow farmers and owners of countryside areas to exclude liability to day-trippers. The land is occupied for 'business purposes': namely, farming or forestry. But any duty owed to entrants coming to the land to have a picnic and so on can be excluded by agreement or notice nonetheless.

CRA 2015 In cases where persons enter premises pursuant to a consumer transaction, the UCTA 1977 provisions just examined do not apply. Instead, the ability of the occupier to exclude liability by way of contract or notice is governed by provisions in the Consumer Rights Act 2015,[131] which were explained when examining defences to negligence in chapter 8.

(B) The Occupiers' Liability Act 1984

(1) Scope of the Act

Liability to trespassers and all other uninvited entrants (such as those using a private right of way)[132] is governed by the Occupiers' Liability Act 1984, section 1 of which provides that the Act:

> shall have effect in place of the rules of common law[133] to determine—
>
> (a) whether any duty is owed by a person as occupier of premises to persons other than his visitors in respect of any risk of their suffering injury on the premises by reason of any danger due to the state of the premises or to things done or omitted to be done on them;
>
> (b) if so, what that duty is.

Although the Occupiers' Liability Act 1984 replaces the rules of common law in relation to an occupier's liability towards uninvited entrants, three exceptional instances fall outside the Act. First, sub-section 1(8) expressly confines liability to personal injuries.

---

[130] Unfair Contract Terms Act 1977, sub-s 1(3)(b).
[131] Consumer Rights Act 2015, ss 62 and 65. See also Consumer Rights Act 2015, sub-s 66(4).
[132] See, eg, *Vodden v Gayton* [2001] PIQR P52.
[133] As to which see *British Railways Board v Herrington* [1972] AC 877.

It follows that the common law rules in respect of damage to a trespasser's (or other uninvited entrant's) personal property survive the enactment. Second, the Act's remit is limited in that the occupier of the *solum* of a public right of way owes no obligation to persons using that right of way.[134] (However, it is arguable that since the Act specifically provides that nothing in its provisions affects any duty otherwise owed to such persons, users of public rights of way are owed the duty of common humanity formulated in *British Railways Board v Herrington*.)[135] Finally, it was held in *Revill v Newbery*[136] that acts of the occupier that are not done in connection with its occupation fall outside the purview of the Act. Put otherwise, liability for acts not affecting the safety of the premises is to be determined according to the common law.[137]

(2) Conditions of liability

Three conditions The 1984 Act is predicated upon a presumption that no duty of care is owed by an occupier to uninvited entrants. An obligation to such persons in respect of any danger due to the state of the premises arises only when three conditions are met.[138] First, the occupier must be aware of the danger or have reasonable grounds to believe it exists. Second, he must have known, or had reasonable grounds to know, that the uninvited entrant either was in, or might come into, the vicinity of the danger. (So, where occupiers had no reason to expect that trespassers were taking shortcuts across their land, no duty arose.[139] And where a trespasser decides to go swimming in a harbour at midnight in mid-winter, the occupier has no reason to suppose that he will be there.)[140] Third, the risk of injury to an uninvited entrant resulting from that danger was one against which, in all the circumstances, the occupier might reasonably be expected to offer the uninvited entrant some protection.

Objective and subjective elements At first sight, the test for the existence of the duty of care imposed by the 1984 Act appears to comprise a mixture of objective and subjective elements. The first and second limbs ostensibly contain both in referring not only to the *individual occupier's* actual knowledge, but also to that knowledge which he ought reasonably to have. However, it has been held that even the second part of the test contains a subjective element. That is, the occupier either must have actual knowledge of the danger and of the presence of a non-visitor *or* must have actual knowledge of the relevant facts from which a reasonable person would draw the relevant inference (even if he does not himself draw that inference).[141] If he knows neither of the danger, nor of the state of affairs, then he will not be liable just because a reasonable occupier would have known of that state of affairs. A landowner who seldom looks around his grounds,

---

[134] Occupiers' Liability Act 1984, sub-s 1(7).
[135] [1972] AC 877. See further J Murphy (1997) 61 Conv 362.   [136] [1996] 1 All ER 291.
[137] However, in *Revill v Newbury* it was said that, for the purposes of the common law, the same principles as those contained in the Occupiers' Liability Act 1984 should be applied: [1996] 1 All ER 291, at 298.
[138] Occupiers' Liability Act 1984, sub-s 1(3).
[139] *White v St Albans City and DC* (1990) *Times*, 12 March.
[140] *Donoghue v Folkestone Properties Ltd* [2003] QB 1008.
[141] *Swain v Natui Ram Puri* [1996] PIQR P442.

and fails to notice the emergence of a danger, could not be held liable, whereas the sub-section would catch a landowner who regularly surveys his premises and turns a blind eye to an obvious source of danger.[142] The third limb is mainly objective in nature, emphasising all the circumstances of the case. However it does not constitute an *entirely* objective test since it demands only that level of protection which reasonably can be expected of the particular occupier.[143] For these purposes, the personal characteristics of the occupier and the limits on his financial resources may be taken as relevant.

(3) Reasonable care

As already noted, sub-section 1(4) of the 1984 Act provides for an obligation 'to take such care as is reasonable in all the circumstances of the case'. Thus, the occupier of an electricity substation is entitled to assume trespassers will not attempt to gain unauthorised entry by scaling both a 13-foot wall and 7-foot spike railings rather than by climbing over a locked metal gate.[144] Relevant circumstances will include the age and capabilities of the entrant,[145] so that greater protection needs to be shown to a child than to an adult trespasser where the danger concerned would be more apparent to the latter than the former.[146] Similarly, the entrant's purpose might be relevant, so that a burglar can expect less by way of protection than, say, an 'innocent' child trespasser.[147] On the other hand, where a burglar is injured because of a negligent act on the part of the occupier, the common law still affords him a remedy. Thus, in *Revill v Newbery* a burglar whom the defendant negligently shot could sue the occupier in negligence even though the case fell outside the 1984 Act.[148]

(4) Effect of warning

General A significant difference between the Occupiers' Liability Act 1984 and the Occupiers' Liability Act 1957 exists in sub-section 1(5) of the later legislation. There it is stipulated that any duty arising under the Occupiers' Liability Act 1984 can 'be discharged by taking such steps as are reasonable in all the circumstances of the case to give warning of the danger concerned or to discourage a person from incurring the risk'. Unlike the position under the 1957 Act, the warning need not enable the uninvited entrant to be or remain safe on the land. If the occupier of a building site with dangerous concealed trenches puts up notices[149] around the perimeter of the site saying 'Danger: Concealed Trench', this would be insufficient to discharge the occupier's duty towards his visitors. But since they make specific mention of 'the danger concerned', as

---

[142] In *Swain v Natui Puri* [1996] PIQR P442, the court added the gloss that an occupier cannot be heard to say that he had deliberately shut his eyes to dangers on his land in order to escape liability: knowledge of glaringly obvious dangers will be imputed to him.

[143] This interpretation seems to be borne out by *Ratcliff v McConnell* [1999] 1 WLR 670, at 680.

[144] *Mann v Northern Electric Distribution Ltd* [2010] EWCA Civ 141.

[145] See *Ratcliff v McConnell* [1999] 1 WLR 670.   [146] *Ratcliff v McConnell* [1999] 1 WLR 670, at 683.

[147] See also *Murphy v Culhane* [1977] QB 94, at 98, where Lord Denning MR suggested *obiter* that the defence of *ex turpi causa* might be available.

[148] The court also refused to entertain D's claim that the defence of *ex turpi causa* should apply.

[149] Note that the Unfair Contract Terms Act 1977 does not apply to the duty created by the 1984 Act and therefore has no impact on the efficacy of such notices so far as they seek to exclude liability.

the Act demands, they would suffice vis-à-vis an uninvited adult entrant.[150] The fact that a warning notice has been read by an uninvited entrant, of itself, will not render that person *volens*,[151] but the Act does provide for the operation of a very similar defence in this context:

> No duty is owed by virtue of this section to any person in respect of risks willingly accepted as his by that person (the question of whether a risk was so accepted to be decided on the same principles as in other cases in which one person owes a duty of care to another).[152]

Obvious dangers There need be no warning of obvious dangers, such as those associated with diving head first into the shallow end of a swimming pool.[153] Whether a danger is obvious or not might vary according to whether the non-visitor is an adult or a child. But just because a non-visitor is a child does not mean that—even allowing for his lesser appreciation of danger—it will never be appropriate in respect of children to treat a given risk as obvious. Obviousness is a question of fact and degree and it is wrong simply to treat all dangers as non-obvious on the basis of a claimant's immaturity.[154]

(5) Limit on liability

As already noted, by virtue of sub-section 1(8) of the 1984 Act, non-visitors are not entitled to sue in respect of property damage occasioned by breach of the duty in section 1. Accordingly, a trespasser who, due to the perilous state of the premises, trips and falls on the occupier's land while snooping about may sue under the Act in respect of his personal injuries but not for the damage caused to his camera.[155]

(6) Rights of way

General Finally, we must consider the provisions inserted into the Occupiers' Liability Act 1984 by the Countryside and Rights of Way Act 2000. As we noted when considering the 1957 Act, those exercising a right of access to open land for recreational purposes under sub-section 2(1) of the 2000 Act are excluded from the category, 'visitors'.[156] Instead, they are non-visitors and are owed a limited duty only under the Occupiers' Liability Act 1984.

---

[150] In relation to an illiterate young child who is allured on to the premises, it is less likely that such a notice would suffice. In any event, he might be classified as a visitor by implied licence.

[151] *Titchener v British Railways Board* [1983] 3 All ER 770.

[152] Occupiers' Liability Act 1984, sub-s 1(6). The difference between this statutory version of *volenti* and its common law cousin lies in the fact that at common law, C, to be *volens*, must accept both the risk of injury *and* the fact that any resulting loss should be his own. Under the 1984 Act, D can raise the defence in sub-s 1(6) on proof of the former alone. Furthermore, properly understood, *volenti* is to be confined to the assumption of risk in relation to future rather than extant dangers: *Morris v Murray* [1991] 2 QB 6, at 17, 28, and 32.

[153] *Ratcliff v McConnell* [1999] 1 WLR 670. On the other hand, the fact that someone takes such foolhardy action does not negate the existence of a duty to take reasonable steps to prevent such persons from doing those things: *Tomlinson v Congleton BC* [2004] 1 AC 46.

[154] *Keown v Coventry Healthcare NHS Trust* [2006] 1 WLR 953 (11-year-old *volens* in respect of dangers of climbing the exterior of a fire escape).

[155] However, he might have an action based on the common law, which remains untouched by the Act in respect of property damage.   [156] Occupiers' Liability Act 1957, sub-s 1(4)(a).

Extent of obligation In determining the obligation owed to those entering the occupier's land on this basis, regard must be had to 'the fact that the existence of that right ought not to place an undue burden (whether financial or otherwise) on the occupier [and to] . . . the importance of maintaining the character of the countryside'.[157] Indeed, the occupier's obligation generally will be excluded in the circumstances governed by the Occupiers' Liability Act 1984, sub-section 1(6A),[158] that is, where there is:

(a) a risk resulting from the existence of any natural feature of the landscape, or any river, stream, ditch or pond whether or not a natural feature, or

(b) a risk of [the claimant] suffering injury when passing over, under or through any wall, fence or gate, except by proper use of the gate or of a stile.

It could be argued that these provisions could be interpreted as conferring greater protection on a trespasser than on someone exercising their right to roam since claims by those exercising the right to roam are barred where their injury results from a natural feature of the landscape, etc. But, in practice, this might do no more than reflect the law as it stands under the 1984 Act. Take, for example, *Tomlinson v Congleton Borough Council*.[159] A trespasser was injured in a lake under the control of the defendant council. But it was held that the council did not owe a duty of care by virtue of section 1 of the 1984 Act as there was no especial danger on the occupier's land, lakes not being inherently dangerous. As Lord Hoffmann put it: '[t]here were no hidden dangers. It was shallow in some places and deep in others, but that is the nature of lakes.'[160]

Suppose the facts were substantially to recur in connection with a lake in the countryside that constituted a natural feature of the land. Any claim based on injury associated with that lake would fail on the basis of sub-section 1(6A). All that the provision has achieved is the same result as in the *Tomlinson* case via a different route (albeit a more certain route that provides occupiers with some degree of reassurance that they need not be especially careful in respect of those exercising the right to roam). It eliminates the need for the occupier to argue that, taking account of 'all the circumstances of the case'—one of which presumably would be that, if the lake happened to be located in an area of natural beauty (which typically attract those exercising the right to roam), it would have been unreasonable to expect him to undermine or diminish the beauty of the land by erecting artificial fences, warning signs, and the like.[161]

The only exceptions to the general exclusion of liability under sub-section 1(6A) of the Occupiers' Liability Act 1984 are those set out in sub-section 1(6C). These relate to dangers either intentionally or recklessly created by the occupier. These exceptions are

---

[157] Occupiers' Liability Act 1984, sub-ss 1A(a), (b).
[158] Inserted by the Countryside and Rights of Way Act 2000, sub-s 13(2).   [159] [2004] 1 AC 46.
[160] [2004] 1 AC 46, at [26].
[161] *Tomlinson v Congleton BC* [2004] 1 AC 46 held that it would have been unreasonable to turn the sandy beaches by the side of the lake that featured in that case into marshland at the cost of the enjoyment of thousands of people who used the beaches for sunbathing. As Lord Hobhouse observed (at [81]): '[it] should never be the policy of the law to require the protection of the foolhardy or reckless few to deprive, or interfere with, the enjoyment by the remainder of society.'

likely to be of little practical significance because there are likely to be few deliberately or recklessly created perils in the countryside in locations that tend to attract walkers. On the other hand, it is not clear why liability remains excluded in relation to reckless omissions to eliminate dangers that occur otherwise than by the occupier's own creation. If, for example, on a known crumbling cliff-top a favourite viewing point reaches the point of imminent collapse, there is no liability for a failure to address that danger.

(C) Common law liability and activities on land

1957 Act An occupier who intentionally harms a person whom he has permitted to be on his premises is answerable for so doing under the law of battery considered in chapter 10. But in addition, the occupier might be under an obligation in the ordinary law of negligence to take reasonable care when conducting certain activities on his land that foreseeably are likely to harm visitors of whose presence he is, or ought to be, aware.[162]

The scope for the residual role of the common law stems from the wording of section 1 of the 1957 Act, providing, first, that the Act 'shall have effect, in place of the rules of common law, to regulate the duty which an occupier of premises owes to visitors in respect of dangers due to the state of the premises *or to things done* or omitted to be done on them'.[163] If it went no further, it would seem that activities—such as driving one's car on the land—would fall within the Act. But it does not stop there: it goes on to provide that the statutory rules also 'regulate the nature of the duty imposed by law *in consequence of a person's occupation or control* of premises'.[164] Therefore, it is arguable that activities on the land that are performed otherwise than as a *consequence* of occupation fall beyond the statute. Thus, driving a tractor on a farm might fall within the Act on the basis that tractor driving will be a normal (and, thus, consequential) act performed by the occupier of a modern arable farm. By contrast, riding a bicycle on the farm could well be seen as an act that is anything but naturally ancillary or incidental to farm occupation.

The fact that there probably is a small residual role for the common law in relation to visitors is doubtless a largely academic point since, as noted earlier, there is very little difference between the common duty of care imposed under the Act and the standard of care demanded by the ordinary law of negligence.

1984 Act So far as the Occupiers' Liability Act 1984 is concerned, however, there are no words equivalent to those located in the 1957 legislation, which might be construed to exclude statutory liability in respect of activities performed on the land. As regards the physical injury of non-visitors, therefore, the pre-existing common law has not survived the passage of the 1984 Act.[165]

---

[162] In *Chettle v Denton* (1951) 95 Sol Jo 802 (D, while shooting game on private land, hit C who was a licensee on the land; D was held liable in negligence in that he would have seen C if he had taken reasonable care).

[163] Occupiers' Liability Act 1957, sub-s 1(1) (emphasis added).

[164] Occupiers' Liability Act 1957, sub-s 1(2) (emphasis added).

[165] See, eg, *Scott v Associated British Ports* 2000 WL 1741511 (youths injured when 'surfing' a ride on a slow-moving goods train).

(D) Liability to those outside one's premises

General The dangers caused by the defective state of premises are not confined to entrants to those premises. Slates falling from roofs, crumbling walls, and dangerous activities carried out on premises are examples of risks just as likely to endanger passers-by and those on adjoining premises. Therefore, the circumstances in which the occupier of premises owes an obligation to such persons require brief consideration. As will be seen in chapter 17, an action in public nuisance sometimes lies in respect of injuries or loss caused on a highway as a result of harmful conditions on adjoining land. But a claimant might just as well sue for personal injuries in negligence in such cases.[166] Furthermore, occupiers are under a general duty to take reasonable care to prevent dangers on their premises damaging persons or property on adjoining premises.[167] This is so whether the danger arises from the disrepair of the premises, or some man-made or natural hazard such as fire caused by lightning striking a tree.[168] Also, where adjoining properties have mutual rights of support, negligently allowing one property to fall into dereliction so as to damage the adjoining premises is actionable in negligence as well as in private nuisance.[169]

Actions against landlords There are two difficult issues affecting the duties of care owed by the occupiers of adjoining premises. First, where a claimant tenant sues his landlord for damage resulting from the defective state of repair of premises retained by the landlord, the case law is confused. Take first *Cunard v Antifyre Ltd*:[170]

> Some defective roofing and guttering, forming part of the premises retained by D, a landlord, fell into a part of the premises let by him to C. As a result, C's wife was injured and C's goods were damaged. Damages in negligence were awarded to both C and his wife.

By contrast, in *Cheater v Cater*[171] the Court of Appeal held that a landlord, who had let a field to a tenant at a time when there was a yew tree on the adjoining premises retained by the landlord, was not liable in negligence when the tenant's horse died through eating leaves from the tree, which was then in just the same state as at the date of the lease. Then, in *Shirvell v Hackwood Estates Co Ltd*,[172] the court doubted *Cunard v Antifyre Ltd*, holding that the workman of a tenant could not recover in negligence from the landlord whose tree on adjoining land fell on him. Finally, came *Taylor v Liverpool Corpn*.[173]

> C, the daughter of a tenant of one of D's flats, was injured by the fall of a chimney stack belonging to these flats into the yard adjoining the premises. D had negligently maintained this chimney, which formed part of the building retained by D.

Stable J found for the claimant in negligence, and did so following *Cunard v Antifyre Ltd* while distinguishing *Cheater v Cater* on the ground that the tenant there had impliedly

---

[166] Eg, *Hilder v Associated Portland Cement Manufacturers Ltd* [1961] 3 All ER 709.
[167] *Hughes v Percival* (1883) 8 App Cas 443.   [168] *Goldman v Hargrave* [1967] 1 AC 645.
[169] *Bradburn v Lindsay* [1983] 2 All ER 408.   [170] [1933] 1 KB 551.
[171] [1918] 1 KB 247 (not cited in *Cunard v Antifyre Ltd*).   [172] [1938] 2 KB 577, at 594–5.
[173] [1939] 3 All ER 329.

agreed to take the risk in respect of danger existing on the premises at that time. The observations in *Shirvell's* case were treated as *obiter* on the basis that no negligence had occurred. In any case, the principle in *Cunard v Antifyre Ltd* would appear to be preferable to the one which affords landlords blanket immunity in respect of retained premises in a state of disrepair.[174]

Damage by third parties The second area of difficulty in delimiting the obligation owed by an occupier to those on adjoining premises relates to damage inflicted on those adjoining premises by third parties. Generally, no duty will be found to lie where vandals or burglars inflict damage on a neighbour's property,[175] even though the wrongdoers' conduct might have been facilitated by a state of disrepair or lax security on the defendant occupier's premises.[176] This approach is in line with the general reluctance on the part of the courts to impose liability on a person who has no special relationship with the relevant third party, for the conduct of that third party.

Section 3 Liability of non-occupiers

An occupier of premises might have immediate control over the state of those premises and the capacity to repair defects in them, but in a number of instances—particularly in relation to structural defects—nothing he has done will have caused the relevant defect. Cracks in a house resulting from inadequate foundations often will be the result of the negligence of the builder and might endanger the occupier as much as any visitor to the property. Parliament passed the Defective Premises Act in 1972 in order to impose on persons providing dwellings a limited responsibility to subsequent purchasers and their families, and to clarify the responsibilities of landlords.

(A) The Defective Premises Act 1972

Primacy of legislation One key feature of *Murphy v Brentwood District Council*[177] (discussed in chapter 4) is that courts should not seek to impose common law rules of liability when Parliament has spoken via the Defective Premises Act 1972. Since *Murphy*, therefore, the primacy of the 1972 Act cannot be doubted, especially since, under sub-section 6(3), its provisions are non-derogable.

Obligation The Defective Premises Act 1972, section 1 imposes on any 'person taking on work for or in connection with the provision of a dwelling' a strict liability to ensure that the work he takes on is 'done in a workmanlike, or, as the case may be, professional manner, with proper materials and so that as regards that work the dwelling will be fit

---

[174] It is submitted that the CA thought wrongly in *Shirvell's* case that the decisions where landlords with no control of defective premises had been held not liable applied in the case before them.

[175] In *P Perl (Exporters) Ltd v Camden LBC* [1984] QB 342 the court did not entirely rule out special circumstances which might give rise to such a duty to adjoining occupiers.

[176] *Smith v Littlewoods Organisation Ltd* [1987] AC 241.   [177] [1990] 2 All ER 908.

for habitation when completed'.[178] Thus, a builder who, reasonably believing that his materials were suitable, used asbestos in roofing materials at a time before the dangers of asbestos were appreciated, still would be in breach of his duty under section 1. The provision covers all those involved in building new homes: from builders and contractors, to architects and developers.[179]

Limits of obligation The Defective Premises Act 1972 is subject to certain restrictions. First, dwellings built under an 'approved scheme' are exempted from the strict liability regime.[180] Second, the limitation period under the 1972 Act begins to run as soon as the dwelling is completed, which might be a considerable time prior to a structural defect manifesting itself. (Defects in foundations, for example, usually take a long time to appear.)[181] By contrast, the limitation period in a negligence action begins to run only when the claimant reasonably should have known of the relevant damage (subject to a long-stop of 15 years after which any action in respect of property damage is barred completely).[182]

Further provisions Further provisions in the Defective Premises Act 1972—in particular sections 3 and 4 concerning the survival of a duty of care after disposal of the premises, and landlords' duties of care where there is an obligation to repair—are also of importance, as we shall see later.[183]

(B) Builders and contractors: physical damage

Current occupiers A builder or contractor actually engaged in construction or repair work on land and premises affixed to that land owes a duty of care[184] to the occupier of the premises, his visitors, and probably to trespassers as well where their presence is foreseeable.[185] Any universal exemption from a duty of care in respect of real property did not survive *AC Billings & Sons Ltd v Riden*,[186] where building contractors were employed to make an alteration to the front part of a house. In the course of this work, the contractors failed to take reasonable care to make access to the house safe and a visitor, Riden, was injured when leaving the house in the hours of darkness. The contractors were held liable in negligence.

---

[178] The section applies to omissions as much as to acts: *Andrews v Schooling* [1991] 3 All ER 723; but it is confined to defects rendering the dwelling (not commercial properties) uninhabitable: *Thompson v Clive Alexander and Partners* (1992) 59 BLR 81.

[179] See the Defective Premises Act 1972, sub-s 1(3) (including local authorities). The fact that all such persons might be liable creates the potential for difficulties in establishing causation. The test to be applied is whether D's breach of the section is a 'significant cause' of the unfitness of the dwelling: *Bayoumi v Protim Services Ltd* [1996] EGCS 187.   [180] Defective Premises Act 1972, s 2.

[181] For an example of the theoretical scope of s 1 made futile by the limitation provisions, see *Rimmer v Liverpool CC* [1985] QB 1.   [182] Under the Latent Damage Act 1986.

[183] See ss 3(B) and 3(F).   [184] *Miller v South of Scotland Electricity Board* 1958 SC (HL) 20.

[185] The contractor might also be the occupier, in which case his liability to trespassers will be governed by the Occupiers' Liability Act 1984. In other circumstances ordinary principles of negligence apply: *Railway Comr v Quinlan* [1964] AC 1054.   [186] [1958] AC 240.

Subsequent occupiers Later decisions held the original builders of a property liable for personal injury (or physical damage to other property) resulting from the negligent construction or repair of buildings both to subsequent occupiers and to their visitors.[187] Thus, if the defendant contractor negligently erects an unsafe roof which later collapses injuring the occupier and his dinner guests, the victims have a claim against the contractor for those injuries. And, if the collapse of the roof also smashes the windows in the adjoining house, the neighbours may sue the contractor also.

Caveat emptor eroded The fact that the landowner also was the builder affords him no immunity from liability in negligence. Most of the content of the maxim *caveat emptor* in relation to the sale of land in this context has been eroded: '[a] landowner who designs or builds a house or flat is no more immune from personal responsibility for faults of construction than a building contractor, or from personal responsibility than an architect, simply because he has disposed of his house or flat by selling or letting'.[188]

Repairs The above-stated principle covers only negligence in the original construction of the building, not inadequate repairs or maintenance conducted by the original owner and vendor. However, the Defective Premises Act, section 3 provides that where:

> work of construction, repair, maintenance or demolition or any other work is done on or in relation to premises, any duty of care owed because of the doing of the work to persons who might reasonably be expected to be affected by defects in the state of the premises by the doing of the work shall not be abated by the subsequent disposal of the premises by the person who owed the duty.

Thus, a botched job in repairing floorboards will create liability to visitors while the owner remains the occupier; and that liability survives for the benefit of subsequent occupiers and their visitors when the owner sells or lets the house.

Omissions But section 3 of the 1972 Act is not comprehensive because it does not cover all possible sources of danger on premises, particularly those caused by omissions. Leaving dangerous refuse on premises and failing to remedy or warn the subsequent occupier about a ruinous defect existing before the vendor came into occupation probably are not covered by the words 'work of construction, repair, maintenance or demolition or any other work'. Thus, the common law principle that there is no duty not to sell or let a ruinous house probably survives, albeit in attenuated form.

Crux of rule It is suggested that the crucial point today is not whether the defendant contractor was the landowner but, rather, what kind of damage resulted from his negligence. If actual physical injury to some person, or separate property, is inflicted as a consequence of his incompetence, that injury is likely to be recoverable just as it would be if the 'guilty' cause of the injury were a negligently manufactured chattel.[189]

---

[187] *Sharpe v ET Sweeting & Sons Ltd* [1963] 2 All ER 455.
[188] *Rimmer v Liverpool CC* [1984] 1 All ER 930, at 938.   [189] See *Murphy v Brentwood DC* [1991] 1 AC 398.

(C) Builders and contractors: other loss

Special relationship No duty of care will be imposed on a builder or contractor in respect of financial loss occasioned by negligent work of construction or repair, save where some 'special relationship' is found to exist between him and the claimant. Thus, developers and contractors owe no obligation in tort in respect of financial losses occasioned to subsequent occupiers of property with whom they have no contractual relationship. *D & F Estates Ltd v Church Commissioners for England*[190] is illustrative:

> D built a block of flats later occupied by C. Crumbling plasterwork caused by D's negligence forced C to expend considerable sums of money on repairs. The House of Lords found that D was not liable for C's loss. By analogy with liability for chattels, D owed a duty to safeguard C against physical damage to person or property caused by negligent construction of the property, but not against loss caused by a defect in the quality of the property itself.

Recoverable physical damage is that which is occasioned to separate property.[191] Damage to the property itself was a mere defect in quality—the property was simply not value for money.

***Murphy* case** Some of the questions left open in *D & F Estates* were answered by the House of Lords in *Murphy v Brentwood District Council*.[192] The *Murphy* case, strictly speaking, relates to the liability of local authorities, but its applicability to builders and contractors was confirmed in *Department of the Environment v Thomas Bates & Son Ltd*.[193] The facts were as follows:

> C had purchased from a construction company a semi-detached dwelling constructed on a concrete raft foundation over an in-filled site. Eleven years later, C noticed cracks in the house which proved to be caused by serious defects in the concrete raft. Repairs which were essential to make the house safe and habitable would have cost £45,000. C could not afford that sum and had to sell the house for £35,000 less than he would have received but for the damage caused by the defective foundations. C sued the local council, whom he alleged had negligently approved the plans for the foundations.

The House of Lords rejected his claim, classifying the damage he suffered as irrecoverable financial loss. When the claimant argued that the nature of the damage to his home posed an immediate and imminent danger to his and his family's health, the Law Lords dismissed that contention as irrelevant since the loss was purely financial. Lord Bridge described the distinction between physical damage and financial loss in this way:[194]

> If a builder erects a structure containing a latent defect which renders it dangerous to persons or property, he will be liable in tort for injury to persons or property resulting from that dangerous defect. But, if the defect becomes apparent before any injury or damage has been caused, the loss sustained by the building owner is purely economic.

---

[190] [1989] AC 177.
[191] See *Bellefield Computer Services Ltd v E Turner & Sons Ltd* [2000] BLR 97. Cf *Baxall Securities Ltd v Sheard Walshaw Partnership* [2001] PNLR 257. [192] [1990] 2 All ER 908.
[193] [1990] 2 All ER 908. [194] [1990] 2 All ER 908, at 926.

Effect of *Murphy* The effect of *Murphy* would seem to be this. Outside a contractual relationship, negligent construction (and presumably repair and extension) of a building results in liability only if actual physical damage is caused to a person or property that is not part of the building. Thus, if defective foundations cause cracks in the walls or threaten damage to any fixture in the building installed by the defendant, the cost of remedying the damage is irrecoverable financial loss. By contrast, if A negligently installs a defective central heating boiler in a building erected by B but which is later bought and occupied by C, and then later still that boiler explodes damaging the building, that loss is recoverable by C against A. A's negligence has caused actual damage to property quite separate from the inherently defective component he installed.

Adjoining land In the *Murphy* case, Lord Bridge suggested a new exception to the general refusal of recovery for financial loss. He said that, where the defect in the building requiring repair threatens damage to adjoining land or the highway:

> the building owner ought, in principle, to be entitled to recover in tort from the negligent builder the cost of demolition, so far as that cost is necessarily incurred in order to protect himself from potential liability to third parties.[195]

This latter proposition does not withstand scrutiny. If one may recover that financial loss occasioned by the need to ensure one's crumbling house does not damage a neighbour's house or crash on to a passer-by on the highway, why is one not able to recover the loss occasioned by the need to ensure that one does not incur similar liability to one's visitors?[196]

Uninhabitable premises Leaving aside the case of purely financial loss, it has also been held, in *Smith v Drumm*,[197] that builders are liable under the Defective Premises Act, section 1 if their work leaves the premises in a state that is not fit for habitation. In this case, the converted flat was left without either electricity or gas and deemed unfit for habitation. Had the work been rectification work (instead of 'construction, conversion or enlargement', in the words of the Act), no duty would have been owed under section 1.[198]

(D) Professional advisers

The strict liability imposed by the Defective Premises Act, section 1 in respect of the construction of buildings is equally incumbent on architects and other professionals involved in the design of the building. Additionally, those professionals owe a duty of care to any

---

[195] [1990] 2 All ER 908.
[196] One difference is that I could 'obviate' that danger by having no visitors. Another is that I could reasonably warn my visitors; but I could not, for example, practicably warn all passers-by who walk beneath a dangerous overhanging gable.   [197] [1996] EGCS 192.
[198] *Jacobs v Morton & Partners* (1994) 72 BLR 92.

person injured on the site in the course of the building work,[199] and to subsequent occupiers of the premises in respect of both their personal safety and damage to property separate from the premises themselves. The reasoning in the *Murphy* case relating to builders applies equally to architects and engineers. Thus, these professionals will not be liable in tort for financial loss arising from the defective nature of the building whether that loss takes the form of the cost of repairs or the diminution in the value of the property.

On subsequent disposal of the premises, surveyors engaged to inspect the property will be liable for any failure to value the property competently or to discover and report on relevant defects in the property. Where the surveyor has been engaged by the building society which is contemplating financing the claimant's house purchase, he will be liable generally, not only to his client (that is, the building society), but to the purchasers also where they have relied on his survey rather than commissioned an independent surveyor.[200] However, where a surveyor is commissioned only to value property, he is not under a duty to report on defects generally, or to advise on possible difficulties with resale of the property.[201]

(E) Local authorities

Local authorities owe duties to tenants and subsequent purchasers of local authority dwellings as builders and contractors. In *Rimmer v Liverpool City Council*[202] the defendants were held liable to a council tenant injuring himself when he fell against a negligently used, thin, glass panel and the glass shattered.

The decision in the *Murphy* case removes from local authorities the greatest potential area of liability for defective premises since it is local authorities that are entrusted with the function of inspecting and approving all building work. Negligent exercise of these powers might result in local people purchasing and living in defective, even dangerous, premises. *Murphy* makes clear, however, that the local authority will not be liable in tort for any financial loss occasioned by the defects in the premises. But would the authority be liable if actual injury was caused to a resident or any of his property that was not an integral part of the premises? The House of Lords suggested that the builder would be so liable. But what if the builder has gone into liquidation? That question was left open by their Lordships.[203] However, while it is true that local authorities are granted inspection powers for the purpose of protecting the health and welfare of local people,[204] it is difficult to characterise this as a duty owed to individuals as opposed to the public more generally (because of an absence of proximity). And why, in any event, should the council be liable for what at bottom is the negligence of a third party, the builder?

---

[199] *Baxall Securities Ltd v Sheard Walshaw Partnership* [2001] PNLR 257 (architect liable for sub-standard roof design causing subsequent water damage). But note, also, that the limited scope of an architect's original instructions will define the extent of his or her liability in tort by confining the extent of the duty of care: *Bellefield Computer Services Ltd v E Turner & Sons Ltd (No 2)* [2002] EWCA Civ 1823.

[200] *Smith v Eric S Bush* [1990] 1 AC 831.   [201] *Sutcliffe v Sayer* [1987] 1 EGLR 155.   [202] [1985] QB 1.

[203] [1990] 2 All ER 908, at 912 and 917.

[204] See *Anns v Merton LBC* [1978] AC 728 per Lord Wilberforce. Note that *Anns* was only overruled as far as recovery for financial loss was concerned.

(F) Landlords

Historically, the liability of landlords for defects arising from disrepair in their premises was limited largely to contractual liability. A person other than the tenant had no remedy, even if the landlord was in breach of a contractual duty to carry out maintenance and repairs.[205] And like vendors, the landlord owed no duty in respect of defects arising before the tenancy was granted. As we have seen, landlords are liable now to tenants, their families, and others injured on the premises just like anyone else in respect of *their* negligent installations or repairs in the premises let by them.[206]

The Defective Premises Act, section 4 established important duties in respect of landlords under an obligation[207] to carry out repairs or maintenance on the premises, or who are empowered to carry out repairs.[208] A landlord owes to all persons who reasonably might be expected to be affected by defects in the state of the premises a duty to take such care as is reasonable in all the circumstances to see that they are reasonably safe from personal injury or from damage to their property caused by the relevant defects.[209] The landlord is liable although he did not know of the defect so long as he ought to have known of it.[210] A defect is relevant if it is one in the state of the premises arising from, or continuing because of, an act or omission by the landlord which constitutes or, if he had had notice of the defect, would have constituted a failure by him to carry out his obligation to the tenant for the maintenance or repair of the premises.[211] The duty is wide: it extends to trespassers and those outside the premises. It applies also where the landlord merely has a right to enter to carry out maintenance or repairs. On the other hand, the duty is not one to make safe premises that are unsafe by virtue of a design defect (rather than a failure to keep those premises in a good state of repair). A defect in design is different from a defect in the performance of a duty to maintain.[212]

The liability of non-occupiers for actual physical damage is fairly extensive, but by no means comprehensive. If an owner knows of a defect in his premises (not created by him) before he sells or lets, but neither repairs it, nor gives warning of the defect, the 1972 Act imposes no liability on him for harm which results after he has disposed of the premises by sale or lease, and there is no liability at common law.[213] A landlord who fails to repair where he has no obligation or power to do so has no liability under either the Act or the common law.

---

[205] But in some circumstances, the Contracts (Rights of Third Parties) Act 1999 might now apply.

[206] *Rimmer v Liverpool CC* [1984] 1 All ER 930; *Boldack v East Lindsey DC* (1998) 31 HLR 41.

[207] This includes statutory obligations.

[208] Defective Premises Act 1972, sub-s 4(4). This extension to the case where the tenant cannot legally insist on a repair, but where the landlord has a power to repair, is important in view of cases like *Mint v Good* [1951] 1 KB 517, deciding that landlords of small houses let on periodic tenancies have such a power.

[209] In the case of children who are injured, however, the landlord is entitled to expect that the parents of the child will take proper precautions to ensure the child's safety: see *B (a child) v Camden LBC* [2001] PIQR P143.

[210] Defective Premises Act 1972, sub-s 4(2).

[211] Defective Premises Act 1972, sub-s 4(3). Failures to remedy such defects are actionable, alternatively, on the basis of common law negligence: see *Targett v Torfaen BC* [1992] 3 All ER 27.

[212] *Alker v Collingwood Housing Association* [2007] 1 WLR 2230.

[213] *Cavalier v Pope* [1906] AC 428; *Bromley v Mercer* [1922] 2 KB 126.

Conclusions

This chapter has considered various issues concerning the liability of those who occupy premises. The law draws a basic distinction between visitor and non-visitor entrants to premises, offering a much more extensive level of protection to the former (under the Occupiers' Liability Act 1957) than to the latter (under the Occupiers' Liability Act 1984). The crucial issue is to work out whether the claimant is one or the other, and this can be complicated by old common law notions such as that (applicable to children) involving the doctrine of allurement. The chapter has considered also the obligations of certain non-occupiers of premises, including landlords, builders, architects, and engineers. Their liability is governed by the Defective Premises Act 1972.

Problem question

Jose and his sister Juanita attend their local school debutant ball held at the Economy Inn Hotel one evening. The signs in the lobby direct them to the room in which the ball is being held. After an hour of dancing, Jose decides that he needs some fresh air. He ventures out to the rear of the hotel, where he sees the hotel pool. The child-proof fence is closed, but Jose (age 12) opens it easily. Although a sign says: 'Hotel Guests Only. All children to be accompanied by their parents', Jose decides that he really needs to cool off and takes off his suit. Unfortunately, the pool is being cleaned by an automatic cleaning device, which crawls along the pool floor. Jose severely hurts his head on the pool cleaner, which he did not see in the darkness, as he dives in to the pool. Juanita (age 18) comes out looking for Jose. She sees that Jose is bleeding in the pool and jumps in to rescue him. Juanita drags Jose out of the pool and over to a deck chair. Under the weight of the two siblings, the deck chair collapses and a mouldy wooden plank also collapses underneath it—causing Juanita to injure her foot. Juanita's iphone falls into the void beneath the planking and she is unable to retrieve it.

Advise Jose and Juanita as to the hotel's liability to them.

 Visit **http://www.oup.com/uk/street15e/** for answer guidance.

Further reading

HOWARTH, 'Negligence after *Murphy*—Time to Re-Think' (1991) 50 *Cambridge Law Journal* 58

JONES, 'The Occupiers' Liability Act 1984—The Wheels of Law Reform Turn Slowly' (1984) 47 *Modern Law Review* 713

Law Commission Report No 75, *Liability for Damage or Injury to Trespassers and Related Questions of Occupiers' Liability* (Cmnd 6428)

MESHER, 'Occupiers, Trespassers and the Unfair Contract Terms Act 1977' (1979) 43 *Conveyancer* 58

MURPHY, 'Public Rights of Way and Private Law Wrongs' (1997) 61 *Conveyancer* 362

SPENCER, 'The Defective Premises Act 1972: Defective Law and Defective Law Reform' (1974) 33 *Cambridge Law Journal* 307 and (1975) 34 *Cambridge Law Journal* 48

PART III

Intentional invasions of interests in the person and property

10

Trespass to the person and related torts

KEY ISSUES

(1) Wide protection of person and liberty
Tort law is highly protective of the body of the person and of her liberty. This is reflected in the torts discussed in this chapter, which provide redress against various interferences with these interests.[1] Protection is available in battery, assault, and false imprisonment, and under the Protection from Harassment Act 1997 following infringement of the protected interest *without* need for proof of harm.[2]

(2) Battery
Battery is any act of the defendant that directly and intentionally (or negligently) causes some physical contact with the claimant's person and without the claimant's consent.

(3) Assault
Assault is any act of the defendant that directly and intentionally (or negligently) causes the claimant reasonably to apprehend the imminent infliction of a battery.

(4) Protection from Harassment Act 1997
Legislation prohibits engagement in a course of conduct amounting to harassment of another and the victim of such conduct has the ability to sue in tort for either damages or an injunction.

(5) False imprisonment
False imprisonment is an act of the defendant which directly and intentionally (or possibly negligently) causes the claimant's confinement within an area delimited by the defendant.

Section 1 Introduction

Battery, assault, and false imprisonment are among the most ancient of torts. Although originally recognised to secure the 'King's peace', today these torts reflect the high value that the common law places on the protection of the body of the person and of her

---

[1] Note, however, that encroachments have been made on the level of protection offered by the common law. See, eg, Criminal Justice Act 2003, s 329, considered in *Adorian v MPC* [2009] 1 WLR 1859, esp. at [7] (Parliament could not have intended the wide measure of immunity against suits brought by persons who committed imprisonable offences at the time of the torts in question).

[2] Eg, *Ashley v CC of Sussex* [2008] 1 AC 962, at [60] (discussing trespass to the person).

liberty. The torts are actionable per se, meaning that there is no need for proof of damage. In recent times, the trespass torts have been complemented by the statutory tort of harassment, which is concerned with repeated acts that a reasonable person would know to be alarming or distressing. Provisions in the European Convention on Human Rights (ECHR) are also of importance.[3] Under the Human Rights Act 1998, section 6, United Kingdom courts must act compatibly with ECHR rights. Articles 2 and 3 respectively guarantee the right to life, and freedom from torture or degrading treatment. Article 5 asserts the right to liberty and security of person, and seeks to ensure that the state cannot detain persons without substantial grounds justifying that deprivation of liberty.[4] Depending on the circumstances, actions for vindication of these rights are available under the 1998 Act either to reinforce the protections offered by the torts to the person or to fill in the gaps where they do not apply.

Section 2 Battery

Battery is any act of the defendant that directly and intentionally or negligently causes some physical contact with the person of the claimant without the claimant's consent. Several key elements of this tort require discussion.

(A) Fault

From the thirteenth century, the courts provided compensation for injuries to the person and to property.[5] A suit in trespass could succeed only where the interference was 'direct' and this remains the case today.[6] But if the injury is caused directly, and is attributable to careless conduct on the part of the defendant, must the claimant frame her action in negligence, or might battery be an option?

(1) Negligently inflicted battery?

Historical position Until the middle of the twentieth century, one would have said with confidence that *both* the torts of battery and negligence were available in cases of direct injuries sustained as a result of careless conduct. This conclusion followed from the fact that, historically, trespass actions would succeed where there was a direct contact unless the defendant could show inevitable accident.[7] In other words, mere carelessness on the defendant's part would not allow her to escape liability in trespass.

Fowler v Lanning The modern confusion surrounding the relationship between negligence and trespass began in *Fowler v Lanning*,[8] which concerned a technical point of law about the burden of proof. In the course of his judgment, Diplock J sought to ensure

---

[3] See, eg, *Olotu v Home Office* [1997] 1 All ER 385.   [4] See Art 5(2)–(5) and Art 6.
[5] See FW Maitland, *The Forms of Action at Common Law* (1909).
[6] *Sterman v E W & W J Moore Ltd* [1970] 1 QB 596.   [7] *Weaver v Ward* (1616) Hob 134.
[8] [1959] 1 QB 426.

that the claimant could not gain an 'unfair' advantage by relying on trespass rather than negligence on the basis that, according to the former tort, the burden of proof would lie with the defendant to disprove any *negligence* on her part, whereas in the latter it was for the claimant to prove a failure in care. In so holding, Diplock J aligned trespass to the person with the hitherto anomalous 'highway rule' that the burden of proof lies on the claimant to show the defendant's negligence.[9]

Letang v Cooper Although *Fowler v Lanning* did not abolish the principle that trespass to the person can be committed negligently, it did leave the claimant with the burden of proving negligence where her injury was caused by negligent conduct. But then came *Letang v Cooper*:[10]

> D negligently drove his car over C's legs while C was sunbathing on the grass car park of a hotel. More than three years later, C sued D. The rules on limitation of actions provided that actions for 'negligence, nuisance or breach of duty' were barred after three years while other tort actions were barred after six years. C relied on trespass in an effort to prevent her action from being time-barred.

The Court of Appeal did not want to reach the supposedly absurd conclusion that an action for negligent trespass would lie while an action for negligence *simpliciter* would not. For their part, Lord Denning MR and Danckwerts LJ insisted that there was no overlap between trespass and negligence. They thought that, if an act was intentional, it would result in trespass (not negligence) liability, and that if an act was negligent it would lead to negligence (not trespass) liability.[11] However, this attempt at doctrinal elegance left no formal place in the law of trespass for intentional but indirect contacts and is problematic for that reason alone. By contrast with it, Diplock LJ thought that trespass could be committed negligently, but that in such cases the claimant must prove *both* the negligence alleged *and* that there was resulting harm.[12] In other words, the claimant would gain no practical advantage from framing his action in trespass rather than negligence.

Utility of negligent trespass In the wake of *Letang v Cooper*, it would appear that actions for negligent trespass effectively have disappeared either in juridical terms (for Lord Denning MR and Danckwerts LJ), or in practical terms (for Diplock LJ). But in academic terms we cannot assert conclusively that trespass has no relevance when negligent conduct is relied on.[13] There might be cases in which a claimant perceives an advantage from framing a claim in trespass rather than in negligence, most probably because of the more generous rules on remoteness of damage. For in negligence law, the defendant is responsible only for injuries that are reasonably foreseeable,[14] whereas in trespass all the damage actually ensuing from the defendant's unlawful act should be recoverable.[15]

---

[9] *Holmes v Mather* (1875) LR 10 Ex 261.   [10] [1965] 1 QB 232.   [11] [1965] 1 QB 232, at 240.
[12] Cf intentional trespass, which is actionable per se.   [13] See F Trindade (1982) 2 OJLS 211.
[14] *The Wagon Mound* [1961] AC 388.
[15] *Williams v Humphrey* (1975) *Times*, 20 February. See also *Allan v New Mount Sinai Hospital* (1980) 109 DLR (3d) 634.

This technical point aside, most modern trespass actions are likely to be based on an intentional act on the part of the defendant.

(2) Meaning of 'intentional act'

This raises a second fundamental question: 'What is meant by "intentional act"?'

Two possibilities In determining the meaning of 'intentional act' in this context, there are two broad possibilities: (1) that D intended only to act in the way that she did; or (2) that D intended *both* to act in the way that she did *and* that the contact with C take place. In most cases, the distinction is of little consequence. If A aims a punch at B and succeeds in striking B, there is nothing to separate A's act (the thrown punch) from its outcome (for example, B's broken nose). But in some circumstances, A might do a thing without intending the outcome. If D aims her rifle at C, then pulls the trigger, there is no doubt that she intended to shoot C. But if D aims her rifle at a partridge on a hunting trip but accidentally shoots C, it is clear that D intended the act (firing the gun) but not the outcome (C's injury). In such circumstances it might be stretching the tort too far to hold D liable in battery. But if D aimed her gun at a third party, T, then pulled the trigger, missing T and shooting C, standing next to T, we might think that D ought to be held liable.

Transferred intent In terms of D's mental state in the first example, there is a genuine accident (possibly even without carelessness on D's part). In the second example, D's act was reckless. This could be the basis upon which the English courts might, like US courts, borrow from the criminal law notion of 'transferred intent' and apply it in tort law.[16] Yet there is but limited support for adopting this approach. In addition to a technically non-binding but supportive first instance decision,[17] there is the argument of principle arising from the fact that battery is both a tort and a crime. Thus, as De Grey CJ observed in *Scott v Shepherd*, 'though criminal cases are no rule for civil ones . . . yet in trespass I think there is an analogy'.[18] In that case there was held to be a battery where D threw a lighted squib into a crowded market place that was tossed from one trader to another before it exploded eventually in C's face. Yet the case is inconclusive because the main issue was whether there was sufficient directness to satisfy the requirements of the tort. Further oblique authority can be discerned in *Haystead v Chief Constable of Derbyshire*.[19] The defendant punched a woman in the face so that she dropped the baby she was holding. He was charged with criminal assault in relation to the baby. Clearly the tortious counterpart of this crime is a battery. The Divisional Court did not consider application of the transferred intent doctrine but did say (with the implication that a battery action might lie) that:

---

[16] Restatement, Torts (2d), § 32. See also WL Prosser (1967) 45 Tex LR 650. In *Livingstone v Ministry of Defence* [1984] NI 356, it was held that where D fired a baton round injuring C it mattered not whether he fired at C or another person—D was liable in battery unless he could prove lawful justification for his act.

[17] *Bici v Ministry of Defence* [2004] EWHC 786, at 71.

[18] (1773) 2 Wm Bl 892, at 899. Cf *Coward v Baddeley* (1859) 4 H & N 478, at 480.

[19] [2000] 3 All ER 890.

> There is no difference in logic or good sense between the facts of this case and one where the defendant might have used a weapon to fell the child to the floor, save only that this is a case of reckless and not intentional battery.

Although the court emphasised the requirement of a sufficiently direct act to ground liability, and although it neglected to address head-on the question of whether the defendant's intention must apply only to her actions, or whether it must extend also to the outcome of those actions, the case does signal an unwillingness to allow defendants to escape liability in such cases.[20]

On balance, then, it seems that there is nascent judicial support for the application of the transferred intent principle in English battery cases. On the other hand, there is a plausible counter-argument that, although certain forms of conduct should be branded morally wrong and deserving of criminal punishment, they might not warrant a remedy in tort where neither motive nor malice normally are relevant in determining liability (as opposed to the amount of damages).[21]

Hostility In cases where contact with the claimant is unproblematic, it is well established that the defendant need not have intended the claimant any harm. Battery is actionable per se—without proof of injury to the claimant. The defendant merely should have understood that her conduct was beyond the bounds of physical contact 'generally acceptable in the ordinary conduct of everyday life'.[22]

In *Wilson v Pringle*,[23] the Court of Appeal held that the claimant must show that the defendant's touching of the claimant was a 'hostile' touching. Yet the term 'hostility' should not be equated with ill-will or malevolence. It means merely that the defendant is doing something to which the claimant might object, something that the claimant might regard as an unlawful intrusion on her rights to physical integrity. Thus, the bare allegation that one 13-year-old boy jumped on another during horseplay was insufficient to establish a battery. Further evidence of intent to injure or cause distress to the claimant had to be shown if liability for battery were to be imposed. Had a grown man engaged in similar conduct, however, the result almost certainly would have been different.

In *F v West Berkshire Health Authority*[24] Lord Goff doubted that the use of the word 'hostile', however defined, was appropriate to describe the necessary state of mind in battery. A surgeon operating on a patient to preserve her life and health might be motivated by her judgment as to the patient's best interests, not hostility towards the patient. Yet if the patient is competent to do so, and has refused to consent to a particular course of treatment, the surgeon commits a battery. Lord Goff preferred the following approach. Any deliberate touching of another's body, beyond the bounds of acceptable everyday conduct, in the absence of lawful excuse, can constitute a battery. Where a person by reason of some permanent or temporary mental incapacity cannot

---

[20] In similar vein see *Livingstone v MOD* [1984] NI 356.

[21] NB *Haystead* was a criminal (not tort) law case! Cf J Gordley, *Foundations of Private Law: Property, Tort, Contract and Unjust Enrichment* (2006), 189ff.   [22] *Collins v Wilcock* [1984] 3 All ER 374, at 378.

[23] [1987] QB 237. Cf *Williams v Humphrey* (1975) *Times*, 20 February.   [24] [1989] 2 All ER 545, at 564.

herself consent to medical or other necessary procedures,[25] the requisite lawful excuse might have to be found in the principle of necessity.

(B) No consent by the claimant

Burden of proof The absence of consent is an element of the cause of action in battery and, consequently, the claimant must prove that she did not acquiesce to contact with her person. At first sight, this might seem rather odd, but any lingering doubt that the burden of proving absence of consent lies on the claimant was laid to rest in *Freeman v Home Office (No 2)*.[26] A prisoner alleged that he had been injected with mood-changing drugs against his will. The judge held that, since the essence of battery is a specific and unpermitted intrusion on the claimant's body, it was for the claimant to establish that he did not agree to the intrusion. This he failed to do.

Rationale Part of the rationale for this approach is that the alternative (treating consent as a defence to liability in battery) would pose potential problems for medical practitioners. Any contact with a patient—for example, in providing vaccinations or examining sore throats with a spatula—prima facie would constitute battery. To escape liability, the doctor would have to justify the intrusion by proving that the patient consented. This might be difficult in cases involving minor procedures where no written consent had been obtained, records were lost, or the practitioner has died.[27] On the other hand, in the context of actions by suspects against the police, or prisoners against prison authorities, casting the burden of proof on the claimant might vitiate the effectiveness of a battery action as a mechanism for vindicating their civil liberties.[28] In such circumstances, cases would turn on the contest between the word of the prisoner and the word of 'respectable' members of society in positions of responsibility.

Treatment in this work Frequently, consent is a fundamental issue—especially in cases of medical trespass. A question might arise of what exactly the patient consented to, or indeed whether she was competent to give consent at all.[29] Logically, as it is for the claimant to prove absence of consent, it might be expected that we should deal with these issues here. But in practice, once the claimant has raised sufficient evidence to cast doubt on the reality of a purported consent, consent is still treated as a defence.[30] For this reason, it is discussed in greater detail in chapter 13, where general defences to the intentional torts are addressed.

---

[25] There is a statutory definition of incapacity in the Mental Capacity Act 2005, ss 2 and 3. The gist is that the defendant is incapacitated when unable to make a decision for himself because of impaired brain function, where the inability to make a decision is to be understood in terms of an inability to understand, retain, or evaluate the information.   [26] [1983] 3 All ER 589, at 594–5 (affd [1984] QB 524).

[27] As had the prison doctor in *Freeman v Home Office (No 2)* [1984] QB 524.

[28] But see *R (on the application of Wilkinson) v Broadmoor Hospital* [2002] 1 WLR 419.

[29] Where medical treatment is administered to a mental patient without her consent, that treatment might nonetheless be justified so long as it does not amount to inhuman or degrading treatment contrary to Art 3 of the European Convention on Human Rights: *R (on the application of Wilkinson) v Broadmoor Hospital* [2002] 1 WLR 419.   [30] The ingredients of consent are discussed in ch 13.

(C) The character of the defendant's act

Positive act There can be no battery unless there is a positive act by the defendant. Merely to obstruct the entrance to a room by standing in someone's way is not enough of itself [31] (although there might be an assault where it is clear that if A tries to pass B, B will attempt forcibly to prevent that happening).[32] Also, no battery is committed if an incident occurs involving contact over which the defendant has no control.[33]

Unpermitted contact There can be no battery unless there is contact with the claimant. But is any contact, however slight, enough? Lord Goff has suggested that battery protects a person 'not only against physical injury but against any form of physical molestation'.[34] This formulation provides a guide as to the kind of conduct that courts hold to be tortious, so long as the word 'molestation' is read broadly. Such a reading explains why spitting in someone's face is battery, while touching another accidentally in a crowd is not. It also explains the view of Holt CJ 'that the least touching of another in anger is battery' but that 'if two or more meet in a narrow passage, and without any . . . design of harm, the one touches the other gently, it is no battery'.[35] The courts cannot, and should not be expected, to give remedies against these unavoidable contacts in everyday life, and thus the second quoted statement can be classed as an example of a permitted contact.[36] Battery, then enables a person to seek redress against all unpermitted contacts amounting to 'molestation', irrespective of whether there is any physical harm.[37] So, taking fingerprints,[38] spitting in another's face,[39] and cutting another's hair against her will[40] are batteries.

Directness As with all trespasses to the person, the requirement of directness applies in battery. It is not enough that the act 'causes' the contact. Contact must follow immediately from the defendant's act;[41] or at least be a continuation of it.[42] This is to say that there must be no significant act of volition between D's act and the eventual contact with C's body. It is battery where A strikes B's horse so that the horse bolts, throwing B to the ground,[43] or where D punches a third party so that injury results to C.[44] It is a

---

[31] *Innes v Wylie* (1844) 1 Car & Kir 257, at 263. A motorist who accidentally drives his car on to a police constable's foot while he is parking commits no battery, but does commit a battery if he then ignores the constable's plea to 'Get off my foot': *Fagan v MPC* [1969] 1 QB 439 (criminal case).

[32] *Hepburn v CC of Thames Valley Police* [2002] EWCA Civ 1841.

[33] See *Gibbons v Pepper* (1695) 2 Salk 637; *Holmes v Mather* (1875) LR 10 Exch 261.

[34] See *F v West Berkshire HA* [1989] 2 All ER 545, at 563.   [35] *Cole v Turner* (1704) 6 Mod Rep 149.

[36] This explains, too, the dictum in *Tuberville v Savage* (1669) 1 Mod Rep 3 to the effect that striking another on the breast in discourse is not actionable. Cf *Donnelly v Jackman* [1970] 1 All ER 987.

[37] *Ashley v CC of Sussex* [2008] 1 AC 962, at [60].

[38] *Dumbell v Roberts* [1944] 1 All ER 326, at 330; *Callis v Gunn* [1964] 1 QB 495.

[39] *R v Cotesworth* (1704) 6 Mod Rep 172.

[40] *Forde v Skinner* (1830) 4 C & P 239. Cf *Nash v Sheen* (1953) *Times*, 13 March.

[41] *Leame v Bray* (1803) 3 East 593, at 603.   [42] *Scott v Shepherd* (1773) 2 Wm Bl 892, at 899.

[43] *Dodwell v Burford* (1669) 1 Mod Rep 24.

[44] *Haystead v CC of Derbyshire* [2000] 3 All ER 890 (*obiter*).

trespass to the person to overturn a chair in which the claimant is sitting.[45] Finally, it is battery for a ship to ram another despite the effect of the current.[46]

If battery protected against insult generally, and not merely against bodily infringement, then any intentional contact with anything closely attached to, or associated with, the person of the claimant conceivably could be treated as battery. This point was explored in *Pursell v Horn*,[47] which decided that throwing water on to clothes which the claimant was wearing was not necessarily battery. But it is probably going too far the other way to suggest that contact with things attached to the claimant can constitute battery only if there is a transmission of force to the body of the claimant.[48] The guide should be whether the action constitutes molestation. The protection from insult or indignity afforded by the tort of battery is limited to insult or indignity arising from the touching.[49]

(D) Damages

Trespass being actionable per se, damages can be awarded even when the claimant suffers no tangible harm.[50] This reflects the importance with which the law treats the autonomy of the person and the affront to personal dignity that frequently arises from battery (and from the other trespasses to the person considered in this chapter).[51] Furthermore, it seems that, once the tort is proved, consequential loss in respect of goods, as well as the personal injury sustained, can be recovered.[52] And the courts can award additional damages also on account of insult or injury to feelings in respect of a battery that has caused harm.[53]

Section 3 Assault

Definition Although an assault will be committed often just before a battery, it makes sense to deal with assault second in this chapter because the tort's definition refers to battery. An assault is any act of the defendant that directly and intentionally or negligently[54] causes the claimant reasonably to apprehend the imminent infliction of a battery. The law of assault is substantially similar to the law of battery except that, in assault, a reasonably held apprehension of contact (rather than contact itself) must be established. Usually when there is a battery there will be an assault, but not, for instance,

---

[45] *Hopper v Reeve* (1817) 7 Taunt 698.   [46] *Covell v Laming* (1808) 1 Camp 497.

[47] (1838) 8 Ad & El 602.

[48] 'It must imply personal violence': *Pursell v Horn* (1838) 8 Ad & El 602, at 604. In *R v Day* (1845) 1 Cox 207 Parke B held that it was the crime of battery to slit with a knife a victim's clothes.

[49] Thus, an unwanted kiss is actionable: see also F Trindade (1982) 2 OJLS 211, at 225.

[50] *Ashley v CC of Sussex* [2008] 1 AC 962, at [60].   [51] See P Cane, *Key Ideas in Tort Law* (2017), 25–6.

[52] *Glover v London and South Western Rly Co* (1867) LR 3 QB 25.

[53] *Loudon v Ryder* [1953] 2 QB 202. There is doubt as to whether such damages are available in cases where the battery does not occasion any physical harm. Cf Riot Compensation Act 2016, ss 1 and 8.

[54] By analogy with battery, it would seem to accord with principle to include foreseeable though unintended harm (although actual decisions are lacking).

when a person is hit from behind. To shake a fist under the claimant's nose, to aim a blow at her which is intercepted, to surround her with a display of force,[55] or to point a loaded gun at her, is to assault her. Clearly, if the defendant by her act intends to commit a battery and the claimant apprehends it, it is an assault. Within the tort of assault what must be apprehended, however, is actual physical contact. Photographing a person against her will is not an actionable assault.[56]

Objective test The origins of this tort are evident when one asks whether to brandish an unloaded pistol is an assault. In *Stephens v Myers*, Tindal CJ said that 'it is not every threat, when there is no actual physical violence, that constitutes an assault, there must, in all cases, be the means of carrying the threat into effect'.[57] Thus, in 1840, it was said still that pointing an unloaded gun at the claimant was not assault because the defendant could not have intended a battery.[58] These cases have not been overruled, but in criminal law such an act is an assault.[59] Reasoning by analogy, it is submitted that a modern court would reach the equivalent conclusion in tort. The gist of the tort of assault is an act which would cause a reasonable person to apprehend an imminent battery.[60] The test for what constitutes reasonable apprehension of an imminent battery is objective not subjective, and a reasonable person could not be expected to know that the gun was not loaded. Conversely, if the claimant is paranoid and perceives the defendant's innocuous waving of her hand in the air during conversation as a threat, there is no assault.

Capacity to commit battery Where interventions of the police, or other protective intrusions, ensure that persons *cannot* carry out threats of violence and abuse, no assault is committed. Thus, where working miners were driven into their collieries on buses with police guards, the threats yelled at them by striking miners were not assaults.[61] The claimants could not reasonably have apprehended that those threats would be carried out there and then and, thus, fell outside the scope of this tort. It is clear as such that the tort of assault provides limited protection only from the infliction of mental anxiety.

Words At one time it was thought that mere words could not constitute an assault,[62] but the rule is now otherwise. According to the House of Lords in *R v Ireland*,[63] words that instil a reasonable fear of an imminent battery amount to a tortious assault for '[the] means by which persons of evil disposition may intentionally or carelessly cause

---

[55] *Read v Coker* (1853) 13 CB 850.

[56] *Murray v MOD* [1985] 12 NIJB 12. On the other hand, publishing such photographs might give rise to an action based on the misuse of private personal information. See *Campbell v MGN* [2004] 2 AC 457 and ch 22.

[57] (1830) 4 C & P 349, at 349–50. In *Osborn v Veitch* (1858) 1 F & F 317 it was held that to point a loaded gun at half-cock at C was an assault but this was because there was 'a present ability of doing the act threatened', the cocking of the gun taking just a split second.   [58] *Blake v Barnard* (1840) 9 C & P 626.

[59] *R v St George* (1840) 9 C & P 483.

[60] 'Imminent' simply means 'immediate': *Mbasogo v Logo Ltd (No 1)* [2007] QB 846, at [81].

[61] *Thomas v NUM* [1985] 2 All ER 1, at 24.

[62] See *R v Meade and Belt* (1823) 1 Lew CC 184, at 185, where it was said *obiter*, that 'no words or singing are equivalent to an assault'.   [63] [1998] AC 147.

another to fear immediate and unlawful violence vary according to the circumstances'.[64] On the other hand, words accompanying an act might explain away or treat as conditional what otherwise would be an assault. Thus, there was no assault in an ancient case where the defendant with his hand on his sword said: '[i]f it were not assize-time, I would not take such language from you'.[65]

Silence Traditionally, there always has been an element of 'physicality' in assault cases, and this appears to be a sensible requirement in a tort which is supplementary to battery in protecting the body, autonomy and dignity of the person. However, in *R v Ireland*,[66] the House of Lords went so far as to hold that silence over the telephone could support a criminal conviction and, possibly, an action in the tort of assault. In hindsight, this development appears to have been unnecessary, given the passage of the Protection from Harassment Act 1997, and it is submitted that tort law should not follow the *Ireland* case.

Section 4 Intentional infliction of harm

For more than a century, the trespass to the person torts have been accompanied by a tort based on the intentional infliction of harm.

Seminal case This action on the case arose from *Wilkinson v Downton*:[67]

> C was told by D, who knew it to be untrue, that her husband had been seriously injured in an accident. Believing this, she suffered nervous shock resulting in serious physical illness, and was held to have a cause of action.

Wright J held the defendant, a practical joker, liable on the basis that he had 'wilfully done an act calculated to cause physical harm to the plaintiff . . . which in fact caused physical harm to her'.[68] But it was by no means clear that the defendant actually had intended the harm caused. For this reason, Wright J explained a little later in his judgment that this intention might need to be *imputed*, and his Lordship went on to impute such to the defendant. But this seems a rash step given that the defendant intended only to play a joke. The defendant's act was more redolent of negligence even though the joke was played intentionally. And, as McPherson J observed in *Carrier v Bonham*:[69]

> Most everyday acts of what we call actionable negligence are in fact wholly or partly a product of intentional conduct. Driving a motor vehicle at high speed through a residential area is an intentional act even if injuring people or property on the way is not a result actually intended. *Wilkinson v Downton* is an example of that kind.[70]

---

[64] [1998] AC 147, at 166. The case centred on telephone calls, but unless a call is made from a mobile phone just outside C's house, it seems contrary to principle to embrace such a case within assault, given the want of an imminent battery.

[65] *Tuberville v Savage* (1669) 1 Mod Rep 3.   [66] [1998] AC 147.

[67] [1897] 2 QB 57; 66 LJQB 493. The Court of Appeal later applied the decision in *Janvier v Sweeney* [1919] 2 KB 316. See C Witting (1998) 21 UNSWLJ 55.

[68] [1897] 2 QB 57, at 58.   [69] [2001] QCA 234.   [70] [2001] QCA 234, at [27].

He then went on to note that 'the expression calculated . . . is one of those weasel words that is capable of meaning either *subjectively contemplated and intended* or, *objectively likely to happen*', before concluding that in *Wilkinson v Downton* those words were 'being used in the latter, not the former sense'.[71] In short, he recast the decision as a negligence case. And this, it is submitted, is the better way in which *that case* should be understood, given that it was highly improbable that the practical joker had *subjectively intended* anything more than fleeting or, at most, short-term, distress. What was crucial to Wright J's *particular decision* was the likelihood of harm occurring from the joke (which is a central question posed in negligence cases).[72]

Re-classification of seminal case There is a historical explanation as to why *Wilkinson v Downton* has been presented as a kind of intentional tort *sui generis*. The fleeting and insubstantial nature of the 'harm' actually intended by the defendant (as opposed to that which actually occurred) would not, at the time, have sufficed to found an action on the case. The Privy Council decision in *Victorian Railways Commissioners v Coultas*[73] had prohibited recovery for nervous shock induced by negligence. Thus, it is probably partly for this reason that Wright J preferred to impute to the defendant an intention to 'produce some effect *of the kind* that was [actually] produced',[74] even though *that kind of harm* almost certainly was never in the defendant's mind. In the light of the more generous, modern approach to cases of psychiatric harm,[75] it seems high time that we abandon Wright J's historically rooted legal fiction, and reclassify *Wilkinson v Downton* as a negligence case in which the defendant failed to take appropriate care to avoid causing psychiatric harm to the claimant. Strong support for this reclassification of *the actual decision* in *Wilkinson v Downton* can be taken from the discussion of the House of Lords in *Wainwright v Home Office*.[76]

Utility of principle Notwithstanding these comments, it would be a mistake to discard *Wilkinson v Downton* wholesale.[77] This is because there are many intentional acts besides the spoken word that can cause harm *indirectly* and thus defy classification as forms of trespass. And without the rule in *Wilkinson v Downton*, it is debatable whether there would be a cause of action.[78] Thus, putting poison in another's tea, or digging a pit into which it is intended that another should fall, are not trespasses, but might be brought within the *stated* rule in *Wilkinson v Downton*. Furthermore, there are ancient cases declaring that it is a tortious act deliberately to set spring guns or other mechanical devices with the intention of injuring trespassers which can be explained according to Wright J's principle.[79] And the form of liability embodied in these cases is very similar

---

[71] [2001] QCA 234, at [25].   [72] See, eg, *Bolton v Stone* [1951] AC 850.

[73] (1888) 13 App Cas 222.   [74] [1897] 2 QB 57, at 59.

[75] See, eg, *Alcock v CC of South Yorkshire* [1992] 1 AC 310.

[76] [2004] 2 AC 406, at [47].   [77] Cf N McBride and R Bagshaw, *Tort Law* (2005), 68–9.

[78] Another point is that actions that might fail in negligence because the loss is regarded as too remote might succeed under the rule in *Wilkinson v Downton* (assuming that the trespass rules on remoteness of damage apply to that tort).

[79] *Deane v Clayton* (1817) 7 Taunt 489; *Bird v Holbrook* (1828) 4 Bing 628. Cf *Townsend v Wathen* (1808) 9 East 277.

to that found in the US 'prima facie tort' cases.[80] The only other way of dealing with such cases would be to allow negligence suits based on intentional and reckless conduct. And while this is not per se objectionable,[81] it does run up against the objection that, in *Letang v Cooper*,[82] Lord Denning MR and Danckwerts LJ made a strenuous effort to keep apart negligence and the intentional torts against the person.

For a time, during the mid-1990s, it looked as though the principle would be extended beyond the protection of physical and mental health, to the protection from harassment.[83] Yet dicta by the Court of Appeal in *Wong v Parkside Health NHS Trust*[84] halted this expansion of the tort in its tracks. In cases of distress falling short of negligently inflicted psychiatric harm or assault, the preferred route to redress was thought to be the Protection from Harassment Act 1997.[85]

However, in *O v Rhodes*[86] the Supreme Court affirmed the existence of a tort of intentional infliction of harm based upon *Wilkinson v Downton*:

> A claim was brought on behalf of an 11-year-old boy who suffered from learning and other disorders against his father, a pianist who intended to publish a 'harrowing' autobiography. The autobiography detailed matters including the sexual abuse committed by a sports coach against the defendant when he was a child. The language used in the book was extremely explicit and it was argued that, should the claimant learn of the essential facts detailed in it, it was likely to cause him psychological harm. An injunction was sought to prevent publication.

Although the claim was rejected, the Supreme Court upheld the underlying principle[87] and clarified the elements of the tort. The tort has the following elements:[88] first, a conduct element comprising actions or words directed towards the claimant or an ascertainable group of persons that includes the claimant. (Lords Neuberger and Wilson would have specified, further, that the conduct be of an outrageous or extreme nature in order not to impede ordinary discourse, including heated and unpleasant arguments.)[89] Second, the tort has an intention element subsisting in *deliberately causing either*

---

[80] See, eg, K Vandervelde (1991) 79 Kentucky LJ 519; C Witting (1999) 25 Mon ULR 295.

[81] For the suggestion that the tort of negligence logically embraces *intentional* wrongs, see J Murphy (2007) 27 OJLS 509.   [82] [1965] 1 QB 232.

[83] *Khorasandjian v Bush* [1993] QB 727 looked for a time as though it might be taking the rule in *Wilkinson v Downton* into new territory: the protection of privacy with no requirement of mental or physical harm. See also *Burris v Azadani* [1995] 1 WLR 1372.   [84] [2001] EWCA Civ 1721.

[85] Three factors serve to make the intentional infliction of harm tort preferable to an action under the 1997 Act. First, where C's complaint turns on a one-off incident rather than a 'course of conduct', as is required by the Act (see section 5 of this chapter), C might need to invoke the rule. Second, although there is no specific timeframe under the Act within which the relevant 'course of conduct' must take place, 'the fewer the occasions and the wider they are spread, the less likely it would be that a finding of harassment can reasonably be made [under the Act]': *Lau v DPP* [2000] 1 FLR 799, at [15]. Third, in cases involving persons who formerly shared an affectionate bond, pestering conduct that falls short of stalking might prove inadequate for the purposes of invoking the Act: see *R v Hills* [2001] 1 FCR 569, at [31]. But see now Crime and Security Act 2010, s 24.

[86] [2016] AC 219.   [87] [2016] AC 219, at [42].

[88] The author has split the Supreme Court's three elements into four for reasons which should be apparent.

[89] [2016] AC 219, [74] and [110] respectively.

physical harm or severe mental distress to the claimant. In underlining this requirement, the court explained that neither the idea of imputed intention, which held sway in the *Wilkinson v Downton* era, nor that of recklessness as to the causation of harm would be sufficient.[90] Third, the tort has a consequence element, which subsists in either physical harm or a *recognised psychiatric illness* (not just distress).[91] Fourth, the defendant should have no justification or reasonable excuse for her conduct.[92] A justification consists in reasons which entail that the defendant's actions were not wrongful in the circumstances of the case, while an excuse is a special ground for not imposing liability *despite* her actions being wrongful.[93] On the facts, the Supreme Court held that the elements of the tort were not satisfied because: the publication of the defendant's book was for a wide audience and not relevantly directed at the claimant; there was no intention to harm the claimant; and publication was justified, for example in the defendant's right to tell his story to the world.

So, what sort of conduct is likely to fall within the revamped tort of intentional infliction of harm? Bagshaw seems to be correct in asserting that the tort is 'of more use against bullies, those who act intending to make their victims' lives miserable, than against foolish pranksters who miscalculate the consequences of practical jokes'.[94]

Section 5 Protection from Harassment Act 1997

This Act creates two criminal offences. The first offence that we consider, created by subsection 1(1), is the general offence of harassing another person. Conduct amounting to harassment of another person[95] is a criminal offence unless justifiable for the purpose of detecting or preventing crime, or authorised by law, or, in the particular circumstances, the conduct was reasonable. By virtue of section 2, the victim[96] of such harassment, be it actual or apprehended, is granted a right to sue in tort—either for damages or for an injunction.[97] The tort has proven to be attractive not only in the household and workplace contexts, but also in controlling oppressive commercial behaviour towards debtors and the like.

---

[90] [2016] AC 219, at [87].   [91] [2016] AC 219, at [73].

[92] Although the court seems to be saying that the claimant bears the burden of proving no justification or reasonable excuse ([2016] AC 219, at [74]), this would be surprising because these are defences.

[93] This is the usual way in which the distinction is drawn (see C Witting (1998) 21 UNSWLJ 55, 67), but note that modern writers on criminal law are reluctant to adopt it: eg, AP Simester et al, *Simester and Sullivan's Criminal Law* (5th edn, 2013), 677.   [94] R Bagshaw (2015) 76 SLR 55, 55.

[95] A corporate entity cannot claim under the Act (although individual employees targeted by the harassment can do so): *Daiichi Pharmaceuticals UK Ltd v Stop Huntingdon Animal Cruelty* [2004] 1 WLR 1503.

[96] The victim can sue whether the intended target or a 'collateral' victim. As to the latter, in *Levi v Bates* [2015] 3 WLR 769, at [34], the Court of Appeal held that the protection of the 1997 Act extends 'to those other persons who are foreseeably, and directly, harmed by the course of targeted conduct of which complaint is made, to the extent that they can properly be described as victims of it'. Collateral victims are likely to include spouses and others who are 'in the way' when harassment occurs.

[97] Protection from Harassment Act 1997, sub-s 3(1). Where an injunction is sought, the civil standard of proof applies: *Jones v Hipgrave* [2005] 2 FLR 174.

Course of conduct The 1997 Act requires there to have been a course of conduct—that is, conduct on at least two occasions.[98] One-off incidents of harassing conduct do not fall within the statute.[99]

Harassment The Act defines harassment to include alarming persons and causing them distress,[100] but is no more explicit than that. In *Hayes v Willoughby*, Lord Sumption asserted that the concept of harassment is 'well understood', consisting in 'a persistent and deliberate course of unreasonable and oppressive conduct, targeted at another person, which is calculated to and does cause that person alarm, fear or distress'.[101] The courts are alive to the fact that harassing conduct might occur on a scale from the innocuous to the severe. In *Majrowski v Guy's and St Thomas' NHS Trust*, Lord Nicholls drew a contrast between 'conduct which is unattractive, even unreasonable, and conduct which is oppressive and unacceptable'.[102] In this light, it has been said that it will be more difficult to rely on pestering that occurs following a relationship breakdown than on stalking.[103] This is borne out by *R v Curtis*, where the Court of Appeal held that there was conduct of insufficient gravity in a domestic relationship characterised by 'spontaneous outbursts of ill-temper and bad behaviour, with aggression on both sides . . . interspersed . . . with considerable periods of affectionate life'.[104]

In determining what amounts to harassment, the context will be important. Thus, '[w]hat might not be harassment on the factory floor or in the barrack room might well be harassment in the hospital ward and vice versa'.[105] To take another example, the bringing of legitimate litigation cannot be complained of. But the commencement and abandonment of successive lawsuits for the recovery of rental arrears, caused by council ineptitude, provides an arguable case of harassment.[106] The provision applies where creditors apply pressure for repayment of debts through computer-generated telephone calls,[107] and can arise from 'unintended', computer-generated demands for payment—as in *Ferguson v British Gas*, where the claimant businesswoman was repeatedly

---

[98] Protection from Harassment Act 1997, sub-s 7(3). This might include a series of newspaper articles, or a series of threatening letters from someone unknown to C, or a series of threatening emails: see *Thomas v News Group Newspapers* [2002] EMLR 78; *R v Colohan* [2001] 2 FLR 757; *Potter v Price* [2004] EWHC 781. The award of both aggravated and exemplary damages in harassment cases against relevant media defendants for the publication of news-related material is now subject to Crime and Courts Act 2013, ss 34–42, considered in ch 21.

[99] See also Equality Act 2010, s 26, creating offences in relation to, inter alia, harassment 'related to a relevant protected characteristic' and 'unwanted conduct of a sexual nature'; and Anti-social Behaviour, Crime and Policing Act 2013, ss 22, 35, 43, and 59, creating a range of orders available in circumstances of harassment.

[100] Protection from Harassment Act 1997, sub-s 7(2).   [101] [2013] 1 WLR 935, at [1].

[102] [2007] 12 AC 224, at [30]. As to 'unattractive' conduct, it has been said that one must put up with a certain amount of annoyance and irritation in modern society: *Shakil-Ur-Rahman v ARY Network Ltd* [2017] 4 WLR 22, at [113].

[103] *R v Hills* [2001] 1 FCR 569, at [31]. But note the potential availability of domestic violence protection notices under Crime and Security Act 2010, s 24.   [104] [2010] 1 WLR 2770, at [32].

[105] *Sunderland CC v Conn* [2008] IRLR 324, at [12].   [106] *Allen v LB of Southwark* [2008] EWCA Civ 1478.

[107] *Roberts v Bank of Scotland plc* [2013] EWCA Civ 882.

threatened that, unless payment were made, credit-rating agencies would be told that she had not paid her gas bills.[108]

Knows or ought to know The defendant's conduct can constitute actionable harassment only if she knows or ought to know that her acts amount to harassment.[109] The latter, objective element of the test would appear to be satisfied in most cases where the court finds that there was harassment. In deciding this, no account is to be taken of any mental deficiency on the defendant's part. Thus, a schizophrenic who sends threatening letters to a local MP is not exempt.[110]

Preventing or detecting crime The Protection from Harassment Act 1997, sub-section 1(3), creates a defence to an action for harassment, inter alia, where the defendant shows 'that it was pursued for the purpose of preventing or detecting crime'. While the defence is enlivened only where the defendant has a genuine belief that her actions are required to prevent or detect crime, in *Hayes v Willoughby* it was interpreted as importing the further requirement that the defendant's belief be rational in the sense that there be a 'logical connection between the evidence and the ostensible reasons for the decision, and . . . an absence of arbitrariness' and capriciousness.[111] The requirement of rationality was thought to be necessary in order to deal with 'cranks' and 'obsessives' who engage in harassing conduct in the 'genuine belief that they are preventing crime'.[112]

Further offence The second offence contained in the 1997 Act, sub-section 1(1A), arises where the defendant pursues a course of conduct that involves harassment of two or more persons, and this harassment is intended to persuade any person *either* not to do something she is entitled or obliged to do, *or* to do something that she is not obliged to do. In respect of this provision, there is no right to sue for damages, but an injunction may be sought.[113] The test of what the defendant knows or ought to know will be the effect of her conduct applies equally to this offence.[114]

Section 6 False imprisonment

False imprisonment involves an act of the defendant which directly and intentionally (or possibly negligently) causes the confinement of the claimant within an area delimited by the defendant. The tort protects the claimant's interests in freedom from

---

[108] [2010] 1 WLR 785 (action to strike out). Despite increased use of the Act in consumer cases, the Law Commission has recommended new legislation to cover aggressive consumer practices: Law Commission, *Consumer Redress for Misleading and Aggressive Practices: A Joint Consultation Paper* (Law Com Consultation Papers Nos 199 and 149, 2011).

[109] For these purposes D ought to know that which a reasonable person in possession of the same information would know: Protection from Harassment Act 1997, sub-s 1(2). The test is a purely objective one: *Banks v Ablex Ltd* [2005] ICR 819, at [20]. [110] *R v Colohan* [2001] 2 FLR 757, at [21].

[111] [2013] 1 WLR 935, at [14]. [112] [2013] 1 WLR 935, at [13].

[113] Protection from Harassment Act 1997, s 3A.

[114] Protection from Harassment Act 1997, sub-s 1(1A).

confinement and in liberty more generally. Usually, when there is a false imprisonment there will be an assault or battery also, but not, for example, when A voluntarily enters a room and B then locks the door, trapping A inside.

There is a substantial overlap between the protection of liberty offered by this tort and the protection available under the ECHR, Article 5(1). The provision lays down a 'positive obligation' on the part of signatory states to 'protect the liberty of those within' their jurisdictions.[115] It is said to be 'in the first rank of the fundamental rights that protect the physical security of an individual'.[116] There must be more than a mere restriction of liberty by the state; there must be a deprivation of liberty.[117] In keeping with the courts' modern view that the presence of an ECHR prohibition does not necessarily require adaptation by the common law of torts, it has been held that gaps in the law of false imprisonment need not be filled in order to ensure the UK's compliance with Article 5.[118] Thus, a remedy might be available under this provision where the claimant would fail in common law false imprisonment.[119]

In the most extreme cases, where the claimant has been held in a state of 'slavery or servitude', an additional cause of action is available under the Modern Slavery Act 2015, which permits the making of a 'slavery reparation order'.[120]

(A) Fault

Intention Normally false imprisonment arises from 'intentional' acts in the sense that the defendant must intend to act in a way which is at least substantially certain to effect the confinement. There is no need to show malice. Indeed, even where the defendant acts in good faith, she might be liable for her intentional confinement of the claimant. Thus, in *R v Governor of Brockhill Prison, ex p Evans (No 2)*,[121] a prison governor who calculated the claimant's release date in accordance with the law as understood at the time of her conviction was held liable when a subsequent change in the interpretation of the law meant that the prisoner should have been released 59 days earlier. However, since the governor was *obliged* to detain the claimant until the law applicable to the calculation of the prisoner's release date was re-interpreted—on which date she was duly released—it is difficult to see why the governor could not have relied on the defence of necessity.[122] Of course, if the law were to have been re-interpreted *before* the actual

---

[115] *Stanev v Bulgaria* (2012) 55 EHRR 696, at [120]. This means that 'criminal and civil law sanctions which operate retrospectively after arbitrary deprivation of liberty has occurred . . . are insufficient to discharge the state's positive obligation': *Staffordshire CC v K* [2017] 2 WLR 1131, at [75].

[116] *McKay v United Kingdom* (2006) 44 EHRR 827, at [30].

[117] *Secretary of State for the Home Department v AP* [2011] 2 AC 1, at [2]; *Austin v Commissioner of Police* [2009] 1 AC 564, at [16].　　　　　　　　　[118] *Zenati v Comr of Police* [2015] QB 758, at [51]–[54].

[119] Eg, *HL v UK* (2005) 40 EHRR 32; *Surrey CC v P* [2014] 2 WLR 642.　　　[120] Sections 1 and 8.

[121] [2001] 2 AC 19. Cf *Olotu v Home Office* [1997] 1 WLR 328.

[122] Their Lordships noted that this involved a hardship to the governor, but felt that it was outweighed by the hardship that would otherwise be done to C were she unable to sue. What perhaps ought to happen, then, is to extend the legislation that currently allows compensation for miscarriages of justice—namely, the Criminal Justice Act 1988, s 133—to cases like *Evans* (for it currently only applies to cases where an innocent prisoner was wrongly convicted). *Evans* now casts doubt on the decision in *Percy v Hall* [1997] QB 924, where C was held to be unable to sue in respect of arrests made under byelaws that were later declared void for uncertainty.

release date, it would have been proper that the detainee should be able to sue because an honest mistake as to the right to continue detention 'does not excuse a trespass to the person':[123] the requisite intention to detain will be present and that is all that counts in the absence of a recognised justification (such as necessity).

The *Brockhill Prison* case is an example of errors ostensibly on the part of the prison governor. In *Quinland v Governor of Swaleside Prison*,[124] by contrast, it was more clearly judicial error in stating the sentence to be three months longer than it ought to have been that caused the claimant to be improperly detained. The Court of Appeal stated that, since the prisoner was detained unduly by virtue of a *court order*, there would be no remedy apart from the correction of the arithmetical error that had occurred in adding together the various periods of confinement attributable to the offences of which the claimant had been convicted.

Negligence In principle, negligence ought to be enough to engage liability for false imprisonment. Accordingly, if a person locks a door, being unaware of the presence of somebody in the room and not having checked, this should suffice. On the other hand, a remedy was made available in one case under the auspices of the tort of negligence, but not false imprisonment, when a prisoner negligently was detained for a period that exceeded that authorised by the court.[125] This suggests that the courts might take a dim view of any claim based on 'negligent false imprisonment'.[126]

(B) Character of the defendant's act

Total restraint The courts insist upon total (as opposed to partial) restraint of the person.[127] Thus, to prevent a person from crossing a bridge except by making a detour around a portion of the bridge which has been closed off is not false imprisonment. Nor is it false imprisonment if A is able to escape confinement by a nominal trespass on the land of a third party.[128] So long as there is a total restraint, a tort is committed and the shortness of the duration will be taken into account when calculating damages.[129]

Place of confinement Although under the rules of false imprisonment confinement must be total, it need not be in a 'prison' as the name of the tort would suggest. While preventing the claimant from landing in England from mainland Europe would not be a false imprisonment,[130] it is more likely that the tort would be committed were the

---

[123] *Hepburn v CC of Thames Valley Police* [2002] EWCA Civ 1841.

[124] [2003] QB 306.   [125] *Clarke v Crew* [1999] NLJR 899.

[126] A 'dim view' is apparent in *obiter* comments in *Iqbal v Prison Officers Assocn* [2010] QB 732, at [71]–[72].

[127] Partial restraint was the subject of an action on the case, on proof of damage: *Wright v Wilson* (1699) 1 Ld Raym 739; *Bird v Jones* (1845) 7 QB 742, at 752.

[128] *Wright v Wilson* (1699) 1 Ld Raym 739; the court thought that a special action on the case would lie.

[129] *Walker v Comr of Police* [2015] 1 WLR 312 (restraint of a few seconds; damages of £5).

[130] But in *Kuchenmeister v Home Office* [1958] 1 QB 496, it was held to be imprisonment for immigration officers to prevent an alien from proceeding from an airport to an aircraft and from embarking on it, even though the Aliens Order 1953 authorised them to prescribe limits within which he must remain.

claimant to be restrained from leaving, say, the Isle of Man. Certainly, one might be confined in a mine,[131] in a house,[132] in a doorway,[133] or even in a vehicle.[134] The important point is that the defendant must fix boundaries to the area of confinement. As Coleridge J said in *Bird v Jones*:[135]

> Some confusion seems . . . to arise from confounding imprisonment of the body with mere loss of freedom . . . . Imprisonment . . . includes the notion of restraint within some limits defined by a will or power exterior to our own.

Lord Denman CJ, in his dissenting judgment in the same case, said:[136]

> As long as I am prevented from doing what I have a right to do, of what importance is it that I am permitted to do something else? . . . . If I am locked in a room, am I not imprisoned because I might effect my escape through a window, or because I might find an exit dangerous or inconvenient to myself, as by wading through water . . .?

Although this contention was rejected so far as the adequacy of a partial restraint is concerned, it is suggested that, if someone can escape only at the risk of personal injury, or if it is otherwise unreasonable[137] for her to escape, false imprisonment arises.

On the other hand, the barriers need not be physical. Thus, when a Commissioner in Lunacy wrongfully used his authority to dissuade the claimant from leaving his office, he was liable in false imprisonment.[138] By contrast, where a voluntary mental patient is restrained only in the sense that she would be compulsorily detained under mental health legislation *if she attempted to leave*, there is, according to House of Lords authority, no false imprisonment for the purposes of English tort law.[139] This is because the tort turns on actual, not merely potential or conditional, imprisonment.[140] (When the case was taken to Strasbourg, however, the European Court of Human Rights (ECtHR) held that there was a contravention of Article 5(1) of the ECHR.[141] In *Surrey CC v P*, the Supreme Court appears to have accepted the ECtHR analysis of this issue, emphasising in proceedings concerned with the Mental Capacity Act 2005 that the fact of deprivation is to be determined objectively, and arises where there is 'continuous supervision and control and lack of freedom to leave'.[142] This is so whether or not the person detained has the desire to leave. Lord Kerr stated that 'deprivation of liberty is not solely dependent on the reaction or acquiescence of the person whose liberty is curtailed'.[143])

---

[131] *Herd v Weardale Steel, Coal and Coke Co Ltd* [1915] AC 67.
[132] *Warner v Riddiford* (1858) 4 CBNS 180.   [133] *Walker v Comr of Police* [2015] 1 WLR 312.
[134] *Burton v Davies* [1953] QSR 26 (driving a car at such a speed as to prevent a passenger from alighting is false imprisonment).
[135] (1845) 7 QB 742, at 744.   [136] (1845) 7 QB 742, at 754–5.
[137] If A removes B's bathing costume in a swimming pool and B does not leave the pool until she has found someone to lend her another costume, is she falsely imprisoned?
[138] *Harnett v Bond* [1925] AC 669.
[139] *R v Bournewood Community and Mental Health NHS Trust, ex p L* [1999] 1 AC 458.
[140] But note the dissenting view of Lord Steyn ([1999] 1 AC 458, at 495) that it was a 'fairy tale' to suggest that the patient was free to leave.   [141] *HL v UK* (2005) 40 EHRR 32.
[142] [2014] 2 WLR 642, at [63].
[143] [2014] 2 WLR 642, at [76]. See also *Staffordshire CC v K* [2017] 2 WLR 1131.

Threat of force Restraint on movement, even by a mere *threat* of force that intimidates a person into compliance, is false imprisonment. This is to say that a restraint achieved by a mere assertion of authority is enough, which is what occurred in a case involving wrongful arrest by the police where no touching took place.[144] The claimant need not risk retaliation by resisting the defendant, even though she is *entitled* to use reasonable force to resist unlawful restraint.[145]

Prisoners Once a person is lawfully detained, changes in the conditions of her detention will not render it unlawful. In a series of cases, prisoners argued that detention in intolerable or unsanitary cells constitutes false imprisonment. The House of Lords rejected their claims.[146] Once a prisoner is lawfully imprisoned by virtue of the Prison Act 1952, she no longer enjoys any 'residual liberty' vis-à-vis the governor of the prison (and those officers acting in accordance with the governor's instructions), and the governor is entitled to restrain and define her movements.[147] This does not mean, however, that a prisoner subjected to intolerable hardship is remediless. In appropriate circumstances, she might have an action for assault and battery, for misfeasance in public office,[148] or, if the conditions of confinement affect her health, in negligence. It is suggested that a similar analysis may be applied to detention by police officers who retain the right to detain (albeit not in the unlawful manner). For, if a remedy in false imprisonment lay, once an arrested person could establish that the conditions of her detention rendered her further detention unlawful, the logical consequence would be that, from that moment on, she could go free, using reasonable force to effect her escape if necessary.

In *Olotu v Home Office* it was held that a person held on remand beyond the statutory time limit could not sue the prison authorities for false imprisonment.[149] The claimant was lawfully in the custody of the prison governor and only an order of the Crown Court could secure her release. The failure of the Crown Prosecution Service to bring her to trial, or arrange her release on bail, and her own surprising failure to apply for bail, did not affect the validity of her detention. The claimant's right was not a right to be released from prison per se, but a right to an order of the court releasing her on bail. In similar terms, a failure by the Parole Board to arrange an expeditious parole hearing for a prisoner does not permit a claim in false imprisonment for the period of the delay (although a claim under Article 5(1) of the European Convention might lie in 'exceptional circumstances' where the 'prisoner's continued detention had become arbitrary');[150] and a similar conclusion has been reached with respect to a failure by

---

[144] *Walker v Comr of Police* [2015] 1 WLR 312, at [23].   [145] *R v McKoy* [2002] EWCA Crim 1628.

[146] *R v Deputy Governor of Parkhurst Prison, ex p Hague* [1992] 1 AC 58. But note the *obiter* suggestion in *Toumia v Evans* [1999] Prison LR 153 that it is arguable that a gaoler who locks a prisoner in his cell in violation of the governor's orders may be liable under this tort.

[147] See *R v Deputy Governor of Parkhurst Prison, ex p Hague* [1992] 1 AC 58, at 164 and 176–8; *Iqbal v Prison Officers Assocn* [2010] QB 732.

[148] However, this would require proof of malice: *Three Rivers DC v Bank of England (No 3)* [2000] 2 WLR 1220.

[149] [1997] 1 WLR 328. See also *Quinland v Governor of Swaleside Prison* [2002] 3 WLR 807.

[150] *R (on the application of Sturnham) v Parole Board* [2013] 2 AC 254, at [13]. See also *Zenati v Comr of Police* [2015] QB 758, at [16] and [20].

a prison authority to release a prisoner into home detention curfew once he became eligible to be considered for this.[151]

Executive detention The Crown is liable in false imprisonment for executive detentions of persons subject to deportation orders, which become unlawful as a result of breaches of public law duties. In *R (Lumba and Mighty) v Secretary of State for the Home Department*, a material breach lay in the application of a secret and unlawful policy for detention, rather than the published policy.[152] Liability was held to arise even where the claimants inevitably would have been detained were the published criteria for detention applied because of the risk that they would abscond and commit offences. Lady Hale justified this result by stating that the 'law requires that decisions to detain should be made on rational grounds and in an open and transparent way and not in accordance with arbitrary rules laid down by Government and operated in secret'.[153] In *Kambadzi v Secretary of State for the Home Department*, the breach lay in a procedural failure to review the continuing detention of the applicant on the regular basis indicated within published policy guidelines. The system of review was characterised as 'integral to the lawfulness of the detention'.[154] In this case, Lords Brown and Rodger dissented, arguing (cogently, it is suggested) that '[t]heir Lordships in *Christie v Leachinsky* would . . . be astonished at the suggestion that any failure to give effect to a self-imposed requirement for periodic review of the continuing detention of those awaiting deportation . . . renders that detention unlawful'.[155]

Directness False imprisonment must result from an act of the defendant which deprives the claimant of her liberty directly.[156] So, it is not false imprisonment to cause a person to be temporarily detained in an asylum by making false statements to the authorities about her behaviour, it being the latter who exercise the restraint.[157] Again, prison officers do not falsely imprison prisoners who are scheduled for daily release from their cells (but are to remain within the confines of the prison) after the officers have gone suddenly on strike that day.[158]

Positive act A false imprisonment normally will result from some positive act;[159] but in *Herd v Weardale Steel, Coal and Coke Co*[160] the question was whether there might be liability in respect of a mere omission:

---

[151] *McCreaner v Ministry of Justice* [2015] 1 WLR 354, esp. at [33] and [35].
[152] [2012] 1 AC 245.   [153] [2012] 1 AC 245, at [205].
[154] [2011] 1 WLR 1299, at [87].
[155] [2011] 1 WLR 1299, at [108].
[156] *Iqbal v Prison Officers Assocn* [2010] QB 732, at [24], [69], and [77]–[78].
[157] But an action on the case lay against a medical practitioner, who negligently certified that C was insane, whereupon she was detained in a mental hospital: *De Freville v Dill* (1927) 96 LJKB 1056.
[158] *Iqbal v Prison Officers Assocn* [2010] QB 732; J Varuhas [2010] CLJ 438.
[159] Cf *Iqbal v Prison Officers Assocn* [2010] QB 732, at [21] and [35].
[160] [1913] 3 KB 771 (affd [1915] AC 67).

> C, a miner employed by Ds, descended into the mine in pursuance of his contract of employment. During his shift, C requested that Ds carry him to the surface in their cage. In refusing this request, Ds committed no breach of contract: their contractual obligation was to transport C to the surface at the end of his shift. The action in false imprisonment failed also.[161]

This case is authority for the proposition that failure to provide a means of egress from premises is not a tort when there is no duty to provide it. Thus, if A falls down B's mine while trespassing on B's land, it is not false imprisonment should B refuse to bring her to the surface in her lift. What the *Herd* case left undecided, however, is whether the failure to carry out a duty—contractual or otherwise—might constitute false imprisonment even though there has been no relevant positive act on the part of the defendant. Here we might note that the House of Lords in *R v Governor of Brockhill Prison, ex p Evans (No 2)*[162] made it clear that the tort is committed where an obligation to release a prisoner who has served his full term is not fulfilled on time. This general approach is fortified by the executive detention case of *Kambadzi v Secretary of State for the Home Department*, already discussed.

Burden Where a direct and intentional confinement can be shown, the burden of proof is upon the defendant to justify that confinement.[163] If this burden cannot be discharged, the defendant is liable no matter how short the period of detention. As mentioned earlier, the length of time imprisoned is a matter for damages.

(C) Knowledge of the claimant

There is no requirement that the claimant alleging false imprisonment be aware of the restraint on her freedom at the time of confinement. In *Meering v Grahame-White Aviation Co*,[164] a man persuaded by works police to remain in an office, but unaware that had he tried to leave he would have been prevented from doing so, successfully recovered damages for his imprisonment. The House of Lords in *Murray v Ministry of Defence*[165] endorsed the result, stating that actual knowledge of detention is not a necessary element of false imprisonment. According to Lord Griffiths, proof of a total restraint should suffice. He said:

> The law attaches supreme importance to the liberty of the individual and if he suffers a wrongful interference with that liberty it should remain actionable even without proof of special damage.[166]

It would seem to follow from this that, if a 'prisoner' has a reasonable means of escape at her disposal, but does not know of it, there will be a false imprisonment. However, the 'prisoner' might need to show that a reasonable person would not have known of the escape route, either.

---

[161] Cf *Robinson v Balmain New Ferry Co Ltd* [1910] AC 295, at 299: 'There is no law requiring the defendants to make the exit from their premises gratuitous to people who come there upon a definite contract which involves their leaving the wharf by another way.'

[162] [2001] 2 AC 19. Cf *Olotu v Home Office* [1997] 1 WLR 328.

[163] *R (Lumba and Mighty) v Secretary of State for the Home Department* [2012] 1 AC 245, at [64].

[164] (1919) 122 LT 44.   [165] [1988] 2 All ER 521.   [166] [1988] 1 WLR 692, at 704.

(D) Who is liable for a false imprisonment?

When deciding who can be sued for false imprisonment, the usual question is: who was 'active in promoting and causing' the confinement?[167] Often, this issue arises when a person is detained and charged for an offence where the arrest is unjustified by law.[168] (The separate question of lawful arrest as a defence is examined in chapter 13.) Giving information to the police, on the basis of which a police officer exercises her own judgement and arrests the claimant, does not impose on the informer responsibility for that arrest, however likely it is that an arrest will ensue from the information proffered. Thus, a store detective was not liable when the claimant was arrested on the basis of information which she gave to police officers, even though her information proved to be erroneous.[169] Even signing the charge sheet at the police station will not necessarily render the private citizen liable for the claimant's detention.[170] It must be shown that the claimant's detention was truly the act of the defendant rather than of the police. So, where a police officer refused to take the claimant into custody unless the defendant charged him and signed the charge sheet, the defendant, not the police officer, was held responsible for that detention.[171]

If the defendant wrongfully delivers the claimant into custody and then the magistrate remands the claimant, the defendant is answerable in false imprisonment for damages only up to the time of the judicial remand. Once a judicial act interposes, liability for false imprisonment ceases.[172]

It is important to distinguish false imprisonment from malicious prosecution. The latter is a tort concerned with the abuse of the judicial process, and which, unlike false imprisonment, calls for proof of malice and of absence of reasonable cause.[173] Therefore, if A wrongfully places a complaint against B before a magistrate, who then issues a warrant or tries her forthwith or remands her, A has not committed the tort of false imprisonment[174]—even if the magistrate has no jurisdiction.[175]

(E) Damages

General Like the other intentional torts considered in this chapter, false imprisonment is actionable without proof of damage.[176] In addition to damages for loss of liberty, the

---

[167] *Aitken v Bedwell* (1827) Mood & M 68.

[168] See *Pike v Waldrum and P & O Navigation Co* [1952] 1 Lloyd's Rep 431 on the liability of naval authorities and a ship's captain for the arrest of a seaman.

[169] *Davidson v CC of North Wales* [1994] 2 All ER 597. See also *Gosden v Elphick* (1849) 4 Exch 445.

[170] *Sewell v National Telephone Co* [1907] 1 KB 557; *Grinham v Willey* (1859) 4 H & N 496.

[171] *Austin v Dowling* (1870) LR 5 CP 534. See also *Ansell v Thomas* [1974] Crim LR 31, where it was recognised that a person might be liable in false imprisonment either because she herself effected the arrest or—in line with the general principle that she who instigates another to commit a tort is a joint tortfeasor—because she actively promoted the arrest of another.

[172] *Ahmed v Shafique* [2009] EWHC 618, at [78]; *Lock v Ashton* (1848) 12 QB 871.

[173] See ch 23.   [174] *Brown v Chapman* (1848) 6 CB 365.   [175] *West v Smallwood* (1838) 3 M & W 418.

[176] *R (Lumba and Mighty) v Secretary of State for the Home Department* [2012] 1 AC 245, at [64], [197], [212], [252], and [343]; *Kambadzi v Secretary of State for the Home Department* [2011] 1 WLR 1299, at [55] and [74]; *Murray v Ministry of Defence* [1988] 1 WLR 692, at 701–2.

court may compensate for injury to feelings and loss of reputation.[177] In *R (Lumba and Mighty) v Secretary of State for the Home Department*, the Supreme Court held that, where false imprisonment has occurred and the claimant was aware of the restraint, damages are to be more than nominal in nature. But there is no separate head of 'vindicatory' damages.[178]

Nominal damages In cases of unlawful executive detention where the defendant authority would have had the right to detain if it had applied the proper policy, it has been held by way of exception that damages may be merely nominal.[179] 'The amount of compensation to which a person is entitled must be affected by whether he would have suffered the loss and damage had things been done as they should have been done.'[180]

Aggravated damages Aggravated damages might be awarded where the claimant has been humiliated during her false imprisonment by the police,[181] although there is a suggestion that this should happen in 'exceptional cases' only.[182]

Exemplary damages Exemplary damages are exceptional. They are granted only where the sum of basic and aggravated damages is inadequate to punish the defendant for oppressive and arbitrary behaviour. An award of exemplary damages constitutes a windfall for the claimant and the amount awarded must be no more than is sufficient to communicate disapproval of relevant behaviour.

Human Rights Act Quite apart from the common law, an action might lie under the Human Rights Act 1998 in respect of a breach of the Article 5 right to liberty. In such cases, the court is required to grant damages that provide 'just satisfaction' to the claimant.[183] This is a vindicatory award and need not, in principle, be limited to the same compensatory figure that would be awarded under the nominate tort of false imprisonment. For even though there will be some degree of overlap between an action premised on Convention rights and one based on the common law, the two are not coextensive.[184] If, however, a claimant does pursue a remedy under the 1998 Act, she must demonstrate a causal link between the breach of Article 5 and her detention.[185]

---

[177] *Hook v Cunard Steamship Co Ltd* [1953] 1 All ER 1021.

[178] On this latter point: [2012] 1 AC 245, at [101], [170], [195], [236]–[237], and [335].

[179] *R (Lumba and Mighty) v Secretary of State for the Home Department* [2012] 1 AC 245, at [71] and [161].

[180] *Kambadzi v Secretary of State for the Home Department* [2011] 1 WLR 1299, at [74]. See also ibid at [89].

[181] See *Wainwright v Home Office* [2002] 3 WLR 405 (affd [2004] 2 AC 406).

[182] *Richardson v Howie* [2005] PIQR Q3, at [23].

[183] Human Rights Act 1998, sub-s 8(3). For further details see *R (on the application of Sturnham) v Parole Board* [2013] 2 WLR 1157; *R (on the application of KB) v Mental Health Review Tribunal* [2004] QB 936.

[184] Cf the Human Rights Act 1998, sub-s 8(3), which requires the court to take into account 'any other relief or remedy granted' and the analogous decision in *Merson v Cartwright* [2005] UKPC 38.

[185] *R (on the application of Richards) v Secretary of State for the Home Department* [2004] EWHC 93.

Conclusions

This chapter has considered ways in which the law of torts protects bodily and dignitary interests as well as interests in autonomy. The three trespass torts of battery, assault, and false imprisonment have some overlap in their operation, and each is constructed upon elements of fault and directness of interference with the claimant's interests. These torts are supplemented by the Protection from Harassment Act 1998 (a statutory tort) and the intentional infliction of harm tort, the latter being revived recently by the UK Supreme Court, although it has been given a narrow compass because of the strict insistence upon the presence of intention to harm—recklessness in the causation of harm will not do.

Problem question

Zain was having trouble paying his electricity bills, issued by his supplier Zapper Electricity. When he was two months in arrears, an agent came to turn off the supply of electricity at his flat. This was unlawful. Zain told the agent that, if he did not turn the electricity back on, Zain would ensure that the agent 'would need to call a cab to get home'. The agent held up his wrench as he made his way past Zain in the stairway and left the flats quickly thereafter. Zain spent two days in his flat, which was freezing cold. The next morning two demands for payment of the electricity bill were pushed through his letter box. The letters stated that, if payment were not received immediately, Zain would be 'prosecuted to the full extent of the law'. Furious at having received these letters of demand, Zain made his way to the nearest branch of Zapper Electricity. When he was there, he was invited by the manager to have a 'discussion' about the unpaid bills. The branch manager, Phil, asked Zain whether he wanted a cup of coffee. Zain responded that he did. On his way out of the room, Phil said he would lock the door—just to make sure that Zain did not wander off before the matter of the unpaid bills was resolved. Phil was gone for ten minutes because he had to answer a call before making the coffee. While he was gone, Zain looked for a means of escape. He chose not to climb out of the window—because the room was located on the second floor of the Zapper branch building.

Advise the parties as to the availability of any actions for torts to the person.

 Visit **http://www.oup.com/Uk/Street15e/** for answer guidance.

Further reading

BEEVER, 'Transferred Malice in Tort Law?' (2009) 29 *Legal Studies* 400

CANE, '*Mens Rea* in Tort Law' (2000) 20 *Oxford Journal of Legal Studies* 533

FINNIS, 'Intention in Tort Law' in Owen (ed), *Philosophical Foundations of Tort Law* (1995)

PROSSER, 'Transferred Intent' (1967) 45 *Texas Law Review* 650

TRINDADE, 'Intentional Torts: Some Thoughts on Assault and Battery' (1982) 2 *Oxford Journal of Legal Studies* 211

11

Wrongful interference with goods

KEY ISSUES

(1) Wide protection of interests in goods
The common law offers a wide degree of protection not just to the body, but to other physical interests—in this case, to interests in goods.

(2) Focus on possession
Protection is offered to those who are owners of goods (especially in negligence and the residual actions on the case), but the main interest protected by the torts of trespass and conversion examined in this chapter is that of possession of goods. Possession arises where there is sufficient evidence of both an intention by the claimant to exercise control over goods on his own behalf and actual, subsisting control.

(3) Trespass to goods
The action in trespass to goods arises where there has been an intentional or negligent direct interference with goods in the claimant's possession at the time of the trespass.

(4) Conversion
The action in conversion arises where the defendant has dealt with goods intentionally in a manner that constitutes a denial of the claimant's rights. The action can be brought by the claimant where the claimant had actual possession or an immediate right to possession of the goods.

(5) Remedies
The remedies available for torts to goods (including relevant actions in negligence) are governed by the Torts (Interference with Goods) Act 1977.

Section 1 Introduction

The law protects persons whose title to, or possession of, goods is interfered with, or whose goods are damaged by intentional conduct, although this is not done in any systematic way. The major torts to goods of trespass and conversion protect interests in possession. Possession arises where there is sufficient evidence of both an intention by the claimant to exercise control over goods on his own behalf and actual, subsisting control.[1] In addition, where goods are lost or damaged as a result of the defendant's

---

[1] *JA Pye (Oxford) Ltd v Graham* [2003] 1 AC 419, at [40]; *Mainline Private Hire Ltd v Nolan* [2011] EWCA Civ 189, at [2]. For more detail, see below.

breach of a duty of care, an action may lie in negligence. The Torts (Interference with Goods) Act 1977 introduces a collective description 'wrongful interference with goods'[2] to cover trespass to goods, conversion, negligence resulting in damage to goods or an interest in goods, and any other tort insofar as it results in damage to goods or to an interest in goods. This is done to facilitate common treatment of remedies and procedure respecting all torts to goods.

Section 2 Trespass to goods

The action for trespass to goods affords a remedy where there has been an intentional or negligent direct interference with goods in the claimant's possession at the time of the trespass, whether that be by taking the goods from him, or by damaging the goods without removing them. But it is of no help where the relevant interference with the goods was indirect; nor is it likely to be of assistance where the goods were not in the possession of the claimant. The tort protects several interests: the claimant's interest in the possession of his goods; his interest in the physical condition of the goods; and the inviolability of goods, so that meddling with the goods, such as wrongful wheel clamping will constitute trespass to goods.[3]

(A) Title to sue

General In order to prove title to sue, the claimant must be in possession of the goods at the time of the interference. Possession connotes both the power of exercising physical control and the intention to exercise such control on his own behalf.[4] Whether the claimant is the owner is immaterial. If A finds goods one day, B's snatching them from him the next day would constitute trespass. But, if E and F come across unclaimed goods, and in a scuffle for them E snatches them from F's hand, F has no possession upon which to found a suit in trespass.[5] Although these points are tolerably clear, the courts have held also that 'constructive possession' provides sufficient title to sue in trespass. A cyclist leaving his cycle outside a shop remains in possession of it but, if a thief rides away on it, the thief then has possession although he obtained it wrongfully.[6] It has been held also that a claimant who left his car at a garage to be repaired, where it was wrongfully removed from the forecourt, had a good title to sue.[7]

In *Johnson v Diprose*, Lord Esher held that there would be sufficient title to sue if the claimant had 'a legal right to the immediate possession' of goods.[8] Any bailee, even a

---

[2] Torts (Interference with Goods) Act 1977, s 1.

[3] *Vine v Waltham Forest LBC* [2000] 1 WLR 2383.

[4] *JA Pye (Oxford) Ltd v Graham* [2003] 1 AC 419, at [40]; *Mainline Private Hire Ltd v Nolan* [2011] EWCA Civ 189, at [2].   [5] *Peachey v Wing* (1826) 5 LJOSKB 55.

[6] *Costello v CC of Derbyshire Constabulary* [2001] 1 WLR 1437 (confirms that a thief can sue; thus the police who detain a stolen car are liable to C (not actually the thief) when they are unable to identify the real owner).

[7] *Wilson v Lombank* [1963] 1 All ER 740.

[8] *Colwill v Reeves* (1811) 2 Camp 575.

gratuitous one,[9] can sue in trespass. The Crown could sue therefore in respect of the loss of Post Office mail.[10] A bailor does not have possession and therefore ordinarily cannot sue in trespass for an act done to the goods bailed.[11] If, however, the bailor has an immediate right to possession as in the case of a bailment at will—for example, where a young man had lent his car to his girlfriend while he was on holiday[12]—he may then sue.[13]

Exceptions There are two significant exceptions to the rule that possession is essential. First, the title of executors or administrators relates back to the death of the deceased, and this entitles them to sue for a trespass between the date of the death and the date of the grant.[14] Second, it can be assumed that all trustees may sue for trespass to goods in the hands of the beneficiary on the basis that they share possession with him.[15]

(B) Character of the defendant's act

Interference Trespass involves a direct interference with goods, meaning that there is no significant act of volition between what the defendant does and the relevant interference. The 'interference' might arise in a number of ways. It is trespass to goods to beat a dog,[16] to cut and take away trees,[17] and to wheel-clamp unlawfully.[18] Whether the goods are capable of being stolen is irrelevant.[19] Taking goods out of the possession of another,[20] moving them from one place to another,[21] and even bringing one's person into contact with them[22] each have been held to be trespass.

Directness There can be no trespass if the interference is indirect.[23] Thus, although he who mixes a drug with the feed of a racehorse commits a trespass to the feed, he does not commit a trespass to the racehorse when it is later given the feed.[24] Moreover, to lock the room in which the claimant has his goods is not a trespass to them.[25]

Actionable per se? A dictum of Lord Blanesburgh in *Leitch & Co Ltd v Leydon*[26] is often cited to support the view that trespass to goods is always actionable per se. But

---

[9] *Rooth v Wilson* (1817) 1 B & Ald 59.

[10] *Attersoll v Stevens* (1808) 1 Taunt 183; *The Winkfield* [1902] P 42.

[11] *Gordon v Harper* (1796) 7 Term Rep 9; *Ward v Macauley* (1791) 4 Term Rep 489.

[12] *O'Sullivan v Williams* [1992] 3 All ER 385.

[13] *Lotan v Cross* (1810) 2 Camp 464; *Penfolds Wines Pty Ltd v Elliott* (1946) 74 CLR 204, at 226–8.

[14] *Tharpe v Stallwood* (1843) 5 Man & G 760.   [15] See *Barker v Furlong* [1891] 2 Ch 172 (conversion).

[16] *Wright v Ramscot* (1667) 1 Saund 84.   [17] *Heydon v Smith* (1610) 2 Brownl 328.

[18] *Vine v Waltham Forest LBC* [2000] 1 WLR 2383. It is unlawful to clamp without a licence: see the Private Security Industry Act 2001, sub-s 3(2)(j).   [19] [1948] 2 KB 311, at 322.

[20] *Brewer v Dew* (1843) 11 M & W 625.

[21] *Kirk v Gregory* (1876) 1 Ex D 55; *Fouldes v Willoughby* (1841) 8 M & W 540, at 544–5.

[22] *Fouldes v Willoughby* (1841) 8 M & W 540, at 549 (*obiter*): 'Scratching the panel of a carriage would be a trespass.'

[23] *Covell v Laming* (1808) 1 Camp 497. Just as in trespass to the person, there will always be difficult questions of where directness ends and indirectness begins. See, eg, *White v Withers LLP* [2010] 1 FLR 859.

[24] *Hutchins v Maughan* [1947] VLR 131.   [25] *Hartley v Moxham* (1842) 3 QB 701.

[26] [1931] AC 90, at 106.

technically the matter was left undecided in that case. Some, on the other hand, state that there is clear authority for the proposition that trespass is actionable per se, but only where there is a dispossession of the claimant. Yet in *Kirk v Gregory*,[27] a woman who moved rings belonging to a man who had just died from one room in his house to another was held liable in nominal damages for this. This case has been treated as consistent with this latter view, but an asportation (or moving) of the goods is not necessarily a dispossession.[28] If, in gently reversing my car, I touch the bumper of another car, the brake of which has not been applied, and, without damaging it, cause it to move a few inches, I have not dispossessed the owner, though I have asported it.

A question arose in *White v Withers LLP* as to the extent to which the law will, in modern times, tolerate actions in trespass to goods which do not involve interferences of a substantial nature:[29]

> D was a law firm which had been provided by C's wife with C's financial and personal papers for the purposes of divorce proceedings. C had not known of or consented to this action. D had the papers photocopied and returned to C only after significant delay.

Sedley LJ appeared doubtful (on an application to strike out) that a technical breach of the '*Hildebrand* rules',[30] which governed a spouse's ability lawfully to photocopy such documents without consent, would sound in damages. Furthermore, he stated: 'The claim for a shilling in damages in order to prove a point and obtain an award of costs is history.'[31] But there are good reasons for making all trespasses to goods actionable per se, and such an approach is consistent with the bulk of the authorities as well as general principle in the trespass torts. Otherwise the law would leave remediless the perhaps not oversensitive person who declined to wear her Armani blouse again after her flat-mate had 'borrowed' it to wear to a party. Perhaps the correct question, in step with other trespasses, is whether the relevant touching was beyond what is acceptable in everyday life.[32] Picking up and admiring a friend's Armani blouse might not be so objectionable as wearing it without her permission. That said, a clear rule is better than an unclear rule.

(C) Fault

The problem of whether there is liability for trespasses which are neither intentional nor negligent has been examined in chapter 10. The same approach is taken in this context so that there is no liability in respect of an act that is neither intentional nor negligent.[33] There is, then, no liability for a simple accidental trespass to goods.[34] But, if the defendant intended to interfere, his trespass is intentional even though he did not know that his act amounted to a trespass (for example, if he believed the goods to be his own).

---

[27] (1876) 1 Ex D 55.   [28] Cf *Burroughes v Bayne* (1860) 5 H & N 296, at 305–6.
[29] [2010] 1 FLR 859. The issue in conversion is different, the court having to find a dealing seriously inconsistent with the rights of another.   [30] *Hildebrand v Hildebrand* [1992] 1 FLR 244.
[31] [2010] 1 FLR 859, at [72]. See also ibid, at [61].
[32] Cf trespass to the person: *F v West Berkshire HA* [1989] 2 All ER 545.
[33] *National Coal Board v J E Evans & Co (Cardiff) Ltd* [1951] 2 KB 861.
[34] See *Manton v Brocklebank* [1923] 2 KB 212, at 229.

(D) Other matters

'Trespass to goods' is included in the definition of a 'wrongful interference with goods' within the Torts (Interference with Goods) Act 1977.[35] Thus, by virtue of the Act's express application the defence of *jus tertii* (that the claimant cannot sue because better title to the goods existed in a third person) is no longer available,[36] and the statutory rules regarding co-ownership apply, as do all forms of relief provided by that Act in appropriate cases (all considered in this chapter).[37]

(E) Damages

Where the claimant has been deprived of goods, he is entitled to their value by way of damages. A claimant may recover general damages for loss of use of goods (as distinct from special damages for loss of profits from the goods) although he would not have been using them during the period within which he has been deprived of their use.[38] The provisions of the Torts (Interference with Goods) Act 1977, considered below, apply in this context.

Section 3 Conversion

Origins The action for *conversion* (originally called trover) developed upon a legal fiction.[39] The original form of the pleadings alleged that the defendant had found the claimant's chattels and had wrongfully converted them to his own use.[40] The allegation of finding could not be contested and the essence of the tort became the wrongful conversion of the goods to the use of the defendant.

Definition Conversion involves an intentional[41] dealing with 'goods'[42] that is seriously inconsistent with the possession or right to immediate possession of another person. The tort protects the claimant's interest in the dominion and control over his goods (so long as the interference occurs in England or Wales).[43] It does not protect his interest

---

[35] Torts (Interference with Goods) Act 1977, sub-s 1(b).

[36] Torts (Interference with Goods) Act 1977, sub-s 8(1). Sub-section 11(1) excludes contributory negligence as a defence in proceedings based on intentional trespass.

[37] Torts (Interference with Goods) Act 1977, sub-s 10(1).   [38] *The Mediana* [1900] AC 113, at 117–18.

[39] Short histories can be found in S Douglas [2009] CLJ 198; SFC Milsom [1954] CLJ 105; B Simpson (1959) 75 LQR 364. For comprehensive treatment, see S Green and J Randall, *The Tort of Conversion* (2009).

[40] The courts wished to encourage the use of conversion but could not do so unless there were some (fictional) reason for which the torts in trespass *de bonis asportatis* and replevin did not apply. 'Loss and finding was convenient . . . and over time became standard': S Green and J Randall, *The Tort of Conversion* (2009), 13. The 'need' for an allegation of losing and finding was abolished by the Common Law Procedure Act 1852, s 49.

[41] At common law an act of conversion had to be a voluntary act; hence the need to make the wrongful loss or destruction of goods by a bailee in breach of duty a statutory conversion once detinue was abolished.

[42] The term 'goods' is used as a matter of convenience. Technically, conversion is based on property and possession, but it is limited to tangible, movable property. See S Green (2008) 71 MLR 114 and discussion in section 3(B).   [43] *Mazur Media Ltd v Mazur Media GmbH* [2005] 1 Lloyd's Rep 41.

in their physical condition. This is why the tort is so much concerned with problems of title to personal property.[44]

Relationship with trespass As seizing goods and carrying them away is clearly a wrongful conversion of goods, conversion often is available concurrently with trespass. But merely moving or damaging goods without converting them to the defendant's own use remains remediable in trespass alone.[45]

(A) Title to sue

The claimant must have *either* possession *or* the right to immediate possession in order to sue.[46] Equitable rights do not suffice;[47] indeed the law on conversion favours possession at the expense of ownership. Thus, if a landlord has rented out furnished accommodation for a fixed term and a third party commits an act of conversion in respect of some of the furniture, the landlord has no right to sue in conversion but the tenant might have such a right.[48]

(1) Bailment

Where goods have been entrusted to another so as to create a bailment relationship, the bailee can sue third parties in conversion.[49] If the bailment is determinable at will, the bailor may sue also because he is deemed to have an immediate right to possession.[50] A bailment that originally gave to the bailor no immediate right to possess may become a bailment at will. *Manders v Williams*[51] is illustrative:

> C supplied porter in casks to a publican on condition that he was to return the empty casks within six months. It was held that C could sue a sheriff who seized some empty casks (within six months of their being supplied) in connection with a debt owed by the publican. Under the contract, once the casks were empty, the publican became a bailee at will, whereupon C was entitled to immediate possession.

---

[44] The tort appears to be actionable without proof of special damage: *Hiort v London and NW Rly Co* (1879) 4 Ex D 188. See discussion in text that follows.

[45] *Bushel v Miller* (1718) 1 Stra 128; *Fouldes v Willoughby* (1841) 8 M & W 540.

[46] *The Future Express* [1993] 2 Lloyd's Rep 542; *Gordon v Harper* (1796) 7 Term Rep 9. See also N Curwen [2004] Conv 308. A contractual right to immediate possession of goods is a sufficient interest to sue: *Islamic Republic of Iran v Barakat Galleries Ltd* [2008] EWCA Civ 1374, at [30].

[47] *Hounslow LBC v Jenkins* [2004] EWHC 315. 'The reason for equitable interests being an insufficient basis for title to sue in Conversion is very simple: an equitable interest is not a possessory interest per se': S Green and J Randall, *The Tort of Conversion* (2009), 104.

[48] *Gordon v Harper* (1796) 7 Term Rep 9 and see: *Roberts v Wyatt* (1810) 2 Taunt 268; *City Motors (1933) Pty Ltd v Southern Aerial Super Service Pty Ltd* (1961) 106 CLR 477.

[49] The bailment gives him the right to possession of the goods for the period of the bailment. In *The Winkfield* [1902] P 42, the Postmaster-General, as bailee, could recover the full value of mail lost through D's wrongdoing.

[50] As the bailment can be terminated at will, the owner retains the right to demand the goods back instantly: *Nicolls v Bastard* (1835) 2 Cr M & R 659; *Kahler v Midland Bank Ltd* [1950] AC 24, at 56.

[51] (1849) 4 Exch 339.

Where a bailor and bailee enjoy concurrent rights to sue in conversion, they cannot both exercise those rights and so obtain double recovery against the defendant.[52] The successful claimant who sues first must then account to the other for the proportion of the damages representing his interest in the property. So, where the owner of a car had lent the vehicle to his girlfriend, and the car was damaged while in her possession, his successful claim for damages based on his right to recover the car at will precluded a second action by the girlfriend, albeit she had possession of the car at the time the damage was done.[53]

In many cases, however, the crucial issue for the bailor who owns the goods is whether he enjoys a right to immediate possession: is the bailment, or has it become, a bailment at will? Or has some wrongful act of the bailee ended the bailment? If a bailee commits a wrongful act that can be deemed to terminate the bailment, the bailor may sue. Sale of the goods by the bailee ordinarily will terminate the bailment and the bailor can sue either the bailee or the third party.[54] Destruction of the goods[55] or dealing with them in a manner wholly inconsistent with the terms of the bailment[56] will have the same result. Thus, often it will be a matter of interpreting the contract to decide whether a particular act of the bailee determines the bailment, or makes it determinable at will.[57] This is true especially in the case of hire-purchase agreements which normally prohibit the hirer from selling or otherwise disposing of the goods,[58] and empower the owner to terminate the agreement if the prohibition is disregarded. If, for example, the agreement dispenses with notice of termination to the hirer, the owner can sue a party who purchases from the hirer in unwitting contravention of such a prohibition.[59] Consider *Whiteley Ltd v Hilt*:[60]

> A hire-purchase agreement allowed the hirer to purchase a piano after payment of the final instalment. It did not prohibit her from transferring the piano during the hiring period. The owners had no cause of action against the transferee, who had paid all the instalments that remained owing.

This can be compared with *Belsize Motor Supply Co v Cox*:[61]

> The owners were authorised to end the agreement if the hirers parted with possession of the hired goods. It was held that (i) the owners could recover from a pledgee of the hirer only the instalments that were owing still; and (ii) that the agreement continued in force despite the transfer of the goods.

---

[52] *Nicolls v Bastard* (1835) 2 Cr M & R 659 (once one has sued, the case is closed).

[53] *O'Sullivan v Williams* [1992] 3 All ER 385.

[54] *Cooper v Willomatt* (1845) 1 CB 672; *Scotland v Solomon* [2002] EWHC 1886.

[55] *Bryant v Wardell* (1848) 2 Exch 479, at 482.

[56] *Plasycoed Collieries Co Ltd v Partridge, Jones & Co Ltd* [1912] 2 KB 345, at 351. Presumably, this does not extend to excess of permitted user.

[57] But the contractual terms are not always determinative—the actions of the bailor and bailee are also relevant in determining the true position: *Mainline Private Hire Ltd v Nolan* [2011] EWCA Civ 189.

[58] It is standard practice in hire-purchase agreements, by express terms, to make the benefits of the hirer's option to purchase unassignable: *Helstan Securities Ltd v Hertfordshire CC* [1978] 3 All ER 262.

[59] *Union Transport Finance Ltd v British Car Auctions Ltd* [1978] 2 All ER 385.   [60] [1918] 2 KB 808.

[61] [1914] 1 KB 244; *Wickham Holdings Ltd v Brooke House Motors Ltd* [1967] 1 All ER 117.

In effect, the courts treat hire-purchase agreements as *sui generis* in that they are regarded as creating a proprietary interest separate from the contractual interest under the bailment agreement.[62]

(2) Lien and pledge

Lien In certain cases where goods are entrusted to another to carry out particular services (for example, repairs or storage), the person in possession acquires a lien over the goods. Ordinarily he will be entitled to retain the goods until he is paid for the services.[63] But if title to the goods has passed to some third party (now the claimant), and the defendant who is holding the goods knows this, the defendant loses his right to retain the goods and must deliver them up to the claimant.[64] The holder of a lien has a sufficient possessory interest to sue in conversion. But if a lien holder once wrongfully parts with possession of the goods, he loses his lien, and his act is a conversion which itself ends the bailment and entitles the owner to sue him.[65]

Pledge A pledge (that is, the deposit of goods as security for a debt), however, confers something more than a lien. It confers a power to sell in default of payment on the agreed date. So, in *Donald v Suckling*[66] it was held that a re-pledge by the pledgee did not end the pledge and the original pledgor could not sue the second pledgee without tendering the sum owing. Similarly, the assignee of a pledgor cannot sue the pledgee who sells the goods because, until the sum owing is paid, there is no immediate right to possession.[67]

(3) Sale

Often, it is difficult to discover which of the parties to a contract for the sale of goods has an interest sufficient to support an action in conversion. The crucial question is whether, at the date of the alleged conversion, the buyer has a sufficient right to immediate possession.[68] In *Empresa Exportadora de Azucar v IANSA*,[69] the claimants had contracted to buy, and had paid for, two cargoes of sugar to be shipped to them in Chile by the defendants from Cuba. On the orders of the Cuban Government, after a military takeover in Chile, the ship discharging the first cargo sailed away with the cargo only partially unloaded and the second ship was diverted back to Cuba part way through its voyage. The buyers were held to have had an immediate right to possession of both the partially unloaded cargo and the diverted cargo and succeeded in conversion against the sellers.

Sales on credit terms pose greater difficulties. In *Bloxam v Sanders*[70] it was held that, where goods were sold on credit, the buyer ordinarily could sue the seller in conversion if he wrongfully sold the goods to a third party, but that, if the seller exercised his right

---

[62] Cf *Karflex Ltd v Poole* [1933] 2 KB 251, at 263–4; *On Demand Information plc v Michael Gerson (Finance) plc* [2001] 1 WLR 155, at 171; *VFS Financial Services (UK) Ltd v Euro Auctions (UK) Ltd* [2007] EWHC 1492.
[63] See A Bell, *Modern Law of Personal Property* (1989), ch 6.
[64] *Pendragon plc v Walon Ltd* [2005] EWHC 1082.   [65] *Mulliner v Florence* (1878) 3 QBD 484.
[66] (1866) LR 1 QB 585.   [67] *Halliday v Holgate* (1868) LR 3 Exch 299.
[68] See, eg, *Wood v Bell* (1856) 5 E & B 772.   [69] [1983] 2 Lloyd's Rep 171.   [70] (1825) 4 B & C 941.

of stoppage *in transitu* upon the buyer becoming insolvent, the buyer could no longer sue. In the absence of credit terms, the buyer, although he might have property in the goods, has no right to immediate possession until he tenders the price.[71]

(4) Licensee

Sometimes a licensee may be able to sue in conversion. In *Northam v Bowden*[72] the claimant had a licence to prospect certain land for tin, and the defendant, without permission, carted away some of the soil on this land. It was held that 'if the claimant had a right to the gravel and soil for the purpose of getting any mineral that could be found in it, he had such a possession of the whole as entitled him to maintain an action for its conversion against a wrongdoer.'[73] Apart from such cases of *profits à prendre*, licensees of goods are bailees and call for no separate treatment.

(5) Finders

The rule that possession is sufficient to ground a claim in conversion means that, in certain circumstances, someone who finds a chattel can keep it and protect his right to do so against third parties.[74] In *Armory v Delamirie*,[75] a chimney sweep's boy who found a jewel was able to sue when the goldsmith's apprentice to whom he had handed the jewel for valuation refused to return it. The rules were settled in *Parker v British Airways Board* although, as Donaldson LJ pointed out, their application to particular cases is often difficult:

> The finder of a chattel acquires rights over it if the true owner is unknown and the chattel appears to have been abandoned or lost and he takes it into his care and control. He acquires a right to keep it against all but the true owner or one who can assert a prior right to keep the chattel which was subsisting at the time when the finder took the chattel into his care and control.[76]

On the other hand, any employee or agent who finds goods in the course of his employment is deemed to do so on behalf of his employer, who acquires a finder's rights. Anyone with finder's rights has an obligation to take reasonable steps to trace the true owner.[77]

Finally, an occupier of land or a building has rights superior to those of a finder over goods in, under, or attached to that land or building. Thus, a medieval gold brooch buried eight inches under the soil in a public park found by the use of a metal detector,[78] and a prehistoric boat embedded in the soil six feet below the surface,[79] belonged to the respective landowners. Similar rules apply to ships, vehicles, and aircraft. Yet an occupier of premises has rights superior to those of a finder over goods upon or in, but not

---

[71] Cf *Chinery v Viall* (1860) 5 H & N 288.   [72] (1855) 11 Exch 70.   [73] (1855) 11 Exch 70, at 73.
[74] R Hickey, *Property and the Law of Finders* (2010).   [75] (1722) 1 Stra 505.
[76] [1982] QB 1004, at 1017.
[77] Cf R Hickey, *Property and the Law of Finders* (2010), 4, summarising the thesis that 'English law can . . . be shown to encourage a finder to act in favour of the loser, but it does not do so by imposing a specific obligation.'
[78] *Waverley BC v Fletcher* [1996] QB 334. See also *South Staffordshire Water Co v Sharman* [1896] 2 QB 44.
[79] *Elwes v Brigg Gas Co* (1886) 33 Ch D 562.

attached to, the premises only if, before the finding, he has manifested an intention to exercise control over the building and the things which may be upon it or in it.[80]

(6) *Jus tertii* (third party rights)

By virtue of the Torts (Interference with Goods) Act 1977,[81] the defendant in an action for conversion or other wrongful interference is entitled to prove that a third party has a better right than the claimant with respect to all or any part of the interest claimed by the claimant. The aims of this provision are to avoid a multiplicity of actions by allowing interested third parties to apply to be joined in actions, to protect defendants against the risk of being liable to two different claimants in respect of the same interference, and to limit the claimant's damages to his actual loss. The relevant date for ascertaining the interest of the third party is the date of the alleged conversion.[82]

(B) The subject matter

In principle, any goods can be converted. But troublesome issues have arisen in two areas concerning human bodily products and choses in action.

Human bodily products The trend appears to be towards permitting actions of conversion regarding human bodily products, although the law is still in a state of development. In *Dobson v North Tyneside Health Authority*,[83] the claimants' daughter's brain was removed after she had died in hospital. The brain was initially stored at the second defendant's hospital, but subsequently disposed of. The claimants sued in conversion, alleging that the defendants' failure to keep and preserve the brain deprived them of the opportunity to discover whether the deceased's tumours were benign or malignant. The Court of Appeal dismissed the claim for conversion, reaffirming the principle that generally there is no property right in a corpse, or its parts. Only where some significant process has been undertaken to alter that body, or preserve it for scientific or exhibition purposes, can any title to the body be claimed.[84]

Dobson expressly addressed property in tissue and organs taken from the dead. But *obiter dicta* in the case suggest that a similar approach should be taken in relation to products taken from living human bodies. Indeed, the fact that the Human Tissue Act 2004, section 32 prohibits commercial dealings in organs for transplant has been argued to be indicative of 'a legislative intent to preclude actions for damages reckoned by their value'.[85]

More recently, the Court of Appeal in *Yearworth v North Bristol NHS Trust*[86] considered the status of stored sperm. Although the claims for accidental destruction of the

---

[80] *Parker v British Airways Board* [1982] QB 1004.
[81] Torts (Interference with Goods) Act 1977, sub-s 8(1).   [82] *De Franco v MPC* (1987) *Times*, 8 May.
[83] [1996] 4 All ER 474.
[84] *AB v Leeds Teaching Hospital* (2004) 77 BMLR 145. So, a museum possessing a valuable Egyptian mummy can assert a claim to that mummy, and, apparently, doctors who deliberately preserved a two-headed foetus could maintain a similar claim: *Doodeward v Spence* (1908) 6 CLR 406.
[85] *Clerk and Lindsell on Torts* (2006), 1024.   [86] [2010] QB 1.

sperm brought by men who had entered into agreements[87] with the defendant Health Trust for its storage were for negligence, the case points towards the availability of an action in conversion. An important issue was whether the loss of the sperm constituted damage to the men's property.[88] The court concluded that, although the Human Tissue Act 2004 circumscribed the ability of the men to direct the use of their stored sperm, they had property in it. Steps in the chain of reasoning included the following. First, 'a distinction between the capacity to own body parts or products which have, and which have not, been subject to the exercise of work or skill is not entirely logical'.[89] Second, the men alone generated by their bodies and ejaculated the sperm. Third, the 'sole object of their ejaculation of the sperm was that, in certain events, it might later be used for their benefit'.[90] Fourth, the men retained absolute negative control over the use of the sperm in that they could direct that it not be used in certain ways. Moreover 'the Act recognises in the men a fundamental feature of ownership, namely that at any time they can require the destruction of [the stored] sperm'.[91] The court concluded that the defendant was liable for losses in tort and for breach of a bailment agreement. 'The law of bailment provides them with a remedy under which, in principle, they are entitled to compensation for any psychiatric injury (or actionable distress) foreseeably consequent upon the breach.'[92]

Given the reasoning and the result in *Yearworth*, it is not surprising that it has been argued that an action must now lie in conversion for damage to or destruction of sperm[93]—and presumably other bodily parts or products capable of designation as property where brought by their 'originators'.[94] The difficulty, such as it is, would lie in proving possession, or an immediate right to possession of the sperm, stored at a hospital.

Choses in action Although cheques are of value only as *choses in action*, the courts have allowed the full value represented by them to be recovered in conversion except where altered so as to become worthless pieces of paper.[95] So, where bankers do not handle actual cash, but merely make the appropriate account entries, the courts treat the conversion as being of the cheque under which the money was transferred, and the value as the sum represented by the cheque.[96] This doctrine, applicable to all negotiable instruments, shows that conversion might lie in respect of rights in intangible property. But this is not the limit. In *Bavins Jnr and Sims v London and South Western Bank*,[97] the Court of Appeal thought that the full value of a non-negotiable document evidencing a debt could be recovered in an action for conversion. Equally, any intangible right that

---

[87] These were not for consideration; thus no suit could be brought for breach of contract. Claims included damages for psychiatric injury following the accidental destruction of the sperm.
[88] [2010] QB 1, at [14]–[15] and [26].   [89] [2010] QB 1, at [45-d].   [90] [2010] QB 1, at [45-f].
[91] [2010] QB 1, at [45-f].   [92] [2010] QB 1, at [58].   [93] C Hawes (2010) 73 MLR 130.
[94] The wider applicability of the principle from this case is foreshadowed in the judgment itself: see [2010] QB 1, at [45-f] (example of severed finger). Commentators have presumed that claims may now be made with respect to human tissue in general: SHE Harmon and GT Laurie (2010) 69 CLJ 476.
[95] *Smith v Lloyd's TSB Group plc* [2001] QB 541.
[96] *Lloyds Bank v Chartered Bank of India, Australia and China* [1929] 1 KB 40, at 55–6.
[97] [1900] 1 QB 270.

is represented in the ordinary course of business by a special written instrument, even though not negotiable, seems to be recoverable. Thus, a life insurance policy[98] or a guarantee[99] might be converted.

In *OBG Ltd v Allan*,[100] the House of Lords was faced with the argument that the tort of conversion should be extended beyond the document cases just referred to so as to encompass a chose in action in the form of debts and contractual liabilities.[101] By a majority, the House rejected extension of the tort beyond those cases in which rights are recorded in a document.[102] Lord Hoffmann saw the document cases as consistent with the *historical development* of conversion as protective of tangibles only and (implicitly) saw any further extension as altering the nature of the tort. This was countered by strong arguments from the dissentients Lord Nicholls and Baroness Hale, who saw the *logic* of extending the tort. Lord Nicholls thought that:

> The existence of a document is essentially irrelevant. Intangible rights can be misappropriated even if they are not recorded in a document. In principle an intangible right not recorded in writing may merit protection just as much as a right which is recorded in this way.[103]

This is the preferable view. It recognises that a document is to be treated ordinarily as nothing more than evidence of a right; it is not conclusive proof of a right.[104] Relevant rights, these days, are just as likely to be recorded electronically as in 'hard copy' form.[105] Moreover, as Baroness Hale observed, 'it makes no sense that the Defendants should be strictly liable for what is lost on the tangible assets but not for what was lost on the intangibles'.[106]

(c) Type of act

Save for the statutory conversion created by the Torts (Interference with Goods) Act 1977, sub-section 2(2), conversion arises only if there is *positive conduct* that interferes with the claimant's goods. *Ashby v Tolhurst*[107] is illustrative:

> A third party had driven away C's car, which he had left in D's car park. At trial, C gave evidence that the attendant told him that he had 'given' the car to the third party. His case in conversion rested upon the assertion that this word 'imports that the attendant took some active step to place this thief in possession of the motor car' but it was found 'impossible to collect that meaning out of the words'. There was no conversion.

---

[98] *Wills v Wells* (1818) 2 Moore CP 247; *Watson v MacLean* (1858) EB & E 75.

[99] *M'Leod v M'Ghie* (1841) 2 Man & G 326.   [100] [2008] 1 AC 1.

[101] These were property because they were 'transferable and therefore had an exchange value': S Green (2008) 71 MLR 114, at 118.   [102] [2008] 1 AC 1, at [94], [271], and [321].

[103] [2008] 1 AC 1, at [230].

[104] There are exceptions to this, eg, Statute of Frauds Amendment Act 1828, s 6.

[105] Yet no torts to goods are available with respect to the interference with such: *Environment Agency v Churngold Recycling Ltd* [2014] EWCA Civ 909. See critique of the rule in S Green (2008) 71 MLR 114, 117.

[106] [2008] 1 AC 1, at [311]. See also S Green and J Randall, *The Tort of Conversion* (2009), ch 5. Contra A Tettenborn, 'Intentional Interference with Chattels' in C Sappideen and P Vines (eds), *Fleming's the Law of Torts* (2011), 68.   [107] [1937] 2 KB 242.

If the defendant deals with the goods in a manner which interferes with the claimant's possession or immediate right to possession, his act will constitute conversion, even if he does not 'intend to challenge the property or possession of the true owner'.[108] In other words, liability is strict and it matters not that the defendant commits a conversion by mistake or in good faith.[109] So, vis-à-vis the true owner, it is no defence for an auctioneer, after selling goods on behalf of a client, honestly delivering them to the buyer, and paying the proceeds of sale to his client, to say that he was unaware that his client did not own the goods.[110] On the other hand, if the auctioneer simply redelivers the goods to the apparent owner, there is no conversion since redelivery (as opposed to sale) changes only the position of the goods, not the property in them.[111]

(D) Examples of actions amounting to conversion

In some instances, especially those involving a sale of goods, it is clear that the act is sufficiently inconsistent with the rightful possessor's rights to be conversion. In many other instances, however, it is a matter of fact and degree whether the court will treat the act as sufficiently inconsistent with the possessor's rights to be conversion. This is true particularly in the case of physical damage to the goods and breach of bailment. Regrettably, the courts have not spelt out fully the factors which go to the exercise of their judgement. But the most important are probably the extent and duration of the control or dominion exercised over the goods, the amount of damage to the goods, and the cost and inconvenience to the rightful possessor.[112]

(1) Taking goods or dispossessing

To steal, or to seize under legal process without justification,[113] certainly is conversion. If, after lopping off the branches of his neighbour's apple tree when they overhang his land, a householder appropriates the fruit, he commits conversion also.[114] To take goods out of the possession of another might be to convert them. However, merely to move goods from one

---

[108] *Caxton Publishing Co Ltd v Sutherland Publishing Co* [1939] AC 178, at 202; *Douglas Valley Finance Co Ltd v S Hughes (Hirers) Ltd* [1969] 1 QB 738.

[109] *Fowler v Hollins* (1872) LR 7 QB 616, at 639 (affd sub nom *Hollins v Fowler* (1875) LR 7 HL 757; flld in *Union Transport Finance Ltd v British Car Auctions Ltd* [1978] 2 All ER 385; *RH Willis & Son v British Car Auctions Ltd* [1978] 2 All ER 392). See also *OGB Ltd v Allan* [2008] 1 AC 1, at [95] and [311]. The policy reason for this is to ensure that those who deal with goods first ascertain title to them: S Green and J Randall, *The Tort of Conversion* (2009), 71–3.

[110] *Consolidated Co v Curtis & Son* [1892] 1 QB 495. In *Moorgate Mercantile Co Ltd v Finch and Read* [1962] 1 QB 701, the borrower of a car had it confiscated upon conviction for carrying in it watches not declared to Customs. This was held to be a conversion, for the confiscation was the result of his intentional act of carrying the watches in the car. See also *Chubb Cash Ltd v John Crilley & Son* [1983] 2 All ER 294. Contra S Douglas [2009] CLJ 198, at 216.   [111] *Marcq v Christie Manson and Wood Ltd* [2004] QB 286.

[112] As indicated, conversion is a tort of strict liability. This said, intention is sometimes important in characterising the nature of the defendant's act: S Green and J Randall, *The Tort of Conversion* (2009), 68. However, this factor is not mentioned in the body of the text so as to avoid unnecessary confusion.

[113] *Tinkler v Poole* (1770) 5 Burr 2657; *Burton v Hughes* (1824) 2 Bing 173; *Chubb Cash Ltd v John Crilley & Son* [1983] 2 All ER 294.   [114] *Mills v Brooker* [1919] 1 KB 555.

place to another is not conversion.[115] Thus, where a porter moved another's goods in order to reach his own, and negligently failed to replace them, he was not liable for their subsequent loss.[116] It might be conversion, however, if goods are moved to an unreasonable place with an intrinsic risk of loss. In *Forsdick v Collins*,[117] for instance, the defendant came into possession of land on which the claimant had a block of Portland stone and its removal by the defendant 'to a distance' was held to be a conversion. A deprivation of goods that is more than a mere moving, in that it deprives the claimant of their use for however long, will be conversion,[118] as will forcing the claimant to hand over goods under duress.[119]

(2) Destroying or altering

To destroy goods is to convert them, if the destruction is voluntary.[120] The quantum of damage constituting destruction for this purpose is a question of degree, but mere damage is not conversion.[121] A change of identity not amounting to destruction is enough. For example, to draw out part of a vessel of liquor and fill it with water is conversion.[122] If goods are used for a purpose which eliminates their utility as goods in their original form—for example, making a fur coat from animal skins—this is conversion.[123] But it is not conversion to bottle another's wine in order to preserve it.[124]

(3) Using

To use goods as one's own ordinarily is to convert them. Thus, it was conversion for a person to whom carbolic acid drums were delivered by mistake to deal with them as his own by pouring the contents into his tank.[125] Equally, a claim 'would not be defeated by the fact that the defendant whom he sues for the misuse of his temporary dominion of the property claims to be an agent for someone else'.[126] However, a mere misuse by a bailee, unaccompanied by any denial of title, is not a conversion, although it might constitute some other tort.[127]

(4) Receipt, disposition, and delivery

Voluntarily[128] to receive goods in consummation of a transaction intended by the parties to give to the recipient some proprietary rights in the goods can be a conversion

---

[115] *Fouldes v Willoughby* (1841) 8 M & W 540.   [116] *Bushel v Miller* (1718) 1 Stra 128.
[117] (1816) 1 Stark 173.   [118] *Empresa Exportadora de Azucar v IANSA* [1983] 2 Lloyd's Rep 171.
[119] *Grainger v Hill* (1838) 4 Bing NC 212.
[120] Purely accidental destruction is not conversion: *Simmons v Lillystone* (1853) 8 Exch 431.
[121] *Fouldes v Willoughby* (1841) 8 M & W 540, at 549.   [122] *Richardson v Atkinson* (1723) 1 Stra 576.
[123] *Jones v de Marchant* (1916) 28 DLR 561 (approved in *Foskett v McKeown* [2001] 1 AC 102). In such cases, the owner of the materials becomes the owner of the product if the material can be wholly or substantially identified in the product: *Glencore International AG v Metro Trading International Inc* [2001] 1 Lloyd's Rep 284.
[124] *Philpott v Kelley* (1835) 3 Ad & El 106.
[125] *Lancashire and Yorkshire Rly Co v MacNicoll* (1918) 88 LJKB 601.
[126] *Morison v London County and Westminster Bank Ltd* [1914] 3 KB 356, at 386 (*obiter*).
[127] *Lee v Atkinson and Brooks* (1609) Yelv 172 (approved in *Donald v Suckling* (1866) LR 1 QB 585, at 615 by Blackburn J, who said that if the act is repugnant to the bailment, it is conversion, but 'where the act, though unauthorised, is not repugnant to the contract as to show a disclaimer' it is not). See also *BMW Financial Services (GB) Ltd v Bhagawani* [2007] EWCA Civ 1230; *Penfolds Wines Pty Ltd v Elliott* (1946) 74 CLR 204.
[128] Receipt by an involuntary bailee is not conversion.

actionable by the owner.[129] It has been held to be a conversion for a purchaser so to receive goods from someone who has no title.[130] If, however, the defendant receives the goods in good faith for the purposes of storage or transport,[131] he does not commit conversion because there is no assertion of a proprietary interest in the goods. Receipt of goods by way of pledge is conversion if the delivery is conversion.[132]

In relation to disposition and delivery, generally there is no conversion where a person agrees to sell goods to which he has no title but does not transfer possession of them. This is because bargain and sale are void if the seller has no rights in the goods.[133] On the other hand, a person who without lawful authority disposes of goods with the intention of transferring title to another and does deliver the goods thereby commits a conversion. A sale and a pledge[134] can each constitute such a disposition. In *Syeds v Hay*,[135] for example, a sea captain was liable for delivering goods to another in the wrongful belief that he had a lien over them.

(5) Mis-delivery by carrier

A carrier[136] or warehouseman[137] who delivers goods to the wrong person by mistake commits a conversion, whether or not his mistake is innocent. But failure to deliver because the goods have been lost or destroyed by accident or carelessness is not conversion.[138] Nor is it conversion for a bailee[139] or pledgee[140] without notice of the claim of the true owner to return goods to the person from whom he received them.

(6) Refusal to surrender on demand

A refusal to surrender goods upon lawful and reasonable demand is a conversion.[141] This rule covers the situation where the possession of the defendant originally was lawful. It may be invoked, for example, where the receipt is not itself actionable. The most important case since the abolition by the Torts (Interference with Goods) Act 1977 of the old action in detinue (a tort permitting an action for return of specific goods after a wrongful refusal to do so) is *Howard E Perry & Co Ltd v British Railways Board*:[142]

> Fearing industrial action by their employees during a steelworkers strike, Ds refused to surrender to Cs steel belonging to Cs held in Ds' depots. Ds admitted that Cs were entitled to immediate possession and it was held that their refusal to allow Cs to enter the depots and collect the steel was wrongful.

---

[129] Cf *M'Combie v Davies* (1805) 6 East 538, at 540.   [130] *Farrant v Thompson* (1822) 5 B & Ald 826.

[131] *Hollins v Fowler* (1875) LR 7 HL 757, at 767.   [132] Sale of Goods Act 1979, sub-s 11(2).

[133] *Lancashire Waggon Co v Fitzhugh* (1861) 6 H & N 502; he might, however, be liable for malicious falsehood: see ch 14.   [134] *Parker v Godin* (1728) 2 Stra 813.

[135] (1791) 4 Term Rep 260. But if someone entrusts another with a chattel to be used by him, the bailor impliedly authorises the bailee to allow a lien for the cost of necessary repairs to be created over it: *Green v All Motors Ltd* [1917] 1 KB 625; *Tappenden v Artus* [1964] 2 QB 185.   [136] *Youl v Harbottle* (1791) Peake 68, NP.

[137] *Devereux v Barclay* (1819) 2 B & Ald 702.

[138] *Owen v Lewyn* (1672) 1 Vent 223; *The Arpad* [1934] P 189, at 232.

[139] *Hollins v Fowler* (1875) LR 7 HL 757, at 767. Otherwise the bailee would be in an impossible position, for if he retained the goods he could not plead a title paramount of which he was unaware.

[140] *Union Credit Bank Ltd v Mersey Docks and Harbour Board* [1899] 2 QB 205.

[141] *Marcq v Christie Manson and Wood Ltd* [2004] QB 286; *Isaack v Clark* (1615) 2 Bulst 306, at 310.

[142] [1980] 2 All ER 579.

There is a large amount of case law on this topic, but the principles are quite simple. Even if the defendant no longer has possession at the time of the demand and refusal, it is no defence for him to prove that, prior to the accrual of the claimant's title, he parted with them wrongfully.[143] On the other hand, the defendant may postpone surrender until after he has had a reasonable time in which to confirm the title of the claimant,[144] or, if he is an employee, to consult his employer.[145] What is reasonable is a question of fact. Many factors might be relevant—the time of the demand, the expense and inconvenience of immediate compliance, the knowledge on the part of the defendant of the claimant's title, and of his identity, and whether the defendant has conveyed adequately to the claimant the grounds for his temporary refusal. An estoppel may sometimes operate to prevent the defendant from setting up facts which otherwise would have justified a refusal.[146]

If an auctioneer redelivers goods to their apparent owner after he has failed to sell them, he cannot be held liable in conversion upon the suit of the rightful possessor so long as his redelivery was made in good faith and without knowledge of the true owner's title.[147]

(7) Goods lost or destroyed

At common law there could be no conversion where there was no voluntary act. The Torts (Interference with Goods) Act 1977, sub-section 22 therefore provides that:

> An action lies in conversion for loss or destruction of goods which a bailee has allowed to happen in breach of his duty to his bailor (that is to say it lies in a case which is not otherwise conversion, but would have been detinue before detinue was abolished).

Bailees are required to take reasonable care of goods in their keeping and are liable for their loss or destruction unless they can disprove fault;[148] but they are not insurers of the goods. In *Sutcliffe v Chief Constable of West Yorkshire*[149] an arson attack destroyed the claimant's car, which had been seized lawfully by the police and which was held thereafter in a police station yard. The Court of Appeal dismissed the claimant's claim for conversion. The attack was unprecedented, and in respect of the claimant's property the defendant had done all that was reasonable to take care of the vehicle.

Denial of title of itself is not conversion.[150] However, there might be conversion of goods although the defendant has not physically dealt with them,[151] or been in

---

[143] *Bristol and West of England Bank v Midland Rly Co* [1891] 2 QB 653.
[144] *Clayton v Le Roy* [1911] 2 KB 1031.   [145] *Alexander v Southey* (1821) 5 B & Ald 247.
[146] *Seton, Laing & Co v Lafone* (1887) 19 QBD 68; *Henderson & Co v Williams* [1895] 1 QB 521.
[147] *Marcq v Christie Manson and Wood Ltd* [2004] QB 286.
[148] Ordinarily, a bailee will be liable unless he disproves fault: *Houghland v RR Low (Luxury Coaches) Ltd* [1962] 1 QB 694. An involuntary bailee is not liable for failure to return merely because he has lost the goods: *Howard v Harris* (1884) 1 Cab & El 253. However, he is liable if he destroys or damages the goods. If the bailee is unaware that the goods on his premises are not his property (ie, he is an 'unconscious bailee'), he is under a duty to exercise reasonable care to ascertain that they were his own before he destroys them: *AVX Ltd v EGM Solders Ltd* (1982) *Times*, 7 July.   [149] [1996] RTR 86.
[150] Torts (Interference with Goods) Act 1977, sub-s 11(3).
[151] *Van Oppen & Co Ltd v Tredegars Ltd* (1921) 37 TLR 504.

physical possession of them,[152] if his acts deprive the claimant of his right to possession or amount to a substantial interference with that right.[153] But a mere threat to prevent an owner in possession from removing his goods of itself will not amount to conversion.[154]

Where goods are left on land and occupier B acquires the land on which the goods lie from occupier A, then, if occupier B refuses to allow the rightful possessor to enter the land and retrieve them, the refusal is not necessarily conversion.[155] It might become conversion, however, if occupier B himself asserts any right in respect of the goods,[156] or denies the claimant the right to possession for a period which is plainly indefinite.[157] But this needs to be established as a question of fact.

(E) Conversion as between co-owners

The Torts (Interference with Goods) Act 1977, sub-section 101 provides that co-ownership[158] is no defence to an action founded on conversion where the defendant, without the authority of the other co-owner, destroys the goods, or disposes of them in a way giving a good title to the entire property in the goods, or otherwise does anything equivalent to the destruction of the other interest in the goods. Thus, a partner who paid cheques into a third person's bank account was, by excluding his co-owner's right to enjoy the proceeds, liable for conversion.[159] However, a co-owner cannot be sued for conversion if he merely makes use of the common property in a reasonable way.[160] Nor was there necessarily a conversion where the co-owner took and kept the goods.[161] The law requires a destruction of the goods or something equivalent to it.[162] The Torts (Interference with Goods) Act 1977, sub-section 101 provides, further, that it is no defence to an action founded on conversion where the defendant, without the authority of the other co-owner, purports to dispose of the goods in such a way as would give a good title to the entire property in the goods if he were acting with the authority of all the co-owners of the goods.

---

[152] Eg, *Oakley v Lyster* [1931] 1 KB 148.

[153] *Lancashire and Yorkshire Rly Co, London and NW Rly Co and Graeser Ltd v MacNicoll* (1918) 88 LJKB 601; *Oakley v Lyster* [1931] 1 KB 148, at 156; *Club Cruise Entertainment and Travelling Services Europe BV v Department for Transport* [2008] EWHC 2794, at [51].   [154] *England v Cowley* (1873) LR 8 Exch 126.

[155] *Wilde v Waters* (1855) 24 LJCP 193, at 195; *British Economical Lamp Co Ltd v Empire Mile End Lane Ltd* (1913) 29 TLR 386.

[156] *Walker v Clyde* (1861) 10 CBNS 381; *H E Dibble Ltd v Moore* [1970] 2 QB 181.

[157] *Howard E Perry & Co Ltd v British Rlys Board* [1980] 2 All ER 579, at 583; *Bryanston Leasings Ltd v Principality Finance Ltd* [1977] RTR 45.

[158] Note the Sale of Goods Act 1979, ss 20A and 20B, whereby a buyer of a quantity of goods forming part of a larger bulk becomes a proportionate co-owner of those goods.

[159] *Baker v Barclays Bank Ltd* [1955] 2 All ER 571.

[160] As, for instance, by cutting grass and making hay in the common field (*Jacobs v Seward* (1872) LR 5 HL 464).

[161] The bailee of common property from one co-owner is not guilty of conversion if he refuses to deliver the property on the demand of another co-owner (*Atwood v Ernest* (1853) 13 CB 881; *Harper v Godsell* (1870) LR 5 QB 422), unless the latter has a special property in the entire chattel (*Nyberg v Handelaar* [1892] 2 QB 202).

[162] *Morgan v Marquis* (1853) 9 Exch 145; *Baker v Barclays Bank Ltd* [1955] 2 All ER 571.

(F) Damages

(1) General principles

Market value In conversion, the claimant is entitled to be compensated to the extent of the value to him of the goods of which he has been deprived. The prima facie measure of damages is the market value of the goods at the time of conversion.[163] Where goods are of a kind which readily can be bought in the market, the actual market value will be the appropriate measure; otherwise the replacement value in a comparable state,[164] or the original cost minus depreciation will be the standard. It is for the defendant to argue that the appropriate compensatory figure is a lower one.[165]

Consistent with this, the manufacturer of goods who has a contract for their sale prima facie is entitled to the sale value of the goods, including the profit component. It is for the defendant to prove that alleged loss of profits will be recouped by alternative sales.[166] 'It is not for the Claimant to prove a negative, that he has not recouped the profit by a substitute sale, but for the Defendant to prove a positive, that the profit has been recouped and thus the loss of profit not suffered after all.'[167]

Where a negotiable instrument or other document ordinarily representing a *chose in action* is converted, the value which the document represents, and not merely its value as a piece of paper, is the basis of the quantum of damages. But, as indicated earlier, a purely intangible *chose in action* cannot be converted.[168]

Mitigation Once a claim for conversion has accrued, it is not open to the claimant to delay the issue of his writ and thereby base his action on a subsequent demand and refusal—the duty to mitigate damages operates.[169] Mitigation requires that the claimant does what is reasonable in order to limit his loss. Reasonable costs of mitigation are recoverable by the claimant.[170]

Remoteness Remoteness of damage is determined by the common law. The test is one of reasonable foreseeability.[171]

(2) Further heads of damage

A rule basing damages on the value at the date of conversion can be seen to work to the claimant's benefit in certain circumstances. If the goods decrease in value between

---

[163] *Kuwait Airways Corpn v Iraqi Airways Co (Nos 4 and 5)* [2002] 2 AC 883, at [67]; *Zabihi v Janzemini* [2009] EWCA Civ 851, at [43].

[164] *J & E Hall Ltd v Barclay* [1937] 3 All ER 620; *Wilson v Robertsons (London) Ltd* [2006] EWCA Civ 1088, at [43]–[44].

[165] *Sony Computer Entertainment UK Ltd v Cinram Logistics UK Ltd* [2008] 2 CLC 441, at [37], [45]–[46], and [49].   [166] *Sony Computer Entertainment UK Ltd v Cinram Logistics UK Ltd* [2008] 2 CLC 441.

[167] [2008] 2 CLC 441, at [49]. It is more doubtful in what circumstances a buyer who does not recover his goods can claim a *loss of resale profit*: *Strand Electric and Engineering Co Ltd v Brisford Entertainments Ltd* [1952] 2 QB 246, at 255.   [168] *OBG Ltd v Allan* [2001] 1 AC 1.

[169] *Empresa Exportadora de Azucar v IANSA* [1983] 2 Lloyd's Rep 171; *Uzinterimpex v Standard Bank* [2008] 2 CLC 80.   [170] S Green and J Randall, *The Tort of Conversion* (2009), 205.

[171] *Saleslease Ltd v Davis* [1999] 1 WLR 1664; *Kuwait Airways Corpn v Iraqi Airways Co (Nos 4 and 5)* [2001] 3 WLR 1117.

the date of the conversion and the date of judgment, the claimant still may recover the value at the date of conversion.[172] However, the general rule is not immutable. The normal purpose of an award of damages is to compensate the claimant for the loss he actually sustains.[173] Thus, the market value (even where ascertainable) at the *date of conversion* will not necessarily mark the top limit of damages recoverable in the following instances.

Rise in market The first departure from the ordinary rule applies where the market value of the goods rises between the date of the cause of action and *trial*.[174] If the act of conversion relied on by the claimant is a sale, and by the time when the claimant knows or ought to know of the sale the value has increased, the claimant can recover that higher value.[175]

Special damage Whether or not the claimant incurs pecuniary loss as a direct consequence of the conversion, he may recover *special damages* in addition to the market value of the goods. For example, a worker deprived of his tools recovered loss of wages,[176] and the owner of a converted pony could claim the cost of hiring another.[177] In *Strand Electric and Engineering Co Ltd v Brisford Entertainments Ltd*[178] (a detinue case), it was held to be irrelevant that the claimants would not have been able to hire out for the whole period of that wrongful detention those goods that the defendants wrongfully failed to return. This is because the usual 'but for' test of causation does not apply in conversion.[179] Similarly, in *Kuwait Airways Corp v Iraqi Airways Co (Damages)*,[180] it was held that the claimant was not bound to show any actual or probable loss associated with the wrongful retention of aircraft parts. The claimant was entitled to damages representing a reasonable sum by way of hire or rent. On the other hand, there will be a time limit to the period for which he can claim a loss of hire because there will come a time when he will be expected to obtain an alternative chattel to hire out.[181]

Loss of use Since the effect of a judgment for damages is to transfer the title to the defendant,[182] it follows that the court will not award damages both for loss of use and for the value of the goods where the effect would be double compensation. The capacity for profitable use is part of the value of the goods. Thus, where the defendant converted manufacturing plant belonging to the claimant, he was liable for the value of the plant when converted but not for loss of use between that date and trial.[183] On the other hand,

---

[172] *Rhodes v Moules* [1895] 1 Ch 236. See also *Solloway v McLaughlin* [1938] AC 247 and *BBMB Finance v Eda Holdings Ltd* [1991] 2 All ER 129.

[173] *Brandeis Goldschmidt & Co v Western Transport Ltd* [1981] QB 864; *IBL Ltd v Coussens* [1991] 2 All ER 133.

[174] *Trafigura Beheer BV v Mediterranean Shipping Co SA* [2007] 2 CLC 379, at [38]–[41].

[175] *Sachs v Miklos* [1948] 2 KB 23.   [176] *Bodley v Reynolds* (1846) 8 QB 779.

[177] *Davis v Oswell* (1837) 7 C & P 804.

[178] [1952] 2 QB 246 (affd in *Inverugie Investments v Hackett* [1995] 3 All ER 841).

[179] *Kuwait Airways Corpn v Iraqi Airways Co (Nos 4 and 5)* [2001] 3 WLR 1117.

[180] [2004] EWHC 2603.   [181] *Greer v Alstons Engineering Sales and Services Ltd* [2003] UKPC 46.

[182] *Ellis v John Stenning & Son* [1932] 2 Ch 81.   [183] *Re Simms, ex p Trustee* [1934] Ch 1.

if the defendant wrongfully detains goods and later sells them, it seems that, in addition to their value, the claimant can recover for the *loss of use* from the date of the unlawful detention until sale,[184] and indeed until the claimant had a reasonable opportunity to buy a replacement after learning of that sale,[185] but not for loss of use until trial.

Exemplary damages If the general preconditions necessary for an award of *exemplary damages* (discussed in chapter 26) are satisfied, such damages can be claimed in conversion.[186]

(3) Avoidance of over-compensation

Courts will be assiduous not to over-compensate the claimant. Thus, the following further points must be borne in mind:

Improvements to goods If the defendant converts the claimant's goods and then *increases their value*, ordinarily the claimant cannot recover that increased value.[187] Thus, where the defendant converted a partially built ship which he completed at his own expense, the claimant was entitled to recover the market value of the completed ship less the expense incurred by the defendant in completing it.[188] Where the act of conversion relied on takes place after improvement of goods, sub-section 61 of the 1977 Act applies. If the defendant has improved the goods in the mistaken but honest belief that he had a good title to them, an allowance is made for the extent to which (at the time at which the goods fall to be valued in assessing damages) the value of the goods is attributable to the improvement. If, for example, the improver is sued for later selling the goods, the statutory allowance applies.[189] Purported purchasers of goods improved by another enjoy a similar allowance, provided again that the purchaser acted in good faith.[190] Subsequent purchasers enjoy the same protection.[191] Thus, an eventual buyer in good faith of a stolen car when sued by the true owner will have damages reduced to reflect improvements made to it since the theft.

Interest Where the court orders that the defendant pay damages representing the increased value, as at the date of judgment, of goods converted, this will not be accompanied by an *award of interest on the loss of use of money* that would have been obtained by the claimant on an earlier sale of those goods. To award interest in such a case would lead to a 'double benefit'.[192]

Temporary deprivations Although detinue was abolished by sub-section 21 of the Torts (Interference with Goods) Act 1977, section 3 of that Act preserved the remedies

---

[184] *Strand Electric and Engineering Co Ltd v Brisford Entertainments Ltd* [1952] 2 QB 246, at 255.
[185] *Re Simms, ex p Trustee* [1934] Ch 1, at 30.   [186] *Borders (UK) Ltd v MPC* [2005] EWCA Civ 197.
[187] *Caxton Publishing Co Ltd v Sutherland Publishing Co* [1939] AC 178; *Greenwood v Bennett* [1973] QB 195.
[188] *Reid v Fairbanks* (1853) 13 CB 692.   [189] And see *Munro v Willmott* [1949] 1 KB 295.
[190] Torts (Interference with Goods) Act 1977, sub-s 6(2).
[191] Torts (Interference with Goods) Act 1977, sub-s 6(3).
[192] *Trafigura Beheer BV v Mediterranean Shipping Co SA* [2007] 2 CLC 379, at [42]–[43].

for what previously would have been detinue by making them available in conversion.[193] The approach under the Act was set out in *IBL Ltd v Coussens*.[194] The Court of Appeal held that, in cases of temporary deprivation of property, where no irreversible act of conversion is committed evidence must be adduced as to the true loss suffered by the rightful possessor. The measure of damages was not to be fixed arbitrarily at either the date of conversion or the date of judgment.

Return of goods If the defendant returns the goods before trial, the court will reduce damages in conversion by the amount of their value at that time.[195] In short, the court will not enforce a sale on the defendant and, 'subject to the payment of costs and special damages (if there are any) an action for damages for conversion can always be stayed if the defendant offers to hand over the property in dispute'.[196] Where goods acquired by the claimant for use in a manufacturing process have been wrongfully detained but later returned, the claimant must show that a loss of profit or other pecuniary loss has resulted from the detention.[197] If he fails to prove that he would have used the goods at any time before their return, he cannot recover the fall in their market value over the period of their detention and can receive only nominal damages.[198] Of course, it will be otherwise where he purchased the goods for resale during the period of detention.[199]

Hire purchase In the case of a conversion of goods that are the subject of a *hire purchase agreement*, the interest of the owner and rightful possessor in the goods is diminished by the extent to which payments have been made under the agreement. Its interest is in the value of the outstanding payments. Damages will be reduced accordingly.[200]

(G) Other remedies

The Torts (Interference with Goods) Act 1977 introduced common remedies for all forms of 'wrongful interferences with goods'. Section 3 provides that, in proceedings for conversion or any other chattel tort against a person in possession or control of the goods, the following relief may be given as far as is appropriate:[201] (1) an order for delivery and for payment of any consequential damages;[202] (2) an order for delivery of the goods, but giving the defendant the alternative of paying damages by reference to the value of the goods, together in either alternative with payment of any consequential

---

[193] *Hillesden Securities Ltd v Ryjak Ltd* [1983] 2 All ER 184.   [194] [1991] 2 All ER 133.
[195] *Fisher v Prince* (1762) 3 Burr 1363; *Solloway v McLaughlin* [1938] AC 247.
[196] *USA and Republic of France v Dollfus Mieg et Compagnie SA and Bank of England* [1952] AC 582, at 619.
[197] *Brandeis Goldschmidt & Co Ltd v Western Transport Ltd* [1981] QB 864, at 870; *Williams v Peel River Land and Mineral Co Ltd* (1886) 55 LT 689, at 692–3.
[198] *Williams v Peel River Land and Mineral Co Ltd* (1886) 55 LT 689, at 692–3; *Bryanston Leasings Ltd v Principality Finance Ltd* [1977] RTR 45; *Brandeis Goldschmidt & Co Ltd v Western Transport Ltd* [1981] QB 864, at 871.   [199] *Brandeis Goldschmidt & Co Ltd v Western Transport Ltd* [1981] QB 864, at 873.
[200] *Wickham Holdings Ltd v Brooke House Motors Ltd* [1967] 1 WLR 295; *VFS Financial Services (UK) Ltd v Euro Auctions (UK) Ltd* [2007] EWHC 1492, at [103].
[201] Torts (Interference with Goods) Act 1977, sub-s 3(1). See *Secretary of State for Defence v Guardian Newspapers Ltd* [1985] AC 339.   [202] Torts (Interference with Goods) Act 1977, sub-s 3(2)(a).

damages;[203] or (3) damages.[204] The first alternative, involving an order for delivery up, is at the discretion of the court.[205] The attitude of the courts is that such an order should not be made with respect to ordinary articles of commerce with no special interest or value to the claimant.[206]

Section 4 Residuum

There are many circumstances where the violation of interests in goods is not protected by trespass, conversion, or even the tort of negligence. Trespass and conversion are especially restrictive in that they are not available to a claimant who neither possesses nor has an immediate right to possess the goods. Yet the case of *Mears v London and South Western Rly Co*[207] has firmly established that if goods are destroyed or damaged, the owner may sue without having possession or an immediate right to possess. The rule benefits, for example, a bailor, a purchaser where the vendor has a lien for unpaid purchase money, and a mortgagee. He must prove damage to his interest; taking the goods from the possessor without affecting title is insufficient. Presumably, the act complained of must be wrongful in that it is one which, had the claimant had possession of the chattel (or the immediate right to it), it would have grounded a suit in trespass or conversion.

Conclusions

This chapter has considered ways in which the law of torts protects interests in goods. For the most part, protection is focused upon the claimant's possession or immediate right to possession—which gives title to sue. Trespass to goods is available in cases of intentional or negligent and direct interferences with goods and the better view is that the tort is actionable per se (without proof of damage). Conversion is a much more complex tort, the thrust of which arises in actions by the defendant which constitute a denial of the claimant's *rights* to possession and control over goods. Although the rules regarding calculation of damages for conversion are voluminous, the starting point is the market value of the goods converted.

Problem question

Jenny was visiting a market on her day off and the following events occurred: Jenny entered shop A and when on the first floor she picked up two silk scarves, which she

---

[203] Torts (Interference with Goods) Act 1977, sub-s 3(2)(b).

[204] Torts (Interference with Goods) Act 1977, sub-s 3(2)(c).

[205] But the claimant may elect as between the second and third remedies where the first is not ordered: Torts (Interference with Goods) Act 1977, sub-s 3(3)(b).

[206] *Whiteley Ltd v Hilt* [1918] 2 KB 808, at 809; *Tanks and Vessels Industries Ltd v Devon Cider Co Ltd* [2009] EWHC 1360, at [55]–[56].   [207] (1862) 11 CBNS 850.

thought that she would buy. However, while carrying the red scarf around the shop, she tore it on an exposed nail in a wall. She decided to leave both that scarf and a blue scarf inside an ornamental vase on the third floor of the shop. Jenny then went into shop B, which sold alcohol. Jenny found a table with 30 sample cups of absinthe on it. Although Jenny realised that customers were invited to try a single sample cup, she drank ten of the sample cups of absinthe. Again, Jenny thought that she would buy a bottle of the absinthe. Feeling a little tipsy, she placed it in her shopping bag. Later, Jenny's partner came to collect her from shop B. Jenny forgot to pay for the bottle of absinthe on her way out of the store.

Advise Jenny as to any torts to goods that she might have committed.

 Visit **http://www.oup.com/uk/street15e/** for answer guidance.

Further reading

CURWEN, 'The Remedy in Conversion: Confusing Property and Obligation' (2006) 26 *Legal Studies* 570

DOUGLAS, 'The Nature of Conversion' (2009) 68 *Cambridge Law Journal* 198

DOUGLAS, *Liability for Wrongful Interferences with Chattels* (2011)

DOUGLAS, 'The Scope of Conversion: Property and Contract' (2011) 74 *Modern Law Review* 329

GREEN, 'Theft and Conversion—Tangibly Different?' (2012) 128 *Law Quarterly Review* 564

GREEN AND RANDALL, *The Tort of Conversion* (2009)

HICKEY, *Property and the Law of Finders* (2010)

MILSOM, 'Not Doing is No Trespass' [1954] *Cambridge Law Journal* 105

PALMER, 'The Application of the Torts (Interference with Goods) Act 1977 to Actions in Bailment' (1978) 41 *Modern Law Review* 629

SIMPSON, 'The Introduction of the Action on the Case for Conversion' (1959) 75 *Law Quarterly Review* 364

TETTENBORN, 'Conversion, Tort and Restitution' in Palmer AND McKendrick (eds), *Interests in Goods* (1998)

12

Trespass to land

KEY ISSUES

(1) Wide protection of possession of land
The law offers a wide degree of protection for those in possession of land—that is, to those with both exclusive occupation of land and the intention to exclude the world at large.

(2) Possession
The possessor of the surface of land is in deemed possession of all the substrata directly below it and of the airspace directly above it insofar as the latter is necessary for the use and enjoyment of the land and any structures upon it.

(3) Elements of trespass
Trespass to land occurs where the defendant directly and either intentionally or negligently interferes with the claimant's possession of land and is actionable without proof of damage. The action can be defeated by proof of a licence to be on the land or by some other justification.

(4) Remedies
Remedies for trespass include injunctions, actions for the recovery of land, and damages.

Section 1 Trespass

This tort protects the interest of the claimant in having her land free from the unjustified physical intrusion of another. Because of this emphasis on physical interference with possession, it follows that it is not the function of the tort to protect ownership. Nonetheless, the purpose of many lawsuits in trespass is not the recovery of damages but, rather, the settlement of disputed rights over land, and a judgment might be backed by the sanction of an injunction if the action succeeds. Furthermore, the use of this action in tort as a means of resolving disputes over title has been facilitated by the rule that trespass is actionable per se.[1]

---

[1] *Bush v Smith* (1953) 162 EG 430.

(A) Title to sue

Possession It is possession of land that entitles a claimant to sue in trespass. The leading case on what constitutes possession is *JA Pye (Oxford) Ltd v Graham*.[2] In the House of Lords, Lord Browne-Wilkinson indicated that possession requires two elements: factual possession *plus* the intention to possess. In relation to the critical second element he approved[3] a dictum in *Powell v McFarlane* that there must be an intention 'to exclude the world at large, including the owner with the paper title if he be not himself the possessor, so far as is reasonably practicable and so far as the processes of the law will allow'.[4] As will be explained now, possession might arise in a number of circumstances.

Recognised interests in land If the claimant has a legal estate and exclusive possession she may sue in trespass. But at the same time, the tenant (not the landlord) can sue if a third party trespasses on the land demised;[5] the owner of an equitable interest with possession can sue;[6] and a statutory possession will found a trespass action also.[7]

Lesser interests in land It has been held that 'a person may have such a right of exclusive possession of property as will entitle him to bring an action for trespass against the owner of that property but which confers no interest whatever in the land'.[8] Those whose interests fall short of a lessee's may be able to sue in trespass also if they have exclusive occupation. Thus, whether a lodger can sue in trespass would depend, on the facts, on her having had exclusive occupation—in other words, it would be relevant whether she had an outdoor key and could bar access to the rooms.[9] Further, in *National Provincial Bank Ltd v Ainsworth*,[10] the House of Lords held that a deserted wife at that time had only a personal, but no proprietary, interest in the matrimonial home. Nonetheless, Lord Upjohn held that, because she had exclusive occupation, she could bring proceedings against trespassers.

New interests in land In *Hill v Tupper*[11] the facts were as follows:

> X Co leased to C certain land, which adjoined X Co's canal. C was given also 'the sole and exclusive rights' to rent out pleasure boats for use on the canal. Subsequently, D set up a

---

[2] [2003] 1 AC 419. See also *Roberts v Swangrove Estates Ltd* [2008] Ch 439, at [33].

[3] *Roberts v Swangrove Estates Ltd* [2008] Ch 439, at [42].   [4] (1979) 38 P & CR 452.

[5] *Cooper v Crabtree* (1882) 20 Ch D 589. C with an *interesse termini* could not sue if she never took possession: *Wallis v Hands* [1893] 2 Ch 75.

[6] *Mason v Clarke* [1955] AC 778. Another example is *Loudon v Ryder* [1953] 2 QB 202, where C was entitled to the premises under a declaration of trust only and yet recovered damages for trespass to the land. A beneficiary under a trust for sale may also sue: *Bull v Bull* [1955] 1 All ER 253, at 255 (*obiter*).

[7] *Cruise v Terrell* [1922] 1 KB 664; *Lewisham BC v Maloney* [1948] 1 KB 50.

[8] *Marcroft Wagons Ltd v Smith* [1951] 2 KB 496, at 501. *Brown v Brash and Ambrose* [1948] 2 KB 247 and *Thompson v Ward* [1953] 2 QB 153 show that a statutory tenant who leaves her premises even for a period of five to ten years with the intention of eventually returning there has the right to sue in trespass. It is sufficient, eg, if she installs someone as licensee yet signals her intention to return by, say, leaving furniture there.

[9] *Lane v Dixon* (1847) 3 CB 776; *Monks v Dykes* (1839) 4 M & W 567; *Helman v Horsham and Worthing Assessment Committee* [1949] 2 KB 335, at 347; *R v St George's Union* (1871) LR 7 QB 90.

[10] [1965] AC 1175.   [11] (1863) 2 H & C 121.

rival concern, whereupon he was sued in trespass by C. C conceded that X Co could sue D in trespass, but C argued that he could sue as well.

Since the claimant's concession was tantamount to an admission that he did not have exclusive occupation, the court dismissed the action. However, it did add that, if a claimant could show that her interest amounted to a new species of property right, she would succeed, subject to the caveat that it was not the policy of the law to allow the courts to create new rights in land. However, in *Manchester Airport plc v Dutton* a licensee who had not yet entered into occupation was entitled to eject trespassers who had set up a protest camp. As Laws LJ explained: 'a licensee not in occupation may claim possession against a trespasser if that is a necessary remedy to vindicate and give effect to such rights of occupation as by contract with his licensor he enjoys'.[12] On the other hand, it was made clear that an action for damages would not have been available on those facts. The action was limited to exercising a superior right in the land in order to gain possession.

Relative title   Generally, it is no defence to a trespasser that the claimant's possession of the land is unlawful. The simple fact of possession normally is enough.[13] But, as against the true owner, the rule is different. In *Delaney v TP Smith Ltd*,[14] the claimant entered premises held under a lease that was unenforceable because there was no memorandum in writing as required by the Law of Property Act 1925, section 40. That being the case, he was unable to sue his landlord in trespass for ejecting him. Two extracts from earlier cases that were cited are important here:

A mere trespasser cannot, by the very act of trespass, immediately and without acquiescence, give himself what the law understands by possession against the person whom he ejects, and drive him to produce his title, if he can, without delay, reinstate himself in his former possession.[15]

   If there are two persons in a field, each asserting that the field is his, and each doing some act in the assertion of the right of possession, and if the question is, which of those two is in actual possession, I answer, the person who has the title is in actual possession, and the other is a trespasser.[16]

Regaining possession   If a claimant has a right to immediate possession of the land, she can seek a summary remedy to obtain possession[17] or, if she has entered upon the

---

[12]   [2000] 1 QB 133, at 150. See also *Hounslow LBC v Twickenham Garden Developments Ltd* [1971] Ch 233, at 257.

[13]   *Graham v Peat* (1801) 1 East 244. In *Mason v Clarke* [1955] AC 778, Visc. Simonds and Lord Oaksey held that the bare possession of a *profit à prendre* was enough to found an action in trespass.

[14]   [1946] KB 393.

[15]   *Browne v Dawson* (1840) 12 Ad & El 624, at 629. (In *Portland Managements Ltd v Harte* [1977] QB 306, it was held that if C proves ownership and her intention to resume possession, the onus is on D to prove that she is not a trespasser.)

[16]   *Jones v Chapman* (1847) 2 Exch 803, at 821 (appd in *Lows v Telford* (1876) 1 App Cas 414, at 426).

[17]   Civil Procedure Rules, r 55.21.

land already, sue for trespasses committed by third parties between the date of accrual of her right of possession and the actual date of her entry.[18] This is called 'trespass by relation'. It operates according to the legal fiction whereby, upon her entry on to the land, the party entitled to possession is deemed to have been in possession from the date of her right to such possession accruing.

No possession Although damages in trespass are not available to those without possession whose interests in land are violated, such persons are not entirely without a remedy. Ordinarily, a landlord will have contractual rights against tenants who damage her interest—for example, by allowing the premises to fall into disrepair—and the law of property also will afford a tort remedy to a landlord who establishes that her tenant has damaged the reversionary interest.[19]

If a third party violates a non-possessory interest in land, an action derived from the old action on the case may lie. The claimant must prove 'such permanent injury as would be necessarily prejudicial to the reversioner.'[20]

(B) Subject matter of the action

Surface and soil The tort is trespass *to land*. So merely walking on the surface of the claimant's land is enough to constitute the tort of trespass. Trespass arises also for interferences with anything attached to the soil and capable of being separately possessed such as grass[21] or crops,[22] or a *profit à prendre* (for example, a fishery).[23]

Layers of interest Possession of land can be separated horizontally, in layers as it were, so that, for instance, A possesses the pasturage, B the surface and subsoil, and C the minerals underneath. Each of them may sue if the subject matter of her possession is invaded. Highway authorities, for example, often have the surface of streets vested in them by statute. This being so, it is those authorities (and not the owners of the subjacent or adjoining land)[24] that can sue for surface trespasses, such as breaking up the street,[25] or erecting structures on the highway.[26] Yet a highway is subject to a public right of way.[27] Thus, if a person uses a highway for purposes other than those 'reasonably

---

[18] *Barnett v Earl of Guildford* (1855) 11 Exch 19.

[19] Landlord–tenant relationships of this kind are dealt with in textbooks on real property.

[20] *Baxter v Taylor* (1832) 5 B & Ad 72, at 75.   [21] *Richards v Davies* [1921] 1 Ch 90, at 94–5.

[22] *Wellaway v Courtier* [1918] 1 KB 200; *Monsanto v Tilly* [2000] Env LR 313.

[23] The principle does not, however, extend to an easement: see *Paine & Co v St Neots Gas and Coke Co* [1939] 3 All ER 812.

[24] In *Hubbard v Pitt* [1976] QB 142, Lord Denning held that, where the surface of a pavement was vested in the local highway authority the adjoining owner could not sue for trespass to the pavement.

[25] *Hyde Corpn v Oldham, Ashton and Hyde Electric Tramway Ltd* (1900) 64 JP 596.

[26] *Sewai Jaipur v Arjun Lal* [1937] 4 All ER 5. See also *Tunbridge Wells Corpn v Baird* [1896] AC 434; *Cox v Glue* (1848) 5 CB 533.

[27] *Rangeley v Midland Rly Co* (1868) 3 Ch App 306; *R (on the application of Smith) v Land Registry* [2010] QB 413, at [8]–[9] and [16].

incident[al] to its user'[28] as a highway (which might include a peaceful demonstration),[29] her act is a trespass. The purpose need not be unlawful in itself.

Subterranean interests Trespass arises where the defendant uses a cave beneath the surface of land, drives building foundations through the soil, tunnels beneath the surface, or mines there. In the absence of specific provision to the contrary, the owner of the surface is presumed to own that which is underground. This was affirmed by the Supreme Court in *Bocardo SA v Star Energy UK Onshore Ltd*:[30]

> D had been granted a licence under statute to search for, bore for, and get petroleum otherwise vested in the Crown. In order to extract the maximum amount of petroleum from the underground reservoir, D drilled diagonally from an external entry point with pipes that ran under C's land. D's operations took place at a depth of no less than 800 feet under C's land. However, D sought no permission for this and C claimed damages for trespass.

The Supreme Court considered the validity of the proposition that the owner of land is 'entitled to the surface itself and everything below it down to the centre of the earth'.[31] It held that the proposition represents the law, insofar as it is sensible to apply it.[32] This is because 'anything that can be touched or worked must be taken to belong to someone' and there is no better claimant to substrata than the owner of the surface above it.[33] In turn, this means that the person who has lawful possession of the surface has lawful possession of the earth and minerals below also, insofar as these have not been alienated to another.[34] It matters not that C or her licensees are making no use of the substrata.[35] Trespass was proved on the facts.

Airspace Possession of land does *not* entitle the possessor to all the airspace above it.[36] Trespass will lie, rather, for invasions of that portion of the airspace necessary for the ordinary use and enjoyment of the land and the structures upon it.[37] Consistently with this, an aircraft does not infringe any of the claimant's rights to airspace when flown above a reasonable height over her land for the purpose of photographing it.[38] The Civil

---

[28] *Liddle v Yorkshire (North Riding) CC* [1934] 2 KB 101, at 127; *R (on application of Smith) v Land Registry* [2010] QB 413, at [16].

[29] *DPP v Jones* [1999] 2 AC 240, at 256, per Lord Irvine LC saying: 'the law should not make unlawful what is commonplace and well accepted'.   [30] [2011] 1 AC 380.

[31] Eg, *Rowbotham v Wilson* (1860) 8 HL Cas 348, at 360.

[32] Beyond a relatively shallow point in the earth's crust, pressure and heat make any human activity impossible: JG Sprankling (2008) 55 UCLA LR 979, at 993, fn 84.

[33] [2011] 1 AC 380, at [26]–[27].   [34] [2011] 1 AC 380, at [27]–[31].   [35] [2011] 1 AC 380, at [35].

[36] *Bocardo SA v Star Energy UK Onshore Ltd* [2011] 1 AC 380, at [26], affirming *Baron Bernstein of Leigh v Skyviews & General Ltd* [1978] QB 479.

[37] *Kelsen v Imperial Tobacco Co of Great Britain and Ireland Ltd* [1957] 2 QB 334; *Anchor Brewhouse Developments v Berkley House Docklands Developments Ltd* (1987) 284 EG 625. The possessor of land has rights to all of the relevant airspace directly above her land. Thus, it is not possible for a person to adversely possess a portion of that airspace: *Stadium Capital Holdings (No 2) Ltd v St Marylebone Property Co plc* [2009] EWHC 2942, at [26] (*obiter*).

[38] That is, the height necessary for ordinary use and enjoyment of land and structures upon it: *Baron Bernstein of Leigh v Skyviews and General Ltd* [1978] QB 479, at 488.

Aviation Act 1982 provides, moreover, that, with the exception of aircraft[39] belonging to, or exclusively employed in, the service of Her Majesty,[40] no action shall lie in respect of trespass or nuisance by reason only of the flight of an aircraft over any property at a height above the ground, which, having regard to weather and other circumstances of the case, is reasonable.[41] Subject to the same exception, the owner of an aircraft is liable for all material loss or damage to persons or property caused by that aircraft, whether in flight, taking off[42] or landing, or by a person in it or articles falling from it, without proof of negligence or intention or other cause of action.[43]

(C) Types of act that constitute trespass

Directness As with all forms of trespass, the interference with land must be direct, meaning that there is no significant act of volition between what the defendant does and the interference. Removing doors and windows,[44] re-building a party (shared) wall,[45] placing a ladder against a wall,[46] or driving nails into it,[47] or encouraging a dog to run on to a person's land[48] are all trespasses. Directly causing foreign matter[49] to enter or come into physical contact with the land of the claimant is a trespass also. But in all cases the intrusion on to the claimant's land must result from some act or omission on the part of the defendant, or persons for whom she is responsible.

The difficulty with drawing the line between 'direct' and 'indirect' interferences is illustrated by two cases. In *Gregory v Piper*,[50] it was held to be trespass where rubbish placed near the claimant's land, on drying, rolled on to it by operation of natural forces. By contrast, in *British Waterways Board v Severn Trent Water Ltd*[51] it was made clear that an action may be brought only by the riparian right owner in respect of the direct fouling of a river or other watercourse, but that an action would not lie in respect of the fouling of adjoining land. Again, a claimant landowner who complains that the

---

[39] Protected 'flights' need not cover lateral ground: *Peires v Bickerton's Aerodromes Ltd* [2017] 1 WLR 2865 (rise and descent of helicopters).   [40] Civil Aviation Act 1982, sub-ss 49(3) and 76(1).

[41] Civil Aviation Act 1982, sub-s 76(1). The sub-section applies to all flights which are at a reasonable height and comply with statutory requirements. But the ordinary liabilities in trespass or nuisance would arise for any other wrongful activity carried on by or from the aircraft, such as deliberate emission of vast quantities of smoke that polluted C's land: *Baron Bernstein of Leigh v Skyviews and General Ltd* [1978] QB 479, at 489.

[42] The ordinary common law applies to accidents caused by the aircraft, while taxiing for take-off: *Blankley v Godley* [1952] 1 All ER 436.   [43] Civil Aviation Act 1982, sub-s 76(2).

[44] *Lavender v Betts* [1942] 2 All ER 72. But this does not apply to D turning off the gas and electricity at the meter in her cellar, for the purpose of evicting the tenant of rooms on an upper floor, because the consequence is indirect: *Perera v Vandiyar* [1953] 1 All ER 1109.   [45] *Rashid v Sharif* [2014] EWCA Civ 377.

[46] *Westripp v Baldock* [1938] 2 All ER 779 (affd [1939] 1 All ER 279).

[47] *Simpson v Weber* (1925) 133 LT 46.

[48] *Beckwith v Shordike* (1767) 4 Burr 2092. But note *League against Cruel Sports Ltd v Scott* [1986] QB 240, where it was held that the intrusion of D's hounds on to C's land does not necessarily constitute a trespass by D: C must prove that D either intended the hounds to enter C's land, or that D negligently failed to exercise suitable control over the hounds.

[49] Perhaps anything having size or mass, including gases, flames, beams from searchlights and mirrors, but not vibrations.   [50] (1829) 9 B & C 591.

[51] [2002] Ch 25. This decision is more in line with existing authority such as *Southport Corpn v Esso Petroleum Co Ltd* [1954] 2 QB 182, at 195–6, where discharge of oil from a ship, which, when carried by tide on to C's foreshore, was held not to constitute a trespass, because it involved consequential, not direct, damage.

defendant has erected a spout to drain away water from the eaves of the defendant's house, as a result of which water has dripped on to the claimant's adjoining land, can sue in nuisance only, not in trespass, because of the indirectness of the interference.[52]

Continuing trespass Simply to enter another's land is a trespass.[53] But such an entry might be an assertion of title, in which case an action in trespass, in effect, will determine who has title.[54] To remain on the land after a trespassory entry thereon is in itself a trespass also known as a 'continuing trespass'. Similarly, if A places goods on B's land and is sued successfully by B in trespass for this act, she is liable to further actions in trespass for the continued presence of the goods on the land if she fails thereafter to remove them.[55] If, on the other hand, she merely digs a hole, or removes goods—that is, if she does not wrongfully allow anything to remain on the land—the fact that the harm occasioned continues is not enough to make it a continuing trespass; damages can be recovered only once for such a trespass.[56] In short, there is a continuing trespass only when that which continued after the first action is a trespass itself.

Expiration of tenancy If a tenant, with the consent of the landlord, stays on at the expiration of her term so that she thereby becomes a tenant either from year to year or at will, her remaining there is not an act of trespass so long as the tenancy has not been properly ended.[57] If, however, she is a mere tenant at sufferance (remaining without the permission of the landlord) the landlord may enter and demand possession and sue in trespass.[58] But, since the termination of a tenancy does not coincide exactly with the claimant assuming possession, it follows that a time lag almost always exists before an action can be brought.

Termination of licence A person who is on land with the permission of the possessor has been held to be a trespasser if she remains there for an unreasonable time after the permission ends.[59] It has been held also that:

> [w]hen a householder lives in a dwelling-house to which there is a garden in front and does not lock the gate of the garden, it gives an implied licence to any member of the public who has lawful reason for doing so to proceed from the gate to the front door or back door, and to inquire whether [s]he may be admitted and to conduct [her] lawful business.[60]

---

[52] *Reynolds v Clark* (1725) 2 Ld Raym 1399. Cf *Lemmon v Webb* [1894] 3 Ch 1, at 24: the encroachment of boughs and roots of trees is not trespass, but a nuisance.

[53] A squatter—ie, 'one who, without any colour of right, enters on an unoccupied house or land, intending to stay there as long as he can'—is a trespasser: *McPhail v Persons (Names Unknown)* [1973] Ch 447, at 456.

[54] If D has not entered, it will normally be impossible to use an action in trespass as a means of settling a dispute in title.

[55] *Holmes v Wilson* (1839) 10 Ad & El 503. The landowner is prima facie entitled to an injunction even where the acts complained of cause no harm: see *Patel v WH Smith (Eziot) Ltd* [1987] 1 WLR 853; *Harrow LBC v Donohue* [1993] NPC 49. [56] *Clegg v Dearden* (1848) 12 QB 576.

[57] *Dougal v McCarthy* [1893] 1 QB 736, at 739–40; *Meye v Electric Transmission Ltd* [1942] Ch 290.

[58] If the deceased tenant's widow remains there after his death she, too, can be sued in trespass: *Thompson v Earthy* [1951] 2 KB 596. [59] *Minister of Health v Bellotti* [1944] KB 298.

[60] *Robson v Hallett* [1967] 2 QB 939, at 953–4. In *Brunner v Williams* (1975) 73 LGR 266, a weights and measures inspector was held to have no implied licence to enter C's garden to see whether a coal dealer was infringing the Weights and Measures Act 1963; all he may do is go to C's door and ask permission.

If the licence is withdrawn, she is not a trespasser during the reasonable time which she takes to leave the premises, but will become so thereafter.[61]

Where the claimant has acquired possession and the trespass continues, a lawsuit may be brought. *Konskier v B Goodman Ltd*[62] is illustrative:

> D, a builder, had permission from the possessor of a building to leave rubbish there while demolishing part of it. During the term of this licence, C became tenant of the building and was entitled to recover in trespass from the builder when the latter did not remove the rubbish after the expiry of the licence.

Further examples *Watson v Murray & Co* provides an illustration of the types of act that constitute trespass to land:[63]

> Ds, who were sheriff's officers, seized goods in C's shop under writs of execution. It was held that each of the following acts amounted to trespass: locking C's premises so as to exclude her therefrom when they had lotted the goods for the purpose of a sale; opening her premises for a public viewing of the goods; affixing posters on her premises.

(D) Fault requirement

It will not avail the defendant that she innocently thought that she was on her own land.[64] Mistake is no defence in trespass. On the other hand, there is no liability if the entry was totally involuntary. Thus, for example, a person who is carried on to the claimant's land by a third party is not liable in trespass.[65] Also, *Letang v Cooper*[66] notwithstanding, it must be assumed that a negligent unintentional act of trespass is enough.[67] Thus, if A intentionally throws a stone on to C's land and, as she should have foreseen, it ricochets on to B's land, this probably is trespass to B's land as well as C's.

Section 2 Defences

(A) Justification

Occasionally it will be possible to show legal justification for one's presence on another's land. In such circumstances, there is no actionable trespass. For example, under the Countryside and Rights of Way Act 2000 rights are conferred to enter land to make

---

[61] *Robson v Hallett* [1967] 2 QB 939, at 953–4.

[62] [1928] 1 KB 421. Presumably, D's successor in title to the chattels would also be liable in trespass for knowingly allowing them to remain on C's land.   [63] [1955] 2 QB 1.

[64] *Basely v Clarkson* (1681) 3 Lev 37; *Nelson v Nicholson* (2001) *Independent*, 22 January.

[65] *Smith v Stone* (1647) Style 65. But note that entering the land of others pursuant to threats is no defence for such an entry and will be regarded as having been voluntary: *Gilbert v Stone* (1647) Style 72.

[66] [1965] 1 QB 232. For discussion see ch 10.

[67] Certainly in *League against Cruel Sports Ltd v Scott* [1986] QB 240, Park J expressed the view that liability in trespass could ensue from the negligent failure of D to control hounds properly so that they enter C's land.

arrangements for the general public to have access to open countryside. In such circumstances, no tort is committed so long as the entrant complies with the specified statutory restrictions within which she must act.[68] Equally, in certain circumstances police officers are permitted to enter land to make an arrest and to search the premises following such an arrest[69] and private individuals have certain similar common law rights to enter another's land to abate a nuisance or reclaim wrongfully taken personal property.

In fact, there are many forms of justification—whether originating in statute or ancient rules of common law—that are too numerous to list here.[70] It suffices to note two general principles: (1) that a recognised legal authority to enter another's land defeats any prospective trespass action; and (2) that a distinction must be drawn between an absolute right to do an act and a mere power to do an act which the defendant elected to do in a fashion that involved an avoidable trespass.[71]

(B) Licence

Where the defendant can claim a positive easement over land (that is, a right enjoyed by one owner of land over the land of another, such as a right of way), she has a defence to an action in trespass.[72] Alternatively, the defendant might raise the defence of licence where the claimant landowner has granted her permission, whether express or implied, to enter the land. Such licences do not require that the entrant be granted any proprietary rights in respect of the land; permission to be there suffices. On the other hand, if the entrant exceeds the permission conferred by the licence, she becomes a trespasser. Thus, if A is granted permission to enter B's land for the purposes of photographing wildlife, she may not fish in B's lake without becoming a trespasser. Similarly, if the landowner revokes the licence, the entrant may not remain on her land. And this is so regardless of whether the licence was conferred gratuitously or by virtue of a contract.[73]

(C) Search warrants

Under the Police and Criminal Evidence Act 1984, section 8, magistrates have, in certain circumstances, the power to grant search warrants.[74]

---

[68] See the Countryside and Rights of Way Act 2000, s 2.

[69] Police and Criminal Evidence Act 1984, ss 17–18.

[70] For full details, see *Clerk and Lindsell* (20th edn, 2010), paras 19–37 *et seq*.

[71] In *British Waterways Board v Severn Trent Water Ltd* [2002] Ch 25 it was stressed that, while a statute authorised certain waterworks, it did not confer impliedly upon D a right to discharge surplus water into another's watercourse. The court adverted to the crucial difference between mere *convenient* ways of carrying out statutory operations and methods that are *necessary*.

[72] See, eg, *Donovan v Rana* [2014] 1 P&CR 23.

[73] Revocation of a contractual licence, it seems, does not require mutually agreed contractual variation. Any complaint about such revocation—effectively a breach of contract—must be pursued under the law of contract: see *Wood v Leadbitter* (1845) 13 M & W 838.

[74] For full details, see *Clerk and Lindsell* (20th edn, 2010), paras 19–61 *et seq*.

Section 3 Remedies

(A) Damages

The claimant is entitled to full reparation for her loss. Generally, the depreciation in selling value will be an adequate measure for destruction of, or damage to, land and buildings. On occasion, though, the claimant can recover special damages also, such as the cost of replacement premises[75] or business profits.[76] Equally, where the cost of reinstatement or repair exceeds the diminution in the property's value, those costs may be awarded as damages provided expenditure on reinstatement and repair is reasonable.[77] For these purposes, reasonableness is to be gauged by applying cost–benefit analysis not only to the reinstatement sought, but also to other available options (including halfway-house solutions and the simple payment of damages).[78] Whatever the court's conclusion, the cost of repair will provide important evidence of the claimant's loss, especially where there is no market in which the value of the property can be ascertained, or where the claimant can prove that it was reasonable to have the property restored.[79] All measures of damages—whether based on market value or replacement cost—are subordinate to the general and overriding tort principle of restoring the claimant to the same position she would have occupied had the tort not been committed.[80]

The measure of damages for wrongful occupancy of land (*mesne profits*) generally is assessed in terms of the reasonable rental value of the land during the time of the defendant's occupancy.[81] So, in *Inverugie Investments Ltd v Hackett*,[82] the claimants were awarded the equivalent of the letting value of the whole of the holiday apartment block wrongfully occupied by the defendant trespassers, even though in practice only about 35–40% of the apartments were rented out. The claimants were entitled to compensation for the wrongful use of their property, regardless of whether they had suffered any actual loss from being deprived of the use of that property and regardless of whether the defendants had benefited in fact from their wrongdoing. Likewise, in the case of a trespass to the claimant's airspace caused by the erection of an advertising hoarding, it is possible for the claimant to obtain what would be a reasonable fee for the use of that hoarding representing its letting value.[83] However, *Davies v Ilieff*[84] provides an important qualification to this approach in that, if the premises concerned are

---

[75] *Dominion Mosaics and Tile Co v Trafalgar Trucking Co* [1990] 2 All ER 246.

[76] *Watson v Murray & Co* [1955] 2 QB 1. Cf *Dunn v Large* (1783) 3 Doug KB 335.

[77] *Heath v Keys* [1984] CLY 3568. Damages based on the cost of repair are only available when C does in fact intend to carry out repairs: *Perry v Sidney Phillips & Son* [1982] 3 All ER 705.

[78] *Bryant v Macklin* [2005] EWCA Civ 762.   [79] See *Hutchinson v Davidson* 1945 SC 395.

[80] *Farmer Giles Ltd v Wessex Water Authority* [1990] 18 EG 102.

[81] *Swordheath Properties Ltd v Tabet* [1979] 1 WLR 285, at 288; *Jones v Merton LBC* [2001] 1 WLR 1269, at [24].

[82] [1995] 1 WLR 713. See also *Whitwham v Westminster Brymbo Coal and Coke Co* [1896] 1 Ch 894 (affd [1896] 2 Ch 538).

[83] *Stadium Capital Holdings (No 2) Ltd v St Marylebone Property Co plc* [2010] EWCA Civ 952, at [13]. See also *Eaton Mansions (Westminster) Ltd v Stinger Compania de Inversion SA* [2013] EWCA Civ 1308, at [21] (fee for the period of the trespass only); *Enfield LBC v Outdoor Plus Ltd* [2012] EWCA Civ 608 (awarding damages not on the basis of mesne profits, because of the absence of a relevant market, but on the basis of a hypothetical negotiation).   [84] 2000 WL 33201551.

the claimant's home (rather than merely commercial residential premises), the court should add to the ordinary letting value a sum in general damages to reflect the insult of the trespass.

Where goods such as coal, minerals, or trees are severed from the land, the measure of damages depends on whether the act is wilful or innocent.[85] If the defendant's severance is innocent, the claimant's damages amount to the value of the goods in their raw state (for example, coal still in a seam) minus the cost of severance and removal.[86] If the act is wilful, however, the claimant's damages will reflect the market value of the goods when they first became a chattel minus only the cost of removal—for example, hauling coal to the surface—but not the cost of severance.[87]

Finally, it is to be noted that aggravated damages potentially are available in the case of a trespass to land, where the interference with possession was high-handed, insulting, or oppressive.[88] And exemplary damages might (in rare cases) be available also, for example in the case of a tenant who is unlawfully evicted by her landlord.[89]

(B) Injunctions

Injunctions, even of the interim variety, are available in the case of continuing trespasses to restrain the trespasser.[90] And mandatory injunctions can be obtained in order to require a trespasser to restore the land to its former state. In *Nelson v Nicholson*,[91] for example, the facts were these:

> Cs had resolved a boundary dispute with their neighbours, but it became apparent that Ds had planted a leylandii hedge on Cs' land. They conceded that this constituted a trespass. Cs then sought a mandatory injunction to require Ds to remove the hedge since they could not do so themselves under the terms of a restrictive covenant that prevented them from removing any fence, hedge, tree, or shrubs within 30 feet of the boundary between the two plots of land.

Despite the defendants proposing an undertaking whereby the defendants would keep the hedge trimmed to a height no greater than seven feet, the court granted the injunction, making the point that the proposed undertaking would not bind the defendants' successors in title.

Finally, a *quia timet* injunction may be granted to restrain the prospective trespasser; that is, where a trespass is merely threatened. Thus, in one case where the owners of

---

[85] 'Wilful' includes 'fraudulent'; whether it includes 'negligent' is doubtful: *Wood v Morewood* (1841) 3 QB 440; *Re United Merthyr Collieries Co* (1872) LR 15 Eq 46. In *Trotter v Maclean* (1879) 13 Ch D 574, at 587, Fry J said (*obiter*) that the burden of proving wilfulness is on C.

[86] *Jegon v Vivian* (1871) 6 Ch App 742.

[87] *Martin v Porter* (1839) 5 M & W 351; *Morgan v Powell* (1842) 3 QB 278.

[88] *Stanford International Bank Ltd v Lapp* [2006] UKPC 50, at [39] (*obiter*). In *Bisney v Swanston* (1972) 225 EG 2299, D put a trailer on C's land so as to interfere with C's business as much as possible. As well as damages for loss of business, aggravated damages were awarded against D for intending to interfere with malice and spite.

[89] *Drane v Evangelou* [1978] 2 All ER 437. See also *Ramzan v Brookwide Ltd* [2012] 1 All ER 903, at [80]–[83].

[90] *Patel v WH Smith (Eziot) Ltd* [1987] 1 WLR 853.   [91] (2001) *Independent*, 22 January.

certain incinerators anticipated a trespass by environmental protestors, an injunction was granted to prevent the trespass from occurring.[92]

(C) Recovery of land

The person entitled to possession may use reasonably necessary force to remove a trespasser.[93] But in many instances the rightful occupant might prefer to pursue an action for recovery of land. In order to succeed, the claimant must demonstrate the relative weakness of the defendant's possessory rights. In other words, the claimant need not show that she has perfect title, merely a better title than the defendant. The clearest modern authority on this remedy is *Manchester Airport plc v Dutton*:[94]

> Manchester Airport needed to remove certain trees in neighbouring woods and it was granted a licence by the owner to 'enter and occupy the woods' to do so. Prior to this, however, protestors had occupied the woods. In order to carry out the work, the airport sought an order for possession against the protestors.

Although Manchester Airport was not the owner of the woods, the Court of Appeal nonetheless granted the order on the basis that the airport had a superior right to occupation than the protestors. What was significant was the fact that the owner had included in the licence a right of occupation. Accordingly, in the ostensibly similar case of *Countryside Residential (North Thames) Ltd v Tugwell*,[95] the court refused such an order on the grounds that the licence in question merely conferred permission to carry out work on the land, but not a right to occupy it.

Conclusions

In this chapter, we have seen that the possessor of the surface of land is in deemed possession of all the substrata directly below it and of the airspace directly above it insofar as the latter is necessary for the use and enjoyment of the land and any structures upon it. The law offers generous protection for those in possession of land—that is, to those with both exclusive occupation and the intention to exclude the world at large. Trespass to land occurs where the defendant directly and either intentionally or negligently interferes with the claimant's possession of land and is actionable without proof of damage. The action can be defeated by proof of a licence to be on the land or by some other justification. Remedies for trespass include injunctions, actions for the recovery of land, and damages.

---

[92] *Hampshire Waste Services Ltd v Intending Trespassers upon Chineham Incinerator* [2004] Env LR 9.
[93] *Hemmings v Stoke Poges Golf Club* [1920] 1 KB 720.   [94] [2000] 1 QB 133.
[95] [2000] 34 EG 87.

Problem question

Ziwei decided to rebuild a brick wall at the end of his rear garden, which, while standing wholly on his own property, formed a barrier between his and the adjoining property owned by Dahlia. While Ziwei was pulling down the old wall, some bricks fell over onto Dahlia's property. A plastic cup that Ziwei drank from also blew over into Dahlia's garden. Ziwei retrieved both the bricks and the plastic cup as quickly as he could. Later that day, Dahlia decided that she would investigate what was going on at the bottom of her garden. Because Dahlia was housebound with meningitis, she launched a small drone, which flew over Ziwei's house. The drone got caught up in one of Ziwei's trees. Later that day the drone fell onto Jo-Beth's neighbouring land. In the late evening, a gas meter reader from the energy supplier Blast Gases plc came onto Ziwei's property in order to read the gas meter. This was a mistake on the meter reader's part because he had meant to check Jo-Beth's meter.

Advise the parties on potential trespasses to land.

 Visit **http://www.oup.com/uk/street15e/** for answer guidance.

Further reading

BIRTS, *Remedies for Trespass* (1990)
DORFMAN AND JACOB, 'The Fault of Trespass' (2015) 65 *University of Toronto Law Journal* 48
HOWELL, '"Subterranean Land Law": Rights Below the Surface of Land' (2002) 53 *Northern Ireland Law Quarterly* 268
SPRANKLING, 'Owning the Center of the Earth' (2008) 55 *UCLA Law Review* 979

13

Defences to intentional torts against the person or property

KEY ISSUES

(1) Three types of defence
Tort law provides for a wide range of defences to the intentional torts against the person or property. Defences to these torts can be placed within a threefold system. The first category consists of 'absent element defences', which are denials of one or more of the elements of the tort in which the claimant sues. The second category comprises 'justification defences', which release the defendant from liability on the ground that he acted reasonably, and thus not wrongfully, in committing a tort. The third category contains public policy defences, which exempt the defendant from responsibility even though he committed a tort for no good reason. They exist in recognition of the fact that unjustified tortfeasors sometimes must be released from liability to further social goals external to the law of torts.

(2) Absent element defences
Consent is an absent element defence to the intentional torts because the absence of consent is an element of these wrongs. The

doctrines of inevitable accident, involuntariness, and physical compulsion are absent element defences also.

(3) Justification defences
The paradigmatic justification defence is self-defence, which releases persons who use necessary and proportionate force to defend themselves against an aggressor or putative aggressor from liability. An array of other justification defences exist which are variations on the theme of self-defence, including defence of another person, defence of one's property, recapture of land or chattels, and arrest.

(4) Public policy defences
Tort law recognises numerous public policy defences, one of the most significant of which is illegality. This defence prevents claimants injured by a tort from recovering compensation where they were committing a serious criminal offence at the time of the defendant's tort and their criminal conduct contributed to their damage.

Section 1 Introduction

Significance of defences This chapter considers the most significant defences to liability arising in the intentional torts against the person or property. It must not be thought, however, that these defences apply only to these torts. Many of them—for example, consent, statutory authority, and illegality—apply throughout the tort law universe. Nevertheless, the defences under consideration are important in the present context particularly because the key question in proceedings for the intentional torts often is whether the defendant has an answer to liability. For example, most claims in false imprisonment turn on whether the detention of the claimant was justified, rather than on whether the definitional elements of this tort are present. The importance of justification defences to false imprisonment is reflected in the European Convention on Human Rights (ECHR). Article 5 of the Convention protects the rights to liberty and security of the person in just ten words: 'Everyone has the right to liberty and security of person.' By contrast, over a page of text is devoted to articulating the circumstances in which interfering with these rights is justifiable. In short, defences are crucial in defining when liability arises in the intentional torts.

Three categories Defences to liability in the intentional torts can be organised within three categories.[1] First, there are denials of one or more of the elements of the tort in which the claimant sues. These defences will be called 'absent element defences'.[2] Second, there are justification defences, which operate to release a defendant from liability on the ground that his actions were not wrongful in the circumstances, although technically he committed a tort. Finally, there are public policy defences. These are defences that exempt the defendant from liability even though he committed a tort without justification. They exist in recognition of the fact that sometimes it is necessary to release unjustified tortfeasors from liability in order to advance some important social goal that is external to tort law. Justification defences and public policy defences may be referred to collectively as 'affirmative defences', since they exempt the defendant from liability even though he committed a tort.

Implications This classification of defences has important implications. For example, it bears upon the allocation of the burdens of pleading and proof. Absent element defences are denials by the defendant that he committed a tort. Accordingly, the claimant carries the burden of negating these defences in his pleadings and in the evidence. By contrast, justifications and public policy defences are affirmative defences; they are for the defendant to plead and prove. Arguably, this classification affects also the permissibility of resisting a defendant. A defendant who has an absent element defence commits no tort. His conduct is lawful (unless, of course, it constitutes a crime or another type of civil wrong). In principle, therefore, others should not generally interfere with

---

[1] J Goudkamp, 'A Taxonomy of Tort Law Defences' in S Degeling, J Edelman, and J Goudkamp (eds), *Torts in Commercial Law* (2011), ch 19.

[2] The terminology is borrowed from PH Robinson, *Structure and Function in Criminal Law* (1997), 12.

his conduct. Doing so is likely to be tortious. The same may hold for justifications. A defendant who is justified (for example, is acting in self-defence) acts in a way that is not wrongful. Arguably, therefore, a justified defendant should not be resisted. In contrast, generally speaking, those who can avoid liability only because of the application of a public policy defence may be resisted. This is because their conduct is unreasonable and typically objectionable.

Section 2 Absent element defences

Recall that absent element defences are contentions by the defendant that one or more of the elements of the tort in which the claimant sues is absent. A selection of absent element defences is discussed here.

(A) Involuntariness

No tort is committed by a defendant whose impugned behaviour is involuntary. For example, if the defendant's leg hits the claimant as a result of a muscle spasm, the defendant has not acted tortiously. Which element, exactly, is negated where the defendant's movements in issue were involuntary? The courts[3] and commentators[4] routinely characterise the plea of involuntariness as a denial of fault. This treatment is to some extent understandable as a person is not, except in relatively uncommon circumstances, at fault for his involuntary movements.[5] The better view, however, is that there must be some other element that is unsatisfied if the defendant's movements in question were involuntary. This is because involuntariness prevents liability from arising in strict liability torts. It follows that all torts incorporate what may be called an 'conduct element'. It is this element that is targeted by a plea of involuntariness.

(B) Physical compulsion

Suppose that A grabs hold of B's hand and uses it to hit C. B is not liable to C in battery[6] (although A is of course liable). This is because the conduct element of battery is not present. It is important to distinguish the plea of physical compulsion from that of duress.[7] Physical compulsion involves a third party using the defendant's body to commit a tort. Duress (which is not a defence) entails the defendant acting tortiously in consequence of threats made by a third party.

---

[3] See, eg, *Sik v Lajos* [1962] SASR 146, at 150; *Smith v Lord* [1962] SASR 88, at 94–5.

[4] See, eg, Restatement (Third) of Torts: Liability for Physical and Emotional Harm at § 11(b), cmt d.

[5] D will be at fault for his involuntary movements if he could have avoided the movements by taking reasonable care. Thus, a person who experiences an epileptic fit will be at fault if he negligently failed to take his anti-convulsant medication as prescribed by his doctor.

[6] This example is taken from *Ward v Weaver* (1616) Hob 134, at 134; 80 ER 284, at 285.

[7] Duress is discussed later.

(C) Inevitable accident

The law treats an accident as inevitable if it could not have been avoided by taking reasonable care and was not intended by the defendant. Since the intentional torts require proof that the defendant acted intentionally or negligently, the plea of inevitable accident is an absent element defence to these causes of action. It is an assertion by the defendant that he was not at fault.

(D) Consent

In the intentional torts, the absence of consent[8] is part of the cause of action.[9] Accordingly, consent is an absent element defence to these wrongs. The fact that the issue of consent is internalised within the definitions of the intentional torts, rather than treated as an affirmative defence, sends an important message: that it is not wrong merely to touch other people or their property. Coming into contact with another person or their property is wrong only when it is non-consensual. This seems to be the correct position for the law to adopt, particularly in relation to sexual batteries. Were a sexual battery constituted simply by proof of sexual intercourse, that would imply that all sexual intercourse is wrong. This would not conform to the prevailing sexual morality in contemporary society. In the usual case, sexual intercourse is wrong only when it is non-consensual.

(1) Generally

Express or implied Consent in the context of the intentional torts may be given expressly or inferred from conduct. For example, a boxer's consent to being punched is implicit in his getting into the ring. Likewise, a teenager engaged in horseplay with a friend cannot complain if he is injured by his friend so long as the latter stays within the tacitly agreed rules of that horseplay.[10] Similarly, a footballer consents not only to those tackles permitted by the rules, but probably to those tackles that involve a technical breach of the rules of the game as well. Where, however, an opponent commits a 'professional foul', the conduct involved is beyond that to which the player agreed when embarking on the game.[11]

Determining what can be inferred from conduct can be difficult and it is inevitable that there will be borderline cases. In *Arthur v Anker*,[12] the Court of Appeal held that, where a person had parked his car unlawfully on another's land knowing that the latter

---

[8] See P Western, *The Logic of Consent: The Diversity and Deceptiveness of Consent as a Defence to Criminal Conduct* (2004).

[9] This is the rule in relation to trespass to the person in England (*Freeman v Home Office (No 2)* [1984] 2 WLR 130, affd [1984] QB 524), New Zealand (*H v R* [1996] 1 NZLR 299, at 305) and USA (*Ford v Ford* 10 NE 474, at 475 (1887)). However, in Australia and Canada, at least in relation to certain trespasses to the person, consent is an affirmative defence (*Marion's Case* (1992) 175 CLR 218, at 310–11).

[10] *Blake v Galloway* [2004] 1 WLR 2844.   [11] *Condon v Basi* [1985] 1 WLR 866.

[12] [1997] QB 564.

asserted a right to wheel-clamp trespassing vehicles and charge for their release, he had impliedly consented not only to the otherwise unlawful detention of his car (so that there was no trespass to goods), but also to being required to pay a reasonable fee to ensure the unclamping of the vehicle. *Arthur v Anker* can be contrasted to *Vine v Waltham Forest London Borough Council*,[13] where it was held that, if the release fee is exorbitant, consent to its payment cannot be implied if the person parking the car does not actually see the sign (even if the sign was both prominently posted and clear in its terms).

Class of act Unless the claimant's consent relates to the class of act complained of, it will not prevent liability from arising. For example, the consent of an occupier to a repairer entering his house to fix his boiler would not stop the repairer from being held liable in battery if she has sexual intercourse with the occupier. However, the claimant's consent need not correspond exactly to the defendant's act. Thus, as already noted, in the context of a contact sport consent generally to the prospect of blows being struck will furnish the defendant with an answer to liability.[14] It need not be shown that the claimant consented to the precise number of blows that were delivered. Of course, determining the generality of the claimant's conduct in a given case can be difficult. Each case will turn on its own facts.

Subjective or objective test? Consent is a state of mind on the part of the claimant. However, the law is yet to determine definitively whether the claimant's mental state is ascertained subjectively or objectively. If a subjective test is adopted, consent will be present only when the claimant in fact agreed to the defendant's contact with his person or property. On an objective test,[15] what was actually running through the claimant's mind at the time is not relevant. What matters is whether the reasonable person would conclude, based on an assessment of the claimant's conduct, that the claimant consented to the contact. A subjective test is more favourable to claimants and promotes rights to personal security. An objective test gives greater weight to the interest in freedom of action. However, the difference between these alternatives is probably not very great in practice. This is because, even if a subjective test is used, the main guide that the court has to the claimant's mental state is his conduct.

Vitiation of consent Fraud or deception can vitiate consent. For example, if D impersonates C's partner and C has sexual intercourse with D believing him to be her partner, C's consent to the intercourse will be vitiated.[16] More complex is the situation where one person has sexual intercourse with another and infects the latter with a sexually transmitted disease. In such a scenario, there are two issues at stake: (1) whether the second person consents to sexual intercourse; and (2) whether that person consents to the risk of being infected with the disease. Consent to sexual intercourse does not

---

[13] [2000] 1 WLR 2383. [14] *Blake v Galloway* [2004] 1 WLR 2844, at [20].

[15] An objective test is supported by *Bennett v Tugwell* [1971] 2 QB 267, at 273.

[16] Sexual Offences Act 2003, sub-s 76(2)(b). This is a criminal law statute. But it reflects the position in tort law.

mean that there is consent to the risk of infection. Hence, a person who has consensual sexual intercourse with another without telling the latter that he is carrying a sexually transmitted disease will not be liable in battery in respect of the intercourse but might be liable in battery as a result of any infection that occurs.[17] Also difficult is the case in which the defendant's motive is in question. Suppose that a male police officer 'cuddles' a distressed female victim of crime whom he is questioning. If he puts his arms around her purely in an attempt to ameliorate some of the stress caused by the occasion, and she welcomes such comforting, there will be no battery. But what if he does it for prurient reasons that become evident later? The criminal law may render the police officer guilty of an offence on the basis that he deceived the complainant as to the nature or purpose of the act.[18] But it is undecided whether a claimant's consent is vitiated in tort.[19] On the one hand, tort law typically ignores the defendant's motive.[20] On the other hand, it seems objectionable for the police officer in the scenario to avoid civil responsibility.

Consent that is obtained under duress is no consent at all.[21] For example, a woman who 'agrees' to sexual intercourse with the defendant owing to threats of violence made against her by the defendant does not consent to intercourse.[22] A display of authority may constitute duress. So, for instance, where a police officer, without formally arresting or charging a suspect, asks him with an authoritative air to accompany him to the police station,[23] the claimant might not be treated as having consented. Likewise, if the claimant is so drunk as to be incapable of consenting, any putative consent is treated as invalid.[24]

Effect of consent The overriding interest of the state in maintaining order means that consent is not necessarily an answer to criminal liability. Thus, the consent of a person to the infliction of actual bodily harm is ineffective in the criminal law unless it is caused for a good reason (such as life-saving surgery).[25] Tort law takes a different approach. As it is concerned with private rather than public interests, consent always prevents liability in tort from arising. It is irrelevant that the act consented to results in the infliction of serious harm for inadequate reasons. It has been held, for example, that a person can consent to the risk of being fatally shot[26] or to being injured in a bar fight.[27]

---

[17] *R v Dica* [2004] QB 1257. See also *R v EB* [2007] 1 WLR 1567.

[18] Sexual Offences Act 2003, sub-s 76(2)(a).   [19] *KD v CC of Hampshire* [2005] EWHC 2550 (QB).

[20] 'Although the rule may be otherwise with regard to crimes, the law of England does not . . . take into account motive as constituting an element of civil wrong': *Allen v Flood* [1898] AC 1, at 92.

[21] Yet in *Latter v Braddell* (1881) 50 LJQB 448, a servant who complied, crying and under protest, with an order of her mistress that she be medically examined to determine whether she was pregnant, was held to have consented. See also *Centre for Reproductive Medicine v U* [2002] EWCA Civ 565.

[22] Cf Sexual Offences Act 2003, sub-s 75(2)(a).

[23] *Warner v Riddiford* (1858) 4 CBNS 180; 140 ER 1052.

[24] *R v Bree* [2008] QB 131.

[25] The leading decision is *R v Brown* [1994] 1 AC 212, which was held not to have violated ECHR, Art 8: *Laskey, Jaggard and Brown v UK* (1997) 24 EHRR 39.

[26] *Murphy v Culhane* [1977] QB 94. Consider also *Lane v Holloway* [1968] 1 QB 379.

[27] *Bain v Altoft* [1967] Qd R 32, at 41. The Restatement (Second) of Torts § 892C provides that consent bars recovery unless the conduct concerned was criminalised in order to protect the individual consenting to it.

Effect of mistake Difficult issues arise where the defendant mistakenly believed that the claimant consented to contact with his person or property. In the criminal law, a reasonable mistake as to the victim's consent precludes liability for rape.[28] Tort law's position on this issue is unclear. Arguably, however, tort law should adopt a rule that is less favourable to defendants than the criminal law. Unlike the criminal law, which favours the interests of the defendant, in tort law neither party has a privileged position. If correct, this would result in defendants being denied any leeway in consequence of a mistaken belief in consent.[29]

(2) Consent to medical treatment

The law concerning consent to medical treatment is voluminous and intricate.[30] In order to provide a broad outline, it is necessary to distinguish between four classes of patient: adults with capacity to consent; children; patients suffering from mental incapacity and receiving treatment under the Mental Health Act 1983; and patients lacking capacity but falling beyond the scope of the Mental Health Act 1983. As we shall see, however, these categories are not watertight. There is some degree of overlap between them.

(a) Adults with capacity to consent

Basis in self-determination Any non-consensual physical contact with a competent adult patient prima facie is a battery.[31] This reflects the fundamental right to self-determination. As Cardozo J put it in *Schloendorff v Society of New York Hospital*:[32] 'Every human being of adult years and sound mind has a right to determine what shall be done with his own body.' As in other contexts, consent need not be written and may be implied from conduct, such as holding out one's arm to receive an injection. However, where surgery or more serious invasive treatment is contemplated, patients usually will be asked to sign a form agreeing to the procedure.

Explanation of treatment required A patient's consent to medical treatment is ineffective unless he is provided with an adequate explanation of the broad nature of what is to be done to him.[33] But a mere failure to warn the patient of the risks or side-effects of the treatment proposed will not vitiate the patient's consent.[34] At most it will constitute a breach of the doctor's duty to give the patient proper advice and will be actionable as negligence subject to the requirement that the patient suffer damage.[35] Only

---

[28] Sexual Offences Act 2003, s 1.

[29] The decision in *Ashley v CC of Sussex Police* [2008] 1 AC 962 supports this analysis.

[30] See, eg, A Mclean, *Autonomy, Informed Consent and Medical Law: A Relational Challenge* (2009); M Brazier and E Cave, *Medicine, Patients and the Law* (4th edn, 2007), ch 6.

[31] *In re F (Mental Patient: Sterilisation)* [1990] 2 AC 1.

[32] 105 NE 92, at 93 (1914).

[33] *Chatterton v Gerson* [1981] QB 432, at 443.

[34] The bringing of actions in battery where the essence of the claim is inadequate advice was deplored in *Sidaway v Board of Governors of the Bethlem Royal Hospital and the Maudsley Hospital* [1985] AC 871, at 883.

[35] See chapter 6, section 3(C), esp. discussion of *Montgomery v Lanarkshire Health Board* [2015] 1 AC 1430.

when the defendant actively misleads the patient will a claim in battery normally be available.[36]

Absence of consent Where it is uncertain whether a patient with full understanding freely rejected life-saving treatment, it is lawful for doctors to err on the side of preserving life.[37] If, however, the patient makes it clear that he does not wish to receive treatment, his wishes must be respected.[38] Thus, if a competent patient requests that his ventilator be disconnected, those providing care must oblige.[39]

(b) Children

Ability to consent Family Law Reform Act 1969, sub-section 8(1) provides that a minor over the age of 16 may consent to medical treatment. The consent of such children is on par with that of competent adults. In the case of children under the age of 16, the Act preserves the common law rule that, provided the individual child is mature enough to make his own decision on the treatment proposed, the child can give an effective consent.[40] Thus, an attempt in *Gillick v West Norfolk and Wisbech Area Health Authority*[41] to ensure that no girl under the age of 16 lawfully could be prescribed the contraceptive pill without parental agreement failed. The House of Lords held that, if such a girl seeking contraception or an abortion should refuse adamantly to consult her parents, the doctor may lawfully treat her provided that he is satisfied that she has sufficient understanding of what is involved in the treatment and its implications for her.

Refusal of treatment While a 'Gillick-competent' child who is not yet 16 can provide effective consent to treatment, the position is otherwise with respect to the *refusal* of treatment, at least in certain situations. In *Re W (a minor) (medical treatment: Court's jurisdiction)*,[42] the Court of Appeal held that it had jurisdiction to order that medical treatment for anorexia nervosa be provided to a 'Gillick-competent' child suffering from anorexia nervosa against her wishes. The court held that account should be taken of the child's wishes, but that it could override them where to do so is in the child's best interests.

Parental consent In the case of very young children, parental consent to treatment is effective to authorise treatment that is beneficial to the child.[43] No battery is committed therefore when a doctor vaccinates a protesting four-year-old if his parent has given

---

[36] See *Appleton v Garrett* [1996] PIQR P1 (dentist withheld essential information from patients). See also *R v Tabassum* [2000] 2 Cr App R 328 (D, who performed breast examinations, misled victims into believing that he had medical qualifications: liable). Cf *R v Richardson* [1999] QB 444 (a dentist who provided treatment although she had been suspended from practice not liable for assault, despite her patients being unaware of her suspension).

[37] *In re T (Adult: Refusal of Treatment)* [1993] Fam 95.

[38] See Mental Capacity Act 2005, ss 24–6, which makes provision for advance decisions to refuse treatment to be made.

[39] *Ms B v An NHS Hospital Trust* [2002] 2 FCR 1.   [40] Sub-section 8(3).

[41] [1986] AC 112.   [42] [1993] Fam 64.

[43] *Gillick v West Norfolk and Wisbech AHA* [1986] AC 112, at 166–7.

consent. Where the procedure proposed is not clearly and unequivocally beneficial to the child, however, parental consent alone might not be sufficient. In such cases—including, for example, sterilisation—the authorisation of the court must be sought, especially before serious and irreversible surgery is performed.[44]

(c) Patients lacking capacity and falling within the scope of the Mental Health Act 1983

Where patients are mentally disordered, the terms under which they may be cared for and treated are governed primarily by the Mental Health Act 1983.[45] The details of this statute[46] cannot be given here. It suffices to note that the Act makes provision for treatment according to a complex method encompassing many procedural and substantive safeguards.

(d) Patients lacking capacity but falling outside the Mental Health Act 1983

The position in relation to patients who lack capacity but who are not mentally disordered (for example, competent but unconscious patients) and hence fall beyond the scope of the Mental Health Act 1983 is determined by the Mental Capacity Act 2005. Again, a detailed account of this legislation is beyond the ambit of this book. However, it is noted that the Act puts in place a presumption of capacity[47] that is ousted only if the patient is shown on the balance of probabilities to lack capacity (judged according to the patient's ability to understand, retain, and use information relevant to a treatment decision and to communicate his decision).[48] Where the person lacks capacity, he may be treated if the person providing treatment reasonably believes it to be in the patient's best interests, subject to certain safeguards (concerning matters such as known previous wishes and religious beliefs).[49]

Section 3 Justification defences

Justification defences are defences that exempt persons from liability where they act reasonably in committing a tort and where their actions should not be viewed, in the circumstances, as wrongful. Many of these defences are instances of self-help, that is to say, situations where the law allows persons to solve their own problems by committing torts rather than resorting to litigation. Given the law's generally dim view of self-help, the circumstances in which it is allowed are defined narrowly. This is because courts fear that steps taken in self-help might result in (further) violence. As Edmund Davies LJ said in *Southwark London Borough Council v Williams*:[50]

---

[44] *Re B (a minor) (Wardship: Sterilisation)* [1988] AC 199, at 205; *Practice Note (Sterilisation: minors and mental health patients)* [1993] 3 All ER 222.

[45] Sub-s 1(1). [46] This Act was amended by the Mental Health Act 2007.

[47] Mental Capacity Act 2005, sub-s 1(2). [48] Mental Capacity Act 2005, sub-s 3(1).

[49] Mental Capacity Act 2005, ss 4–6.

[50] [1971] Ch 734, at 745–6. See also *R v Burns* [2010] EWCA Crim 1023, at [11]–[14].

> [T]he law regards with the deepest suspicion any remedies of self-help, and permits these remedies to be resorted to only in very special circumstances. The reason for such circumspection is clear—necessity can very easily become simply a mask for anarchy.

(A) Prevention of crime

The Criminal Law Act 1967, section 3 absolves of liability persons who use reasonable force to prevent the commission of any offence recognised by domestic law.[51] This justification defence[52] overlaps significantly with the defences of self-defence and defence of another person. However, unlike the latter defences, section 3 applies only where the defendant is preventing a 'crime'. Accordingly, in contrast with the common law defences just mentioned, section 3 probably does not insulate a defendant from liability for restraining a mentally disordered aggressor or a child under the age of ten,[53] since such persons are not criminally responsible for their acts.

(B) Self-defence

A battery may be justified on the ground of self-defence.[54] In order to establish this defence, the defendant must prove that it was necessary to use force to repel an attack by the claimant or to prevent or terminate a false imprisonment[55] and that the amount of force used was reasonable.

Necessity The necessity requirement means that the defence will be unavailable unless physical force was the only realistic means of avoiding the threat posed by the claimant. Suppose, for example, that a defendant could prevent the claimant from murdering him either by shooting the claimant or by closing and locking a door between him and the claimant. If the defendant opted to shoot the claimant, self-defence would be excluded because it would be unnecessary do this in order for the defendant to save himself.

The criterion of necessity dictates that the threat posed by the claimant must be reasonably imminent. This is because threats that are not proximate can be neutralised other than by using defensive force, such as by seeking help from the authorities. In other words, the defence of self-defence does not create a privilege to commit pre-emptive strikes. Of course, this does not mean that the defendant has to wait until he is struck before it is permissible to use defensive force. This would not make sense for, on occasion, the opportunity for the defendant to save himself might be lost if he does not act first. Thus, the law permits the defendant to strike before the claimant if doing so

---

[51] Preventing breaches of international law does not qualify: *R v Jones* [2007] 1 AC 136.

[52] See also the analogous defence in Education Act 1996, sub-s 550A(1) (teachers can use force against a pupil to prevent the commission of an offence, among other things).

[53] Criminal responsibility begins at the age of ten: Crime and Disorder Act 1998, s 34.

[54] See J Goudkamp (2010) 18 TLJ 61.

[55] This includes an unlawful arrest: *Codd v Cabe* (1875–1876) LR 1 Ex D 352; *R v McKoy* [2002] EWCA Crim 1628.

is necessary.[56] The point is that the defence is unavailable if the threat is so distant that it is speculative. The necessity limb means also that force that comes after a threat has passed will not amount to self-defence.

Reasonableness The reasonableness limb is concerned with whether the amount of force used by the defendant was proportionate to the threat posed by the claimant. What constitutes reasonable force is a question of fact to be determined in the light of the circumstances. It will be relevant to consider, among other things, how the defendant resisted the claimant, whether a weapon was used, and the number of times that the claimant was struck.[57] It is not a question simply of comparing the evil of the response with the evil of the attack. Suppose that A pins B against a wall and repeatedly kisses her against her will. The only means by which B can compel A to desist is by lacerating his hands with a pair of scissors that she is holding. It is not certain that the defence of self-defence will fail simply because the wounding is more severe than the unwanted kisses. Similarly, suppose that E attempts to rape F and that the only way that F can prevent this is to use lethal force. F probably would be permitted to kill E even though, in doing so, she was causing more harm than that with which she was threatened. It should also be noted that, although self-defence is a type of self-help, the courts usually are generous to the defendant in determining whether the amount of force that he used was proportionate. This is because acts of self-defence normally are carried out under extreme circumstances. As Holmes J observed: 'Detached reflection cannot be demanded in the presence of an uplifted knife.'[58]

Mistake Self-defence will be available to a defendant who uses force against an innocent person whom he mistook for an aggressor provided that his mistake was reasonable and the requirements of necessity and proportionality are satisfied according to the world as perceived by the defendant. This principle was established in *Ashley v Chief Constable of Sussex Police*,[59] which featured a police officer fatally shooting a man whom he believed mistakenly was reaching for a weapon. The deceased's estate and his dependants sued the defendant, alleging that he was vicariously liable for the officer's conduct. The House of Lords ruled that self-defence is unavailable when the defendant's mistake as to the necessity for defensive force was unreasonable. This was on the basis that requiring mistakes to be reasonable strikes a fair balance between the interests of both claimants and defendants.

---

[56] *Dale v Wood* (1822) 7 Moore CP 33 (though on the facts D's response was greater than what was warranted).

[57] Whether or not D had an opportunity to retreat may not be relevant. In the criminal law context, there is no duty to retreat: *R v Bird* [1985] 1 WLR 816; A Ashworth, *Principles of Criminal Law* (6th edn, 2009), 120–1.

[58] *Brown v US* 256 US 335 at 343 (1921). See also *Reed v Wastie* [1972] Crim LR 221 ('one does not use jewellers' scales to measure reasonable force'); *Cross v Kirkby* (2000) *Times*, 5 April ('the law does not require that [D] measure the violence to be deployed with mathematical precision'). See also the Criminal Justice and Immigration Act 2008, sub-s 76(7)(a) ('a person acting for a legitimate purpose may not be able to weigh to a nicety the exact measure of any necessary action').

[59] [2008] 1 AC 962.

(C) Defence of another person

The early common law, which saw the exercise of defensive force as a significant threat to the maintenance of law and order, only permitted persons who stood in certain relationships (such as one of employment) with a person confronted by an aggressor to come to that person's aid.[60] Today, the plea of defence of others probably is not limited to any specific relationships.[61] Anyone who takes necessary and proportionate defensive measures to save another from an aggressor should be entitled to it. However, it is conceivable that the relationship between the defendant and the person whom he defended might be relevant to whether the force was proportionate.

(D) Defence of one's property

Possession required Where necessary to do so, one may use reasonable force to defend property in one's possession against any person committing or threatening to commit a trespass to it. But the defendant must have such possession of the property in question as would enable him to sue the claimant in trespass. Thus, the captain of a cricket club who removed the claimant from a field on account of his disruptive behaviour was liable because he did not have possession of the field.[62] A lack of possession was crucial in *Scott v Matthew Brown & Co Ltd*[63] also, where the defendant was on a plot of land merely as a result of ejecting the claimant, the true owner, by an act of trespass. The claimant re-entered the property and the defendant forcibly removed him. The defendant was held not to have sufficient possession to sue in trespass, and therefore had no defence to liability in battery. If the defendant has a right to possession, but not actual possession, he may have some other defence, such as recapture of land or chattels,[64] but he cannot plead successfully that he was defending his property.

Reasonable force To remain on land after the occupier's consent has been withdrawn is a trespass. Likewise, it is a trespass for a passenger to refuse to alight from a vehicle if its owner rescinds his agreement to the passenger's presence in it. Therefore, the defence of protecting property may be invoked by those who use reasonable force to eject such persons.[65] A threatened intrusion is sufficient to trigger the defence; so if the claimant has taken the key of the defendant's car and is about to enter it, the defendant is entitled to resist this potential trespass. As with self-defence, if the defendant reasonably believes that force is necessary to prevent a trespass, he may use force, although he

---

[60] *Seaman v Cuppledick* (1614) Owen 150; 74 ER 966; *Tickell v Read* (1773) Lofft 215; 98 ER 617; *Barfoot v Reynolds* (1733) 2 Str 953; 93 ER 963.

[61] *Goss v Nicholas* [1960] Tas SR 133 (stranger).

[62] *Holmes v Bagge and Fletcher* (1853) 1 El & Bl 782; 118 ER 629.

[63] (1884) 51 LT 746. See also *Dean v Hogg and Lewis* (1824) 10 Bing 345; 131 ER 937 (hirer of steamboat lacked sufficient possession).

[64] See section 3(F).

[65] *Green v Bartram* (1830) 4 Car & P 308; 172 ER 717; *Moriarty v Brooks* (1834) 6 Car & P 684; 172 ER 1419; *R v Burns* [2010] 1 WLR 2694.

is mistaken in thinking it to be necessary. Whether force is necessary and reasonable depends on the facts. It may be relevant to consider, among other things, whether the defendant requested the claimant to cease the interference with his rights before apply-ing force. The use of force will be unnecessary if the claimant would have ceased his interference with the defendant's property rights following a verbal request from the defendant.[66] However, a defendant is not required to make such a request when to do so would be obviously futile.[67]

Justifying use of force As the law does not generally value interests in property as highly as those in bodily security,[68] all other things being equal the use of force in defence of the former is harder to justify than in the case of self-defence.[69] Firing a shot-gun at a burglar breaking into a garden shed, but who shows no overt sign of violence towards the owner, was held in *Revill v Newbery*[70] to be unreasonable. Might it be, then, that unless the claimant resists his expulsion so as to bring the rules of self-defence into play, the courts will treat force likely to cause death or serious bodily harm as unjustifi-able in the defence of property?[71]

Use of an instrument The courts have had to consider often the extent to which it is permissible for a defendant to use mechanical devices or barriers to protect his prop-erty.[72] The test is one of reasonableness. Thus, attempting to deter intruders by placing barbed wire or spiked railings on the confines of one's land ordinarily will be reason-able. On the other hand, it is unreasonable to set without notice spring guns or such other devices that are calculated to kill or cause grievous bodily harm.[73] Where dogs (or, theoretically, other animals) are used to protect one's property, the relevant rules concerning the defence of one's property are contained in the Animals Act 1971. Under that Act, a person is not liable:[74]

---

[66] Some old cases suggest that a request must be made before it is permissible to use force: see, eg, *Green v Goddard* (1702) 2 Salk 641; 91 ER 540.

[67] *Tullay v Reed* (1823) 1 Car & P 6; 171 ER 1078; *Polkinhorn v Wright* (1845) 8 QB 197.

[68] In *Southport Corp v Esso Petroleum Co Ltd* [1953] 3 WLR 773, at 779, Devlin J said that '[the] safety of human lives belongs to a different scale of values from the safety of property. The two are beyond comparison.' But in relation to injunctive relief, this hierarchy of interests seems to be inverted, with property rights receiv-ing more robust protection: see J Murphy (2007) 27 OJLS 509.

[69] See R Posner (1971) 14 J Law & Econ 201.

[70] [1996] QB 567. See also *Collins v Renison* (1754) Say 138; 96 ER 830; *Moriarty v Brooks* (1834) 6 C & P 684; 172 ER 1419.

[71] As to when killing intruding animals is justifiable, see *Hamps v Darby* [1948] 2 KB 311. See also Animals Act 1971, ss 7 (detention of trespassing livestock) and 9 (destruction of dogs that worry livestock).

[72] See generally FH Bohlen and JJ Burns (1926) 35 Yale LJ 525.

[73] *Bird v Holbrook* (1828) 4 Bing 628; 130 ER 911. Consider also the Offences against the Person Act 1861, s 31. In *AG's Reference (No 2 of 1983)* [1984] QB 456, D had armed himself with petrol bombs to repel rioters who had earlier smashed into his shop. He had been charged with unlawfully being in possession of an explo-sive device. It was held that D was entitled to acquittal if his object was to protect his family or his property from an imminent attack and he believed that it was both necessary and reasonable to use the petrol bombs to meet the force used by any attackers.

[74] Sub-section 5(3) (considered in *Cummings v Grainger* [1977] QB 397). See further the chapter contained in the Online Resources.

> for any damage caused by an animal kept on any premises or structure to a person tres-
> passing there, if it is proved either—(a) that the animal was not kept there for the pro-
> tection of persons or property; or (b) (if the animal was kept there for the protection of
> persons or property) that keeping it there for that purpose was not unreasonable.

(E) Defence of another's property

According to Blackstone, it is a defence to use reasonable force to protect the property of other members of one's household.[75] It is unclear, however, whether this remains the case today. It is difficult to reconcile this proposition with the requirement that only those with sufficient possession of property to enable one to sue for a trespass commit-ted against it may exercise defensive force in respect of it.[76]

(F) Recapture of land or goods

Land A person who enters land in respect of which he has a right of possession and who uses no more force than reasonably necessary in order to evict a trespasser will have a defence in an action brought by the trespasser for battery and interference with his goods.[77] It is unnecessary for such an individual to bring proceedings for possession, although the practicality of obtaining judicial relief will be relevant to whether forcibly re-entering the land was reasonable. This defence is closely related to the defence of property defence. It too is justificatory in nature.[78]

Goods Tort law recognises a defence of recapture of goods also.[79] Unfortunately, a paucity of modern authority renders it difficult to describe with precision the scope of this answer to liability. Old cases hold, however, that one who has been dispossessed of goods may use reasonable force to retake them.[80] It is permissible also for a defendant to enter the claimant's land if doing so is necessary to reclaim goods.[81] So, for example, if an apple falls from a tree on the defendant's land and lands on the claimant's property, the defendant is entitled to enter the claimant's land to retrieve it if doing so is reasonable in the circumstances. For example, the defence will not lie where the defendant breaks into the stables of an innocent person in which his horse was placed by a third party.

(G) Abatement

The doctrine of abatement is a defence to liability in trespass to land. It applies where a person takes reasonable steps to ameliorate or terminate a nuisance.[82] This rule's

---

[75] W Blackstone, *Commentaries on the Laws of England*, vol 3 (1769), at 3.

[76] This requirement is discussed in section 3(D).

[77] *Hemmings v Stoke Poges Golf Club Ltd* [1920] 1 KB 720; *Manchester Airport plc v Dutton* [2000] QB 133.

[78] The defence has been abrogated where the trespasser is a tenant who has held over: Protection from Evic-tion Act 1977, s 2.

[79] See C Branston (1912) 28 LQR 262; C Hawes (2006) 12 Cant LR 253.

[80] *Blades v Higgs* (1865) 11 HL Cas 621; 11 ER 1474; *Anthony v Haney and Harding* (1832) 8 Bing 186; 131 ER 372.

[81] *Patrick v Colerick* (1838) 3 M & W 483; 150 ER 1235.

[82] Eg, chopping off branches of overhanging trees: *Lemmon v Webb* [1895] AC 1.

resemblance to the plea of defence of one's property is obvious and, like that defence, it is a justification. This is because it extends only to objectively warranted steps taken to reduce a nuisance or to bring one to an end. It will be forfeited if, for instance, one uses disproportionate force to eliminate the nuisance,[83] if the more prudent course of action would have been to request the occupier of the land on which the nuisance was situated to terminate it,[84] or if one delayed to such an extent before taking steps to address the nuisance that one could have waited for relief through 'the slow progress of the ordinary forms of justice'.[85]

(H) Statutory authority

Public bodies and officials invariably are empowered or obliged to perform particular acts. If they commit a tort while undertaking conduct they are authorised or under a duty to engage in, they might have a defence to liability.[86] Whether or not they enjoy a defence depends upon the construction of the statute that conferred or created the relevant powers or duty—which is a matter of interpretation.[87] Any defence that is found to exist usually will be held only to insulate the defendant from liability in respect of torts that could not have been avoided by taking reasonable care.[88] Such defences are justificatory in nature. A statute may confer an immunity also. However, courts are slow to discover immunities owing primarily to the fact that they ignore the extent to which the claimant's rights are infringed.

In determining whether Parliament intended to create a defence, the presence of a provision in the Act for compensating those injured by the activity might be material. It is important to look also at the nature of the power or duty. Powers to execute some particular work, or to carry on some particular undertaking (such as building a reservoir or a gasworks), 'are, in the absence of clear provision to the contrary in the Act, limited to the doing of the particular things authorised without infringement of the rights of others, except in so far as any such infringement may be a demonstrably necessary consequence of doing what is authorized to be done'.[89] If, however, a public body is required to execute a variety of works at its discretion (many of which are likely to affect private rights), the body rarely will be permitted to infringe those rights unless respecting the rights concerned would prevent it from doing the very thing it was set up to perform.[90]

---

[83] Such as demolishing a house simply because it was used as a brothel: *Ely v Supervisors of Niagara County* 36 NY 297 (1867).

[84] *Lagan Navigation Co v Lambeg Bleaching, Dyeing and Finishing Co Ltd* [1927] AC 226.

[85] W Blackstone, *Commentaries on the Laws of England*, vol 3 (1769), 6.

[86] *Hammersmith and City Rly Co v Brand* (1869–1870) LR 4 HL 171.

[87] *Inland Revenue Commissioners v Rossminster Ltd* [1980] AC 952 is an example of problems of statutory construction.

[88] *Manchester Corp v Farnworth* [1930] AC 171; *Tate & Lyle Industries Ltd v Greater London Council* [1983] 2 AC 509; *Geddis v Bann Reservoir Proprietors* (1877–1878) LR 3 App Cas 430.

[89] *Marriage v East Norfolk River Catchment Board* [1950] 1 KB 284, at 307; *British Waterways Board v Severn Trent Water Ltd* [2002] Ch 25.

[90] *Marriage v East Norfolk River Catchment Board* [1950] 1 KB 284, at 307–8.

(I) Public necessity

Elements The defence of public necessity exists in order to permit the commission of torts to preserve important public interests from danger.[91] It is available in the following circumstances: (1) there is an actual or apparent danger to a public interest;[92] (2) the danger was imminent;[93] (3) the steps taken to protect the public interest from the danger were reasonable;[94] and (4) the defendant was not at fault for creating the threat.[95]

Use of force The key difference between the defence of public necessity and the defensive force defences is that the latter presuppose that the claimant is a wrongdoer whereas the former contemplates the infliction of harm upon an innocent person. Unsurprisingly, therefore, the defence of public necessity gives greater weight to the interest of the victim of the tort than the defensive force justifications and authorises a lower level of force as a result. For example, whereas it is permissible to use lethal force in self-defence if one is confronted by a risk of death or serious bodily injury, it is doubtful that such harm can be inflicted pursuant to the defence of public necessity. Indeed, it is questionable whether public necessity allows a person to cause personal injury. Virtually all cases in which it has succeeded involved the destruction of property.

Illustrations Classic examples of torts that will not be actionable on the ground that they were committed out of public necessity include entering another's land to erect fortifications on it for the defence of the realm[96] or to fight fires,[97] throwing cargo overboard in order to prevent a ship from sinking,[98] and destroying clothing infected with a virulent disease.[99] The defence has been invoked also to justify restraining a crowd of protestors in the interests of public safety[100] and firing a tear gas cylinder into a shop in order to flush out a dangerous psychopath.[101] The defence was of considerable importance in the past in determining when medical treatment could be provided to a mentally disordered person.[102] Such cases are now governed by primary legislation.[103] The detailed provisions of this legislation are beyond the scope of this book.

---

[91] See JA Cohan (2007) 83 ND L Rev 651.

[92] *Cope v Sharpe (No 2)* [1912] 1 KB 496.

[93] The defence does not apply, therefore, for the benefit of homeless persons who squat in unoccupied premises since they face no immediate peril: *Southwark LBC v Williams* [1971] Ch 734.

[94] *Cope v Sharpe (No 2)* [1912] 1 KB 496.

[95] *Rigby v CC of Northamptonshire* [1985] 1 WLR 1242; *Esso Petroleum Ltd v Southport Corp* [1956] AC 218, at 242.

[96] *The Case of the King's Prerogative in Saltpetre* (1606) 12 Co Rep 12; 77 ER 1294 (*obiter*).

[97] *Dewey v White* (1827) Mood & M 56; 173 ER 1079 (firemen justified in throwing down the claimant's chimney because of the risk that it would fall on the highway); cf *Burmah Oil Co (Burma Trading) Ltd v Lord Advocate* [1965] AC 75, at 164–5. Fire brigades now have statutory authority to do such things (Fire Services Act 1947, s 30).

[98] *Mouse's Case* (1608) 12 Co Rep 63; 77 ER 1341.   [99] *Seavey v Preble* 64 Me 120 (1874).

[100] *Austin v MPC* [2008] QB 660 (defence not considered on appeal: [2009] 1 AC 564).

[101] *Rigby v CC of Northamptonshire* [1985] 1 WLR 1242.

[102] See, eg, *R v Bournewood Community and Mental Health NHS Trust* [1999] 1 AC 458.

[103] The most important statutes are the Mental Health Act 1983, the Mental Health (Patients in the Community) Act 1995, and the Mental Capacity Act 2005.

(J) Arrest

The powers of arrest conferred on constables and, to a limited extent, on private citizens, are among the most important of the defences. The Human Rights Act 1998 requires that the power of arrest meet the principles set out in Article 5 ECHR, which guarantees a right to liberty and security.

(1) By a constable with a warrant

A constable is justified in using reasonable force to arrest a person under a warrant.[104] Even if there is a 'defect of jurisdiction' in the magistrate who issued the warrant, the constable is exempt from liability.[105] Thus, a constable is not liable if he obeys even an 'invalid or unlawful warrant'.[106] Obedience to the warrant is always central: thus he is liable if he arrests the wrong person or acts outside his jurisdiction.[107] If he does not have the warrant in his possession, he must produce it on demand as soon as it is practicable to do so.[108]

(2) By a constable without a warrant

The power of arrest without a warrant is governed by the Police and Criminal Evidence Act 1984, section 24, which provides that a constable may arrest without a warrant: (1) anyone who is committing, is about to commit, or has committed an offence; and (2) anyone whom he has reasonable grounds for suspecting is committing, is about to commit, or has committed an offence. Furthermore, a constable can make an arrest under section 24 only if he believes that it is necessary for one or more prescribed reasons. These reasons relate to matters such as ascertaining the name and address of the person in question, preventing the infliction of physical injury (either to the person in question or to some third party), protecting a child, and facilitating the swift investigation of the offence or conduct of the person in question. Section 24 protects from liability constables who make an arrest as a consequence of a reasonable but mistaken belief that the person arrested was an offender.[109]

(3) Arrest by a private citizen

A person other than a constable may arrest anyone in the act of committing (or reasonably suspected to be committing) an indictable offence.[110] Here, private citizens act at their peril; for if, despite appearances, no offence has been committed, they are likely to be liable in false imprisonment.[111] Just as with constables, private citizens may arrest another only where they believe on reasonable grounds that an arrest is necessary according to a list of statutory reasons; but, in addition, it must appear also to the person making the arrest that it is not reasonably practicable for a constable to make that arrest instead.

---

[104] See also Anti-social Behaviour, Crime and Policing Act 2014, s 4 (power of arrest in circumstances of anti-social behaviour).

[105] Constables Protection Act 1750, s 6.

[106] *McGrath v CC of RUC* [2001] 2 AC 73; *Horsfield v Brown* [1932] 1 KB 355, at 369.

[107] As to constables' jurisdiction see the Magistrates' Courts Act 1980, sub-s 125(2).

[108] Access to Justice Act 1999, sub-s 96(4).

[109] Eg, *Alanov v CC of Sussex Police* [2012] EWCA Civ 234.

[110] Police and Criminal Evidence Act 1984, sub-s 24A(1).

[111] *R v Self* [1992] 1 WLR 657 (a store detective arrested a customer whom she saw putting a bar of chocolate in his pocket; the customer was acquitted of theft and the arrest was found to be unlawful).

(4) Breach of the peace

The common law permits both constables and private citizens to arrest without warrant a person committing a breach of the peace or a person who, having committed one, reasonably is believed to be about to renew that breach.[112] Equally, there is a common law power to intervene where an imminent breach of the peace reasonably is apprehended.[113] Exceptionally, a person may be detained without a formal arrest in order to prevent or terminate a breach of the peace.[114]

(5) Reasonable grounds for suspicion

The powers of arrest considered so far make frequent reference to reasonable grounds for suspicion about the actual or imminent commission of an offence. It is important to note two things: that reasonable grounds for suspicion are to be judged as a question of fact in each case and that the basic test is whether, in all the circumstances, the information available to the person making the arrest, at the time of the arrest, was sufficient to give rise to reasonable grounds for suspicion.

(K) Entry, search, and seizure

In addition to the power of constables to seek a search warrant from a magistrate, the Police and Criminal Evidence Act 1984 confers on constables powers far greater than those ill-defined powers enjoyed by the police at common law to enter premises, to search persons and property, and to seize evidence.[115] The exercise of these powers will provide a defence in an appropriate case to actions for trespass whether to land, person, or goods, and to actions for conversion.

(L) Discipline

The two main contexts in which torts may be committed to discipline others concern children and unruly passengers on ships and aircraft.

(1) Children

(a) Force used by those with parental responsibility

Those with parental responsibility for a child[116] have the right to chastise the child provided that only reasonable corrective force is used.[117] By legislative fiat, the infliction of

---

[112] *Timothy v Simpson* (1835) 1 Cr M & R 757; 149 ER 1285; *Bibby v CC of Essex* (2000) 164 JP 297. Police are not entitled to arrest for obstruction of an officer in the execution of his duty unless the disturbance caused, or was likely to cause, a breach of the peace: *Wershof v MPC* (1979) 68 Cr App R 82.

[113] *Foulkes v CC of Merseyside Police* [1998] 2 FLR 798.

[114] *Albert v Lavin* [1982] AC 546.   [115] See also Criminal Justice and Police Act 2001, ss 50–1.

[116] See generally H Keating (2006) 26 LS 394; J Scutt (2009) 28 U Tas L Rev 1.

[117] In *R v H (assault of child: reasonable chastisement)* [2001] 2 FLR 431 it was held that reasonableness will be judged by reference to the nature and context of D's behaviour, the duration of D's behaviour, the physical and mental consequences to the child, the age and personal characteristics of the child, and the reasons given by D for administering the punishment.

'actual bodily harm' is unreasonable.[118] Parents are justified in detaining their children also to punish them provided that such detention is reasonable in all of the circumstances[119] and so long as it does not breach Article 3 ECHR, which prohibits inhuman and degrading treatment.

(b) Force used by schoolteachers and others responsible for children or for their training and education

At one time, schoolteachers were afforded a broad privilege to use reasonable force to correct children under their tutelage.[120] Nowadays, not least because of the passage of the Human Rights Act 1998, the ability of persons other than parents to discipline children by using force against them, by detaining them, or by confiscating their property is limited.[121] Education Act 1996, section 548, for example, prohibits use of corporal punishment in both state and independent schools.[122] Similar rules apply to children in community homes[123] and in local authority foster placements.[124] That said, teachers continue to enjoy a residual privilege, the precise scope of which is unclear.

(2) Passengers on vessels

The captain of a ship may use reasonable force against passengers who commit 'some act calculated in the apprehension of a reasonable [person] to interfere with the safety of the ship or the due prosecution of the voyage',[125] provided that he believes that using force is necessary to prevent the act concerned.[126] A captain is not justified, therefore, in detaining a passenger in his cabin because the passenger thumbed his nose to him and did not apologise.[127] A similar power exists in favour of the captain of an aircraft in flight where a person is jeopardising or likely to jeopardise the safety of the flight or persons on board.[128]

Section 4 Public policy defences

Public policy defences are defences that release the defendant from liability although he committed a tort for no good reason. They exist in order to advance some important goal external to tort law.

---

[118] Under the Children Act 2004, sub-s 58(3), any battery of a child that causes 'actual bodily harm' cannot be justified under the reasonable chastisement principle. See further D Ormerod, *Smith & Hogan: Criminal Law* (12th edn, 2008), 606–8.

[119] *R v Rahman* (1985) 81 Cr App R 349.

[120] Eg, *Fitzgerald v Northcote* (1865) 4 F & F 656; 176 ER 734; *Ryan v Fildes* [1938] 3 All ER 517.

[121] See generally Education and Inspections Act 2006, Pt 7.

[122] The Act's extension to independent schools, not merely in respect of state-funded pupils, was made clear in *R (on the application of Williamson) v Secretary of State for Education and Employment* [2002] 1 FLR 493.

[123] Children's Homes Regulations 1991 (SI 1991/1506), reg 8(2)(a).

[124] Foster Placement (Children) Regulations 1991 (SI 1991/910), Sch 2, para 5.

[125] *Aldworth v Stewart* (1866) 4 F & F 957, at 961; 176 ER 865, at 868.

[126] *Hook v Cunard Steamship Co Ltd* [1953] 1 WLR 682.

[127] *Aldworth v Stewart* (1866) 4 F & F 957; 176 ER 865.   [128] Civil Aviation Act 1982, s 94.

(A) Illegality

Public policy The defence of illegality was encountered earlier in the context of the tort of negligence.[129] In relation to that tort, it operates as an absent element defence as it denies the existence of a duty of care. Illegality is an answer also to the intentional torts, but is not regarded as an absent element defence to such torts because they do not require a duty of care. Rather, it is a public policy defence since it falls for consideration only after one of these torts is shown to have been committed, and is insensitive to the justifiability of the defendant's impugned conduct.

Revill v Newbery Regrettably, the courts have not said clearly when a claim in the intentional torts will fail for illegality. An important decision is *Revill v Newbery*,[130] which was mentioned earlier.[131] Recall that the claimant burglar was shot by the defendant occupier while he tried to break into the latter's shed. The occupier's defence of illegality failed. The Court of Appeal held that, if the illegality defence applied, it would effectively render the claimant an outlaw and that the legislature, in enacting the Occupiers' Liability Act 1984, which mollified the harsh view that the common law took of the rights of trespassers, implicitly discountenanced such a result.

Cross v Kirkby A different approach was taken in *Cross v Kirkby*.[132] The claimant was a hunting protester. He attacked the defendant, a farmer on whose land he was trespassing for the purpose of disrupting a hunt, with a baseball bat. The defendant wrested the bat from the claimant and used it against him. In resisting an action in battery, the defendant relied on the illegality defence. The Court of Appeal stressed the need to consider whether the claimant's injury was 'closely connected or inextricably bound up' or 'interwoven or linked' with his illegal conduct. In the event, the court held the connection was sufficiently close to enliven the defence. The court attempted to explain the different outcome in *Revill* by asserting that the injury suffered by the claimant in that case was not sufficiently interwoven with his offence. However, it was not made clear why this was so.

Lane v Holloway A third test was developed in *Lane v Holloway*.[133] The claimant was an elderly man who provoked the defendant, who was younger and much stronger, by insulting his wife and by striking him on the shoulder (a minor criminal assault). The defendant retaliated with a powerful punch that caused the claimant serious injury. The claimant brought proceedings in battery for this injury. The defence of illegality failed. The Court of Appeal thought that it was significant that the force of the defendant's punch was disproportionate to the gravity of the claimant's offending.

Summary Although no definitive test regarding the defence of illegality emerges from these decisions, they establish two general principles. First, the mere fact that the

---

[129] See ch 8.   [130] [1996] QB 567.   [131] See section 3(D).
[132] [2000] All ER (D) 212.   [133] [1968] 1 QB 379.

claimant was acting unlawfully at the time of the defendant's tort will not prevent liability from arising. For example, the defence of illegality will not succeed simply because the claimant was in possession of illegal drugs at the time at which he was beaten by the defendant. Some connection between the illegal act and the damage is essential. Second, trivial offending will not enliven the defence. Only offences entailing moral turpitude[134] will suffice, although exactly how serious the offending must be before the defence will be enlivened is unclear.

Criminal Justice Act The Criminal Justice Act 2003, section 329[135] applies where the claimant sues in trespass to the person and he was convicted of an imprisonable offence in respect of conduct committed at the time of the tort. Where it applies, the defendant will enjoy a defence when the following conditions are satisfied: (1) his act was not grossly disproportionate; (2) he believed that the claimant was about to commit an offence; and (3) that it was necessary to act to protect himself or his property, to protect the person or property of a third party, or to apprehend the claimant. This section probably adds little to the protection given to defendants by virtue of the defensive force defences and that of illegality.

(B) Prior private prosecution

Suppose that the claimant brings a private prosecution against the defendant for assault and battery. Irrespective of the outcome of the prosecution, the fact that the prosecution was brought provides the defendant with a defence to any civil liability that he may otherwise have incurred in respect of the act on which the prosecution was based.[136] The apparent rationale for this defence[137] is that it would be wasteful and unjust to permit the claimant to pursue the defendant in the civil sphere in light of the prior prosecution.

(C) Judicial acts

Judicial officers generally enjoy immunity in tort.[138] For example, a judge is not liable in trespass to the person in respect of acts taken against a convicted criminal in the execution of his orders. However, where a judicial order results in an arrest or detention in contravention of the principles embodied in Article 5 ECHR, an action for damages may lie under the Human Rights Act 1998, section 9.

---

[134] Sufficiently immoral but lawful acts might also be sufficient.

[135] Considered in *Adorian v MPC* [2009] 1 WLR 1859; J Spencer (2010) 69 CLJ 19.

[136] Offences against the Person Act 1861, ss 44–5.

[137] The Law Commission recommended that this defence be abolished: Law Commission, *Legislating the Criminal Code: Offences against the Person and General Principles*, Report 218 (1993), at 138 [12.2]. In *Wong v Parkside Health NHS Trust* [2003] 3 All ER 932, at 939 [16], Hale LJ described it as 'anomalous'.

[138] The law in this connection is complex: see A Olowofoyeku, *Suing Judges: A Study of Judicial Immunity* (1993), ch 2. See also J Murphy (2013) 33 LS 455.

Section 5 Non-defences

In this section, a number of non-defences to liability arising in the intentional torts to the person and to property will be mentioned briefly.

(A) Provocation

The fact that the defendant was provoked into attacking the claimant is not a defence to liability in battery. However, it is a factor that can reduce awards of exemplary damages[139] and, possibly, compensatory damages.[140]

(B) Private necessity

The defence of public necessity[141] was discussed earlier.[142] Recall that it applies where the defendant commits a tort in order to protect a greater public interest from an imminent risk of harm. Private necessity involves the defendant acting tortiously in order to safeguard an interest of his own from a sudden emergency. Unlike public necessity, private necessity is probably not a defence.[143] In the US case of *Vincent v Lake Erie Transportation Co*,[144] the facts were as follows:[145]

> The SS *Reynolds*, which was owned by the defendant, was moored at the claimant's dock. A fierce storm spontaneously developed. The captain of the *Reynolds* signalled for a tugboat to assist her to leave the dock. But no tugboat operator was prepared to help, owing to the ferocity of the storm. Accordingly, the captain of the *Reynolds* decided that the ship should remain docked. (Had the captain cast off, the *Reynolds* would probably have been destroyed.) The storm repeatedly threw the *Reynolds* against the dock. The claimant sued the defendant in negligence and trespass in respect of the damage caused to the dock.

The court rejected the claim in negligence on the ground that the captain acted reasonably but found for the claimant in the action in trespass. Although private necessity is not a defence to the intentional torts, it seems that it is a tort to resist a person who acts out of private necessity.[146] It is for this reason that it is sometimes said that private necessity is an 'incomplete privilege'.

---

[139] *Fontin v Katapodis* (1962) 108 CLR 177, approved in *Lane v Holloway* [1968] 1 QB 379.
[140] Consider *Murphy v Culhane* [1977] QB 94, at 98; *Cassell & Co Ltd v Broome* [1972] AC 1027, at 1071; *Wilson v Bobbie* (2006) 394 AR 118. See further A Nadel (1985) 35 ALR 4th 947.
[141] An exhaustive review of the case law is provided in JA Cohan (2007) 83 ND L Rev 651.
[142] See section 3(I).
[143] Cf *Cope v Sharpe (No 2)* [1912] 1 KB 496 (D, who burned heather on C's land in order to prevent a fire on C's land from spreading to land on which D's master had shooting rights exempted from liability).
[144] 124 NW 221 (1910).
[145] See F Bohlen (1926) 39 Harv L Rev 307; RE Keeton (1959) 72 Harv L Rev 401, at 410–18; GC Christie (1999) 48 Duke LJ 975; D Klimchuk (2001) 7 Legal Theory 59.
[146] *Ploof v Putnam* 71 A 188 (1908).

(C) Duress

Gilbert v Stone[147] held that duress is not an answer to liability in tort. In this case, 12 bandits threatened to kill the defendant if he did not help them to steal the claimant's horse. The defendant yielded to this threat and was sued by the claimant in trespass. The fact that the defendant's acts were coerced was no defence.[148] The outcome would have been different if the bandits had carried or pushed the defendant on to the claimant's land.[149] This would be a case of physical compulsion rather than duress.

(D) Mistake

In previous chapters it was observed that mistake[150] is not a defence to liability arising in the intentional torts.[151] If the defendant drove his tractor on to the claimant's land, the fact that he believed mistakenly that the land was his own, or that the occupier consented to his entry, will not negate the tort of trespass to land. This is so even if the mistake was made reasonably. Analogous comments can be made about conversion. An auctioneer who sells a stolen chattel is liable in this tort even if he believed that the vendor owned the goods. The reasonableness of his mistake is irrelevant. Likewise, it is a battery to touch another person who does not consent. It is (probably) no answer to liability that the defendant believed that the claimant was consenting.[152] Although mistake per se is not a defence to the intentional torts, it might be relevant to know in the context of some defences whether the defendant was mistaken as to some fact. For example, as discussed earlier, a defendant who uses defensive force against a person whom he mistakenly believes is an aggressor may be entitled to the defence of self-defence if his mistake is reasonable.[153]

(E) Insanity

Unlike the position in the criminal law, insanity[154] is not a defence to liability in tort.[155] Mentally disordered defendants have been held liable in battery,[156] false imprisonment,[157] and trespass to land[158] and trespass to goods.[159] A question arises as to whether it is fair to hold the insane liable for their torts. To the extent that liability in tort is a sanction, it seems unjust to impose liability on mentally disordered persons. However, the counterargument is that tort law is concerned primarily with the maintenance of

---

[147] (1641) Aleyn 35; 82 ER 902.

[148] The courts have had little to say about *Gilbert*. Holmes J was agnostic on whether it was correctly decided: eg, *The Eliza Lines* 199 US 119, at 130–1 (1905).

[149] See section 2(B). [150] See CB Whittier (1902) 15 Harv L Rev 44; FA Trindade (1982) 2 OJLS 211.

[151] See chs 10–12.

[152] McBride asserts that the position would be otherwise if C induced D to believe that he was consenting: N McBride (2008) 67 CLJ 461, at 462–3.

[153] See section 3(A). [154] See J Goudkamp (2011) OJLS 727.

[155] *Weaver v Ward* (1616) Hob 134; 80 ER 284. [156] *Morriss v Marsden* [1952] 1 All ER 925.

[157] *Krom v Schoonmaker* 3 Barb 647 (1848). [158] *Re Meyer's Guardianship* 261 NW 211 (1935).

[159] *Morse v Crawford* 17 Vt 499 (1845).

proper standards of interaction between persons, focussed upon their external acts (as we saw in chapter 1), and with redressing those who have been injured by substandard and unjustified conduct.

(F) Infancy

The fact that the defendant was an infant at the time of committing a tort is not a defence.[160] As Lord Keynon CJ said in *Jennings v Rundall*, 'if an infant commit an assault, or utter slander, God forbid that he should not be answerable for it in a Court of Justice'.[161] This rule is controversial, but might be justified according to the reasoning used to justify the fact that insanity is no defence in tort law.

(G) Contributory negligence

This defence does not apply to trespass to the person.[162] Thus, if A goads B into attacking him, A's damages will not be apportioned for his contributory negligence. Nor is contributory negligence a defence in the context of conversion or trespass to goods.[163]

Conclusions

In this chapter, we have seen that tort law provides a wide range of defences to intentional torts against the person or property. 'Absent element defences' are denials of one or more of the elements of the tort in which the claimant sues. For example, the plea of consent is an absent element defence to the intentional torts because the absence of consent is an element of these wrongs. The doctrines of inevitable accident, involuntariness, and physical compulsion are absent element defences also. 'Justification defences' release the defendant from liability on the ground that he acted reasonably, or without wrongdoing, in committing a tort. For example, self-defence releases from liability persons who use necessary and proportionate force in order to defend themselves against an aggressor or putative aggressor. An array of other justification defences exist which are variations on the theme of self-defence, including defence of another person and defence of one's property. Public policy defences exempt the defendant from responsibility in tort even though he committed a tort for no good reason. They exist in recognition of the fact that unjustified tortfeasors sometimes must be released from liability in order to further social goals external to the law of torts. One of the most significant is that of illegality, which prevents claimants injured by a tort from recovering compensation where they were committing a serious criminal offence at the time of the defendant's tort and their criminal conduct contributed to their damage.

---

[160] *Ellis v D'Angelo* 253 P 2d 675 (1953) (four-year-old capable of being held liable for battery). Consider also *Hackshaw v Shaw* (1984) 155 CLR 614, at 664.

[161] (1799) 8 TR 335, at 337; 101 ER 1419, at 1421–2.

[162] *Co-operative Group (CWS) Ltd v Pritchard* [2012] QB 320. See further J Goudkamp (2011) 127 LQR 518.

[163] Torts (Interference with Goods) Act 1977, sub-s 11(1).

Problem question

Bill, an elderly man, was crossing the road. Chris saw a car approaching Bill very quickly and believed that Bill was about to be run over. Chris ran over to Bill and pulled him hard towards the pavement. Bill stumbled over and was hurt. The evidence was that the car that Chris was concerned about was a high-performance vehicle with excellent braking ability. Its driver would have had no difficulty in avoiding Bill. Chris called a taxi, using Bill's phone, in order to get Bill to a doctor. Chris accompanied Bill to the hospital but forgot to give Bill's phone back to him. Bill needed to have several stitches just above his eye. While Dr Xog was inserting the stitches, he suffered a sudden bout of sneezing. Dr Xog's hand jerked with his first sneeze and he injured Bill further with a needle. Nurse Zelda grabbed the needle from Dr Xog who, irrationally fearing that Zelda presented a threat to Bill, pushed her away against the wall. Zelda suffered a broken collar bone as a result.

Advise the parties by briefly stating which intentional torts might have been committed and the potential defences to them.

 Visit **http://www.oup.com/uk/street15e/** for answer guidance.

Further reading

BRUDNER, 'A Theory of Necessity' (1987) 7 *Oxford Journal of Legal Studies* 339

DESCHEEMAEKER, 'Tort Law Defences: A Defence of Conventionalism' (2014) 77 *Modern Law Review* 493

GILLES, 'Inevitable Accident in Classical English Tort Law' (1994) 43 *Emory Law Journal* 575

GOUDKAMP, 'Insanity as a Tort Defence' (2011) 31 *Oxford Journal of Legal Studies* 727

GOUDKAMP, *Tort Law Defences* (2013)

HAWES, 'Reception of Chattels: The Use of Force against the Person' (2006) 12 *Canterbury Law Review* 253

KEATING, 'Protecting or Punishing Children: Physical Punishment, Human Rights and English Law Reform' (2006) 26 *Legal Studies* 394

LAW COMMISSION, *Illegality Defence*, Report 320 (2010)

POSNER, 'Killing or Wounding to Protect a Property Interest' (1971) 14 *Journal of Law and Economics* 201

SUGARMAN, 'The "Necessity" Defense and the Failure of Tort Theory: The Case against Strict Liability for Damages Caused while Exercising Self-Help in an Emergency' (2005) *Issues in Legal Scholarship* (online journal)

PART IV
Misrepresentation-based and 'economic' torts

14

False representations

KEY ISSUES

(1) Torts based on false statements protective of financial interests
This chapter considers torts protective of the claimant's financial interests from improper actions of others. The unifying feature is a false representation. In most cases, 'the defendant seeks to make a gain which properly belongs to the claimant'.[1]

(2) Deceit
The tort of deceit occurs where the defendant makes a representation knowing of its falsity, or without belief in its truth, or recklessly, careless whether it be true or false, with the intention that the claimant should act in reliance upon it, which causes damage to the claimant in consequence of her reliance upon it.

(3) Passing off
The tort of passing off occurs where the defendant makes, in the course of trade, a false representation that is calculated to deceive the claimant's customers or clients in a way which is really likely to be damaging to the claimant's goodwill. There is no need to prove an intention to harm. The focus is upon the likely effect, objectively considered, of the misrepresentation upon the claimant's goodwill.

(4) Malicious falsehood
The tort of malicious falsehood occurs where the defendant makes a false representation disparaging of the claimant's interest in property, the quality of her goods, or her fitness to offer services, which is maliciously published and really likely to cause, and which does actually cause, damage to the claimant's goodwill.

Section 1 Background to misrepresentation-based and 'economic' torts

Context The law of torts affords generous protection from deliberate interferences with personal integrity, goods, and land by means of the torts discussed in Part III of this book. By contrast, the protection afforded to interests one has in one's livelihood, business, and trade is far less comprehensive. To be sure, these interests frequently are protected *indirectly*—that is, where financial losses are *consequential* in nature, such as

---

[1] H Carty, *An Analysis of the Economic Torts* (2nd edn, 2010), 3.

when a deliberate interference with the claimant's body results in injury and deprivation of employment income. But the question is whether there should be recovery for financial losses where these are the primary losses that the claimant suffers. In chapter 4, we saw that rules for recovery of *negligently* inflicted financial losses are highly circumscribed. There must be a prior duty of care relating to the financial interests in question. Duties of care are confined mainly to professional and other formal dealings between persons. Moreover, recovery in negligence is limited by the rule of remoteness, which means that types of loss must have been foreseeable in the circumstances of the case.

Specific actions At present, English law offers no *general* protection against financial losses where these losses are brought about intentionally by the defendant. One reason for this is that the House of Lords' decision in *Allen v Flood*[2] indicated a preference for an abstentionist approach to the intentional infliction of such harm as between business or industrial rivals. Liability, their Lordships suggested, should be imposed only where financial losses were inflicted in ways that involve recognised unlawful means. This reflected an underlying concern about adjudication over what essentially are seen to be matters of business *competition*. In *Ware and de Freville Ltd v Motor Trade Association*, Atkin LJ explained the abstentionist position:

> [T]he right of the individual to carry on his trade or profession or execute his own activities, whatever they may be, without interruption, so long as he refrains from tort or crime, affords an unsatisfactory basis for determining what is actionable, in as much as the right is conditioned by a precisely similar right in the rest of his fellow men. Such co-existing rights do in a world of competition necessarily impinge upon one another . . . . The true question is, was the power of the [claimant] to carry on his trade etc, interrupted by an act which the law deems wrongful.[3]

English law favours 'free competition', which is seen as inconsistent with any assumption that the interest in pursuing business activities or a trade is entitled to absolute legal protection. However, this is *not* to say that there are no rules at all against intentional (and certain other) interferences with financial (or 'economic') interests. The causes of action to be considered in this chapter and chapter 15 arise from *specific circumstances* in which the law grants a remedy because the practices to which they attach are unacceptable[4]—whether occurring in the course of competition or not. In this chapter, we consider cases based upon forms of *misrepresentation* which permit recovery of financial losses. In chapter 15, we consider the 'general economic torts', among which interference with another's business generally is tortious only so long as, at some point in the chain of causative events, an *independently unlawful* act is committed. The one exception to this proposition is the tort of simple conspiracy, whose touchstones are malicious purpose and combination.

---

[2] [1898] AC 1, at 14.   [3] [1921] 3 KB 40, at 79.

[4] Eg, *Fenty v Arcadia Group Brands Ltd (t/a Topshop)* [2015] 1 WLR 3291 (no action in passing off where fair competition involved).

Caveats Having set out the parameters of the forthcoming discussion in this way, some important caveats are in order. The first is that many writers on these matters consider the 'lumping together' of the torts considered in this and chapter 15 as wrong-headed, given that there are few general characteristics that unite them.[5] The features that they share are some kind of intention to harm, causation of loss, and the tendency to be pleaded in the area of business and trade activity. The second is that arguments appear in the literature which demonstrate either the potential for, or the actuality of, the application of one or more of the relevant torts to cases in which the primary losses suffered are not financial, but something else—such as psychiatric illness or distress, or interference with autonomy rights.[6] Indeed, the present writer himself has argued that there appear to be few reasons for restricting recovery of intention-based torts to cases of financial losses.[7] In this respect, what we are waiting for is a clearer indication from higher appellate courts that the torts examined in these two chapters are of more general operation. When that point comes, a serious reorganisation of the subject matter might be called for.

Section 2 Deceit

History There has been a writ of deceit since 1201. Whether early authorities were founded on contract, equity, or tort is not entirely clear. However, for more than two centuries, deliberately false representations on which the claimant is induced to, and does, rely to her detriment have been actionable under the tort of deceit.[8] The seminal decision was *Pasley v Freeman*,[9] in which the defendant falsely misrepresented to the claimant that X was a person to whom the claimant might safely sell goods on credit. The claimant suffered loss by relying on this representation and was held to have an action on the case for deceit.

Elements Subsequently, in *Derry v Peek*, the tort of deceit was defined in terms of several key elements: a false representation made '(1) knowingly, or (2) without belief in its truth, or (3) recklessly, careless whether it be true or false',[10] with the intention that the claimant should act in reliance upon the representation, which causes damage to her in consequence of her reliance upon it. These matters need to be proved to the ordinary civil standard, that is, on the balance of probabilities.[11]

(A) False representations

General The core of deceit concerns representations which are misleading as to facts or states of affairs. Usually the representation will consist of written or spoken words.

---

[5] Eg, NJ McBride and R Bagshaw, *Tort Law* (4th edn, 2012), 656.
[6] See more specific references in the footnotes of chapters 15 and 16.
[7] C Witting (1999) 25 Mon ULR 295.   [8] *Pasley v Freeman* (1789) 3 Term Rep 51.
[9] (1789) 3 Term Rep 51.   [10] (1889) 14 App Cas 337, at 374.
[11] *Re B (Children)* [2009] 1 AC 11, at [10]–[15].

But any conduct calculated to mislead will suffice[12]—for example, turning back the mileage indicator on a car's odometer prior to negotiating its sale. The court will determine 'what a reasonable person would have inferred was being implicitly represented by the representor's words and conduct' when viewed in context.[13] The representation need not emanate from the defendant: '[w]here the defendant has manifestly approved and adopted a representation made by some third person' she may herself be held to commit the tort.[14]

Incomplete representations of fact   Active concealment of the truth, whereby the claimant is prevented from getting information which she otherwise would have got, is a sufficient misrepresentation although no positive statement is made.[15] Equally, although mere non-disclosure is not enough for this tort,[16] a statement which is misleading because it is incomplete might be actionable. Thus, Lord Cairns held in *Peek v Gurney*:[17] 'there must . . . be some active misstatement of fact, or, at all events, such a partial and fragmentary statement of fact, as that the withholding of that which is not stated makes that which is stated absolutely false'. More recently, the Court of Appeal in *Mellor v Partridge* held that liability arises for withholding facts that are or might be material to the matter in question.[18]

Ambiguity in representation   Where a statement is simultaneously capable of bearing both a true and a false interpretation, and the defendant knows of the false one, there is a false representation for present purposes.[19]

Representations becoming false   Where a defendant's statement *was accurate* when made but, owing to a change of circumstances of which the defendant has become aware, it ceases to be accurate, there is an actionable misrepresentation if the defendant, by remaining silent, induces the claimant to act to her detriment on the basis of the original statement. Consider *Incledon v Watson*:[20]

> In an advertisement for the sale of his school, D stated the number of scholars at that time. That statement was not proved to be inaccurate. During the course of negotiations, the number decreased. C, who bought on the faith of the representation, and who was not informed of the reduction in numbers, was held to have an action in deceit for damages.

---

[12] Cf *R v Barnard* (1837) 7 C & P 784.   [13] *Mellor v Partridge* [2013] EWCA Civ 477, at [177].
[14] *Bradford Third Equitable Benefit Building Society v Borders* [1941] 2 All ER 205, at 211; *Webster v Liddington* [2014] EWCA Civ 560, at [46]–[47].   [15] Cf *Schneider v Heath* (1813) 3 Camp 506.
[16] There is generally no duty of candour. Even in the exceptional case of insurance contracts, avoidance of the contract (rather than an action in deceit) is the appropriate remedy: *Banque Keyser Ullmann SA v Skandia (UK) Insurance Co Ltd* [1990] 1 QB 665; *HIH Casualty and General Insurance Ltd v Chase Manhattan Bank* [2001] 2 Lloyd's Rep 483.
[17] (1873) LR 6 HL 377, at 403. See also *Banque Financière de la Cité v Westgate Insurance Co Ltd* [1990] 2 All ER 947.   [18] [2013] EWCA Civ 477, at [22].
[19] *Smith v Chadwick* (1884) 9 App Cas 187, at 201. If the court construes documents as false, but is not satisfied that D intended to give them that false meaning, she is not liable in deceit: *Gross v Lewis Hillman Ltd* [1970] Ch 445.   [20] (1862) 2 F & F 841. See also *Jones v Dumbrell* [1981] VR 199.

The case illustrates that what counts is that the statement must be false when the claimant acts upon it.[21] In similar terms to the rule just stated, where a statement was made by the defendant who *believed* it then to be accurate, but who later learns of its falsity but does not disclose this to the claimant who subsequently relies on it, there is an actionable misrepresentation.[22]

(B) Knowledge of falsity

Lack of honest belief In order for the defendant to be liable, she must have made the statement knowingly, or without belief in its truth, or recklessly, careless whether it be true or false. In short, the claimant must prove that the defendant did not honestly believe the statement to be true.[23] Importantly, there is no tort of deceit merely because the claimant does not have reasonable grounds for believing the truth of her statement.[24] The facts of *Derry v Peek* illustrate how onerous the burden of proof can be:

> A company was empowered by private Act to run trams by animal power, or, if the consent of the Board of Trade was obtained, by steam power. The directors, believing that the Board of Trade would give this consent as a matter of course (since the Board of Trade raised no objection when the plans were laid before it) issued a prospectus saying that the company had the ability to run trams by steam power. Relying on this prospectus, the respondent bought shares in the company. The Board of Trade eventually refused its consent, and later the company was wound up.

The House of Lords held that an action in deceit against the directors failed because the respondent established no want of honest belief on the part of any director,[25] and it has since been stated that the absence of any injurious intent—though motive is technically immaterial in deceit—nonetheless might constitute good evidence of an honest belief in the truth of a statement.[26]

Procedure In light of the seriousness of an allegation of fraud, courts have insisted upon a special rule for legal counsel: namely, that before counsel puts her signature to an allegation of fraud, she must receive instructions to do so and have evidence before her to make good the allegation.[27] Moreover, where the defendant to a claim based on fraud is called as a witness at trial, the specific allegation of fraud must be put to her. Failure to do so might lead to a finding of fraud being overturned on appeal.[28]

---

[21] Cf *Briess v Woolley* [1954] AC 333.

[22] *Brownlie v Campbell* (1880) 5 App Cas 925, at 950 (*obiter*); *Templeton Insurance Ltd v Motorcare Warranties Ltd* [2010] EWHC 3113 (Comm), at [168].

[23] Although C need not shoulder a criminal standard of proof, her burden of proving fraud is stricter than that of the ordinary civil standard: see *Hornal v Neuberger Products Ltd* [1957] 1 QB 247.

[24] See, eg, *Niru Battery Manufacturing Co v Milestone Trading Ltd* [2004] QB 985.

[25] But see now the Financial Services and Markets Act 2000, s 90A and Sch 10 (statutory liability for false prospectuses); HM Treasury, *Extension of Statutory Regime for Issuer Liability* (2008).

[26] *Barings plc v Coopers & Lybrand (No 5)* [2002] PNLR 823.

[27] *Medcalf v Mardell* [2002] 3 All ER 721.   [28] *Haringey LBC v Hines* [2011] HLR 6, at [39].

(C) Intention to deceive

Meaning of intention In deceit cases, the claimant must prove that the statement was 'made with the intention that it should be acted upon by the claimant, or by a class of persons which will include the claimant'.[29] Lord Cairns in *Peek v Gurney*[30] might be taken as saying that the claimant must prove that the defendant 'intended'—in the sense that she desired or had the purpose—that the claimant should act on the statement. However, intention is interpreted best in the way in which it often is used in torts: the misrepresentation should be calculated, or its necessary consequence should be, to induce the claimant.[31] Thus, a deceit action may be based on an advertisement in a newspaper if the claimant shows that she was one of a class of persons at whom the advertisement was directed.[32]

Imputed intention A misrepresentation need not be communicated to the claimant by the defendant, provided that the defendant intended that it should be communicated to her and that she should rely on it.[33] Furthermore, *Pilmore v Hood*[34] seems to support the imputation of such intention:

> A, who was negotiating the sale of a public house to B, made false representations to B concerning its revenue. The transaction fell through. To A's knowledge, B passed on to C these false statements. A then sold to C without correcting these statements and was held liable in deceit.

Motive irrelevant The claimant must have been influenced in the manner intended. Therefore, if company promoters issue a prospectus to the claimant, who buys shares (not by subscribing to the issue, but by purchasing on the after-market), and the prospectus was not calculated to influence market dealings, no action will lie.[35] The motive of the defendant is irrelevant. That being so, it was no excuse that the defendant who made a false statement about some company shares genuinely believed that investment in that company would be advantageous to the claimant,[36] or that the defendant did not intend the claimant to suffer any loss in consequence of the misrepresentation.[37] On the other hand, promoters will be liable where they issue false information about a company in order to inflate the market value of shares in that company for their personal gain.[38]

---

[29] *Bradford Third Equitable Benefit Building Society v Borders* [1941] 2 All ER 205, at 211.

[30] (1873) LR 6 HL 377.

[31] *Polhill v Walter* (1832) 3 B & Ad 114; *Richardson v Silvester* (1873) LR 9 QB 34. But note the rejection by the Supreme Court of this kind of formulation in another intentional tort context: *O v Rhodes* [2016] AC 219 (considered in chapter 10).

[32] *Richardson v Silvester* (1873) LR 9 QB 34 (C misled by a false advertisement in the press that a farm was for sale).   [33] *JD Wetherspoon plc v Van De Berg & Co Ltd* [2007] PNLR 28, at [384].

[34] (1838) 5 Bing NC 97. See also *Langridge v Levy* (1837) 2 M & W 519.

[35] *Peek v Gurney* (1873) LR 6 HL 377 had similar facts. Cf *Andrews v Mockford* [1896] 1 QB 372. The Stock Exchange now makes a public advertisement of an issue a condition precedent to the grant of a market quotation, and intention to induce marketing dealings presumably will now be imputed.

[36] *Smith v Chadwick* (1884) 9 App Cas 187, at 201.

[37] *Brown, Jenkinson & Co Ltd v Percy Dalton (London) Ltd* [1957] 2 QB 621.

[38] *Possfund Custodian Trustee Ltd v Diamond* [1996] 2 All ER 774.

(D) Reliance of the claimant

Influenced the claimant The claimant must prove that the defendant's misrepresentation both influenced her[39] and caused her to act to her own prejudice as she did.[40] The action lies even if the misrepresentation was only one of several factors impinging on the claimant's mind.[41] And, if the court is satisfied that the false statement was 'actively present to her mind' when the claimant acted, it matters not what the claimant would have done if told the truth. Thus, it is not germane to enquire whether the claimant, knowing the facts, would have entered into the same transaction.[42]

Materiality Sometimes, courts say that the misrepresentation must be material.[43] However, this does not appear to be a separate requirement of the tort.[44] It appears more accurate to say that, where the statement is 'of such a nature as would be likely to induce a person to enter into a contract, it is a fair inference of fact that [s]he was induced to do so by the statement'.[45] In other words, the material nature of the representation creates a presumption of reliance. This presumption can be rebutted by evidence to the contrary.

Claimant's state of mind Although the claimant's knowledge of falsity would negate reliance, mere suspicion of falsity is not sufficient.[46] Moreover, the fact that the claimant acted foolishly is of no moment, because, first, the claimant's act of reliance need not be of the precise kind intended by the defendant[47] and, second, there is no scope for invoking the defence of contributory negligence in the tort of deceit[48] (although the latter rule has been argued to be inconsistent with the presence of the normal tort law obligation of the claimant to mitigate her loss).[49]

Opinions Sometimes, it is doubted whether a misrepresentation of an opinion is actionable, usually on the basis that an opinion is not falsifiable in the way that a statement of fact is. Thus, there can be legitimate dispute over opinions in a way which is not possible regarding 'hard facts'. However, courts have long recognised that there might

---

[39] *Downs v Chappell* [1996] 3 All ER 344. Murphy thus characterises the wrongfulness of deceit in its interference with decision-making autonomy: J Murphy (2016) 75 CLJ 301, 321. This is one of the reasons for which he believes that it is a 'gross mischaracterisation' to call deceit nothing more than an 'economic tort': ibid 322.

[40] *Smith v Chadwick* (1884) 9 App Cas 187; *MacLeay v Tait* [1906] AC 24; *Dadourian Group Int'l Inc v Simms* [2009] 1 Lloyd's Rep PN 601, at [99]–[101]. There must be some conduct of C's in reliance on the representation. Harmful effects produced directly on C (eg, if the false statement causes her to be ill) are not the subject of a claim for this tort, even though C does not recover in the same action for loss suffered through acts performed in reliance: *Wilkinson v Downton* [1897] 2 QB 57.

[41] *Cassa di Risparmio della Republicca di San Marino SpA v Barclays Bank Ltd* [2011] EWHC 484 (Comm), at [468].   [42] *Dadourian Group International Inc v Simms* [2009] 1 Lloyd's Rep PN 601, at [107].

[43] *Downs v Chappell* [1996] 3 All ER 344, at 351.

[44] See, eg, statement of elements in *Eco3 Capital Ltd v Ludsin Overseas Ltd* [2013] EWCA Civ 413, at [77].

[45] *Smith v Chadwick* (1884) 9 App Cas 187, at 196.   [46] *Conlon v Simms* [2008] 1 WLR 484, at 514.

[47] *Goose v Wilson Sandford & Co (No 2)* [2001] Lloyd's Rep PN 189.

[48] *Standard Chartered Bank v Pakistan National Shipping Corpn (Nos 2 and 4)* [2003] 1 AC 959. On the other hand, a C who is aware of the falsity and, perhaps also one who is misled by any patent defect, cannot recover damages. Cf *Horsfall v Thomas* (1862) 1 H & C 90.   [49] J Murphy (2016) 75 CLJ 301, 324ff.

be liability in cases of opinion where the defendant has misrepresented what her true opinion is—which itself is a matter of fact.[50] Obviously, this presents a rather tenuous basis for determining susceptibility to suit. For this reason, courts rarely deny liability in deceit simply because the representation is an opinion. A number of factors are taken into account. In the case of a vendor who describes her house as 'highly desirable and commodious', no liability arises both because purchasers understand the maxim 'buyer beware' and because they can make up their own minds. Again, a statement by a ratings agency that a complex financial instrument is 'AAA' is said to be an opinion, and not a representation as to default probabilities that could be relied upon by the instrument's purchaser.[51] If both parties have equal access to information about the subject matter, no action is likely to lie. But when the opinion, for example about the risk attached to a financial instrument, purports to impart information to another who is not on an equal footing,[52] or where it is provided without reasonable grounds such as to evidence dishonesty,[53] an action is possible.

Future intention Intentions as to the future give rise to similar issues and a similar outcome as to actionability. If a defendant promises to do something and fails to carry out her promise, the claimant ordinarily will look to the law of contract for her remedy. Courts are right to be concerned to ensure that claimants in the tort of deceit do not seek to side-step ordinary contract rules. If, however, the defendant lacks either the will or the ability to carry out the promise at the time of her statement, there is a misrepresentation capable of amounting to deceit. Again, the courts have recognised that 'that which is in form a promise may be in another aspect a representation'.[54] Thus, it was actionable to state in a company's invitation to the public to subscribe to an issue of debentures that the loan was being arranged in order to improve buildings, when the real purpose was to discharge existing liabilities.[55]

Law The same general principles applicable to statements of opinion govern statements of law.[56] If the representations refer to legal principles, as distinct from the facts on which those principles operate,[57] and the parties are on an equal footing, those representations are expressions of belief only and of the same effect as expressions of opinion between parties on an equal footing. In other cases where the defendant professes legal knowledge beyond that of the claimant (most usually when she has practised law), the potential arises for an action in deceit. However, liability is likely

---

[50] Eg, *Bisset v Wilkinson* [1927] AC 177, at 182.

[51] *Cassa di Risparmio della Republicca di San Marino SpA v Barclays Bank Ltd* [2011] EWHC 484 (Comm), at [265]–[266].

[52] *Cassa di Risparmio della Republicca di San Marino SpA v Barclays Bank Ltd* [2011] EWHC 484 (Comm), at [217]. See also *Springwell Navigation Corp v JP Morgan Chase Bank* [2010] 2 CLC 705, at [122] (concerning Misrepresentation Act 1967).

[53] *Cassa di Risparmio della Republicca di San Marino SpA v Barclays Bank Ltd* [2011] EWHC 484 (Comm), at [267].   [54] *Clydesdale Bank Ltd v Paton* [1896] AC 381, at 394.

[55] *Edgington v Fitzmaurice* (1885) 29 Ch D 459.

[56] *West London Commercial Bank Ltd v Kitson* (1884) 13 QBD 360.

[57] These are not water-tight categories: *Kleinwort Benson Ltd v Lincoln City Council* [1999] 2 AC 349.

to arise in clear cases of misrepresentation of the law only, given the often contentious nature of legal rules.

(E) Loss

Heads of damage Being an action on the case, there is no cause of action in deceit unless the claimant proves that she sustained loss or damage.[58] And while, ordinarily, the damages will be for financial loss (including loss of alternative opportunities to invest money),[59] damages for personal injuries[60] and for loss of property[61] are recoverable in principle. Where the claimed loss is that of an alternative opportunity to invest money, the court will be assisted by evidence of a specific contemplated transaction, but evidence of genuinely available alternatives is sufficient.[62]

Consequential losses The claimant is entitled to recover for all the actual damage directly flowing from the fraud, even if not all of it was foreseeable.[63] For example, if she is induced by fraud to buy business property, she can claim not only the difference between the price paid and the market value[64] but also for expenses reasonably incurred in trying to run the business fraudulently sold to her,[65] interest on loans entered into to facilitate the purchase of the property,[66] and the loss of the profit which she might reasonably have earned but for the defendant's deceit.[67]

Aggravated and exemplary damages It is unclear whether exemplary damages can be awarded in deceit;[68] but in the light of the decision in *Kuddus v Chief Constable of Leicestershire*,[69] such damages ought to be available. By contrast, aggravated damages definitely can be obtained in deceit.[70]

---

[58] Damage need not be proved in order to obtain rescission: *Goldrei Foucard & Son v Sinclair and Russian Chamber of Commerce in London* [1918] 1 KB 180, at 192; *Lemprière v Lange* (1879) 12 Ch D 675.

[59] *Parabola Investments Ltd v Browallia Cal Ltd* [2011] QB 477, at [38].

[60] *Langridge v Levy* (1837) 2 M & W 519; *Graham v Saville* [1945] 2 DLR 489.

[61] *Mullett v Mason* (1866) LR 1 CP 559.

[62] See, eg, *Parabola Investments Ltd v Browallia Cal Ltd* [2011] QB 477; *Nationwide Building Society v Dunlop Haywards Ltd* [2010] 1 WLR 258.

[63] *Smith New Court Securities Ltd v Citibank NA* [1997] AC 254. See, eg, *AIC Ltd v ITS Testing Services (UK) Ltd* [2005] EWHC 2122.

[64] *OMV Petrom SA v Glencore International AG* [2016] 2 Lloyd's Rep 432. Cf A Summers and A Kramer (2017) 133 LQR 41.

[65] *Doyle v Olby (Ironmongers) Ltd* [1969] 2 QB 158; *Banque Bruxelles Lambert SA v Eagle Star Insurance Co Ltd* [1997] AC 191.

[66] *Archer v Brown* [1985] QB 401 (loss resulting from C's impecuniosity did not prevent its recovery).

[67] *East v Maurer* [1991] 2 All ER 733; *Clef Aquitaine Sarl v Laporte Materials (Barrow) Ltd* [2001] QB 488; *Parabola Investments Ltd v Browallia Cal Ltd* [2011] QB 477.

[68] *Mafo v Adams* [1970] 1 QB 548; *Archer v Brown* [1985] QB 401; *Metall und Rohstoff AG v ACLI Metals (London) Ltd* [1984] 1 Lloyd's Rep 598. See more generally, Law Commission, *Exemplary, Aggravated and Restitutionary Damages* (Law Com No 247,1997). [69] [2002] 2 AC 122.

[70] *Archer v Brown* [1985] QB 401; *Saunders v Edwards* [1987] 2 All ER 651; *Shaw v Sequence (UK) Ltd* [2004] EWHC 3249.

(F) Agency

Agency rules relevant Agency is generally of little relevance in the law of torts, but deceit provides an exception to this rule. The key question in relation to liability for deceit by agents generally is whether the false representation was made within the scope of the agent's actual or ostensible authority.[71] Liability arises where the representation as to the agent's authority in respect of the transaction was relied upon by the third party claimant; this involves no question of reasonableness of reliance.[72]

Direct liability The principal is *directly* liable for misrepresentations which she expressly or ostensibly authorises, including those made by persons acting for her in relation to a particular transaction—for example, an estate agent or broker. A principal who expressly authorises a statement which she and the agent know to be untrue is liable with the agent as a joint tortfeasor. (She is vicariously liable for statements known to be untrue by the agent, and will further be liable where one agent passes on to another information which she knows to be false in order that the second 'innocent' agent will pass it on to the claimant, who then acts on it to his detriment.[73])

Scope of liability In *Armagas Ltd v Mundogas SA, The Ocean Frost,* Lord Keith explained the scope of a principal's liability for deceit thus:

> [T]he question is whether the circumstances under which a servant has made a fraudulent representation which has caused loss to an innocent party contracting with him are such as to make it just for the employer to bear the loss. Such circumstances exist where the employer by words or conduct has induced the injured party to believe that the servant was acting in the lawful course of the employer's business. They do not exist where such belief, although it is present, has been brought about through misguided reliance on the servant himself, when the servant is not authorised to do what he was purporting to do, when what he is purporting to do is not within the class of acts that an employee in his position is usually authorised to do and when the employer has done nothing to represent that he is authorised to do it.[74]

Alternative approach An alternative approach may admit of liability for false representations made opportunistically by the agent in a context that was closely connected to her position as the principal's agent.[75] In such a case, the court is said to be entitled to adopt a 'broad approach' to the liability of the principal.[76]

---

[71] *Armagas Ltd v Mundogas SA* [1986] AC 717, at 780–1; *Quinn v CC Automotive Group Ltd* [2010] EWCA Civ 1412, at [19].

[72] *Quinn v CC Automotive Group Ltd* [2010] EWCA Civ 1412, at [23].

[73] *London County Freehold and Leasehold Properties Ltd v Berkeley Property and Investment Co Ltd* [1936] 2 All ER 1039 (as explained in *Anglo-Scottish Beet Sugar Corpn Ltd v Spalding UDC* [1937] 2 KB 607).

[74] [1986] AC 717, at 781.

[75] *Quinn v CC Automotive Group Ltd* [2010] EWCA Civ 1412, at [21], following approach in *Lister v Hesley Hall Ltd* [2002] 1 AC 215.   [76] *Quinn v CC Automotive Group Ltd* [2010] EWCA Civ 1412, at [22].

Section 3 Passing off

Elements The action for deceit affords a remedy to persons who are direct targets of fraudulent misrepresentation. By contrast, the tort of passing off involves a three-party structure featuring a misrepresentation by which A passes off her goods as those of a rival, B, with a view to inducing B's customers to believe that the goods were produced or endorsed by B, so that she can take advantage of B's goodwill.[77] Although a broader formulation of the tort has been used (going beyond protection of goodwill),[78] the above formulation has regained prominence[79] and, in accordance with it, this section will examine its essential elements of misrepresentation, goodwill, and damage.[80]

(A) Misrepresentation

The first requirement in any passing off action is that the defendant must have made a material misrepresentation, whether express or implied.[81] This must lead, or be likely to lead, the public to believe that the goods offered by the defendant are those of the claimant.[82] The failure to point to a misrepresentation is fatal because, as Lloyd J stated in *HFC Bank plc v Midland Bank plc*, 'people make assumptions, jump to unjustified conclusions [and] these are cases of non-actionable confusion'.[83]

(1) Kinds of misrepresentation

Misrepresentations can take many forms, and various titles may be applied to the different kinds.[84] They include the following forms:

(a) Marketing a product as that of the claimant

For A to market her product claiming falsely that it is the claimant, B's, product is passing off.[85]

(b) Using the claimant's name

To engage in the same line of business as the claimant and to use a similar name might be passing off, even though the name being used is a genuine family name.[86] So long as

---

[77] The rule has been said to extend to the offer of services: eg, *Fenty v Arcadia Group Brands Ltd (t/a Topshop)* [2015] 1 WLR 3291, at [34].

[78] Eg, *Erven Warnink BV v J Townend & Sons (Hull) Ltd* [1979] AC 731.

[79] Eg, *Starbucks (HK) Ltd v British Sky Broadcasting Group (No 2)* [2015] 1 WLR 2628; *Reckitt & Colman Products Ltd v Borden Inc* [1990] RPC 340, at 341; *Fenty v Arcadia Group Brands Ltd (t/a Topshop)* [2015] 1 WLR 3291, at [33].

[80] Cf P Johnson and J Gibson (2015) 131 LQR 476 (arguing that the extent of the tort might need to be pared back in cases of subject matter overlap with the Unfair Commercial Practices Directive (2005/29/EC)).

[81] *Fenty v Arcadia Group Brands Ltd (t/a Topshop)* [2015] 1 WLR 3291, at [45]; *Boehringer Ingleheim KG v Swingward Ltd* [2004] EWCA Civ 129, at [2]; H Carty, *An Analysis of the Economic Torts* (2nd edn, 2010), 236.

[82] *Fenty v Arcadia Group Brands Ltd (t/a Topshop)* [2015] 1 WLR 3291, at [33].

[83] [2000] FSR 176, at 201.

[84] See, eg, H Carty, *An Analysis of the Economic Torts* (2nd edn, 2010), 237–49.

[85] *Lord Byron v Johnston* (1816) 2 Mer 29; *CG Vokes Ltd v F J Evans and Marble Arch Motor Supplies Ltd* (1931) 49 RPC 140.

[86] *Tussaud v Tussaud* (1890) 44 Ch D 678; *Boswell-Wilkie Circus (Pty) Ltd v Brian Boswell Circus (Pty) Ltd* [1985] FSR 434.

all of the elements of the tort are present, it is no barrier to liability that the defendant's use is bona fide,[87] the issue being whether the claimant had established goodwill in her business before the defendant set up. The scope for competing claims by bona fide users is reduced to some extent by the rule that a company does not acquire and incorporate the individual rights of its promoters to carry on business under their names.[88]

(c) Using the claimant's trade name

Trade names   To use the claimant's trade name—that is, the designation adopted by the claimant to identify goods or services she markets or supplies—can constitute misrepresentation for the purposes of this tort. Examples of this include: describing and selling sauce as 'Yorkshire Relish';[89] and using internet domain names that closely resemble (or incorporate parts of) those used by C.[90]

Fancy names   Courts are more willing to protect the use of 'fancy' names which do not describe the quality of the goods—for example, 'Apollinaris'.[91] It has been suggested, however, that a person originally entitled to protection for a fancy name might lose that right if the name later becomes a mere description of the type of product rather than a word associated with the claimant's goods.[92] Yet no case confirms this,[93] and the attempt failed in *Havana Cigar and Tobacco Factories Ltd v Oddenino*:[94]

> C was the original manufacturer of Corona cigars. D supplied other cigars described as Corona cigars. C successfully sued in passing off, the court rejecting D's argument that the word no longer described a brand of cigar, but only a particular size of cigar.

Descriptions   If the trade name merely describes the goods or their characteristics, ordinarily the claimant cannot prevent others from using it. For example, the terms 'vacuum cleaner',[95] 'cellular textiles',[96] and 'shredded wheat'[97] may be used with impunity. A heavy burden of proof is cast on the claimant who seeks to establish that a name which is merely descriptive of the product has acquired a technical secondary meaning, so exclusively associated with the claimant's own product that its use by others is calculated to deceive purchasers. This burden was discharged nonetheless by the makers of 'Camel Hair Belting' in *Reddaway v Banham*.[98] The task is a little easier when

---

[87]   *Parker-Knoll Ltd v Knoll International Ltd* [1962] RPC 265; *WH Allen & Co v Brown Watson Ltd* [1965] RPC 191.
[88]   *Tussaud v Tussaud* (1890) 44 Ch D 678. Nor has a foreign company a right to set up in England in competitive business with C, a company of the same name: *Sturtevant Engineering Co Ltd v Sturtevant Mill Co of USA Ltd* [1936] 3 All ER 137.   [89]   *Powell v Birmingham Vinegar Brewery Co* [1896] 2 Ch 54.
[90]   *Tesco Stores Ltd v Elogicom Ltd* [2006] EWHC 403; *Global Projects Management Ltd v Citigroup Inc* [2005] EWHC 2663.   [91]   *Apollinaris Co Ltd v Norrish* (1875) 33 LT 242.
[92]   Eg, *Ford v Foster* (1872) 7 Ch App 611 (*obiter*).
[93]   *GH Gledhill & Sons Ltd v British Perforated Toilet Paper Co* (1911) 28 RPC 429.
[94]   [1924] 1 Ch 179. The same outcome was reached in *Antec International Ltd v South Western Chicks (Warren) Ltd* [1998] 18 LS Gaz R 32.
[95]   *British Vacuum Cleaner Co Ltd v New Vacuum Cleaner Co Ltd* [1907] 2 Ch 312.
[96]   *Cellular Clothing Co v Maxton and Murray* [1899] AC 326.
[97]   *Canadian Shredded Wheat Co Ltd v Kellogg Co of Canada Ltd* [1938] 1 All ER 618.   [98]   [1896] AC 199.

the descriptive words connect the product with the place of its manufacture. Thus, the manufacturers of 'Glenfield Starch',[99] 'Stone Ales',[100] and 'Chartreuse liqueurs'[101] all succeeded in passing-off actions.

(d) Using the claimant's trade mark

Historically it was tortious to use the claimant's trade mark—that is, a design, picture, or other arrangement affixed by her to goods which she markets so as to identify them with her.[102] And although the Trade Marks Act 1994 creates separate rights of action in respect of trade mark infringements, sub-section 2(2) of that Act preserves the common law action of passing off in respect of trade marks. That it does so might prove valuable where the claimant fails to prove registration, or where registration does not extend to the goods in question or is invalid. In such cases, the statutory action for infringement of the claimant's trade mark will fail and it will be necessary to have recourse to the common law action. An example is given by *Lumos Skincare Ltd v Sweet Squared Ltd*,[103] in which the claimant had registered a mark in respect of high-end beauty anti-ageing products and the defendants sold cheap nail-care products under a substantially similar mark. The Court of Appeal awarded an injunction because the products were sold in similar markets, in that: products of these kinds frequently were sold by the same companies; and that these particular products could be purchased through some of the same beauty salons.[104]

(e) Imitating the appearance of the claimant's goods

Particular source To imitate the appearance of the claimant's goods may be passing off, although it might be difficult to prove that mere imitation sufficiently impacts upon goodwill.[105] The question will be whether the shape and other characteristics of goods have come to denote a particular source in the relevant market.[106] This criterion was satisfied where, for over 30 years, claimants had marketed lemon juice in a distinctive yellow, plastic squeeze-pack shaped like a natural lemon that the defendants sought to emulate.[107] It was satisfied also in the case of a manufacturer which sought to sell vacuum cleaners that, although not anthropomorphised to the extent of the claimant's products, were to feature a bowler hat-shaped lid.[108]

Mere functional characteristics If the appearance complained of is dictated by functional considerations—for example, the purpose or performance of goods, or simplicity in handling or processing them—the courts will be reluctant to interfere. An action

---

[99] *Wotherspoon v Currie* (1872) LR 5 HL 508.   [100] *Montgomery v Thompson* [1891] AC 217.
[101] *Rey v Lecouturier* [1908] 2 Ch 71 (affd *sub nom Lecouturier v Rey* [1910] AC 262).
[102] *Millington v Fox* (1838) 3 My & Cr 338; *Singer Machine Manufacturers v Wilson* (1877) 3 App Cas 376, at 391–2.
[103] [2013] EWCA Civ 590.   [104] [2013] EWCA Civ 590, at [76] and [85].
[105] The case will be stronger where, eg, a similar name is used for goods. See *Massam v Thorley's Cattle Food Co* (1880) 14 Ch D 748. See also C Monaghan (2010) 31 *Company Lawyer* 184.
[106] *Numatic International Ltd v Qualtex UK Ltd* [2010] EWHC 1237 (Ch), at [39].
[107] *Reckitt & Colman Products Ltd v Borden Inc* [1990] 1 All ER 873.
[108] *Numatic International Ltd v Qualtex UK Ltd* [2010] EWHC 1237 (Ch).

to prevent the defendant's use of the normal shape of a shaving stick container failed accordingly.[109] Yet the manufacturer of laundry bleach which had a knobbed stick through the middle of the container was able to prevent the defendant from marketing a product similar in appearance, since it satisfied the court that this appearance was more than merely functional. The defendant was at liberty to have a stick in its product, but not one of the same 'get-up' as the claimant's.[110] Protection will not be afforded where the defendant's product merely is similar to the claimant's in particulars which are common to all types of that product.[111]

(f) Selling goods inferior to claimant's goods, thereby misleading the purchaser

A defendant must not sell goods which are in fact, and are described as, the goods of the claimant, but which are of a quality inferior to the claimant's normal, new, and current product, in such a way as to cause prospective purchasers to believe that the goods are the claimant's normal, new, and current product. Thus, the manufacturers of Gillette razor blades obtained an injunction restraining the defendant from selling used Gillette blades as 'genuine' ones.[112] On the other hand, a general dealer in a working-class area who advertised in his shop 'All types of electric lamps and fittings at cut prices' was not liable in passing off to the manufacturers of Osram lamps for selling old Osram lamps because it was not established that his acts were calculated to deceive the public into thinking that new lamps were being offered for sale.[113] Judicial reluctance to decide the respective merits of various products[114] led to a denial of a remedy in *Harris v Warren and Phillips*:[115]

> The publishers of a songwriter, who had recently attained fame, were unable to restrain D from passing off as new work the writer's early work (in which D had the copyright, and which, it was contended, was of greatly inferior quality to her latest work). The court held that it could draw no sharp dividing line between the quality of her early and more recent songs.

(g) False advertising

False advertising can also amount to passing off as the following illustrations reveal:

> In *Cadbury Schweppes Pty Ltd v Pub Squash Co Pty Ltd*,[116] C successfully launched a new canned lemon drink with a big media advertising campaign. The following year, D launched a similar drink with a media campaign in which D imitated the slogans and visual images of C's advertising. It was held that such advertising could be passing off, but the action failed: C failed to prove that there had been a confusing misrepresentation.
>
> In *Masson Seeley & Co Ltd v Embosotype Manufacturing Co*,[117] D deliberately created a market for their goods by copying C's catalogue so as to induce the public to believe that

---

[109] *JB Williams Co v H Bronnley & Co Ltd* (1909) 26 RPC 765.

[110] *William Edge & Sons Ltd v William Niccolls & Sons Ltd* [1911] AC 693.

[111] *Jamieson & Co v Jamieson* (1898) 14 TLR 160.

[112] *Gillette Safety Razor Co and Gillette Safety Razor Ltd v Franks* (1924) 40 TLR 606.

[113] *General Electric Co and British Thomson-Houston Co v Pryce's Stores* (1933) 50 RPC 232.

[114] Cf *White v Mellin* [1895] AC 154.   [115] (1918) 87 LJ Ch 491.

[116] [1981] 1 All ER 213. Cf *United Biscuits (UK) Ltd v Asda Stores Ltd* [1997] RPC 513.

[117] (1924) 41 RPC 160. Cf *Purefoy Engineering Co Ltd v Sykes Boxall & Co Ltd* (1955) 72 RPC 89.

goods offered by D were those of C. C's customers normally ordered goods by reference to certain key words in the catalogue, and D used the same artificial words in their catalogue. Although D's goods were inferior to those sold by C, this was held to be passing off.

In *Associated Newspapers plc v Insert Media Ltd*,[118] D arranged to insert advertising material into C's newspapers without their authority. Readers would assume that the newspaper had sanctioned the inserts, with consequent potential damage to C's reputation and goodwill. D's conduct was found to constitute a misrepresentation amounting to passing off.

On the other hand, if the defendant merely makes inflated claims about her own product, a rival cannot sue for passing off even though she suffered loss thereby.[119]

(h) Character merchandising

Character merchandising allows great profits to be made from exploiting the popularity of film stars, television characters, singers, sportsmen, and others. Thus, to give an example, children's cartoons have spawned industries of their own. Having seen the Teenage Mutant Ninja Turtles on television, child viewers pestered their parents for Turtle paraphernalia such as Turtle mugs. In recognition of the fact that unlicensed distributors would try to cash in on the craze, an injunction was granted in *Mirage Studios v Counter-Feat Clothing* to prevent unauthorised use of the 'Turtle' connection.[120] Since that case, actions for passing off have become frequent in cases of character merchandising. The action is available where the claimant is able to demonstrate that the representation was such as to mislead members of the public that a celebrity or character had endorsed the goods in circumstances where they wished to buy endorsed goods.[121] But courts take judicial notice of the fact that, often, consumers simply wish to purchase goods featuring the relevant likeness, so that there can be no *presumption* of a misleading representation.

(2) Representation must be likely to deceive the claimant's customers

Substantial number would be misled The misrepresentation must be made either to prospective customers of the claimant or to ultimate consumers of goods or services supplied by her.[122] It must be likely to deceive them in a way which is 'really likely to be damaging to the Claimant's goodwill'.[123] Likelihood of deceit is a question of law. The judge must decide on the balance of probabilities whether a substantial number of actual or potential customers would be misled by the representation.[124] This is not just

---

[118] [1991] 3 All ER 535.   [119] *BBC v Talksport Ltd* [2001] FSR 53.

[120] [1991] FSR 145. See also *BBC Worldwide Ltd v Pally Screen Printing Ltd* [1998] FSR 665.

[121] *Fenty v Arcadia Group Brands Ltd (t/a Topshop)* [2015] 1 WLR 3291; *Lumos Skincare Ltd v Sweet Squared Ltd* [2013] EWCA Civ 590.

[122] *Erven Warnink BV v J Townend & Sons (Hull) Ltd* [1979] AC 731, at 742. As regards foreign-based companies, the claimant 'must establish that it has actual goodwill in this jurisdiction, and that such goodwill involves the presence of clients or customers in the jurisdiction for the products or services in question': *Starbucks (HK) Ltd v British Sky Broadcasting Group (No 2)* [2015] 1 WLR 2628, at [47].

[123] *Phones 4U Ltd v Phone4u.co.uk Internet Ltd* [2006] EWCA Civ 244, at [19].

[124] *Lumos Skincare Ltd v Sweet Squared Ltd* [2013] EWCA Civ 590, at [64]; *Arsenal Football Club plc v Reed* [2001] RPC 922; *Neutrogena Corpn v Golden Ltd* [1996] RPC 473.

a matter of 'counting heads'. Rather, the issue is determined 'relative to the product and market in question'.[125] To an extent, then, each case must be decided on its own facts. In assessing the matter, the court will take account of who the likely customers for the product or service are.[126] Thus, although the ordinary standard to be applied is that of the unwary member of the public,[127] if the particular trade is with experts, the test must be whether such an expert is likely to be deceived.[128]

Right way round In *Woolley v Ultimate Products Ltd*, Arden LJ stated what has been implicit in the case-law:

> Members of the public must be confused into believing that the goods of the defendant are goods of the claimant. It is not enough for them to be misled into thinking that goods of the claimant are goods of the defendant. This is 'the wrong way round' or 'reverse misrepresentation', as I shall call it. It may suffice for trade mark infringement but not for passing off.[129]

This matter can be determined by examining whether the claimant has the established reputation for such things as quality, innovation, service, or value for money, the defendant being the interloper.

Knowledge of name not essential It is not essential that the person deceived should know the name of the claimant: it is enough 'if a person minded to obtain goods which are identified in h[er] mind with a certain definite commercial source is led by false statements to accept goods coming from a different commercial source'.[130] If the public would not in any sense be confused, there is no tort.[131]

Different fields of activity Even when the parties have no common field of activity, an action might lie provided that likely injury to goodwill is established. Thus, a moneylender who sets up in trade under the same name as an established bank can be restrained on the ground that it would endanger the bank's reputation if it were thought also to be a moneylender.[132] And *The Times* newspaper obtained an injunction against the defendant who represented it to be his principal or business associate in his cycle dealer business.[133] However, Granada TV could not prevent Ford from calling a new model 'Granada', for there was neither a connection nor association between the two activities, nor any proved confusion of the public.[134]

---

[125] *Woolley v Ultimate Products Ltd* [2012] EWCA Civ 1038, at [5]. See also *Lumos Skincare Ltd v Sweet Squared Ltd* [2013] EWCA Civ 590, at [64].   [126] *Bollinger v Costa Brava Wine Co Ltd* [1961] 1 All ER 561.

[127] *Reckitt & Colman Products Ltd v Borden Inc* [1990] 1 All ER 873, at 888.

[128] *Singer Manufacturing Co v Loog* (1882) 8 App Cas 15.   [129] [2012] EWCA Civ 1038, at [6].

[130] *Plomien Fuel Economiser Co Ltd v National School of Salesmanship Ltd* (1943) 60 RPC 209, at 214. The same applies even though the drug passed off by imitating get-up was sold on prescription only so that the public had no choice of supplier: *F Hoffman-La Roche & Co AG v DDSA Pharmaceuticals Ltd* [1969] FSR 410.

[131] Examples of failure for this reason include *Cadbury Schweppes Pty Ltd v Pub Squash Co Pty Ltd* [1981] 1 All ER 213 and *Newsweek Inc v BBC* [1979] RPC 441.

[132] *Harrods Ltd v R Harrod Ltd* (1923) 40 TLR 195.   [133] *Walter v Ashton* [1902] 2 Ch 282.

[134] *Granada Group Ltd v Ford Motor Co Ltd* [1973] RPC 49.

Groups of traders Where the misrepresentation relates to a product produced by a group of traders, rather than a single claimant, the group must establish that they constitute a distinctive class of traders who have built up goodwill by the use of a particular name or description of goods. Thus, the French producers of champagne succeeded by establishing that they all operated from the Champagne region in France.[135]

(3) Representation in the course of a trade

The representation must be made in the course of a trade. Trade is defined liberally and includes pursuit of a profession[136] and a person's interest in his literary and performance rights.[137] The tort is available even to protect the name of a political party where it can demonstrate that it has valuable property in the form of the goodwill in its name.[138]

(4) Intention to deceive not required

By contrast with the tort of deceit, proof of intention to deceive is not essential.[139]

(B) Goodwill

Definition and ambit In *AG Spalding & Bros v AW Gamage Ltd*,[140] Lord Parker stated that the tort protects goodwill—that is, 'the attractive force that brings in custom'.[141] The tort of passing off is protective of the trader's goodwill earned through the sale of goods or services.[142] Goodwill is said to be 'local in character and divisible' in the sense that separate goodwill attaches in each market where the business is carried on.[143] A market exists where there are customers among the local general public.[144] Goodwill must exist in the use of the claimant's mark or name immediately before the introduction of the defendant's goods or services to the relevant market.[145] No claim will be available for damage to goodwill where the goodwill is of trivial proportions.[146]

---

[135] *J Bollinger v Costa Brava Wine Co* [1960] Ch 262.

[136] *Society of Incorporated Accountants v Vincent* (1954) 71 RPC 325.

[137] See *Lord Byron v Johnston* (1816) 2 Mer 29; *Hines v Winnick* [1947] Ch 708; *Illustrated Newspapers Ltd v Publicity Services (London) Ltd* [1938] Ch 414.   [138] *Burge v Haycock* [2002] RPC 553.

[139] *Baume & Co Ltd v A H Moore Ltd* [1958] Ch 907. See explanation in CA Banfi [2011] CLJ 83, at 93.

[140] (1915) 84 LJ Ch 449.

[141] Echoing *IRC v Muller & Co's Margarine Ltd* [1901] AC 217, at 223–4. Goodwill is said to be different from reputation, although it is built upon reputation and other factors: *Starbucks (HK) Ltd v British Sky Broadcasting Group (No 2)* [2015] 1 WLR 2628, at [59], citing C Wadlow, *The Law of Passing-Off: Unfair Competition by Misrepresentation* (4th edn, 2011), para 3–131. See also CL Saw [2010] JBL 645, 658–9.

[142] *Star Industrial Co Ltd v Yap Kwee Kor* [1976] FSR 256, at 269.

[143] *Star Industrial Co Ltd v Yap Kwee Kor* [1976] FSR 256, at 269. See also *Starbucks (HK) Ltd v British Sky Broadcasting Group (No 2)* [2015] 1 WLR 2628, at [55].

[144] *Hotel Cipriani SRL v Cipriani (Grosvenor Street) Ltd* [2010] EWCA Civ 110, at [106]. A debate exists about how this should be proved: see CL Saw [2010] JBL 645.

[145] *Starbucks (HK) Ltd v British Sky Broadcasting Group (No 2)* [2015] 1 WLR 2628, at [16]; *Hotel Cipriani SRL v Cipriani (Grosvenor Street) Ltd* [2010] EWCA Civ 110, at [90].

[146] *Knight v Beyond Properties Pty Ltd* [2007] EWHC 1251 (Ch), at [27]; *Sutherland v V2 Music Ltd* [2002] EMLR 568, at [22].

Goods of a locality Nearly all the examples so far given constitute passing off in the form of inducing consumers to believe that they are purchasing the claimant's products. But passing off extends beyond such cases. This theme was picked up in *J Bollinger v Costa Brava Wine Co Ltd*:[147]

> D marketed 'Spanish Champagne', a sparkling Spanish wine. C was one of several manufacturers of champagne in the Champagne region of France. The court found that members of the public bought D's wine in the mistaken belief that they were buying champagne from the vineyards of Champagne. It was held D had committed the tort of passing off.

Crucially, Danckwerts J held that the description 'champagne' was part of the claimants' goodwill and a *right of property*. A group of persons producing goods in a certain locality and naming those goods by reference to that locality were entitled to protection against competitors who sought to cash in on their goodwill and reputation by attaching that name to a product originating from a different locality and with which the competing product has no rational association.[148]

Distinctive class The limitation to goods produced in a certain locality was considered immaterial in *Erven Warnink BV v J Townend & Sons (Hull) Ltd.*[149] Dutch traders recovered for the loss in their business resulting from the defendants' misleading appropriation of the name 'Advocaat' for their different and cheaper alcoholic egg drink. The crucial issues were that there was a 'distinctive class of goods' and that those goods were marketed in England by a class of persons whose product was genuinely indicated by the use of the name 'Advocaat'. This approach continues to be followed,[150] although it has been observed that the more general and descriptive the name of the goods (or services), the more difficult it will be to establish the reputation and goodwill of the claimant in the use of the name.[151] The name must be distinctive of a certain class of goods (or services).[152]

(C) Damage

A passing-off action can be brought even where no damage can be proved.[153] Although desirable, it is unnecessary to prove that any members of the public actually were deceived. Thus, where the defendant had done no more than sell to middlemen who were not deceived themselves, the action still lay where it was to be expected that the

---

[147] [1960] Ch 262 (flld in *Vine Products Ltd v Mackenzie & Co Ltd* [1969] RPC 1).

[148] See also *Chocosuisse Union des Fabricants Suisses de Chocolat v Cadbury Ltd* [1998] RPC 117.

[149] [1979] AC 731.

[150] Eg, *Fenty v Arcadia Group Brands Ltd (t/a Topshop)* [2015] 1 WLR 3291, at [33].

[151] Eg, *Office Cleaning Services v Westminster Window and General Cleaners* [1946] 63 RPC 39; [1944] 2 All ER 269, at 271.

[152] *Diageo North America Inc v Intercontinental Brands Ltd* [2010] EWCA Civ 920, at [24] and [28]; contra *Phones 4U Ltd v Phone4u.co.uk Internet Ltd* [2006] EWCA Civ 244, at [25].

[153] *Draper v Trist* [1939] 3 All ER 513; *Procea Products Ltd v Evans & Sons Ltd* (1951) 68 RPC 210.

defendant's act was calculated in due course to cause confusion in the minds of the purchasing public.[154] The likelihood of damage suffices.[155] The crucial test is whether a false representation has been made in fact, fraudulently or otherwise,[156] and whether this foreseeably will result in consumers being misled.[157] Damage subsists in reduced profitability because of, inter alia, diversion of sales and reduced fee-earning opportunities, including that which flows from the misuse of the likeness of a famous person for the purposes of a false endorsement.[158] It has been said also that damage might inhere in diminution of goodwill or damage to reputation[159]—although this might be of most importance in cases where the claimant has sold her business at an undervalue, thereby crystallising a loss.

(D) Defences

None of the general defences to torts that might apply call for special attention here; but it is worth noting that consent probably is the most important of them.[160]

(E) Remedies

(1) Injunction

This remedy is often the most important to the claimant. As always, it is awarded at the discretion of the court, and often the actual form of the injunction is one of the most contested points in the litigation.[161] If the defendant's conduct is calculated to divert customers, even though no sale has occurred, an injunction will lie to prevent the apprehended wrong.[162]

(2) Damages

Common law In the archetypal case, claimants recover damages for the loss of profits sustained in consequence of customers being diverted from them to the defendant. But it is not per se in respect of such loss that they may claim. Rather, all loss must be referable to goodwill, which lies at the heart of the classic trinity. But goodwill has been

---

[154] *Draper v Trist* [1939] 3 All ER 513. See also *Lumos Skincare Ltd v Sweet Squared Ltd* [2013] EWCA Civ 590.

[155] *HP Bulmer Ltd and Showerings Ltd v J Bollinger SA* [1978] RPC 79. Note, however, that it might be more accurate to speak of a spectrum of differing requirements for proof of damage: H Carty, *An Analysis of the Economic Torts* (2nd edn, 2010), 258.

[156] Indeed, in *Gillette UK Ltd v Edenwest Ltd* [1994] RPC 279 it was held that innocence on the part of D was no defence to an action for damages against her.

[157] *AG Spalding & Bros v AW Gamage Ltd* (1915) 84 LJ Ch 449, at 452. For cases where there was no confusion, see *Grand Hotel Co of Caledonia Springs v Wilson* [1904] AC 103; *Office Cleaning Services Ltd v Westminster Office Cleaning Association* (1944) 61 RPC 133 (affd (1946) 63 RPC 39).

[158] *Irvine v Talksport Ltd (Damages)* [2003] 2 All ER 881.

[159] *Woolley v Ultimate Products Ltd* [2012] EWCA Civ 1038, at [8].

[160] *Ex turpi causa* is a defence: *Lee v Haley* (1869) 5 Ch App 155; *Ford v Foster* (1872) 7 Ch App 611, at 630–1.

[161] In the absence of a threat to continue the acts complained of, the courts may grant a declaration but not an injunction (though giving liberty to apply for an injunction, eg, if D does continue): *Treasure Cot Co Ltd v Hamley Bros* (1950) 67 RPC 89.   [162] *Reddaway v Bentham Hemp-Spinning Co* [1892] 2 QB 639, at 648.

recognised as capable of being harmed in several ways beyond mere diversion of customers. Loss of business reputation,[163] restriction of the claimant's expansion potential (within limits),[164] and dilution (of the effectiveness of distinctive symbols)[165] are some examples.

Equity The alternative to the common law inquiry into damages is the equitable remedy of an account of the profits made by the defendant by virtue of the passing off.[166] There are dicta to the effect that an account of profits will not be directed for such period as the defendant's action was innocent.[167] It is uncertain whether more than nominal damages may be awarded when the defendant neither knew nor ought to have known[168] that she was committing the tort of passing off.[169]

Section 4 Malicious falsehood

General Passing off generally prevents competitors from using false representations to cash in on the claimant's goodwill. By contrast, malicious falsehood affords a remedy where business reputations are maliciously disparaged even though no aspersion is cast upon the character of an individual sufficient to give rise to a cause of action in defamation.[170] The tort protects interests in goodwill and business reputation,[171] its essence being that the defendant's lies cause financial loss to the claimant. The Court of Appeal set out the parameters of this tort as follows:

> [A]n action will lie for written or oral falsehoods . . . where they are maliciously published, where they are calculated in the ordinary course of things to produce, and where they do produce, actual damage.[172]

(A) Interests protected

Originally, this tort protected persons against unwarranted attacks on title to land which might hamper its disposal.[173] Hence, it was called 'slander of title'.[174] Later, it was held applicable to goods, and in that context the tort was called 'slander of goods'.[175] And before the end of the nineteenth century, *Ratcliffe v Evans*[176] made

---

[163] *AG Spalding and Bros v AW Gamage Ltd* (1918) 35 RPC 101; *Treasure Cot Co Ltd v Hamley Bros* (1950) 67 RPC 89.

[164] *Alfred Dunhill Ltd v Sunoptic SA* [1979] FSR 337; *LRC International v Lilla Edets Sales Co* [1973] RPC 560.

[165] *Taittinger SA v Allbev Ltd* [1993] FSR 641.

[166] In computing this profit, sales by D to middlemen can be considered, although the middlemen were not deceived, and had not passed the goods on to the public: *Lever v Goodwin* (1887) 36 Ch D 1.

[167] *Edelsten v Edelsten* (1863) 1 De GJ & Sm 185, at 199.

[168] This is what 'innocent' means: *Edward Young & Co Ltd v Holt* (1947) 65 RPC 25.

[169] *Draper v Trist* [1939] 3 All ER 513; *Marengo v Daily Sketch and Sunday Graphic Ltd* (1948) 65 RPC 242, at 251.   [170] See H Carty, *An Analysis of the Economic Torts* (2nd edn, 2010), ch 10.

[171] *CHC Software Care Ltd v Hopkins & Wood* [1993] FSR 241.

[172] *Ratcliffe v Evans* [1892] 2 QB 524, at 527.   [173] See FH Newark (1944) 60 LQR 366.

[174] Eg, *Gerard v Dickenson* (1590) Cro Eliz 196.

[175] *Malachy v Soper* (1836) 3 Bing NC 371. Cf *Green v Button* (1835) 2 Cr M & R 707.   [176] [1892] 2 QB 524.

it clear that the tort could be committed whenever false representations are made about a business. Indeed, it appears to be applicable wherever one's financial interests are threatened, whether these are *commercial* or not.[177] Although the tort has been referred to by many names,[178] the term 'malicious falsehood' is preferred here because it is the generic term used in the Defamation Act 1952.[179] Any type of interest in land, whether vested in possession or not,[180] is protected. Trade marks,[181] patents,[182] trade names,[183] copyright,[184] and company shares[185] can be the subject of actionable disparagements.

(B) Disparagement

General Most, but not all, cases of malicious falsehood involve disparagement.[186] It is a disparagement if there is some misstatement as to the extent of the claimant's interest in her property, as to the quality of her goods, or as to her fitness to offer services. Where a statement is capable of being read in a number of ways, at least one of which is not disparaging of the claimant's title, goods, or business, there is no requirement that the court settle upon a 'single meaning' as in the law of libel; the court will consider 'every reasonably available meaning, damaging or not' and the impact of the statement in the round.[187]

Infringement proceedings A threat of proceedings for infringement of a patent[188] or a trade mark[189] may be enough to enliven the action.

Comparative merit of goods An assertion by way of mere 'puffery' that the defendant's goods are better than the claimant's, is not actionable[190] unless the defendant's claims are couched in terms of verifiable facts, and those facts can be shown to be untrue, in which case an action will lie.[191] The test is whether a reasonable person would take the claim that denigrates the claimant's goods as one made seriously.[192] In such cases, the courts will not decide the relative merits of competing products.[193]

---

[177] *Kaye v Robertson* [1991] FSR 62; *Joyce v Sengupta* [1993] 1 All ER 897. In so saying, the demarcation between malicious falsehood and defamation was partly blurred. See also T Gibbons (1996) 16 OJLS 587.

[178] See H Carty, *An Analysis of the Economic Torts* (2nd edn, 2010), 200–3.

[179] Defamation Act 1952, s 3.   [180] *Vaughan v Ellis* (1608) Cro Jac 213.

[181] *Greers Ltd v Pearman and Corder Ltd* (1922) 39 RPC 406.   [182] *Wren v Weild* (1869) LR 4 QB 730.

[183] *Royal Baking Powder Co v Wright, Crossley & Co* (1900) 18 RPC 95.

[184] *Dicks v Brooks* (1880) 15 Ch D 22.   [185] *Malachy v Soper* (1836) 3 Bing NC 371.

[186] H Carty, *An Analysis of the Economic Torts* (2nd edn, 2010), 203.

[187] *Cruddas v Calvert* [2014] EMLR 5, at [32]; *Ajinomoto Sweeteners Europe SAS v Asda Stores Ltd* [2011] QB 497.

[188] *Mentmore Manufacturing Co Ltd v Fomento (Sterling Area) Ltd* (1955) 72 RPC 157.

[189] *Colley v Hart* (1890) 44 Ch D 179, at 183.

[190] *Young v Macrae* (1862) 3 B & S 264; *Hubbuck & Sons v Wilkinson, Heywood and Clark* [1899] 1 QB 86.

[191] *De Beers Abrasive Products Ltd v International General Electric Co of New York Ltd* [1975] 2 All ER 599; *DSG Retail Ltd v Comet Group plc* [2002] FSR 58.

[192] *De Beers Abrasive Products Ltd v International General Electric Co of New York Ltd* [1975] 2 All ER 599, applied in *Vodafone Group plc v Orange Personal Communications Services Ltd* [1997] FSR 34.

[193] *White v Mellin* [1895] AC 154.

Further illustrations In *Joyce v Sengupta*[194] the defendant newspaper published an article insinuating that the claimant had abused her position as lady's maid to the Princess Royal in order to steal personal letters from her employer. The claimant argued that the article might well prejudice her future employment prospects and her malicious falsehood claim was allowed to proceed. In *Joyce v Motor Surveys Ltd* the facts were as follows:[195]

> C became the tenant of one of D's lock-up garages in order to have premises at which he could be registered as a tyre dealer. D subsequently wished to evict C in order to sell the entire property with vacant possession. D therefore told the Post Office not to forward any more mail to him at that address, and told the tyre manufacturers' association that he was no longer trading there. D's conduct was held to constitute malicious falsehood.

Similarly, the action succeeded in the case of a false statement in the defendant's newspaper that the claimant had ceased to carry on business.[196] Finally, a false statement by a newspaper owner that the circulation of his newspaper greatly exceeded that of the claimant's rival newspaper was held to be capable of being tortious.[197]

(C) False statement

The claimant must establish that the disparaging statement was untrue.[198] The statement must be a false one *about the claimant, her property, or her business*; it is not enough that just any false statement resulted in harm to the claimant. Thus, whilst the disparaging statement need not identify the claimant personally, it must at least indirectly refer to her or her interests.[199] In addition, the false statement must be such as is 'calculated' to cause harm[200] in the sense that it is of its nature 'really likely' to cause harm to the claimant's goodwill.

(D) Publication

Because the essence of the tort is the effect produced by the false statement on persons entering into relations with the claimant, the falsehood must be published to persons other than the claimant.[201] It is clear that the defendant is liable for a re-publication that is the natural and probable result of her original publication.[202] Whether a negligent or accidental publication is sufficient is undecided.

---

[194] [1993] 1 All ER 897.   [195] [1948] Ch 252.

[196] *Ratcliffe v Evans* [1892] 2 QB 524; *Danish Mercantile Co v Beaumont* (1950) 67 RPC 111.

[197] *Lyne v Nicholls* (1906) 23 TLR 86. Cf *Evans v Harlow* (1844) 5 QB 624.

[198] *Royal Baking Powder Co v Wright, Crossley & Co* (1900) 18 RPC 95, at 99. And see also *Joyce v Sengupta* [1993] 1 All ER 897, at 901. Note that where the statement is 'not obviously untrue', no action will lie: *MacMillan Magazines Ltd v RCN Publishing Co Ltd* [1998] FSR 9.

[199] *Marathon Mutual Ltd v Waters* [2009] EWHC 1931 (QB), at [9-c]; H Carty, *An Analysis of the Economic Torts* (2nd edn, 2010), 204.

[200] *Ratcliffe v Evans* [1892] 2 QB 524, at 527; *Kaye v Robertson* [1991] FSR 62, at 67.

[201] Cf *Malachy v Soper* (1836) 3 Bing NC 371.

[202] *Cellactite and British Uralite Ltd v HH Robertson & Co* (1957) *Times*, 23 July.

(E) Malice

Since malice is always required to ground liability for this tort, it follows that good faith on the part of the defendant will be a good defence.[203] But whether the absence of good faith should be taken necessarily to imply the presence of malice is unclear due to the different tests for malice that have been put forward from time to time. Malice has been defined as 'intention to injure',[204] 'improper motive',[205] and 'want of honest belief in the truth of the statement'.[206] The courts have not indicated a preference for any one of these definitions ahead of the others.[207] Thus, while the House of Lords in *White v Mellin*[208] held that either an intention to injure or knowledge of the falsity of the statement would suffice, Lord Coleridge LCJ was of the view in *Halsey v Brotherhood* that mere 'want of *bona fides*' would suffice.[209] The defendant is potentially liable if her primary purpose was to damage the claimant's business, even, it seems, although she was acting also for the benefit of her own interests.[210] But malice will be difficult to prove where statements disparaging of the claimant's goods are made against a background of competition for customers and a belief by the defendant in the superiority of its own product, which it attempts to prove, for example, through comparative demonstrations of safety.[211]

(F) Damage

Common law The claimant must prove that the false statement caused her financial loss.[212] A debatable issue has been whether the requirement that special damage has to be proved can be discharged by showing general loss of custom without adducing evidence that particular customers have withdrawn their business in consequence of the falsehood.[213] Whether evidence of general loss of business will be sufficient depends on 'the nature and circumstances of the falsehood'.[214] For example, a claimant cannot be expected to identify individuals affected by a statement in a newspaper. Evidence of general business loss will be acceptable in such a case. The same rule has

---

[203] *Spring v Guardian Assurance plc* [1994] 3 All ER 129; *Kingspan Group plc v Rockwool Ltd* [2011] EWHC 250 (Ch), at [240].

[204] *Steward v Young* (1870) LR 5 CP 122, at 127.   [205] *Balden v Shorter* [1933] Ch 427, at 430.

[206] *Greers Ltd v Pearman and Corder Ltd* (1922) 39 RPC 406, at 417.

[207] Indeed, *British Railway Traffic and Electric Co v CRC Co and LCC* [1922] 2 KB 260 is one of the few cases where the court has held that some particular type of these variants of malice has to be proved. Equally, on only the non-binding authority of a first instance judge, it has been suggested that malice in this context bears the same meaning as in the context of defamation law: *Dorset Flint & Stone Blocks Ltd v Moir* [2004] EWHC 2173.

[208] [1895] AC 154, esp. at 160. Cf *Shapiro v La Morta* (1923) 130 LT 622, at 628 and *Greers Ltd v Pearman and Corder Ltd* (1922) 39 RPC 406, at 417–18.

[209] (1881) 19 Ch D 386, at 388. Cf *Wren v Weild* (1869) LR 4 QB 730.

[210] The *ratio* of *Joyce v Motor Surveys Ltd* [1948] Ch 252 is supported in *Alcott v Millar's Karri and Jarrah Forests Ltd* (1904) 91 LT 722, at 723. Cf *Mentmore Manufacturing Co Ltd v Fomento (Sterling Area) Ltd* (1955) 72 RPC 157.   [211] See, eg, *Kingspan Group plc v Rockwool Ltd* [2011] EWHC 250 (Ch).

[212] *Ajello v Worsley* [1898] 1 Ch 274; *Shapiro v La Morta* (1923) 130 LT 622; *Allason v Campbell* (1996) *Times*, 8 May. When the damage complained of is physical injury, this tort is presumably not applicable and *O v Rhodes* [2016] AC 219 must be relied on. Cf *Guay v Sun Publishing Co Ltd* [1952] 2 DLR 479 (affd [1953] 4 DLR 577).   [213] *Malachy v Soper* (1836) Bing NC 371 decided that the tort is not actionable per se.

[214] *Ratcliffe v Evans* [1892] 2 QB 524, at 533.

been extended to a circular to customers where the circular was reasonably likely to cause a decline in business.[215] On the other hand, a claimant who complained that the defendants had stated in their newspaper that his house was haunted, but who neither produced witnesses giving evidence that the statement had influenced them to the detriment of the claimant, nor showed that the house had depreciated in value as a result of it, failed.[216] The expenses of bringing litigation in order to remove a cloud hanging over the title caused by the defendant's statement are to be treated as special damage.[217]

Statutory intervention   The difficulties inherent in proving actual loss caused actions for malicious falsehood to become extremely rare.[218] In consequence, the common law rules on damage have been modified by the Defamation Act 1952, section 3 of which provides:

> In an action for slander of title, slander of goods or other malicious falsehood, it shall not be necessary to allege or prove special damage—(a) if the words upon which the action is founded are calculated to cause pecuniary damage to the [claimant] and are published in writing or other permanent form;[219] or (b) if the said words are calculated to cause pecuniary damage to the [claimant] in respect of any office, profession, calling, trade or business[220] held or carried on by him at the time of the publication.[221]

For the purpose of this section, 'calculated to cause pecuniary damage' means harm that is objectively likely or probable.[222] And as a result of the section, in the vast majority of cases concerning this tort it will not be necessary to prove special damage.[223] This is important given doubts as to whether an injunction could be obtained before commencement of the Act where damage was merely likely to accrue.[224] However, where the court is not satisfied that any substantial loss either has occurred or is likely to occur, no substantial tort has been committed and the court might strike out the claim as an abuse of process.[225]

Consequential financial loss   A loss of sales might have a further impact upon profitability. In the case of a small car manufacturer, for example, there might be increases in the unit costs of manufacture and distribution and there is dictum that these are

[215]   *E Worsley & Co Ltd v Cooper* [1939] 1 All ER 290. Cf *Lyne v Nicholls* (1906) 23 TLR 86.
[216]   *Barrett v Associated Newspapers Ltd* (1907) 23 TLR 666.   [217]   *Elborow v Allen* (1622) Cro Jac 642.
[218]   This was the view expressed in *Joyce v Sengupta* [1993] 1 All ER 897.   [219]   This includes broadcasting.
[220]   These words probably have the same meaning here as in the context of defamation.
[221]   Note, too, that in *Joyce v Sengupta* [1993] 1 All ER 897 the court said that the Defamation Act 1952, s 3 is not confined to nominal damages.
[222]   *IBM v Web-Sphere Ltd* [2004] EWHC 529.
[223]   C who relies on the Defamation Act 1952, s 3 is not allowed to prove special damage unless she has specifically pleaded it: *Calvet v Tomkies* [1963] 3 All ER 610.
[224]   *Dunlop Pneumatic Tyre Co Ltd v Maison Talbot* (1904) 20 TLR 579. Cf *White v Mellin* [1895] AC 154, at 163–4 and 167. Note that *Easycare Inc v Bryan Lawrence & Co* [1995] FSR 597 establishes that the normal rules applicable to the granting of interlocutory injunctions do not apply in cases of malicious falsehood.
[225]   *Tesla Motors Ltd v British Broadcasting Corporation* [2013] EWCA Civ 152, at [48]–[50], citing *Jameel v Dow Jones & Co Inc* [2005] QB 946; *Citation plc v Ellis Whittam Ltd* [2013] EWCA Civ 155, at [33]–[34].

recoverable.[226] In the case of a seller of goods, there might be recovery for increases in the costs of storage and other consequential financial losses.[227]

Non-financial loss The financial loss inflicted on the claimant by the falsehood might be accompanied by mental distress and injury to feelings.[228] The Court of Appeal in *Joyce v Sengupta*[229] suggested that injury to feelings was not per se recoverable. But Sir Michael Kerr suggested that, within general damages, an award of aggravated damages might partly reflect the injury to the claimant's feelings and dignity. The award of both aggravated and exemplary damages in malicious falsehood cases against relevant media defendants for the publication of news-related material is now subject to Crime and Courts Act 2013, sections 34–42, considered in chapter 21.

(G) Defences

In those circumstances where a defendant in defamation could plead legislative immunity or absolute privilege—for example, in relation to statements in judicial proceedings—the same defence will be available here. Formerly, it might have been apt to say that the defences of qualified privilege in defamation were similarly applicable, but the requirement of malice in this tort defeats any such claim.

(H) Malicious falsehood and defamation

Overlapping actions There are clear similarities between malicious falsehood and the related tort of defamation.[230] It is apparent, for example, that there are occasions when the claimant has a choice between the two. In *Joyce v Sengupta*, where the claimant argued that allegations that she had stolen from the Princess Royal constituted a malicious false-hood threatening her employment prospects, the defendants contended that her proper remedy lay in defamation. By electing to sue in malicious falsehood, the claimant was able to obtain legal aid (which was unavailable in defamation)[231] and the defendant lost the right to trial by jury. The Court of Appeal refused to strike out the claimant's claim. There is no principle of law that a claimant must pursue the most appropriate remedy. Following *Joyce v Sengupta* she is entitled to elect the action that best suits her. As long as one has an arguable case that defamatory allegations will damage one's financial prospects as well as one's reputation, one may choose whether to sue in defamation or in malicious falsehood.

Differences That said, four key differences can be identified between malicious false-hood and defamation.[232] First, X cannot defame Y unless the statement casts aspersions

---

[226] *Tesla Motors Ltd v British Broadcasting Corporation* [2013] EWCA Civ 152, at [37].

[227] *Tesla Motors Ltd v British Broadcasting Corporation* [2013] EWCA Civ 152, at [37].

[228] In *Fielding v Variety Inc* [1967] 2 QB 841, Lord Denning stated that damages for injured feelings were not recoverable for the tort of malicious falsehood. [229] [1993] 1 All ER 897.

[230] See T Gibbons (1996) 16 OJLS 587. [231] And is nowadays also unavailable in malicious falsehood.

[232] The Court of Appeal has noted differences in the operation of the torts and indicated its contentment with this: *Ajinomoto Sweeteners Europe SAS v Asda Stores Ltd* [2011] QB 497, at [43].

on Y's character, whereas other classes of untruth—such as false statements about Y's business—will suffice in malicious falsehood. This might have repercussions in terms of the relationship of the tort to Article 10 ECHR.[233] Second, whereas defamation actions are confined by the single meaning rule, no such restriction affects malicious falsehood.[234] Third, in defamation, the burden of proof lies with the defendant to establish the truth of a defamatory statement, whereas in malicious falsehood it rests with the claimant to show that the defendant's statement was untrue. And, finally, while malice is a prerequisite to suing in malicious falsehood, it is not in defamation.

Conclusions

This chapter has considered torts protective of the claimant's business and financial interests from false representations. The tort of deceit occurs where the defendant makes a representation knowing of its falsity, or without belief in its truth, or recklessly, careless whether it be true or false, with the intention that the claimant should act in reliance upon it, which causes damage to the claimant in consequence of his reliance upon it. The tort of passing off occurs where the defendant makes, in the course of trade, a false representation that is calculated to deceive the claimant's customers or clients in a way which is likely to be damaging to the claimant's goodwill. There is no need to prove an intention to harm. The focus is upon the likely effect, objectively considered, of the misrepresentation upon the claimant's goodwill. The tort of malicious falsehood occurs where the defendant makes a false representation disparaging of the claimant's interest in property, the quality of her goods, or her fitness to offer services, which is maliciously published and likely to cause, and which does actually cause, damage to the claimant's goodwill.

Problem question

Gabriella operates a market stall in Zanesville. She sells cupcakes in the shape of love hearts. These cupcakes resemble those of the famous brand manufactured by Zanesville manufacturer Lovecakes Ltd. Indeed, the Lovecakes cupcakes were Gabriella's inspiration for going into small business. Just to make sure that her cupcakes are similarly attractive, Gabriella adds a hint of pumpkin seed to them. Jorge attends the Zanesville market and sees Gabriella's stall. Gabriella's sister Monica is selling the cupcakes on the day in question. Jorge is interested in a commercial arrangement to acquire large quantities of cupcakes. Jorge asks Monica whether she would be able to supply on a commercial scale. Monica says that this should be 'no problem'. In fact, Monica has no idea whether Gabriella can do this. Jorge also asks whether the cupcakes have any preservatives in

---

[233] *Charterhouse Clinical Research Unit Ltd v Richmond Pharmacology Ltd* [2003] EWHC 1099, at [14].
[234] Eg, *Cruddas v Calvert* [2014] EMLR 5.

them. Monica rings up Gabriella to ask about this. Gabriella tells Monica that she can make the cupcakes without preservatives—although she does use preservatives at the moment. Monica tells Jorge that the cupcakes are 'preservative free'. Jorge enters into an agreement for the purchase of 15000 cupcakes a month. Gabriella is unable to supply more than 5000. Jorge discovers also that the cupcakes that he purchases contain preservatives. Jorge's business reputation is badly affected by these events.

Advise Lovecakes and Jorge as to the availability of misrepresentation-based torts against Gabriella.

 Visit **http://www.oup.com/uk/street15e/** for answer guidance.

Further reading

BEVERLEY-SMITH AND BARROW, 'Talk that Tort . . . of Passing Off: Rihanna, and the Scope of Actionable Misrepresentation' [2014] *European Intellectual Property Review* 57

CARTY, *An Analysis of the Economic Torts* (2nd edn, 2010), chs 9–12

MURPHY, 'Misleading Appearances in the Tort of Deceit' (2016) 72 *Cambridge Law Journal* 301

NEWARK, 'Malice in Actions on the Case for Words' (1944) 60 *Law Quarterly Review* 366

SAW, 'Goodwill Hunting in Passing Off: Time to Jettison the Strict "Hard Line" Approach in England?' [2010] *Journal of Business Law* 645

15

The general 'economic' torts

KEY ISSUES

(1) Variegated torts
As suggested in chapter 14, the so-called 'general "economic" torts' comprise a variegated group of torts with few features in common apart from an element of intention, the causation of loss, and the tendency of the courts to apply them in business and other financial settings. However, there are strong arguments for the proposition that a number of them should not be confined to cases of financial loss alone because they have a greater role in protecting autonomy, preventing abuses of rights to act, and/or filling in gaps left by other torts and causes of action.

(2) Outlines
In the circumstances, we introduce these torts with a simple list of definitions. Inducing breach of contract occurs where a defendant knowingly and intentionally induces a third party to break his contract with the claimant so that the breach causes the claimant to suffer loss; the unlawful means tort is enlivened where there is an intention to cause loss by the use of unlawful means and loss is so caused; lawful means conspiracy comprises a combination to use lawful means for the predominant purpose of injuring another where such injury occurs; unlawful means conspiracy has similar combination and loss elements, but otherwise comprises an intention to use unlawful means in order to injure another; finally, intimidation occurs with the use of an unlawful threat successfully to compel another to act (or refrain from acting) in a particular manner that will cause harm.

Section 1 Introduction

This chapter examines the five general 'economic' torts: viz, inducing breach of contract, causing loss by unlawful means, lawful means conspiracy, unlawful means conspiracy, and intimidation. Although each of these torts has the imprimatur of the House of Lords,[1] the foundations of the third and fourth appear to be less secure than those of

---

[1] Eg, *Total Network v Revenue and Customs Commissioners* [2008] 1 AC 1174; *OBG Ltd v Allan* [2008] 1 AC 1.

the others. Moreover, close analysis of the torts of lawful means conspiracy and intimidation reveal that, while they might serve to protect financial interests, they are not designed specifically to do this; indeed, they appear to serve a wider role in protecting autonomy, preventing abuse of rights, and/or filling in gaps left by other torts or causes of action.[2] This last point reflects the point made in chapter 14 that the correctness of collectively labelling the five torts as 'economic torts' increasingly is being questioned. However, no clear alternative way of organising their discussion presents itself yet. In the circumstances, this chapter continues with the conventional ordering of the torts.

Section 2 Inducing breach of an existing contract

(A) Introduction

Origins Inducing breach of contract has its origins in *Lumley v Gye*,[3] the alleged facts of which were as follows:

> A famous opera singer was contracted to sing at C's theatre *and nowhere else*, but she was not C's servant. C claimed that D, who knew of the contract,[4] had induced the singer to break it so that she would sing at D's theatre instead.

The court held that on these facts the defendant would have committed a tort in respect of which the claimant would be entitled to a remedy. (However, the defendant was able to show that he honestly believed that the opera singer was entitled to terminate her contract with the claimant.) The case established that a tort will be committed if a defendant knowingly and intentionally induces a third party to break his contract with the claimant with the result that the breach causes the claimant to suffer loss.[5] Since that time, a qualification has become clear in that a defendant will have a defence to the tort if able to establish that his inducing the breach of contract was justified. Six important issues require consideration: inducement, breach, knowledge, intention, loss, and justification.

Secondary liability Before considering these elements, however, it should be noted that liability for this tort is not primary but secondary: that is, the tortfeasor is a sort of accessory to the primary legal wrong committed by the contract breaker. It is worth bearing this in mind when attempting to distinguish this tort from the other general economic torts. It was the neglect of this point that led to so much of the confusion that bedevilled the development of the economic torts during the twentieth century.[6] It is

---

[2] See, eg, J Murphy (2014) 77 MLR 33; JW Neyers, 'Explaining the Inexplicable? Four Manifestations of Abuse of Rights in English Law' in D Nolan and A Robertson (eds), *Rights and Private Law* (2011), ch 11; N Tamblyn [2013] Sing JLS 158; N Tamblyn (2015) 23 Tort LR 1.

[3] *Lumley v Gye* (1853) 2 E & B 216.

[4] C failed at the subsequent trial, the jury finding that D did not believe the contract between C and Wagner to be binding: see S Waddams (2001) 117 LQR 431.

[5] This principle was confirmed a generation later in *Bowen v Hall* (1881) 6 QBD 333.

[6] For an account of the content and contours of the general economic torts prior to *OBG v Allan*, see H Carty, *An Analysis of the Economic Torts* (2nd edn, 2010), chs 2–8.

worth noting also that calling it accessory liability *does not* enable us to label the inducer a *joint tortfeasor* for the simple reason that he is an accessory to a breach of contract, not a tort.

(B) Elements of the tort

(1) Inducement

Prior to the House of Lords' decision in *OBG Ltd v Allan*,[7] a measure of confusion had crept into the law on what, for the purposes of this tort, could be regarded as inducement. For example, in one strain of cases,[8] it was thought that mere prevention of performance would count. In another, it was held that mere inconsistent dealings would suffice. As Jenkins LJ put it in *Thomson & Co Ltd v Deakin*: 'if a third party, with knowledge of a contract between the contract breaker and another, had dealings with the contract breaker which the third party knows to be inconsistent with the contract, he has committed an actionable interference'.[9] However, the thrust of *OBG Ltd v Allan* was that orthodoxy should be restored and that the tort should revert to its original conception in *Lumley v Gye*. So, for Lord Nicholls, it was 'evident that application of the *Lumley v Gye* tort to a "prevention" case was unfortunate [since] [t]here is a crucial difference between cases where the defendant induces a contracting party not to perform his contractual obligations and cases where the defendant prevents a contracting party from carrying out his contractual obligations'.[10] And while Lord Hoffmann's speech was less clear-cut, nonetheless he identified as the basis of the original decision in *Lumley v Gye* the fact that 'a person . . . procures another to commit a wrong'.[11] If one adds to this the fact that Arden LJ has since stated that '[t]he tort of inducing a breach of contract is committed when a person, with the requisite knowledge and intention . . . *procures or persuades* another person to breach his contract with a third party',[12] it seems safe to state that prevention of performance and mere inconsistent dealing no longer are seen as adequate. What this tort requires is direct inducement along the lines of active persuasion or positive encouragement to commit a breach.

(2) Breach

Enforceable contracts Any valid and enforceable contract can found an action for this tort.[13] But if the contract was void or voidable and therefore unenforceable any putative procurement of its breach is not actionable.[14] The relevant breach need not be of a

---

[7] [2008] 1 AC 1.

[8] See, eg, *Torquay Hotel Co Ltd v Cousins* [1969] 2 Ch 106; *Merkur Island Shipping Corpn v Laughton* [1983] 2 AC 570. [9] [1952] Ch 646, at 694.

[10] [2008] 1 AC 1, at [178].

[11] [2008] 1 AC 1, at [3]. Cf his focus on the causation of breach via 'encouragement, threat, persuasion and so forth' at [36]. [12] *Meretz Investments NV v ACP Ltd* [2008] Ch 244, at [86] (emphasis added).

[13] Cf *Thomson & Co Ltd v Deakin* [1952] Ch 646, at 677; *Findlay v Blaylock* 1937 SC 21.

[14] *Proform Sports Management Ltd v Proactive Sports Management* [2007] 1 All ER 542; *Shears v Mendeloff* (1914) 30 TLR 342 (contracts involving minors); *Said v Butt* [1920] 3 KB 497 (mistake); *Joe Lee Ltd v Lord Dalmery* [1927] 1 Ch 300 (gaming).

primary term of the contract. As the Court of Appeal made clear in *Law Debenture Trust Corpn v Ural Caspian Oil Corporation*,[15] breach of even the secondary contractual duty to pay damages when a primary contractual obligation has been broken can give rise to tortious liability.[16] It would seem to follow from this that, even if the defendant is not responsible for the initial breach of a contract, he will be liable in tort still if he is responsible for procuring the continuing breach of a subsisting contract the obligations of which are ongoing at the time of the inducement.[17] Thus, where the defendant engaged a servant in ignorance of an existing contract of service between the servant and the claimant, he could not escape liability after continuing to employ the servant after learning the facts.[18]

Implied terms The breach of implied terms will suffice also, as *Hivac Ltd v Park Royal Scientific Instruments Ltd*[19] demonstrates.[20] The claimant had been the only English maker of midget valves for hearing aids. Setting up in competition, the defendant employed some of the claimant's staff in their spare time. It was held that an implied term must be read into the engagement of these staff that the latter should not compromise their fidelity to the claimant by doing things which would injure the claimant's business. In view of the fact that the claimant had a monopoly on this type of work, and the staff held a monopoly over the relevant skill, an injunction restraining the inducement of breach could be obtained.

Actionability not required According to *Torquay Hotel Co Ltd v Cousins*,[21] the breach need not be actionable:

> An injunction was granted against Ds who, in the course of industrial action, were attempting to stop a supplier from fulfilling his contract with C. The contract expressly exempted either party from liability for events beyond their control—such as labour disputes—if those events led to a failure to perform.

The Court of Appeal interpreted the clause as 'an exception from liability for non-performance rather than an exception from the obligation to perform'.[22] Accordingly, the defendant's conduct still constituted the procurement of a breach, and the claimant still suffered loss (albeit loss that was not actionable under the contract). The logic of this reasoning seems sound enough even if in other respects (exposed by their Lordships in *OBG Ltd v Allan*) the decision in the *Torquay Hotel* case was flawed.

Lawful terminations Inducing someone to give proper notice in order to terminate a contract lawfully cannot give rise to a tort action.[23] Similarly, if a contract is

---

[15] [1995] Ch 152.   [16] [1994] 3 WLR 1221, at 1235.
[17] *Smithies v National Association of Operative Plasterers* [1909] 1 KB 310.
[18] *Blake v Lanyon* (1795) 6 Term Rep 221; *Fred Wilkins & Bros Ltd v Weaver* [1915] 2 Ch 322. Cf *Read v Friendly Society of Operative Stonemasons* [1902] 2 KB 88, at 95 (on appeal [1902] 2 KB 732). See also *Jones Bros (Hunstanton) Ltd v Stevens* [1955] 1 QB 275.   [19] [1946] Ch 169.
[20] See also *Lonmar Global Risks Ltd v West* [2011] IRLR 138.   [21] [1969] 2 Ch 106.
[22] [1969] 2 Ch 106, at 143.
[23] See, eg, *Boxfoldia Ltd v National Graphic Association (1982)* [1988] ICR 752; *Thomson & Co Ltd v Deakin* [1952] Ch 646.

determinable by either party at will, it is not actionable if the defendant induces a party to determine that contract.[24] This is because there has been no breach, but merely a lawful termination of the contract.

Strikes Giving notice of a forthcoming strike is not notice to terminate, but, rather, notice of a forthcoming breach of contract. It follows that, where there is a no-strike clause in the contract, inducing a strike will amount to inducing breach of contract.[25] Union officials inducing strike action thus are prima facie open to tort liability. In reality, however, they enjoy certain statutory immunities as a matter of employment law. (These immunities fall beyond the scope of this book.)

(3) Knowledge of the contract

Lumley v Gye was clear that the defendant must have known of the contract between the claimant and the contract breaker. This was reiterated in *Mainstream Properties v Young*,[26] an appeal heard together with *OBG Ltd v Allan*:

> D had supplied two of C's employees with funding that enabled them to pursue a personal property development project which initially had been offered to C (a property development company). In pursuing such a project for independent gain, the employees were in breach of their employment contracts with C. D knew that they worked for C and what C's line of business was. Therefore, he could not deny his awareness of the obvious potential conflict of interest. Nonetheless, because the employees had assured D that there would be no breach of contract if they pursued the project, D escaped liability on the footing that he did not know subjectively that there would be a breach of contract.

The defendant was doubtless foolish to believe the employees' lies, but believe them he did. This, Lord Hoffmann said, was enough to exculpate him on the basis that he honestly did not believe that the employees' acts would be in breach of contract and that he was procuring a breach of contract. He said:

> It is not enough that you know that you are procuring an act which, as a matter of law or construction of the contract, is a breach. You must actually realise that it will have this effect. Nor does it matter that you ought reasonably to have done so.[27]

In the light of this passage, it might be thought that nothing short of actual knowledge would suffice. However, both Lord Hoffmann and Lord Nicholls were prepared to countenance an exception where the defendant deliberately turns a blind eye to facts that would reveal the breach of contract. In their view, a defendant cannot escape liability if he consciously avoids enquiring into a case in order to avoid an inconvenient truth. Thus, as Lord Denning pointed out in *Emerald Construction Co Ltd v Lowthian*[28]—a case where union officials threatened a building contractor with a strike unless he terminated a sub-contract for the supply of labour—the defendants knew that there was a contract because they wanted it broken. So, '[e]ven if they did not know the actual

---

[24] *McManus v Bowes* [1938] 1 KB 98.   [25] *Rookes v Barnard* [1964] AC 1129.
[26] [2008] 1 AC 1.   [27] [2008] 1 AC 1, at [39].   [28] [1966] 1 WLR 691.

terms of the contract, but had the means of knowledge—which they deliberately dis-regarded—that would be enough'.[29] It should be noted, however, that the defendant in *Mainstream Properties* had not turned a blind eye. He had been lied to, and he honestly believed those lies to the effect that no breach would occur.

(4) Intention

The need for intention in the tort of inducing breach of contract was asserted forcefully in *OBG Ltd v Allan*. For Lord Nicholls, the defendant 'is liable if he intended to persuade the contracting party to breach the contract'.[30] Lord Hoffmann, while equally certain of the need for intention, believed that it could be identified in one of two ways: by refer-ence to whether a breach of contract was intended as an end in itself, or by reference to whether it was sought as a means to an end (such as, say, endeavouring somehow to aug-ment the defendant's own market position).[31] Importantly, both Law Lords stopped short of insisting that the defendant should have intended the breach to result in harm to the claimant. It was enough that a breach was intended. That being so, there was no absence of the requisite intention in one case in which the defendant union believed that calling a strike of their members ultimately would be to the financial benefit of the mine owner by forcing up the price of coal.[32] On the other hand, nothing in this case should be seen as undermining the additional requirement for this tort that damage actually be suffered.

(5) Harm

In order to be able to invoke this tort, the claimant must suffer loss of a more than nominal kind by virtue of the breach of contract.[33] If the breach is of a kind that, 'in the ordinary course of business', will cause damage, loss may be inferred from the circum-stances.[34] If the breach is not of this kind, loss will have to be proved; and this might be no easy matter, as is illustrated by *Jones Bros (Hunstanton) Ltd v Stevens*:[35]

> D continued to employ a servant after learning that the servant, in entering into his employment, was breaking his contract with C. It was shown, however, that the servant would not have returned to C's employment in any event. C's action failed because no damage had been occasioned.

In cases where the claimant's loss depends upon what, but for the tort, a third party would have done in the future, courts will entertain an award of damages for the loss of a chance. Thus, in *McGill v Sports and Entertainment Media Group*:[36]

> Pursuant to an oral agreement, the claimant football agent had represented a professional football player in negotiations for a lucrative transfer deal. Before signing with the new club, the footballer was induced by the defendants to have them represent him as agents. The claimant argued that, thereby, he had lost the chance of a substantial agent's fee from

---

[29] [1966] 1 WLR 691, at 700–1.   [30] [2008] 1 AC 1, at [192].   [31] [2008] 1 AC 1, at [43].
[32] *South Wales Miners' Federation v Glamorgan Coal Co Ltd* [1905] AC 239.
[33] *Greig v Insole* [1978] 1 WLR 302, at 332.
[34] *Exchange Telegraph Co Ltd v Gregory & Co* [1896] 1 QB 147; *Goldsoll v Goldman* [1914] 2 Ch 603 (on appeal [1915] 1 Ch 292); *Bents Brewery Co Ltd v Hogan* [1945] 2 All ER 570.
[35] [1955] 1 QB 275.   [36] [2017] 1 WLR 989.

the new club, which might have been secured had he been able to formalise his agency contract with the player as required by Football Association rules. The reason for which the matter was argued on the basis of a lost chance was that the player had had an aversion to entering into formal agency agreements after having previously entered one pursuant to which he became liable for taxation of a benefit in kind.

The Court of Appeal held the claimant to be eligible for an assessment of damages for his lost chance of securing the written contract and the agency fee pursuant to principles established in *Allied Maples Group Ltd v Simmons and Simmons*[37] (in line with the rules in negligence examined in chapter 6).

Under the rules governing recovery for inducing breach of contract, there appears to be a remoteness test based on reasonable foreseeability of harm with respect to this tort.[38] Moreover, so long as ordinary losses (such as financial loss) can be identified, it seems that aggravated damages may be recovered also in circumstances where the breach was intended to inflict 'humiliation and menace'.[39]

(6) Justification

OBG Ltd v Allan[40] has affirmed that the inducement of a breach of contract might be capable of justification. As yet, the courts have not laid down any settled test for this defence; but the dictum of Romer LJ in *Glamorgan Coal Co Ltd v South Wales Miners' Federation* is widely cited:[41]

[R]egard might be had to the nature of the contract broken; the position of the parties to the contract; the grounds for the breach; the means employed to procure the breach; the relation of the person procuring the breach to the person who breaks the contract; and the object of the person in procuring the breach.

In that case it was held that the defendants were not justified in calling the miners out on strike in order to keep up the price of coal by which the miners' pay was regulated.[42] The breach by a claimant of his contract with the defendant will not justify the defendant in inducing a third party to break his contract with the claimant.[43] On the other hand, *Brimelow v Casson* is one of the rare cases in which the defence has succeeded:[44]

D represented various theatrical unions, and C owned a touring theatrical company. D induced a theatre manager to break his contract with C because C was paying such low wages to his company that some performers were compelled to resort to prostitution. The interest that D had in maintaining professional theatrical standards was held to justify D procuring the breach.

---

[37] [1995] 1 WLR 1602.   [38] *Boxfoldia Ltd v NGA (1982)* [1988] IRLR 383.

[39] *Pratt v BMA* [1919] 1 KB 244.   [40] [2008] 1 AC 1, at [193].

[41] [1903] 2 KB 545, at 574–5 (approved in *South Wales Miners' Federation v Glamorgan Coal Co Ltd* [1905] AC 239, at 252).

[42] Cf *Temperton v Russell* [1893] 1 QB 715, where trade union officials were not justified in interfering in order to enforce certain conditions of labour in a particular trade; *Read v Friendly Society of Operative Stonemasons of England, Ireland and Wales* [1902] 2 KB 88.

[43] *Smithies v National Association of Operative Plasterers* [1909] 1 KB 310.

[44] [1924] 1 Ch 302. Yet Simonds J in *Camden Nominees Ltd v Forcey* [1940] Ch 352 treated that decision (at 366) as being based on the separate ground of *ex turpi causa*.

Notwithstanding this decision, the defence of justification is unlikely to be widely invoked. Certainly, it has been held that the role for justification is highly exceptional in relation to procuring a breach of contract.[45] There is a simple reason for this: the interest in maintaining the security of contracts almost always outweighs that of protecting free trade.

Section 3 Causing loss by unlawful means

(A) Introduction

For a time, this tort was conceived in terms of 'interfering with the trade or business of another person by doing unlawful acts'.[46] These days, however, the accepted name for the tort is 'causing loss by unlawful means'.[47] Owing to its patchy history, it is to the House of Lords' milestone decision in *OBG Ltd v Allan* that we must turn in order to tease out its essential ingredients. Although this can be done with more confidence than was formerly possible, several ambiguities in the law remain that will require consideration by the courts on future occasions. With this in mind, we turn first to consider those elements of the tort that can with certainty be claimed to be necessary to its invocation: unlawful means, intention, and harm. Thereafter, we shall examine the lingering uncertainties.

(B) Elements of the tort

(1) Intention

Just as with inducing breach of contract, intention is central to the tort of causing loss by unlawful means. However, whereas in the former the defendant must intend to bring about a mere breach of contract (which might or might not result in loss), in this tort the relevant intention is one to cause loss (as opposed to breach of contract) as an end in itself, or as a means to an end (eg, securing a competitive advantage).[48] Whether it makes more sense for the law to adopt a test based on targeted harm is a moot point. Certainly, some writers are of the view that orthodoxy demands a narrow view of intention: one that sees a specific aim of the defendant's act being the infliction of harm on the claimant as an end in itself.[49] The test propounded in *OBG Ltd v Allan*, by contrast, goes further: it also embraces acts designed to cause harm as a means to some ulterior end (such as self-enrichment). And since Lord Nicholls was content to adopt the same test as Lord Hoffmann as regards intention, it is fairly safe to conclude that, whatever

---

[45] *SOS Kinderdorf International v Bittaye* [1996] 1 WLR 987, at 994.

[46] *Merkur Island Shipping Corpn v Laughton* [1983] 2 AC 570, at 608.

[47] It is the term used repeatedly in *OBG v Allan* (though not always by Lord Nicholls) and by the Court of Appeal in *Meretz Investments NV v ACP Ltd* [2008] Ch 244.   [48] *OBG v Allan* [2008] 1 AC 1, at [62].

[49] For details of these writers and the cases on which they ground their analyses, see H Carty, *An Analysis of the Economic Torts* (2nd edn, 2010), 80–2.

the balance of arguments regarding the need for, or rejection of, a targeted harm test, the law is now clear on this matter.

(2) Unlawful means

Meaning The question of what constitutes 'unlawful means' in the context of the economic torts has been a controversial issue. However, for the purposes of the present tort, it is now possible to state with some confidence what will be taken to amount to unlawful means. According to Lord Hoffmann in *OBG Ltd v Allan*, unlawful means generally should be taken to constitute 'acts against a third party . . . [that] are actionable by that third party'.[50] Examples would include breaches of contract, common law torts,[51] any actionable breach of statutory duty, and (probably) breaches of equitable obligations.[52] One qualification is 'that they will also be unlawful means if the only reason why they are not actionable is because the third party has suffered no loss'.[53] He then gave as an example *National Phonograph Co Ltd v Edison-Bell Consolidated Phonograph Co Ltd*.[54] In that case the defendant intentionally caused loss to the claimant by fraudulently inducing a third party to act to the claimant's detriment. Importantly, however, the party who was actually defrauded *did not* suffer any loss. Nonetheless, the fact that the third party had been induced to act in the way that he did was sufficient to constitute unlawful means.

Two general points can be made about this conception of unlawful means. The first is that, because the tort requires an actionable (or potentially actionable) wrong to be committed against an intermediary, the tort of causing loss by unlawful means *always* involves three parties. This distinguishes it from the torts of intimidation and unlawful means conspiracy where two-party liability is at play. The second point is that there now seems little to ground either Lord Nicholls' dissenting view that the term unlawful means 'embraces all acts a defendant is not permitted to do whether by the civil or criminal law',[55] or the idea that an agreement made in restraint of trade will suffice. In respect of the latter, it seems we must now regard as wrong earlier cases[56] suggesting that such agreements—which are void and therefore legal nullities—would constitute unlawful means.

Financial interest In *OBG Ltd v Allan*, Lord Hoffmann was not content to control liability for this tort by virtue of a restrictive conception of unlawful means—one which entails only (potentially) actionable civil wrongs. He also insisted that the third party must be one in whom the claimant has a financial interest and that, bearing in mind

---

[50] [2008] 1 AC 1, at [49].

[51] Intimidation is a prime candidate here since this tort necessarily involves D coercing X into acting in a particular way, including those that harm C: see, eg, *Rookes v Barnard* [1964] AC 1129.

[52] See, eg, *Jarman & Platt Ltd v I Barget Ltd* [1977] FSR 260; *Indata Equipment Supplies Ltd v ACL Ltd* [1998] FSR 248, at 264. Cf *AI Enterprises Ltd v Bram Enterprises Ltd* [2014] SCC 12 (advocating a narrow approach and specifically excluding breaches of statute).   [53] [2008] 1 AC 1, at [49].

[54] [1908] 1 Ch 335. See also *Lonrho plc v Fayed* [1990] 2 QB 479, at 489.

[55] [2008] 1 AC 1, at [162].

[56] Eg, *Daily Mirror Newspapers Ltd v Gardner* [1968] 2 QB 762; *Associated British Ports v TGWU* [1989] ICR 557.

this interest, the unlawful means must cause loss to the claimant by interfering with the third party's liberty to deal with the claimant. The importance of this rider is that it enabled his Lordship to leave intact two cases involving the infringement of intellectual property rights (which, naturally, would be actionable wrongs in the hands of the intellectual property rights holders). The first was *RCA v Pollard*;[57] the second, *Oren v Red Box Toy Factory Ltd.*[58] At the heart of both cases was the fact that the defendant's infringement of a third party's intellectual property right resulted in harm to a claimant who was an exclusive licensee (ie, the only person permitted lawfully to exploit the intellectual property in question). In both cases, the defendant's infringement of the third party's intellectual property right did 'nothing which affected the relations between the owner and the licensee' and, therefore, fell outside the strictures of Lord Hoffmann's rider in *OBG*. We might note *en passant* that it would not have been necessary to introduce the rider had the House of Lords made the test for intention for this tort one of targeted harm.[59]

(3) Harm

'Causing loss' One thing that has never been in doubt is that the claimant must be able to show that he has suffered harm in order to invoke this tort. But quite what form that harm should take was undecided prior to the House of Lords' decision in *OBG Ltd v Allan*. According to some of the earlier case law, the tort concerned interference with trade or business.[60] Nowadays, however, the preferred name for the tort simply is that of causing loss by unlawful means.[61]

Financial interests However the simple reference to 'causing loss' is apt to mislead as to the kind of harm that can support liability. This is because Lord Hoffmann's rider on unlawful means makes it clear that the tort protects only financial interests. (Recall his insistence that the third party through whom the claimant is injured must be someone 'in whom the claimant has an economic interest'.) What we are left with, then, is a tort of causing loss to financial interests by unlawful means: a tort with a wider range of application than one that simply protects trade or business, but a tort of insufficient scope to encompass, say, physical injury. That being so, if A intimidates B so that B desists from buying C's house from him, it is probable the tort could be invoked even though C is not a commercial property dealer. Conversely, however, if A intimidates B into punching C, this tort is not engaged.[62]

Other interests Whether it is appropriate for the tort's remit to be limited by reference to financial interests is an interesting question. An argument can be made for using

---

[57] [1983] Ch 135.   [58] [1999] FSR 785.

[59] For a full account, see H Carty, *An Analysis of the Economic Torts* (2nd edn, 2010), 97.

[60] See the 12th edition of this book for examples.

[61] See *Meretz Investments NV v ACP Ltd* [2008] Ch 244.

[62] There is, however, the possibility of being held jointly liable along with the party intimidated on the basis that he *procured* the commission of a battery, for procuring the commission of a tort is a settled basis for the imposition of joint liability: see, eg, *Wah Tat Bank Ltd v Chan* [1975] AC 507.

this tort as a platform for the 'development of general principles of liability in respect of harm suffered intentionally'.[63] At the heart of such a development would be two main considerations: (1) the infliction of intentional harm;[64] and (2) the requirement that unlawful means be used. These factors do not dictate the limitation of this tort to cases in which financial harm has been caused. Nor is it easy to see why financial interests—which are generally found at the bottom end of the hierarchy of protected interests in tort law—should be singled out for special treatment. Indeed, a cogent argument can be made that this tort could become a 'general principle of liability in respect of harm inflicted intentionally as a counterpart to the generalisation of the reasonable care or reasonable behaviour standard in the non-intentional sphere'.[65]

(4) Justification

A matter not directly considered by the House of Lords in *OBG Ltd v Allan* is whether a defence of justification can be raised in relation to this tort. Academic views on the matter are divided. But the present submission is that, so long as the test for unlawful means is that of an actionable (or potentially actionable) civil wrong, there is no conceptual space for the putative defence of justification to occupy. To explain: if the general law says that the unlawful means in a certain case constitute an actionable tort, that carries with it the idea that what the defendant did was not excusable by reference to the general law on tort law defences. That being the case, there is no obvious reason why a more specious defence should be crafted simply to suit this tort. In any event, it is hard to disclaim the idea that 'there can be no justification for a civil wrong'.[66]

Section 4 Lawful means conspiracy

(A) Introduction

Tortious conspiracy takes two forms. The first form—sometimes called 'simple conspiracy'—is that of lawful means conspiracy. It is styled thus because of the absence of any requirement that the defendant must show the use of unlawful means on the part of the conspirators. Many consider the tort to be highly anomalous,[67] despite the fact it occupies its place within the common law on the repeated authority of the House of Lords.[68] It is said to be (1) the fact of combination; in tandem with (2) the intentional

---

[63] P Sales and D Stilitz (1999) 115 LQR 411, 436.
[64] *Associated British Ports v TGWU* [1989] ICR 557. In this case Stuart-Smith LJ made it clear (at 586) that 'deliberate and intended damage' is required. That view also appears in: *Douglas v Hello! Ltd (No 6)* [2006] QB 125; *Mainstream Properties v Young* [2005] EWCA Civ 861.
[65] P Sales and D Stilitz (1999) 115 LQR 411, 430.
[66] *Shearson Lehman Hutton Inc v Maclaine Watson & Co* [1989] 2 Lloyd's Rep 570, at 633.
[67] In *Lonrho Ltd v Shell Petroleum Co Ltd (No 2)* [1982] AC 172 the HL recognised simple conspiracy as a 'highly anomalous cause of action', but one too well established to be discarded.
[68] *Mogul Steamship Co v McGregor* [1892] AC 25; *Quinn v Leathem* [1901] AC 945; *Crofter v Veitch* [1942] AC 435.

infliction of harm; in furtherance of (3) an illegitimate purpose that renders the conspirators' acts tortious.

(B) Elements of the tort

(1) Combination

The requirement of combination generally is straightforward. Combinations with which the tort of conspiracy is concerned can take many forms. Examples include traders combining to ward off the competition of a rival trader;[69] trade union officials combining to compel an employer to dismiss a non-union employee;[70] an employers' federation and a trade union combining to deprive a worker belonging to another union of his job so as to promote collective bargaining in the industry concerned;[71] and employees collectively threatening a strike unless the employer dismissed a worker belonging to another union.[72]

Directors and their company can conspire together since the company is a separate legal entity.[73] However, to establish such a conspiracy, it is essential to identify the relevant 'mind and will' of the company (normally found in the director who had management or control over the particular act in question).[74] The relevant mind and will of the company will be located in different people for different purposes (often discoverable from the company's articles of association).[75]

(2) Preponderantly illegitimate purpose

Exceptional form of liability The second ingredient of this tort is that of illegitimate purpose. The claimant must prove that the parties combining against him were preponderantly seeking to secure an illegitimate end. In other words, it is the fact that the conspirators' acts are animated by an injurious motive that is pivotal. In this respect, the tort of lawful means conspiracy contradicts the fundamental proposition in *Allen v Flood*[76] that motive alone cannot render illegal that which would otherwise be legal conduct. The contradiction inheres in the fact that, in lawful means conspiracy, defendants effectively are being held liable for doing in combination that which any one of them would be within their rights to do if acting alone. Nonetheless, as one judge has explained, the requirement of preponderantly harmful motive is intended to secure the proper 'balance between the defendant's right to exercise his lawful rights and the plaintiff's right not to be injured by an injurious conspiracy'.[77]

Proof of predominant purpose Much as it is an easy thing to state that the defendants' acts must be preponderantly calculated to achieve an illegitimate purpose, it might be

---

[69] *Mogul Steamship Co v McGregor, Gow & Co* [1892] AC 25.   [70] *Quinn v Leathem* [1901] AC 495.
[71] *Reynolds v Shipping Federation Ltd* [1924] 1 Ch 28.   [72] *White v Riley* [1921] 1 Ch 1.
[73] *Belmont Finance Corpn Ltd v Williams Furniture Ltd* [1979] Ch 250. And see *Taylor v Smyth* [1991] 1 IR 142 (conspiring with companies under D's control).
[74] *El Ajou v Dollar Land Holdings plc* [1994] 2 All ER 685. See also *Bilta (UK) Ltd (in liq) v Nazir* [2015] 2 WLR 1168 ff (discussion of attribution in context of a claim of *ex turpi causa*).
[75] *Meridian Global Funds Management Asia Ltd v Securities Commission* [1995] 3 All ER 918, at 923.
[76] [1898] AC 1.   [77] *Crofter v Veitch* [1942] AC 435, at 462.

rather difficult to establish this. *Crofter Hand Woven Harris Tweed Co Ltd v Veitch*[78] exemplifies the problem:

> Cs produced tweed cloth on an island in the Outer Hebrides. Only the weaving of their cloth took place on the island; they imported yarn from the mainland. Other firms had their cloth spun as well as woven on the island. Ds were officials of the union to which most of the spinners employed in the island mills belonged. Their employers informed Ds that the competition of Cs prevented them from raising wages. Ds (assumed by some of their Lordships to be acting in combination with the mill-owners) instructed dockers at the island's port to refuse to handle yarn imported from the mainland and consigned to Cs. Without breaking their contracts of employment, the dockers (who were members of the same union as Ds) consented. Cs sought to stop this embargo on the ground that it was an actionable conspiracy. They failed. The House of Lords held that the predominant purpose of the combination was the legitimate promotion of Ds' own interests.

Inevitable consequences An issue arises where the defendants are aware that damage to the claimant is an inevitable consequence of their collective action. But being aware of an inevitable consequence cannot be taken to be synonymous with having that consequence as one's predominant purpose. The House of Lords made this point in *Lonrho Ltd v Shell Petroleum Co Ltd (No 2)*:[79]

> Ds breached sanctions orders against the 'illegal' regime in Rhodesia, substantially increasing their profits at C's expense. Rejecting the claim in conspiracy, the House of Lords found that, even if unlawful means were used to further the conspiracy, no liability arose unless Ds acted 'for the purpose not of protecting their own interests but of injuring the interests of [C]'.[80]

Absence of predominant purpose Once the bona fides of the defendants are established, it is irrelevant that the damage inflicted to secure their purposes is disproportionately severe.[81] Nor does it matter that the defendants are glad as an incidental matter to see the claimant suffer a loss.[82] Furthermore, there is no need for the conspirators to share a common, justificatory, predominant purpose: 'it is sufficient if all the various combining parties have their own legitimate trade or business interests to gain, even though these interests may be of differing kinds'.[83] This dictum tends to limit considerably the practical utility of this tort, since most people have individual (as opposed to collective) interests to pursue.

---

[78] [1942] AC 435, at 462.   [79] [1982] AC 173.   [80] [1982] AC 173, at 189.

[81] *Crofter Hand Woven Harris Tweed Co Ltd Veitch* [1942] AC 435, at 447. Cf *Trollope & Sons v London Building Trades Federation* (1895) 72 LT 342.

[82] In *Crofter Hand Woven Harris Tweed Co Ltd v Veitch* [1942] AC 435, Lord Wright said (at 471): 'I cannot see how the pursuit of a legitimate practical object can be vitiated by glee at the adversary's expected discomfiture.' Cf ibid at 444–5 and 450. Yet the court must inquire into the state of knowledge of Ds whenever it is relevant for the ascertainment of their purpose: *Huntley v Thornton* [1957] 1 All ER 234; *Bird v O'Neal* [1960] AC 907.

[83] *Crofter Hand Woven Harris Tweed Co Ltd v Veitch* [1942] AC 435, at 453. Cf *McKerman v Fraser* (1931) 46 CLR 343.

(3) Harm

It is the securing of the defendants' preponderantly illegitimate purpose that forms the gist of this tort. Accordingly, resulting harm on the part of the claimant is an essential requirement, and it has been held that 'a plaintiff in a civil action for conspiracy must prove actual pecuniary loss'.[84]

Section 5 Unlawful means conspiracy

(A) Introduction

The main difference between unlawful and lawful means conspiracy is the obvious one that, in the former, the claimant must show that the defendant used unlawful means to cause harm to the claimant. Another difference is that, in unlawful means conspiracy, the defendant's principal motive is irrelevant. Thus, in *Lonrho v Fayed*,[85] Lord Bridge affirmed that, although both forms of civil conspiracy involve intention to harm, in unlawful means conspiracy that intention need not be the defendant's predominant purpose. Indeed, his Lordship explained that, even if the defendants can show that their main purpose was to protect or advance their own interests, this will not prevent their liability.

The question is whether there is a need for unlawful means conspiracy. If A and B combine to do something tortious to C, their liability could be dealt with as an issue of joint tortfeasance. However, if the unlawful means by which loss is inflicted on C do *not* amount to a tort, the joint tortfeasance doctrine has no application. That being the case, the independent vitality of this tort can be ascertained only by reference to what counts as unlawful means. This, and the other chief ingredients of the tort, need, therefore, to be elucidated.

(B) Elements of the tort

(1) Combination

Just as with lawful means conspiracy, this tort demands that there be combination between the conspirators. However, whereas conspirators in the lawful means version of the tort need not share the same purpose, the conspirators in unlawful means conspiracy must pursue a 'common design'.[86] A mere association with a primary tortfeasor (or with an extant group of conspirators) will not suffice.[87] Thus, in one case[88] in which X sold recording equipment and Y used it to tape copyright material, there was no prospect of X being held liable for the commission of this tort since X had an interest only in selling the recording equipment and was indifferent to the uses

---

[84] *Lonrho v Fayed (No 5)* [1993] 1 WLR 1489, at 1494.   [85] [1992] 1 AC 448.
[86] *Rookes v Barnard* [1964] AC 1129, at 1211.   [87] *Sandman v Panasonic UK Ltd* [1998] FSR 651.
[88] *CBS Songs Ltd v Amstrad* [1998] AC 1013.

to which it was put after it had been sold. It has been held, further, that a common design is to be identified in concerted action done in furtherance or pursuit of a common purpose.[89]

(2) Intention

While there is no doubt that the tort of unlawful means conspiracy requires proof of intention, the meaning of 'intention' in this context has proven to be somewhat elusive. In the past, there was no settled view.[90] Nor was there a single test of intention to emerge from *Total Network v Revenue and Customs Commissioners*.[91] Lord Walker adopted the ends/means test propounded in *OBG Ltd v Allan* (and discussed earlier),[92] while Lords Hope and Mance favoured a test of targeted harm.[93] Since then, the Court of Appeal has suggested twice that the appropriate test of intention in relation to unlawful means conspiracy involves the *OBG Ltd v Allan* test.[94] In either case, where the claimants comprise a *group* of persons, it must be possible to connect the defendant's intentions to their sufferance of harm with some specificity. Although clear guidance has not been given on the matter, this would seem to require that the individual members of the group be known *and* that it be probable that each will suffer loss as a result of the defendants' use of unlawful means.[95] These matters could not be proven in a case brought by hundreds of shippers of airfreight against airlines found to have colluded in setting airfreight costs, especially because there was every likelihood that the shippers could pass the costs on down the chain of customers.[96]

(3) Unlawful means

Total Network The 'concept of unlawful means, as used in the tort of conspiracy to injure by unlawful means, marks the boundaries within which hostile action taken by combinations of persons who intend to inflict harm on a claimant will be regarded as legitimate and lawful, despite their hostile intention'.[97] As noted already, if 'unlawful means' is treated as a mere synonym for some or other tort, then unlawful means conspiracy amounts to no more than an instance of joint tortfeasance. If, however, unlawful means is a term that is to be construed more broadly, the tort does possess free-standing significance. The leading case is *Total Network v Revenue and Customs Commissioners*:

> D had been involved in a complex financial scam known as a carousel fraud. Its point was to cheat the Inland Revenue out of VAT. Importantly, the carousel fraud involved no known tort; but it did amount to the common law crime of defrauding the Inland

---

[89] *Unilever plc v Chefaro* [1994] FSR 135.

[90] Cf the different tests applied in: *Ware and De Freville v Motor Traders Association* [1921] 3 KB 40; *Lonrho v Fayed* [1992] 1 AC 448.   [91] [2008] 1 AC 1174.

[92] [2008] 1 AC 1174, at [100]. The same approach was adopted by the Court of Appeal in *Meretz Investments NV v ACP Ltd* [2008] Ch 244.   [93] [2008] 1 AC 1174, at [44] and [120], respectively.

[94] *Meretz Investments NV v ACP* [2008] Ch 244, at [146]; *Berryland Books Ltd v BK Books Ltd* [2010] EWCA Civ 1440, at [48].

[95] See *Emerald Supplies Ltd v British Airways plc (Nos 1 & 2)* [2016] Bus LR 145, at [167]–[170].

[96] *Emerald Supplies Ltd v British Airways plc (Nos 1 & 2)* [2016] Bus LR 145, at [170]. See also *WH Newson Holdings Ltd v IMI plc* [2014] Bus LR 156.

[97] *JSC BTA Bank v Ablyazov* [2017] QB 853, at [47].

> Revenue. The Revenue was unable to recover the lost VAT by recourse to any statute, so it turned, instead, to the tort of unlawful means conspiracy. The House of Lords found in its favour, holding that the criminal acts of the conspirators were sufficient unlawful means on which to found a cause of action.

The House of Lords in *Total Network* undoubtedly breathed new life into unlawful means conspiracy. In so doing, it alighted upon a conception of 'unlawful means' wide enough to embrace not merely (potentially) actionable civil wrongs, but criminal acts as well.

Caveat   However, the House of Lords in *Total Network* was *not willing* to treat *all* crimes as 'unlawful means'. Rather, it was insistent that criminal conduct which was 'wrongful for reasons which have nothing to do with the damage inflicted on the claimant' would not suffice.[98] Thus, although the crime of defrauding the Inland Revenue obviously had as its objective the protection of the claimant, this could not be said of all criminal offences—especially those which can be described as mere regulatory offences and which derive from statutes that have nothing to do with the protection of the interests or well-being of anyone in particular.[99] Unfortunately, their Lordships considered it 'unwise to attempt to lay down any general rule',[100] so whether any given crime will constitute unlawful means needs to be decided on a case-by-case basis.

Contempt of court   In more recent times, the Court of Appeal has accepted in *JSC BTA Bank v Ablyazov* that unlawful means extends to civil contempts of court by breaches of court orders.[101] Such contempts are not actionable at the instance of adversely affected parties unless they are deployed as part of an unlawful means conspiracy.

(4) Harm

Financial losses   In the tort of lawful means conspiracy a claimant must prove actual pecuniary loss. Although this proclamation was made in a case of lawful means conspiracy,[102] it is couched in terms broad enough to encompass also cases of unlawful means conspiracy. Bearing in mind that *Total Network* was dealt with on the basis of unlawful means conspiracy being an economic tort, there is no apparent reason to proceed on any other basis. Indeed, it has been held that injury to reputation falls beyond the scope of this tort.[103]

Additional harm-doing   A final point is that, in any case in which a conspirator joins an existing conspiracy, and thus helps add to the injury that has been visited upon the claimant already, that 'new' conspirator will be liable only for participation in inflicting harm that is suffered *after* the time he joined. He cannot be held liable for prior losses.[104]

---

[98]   [2008] 1 AC 1174, at [119].
[99]   This is not to say that statutory offences will *never* suffice: see [2008] 1 AC 1174, at [45] and [95].
[100]   [2008] 1 AC 1174, at [96].   [101]   [2017] QB 853, at [48].
[102]   *Lonrho v Fayed (No 5)* [1993] 1 WLR 1489, at 1494.
[103]   *Lonrho v Fayed (No 5)* [1993] 1 WLR 1489, at 1509.
[104]   *Bank of Tokyo-Mitsubishi UFJ Ltd v Baskan Gida Sanayi Ve Pazarlama AS* [2009] EWHC 1276 (Ch).

Section 6 Intimidation

(A) Introduction

Leading cases Intimidation involves the defendant using an unlawful threat success-fully to compel another to act (or refrain from acting) in a particular manner that will cause harm.[105] In the leading case of *Rookes v Barnard*,[106] the tort was considered to exist in two forms: a two-party form (where the claimant is the person actually intimi-dated) and a three-party form (where the claimant is someone at whom the defendant strikes through his intimidating an intermediary into acting to the claimant's detri-ment). However, since then, the two versions of the tort have been reconsidered, re-conceptualised, and repackaged. In *OBG Ltd v Allan*, the House of Lords was clear that the three-party version of the tort was but a mere sub-species of the tort of causing loss by unlawful means. Furthermore, Lord Hoffmann also cast doubt on the continued vitality of the two-party version,[107] though he stopped short of declaring it completely moribund. That being so, it is submitted that the two-party version of the tort survived the decision in *OBG v Allan*.

Limited use One factor that serves to shrink the practical importance of the two-party version of this tort is the Protection from Harassment Act 1997. Under sub-section 3(2) of that Act, damages are available not only for any anxiety caused by harassment of the victim, but also in respect of any financial loss resulting from that harassment. Thus, if harassment is of an intimidatory nature, so long as there has been the requisite course of conduct demanded by that Act, the claimant may well rely on the statute rather than the common law in seeking a remedy.

(B) Elements of the tort

(1) Unlawful threats

Threats Intimidation is committed whenever an unlawful threat is used deliberately[108] and successfully in order to cause another to do something they would not otherwise do, or refrain from doing something that they would otherwise do with the result (in either case) that harm is thereby caused.[109]

Unlawfulness In terms of the unlawfulness of the conduct threatened, the early author-ities on intimidation involved threats of violence.[110] But the modern tort of intimidation

---

[105] *News Group Newspapers Ltd v SOGAT '82 (No 2)* [1987] ICR 181.   [106] [1964] AC 1129.

[107] [2008] 1 AC 1, at [61]. He thought two-party intimidation raised 'altogether different issues' from those that had been considered central to his attempt to rationalise the economic torts in *OBG v Allan*. But his rea-soning is questionable. For, if the two-party version ought not to be seen as a tort (ie, an actionable or poten-tially actionable wrong), where are the unlawful means for the three-party version he was content to subsume within the unlawful means tort?

[108] *Chet Camp Fisheries Co-operative Ltd v Canada* (1995) 123 DLR (4th) 121, at 127.

[109] See *Hodges v Webb* [1920] 2 Ch 70; *J T Stratford & Sons Ltd v Lindley* [1965] AC 269.

[110] For a modern example see *Godwin v Uzoigwe* [1993] Fam Law 65.

is by no means confined to threats of this kind. Indeed it was defined in considerably broader terms than this in *Rookes v Barnard*,[111] where the facts were as follows:

> C was an employee of the airline BOAC who had resigned from his trade union. Ds were union officials. They threatened BOAC that all union members employed at BOAC would strike unless C were dismissed. BOAC consequently gave C notice and (lawfully) dismissed him. The House of Lords held that the breach of contract threatened by the union members was a sufficiently unlawful form of conduct to substantiate the tort.

Just a few years after the decision in *Rookes v Barnard*, Lord Denning ventured to suggest that any threat of 'violence, or a tort, or a breach of contract'[112] would amount to an unlawful threat for the purposes of this tort: the key being that, in each case, the defendant would be threatening to do something that he was not entitled lawfully to do. Indeed, as Lord Reid put it in *Rookes* itself: 'so long as the defendant only threatens what he has a legal right to do he is on safe ground'.[113]

Relationship with contract   However, the fact that *Rookes* established that a threat to break a contract would constitute an unlawful threat raised an interesting question about whether the tort was thus set up to usurp the ground occupied by contract law in a case of two-party intimidation. In particular, there might be a tension between the tort of intimidation and the doctrines of anticipatory breach and duress (depending on the nature of the threat). Quite how these potential tensions should be resolved is still underexplored in judicial terms (though academics have not shied away from offering a view[114]). The best judicial guide that exists is probably *Kolmar Group AG v Traxpo Enterprises Pvt Ltd*,[115] in which Christopher Clarke J held in a two-party setting that a threat to break a contract should sound in tort and result in an award of damages for intimidation.

Statutory and equitable obligations   A threat to commit a criminal act of violence will suffice always for the purposes of the tort of intimidation; but a threat to commit a breach of a penal statute is not per se sufficient: the statute must be intended to create private rights.[116] Following the logic of this, a threat to breach an equitable obligation might be sufficient.[117] But what is certainly clear is that words of idle abuse, or words of advice or warning, should not be regarded as threats of the requisite 'or else I will do X' variety.[118]

(2) Intention

The defendant must intend his threat to cause harm to the claimant. So, for example, in *News Group Newspapers Ltd v SOGAT '82 (No 2)*, Stuart-Smith J insisted that the

---

[111] [1964] AC 1129.   [112] *Morgan v Fry* [1968] 2 QB 710, at 724.
[113] *Rookes v Barnard* [1964] AC 1129, at 1168–9. See also *Hardie and Lane Ltd v Chilton* [1928] 2 KB 306 and *Ware and De Freville Ltd v Motor Trade Association* [1921] 3 KB 40.
[114] See, eg, R Bigwood (2001) 117 LQR 376.   [115] [2010] 2 Lloyd's Rep 653.
[116] *Lonrho Ltd v Shell Petroleum Co Ltd (No 2)* [1982] AC 173.
[117] *Dixon v Dixon* [1904] 1 Ch 161. See also *AS v Murray* [2013] NSWSC 733.
[118] See: *News Group Newspapers Ltd v SOGAT '82 (No 2)* [1987] ICR 181, at 204 ('idle abuse'); *Conway v Wade* [1909] AC 506, at 510 (warnings); and *J T Stratford & Sons Ltd v Lindley* [1965] AC 269 (advice).

claimant 'must be a person whom [the defendant] intended to injure'.[119] Since the House of Lords effectively has subsumed cases of three-party intimidation within the tort of causing loss by unlawful means, it must follow that the test for 'intention' in two-party intimidation cases is the same as that used in the unlawful means tort. The reason why this must follow can be explained in stages: if X threatens Y that, unless Y dismiss Z from his workforce, X will take unlawful action against Y, we know that this would, prior to *OBG Ltd v Allan*, enable Z to sue X on the basis of three-party intimidation. This is effectively what happened in *Rookes v Barnard*. We may also suppose, however, that employer Y is as dismayed to lose his former star employee Z, as Z is to lose his job. In other words, the self-same threat made by X to Y could just as well form the basis of an action for two-party intimidation. Given this, it would seem entirely indefensible to have a different test of intention depending on which person—Y or Z—was bringing the action. That being so, we might reasonably conclude that the test of whether the defendant intended to injure the claimant is the same in two-party intimidation as it is in the tort of causing loss by unlawful means. Now, since the test of intention is likely to be regarded as the ends/means test promulgated in *OBG Ltd v Allan*, a further potential tension between this tort and the law of contract arises. Suppose A threatens a breach of contract with B intending not just to disappoint B's immediate contractual expectations but also to bring about B's entire financial ruin. Suppose also that the prospect of bringing about B's ruination has only come to A's attention *since the formation of the contract*. In such circumstances, it is entirely possible that the damages available for intimidation would stretch beyond what would be available by reference to the remoteness rules in contract.[120] It is also conceivable that the intentional infliction of harm required by this tort may bring the prospect of exemplary damages into play.[121]

(3) Damage

Position unclear It has never been entirely clear for what kinds of damage one can sue in the tort of intimidation. The cases abound with statements like Lord Denning's proclamation that '[it is] the person damnified by the compliance [with the threat]' that can sue.[122] But unfortunately, such vacuous statements do not really limit or explain the kinds of damage in respect of which this tort can be invoked. All that can be said with confidence is that the types of harm that will be actionable *are not* limited to financial losses. So much is clear from *Godwin v Uzoigwe*,[123] in which case a young woman was intimidated not into suffering financial loss, but into working as a virtual slave in the home of the appellants.

Suggested approach Bearing in mind the lack of clear authority on what constitutes actionable harm for the purposes of this tort, two suggestions are made here.[124] The first is that intimidation is not *in the strict sense* a specifically economic tort (*Godwin* would

---

[119] [1987] ICR 181, at 204.

[120] In contract, the remoteness test is set according to things foreseeable by *both parties* at the time of the making of the contract.   [121] *Kuddus v CC of Leicestershire Constabulary* [2001] 2 WLR 1789.

[122] *Morgan v Fry* [1968] 2 QB 710, at 724.   [123] [1993] Fam Law 65.

[124] These suggestions have been followed up by a previous author of this work: J Murphy (2014) 77 MLR 33.

be inexplicable if it were). The second is that the gist of the tort is an infringement of the victim's right to free agency/autonomy, and that when financial loss occurs as a consequence, this is the best metric according to which the value of the infringed right can be measured. The cases are certainly littered with references to coercion; and it is one's autonomy, one's right to choose for oneself what one will do or desist from doing, that is infringed when one's will is overborne by intimidation. The mere making of a threat will not amount to intimidation. There must also be compliance, and it is the fact of this compliance in conjunction with the consequential harm to which this compliance gives rise that makes intimidation actionable.

This view is at loggerheads with the understanding of what makes intimidation unlawful proffered by perhaps the leading authority on this area of the law, according to whom what makes intimidation unlawful is the fact that 'threatened unlawful acts are equated with the unlawful acts themselves'.[125] But this latter view can hardly be right given that two-party intimidation is a tort that can be committed by virtue of a threatened breach of contract. If the threat were equated with an actual breach of contract, it would be hard to see why the intimidation in such a case should be regarded as a tortious (not contractual) wrong.

Advantage of suggested approach One (arguably) advantageous consequence of refusing to equate the threat with the actual act threatened, and preferring instead to see the infringement of autonomy as the gist of the tort, is the fact that it would enable a case of intimidation to be grounded even if the act threatened were not to be directed at the person threatened. Thus, if A threatened to shoot B's son if B did not comply with A's demand, A might perfectly well be regarded as having been coerced into acting the way that he did without ever being the immediate, prospective victim of the act threatened.

Conclusions

This chapter has examined what are, fairly loosely, referred to as the 'general economic torts'. What unites them is that they are all torts enlivened by the presence of some kind of intention in the defendant, that they involve the actual causation of loss, and that they have tended to be argued in cases involving business and financial disputes. An increasing amount of effort is being put into understanding these torts by both courts and scholars. The result seems to be an increasing recognition that a number of these torts should be freed from the limiting context of business and financial loss. While the unlawful means tort seems to capture a salient legal principle, we may yet discover within the 'economic torts' other, even more general, principles related, for example, to the causation of intended harm or to the abuse of rights, which are of a wider relevance.

---

[125]   H Carty, *An Analysis of the Economic Torts* (2nd edn, 2010), 120.

Problem question

Gems Ltd is in the business of selling precious stones. Business has been difficult lately. In order to boost business, Gems looks for new sources of precious stones that are cheaper to procure. Although illegal under the Economic Sanctions Act 2011, Gems agrees to source its diamonds from the Congo. Gems' director Sally flies to Congo in order to seal a deal. Her main concern is to undercut the prices offered by a rival business, Plus Diamonds Ltd. Sally's strategy is an instant success. Gems' newfound ability to sell low-cost diamonds at a greater level of profit reinvigorates Gems' business. It has the intended effect, as well, of reducing Plus Diamonds' profitability. Sally is able to persuade several of Plus Diamonds' employees to come and work for it. These employees faced dismissal at Plus Diamonds and sought to secure their employment status. One of those employees, Max, is an expert cutter whose services cannot easily be replaced by Plus Diamonds. Moreover, Plus Diamonds has had to renege on contracts with its sales agents. Plus Diamonds has offered the sales agents new contracts at a much lower rate of commission.

Advise Plus Diamonds and its agents as to any actions they might have for commission by Sally and/or Gems of the general economic torts.

 Visit http://www.oup.com/uk/street15e/ for answer guidance.

Further reading

BAGSHAW, 'Inducing Breach of Contract' in Horder (ed), *Oxford Essays in Jurisprudence, 4th Series* (2000)

CARTY, *An Analysis of the Economic Torts* (2nd edn, 2010)

DEAKIN AND RANDALL, 'Rethinking the Economic Torts' (2009) 72 *Modern Law Review* 519

LEE, 'Civil Conspiracy in the Corporate Context' (2016) 23 *Torts Law Journal* 257

MURPHY, 'Understanding Intimidation' (2014) 77 *Modern Law Review* 33

NEYERS, 'The Economic Torts as Corrective Justice' (2009) 17 *Torts Law Journal* 1

O'SULLIVAN, 'Unlawful Means Conspiracy in the House of Lords' (2008) 67 *Cambridge Law Journal* 459

SALES AND STILITZ, 'Intentional Infliction of Harm by Unlawful Means' (1999) 115 *Law Quarterly Review* 411

TAMBLYN, 'Lawful Act Conspiracy: Malice and Abuse of Rights' [2013] *Singapore Journal of Legal Studies*

WADDAMS, 'Johanna Wagner and the Rival Opera Houses' (1998) 117 *Law Quarterly Review* 431

WITTING, 'Intra-Corporate Conspiracy: An Intriguing Prospect' (2013) 72 *Cambridge Law Journal* 178

PART V
Torts involving strict or stricter liability

The common element in the torts discussed in this Part is that a defendant who is not merely being held accountable for the acts of an employee need not have committed the act complained of either intentionally or negligently. They are often referred to as torts of strict liability; yet as chapters 16–19 reveal, the liability threshold in some of these torts is less strict than that in others. This being so, it is better to see only some of these torts as involving pure strict liability, while the others impose merely stricter liability than that which characterises the archetypal, fault-based tort of negligence.

16

Product liability

KEY ISSUES

(1) Two strands of liability
Liability for a defective product that injures or causes damage to property other than that which is defective arises both in negligence and under the Consumer Protection Act 1987. The former is a fault-based form of liability; the latter is strict liability for defects—that is, liability that arises regardless of fault. Actions are available to the purchasers of goods, to users, and to bystanders.

(2) Tort of negligence
Liability for a failure to take care in the manufacture of a product causing personal injury was established in *Donoghue v Stevenson*.[1] It has been extended since to include others involved in the life cycle of products, including assemblers, repairers, testers, and certain

suppliers. In some cases, there might be an obligation to recall unsafe products.

(3) Limitations of negligence
The burden is upon the claimant to prove fault when suing in negligence and this can be a real hurdle, especially in cases of design defects.

(4) Consumer Protection Act 1987
The claimant is likely to find it more advantageous to bring an action for a defective product under the Act because it does not require proof of fault. The Act creates liability in producers and importers of products that are defective in that their safety is not such as consumers generally are entitled to expect and which thereby cause injury or damage to other property. A number of statutory defences to liability are available.

Section 1 Introduction

History The complex history of liability for loss or injury caused by defective products[2] illustrates well the gradual development and changing perceptions of the role of tort law and its interrelationship with the law of contract. The classical common law stance

---

[1] [1932] AC 562.

[2] See generally G Howells, *Product Liability* (2000); D Fairgrieve (ed), *Product Liability in Comparative Perspective* (2005). For developments in the US, see JCP Goldberg and B Zipursky, *The Oxford Introductions to US Law: Torts* (2010), ch 10.

towards faulty or useless goods was that of *caveat emptor*—let the buyer beware. The person buying goods was expected either to take steps to ensure that the goods were safe for use and value for money, or to make contractual arrangements which would provide her with a remedy should the goods prove to be defective. If she failed to protect herself, she would bear any resulting loss. In 1893, Parliament gave some protection to purchasers of goods via the first Sale of Goods Act. Then, in 1932, the House of Lords held in *Donoghue v Stevenson*[3] that the ultimate user of a product, in certain circumstances, would be able to sue in negligence the manufacturers of a product causing injury to her person or property. The extent of manufacturers' negligence liability has been further developed since and refined by the courts.

Legislative interventions In the meantime, Parliament strengthened the contractual rights of purchasers of goods[4] and services[5] with increasingly interventionist consumer protection laws.[6] And, in respect of certain types of goods, the criminal law was used to promote safety standards, and an action for breach of statutory duty[7] was created to allow individuals injured by goods in the specified categories to recover compensation from the manufacturers. Thus, by 1987 little survived of the *caveat emptor* principle. The social and legal climate had changed, but there was a confusing multiplicity of potential remedies available under a range of limited causes of action. Furthermore, the difficulty of proving negligence had become especially problematic in relation to products. Several official bodies[8] advocated therefore that manufacturers be made strictly liable for defective products.[9] The final victory for proponents of strict liability was won when on 25 July 1985 the Council of the European Communities issued a Directive[10] requiring all member states to implement a regime of strict liability for defective products. The UK Government responded by enacting the Consumer Protection Act 1987. The Act leaves untouched contractual claims against the retailer, the action in negligence, and, where appropriate, actions for breach of statutory duty. But the Act provides for claims in relation to personal injury and damage to private property only. Damage to business property and financial loss resulting from defective products are outside its remit.

Section 2 Consumer protection and the changing common law

(A) The limitations of contract law

Legislation The primary means invoked to protect consumers against faulty goods has traditionally been the law of contract. Today, the Sale of Goods Act 1979 and the

---

[3] [1932] AC 562.   [4] See the Sale of Goods Act 1979.
[5] See the Supply of Goods and Services Act 1982. Note also the Unfair Contract Terms Act 1977.
[6] Domestic consumer protection legislation has been strengthened further by the European Directive on Unfair Terms in Consumer Contracts 1993.   [7] Consumer Protection Act 1987, s 41.
[8] See *Law Commission Report on Liability for Defective Products* (1977); *Royal Commission on Civil Liability and Compensation for Personal Injury* (1978) (Cmnd 7054–1).
[9] For the reasons and relevant history, see the 10th edition of this book.   [10] 1985/374/EEC.

Consumer Rights Act 2015 incorporate into contracts of sales terms that require that they be of satisfactory quality[11] and fit for purpose.[12] The Supply of Goods and Services Act 1982 implies an identical term into contracts for services in the course of which goods are supplied.[13] Thus, if in the course of private dental treatment a dentist provides her patient with dentures which crumble within the week, it matters not whether any contract of sale for the dentures exists. The patient clearly had a contract for services under which unsuitable dentures were supplied. The statutory terms cannot be excluded against the consumer, liability is strict, and it is not limited to protection against injury to the person or property.

Problem of privity However, there are limitations to the effectiveness of contract as a means of general consumer protection against defective goods. These arise from the rules of privity of contract. A person who is not a party to a contract generally cannot benefit from that contract. So, if one receives as a gift an electric blanket bought by a friend, one has no contractual right to sue the retailer if it proves to be faulty; and where one purchases the faulty blanket oneself and the retailer goes out of business, one has no contractual claim against the wholesaler.[14] The Contracts (Rights of Third Parties) Act 1999 is unlikely to be of much use in this context, for that Act only confers rights on third parties in respect of whom it is clear that the contract was designed to confer a benefit and who are identified by name, class, or description in the contract.[15]

A number of devices have been used occasionally to evade the consequences of rules of privity. In *Lockett v Charles*,[16] for instance, a wife whose husband bought her a restaurant meal was able to claim for her food poisoning on the basis that her husband had acted as her agent. But the circumstances allowing for an inference of agency are limited. The same is true of the other devices that have been employed to avoid the privity rule. Thus, it is to tort law that a claimant generally must look if she did not purchase the product herself.

(B) The action for negligence

Restrictive attitude The development of liability in negligence for defective goods began with *Dixon v Bell*,[17] where a master, who entrusted a loaded gun to his young servant, was found liable to a third party injured by the servant firing the gun on the ground that the goods 'were in a state capable of doing mischief'. However, the court in

---

[11] Consumer Rights Act 2015, s 9; Sale of Goods Act 1979, sub-s 14(2). Under the 1979 Act, satisfactory quality means 'the standard that a reasonable person would regard as satisfactory taking into account any description of the goods, the price (if relevant) and all the other relevant circumstances'. So, an electric blanket that fails to heat a bed as expected would incur liability as easily as one that causes an electric shock or fire.

[12] Consumer Rights Act 2015, s 10; Sale of Goods Act 1979, sub-s 14(3).

[13] Supply of Goods and Services Act 1982, s 4.

[14] There may, however, be a collateral contract with the manufacturer to the effect that any guarantee given is effective in the hands of the ultimate purchaser. But even if there is no such collateral contract, Art 6 of Directive 1999/44/EC requires that manufacturers' guarantees should be legally enforceable.

[15] Contracts (Rights of Third Parties) Act 1999, sub-ss 1(1)(b) and (3).

[16] *Lockett v A & M Charles Ltd* [1938] 4 All ER 170.   [17] (1816) 5 M & S 198.

Langridge v Levy[18] declined an invitation to deduce from *Dixon v Bell* a general principle of liability for putting into circulation things 'of a dangerous nature'. In *Winterbottom v Wright*,[19] the driver was injured as a result of a defect in a coach. His action against the defendant (who supplied his employers with coaches and horses) failed because of privity of contract: the claimant could not take advantage of express terms in the contract as to the repair and maintenance of the coach. But what the court in *Winterbottom* failed to assess was the possibility of a separate and independent obligation arising in the tort of negligence.

Goods dangerous in themselves   Between 1851 and 1932, courts continued to deny any general duty to take care in the manufacture and distribution of goods, although some exceptional cases did hold that a duty existed. Eventually, liability was recognised in relation to: goods 'dangerous in themselves';[20] and known defects of which no warning was given by the supplier.[21] In addition, occupiers were held liable to their invitees in respect of appliances on their premises which proved to be defective.[22] The boundaries of these instances of liability for defects were unclear, and the need to prove knowledge of the defect in the second category frequently was fatal to the success of a claim.

Donoghue v Stevenson   The decision of the House of Lords in *Donoghue v Stevenson*[23] heralded a new age:

> C drank ginger beer manufactured by D, which a friend bought in a bottle from a retailer and gave to C. The bottle contained the decomposed remains of a snail which were not, and could not, be detected (as the bottle was opaque) until most of the ginger beer had been consumed. C became ill as a result and sued D. The House of Lords had to decide whether the facts disclosed a cause of action. They found for C by a majority of three to two.

Lord Atkin held that:

> a manufacturer of products, which he sells in such form as to show that he intends them to reach the ultimate consumer in the form in which they left him with no reasonable possibility of intermediate examination, and with the knowledge that the absence of reasonable care in the preparation or putting up of the products will result in an injury to the consumer's life or property, owes a duty to the consumer to take that reasonable care.[24]

Others among their Lordships in the majority had various reasons for reaching the same result.

---

[18] (1837) 2 M & W 519. The court nevertheless found for C on the ground of fraud.
[19] (1842) 10 M & W 109.   [20] See *Longmeid v Holliday* (1851) 6 Exch 761.
[21] *Heaven v Pender* (1883) 11 QBD 503, at 517; *Clarke v Army and Navy Co-operative Society* [1903] 1 KB 155.
[22] *Heaven v Pender* (1883) 11 QBD 503.   [23] [1932] AC 562.
[24] [1932] AC 562, at 599. This proposition will be called the 'narrow rule' in the case; and the 'neighbour principle', the broad rule.

(1) Range of defendants

Although Lord Atkin imposed liability on manufacturers only, later case law extended liability to, among others, assemblers,[25] repairers,[26] and suppliers of drinking water.[27] Mere suppliers of goods have been held liable also where their function went beyond simple distribution. For example, a car dealer selling vehicles reconditioned by him[28] and a retail chemist[29] failing to observe the manufacturers' instructions to test the product before labelling it were liable to injured users. Indeed, wherever the circumstances are such that a supplier normally would be expected to check a product, a duty to do so frequently is imposed. Second-hand car dealers will be expected to check the steering on used cars.[30] Wholesalers who fail to test a hair dye of dubious provenance will be held negligent also.[31]

A number of categories of person owing a common law duty of care will shoulder responsibility for compensating victims of defective products under the Consumer Protection Act 1987 as well. But this is not so of all those owing a common law duty of care. For example, suppliers failing to carry out tests can avoid liability under the statute simply by naming the person who supplied the goods to them. Repairers are beyond the scope of the statute.

(2) Products

Today, the term 'products' includes not only food and drink[32] but any product in normal domestic use. Underwear,[33] hair dye,[34] computer software,[35] installations in houses,[36] exterior staircases,[37] and motor cars[38] have been treated as proper subjects of a duty of care. Pre-*Donoghue v Stevenson* distinctions[39] between products 'dangerous in themselves' and other goods largely can be disregarded now.[40] The distinction remains relevant only in that the greater the potential danger inherent in a product, the more stringent must be the precautions to protect the user against injury or loss.[41]

(3) Ultimate 'consumer'

It follows from what has been said about the courts' willingness to expand negligence liability since *Donoghue v Stevenson* that a wide range of claimants may sue for injuries caused by defective products. Thus, in *Barnett v H and J Packer & Co*,[42] the proprietor

---

[25] *Malfroot v Noxal Ltd* (1935) 51 TLR 551.   [26] *Haseldine v C A Daw & Son Ltd* [1941] 2 KB 343.

[27] *Read v Croydon Corpn* [1938] 4 All ER 631; *Barnes v Irwell Valley Water Board* [1939] 1 KB 21.

[28] *Herschtal v Stewart and Ardern Ltd* [1940] 1 KB 155.   [29] *Kubach v Hollands* [1937] 3 All ER 907.

[30] *Andrews v Hopkinson* [1957] 1 QB 229. See also *Fisher v Harrods Ltd* [1966] 1 Lloyd's Rep 500.

[31] *Watson v Buckley, Osborne Garrett & Co Ltd* [1940] 1 All ER 174.

[32] *Barnes v Irwell Water Board* [1939] 1 KB 21.   [33] *Grant v Australian Knitting Mills Ltd* [1936] AC 85.

[34] *Watson v Buckley, Osborne, Garrett & Co Ltd* [1940] 1 All ER 174.

[35] *St Albans City and DC v International Computers Ltd* [1996] 4 All ER 481.

[36] *Haseldine v C A Daw & Son Ltd* [1941] 2 KB 343.   [37] *Targett v Torfaen BC* [1992] 3 All ER 27.

[38] *Herschtal v Stewart and Ardern Ltd* [1940] 1 KB 155.

[39] See *Dominion Natural Gas Co Ltd v Collins and Perkins* [1909] AC 640.

[40] See *Billings (AC) & Sons Ltd v Riden* [1958] AC 240.

[41] But that must not be construed as a rule distinct from negligence that there is a separate class of dangerous things which D must keep safe at her peril. See *Read v J Lyons & Co Ltd* [1947] AC 156, at 172–3.

[42] [1940] 3 All ER 575. Cf *Mason v Williams and Williams Ltd and Thomas Turton & Sons Ltd* [1955] 1 All ER 808.

of a sweet shop who was injured by a piece of metal protruding from a sweet recovered damages from the manufacturers. And in *Stennett v Hancock and Peters*[43] a bystander was able to sue after a defendant garage owner negligently reassembled the flange on the wheel of a lorry so that the flange came off, mounted the pavement, and injured him. The defendant was held liable for his negligent repair. In neither case was the claimant strictly a 'consumer'.

(4) Gratuitous supply

There seems to be no reason why the rule should not apply even where there is no sale of goods distributed in the course of a business, for example, where manufacturers supply free samples.[44] The liability for goods supplied in a domestic or social context is more disputable. Would a person who baked a fish pie for a charity fair be liable to the person who bought it, ate it, and succumbed to food poisoning? Would she be liable to her own children who ate a second pie made for their dinner?[45]

(5) Intermediate examination

Lord Atkin envisaged that a manufacturer should be liable where she intended her products 'to reach the ultimate consumer in the form in which they left' her 'with no reasonable possibility of intermediate examination'. If the rule is to apply, 'the customer must use the article exactly as it left the maker, that is in all material features, and use it as it was intended to be used'.[46] The effect of intermediate examination seems, therefore, to be this: if someone in the place of the manufacturer reasonably would contemplate that the defect in the goods would remain there at the time of their use by the claimant despite their passing through the hands of intermediaries, still she is liable.[47] The test is not whether intermediate examination is possible.[48] However, where an intermediary does test and certify a product as safe, she herself may incur negligence liability.[49]

This test with respect to defective goods is stricter than it might be for other forms of negligence. *Clay v A J Crump & Sons Ltd*[50] illustrates the point:

> Under the supervision of an architect, D, demolition contractors were demolishing a building and builders were to construct a new one. On D's advice a wall was left standing on the site. Subsequently, it collapsed on to C, an employee of the builders. D pleaded that the demolition contractors and their employees had had the opportunity of intermediate examination.

---

[43] [1939] 2 All ER 578.   [44] See *Hawkins v Coulsdon and Purley UDC* [1954] 1 QB 319, at 333.

[45] The narrow rule in *Donoghue v Stevenson* is probably inapplicable to gratuitous transfers. There are cases where liability has been established in respect of dangers known to the transferor: see, eg, *Hodge & Sons v Anglo-American Oil Co* (1922) 12 Ll L Rep 183; *Hurley v Dyke* [1979] RTR 265. Where the defect is not known to the transferor, however, there seems no reason in principle why the *broad rule* should not apply to gratuitous transfers.   [46] *Grant v Australian Knitting Mills Ltd* [1936] AC 85, at 104.

[47] [1936] AC 85, at 105; *Haseldine v C A Daw & Son Ltd* [1941] 2 KB 343, at 376. And see *Nitrigin Eireann Teoranta v Inco Alloys* [1992] 1 All ER 854.

[48] *Dransfield v British Insulated Cables Ltd* [1937] 4 All ER 382, holding the opposite, is best regarded as wrongly decided.

[49] *Perrett v Collins* [1998] 2 Lloyd's Rep 255.   [50] [1964] 1 QB 533.

This was held to be a case not of the narrow products rule but of the broad principle, so that the intermediate examination principle did not apply to defeat the claimant's claim against the architect.

(6) Preparation or putting up

There may be liability for a defect in the design of a product,[51] in the container, and/or in the labelling of the package.[52]

(7) Continuing duty of care

What if the product when first put on the market was not manufactured with any lack of care? Imagine that, at that time, on all the reasonably available evidence, the manufacturers could have discovered no defect in their product. Suppose, however, that evidence later transpires of risks to person or property posed by a latent defect. Do the manufacturers then owe any duty (1) to attempt to recall the goods; and/or (2) to warn consumers of the danger? It is clear that, even though originally the design of a product was undertaken with all due care, once a design defect becomes patent, the manufacturer is liable in negligence if she continues to produce and market the unsafe product.[53] In respect of unsafe products already in circulation, a continuing duty of care is owed to do whatever is reasonable to recall the defective product and warn users of the risk the defect might pose to their health and/or property.[54] As regards the duty to warn, it might be sufficient if the manufacturer passes the warning on to the intermediary (in that case, a doctor) who supplied the consumer (a patient) with the product rather than warning the consumer directly.[55] So far as the duty to recall goes, the recall procedure must be conducted non-negligently itself if further liability is to be avoided.[56]

(8) Recoverable loss

The duty of care in respect of defective products, in general, remains limited to a duty to avoid inflicting injury to the ultimate consumer's life or other property.[57] No liability is imposed in respect of damage to the defective product itself. Thus, if pistons in a car's engine fail causing further damage to the engine, there is no liability imposed in respect of that further damage.[58] This is purely financial loss and generally is not recoverable in negligence (as we saw in chapter 4).[59] It is only where non-integral parts of a car malfunction and cause further damage—such as a CD player that overheats and causes

---

[51] *Hindustan Steam Shipping Co Ltd v Siemens Bros & Co Ltd* [1955] 1 Lloyd's Rep 167.

[52] *Kubach v Hollands* [1937] 3 All ER 907.   [53] *Wright v Dunlop Rubber Co Ltd* (1972) 13 KIR 255.

[54] *Hobbs (Farms) v Baxenden Chemicals* [1992] 1 Lloyd's Rep 54; *Walton v British Leyland UK Ltd* (1978) *Times*, 13 July; *Rivtow Marine Ltd v Washington Ironworks* (1974) 40 DLR (3rd) 530.

[55] *Hollis v Dow Corning Corpn* (1995) 129 DLR (4th) 609.

[56] *McCain Foods Ltd v Grand Falls Industries Ltd* (1991) 80 DLR (4th) 252.

[57] The property damage must arise from a use to which D might reasonably have expected the property to be put. There was no liability where a waterproofing compound was lost when pails manufactured by D melted in the intense heat of Kuwait: *Aswan Engineering Establishment Co v Lupdine Ltd* [1987] 1 All ER 135.

[58] Analogy drawn from *Hamble Fisheries Ltd v Gardner & Sons Ltd, The Rebecca Elaine* [1999] 2 Lloyd's Rep 1.

[59] Eg, *Simaan General Contracting Co v Pilkington Glass Ltd (No 2)* [1988] QB 758; *Aswan Engineering Establishment Co v Lupdine Ltd* [1987] 1 All ER 135.

a fire—that an action *might* lie.[60] It would be inapt to conceive of a car without tyres; therefore the tyres are merely parts of an overall defective product. But where an accessory such as a CD player is added, it is possible to talk of product A (the CD player) damaging product B (the car). This example should not be confused, however, with a case in which defective product A is combined with product B to make product C—for example, where two products (a gas and a liquid) are combined to make a carbonated drink. In such a case it is inappropriate to talk of product A damaging product B. Instead, there is merely the production of a defective product, product C, in respect of which the defects are to be treated as irrecoverable, purely financial loss.[61]

(9) Proving negligence

Burden on claimant   The scope of liability for negligent manufacture, distribution, and repair that has evolved is now very considerable. Yet it is in the formidable task of proving a failure in care that claimants confront their greatest challenge. Frequently, this is difficult for a consumer or bystander to prove against a manufacturer.[62] The consumer's difficulties might be compounded further by problems of proving causation (for example, in claims relating to generic drugs). Yet the burden of proof remains with the claimant. As Lord Macmillan said in *Donoghue v Stevenson*: 'There is no presumption of negligence in such a case . . . nor is there any justification for applying the maxim *res ipsa loquitur*.'[63]

Inferences   However, the Privy Council modified this rigid approach in *Grant v Australian Knitting Mills Ltd*.[64] The claimant was concerned to prove that the dermatitis he contracted was caused by the presence of invisible excess sulphites in the underwear he purchased, which was made by the defendants. It was explained that the test was whether, on the balance of probabilities, it was a reasonable inference to be drawn from the evidence that the harm was so caused.[65] On the issue of negligence, it was said that:

> if excess sulphites were left in the garment, that could only be because someone was at fault. The appellant is not required to lay his finger on the exact person in all the chain who was responsible, or to specify what he did wrong. Negligence is found as a matter of inference from the existence of the defects taken in connection with all the known circumstances.[66]

Where the presence of the defect (in combination with the known circumstances) gives rise to an inference of negligence against the manufacturers, the burden shifts to the defendant to rebut that inference. This might be done either by pinpointing the exact cause giving rise to the defect and establishing that it does not arise from any failure in care, or by the manufacturer producing evidence as to its system and establishing

---

[60] For an analogous application of this so-called 'complex structure' approach, see *Jacobs v Moreton & Partner* (1994) 72 BLR 92.

[61] *Bacardi-Martini Beverages Ltd v Thomas Hardy Packaging Ltd* [2002] 1 Lloyd's Rep 62. See also, A Tettenborn [2000] LMCLQ 338.   [62] See G Schwartz (1991) 43 Rutgers LR 1013.

[63] [1932] AC 562, at 622.   [64] [1936] AC 85.   [65] [1936] AC 85, at 96–7.

[66] [1936] AC 85, at 101. Thus, where there is no evidence of a defect at the time of manufacture, and there exist several alternative explanations of why a malfunction occurred, liability will not be imposed on a manufacturer: see *Evans v Triplex Safety Glass Co Ltd* [1936] 1 All ER 283. Cf *Carroll v Fearon* [1998] PIQR P416.

that the system was consistent with taking due care. In *Daniels and Daniels v R White & Sons Ltd and Tabbard*,[67] the claimant was seriously injured when he drank lemonade containing a large quantity of carbolic acid. Presumably, the acid came from the washing process used by the defendant manufacturer. The judge accepted evidence of the precautions taken by the defendants to avoid such residues and found that the claimants had failed to prove negligence.

Design defects The problems faced by the claimant are compounded where the relevant defect is not a manufacturing defect but a design defect.[68] Design defects occur where the basic design of the product proves to be inherently dangerous. Although a manufacturing defect—where something goes wrong that does not normally go wrong—allows the possibility of the court inferring negligence, a similar inference cannot be made with respect to a design defect. In design cases, the claimant must prove (1) that the manufacturer should have been aware of the risk of the defect; and (2) that it reasonably could have avoided the defect. The issue all too often becomes one of whether, at the time the product was put on the market, scientific and technical knowledge available to the manufacturer should have enabled it to identify the danger. The classic example of the difficulties posed in this connection arises in the medical context where a drug is first marketed without foresight of its possible repercussions, but in the firm belief (based on the best available scientific knowledge) that it is safe. In such cases, an action in negligence requires a claimant to prove that, according to the state of scientific knowledge at the time of marketing, the manufacturer should have recognised the risk.[69]

(10) Proving causation

The next problem faced by the claimant is that of proving causation. Normally, this is done in accordance with the 'but for' test.[70] But in relation to certain types of product—especially pharmaceutical products—difficulties can arise.[71] Frequently the claimant will be suffering from an illness already. Where the claimant's condition deteriorates, or she suffers the onset of a related illness, the question is whether the drug caused the additional illness. Similarly, it is one thing to allege that a drug has caused injurious side-effects, but another to prove that it has done so. Thus, in *Loveday v Renton*[72] the action failed because it could not be proved on the balance of probabilities that the claimant's brain damage had been caused by the administration of the pertussis vaccine. This was despite the fact that it was known that the pertussis vaccine *could* cause brain damage in children. On the other hand, the courts need not abandon common sense. So in *Best v Wellcome Foundation Ltd*,[73] for example, the Irish Supreme Court held that

---

[67] [1938] 4 All ER 258.

[68] The construction/design dichotomy was rejected as an analytical device in *A v National Blood Authority* [2001] 3 All ER 289. But why? In terms of both conceptual distinctiveness and practical repercussions, the two are readily distinguishable.

[69] While it is very difficult to establish negligence in design defects, it is not absolutely impossible: see *Independent Broadcasting Authority v EMI Electronics and BICC Construction Ltd* (1980) 14 BLR 1.

[70] See ch 7.   [71] See, eg, A Porat and A Stein, *Tort Liability under Uncertainty* (2000).

[72] [1990] 1 Med LR 117.   [73] [1994] 5 Med LR 81.

causation could be inferred from the facts that the first sign of the claimant's brain dam-age followed closely on the heels of the administration of the pertussis vaccine and that there was no other plausible explanation of its cause.

Another danger for the claimant lies in the fact that, where it has developed suffi-cient knowledge that goods manufactured by the defendant are faulty *before* injury or damage to other property occurs, it might be unable to prove causation of that injury or damage. This might be because, in the case of a protective device such as an alarm system, the claimant with knowledge of the fault no longer can be said to be relying upon its protection, or, more generally, because the claimant's own conduct in respond-ing to its knowledge of the fault constitutes a *novus actus interveniens*[74] (as to which, see chapter 7). In less serious cases, the claimant might be subject to a reduction in damages for contributory negligence.[75]

(C) Action for breach of statutory duty

Before considering the strict liability regime contained in the Consumer Protection Act 1987, brief mention must be made of the possibility of an action for breach of statutory duty in respect of certain limited categories of goods. The Secretary of State has the power to make safety regulations prescribing detailed rules as to, among other things, the design, manufacture, and packaging of specified classes of goods.[76] Breach of such regulations is a criminal offence.[77] But the Consumer Protection Act 1987, section 4 also provides that an individual injured by a breach of the regulations will have an action for breach of statutory duty.[78] The regulations cover a limited class of goods only and the action for damages is dependent upon the defect in the goods having derived from breach of the regulations. The action is subject to the due diligence defence in section 39.

Section 3 The strict liability regime

(A) The Consumer Protection Act 1987

Three prefatory points must be borne in mind when considering the 1987 Act. First, the regime it contains derives from the European Union Directive of 12 July 1985.[79] And although the Directive allows for some variation in the rules throughout mem-ber states, the basic regime throughout the Union is the same. UK manufacturers

---

[74] *Howmet Ltd v Economy Devices Ltd* [2016] EWCA Civ 847, at [92]–[96] and [119], respectively. See also dictum in *D&F Estates Ltd v Church Comrs for England* [1989] 1 AC 177, at 208.

[75] *Howmet Ltd v Economy Devices Ltd* [2016] EWCA Civ 847, at [126].

[76] Consumer Protection Act 1987, s 41.

[77] See General Product Safety Regulations 2005 (SI 2005/1803).

[78] Note that it is only breach of specific safety regulations that gives rise to an action for breach of statutory duty and not infringement of the general safety duty provided for by the Consumer Protection Act 1987, s 10.

[79] 1985/374/EEC.

are subjected to the same strict liability rules as their European competitors.[80] Second, industry in the UK—particularly the pharmaceutical industry—persuaded the Government to adopt the controversial 'development risks' defence despite official reports on product liability advising against such a course of action. (As we shall see, the defence does much to undermine the strictness of liability under the Act.) Third, although it was possible to give direct statutory effect to the law, that was not done. Thus, where the interpretation of the 1987 Act is in doubt, it should be construed in the light of the Directive. And should there be any serious conflict between the provisions of the Act and the Directive, the dispute ultimately might have to be decided by the Court of Justice of the European Union.[81] That said, there is clear domestic judicial support for the view that the wording of the Directive should prevail in such cases.[82]

(B) Who can sue under the act?

Wherever a defect in a product wholly or partly causes death or personal injury, the victim or her dependants may sue under the Act.[83] The injured individual need not be a purchaser or even a direct user of the faulty goods. If defective brakes in a new car bought by A suddenly fail causing a road accident in which A, her passenger B, and C, a pedestrian, are injured seriously, all three can sue the car's manufacturer. Where a defective product causes damage to a baby before birth, the baby's representative may sue later in respect of its disabilities.[84] Moreover, although the Act is aimed primarily at protection against personal injuries and death, consumers can invoke its provisions also where a product causes damage to private property (including land) provided the amount to be awarded to compensate for that damage exceeds £275.[85] Damage to the product itself is excluded expressly;[86] and other forms of purely financial loss also clearly are irrecoverable.[87]

(C) On whom is strict liability imposed?

General Liability is not limited to manufacturers alone. Essentially, all those involved in the primary production and marketing of goods are made liable. Repairers and distributors who may owe consumers a duty of care at common law are generally outside

---

[80] Notably, the Court of Justice of the European Union has held that member states may not implement rules more stringent than those contained in the Directive (*European Commission v France* Case C–52/00, 25 April 2002), nor may they retain pre-existing rules that are more stringent than those in the Directive (*Sanchez v Medicina Asturiana SA* Case C–183/00, 25 April 2002).

[81] Interestingly, in *European Commission v UK* Case C–300/95 [1997] All ER (EC) 481, the Commission refused to accept that the UK's adoption of the development risk defence is, despite plausible arguments to the contrary, incompatible with Art 7 of the Directive.

[82] See *A v National Blood Authority* [2001] 3 All ER 289, at 297.

[83] Consumer Protection Act 1987, sub-s 2(1).   [84] Consumer Protection Act 1987, sub-s 6(3).

[85] See the Consumer Protection Act 1987, sub-s 5(4). By sub-s 5(3) property used for business purposes is excluded. See J Bell (1992) 20 Anglo-Am LR 371.   [86] Consumer Protection Act 1987, sub-s 5(2).

[87] Financial loss consequent upon physical injury or damage to private property should in principle, however, be recoverable.

the scope of the strict liability regime. The Act imposes liability on the following categories of persons:

Producers Liability is imposed on 'producers';[88] and producers are defined as: (a) manufacturers;[89] (b) in the case of products which are not made, but won or abstracted (for example, coal and minerals) the person who won or abstracted the product;[90] and (c) in respect of products which are neither made, nor won or abstracted (for example, crops), but where essential characteristics of the product are attributable to an industrial or other process, the person carrying out that process.[91]

Brands Liability is imposed on any person who brand names a product or by other means holds herself out as a producer.[92] This does not necessarily mean, however, that if you buy a food processor at Marks & Spencer which bears the brand name 'St Michael', and a part of the machine flies off and injures you, you may sue Marks & Spencer on this basis. Simply placing the 'St Michael' stamp on the processor probably is insufficient, since the company must hold itself out as having actually produced the product.

Importers Liability is imposed on any person importing a product into Europe from outside Europe.[93] Had you bought a Japanese food processor you need not concern yourself with the intricacies of suing in Japan; you can proceed against whichever Europe-based person imported it into Europe.

Component manufacturers The Directive expressly defines manufacturers of component parts as 'producers' so they are subject to strict liability too.[94] The Act achieves the same end by more tortuous means: namely, defining 'product' so as to embrace component parts.[95] The effect is illustrated simply. Should defective brakes in a new car fail causing personal injuries, the injured person may sue both the 'producer' of the finished product (the car manufacturer) and the 'producer' of the defective component (the manufacturer of the brakes). However, sub-section 1(3) provides that a supplier of the finished product shall not be deemed to be liable for defects in all component parts simply because she cannot name the actual manufacturer of each and every component.

Distributors Liability is also potentially imposed on distributors. Sub-section 2(3) provides that any supplier of a product will be liable to the injured person *unless* she complies with a request to name, within a reasonable time, the person supplying her with

---

[88] Consumer Protection Act 1987, sub-s 2(2)(a).   [89] Consumer Protection Act 1987, sub-s 1(2)(a).
[90] Consumer Protection Act 1987, sub-s 1(2)(b).
[91] Consumer Protection Act 1987, sub-s 1(2)(c). The cumbersome definition of this category of producer is explained by reference to the former exemption of primary agricultural produce from the regime instituted by the 1987 Act. This exemption was removed by the Consumer Protection Act 1987 (Product Liability) (Modification) Order 2000 (SI 2000/2771) giving effect to Directive 1999/34/EC.
[92] Consumer Protection Act 1987, sub-s 2(2)(b).
[93] Consumer Protection Act 1987, sub-s 2(2)(c). Note that a person importing a product into the UK from another member state is not made strictly liable under the Act. She might, however, be liable in negligence.
[94] Art 3(1).   [95] See the Consumer Protection Act 1987, sub-s 1(2).

the product. (Recall that a consumer might not know the identity of a manufacturer in a long chain of supply.) Compliance is not present where the supplier merely confirms that it is not the manufacturer without naming the manufacturer.[96]

In *O'Byrne v Sanofi Pasteur MSD Ltd*,[97] the Court of Justice of the European Union held upon a reference that pursuant to Articles 3 and 11 of the Directive it was open to a national court to treat a distributor of goods as the producer where the distributor is both a wholly owned subsidiary of the manufacturer and under the control of the manufacturer in that the latter determines when goods are put into circulation. It held that the separate legal status of the two entities was not to 'influence' the court and that 'the fact that the products are invoiced to a subsidiary company and that the latter, like any purchaser, pays the price, is not conclusive'.[98] The Supreme Court later held in *O'Byrne v Aventis Pasteur SA* that the UK distributor of a drug was a correct defendant to proceedings brought by an infant claimant and that there was no need to rely upon the power of substitution available under the Limitation Act 1980 to substitute the French manufacturer for the distributor.[99] The court explained:

> If [the manufacturer] APSA was indeed in a position to decide when the product was to be distributed, then [the distributor] APMSD would be integrated into the manufacturing process and so tightly controlled by APSA that proceedings against APMSD could properly be regarded as proceedings against the parent company, APSA.[100]

(D) Products

'Products' are defined in the Act[101] as 'any goods or electricity' and include component parts, certain substances,[102] and agricultural crops. In earlier drafts of the Directive, blood and human tissue were expressly excluded from the Directive, but it has been held since that blood and blood products do fall within its compass, even though the Directive and the Act are silent on the matter.[103] By contrast, the Act does not cover immovable property—that is, land and fixtures on land.[104] But products which become fixtures within immovable property—for example, central heating boilers—probably are within the scope of the Act.[105]

---

[96] *O'Byrne v Aventis Pasteur SA* Case C–358/08 (2009) 113 BMLR 1, at [57].

[97] *O'Byrne v Sanofi Pasteur MSD Ltd* Case C–127/04 (2006) 91 BMLR 175.

[98] *O'Byrne v Sanofi Pasteur MSD Ltd* Case C–127/04 (2006) 91 BMLR 175, at [30]–[31] (affd *O'Byrne v Aventis Pasteur SA* Case C–358/08 (2009) 113 BMLR 1). This would allow a national court, where appropriate, to substitute the parent company for the subsidiary in proceedings commenced in time against the subsidiary. For our purposes, the important point is obviously that a suit against the subsidiary is of itself *sufficient* for the purposes of the Directive (and the Consumer Protection Act 1987).

[99] *O'Byrne v Aventis Pasteur SA* [2010] 1 WLR 1412.

[100] [2010] 1 WLR 1412, at [34]. In other words, proceedings against the subsidiary were sufficient for the purposes of the Act.   [101] Consumer Protection Act 1987, sub-s 1(2).

[102] Eg, blood and blood products: see *A v National Blood Authority* [2001] 3 All ER 289.

[103] *A v National Blood Authority* [2001] 3 All ER 289.

[104] Liability for defectively constructed buildings remains subject to the general rules of negligence and the Defective Premises Act 1972.

[105] See the Consumer Protection Act 1987, sub-s 45(1) and Art 2 of the Directive.

(E) Defining 'defect'

Defect, not cause of defect Proof that a product resulted in injury is not sufficient to establish liability. The claimant must show also that *a defect in the product* caused the injury. So long as a defect is proved, there is no need for the claimant to prove the cause of the defect.[106] That is for the defendant to investigate and remedy. Carelessness per se is irrelevant. Thus, if a chef is badly cut when the blade from her new food processor flies off the machine, she will succeed in her claim simply on proof of the obvious: that the processor is unsafe and defective.

Definition 'Defect' is defined in section 3 of the Act in terms that there is a defect in a product if the safety of that product is not such as persons generally are entitled to expect.[107] It is important to note that the standard that a person is entitled to expect—perfection in some circumstances—might transcend the standard they do *in fact* expect.[108] In assessing what persons generally are entitled to expect, sub-section 3(2) provides that all the circumstances are to be taken into account, including:

(a) the manner in which, and purposes for which, the product has been marketed, its getup, the use of any mark in relation to the product and any instructions for, or warnings with respect to, doing or refraining from doing anything with or in relation to the product;

(b) what might reasonably be expected to be done with or in relation to the product; and

(c) the time when the product was supplied by its producer to another;

and nothing in this section shall require a defect to be inferred from the fact alone that the safety of a product which is supplied after that time is greater than the safety of the product in question.

It remains for the claimant to prove that, taking into account the criteria outlined in section 3, the product is defective. Hardly any product is entirely safe and free of risk. The test is whether the risk to person and property posed by the product in the context of its common use or uses exceeds what is generally acceptable. Take the example of a sharp knife marketed as a kitchen knife for chopping vegetables and packaged so as to be reasonably child-proof on display. If the knife cuts off the tip of one's finger, one cannot claim that the injury resulted from a defect. A sharp cutting edge is a risk one accepts as the price for a knife which does its job. But if the same knife were marketed as a 'Marvellous Magic Dagger' and a child should cut herself, the defect would be easier to prove: a risk to children in such a product (clearly aimed at children) would be generally unacceptable. Ultimately, the question is one of whether the manufacturer ought to issue a warning as to dangers one would not expect the product to present. If the danger is both obvious and inherent, and if it is part and parcel of what the consumer would expect, there is no defect. Thus, hot coffee which carries the inevitable potential to scald is not a defective product.[109]

---

[106] *Ide v ATB Sales Ltd* [2009] RTR 8, at [19].   [107] See generally A Stoppa (1992) 12 LS 210.
[108] See *A v National Blood Authority* [2001] 3 All ER 289.
[109] *B v McDonald's Restaurants Ltd* [2002] EWHC 409.

Risk–benefit The test for a defect set out in sub-sections 3(2)(a) and (b) might involve the courts in risk–benefit analysis. This can be illustrated by examples of liability for drugs.[110] Imagine a new and effective antibiotic is introduced. In 99.5% of cases it works well with fewer side-effects than other antibiotics. But 0.5% of consumers develop serious kidney damage caused by the drug. If an identifiable group of persons should or could have been foreseen as susceptible to damage, the failure to warn doctors of the potential allergic reaction might conclude the issue of defect.[111] But in cases where no such reaction is foreseeable, much might turn on the nature of the drug and the condition it is designed to combat. Thus, while a minor new tranquilliser posing a risk of liver damage to a very small group probably would be found defective, an AIDS drug designed to prolong sufferers' lives probably would justify a much higher degree of risk to life and health. Where the consumer of the drug faces a prospect of almost certain and painful death, any product offering a realistic hope of cure or palliation generally may be thought acceptable, even if it is inherently dangerous to some of its users. Existing chemotherapy treatments, for example, fit this analysis.

Relevant time Sub-section 3(2)(c) of the Act warrants separate consideration. It has two main implications. First, the time when the product was put into circulation obviously is relevant to determine whether the defect was inherent in the product or merely the result of 'fair wear and tear'. Thus, when a child-seat is eight years old and has been used by three different children, can it be expected to be as safe as when new?[112] Second, sub-section 3(2)(c) provides also that safety standards must be judged by the generally acceptable standards at the time at which the product was put on the market, and not with hindsight, according to standards prevailing when the claim reaches court. Thus, a very old car without rear seat belts ought not to be regarded as defective *purely because* of that absence.

In *Pollard v Tesco Stores Ltd*,[113] the Court of Appeal held that the question of what persons generally are entitled to expect could be determined without reliance upon a published technical standard existing at the time of the accident. The case concerned the ease with which a young child could open a bottle of dishwasher powder. A British Standard established the torque which such a bottle should have required to be opened. Yet this was not decisive, in part for the obvious reason that most members of the public would not have any knowledge of the BS torque measure.[114] The court set the relevant expectation as being that the bottle should be 'more difficult to open than an ordinary screw top', which it was, and so there was no defect.[115]

In relation to construction and presentation defects, strict liability probably will be easy to establish. Where the manufacturing process breaks down—for example, where snails get into ginger beer bottles—the product will be patently defective. Equally, where

---

[110] See C Newdick (1985) 101 LQR 405. For a more straightforward example, see *Piper v JRI Manufacturing Ltd* (2006) 92 BMLR 141.

[111] By analogy with *A v National Blood Authority* [2001] 3 All ER 289, and the emphasis placed on strict liability in that case, it is conceivable that even a 0.05% risk would not excuse the manufacturer from liability.

[112] See Clark (1985) 48 MLR 325.

[113] [2006] EWCA Civ 393, criticised in D Fairgrieve and G Howells (2007) 70 MLR 962, at 973.

[114] [2006] EWCA Civ 393, at [16]–[18].   [115] [2006] EWCA Civ 393, at [18].

instructions on use are inadequate, or warnings as to use fail to make the consumer safe, a defect will be easy to establish.[116] The need to engage in a rigorous examination of risks and benefits of a product generally will be reserved for design defects[117] where the implications for industry of design defects potentially are much more profound.[118]

The question of what the defendant could (reasonably or otherwise) have done to eliminate or reduce the risks will be irrelevant under the 1987 Act.

(F) General defences

Statutory defences The Consumer Protection Act 1987, section 4 provides several defences to strict liability. They include the following:

(1) The defect is attributable to compliance with any requirement imposed by legislation (whether domestic or European).[119] The defence is not available where there are no statutory rules on how the product is to be made, but there are rules requiring licensing of the product by a public body before it can be marketed.

(2) The defendant proves she never supplied the product to another[120]—for example, if experimental drugs are stolen from a drug company's laboratory and sold by the thieves.

(3) The defendant did not supply the goods in the course of business.[121] Thus, the defendant is not strictly liable for defects in the food she serves to colleagues at a dinner party.

(4) The defendant proves that the defect did not exist in the product when it was supplied by the defendant to another.[122] Thus, a chocolate manufacturer would not be liable for chocolates injected with poison on the supermarket shelves by some third party.

(5) Where the defendant makes components, she will not be liable where the defect arose in the finished product and was caused by the faulty design of the finished product or inadequate installation of D's component into the finished product by the manufacturers of that product.[123]

Contributory negligence In addition to the defences provided for by section 4 of the Act, sub-section 6(4) provides that the contributory negligence of the consumer is a defence under the Act. Two difficult questions arise, however. The Law Reform

---

[116] If, however, a warning leaflet is lost, or a consumer chooses not to replace a lost leaflet, the manufacturer cannot be held responsible: *Worsley v Tambrands Ltd* [2000] PIQR P95.

[117] See, eg, *Abouzaid v Mothercare (UK) Ltd* 2000 WL 1918530, where Pill LJ thought the question for the court was one of whether the public could legitimately expect a higher degree of safety from the product than that which was actually present.

[118] Compensating ten victims of a freak construction defect is a less daunting prospect than compensating the thousands who have suffered injury before a design defect became patent.

[119] Consumer Protection Act 1987, sub-s 4(1)(a); eg, drugs which must be licensed under the Medicines Act 1968.　　　　　　　　　　　　　　　　　　　[120] Consumer Protection Act 1987, sub-s 4(1)(b).

[121] Consumer Protection Act 1987, sub-s 4(1)(c).　　[122] Consumer Protection Act 1987, sub-s 4(1)(d).

[123] Consumer Protection Act 1987, sub-s 4(1)(f).

(Contributory Negligence) Act 1945 provides that when a finding of contributory negligence is made, apportionment of responsibility between the claimant and defendant (and hence the level of damages) is based on relative fault. But where the defendant is strictly liable, and the claimant has been careless of her own safety, does this mean that the claimant generally will have to bear the lion's share of responsibility, or will the courts have to revert to considering evidence of want of care on the part of the defendant?

More problematic still is the matter of defining the circumstances in which a product that is put to improper use is evidence of contributory negligence. Imagine a stepladder is bought for cleaning windows. The 17-year-old daughter of the purchaser uses it to build an assault course. After a 14-stone friend of hers has thundered across it, the wood cracks as the daughter herself is on the ladder. She falls and breaks a leg. Is she guilty of a degree of contributory negligence, or was the ladder put to a use that it generally would not be expected to withstand (in which case it may not even have been defective)?

(G) The 'development risks' defence

Statutory defence The incorporation of the development risks defence[124] into the Act via sub-section 4(1)(e) is the most controversial part of the legislation. Permitting member states to incorporate such a defence was a compromise by the European Community in order to end the long-drawn-out process of agreeing to implement strict liability at all. Sub-section 4(1)(e) provides that a defendant shall not be liable where she can show:

> that the state of scientific and technical knowledge at the relevant time was not such that a producer of products of the same description as the product in question might be expected to have discovered the defect if it had existed in his products while they were under his control.

Effect The effect of the defence can be explained as follows. Consider a drug-induced injury. A claimant establishes that the product fails to comply with society's legitimate expectations for the safety of that type of product. This means she proves that the risks created by the drug outweigh its potential benefits. The defendant may escape liability still by virtue of the 'development risks' defence if she can prove that the nature of the defect was such that, at the time she marketed the drug,[125] the very best available scientific and technical knowledge[126] would not have revealed

---

[124] See generally C Newdick (1988) 47 CLJ 455; (1992) 20 Anglo-Am LR 309.

[125] It will not, once and for all, be enough simply to establish that at the time the design was first put on the market the defect was not discoverable. Once the defect becomes apparent, any further marketing of batches of the drug will engage liability both under the Act and in negligence: see *Wright v Dunlop Rubber Co Ltd* (1972) 13 KIR 255.

[126] The development risks defence in Art 7(e) of the Directive is defined in terms of 'the state of scientific and technical knowledge at the time when he put the product into circulation was not such as to enable the existence of the defect to be discovered'. There is no reference to whether a 'producer of products of the same description might be expected to have discovered the defect' as in the Consumer Protection Act 1987, sub-s 4(1)(e). But notwithstanding the seemingly more generous test under the Act, relevant case law points to what is unknown to the world of science rather than merely what is unknown to the defendant: see *Richardson v LRC Products Ltd* [2000] Lloyd's Rep Med 280; *A v National Blood Authority* [2001] 3 All ER 289.

the defect.[127] Imagine, for example, that a drug has been developed to alleviate sickness during pregnancy. Imagine further that it leads to unforeseen disabilities in the children born subsequently. In such circumstances, the development risks defence would confer one significant advantage on the parents of the injured babies. In negligence they would have to prove that the defendants should have foreseen the risk. But under the statute, the onus is on the defendants to prove that they could not have anticipated the danger. That being the case, self-interest impels manufacturers to disclose all reports of tests on a product as well as the expert opinion made available to them.

(H) Causation

Burden of proof The burden of proof rests with the claimant to show that there was a 'defect' in the product, and that the relevant injury or damage was wholly or partly caused by that defect.[128]

Improper use Often, the burden of proof presents a problem in establishing causation where an improper or unexpected use of the product leads to the claimant's injury: is it the improper use or the defect which caused the injury? Consider the following difficult scenarios:

(1) A new antibiotic is marketed. Information to doctors includes a warning not to prescribe the drug to pregnant women. The drug is available on prescription only. Dr X prescribes the drug for Y. Y feels better the next day. Y discontinues the tablets and gives the remainder to her colleague Z who is ten weeks pregnant. Z takes the tablets and her baby is born seriously damaged.[129]

(2) A trendy student buys a lurid pink dye in a dressmaking shop. She uses it to dye her hair and suffers acute dermatitis as a result.[130]

(3) A wealthy businessperson buys domestic heaters and installs them in her swimming pool. One heater explodes, destroying the pool.

Intermediate examination However, one causation issue is clear. Intermediate examination of the product will no longer exculpate the manufacturer from liability for defects in the product existing at the time that she put the product into circulation. That

---

[127] It follows that if a risk is known, or ought to be known, in the light of accessible information, the defence is not available: *A v National Blood Authority* [2001] 3 All ER 289.

[128] See the Consumer Protection Act 1987, sub-s 2(1) and Art 4 of the Directive. Causation may be inferred from the facts by a process of eliminating non-causes, so long as the remaining cause is not one which is improbable in nature: *Ide v ATB Sales Ltd* [2009] RTR 8, distinguishing *Rhesa Shipping Co SA v Edmunds* ('*The Popi M*') [1985] 1 WLR 948.

[129] Questions of causation can be seen from this example to be inextricably bound up with the definition of a 'defect'. D could argue that the manner in which the product was marketed as a 'prescription only' drug, with appropriate information supplied to GPs, rendered it acceptably safe.

[130] Should dye intended for use on materials be marked 'Not to be used on the hair'?

some third party might share liability for the injury to the claimant is relevant only to the issue of contribution between the tortfeasors.[131]

Identifying manufacturer Equally, certain factual difficulties associated with causation for the consumer seeking to identify and sue the manufacturer will be alleviated largely by the obligation on each supplier to name her supplier or be deemed strictly liable herself.[132] Only where the last party identified, moving back up the chain, is bankrupt will problems arise.

Market share liability In the US, claims have been litigated where the actual manufacturer of the product—a generic drug—injuring the claimant cannot be traced. US courts have held that liability should be apportioned between all companies manufacturing the drug in proportion to their share in the market for that drug.[133]

(I) Limitation

Rules Actions under Part I of the Consumer Protection Act 1987 are subject to the usual limitation periods with the exception of two special periods of limitation. First, the action must be brought within three years of the date on which injury or damage was suffered by the claimant, or, if later, the date on which the claimant becomes aware of the injury or damage.[134] Only in the case of personal injuries does the court have a discretion to override that three-year period. Second, no action may be brought in any circumstances more than ten years from the date on which the defendant supplied the relevant product to another.[135]

Reason for long-stop The reason for the provision on which the latter rule is based (Article 11 of the Directive) has been explained by the Court of Justice of the European Union as to do, inter alia, with the need for an appropriate balancing between the interests of, on the one hand, injured claimants and, on the other hand, defendant producers, which are subject to a strict liability regime that represents 'a greater burden than under a traditional system of liability'.[136] The long-stop period is designed to ensure legal certainty, the ability of a producer to insure against liability, and also to ensure continued innovation in industries such as the pharmaceutical industry.[137] Claims such as those brought before the courts in the US by several young women who had developed

---

[131] See Art 8(1) of the Directive. Contribution is not limited to tortfeasors but is available between all persons liable for the same damage: see the Civil Liability (Contribution) Act 1978 discussed in ch 25. Retailers liable to purchasers for breach of the implied conditions of the contract of sale may also seek a contribution from the manufacturers.   [132] See the Consumer Protection Act 1987, sub-s 2(3).

[133] See *Sindell v Abbott Laboratories* 26 Cal 3d 588 (1980). See also A Porat and A Stein, *Tort Liability under Uncertainty* (2001); C Newdick (1985) 101 LQR 405.

[134] For example, a person who took a particular drug in 2006 but only became aware of the kidney damage caused by that drug in 2011.

[135] As to time of supply, see the earlier discussion of *O'Byrne v Aventis Pasteur SA* [2010] 1 WLR 1412.

[136] *O'Byrne v Aventis Pasteur* Case C–358/08 (2009) 113 BMLR 1, at [41]–[42].

[137] *O'Byrne v Aventis Pasteur* Case C–358/08 (2009) 113 BMLR 1, at [41]–[42] and [46].

cervical cancer as a result of a drug (DES) taken by their mothers in pregnancy therefore could not have been brought under the 1987 Act. In this country, the young women would have had to fall back on the common law action for negligence.

Conclusions

This chapter has considered the law of torts insofar as it relates to products that cause injury. The law of negligence applies in this setting. Today, a manufacturer owes a duty of care to a consumer, which arises whether there was an opportunity for intermediate examination of the goods or not. A duty of care is owed by several other parties involved in the chain of distribution. In most cases, however, the claimant will prefer to bring action under the Consumer Protection Act 1987. This legislation creates a cause of action against producers for the supply of defective goods. So the claimant need only prove defect and injury—there is no need to prove negligence on the part of the defendant. One shortcoming of the 1987 Act is the wide development risks defence.

Problem question

Cooters' Scooters sells imported scooters and accessories. One scooter is the 'Model 40', which is manufactured in Moldova (a country outside the EU). These are electric-powered scooters—although their battery life has proved very short. Phileas buys a Model 40 for his daughter Freya. Freya rides it around for a while when, all of a sudden, the battery expires and the scooter comes to a sudden stop. This particular Model 40 was found to have a brake which activated automatically upon a loss of battery power—although this problem was not found in any other Model 40 tested. The result of the sudden expiration of the battery and activation of the brake on Freya's Model 40 was that she was thrown off her scooter while crossing a road. Freya sustained a broken wrist and ripped her shirt. She also dropped her mobile phone, the glass surface of which shattered. As a result of this incident, Phileas had to rush Freya to hospital and was unable to obtain a valuable contract for the sale of the honey that he makes on weekends.

Advise Phileas and Freya as to their rights under product liability laws.

 Visit **http://www.oup.com/uk/street15e/** for answer guidance.

Further reading

BELL, 'Product Liability Damages in England and Wales' (1992) 20 *Anglo-American Law Review* 371

CLARK, 'The Conceptual Basis of Product Liability' (1985) 48 *Modern Law Review* 325

FAIRGRIEVE AND GOLDBERG, *Product Liability* (3rd edn, 2018)

FAIRGRIEVE AND HOWELLS, 'Rethinking Product Liability: A Missing Element in the European Commission's Third Review of the Product Liability Directive' (2007) 70 *Modern Law Review* 962

GOLDBERG AND ZIPURSKY, *The Oxford Introductions to US Law: Torts* (2010), ch 10

NEWDICK, 'Liability for Defective Drugs' (1985) 101 *Law Quarterly Review* 405

NEWDICK, 'The Future of Negligence in Product Liability' (1987) 104 *Law Quarterly Review* 288

NEWDICK, 'The Development Risks Defence of the Consumer Protection Act 1987' (1988) 47 *Cambridge Law Journal* 455

STAPLETON, *Product Liability* (1994)

STOPPA, 'The Concept of Defectiveness in the Consumer Protection Act 1987' (1992) 12 *Legal Studies* 210

TETTENBORN, 'Components and Product Liability' [2000] *Lloyds Maritime and Commercial Law Quarterly* 338

17

Nuisance

KEY ISSUES

(1) Two torts
There are two torts that fall under the rubric of nuisance law. The first, which turns on the infringement of private rights, is the tort of private nuisance. The second, which turns on the infringement of rights shared with the public in general, is public nuisance.

(2) Private nuisance and protected interests
The tort of private nuisance protects rights in the physical integrity of land and in its use and enjoyment.

(3) Private nuisance and strict liability
In theory, liability for private nuisance is strict; liability arises regardless of fault where harm of the requisite kind has been suffered. However, one of the characteristics of the requisite harm—that it be an unreasonable interference with the claimant's rights in or over land—

tends to confuse. This is because, in deciding whether there has been such an interference, it is material to consider whether the defendant engaged in an unreasonable user of his own land. That being the case, the impression might arise that liability for this tort is governed by a fault-based standard. This appearance can be reinforced by reference to the test for remoteness of damage (ie, whether the harm suffered was of a reasonably foreseeable kind). However, these matters do not detract from the essential strict liability of the tort.

(4) Public nuisance
There are two key elements of public nuisance: viz (1) the infringement of a public right; and (2) proof that the claimant has suffered harm to a markedly greater degree than other persons.

Section 1 Introductory observations

(A) Scope of nuisance law

Two torts This chapter deals with two torts: public nuisance and private nuisance. Though both are actionable under the civil law, the commission of a public nuisance has a unique character in tort law and, therefore, must be considered separately. The greater part of the chapter is concerned with the more prevalent tort of private nuisance.

Definition A private nuisance is any activity or state of affairs causing a substantial and unreasonable interference with a claimant's land or his use or enjoyment of that land. From this definition we can discern three kinds of interest to which nuisance law affords protection:[1] the protection of land per se; the protection of the use of land; and the protection of the enjoyment of land. In each case, the damage must be referable to the land, and not merely to goods which happen to be on the land[2] or particular activities undertaken there. It follows from this that not every interference caused by A to B will amount to an actionable nuisance. Instead, the law calls for reasonable tolerance between neighbours as regards the uses to which each puts his land.[3] Indeed, from time to time, it is almost inevitable that each neighbour will put his land to a use that causes some irritation to the other.[4] It would be absurd for the law to allow an action for every minor irritation so caused, for it would circumscribe unjustifiably the freedom to enjoy one's own land. It is for this reason that the law of nuisance insists not simply that there be an interference with the claimant's land in one of the senses mentioned, but also that that interference be both *substantial and unreasonable*.[5]

Activities covered The range of activities that can give rise to an action in nuisance are manifold. They include the emission of noxious fumes, smoke, heat, and noise, or the generation of violent vibrations. But not every instance of smoke or noise emission will sustain an action: it is impossible to characterise any of the activities just listed as inevitably amounting to a nuisance. At most, all that can be said is that each has the *potential* to constitute a nuisance. Imagine, for example, that a neighbour's very young child manages momentarily to turn a stereo system up to full volume. Naturally, the noise will create a disturbance until the neighbour turns it back down again. In such an instance it would be an unjust law that characterised such a fleeting disturbance as an actionable nuisance, and it would be difficult to say that the disturbance caused by a momentary increase in volume was either substantial or unreasonable.

Context dependent While the rigours of the law of nuisance are tempered in this way, there are no precise thresholds beyond which any given disturbance becomes either substantial or unreasonable. The concepts of magnitude and unreasonableness are context dependent;[6] and their assessment depends upon a series of factors explored later in this chapter. One point worthy of note, however, is that, unlike the law of negligence,

---

[1] Though the enjoyment of land and the use of land might, at one level, be seen as distinct interests, they are interrelated: see, eg, *Dodds Properties v Canterbury CC (Kent) Ltd* [1980] 1 All ER 928.

[2] In *Anglian Water Services Ltd v Crawshaw Robbins & Co Ltd* [2001] BLR 273, at [142], Stanley Burnton J opined (in relation to a disrupted gas supply) that 'it is possible to regard the interruption to the supply of gas as an interference with the use of gas appliances rather than with a use of land [since replacement electrical appliances can be obtained]'. But this seems a tenuous distinction.

[3] See, eg, in *Bamford v Turnley* (1862) 3 B & S 66, Bramwell B described nuisance as 'A rule of give and take, live and let live'. As an alternative, in *Hughes v Riley* [2006] 1 P & CR 29, at [29], Chadwick LJ described it as a principle of 'good neighbourliness … [which] involves reciprocity'.

[4] See, eg, a twenty-first-birthday celebration that goes on until late at night.

[5] The *magnitude* and *unreasonableness* of an interference are not mutually exclusive.

[6] *Sturges v Bridgman* (1879) 11 Ch D 852.

reasonableness in nuisance refers not to the defendant's conduct, as such, but to the *out-come* of his conduct. We are not concerned strictly with whether the defendant passes the 'reasonable person test' (in the sense of taking reasonable care to avoid causing harm) that is central to negligence. Rather, we are concerned to assess the reasonable-ness of the harm occasioned to the claimant.[7] Thus, as Lindley LJ observed in *Rapier v London Tramways Co*: 'If I am sued for nuisance, and nuisance is proved, it is no defence to say and to prove that I have taken all reasonable care to prevent it.'[8] On the other hand, it would be wrong to assume that the reasonableness of the defendant's conduct is an irrelevant consideration (especially where what is in question is whether the defend-ant has adopted or continued a nuisance),[9] for there exists an immutable relationship between the unreasonableness of what the defendant does and the unreasonableness of the interference thereby caused to the claimant. Disturbances caused by malice[10] or reckless disregard for one's neighbour—such as persistently playing a musical instru-ment in the small hours of the morning—as opposed to those caused innocently and unavoidably[11] clearly are unjustifiable.

Recoverable damage As originally conceived, the law of nuisance was not designed to cover personal injuries. It was concerned with acts or omissions[12] causing violations of interests in or over land.[13] For a time, however, it was thought that personal injuries were actionable in nuisance. Then, in *Hunter v Canary Wharf Ltd*, the House of Lords reaffirmed that such injuries are not recoverable in private nuisance but rather in negli-gence.[14] The fact that the law has fluctuated on this point demonstrates that the bound-aries of the law of nuisance are by no means fixed or easy to identify.[15] This is in large part because, to a considerable extent, the tort of negligence has subsumed important elements of nuisance law.

Injunctions A final characteristic of the tort of nuisance is that the normal remedy sought by the claimant is an injunction rather than damages. His main concern, when subjected to the persistent late-night trumpet playing of his neighbour, for example, is that his neighbour should desist. But, as we shall see, an injunction might be refused even though an actionable nuisance can be proven. Later in this chapter, we shall see that the courts have developed a series of factors to which they will have regard in

---

[7] *Walter v Selfe* (1851) 4 De G & Sm 315.

[8] [1893] 2 Ch 588, at 600. See also *Halsey v Esso Petroleum Co Ltd* [1961] 2 All ER 145.

[9] See, eg, *Leakey v National Trust* [1980] QB 485; *Transco plc v Stockport MBC* [2004] 2 AC 1, at [96] (sug-gesting an overlap between negligence and nuisance law).

[10] Eg, *Hollywood Silver Fox Farm Ltd v Emmett* [1936] 2 KB 468. In *Hunter v Canary Wharf Ltd* [1997] 2 All ER 426, at 465, Lord Cooke expressed the view (*obiter*) that the 'malicious erection of a structure for the purpose of interfering with television reception should be actionable in nuisance'.

[11] Eg, *Moy v Stoop* (1909) 25 TLR 262.

[12] Nuisance can be grounded on either nonfeasance or misfeasance: see *Goldman v Hargrave* [1967] 1 AC 645.

[13] For origins of the tort, see J Murphy (2004) 24 OJLS 643.   [14] [1997] 2 All ER 426, at 438 and 442.

[15] In *Sedleigh-Denfield v O'Callaghan* [1940] AC 880, at 903, Lord Wright commented that: 'The forms which nuisance may take are protean ... many reported cases are no more than illustrations of particular mat-ters of fact which have been held to be nuisances.'

considering the award of injunctive relief to those who can prove the commission of a nuisance.

(B) Nuisance and environmental law

Limited protection Nuisance law plays only a limited role in the protection of the environment.[16] The fact that there has been a steady growth in popular concern for the protection of the environment has resulted in the implementation of a number of statutes imposing a system of regulation that renders the common law very much a secondary means of protection. As Lord Goff put it:

> [S]o much well-informed and carefully structured legislation is now being put in place to effect environmental protection … [that] there is less need for the courts to develop a common law principle to achieve the same end, and indeed it may be undesirable that they should do so.[17]

The point is that many of the sorts of conduct that would formerly have sounded in nuisance (and nuisance alone) are now covered by statutes such as the Clean Air Act 1993 and the Environmental Protection Act 1990.[18] The implementation of such legislation has meant that it is easier and more effective to pursue a grievance via the local environmental health officers (who can prosecute 'statutory nuisances') than through the courts, where costs might be high.

Planning laws A further, related cause of the diminution in the number of nuisance actions has been the effect of planning legislation. Essentially, the requirement that planning permission be obtained prior to a change in use of existing premises, or the construction of new ones, has meant that some potential nuisances have been avoided. Thus, where a person is denied the planning permission to turn his house into a small printing works, the obvious potential for disturbance to a neighbour caused by vibrations is curtailed. In such cases, nuisance law has no direct role to play.

Residual role It would be wrong to assume, however, that nuisance is a redundant tort in the environmental and planning context. It retains the potential to perform several useful functions.[19] When a nuisance case is decided in favour of the claimant, the effect of the judgment might be to establish standards in relation to, say, pollution control, which are additional to those contained in environmental and planning statutes. Moreover, the tort can operate as an enforcement procedure supplemental to those contained in relevant statutes and, thereby, retains its deterrent potential.

---

[16] See J Murphy, 'Noxious Emissions and Common Law Liability—Tort in the Shadow of Regulation' in J Lowry and R Edmunds (eds), *Environmental Protection and the Common Law* (1999).

[17] *Cambridge Water Co Ltd v Eastern Counties Leather plc* [1994] 2 AC 264, at 305.

[18] For an account of these and other statutory nuisances, see J Murphy, *The Law of Nuisance* (2010), ch 8.

[19] See D Nolan, 'Nuisance, Planning and Regulation: The Limits of Statutory Authority' in A Dyson et al, *Defences in Tort* (2015), ch 10.

(C) Nuisance and other torts

Nuisance is not the only tort that has a role to play in the protection of interests in land. Indeed, there are a number of further torts to consider.

Relation to negligence There is considerable overlap between nuisance and negligence. As Lord Wilberforce remarked in *Goldman v Hargrave*, a nuisance 'may comprise a wide variety of situations, in some of which negligence plays no part, in others of which it is decisive'.[20] For example, if I were to light a fire next to my neighbour's fence and leave it unattended, I might be held liable in either negligence or nuisance if the fire were to spread to his fence or shrubs. Indeed, in one case where the action was framed both in negligence and nuisance, the judge, in dismissing the negligence claim, stated that he 'need not discuss the alternative claim based on nuisance ... [since the latter] cannot be established unless negligence is proved'.[21] On a practical level, there is a choice often in terms of the way in which a claimant may frame his action. But on a jurisprudential level, a question arises as to why, when nuisance protects interests in the enjoyment of land, it is necessary to extend the boundaries of negligence to cover similar situations—especially at a time when the judicial trend is to restrain carefully the growth of negligence. Another question is whether nuisance law ought to be reined in and restored to its origins as a strict liability tort protecting only the amenities associated with land ownership.[22]

Relation to *Rylands* If the interface between negligence and nuisance leads to some difficult questions about the extent of nuisance liability, these have been compounded by similar questions concerning the relationship between nuisance and the rule in *Rylands v Fletcher*[23] (discussed in chapter 18). In juridical terms, the two torts can be distinguished.[24] Yet they share a number of common features which have been taken by the courts to form the basis for the mistaken idea that the rule in *Rylands v Fletcher* was derived from the law of nuisance.[25]

Relation to trespass Trespass to land concerns direct rather than consequential harm and, therefore, might be distinguished from nuisance in both juristic and factual terms. For example, in being actionable per se, trespass does not require the claimant to prove damage.[26] Thus, in *Kelsen v Imperial Tobacco Co (of Great Britain and Ireland) Ltd*, where a sign erected by the defendants projected into the air space above the claimant's shop, it was held that the sign constituted a trespass but not a nuisance since 'the presence of this sign ... caused no inconvenience and no interference with the [claimant's] use of

---

[20] [1967] 1 AC 645, at 657.

[21] *Bolton v Stone* [1951] AC 850, at 860. This point was endorsed by Lord Reid in *The Wagon Mound (No 2)* [1967] 1 AC 617, at 640: 'the similarities between nuisance and [negligence] ... far outweigh any differences'.

[22] See C Gearty [1989] CLJ 214.   [23] (1866) LR 1 Exch 265.

[24] See *Leakey v National Trust* [1980] QB 485; D Nolan (2005) 121 LQR 421; J Murphy (2004) 24 OJLS 643.

[25] See, eg, *Cambridge Water Co Ltd v Eastern Counties Leather plc* [1994] 2 AC 264, at 298; FH Newark (1949) 65 LQR 480.   [26] *Stoke-on-Trent Council v W & J Wass Ltd* [1988] 3 All ER 394.

his air'.[27] On the other hand, where damage occurs as a result of a trespass, 'it makes no difference to the result' whether the action is framed in trespass or in nuisance.[28]

Overlapping torts The fact that some degree of overlap exists between nuisance and other torts makes it difficult to classify any of them purely on the basis of the interest protected. If, for example, a neighbour's land is damaged because of an overflow of water, much will depend upon: the directness of the invasion (central to trespass);[29] the role of fault (crucial in 'state of affairs' nuisance cases);[30] and whether the invasion was attributable to a foreseeably injurious escape (which lies at the heart of *Rylands v Fletcher* liability).[31]

Section 2 Title to sue

We now move to a formal consideration of each of the elements of the tort of private nuisance.

Proprietary interest Reflecting the fact that nuisance law traditionally has protected interests in land, the conventional approach has been to allow only those with a sufficient proprietary interest to sue.[32] In *Malone v Laskey*,[33] a homemaker was injured when vibrations generated by the defendant caused an iron bracket designed to support a lavatory cistern to fall off the wall and on to her head. Her claim in nuisance failed because she had no legal or equitable interest in the land. Fletcher Moulton LJ observed: 'a person who is merely present in the house cannot complain of a nuisance'.[34] The point was endorsed by Lord Simmonds in *Read v J Lyons & Co Ltd* when he said: 'he alone has a lawful claim who has suffered an invasion of some proprietary or other interest in land'.[35] Moreover, the significance of a proprietary interest was reaffirmed forcefully in *Hunter v Canary Wharf Ltd*,[36] where Lord Goff said:

> an action in private nuisance will only lie at the suit of a person who has a right to the land affected. Ordinarily such a person can only sue if he has the right to exclusive possession of the land, such as a freeholder or tenant in possession, or even a licensee with exclusive possession ... . But a mere licensee on the land has no right to sue.[37]

Notwithstanding the consistency with which the proprietary interest requirement has been endorsed, some uncertainty remains. For this reason, the law is set out under two sub-headings: the first dealing with established claimants and the second dealing with more controversial claimants.

---

[27] [1957] 2 QB 334, at 343. Cf *Smith v Giddy* [1904] 2 KB 448 (nuisance where D allowed his trees to overhang C's land and stymie growth of C's fruit trees).

[28] *Home Brewery Co v William Davies & Co (Loughborough) Ltd* [1987] QB 339, at 354.

[29] *Preston v Mercer* (1656) Hard 60.   [30] *Sedleigh-Denfield v O'Callaghan* [1940] AC 880.

[31] (1868) LR 3 HL 330.   [32] *Hunter v Canary Wharf Ltd* [1997] AC 655, at 702.

[33] [1907] 2 KB 141.   [34] [1907] 2 KB 141, at 153–4.

[35] *Read v J Lyons & Co Ltd* [1946] 2 All ER 471, at 482.

[36] [1997] AC 655. The sole dissent was voiced by Lord Cooke.   [37] [1997] AC 655, at 688.

(A) Established categories of claimant

(1) Those in exclusive possession of land

In the light of what Lord Goff said in the *Hunter* case, there can be no doubt that free-holders possess title to sue in private nuisance. Leaseholders also can be regarded as possessing a sufficient proprietary interest, given that their Lordships were prepared to countenance claims by resident tenants enjoying exclusive possession.[38] Their Lordships saw exclusive possession as the main criterion.[39] So, while a licensee with such possession will be able to sue in nuisance,[40] a claimant with a lesser form of possessory entitlement will not.[41]

One final category of occupier worthy of mention is the successor in title to land afflicted by a continuing nuisance. Such persons are entitled to sue in nuisance even though the interference began prior to their acquisition of the property afflicted.[42] For example, in *Delaware Mansions Ltd v Westminster City Council*,[43] the claimants were freehold owners of certain flats. At the time damage was first occasioned by the encroachment of the defendant's tree roots, the claimants were not the freehold owners. But, since the defendants had taken no remedial action so that the nuisance was a continuing one, the flat owners were able to sue in respect of the physical damage caused.

(2) Reversioners

Another well-settled category of claimant with the right to sue in private nuisance is that of reversioners. But reversioners cannot sue for all nuisances. They may sue only in respect of damage caused to their reversionary interest. Short-term nuisances that are capable only of affecting tenants currently in occupation will not ground an action by a reversioner. That said, it is going too far to suggest that only a permanent injury to the reversion will suffice. Although Parker J made mention of permanent injuries in *Jones v Llanrwst UDC (No 2)*,[44] he offered a qualified notion of what amounts to permanency for these purposes:

> I take 'permanent' in this connection to mean such as will continue indefinitely unless something is done to remove it. Thus a building which infringes ancient lights is permanent within the rule, for, though it can be removed before the reversion falls into possession, still it will continue until it be removed. On the other hand, a noisy trade and the exercise of an alleged right of way are not in their nature permanent within the rule, for they cease of themselves, unless there be someone to continue them.[45]

In accordance with this principle, a reversioner may sue where an adjoining landowner constructs a house, the eaves of which project over his land and discharge rainwater on

---

[38] [1997] AC 655, at 688 and 724.

[39] See also *Pemberton v Southwark LBC* [2000] 1 WLR 1672. See also *Foster v Warblington UDC* [1906] 1 KB 648; *Newcastle-Under-Lyme Corpn v Wolstanton Ltd* [1947] Ch 92.

[40] *Newcastle-Under-Lyme Corpn v Wolstanton Ltd* [1947] Ch 92; *Hunter v Canary Wharf Ltd* [1997] AC 655.

[41] *Jan de Nul (UK) v NV Royale Belge* [2000] 2 Lloyd's Rep 700 (C had no exclusive right to possession).

[42] *Masters v Brent LBC* [1978] QB 841, at 848. Where the damage caused by a nuisance remains, but the original nuisance has ceased to operate, only the original owner can sue: *Jeffries v Williams* (1850) 5 Exch 792.

[43] [2002] 1 AC 321.   [44] [1911] 1 Ch 393, at 404.   [45] [1911] 1 Ch 393, at 404.

to it.[46] Similarly, physical damage caused to the reversioner's buildings will afford him a cause of action.[47] But no such action lies where the nuisance complained of comprises mere temporary annoyance caused by the emission of smoke.[48]

(3) Those with easements and *profits à prendre*

As Lord Goff observed in *Hunter v Canary Wharf Ltd*, '[n]uisance is a tort against land, including interests in land such as easements and profits'.[49] In the case of a *profit à prendre* (that is, a right to take produce from another's land)[50] the claimant can sue without the need to prove that he holds title to the land affected[51] because the person with a *profit à prendre* 'has such possessory rights that he can ... maintain an action on the case for nuisance at common law for such an interference with his right as is proved'.[52] By contrast, easements always are connected to land and the claimant must be able to show his proprietary or possessory right to the dominant (ie benefitting) tenement; for, by definition, he can never have title to the servient tenement burdened by the easement.[53] Furthermore, it is clear that no claim will lie in respect of a trifling interference with an easement, for the claimant 'cannot complain, unless he can prove an obstruction which injures him'.[54]

(B) More doubtful cases

(1) Spouses in possession of 'home rights'?

If the facts of *Malone v Laskey* were to arise again today, it is by no means certain that the same decision would be reached. This is because the Family Law Act 1996, section 30 confers upon spouse (or civil partner) X (who has no proprietary interest in the home) certain rights known as 'home rights' *so long as* his or her spouse (or civil partner) does have a proprietary right to the home. The question is whether these 'home rights' are sufficient to confer upon X a sufficient possessory interest to ground a nuisance action. The Family Law Act, section 30 makes plain that X has a right not to be evicted by his or her spouse or civil partner (if X currently is in occupation).[55] It states also that X will have a right, so long as the *leave of the court has been given*, to enter and occupy the home.[56] Clearly, the section aims to secure the occupation rights of non-owning spouses and civil partners. But this does not mean necessarily that such rights suffice for the purpose of the *locus standi* rule in nuisance law. It can be argued that the first of the two rights conferred—the right not to be evicted or excluded from the home *by*

---

[46] *Tucker v Newman* (1839) 11 Ad & El 40.
[47] *Meux's Brewery Co v City of London Electric Lighting Co* [1895] 1 Ch 287.
[48] *Simpson v Savage* (1856) 1 CBNS 347.   [49] [1997] AC 655, at 702.
[50] For example, a public right to fish in the sea and in tidal waters.
[51] *Nicholls v Ely Beet Sugar Factory Ltd (No 1)* [1931] 2 Ch 84, at 88.
[52] *Fitzgerald v Firbank* [1897] 2 Ch 96, at 101–2.
[53] *Paine & Co Ltd v St Neots Gas & Coke Co* [1939] 3 All ER 812, at 823–4.
[54] *Thorpe v Brumfitt* (1872–73) LR 8 Ch App 650, at 656.   [55] Family Law Act 1996, sub-s 30(2)(a).
[56] Family Law Act 1996, sub-s 30(2)(b).

the other spouse or civil partner—probably is insufficient because the right is a right as against the other adult occupant. It is more in the nature of a personal right than a proprietary right. As regards the second of the two rights—the right to enter and occupy the dwelling house with the leave of the court—it can be argued that there is no automatic right held by the relevant spouse or civil partner (given that the leave of the court must have been obtained). But once such leave has been granted, it could be seen as possessing a sufficiently proprietary character.

(2) Claimants suffering personal injuries, damage to goods, or financial loss

Personal injuries It was held in *Hunter v Canary Wharf Ltd*[57] that personal injuries are not, per se, recoverable in an action for private nuisance. Nonetheless, an action will lie where 'the injury to the amenity of the land consists in the fact that persons on it are liable to suffer inconvenience, annoyance or illness'.[58] The point is one of emphasis. To be recoverable, the personal injury must be seen in terms of a diminution in the capacity of the land to be enjoyed. That being so, where defective wiring in a neighbouring house causes a fire that spreads to the claimant's house, the claimant should be allowed to recover not only for the damage caused to his house but also for any burns he sustains because it is not only the land, but also the amenity of the land (in terms of the ability to live there free from burns) that has been affected. The matter has resonance when quantifying damages: 'the reduction in amenity value is the same whether the land is occupied by the family man or the bachelor ... the quantum of damages in private nuisance does not depend on the number of those enjoying the land in question'.[59] In other words, there will be no simple multiplication of damages just because more than one person is affected.[60] Yet, if the nuisance does affect a whole family, 'the experience of the members of that family is likely to be the best evidence available ... upon which the financial assessment of diminution of amenity value must depend'.[61]

Goods So far as damage to goods is concerned, it is also reasonably well established that private nuisance affords a remedy. In *Midwood & Co Ltd v Manchester Corpn*,[62] for example, damages were awarded for loss of stock in trade; while in *Halsey v Esso Petroleum Co Ltd*[63] they were awarded for damage to washing on a clothes line. Notwithstanding the fact that in *Hunter* their Lordships staunchly reasserted the principle that nuisance is a tort to *land*, it was stated explicitly that an action in respect of *consequential* damage to goods is recoverable.[64]

Financial loss As Lord Hoffmann recognised in the *Hunter* case, consequential financial loss in the form of the claimant's inability to use the land for the purposes of his business is recoverable.[65] Beyond this, matters are more opaque. In two cases[66] decided under the

---

[57] [1997] 2 All ER 426, at 442.   [58] [1997] 2 All ER 426, at 452.   [59] [1997] 2 All ER 426, at 442.
[60] But note that personal injuries are recoverable in the tort of public nuisance (see section 8).
[61] *Dobson v Thames Water Utilities Ltd* [2010] HLR 9, at [33].   [62] [1905] 2 KB 597.
[63] [1961] 2 All ER 145.   [64] [1997] 2 All ER 426, at 452.   [65] [1997] 2 All ER 426, at 452.
[66] *British Celanese Ltd v A H Hunt (Capacitors) Ltd* [1969] 2 All ER 1252; *Ryeford Homes Ltd v Sevenoaks DC* [1989] 2 EGLR 281.

rule in *Rylands v Fletcher* it has been suggested that, in principle, it is possible to recover for purely financial loss. Since Lord Goff's view in *Cambridge Water Co Ltd v Eastern Counties Leather plc*[67] was that the rule in *Rylands v Fletcher* was a tort derived from nuisance, it could be argued that there should be no objection to purely financial loss being recovered in the latter tort, too, *so long as* it arises out of an interference with the amenity of the land.[68]

Section 3 Who can be sued?

A person is liable in nuisance only if he bears 'some degree of personal responsibility' for it.[69] Such persons can be identified under three main heads—viz, as creators/authorisers, occupiers, or landlords.

(A) Creators and authorisers

Creation If the actual wrongdoer is invested with the management and control of the premises from which nuisance emanates, he is liable irrespective of whether he is an occupier of those premises in the normal sense of the word.[70] Indeed, even though the person who created the interference was *not* in occupation or control of the premises from which a nuisance emanated at the time of the interference, but merely created it with the authority of the occupier, he might be liable still.[71] And he will not be excused simply because he lacks the right to enter the premises in order to abate it.[72]

Where the interference complained of arises from a 'state of affairs' that was created by the defendant,[73] he will be liable (even though his *initial* conduct does not amount to a nuisance) so long as harm to the claimant is a foreseeable consequence of that initial conduct. Thus, he who plants poplar trees—itself an innocuous act—is liable in nuisance in respect of the indirect harm caused by their roots spreading under neighbouring land.[74] Equally, liability arises for foreseeable damage that ensues from keeping defective electric mains.[75] Where, on the other hand, the defendant creates a state of affairs that will not foreseeably result in a nuisance, no liability arises. Thus, in *Ilford Urban District Council v Beal*:[76]

> D erected a retaining wall along the bank of a river. Because the wall was not constructed in accordance with best engineering practice it was later undermined by the river. This

---

[67] [1997] 2 All ER 426.

[68] Cf *obiter* that the cost of replacement cooking facilities necessitated by a disturbed gas supply is irrecoverable: *Anglian Water Services Ltd v Crawshaw Robbins & Co Ltd* 2002 WL 31523191, at [124].

[69] *Sedleigh-Denfield v O'Callaghan* [1940] AC 880, at 897.

[70] *Hall v Beckenham Corpn* [1949] 1 KB 716.   [71] *Southwark LBC v Tanner* [2001] 1 AC 1.

[72] *Thompson v Gibson* (1841) 7 M & W 456. In *Southport Corpn v Esso Petroleum Co Ltd* [1953] 2 All ER 1204, at 1207, Devlin J said *obiter*: 'I can see no reason why … if the defendant as a licensee or trespasser misuses someone else's land, he should not be liable for a nuisance.'

[73] Cf circumstances in which D only inherits or continues a state of affairs produced by a third party. In such cases, D's liability attaches because of his failure to remedy the potentially injurious state of affairs: see *Delaware Mansions Ltd v Westminster CC* [2002] 1 AC 321.

[74] *Butler v Standard Telephones and Cables Ltd* [1940] 1 KB 399; *McCombe v Read* [1955] 2 QB 429.

[75] *Midwood & Co Ltd v Manchester Corpn* [1905] 2 KB 597.   [76] [1925] 1 KB 671.

undermining caused the wall to move forward a foot or two where it came to press against, and cause damage to, C's sewer. C neither knew, nor ought to have known, about the presence of the sewer. The damage to the sewer, therefore, was unforeseeable and D was held not liable in nuisance.

Although the key to liability in such cases is the remoteness of the injurious consequences of the defendant's initial conduct, it is not always easy to distinguish those cases in which the defendant genuinely created the dangerous state of affairs from those in which he failed merely to remedy it. The point can be illustrated by reference to *Goldman v Hargrave*,[77] in which the defendant failed to deal adequately with a red gum tree that caught fire after being struck by lightning. The Privy Council held that the defendant's method of dealing with the fire gave rise to a foreseeable risk of the embers rekindling and the fire spreading to the claimant's land (as in fact occurred). It is not wholly clear whether the defendant's wrongdoing amounted to misfeasance (in that he dealt inappropriately with a burning tree, thereby creating a risk to his neighbour) or nonfeasance (in that he failed to avert an extant risk of fire spreading). Had the tree not been felled in the manner adopted by the defendant, the fire might never have rekindled and spread to the defendant's land. On the other hand, had the tree not been struck by lightning in the first place, a hazardous state of affairs would never have arisen on the defendant's land. Whether cases such as this are better seen as involving misfeasance or nonfeasance is not easy to determine.[78]

Authority In accordance with ordinary principles, anyone who authorises another to commit a nuisance is liable himself.[79] So, for example, a local authority is liable when it authorises the use of its land as a go-kart circuit given that a nuisance is the known and inevitable consequence.[80] And a landlord is liable when it authorises the use of its land for an inevitable nuisance even though the lease contains a covenant against the commission of nuisances.[81] Indeed, it is only the authorisation of conduct that inevitably will cause a nuisance that enables the court to treat the landowner as though he had caused the interference *himself*. Thus, it was held in *Hussain v Lancaster City Council*[82] that, since acts of harassment against local shopkeepers had no direct connection with the tenants' use of the premises they rented from the defendants, nuisance liability could not be imposed on the defendants. The council could be held liable only in respect of uses of the tenants' council houses that they had authorised and that had caused a nuisance.[83] So, if land is let by a local authority to persons who might *or might not* cause a nuisance, there is no liability because nuisance is not inevitable.[84] Nor will a

---

[77] [1967] 1 AC 645.   [78] In the eventuality, the Privy Council treated *Goldman* as a nonfeasance case.

[79] *Lawrence v Fen Tigers (No 2)* [2015] AC 106.   [80] *Tetley v Chitty* [1986] 1 All ER 663.

[81] *Lawrence v Fen Tigers (No 2)* [2015] AC 106, at [17].

[82] [1999] 4 All ER 125. Cf *Lippiatt v South Gloucestershire Council* [1999] 4 All ER 149.

[83] But this decision comes close to supporting the untenable proposition that a nuisance requires an improper use of D's land (on which see *LE Jones (Insurance Brokers) Ltd v Portsmouth CC* [2003] 1 WLR 427).

[84] *Lawrence v Fen Tigers (No 2)* [2015] AC 106, at [15]; *Smith v Scott* [1973] Ch 314. Cf *Lippiatt v South Gloucestershire Council* [1999] 4 All ER 149.

local authority be liable if it lets premises in poorly soundproofed buildings to tenants who cause annoyance to others simply by using them in the normal way.[85]

(B) Occupiers

The occupier of premises will be liable in respect of nuisances that he has created. But he might be liable in other circumstances as well. In the main, the cases turn on the occupier having 'adopted' or 'continued' the nuisance by failing to take reasonable steps to remedy a potential hazard on land that he occupies. Broadly speaking, an occupier *adopts* a nuisance if he makes use of an 'erection, building, bank or artificial contrivance which constitutes the nuisance', whereas he *continues* the nuisance if he, with '[actual] knowledge or presumed knowledge of its existence, fails to take any reasonable means to bring it to an end'.[86] In determining what amounts to reasonableness, the court *may* have regard to his limited financial and other resources,[87] especially if the defendant has had the state of affairs involuntarily thrust upon him.

So far as the liability of occupiers for nuisance is concerned, there are five main categories of case to consider. And in doing so, it is worth noting that the first three categories apparently would apply in respect not just of persons in control of the land, but of persons in control of the hazard alone.[88]

(1) Acts of a trespasser

If the dangerous state of affairs on the defendant's land is created by a trespasser, so long as the occupier knows or ought to know about it, he is liable in nuisance in respect of damage caused to his neighbour. The leading case is *Sedleigh-Denfield v O'Callaghan*:[89]

> A drainage pipe had been laid by a trespasser. Initially, the defendant occupiers had no knowledge of it. But later, when they discovered it, the defendants used the pipe to drain excess water from their own land. Due to misplaced grating, the pipe became blocked. The defendants' servant—who had been responsible for periodically maintaining the drainage system—ought to have noticed the risk of flooding that it posed. But he did not notice it, and the blocked pipe caused water to overflow on to the claimant's premises.

In finding the defendant liable, the House of Lords stressed the importance of the defendant's (presumed) knowledge of the risk:

> An occupier is not *prima facie* responsible for a nuisance created without his knowledge and consent. If he is to be liable a further condition is necessary, namely, that he had knowledge or means of knowledge, that he knew or should have known, of the nuisance in time to correct it.[90]

---

[85] *Southwark LBC v Tanner* [2001] 1 AC 1.   [86] *Sedleigh-Denfield v O'Callaghan* [1940] AC 880, at 894.
[87] But not always, see *Abbahall v Smee* [2003] 1 All ER 465.
[88] *Jones Ltd v Portsmouth CC* [2003] 1 WLR 427.   [89] [1940] AC 880.
[90] [1940] AC 880, at 904. See also *Lippiatt v South Gloucestershire Council* [1999] 4 All ER 149.

It is important to distinguish cases such as *Sedleigh-Denfield* from two further kinds of case; first, from those such as *Smith v Littlewoods Organisation Ltd*,[91] where there was no liability where the trespassers had, *in the absence of actual or presumed knowledge* on the part of the defendants, caused a fire in the defendants' disused cinema which spread to the claimant's property; second, from those where the third party merely uses the defendant's land as a means of gaining access to the claimant's land rather than, as in *Sedleigh-Denfield*, where the third party's mischievous act or omission actually occurs on the defendant's land. In such cases, it has been held that the defendant will be free of any general liability in respect of the acts of such third parties.[92] A final point is that, where the defendant's failure to abate a nuisance can be attributed to a pre-existing duty on his part to consult the interested parties before any remedial steps permissibly can be taken, the defendant's inaction will not be taken to be an unreasonable failure to erase the menacing state of affairs.[93]

(2) Overwhelming acts of nature

If a dangerous state of affairs arises on the defendant's land due to an act of nature of which the occupier knows or ought to know, he is liable in nuisance if damage occurs to a neighbouring landowner. In *Goldman v Hargrave*, the facts of which we have noted already, the Privy Council extended the rule in *Sedleigh-Denfield v O'Callaghan*—that an occupier must take reasonable steps to remedy a potentially hazardous state of affairs—to cases in which the danger arises by an overwhelming act of nature. However, Lord Wilberforce added the important qualification that the reasonableness of the defendant's attempts to avert such a danger must be judged in the light of his financial and other resources:

> [T]he law must take account of the fact that the occupier on whom the duty is cast has, *ex hypothesi*, had this hazard thrust upon him through no seeking or fault of his own. His interest and his resources, whether physical or material, may be of very modest character ... . A rule which required of him in such unsought circumstances in his neighbour's interest a physical effort of which he is not capable, or an excessive expenditure of money, would be unenforceable or unjust.[94]

Although *Goldman* is a Privy Council decision, its underlying rationale was adopted in the English case of *Leakey v National Trust for Places of Historic Interest or Natural Beauty*.[95] There, the defendants owned land on which stood a large mound of earth that they knew to be prone to subsidence. When, following a particularly dry summer which caused cracks to appear in the earth, the mound gave way causing damage to the claimant's houses, the Court of Appeal held the defendants liable for the landslip.[96]

---

[91] [1987] AC 241.   [92] *P Perl Exporters Ltd v Camden LBC* [1984] QB 342.

[93] *Page Motors Ltd v Epsom and Ewell BC* (1981) 80 LGR 337.

[94] [1967] 1 AC 645, at 663. This might be seen as undermining the supposed strictness of nuisance liability. On the other hand, it might be seen as being a not unreasonable user of the land (and, therefore, a not unreasonable interference).   [95] [1980] QB 485.

[96] But note that where D's *nonfeasance* is in issue, the court's expectations of him will diminish: *Holbeck Hall Hotel Ltd v Scarborough BC* [2000] 2 All ER 705.

Although the defendants had given permission to the claimant to abate the cause of the nuisance, they themselves had done nothing to remove the danger.[97]

(3) Nuisances created by independent contractors

An employer is vicariously liable for nuisances created by an employee in the course of his employment.[98] But as regards independent contractors, the defendant is liable only in respect of their failure to take precautions if, as Slesser LJ held in *Matania v National Provincial Bank Ltd and Elevenist Syndicate Ltd*,[99] 'the act done is one which in its very nature involves a special danger of nuisance being complained of'. In that case, the occupier of the first floor of a building was held liable to the superjacent occupiers in respect of the dust and noise generated by the alteration works carried out by the independent contractors he had employed.

The nature of an occupier's liability for independent contractors was stated more widely by Cockburn CJ in *Bower v Peate* (a non-delegable duty case), when holding a principal liable for his independent contractor's withdrawing support from the buildings of the claimant:

> a man who orders a work to be executed, from which, in the natural course of things, injurious consequences to his neighbour must be expected to arise … is bound to see to the doing of that which is necessary to prevent the mischief, and cannot relieve himself of his responsibility by employing someone else.[100]

(4) Acts of a licensee

In *Cocking v Eacott*,[101] the Court of Appeal held that the owner of land who has licensed another to be there on terms which are not those of a tenancy, so that the owner retains possession and control of the land and cannot be excluded from it, is eligible to be called the occupier of the land and is liable for nuisances created by the licensee of which he has knowledge. On the facts, the defendant had permitted her daughter to reside in a terrace house rent-free but retained full control. She was held jointly liable for the daughter's nuisances which arose from the excessive barking of her dogs, which the defendant did nothing to abate.

(5) Acts of a previous occupier

If the predecessor of the defendant occupier created a hazardous state of affairs and the defendant knows or ought to know of its existence then, according to Scrutton LJ in *St Anne's Well Brewery Co v Roberts*,[102] he is liable in respect of any damage to which it gives rise. Even if the construction created by the occupier's predecessor in title did not

---

[97] But note that it is doubtful whether liability arises for the presence of animals *ferae naturae* or failure to remove them: *Farrer v Nelson* (1885) 15 QBD 258; *Seligman v Docker* [1949] Ch 53.

[98] *Spicer v Smee* [1946] 1 All ER 489, at 493 (*obiter*).   [99] [1936] 2 All ER 633, at 646.

[100] (1876) 1 QBD 321, at 326. Followed in *Spicer v Smee* [1946] 1 All ER 489, at 495.

[101] [2016] QB 1080.

[102] (1928) 140 LT 1 (part of an ancient wall collapsed damaging C's inn but, on the facts, D was found not liable because he lacked constructive knowledge that the wall was likely to collapse).

pose a threat at the time of its creation, that person might be held liable nonetheless in respect of any hazards it gives rise subsequently to so long as he knew, or ought to have known, that such a threat was posed.[103]

(C) Landlords

Landlords' liability We have already seen that a landlord will be liable for the commission of a nuisance where he creates the nuisance or where he authorises his tenant to commit it.[104] With respect to nuisances created by tenants, in *Lawrence v Fen Tigers (No 2)* Lord Neuberger stated that questions concerning the landlords' liability for participation would be examined by reference to conduct occurring after the grant of the lease, although the matter 'may take colour from the nature and circumstances of the grant and what preceded it'.[105] There must be acts of actual participation; 'the fact that a landlord does nothing to stop or discourage a tenant from causing a nuisance cannot amount to "participating" in the nuisance'.[106]

But there are further situations that call for discussion in which the landlord may be held liable *qua landlord* (and not as creator). First, if at the date of letting the landlord knows or ought to know of the condition giving rise to the actionable nuisance, he will be liable despite the tenancy if he has not taken a covenant to repair the premises from the tenant.[107] According to *Wilchick v Marks and Silverstone*, a landlord ought to know not only of those defects that are patently obvious but also of those that are capable of being discovered by use of reasonable care.[108] Second, a landlord will be liable for dangerous conditions that arise from want of repair during the tenancy if he has covenanted to perform such repairs,[109] reserves the right to enter and repair,[110] or has an implied right to enter and repair.[111] Furthermore, where the landlord's premises are situated on a highway, he will be liable to both neighbouring landowners and passers-by regardless of whether the want of repair is attributable to the landlord's negligence.[112] Finally, there are certain circumstances in which a landlord does something to the premises that leads inevitably to a nuisance if the premises are occupied so that he will be liable *rather than the tenants*. In *Toff v McDowell*,[113] for example, the tenants had used the premises in a perfectly normal fashion but, because the landlord

---

[103] *Bybrook Barn Garden Centre Ltd v Kent CC* [2001] Env LR 30.

[104] See, eg, *Lawrence v Fen Tigers (No 2)* [2015] AC 106; *Lippiatt v South Gloucestershire Council* [1999] 4 All ER 149.   [105] [2015] AC 106, at [20].

[106] *Lawrence v Fen Tigers (No 2)* [2015] AC 106, at [22].

[107] *Todd v Flight* (1860) 9 CBNS 377; *Gandy v Jubber* (1864) 5 B & S 78 (revd (1865) 9 B & S 15); *Bowen v Anderson* [1894] 1 QB 164.   [108] [1934] 2 KB 56, at 67–8.

[109] *Payne v Rogers* (1794) 2 Hy Bl 350. Where there is no such covenant, the landlord will not be liable for adopting or continuing a nuisance if it is attributable to defective construction of the premises: *Jackson v JH Watson Property Investment Ltd* [2008] 11 EG 94.

[110] *Wilchick v Marks and Silverstone* [1934] 2 KB 56; *Heap v Ind Coope and Allsopp Ltd* [1940] 2 KB 476; *Spicer v Smee* [1946] 1 All ER 489.   [111] *Mint v Good* [1951] 1 KB 517.

[112] *Wringe v Cohen* [1940] 1 KB 229 (flld in *Mint v Good* [1951] 1 KB 517).

[113] (1993) 25 HLR 650. To similar effect, see *Stannard v Charles Pitcher Ltd* [2002] BLR 441.

had taken up the floor covering, anyone occupying the premises subsequently would sound unbearably loud to the subjacent claimant. The landlord was held liable and directed to replace the flooring.[114]

Tenants' liability As regards the liability of a tenant, he is liable in nuisance for damage arising from a failure to effect repairs if he has covenanted to repair the premises.[115] On the other hand, the mere fact that the landlord has covenanted to repair the premises will not, ipso facto, exonerate the tenant from nuisance liability.[116] As Lawrence LJ explained in *St Anne's Well Brewery Co v Roberts*:[117]

> Any bargain made [as to who] should perform that obligation may give rise to rights as between the two contracting parties, but does not, in my judgment, in any way affect any right of third parties, who are not parties or privy to such contract.

Section 4 The bases of nuisance liability

Under the definition of nuisance offered earlier, a claimant must prove a substantial interference either with his land, or with the use or the enjoyment of his land; and he must demonstrate also that the interference was an unreasonable one. The factors taken into account by the courts in assessing both the magnitude and reasonableness of an interference are both manifold and intricately interconnected.

(A) Substantial interference

Before a claimant can succeed in a nuisance action, he must be able to prove that he has suffered damage; nuisance is not a tort which is actionable per se. Since the law of nuisance protects not just against physical damage to land, but against interferences with the use or enjoyment of it also, it is apparent that we require a definition of damage that embraces both tangible and intangible interferences. Thus, in addition to physical harm to land, our concept of damage must embrace those cases in which the claimant's complaint related to, say, the emission of unpleasant smells, or the generation of loud noise; in short, with things that represent 'sensible discomfort',[118] which are interferences with the amenities associated with occupation of land.

Although, for the purposes of nuisance, both physical damage and disturbances to the enjoyment of land are actionable, it does not follow that we need not distinguish between the various kinds of interference. Indeed, the case law requires us to treat material harm quite differently from interferences with amenities.

---

[114] Cf *Southwark LBC v Tanner* [2001] 1 AC 1 (D had not done anything to the rented premises so as to render a disturbance to C inevitable: D was not liable).

[115] *Brew Bros Ltd v Snax (Ross) Ltd* [1970] 1 QB 612.

[116] *Wilchick v Marks and Silverstone* [1934] 2 KB 56.   [117] (1928) 140 LT 1, at 8.

[118] *Hunter v Canary Wharf Ltd* [1997] 2 All ER 426, at 452.

(1) Interference with the use or enjoyment of land

Give and take As regards interference with the use or enjoyment of land (amenity nuisance), the law requires give and take on the part of neighbouring land owners. This principle was encapsulated in *Sedleigh-Denfield v O'Callaghan* by Lord Wright when he said that '[a] balance has to be maintained between the right of the occupier to do what he likes with his own [land], and the right of his neighbour not to be interfered with'.[119] It is implicit in this that, as between neighbours, some measure of interference with the use and enjoyment of each other's land is permissible. Only a *substantial* interference with a claimant's amenities can constitute a nuisance. As Lord Selbourne said in *Gaunt v Fynney*: '[a] nuisance by noise … is emphatically a question of degree … . Such things to offend against the law must be done in a manner which, beyond fair controversy, are to be regarded as excessive'.[120] The same rule, that the nuisance must be substantial, applies in respect of other amenities. So, for example, an interference with the right to the free passage of light—acquired by grant or prescription[121]— amounts to a nuisance only when it deprives the claimant of 'sufficient light, according to the ordinary notions of mankind, for the comfortable use and enjoyment of his house'.[122]

Substantial infringement A key issue is when an interference with amenities amounts to a substantial infringement of the claimant's interests. The claimant's health need not have suffered;[123] indeed, the loss of a single night's sleep has been held to be sufficient to constitute a nuisance.[124] So too has the use of adjoining premises for the purposes of prostitution.[125] The question is one of fact, to be determined on a case-by-case basis. Not every interference will constitute a nuisance, and an interference that comprises a nuisance in one context might not do so in another.[126] The most commonly cited formulation of the rule by which the interference is to be adjudged substantial is that of Knight Bruce VC in *Walter v Selfe*:[127]

> [O]ught this inconvenience to be considered in fact as more than fanciful, more than one of mere delicacy or fastidiousness, as an inconvenience materially interfering with the ordinary comfort physically of human existence, not merely according to elegant or dainty modes and habits of living, but according to plain and simple notions among the English people?

Over the years, the courts have tended to assess the seriousness of an interference by reference to two main considerations: the claimant's sensitivity and the locality in which the alleged nuisance occurs. Neither of these factors is conclusive of whether an interference is sufficiently substantial to constitute nuisance; they merely are *relevant* considerations which ought to be taken into account in amenity nuisance cases.

---

[119] [1940] AC 880, at 903; *Delaware Mansions Ltd v Westminster CC* [2002] 1 AC 321.

[120] (1872) 8 Ch App 8, at 11–12.

[121] English common law recognises no automatic right to light, and such a right can only be acquired in connection with a building: *Harris v de Pinna* (1886) 33 Ch D 238.

[122] *Colls v Home and Colonial Stores* [1904] AC 179, at 208.

[123] *Crump v Lambert* (1867) LR 3 Eq 409, at 412.   [124] *Andreae v Selfridge & Co Ltd* [1938] Ch 1.

[125] *Thompson-Schwab v Costaki* [1956] 1 All ER 652. See also *Laws v Florinplace Ltd* [1981] 1 All ER 659 (sex shop established in a residential area).   [126] *Sturges v Bridgman* (1879) 11 Ch D 852.

[127] (1851) 4 De G & Sm 315, at 322.

(a) The sensitivity of the claimant

Rule If the activity of which the claimant complains only disturbs the use or enjoyment of his land because he carries on a 'delicate trade', heightening his sensitivity to interference, then the interference complained of will not amount to an actionable nuisance. 'A man cannot increase the liabilities of his neighbour by applying his own property to special uses';[128] he will be able to claim only when a claimant of ordinary sensitivity would be able to sue.[129] Take, for example, *Robinson v Kilvert*:[130]

> A landlord, who remained in occupation of the cellar, let the floor above it to C. Because of the landlord's business it was necessary for the cellar to be dry and hot. Cellar heat passed through the ceiling to the floor above, which C used as a paper warehouse, and caused damage to paper.

The court rejected the claimant's application for an injunction to restrain the landlord from keeping his cellar so hot. It was only the fact that the claimant was engaged in an 'exceptionally delicate trade' that caused him to suffer loss.

Radio and television Similarly, in *Bridlington Relay Ltd v Yorkshire Electricity Board* the defendants' power line interfered with the claimant's business of providing a subscription radio and television relay service. It was said *obiter* that, because interference with the recreational amenity of television viewing was not a substantial interference with the use and enjoyment of land, the claimants could not sue for the business interference complained of: 'the claimants could not succeed in a claim for damages for nuisance if … an ordinary receiver of television by means of an aerial mounted on his house could not do so'.[131] That case was decided in 1965, when television ownership was comparatively rare. These days, television viewing is far less easily classified as an unusually sensitive activity. Indeed, if the same facts were to arise today, it is possible that the court would hold there to be a nuisance.[132] Such a possibility was not ruled out in *Hunter v Canary Wharf Ltd*, where Lords Goff and Cooke suggested that, in certain circumstances, an action for this kind of interference might lie. However, in refusing to award damages to the claimants, Lord Goff stated that, while interferences with television reception 'might in appropriate circumstances be protected', it was also the case that 'more is required than the mere presence of a neighbouring building to give rise to an actionable private nuisance'.[133]

Businesses *McKinnon Industries Ltd v Walker*[134] provides an example where liability was established. Damage to the claimant's commercially grown orchids caused by the emission of sulphur dioxide gas from the defendant's factory was held to be actionable since it amounted to a non-remote consequence of what had been proved already to be

---

[128] *Eastern and South African Telegraph Co Ltd v Cape Town Tramways Companies Ltd* [1902] AC 381, at 393.
[129] Though the hypersensitivity rule is well established, the fact that C must suffer a foreseeable kind of harm might limit its practical import: *Network Rail Infrastructure Ltd v CJ Morris* [2004] Env LR 41, at [35].
[130] (1889) 41 Ch D 88.   [131] [1965] Ch 436, at 446.
[132] As in Canada: see *Nor-Video Services Ltd v Ontario Hydro* (1978) 84 DLR (3d) 221, at 231.
[133] [1997] 2 All ER 426, at 432.   [134] [1951] 3 DLR 577.

a nuisance. That said, the fact that the claimant has suffered appreciable financial loss should not be taken, of itself, to amount to a substantial interference.[135] The infliction of such business losses will be taken into account in deciding whether the interference with the use and enjoyment of land *as a whole* was substantial.[136]

(b) Location of the claimant's premises

General The locality in which the claimant's premises are situated is a second factor relevant to determining whether an interference is sufficiently substantial to amount to a nuisance. A 'locality' is an area which might comprise, for example, 'a set of two or three adjoining streets' and which can be characterised (typically) as residential, commercial, industrial, or mixed use.[137] The expectations of the claimant, in terms of comfort, peace, and quiet, are likely to vary according to the location of his house or business. The point was made succinctly in *Sturges v Bridgman*,[138] where a physician complained about the noise generated by a neighbouring confectioner who was operating a pestle and mortar. Thesiger LJ held that the court should take account of the fact that the locale consisted largely of medical specialists' consulting rooms since:

> [w]hether anything is a nuisance or not is a question to be determined, not merely by an abstract consideration of the thing itself, but in reference to its circumstances; what would be a nuisance in Belgrave Square would not necessarily be so in Bermondsey; and where a locality is devoted to a particular trade ... [a court] would be justified in finding, and may be trusted to find, that the trade ... is not an actionable wrong.[139]

In determining the character of a locality, the Supreme Court in *Lawrence v Fen Tigers Ltd* held that the court is to *take into account* the defendant's own activities, unless they are unlawful (such as where they constitute a nuisance) in determining whether a substantial interference has occurred.[140] This has been acknowledged to create a circular test,[141] given that character itself is relevant to whether the defendant's activities constitute a nuisance. In such circumstances, Lord Neuberger thought it would help to keep in mind the fact that the issue can be decided by use of an 'iterative process'[142] (although this did not provide much comfort to Lord Carnwath).[143] This, it is submitted, is not the appropriate test. The appropriate test is to *compare* the defendant's use of land with that of *all others* in the locality, so as to determine whether the defendant's use 'stands out'.[144]

Although locality is relevant in deciding amenity nuisance cases, it is not necessarily a conclusive consideration. Thus, while locality provided a compelling reason for the decision in *Adams v Ursell*[145]—where a fish and chip shop established in a fashionable

---

[135] See *Victoria Park Racing and Recreation Grounds Ltd v Taylor* (1937) 58 CLR 479.

[136] *Thompson-Schwab v Costaki* [1956] 1 All ER 652.

[137] S Steel (2017) 76 CLJ 145, 148 citing *Laws v Florinplace* [1981] 1 All ER 659 and *Murdoch v Glacier Metal Co Ltd* [1988] Env LR 732, at 733.　　　　　[138] (1879) 11 Ch D 852.

[139] (1879) 11 Ch D 852, at 865.　　　[140] [2014] AC 822, at [63]–[66].　　　[141] [2014] AC 822, at [71].

[142] [2014] AC 822, at [72].　　　[143] [2014] AC 822, at [190].

[144] This seems to have been the approach advocated by Lord Mance: [2014] AC 822, at [164]. Cf D Nolan, 'Nuisance, Planning and Regulation: The Limits of Statutory Authority' in A Dyson et al (eds), *Defences in Tort* (2015), 191 (incl. fn 57).

[145] [1913] 1 Ch 269. See also *Thompson-Schwab v Costaki* [1956] 1 All ER 652 (brothel in high-class street).

street was held to be a nuisance—it was not determinative in *Rushmer v Polsue and Alfieri Ltd*,[146] where printing presses were used at night in a printing district.

Changing character The character of a locality is susceptible to change over time. Thus, the fact that an area was at one time wholly residential does not mean that the residents will be entitled always to a very high standard of peace and quiet. This gives rise to the question whether planning permission is relevant in determining character. In *Lawrence v Fen Tigers Ltd*, Lord Neuberger noted that the grant of planning permission has a limited effect. 'All it means is that a bar to the use imposed by planning law, in the public interest, has been removed.'[147] Absent 'express or implied statutory authority to commit a nuisance … there is no basis … for using such a statutory scheme to cut down private law rights'.[148] Although the terms of planning permission might serve as a starting point for discussions about whether the defendant's activities amount to a nuisance, the matter is for the court to decide[149] and is a question of fact and degree.[150] It is the *implementation* of planning permission, through new or different uses of land, which might entail a change in the character of a locality.[151]

(2) Material damage to land

General So far we have been concerned with what amounts to a substantial interference with the use or enjoyment of land (otherwise known as 'amenity nuisance'). In this section, we consider cases in which the activity complained of causes actual physical damage to the claimant's land. Relevant kinds of nuisance include collapses of the defendant's property on to the claimant's land,[152] drenching or flooding,[153] the encroachment of roots,[154] vegetation damage caused by the emission of noxious fumes,[155] and vibration damage.[156] In such cases, the court will approach the question of substantial interference rather differently from where the claimant complains of amenity nuisance.

Character not relevant To begin with, where physical damage to property arises, the character of the district in which the claimant's land lies is *not* a material factor in assessing the gravity of the interference. In *St Helen's Smelting Co v Tipping*[157]—a case in which the claimant's shrubs had been damaged by fumes emitted from the defendants' copper-smelting plant—Lord Westbury held that:

> It is a very desirable thing to mark the difference between an action brought for a nuisance upon the ground that the alleged nuisance produces material injury to the property, and

---

[146] [1906] 1 Ch 234 (affd [1907] AC 121).   [147] [2014] AC 822, at [89].

[148] *Barr v Biffa Waste Services Ltd* [2003] QB 455, at [46]; cited with approval in *Lawrence v Fen Tigers Ltd* [2014] AC 822, at [92]. See also *Wheeler v JJ Saunders Ltd* [1995] 2 All ER 697.

[149] *Lawrence v Fen Tigers Ltd* [2014] AC 822, at [96].

[150] *Watson v Croft Promo Sport Ltd* [2009] EWCA Civ 15, at [24].

[151] D Nolan, 'Nuisance, Planning and Regulation: The Limits of Statutory Authority' in A Dyson et al, *Defences in Tort* (2015), 190.   [152] *Wringe v Cohen* [1940] 1 KB 229. Cf *Sack v Jones* [1925] Ch 235.

[153] *Sedleigh-Denfield v O'Callaghan* [1940] AC 880; *Hurdman v NE Rly Co* (1878) 3 CPD 168; *Broder v Saillard* (1876) 2 Ch D 692.   [154] *Masters v Brent LBC* [1978] QB 841.

[155] *St Helen's Smelting Co v Tipping* (1865) 11 HL Cas 642; *Manchester Corpn v Farnworth* [1930] AC 171.

[156] *Grosvenor Hotel Co v Hamilton* [1894] 2 QB 836.   [157] (1865) 11 HL Cas 642.

> an action … on the ground that the thing alleged … is productive of personal discomfort. With regard to the latter … a nuisance must undoubtedly depend greatly on the circumstances of the place where the thing complained of actually occurs. But where [physical damage is caused] … there unquestionably arises a very different consideration.[158]

One difficulty that arises from the fact that location is irrelevant is that physical damage and interference with amenities often arise simultaneously, without any clear distinction between the two. If, for example, vibrations cause plaster to break off my walls, those same vibrations probably will affect adversely the comfort and enjoyment of my home as well. Furthermore, the fact that the defendant engages in such a disturbing enterprise is likely to cause a diminution in the value of my house, which is not easy to classify as either an amenity nuisance or physical damage.[159] Notwithstanding these problems, courts have made some attempts to clarify the meaning of 'material damage'. A dictum of Lord Selbourne suggests that it is enough if science can trace a deleterious physical change in the property.[160] However, because it can be difficult to distinguish between amenity nuisances and those involving physical damage, it is preferable not to ignore the locality issue in all but the most clear-cut cases.

Materiality Just as in the case of amenity nuisance, it is important also to establish in physical damage cases that the nuisance complained of is substantial in nature. Hence, in *Darley Main Colliery Co v Mitchell*[161] it was held that minor subsidence (though identifiable and tangible) which caused the claimant no appreciable harm was not an actionable nuisance.

(3) Interference with servitudes

For the sake of completeness, we ought to note a final category of damage that technically can form the basis of a nuisance action. It involves interferences with servitudes such as the right to light and air, and the right to support of land and buildings. The rules in relation to these rights are more suitably the subject matter of a textbook on land law than one on tort.

(B) Unreasonableness

There is perhaps no more confusing matter in the law of private nuisance than the role played by unreasonableness in the ascription of liability. Conceivably, unreasonableness could relate to one or both of two issues: the conduct of the defendant and the

---

[158] (1865) 11 HL Cas 642, at 650.

[159] Although the drop in value of the property is a form of financial loss, it seems implicit from *Bone v Seale* [1975] 1 All ER 787 that such loss should be treated as property damage (given that the court treated it separately from the award for the amenity nuisance). Does this mean that diminution in value is to be regarded, in nuisance, as physical damage? If so, it could be argued that *all* amenity cases involve at least some element of physical damage according to this conception (which is the one favoured in *Hunter v Canary Wharf Ltd* [1997] 2 All ER 426).   [160] *Gaunt v Fynney* (1872) 8 Ch App 8, at 11–12.

[161] (1886) 11 App Cas 127.

nature of the interference with the claimant's land. Properly understood, it is the inter-ference, rather than the defendant's conduct, which must be unreasonable.[162] This does not mean, however, that the nature of the defendant's conduct is irrelevant, since the unreasonableness of the defendant's user will impact upon the court's characterisation of the nature of the interference. Imagine, for example, that I regularly fire a gun on my land in order to control vermin posing a threat to my crops. The level of noise made by the gun is precisely the same as if I were firing it out of wantonness. And since the sound level remains constant, so does the degree of disturbance that I cause my neighbour. In only the latter case, however, might a judge declare there to be a nuisance on the basis that the shooting in that instance was completely unwarranted. In the former case, where the shooting was reasonable in order to effect pest control, the judge easily might reach the opposite conclusion. The difference between the two cases lies in the way in which we characterise the nature of the interference (albeit by reference to the nature of the defendant's conduct). Yet not in every case in which the defendant acts unreasonably will he be liable in nuisance; for the disturbance must still be substantial. So, for example, if I play my stereo late at night and at full volume, I will not be liable in nuisance to my neighbour if she is almost entirely deaf and hears virtually nothing. The interference in such a case will be regarded as *de minimis*. As McNeill J insisted in *Tetley v Chitty*, the claimant must be able to demonstrate 'a real interference with *his* use and enjoyment of his premises'.[163] The italicised words make it clear that there needs to be a subjective disturbance. So, it will not matter in such cases that every unreasonable user that gives rise to an interference *necessarily* will give rise to an unreasonable interfer-ence. The fact that the interference is not *subjectively substantial* will defeat the claim.

There are several factors that the courts typically will take into account in deciding whether the interference is unreasonable:

(1) The seriousness of the interference

Generally, the more serious an interference with the claimant's interests, the more likely it is that the interference will be regarded as unreasonable. In turn, the seriousness of the interference is influenced by four factors: the duration of the harm; the extent (or degree) of the harm; the character of the harm; and the social value of the use interfered with.

(a) The duration of the harm

The persistence of an interference has a direct bearing on its reasonableness. In general terms, the more persistent an interference, the more likely it is that the court will deem it to be unreasonable. Self-evidently, it is much less reasonable to expect one's neigh-bours to tolerate a nauseating smell that is more or less permanent than one that lasts for just a few moments.[164] It follows from this that nuisances normally involve ongoing

---

[162] See, eg, *Sampson v Hodson-Pressinger* [1981] 3 All ER 710 (ordinary use of badly constructed premises caused intolerable noise to neighbours held to be a nuisance). See also *Toff v McDowell* (1993) 25 HLR 650.

[163] [1986] 1 All ER 663, at 665. In *Bradford Corpn v Pickles* [1895] AC 587, at 601, Lord Macnaghten stated that no action would lie '[if]the act … gives rise merely to damage without legal injury'. See also *Crown River Cruises Ltd v Kimbolton Fireworks Ltd* [1996] 2 Lloyd's Rep 533.

[164] See *Hirose Electrical UK Ltd v Peak Ingredients Ltd* [2011] EWCA Civ 987.

interferences as opposed to those which are merely transitory or isolated.[165] In some circumstances, however, even isolated or transitory interferences are actionable. For example, if the interference complained of is an isolated event but it causes physical damage, the courts appear willing to allow claims in nuisance so long as the damage arose out of a dangerous 'state of affairs'.[166] In *Spicer v Smee*—a case in which defective electrical wiring in the defendant's premises resulted in the claimant's bungalow being destroyed by fire—Atkinson J put the matter thus: 'A private nuisance arises out of a state of things on one man's property whereby his neighbour's property is exposed to danger.'[167] Similarly, in *Midwood & Co Ltd v Manchester Corpn*,[168] where an accumulation of inflammable gas caused an explosion to occur which set fire to the claimant's premises, the court held there to be a nuisance by focusing upon the prevailing state of affairs. (Nevertheless, it is arguable that these cases would have been better brought in negligence.)

Though it is a pre-condition of liability in respect of an isolated event that it arose from a dangerous state of affairs on the defendant's land, it is important to be clear that damages are awarded only for the harm caused. Nothing can be recovered in connection with the menacing state of affairs, per se, for this is merely a prerequisite for, and not the basis of, the defendant's liability. Nuisance law insists that the claimant must demonstrate that he has suffered actual damage.

(b) The extent of the harm

Whether an interference is serious (and hence unreasonable) must be assessed in the light of its impact on the defendant. Whenever I play my piano, I generate a level of noise that might be moderately irksome to my neighbour; but he might easily block it out with some headphones. On the other hand, if I were to play my trombone, it would generate much more noise and be likely to remain heard and cause disturbance no matter what steps my neighbour might take. The relationship between the degree of interference and its unreasonableness is clear therefore: the louder I play an instrument, or the more odious the smell that my business generates, the more likely it is that the court will find the interference thereby caused to be not only substantial, but also unreasonable.

On the other hand, the gravity of the harm caused must not be assessed on a purely objective basis (for example, by reference only to the loudness of my trumpet playing). There is an important role also for a subjective element in the assessment of whether the interference was unreasonable. Although there is usually a correlation between the magnitude of an interference and its unreasonableness, this is not always the case.

---

[165] Thus, in *Cunard v Antifyre Ltd* [1933] 1 KB 551, where some of D's roofing fell into C's premises. Talbot J stated (at 557) that: 'nuisances, at least in the vast majority of cases, are interferences for a substantial length of time'.

[166] *Midwood & Co Ltd v Manchester Corpn* [1905] 2 KB 597; *Spicer v Smee* [1946] 1 All ER 489. Note, too, that ongoing, but rather short, interferences can be nuisances: see, eg, *Crown River Cruises Ltd v Kimbolton Fireworks Ltd* [1996] 2 Lloyd's Rep 533. [167] [1946] 1 All ER 489, at 493.

[168] [1905] 2 KB 597. See also *Stone v Bolton* [1949] 2 All ER 851; *British Celanese Ltd v A H Hunt (Capacitors) Ltd* [1969] 2 All ER 1252.

Where, for example, I play my trombone late at night generating, say, 85 decibels of noise, nine times out of ten this would be considered a very substantial (and hence unreasonable) disturbance to my next-door neighbour. Where, however, my neighbour is practically deaf, he might hear the trombone only faintly. Accordingly, despite the *objective* loudness of my playing, it will not be perceived *subjectively* to be an unreasonable interference. And, as we have already seen, the claimant must show that *he* has suffered a substantial interference, for 'the law does not regard trifling and small inconveniences, but only regards sensible inconveniences which sensibly diminish the comfort … *of the property which is affected*'.[169]

(c) The character of the harm

As mentioned earlier, for the purposes of nuisance law, harm might take the form either of physical damage to land or an interference with the use and enjoyment of it. Although both forms are actionable, physical injury generally is regarded as being of a more serious kind than interferences with a claimant's amenities. Indeed, the distinction drawn in *St Helen's Smelting Co v Tipping* between physical damage and amenity nuisance[170] has been taken by some commentators to support the proposition that physical injury is actionable regardless of whether the defendant's user of his land was objectively reasonable.[171] This proposition probably goes too far,[172] but it does draw attention to the fact that, even in the context of nuisance, the English courts remain wary of finding liable trifling personal discomforts falling short of physical injury.[173] The central issue is whether the interference is unreasonable.[174] So, in clear cases of physical injury—which can easily be proven and quantified in terms of damages, and which sit towards the top end of the hierarchy of protected interests in tort law—it is simpler for the courts to find that the interference complained of was unreasonable than in cases of personal discomfort or annoyance.[175] Consequently, physical violations of the claimant's land are tolerated far less readily than disruptions to the peaceful enjoyment of it.

(d) Social value of the use interfered with

The final factor that can affect the seriousness of the harm is the nature of the use to which the claimant puts his land. Where the claimant uses his land in such a way that it can be classified as socially useful, it is more likely that the disruptive interference about which a complaint has been made will be regarded as serious. In *Smith v Giddy*, for example, branches on the defendant's trees which overhung the claimant's land and

---

[169] *St Helen's Smelting Co v Tipping* (1865) 11 HL Cas 642, at 654 (emphasis added). See also *Sturges v Bridgman* (1879) 11 Ch D 852, at 863: '[where the interference is of] so trifling a character, that, upon the maxim *de minimis non curat lex*, we arrive at the conclusion that the defendant's acts would not have given rise to [liability]'.   [170] *St Helen's Smelting Co v Tipping* (1865) 11 HL Cas 642, at 650.

[171] A Ogus and GM Richardson [1977] CLJ 284, 297.

[172] See *Ellison v Ministry of Defence* (1996) 81 BLR 101.

[173] See the observations of Lord Hoffmann in *Hunter* (noted, at the beginning of this chapter).

[174] See, eg, *Watt v Jamieson* 1954 SC 56, at 58 where Lord President Cooper held that the key question was 'whether what he was exposed to was *plus quam tolerabile*'.

[175] As Lord Selborne put it in *Gaunt v Fynney* (1872) 8 Ch App 8, at 11–12: '[amenity nuisance] is much more difficult to prove than when the injury complained of is the demonstrable effect of a visible or tangible cause'.

prevented his commercially cultivated fruit trees from growing properly were held to be a nuisance, whereas it was stated *obiter* that, had the claimant not been growing such trees, the mere blockage of light would not have been actionable.[176]

(2) Use of the defendant's land

Nuisance liability depends upon there being an unreasonable interference with the claimant's interests, rather than there being unreasonable conduct per se on the defendant's part. However, there is a fundamental relationship between the reasonableness of the interference and the (un-)reasonableness of the user or activity. The fact that one is engaged in an unreasonable user ipso facto will render any interference caused equally unreasonable: an interference that is caused by an unjustifiable activity cannot itself be justified.[177] As Lord Goff noted in *Cambridge Water Co Ltd v Eastern Counties Leather plc*, the converse is true also: 'if the user is reasonable the defendant will not be liable for consequent harm to his neighbour's enjoyment of his land'.[178] It follows that the question of negligent conduct is a highly relevant consideration, not in itself, but because of its impact on the characterisation of the interference caused. Much can turn on the burden of proof, for, as the Court of Appeal explained in *Marcic v Thames Water Utilities Ltd*:

> Once a claimant has proved that a nuisance has emanated from land in the possession or control of the defendant, the onus shifts to the defendant to show that he has a defence to the claim, whether this be absence of 'negligence' in a statutory authority case or that he took all reasonable steps to prevent the nuisance [in other cases].[179]

In assessing the reasonableness of the defendant's user the courts resort to a further range of factors. The following comprise the more important of these:

(a) The defendant's motive

Motive relevant The court will take into account the main purpose of the defendant's activity. Where the defendant's primary aim is to injure his neighbour, his malicious motives might render the interference unreasonable.[180] In *Christie v Davey*,[181] for example, the claimants' action lay in respect of noises being made by their defendant neighbours. Central to North J's judgment that the noises were a nuisance was the fact that they were made 'deliberately and maliciously for the purpose of annoying the [claimants]'.[182] Similarly, in *Hollywood Silver Fox Farm Ltd v Emmett*,[183] the court held the firing of guns to be actionable where done out of spite, with the object of interfering with the claimant's breeding of silver foxes. Having said as much, it is not the unreasonableness of the defendant's conduct, per se, that is of concern. Rather, it is the fact that this

---

[176] [1904] 2 KB 448.

[177] Though the unreasonableness of the user will confirm the unreasonableness of the interference, it does not follow that all unreasonable users will result in liability; eg, an unreasonable user that causes minimal interference will not be actionable: the interference must also be substantial.   [178] [1994] 2 AC 264, at 299.

[179] [2002] QB 929, at [85] (revd on appeal on different points of law: [2004] 2 AC 42).

[180] Cf *Bradford Corpn v Pickles* [1895] AC 587.   [181] [1893] 1 Ch 316.   [182] [1893] 1 Ch 316, at 326.

[183] [1936] 2 KB 468.

has a direct impact on the reasonableness of the interference. This is consistent with the definition of nuisance offered at the beginning of this chapter, which does not stipulate unreasonable conduct—for this would blur the distinction between negligence and nuisance liability—but, instead, an unreasonable interference.

Social objectives Wanton ill-conduct serves no socially useful function. It necessarily amounts to an unreasonable user, and has the inevitable effect of rendering unreasonable any interference thereby caused to the claimant. However, where the defendant's activity does possess some social utility, and it is this social utility that motivates the defendant, the court will be less inclined to declare any resulting interference unreasonable. For example, in *Harrison v Southwark and Vauxhall Water Co*,[184] the useful nature of the defendants' construction work was a reason why the claimant's action was dismissed. The country must have power stations, factories, and smelting works. By contrast, the need for motorcycle speedway tracks or racecourses is much less pressing and, consequently, such activities much more readily form the basis of successful nuisance actions.[185]

(b) Fault

Wagon Mound The undoubted role that fault can play in determining nuisance liability raises one of the most difficult questions in tort: is nuisance liability strict or fault-based? To answer this question, we must identify both the function served by identifying fault on the part of the defendant and its limited use. Much of the confusion that surrounds these issues stems from a passage in Lord Reid's Privy Council speech in *The Wagon Mound (No 2)*, where he said:

> Nuisance is a term used to cover a wide variety of tortious acts or omissions and in many negligence in the narrow sense is not essential. An occupier may incur liability for the emission of noxious fumes or noise although he has used the utmost care in building and using his premises ... . [And yet,] although negligence may not be necessary, *fault of some kind is almost always necessary* and fault generally involves foreseeability.[186]

At first sight, this passage might appear either intractable or inherently self-contradictory. Negligence is the archetypal fault-based tort. How then can it be asserted that while negligence is not required, fault is almost invariably a pre-condition of liability? The answer lies in Lord Reid's qualification that it is only *negligence in the narrow sense* that need not be shown. 'Negligence in the narrow sense' refers to no more than a failure to meet the standard of conduct of the reasonable person. Furthermore, although one undertakes an enterprise with all possible caution, one can seldom guarantee that certain, *foreseeable*, adverse consequences will not arise. For example, I might drive my car in the winter with all due care but be unable to prevent a collision with another car after skidding on a patch of 'black ice'. Although it could not be said that my driving was below the standard of the reasonable driver and, thus, negligent, it still might be said

---

[184] [1891] 2 Ch 409, at 414.   [185] See, eg, *A-G v Hastings Corpn* (1950) 94 Sol Jo 225.
[186] [1967] 1 AC 617, at 639 (emphasis added).

that I was at fault in the different sense that I knowingly took the risk of such an occurrence by deciding to drive in the first place. The element of fault in this second sense derives from the foreseeability of an accident, even though I drive to an exemplary standard. It is submitted that it is this notion of fault that Lord Reid considered to be crucial to nuisance liability.

Cambridge Water The question whether nuisance involves strict or fault-based liability was revisited by the House of Lords in *Cambridge Water Co Ltd v Eastern Counties Leather plc*.[187] Lord Goff, with whom the other Law Lords agreed, offered a similar interpretation of the role of fault to the one suggested here. He said:

> [T]he fact that the defendant has taken all reasonable care will not of itself exonerate him ... . But it by no means follows that the defendant should be held liable for damage of a type which he could not reasonably foresee; and the development of the law of negligence in the past 60 years points strongly towards a requirement that such foreseeability be a prerequisite of liability in damages for nuisance, as it is of liability in negligence.[188]

This passage makes it clear that liability in nuisance is strict in the sense that a defendant might be found liable regardless of the care he took in doing what he did to avoid causing harm. But this does not exclude a residual role for fault in the second sense: that is, that liability will attach only to those uses of land that involve a foreseeable risk of harm.[189]

(c) Location of the defendant's premises

Just as the location of the *claimant's* premises is important in determining what constitutes a 'substantial interference' in cases of amenity nuisance, so too is the location of the *defendant's* premises important in assessing the reasonableness of the defendant's conduct. Put simply, we are concerned with the question 'What is it reasonable to do?' and not with the question (relevant when considering the location of the claimant's premises) 'What is it reasonable to put up with?' Thus, in addition to considering the usefulness of the defendant's activity, we must consider also whether it is being carried on in a suitable locality. In this connection, the courts have recognised the national policy of segregating different uses of land and have furthered this policy by taking into account whether the defendant is putting his land to a use compatible with the main use to which land in that area usually is put. To take an example, the operation of a chemicals works would not be considered in every conceivable instance to be an unreasonable use of land. If it were operated in a residential area, it could be so regarded; but if the factory were located in an industrial area, the activity probably would be considered reasonable.[190]

---

[187] [1994] 2 AC 264.   [188] [1994] 2 AC 264, at 300.

[189] See, eg, *Leakey v National Trust* [1980] QB 485, at 526; *Delaware Mansions Ltd v Westminster CC* [2002] 1 AC 321 (foreseeable root encroachment: D liable).

[190] It was decided in *Ball v Ray* (1873) 8 Ch App 467 that converting part of a house in a residential street into stables caused an unreasonable interference. But a similar degree of interference caused by a piano being played, or crying children, would not be a nuisance: see *Moy v Stoop* (1909) 25 TLR 262.

(d) The kind of user

A penultimate factor that can influence the court's view of the reasonableness of the defendant's user is the kind of activity in which he is engaged. If my neighbour disturbs me by operating a noisy printing press in order to produce illegal pornographic material, his activity can never be justified, for the activity is illegal and thus unreasonable. Illegal and extremely dangerous enterprises[191] by definition are unreasonable users of land and, apart from the criminal aspects of such activities, any disturbances they cause will be regarded as unreasonable *regardless* of motive.[192] By contrast, if the defendant is responsible for doing something that is socially useful, this might temper the court's willingness to find his user to be unreasonable and help persuade the court not to grant injunctive relief even if it finds the activity to be a nuisance.[193]

(e) Practicability of preventing or avoiding the interference

It will be material always to ask whether the defendant, by taking reasonable, practicable steps to prevent the interference, still could have achieved his purpose without interfering with the claimant's use of his land. If, without excessive expenditure, a factory owner could install equipment that would prevent him causing a disturbance to his neighbours, a court might treat this as conclusive that the defendant's user was unreasonable. In *Andreae v Selfridge & Co Ltd*, for example, where building operations that were generating noise and dust interfered with the comfortable enjoyment of a neighbour's hotel, it was held that the defendants who had undertaken an ostensibly reasonable user of the land were under a duty nonetheless:

> to take proper precautions, and to see that the nuisance is reduced to a minimum. It is no answer for them to say: 'But this would mean that we should have to do the work more slowly than we would like to do it, or it would involve putting us to some extra expense.'[194]

On the other hand, in one case involving young children whose crying often caused a disturbance to the claimant, there was no liability as there was no evidence that the children had been neglected or suffered from a want of care.[195] What was crucial to this finding was the actual ability of the defendant to eradicate or minimise the interference. This principle was endorsed in *Leakey v National Trust* where, despite the defendants ultimately being found liable in respect of an earth-slide from their land, the Court of Appeal declared that the extent of the defendant's duty to minimise any interference and the question of whether he has fulfilled that duty might depend on the defendant's financial resources.[196] Similarly, in *Holbeck Hall Hotel Ltd v Scarborough Borough*

---

[191] For instance, the storing of large quantities of high explosives in a private, terraced house.

[192] In *Cambridge Water Co Ltd v Eastern Counties Leather plc* [1994] 2 AC 264, at 298, Lord Goff identified that unreasonable land use is not necessarily to be equated with negligent land use, though the latter will always be good evidence of the former.

[193] *Dennis v Ministry of Defence* [2003] Env LR 34 (noise from RAF training aircraft a nuisance, but damages only were awarded, and continuance of the nuisance permitted).

[194] [1938] Ch 1, at 9–10. See also endorsement of this approach in *Southwark LBC v Tanner* [2001] 1 AC 1.

[195] *Moy v Stoop* (1909) 25 TLR 262.

[196] [1980] QB 485, at 526. Cf the wholly objective standard that applies in cases of public nuisance: *Wandsworth LBC v Railtrack plc* [2002] QB 756.

Council,[197] the Court of Appeal stated that, in cases involving naturally occurring nuisances—in this case landslips—the defendants' duty would be restricted in part by their ability to avert the nuisance. The Court of Appeal has held also that, where the defendant and claimant would both benefit from works done to avoid a nuisance, they should contribute to the cost of those works in proportion to their respective benefit.[198]

Section 5 Must the interference emanate from the defendant's land?

The land from which the interference has its source normally will be in the ownership or control of the defendant. Indeed, insofar as nuisance law is designed to provide a means of regulating competing land uses, it might be argued that land ownership on the part of the defendant is as important as the requirement that the claimant have a proprietary interest.[199] Nonetheless, dicta abound to the effect that the defendant need not be the owner of the land from which the nuisance emanates. Thus, in *Sedleigh-Denfield v O'Callaghan* Lord Wright declared 'the ground of responsibility' to be merely 'the possession and control of the land from which the nuisance proceeds'.[200] And in *Halsey v Esso Petroleum Co Ltd*[201] the defendants were held liable even in respect of the noise generated by their lorries driving along a public street late at night.

Section 6 Defences

(A) Statutory authority

General Many activities which interfere with the enjoyment of land are carried out by public or private enterprises in pursuance of an Act of Parliament. The fact that the activity giving rise to the interference complained of is authorised by statute is the single most important defence in the law of private nuisance. Whether the activity complained of is authorised by statute, and whether any potential nuisance action is defeated, is a matter of statutory interpretation. In *Allen v Gulf Oil Refining Ltd*[202] the facts were as follows:

> D was authorised by statute compulsorily to acquire land near Milford Haven for the purpose of constructing and operating an oil refinery. C complained that the smell, noise, and vibrations made by the refinery constituted a nuisance. D pleaded the defence of statutory authority.

[197] [2000] 2 All ER 705. The court emphasised that liability in cases of this type involved nonfeasance and that, therefore, the duty to minimise or avoid an interference to C could be restricted. Their Lordships even considered, *obiter*, that issuing a warning to C of a known natural danger might suffice.

[198] *Abbahall v Smee* [2003] 1 All ER 465, at [41] (D and C lived beneath a common roof which needed repairs).

[199] In *Miller v Jackson* [1977] QB 966, at 980, Lord Denning MR proclaimed that, '[it] is the very essence of a private nuisance that it is the unreasonable use by a man of *his land* to the detriment of his neighbour' (emphasis added).   [200] [1940] AC 880, at 903.

[201] [1961] 2 All ER 145.   [202] [1981] AC 1001.

The House of Lords held that the claimants first would have to establish a nuisance, and that the change in the local environment caused by authorising the operation of the refinery was relevant to that issue.[203] If a nuisance could be established, then the company had to prove that it was an inevitable result of carrying on a refinery there.[204]

Due diligence required The defendant must use all due diligence in performing the activity authorised by statute.[205] If he fails so to do, he will be held to have exceeded the level of damage for which he was granted immunity by the statute.[206] So, in *Tate & Lyle Industries Ltd v Greater London Council*[207] the defendants were held liable in public nuisance where reasonable care in the design and erection of new ferry terminals, which statute had authorised them to build, would have partially avoided the siltation of the River Thames which damaged the claimants' business.

Permissive powers If the statute merely confers a permissive power to do something, or planning permission is granted, then the power must be exercised so as *not* to interfere with private rights.[208]

(B) Prescription

General The right to do something that would otherwise constitute private nuisance may be acquired as an easement (or perhaps some lesser right)[209] by way of prescription. The most common way of acquiring an easement is by 20 years' overt user. Overt use means that 'time does not run … until the activities of the owner (or occupier) of the putative dominant land can be objected to by the owner of the putative servient land'.[210] The use need not be continuous over that time;[211] but it seems that a fairly pervasive use is required. One may acquire the right do such things as discharge surface water,[212] or rainwater from the eaves of one's house,[213] or emit sound-waves (that is, noise)[214] on to a neighbour's land. Any easement so created will run with the land and bind successors in title.[215]

---

[203] But note: an injunction can exceptionally be obtained to restrain D from engaging in a land use authorised by planning permission: *Wheeler v JJ Saunders Ltd* [1995] 2 All ER 697.

[204] The House of Lords followed its earlier decision in *Manchester Corpn v Farnworth* [1930] AC 171 (power station established by statute emitted poisonous fumes that damaged C's fields).

[205] *Marcic v Thames Water Utilities Ltd* [2004] 2 AC 42.

[206] In fact, frequently it is the case that while common law damages are precluded by the statute, statutory compensation for interference is available: D Nolan, 'Nuisance, Planning and Regulation: The Limits of Statutory Authority' in A Dyson et al (eds), *Defences in Tort* (2015), 187.

[207] [1983] 2 AC 509. See also *Department of Transport v NW Water Authority* [1984] AC 336.

[208] *Lawrence v Fen Tigers Ltd* [2014] AC 822, at [99]; *Metropolitan Asylum District Managers v Hill* (1881) 6 App Cas 193. See JE Penner (1993) 5 J Env L 1, 24–5.   [209] *Lawrence v Fen Tigers Ltd* [2014] AC 822, at [32].

[210] *Lawrence v Fen Tigers Ltd* [2014] AC 822, at [42].

[211] *Lawrence v Fen Tigers Ltd* [2014] AC 822, at [37], citing *Carr v Foster* (1842) 3 QB 581, at 586–8.

[212] *A-G v Copeland* [1902] 1 KB 690.   [213] *Thomas v Thomas* (1835) 2 Cr M & R 34.

[214] *Lawrence v Fen Tigers Ltd* [2014] AC 822, at [33].

[215] *Lawrence v Fen Tigers Ltd* [2014] AC 822, at [34].

Limits If the user is prohibited by statute, it cannot be claimed as a prescriptive right.[216] Equally, 'acts which are *neither preventable nor actionable* cannot be relied upon to found an easement'.[217] So, where a confectioner for more than 20 years had made certain noises on his land through the operation of his equipment, which then, for the first time, interfered with the claimant doctor's user of his land, the defendant could not plead a prescriptive right.[218] As there had been no invasion of a legal right before the consulting room was built, until then there were no steps that the claimant could have taken to prevent the interference.

(C) The claimant's conduct

Coming to the nuisance It is no defence that the claimant came to the nuisance by occupying the land adjoining it and using it *in the same way* as his predecessor.[219] Although it had been assumed that the rule would be the same in the case where the claimant's use of the land is different from that of his predecessor,[220] this further rule has been doubted by the Supreme Court. Thus, a defence *might* be available where the claimant has 'changed the use of, or built on, her land [so] that the defendant's pre-existing activity is claimed to have become a nuisance'.[221]

Mitigation When a nuisance arises, the claimant has the normal obligation in tort to take reasonable steps to mitigate his loss. For instance, he should take reasonable steps to minimise the damage when his land is flooded in consequence of his neighbour's tortious conduct. The ordinary principles of causation apply in nuisance law and, if the nuisance is caused by the claimant's own acts, he cannot recover.[222]

Consent The defences of consent and assumption of risk are available also. *Pwllbach Colliery Co Ltd v Woodman*[223] illustrates the operation of the consent defence:

> A lessor allowed his lessee to mine for coal. The issue was whether he could complain when the lessee's non-negligent operations caused coal dust to be deposited on other land owned by the lessor.

The House of Lords held that only if the terms of the lease could be construed as authorising a nuisance was there any defence. On the facts, the nuisance was not a necessary consequence of carrying on that trade and there had been no express authorisation of the nuisance in the lease. Therefore, the defence of consent failed.

---

[216] *Liverpool Corpn v H Coghill & Son Ltd* [1918] 1 Ch 307.

[217] *Sturges v Bridgman* (1879) 11 Ch D 852, at 863 (emphasis added).

[218] *Sturges v Bridgman* (1879) 11 Ch D 852.

[219] *Bliss v Hall* (1838) 4 Bing NC 183; *Miller v Jackson* [1977] QB 966 (no defence to a cricket club that the ground first became a nuisance when C built premises close to it); *Lawrence v Fen Tigers Ltd* [2014] AC 822, at [51].   [220] *Sturges v Bridgman* (1879) 11 Ch D 852.

[221] *Lawrence v Fen Tigers Ltd* [2014] AC 822, at [58].

[222] Cf the case in public nuisance: *Almeroth v Chivers & Sons Ltd* [1948] 1 All ER 53.

[223] [1915] AC 634.

As regards the assumption of risk, *Kiddle v City Business Properties Ltd*[224] is a case in point. The claimant complained of the damage caused to his shop when flooding occurred from the gutter carrying water from a part of the premises retained by the defendant landlord without negligence on the defendant's part. It was held that the tenant took the premises as he found them, and must be deemed to have run this risk. Accordingly, his action in nuisance failed.

Contributory negligence Contributory negligence on the part of the claimant might be raised as a defence to an action in nuisance; at least where the nuisance arises out of negligent conduct.[225]

(D) Other defences

As we saw earlier, an occupier who unreasonably fails to avert a danger to his neighbour arising out of an overwhelming act of nature will be liable in nuisance. Where, however, there is an occurrence alleged by the claimant to be a nuisance, which in truth is an inevitable accident, no liability will attach.[226] But it is no defence that the act of the defendant would not have been a nuisance but for the acts of others, provided that the defendant knew what the others were doing.[227]

Section 7 Remedies

(A) Damages

Full compensation In the law of nuisance, the successful claimant is entitled to full compensation for his loss. Where, for instance, a house (or a crop or something analogous)[228] is destroyed or damaged, the claimant can recover the difference between the monetary value to him of his interest (whether he is the landlord, tenant, or otherwise) before and after the event.[229] Where business loss is suffered in consequence of the interference, whether by loss of custom[230] or the cost of moving elsewhere,[231] this is recoverable also. However, where a hotel owner complained of loss of custom caused by nearby building operations, the Court of Appeal reversed an award of damages to the full extent of loss of custom, holding that a certain amount of the interference was reasonable in the circumstances, although likely to lead to some loss of custom. Therefore, the court assessed what proportion of the business loss was attributable to that excess of noise and dust which alone was actionable.[232]

---

[224] [1942] 1 KB 269.

[225] There is *obiter* to this effect in the public nuisance case of *Trevett v Lee* [1955] 1 All ER 406, at 412.

[226] *Tennent v Earl of Glasgow* (1864) 2 M 22.   [227] *Thorpe v Brumfitt* (1873) 8 Ch App 650.

[228] See *Marquis of Granby v Bakewell UDC* (1923) 87 JP 105 (destruction of fish).

[229] *Moss v Christchurch RDC* [1925] 2 KB 750. The law does not grant damages based on the cost of restoring the damaged property to its prior state *if* C has no genuine interest in such restoration: *CR Taylor (Wholesale) Ltd v Hepworths Ltd* [1977] 2 All ER 784.   [230] *Fritz v Hobson* (1880) 14 Ch D 542.

[231] *Grosvenor Hotel Co v Hamilton* [1894] 2 QB 836, at 840.

[232] *Andrae v Selfridge & Co Ltd* [1938] Ch 1.

Continuing interference The amount to be awarded by way of damages increases the longer the nuisance continues. But the law does not treat this as the continuance of the original nuisance complained of, but rather as a new and distinct nuisance. Thus, in a case where a defendant imposed a strain on the claimant's wall by piling earth against it and was sued in nuisance, it was stated that 'a fresh cause of action arises as each brick topples down, and that there is a continuing cause of action until the root of the trouble is eradicated'.[233] Whether the continuance of the interference is characterised as a fresh nuisance or as a prolongation of the original one is largely immaterial so far as the claimant is concerned.[234] He is much more interested in having the nuisance abated and, in most cases, will seek an injunction.

Foreseeability In *The Wagon Mound (No 2)*,[235] the Privy Council held that, in public nuisance, it is not enough that the damage is a direct consequence of the wrongful act; it must be a foreseeable consequence. *Obiter dicta* in the case assert this rule to be applicable to private nuisance also.

Damages in lieu The court has a statutory power[236] to grant damages in lieu of an injunction (thus enabling it to make an award that takes account of future as well as past harm). In *Shelfer v City of London Electric Lighting Co (No 1)*,[237] Smith LJ stated that the court could award damages in lieu where (1) the injury to the claimant is small; (2) it is quantifiable in money terms; (3) it is capable of being adequately compensated in money; and (4) it would be oppressive to the defendant to grant an injunction.[238] Although this case remains a useful authority, the Supreme Court ruled in *Lawrence v Fen Tigers Ltd* that it provides no more than a guide to structure thinking. It is for the defendant to convince the court that damages would be the appropriate remedy. In considering the matter, the court has a measure of flexibility and should consider all of the circumstances.[239] The court is able to consider wider matters of public interest, including, on the one hand, any businesses that might be forced to close down should an injunction go and, on the other hand, the interests of all others in the neighbourhood who are affected by the impugned activity.[240]

(B) Injunction

General An injunction is an order from the court directing the defendant to desist from the future commission of a tortious act. It is the remedy most often sought in nuisance cases and is granted on what is often (but inaccurately) described as being a discretionary basis. Thus, even where the claimant can establish an actionable claim, he might be refused an

---

[233] *Maberley v Henry W Peabody & Co of London Ltd* [1946] 2 All ER 192, at 194. See adoption of this approach in *Delaware Mansions Ltd v Westminster CC* [2002] 1 AC 321.

[234] It can, however, be a concern to D, who merely continues a nuisance begun by his predecessor. Yet where the nuisance has caused harm of a kind that now requires remedial work, the courts will award damages that reflect the cost of that remedial work regardless of whether some of the harm was occasioned prior to D 'inheriting' the nuisance: *Delaware Mansions Ltd v Westminster CC* [2002] 1 AC 321, at [38].

[235] [1967] 1 AC 617.   [236] Senior Courts Act 1981, s 50.   [237] [1895] 1 Ch 287, at 322–3.

[238] This means, in effect, that D buys the right to commit the nuisance.

[239] [2014] AC 822, at [119]–[123] and [239].   [240] [2014] AC 822, at [124].

injunction. Broadly, there are two factors which influence the courts in deciding whether or not to grant an injunction: the gravity of the interference and the public interest.[241]

Gravity The courts tend to view occasional interferences as insufficiently substantial to warrant the grant of an injunction. Take, for example, *Cooke v Forbes*:[242]

> C used a bleaching chemical in making cocoa-nut matting. Occasionally, emission of a noxious chemical from D's plant damaged C's manufactures. Without prejudice to a claim in damages, the court refused an injunction because the interference was occasional only.

However, where there is an ongoing interference with the claimant's legal right—for example, his right to light—the courts presumptively will grant an injunction and be prepared to substitute damages for the injunction in exceptional circumstances only.[243]

Public interest The *Fen Tigers* case has affirmed the relevance of the public interest in determining the appropriateness of either an injunction or damages in lieu. An example of the role that can be played by the public interest is evident in *Wheeler v JJ Saunders Ltd*. In that case, the nuisance was caused by the defendant running a pig farm. In relation to the application for an injunction, Peter Gibson LJ said: 'I can well see that in such a case the public interest must be allowed to prevail and that it would be inappropriate to grant an injunction.'[244]

Dual awards The fact that the claimant's chief concern is with the future abatement of the nuisance does not mean that he will not seek damages also in respect of the past harm that he has suffered. In consequence, the law of nuisance is complicated by the fact that the claimant often will seek two remedies at once.[245] Of particular note in this context is the Canadian decision that, where both remedies are granted, any damages must not include an element in respect of permanent depreciation in the claimant's land: it is to be presumed that the injunction will be obeyed and that the value of the land will not further depreciate.[246]

Section 8 Public nuisance

(A) Nature of public nuisance

In *R v Rimmington; R v Goldstein*,[247] the House of Lords adopted the definition of public nuisance offered in *Archbold*, which states that:

> A person is guilty of a public nuisance ... who (a) does an act not by law, or (b) omits to discharge a legal duty, if the effect of the act or omission is to endanger the life, health,

---

[241] For a fuller account of the principles, see J Murphy, *The Law of Nuisance* (2010), ch 6.

[242] (1867) LR 5 Eq 166. Once C has established that a substantial interference has occurred, and is likely to recur, the burden is on D to show special circumstances why an injunction should not be granted: *McKinnon Industries Ltd v Walker* (1951) 3 DLR 577, at 581.   [243] *Regan v Paul Properties Ltd* [2006] 3 WLR 1131.

[244] [1995] 2 All ER 697, at 711. Cf *Kennaway v Thompson* [1981] QB 88.

[245] *Lawrence v Fen Tigers Ltd* [2014] AC 822, at [247].   [246] *Macievich v Anderson* [1952] 4 DLR 507.

[247] [2006] 1 AC 456.

> property or comfort of the public, or to obstruct the public in the exercise or enjoyment of [common] rights.[248]

Although this is a broad definition of an ostensible tort, in truth the cause of action for public nuisance is confined in various ways. First, it is essential that there be an infringement of a public right. That being so, the accused in *R v Rimmington*, who sent over 500 abusive postal packages to different recipients, could not be held guilty of public nuisance.[249] Second, the cause of action tends to be pleaded successfully in a narrow range of situations (to be surveyed below) where public rights have been substantially impeded. The resulting impediments have been characterised as involving interferences with individual rights of free movement and autonomy.[250] Third, public nuisance may ground a civil action in three ways: by a relator action (brought in the name of the Attorney General on behalf of a private citizen to suppress underlying criminal activity of the defendant); by a local authority under the Local Government Act 1972; or by an action for damages in tort brought by a private citizen who has suffered 'special damage'.

(1) The relator action

If the defendant is responsible for a nuisance that affects a large number of citizens but fails to occasion any of them special damage, then an individual citizen may seek to persuade the Attorney General to suppress the defendant's activity on his behalf by way of a relator action for an injunction. To do so, the elements of the crime of public nuisance must be established. In practice, this method of obtaining injunctive relief is seldom used. This is explained in large part by the fact that the Attorney General is unlikely to entertain an application for a relator action where the victim has not experienced special harm; and where special harm has been suffered, the victim is entitled to bring a civil action in his own name.

(2) Local authority applications

Under the Local Government Act 1972, section 222, a local authority is empowered to bring proceedings in its own name for injunctive relief where it considers it 'expedient to do so for the promotion and protection of the interests of the inhabitants'. This provision extends to injunctive relief to prevent a public nuisance. Thus, in *Nottingham City Council v Zain (a minor)*,[251] it was held that an injunction could be sought to exclude a known drug-dealer from one of the city council's housing estates.

(3) Civil actions for 'special damage'

Two situations There are two situations in which a private citizen may bring a civil action for public nuisance. The first is said to arise where the defendant is responsible

---

[248] J Richardson, *Archbold: Criminal Pleading, Evidence and Practice* (2010), 2864.

[249] [2006] 1 AC 456, at [6]. Drawing an analogy with abusive phone calls, Lord Rodger said (at [48]): 'no such individual call can become a criminal public nuisance merely by reason of the fact that it is one of a series'.

[250] See A Ripstein, *Force and Freedom: Kant's Legal and Political Philosophy* (2009), 261–2; JW Neyers (2017) 76 CLJ 87.   [251] [2002] 1 WLR 607.

for an interference which bears the characteristics of a private nuisance *except* that it affects a much greater number of people.[252] And here, just as in private nuisance, it is not a prerequisite that the act itself be unlawful: the nuisance derives from the detrimental effect of the act complained of. The second concerns cases where the interference would not bear the key characteristics of a private nuisance in that it does not affect the claimant's land, or his use or enjoyment of that land. Instead, the nuisance in such cases amounts to an inconvenience occasioned to the public generally but causes special damage to the claimant (that is, damage beyond that suffered by other members of the public). Such nuisances typically involve obstructing, or creating dangers on, highways and waterways as well as interferences with *profits à prendre*.[253]

Special damage Crucial to both kinds of public nuisance is the requirement that the claimant must suffer, or be at risk of, 'special damage'. While it is difficult to supply a precise definition of special damage, it is possible to advert to a number of established categories of such loss. Financial loss stemming from loss of business or custom, where the injury was of a 'substantial character, not fleeting or evanescent' has long been recognised as such a category.[254] But where other members of the public have suffered financial loss also, it is more difficult for the claimant to establish special damage, for he is able only to show the same kind of damage as that suffered by the others[255] and therefore might obtain no remedy.[256] In addition to financial loss, property damage[257] and personal injury[258] have been held to constitute special damage. So too have causing inconvenience or delay, provided that the harm caused to the claimant is substantial and appreciably greater in extent than any suffered by the general public.[259] Thus, in one case, a claimant could recover in public nuisance both for damage to his vehicle on the highway and for interference with peaceful sleep in his adjoining house.[260]

Circumstances giving rise to special damage Waterways and *profits à prendre* to one side, the majority of public nuisance cases arise where the defendant either

---

[252] The required number of people will vary from case to case; and if the public right at stake is enjoyed by a relatively small number of people, this will not prevent there being a public nuisance: *Jan de Nul (UK) Ltd v NV Royal Belge* [2002] 1 Lloyd's Rep 583. Examples include driving lorries through residential streets: *Gillingham BC v Medway (Chatham) Dock Co Ltd* [1993] QB 343; blasting from a quarry causing vibrations, etc: *A-G (on the relation of Glamorgan CC and Pontardawe RDC) v PYA Quarries Ltd* [1957] 2 QB 169; holding 'acid-house parties': *R v Shorrock* [1994] QB 279. But this formulation of the tort has been criticised: JW Neyers [2017] 76 CLJ 87.   [253] JW Neyers [2017] 76 CLJ 87, 97.

[254] *Benjamin v Storr* (1874) LR 9 CP 400, at 407 (C's coffee shop lost custom when D parked horse-drawn vans outside his premises); *Lyons, Sons & Co v Gulliver* [1914] 1 Ch 631; *Blundy Clark & Co Ltd v London and NE Rly Co* [1931] 2 KB 334. See also *Caledonian Rly Co v Walker's Trustees* (1882) 7 App Cas 259 (depreciation in the value of land) and *Tate and Lyle Industries Ltd v GLC* [1983] 2 AC 509 (cost of dredging silted-up river in order to continue use of a ferry).   [255] *Martin v LCC* (1899) 80 LT 866.

[256] *Ricket v Directors etc of the Metropolitan Rly Co* (1867) LR 2 HL 175, at 190 and 199. But that this case did not overturn *Wilkes* is clear from *Blundy Clarke & Co v London and NE Rly Co* [1931] 2 KB 334 and *Colour Quest Ltd v Total Downstream UK plc* [2009] 1 CLC 186.

[257] *Halsey v Esso Petroleum Co Ltd* [1961] 2 All ER 145.

[258] *Castle v St Augustine's Links Ltd* (1922) 38 TLR 615.

[259] *Walsh v Ervin* [1952] VLR 361; *Boyd v Great Northern Rly Co* [1895] 2 IR 555.

[260] *Halsey v Esso Petroleum Co Ltd* [1961] 2 All ER 145.

creates a danger on or obstructs[261] the highway[262] or the adjacent pavement.[263] There is a long line of cases that establishes liability in public nuisance for rendering the highway unsafe in respect of walls,[264] fences,[265] windows,[266] etc that fall on to the highway from adjoining premises. But other examples include leaving dangerous articles such as defective cellar flaps or unlighted scaffolding there,[267] or conducting operations off the highway which menace the safety of those upon it.[268] Where all that occurs is a blockage of the highway, in principle it should be users of the highway whose right to use the highway has been infringed, rather than shopkeepers who suffer a consequential loss in trade, who can sue. (However, the aberrant decision in *Wilkes v Hungerford Market Co*[269] points the other way, and it has been rightly criticised by subsequent judges for doing so.[270])

Although an obstruction of the highway is only partial, it might give rise nonetheless to liability in public nuisance. As Lord Evershed MR explained in *Trevett v Lee*: '[a]n obstruction is something which permanently or temporarily removes the whole *or part of the highway* from public use.'[271] Accordingly, where a vehicle is parked in such a way as to narrow significantly the width of the road, its owner may be held liable in public nuisance.[272] The obstruction need not be caused by vehicles. A crowd—such as workers picketing an employer's premises—might just as easily obstruct the highway and form the basis of an action in public nuisance.[273] But where a demonstration or picket takes place peacefully, the obstruction prima facie will be considered a reasonable (and thus non-actionable) use of the highway.[274] Moreover, temporary and reasonable obstructions of the highway will not attract liability. Consider *Trevett v Lee*:[275]

> Ds, who had no mains connection, laid a hose pipe across the highway in a time of drought in order to obtain a water supply from the other side of the road. C, who tripped over it and suffered injury, failed in an action for public nuisance since Ds' user of the highway was reasonable 'judged both from their own point of view and from the point of view of the other members of the public'.[276]

Statutory duties A final point worth noting in this context is that, where the claimant alleges public nuisance because the matter in question, although regulated by statute, is not so regulated so as to confer an action for breach of statutory duty, the courts will

---

[261] Whether there is an obstruction is a question of fact: *Harper v G N Haden & Sons* [1933] Ch 298.

[262] The same principles apply to navigable waterways: *Tate & Lyle Industries Ltd v GLC* [1983] 2 AC 509; *Rose v Miles* (1815) 4 M & S 101.   [263] *Ellis v Sheffield Gas Co* (1853) 2 E & B 767.

[264] *Mint v Good* [1951] 1 KB 517.   [265] *Harrold v Watney* [1898] 2 QB 320.

[266] *Leanse v Lord Egerton* [1943] KB 323.   [267] *Penny v Wimbledon UDC and Iles* [1899] 2 QB 72.

[268] *Castle v St Augustine's Links* (1922) 38 TLR 615 (C lost an eye when a golf ball smashed the window of his car). Cf *Stone v Bolton* [1950] 1 KB 201 (a cricket ball escaping the cricket ground was not a public nuisance as it was an isolated event).   [269] (1835) Bing NC 281.

[270] See, eg, *Ricket v Directors etc of the Metropolitan Rly Co* (1867) LR 2 HL 175, at 190 and 199.

[271] *Trevett v Lee* [1955] 1 All ER 406, at 409 (emphasis added).

[272] *A-G v Gastonia Coaches Ltd* [1977] RTR 219; *Dymond v Pearce* [1972] 1 QB 496.

[273] *News Group Newspapers Ltd v SOGAT '82 (No 2)* [1987] ICR 181.   [274] *DPP v Jones* [1999] 2 AC 240.

[275] [1955] 1 All ER 406. Whether it is a defence to say that the obstruction is reasonable because it is for the public benefit is unsettled. Compare *R v Russell* (1827) 6 B & C 566 (held to be a defence) and *R v Ward* (1836) 4 Ad & El 384.   [276] *Trevett v Lee* [1955] 1 All ER 406, at 412.

be slow to provide a common law remedy where Parliament did not see fit to create a statutory one.[277]

(B) The relationship between public nuisance and private nuisance

There has been some confusion about the relationship between public nuisance and private nuisance. For example, since it was recognised that private nuisance protected householders from the nauseous smells generated by their neighbours, it was thought that public nuisance ought logically to be applicable in cases involving the de-pasturing of pigs in towns and cities,[278] and otherwise infiltrating the air on highways with 'noisome and offensive stinks and smells'.[279] However, while such extensions might have been justifiable, there is no basis for the oft-made claim that there is a sub-category of public nuisance which 'overlaps with private nuisance and consists of those cases which satisfy the requirements of that tort but affect a much larger number of people than is usual in a private nuisance action'.[280] The reason the claim is groundless lies in the fact that, while private rights animate the law of private nuisance, a different category of rights—namely, public rights which are not a mere amalgam of multiple private rights—underpins the law of public nuisance.[281] There is an important difference. Private rights are personal to each of us whereas public rights are not. So, although Romer LJ once said that 'a normal and legitimate way of proving a public nuisance is to prove a sufficiently large collection of private nuisances',[282] the House of Lords has held this approach to be wrong. Using the example of multiple obscene phone calls, the House observed that 'each telephone call affects only one individual … [and] no such individual call can become a criminal public nuisance merely by reason of the fact that it is one of a series'.[283] Each and every call lacks the essential element of common injury: that is, the infringement of a *public* right.[284] On top of this difference, a distinction can be made between the kinds of interests protected by private and public nuisance since these do not overlap precisely. For example, while an action for private nuisance will be confined to interests in or over land, and will not accommodate actions in respect of personal injuries,[285] the same is not true of public nuisances. Indeed, *In re Corby Group Litigation*[286] held that personal injuries *are* compensable in public nuisance.

---

[277] *Ali v Bradford City MDC* [2011] RTR 20; *Wilkinson v York CC* [2011] EWCA Civ 207, at [9].

[278] *R v Wigg* (1705) 2 Ld Raym 1163.   [279] *R v White and Ward* (1757) 1 Burr 333.

[280] RA Buckley, *The Law of Nuisance* (1996), 67. This is not to say that any given case will not support an action in both private and public nuisance: see, eg, *Halsey v Esso Petroleum Co Ltd* [1961] 2 All ER 145. Nor are actions for public nuisance and negligence necessarily mutually exclusive: see, eg, *Dymond v Pearce* [1972] 1 QB 496.   [281] *R v Rimmington; R v Goldstein* [2006] 1 AC 459, at [44].

[282] *A-G v PYA Quarries* [1957] 2 QB 169, at 187. See also at 191.

[283] *R v Rimmington; R v Goldstein* [2006] 1 AC 459, at [48] and [58].

[284] In order to infringe a public right in such a way as to cause a public nuisance, there must be interference with its use to an unreasonable degree: *Westminster CC v Ocean Leisure Ltd* [2004] EWCA Civ 970. Insofar as personal injuries are recoverable (on which see *In re Corby Group Litigation* [2008] EWCA Civ 463), it is to be inferred that a *public* right to reasonable safety exists.   [285] *Hunter v Canary Wharf Ltd* [1997] AC 655.

[286] [2008] EWCA Civ 463, at [22]–[24].

(C) Remedies in public nuisance

(1) Injunction

As we have already seen, where the victim of a public nuisance cannot establish special damage, a relator action for an injunction may be brought by the Attorney General on his behalf. Alternatively, under the Local Government Act 1972, section 222, a local authority may seek an injunction to secure 'the promotion and protection of the interests of the inhabitants'. Finally, individual applicants relying on their special damage are able to obtain injunctions in public nuisance.[287]

(2) Damages

Heads of damage Most commonly, a claim in public nuisance will be for damages in respect of personal injuries or for financial losses sustained by people using a public highway.[288] In addition occupiers of premises adjoining the highway may recover in public nuisance when they suffer special damage as a result of a nuisance on a highway. And this is the case even though the damage complained of is not suffered by them qua users of the highway. For example, shopkeepers have succeeded in this tort where access to their premises has been interfered with,[289] or where their customers have been subjected to noxious smells and darkened rooms as a result of the parking of horses and carts outside their premises.[290]

Remoteness It is clear from *The Wagon Mound (No 2)*[291] that damages are available *subject to* the familiar remoteness of damage principle. That is, the claimant will recover only so far as the defendant ought to have foreseen the type of loss suffered by the claimant. In that case, the claimant's ship was damaged in a fire caused by the defendant carelessly allowing oil to overflow from the defendant's ship into the waters of Sydney Harbour. The defendant was held liable in public nuisance, but only because the fire on the claimant's ship was held to be a foreseeable consequence of the defendant's wrongful act. By contrast, in *Savage v Fairclough*,[292] a pig farmer who had relied on the advice of an expert agronomist was held not liable in respect of the ensuing pollution of the claimant's water since such pollution had not in fact been foreseen, nor had it been reasonably foreseeable.

Further limits Two further limitations exist with respect to the quantum of damages. First, no matter how reprehensible the public nuisance, exemplary damages will never be available.[293] Second, an award of damages can be reduced or excluded altogether by operation of the defences of contributory negligence or *volenti non fit injuria*, respectively.[294]

---

[287] *Spencer v London and Birmingham Rly Co* (1836) 8 Sim 193.
[288] Note, however, that the creation of a mere hazard on the highway might suffice: *Wandsworth LBC v Railtrack plc* [2002] QB 756 (excessive pigeon droppings).   [289] *Fritz v Hobson* (1880) 14 Ch D 542.
[290] *Benjamin v Storr* (1874) LR 9 CP 400.   [291] [1967] 1 AC 617.   [292] [2000] Env LR 183.
[293] *Gibbons v South West Water Services Ltd* [1993] QB 507, at 531.
[294] *Dymond v Pearce* [1972] 1 QB 496.

Conclusions

This chapter has considered two torts with quite different operations—although they are complementary in that they both deal with 'uses of land'. The tort of private nuisance is concerned with interferences with private land, while public nuisance is concerned with interferences with public rights over the use of land that impact upon particular individuals in extraordinary ways. The former tort is much more prevalent than the latter. Private nuisance occurs where there is physical interference with neighbouring land or interference with the amenity value of that land. In order to be able to claim in nuisance, it is necessary for the claimant to have a proprietary or possessory interest in the affected land. Private nuisance is a strict liability tort in that it does not depend upon proof of fault in the defendant.

Problem question

Rollerrama Ltd operates a roller-skating rink on the outskirts of Pleasantville. Although the rink used to be some 500 metres away from the nearest houses, the local council has given permission for housing construction in the area and these days the roller-skating rink is surrounded by new-build houses constructed at low cost. The construction of the houses has coincided with a revival in children's interest in roller-skating. Rollerrama conducts skate nights on Fridays, Saturdays, and Sundays. These feature loud music from the 1970s and flashing disco lights. In order to advertise its skate nights, Rollerrama projects colourful light beams into the night sky. This disturbs Fred and Mary and their dogs, who live 100 metres away in a new-build home. Fred and Mary's dogs bark throughout the duration of the skating events. In turn, Barney is unable to sleep in his new-build home situated next to Fred and Mary's. In order to let Fred and Mary know that he is not sleeping very well, Barney himself makes a barking sound at night—just after Rollerrama closes. As a result, Fred and Mary are awoken just as they are nodding off to sleep at 1 am.

Advise the parties as to the commission of any potential nuisances.

 Visit **http://www.oup.com/uk/street15e/** for answer guidance.

Further reading

CROSS, 'Does only the Careless Polluter Pay? A Fresh Examination of the Nature of Private Nuisance' (1995) 111 *Law Quarterly Review* 445

GEARTY, 'The Place of Nuisance in the Modern Law of Torts' (1989) 48 *Cambridge Law Journal* 214

LEE, 'What is Private Nuisance?' (2003) 119 *Law Quarterly Review* 298

LEE, 'Personal Injury, Public Nuisance and Environmental Regulation' (2009) 20 *King's Law Journal* 12

MURPHY, *The Law of Nuisance* (2010)

NEYERS, 'Reconceptualising the Tort of Public Nuisance' (2017) 76 *Cambridge Law Journal* 87

NOLAN, 'Nuisance, Planning and Regulation: The Limits of Statutory Authority' in Dyson, Goudkamp, and Wilmot-Smith (eds), *Defences in Tort* (2015)

SPENCER, 'Public Nuisance—A Critical Examination' (1989) 48 *Cambridge Law Journal* 55

STEEL, 'The Locality Principle in Private Nuisance' (2017) 76 *Cambridge Law Journal* 145

STEELE, 'Private Law and the Environment: Nuisance in Context' (1995) 15 *Legal Studies* 236

TROMANS, 'Nuisance—Prevention or Payment?' (1982) 41 *Cambridge Law Journal* 87

18

The rule in *Rylands v Fletcher*

KEY ISSUES

(1) Elements of the rule
In order to have a cause of action under the rule in *Rylands v Fletcher*, a claimant must show that: (1) the thing causing damage had been kept or collected on land owned by, or under the control of, the defendant; (2) it is of a kind that foreseeably will cause harm upon its escape; (3) there has been a non-natural use (which is not the same as a merely unreasonable use) of land; and (4) there has been an escape of the thing.

(2) Comparison with other torts
There is some doubt about the discrete nature of this action. The ascendant view is that the rule in *Rylands v Fletcher* is merely a sub-branch of the law of private nuisance. The rule is seen as a spur of nuisance law that deals only with one-off occurrences. There is a somewhat less popular view also that the

rule in *Rylands v Fletcher* ought to be subsumed within the general law of negligence. But these views conflict with orthodoxy.

(3) Strict liability
An issue arises whether this tort is truly an instance of strict liability in tort. The greatest doubt as to whether liability is truly strict in this context inheres in what is implied by the test for remoteness of damage in this tort as well as some of the defences that are available.

(4) Interests protected
A final key issue concerns the kinds of loss or harm that are actionable under the rule in *Rylands v Fletcher*. If the idea is pressed hard that it is a mere sub-branch of the law of nuisance, then certain forms of harm—in particular physical injury to the person—ought not to be viewed as actionable.

Section 1 Introduction

Origins The rule in *Rylands v Fletcher*[1] probably is the best known example of an ostensibly 'strict liability'[2] tort in English law and it derives from the nineteenth-century case of that name:

---

[1] (1866) LR 1 Exch 265 (affd (1868) LR 3 HL 330).
[2] Recall from ch 1 that this implies that liability arises regardless of fault. There are reasons to doubt the extent of the strictness of the liability, as will be seen in the text that follows.

> Ds employed independent contractors to build a reservoir on their land. Through the neg-
> ligence of the independent contractors, disused shafts upon the site which communicated
> with C's mine beneath the reservoir were not blocked up. On the filling of the reservoir, the
> water escaped down the shafts and flooded C's mine.

Although the defendants were themselves neither negligent nor vicariously liable for
the negligence of their independent contractors,[3] they were held liable both by the
Court of Exchequer Chamber and the House of Lords. Blackburn J, delivering the judgment of the Court of Exchequer Chamber, said:

> [A] person who for his own purposes brings on his lands and collects and keeps there any-
> thing likely to do mischief if it escapes, must keep it in at his peril, and if he does not do so,
> is *prima facie* answerable for all the damage which is the natural consequence of its escape.[4]

Lord Cairns in the House of Lords broadly agreed with this judgment, but he restricted
the scope of the rule to instances where the defendant had engaged in 'a non-natural
use' of the land.[5] Though seemingly innocuous at the time, this addition to Blackburn
J's formulation of the rule gave rise to one of the most vexed questions in relation to
Rylands v Fletcher liability: what is 'a non-natural use' of land? As we shall see in section
4 of this chapter, there is still no clear answer to this question.

Blackburn J did not consider himself to be making new law. The following quotation
encapsulates his thinking:

> The general rule, as above stated, seems on general principle just. The person whose grass
> or corn is eaten down by the escaping cattle of his neighbour, or whose mine is flooded by
> the water from his neighbour's reservoir, or whose cellar is invaded by the filth of his neigh-
> bour's privy, or whose habitation is made unhealthy by the fumes and noisome vapours of
> his neighbour's alkali works, is damnified without any fault of his own; and it seems but rea-
> sonable and just that the neighbour, who has brought something on his own property which
> was not naturally there, harmless to others so long as it is confined to his own property, but
> which he knows to be mischievous if it gets on his neighbour's, should be obliged to make
> good the damage which ensues if he does not succeed in confining it to his own property.[6]

General theory denied Yet, close though the analogy with nuisance might appear,[7]
the fact remains that *Rylands v Fletcher* was the starting point for a form of liability
which, as developed by the courts in subsequent decisions, was wider and quite different in kind from any that preceded it.[8] Indeed, this extension of liability gave rise
to speculation about whether or not some comprehensive theory of strict liability for
harm caused to persons by ultra-hazardous things was being formulated. Whatever

---

[3] For discussion of vicarious liability and liability in relation to independent contractors, see ch 24.
[4] (1866) LR 1 Exch 265, at 279–80.   [5] (1866) LR 1 Exch 265, at 338–40.
[6] (1866) LR 1 Exch 265, at 280.
[7] For an early account of the relationship between liability in nuisance and liability under the rule in *Rylands
v Fletcher*, see FH Newark (1945) 65 LQR 480. See also *Cambridge Water Co Ltd v Eastern Counties Leather plc*
[1994] 2 AC 264, at 298; *Transco v Stockport MBC* [2004] 2 AC 1, at [9]. For criticism, see J Murphy (2004) 24
OJLS 643.   [8] See, eg, D Nolan (2005) 121 LQR 421.

attraction it might once have had, such a theory is no longer tenable after the interpretation put upon *Rylands v Fletcher* by the House of Lords in *Read v J Lyons & Co Ltd*[9] There, the facts were as follows:

> The appellant, while working in the respondent's factory, was injured by an explosion there. No allegation of negligence was made by her against the respondents. The basis of her claim was that the respondents carried on the manufacture of high-explosive shells, knowing that they were dangerous things.

The ground for the decision in favour of the respondents was that the rule in *Rylands v Fletcher* does not apply unless there has been an escape from a place where the defendant has occupation or control over land to a place outside her control.[10] But the importance of the case does not end there. *Read v J Lyons & Co Ltd* constituted a denial of a general theory of strict liability for ultra-hazardous activities; there is liability for non-negligent escapes only where the several preconditions for *Rylands v Fletcher* liability (considered in the following sections) are satisfied. Where these preconditions are not met, the claimant's case can be formulated neither in terms of the intentional or negligent conduct of the defendant.

Utilisation and decline Perhaps the most remarkable characteristic of this rule, early in its life, was its fluidity. Stated in very broad terms by Blackburn J, it was at once modified in the case itself by the House of Lords, which confined it to instances involving a 'non-natural use' of land. Thereafter, it was widely utilised. Often cases properly sounding in nuisance alone were brought within the fold of *Rylands v Fletcher*. The rule was given even greater elasticity by the interpretation of 'non-natural use' by the Privy Council in 1913, which considered it to mean 'some special use bringing with it increased danger to others, and [which] must not merely be the ordinary use of the land or such a use as is proper for the general benefit of the community'.[11] Even after 1913, the rule in *Rylands v Fletcher* continued to be invoked freely; and often it was not sufficiently sharply distinguished from nuisance.[12] Then, in 1947, came something of a volte-face in the shape of *Read v J Lyons & Co Ltd*.[13] There, it was made clear that the earlier decisions

---

[9] [1945] KB 216 (affd [1947] AC 156). In *Transco v Stockport MBC* [2004] 2 AC 1, emphasis was placed on extraordinary uses of land. Yet such uses do not require an ultra-hazardous agent to have been accumulated. It was only Lord Bingham (at [11]) who took the view that the operation of the rule hinged on an especially dangerous agent. Those agreeing with Lord Bingham *also* signalled their agreement with Lord Hoffmann's approach, which was markedly different.

[10] There are *obiter dicta* to the effect that the escape of a dangerous thing from D's chattel, located on a highway (*Rigby v CC of Northamptonshire* [1985] 1 WLR 1242, at 1255) or from her vessel, situated on a navigable waterway (*Crown River Cruises Ltd v Kimbolton Fireworks Ltd* [1996] 2 Lloyd's Rep 533) is sufficient to give rise to *Rylands* liability. However, these *dicta* are difficult to sustain both in principle, and in the light of existing authority: see *Jones v Festiniog Rly Co* (1868) LR 3 QB 733; *Powell v Fall* (1880) 5 QBD 597; *West v Bristol Tramways Co* [1908] 2 KB 14. Such actions should sound in negligence, not *Rylands v Fletcher*—which has always been a land-based tort—*unless*, as in the three cases cited, D has a statutory right to occupation of the public thoroughfare.   [11] *Rickards v Lothian* [1913] AC 263, at 280.

[12] The most authoritative statement of the continuing affinity between the two torts is set out in *Cambridge Water Co Ltd v Eastern Counties Leather plc* [1994] 2 AC 264, at 298–9 (Lord Goff). The remaining four Law Lords concurred.   [13] [1945] KB 216, at 247.

of the lower courts, which had appeared to extend the original rule, henceforth must be closely scrutinised before they could be accepted as good authorities.

Section 2 'Things' within the rule

Damage on escape Blackburn J spoke of 'anything likely to do mischief if it escapes'. These things must not summarily be described as 'dangerous' and then equated (and, in turn, confused) with those things which have been considered 'dangerous' in the context of negligence. Indeed, it would be wise to eschew the word 'dangerous' altogether since it is an inherently protean concept. A simple example of the need for caution in this context can be supplied by reference to the mischievous 'thing' in *Rylands v Fletcher* itself—namely, water. Water is not 'dangerous' per se. Yet, as Du Parcq LJ observed in the Court of Appeal in *Read v J Lyons & Co Ltd*,[14] what matters is whether the thing is likely to do damage on escaping to other land.[15] Whether or not this involves personal danger is quite irrelevant. Thus, filth and water are both 'things' caught by the rule even though they are not inherently dangerous.

Independent movement In *Read v J Lyons & Co Ltd*, counsel argued that the thing must have the 'capacity for independent movement'[16] as well as being a potential cause of harm. So, for example, glass would be outside the rule. Provided that an extension is made to include a thing likely to give off something such as a gas, which itself has the capacity for independent movement, this contention has much to commend it in describing many of the 'things' covered by the rule in *Rylands v Fletcher*, and there is some (albeit limited) support for it in the cases.[17]

Examples Things which have been held to be capable of giving rise to *Rylands v Fletcher* liability include water,[18] sewage,[19] gas likely to pollute water supplies,[20] things likely to give off noxious gases or fumes,[21] electricity,[22] explosives,[23] and things likely to cause fires[24] (including in a motor vehicle whether the tank contains,[25] or is empty of,[26] petrol), and slag heaps.[27] Cases holding planted yew trees[28] and chair-o-planes[29] to be within the

---

[14] [1945] KB 216, at 247.   [15] Cf *Read v J Lyons & Co* [1947] AC 156, at 176.

[16] [1947] AC 156, at 158.

[17] Eg, *Wilson v Newberry* (1871) LR 7 QB 31, at 33, per Mellor J: 'things which have a tendency to escape and to do mischief'.

[18] *Rylands v Fletcher* (1868) LR 3 HL 330; *Western Engraving Co v Film Laboratories Ltd* [1936] 1 All ER 106.

[19] *Humphries v Cousins* (1877) 2 CPD 239.   [20] *Batchellor v Tunbridge Wells Gas Co* (1901) 84 LT 765.

[21] *West v Bristol Tramways Co* [1908] 2 KB 14; *Halsey v Esso Petroleum Co Ltd* [1961] 2 All ER 145 (acid smuts).

[22] *National Telephone Co v Baker* [1893] 2 Ch 186.

[23] *Rainham Chemical Works Ltd v Belvedere Fish Guano Co* [1921] 2 AC 465; *Rigby v CC of Northamptonshire* [1985] 1 WLR 1242 (CS gas canisters).

[24] *Jones v Festiniog Rly Co* (1868) LR 3 QB 733 (sparks from railway engine); *Balfour v Barty-King* [1956] 2 All ER 555 (blowlamp) (affd on other grounds [1957] 1 QB 496).

[25] *Musgrove v Pandelis* [1919] 2 KB 43 (doubted in *Gore v Stannard (trading as Wyvern Tyres)* [2014] QB 1, at [146] (Lewison LJ)).   [26] *Perry v Kendricks Transport Ltd* [1956] 1 All ER 154.

[27] *Kennard v Cory Bros & Co Ltd* [1921] AC 521.

[28] *Crowhurst v Amersham Burial Board* (1878) 4 Ex D 5.   [29] *Hale v Jennings Bros* [1938] 1 All ER 579.

rule probably are sound, so long as there is movement of the mischievous thing beyond the boundary of the land under the defendant's control. A final and interesting illustration of the kind of 'things' that fall within the rule is supplied by *A-G v Corke*.[30] There it was held that the owner of land who allowed caravan dwellers to live on that land was answerable under the rule for the interferences which they perpetrated on adjoining land.[31] However, whether a decayed and rusty wire fence[32] and a flag-pole[33] have been rightly regarded as being within the rule is doubtful.

Fire Although it has been held that the rule in *Rylands v Fletcher* is applicable to cases involving the outbreak of fire,[34] the salience of the proposition must be doubted following the decision of the Court of Appeal in *Gore v Stannard (trading as Wyvern Tyres)*,[35] the facts of which were as follows:

> D operated a tyre sales business on a light industrial estate. An estimated 3,000 tyres were stored on the premises. Although the tyres were not easily set alight, an electrical fault caused a fire, which caught hold of the tyres, and the fire spread to cause damage to the claimant's neighbouring premises.

It was held that an action under *Rylands v Fletcher*, although available in cases of fire,[36] was not established on the facts because the defendant had not brought anything on to land which made his use of the land non-natural and because the tyres themselves had not escaped.[37] Ward LJ underlined how difficult it would be to bring a fire case within the principles (for the same reasons applicable on the facts).[38] Lewison LJ, in a compelling judgment, went even further so as to rule that such cases were not even theoretically available.[39]

Brought onto land The last characteristic of those 'things' whose escape might give rise to liability under the rule is that they must have been brought on to the land by the defendant. This final characteristic applies only to 'things artificially brought or kept upon the defendant's land'.[40]

Section 3 Parties

(A) Who may be sued?

Persons bringing things onto land Blackburn J said that the rule applies to a 'person who for his own purposes brings on his lands and collects and keeps there' the thing in question. The thing might or might not be something which in its nature is capable

---

[30] [1933] Ch 89. In *Smith v Scott* [1973] Ch 314 (undesirable tenants were held to be outside the rule, because a landlord has no 'control' over them).

[31] On similar facts, liability has also been imposed in private nuisance: see *Lippiatt v South Gloucestershire Council* [1999] 4 All ER 149. [32] *Firth v Bowling Iron Co* (1878) 3 CPD 254.

[33] *Shiffman v Venerable Order of the Hospital of St John of Jerusalem* [1936] 1 All ER 557.

[34] *LMS International Ltd v Styrene Packaging & Insulation Ltd* [2006] TCLR 6. [35] [2014] QB 1.

[36] [2014] QB 1, at [47] and [53]. [37] [2014] QB 1, at [50], [53], and [68]. [38] [2014] QB 1, at [48].

[39] [2014] QB 1, esp. at [109], [112], and [145]. [40] *Bartlett v Tottenham* [1932] 1 Ch 114, at 131.

of being naturally there: what matters is whether the particular thing has been accumulated there in fact. Therefore, if water flows from A's underground tunnels into B's mines, whether by force of gravitation or by percolation, A is not liable under the rule in *Rylands v Fletcher* for that escape if the water was on A's land naturally and she did nothing to accumulate it there.[41] On the other hand, there was liability in *Rylands v Fletcher* itself because steps had been taken by the defendants to accumulate the water on their land by constructing the reservoir.[42] The cases where flooding of neighbouring land results from pumping or diverting water from the land of the defendant to that of the claimant may be nuisance, or even perhaps trespass. But they cannot be within the rule in *Rylands v Fletcher* if the defendant has not artificially accumulated the water.[43] Similarly, the escape of rocks is outside the rule since there has been no accumulation.[44] If, however, rocks are blasted in quarrying, there may be liability for accumulating the explosives.[45]

Licensees In *Rainham Chemical Works Ltd v Belvedere Fish Guano Co Ltd*,[46] the facts were as follows:

> A and B contracted with the Ministry of Munitions to manufacture explosives on their land. They formed a limited company, C Ltd, and arranged for C Ltd to perform this contract on the land of A and B. Thus, C Ltd was the licensee of A and B. Neighbouring landowners suffered damage to their land caused by an explosion on the land of A and B while C Ltd was using it, and they sued C Ltd as well as A and B.

The House decided that a licensee who accumulates something on the land of another is liable for the consequences of that accumulation.[47] It was held, further, that those who remain in occupation of land are liable also to landowners injured by the escape of that which their licensee accumulates in discharge of a contractual duty owed by the occupiers to a third party. Moreover, Lord Sumner stated (*obiter*) that, if 'they [A and B] . . . simply suffered others to manufacture upon the site which they nevertheless continued to occupy' they would be liable for the consequences of an escape.[48]

On the other hand, Eve J in *Whitmores (Edenbridge) Ltd v Stanford*[49] held that a landowner, upon whose land some other person had a prescriptive right to accumulate water for his own purposes, would not be liable under the rule.

---

[41] *Wilson v Waddell* (1876) 2 App Cas 95.

[42] And in *Broder v Saillard* (1876) 2 Ch D 692, where the water was brought on to the land in connection with the stabling of D's horses.

[43] Eg, *Palmer v Bowman* [2000] 1 All ER 22; *Baird v Williamson* (1863) 15 CBNS 376. Cf *Hurdman v North Eastern Rly Co* (1878) 3 CPD 168.   [44] *Pontardawe RDC v Moore-Gwyn* [1929] 1 Ch 656.

[45] *Miles v Forest Rock Granite Co (Leicestershire) Ltd* (1918) 34 TLR 500. If it is not the explosives, but the rocks which have escaped, then presumably there needs to be an analogy drawn with those cases in which D accumulates agent X but X gives off a gas which escapes, in which case there can be liability: see, eg, *Wilson v Newberry* (1871) LR 7 QB 31.   [46] [1921] 2 AC 465.

[47] However, where over 20 years had elapsed since the licensee had acquired the right to enter and accumulate water there, he was held not to be accountable for the escape of water, if he no longer had control of the land: *Westhoughton Coal and Cannel Co Ltd v Wigan Coal Corpn Ltd* [1939] Ch 800.

[48] [1921] 2 AC 465, at 480.   [49] [1909] 1 Ch 427.

The extent to which an occupier is liable in respect of the accumulations of her licensees cannot be regarded as entirely settled, but it is relevant to observe that in *Rylands v Fletcher* Blackburn J spoke only of a person who for her 'own purposes' brings things on to her land.[50] Thus, a local authority which is required by statute to permit the discharge of sewage into its sewers is treated as responsible for the accumulation of that sewage.[51]

Authority A person who authorises another to commit a tort is normally herself liable for that tort. Thus, a lessor is liable in nuisance if she lets land for a particular purpose in such circumstances that she is taken necessarily to have authorised the interference which the lessee in consequence causes.[52] There were *obiter dicta* in *Rainham Chemical Works Ltd v Belvedere Fish Guano Co Ltd* to the effect that the same rule applies in *Rylands v Fletcher* cases—in short, that a defendant might be liable although she does not occupy the land, if she has authorised another to accumulate something on it, when the thing so accumulated later escapes.[53]

Omissions What happens where the accumulation is not on the land owned or occupied by the defendant? In *Rigby v Chief Constable of Northamptonshire* Taylor J, relying on a passage in the then current edition of *Clerk and Lindsell on Torts*, suggested (*obiter*) that, so far as he could see, there was 'no difference in principle between allowing a man-eating tiger to escape from your land onto that of another and allowing it to escape from the back of your wagon parked on the highway'.[54] It is submitted that this view is wrong. How can the requirements that there be an artificial accumulation on, and a non-natural use of, the defendant's land be satisfied if both the accumulation and escape take place elsewhere? The preferable view is that such cases should be actionable, if at all, as negligent omissions.[55] The rule in *Rylands v Fletcher* is a well-established land-based tort, yet the focus is on land owned by, or under the control of, the defendant.[56]

(B) Who may sue?

Owners It is clear that this rule permits a landowning claimant, as in *Rylands v Fletcher* itself, to sue in respect of damage to land. Similarly, in relation to damage to chattels, Blackburn J later allowed a claim where sparks from a railway engine set fire to a haystack;[57] and several other cases support the proposition that liability for damage to goods is recoverable.[58]

---

[50] (1866) LR 1 Exch 265, at 279.   [51] *Smeaton v Ilford Corpn* [1954] Ch 450.   [52] See ch 17.

[53] [1921] 2 AC 465, at 476 and 489.   [54] [1985] 1 WLR 1242, at 1255.

[55] Negligent omissions are actionable infrequently, but creating an obvious source of danger that is liable to be 'sparked off' by a third party might give rise to negligence liability: see *Topp v London Country Bus (South West) Ltd* [1993] 1 WLR 976.   [56] See J Murphy (2004) 24 OJLS 643. Cf *Read v Lyons* [1947] AC 156, at 173.

[57] *Jones v Festiniog Rly Co* (1868) LR 3 QB 733. Cf *Cattle v Stockton Waterworks Co* (1875) LR 10 QB 453, at 457. See also discussion of *Gore v Stannard (trading as Wyvern Tyres)* [2014] QB 1, above.

[58] Eg, *Midwood & Co Ltd v Manchester Corpn* [1905] 2 KB 597; *Musgrove v Pandelis* [1919] 2 KB 43; *Collingwood v Home and Colonial Stores Ltd* [1936] 3 All ER 200. Cf *Read v J Lyons & Co* [1947] AC 156, at 169, and *Transco v Stockport MBC* [2004] 2 AC 1 (*obiter*).

Injured persons But what of those who suffer no such property damage, but merely personal injuries? Arguably, the question needs to be addressed in two stages.[59] First, where the claimant is an occupier of land, *Hale v Jennings Bros* is a Court of Appeal authority enabling occupiers to recover in respect of personal injuries.[60] There, a tenant of a stall at a fair suffered personal injuries as the result of an escape of the defendant's chair-o-plane. She was held to have a good cause of action based on *Rylands v Fletcher*.

Second, we must consider the position of the claimant who suffers personal injury without any such proprietary interest. Here, the law is less clear, both in relation to the general question of whether such persons have a right to sue at all[61] and in relation to the narrower question whether they may sue in respect of personal injuries. In both *Perry v Kendricks Transport Ltd*[62] and *British Celanese Ltd v AH Hunt (Capacitors) Ltd*[63] it was suggested, *obiter*, that even those with no proprietary interests are able to bring an action for personal injuries under the rule in *Rylands v Fletcher*. Certainly, there was nothing in Blackburn J's judgment in *Rylands* to prohibit such a possibility. Indeed his Lordship envisaged liability in respect of '*all the damage* which is the natural consequence of the escape'.[64] On this basis, it might be argued that a proprietary interest in land is not (and never has been) a prerequisite to recovery under this tort.[65] On the other hand, the House of Lords has twice stressed (wrongly, it is submitted) the fact that the rule in *Rylands v Fletcher* derives from, and is a sub-species of, private nuisance.[66] That being the case, on the present standing of English law, the rule in *Rylands v Fletcher*, like the law of private nuisance, would seem to be available only to those who possess a proprietary interest in the land affected by the escape.[67]

Preferable rule In the absence of clear authority, it is submitted that the view that anyone suffering personal injury may recover is to be preferred since the closeness between nuisance and *Rylands v Fletcher* is apt to be overstated—as we shall see later in this chapter. Moreover, there is a sense in which the distinction between personal injuries

---

[59] The most recent ultimate appellate court pronouncement on the question is in the *Transco* case. Lords Bingham and Hoffmann stated, *obiter*, that the rule does not permit claims for personal injuries or death. But as the following discussion reveals, this approach is highly suspect.   [60] [1938] 1 All ER 579.

[61] See *McKenna v British Aluminium Ltd* [2002] Env LR 30, at [20]–[28], where Neuberger J questioned, in the context of a striking out action, (1) whether the increasingly close relationship between nuisance and the rule in *Rylands v Fletcher* meant that the proprietary entitlement rule in nuisance applied also to *Rylands v Fletcher*; and (2) assuming it did, whether it was a sustainable rule in the wake of the enactment of the Human Rights Act 1998.

[62] [1956] 1 All ER 154.   [63] [1969] 2 All ER 1252.   [64] (1866) LR 1 Exch 265, at 279.

[65] Cf *Hunter v Canary Wharf Ltd* [1997] 2 All ER 426.

[66] *Cambridge Water Co Ltd v Eastern Counties Leather plc* [1994] 2 AC 264; *Transco v Stockport MBC* [2004] 2 AC 1, at [9], [52], and [92].

[67] See *Hunter v Canary Wharf Ltd* [1997] AC 655 (on nuisance) and *Transco v Stockport MBC* [2004] 2 AC 1, at [11], [47], and [68] (on the rule in *Rylands v Fletcher*). In both cases, however, this approach is difficult to reconcile with Art 8 of the European Convention on Human Rights, which affords all citizens an equal right to respect for their private lives. This point was recognised in *McKenna v British Aluminium Ltd* [2002] Env LR 30. In addition, a further weakness is that the approach conflates nuisance law with the rule in *Rylands v Fletcher* without any heed to the historical fact that, in nuisance, the emphasis is placed on C having a proprietary interest, whereas under *Rylands v Fletcher* the emphasis rests upon D's property (or, at least, property under D's control): it is on *D's land* that an accumulation must occur, and from *D's land* that there must be an escape.

and property damage is not always easy to sustain in this context, since, in the case of personal injury to the occupier or holder of a proprietary interest, injury to the person might be seen to merge into a general injury to the proprietary interest as a whole by way of a diminution in the amenity value of the land.[68]

Financial losses A final question is whether the claimant who suffers purely financial loss is able to claim for her losses under the rule in *Rylands v Fletcher*. Here too the law is somewhat uncertain. *Weller & Co v Foot and Mouth Disease Research Institute*[69] held that the escape of a virus was not actionable by the claimant, a cattle auctioneer, when it caused a loss of profit to his business after making a third party's cattle unsaleable. But, in *Ryeford Homes v Sevenoaks District Council*,[70] the possibility of recovery for financial loss was not ruled out. Judge Newey QC expressed the view that purely financial loss was recoverable *in principle* under the rule in *Rylands v Fletcher* so long as it was 'a sufficiently direct result of an escape of water from sewers'.[71] This view is thought to be correct and it is entirely consistent with both Blackburn J's judgment in *Rylands v Fletcher* and the decision in the *Weller* case.[72]

Section 4 The non-natural use of land

Initial interpretation Blackburn J said that the rule applied only to a thing 'which was not naturally there'.[73] In the House of Lords, Lord Cairns used more ambiguous words[74] which have since been construed as meaning that the defendant is answerable only if, in bringing the thing on to her land,[75] she is making 'a non-natural use' of the land. The expression 'non-natural use' is very flexible and the courts are afforded a great deal of latitude in construing whether the defendant has engaged in a 'non-natural use'. The form in which Lord Moulton expressed this rule on behalf of the Privy Council in *Rickards v Lothian* emphasised this flexibility.[76] He said: '[it] must be some special use bringing with it increased danger to others, and must not merely be the ordinary use of the land or such a use as is proper for the general benefit of the community'.[77] Viscount Simon in *Read v J Lyons & Co Ltd* thought this statement to be 'of the first importance'[78] and Lord Porter said:

---

[68] See the analysis of *Hunter v Canary Wharf* in ch 17.

[69] [1966] 1 QB 569. See also, in similar vein, *Cattle v Stockton Waterworks Co* (1875) LR 10 QB 453 (escape of water which made it more expensive for C to carry out his contract to construct a tunnel; not actionable).

[70] [1989] 2 EGLR 281.

[71] On the facts, however, D was able to invoke the defence of statutory authority (as to which, see section 7).

[72] The fact that the auctioneer's loss in *Weller* was contingent upon the cattle owners' loss rendered the loss of profit from the would-be auctions an *indirect*, and hence irrecoverable, financial loss.

[73] In *Read v Lyons* [1947] AC 156, at 166, Visc. Simon described this as 'a parenthetic reference to' the test of Lord Cairns.   [74] (1868) LR 3 HL 330, at 337–40.

[75] What matters is whether the accumulation (as distinct from the escape) is a non-natural use: *Read v Lyons* [1947] AC 156, at 186.   [76] [1913] AC 263, at 280.

[77] [1913] AC 263, at 280. It has since been qualified that this means the 'national community as a whole': *Ellison v Ministry of Defence* (1996) 81 BLR 101, at 119.   [78] [1947] AC 156, at 169.

> each seems to be a question of fact subject to a ruling of the judge as to whether . . . the particular use can be non-natural, and in deciding this question I think that all the circumstances of the time and place and practice of mankind must be taken into consideration so that what might be regarded as . . . non-natural may vary according to those circumstances.[79]

Current interpretation The current tendency is to interpret 'non-natural use' narrowly, and earlier cases might no longer be followed. For instance, despite the contrary House of Lords' decision in *Rainham Chemical Works Ltd v Belvedere Fish Guano Co*,[80] in *Read v J Lyons & Co Ltd* it was doubted whether building and running a munitions factory on land in wartime was a non-natural use.[81] Similarly, despite the words of Lord Moulton in *Rickards v Lothian* concerning uses that bring a 'general benefit to the community', Lord Goff denied that the generation of employment for a local community was sufficient to transform the storage of chemicals used in the tanning industry into a natural use of the land. He stated that he was not:

> able to accept that the creation of employment as such, even in a small industrial complex, is sufficient of itself to establish a particular use as constituting a natural or ordinary use of land.[82]

Beyond this, his Lordship offered little to clarify the meaning of the term 'non-natural use'. Instead of taking the opportunity to do so in *Cambridge Water*, he declined to say more than that he did not consider it necessary to redefine the phrase in that context since 'the storage of chemicals on industrial premises should be regarded as *an almost classic case* of non-natural use'.[83]

Thus it fell to the House of Lords in *Transco v Stockport MBC* to clarify this troublesome phrase. There—in holding that the supply of pressurised water to 66 flats constituted a natural use of land so that there could be no liability for the effects of a burst pipe—Lord Bingham offered the following thoughts.

> I think it is clear that ordinary user is a preferable test to natural user, making it clear that the rule in *Rylands v Fletcher* is engaged only where the defendant's use is shown to be extraordinary and unusual. This is not a test to be inflexibly applied: a use may be extraordinary and unusual at one time or in one place but not so at another time or in another place .... [T]he question is whether the defendant has done something out of the ordinary in the place and at the time when he does it. In answering that question, I respectfully think that little help is gained (and unnecessary confusion perhaps caused) by considering whether the use is proper for the general benefit of the community.[84]

By contrast, in the same case Lord Hoffmann was of the view that a test based on ordinary user was rather vague and preferred a test based on increased risk.[85] And confusingly, various other members of the House of Lords agreed with both analyses of the problem without indicating a preference for either one. That being so, a certain haze

---

[79] [1947] AC 156, at 176.   [80] [1921] 2 AC 465.   [81] [1947] AC 156, at 169–70 and 173.
[82] [1994] 1 All ER 53, at 79.   [83] [1994] 1 All ER 53, at 79 (emphasis added).
[84] [2004] 2 AC 1, at [11].   [85] [2004] 2 AC 1, at [37].

continues to overhang the definition of non-natural use, with some courts preferring to use the concept of reasonable use instead.[86]

Illustrations of natural use The following instances have been held to be natural uses of land: growing trees planted by the defendant, so long as they are not poisonous;[87] lighting a fire in the fireplace of a house;[88] using a hot wire-cutter in proximity to flammable material;[89] storing large quantities of tyres on an industrial estate;[90] storing metal foil in a factory;[91] installing necessary wiring for electric lighting;[92] water-pipe installations in buildings;[93] supplying gas to flats in a tower block;[94] working mines and minerals on land;[95] and building or pulling down walls.[96]

Non-natural uses By contrast, the following activities have been held to constitute non-natural uses of land: storing water, gas, electricity, and the like in *abnormal or excessive* quantities;[97] the storage of *ignitable* material in a barn;[98] and the use of a blow-lamp to thaw pipes *in a loft*.[99] But it is difficult to resist the conclusion that the current notion of a 'non-natural use' is both narrow and becoming narrower as technology develops and further commercial uses of land become accepted, so as to greatly restrict the scope of the rule in *Rylands v Fletcher*.

Section 5 Escape

Defendant's occupation or control According to the orthodox view, an explosion which injures a claimant within the factory where the explosion occurs is outside the rule since there must be an 'escape from a place where the defendant has occupation of, or control over, land to a place which is outside his occupation or control'.[100] By contrast, where something escapes from one place of entertainment in a fairground to a stall

---

[86] See, eg, *Arscott v Coal Authority* [2005] Env LR 6, at [29].   [87] *Noble v Harrison* [1926] 2 KB 332.

[88] *Sochaski v Sas* [1947] 1 All ER 344. Ditto holding a torch, at the top of the opening of a grate in order to test chimney draught: *J Doltis Ltd v Isaac Braithwaite & Sons (Engineers) Ltd* [1957] 1 Lloyd's Rep 522.

[89] *LMS International Ltd v Styrene Packaging & Insulation Ltd* [2005] EWHC 2065.

[90] *Gore v Stannard (trading as Wyvern Tyres)* [2014] QB 1.

[91] *British Celanese Ltd v A H Hunt (Capacitors) Ltd* [1969] 2 All ER 1252; *Mason v Levy Auto Parts of England Ltd* [1967] 2 QB 530 (doubted in *Gore v Stannard (trading as Wyvern Tyres)* [2014] QB 1, at [162]–[164]).

[92] *Collingwood v Home and Colonial Stores Ltd* [1936] 3 All ER 200.

[93] *Rickards v Lothian* [1913] AC 263; *Tilley v Stevenson* [1939] 4 All ER 207.

[94] *British Gas plc v Stockport MBC* [2001] Env LR 44.   [95] *Rouse v Gravelworks Ltd* [1940] 1 KB 489.

[96] *Thomas and Evans Ltd v Mid-Rhondda Co-operative Society Ltd* [1941] 1 KB 381; *St Anne's Well Brewery Co v Roberts* (1928) 140 LT 1.

[97] *Northwestern Utilities Ltd v London Guarantee and Accident Co Ltd* [1936] AC 108; *Western Engraving Co v Film Laboratories Ltd* [1936] 1 All ER 106 (water in unusual quantities brought on to land for manufacturing purposes of D). In *Transco*, the House of Lords expressly distinguished the substantially greater amount of water stored in *Rylands v Fletcher*.

[98] *E Hobbs (Farms) Ltd v Baxenden Chemical Co Ltd* [1992] 1 Lloyd's Rep 54.

[99] *Balfour v Barty-King* [1956] 2 All ER 555 (affd on other grounds [1957] 1 QB 496).

[100] *Read v J Lyons & Co* [1947] AC 156, at 168.

tenanted by another fairground operative (but still within the fairground), apparently there *is* a sufficient escape.[101]

Licence In *Midwood & Co Ltd v Manchester Corpn*,[102] an explosion in a cable belonging to, and laid by, the defendant in the highway caused inflammable gas to escape into the claimant's nearby house and set fire to its contents. There was held to be a sufficient escape to fall within the rule in *Rylands v Fletcher*. Then, in *Charing Cross Electric Supply Co v Hydraulic Power Co*,[103] the Court of Appeal, relying on the *Midwood* case, held that there was a sufficient escape when water from a main, laid by the defendants under the highway, escaped and damaged the claimant's electric cable which was near to it and under the same highway. In *Read v J Lyons & Co Ltd*, the House of Lords did not overrule these cases, but pointed out that there was, in each of them, an escape on to property over which the defendant had no control, from a container which the defendant had a licence to put in the highway.[104] On the other hand, the proposition that the rule extends to cases where the defendant has no such licence in respect of a public thoroughfare is thought to be wrong.[105]

What must escape The traditional assumption has been that the actual harm wrought by the escape need not be caused immediately by the thing accumulated. So, for example, it was held in *Kennard v Cory Bros & Co* that, where parts of a coal slag heap escaped and their pressure on a third party's quarry spoil caused that spoil to damage the claimant's land, the escape requirement of the rule in *Rylands v Fletcher* was satisfied.[106] However, in *Gore v Stannard (trading as Wyvern Tyres)*,[107] considered earlier, the Court of Appeal held that there was no liability on the part of a tyre seller in storing a large number of tyres on his premises, which subsequently caught fire. There was no escape of any tyres from the premises and the escape of the fire was held to be insufficient. It is respectfully submitted that the decision, although correct, was not supportable on this particular basis.[108]

Section 6 Foreseeability of harm

Since the important decision in the *Cambridge Water* case, it is clear that foreseeability of harm is required if a claimant is to succeed in an action based on the rule in *Rylands v Fletcher*. The facts in that case were as follows:

---

[101] This point was essential to the decision in *Hale v Jennings Bros* [1938] 1 All ER 579. Similarly, an escape to the lower part of the same building is sufficient: *J Doltis Ltd v Isaac Braithwaite & Sons (Engineers) Ltd* [1957] 1 Lloyd's Rep 522. The key to these cases appears to be an escape on to land under another's control, regardless of property ownership on D's part.   [102] [1905] 2 KB 597.

[103] [1914] 3 KB 772.   [104] [1947] AC 156, at 177. Cf ibid at 168 and 183.

[105] See the *obiter* suggestion in *Rigby v CC of Northamptonshire* [1985] 1 WLR 1242, at 1255 to this effect. See also *Crown River Cruises Ltd v Kimbolton Fireworks Ltd* [1996] 2 Lloyd's Rep 533 (escape from a vessel on a navigable waterway).

[106] [1921] AC 521, at 538.   [107] [2014] QB 1.   [108] See also comment by S Tofaris (2013) 72 CLJ 11.

Solvents which had been used by Ds in their tannery for many years had a history of being spilt on to the floor of Ds' factory. From there, they seeped into a natural ground-water source drawn upon by C in order to fulfil its statutory duty to supply drinking water to the inhabitants of Cambridge. The seepage caused the water to become contaminated to the extent that it was unwholesome according to European Community standards. No one had supposed that this contamination would take place, mainly because of the volatility of the solvents which it had been thought had simply evaporated from Ds' factory floor.

A unanimous House of Lords held the defendants not liable on the basis of the unforeseeability of the harm caused to the claimant's water supply. Lord Goff stated that 'foreseeability of damage of the relevant type should be regarded as a prerequisite of liability in damages under the rule'.[109] However, his Lordship failed to make clear whether damage had to be foreseeable (1) in terms of the *kind* of harm alone; or (2) in terms of *both* an escape occurring *and* harm being thereby caused. But since then it has been made clear that it is the former that is required. As Lord Bingham put it in the *Transco* case:

It must be shown that the defendant has done something which [s]he recognised, or judged by the standards appropriate at the relevant place and time, he ought reasonably to have recognised, as giving rise to an exceptionally high risk of danger or mischief if there should be an escape, however unlikely an escape may have been thought to be.[110]

Section 7 Defences

(A) Statutory authority

Sometimes, public bodies storing water, gas, electricity, and the like are by statute exempted from liability so long as they have taken reasonable care. It is a question of statutory interpretation whether (and, if so, to what extent) liability under the rule in *Rylands v Fletcher* has been excluded. Only if there is a statutory *duty* (as opposed to a mere *permission*) to perform the hazardous activity will there be a defence. *Smeaton v Ilford Corporation*[111] is illustrative:

Sewage accumulated by Ds in their sewers overflowed on to the land of C in circumstances held to constitute neither nuisance nor negligence. According to the Public Health Act 1936, section 31, under which Ds had acted in receiving the sewage: 'A local authority shall so discharge their functions . . . as not to create a nuisance.' In interpreting this to mean that Ds were absolved from liability because they were *obliged* to fulfil the duty without creating a nuisance, the court held that Ds had a defence under the statute to an action based on *Rylands v Fletcher*.

---

[109] [1994] 1 All ER 53, at 75.
[110] [2004] 2 AC 1, at [10]. This echoes Lord Goff in *Cambridge Water* (see [1994] 1 All ER 53, at 71) and *Hamilton v Papakura DC* [2002] UKPC 9, where the Privy Council also emphasised the need to establish the foreseeability of the relevant damage.   [111] [1954] Ch 450.

Green v Chelsea Waterworks Co[112] provides a further example of the statutory author-ity defence in operation. In that case, there was no liability when a water main burst because the waterworks company was under *a statutory obligation* to keep the mains charged at high pressure, making a damaging escape an inevitable consequence of any non-negligent burst. By contrast, in *Charing Cross Electricity Co v Hydraulic Power Co*,[113] the defendant had a statutory permission (but no obligation) to keep its water mains charged at high pressure. On this basis, no immunity from liability could be claimed.

(B) Necessity

If an intentional release of a substance could ground liability under the rule in *Rylands v Fletcher*, then the defence of necessity ought, in principle, to be available in this tort.[114] However, it is probably better to treat such cases as trespass cases in which the defence of necessity is well established.[115] Certainly, in one first instance case in which police officers had fired CS gas canisters into the claimant's shop in order to flush out a psycho-path, it was suggested that trespass would be the appropriate cause of action.[116]

(C) Consent of the claimant

If the claimant has permitted the defendant to accumulate the thing the escape of which is complained of, then she cannot sue if it escapes.[117] For the purposes of this defence, implied consent will suffice. Thus, a person becoming the tenant of business premises at a time when the condition or construction of adjoining premises is such that an escape is likely to ensue is deemed to have consented to the risk of such an event actually hap-pening. This defence was the crux of *Kiddle v City Business Properties Ltd*,[118] where an overflow of rainwater from a blocked gutter at the bottom of a sloping roof in the possession of the landlord, and above the tenant's premises, damaged the stock in the tenant's premises.[119]

If the accumulation benefits both claimant and defendant, this is an important ele-ment in deciding whether the claimant is deemed to have consented.[120] Therefore, where rainwater is collected on the roof for the benefit of the several occupants of a

---

[112] (1894) 70 LT 547.   [113] [1914] 3 KB 772.

[114] On the basis of the assumption that the rule in *Rylands v Fletcher* could apply to deliberate releases, this point was conceded in *Rigby v CC of Northamptonshire* [1985] 1 WLR 1242, at 1255. However, the judge was of the view that the rule should not be applied to deliberate releases.

[115] On the defence of necessity, see ch 13.

[116] *Rigby v CC of Northamptonshire* [1985] 1 WLR 1242, at 1255.

[117] *Kennard v Cory Bros & Co Ltd* [1921] AC 521.   [118] [1942] 1 KB 269.

[119] The principle of implied consent does not apply, however, where C and D are not in a tenant–landlord relationship: *Humphries v Cousins* (1877) 2 CPD 239.

[120] *Peters v Prince of Wales Theatre (Birmingham) Ltd* [1943] KB 73. Where C has, by inference, consented to receiving the benefit of D's watercourse, but contends he has not consented to a negligent accumulation of water, C must prove negligence: *Gilson v Kerrier RDC* [1976] 3 All ER 343.

building,[121] or where a water-closet is installed,[122] or water pipes are fitted,[123] the various occupants are presumed to have consented. On the other hand, the defence does not seem to be available as between a commercial supplier of gas (in respect of gas mains under the highway) and a consumer in premises adjoining the highway.[124] In any event, an occupier will not be presumed to have consented to installations being left in a dangerously unsafe state.[125]

(D) Contributory negligence and related matters

Where the claimants worked a mine under the defendant's canal, and had good reason to know that they would cause the water from the canal to escape thereby into this mine, it was held that the claimants could not invoke the rule in *Rylands v Fletcher* when the water actually escaped and damaged their mine. Cockburn CJ described the matter thus: 'the plaintiffs saw the danger and may be said to have courted it'.[126] Where the claimant is contributorily negligent, the apportionment provisions of the Law Reform (Contributory Negligence) Act 1945 will apply. In addition, as was said in *Eastern and Southern African Telegraph Co Ltd v Cape Town Tramways Co Ltd*, 'a man cannot increase the liabilities of his neighbour by applying his own property to special uses, whether for business or pleasure'.[127] In that case, the claimant, who complained that the defendant's tramways caused electrical interference with the receipt of messages through his submarine cable, failed in his action because no damage to the cable itself was caused. The claimant suffered loss only because he relied on the cable for the transmission of messages.[128]

(E) Act of a third party: the rule in *Rylands v Fletcher* or negligence?

Foreseeable actions What must be considered next is whether it is a defence that, although the defendant brought the thing on to her land, it has escaped only through the act of a third party. It is evident from *Rylands v Fletcher* itself that the defendant is liable for an escape attributable to her independent contractors. Further, there is weighty support for the proposition that the defendant is liable for escapes caused by any other third party where the defendant reasonably ought to have foreseen the act of that third party and had enough control of the premises to be able to prevent it. Accordingly, the proprietor of a chair-o-plane was held liable for the escape of a chair caused by a passenger

---

[121] *Carstairs v Taylor* (1871) LR 6 Exch 217.   [122] *Ross v Fedden* (1872) LR 7 QB 661.

[123] *Anderson v Oppenheimer* (1880) 5 QBD 602 (the reasoning is muddled, but this is the most likely basis of the decision).

[124] *Northwestern Utilities Ltd v London Guarantee and Accident Co Ltd* [1936] AC 108, at 120.

[125] *A Prosser & Sons Ltd v Levy* [1955] 3 All ER 577.

[126] *Dunn v Birmingham Canal Navigation Co* (1872) LR 7 QB 244, at 260 (affd LR 8 QB 42).

[127] [1902] AC 381, at 393. Cf *Hoare & Co v McAlpine* [1923] 1 Ch 167, which left open the question whether C, who complains that his buildings have been damaged, could be met by the plea that they were damaged only because they were dilapidated buildings having insecure foundations.

[128] This decision is better understood in terms of C's loss not being a sufficiently direct consequence of the escape.

tampering with it;[129] the owner of a flag-pole was liable also when small children caused the pole to fall and injure the claimant.[130] Similarly, a gas company laying a main in a highway was liable for damage caused by an explosion of gas when the surrounding earth subsided due to a third party's subjacent mines.[131]

Examples of no liability On the other hand, in *Rickards v Lothian*, the defendant was not liable where flooding of the claimant's premises was caused by an unknown third party who maliciously had turned on a water tap in the defendant's premises and blocked the waste pipe of the lavatory basin.[132] Nor was there liability in *Box v Jubb*, where the defendant's reservoir overflowed when a third party, conducting operations higher up the stream supplying it, discharged downstream an unusually large volume of water without any warning.[133]

There has been a tendency—an example of which is *Perry v Kendricks*[134]—for the preceding two cases to be taken to support the view that, once the defendants have proved that the escape was due to the act of a stranger 'they avoid liability, unless the claimant can go on to show that the act which caused the escape was an act of the kind which the owner could reasonably have contemplated and guarded against.'[135] However, it is submitted that, although the case law supports such a proposition, it has been somewhat misguided in its approach. Thus, while it is not suggested that the actual decisions in the two cases are wrong, the legal doctrine according to which they ought to have been decided is mistaken: by nature they are more in line with negligence, not *Rylands*, principles. The reasoning for this assertion is as follows.

Explanation Since the rule in *Rylands v Fletcher* is a strict liability tort, it follows that negligence in the narrow sense (that is, the breach of a duty to take reasonable care) should play no part in determining liability. This much was made clear by Lord Goff in *Cambridge Water v Eastern Counties Leather plc* when he said: 'the defendant will be liable for harm caused to the claimant by the escape, notwithstanding that he has exercised all reasonable care and skill to prevent the escape from occurring'.[136] Similarly, in *Transco v Stockport MBC*, Lord Hoffmann stressed the immateriality of the fact that

---

[129] *Hale v Jennings Bros* [1938] 1 All ER 579.

[130] *Shiffman v Venerable Order of the Hospital of St John of Jerusalem* [1936] 1 All ER 557, at 561 (*obiter* regarding *Rylands v Fletcher*).

[131] *Hanson v Wearmouth Coal Co Ltd and Sunderland Gas Co* [1939] 3 All ER 47.

[132] *Rickards v Lothian* [1913] AC 263.

[133] (1879) 4 Ex D 76. Cf *Black v Christchurch Finance Co Ltd* [1894] AC 48. Analogous cases to those last cited are those suggesting that there is no liability where an unobservable defect of nature causes the escape, or where there is flooding because a rat gnaws through a water cistern: *Carstairs v Taylor* (1871) LR 6 Exch 217.

[134] [1956] 1 All ER 154.

[135] [1956] 1 All ER 154, at 161 (Parker LJ). Likewise, Jenkins LJ held (at 160) that once the act of a stranger is made out, 'one reaches the point where the claim based on *Rylands v Fletcher* merges into the claim in negligence'.

[136] See *Smith v Littlewoods Organisation Ltd* [1994] 1 All ER 53, at 71. In Australia, this tort has been abandoned and replaced by a 'non-delegable duty' in negligence: *Burnie Port Authority v General Jones Pty Ltd* (1994) 120 ALR 42.

the defendant could not reasonably have foreseen an escape.[137] In other words, and contrary to the view in *Perry v Kendricks* just quoted, it should not matter whether the defendant 'could reasonably have contemplated and guarded against' the intervention of a third party. The better approach is to say that such reasoning has nothing to do with the rule in *Rylands v Fletcher*. In essence, these cases do not involve a failure to control (that is, keep in) a dangerous thing (*Rylands*); instead they centre upon the question whether there was a failure to control the unforeseeable harmful acts of third parties (negligence).[138]

Deliberate discharges The rule in *Rylands v Fletcher* (concerned with escapes) is to be contrasted with deliberate discharges of the dangerous thing on to another's land. Those cases—at least where the discharge is by the person who accumulated the thing—should sound in trespass.[139]

(F) Overwhelming act of nature

This defence has received a prominence out of all proportion to its practical importance. It arises only where an escape is caused through natural causes and without human intervention, in 'circumstances which no human foresight can provide against, and of which human prudence is not bound to recognise the possibility'.[140] Thus, the defence succeeded in *Nichols v Marsland*[141] where a most violent thunderstorm caused flooding. Yet the defence was put in its proper perspective by the House of Lords in *Greenock Corpn v Caledonian Rly Co*,[142] where an extraordinary and unprecedented rainfall was held in similar circumstances not to be an overwhelming act of nature. The explanation of the *Nichols* case was that the jury in *Nichols* found that no reasonable person could have anticipated the storm and the court would not disturb this finding of fact.

The problem with the way in which the defence has been construed by the courts is that they make its incidence referable to reasonable foresight of the cause of an escape. On one construction, this tends to undermine the strictness of *Rylands* liability because it makes the defendant's liability depend, like the unforeseeable acts of a third party just considered, upon the existence of fault.[143] However, a second (and preferable) construction of the defence is possible. This involves requiring that an overwhelming act of nature be beyond *all*, not just reasonable, human foresight. According to this construction, we are not excusing the defendant because the natural event causing the escape was beyond what reasonably could have been foreseen; instead, we are concerned with identifying the truly unique and freak occurrence (which should be distinguished from

---

[137] [2004] 2 AC 1, at [27].

[138] [1987] 1 All ER 710. See also *Topp v London Country Bus (South West) Ltd* [1993] 1 WLR 976.

[139] *Rigby v CC of Northamptonshire* [1985] 1 WLR 1242, at 1255.

[140] A definition of Lord Westbury in *Tennent v Earl of Glasgow* (1864) 2 M 22, at 26–7 (flld in *Greenock Corpn v Caledonian Rly Co* [1917] AC 556).

[141] (1876) 2 Ex D 1.   [142] [1917] AC 556.

[143] If this construction is accepted, the failure to prevent the escape ought to sound in negligence instead.

the highly unusual—but not unknown—event).[144] On this basis, it might be argued that few phenomena beyond earthquakes and tornadoes are likely to constitute an overwhelming act of nature for the purposes of this defence. Certainly, the paucity of occasions on which the defence has succeeded would tend to vindicate this view.

Section 8 Nuisance and the rule in *Rylands v Fletcher*

The *Cambridge Water* case suggested that the rule in *Rylands v Fletcher* properly is to be considered a sub-branch of the law of nuisance. However, there are a number of bases on which this understanding can be refuted.

Different foci To begin with, although they are both land-based torts, the focus in private nuisance is on the land in which the claimant has a proprietary interest.[145] By contrast, under the rule in *Rylands v Fletcher,* the focus is upon the land owned or controlled by the defendant; there is no requirement for the purposes of this tort that the claimant should have a proprietary interest in any land at all.[146] Similarly, while the escape must be from the defendant's land in *Rylands v Fletcher*, there is no requirement in private nuisance that the defendant be an occupier of land.[147]

Damages for personal injury Second, although the House of Lords made clear in *Hunter v Canary Wharf Ltd*[148] the fact that personal injuries could not be recovered under the tort of private nuisance, there is no such prohibition in operation under the rule in *Rylands v Fletcher*, as cases such as *Hale v Jennings Bros*[149] illustrate.

Artificiality vs unreasonableness Third, a use of land might be artificial (and therefore non-natural, so as to fall within the rule in *Rylands v Fletcher*) without being unreasonable (so as to satisfy the unreasonable user test in private nuisance). Thus, while no one seriously would consider the building of a reservoir to be unreasonable (given the importance to society of water storage), no one would consider a reservoir to be anything other than an artificial construction either. Furthermore, while the reasonableness of the defendant's user is a relevant *factor* that may be taken into account in assessing nuisance liability, it is not a *precondition* of liability since it is only the unreasonableness

---

[144] To allow reasonable foreseeability of the abnormal event to play a part in defining the defence is to suggest that foresight of such events is a factor which determines prima facie liability. And while, in the wake of *Cambridge Water* it is clear that foreseeability is a relevant factor in a *Rylands* action, it operates only to characterise the kind of harm, for which D would otherwise be prima facie liable, as too remote. If foreseeability of the 'freak' event were to play a part in defining this defence, however, it would operate at the level of the *definition* (as opposed to *limitation*) of prima facie liability. (For *obiter* support, see *Ellison v Ministry of Defence* (1996) 81 BLR 101.)

[145] *Hunter v Canary Wharf Ltd* [1997] 2 All ER 426.   [146] *Hale v Jennings Bros* [1938] 1 All ER 579.

[147] *LE Jones (Insurance Brokers) v Portsmouth CC* [2003] 1 WLR 427.   [148] [1997] 2 All ER 426.

[149] [1938] 1 All ER 579.

of the interference that ultimately counts.[150] By contrast, the non-natural use of land is absolutely central to *Rylands* liability. The House of Lords insisted on this in their amendment of the rule promulgated by Blackburn J.

Responsibility for contractors Fourth, the occupier of land is liable under the rule in *Rylands v Fletcher* for the accumulations and escapes caused by independent contractors. By contrast, in private nuisance, the liability for independent contractors is markedly less extensive.[151]

Further matters Beyond these instances it is difficult to state with certainty further circumstances where the distinction between nuisance and the rule in *Rylands v Fletcher* exists. But this does not mean that such distinctions cannot be suggested. For example, it is generally accepted that *Rylands v Fletcher* cases turn on isolated escapes, whereas in nuisance cases the interference is normally supposed to be an ongoing one.[152] That being so, it becomes difficult to square the 'state of affairs' nuisance cases[153] with nuisance law orthodoxy. And if these cases are truly anomalous, a further distinction—based on persistence *versus* one-off escape—comes into being.

Conclusions

This chapter has considered a rule of strict liability relating to land usage. In order to have a cause of action under the rule in *Rylands v Fletcher*, a claimant must show that: the thing causing damage had been kept or collected on land owned by, or under the control of, the defendant; it is of a kind that will foreseeably cause harm upon its escape; there has been a non-natural use of land; and there has been an escape of the agent. Liability arises for foreseeable kinds of loss only. The rule is seen by courts as a spur of nuisance law that deals only with one-off occurrences.

Problem question

Glug Ltd operates a glue factory in Pleasantville. It keeps animals there which are slaughtered in order to make glue. The stink created by dead horses travels downwind and affects local houses. During the summer months, the smell attracts flies, wasps, and locusts, which swarm around the glue factory and fly over neighbouring houses. Late one summer night, there is a malfunction in Glug Ltd's glue storage tank. Glue pours out of the tank and floods local homes. Although inhabitants are able to escape, the

---

[150] See, eg, *Sampson v Hodson-Pressinger* [1981] 3 All ER 710, where the ordinary use of premises which, as a result of poor construction, caused intolerable noise to be perceived in adjoining premises was held to be a nuisance. See also *Toff v McDowell* (1993) 25 HLR 650.

[151] See ch 17.   [152] Cf FH Newark (1949) 65 LQR 480, at 488.

[153] See, eg, *Midwood & Co Ltd v Manchester Corpn* [1905] 2 KB 597. But for compelling criticism, see D Nolan (2005) 121 LQR 421.

glue sets, causing massive dislocation. A couple of dead horses are found in Mavis's back garden, solidified in glue.

Advise Mavis as to whether she has any rights against Glug Ltd under the tort in *Rylands v Fletcher*.

 Visit **http://www.oup.com/uk/street15e/** for answer guidance.

Further reading

HALL, 'An Unsearchable Providence: The Lawyer's Concept of Act of God' (1993) 12 *Oxford Journal of Legal Studies* 227

MURPHY, 'The Merits of *Rylands v Fletcher*' (2004) 24 *Oxford Journal of Legal Studies* 643

NOLAN, 'The Distinctiveness of *Rylands v Fletcher*' (2005) 121 *Law Quarterly Review* 421

OLIPHANT, '*Rylands v Fletcher* and the Emergence of Enterprise Liability in the Common Law' [2004] *European Tort Law* 81

STANTON, 'The Legacy of *Rylands v Fletcher*' in Mullany and Linden(eds), *Torts Tomorrow: A Tribute to John Fleming* (1998)

WILKINSON, '*Cambridge Water Company v Eastern Counties Leather plc*: Diluting Liability for Continuing Escapes' (1994) 57 *Modern Law Review* 799

WILLIAMS, 'Non-Natural Use of Land' (1973) 32 *Cambridge Law Journal* 310

19

Breach of statutory duty

KEY ISSUES

(1) Deciding when rights of action exist
The simple fact that the defendant is in breach of an obligation imposed upon him by a statute (a 'statutory duty') does not automatically confer a right of action on persons adversely affected by it. If the statute does not provide expressly that an action can be brought, the issue is resolved as a matter of statutory interpretation. The statute must reveal a parliamentary intention either to (i) create an obligation for the benefit of the claimant (or a class to which the claimant belongs); or (ii) create a public right that is actionable by the claimant upon breach of the duty *because* the claimant suffers more severe harm than the public in general.

(2) The statute must envisage both the claimant and the kind of loss suffered
To succeed in an action for breach of statutory duty, the claimant must prove *both* that he was intended to be protected by the duty *and* that the protection was aimed at preventing the kind of loss he suffered.

(3) What is needed to establish a breach of duty might vary
Sometimes liability for breach of statutory duty will be strict (thus exonerating the claimant from proving fault or intention), while on other occasions proof of fault is required. In certain circumstances, the Social Action, Heroism and Responsibility Act 2015 and the Compensation Act 2006 cut down on the availability of actions.

(4) Breach of statutory duty will not ground an action for negligence
The mere existence of a statutory duty will not support an action for common law *negligence* should the obligation in question be undertaken carelessly. The statutory duty might create a relationship from which a common law duty can be imposed; but it is the relationship (not the statutory duty) that is critical in such cases.

Section 1 Introduction

General As an exceptional matter, a person suffering injury or loss as a result of a violation of a statutory obligation might have an action in tort in respect of that injury or loss—commonly called an action for 'breach of statutory duty'. The early cases on the tort rested on the broad principle that, whenever a violation of a statute caused damage to an individual's interests, a right of action in tort arose.[1] Leading nineteenth-century decisions[2] markedly restricted the scope of the tort, however, and required that anyone claiming for breach of statutory duty establish that the legislature intended that a violation of his right or interest should result in tort liability.

Broader formulation Lord Denning MR attempted (unsuccessfully) to resurrect the broader principle in *Ex parte Island Records Ltd*,[3] arguing that, '[if] a private right is being interfered with by a criminal act, thus causing or threatening to cause him special damage over and above the generality of the public, then he can come to the court as a private individual and ask that his private right be protected.'[4] Had this 'Denning principle' taken root, it would have transformed the action for breach of statutory duty and opened the way for greater protection of individual interests by tort law in two crucial respects. First, in respect of damage to financial and business interests, claimants could have taken advantage of the extensive provision made by statute to regulate the economy in order to obtain compensation for losses falling outside the compass of the economic torts.[5] Second, citizens aggrieved by the failure of public authorities to fulfil obligations designed to protect their welfare could have sought extensive redress from central and local government.

Narrower formulation House of Lords decisions in *Lonrho Ltd v Shell Petroleum Co Ltd (No 2)*[6] and *X v Bedfordshire County Council*,[7] however, appear to have stifled development of the action for breach of statutory duty. The claimant in *Lonrho* was an oil company which had suffered losses after complying with UK Government sanction orders prohibiting trade with the illegal regime in Rhodesia, while its competitors had violated those orders. Relying on *Ex parte Island Records Ltd*, the claimants sought to sue their competitors for breach of the orders. The House of Lords rejected the 'Denning principle',[8] reasserting that the general rule in a claim for breach of statutory duty is that, 'where an Act creates an obligation and enforces performance in a specified manner, . . . that performance cannot be enforced in any other manner.'[9] Where the only manner of enforcing performance for which the Act provides is the criminal process, there are two classes of exception to this general rule. The first is where 'on the true construction of the Act it is apparent that the obligation or prohibition was imposed for the *benefit of*

---

[1] *Couch v Steel* (1854) 3 E & B 402 was the last important case resting on the old broad principle.

[2] *Atkinson v Newcastle and Gateshead Waterworks Co* (1877) 2 Ex D 441; *Groves v Lord Wimborne* [1898] 2 QB 402.   [3] [1978] Ch 122.

[4] [1978] Ch 122, at 139.

[5] According to a majority of the House of Lords in *OBG v Allan* [2008] 1 AC 1, the breach of a regulatory statute shall not be taken to amount to unlawful means for the purposes of the tort of causing financial loss by unlawful means.   [6] [1982] AC 173.

[7] [1995] 2 AC 633.

[8] Technically, the *Lonrho* case involved a claim for damages, whereas in *Ex p Island Records* injunctive relief was sought. The Court of Appeal later clarified that it makes no difference which type of remedy is sought: *RCA Corp v Pollard* [1983] Ch 135.

[9] *Morshead Mansions Ltd v Di Marco (No 2)* [2014] 1 WLR 1799, at [25], citing *Doe d Bishop of Rochester v Bridges* (1831) 1 B & Ad 847, at 859.

a particular class of individuals'.[10] The second is where the statute creates a *public right and* an individual member of the public *suffers damage* which is 'particular, direct and substantial damage other and different from that which is common to the rest of the public'.[11] Lonrho's claim fell outside both exceptions. Sanctions orders prohibiting trade with Rhodesia were intended to end all trade and bring down the illegal regime. They were not imposed for the benefit of any class to which Lonrho belonged; nor did they create a public right.

Health and safety The tort of breach of statutory duty had its greatest impact in the area of health and safety legislation by providing actions for compensation where breaches of relevant legislation resulted in personal injuries. However, the width of the tort was reduced following amendments in 2013 to the Health and Safety at Work etc Act 1974, section 47. Under the new formulation of that provision, breaches of duty imposed by either statutory provisions or statutory instruments 'shall not be actionable except to the extent that regulations' so provide. The result is that the potential for such actions 'in the field of health and safety regulation has been severely restricted'.[12] When examining whether there is an implied statutory intention in *other* legislation to create rights of private action, the fact that the relevant provisions were intended to protect bodily integrity is viewed now as a factor that is favourable to the claimant's case; but this positive factor is treated as no more than one thing to be taken into account among all other relevant factors.[13]

Rule In order to succeed in a claim for breach of statutory duty under the modern rule, the claimant must establish the following matters: (1) a statutory obligation imposed upon the defendant; (2) a parliamentary intention to permit private persons a cause of action; (3) the claimant's being a proper person to bring such a cause of action; (4) breach of the statutory duty; (5) causation of harm of the type contemplated by the statute; and (6) absence of a defence. It is to these factors that we now turn before comparing the present cause of action with others that might be available to the claimant.

Section 2 Statute imposes an obligation

Mandatory obligation The statutory provision in question (whether an Act of Parliament or delegated legislation) must impose a *mandatory* obligation (or 'duty') on the defendant if the action is to lie. The creation of a criminal offence prohibiting members of the public from engaging in certain conduct is insufficient,[14] as is the conferral of a mere power to act.

---

[10] [1982] AC 173, at 186.

[11] [1982] AC 173, at 186, citing *Benjamin v Storr* (1874) LR 9 CP 400, at 407. These alternatives were affirmed in *Morshead Mansions Ltd v Di Marco (No 2)* [2014] 1 WLR 1799, at [25].

[12] K Oliphant (ed), *The Law of Tort* (3rd edn, 2015), [15.7].

[13] *Morison Sports Ltd v Scottish Power UK Ltd* [2010] 1 WLR 1934, at [41] (also mentioning property damage).   [14] *Lonrho Ltd v Shell Petroleum Co Ltd (No 2)* [1981] 2 All ER 456.

On the defendant In *Campbell v Peter Gordon Joiners Ltd*,[15] the Supreme Court considered what type of liability arose under the Employers' Liability (Compulsory Insurance) Act 1969 for failures to insure employees against injury. The main issue concerned *who* was under the statutory obligation in question—which in this case was placed upon the company and *not* upon its directors personally. Lord Carnwath said:

> The essential starting point . . . is an obligation created by statute, binding on the person sought to be made liable. There is no suggestion in [the authorities] that a person can be made indirectly liable for breach of an obligation imposed by statute on someone else. It is no different where an obligation is imposed on a company. There is no basis for looking through the corporate veil to the directors [*sic*] or other individuals through whom the company acts … . [D]irectors are not in general liable for the tortious actions of the company.[16]

This issue about suing the correct defendant has been raised most frequently in actions by workers against their employers where they have been injured by some act or omission of *fellow workers*. In such cases, it can be difficult to decide whether the duty is imposed on the employer or on those fellow workers. For example, in *Harrison v National Coal Board*[17] statute imposed various duties relating to the running of mines. The House of Lords held that, when expressed impersonally, the duties were to be understood as binding mine owners. But where the duties were personal—such as duties relating to shot-firing—they were to be treated as binding individual shot-firers alone.

Non-delegability Once the statute has been interpreted to impose a duty on the employer, the general principle is clear: the duty will be non-delegable. Thus 'the owner cannot relieve himself of his obligation by saying that he has appointed reasonably competent persons and that the breach is due to negligence on their part'.[18] Therefore, it would be no defence to an employer of a worker injured by an unfenced machine that the foreman has failed to carry out the employer's instructions to install a fence. The rule is the same where an independent contractor engaged by the employer has neglected the duty.[19]

Section 3 Parliamentary intention to permit actions

The success or failure of any attempt to frame an action for breach of statutory duty will turn on parliamentary intention. As Lord Steyn observed in *Gorringe v Calderdale MBC*, 'the central question is whether from the provisions and structure of the statute

---

[15] [2016] AC 1513.

[16] [2016] AC 1513, at [13] and [18]. Note that it is incorrect to speak of veil-piercing against directors because they are not protected by limited liability: CA Witting, *Liability of Corporate Groups and Networks* (2018), ch 10.   [17] [1951] AC 639.

[18] *Lochgelly Iron and Coal Co v M'Mullan* [1934] AC 1, at 13.

[19] *Hosking v De Havilland Aircraft Co Ltd* [1949] 1 All ER 540; *Braham v J Lyons & Co Ltd* [1962] 3 All ER 281. Cf *Hole v Sittingbourne and Sheerness Rly Co* (1861) 6 H & N 488.

an intention can be gathered to create a private law remedy'.[20] An action for breach of statutory duty will lie only if the court finds that Parliament intended to confer a right to compensation on an individual injured by breach of that duty.[21] It is not enough to show that a statute was designed to protect the claimant in some general sense. Loss or injury of a recognised type must be shown, as must the intention of Parliament that victims should be entitled to monetary compensation. Thus, in *Hague v Deputy Governor of Parkhurst Prison*,[22] where prisoners alleged that they had suffered injury as a result of being held in solitary confinement in breach of Prison Rules, it was held that mere evidence that the Rules were designed in part to protect prisoners was insufficient to show the required parliamentary intention that they should be able to sue. Lord Jauncey put it this way:

> The Prison Act 1952 . . . covers such wide-ranging matters as central administration, prison officers, confinement and treatment of prisoners, release of prisoners on licence. Its objects are far removed from those of legislation such as the Factories and Coal Miners Acts whose prime concern is to protect the health and safety of persons who work therein.[23]

Only rarely does Parliament *expressly* declare that any breach of the statute should,[24] or should not,[25] be actionable in tort. The Water Act 2003, section 48A[26] is an example of the express creation of a cause of action. It provides an action against persons who abstract water from inland waters or underground strata and thereby cause loss or damage to another person. Under section 2, a 'person who suffers such loss or damage . . . may bring an action against the abstractor'. And, under section 3, '[s]uch a claim shall be treated as one in tort for breach of statutory duty'.

In cases where the courts must consider the claimant's plea of an *implied* intention to create a private law remedy, Hansard can be referred to. Parliamentary intention sometimes can be discerned from a study of the parliamentary debates.[27] Where this is not possible, as Lord Simonds has said: 'the answer must depend on a consideration of the whole Act and the circumstances, including the pre-existing law, in which it was enacted'.[28] The following considerations are no more than guides to the principles that courts may utilise in identifying an implied legislative intention:

---

[20] [2004] 1 WLR 1057. See also, eg, *Hague v Deputy Governor of Parkhurst Prison* [1991] 3 All ER 733, at 705; *Atkinson v Newcastle and Gateshead Waterworks Co* (1877) 2 Ex D 441, at 448; *Pasmore v Oswaldtwistle UDC* [1898] AC 387, at 397.

[21] *Hague v Deputy Governor of Parkhurst Prison* [1991] 3 All ER 733, at 750.

[22] [1991] 3 All ER 733.   [23] [1991] 3 All ER 733, at 750–1.

[24] For examples of Parliament expressly creating a civil remedy for breach of statutory duty see: Water Act 2003, s 48A; Protection from Harassment Act 1997, s 3; Consumer Protection Act 1987, s 41.

[25] See the Health and Safety at Work Act 1974, sub-ss 47(2) (as amended by the Enterprise and Regulatory Reform Act 2013, s 69 and 47(2A).

[26] Considered in *Chetwynd v Tunmore* [2017] QB 188.

[27] See *Richardson v Pitt-Stanley* [1995] QB 123.

[28] *Cutler v Wandsworth Stadium Ltd* [1949] AC 398, at 407.

(A) The state of the pre-existing common law

Sometimes, tort rules in existence before passage of a statute[29] are considered to afford adequate compensation for the losses that arise from activities that it regulates.[30] The statute is taken merely to assist in preventing those kinds of loss[31] and not to confer an additional cause of action. For instance, the need to reduce road accidents is so urgent that there is much legislation regulating road traffic (for example, on seat belt and headlight usage). But persons injured by motorists in breach of statutory duties cannot rely on the statute to sue, they must pursue their common law remedies because ordinary negligence law is seen to afford adequate protection.[32] On the other hand, statutory affirmation of a common law right might make it inevitable that the legislature intends to offer a further remedy for individuals whose rights have been interfered with in a manner proscribed by the statute. Thus, in *Ashby v White*, where the common law right to vote had been confirmed by statute, Holt CJ said:

> And this statute . . . is only an enforcement of the common law; and if the Parliament thought the freedom of elections to be a matter of that consequence, as to give their sanction to it, and to enact that they should be free; it is a violation of that statute, to disturb the [claimant] in this case in giving his vote at an election, and consequently actionable.[33]

(B) Alternative remedies provided by statute

General It has been suggested that, where a statute *fails* to provide any alternative means of enforcement at all in the event of breach of the relevant duty, the claimant has an easier task in establishing that the statute intended an action in tort.[34] But the absence of an alternative remedy is not irrefutable evidence that Parliament intended to grant the claimant redress via an action for breach of statutory duty. Counsel for prisoners claiming damages for breaches of the Prison Rules in *Hague v Deputy Governor of Parkhurst Prison* sought to argue that the absence of any other remedy available to them necessarily meant that an action lay. The House of Lords rejected that contention.[35] According to their Lordships, evidence must be presented on the central question of parliamentary intention in *every case*.

In *Morrison Sports Ltd v Scottish Power plc*, a case in which an alternative remedy *was* made available in certain circumstances but not in others, Lord Rodger opined that 'where Parliament has made specific provision [for remedies] in two sections, the

---

[29] So in *Issa v Hackney LBC* [1997] 1 WLR 956, no claim lay in respect of a statutory nuisance because in 1936, when the relevant Act was passed, virtually all victims of such a nuisance would have been able to recover compensation from their landlords.   [30] See *Richardson v Pitt-Stanley* [1995] QB 123.

[31] Sometimes, as in *Square v Model Farm Dairies (Bournemouth) Ltd* [1939] 2 KB 365 (sale of infected milk), the court might decide that no tort was intended to be created because existing contractual remedies were adequate.   [32] See, eg, *Phillips v Britannia Hygienic Laundry Co* [1923] 2 KB 832.

[33] (1703) 2 Ld Raym 938, at 954. Cf the approach in *Watkins v Secretary of State for the Home Department* [2006] 2 WLR 807 concerning misfeasance in public office.

[34] *Thornton v Kirklees MBC* [1979] QB 626 (overruled on its facts in *O'Rourke v Camden LBC* [1998] AC 188). And see *Booth & Co (Intl) Ltd v National Enterprise Board* [1978] 3 All ER 624.

[35] [1991] 3 All ER 733.

natural inference is that it does not intend there to be a right to damages or compensation for loss or injury caused by other breaches of the statute or of subordinate legislation for which no specific provision is made'.[36] With respect to cases where the alternative remedy is not a suit in damages but something else, its mere availability is not determinative of the issue. As Lord Browne-Wilkinson put it in *X v Bedfordshire County Council*: 'the mere existence of some other statutory remedy is not necessarily decisive'.[37] This is an important statement given that provision frequently is made for bespoke administrative machinery under which a public authority's compliance with its duties might be sought. For example, it might be provided that representations can be made to the relevant Secretary of State (who can order a recalcitrant public body to fulfil its responsibilities);[38] or an appeal procedure might be specified.[39] When examining such cases, the courts will need to be mindful of the extent to which the relevant administrative 'remedy' provides the claimant with a means of obtaining financial redress.[40]

Criminal penalties Where the 'alternative remedy' is the imposition of a *criminal penalty*, the onus will be on the claimant to establish that his claim falls within one of the two exceptions to the general rule of non-actionability set out by Lord Diplock in *Lonrho*.[41] In practice, this will mean usually that he must show that the purpose of the statute was not just to regulate a particular activity in the general public interest, but also to benefit a class of persons to which he belongs.[42] Thus, the existence of criminal penalties in the Factories Acts did not bar concurrent remedies in tort since the statutory obligations were designed specifically to protect workers.[43] By contrast, however, in *Richardson v Pitt-Stanley*[44] a claim against the claimant's employer-company and its directors for failure to comply with provisions of the Employers' Liability (Compulsory Insurance) Act 1969 requiring employers to insure against liability for accidents at work failed. The Court of Appeal held that, in respect of the company, the employee enjoyed a range of remedies at common law enforceable against company assets. If there were no such assets and no valid insurance policy, no additional claim for breach of statutory duty under the 1969 Act would avail the claimant. The substantial criminal penalties under the Act militated against the existence of a civil claim and some slight indication that Parliament did not intend to create such a private right was to be found in Hansard. Moreover, if no civil action for breach of statutory duty was intended against the company, their Lordships thought it highly unlikely that Parliament intended a claim to lie against individual directors (in conformity with the *Morrison Sports* case, considered above).

---

[36] [2010] 1 WLR 1934, at [13].
[37] [1995] 2 AC 633, at 731. See also *Morison Sports Ltd v Scottish Power plc* [2010] 1 WLR 1934, at [29].
[38] See, eg, Children Act 1989, s 84(3) in relation to a local authority's duties to children in care.
[39] See, eg, *Neil Martin Ltd v Revenue and Customs Commissioners* [2008] Bus LR 663.
[40] See, eg, *Phelps v Hillingdon LBC* [2001] 2 AC 619.
[41] *Atkinson v Newcastle and Gateshead Waterworks Co* (1877) 2 Ex D 441.
[42] See, eg, *Todd v Adams* [2002] 2 Lloyd's Rep 293.
[43] *Groves v Lord Wimborne* [1898] 2 QB 402. Breach of the duty to stop at a pedestrian crossing is a rare example of a road safety regulation being interpreted so as to create a right of action in tort: *London Passenger Transport Board v Upson* [1949] AC 155.   [44] [1995] QB 123.

Judicial review The House of Lords in *Cullen v Chief Constable of the Royal Ulster Constabulary*[45] considered cases in which the alternative remedy available to the claimant would be judicial review:

> C was detained in custody under terrorism legislation. Contrary to the Northern Ireland (Temporary Provisions) Act 1987, section 15, C was denied the right to a private consultation with a solicitor. The fact that he was denied this right resulted in no measurable harm to C.

Their Lordships held that the claimant did not have a civil claim for nominal damages based on breach of statutory duty. Material to this decision was the fact that 'the speedy hearing of an application for judicial review . . . is a much more effective remedy for a claimant to seek than an action for nominal damages'.[46] Putting to one side the fact that the accuracy of this statement is questionable, the case law leaves us unclear on whether an action based on breach of statutory duty would have been available if the denial of access to a solicitor had resulted in measurable harm.[47]

(C) Public and private rights

Although the case law is not entirely clear on this, a view exists that a claimant can rely on breach of statutory duty when this infringes a *public right* in a way that causes the claimant to suffer to a much greater degree than other members of the public.[48] In support of this there is Lord Diplock's second exception[49] to the general rule against the actionability of criminal law statutes. However, *dicta* can be found which intimate that this view is no longer tenable. For example, in *X v Bedfordshire County Council* Lord Browne-Wilkinson saw actions for breach of statutory duty *simpliciter* as arising only in favour of 'a limited class of the public'.[50] Indeed, there is a great reluctance to allow a claim for breach of statutory duty against a public authority for failure to provide adequate public services. Claims have failed against health[51] and education ministers[52] for failure to meet their statutory obligations to ensure adequate health care to patients and education for the nation's children, respectively. Claims have failed also when brought against municipal councils for alleged failures to protect children in need.[53] But if the statute creates a public right, which favours all citizens, why object? After all, the law of public nuisance shows that there is nothing wrong with making the infringement of public rights actionable, so long as the claimant suffers to a much greater extent than the generality of the public.

---

[45] [2003] 1 WLR 1763.   [46] [2003] 1 WLR 1763, at [39].

[47] As regards those in the majority, Lord Hutton thought that it would be available (at [41]) while Lord Millett (despite elsewhere signalling his agreement with Lord Hutton) thought it would not (at [69]). Lord Rodger muddied the waters further by agreeing with both of them, while Lords Bingham and Steyn, dissenting, were of the opinion that such an action would lie.

[48] *Phillips v Britannia Hygienic Laundry Co* [1923] 2 KB 832, at 841.

[49] *Lonrho Ltd v Shell Petroleum Co Ltd (No 2)* [1982] AC 173.

[50] [1995] 2 AC 633, at 731. See also *Morison Sports Ltd v Scottish Power UK plc* [2010] 1 WLR 1934, at [40] (need for rule to be protective of a limited class); *O'Rourke v Camden LBC* [1998] AC 188, at 194.

[51] *R v Secretary of State for Social Services, ex p Hincks* (1979) 123 Sol Jo 436.

[52] *Phelps v Hillingdon London Borough Council* [2001] 2 AC 619; *Watt v Kesteven CC* [1955] 1 QB 408.

[53] *X v Bedfordshire County Council* [1995] 2 AC 633.

(D) Nature of interest protected

Bodily integrity The priority afforded to interests in bodily security by tort law was reflected in the willingness of the courts to interpret industrial safety legislation so as to confer a right of action on injured workmen. Breaches of statutory rules to fence machinery in the Factories Act[54] and regulations made for miners' safety by the Mines and Quarries Acts[55] were classic examples of the statutory provisions traditionally supporting tort actions. In such cases, the courts readily found that Parliament envisaged that an injured employee should be able to claim compensation from any employer who failed to provide his workforce with the protection Parliament demanded. Strict liability for injury to employees both offered an incentive to employers to ensure that safety rules were complied with, and meant that the cost of any injury which befell a worker fell on the employer, not the worker. Piecemeal legislation on industrial safety was replaced by an all-embracing statutory regime under the Health and Safety at Work Act 1974, sections 2–9 of which imposed general safety duties on all employers. While breach of those general duties is expressly stated not to be actionable in tort,[56] section 15 empowered the Secretary of State to make specific health and safety regulations for particular industries.[57] Formerly, breaches of these regulations were actionable *unless* the regulation in question provided otherwise. But this is no longer the presumption. As mentioned, the amended section 47 now provides that breaches of statutory duties and of duties imposed by statutory instruments are *not* actionable 'except to the extent that regulations . . . provide'.[58] The irony is that, while legislation now precludes many actions formerly available in the health and safety realm, there has been no such alteration of the law with respect to other interests protected by statute.

Interests in land and goods There are precedents for the protection of interests in land and goods against violation of statute.[59]

Financial loss Even financial losses have been found recoverable where, exceptionally, protection from that kind of loss was within the ambit of the statute. In *Rickless v United Artists Corpn*,[60] the claimants obtained damages for the defendants' unauthorised use of clips from old Peter Sellers films. The Court of Appeal found that violation of the Dramatic and Musical Performers' Protection Act 1958, section 2, prohibiting use of such material without the performer's consent, created a civil right of action. The purpose of the Act was protection of performers' rights and correlative financial interests. Nevertheless, in light of the judiciary's commitment to restricting liability for purely financial loss, very clear evidence that the statute intended to protect against it will be required. Consistent with this approach, the claimant in *Wentworth v Wiltshire County Council*[61] failed in his

---

[54] *Groves v Lord Wimborne* [1898] 2 QB 402.
[55] *Black v Fife Coal Co Ltd* [1912] AC 149; *National Coal Board v England* [1954] AC 403.
[56] Health and Safety at Work Act 1974, s 47(1)(a).
[57] Replacing earlier legislation such as the Factories Acts.
[58] Health and Safety at Work Act 1974, sub-ss 47(2) and (2A).
[59] *Ross v Rugge-Price* (1876) 1 Ex D 269.   [60] [1988] QB 40.   [61] [1993] QB 654.

action to recover for damage to his business caused by disrepair of the adjacent highway. The duty to maintain the highway existed to protect users against personal injury, not to safeguard the profits of traders.

Education and welfare In *X v Bedfordshire County Council*, the House of Lords held that no action for breach of statutory duty arose out of *either* legislation imposing obligations on local authorities to safeguard the welfare of children and protect them from child abuse, *or* legislation requiring local authorities to meet the educational needs of children in their district. Lord Browne-Wilkinson acknowledged that legislation to protect children at risk and to provide for education was designed to benefit those children, but found that it was not Parliament's intention to allow individual children harmed by a local authority's failure to meet its statutory obligations to recover compensation from the public purse. His Lordship noted that no case had been cited before the court where statutory provisions creating a general regulatory scheme to promote social welfare had been held to give rise to a private law claim for damages. He went on to say that:

> [a]lthough regulatory or welfare legislation affecting a particular area of activity does in fact provide protection to those individuals particularly affected by that activity, the legislation is not to be treated as being passed for the benefit of those individuals *but for the benefit of society in general.*[62]

Subsequent to the House of Lords' decision in the *Bedfordshire* case, the claimants pursued their action in the European Court of Human Rights, which held that there had been a breach of Articles 3 and 13 of the European Convention on Human Rights.[63] These Articles provide, respectively, for protection from inhuman or degrading treatment and the right to an adequate remedy under domestic law. However, the Strasbourg court's finding does not affect the action for breach of statutory duty.

(E) Other factors

A number of other factors impact on the courts' readiness to find that Parliament intended that individuals should have actions for compensation for breach of a statutory duty, namely:

Contemplation of legislature It must be shown that Parliament could have envisaged *the circumstances* in which the claimant came to suffer harm. In *Olotu v Home Office*[64] the claimant was remanded in custody for a period exceeding the limit set by Regulations. The court found that the Regulations were designed to achieve expedition in the prosecution of crime and to ensure that accused persons did 'not languish in prison for excessive periods awaiting trial'. Protecting accused persons—the class to which the claimant belonged—was a clear object of the Regulations. However, no claim for breach of statutory duty arose because

---

[62] [1995] 2 AC 633, at 731–2 (emphasis added). See confirmation of this approach in *Phelps v Hillingdon LBC* [2001] 2 AC 619. [63] *Z v UK* (2001) 34 EHRR 97. See also ch 1.
[64] [1997] 1 WLR 328. See also *Issa v Hackney LBC* [1997] 1 All ER 999.

neither Parliament nor the Secretary of State laying down the Regulations would have foreseen a scenario where loss could occur because the Crown Prosecution Service failed to comply with its duty under the Regulations *and* the accused failed to apply for immediate bail.

Precision of language The statutory duty itself must be precise in its terms so as to make enforcing it by way of an action in tort fair to the defendant.[65]

Delegated legislation Finally, if the alleged breach of duty derives not from an Act of Parliament, but from a regulation made under a statute, the following question arises: did the enabling Act empower the minister to make regulations conferring private rights of action on individuals?[66] In answering this question, it is established that where (1) a statute permits a minister to make rules concerned with the safety of a particular class of persons; and (2) the Act empowers the minister also to exempt certain potential defendants from the rules, the inference will be that there was no legislative intention that those rules support an action for breach of statutory duty.[67]

Section 4 Proper claimant

For breach of a statutory duty to give rise to an action in tort (any cases of public right to one side), the claimant must be an individual, or member of a class, that the statute aims to protect. *Knapp v Railway Executive*[68] illustrates the point:

> Railway legislation provided for the maintenance of gates at level crossings. C had stopped his car just short of a closed gate governed by this Act. Somehow the car moved forward, striking the gate and, since the gate had not been fenced properly, it swung into an oncoming train, injuring the driver. The engine driver sued C successfully so he, in turn, sought a contribution from D.

The claimant's action failed because the Act was designed only to protect road users (not engine drivers). As the engine driver could not have sued the defendant directly for breach of statutory duty, it was not liable to make a contribution to the claimant.

Section 5 Breach of the statutory duty

General A typical claim for breach of statutory duty requires only that the claimant prove that the statutory obligation was not fulfilled. This is because liability frequently is strict.[69] In some cases, however, the statute will prescribe that some degree of negligence

---

[65] *Cutler v Wandsworth Stadium Ltd* [1949] AC 398; *X v Bedfordshire CC* [1995] 2 AC 633.

[66] *Hague v Deputy Governor of Parkhurst Prison* [1991] 3 All ER 733. Note the rather different answers to the question from Lords Bridge and Jauncey. See also *Olotu v Home Office* [1997] 1 WLR 328, at 339 and *Todd v Adams* [2002] 2 Lloyd's Rep 293.   [67] *Todd v Adams* [2002] 2 Lloyd's Rep 293, at [25].

[68] [1949] 2 All ER 508. Cf *Lavender v Diamints Ltd* [1949] 1 KB 585.

[69] See, eg, Water Act 2003, s 48A (extracted above in text).

be proven, while in others it will allow the defendant a defence if he shows that avoiding injury to the claimant was not 'reasonably practicable'.[70] Alternatively, where the duty is cast in terms of reasonable practicability, the court might read into the duty a negligence-like element. For example, in *Baker v Quantum Clothing Group*,[71] the employer's workplace had, so far as reasonably practicable, to be made and kept safe. A majority of the Supreme Court held that, whether an employer had discharged this duty was to be judged according to the general knowledge and standards of the time and, thus, by reference to what reasonably might have been foreseen by a reasonable employer. But bearing in mind that two members of the court disagreed, citing a range of cases they thought suggested a stricter interpretation, the case illustrates that great care needs to be exercised in assessing the strictness of any given statutory duty.

In relevant cases, courts must consider the provisions of the SARAH Act 2015 and the Compensation Act 2006 (considered next). The point is that there is *no universal standard* of liability for this tort: one must turn always to the statute in question in order to discover what constitutes a breach of the statutory duty.

SARAH Act Under the Social Action, Responsibility and Heroism Act 2015, when a court is 'determining the steps' that a defendant to a claim for breach of statutory duty ought to have taken in response to risks of harm to others, it must take into account two potential motives: first, whether the defendant was 'acting heroically by intervening in an emergency to assist an individual in danger' (section 4), and, second, whether it (or he) was 'acting for the benefit of society or any of its members' (section 2). Moreover, the court must 'have regard to whether the' defendant 'demonstrated a predominantly responsible approach towards the safety or interests of others' (section 3). These provisions apply also to the tort of negligence, and the first two of them were considered in chapter 6. In the present context, the provisions appear to modify earlier legislation (passed before the SARAH Act) creating statutory duties by requiring, when considering whether a court should find the defendant in breach, that it take these matters into account. In other words, the question of breach is no longer simply about whether the statutory duty has been fulfilled, but about certain circumstances that might explain its non-fulfilment. In cases of non-fulfilment, the court will be able to decide that, for example, because the defendant had been acting 'heroically', no breach permitting a cause of action will be attributed to it (or him). The potential width of this provision will be seen in cases involving pleas related to section 2—which presumably would encompass most statutory authorities and public officials. The potential is for a further reduction in the number of successful cases involving such defendants.

Compensation Act By the Compensation Act 2006, section 1, where a court is considering a claim of breach of statutory duty, it shall, in setting the required standard of care, 'have regard to whether a requirement to take those steps [necessary to meet the statutory duty] might (a) prevent a desirable activity from being undertaken at all, to

---

[70] See, eg, the Highways Act 1980, sub-s 41(1A) of which provides that a highway authority is only required to keep a highway free from snow or ice 'so far as is reasonably practicable'.   [71] [2011] 1 WLR 1003.

a particular extent or in a particular way, or (b) discourage persons from undertaking functions in connection with a desirable activity'. This provision operates in a similar way to the SARAH Act provisions, except that it is not mandatory for a court to take into account the matters stated, but simply permissible.

Section 6 Causation of the type of harm contemplated

Harm Most statutes that permit a tortious cause of action will avail a claimant only where he suffers the particular type of harm or loss envisaged by the Act.[72] However, there are rare instances in which a statute confers a right that is actionable per se. For example, in *Ashby v White*,[73] an interference with the statutory right to vote was held actionable per se.

Type of harm There can be no remedy for breach of a statutory duty unless the claimant's harm fell within the scope of the Act. The leading case is *Gorris v Scott*:[74]

> A statutory order required that those parts of a ship to be occupied by animals should be divided into pens of a specified size. D violated this order on a ship on which he was transporting sheep belonging to C. This violation contributed to C's sheep being washed overboard.

Since the statute was designed to prevent the spread of disease rather than to prevent animals from being drowned, the action for breach of statutory duty failed. In a similar vein, the duty imposed on highway authorities to repair the roads in order to protect users from injury was held not to embrace loss of profit to a local trader.[75]

In the industrial context, too, the House of Lords has held that the statutory duty on an employer to fence every dangerous part of a machine was designed to prevent a worker coming into contact with moving parts of the machine and did not envisage protecting him from injury caused by flying pieces of the machine itself, or the material on which the machine was working.[76] On the other hand, when a bogie was derailed by a stone that had been allowed to fall from the roof of a mine in breach of the defendants' statutory duty, and the claimant was consequently injured, the House of Lords held that 'where the object of the enactment is to promote safety there can be no implication that liability for a breach is limited to one which causes injury in a particular way'.[77] And in *Gerrard v Staffordshire Potteries*[78] the defendant was found liable in respect of a breach of regulations requiring eye protection against any 'reasonably foreseeable risk engaged in the work from particles or fragments thrown off' where a foreign body flew out of a

---

[72] *Chetwynd v Tunmore* [2017] QB 188, at [22].
[73] (1703) 2 Ld Raym 938. Cf *Simmonds v Newport Abercarn Black Vein Steam Coal Co* [1921] 1 KB 616.
[74] (1874) LR 9 Exch 125. But see also *Tasci v Pekalp of London Ltd* [2001] ICR 633.
[75] *Wentworth v Wiltshire CC* [1993] 2 All ER 256.
[76] *Close v Steel Co of Wales Ltd* [1962] AC 367. Cf *Wearing v Pirelli Ltd* [1977] 1 All ER 339.
[77] *Grant v National Coal Board* [1956] AC 649, at 664.   [78] [1995] ICR 502.

jar the claimant was glazing. The statute was designed to safeguard the worker from any object dangerous to the eye in the course of her work.

Causation The claimant 'must in all cases prove his case by the ordinary standard of proof in civil actions: he must show that on a balance of probabilities the breach of duty caused or materially contributed to his injury'.[79] Thus, where it was shown that a steel erector would not have worn a safety belt, even if it had been provided, the House of Lords held that his employers were not liable to him for breach of their statutory duty to provide one.[80] Similarly, where a carpenter fell from a scaffold because the scaffold had been pushed over deliberately by a workmate, it was not the employer's breach of duty that had caused his injury. The employer was required to provide safe equipment and a safe place of work, but the duty incumbent upon him was to ensure only that employees would be safe from foreseeable risks. The deliberate, wanton act of the workmate did not constitute such a risk;[81] it was a *novus actus interveniens* that broke the chain of causation.

Section 7 Defences

(A) Assumption of risk

Wheeler v New Merton Board Mills Ltd[82] decided that *volenti non fit injuria* is not a defence to an action brought by a workman for breach by an employer of his statutory duty—at least where the statute makes the employer liable whether or not his conduct was intentional or negligent. In *ICI Ltd v Shatwell*,[83] the House of Lords approved the *Wheeler* case insofar as employers' statutory duties are concerned; but it added that the defence of *volenti* 'should be available where the employer was not himself in breach of statutory duty and was not vicariously in breach of any statutory duty through the neglect of some person who was of superior rank to the [claimant] and whose commands the [claimant] was bound to obey'.[84] The grounds for the *Wheeler* decision are not obvious. This makes it all the harder, in the absence of any decision outside the sphere of such duties of employers owed to workers, to know whether the defence generally is inapplicable to actions for breach of statutory duty.[85] It might well be contrary to public policy for anybody (not merely employers) to contract out of a duty imposed by an Act of Parliament. If this is so, assumption of risk might never be a defence to this action.

(B) Contributory negligence

The application of this defence is the same as that discussed in chapter 8, subject to the following points. Legislation and regulations designed to protect health and

---

[79] *Bonnington Castings Ltd v Wardlaw* [1956] AC 613, at 620. Cf *McGhee v National Coal Board* [1972] 3 All ER 1008.   [80] *Cummings (or McWilliams) v Sir William Arrol & Co Ltd* [1962] 1 All ER 623.
[81] *Horton v Taplin Contracts Ltd* [2003] ICR 179.   [82] [1965] AC 656.   [83] [1965] AC 656.
[84] [1965] AC 656, at 687.   [85] See *Alford v National Coal Board* [1952] 1 All ER 754, at 757 (*obiter*).

safety often are designed expressly to protect workers against acts or inattention. Accordingly, a 'risky act due to familiarity with the work or some inattention result- ing from noise or strain' will not be contributory negligence,[86] although it might be sufficient negligence to make the employer vicariously liable to a negligently injured third party.[87] Frequently, the employer will have delegated to his employee responsibil- ity for the performance of the statutory duty and that employee will then have been negligent. The House of Lords held in *Boyle v Kodak Ltd*[88] that 'once the [claimant] has established that there was a breach of enactment which made the employer absolutely liable, and that that breach caused the accident, he need do no more'.[89] But, 'if the employer can prove that the only act or default of anyone which caused or contributed to the non-compliance was the act or default of the [claimant] himself, he establishes a good defence'.[90]

In *Boyle v Kodak Ltd* the statutory duty to fix a ladder securely while a storage tank was painted was imposed on both the employers and the employee who was injured through its breach. The Court of Appeal dismissed the action on the ground that the claimant was the sole cause of the accident, but the House of Lords allowed his appeal. The employers had not proved that they had instructed the claimant on how to comply with the regulations. That being so, their breach of statutory duty was a cause of the damage. The significance of the claimant also being in breach of his statutory duty was that it constituted a ground for apportionment of the damages: he was awarded one half. Had the statute imposed the duty on the employers alone, the claimant's damages would not have been reduced, unless the employers proved that the claimant failed to take care for his own safety and was thus contributorily negligent.

(C) Act of a third party

This is no defence where the statute is deemed to impose liability so strict that the defendant is responsible for such acts. In other cases it might be a defence; but every- thing depends on the particular wording and interpretation of the Act.[91]

(D) *Ex turpi causa*

The Court of Appeal has held that the defence of *ex turpi causa non oritur actio* can be invoked in cases where the claimant is relying on a breach of statutory duty.[92]

---

[86] Where the risk has been consciously accepted by the employee, it will, apparently, be contributory negli- gence: see, eg, *Sherlock v Chester CC* [2004] EWCA Civ 201, at [32].

[87] *Staveley Iron and Chemical Co Ltd v Jones* [1956] AC 627, at 648 (explaining the similar decision in *Cas- well v Powell Duffryn Associated Collieries Ltd* [1939] 3 All ER 722). On the difficulty of proving contributory negligence in this tort, see *Westwood v Post Office* [1974] AC 1.

[88] [1969] 2 All ER 439 (applied in *Ross v Associated Portland Cement Manufacturers Ltd* [1964] 2 All ER 452; *Ginty v Belmont Building Supplies Ltd* [1959] 1 All ER 414).   [89] [1969] 2 All ER 439, at 441.

[90] [1969] 2 All ER 439, at 446.   [91] *Cooper v Railway Executive (Southern Region)* [1953] 1 All ER 477.

[92] *Hewison v Meridian Shipping Services Pte Ltd* (2003) 147 SJLB 24 (C's fraudulent concealment of his epilepsy led to the defeat of his claim).

Section 8 Relationship to other actions

Care must be taken to avoid confusion between breach of statutory duty and negligence, albeit in practice claimants often will make concurrent claims for breach of statutory duty and negligence. Lord Browne-Wilkinson offered instructive analysis in *X v Bedfordshire County Council*.[93] Addressing the extent of the defendant local authority's liabilities in tort generally for failures in child care and educational provision, he distinguished between three possible causes of action in tort, as follows:

(A) Breach of statutory duty *simpliciter*

Such a claim 'depends neither on any breach of the [claimant's] common law rights nor on any allegation of negligence by the defendants'.[94] If a private right of action lies for violation of a statute, the claimant has no need to prove negligence. This is the action which we have examined above.

(B) The common law duty of care

The existence of a statutory duty might create a relationship from which a common law duty of care in negligence arises. An example is a relationship created by the statute that is akin, but by no means identical, to that of employer and employee.[95] Importantly, though, it is the relationship created by the statutory duty (as opposed to the statutory duty itself) that forms the basis of the common law duty.[96] But a common law duty will never arise in favour of C2 where it might conflict with the purpose of the statutory duty owed to C1. Thus, in *Jain v Trent Strategic Health Authority*,[97] where a public authority was authorised by statute to protect the residents of a nursing home, the House of Lords held that no common law duty could arise in favour of the owners of the nursing home in respect of the manner in which that power was exercised. Any such common law duty could conflict with the purpose, and thus inhibit the exercise, of the statutory power.

(C) Careless performance of a statutory duty

If it is not established that Parliament intended to create an action for breach of statutory duty in respect of a particular obligation, and if it cannot be established, either, that the circumstances of the claimant's relationship with the defendant gave rise to a common law duty of care, no claim in tort lies simply for the careless performance of a statutory duty. On the other hand, if the claim is founded on another tort—say, private

---

[93] [1995] 2 AC 633, at 731–6. See also *London Passenger Transport Board v Upson* [1949] AC 155, at 168.
[94] *X v Bedfordshire CC* [1995] 2 AC 633, at 731.
[95] *Rice v Secretary of State for Trade and Industry* [2007] ICR 1469.
[96] In *Gorringe v Calderdale MBC* [2004] 1 WLR 1057, Lord Scott said (at [71]): 'the [statutory] duty cannot create a duty of care that would not have been owed at common law'.   [97] [2009] 2 WLR 248.

nuisance—the fact that the statutory duty has been performed negligently will defeat an otherwise extant defence of statutory authority.[98]

Section 9 The 'Eurotort' action

Origins English courts have accepted for some time that directly applicable European Union law can create obligations the breach of which entitles affected persons to sue for the harm thereby caused.[99] In *Francovich v Italy*,[100] the Court of Justice of the European Union broadened the bases of liability by holding that a failure by a member state to implement an EU Directive designed to create rights on the part of particular individuals would also give rise to a claim in damages on the part of those individuals. Strikingly, in *Francovich*, the EU legislation in question was not directly effective, which meant that, in the absence of an action against the state, there would have been no one against whom an action could have been brought. Since then, the European Court has held that the *Francovich* principle applies more widely: where the legislation *is* of direct effect;[101] where the breach of EU law entails a legislative act (not merely an omission);[102] and in respect of administrative decisions.[103]

Elements The conditions that must be satisfied in order to sue according to this 'Eurotort' principle were set out by Lord Slynn in *R v Secretary of State for Transport, ex p Factortame Ltd*. He said:

> Before a member state can be held liable, a national court must find that:
>
> (i) the relevant rule of [EU] law is one which is intended to confer rights on individuals;
> (ii) the breach must be sufficiently serious;
> (iii) there must be a direct causal link between the breach and the loss complained of.[104]

Intention to confer rights The similarity between the first requirement and the test adopted in relation to an action for breach of statutory duty is immediately apparent. This connection between the two forms of action was arguably furthered in *Three Rivers District Council v Bank of England (No 3)*.[105] The House of Lords held that a directive concerning the regulation of credit institutions was designed to harmonise banking practice, rather than to protect depositors. That being so, a failure to comply with the directive did not avail the depositors: the directive was not primarily intended to confer a right of action upon them.

---

[98] *X v Bedfordshire CC* [1995] 2 AC 633, at 728–9.

[99] *Garden Cottage Foods Ltd v Milk Marketing Board* [1984] AC 130.   [100] [1993] 2 CMLR 66.

[101] *Brasserie du Pêcheur SA v Federal Republic of Germany* (Case C–46/93).

[102] *R v Secretary of State for Transport, ex p Factortame Ltd* (Case C–48/93).

[103] *R v Ministry of Agriculture, Fisheries and Food, ex p Hedley Lomas (Ireland)* (Case C–5/94).

[104] [1999] 4 All ER 906, at 916. These conditions derive directly from the decision of the Court of Justice of the EU in *Brasserie du Pêcheur SA v Federal Republic of Germany* (Case C–46/93), at [74].

[105] [2000] 2 WLR 1220.

Sufficiently serious The pivotal phrase 'sufficiently serious' does not necessarily require negligence or fault (although fault might be a material consideration). The seriousness of the breach must be judged in the context of the clarity of the EU rule breached and, where appropriate, the legislative discretion afforded to the member state.[106] Again, there is some similarity with ordinary breach of statutory duty principles.

A unique cause of action Despite these similarities between the Eurotort principle and the breach of statutory duty, there are sufficient differences to identify the Eurotort as a unique cause of action. These have been identified as including the facts that the action is a 'public law tort', different rules of interpretation apply to it, and redress arises because of deficiencies in national law (including statutory law) rather than because national law dictates the availability of redress.[107]

Conclusions

The cause of action for breach of statutory duty is a tort the existence of which derives from the statutory intention to permit damages where the defendant has failed to fulfil a statutory duty. In this sense, it operates where the relevant statute either expressly or impliedly ordains that there shall be an action. The usual cannons of statutory interpretation apply. Where the intention exists and breach occurs, the claimant must prove causation of harm which is of a type within the scope of the statute.

Problem question

The Waterways Act 2010 provides that 'owners of vessels using rivers, canals and other internal navigable waterways shall be guilty of an offence where, through their neglect or breach of duty, they are responsible for blockages of those rivers etc which cause flooding on neighbouring lands'. In Hansard, the responsible Minister is quoted as saying that 'this legislation will bring peace of mind to those residents adjacent to waterways whose factories, businesses and homes are threatened by ship-owner neglect'. The owners of the vessel *Flamin' Rose* were aware of problems with its boiler before a fire broke out in its boiler-room and the vessel sank in the Upper Combucta West canal. Several residents of Upper Combucta West were the subject of the flooding which followed. These floods were not covered by their insurance policies. The residents wish to bring actions against the owners of the *Flamin' Rose* for property damage and for the fall in the market value of homes in the neighbourhood following this incident.

Advise the residents about any claim they might have for breach of statutory duty.

 Visit **http://www.oup.com/uk/street15e/** for answer guidance.

---

[106] *R v Secretary of State for Transport, ex p Factortame Ltd (No 5)* [1999] 4 All ER 906; *Byrne v Motor Insurers Bureau* [2009] QB 66.   [107] P Giliker (2012) 128 LQR 541.

Further reading

BUCKLEY, 'Liability in Tort for Breach of Statutory Duty' (1984) 100 *Law Quarterly Review* 204

FOSTER, 'The Merits of the Civil Action for Breach of Statutory Duty' (2011) 33 *Sydney Law Review* 67

GILIKER, 'English Tort Law and the Challenge of *Francovich* Liability: 20 Years On' (2012) 128 *Law Quarterly Review* 541

STANTON, 'New Forms of the Tort of Breach of Statutory Duty' (2004) 120 *Law Quarterly Review* 324

PART VI

Interests in reputation: defamation

20

Defamation: foundational principles

KEY ISSUES

(1) Competing interests

Reputation is the regard in which others hold a person, injury to which threatens full membership of her community. The law of defamation is to be found at the point at which interests in freedom of expression and reputation intersect. Liability rules reflect the delicate balance struck by the legislature and the courts between these interests.

(2) Libel and slander

Defamation comes in two forms: libel, which generally is in written form; and slander, which generally is oral (although the rules are a little more complicated than that).

(3) Lowering of reputation

Three tests for defamation have been used in the cases. This chapter notes that the eponymous test is whether the impugned statement is such that a substantial and respectable proportion of society would think less well of a person. Supplementary tests used by the courts include the ridicule test and the shun-and-avoid test.

(4) Reference and publication

The defamatory statement must refer adequately to the claimant in order for the claimant to be able to sue upon it. Moreover, it must be published—meaning that it must have come to the attention of third persons.

(5) Serious harm

Following legislative reform, a statement is not defamatory unless its publication has caused or is likely to cause serious harm to the reputation of the claimant. This sets a threshold for all claims. In cases of libel, while no damage need be proved to have occurred, this must (according to the legislation) be likely to arise from the use of the words. In slander, it is still the case that special damage must be proved (with two exceptions where no damage need be proved but which, of their nature, indicate that damage is likely to arise in accordance with the threshold test). Special damage is loss of a material nature.

(6) Defences

Much of the balance between the competing interests of freedom of expression and reputation is struck in the form of the defences available to claims of defamation, which are dealt with in chapter 21.

Section 1 Introduction

Defamation protects the interest that a person has in her reputation. Reputation is the regard in which others hold a person (and not the regard in which she holds herself).[1] All persons are capable of having a valuable reputation, whether high-ranking or living amongst the homeless.[2] Reputation is important in communal life. It expresses a judgement about a person in terms of her worthiness for membership of the community. This judgement is made by reference to the values ostensibly shared by 'right-thinking members of society'.[3] Improper injury to reputation threatens continued full membership of the community, which harms both the individual *and* her community,[4] and provides a reason for the law to intervene. The main test for defamation, thus, looks to determine whether the impugned statement lowers the claimant in the estimation of right-thinking members of society generally. There are two types of defamation: libel—which generally is in written form; and slander—which generally is oral.[5] Slightly different rules are applicable to each. But there is no tort unless the impugned statement has made sufficient reference to the claimant and has been communicated to a third party. The action in defamation is brought to vindicate the claimant's reputation,[6] to compensate,[7] and deter.[8] Such is the protection that the law traditionally has offered to reputation that defamation can be committed in circumstances of strict liability. However, in recent times, the width of the tort has been pared back in a number of ways to be considered in this chapter and in chapter 21.[9]

Historical development In many ways defamation is unique among torts, and it is best understood in the context of its historical development. Until the sixteenth century, the ecclesiastical courts exercised general jurisdiction over defamation. Thereafter, the common law courts developed an action on the case for slander where 'temporal' (as distinct from 'spiritual') damage could be established. Much later, the common law

---

[1] *Thornton v Telegraph Media Group Ltd* [2011] 1 WLR 1985, at [96]; *Ames v Spamhouse Project Ltd* [2015] 1 WLR 3409, at [39].

[2] *Calix v A-G of Trinidad and Tobago* [2013] 1 WLR 3283, 3288–9 (case of malicious prosecution). This is the 'default' position: E Descheemaeker (2009) 29 OJLS 603, 609. See also L McNamara, *Reputation and Defamation* (2007).

[3] See L McNamara, *Reputation and Defamation* (2007), ch 1. Reputation has been theorised on a number of bases, including those involving notions of property, honour, and dignity: D Milo, *Defamation and Freedom of Expression* (2008), ch 2; RC Post (1986) 74 Calif LR 691. The property conception has been rejected by the Court of Appeal: *Rothschild v Associated Newspapers Ltd* [2013] EWCA Civ 197, at [25].

[4] *Reynolds v Times Newspapers Ltd* [2001] 2 AC 127, at 201; D Milo, *Defamation and Freedom of Expression* (2008), 36–7.

[5] It is inaccurate, however, to say that slander is always oral and that libel is always visual. The use of sign language as between two deaf persons, for example, probably is capable of constituting slander. Equally, television broadcasts and public theatre performances of a defamatory nature are, by statute, libellous rather than slanderous: see section 3(B).   [6] *Bewry v Reed Elsevier UK Ltd* [2015] 1 WLR 2565, at [5].

[7] A view exists that vindication is part of what is required to compensate: *Sloutsker v Romanova* [2015] EMLR 27, at [77]. This might well be right.

[8] *Secretary of State for the Environment etc* [2009] 1 WLR 2780; *Sloutsker v Romanova* [2015] EMLR 27, at [96].

[9] This is part of a longer-term trend: see E Barendt, *Freedom of Speech* (2007), ch 6.

courts acquired jurisdiction over libels, too, and they forged a distinction between libel and slander on the basis that damage would be presumed in libel, but that the claimant would have to prove 'special damage'[10] for slander. In the late nineteenth and early twentieth centuries, liability in defamation was extended because of the menace to reputation occasioned by the mass circulation of the new, popular press.

Recent developments The recent history of defamation is marked by continuing conflict between the need to protect the reputation (and privacy) of individuals, on the one hand, and the right to freedom of expression, on the other.[11] The intensity of this conflict has been heightened with the enactment of the Human Rights Act 1998, which gives effect to formal rights with respect to each arising under the European Convention on Human Rights. Thus, the Act gives effect to the Article 8 right to 'private life'. The courts have interpreted the concept of 'privacy' here to encompass a right to reputation.[12] The right is subject to the 'rights and freedoms of others'. One of those conflicting freedoms is that under Article 10, which provides a right to freedom of expression. The provision includes a right to 'impart information and ideas without interference by public authority', but, again, is subject to the rights of others. The right to freedom of expression has been seen to place particular importance upon protection of political speech, artistic expression, and commercial speech.[13]

In *Campbell v MGN*,[14] the House of Lords held that there was no presumption that the Article 10 right to freedom of expression should trump any competing interests, such as the Article 8 right to respect for privacy. It would need to be balanced against those interests.[15] However, there has been a significant movement in English defamation law towards greater protection for freedom of expression, some of this movement being inspired by Article 10. Thus, in *Derbyshire County Council v Times Newspapers Ltd*,[16] the House of Lords ruled that public authorities and governmental bodies were not entitled to sue in defamation. As Lord Keith put it:

> It is of the highest public importance that . . . any governmental body [ ] should be open to uninhibited public criticism. The threat of a civil action for defamation must inevitably have an inhibiting effect on freedom of speech.[17]

---

[10] The phrase 'special damage' is to some extent misleading; 'actual damage' is more accurate: see JA Jolowicz (1960) 18 CLJ 214.   [11] See, eg, E Barendt [1993] PL 449.

[12] See *Cumpănă and Mazăre v Romania* (2005) 41 EHRR 200, at [91]; *Chauvy v France* (2005) 41 EHRR 29, at [70]. The European Court of Human Rights has not been entirely consistent in its jurisprudence on the protection afforded to reputation and has even stated that the 'personal integrity rights falling within the ambit of article 8 are unrelated to the external evaluation of the individual . . . ': *Karako v Hungary* [2011] 52 EHRR 36, at [23].   [13] J Rowbottom (2012) 71 CLJ 355, 369 (arguing for wider protection).

[14] [2004] 2 AC 457.

[15] See also *Joseph v Spiller* [2011] 1 AC 852, at [74]–[79]; *Clift v Slough BC* [2010] EWCA Civ 1484.

[16] [1993] AC 534. Note their Lordship's references to (but not reliance on) the European Convention on Human Rights, Art 10.

[17] [1993] AC 534, at 547. The principle was extended to political parties in the course of an election campaign in *Goldsmith v Bhoyrul* [1997] 4 All ER 268. Other arguments that have been given for protection of expression include those relating to facilitation of truth-finding, access to ideas enabling persons to make up their minds on issues, and expression as both a means of self-fulfilment and a public good: see E Barendt, *Freedom of Speech* (2007), ch 1.

In *O'Shea v MGN Ltd*,[18] it was held that there could be no action in defamation in the case of a model, similar in appearance to the claimant, who featured in advertisements for a pornographic website. One of the reasons for this was the impossible burden that liability would impose upon publishers, should they be required to check for unintended reference to other persons. And, relying on Court of Appeal authority in *Jameel v Dow Jones* which stated the need for the commission of a substantial tort,[19] in *Thornton v Telegraph Media Group Ltd*,[20] Tugendhat J espoused a test of 'seriousness' in the law of defamation so as to reduce the scope for trivial claims. In the view of the Court of Appeal in *Cammish v Hughes*, this was to 'avoid normal social banter or discourtesy ending up in litigation'.[21] The Article 10 right to freedom of expression was used to justify the result in both of these developments. The decision in the *Thornton* case was cited by the Ministry of Justice[22] and in the Explanatory Notes accompanying the Defamation Act 2013[23] as a development justifying the introduction of a statutory requirement of serious harm into the law of defamation.

The move towards greater protection of free expression, and of the ability of the media to report matters of public interest, has been confirmed by other amendments to the law brought about by the Defamation Act 2013 considered in this chapter and in chapter 21.

Section 2 Elements of defamation

Whether a defamation action is framed in libel or slander, the claimant must prove that the statement (whether encompassing words, pictures, gestures, etc)[24] was defamatory. The claimant must show also that the statement refers to her and that it was published to third persons. These elements are now considered.

(A) The meaning of 'defamatory'

(1) Tests of defamation

Ridicule test The classic definition of a defamatory statement is one 'which is calculated to injure the reputation of another, by exposing h[er] to hatred, contempt or ridicule'.[25] This test was used in *Berkoff v Burchill*[26] to hold that a statement that an actor is 'hideous-looking' was capable of meaning that the actor was physically repulsive in a way that would make him the object of ridicule. Although Neill LJ admitted that the

---

[18] [2001] EMLR 943.   [19] [2005] QB 946, at [55].

[20] [2011] 1 WLR 1985 (adopted in *Cammish v Hughes* [2013] EMLR 13; *Tamiz v Google Inc* [2013] EWCA Civ 68, at [50]).   [21] [2012] EWCA Civ 1655; [2013] EMLR 13, at [38].

[22] Ministry of Justice, *Draft Defamation Bill Consultation* (Cm 8020, 2011), 8.

[23] Explanatory Notes to the Defamation Act 2013, [11].

[24] See Defamation Act 2013, s 15 (definition for purposes of the Act).

[25] *Parmiter v Coupland* (1840) 6 M & W 105, at 108; *Emerson v Grimsby Times and Telegraph Co Ltd* (1926) 42 TLR 238.   [26] [1996] 4 All ER 1008, at 1018.

line was not easy to draw, many a commentator believes that the line in this case was drawn in the wrong place. Indeed, it is otherwise clear that being made a laughing stock is not sufficient. In *Blennerhasset v Novelty Sales Services Ltd*,[27] a newspaper advertisement was headed 'Beware of Yo Yo' and implied that Mr Blennerhasset had been placed under supervision in a quiet place in the country by reason of his fascination with the defendant's toy, the Yo Yo. Although the claimant, a stockbroker, showed that his arrival at the Stock Exchange on the day after the publication was greeted with 'jeers, ribaldry and laughter', the statement was held not to be defamatory.[28]

Although the ridicule test is of considerable vintage, argument has been made that it is inconsistent with the general nature of defamation law. The cases appear to protect self-worth (rather than reputation) and are not necessarily susceptible to a defence of truth. For these reasons and others, one scholar has argued that the test ought to be abolished.[29]

Lowering of reputation test In *Sim v Stretch*, Lord Atkin proposed the alternative test of whether 'the words tend to lower the claimant in the estimation of right-thinking members of society generally'.[30] This test creates a legal standard by which to assess the use of language and other communicative acts, which is applied by the court in a similar fashion to the 'reasonable person' test in negligence. The court will establish what it believes would be the reaction of right-thinking persons in general to the impugned statement (which is to say that the issue is a normative and not an empirical one).

The general standards approach is the implicit point of reference in *Sim v Stretch*,[31] although the courts have not been entirely consistent in applying it. In some cases, courts have resorted to a test involving the hypothetical reader who is 'representative of those who would read the publication in question'.[32] This appears to adopt a sectional standard, assessing statements by reference to the values of the relevant subsection of the community. McNamara believes that the sectional standards approach is preferable in a pluralist society—one in which differing views are accepted and in which different views of the same words might be taken.[33] He recognises the potential width of such an approach (which would have a consequent impact upon freedom of expression), but believes that a limit would be reached in cases where such an approach has 'the potential to undermine the liberal presumptive content of "the right-thinking person"'. The sectional standards approach inevitably favours claimants'

---

[27] (1933) 175 LT Jo 393.

[28] On the other hand, so long as it inspires contempt or ridicule, even a caricature can constitute defamation: *Dunlop Rubber Co Ltd v Dunlop* [1921] 1 AC 367.

[29] L McNamara, *Reputation and Defamation* (2007), ch 7.

[30] [1936] 2 All ER 1237, at 1240. In *Rubber Improvement Ltd v Daily Telegraph Ltd* [1964] AC 234, at 285, Lord Devlin said that the test was the effect on the 'ordinary' man, not the 'logical' man. See also *Skuse v Granada Television Ltd* [1996] EMLR 278 and *Berkoff v Burchill* [1996] 4 All ER 1008. Cf *Norman v Future Publishing Ltd* [1999] EMLR 325 (gentle humour short of ridicule is not actionable).

[31] See L McNamara, *Reputation and Defamation* (2007), 117.

[32] *Jeynes v News Magazines Ltd* [2008] EWCA Civ 130, at [14]; *Cammish v Hughes* [2013] EMLR 13, at [32].

[33] L McNamara, *Reputation and Defamation* (2007), chs 5 and 8. Compare *Arab News Network v Al Khazen* [2001] EWCA Civ 118 (*dictum* that lowering of reputation within a particular racial group is insufficient).

actions for defamation. In *Monroe v Hopkins*, Warby J underlined the correctness of the orthodox view, stating that:

> The demands of pluralism in a democratic society make it important to allow room for differing views to be expressed, without fear of paying damages for defamation. Hence, a statement is not defamatory if it would only tend to have an adverse effect on the attitudes to the claimant of a certain section of society.[34]

Indeed, the general standards approach appears even more preferable when the following cases are considered, in which the claimants were each seeking to appeal to a type of moral-relativism. In *Byrne v Deane*,[35] it was held that to impute that a member of a golf club had informed the police about an illegal fruit-machine kept in the club was not defamatory, even though it lowered him in the esteem of his fellow members. A certain sub-section of the community might think badly of police informers, but simply to impute this conduct to someone is not defamatory.[36] Again, in *Myroft v Sleight*[37] there is *dictum* to the effect that, although trade unionists might think less well of a fellow member who crosses a picket, this is not a generally accepted viewpoint and cannot give rise in itself to liability in defamation.

Shun-and-avoid test In addition to the preceding tests for defamation, a third test that has been employed only rarely is the 'shun-and-avoid test'. It was a basis for finding for the claimant in *Youssoupoff v Metro-Goldwyn-Mayer Pictures Ltd*,[38] in which the claimant, a Russian princess, objected to the imputation in a film called 'Rasputin, the Mad Monk' that she had been raped by Rasputin. Although the imputation of having been raped reflected no discredit on the claimant, in invoking the test Slesser LJ stated that the imputation would reduce the princess's 'opportunities of receiving respectable consideration from the world'.[39] The shun-and-avoid test usually is invoked in cases dealing with ascriptive characteristics that entail no moral blameworthiness, such as mental illness.[40] Argument has been made that this test should be abolished because it risks straying from protection of reputation, would seem to validate ideas of inferiority based on ascriptive characteristics, and does not add anything of value to the lowering the claimant test.[41] The counter-argument is that the test is suited to protecting the interest that persons have in their 'formation and maintenance of social relations' in circumstances where '[i]nterference with a person's ability to associate with other people . . . is the most obvious effect of damaging a person's reputation.'[42]

---

[34] [2017] 4 WLR 68, at [50]. Cf GKY Chan (2014) 19 Media and Arts LR 47 (advocating a staged approach).
[35] [1937] 1 KB 818.
[36] *Sim v Stretch* [1936] 2 All ER 1237. On the other hand, not merely the golfing fraternity, but right-thinking persons will (it has been held) think worse of an amateur golfer who allows his name to be used in the advertising of chocolates: *Tolley v JS Fry & Sons Ltd* [1931] AC 333.   [37] (1921) 90 LJKB 883.
[38] (1934) 50 TLR 581.   [39] (1934) 50 TLR 581, at 587.
[40] See *Youssoupoff v Metro-Goldwyn-Mayer Pictures Ltd* (1934) 50 TLR 581, at 587.
[41] L McNamara, *Reputation and Defamation* (2007), ch 6 and 214–16.
[42] D Howarth (2011) 74 MLR 845, 849–52.

Reconciliation of tests English law has not defined the term 'defamatory' with precision.[43] With diffidence, it is suggested that the 'right-thinking' person test is of greatest utility but must be understood in the following way: if a substantial and respectable proportion of society would think less well of a person, then the statement will be construed as defamatory provided that their reaction is not plainly anti-social or irrational.[44]

(2) Scope of defamation

Abuse Defamatory statements frequently have been contrasted with 'mere abuse', which is said not to be actionable. However, to say that abuse is not defamatory is misleading. The cases relied on for this proposition are cases of slander deciding that special damage ordinarily must be proved.[45] The test to be applied to words of abuse is exactly the same as for other allegedly defamatory statements. Thus, it might be defamatory to call a person a habitual drunkard,[46] a villain,[47] or even a black sheep.[48] What matters is the context and manner in which the words are uttered. Thus, a word like 'Mafia' might be understood to describe a close-knit group in a metaphorical, but not defamatory, sense.[49]

Opinion A statement might be defamatory, even though the maker states it, not as fact, but as opinion.[50] One must take into account circumstances of time and place.[51] Thus, in *Slazengers Ltd v C Gibbs & Co*,[52] it was defamatory to state during World War One that the claimant was a German firm that was likely to be closed down. Certain statements that reflect the defendant's honest opinion will fall within a defence to be discussed in chapter 21.

Other illustrations Several further examples might help to illustrate what is, and what is not, defamatory. It is defamatory to impute to a trader, business-, or professional person a lack of qualification, knowledge, skill, or efficiency in the conduct of her trade or business or professional activity (such as a severe attack on the special anaesthetising technique of a practising dental surgeon).[53] By contrast, it is not defamatory per se

---

[43] Gibbons' answer would be to change the basis of the action from damage to reputation to awarding a remedy for unsubstantiated allegations that cause C to be falsely judged: T Gibbons (1996) 16 OJLS 587.

[44] If the words would not in themselves convey to the ordinary person the meaning which a special group of experts would give to them, then this interpretation would not apply (unless an innuendo were pleaded: see section 2(A)(4)(c) because the basic rule that words must be defamatory in their ordinary meaning would not be satisfied: *Mollo v BBC* (1963) *The Times*, 2 February. Nor is it defamatory, without more, for D to say that C is Mr X, even though others have published defamatory articles about Mr X. The libel complained of must be in the statement published by D: *Astaire v Campling* [1965] 3 All ER 666.

[45] Eg, *Thorley v Lord Kerry* (1812) 4 Taunt 355. But in that case, it was explicitly stated (at 365) that, 'for mere general abuse spoken, no action lies'.   [46] *Alexander v Jenkins* [1892] 1 QB 797, at 804.

[47] *Bell v Stone* (1798) 1 Bos & P 331.   [48] *M'Gregor v Gregory* (1843) 11 M & W 287.

[49] *Brooks v Lind* (1997) Rep LR 83 (not defamation to suggest C was associated with a 'Council Mafia').

[50] *Braddock v Bevins* [1948] 1 KB 580.

[51] *Dolby v Newnes* (1887) 3 TLR 393 (a statement at a private dinner party, although not defamatory, might become so if repeated in a magazine).   [52] (1916) 33 TLR 35.

[53] *Drummond-Jackson v British Medical Association* [1970] 1 All ER 1094.

merely to criticise a trader's goods: the trader herself must be attacked for defamation to arise. If, however, one can read into a criticism of the product a criticism of its manufacturer, then the criticism might be defamatory.[54] Thus, to say that a baker's bread is *always unwholesome* is defamatory.[55] But to say that a product does not answer its purpose is not.[56] To say that a trader is bankrupt or insolvent is defamatory;[57] but to say that she has ceased to be in business is not, for it does not reflect unnecessarily on her reputation.[58] It is also not per se defamatory to say that a trader has been put on a stop-list.[59]

(3) Who can be defamed?

Natural persons and companies Either a living person or a company with a commercial reputation might be defamed under English law,[60] so long as their reputation exists at least partly in England.[61] The importance of the protection offered to commercial enterprises by the law of defamation was affirmed in *Jameel v Wall Street Journal Europe SPRL* by Lord Bingham:

> [T]he good name of a company, as that of an individual, is a thing of value. A damaging libel may lower its standing in the eyes of the public and even its own staff, make people less ready to deal with it, less willing or less proud to work for it.[62]

Accordingly, it is defamation to claim that X Co Ltd indulges in black-market activities.[63]

Concerns about corporate claimants The media sees the ability of commercial enterprises to sue for defamation as a powerful inhibition of vigorous criticism of such entities. The threat to sue for libel has a 'chilling effect' on investigations by the media and might allow corrupt practices to remain hidden from the public. Australian legislatures have removed the rights of larger and medium-sized companies to sue for defamation,[64] but this type of reform has not been considered seriously in England.[65] Nevertheless, some limits to the ability of companies to bring actions in defamation do apply. First, the European Court of Human Rights has ruled that large companies must be open to a higher degree of public criticism about their business practices.[66] Second, the ability of

---

[54] *Evans v Harlow* (1844) 5 QB 624.

[55] *Linotype Co Ltd v British Empire Type-Setting Machine Co Ltd* (1899) 81 LT 331, at 331 (*obiter*).

[56] *Evans v Harlow* (1844) 5 QB 624.   [57] *Shepheard v Whitaker* (1875) LR 10 CP 502.

[58] *Ratcliffe v Evans* [1892] 2 QB 524. Nor is it defamatory to say that her business is suffering as a result of competition: *Stephenson v Donaldson & Sons* (1981) 262 EG 148. In some circumstances it may constitute the separate tort of injurious falsehood.

[59] *Ware and De Freville Ltd v Motor Trade Association* [1921] 3 KB 40.

[60] In relation to companies, the statement 'must attack the corporation or company in the method of conducting its affairs, must accuse it of fraud or mismanagement, or must attack its financial position': *South Hetton Coal Co v NE News Association* [1894] 1 QB 133, at 141 (approved in *Jameel v Wall Street Journal Europe SPRL* [2007] 1 AC 359, at [17]).

[61] *King v Lewis* [2005] EMLR 4; *Jameel v Wall Street Journal Europe SPRL* [2007] 1 AC 359, at [17].

[62] [2007] 1 AC 359, at [26]. See also P Coe [2015] JBL 313.

[63] *D & L Caterers Ltd and Jackson v D'Ajou* [1945] KB 364.   [64] See, eg, Defamation Act 2005 (NSW), s 9.

[65] Ministry of Justice, *Draft Defamation Bill Consultation* (Cm 8020, 2011), 52–4. See extended discussion in GKY Chan (2013) 33 LS 264.   [66] *Steel and Morris v United Kingdom* [2005] 41 EHRR 22, at [94].

commercial enterprises to bring actions in defamation is subject to the 'serious financial loss' requirement in the Defamation Act 2013, considered later.[67]

Charities and unions In the *Jameel* case, Lord Craig observed that other organisations not involved in trading for profit, such as charities and trade unions, can be harmed by defamatory statements and might have a right of action. In the case of a charity, his Lordship reasoned that 'it is not only its pocket, due to a loss of income, that is liable to be injured. Injury to its reputation in the eyes of those with whom it must deal to achieve its charitable objects may be just as damaging to the purpose for which it exists.'[68]

Public authorities excluded By contrast to the position regarding companies, the House of Lords held in *Derbyshire County Council v Times Newspapers Ltd*[69] that public authorities cannot invoke defamation law to protect their 'governing reputation':[70]

> Ds had published articles questioning the propriety of C's management of pension funds. The House of Lords struck out the claim, holding that democratically elected government bodies and public authorities should be open to uninhibited public criticism. The 'chilling effect' of libel might prevent publication of matters about which the public ought to be informed.

In effect, then, the right of freedom of expression and freedom of the press (enshrined in Article 10 of the European Convention on Human Rights) outweighed the Council's claim to protection of its reputation.[71] Subsequently, it has been held that political parties are precluded from suing in defamation.[72]

The limitation on suits in libel by public authorities—whether a local council or government ministry—and political parties does not apply to *individual* members of these organisations, where the individual can show that she has been defamed personally.[73] However, a number of points should be kept in mind. First, an English decision demonstrates that difficulty might attend the bringing of a defamation action when 'statements by one candidate about another candidate, or about a person associated with another candidate' are made in the course of an election because these 'are not capable of being understood as anything other than partisan'.[74] Second, the European Court of Human Rights offers a greater degree of freedom of expression in criticising those running for political office than private persons are expected to endure,[75] and English courts must have regard to such jurisprudence. Indeed, as a policy matter uninhibited

---

[67] See sub-section 2(A)(7).   [68] *Steel and Morris v United Kingdom* [2005] 41 EHRR 22, at [96].

[69] [1993] 1 All ER 1011 (overruling *Bognor Regis UDC v Campion* [1972] 2 QB 169).

[70] The question arises whether non-governmental bodies serving a public function should be excluded from bringing actions in defamation by analogy to the reasoning used for judicial intervention in *R v Panel on Takeovers and Mergers, ex parte Datafin plc* [1986] 1 QB 815. At present, the answer appears to be 'no': *Duke v University of Salford* [2013] EWHC 196 (QB).

[71] For critique see ID Loveland (1994) 14 LS 206. Recall, also, that the Convention has all but been incorporated into English law by virtue of the Human Rights Act 1998.

[72] *Goldsmith v Bhoyrul* [1998] QB 459.   [73] Eg, *Bookbinder v Tebbit* (1988) [1989] 1 WLR 640.

[74] See *Crow v Johnson* [2012] EWHC 1982, at [24] (QB).

[75] *Lingens v Austria* (1986) 8 EHRR 407.

criticism might be appropriate when concerning many individuals holding important public offices. (Indeed, the First Amendment to the United States' Constitution has been interpreted to offer a wide scope for defamatory statements about public figures, liability arising only where 'actual malice' can be proved.)[76]

(4) The interpretation of defamatory statements

So far in this chapter, it has been assumed that the meaning of the statement complained of is readily ascertainable. But this is not always so; and there are detailed rules of interpretation that must now be considered.

(a) Ordinary meaning

The initial question in any defamation action is whether the words complained of are capable of bearing a defamatory meaning. In the absence of an allegation that those words possess an extended meaning (as to which, see later), words must be construed in their ordinary and natural sense.[77] In *Capital and Counties Bank Ltd v Henty*, Lord Blackburn stated that the court is required to 'put that meaning on them which the words would be understood by ordinary persons to bear'.[78] And Lord Bramwell explained that 'the question is not what the writer of any alleged libel means, but what is the meaning of the words [s]he has used'.[79]

Whole statement   The whole of the statement must be looked at, not merely that part which the claimant alleges to be defamatory (although it might be relevant to take account of the greater importance of some part of a statement—for example, the headlines of an article in a newspaper).[80] In *Charleston v News Group Newspapers Ltd*,[81] for instance, 'soap opera' actors sued in respect of material published in the defendant's newspaper which depicted the claimants' faces superimposed upon two near-naked torsos. The article printed beneath the picture castigated the makers of a pornographic computer game, which had been used to generate the images. It was held that, taken as a whole, the picture and the article were not capable of being defamatory.[82] On the other hand, where an article contains both a defamatory statement *and* a denial of that statement, the denial does not necessarily neutralise the defamatory comment. As Simon Brown LJ put it in *Mark v Associated Newspapers (No 1)*: 'I find it very difficult to conceive of circumstances in which the mere printing of a denial could of itself be said to constitute an antidote sufficient to neutralise the bane.'[83]

---

[76]   *New York Times v Sullivan* 376 US 254 (1964). See also E Barendt, *Freedom of Speech* (2007), ch 6.

[77]   *Capital and Counties Bank Ltd v George Henty & Sons* (1882) 7 App Cas 741, at 772. See also *Skuse v Granada Television Ltd* [1996] EMLR 278; *Gillick v BBC* [1996] EMLR 267. In *Mitchell v Faber and Faber Ltd* [1998] EMLR 807, Hirst LJ stated (at 811) that, '[i]n deciding whether words are capable of conveying a defamatory meaning the court will reject those meanings which can only emerge as the product of some strained or forced or utterly unreasonable interpretation'.   [78]   (1882) 7 App Cas 741, at 772.

[79]   (1882) 7 App Cas 741, at 790.   [80]   *Shipley v Todhunter* (1836) 7 C & P 680.

[81]   [1995] 2 AC 65.

[82]   For criticism, see *Chakravarti v Advertisers Newspapers* [1998] HCA 37, at [134].

[83]   [2002] EMLR 38.

Context There may be circumstances in which the wider context in which the words are uttered must be taken into account. In *Bookbinder v Tebbit*,[84] for example, the alleged slander was made at a political meeting. The court said that the meaning to be attached to the defendant's words could be affected, among other things, by the form of the question to which the words were an answer or the general course of the speech in issue.

(b) Inferred meaning

Words might have a meaning beyond their literal meaning, which arises by inference or implication—that is, an 'inferred meaning'.[85] This is so when persons are able to 'read between the lines' for the real, substantial meaning of the statement.[86] The claimant must plead inferred meaning separately from allegations involving ordinary, literal meaning. Thus, when a defendant newspaper described a well-known broadcaster as 'bent', the claimant had to set out the meaning of the word on which he relied.[87] If a statement is capable of many different meanings and the claimant does not specify those on which she relies, the defendant is entitled to defend the statement according to any meaning which it reasonably bears.[88] If, in a long article containing many different meanings in relation to her, the claimant fails to plead the meaning(s) on which she relies, the defendant is entitled to have the claimant's statement of claim struck out as disclosing no reasonable cause of action.[89]

Suspicion of guilt Problems can arise with regard to inferred meaning. In *Rubber Improvement Ltd v Daily Telegraph Ltd*,[90] the defendants published an article which stated that the Fraud Squad of the City of London Police were investigating the affairs of the claimants' company. The article was found to be defamatory in its ordinary meaning because the simple statement that the Fraud Squad was inquiring into his affairs might have damaged his reputation even though such investigation did not, per se, impugn his innocence. However, since what was said was true—the Fraud Squad was conducting the investigations mentioned—no action lay.[91] The claimants alleged also that the words were defamatory in a second way: that they included the imputation that there was a basis for suspicion about the way in which the business was conducted. The thrust of the plea was that the imputation of reasonable suspicion (while still consistent with the claimants' innocence) was capable nonetheless of diminishing their trading reputation. On the facts, their Lordships held that the words were not defamatory in this second sense; since there was a distinction between, on the one hand, imputing reasonable

---

[84] [1989] 1 WLR 640.   [85] This terminology is preferred to the term 'false innuendo'.
[86] *Lewis v Daily Telegraph* [1964] AC 234, at 277.
[87] *Allsop v Church of England Newspaper Ltd* [1972] 2 QB 161.
[88] *London Computer Operators Training Ltd v BBC* [1973] 2 All ER 170.
[89] *DDSA Pharmaceuticals Ltd v Times Newspapers Ltd* [1973] QB 21.
[90] [1964] AC 234. But see *Hyams v Peterson* [1991] 1 NZLR 711, where the New Zealand Court of Appeal found that a statement containing words of suspicion could impute guilt.
[91] There is a difference between something being defamatory *simpliciter* and something being defamatory and *actionable*. To be defamatory, the statement must diminish C's reputation; but to be actionable, the statement must also be untrue. In short, both true and false statements might be defamatory, but only the latter may be actionable.

grounds for suspicion and, on the other hand (as here), simply reporting the fact of suspicion.

This crucial distinction between a statement and an imputation of suspicion has been reasserted by the Court of Appeal in *Mapp v News Group Newspapers Ltd*.[92] But it should be noted that the second plea in *Rubber Improvement Ltd* constituted the allegation of inferred meaning and did not require the claimants to adduce evidence of any extrinsic facts which had to be set out in the pleading (such as details of individual readers who would interpret the words in a particular way).

(c) True innuendoes

There might be circumstances in which the claimant alleges that the statement is defamatory because specific facts known to the reader give to the statement a meaning other than, or additional to, its ordinary meaning.[93] This is known as a 'true' or 'legal' innuendo, and here the claimant must plead and prove such facts[94] because the defendant is entitled to know the meaning of the statement on which the claimant relies so that she is able to argue either that, even construed thus the statement is not defamatory, or that it is true of the claimant.

Illustrations Perhaps the most famous example of 'true', or 'legal', innuendoes is Lord Devlin's from *Lewis v Daily Telegraph*,[95] where he stated that 'to say of a man that he was seen to enter a named house would contain a derogatory implication for anyone who knew that the house was a brothel but not for anyone who did not', although it appears that views of such sexual practices are (to a greater or lesser extent) becoming less severe and thus less defamatory. Another example arose in *Cassidy v Daily Mirror Newspapers Ltd*:

> With the authority of Mr C, Ds published a photograph, taken at a race meeting, with the following words underneath: 'Mr C, the racehorse owner, and Miss X, whose engagement has been announced'. Ds published the photograph, not knowing that C was married to the man in question, and having taken no steps to find out whether he was married already.

The defendants were held liable to the claimant for implying she had been living with Mr Corrigan without being married to him. Scrutton LJ stated that 'to say that A is a single man or a bachelor may be capable of a defamatory meaning if published to persons who know a lady who passes as Mrs A . . .'.[96]

Objective test In *Hough v London Express Newspaper Ltd*,[97] the question arose whether a claimant relying on an innuendo has to prove that there was publication to somebody who interpreted the matter in the defamatory sense alleged:

---

[92] [1998] QB 520.   [93] *Slim v Daily Telegraph* [1968] 2 QB 157, at 183.

[94] C must prove that those facts were actually known to some people (*Fullam v Newcastle Chronicle and Journal Ltd* [1977] 1 WLR 651) and that those facts were in existence and known to those people at the time of the publication (*Grapelli v Derek Block (Holdings) Ltd* [1981] 2 All ER 272; *Baturina v Times Newspapers Ltd* [2011] 1 WLR 1526).   [95] [1964] AC 234, at 278.

[96] [1929] 2 KB 331, at 339.   [97] [1940] 2 KB 507.

> D published an account and photograph of the 'curly-headed wife' of a named boxer. C, the boxer's real wife, produced witnesses who gave evidence that they had read the statement to mean that C was not the boxer's wife. In the event, they were not misled into thinking that she was not his wife, nor was any person that was produced as a witness so misled.

It was held that the appropriate test was an objective one. The court found in the claimant's favour: it was enough to prove that there are people who *might* understand the words in a defamatory sense, but no need for 'evidence that some person did so understand them'.[98]

(d) One and only meaning

Where the parties contend that the statement has different defamatory meanings, the judge decides which of those meanings the statement is capable of conveying. Having done that, the judge's task is to take a middle-of-the-road approach to ascertaining the one and only meaning of the defamatory words.[99] Ostensibly, this is the meaning that the hypothetical ordinary reasonable reader of the kind of publication in question would give to the words.[100] In order to determine what such a person would think, the court must take account of the knowledge that they are likely to have had when exposed to the defamatory words. In *Monroe v Hopkins*, for example, when deciding between two defamatory meanings of a posting on Twitter, Warby J took into account such things as the nature of Twitter as a medium of spirited 'conversation' and the immediately surrounding contextual material that accompanied the Tweet complained of.[101] The one and only meaning becomes that with respect to which the judge must apply any pleaded defences.

(5) Immateriality of the defendant's knowledge

A person charged with libel cannot defend herself by showing that she never intended to defame.[102] Nor is it a defence that a person has no actual knowledge that her statement is defamatory. Thus, liability is described as being strict in nature: it matters not whether the defendant could have taken steps to discover that the statement was defamatory. The leading case is *Cassidy v Daily Mirror Newspapers Ltd*,[103] considered earlier, which is authority for the proposition that one might be liable for a statement that one does not recognise to be defamatory. To this strict general rule, however, there are two exceptions—one statutory; one rooted in the common law. These exceptions are discussed in chapter 21.

(6) Presumption of falsity

Assuming that the claimant has proven that a statement is defamatory, the law does not require that she prove that it is 'false'. Rather, in cases involving a statement about factual

---

[98] [1940] 2 KB 507, at 515. See also *Theaker v Richardson* [1962] 1 All ER 229.

[99] *Simpson v MGN Ltd* [2016] EMLR 26, at [15]. See also *Jeynes v News Magazines Ltd* [2008] EWCA Civ 140, at [14].

[100] *Monroe v Hopkins* [2017] 4 WLR 68, at [23]; *McAlpine v Bercow* [2013] EWHC 1342 (QB), at [66].

[101] [2017] 4 WLR 68, at [43]. [102] *E Hulton & Co v Jones* [1910] AC 20, at 23. [103] [1929] 2 KB 331.

matters, the law presumes that the statement is false;[104] that presumption can be rebutted through proof of the statement's truth (as to which see chapter 21). The European Court of Human Rights has accepted that the presumption of falsity is not incompatible with the Article 10 right to freedom of expression.[105]

(7) Serious harm

Threshold of seriousness The Defamation Act 2013, sub-section 1(1), provides that a 'statement is not defamatory unless its publication has caused or is likely to cause serious harm to the reputation of the claimant'. This appears to imply that a statement itself is now seen as defamatory only when it would give rise to serious harm. The serious harm requirement, in turn, sets a threshold of actionability for all claims in defamation. But we must consider how the provision impacts upon cases of libel and slander separately.

In cases of libel, while no damage need be proved to have occurred when commencing an action, the court must be satisfied at the date of trial that serious harm is likely to arise from the use of the words. It would appear that the court should determine this issue by taking account of factors such as: the nature and gravity of the imputations (including whether it is mere innuendo understood by a limited group of persons); the extent of publication (including any prior defamation) and any retraction; and the pre-existing status and reputation of the claimant.

By contrast to the approach suggested above, the Court of Appeal's first major statement about this matter takes a very liberal view of what the legislation requires. In *Lachaux v Independent Print Ltd*,[106] the court held that: (1) the 2013 Act raises the damage threshold from one of substantiality to one of seriousness: no less and no more; (2) a disjunctive approach to the words of sub-section 1(1) can be taken. *If* the court finds that the words used were defamatory, *only then* does the issue of damage arise and *damage can be presumed* as per the common law; (3) although damage is presumed, the claimant must prove that it is or is likely to be serious—which can be done by a process of inference; and (4) in an appropriate case, a defendant disputing the existence or likelihood of serious harm can seek to overturn a finding in favour of the claimant by seeking summary judgment.[107] This approach does not seem to reflect what the statute requires. It is submitted that the *correct* approach was taken by Warby J in the court below, when he stated that 'libel is no longer actionable without proof of damage, and . . . the legal presumption of damage will cease to play any significant role'.[108]

---

[104] For discussion and argument against the presumption, see D Milo, *Defamation and Freedom of Speech* (2008), ch 5. The presumption no longer applies in the US on account of its impact upon freedom of expression: *New York Times v Sullivan* 376 US 254, 279 (1964).

[105] *Steel & Morris v UK* [2005] EMLR 15, at [93]–[94].   [106] [2017] EWCA Civ 1334.

[107] [2017] EWCA Civ 1334, at [70], [72], and [82]. The reaction from law firms has been one of surprise. It appears that an appeal to the Supreme Court has been lodged.

[108] [2015] EWHC 2242 (QB), at [60]. This approach conforms to decisions in *Ames v Spamhouse Project Ltd* [2015] 1 WLR 3409, at [49]; *Cooke v MGN Ltd* [2015] 1 WLR 895, at [37]. Certainly, defamation is not actionable per se in the way that torts such as trespass are actionable without proof of damage and without the need for any damage to be likely.

In cases of slander, *special* damage must be proved. There are two exceptions (relating to imputations of crime and slander of office etc, considered later), but these fall naturally within the requirements of sub-section 1(a) because serious harm is inherent within the relevant words.

Traders The Defamation Act 2013, section 1(b), provides that, in the case of 'a body that trades for profit', serious harm does not arise unless it has caused or is likely to cause the body 'serious financial loss'. Claimants falling within this description include not only businesses that trade goods, but also professional services firms.[109] When considering the losses that such bodies have incurred, a distinction should be drawn here between mere loss of goodwill value (which would be reflected in the value of the business to its owners) and financial loss from lost sales or reductions in a revenue stream, only the latter being actionable.[110] Existing authority indicates that it might be difficult to prove the causal connection between a defamatory statement and any subsequent loss of revenues; this would be so especially in a case where the argument was that an anticipated upward sales trajectory never materialised.[111] As regards slander, what constitutes special damage is considered later.

(B) Reference to the claimant

'In order to be actionable the defamatory words must be understood to be published of and concerning' the claimant.[112] The claimant need not be mentioned in the statement, nor need everyone reading it know that she was referred to; it suffices if ordinary sensible people with knowledge of the facts might reasonably believe that the statement referred to the claimant.[113] Thus, where the defendant publishes a biography about X, and it contains a picture of X together with the claimant *and* a known prostitute, it has been held to be defamatory of the claimant to publish that photograph where the claimant's friends would see the picture and identify him even though he is not actually named in the book.[114] On the other hand, in cases such as this, the damages will be lower where only a small proportion of those who read the book would know that it was defamatory of the claimant.

(1) Class libels

Where a statement defamatory of a class of persons is made, the same test is applied to determine whether individuals within the class may sue. If the class is so small that

---

[109] *Brett Wilson LLP v Person(s) Unknown* [2016] 4 WLR 69, at [26].

[110] See *Collins Stewart Ltd v Financial Times Ltd (No 1)* [2004] EWHC 2337.

[111] See *Tesla Motors Ltd v BBC* [2013] EWCA Civ 152 (case of malicious falsehood).

[112] *Knupffer v London Express Newspaper Ltd* [1944] AC 116, at 121. Cf *Farrington v Leigh* (1987) *Times*, 10 December.

[113] *Morgan v Odhams Press Ltd* [1971] 2 All ER 1156. If D publishes a statement defamatory on its face about someone described but not named, and a later publication by D names C so as to identify the subject to readers of the first article, for the first time, the second publication can be relied on to support the allegation that the first one referred to C: *Hayward v Thompson* [1982] QB 47.

[114] *Dwek v Macmillan Publishers Ltd* [2000] EMLR 284.

persons would believe reasonably that every member of it was targeted, then each may sue.[115] Thus, where proceedings were pending against 17 persons, it was held that one of them could sue a third party who said of them all that 'these defendants helped to murder HF'.[116] A similar rule applies to company directors,[117] given that boards of directors usually have a small number of members. But a statement that 'all lawyers are thieves' would not enable any one member of such a large class to sue.[118]

Even where the class is too large to permit every member to sue, an individual within it may still be able to sue. So, for example, even if the claimant has a very common surname, other facts contained in the statement in question might narrow the class sufficiently for her to be defamed.[119] Of course, if the claimant can show that the statement was especially referable to her, she may sue. Often this will rest on an innuendo that must be pleaded specifically; and the court will order the claimant to give full particulars of the facts on which the claim rests.[120] Two cases illustrate the position. First, *Le Fanu v Malcomson*:[121]

> D published an article suggesting that in certain Irish factories cruelties were practised upon employees. There were circumstances in the article as a whole, including a reference to Waterford, which enabled the jury to identify C's Waterford factory as the one at which the article was aimed. C's action succeeded.

Second, *Knuppfer v London Express Newspaper Ltd*:[122]

> During the war, D's newspaper referred to the Quisling activities of the Young Russian Party. Although the party was international, and had a British branch of 24 members headed by C, the article referred only to the Party's activities in France and the US. But since the total membership was several thousand, each member could not be said to be identified. No facts were proved in evidence that could identify C as being singled out in the article, and his action failed.

(2) Unintentional references to the claimant

The claimant might be defamed even though the defendant did not intend it (but damages are likely to be lower than in cases where reference is intended[123]). In several cases, newspaper proprietors who did not intend to defame the claimant have been held liable. In *Hulton v Jones*,[124] for example, the defendants published a fictional article about 'Artemus Jones'. Ostensibly, the writer of the article did not know of the claimant of that name, who was a former contributor to the newspaper in which it was published. But the managing editor, on reading the article in proof form, had thought at first that

---

[115] *Knuppfer v London Express Newspaper* [1944] AC 116, at 119.

[116] *Foxcroft v Lacy* (1613) Hob 89. See also *Browne v Thomson & Co* 1912 SC 359.

[117] *Aspro Travel Ltd v Owners Abroad Group plc* [1995] 4 All ER 728. See also *Elite Model Management Corp v BBC* [2001] All ER (D) 334 (defamation of company executives may also be defamatory of the company). Cf *Chomley v Watson* [1907] VLR 502, where the true statement 'Either you or Jones stole the money' was held not to be actionable by the innocent party, Jones.

[118] *Eastwood v Holmes* (1858) 1 F & F 347; 175 ER 758, at 759.

[119] *Jameel v Dow Jones & Co Inc* [2005] QB 946.   [120] *Bruce v Odhams Press Ltd* [1936] 1 KB 697.

[121] (1848) 1 HL Cas 637.   [122] [1944] AC 116.

[123] *Bridgmont v Associated Newspapers Ltd* [1951] 2 KB 578.   [124] [1910] AC 20.

the claimant was intended. The defendants were held liable. Similarly, in *Newstead v London Express Newspaper Ltd*,[125] the defendant published an account of the trial for bigamy of 'Harold Newstead, thirty-year-old Camberwell man'. The reporter had included the address and occupation of the Harold Newstead of whom this was a correct report, but the sub-editor deleted it. This want of particularity caused readers to think that the claimant—another Harold Newstead of Camberwell, of about the same age—was meant. It was held to be no defence that the words were true of, and intended to refer to, another.

Impact of HRA Whether cases like these can withstand the passage of the Human Rights Act 1998, with its requirement that the courts develop the common law in accordance with rights enshrined in the European Convention,[126] is questionable. As mentioned, the view was taken in *O'Shea v MGN Ltd* that a requirement that a publisher check whether a model resembles any other person would place too onerous a burden on it. As Morland J put it:

> [T]he strict liability principle should not cover the 'look-alike' situation. To allow it to do so would be an unjustifiable interference with the vital right of freedom of expression disproportionate to the legitimate aim of protecting the reputations of 'look-alikes' and contrary to Article 10.[127]

Much of the reasoning in this case would appear capable of extension to cases where articles are printed in newspapers with no accompanying photograph. For now, however, the Court of Appeal has taken the view that *Hulton v Jones* is compatible with the right to freedom of expression under Article 10.[128]

(C) Publication

(1) General rules

Publication is 'making known the defamatory matter after it has been written to some person other than the person of whom it is written'.[129] The requirement of publication to a third party underlines that the tort protects not an individual's opinion of herself but the estimation in which others hold her. The following illustrations are some guidance on when a court is likely to find publication to a third party. The requirement is satisfied by dictating a letter to a typist,[130] and probably when office staff photocopy a document.[131]

---

[125] [1940] 1 KB 377. And see *Grappelli v Derek Block (Holdings) Ltd* [1981] 2 All ER 272 and *Hayward v Thompson* [1982] QB 47 (effect of later publications identifying the person defamed).

[126] See *Douglas v Hello! Ltd* [2001] QB 967, at [129].   [127] [2001] EMLR 40, at [47].

[128] *Baturina v Times Newspapers Ltd* [2011] 1 WLR 1526.

[129] *Pullman v Walter Hill & Co* [1891] 1 QB 524, at 527.

[130] *Pullman v Walter Hill & Co* [1891] 1 QB 524. The circulation of interdepartmental memoranda within a company is also sufficient publication: *Riddick v Thames Board Mills Ltd* [1977] QB 881.

[131] The official report of *Pullman v Walter Hill & Co* [1891] 1 QB 524 does not expressly state that the press copying in that case was held to be a publication, but Lord Esher MR said in *Boxsius v Goblet Frères* [1894] 1 QB 842, at 849 that the case had so decided, and he was a judge in both cases.

The defendant's publication to her own spouse is not enough,[132] but publication to the claimant's spouse suffices.[133] A correspondent should expect that, in the ordinary course of business, clerks of a businessperson-claimant will open letters addressed to her at her place of business, but not when they are marked 'personal', 'private', etc. She is responsible for the publication to them where the correspondence is not so marked.[134]

Rebuttable presumptions Difficulties of proving publication are eased by certain rebuttable presumptions. If one can prove, for example, that a letter bore the correct address and that it was properly posted, there is a presumption of publication to the addressee.[135] Similarly, postcards and telegrams[136] (though not unsealed letters)[137] are presumed to have been published to Post Office officials.

Illustrations of no liability On the other hand, there is no publication for the purposes of defamation law unless the third party would understand the defamatory meaning of the communication. Thus, a postcard defamatory of, but not known to be referable to the claimant by, persons unaware of the special facts, was held not to be published to Post Office staff.[138] A defendant is not liable for an 'unsuspected overhearing of the words' spoken by her to the claimant.[139] She is not liable where a father opens his son's letter,[140] or the butler opens her employer's unsealed letter.[141] It has been held that a printer does not, by the very act of handing back in a parcel printed handbills to the customer-author, publish those handbills.[142]

(2) Single publication rule

The common law permits a new cause of action every time a person re-publishes a defamatory statement.[143] The Defamation Act 2013, section 8, creates an important exception to the ordinary rule. The 12-month limitation period for bringing actions[144] now runs from the point in time at which a statement is *first* published to the public. So, where there is a subsequent publication by the same person of a statement in substantially the same form, no further cause of action arises. The provision 'replaces the longstanding principle that each publication of defamatory material gives rise to a separate cause of action which is subject to its own limitation period'.[145] The exception

---

[132] *Wennhak v Morgan* (1888) 20 QBD 635.   [133] *Wenman v Ash* (1853) 13 CB 836.
[134] *Pullman v Walter Hill & Co* [1891] 1 QB 524.   [135] *Warren v Warren* (1834) 1 Cr M & R 250.
[136] *Sadgrove v Hole* [1901] 2 KB 1.
[137] *Huth v Huth* [1915] 3 KB 32. It was stated, *obiter*, that had Post Office officials in fact read the letter to check whether it was properly stamped, that would have been publication. Cf *Clutterbuck v Chaffers* (1816) 1 Stark 471 (no publication where D handed to X a folded, unsealed letter which X, without reading or showing it to others, handed to C).
[138] *Sadgrove v Hole* [1901] 2 KB 1. The same applies to cipher messages and messages in foreign languages.
[139] *White v J and F Stone (Lighting and Radio) Ltd* [1939] 2 KB 827.
[140] *Powell v Gelston* [1916] 2 KB 615.   [141] *Huth v Huth* [1915] 3 KB 32.
[142] *Eglantine Inn Ltd v Isaiah Smith* [1948] NI 29.   [143] *Duke of Brunswick v Harmer* (1849) 14 QB 185.
[144] Limitation Act 1980, s 4A.   [145] Explanatory Notes to the Defamation Act 2013, at [60].

responds to the chilling effect that arises under the common law rule with respect to material archived on the internet which prompted 'publishers to [remove] past articles against which complaint was made'.[146]

In determining whether a subsequent publication is 'substantially the same' (rather than 'materially different'), the court will take into account factors including the 'level of prominence that the statement is given' and its 'extent'. Alteration to the meaning of a statement is likely to give rise to a new publication, whereas a mere change in presentation is not likely to do so.[147] In the Explanatory Notes, it is said that:

> A possible example [of material difference] could be where a story has first appeared relatively obscurely in a section of a website where several clicks need to be gone through to access it, but has subsequently been promoted to a position where it can be directly accessed from the home page of the site, thereby increasing considerably the number of hits it receives.

The court retains a discretion to extend the period of time within which actions must be brought, for exercise in exceptional cases.[148] In the view of two commentators, the rule's implementation is likely to be fraught because of the existence of this discretion to extend time:

> Faced with a claimant who argues credibly that a reading of [a] defamatory online publication that took place yesterday, and which might be emulated tomorrow, has had adverse consequences for his or her Article 8 right to reputation, no judge will be able to refuse to lift the limitation period.[149]

(3) Agents and other intermediaries

Agents Often, it is important to know when the defendant can be held responsible for the role of an intermediary in communicating a defamatory statement to third parties. A statement maker *is* liable for the repetition of a defamatory statement by her agent (someone acting on instruction). Thus:

> where a man who makes a request to another to publish defamatory matter, of which, for the purpose, he gives him a statement, whether in full or in outline, and the agent publishes the matter, adhering to the sense and substance of it, although the language be to some extent his own, the man making the request is liable to an action as the publisher.[150]

Other intermediaries It is possible also for the original statement maker to be held responsible for repetition where undertaken by others who are not specifically authorised to repeat the statement. The rule is that, if she intended it to be published to them,

---

[146] A Mullis and A Scott (2014) 77 MLR 87, 103.

[147] See D Hooper, K Waite, and O Murphy [2013] 24 Ent LR 199, 204–5.

[148] Limitation Act 1980, s 32A. See *Bewry v Reed Elsevier UK Ltd* [2015] 1 WLR 2565.

[149] A Mullis and A Scott (2014) 77 MLR 87, 103.   [150] *Parkes v Prescott* (1869) LR 4 Exch 169, at 179.

or ought to have foreseen such publication, she is liable, but not otherwise.[151] In determining this question of fact, the focus is upon the conditions foreseeably prevailing in the place to which the statement is destined.[152] A person who knows that reporters are present when she is making a speech is not responsible thereby for its publication in the press, but she is answerable if she gives the information to them with a view to publication.[153] And when a television broadcast foreseeably invites comment in the next day's newspapers, the maker of the original defamatory statement will be liable for its repetition by the press.[154]

(4) Acquiescence

Failure by a defendant who is able to but does not remove or amend defamatory matter, which is the work of another, amounts to publication by her. Thus, those in charge of a club will be accountable for defamatory matter placed by another on the club notice board if they do not remove it within a reasonable time.[155] The same kind of reasoning has been employed in the next category of cases to be examined, involving the internet.

Internet-based publication   An internet service provider (ISP) is liable prima facie for making available defamatory material on its news server,[156] as is a content provider where permitting the hosting of a blog.[157] This is on the basis that what they do is facilitative and not purely passive. Thus, in *Tamiz v Google Inc*, the Court of Appeal noted of Google's provision of a blogging service:

> Google provides a platform for blogs, together with design tools and, if required, a URL . . . It makes the Blogger service available on terms of its own choice and it can readily remove or block access to any blog that does not comply with those terms (a point of distinction [from a] search engine. . .).[158]

However, liability arises in general only after the point at which the ISP or content provider has been made aware of the presence of the defamatory material and can be negated by action within a reasonable time to remove the material.[159] By contrast to these cases, the Supreme Court of Canada has held that the mere provision of a

---

[151] *Huth v Huth* [1915] 3 KB 32, at 38; *Slipper v BBC* [1991] 1 All ER 165.

[152] *Theaker v Richardson* [1962] 1 All ER 229, at 235 (although Harman LJ refers to likelihood rather than foreseeability).

[153] *Adams v Kelly* (1824) Ry & M 157; *McWhirter v Manning* (1954) *Times*, 30 October.

[154] *Slipper v BBC* [1991] 1 All ER 165. In effect, this decision is no more than an application of the general law of causation; the foreseeable repetition of the statement by the press is too probable to be regarded as a *novus actus interveniens*.

[155] *Byrne v Deane* [1937] 1 KB 818. Compare those cases where the matter is carved in stone, or D is not in control of the place where the libel is exhibited. Here the impracticability/impossibility of avoiding the publication negates any prospect of liability.

[156] *Godfrey v Demon Internet Ltd* [2001] QB 201. Doubt must now be cast on reasoning in *Bunt v Tilley* [2007] 1 WLR 1243.   [157] *Tamiz v Google Inc* [2013] EWCA Civ 68.

[158] *Tamiz v Google Inc* [2013] EWCA Civ 68, at [24].

[159] *Tamiz v Google Inc* [2013] EWCA Civ 68, at [34]–[35].

hyperlink to a webpage which contains defamatory material is not sufficient to give rise to liability on the part of the 'hyperlinker'. Abella J stated that 'it is only when a hyperlinker presents content from the hyperlinked material in a way that actually repeats the defamatory content, should that content be considered to be "published" by the hyperlinker'.[160]

In *Metropolitan International Schools Ltd v Designtechnica Corporation*,[161] the claimant complained about an internet search engine, Google, which yielded responses to a search which were defamatory in nature:

> When entering search terms, the search engine suggested that the user looking for 'Train2Game' also use the term 'scam'. Search terms having been selected, 'snippets' of allegedly defamatory web pages were displayed. All of this followed an automatic process of web-crawling, indexing, and ranking of web pages.

Eady J held there to be no liability based upon these automatic processes alone. Google had not 'caused' in any meaningful sense either the search term suggestion or the snippet to appear on the screen.[162] Moreover, his Lordship expressed reluctance to contemplate actions for the period after Google was *notified*, in circumstances where, although it blocked access to certain offending web pages from its UK search portal, this was not completely effective. (Subsequently, however, the Court of Justice of the European Union has held, in *Google Spain SL v Agencia Española de Protección de Datos*,[163] that Google is a data controller for the purposes of the EU Directive on Data Protection[164] and falls under certain obligations regarding the removal of links to incorrect or irrelevant and outdated information on third-party websites.)

The legislature has provided for certain defences for the operators of websites, to be discussed in chapter 21.

(5) Multiple actors

Under the common law, the newspaper proprietor, writer, printer, and distributors of a defamatory article in a newspaper are each liable for their part in its publication[165] and this rule has been held to be compatible with Article 10 of the European Convention on Human Rights[166] (even though it might be seen as forcing journalists to check scrupulously (or distance themselves from) comments made by others). Under the Defamation Act 2013, section 10, the ability of a claimant now to sue a person other than the author, editor, or commercial publisher of a statement is restricted. This reduces the scope of liability of printers and distributors, although they might still be sued if 'it is not reasonably practicable for an action to be brought against the author, editor or publisher'.

---

[160] *Crookes v Newton* [2011] 3 SCR 269, at [42].   [161] [2011] 1 WLR 1743.

[162] [2011] 1 WLR 1743, at [50]–[51].   [163] Case C–131/12, 13 May 2014.

[164] Council Directive 95/46/EC. See now Council Regulation EU/2016/679 of 27 April 2016 on the protection of natural persons with regard to the processing of personal data.

[165] See *Goldsmith v Sperrings Ltd* [1977] 2 All ER 566.

[166] *Chase v News Group Newspapers Ltd* [2003] EMLR 11. Cf *Thoma v Luxembourg* (2003) 36 EHRR 21 ('a general requirement for journalists to distance themselves from the content of a quotation' would be irreconcilable with the role of the press and thus an infringement of Art 10).

Section 3 Distinguishing libel from slander

(A) Criteria for distinguishing libel from slander

Any medium whereby thought and ideas can be expressed or conveyed may constitute a defamatory publication—words, pictures, gestures,[167] music, and statues are all examples.[168] However, it is the choice of medium that determines whether the defamation is libel or slander; and it is because the rules relating to the two torts differ in some respects that it is necessary to distinguish between them.

Permanent form Anything communicated in permanent form and visible to the eye is libel, and anything temporary is slander. The word 'permanent' should be understood here to mean capable of preservation and, thus, 'lasting indefinitely'. Thus, defamatory books, newspapers, letters, and effigies[169] are all libels, while spoken words are slander. In *Youssoupoff v Metro-Goldwyn-Mayer Pictures Ltd*,[170] the scenes depicted on the screen in a film with sound (a new invention at the time) were held to constitute libel. Yet, the case might be said only to support the view that permanency is an important element in the test for libel. It does not establish that permanency is the sole criterion. Slesser LJ put it thus:

> [S]o far as the photographic part of the exhibition is concerned, that is a *permanent matter to be seen by the eye*, and is the proper subject of an action for libel, if defamatory. I regard the speech which is synchronised with the photographic reproduction and forms part of one complex, common exhibition as an ancillary circumstance, part of the surroundings explaining that which is to be seen.[171]

The case does not settle authoritatively whether a defamatory anecdote in a film is libel. Nor does it tell us whether defamatory remarks on a CD are libel, although the presumption must be that they are both libel, given that they share the characteristics of being capable of preservation and lasting indefinitely. Defamatory material posted on an internet website has been held to be a libel once downloaded in England.[172]

Broadcasting and performance The uncertainty at common law prompted statutory intervention to cover mass media communications. Broadcasting Act 1990, section 166 provides that the publication of any words in the course of any broadcast programme on television or radio shall be treated as publication in a permanent form. Similarly, the Theatres Act 1968 provides that the publication of words in the course of a performance of a play shall also be treated as publication in a permanent form.[173]

---

[167] See *Cook v Cox* (1814) 3 M & S 110, at 114.
[168] Even the lighting of a lamp in the daytime in C's garden, thereby inferring that he keeps a brothel, is caught: *Jefferies v Duncombe* (1809) 2 Camp 3; and perhaps so is police shadowing of C's house.
[169] *Monson v Tussauds Ltd* [1894] 1 QB 671.   [170] (1934) 50 TLR 581.
[171] (1934) 50 TLR 581, at 587 (emphasis added).   [172] *King v Lewis* [2005] EMLR 4.
[173] Section 4. But note that performances given 'on a domestic occasion in a private dwelling' are exempted by s 7 of the Act.

Other statements The forwarding of a typed letter is libel and one for which the writer is accountable on the basis that she authorised her agent to forward it. The reading aloud of a letter written by another, where those to whom it was read were aware that the speaker was reading from the document, was held to be libel in *Forrester v Tyrrell*.[174] The short report of this case does not mention, however, whether the point that it might have been slander was argued.[175] In *Osborn v Boulter*,[176] Scrutton and Slesser LJJ thought that the reading aloud of a document was slander, while Greer LJ was inclined to think it libel. It is submitted that the approach in *Forrester v Tyrrell* is preferable because the defamatory material was both visible and in permanent form. The reading of it simply constituted the means of publication.[177] By contrast, dictation of a letter to a typist can be slander only.[178]

(B) Juridical differences between libel and slander

There are two juridical differences between libel and slander. First, a libel of sufficient seriousness may be punished as a crime, whereas slander is only tortious.[179] Second, under the old law, libel was actionable per se, whereas slander was actionable only upon proof of actual damage, subject to exceptions.[180] Defamation Act 2013, section 1, now provides that a 'statement is not defamatory unless its publication has caused or is likely to cause serious harm to the reputation of the claimant'. This represents a new threshold to be met in cases of libel. In cases of slander, it remains the case that *special* damage must be proved, which is damage that is material in nature (discussed later). Two exceptional cases in which special damage need not be proved (but must be likely to cause serious harm and are of their nature likely to do so) are now discussed.

(C) Cases where slander is actionable without proof of special damage

(1) Imputation of crime

The crime must be one for which the claimant could be imprisoned forthwith. Therefore, the statement that 'I know enough to put you in gaol' is actionable without proof of special damage.[181] Even where the perpetrator of an offence has been arrested, if she can be punished by a fine only (and not by imprisonment), the imputation of the commission of the crime remains

---

[174] (1893) 57 JP 532. MacDermott J followed this decision with reluctance in *Robinson v Chambers (No 2)* [1946] NI 148, where the audience was aware that D was reading out a letter.

[175] If the secretary simply hands or reads the letter back to the person who dictated it, then there can be no defamation, for there has been no publication.   [176] [1930] 2 KB 226.

[177] For additional judicial support for this view, see *Robinson v Chambers (No 2)* [1946] NI 148.

[178] But when the typist listens to a dictaphone, a libel is probably being published.

[179] Of course, spoken words might constitute a crime where the other elements of that crime are present: eg, blasphemy or sedition. See *Gleaves v Deakin* [1980] AC 477.

[180] Although the term 'special damage' is used frequently, this is misleading, as noted earlier, since the phrase has other meanings in other contexts. In fact, the use of the term 'special damage' in this context is to be attributed to the *dictum* of Lord Wensleydale in *Lynch v Knight* (1861) 9 HL Cas 577.

[181] *Webb v Beavan* (1883) 11 QBD 609. This illustration also shows that a general imputation of criminality without reference to a specific offence is sufficient.

outside the exception.[182] And this is the case even though there is a power to commit for non-payment of the fine.[183]

The words of imputation must be clear and unambiguous. If they convey a mere suspicion—for example, of murder—they do not fall within the exception.[184] In addition, in construing the meaning of the words, they must be looked at in context in order to discover what was imputed. This rule is made clear by *Thompson v Bernard*,[185] which illustrates also the obvious point that difficult problems of criminal law might need to be resolved in order to determine whether the facts imputed constituted a crime punishable by imprisonment.

If the claimant has to rely on some secondary meaning of the words spoken, according to *Gray v Jones*,[186] she must prove that they reasonably were capable of being so interpreted. That case lends support also to the view that the risk of social ostracism is one of the reasons for this exception. Having found that the words 'You are a convicted person' reasonably might mean that a crime punishable by imprisonment was imputed, Atkinson J held them to be within the exception because, although they would not place the claimant in jeopardy,[187] they would tend to cause her to be ostracised socially. On the other hand, there have been several cases where something criminal in character, but for technical reasons not punishable in the requisite way, has been held to be outside the rule—presumably because the claimant was not in jeopardy. In *Lemon v Simmons*,[188] for instance, saying that a husband stole from his wife while the couple lived together was held not to impute a crime since, at the time, husbands could not be punishable for such thefts.

(2) Slander in respect of office, profession, calling, trade, or business

Under Defamation Act 1952, section 2:

In an action for slander in respect of words calculated to disparage the [claimant] in any office, profession, calling, trade or business held or carried on by him at the time of the publication, it shall not be necessary to allege or prove special damage, whether or not the words are spoken of the [claimant] in the way of his office, profession, calling, trade or business.

Section 2 nullifies decisions on the prior common law such as *Jones v Jones*,[189] where it was held that an allegation that a headmaster had committed adultery with a school cleaner did not relate to his conduct *in his profession*. Today, such an allegation would be actionable simply because it had prejudicial *effects on* his employment. The statutory exception covers also slanders that impute a want of integrity or corrupt or dishonest conduct in an office. But slanders about persons in honorary positions fall within the exception only if they impute such want of integrity, dishonesty, or incompetence as to justify removal from office.[190]

---

[182] *Hellwig v Mitchell* [1910] 1 KB 609; *Ormiston v Great Western Rly Co* [1917] 1 KB 598.
[183] *Michael v Spiers and Pond Ltd* (1909) 101 LT 352.   [184] *Simmons v Mitchell* (1880) 6 App Cas 156.
[185] (1807) 1 Camp 48.   [186] [1939] 1 All ER 798.
[187] On which see *Jackson v Adams* (1835) 2 Bing NC 402.   [188] (1888) 57 LJQB 260.
[189] [1916] 2 AC 481.   [190] *Robinson v Ward* (1958) 108 L Jo 491.

(D) Special damage and remoteness of damage

Material loss is required if an allegation of special damage is to be substantiated. Examples include loss of employment,[191] the refusal of persons to enter into contracts with the claimant,[192] and the loss of hospitality from friends proved to have provided food or drink on prior occasions.[193] A mere threat of material loss is insufficient.[194]

Psychiatric harm In *Allsop v Allsop*,[195] the claimant suffered physical illness as a result of a slander. This was held not to be special damage. Although bodily harm and mental distress may be taken into account in assessing damages in defamation,[196] *Allsop* must be taken as deciding that special damage in slander must be damage in respect of loss of esteem or association and that the primary purpose of the law of defamation is not to protect against psychiatric harm resulting from the apprehension of the effects of defamatory matter being published to third persons.

Causation In *Slipper v BBC*,[197] allegations in an original broadcast were given wider publicity in newspaper reviews of the programme. The Court of Appeal refused to strike out the part of the claim dealing with that additional damage. While unauthorised repetition might constitute a *novus actus interveniens*, there has never been an absolute rule that the original defamer cannot be held liable for the consequences of such a repetition. Thus, if I write to the Students' Union claiming a colleague is embezzling Student Law Society funds, it is foreseeable that this allegation will be repeated. If the letter had not been sent, but a colleague took it from my desk and sent it to a newspaper, there would be a break in the chain of causation.[198]

Remoteness Despite the fact that, historically, the test for remoteness in defamation was based on 'the natural and necessary consequences' of the defamation,[199] it seems now that the test is the same as in most other areas of tort law. The key question is whether the kind of damage suffered by the claimant was a reasonably foreseeable consequence of the defendant's act.

Section 4 Further matters

Limits to actionability 'Reputation' is treated as a transitory interest since no cause of action will survive the defamed person's death.[200] Furthermore, the defences in defamation serve to make it a contingent interest that sometimes must give way to other,

---

[191] *Coward v Wellington* (1836) 7 C & P 531.   [192] *Storey v Challands* (1837) 8 C & P 234.

[193] *Davies v Solomon* (1871) LR 7 QB 112. The rationale is that the loss of food and drink represents a loss of material value.   [194] *Michael v Spiers and Pond Ltd* (1909) 101 LT 352.

[195] (1860) 5 H & N 534.   [196] (1860) 5 H & N 534, at 539.

[197] [1991] 1 QB 283. See also *Sutcliffe v Pressdram Ltd* [1991] 1 QB 153.

[198] See *Weld-Blundell v Stephens* [1920] AC 956.   [199] *Ward v Weeks* (1830) 7 Bing 211.

[200] See Law Reform (Miscellaneous Provisions) Act 1934, s 1(1). However, defaming a dead person might still constitute a criminal libel.

pressing needs. Much of the balance between the competing interests of reputation and free speech is struck by the defences, which are dealt with in chapter 21.

Conclusions

This chapter has considered the tort of defamation. A prima facie case of defamation arises where the claimant is able to prove that the defendant made a statement with a defamatory meaning (lowering the subject in the eyes of right-thinking people generally), that the statement referred to the claimant, that it was published to at least one other person, and that the statement has caused, or is likely to cause, serious harm to her. Defamatory statements in a permanent form are called 'libels', and those in temporary form (usually oral) are called 'slanders'. For slander, special damage needs to be proved (with two exceptions, involving imputations of crime carrying prison sentences and imputations calculated to disparage the claimant in any office, profession, calling, trade or business).

Problem question

Constable Julie and Constable Steven stop a motorist, Francois, and ask him to get out of his car. A small crowd gathers around Julie, Steven, and Francois as the scene unfolds. Steven says to Francois: 'Excuse me sir, we have reason to believe that this is a stolen motor vehicle. Could you please provide us with your licence while we check with the Station?' After a five-minute conversation over the radio, Steven hands back Francois's licence and says: 'OK Sir, the computer's down at HQ and we'll have to let you go.' Francois shouts out in French: 'I bet you guys were looking for a bit of baksheesh! I've seen cleaner pigs in my grandad's muddy sty!' When Steven asks for a translation, Francois says that he and Julie 'should have a pleasant day'. One member of the small crowd who was watching, Millie (who is five years of age) asks her mum: 'Is that man going to be in trouble?' Millie's mum, Jessica replies: 'Probably will be. He's got a shifty look about him he has. Probably knows what the insides of a jail looks like.'

Advise the two Constables and Francois about any actions in defamation that might be available.

 Visit **http://www.oup.com/uk/street15e/** for answer guidance.

Further reading

BARENDT, *Freedom of Speech* (2007)
CHAN, 'Corporate Defamation: Reputation, Rights and Remedies' (2013) 33 *Legal Studies* 264
CHAN, 'Defamatory Meaning, Community Perspectives and Standards' (2014) 19 *Media and Arts Law Review* 47

COE, 'The Defamation Act 2013: We Need to Talk About Corporate Reputation' [2015] Journal of Business Law 313

DESCHEEMAEKER, 'Protecting Reputation: Defamation and Negligence' (2009) 29 Oxford Journal of Legal Studies 603

GIBBONS, 'Defamation Reconsidered' (1996) 16 Oxford Journal of Legal Studies 587

HOWARTH, 'Libel: Its Purpose and Reform' (2011) 74 Modern Law Review 845

KENYON, 'What Conversation? Free Speech and Defamation Law' (2010) 73 Modern Law Review 697

MCNAMARA, Reputation and Defamation (2007)

MILO, Defamation and Free Speech (2008)

MITCHELL, The Making of the Modern Law of Defamation (2005)

POST, 'The Social Foundations of Defamation Law: Reputation and the Constitution' (1986) 74 California Law Review 691

ROWBOTTOM, 'To Rant, Vent and Converse: Protecting Low Level Digital Speech' (2012) 71 Cambridge Law Journal 355

21

Defences and remedies in defamation

KEY ISSUES

(1) Consent to publication
Consistent with its operation in other torts, it is a defence to defamation that the claimant has consented to the publication of an allegedly defamatory statement concerning him.

(2) Special defences
In addition to consent, there are several other defences that are peculiar to defamation. In general, these attempt to balance the competing interests of freedom of speech and reputation.

(3) Truth
It is a defence to defamation that the statement of the defendant is of a factual nature and that the facts are proved to be true or substantially true.

(4) Offer of amends
It is a defence under statute where the defendant made a statement that he did not know to be defamatory of the claimant and subsequently makes an offer, in writing, correcting and apologising for the statement and where he is willing to publish the correction and pay a sum by way of compensation.

(5) Privilege
Various forms of privilege exist, which protect the defendant from liability in defamation on the occasion on which a statement is made. Privilege is either absolute or qualified in nature. Qualified privilege arises where there is a common interest in publication and the statement is not made with 'malice'.

(6) Public interest
It is a defence to defamation that the statement was on a matter of public interest and that the defendant reasonably believed that its publication was in the public interest. The defence applies to both statements of fact and of opinion.

(7) Honest opinion
It is a defence to defamation that the statement is in the nature of opinion, that it indicated in general or specific terms the factual basis upon which it was made and that it could have been held by an honest person by reference to either facts existing at the time or certain privileged statements published before the opinion. The defence is not available where the defendant did not hold the opinion.

(8) Remedies
Remedies to claims of defamation include damages and injunctions.

Section 1 Consent and assumption of risk

Consent Although opinions vary, the better opinion is that consent is an independent defence in defamation.[1] Someone who telephones a newspaper with false information about himself will not be able to sue in defamation when the newspaper publishes it; but he does not consent to the publication in a newspaper of a story about himself that he told at a parish vestry meeting.[2] Consent might be implied or express, so consent explicitly supplied on a contractual basis defeats a defamation action.[3] On the other hand, implied consent sometimes involves a difficult question of fact about whether a claimant genuinely has consented to the repetition of a defamatory statement. If, for instance, the claimant asked the defendant to repeat it, because he did not understand properly on the first occasion, he would not be consenting. Whether express or implied, consent is narrowly construed in defamation cases.[4]

Assumption of risk The related defence of assumption of risk was applied in *Chapman v Lord Ellesmere*.[5] There the claimant maintained that, even if he had consented to the publication of a report of an inquiry by the Jockey Club, he had not consented to its publication in a form that contained an innuendo against him. The Court of Appeal found for the defendant on the ground that the claimant had agreed to run the risk of the particular form that the statement might take.[6]

Section 2 Truth

(A) Onus

It is no part of the claimant's case to establish that the defendant's statement was untrue: the claimant has merely to prove the publication of a statement defamatory of him. In chapter 20, we saw that the law assumes a defamatory statement to be false. However, if the defendant can prove that his statement was substantially true (or 'justify it' in the old language), he has a complete defence under Defamation Act 2013, sub-section 2(1)—even if he made the statement maliciously.[7] The rationale is that 'the law will not permit a man to recover damages in respect of an injury to a character which he does not . . . possess'.[8] The defendant does not discharge this burden by proving that he honestly believed the statement to be true. He must prove that it was true.[9] If the words impute the commission of a specific offence, it is not enough to prove that the claimant

---

[1] Cf *Russell v Duke of Norfolk* [1949] 1 All ER 109, at 120.   [2] *Cook v Ward* (1830) 6 Bing 409.
[3] *Cookson v Harewood* [1932] 2 KB 478n.   [4] *Howe v Burden* [2004] EWHC 196.
[5] [1932] 2 KB 431.   [6] [1932] 2 KB 431, at 464.
[7] The importance of this defence is explored in E Descheemaeker (2011) 31 LS 1.
[8] *M'Pherson v Daniels* (1829) 10 B & C 263.
[9] *Peters v Bradlaugh* (1888) 4 TLR 414. In this context it is arguable that the European Convention on Human Rights might require a relaxation of this rule where the publication relates to matters of public importance: see Art 8(2).

was suspected of that offence.[10] In order to invoke the defence of truth in these circumstances, the defendant must be able to identify specific conduct on the part of the claimant which grounds such a suspicion.[11]

(B) Meaning

Pleaded case Before deciding whether the defendant can plead truth successfully, one must discover what the statement complained of means.[12] Just as the claimant must plead the meanings he relies on specifically as defamatory, so the defendant pleading truth must 'make it clear to the [claimant] what is the case he is seeking to set up'.[13] Given that the primary meaning of the words and any innuendo form separate heads of claim, in order to succeed the defendant must prove that each is substantially true.[14]

Interpretation Underlying many problems with the defence of truth is the question: 'Does that which is proved to be true correspond with that which the defendant's statement is interpreted to mean?' In *Jameel v Wall Street Journal Europe (No 3)*,[15] the defendant made reference to 'those with potential terrorist ties'. The claimants argued that the words used meant, at the very least, that they reasonably were suspected of having terrorist links. The defendant counter argued that the words implied no more than that there were reasonable grounds to undertake an investigation of whether there were terrorist links in fact (this meaning being one stage removed from what the claimants alleged). The Court of Appeal accepted that both meanings were feasible and held that the issue should be left for a jury to decide.

Allegation of general behaviour In *Wakley v Cooke*,[16] the defendant called the claimant a 'libellous journalist'. He proved that a judgment against the claimant for libel had once been obtained; but because the defamatory statement complained of implied that the journalist habitually libelled people, the defendant failed to prove the truth of his remark.[17]

Allegation of specific conduct In *Bookbinder v Tebbit*,[18] the defendant had alleged at an electoral meeting that the claimant had squandered public money on a campaign to print 'support Nuclear Free Zones' on council stationery. He sought to prove truth by advancing evidence of general financial mismanagement on the part of the claimant,

---

[10] *Rubber Improvement Ltd v Daily Telegraph Ltd* [1964] AC 234, at 274–5.

[11] *Shah v Standard Chartered Bank* [1999] QB 241, at 269–70 (it is not enough to show that the suspicion emanates from a reliable source). The suggestion that this 'conduct rule' places an unjustifiable restriction on the Art 10 right to freedom of expression has been rejected: *Chase v Newsgroup Newspapers Ltd* [2002] EWCA Civ 1772.   [12] See ch 20.

[13] *Lucas-Box v Associated Newspapers Group* [1986] 1 All ER 177. See also *Morrell v International Thomson Publishing Ltd* [1989] 3 All ER 733.

[14] *Watkin v Hall* (1868) LR 3 QB 396, at 402; *Rubber Improvement Ltd v Daily Telegraph Ltd* [1964] AC 234.

[15] [2005] QB 904 (revd on other grounds at [2007] 1 AC 359).   [16] (1849) 4 Exch 511.

[17] On the question whether it is more defamatory of a woman to allege that she has had an extramarital affair with one man rather than another see *Khashoggi v IPC Magazines Ltd* [1986] 3 All ER 577.

[18] [1989] 1 All ER 1169.

who was the leader of the local council. The Court of Appeal struck out those particulars of the pleading of truth. They did not pertain to the very specific 'sting' of the libel. One cannot prove the truth of an express claim of misconduct by generalised evidence of the claimant's behaviour.[19]

(C) Substantial truth

The defence of truth will succeed so long as the statement is substantially true; inaccuracy on minor points of detail does not negate it.[20] Similarly, 'it is unnecessary to repeat every word which might have been the subject of the original comment. As much must be justified as meets the sting of the charge, and if anything be contained in a charge which does not add to the sting of it, that need not be justified'.[21] Consider *Clarke v Taylor*:[22]

> D accused C of taking part in a 'grand swindling concern' at Manchester, and added that '[C] had been at Leeds for one or two days before his arrival in [Manchester] . . . and is supposed to have made considerable purchases there. It is hoped, however, that the detection of his plans in Manchester will be learnt in time to prevent any serious losses from taking place.'

D was able to prove the truth of the statement that C had swindled at Manchester, but not the remainder of the statement. It was held that this was a sufficient plea of truth because the remaining words did not allege any further act of criminality.

Many statements contain both statements of fact and opinion: for example, 'X was drunk again last night; his behaviour was disgusting.' If the defendant relies on the defence of truth in respect of this, he must prove not only that X was drunk but also the accuracy of his claim that X's behaviour was disgusting (insofar as that comment adds to the sting of the libel). If the further statement introduces new matter, or implies the existence of further facts, he must prove those further facts which prove the truth of the terms in which he has described the claimant.[23]

Adoption of statement of another Defamation Act 2013, sub-section 2(1) applies where the defendant adopts the words of another in a way which requires that the truth of the underlying statement be proved. According to the Ministry of Justice *Draft Defamation Bill Consultation* paper:

> [I]f the defendant published a statement which said 'X told me that C murdered Y', the imputation is that C murdered Y. In order to establish the defence, the defendant would need to prove the fact that C murdered Y and not merely that X said that C had done so.[24]

---

[19] Cf *Rothschild v Associated Newspapers Ltd* [2013] EWCA Civ 197, considered later.

[20] Defamation Act 2013, sub-s 2(1). For the equivalent common law rule, see, eg, *Alexander v North Eastern Rly Co* (1865) 6 B & S 340.   [21] *Edwards v Bell* (1824) 1 Bing 403, at 409.

[22] (1836) 2 Bing NC 654.

[23] *Cooper v Lawson* (1838) 8 Ad & El 746. There is sometimes a defence of honest opinion.

[24] Ministry of Justice, *Draft Defamation Bill Consultation* (Cm 8020, 2011), at [27]. Although the consultation paper uses the term 'repetition', this book prefers the term 'adoption' because of the confusion that has arisen regarding to whom 'the repetition rule' refers (the usual understanding being that it refers to the original statement-maker's liability). For the analogous common law position, see *M'Pherson v Daniels* (1829) 10 B & C 263.

Multiple imputations At common law, every material statement had to be proved substantially true. Thus, if the defendant could prove the truth of three 'charges' but not a fourth 'charge', the defence would fail (although proof of three would be relevant in assessing damages). This rule is now modified by the Defamation Act 2013, section 2, which provides:

> (2) Subsection (3) applies in an action for defamation if the statement complained of conveys two or more distinct imputations.
> (3) If one or more of the imputations is not shown to be substantially true, the defence under this section does not fail if, having regard to the imputations which are shown to be substantially true, the imputations which are not shown to be substantially true do not seriously harm the claimant's reputation.

It is important to know, therefore, when multiple 'imputations' arise. An example is provided in the *Draft Defamation Bill Consultation* paper by reference to *Henry v BBC*:[25]

> In that case falsification of waiting list figures and complicity in waiting list fraud was proved but bullying was not proved. Falsification of waiting list figures and bullying are two distinct imputations.[26]

Where distinct allegations are made and the claimant relies only on the allegation that cannot be proved true (with no mention of the statement that can be proved true), the defendant cannot invoke sub-section 2(3).[27] Thus, in *Cruise v Express Newspapers plc*, Brooke LJ observed that: 'It is no defence to a charge that "You called me A" to say "Yes, but I also called you B on the same occasion and that was true".'[28]

Common sting Where multiple defamatory imputations have a common 'sting', they are not to be regarded as separate and distinct and, therefore, do not fall within Defamation Act 2013, sub-section 2(3). The defendant must prove the truth of the 'sting' and it is simply 'fortuitous that what is in fact similar fact evidence is found in the publication'.[29] This was the task for the defendant in *Rothschild v Associated Newspapers Ltd*:[30]

> A newspaper published an article concerning certain unofficial encounters between M, the EU Trade Commissioner, and D, a Russian tycoon. These meetings were facilitated by R (the claimant). Although the article focused upon a dinner in Moscow, M had not been a party to it. The article discussed also a visit by M, D and R to an aluminium smelter in Abakan, Siberia, to which they travelled in D's private jet. M's short stay in Siberia was characterised by 'lavish' hospitality. The Court agreed that the sting of the article was to accuse R of arranging meetings which, given a perceived conflict of interest, would bring M into disrepute.

---

[25] [2006] All ER (D) 124.
[26] Ministry of Justice, *Draft Defamation Bill Consultation* (Cm 8020, 2011), at [29].
[27] [1999] QB 931, at 954.   [28] [1991] QB 931, at 954.
[29] *Polly Peck (Holdings) plc v Trelford* [1986] 2 All ER 84, at 102; *Khashoggi v IPC Magazines Ltd* [1986] 3 All ER 577.   [30] [2013] EWCA Civ 197.

The Court of Appeal held that the article was not concerned with 'one event', but 'contained wider themes'.[31] The common sting could be proved true by reference to the meeting that did take place, so long as the result of proving the truth of this instance of misjudgement was that 'the claimant has no more reputation to lose by force . . . of the published, false accusation'.[32]

(D) Other matters

Complete defence   Truth is a complete defence. Even if the defendant was inspired by malice, or even if, when he made the statements, he did not believe them to be true, his defence is sound so long as they are proved to have been true.

Spent convictions   There is one exception to the above rule. In relation to 'spent' convictions of 'rehabilitated persons', the Rehabilitation of Offenders Act 1974 provides that, after the expiry of certain defined periods—the duration of which differ according to the length of sentence—most convictions become spent, and the convicted person becomes rehabilitated. A person cannot, then, rely upon the truth of the statement that the claimant had been convicted of a relevant offence. Sub-section 8(3) of the Act provides an exception to the general tenor of the legislation according to which convictions become totally spent. It entitles a defendant in a defamation action to adduce evidence of the claimant's conviction; but only so long as the defendant mentions this conviction without malice.[33] The onus of establishing the presence of malice—defined as some spiteful, irrelevant, or improper motive—lies with the claimant.[34]

Persisting in claim of truth   If a defendant wrongly persists in a plea of truth and thereby prolongs the period in which the damage from the publication continues to spread, a greater sum by way of aggravated damages may be awarded against him.[35]

Section 3   Innocent dissemination

Jurisdiction   Prima facie, no action in defamation can be brought with respect to persons who do not fall within the categories of author, editor, or publisher of the statement complained of. Under the Defamation Act 2013, sub-section 10(1), the court has no jurisdiction to hear an action against other persons unless it is 'satisfied that it is not reasonably practicable for an action to be brought against the author, editor or publisher'.[36] If the jurisdiction does arise, then the further rules discussed in this section apply.

---

[31] [2013] EWCA Civ 197, at [34].   [32] [2013] EWCA Civ 197, at [24].

[33] It is arguable that this qualification of the right to adduce evidence of a spent conviction is antithetical to the right to freedom of speech enshrined in Art 10 of the European Convention on Human Rights.

[34] *Herbage v Pressdram Ltd* [1984] 2 All ER 769. For analysis, see Descheemaeker (2011) 31 LS 1, esp. 16–17.

[35] *Cassell & Co Ltd v Broome* [1972] AC 1027, at 1125. For general principles on damages, see later. The one exception to this rule is considered next.

[36] These terms have the same meaning as in Defamation Act 1996, s 1: Defamation Act 2013, sub-s 10(2).

Common law There is still a common law defence based on innocent dissemination.[37] But this has been subsumed largely within the Defamation Act 1996, section 1. Furthermore, because the statutory defence is broader in scope, and normally no less onerous to invoke, it seems that the common law defence is all but otiose nowadays.

Defamation Act 1996 Under sub-section 1(1), a person has a defence if he shows that he was not the 'author, editor or publisher'[38] of the matter complained of, that he took reasonable care in relation to its publication, and that he did not know (or have reason to believe) that what he did caused or contributed to the publication of defamatory matter. As mentioned, the defence is wider than the common law defence of innocent dissemination in that a wider class of persons can use it.[39] But the defendant has a burden and standard of proof that require him to show his innocence as regards knowledge of the defamatory nature of the statement,[40] and that he took reasonable care in relation to his part in its publication. So far as the reasonable care test is concerned, under sub-section 1(5) of the 1996 Act the court is to have regard to three specific factors: (1) the degree of the defendant's responsibility for the content of the statement complained of, or for the decision to publish it; (2) the nature or circumstances of publication;[41] (3) and the previous conduct or character of the author, editor, or publisher.[42]

Operators of websites In chapter 20, we saw that ISPs and web content providers that facilitate the publication of defamatory matter potentially are liable in defamation, at least beyond the point at which they are informed of its presence and fail to remove it. The content provider (Google) in *Tamiz v Google* would not have had a defence under Defamation Act 1996, section 1 because 'following notification it knew or had reason to believe that what it did [in providing a platform for blogging] caused or contributed to the continued publication of the comments.'[43]

The position of 'operators of websites' has been improved under Defamation Act 2013, section 5. A defence arises when the operator can 'show that it was not the operator who posted the statement on the website.'[44] The defence is not available in either of two circumstances. The first circumstance is where the operator 'acted with malice

---

[37] *Metropolitan International Schools Ltd v Designtechnica Corp* [2011] 1 WLR 1743, at [70].

[38] The notion of publisher, for the purposes of the Act, is confined to that of 'commercial publisher'; ie, 'a person whose business is issuing material to the public': sub-s 1(2).

[39] Under sub-s 1(3)(a) of the Act, those involved in the production process or printing of books, newspapers, and magazines are covered. So too are those who distribute information by way of electronic media such as internet users (sub-s 1(3)(c)), those, such as chat-show and phone-in hosts, who broadcast information in live programmes (sub-s 1(3)(d)) and those, such as ISPs, who operate communications systems that are used to transmit defamatory statements (sub-s 1(3)(e)).

[40] Strictly, *Vizetelly v Mudie's Select Library Ltd* [1900] 2 QB 170 required ignorance of *a libel* (a narrower concept than that of a defamatory remark). Thus, the defence is more restrictive than the common law in that knowledge of a defamatory statement (eg, one known to be defamatory, but believed to be true) defeats the defence.

[41] The Act is unclear on what is meant by 'the circumstances of the publication'. Presumably, remarks made about infamous persons would require greater concern than remarks about less-well-known people.

[42] Presumably, here, the standard of care demanded is greater in relation to publishers with a history of producing defamatory material.   [43] [2013] EWCA Civ 68, at [44].

[44] Defamation Act 2013, sub-s 5(2).

in relation to the posting of the statement concerned'.[45] This might be the case 'where, for example, the website operator had incited the poster to make the posting or had otherwise colluded with the poster'.[46] The second circumstance is where the claimant has not been able to identify the person who posted the statement and has given the operator a notice of complaint, following which the operator has failed to respond in accordance with the procedures set out in the regulations.[47] The relevant regulations are the Defamation (Operators of Websites) Regulations 2013.[48] The effect of the latter provisions appears to be that, where the claimant is able to obtain information about the identity of the poster, the website operator can with impunity allow the defamatory material to remain on the website while any litigation runs its course.[49]

Section 4 Offer of amends

The Defamation Act 1996 creates a defence related to an 'offer to make amends'.[50]

No knowledge The defence is available only to those defendants who did not know and had no reason to believe that an impugned statement referred to the claimant and was untrue and defamatory of him.[51] 'Having a reason to believe' in this context requires that the defendant must have been reckless as to the matter and not merely that a reasonable person in his position would have realised that the statement was untrue or defamatory. In other words, the test is a subjective, not objective, one.[52]

Further prerequisites The defence may be invoked only where the offer to make amends is in writing and states that it is such an offer under the 1996 Act.[53] In addition, the offer must satisfy three further prerequisites: it must contain a correction to, and apology for, the original statement; it must state a willingness to publish that correction and apology; and it must make clear that the publisher consents to pay to the aggrieved party such sum as may be agreed between them, or, as may be determined judicially.[54] Where an offer of amends has been made, it probably will serve as significant mitigation.[55]

Acceptance If the offer of amends is accepted, sub-section 3(2) prohibits the aggrieved party from subsequently bringing or continuing defamation proceedings. An offer which has been accepted creates an agreement between the parties, which rarely will be undone

---

[45] Defamation Act 2013, sub-s 5(11).   [46] Explanatory Notes to the Defamation Act 2013, at [42].
[47] Defamation Act 2013, sub-s 5(3).
[48] SI 2013/3028. Readers should also be aware of the Electronic Commerce (EC Directive) Regulations 2002, SI 2002/2013, applicable to 'information society services' (defined as covering 'any service normally provided for remuneration, at a distance, by means of electronic equipment for the processing . . . and storage of data . . . at the request of a recipient of a service': reg 2(1)).
[49] See G Benaim (2013) 24 Ent LR 231, 231–2; A Mullis and A Scott (2014) 77 MLR 87, 100.
[50] Defamation Act 1996, ss 2–4.   [51] Defamation Act 1996, sub-s 4(3).
[52] *Milne v Express Newspapers (No 1)* [2005] 1 WLR 772.   [53] Defamation Act 1996, sub-s 2(3).
[54] Defamation Act 1996, sub-s 2(3), (4).   [55] *Nail v NGN Ltd* [2005] EMLR 12.

by a court even if new facts come to light. In *Warren v Random House Group Ltd*,[56] the Court of Appeal accepted that it had a discretion to undo an agreement, but insisted that this is of narrow compass. The central issue would be whether any special circumstances supported the avoidance of the agreement 'in the sense of circumstances so different from those contemplated or intended to be governed by the undertaking at the time that it was a given that it is appropriate for the undertaker to be released from his promise'.[57]

Non-acceptance If the offer of amends is not accepted, the offer may be invoked nonetheless as a defence in any subsequent defamation proceedings brought by the claimant.[58] For this reason, it is suggested that normally it would be unwise for a claimant to reject an offer of amends. Should he pursue an action in the courts instead, in order for the offer not to constitute a defence, the claimant would have to show, first, that the defendant knew or had reason to believe that the statement referred to the claimant and, second, that it was both false and defamatory.[59]

Other matters The offer of amends defence does not require the alleged defamer to prove his innocence.[60] Accordingly, it effects a significant change in the location of the burden of proof. On the other hand, any defendant wishing to use this defence is debarred from resorting to any other defence (such as truth).[61] This means that he is forced to choose between (1) definitely paying moderate damages (either agreed with the claimant, or judicially determined); and (2) risking paying damages in full if another defence—such as truth—should be held not to be available.

Section 5 Absolute privilege

Certain occasions are deemed to be so important that those making statements upon them are not liable in defamation despite their statements being untrue and even malicious. These occasions—where the public interest in freedom of communication is paramount—invoke an absolute privilege.

(A) Parliamentary proceedings

Under the Bill of Rights 1688, Article 9, the courts for centuries had no jurisdiction to hear evidence of proceedings in Parliament.[62] This immunity was extended beyond statements made in the course of parliamentary proceedings to all reports, papers,

---

[56] [2009] QB 600.   [57] [2009] QB 600, at [26].   [58] Defamation Act 1996, sub-s 4(2).

[59] C bears the burden of proof under Defamation Act 1996, sub-s 4(3), which introduced a statutory presumption of the publisher's innocence, giving him the right to invoke his offer of amends as a defence.

[60] This is now presumed under sub-s 4(3). If the offer is refused, the case will proceed but D may still use the making of the offer as a mitigatory defence (reducing the amount of damages payable) where he (1) knew that the publication was defamatory of C; but (2) reasonably believed that what was said was true: sub-s 4(5).

[61] Defamation Act 1996, sub-s 4(4).

[62] See also *Ex p Wason* (1869) LR 4 QB 573, at 576; Government of Wales Act 2006, s 42. Hence, the frequent challenge by the victim to the MP to repeat outside the House his attacks on the victim's reputation.

votes, and proceedings published by, or under the authority of, either House.[63] The reason for the immunity is to ensure that parliamentary functions are not inhibited 63 by the fear of litigation. The protection is directed to the 'integrity of the legislature's democratic process' and 'is not given for the sake of the individual member.'[64]

Secondary usage The assertion of 'parliamentary privilege' meant not only that parliamentary proceedings could not found an action in defamation, but also that such proceedings could not be relied on in relation to a claim arising out of a non-parliamentary publication. Thus, in one case, the court would not admit evidence of statements contained in Hansard that the claimant sought to introduce in order to demonstrate malice.[65]

Extra-parliamentary statements Comments outside Parliament, even if they refer to earlier privileged statements, ordinarily do not attract absolute privilege.[66] In *Makudi v Triesman*, however, the privilege was held to extend to statements made outside Parliament where they mirrored what was said in Parliament and where they resulted from an undertaking given to a House of Commons Committee. The Court of Appeal accepted the general proposition that the Bill of Rights, Article 9, would be likely to cover extra-parliamentary statements when two conditions are met:

> (1) A public interest in repetition of the Parliamentary utterance which the speaker ought reasonably to serve, and (2) so close a nexus between the occasion of his speaking, in and out of Parliament, that the prospect of his obligation to speak on the second occasion (or the expectation or promise that he would do so) is reasonably foreseeable at the time of the first and his purpose in speaking on both occasions is the same or very closely related.[67]

Waiver Defamation Act 1996, section 13 permits an MP to waive the prohibition on adducing evidence of parliamentary proceedings enshrined in Bill of Rights 1688, Article [68] But where an MP waives that privilege in order to enter evidence of the proceedings of a parliamentary committee (or its findings), the waiver will override the privilege of the House as a whole, and thus entitle the defendant to challenge the parliamentary proceedings in question, and even the findings of a prior parliamentary inquiry into the conduct of the MP in question.[69] It is clear from sub-section 13(5) that it extends not just to parliamentary proceedings per se, but also to evidence contained in documents such as reports produced by parliamentary committees.[70]

---

[63] Parliamentary Papers Act 1840, s 1.   [64] *Makudi v Triesman* [2014] 2 WLR 1228, at [20].

[65] *Church of Scientology of California v Johnson-Smith* [1972] 1 QB 522. See also *Hamilton v Al Fayed* [2001] 1 AC 395.   [66] *Jennings v Buchanan* [2005] 1 AC 115.

[67] [2014] 2 WLR 1228, at [25].

[68] Section 13 operates in favour of MPs only. The waiver enables an MP to vindicate his character in a defamation action by adducing evidence of parliamentary proceedings. It does not, by contrast, allow the MP to adduce evidence from a similar source in order to substantiate the main argument.

[69] *Hamilton v Al-Fayed* [2001] 1 AC 395. Note, however, that *the actual words used* by the MP remain privileged: Defamation Act 1996, sub-s 13(4).   [70] See A Sharland and ID Loveland [1997] PL 113.

(B) Executive matters

In *Chatterton v Secretary of State for India*[71] it was held that a letter from the Secretary of State for India to his Parliamentary Under-Secretary providing material for the answer to a parliamentary question was absolutely privileged. A message from a very senior diplomat to a minister about a commercial matter also falls within the privilege.[72] Beyond this, it is doubtful whether those below the status of minister may claim the privilege[73] and it is unsafe to assume that routine communications between persons not in charge of government departments are within it.

Procedural rule distinguished The absolute privilege on executive matters must not be confused with the procedural rule that the Crown, whether or not it is a party, cannot be compelled in any litigation to produce or disclose the existence of any documents where this would be contrary to the public interest.[74] In practice, because the Crown can decide at its discretion whether to produce such documents, this rule has prevented claimants from maintaining libel suits, even for communications within the civil service that were not absolutely privileged.[75]

(C) Judicial proceedings

Statements made in proceedings before superior and inferior courts of record and magistrates' courts are privileged. The privilege extends to other tribunals recognised by law,[76] provided they are 'exercising functions equivalent to those of an established court of justice'.[77] In cases of doubt, 'the overriding factor is whether there will emerge from the proceedings a determination the truth and justice of which is a matter of public concern'.[78] Thus, select committees of the House of Commons,[79] courts martial,[80] and the disciplinary committee of the Law Society[81] are within the privilege, as is an enquiry before an Inn of Court into the conduct of a barrister,[82] even though the body had no power to issue a subpoena or to take evidence on oath and sits in private.

---

[71] [1895] 2 QB 189. The Parliamentary Commissioner Act 1967, sub-s 10(5) also gives an absolute privilege to the Parliamentary Commissioner for his reports to Parliament and for certain of his communications to MPs; the Local Commissioners have a similar absolute privilege under the Local Government Act 1974, s 32; so, too, does the Legal Services Ombudsman under s 23 of the Courts and Legal Services Act 1990.

[72] *M Isaacs & Sons Ltd v Cook* [1925] 2 KB 391.

[73] *Szalatnay-Stacho v Fink* [1946] 1 All ER 303, at 305 (not considered on appeal: [1947] KB 1).

[74] Crown Proceedings Act 1947, s 28. See also *Schneider v Leigh* [1955] 2 QB 195.

[75] *Home v Bentinck* (1820) 2 Brod & Bing 130; *Beatson v Skene* (1860) 5 H & N 838; and *West v West* (1911) 27 TLR 476, are examples of cases where the rule was successfully used for that purpose.

[76] Either under statute or by royal prerogative of justice: *Lincoln v Daniels* [1962] 1 QB 237.

[77] *O'Connor v Waldron* [1935] AC 76, at 81.　　[78] *Lincoln v Daniels* [1962] 1 QB 237, at 255–6.

[79] In principle, these would seem to have been more properly within the 'legislative privilege', but this is not the basis of *Goffin v Donnelly* (1881) 6 QBD 307. But see now *Rost v Edwards* [1990] 2 QB 460.

[80] *Wilson v Westney* [2001] EWCA Civ 839.　　[81] *Addis v Crocker* [1961] 1 QB 11.

[82] *Lincoln v Daniels* [1962] 1 QB 237.

Administrative proceedings distinguished If the function of the body in question is merely administrative, and it does not determine the rights, guilt, or innocence of anyone, there is no absolute privilege, even though procedures akin to judicial procedures—such as hearing evidence or summoning witnesses—are used.[83] Thus, justices dealing with applications for liquor licensing,[84] official industrial conciliation processes,[85] and complaints to social security adjudication officers[86] have been held to be outside the scope of the privilege.

Necessary link with judicial proceedings The privilege extends to documents initiating[87] or made in the course of judicial proceedings (for example, statements of claim and witness statements).[88] However, documents prepared prior to proceedings that do not have any *necessary* link with those proceedings are not privileged in this way. Accordingly, in a case where a defamatory letter was written by the defendant council to the claimant's solicitor in the course of pre-hearing negotiations, it was held that, since the letter's contents did not have any necessary import for any future legal proceedings, it was inappropriate to allow the defendant to claim a privilege.[89]

Protected parties The privilege is enjoyed by judges,[90] parties, informants,[91] witnesses questioned in relation to a crime,[92] counsel[93] and solicitors,[94] and presumably jurors. Whether others engaged in the proceedings are privileged is doubtful.[95] Certainly, they are not protected where the statement is so irrelevant that it is no longer made by a person qua participant in the proceedings.[96] The privilege is probably lost when the court has no jurisdiction.

---

[83] See, eg, *W v Westminster CC* [2005] 1 FLR 816; *O'Connor v Waldron* [1935] AC 76.

[84] *Attwood v Chapman* [1914] 3 KB 275.   [85] *Tadd v Eastwood* [1985] ICR 132.

[86] *Purdew and Purdew v Seress Smith* [1993] IRLR 77.

[87] But not if the initiating document is wrongly sent to the Bar Council, instead of to an Inn of Court: *Lincoln v Daniels* [1962] 1 QB 237.

[88] See *Lilley v Roney* (1892) 61 LJQB 727; *Revis v Smith* (1856) 18 CB 126; *Taylor v Director of the Serious Fraud Office* [1999] 2 AC 177. The privilege confers a general defence to all torts, and not merely to defamation: *Marrinan v Vibart* [1963] 1 QB 528.

[89] *Waple v Surrey CC* [1998] 1 All ER 624. See also *Daniels v Griffith* [1998] EMLR 489 (no privilege in respect of a defamatory statement (relating to C) given by D to the police, which was later used by a parole board considering C's parole because the parole board was not a court of law).

[90] *Scott v Stansfield* (1868) LR 3 Exch 220.

[91] *Westcott v Westcott* [2008] EWCA Civ 818, although criminal proceedings were never commenced.

[92] *Seaman v Netherclift* (1876) 2 CPD 53. See also *Mahon v Rahn (No 2)* [2000] 4 All ER 41.

[93] *Munster v Lamb* (1883) 11 QBD 588.

[94] *Mackay v Ford* (1860) 5 H & N 792. But in non-contentious matters, a qualified privilege may be sufficient: see *Waple v Surrey CC* [1998] 1 WLR 860.

[95] Doubt arises since judicial immunity may derive from the separate defence of judicial act, not that of privilege: *Hamilton v Anderson* (1858) 3 Macq 363.

[96] In answer to the question: 'Were you at York on a certain day?' a statement by a witness: 'Yes, and AB picked my pocket there', would not be made qua witness if the proceedings were entirely unconnected with AB: *Seaman v Netherclift* (1876) 2 CPD 53, at 57.

(D) Reports of judicial proceedings

Under Defamation Act 1996, section 14, a fair and accurate report of judicial proceedings heard in public and published contemporaneously with those proceedings is absolutely privileged. In *Alsaifi v Amunwa*, Warby J stated that:[97]

> fairness and accuracy are matters of substance not form. A report does not need to be verbatim. It may to an extent be impressionistic. Fairness is to be tested by reference to the impact on the claimant's reputation. Minor inaccuracies will not deprive a defendant of the privilege.

'Contemporaneous' publications include those that appear 'as soon as practicable after publication is permitted',[98] which is unlikely to include those appearing a number of weeks later;[99] and 'judicial proceedings' are specified to mean any proceedings in a UK court, any court outside the UK, and any international court or tribunal established by the UN Security Council or by an international agreement.[100] The privilege is conferred on *all* contemporaneous reports regardless of the medium of publication.

(E) Solicitor–client communications

Closely related to the judicial proceedings privilege is the question of how far statements before trial to solicitors by either clients or witnesses are protected. If the purpose of not restricting the prosecution of judicial proceedings is to be attained, it would be unrealistic to deny to a witness privilege in respect of a proof of his evidence made immediately before trial. Therefore, the House of Lords held in *Watson v M'Ewan* that a witness making a proof after the issue of a writ, but before trial, is absolutely privileged.[101] This extension of the privilege surrounding judicial proceedings is restricted to matters outside the proceedings which are necessary for the administration of justice. It does not extend to a complaint to the Bar Council.[102]

Whether all communications between solicitor and client *should* be privileged is a different matter. Consider *More v Weaver*:[103] in a discussion between solicitor and client on whether a loan should be called in, the claimant was defamed. The discussion bore no relation to any actual or prospective litigation, yet the statement was held to be absolutely privileged. By contrast, in *Minter v Priest*[104] the House of Lords left open the question whether *More v Weaver* had been rightly decided. It is submitted that it was wrongly decided. In the cases which it purported to follow,[105] solicitor–client communications were held to be absolutely privileged only because they referred to judicial proceedings actually pending.

---

[97] [2017] EWHC 1443 (QB), at [63].   [98] Defamation Act 1996, sub-s 14(2).
[99] *Alsaifi v Amunwa* [2017] EWHC 1443 (QB), at [73].   [100] Defamation Act 1996, sub-s 14(3).
[101] [1905] AC 480.   [102] *Lincoln v Daniels* [1962] 1 QB 237.   [103] [1928] 2 KB 520.
[104] [1930] AC 558, at 579.   [105] Eg, *Browne v Dunn* (1893) 6 R 67.

Section 6 Qualified privilege

In certain circumstances, it is thought desirable that reflections on the reputation of another, although untrue, should not give rise to tortious liability provided those reflections were not published with 'malice'. These are occasions of qualified privilege—with respect to which the interest in freedom of speech is more important than the claimant's interest in the protection of her reputation. Generally, the defence is underpinned by the notion that the defendant was under a duty—whether legal, social, or moral—to make the communication complained of.[106] However, since malice—which defeats the defence—can be evidenced in a number of ways, that concept needs to be considered as a preliminary matter.

(A) Malice

(1) Establishing malice

For the purposes of defeating a claim to qualified privilege, 'malice' means making use of the privileged occasion dishonestly or for some improper purpose.

(a) The defendant does not believe in the truth of his statement

By far the most important way of establishing malice (and thereby rebutting the privilege) is to show that the defendant did not believe in the truth of his statement or that he was reckless as to whether it was true or false. Thus, '[i]f a man is proved to have stated that which he knew to be false, no one need inquire further'.[107] That being so, a solicitor who writes that his client has admitted his negligence, when he knows that he has not admitted it, has abused the privilege.[108] Equally, in *Fraser v Mirza*,[109] proof that the defendant blatantly and deliberately lied in parts of the statement complained of was sufficient to establish malice and defeat his claim of privilege. On the other hand, mere proof that the defendant had no reasonable grounds for believing his statement to be true is not enough to rebut the qualified privilege.[110] In *Horrocks v Lowe*,[111] it was held that, if the defendant honestly believed his statement to be true, his privilege would not be lost merely because his conclusion was irrational or borne of unreasoned prejudice. Naturally, mere careless-ness in the choice of one's words is insufficient to establish malice.[112]

Exception There is probably one exception to the rule that a person who does not believe in the truth of a statement forfeits the privilege. Lord Bramwell established this exception thus:

> A person may honestly make on a particular occasion a defamatory statement without believing it to be true; because the statement may be of such a character that on that

---

[106] Eg, *Browne v Dunn* (1893) 6 R 67.
[107] *Clark v Molyneux* (1877) 3 QBD 237, at 247.   [108] *Groom v Crocker* [1939] 1 KB 194.
[109] 1993 SLT 527.
[110] *Clark v Molyneux* (1877) 3 QBD 237. C might, however, be able to circumvent a plea of qualified privil-ege by suing in negligence: *Spring v Guardian Assurance plc* [1995] 2 AC 296.   [111] [1975] AC 135.
[112] *Oliver v CC of Northumbria Police* [2004] EWHC 790.

> occasion it may be proper to communicate it to a particular person who ought to be informed of it.[113]

Although authority is lacking, this exception seems sound in principle. There may be circumstances in which the obligation to communicate the defamatory matter is so pressing that the defendant should be free to do so—particularly where such information as the defendant has is properly requested by another, or where an important interest is subjected to a serious risk of harm if the defendant does not publish the information.

(b) Abuse of the purpose of the privilege

If the defendant does not act for the purpose of protecting that interest for which the privilege is given, he loses it.[114] Thus, even if the defendant believes his statement to be true, where the court is satisfied that his dominant motive was an improper purpose, the privilege will be lost.[115] He must use the occasion in accordance with the purpose for which the occasion arose.[116] Thus, it was held that a letter sent to the BBC by a film company about a film critic would be 'malicious' if its purpose was to stifle criticism.[117]

Causal link Not only must there be an improper motive, that motive must have been a causative factor in the publishing of the defamation. Thus, in *Winstanley v Bampton*, a creditor who wrote a defamatory letter to the commanding officer of the claimant debtor, and believed what he wrote, forfeited his privilege because his indignation and anger had led him to defame the claimant.[118] If, however, the defendant was using the occasion for its proper purpose but happened incidentally to have feelings of resentment towards the claimant, this would not deprive him of the privilege, which is not lost if the ill-will is not the defendant's primary purpose but merely one purpose.[119]

(c) The inclusion of extraneous matter

The introduction of irrelevant matter in a communication might be evidence of malice which will defeat the privilege that would otherwise attach to the communication.[120] On the other hand, where the material is wholly extraneous to the main statement being made, there will be no privilege in the first place and the question whether a qualified privilege is defeated by malice will not arise.[121]

(d) Unreasonable publication to persons outside the scope of the privilege

Malice is present (and rebuts the privilege) if a defendant deliberately slanders another in the presence of persons to whom he has no privilege to communicate the matter

---

[113] *Clark v Molyneux* (1877) 3 QBD 237, at 244.   [114] (1877) 3 QBD 237, at 246.
[115] *Horrocks v Lowe* [1975] AC 135, at 149.
[116] *Royal Aquarium and Summer and Winter Garden Society v Parkinson* [1892] 1 QB 431.
[117] *Turner v Metro-Goldwyn-Mayer Pictures Ltd* [1950] 1 All ER 449, at 457–8.   [118] [1943] KB 319.
[119] *Horrocks v Lowe* [1975] AC 135.   [120] *Adam v Ward* [1917] AC 309.
[121] *Adam v Ward* [1917] AC 309; *Watts v Times Newspapers Ltd* [1997] QB 650.

(even if he has privilege to inform some of those present), or if he publishes in the press when he could have protected his interest by a private communication.[122]

(2) Joint publishers and malice

An agent through whom a person publishes a privileged communication enjoys the same privilege as his principal. Thus, a solicitor has the defence of qualified privilege when he publishes on behalf of his client some matter which his client had a privilege to publish.[123] Correspondingly, if an employee in the course of his employment publishes with malice, the fact that his employer was not personally malicious will not exempt the employer from vicarious liability since the employee who forfeits the privilege does so in the course of his employment.[124] Where each party responsible for a joint publication has an individual right to publish the statement—for example, trustees or members of a committee—each has an independent privilege unaffected by the malice of one or more of the other joint publishers.[125] Sometimes, however, one of the persons sued for the publication is a mere ancillary (for example, a printer or typist). Such an ancillary publisher probably may plead qualified privilege even if all his principals published maliciously. The key question would be whether the ancillary was actuated himself by malice.[126]

(3) Excess of privilege

As mentioned earlier, qualified privilege does not attach to statements that are published in excess of (or beyond) the proper subject matter of the privilege.[127] There might be such excess publication where statements unconnected with the main statement are introduced.[128] Take, for example, *Tuson v Evans*.[129]

> In a letter to C's agent setting out the basis of his claim against C for arrears of rent, D added: 'This attempt to defraud me of the produce of land is as mean as it is dishonest'. This 'wholly unnecessary' addition deprived him of his qualified privilege.

The privilege will be lost also by publishing to *more persons* than is necessary. It was exceeded, for example, when the minutes of a preliminary inquiry by a local authority committee into alleged petrol thefts by employees were placed in the public library. At that stage, ordinary ratepayers did not possess the necessary interest to receive that information.[130] On the other hand, an occasion does not cease to be privileged simply because, for example the defendant publishes: details of alleged sexual abuse of a child to multiple agencies of the state with a role in investigating such allegations and taking appropriate care measures—as his role requires him to do;[131] or to clerks or others in

---

[122] *Oddy v Lord Paulet* (1865) 4 F & F 1009.   [123] *Baker v Carrick* [1894] 1 QB 838.

[124] *Citizens' Life Assurance Co v Brown* [1904] AC 423; *Riddick v Thames Board Mills Ltd* [1977] QB 881.

[125] *Egger v Viscount Chelmsford* [1965] 1 QB 248.   [126] *Egger v Viscount Chelmsford* [1965] 1 QB 248.

[127] *Adam v Ward* [1917] AC 309, at 318, 320–1, and 327.

[128] If the statement, though not in strict logic relevant to the privileged occasion, is reasonably germane to the subject matter, then it is material only as evidence of malice to take the case out of the privilege: *Horrocks v Lowe* [1975] AC 135, at 151.   [129] (1840) 12 Ad & El 733.

[130] *De Buse v McCarthy* [1942] 1 KB 156.

[131] *ABC v CC of West Yorkshire* [2017] EWHC 1650 (QB), at [118].

the reasonable and ordinary course of business practice.[132] The fact that persons are present beyond those to whom there is a duty to make the statement will not curtail the privilege if the ordinary 'business of life could not well be carried on' were such restrictions to be imposed.[133] So, for example, a company does not forfeit its protection if, in order to have circulated a copy of the auditor's report, it sends it to printers, for that is reasonable and necessary.[134]

(B) Instances of qualified privilege

(1) General principle

'[O]riginally and in principle there are not many different kinds of privilege, but rather for all privilege there is the same foundation of the public interest.'[135] All the instances of qualified privilege discussed in what follows exist where the defendant has an interest or duty (whether legal, social, or moral) to communicate intelligence about the claimant to a third party who has a corresponding interest or duty in receiving it.[136] The classic statement on the matter is that of Parke B in *Toogood v Spyring*, observing that the defendant is liable for a defamatory statement:[137]

> unless it is fairly made by a person in the discharge of some public or private duty, whether legal or moral, or in the conduct of his own affairs, in matters where his interest is concerned. If fairly warranted by any reasonable occasion or exigency, and honestly made, such communications are protected for the common convenience and welfare of society; and the law has not restricted the right to make them within any narrow limits.

It is convenient to group our examples of statements afforded qualified privilege as follows: privileged reports, statements which protect an interest, and peer-reviewed academic papers.

(2) Privileged reports

Parliament Fair and accurate reports of proceedings in Parliament or in committees thereof, or fair summaries of those parts of the proceedings which are of special interest,[138] are privileged at common law.[139] These, and other such common law privileges, are preserved by the Defamation Act 1996[140]—even though section 15 and

---

[132] *Boxsius v Goblet Frères* [1894] 1 QB 842; *Edmondson v Birch & Co Ltd and Horner* [1907] 1 KB 371; *Bryanston Finance Co Ltd v De Vries* [1975] QB 703.

[133] *Toogood v Spyring* (1834) 1 Cr M & R 181, at 194.

[134] *Lawless v Anglo-Egyptian Cotton and Oil Co* (1869) LR 4 QB 262.

[135] *Webb v Times Publishing Co Ltd* [1960] 2 QB 535, at 563.

[136] *Adam v Ward* [1917] AC 309. This even covers broad-based internet communications to all the members of a particular religious community if they have sufficient interest in receiving the information: *Hewitt v Grunwald* [2004] EWCA Civ 2959.

[137] (1834) 1 Cr M & R 181, at 193 (approved in *Adam v Ward* [1917] AC 309, at 349).

[138] *Cook v Alexander* [1974] QB 279.

[139] *Wason v Walter* (1868) LR 4 QB 73. For consideration of what constitutes a 'fair and accurate' report, see *Curistan v Times Newspapers Ltd* [2008] EWCA Civ 432, esp. at [26]–[36].

[140] Defamation Act 1996, sub-s 15(4)(b).

Schedule 1 of that Act endeavour to establish a comprehensive range of reports that attract a statutory qualified privilege. The printing or broadcasting[141] of copies of, or extracts from, reports,[142] papers, votes, or proceedings published by authority of either House of Parliament are privileged also independently of the 1996 Act.[143]

Judicial functions Judicial reports remain privileged at common law so long as they are fair and accurate.[144] In view of the different rationale for this privilege, these 'judicial proceedings' (reports of which acquire qualified privilege) are not the same as 'judicial proceedings', reports of which attract absolute privilege.[145] The former is a much broader class of reports. Although a tribunal for the purposes of qualified privilege need not perform 'judicial functions' (in the narrow sense of the term), reports of its proceedings might be privileged provided the public are admitted and the tribunal is not a mere domestic one, such as the Jockey Club.[146] The privilege applies still where the tribunal is considering the case simply in order to discover whether it has jurisdiction, even though it has no such jurisdiction in fact.[147] Yet in *Stern v Piper*,[148] it was held that qualified privilege does not stretch to a report of proceedings that are merely 'pending'.

Schedule 1 By far the most comprehensive list of those reports and statements that are afforded a qualified privilege is contained in Defamation Act 1996, Schedule 1.[149] However, there are limits to this statutory privilege. The Act offers no protection for any 'publication to the public[] of matter which is not of public interest and the publication of which is not for the public benefit'.[150] Nor does it confer a qualified privilege in respect of anything published with malice[151] or illegally.[152]

Privileged without contradiction Reports protected by the 1996 Act fall into two groups: (1) those privileged without any explanation or contradiction;[153] and (2) those privileged subject to explanation or contradiction.[154] In relation to the former category, protection is conferred, broadly, on a worldwide basis. It lies in respect of reports of judicial, legislative, and international organisation proceedings conducted in public,

---

[141] Defamation Act 1952, sub-s 9(1) extends this privilege to those forms of broadcasting to which the Act applies.   [142] Parliamentary Papers Act 1840, s 2.

[143] Including Blue Books and reports of Royal Commissions presented to Parliament: *Mangena v Edward Lloyd Ltd* (1908) 98 LT 640; on appeal (1909) 99 LT 824.

[144] *Furniss v Cambridge Daily News Ltd* (1907) 23 TLR 705, at 706.

[145] For the judicial proceedings covered by absolute privilege, see the Defamation Act 1996, sub-s 14(3).

[146] *Chapman v Lord Ellesmere* [1932] 2 KB 431.

[147] *Usill v Hales* (1878) 3 CPD 319. This case is not an authority on absolute privilege for judicial acts done without jurisdiction.   [148] [1997] QB 123.

[149] The statutory list is too long to be reproduced here.

[150] Defamation Act 1996, sub-s 15(3). In, eg, *Kelly v O'Malley* (1889) 6 TLR 62 irrelevant, defamatory comments made at a public meeting were afforded no privilege.

[151] Defamation Act 1996, sub-s 15(1).   [152] Defamation Act 1996, sub-s 15(4)(a).

[153] Defamation Act 1996, Sch 1, Part I.

[154] Defamation Act 1996, Sch 1, Part II. Reports' include the summary of a press release accompanying a press conference: *McCartan Turkington Breen v Times Newspapers Ltd* [2001] 2 AC 277.

and reports on official publications. Unlike the absolute privilege conferred in relation to reports of judicial proceedings, the protection conferred under section 15 of the 1996 Act applies without requiring the report to be contemporaneous with the judicial proceedings.[155]

Subject to contradiction In relation to the second class of reports covered by section 15—those which are privileged subject to explanation or contradiction—no protection will be afforded if the claimant proves that the defendant, despite a request to publish an explanation or contradiction in a suitable manner,[156] has refused or neglected so to do.[157] The kinds of reports and statements that fall into this second class include those concerning: notices and other matters issued for public information by or on behalf of international organisations and legislatures and governments anywhere in the world; documents made available by courts anywhere in the world; proceedings at public meetings in the UK of local authorities and of commissions and tribunals; proceedings at any public meetings held anywhere in the world; and proceedings at general meetings of listed companies listed on recognised stock exchanges. A recent, novel addition to the list encompasses reports of scientific and academic conferences held anywhere in the world.

(3) Statements to protect an interest

(a) The public interest

(i) Statements by way of help in discovering criminals

Privilege has been held to cover: information given to the police in order to detect crime;[158] and statements made in the course of complaints about police conduct.[159] Presumably, it covers statements made by the police in the course of their inquiries into suspected crimes.

(ii) Statements about the misconduct of public officers

Privilege covers members of the public who bring to the notice of the proper authority any misconduct or neglect of duty on the part of public officers.[160] A defendant who first addresses his complaint about misconduct to his MP will be privileged.[161] However, when the defendant, acting in good faith, complains to the wrong official, he is not privileged.[162]

---

[155] *Tsikata v Newspaper Publishing plc* [1997] 1 All ER 655.

[156] That is, in the same manner as the publication complained of or, alternatively, in a manner that is both reasonable and adequate in the circumstances: Defamation Act 1996, sub-s 15(2).

[157] Defamation Act 1996, sub-s 15(2).   [158] *Padmore v Lawrence* (1840) 11 Ad & El 380.

[159] *Fraser v Mirza* 1993 SLT 527.

[160] Eg, *Harrison v Bush* (1855) 5 E & B 344 (statement to Home Secretary about county magistrate). But see *Blackshaw v Lord* [1984] QB 1: suspicions must be aired to the proper authority and not the public at large unless public safety is at risk.   [161] *R v Rule* [1937] 2 KB 375.

[162] *Hebditch v MacIlwaine* [1894] 2 QB 54; *Beach v Freeson* [1972] 1 QB 14.

(iii) Other statements

The defendant's duty to make a statement about the claimant is sometimes only a moral or social one—for example, to supply a third party with a warning about the claimant.[163] However, this does not prohibit his statement attracting a qualified privilege. That said, in the absence of a legal or contractual duty to make such a statement, the court might be wary of granting a privilege unless the defendant can show a strong relationship—for example, one of friendship—between himself and the third party to whom he feels obliged to make the statement.[164] Furthermore, in establishing the existence of such a duty, the defendant is entitled only to rely on matters that were known to him at the time of publication.[165]

The list of moral and social duties is virtually endless and includes, for example, answers to confidential inquiries about employees,[166] protection by a solicitor of his client's interests,[167] and supplying information about credit.[168] By contrast, the privilege does not cover officious intermeddling by strangers or idle gossip.[169] Consider *Watt v Longsdon*:[170]

> A company director was held to be privileged in passing on to the chairman a report that an employee was associating with another woman and otherwise misconducting himself during his employment overseas, but he was not protected in informing the employee's wife—even if she had an interest in receiving that information.

References When Employer A provides a reference on behalf of one of his (former) employees to Employer B, qualified privilege attaches to it. On the other hand, in the light of the House of Lords' decision in *Spring v Guardian Assurance plc*,[171] this immunity might be of little use since the employee would be entitled to sue in negligence rather than defamation for the loss attributable to a carelessly written reference.

(b) The self-interest of the publisher

Just as self-defence and protection of property are defences in torts against the person and property, a statement made to protect or advance the defendant's interests attracts qualified privilege in defamation.[172] Thus, a creditor may write to an auctioneer to protect his security.[173] Equally, a man who replied to a letter demanding payment of fees for medical services to his wife (who died from scarlet fever) saying 'I shall never pay him unless the law compels me, and that I do not fancy it can, as I could more easily

---

[163] See, eg, *Amann v Damm* (1860) 8 CBNS 597; *S v Newham LBC* (1998) 96 LGR 651.

[164] *Todd v Hawkins* (1837) 8 C & P 88.

[165] *Loutchansky v Times Newspapers Ltd* [2002] QB 321; *GKR Karate (UK) Ltd v Yorkshire Post Newspapers Ltd (No 2)* [2000] EMLR 410.   [166] *Kelly v Partington* (1833) 4 B & Ad 700.

[167] Cf *Baker v Carrick* [1894] 1 QB 838, at 841.

[168] *London Association for Protection of Trade v Greenlands Ltd* [1916] 2 AC 15.

[169] *Coxhead v Richards* (1846) 2 CB 569.   [170] [1930] 1 KB 130.   [171] [1995] 2 AC 296.

[172] *Toogood v Spyring* (1834) 1 Cr M & R 181, at 193; *Aspro Travel Ltd v Owners Abroad Group plc* [1995] 4 All ER 728.   [173] *Blackman v Pugh* (1846) 2 CB 611.

indict Dr S for manslaughter' was held to be privileged.[174] Privilege will extend also to: the publisher's reasonable steps to collect money owing to him;[175] warnings issued to servants about the bad character of their associates;[176] and replies to attacks on the publisher's reputation.[177]

(c) Common interest

There are cases of privilege based on interest where neither the public nor the publisher *alone* has a sufficiently defensible interest for the case to be brought within any of the preceding subheadings. These cases attract a privilege on the basis that the publisher and the recipient of the communication have a 'common interest' in the subject matter of the communication. A common interest of this kind exists between an employer and his employees. Thus, in one case the defendants had posted circulars in such of their premises as would be frequented by their employees, stating that a former employee (the claimant) had been dismissed for neglect of duty. The privilege of common interest was held to extend to the defendants.[178]

The range of matters privileged because they are of common interest are manifold and include speeches by a company shareholder at a shareholders' meeting[179] a statement made by a creditor to another creditor about their debtor,[180] communications by the head of the Bar Council to members of the Bar,[181] and communications within a family on matters affecting the welfare of a member of that family.[182]

In one respect the scope of this privilege has been curtailed by Defamation Act 1952, section 10, which provides that publications, even to a qualified voter, by or on behalf of a candidate at a parliamentary or local government election, are not privileged on the ground that they are material to a question in issue in the election.[183]

(4) Peer-reviewed academic papers

Defamation Act 2013, section 6 provides qualified privilege to peer-reviewed statements in academic or scientific journals. It applies where the statement relates to an academic or scientific matter[184] and where, before publication, 'an independent review' of its merit was conducted. This review must have been undertaken by both an editor (or editors) of the journal and by 'one or more persons with expertise' in the subject area.[185] The privilege attaches also to fair and accurate copies of extracts from, and summaries of, the privileged journal papers.[186] The privilege is lost if the claimant is able to

---

[174] *Stevens v Kitchener* (1887) 4 TLR 159.   [175] *Winstanley v Bampton* [1943] KB 319.

[176] *Somerville v Hawkins* (1851) 10 CB 583.

[177] *Laughton v Bishop of Sodor and Man* (1872) LR 4 PC 495.

[178] *Hunt v Great Northern Rly Co* [1891] 2 QB 189. See also *Bryanston Finance Ltd v De Vries* [1975] QB 703.

[179] *Parsons v Surgey* (1864) 4 F & F 247.   [180] *Spill v Maule* (1869) LR 4 Exch 232.

[181] *Kearns v General Council of the Bar* [2003] 1 WLR 1357.   [182] *Todd v Hawkins* (1837) 8 C & P 88.

[183] *Braddock v Bevins* [1948] 1 KB 580 must now be read in the light of this section. See also *Plummer v Charman* [1962] 3 All ER 823.

[184] Defamation Act 2013, sub-s 6(2). This is intended to include medical and engineering matters: Explanatory Notes to the Defamation Act 2013, at [44].   [185] Defamation Act 2013, sub-ss 6(3) and 6(8).

[186] Defamation Act 2013, sub-s 6(5). See also Defamation Act 1996, s 14A (reports of proceedings of academic or scientific conferences anywhere in the world).

prove malice on the part of the defendant editor or author.[187] Although this privilege is a valuable one, its scope is narrow and would not cover many outlets for academic work such as books and the media.[188] In such cases, defendants must fall back on other defences.

Section 7 Public interest

(A) Modern defence

Defamation Act 2013, section 4 creates a defence of 'publication on a matter of public interest'. The defence is available where the defendant is able to prove that 'the statement complained of was, or formed part of, a statement on a matter of public interest' and that 'the defendant reasonably believed that publishing the statement' was in the public interest.[189] It is available 'irrespective of whether the statement complained of is a statement of fact or a statement of opinion'.[190] The defence replaces the common law *Reynolds* defence, differing from it by omitting an overt requirement of 'responsible journalism'. This aside, the defence is intended to reflect the principles established in *Reynolds* and subsequent case law.[191] The established case law is envisaged by the legislature to be 'a helpful (albeit not binding) guide to interpreting' the provisions.[192]

(B) *Reynolds* and subsequent case law

We begin our consideration of the defence by examining the seminal case law. In *Reynolds v Times Newspapers Ltd*,[193] the facts were as follows:

> A UK newspaper alleged that R, the Irish Prime Minister, had misled the Irish Parliament (Dáil) about matters relating to W, whom his government had appointed as a judge. Concern had arisen over the failure of the Attorney-General's Office to extradite an alleged sexual offender while W was Attorney-General. R gave a speech in the Dáil that was broadly supportive of W, although he had been informed of potential dishonesty concerning W which had not, at that stage, been confirmed. Soon after, R was informed that W in fact had been dishonest about the reasons for delay in the extradition case. R made another statement to the Dáil and expressed regret that W had been appointed. R brought an action for defamation, alleging that the newspaper article had imputed that he had deliberately and dishonestly misled the Dáil by suppressing vital information.

The House of Lords held that newspapers publishing to the world at large were entitled to a variant of qualified privilege on matters of public interest, although the defence failed in this case because the newspaper had not included R's own explanation of

---

[187] Defamation Act 2013, sub-s 6(6).
[188] See comment in A Mullis and A Scott (2014) 77 MLR 87, at 99.
[189] Defamation Act 2013, sub-s 4(1).   [190] Defamation Act 2013, sub-s 4(5).
[191] Explanatory Notes to the Defamation Act 2013, [29].
[192] Explanatory Notes to the Defamation Act 2013, [35]. For doubts about this and other points, see KY Low (2014) 130 LQR 24.   [193] [2001] 2 AC 127.

events. In determining when the defence was available, the court would examine all of the relevant circumstances, which Lord Nicholls stated to include the following:

> 1. The seriousness of the allegation. The more serious the charge, the more the public is misinformed and the individual harmed, if the allegation is not true. 2. The nature of the information, and the extent to which the subject matter is a matter of public concern. 3. The source of the information. Some informants have no direct knowledge of the events. Some have their own axes to grind, or are being paid for their stories. 4. The steps taken to verify the information. 5. The status of the information. The allegation may have already been the subject of an investigation which commands respect. 6. The urgency of the matter. News is often a perishable commodity. 7. Whether comment was sought from the [claimant]. He may have information others do not possess or have not disclosed. An approach to the [claimant] will not always be necessary. 8. Whether the article contained the gist of the [claimant]'s side of the story. 9. The tone of the article. A newspaper can raise queries or call for an investigation. It need not adopt allegations as statements of fact. 10. The circumstances of the publication, including the timing.
>
> This list is not exhaustive. The weight to be given to these and any other relevant factors will vary from case to case.[194]

Lord Nicholls urged that a liberal approach be taken to media stories about political figures. A 'court should be slow to conclude that a publication was not in the public interest and, therefore, the public had no right to know, especially when the information is in the field of political discussion'.[195] Following this decision, it was suggested that the proper benchmark for claiming the privilege was that of 'responsible journalism'.[196]

In *Jameel v Wall Street Journal Europe SPRL*,[197] the House of Lords affirmed its disposition towards greater freedom of discussion of matters of public interest:

> The case concerned a newspaper report which, in factual terms, revealed supposed information that the bank accounts of a Saudi Arabian company and its managing director were being monitored by the Saudi Arabian Monetary Authority in connection with the funding of terrorist organisations. This was taken to mean, at the least, that grounds existed upon which to investigate the involvement of those persons. The report was defamatory, but was found to be in the public interest.

One question was whether the 'responsible journalism' threshold had been met. In discussing this, Lord Bingham stressed that the *Reynolds* factors were not to be seen as a 'series of hurdles to be negotiated by a publisher' in order to invoke the privilege. Rather, the factors consisted of 'matters which might be taken into account'.[198] His Lordship, and others, pointed also to the need of the court to place weight upon 'editorial decisions and judgments made at the time, without the knowledge of falsity which is a benefit of hindsight' where these were considered in nature and not casual or slipshod.[199] In

---

[194] [2001] 2 AC 127, at 205.
[195] [2001] 2 AC 127, at 205. See, eg, *Tsikata v Newspaper Publishing plc* [1997] 1 All ER 655.
[196] Eg, *Bonnick v Morris* [2003] 1 AC 300; *Kearns v General Council of the Bar* [2003] 1 WLR 1357.
[197] [2007] 1 AC 359.   [198] [2007] 1 AC 359, at [33]. See also at [56].
[199] [2007] 1 AC 359, at [33]. See also at [51] and [108].

the result, the House held that the *Reynolds* privilege was available to report the matters in question.

Types of publication Since the decision in the *Reynolds* case, there has been an exponential increase in 'publication' beyond traditional forms. These include much material that is 'self-published' on the internet by way of blogs and the like. In a sign that the courts are aware of the greater ability of the 'average person' to publish on the internet, the Privy Council stated in *Seaga v Harper* [200] that the *Reynolds* privilege is not to be restricted to newspaper publications. Lord Carswell stated that there is 'no valid reason why it should not extend to publications made by any person who publishes material of public interest in any medium', so long as the test of 'responsible journalism' is satisfied.[201] In *Flood v Times Newspapers Ltd*,[202] the Supreme Court agreed that the defence should not be restricted to the media.

Sui generis defence In the *Flood* case, the Supreme Court accepted that the *Reynolds* defence was best described as something other than a form of qualified privilege, given that it arises 'not simply because of the circumstances in which the publication is made, although these can bear on the test of responsible journalism, [but] because of the subject matter of the publication itself'. Furthermore, unlike qualified privilege, there is little real room for consideration of malice.[203]

Rationale Among the arguments in favour of freedom of speech is the argument from democracy. The core of the *Reynolds* privilege is explained by the need for 'a well-informed, politically-sophisticated electorate able to confront government . . . .'[204] Its impact has been described as 'an answer to the "structural" chilling effect of libel law', which is the 'disincentive the law creates against publishing anything at all'. This disincentive arises from the kind of strict liability inherent in establishing a prima facie case of defamation. '*Reynolds* lifts that general disincentive and replaces it with a standard that defendants are capable of meeting in any given case, a standard that "chills" only publication[s] that might fail to meet it.'[205]

(C) Statutory requirements

The Government noted perceived problems with the *Reynolds* privilege, such as lingering uncertainty about its scope (including its applicability beyond mainstream journalism), which had a potentially 'chilling' effect on freedom of expression. There was concern also about the 'complication' of the defence and its costliness to run.[206] The statutory restatement of the defence is intended to reflect many of the common law developments up to the decision of the Supreme Court in *Flood v Times Newspapers Ltd*.[207]

---

[200] [2009] 1 AC 1.   [201] [2008] UKPC 9; [2009] 1 AC 1, at [11].   [202] [2012] 2 AC 273, at [279].
[203] [2012] 2 AC 273, at [27], [38], and [201].   [204] E Barendt, *Freedom of Speech* (2007), 155.
[205] D Howarth (2011) 74 MLR 845, 870–1.
[206] Ministry of Justice, *Draft Defamation Bill Consultation Paper* (Cm 8020, 2011), at [8]–[9].
[207] [2012] 2 AC 273. See Explanatory Notes to the Defamation Act 2013, at [29].

Elements Under the Defamation Act 2013, there are two elements to the defence. As mentioned earlier, these are that 'the statement complained of was, or formed part of, a statement on a matter of public interest' and that 'the defendant reasonably believed that publishing the statement' was in the public interest.[208] The defence is available 'irrespective of whether the statement complained of is a statement of fact or a statement of opinion'.[209]

Public interest The 'public interest' includes, but is not limited to, political matters. It encompasses the conduct of government, public administration and governance of public institutions and state-owned and larger companies.[210] In cases of doubt, relevant factors in determining the public interest are likely to include the status of the claimant (whether he has entered the public arena),[211] the content of the statement (whether it affects 'people at large'),[212] and the context of its publication.[213]

Reasonable belief The Act specifies that, in determining whether the defendant has proven the necessary elements, 'the court must have regard to all the circumstances of the case'.[214] This should mean that many of the *Reynolds* factors remain relevant, especially in determining the reasonableness of the belief that publishing the statement was in the public interest. Indeed, in moving passage of the Bill, Lord McNally emphasised that the issue was to be examined from the perspective of the publisher at the time of publication and that the 'courts will need to look at the conduct of the publisher in deciding' reasonableness of belief.[215] The Act requires, moreover, that the court should 'make such allowance for editorial judgment as it considers appropriate' in determining reasonableness of belief.[216]

Other matters Although the statutory defence does away with any overt requirement of 'responsible journalism' (one of the hallmarks of its common law predecessor), it seems that the continued relevance of the factors that undergirded that requirement obviates any perceived radicalism[217] in the change in the law.[218] The statutory defence precludes consideration of malice also, but this was not an important part of the common law defence.

(D) Reportage doctrine

Common law In addition to the main public interest defence, the courts recognised a subspecies of qualified privilege called 'reportage'. This involved cases in which the

---

[208] Defamation Act 2013, sub-s 4(1).
[209] Defamation Act 2013, sub-s 4(5). The application of the defence to opinions is a departure from prior case law and has the potential to undermine the operation of the defence of honest opinion. See A Mullis and A Scott (2014) 77 MLR 87, 95.
[210] See definition in *Reynolds v Times Newspapers Ltd* [1998] 3 All ER 961 (CA), at 1004.
[211] See *Krone Verlag GmbH & Co KG v Austria* (2003) 36 EHRR 57, at [37].
[212] *London Artists v Littler* [1969] 2 QB 375, at 391.
[213] D Milo, *Defamation and Freedom of Speech* (2008), 96.   [214] Defamation Act 2013, sub-s 4(2).
[215] HL Deb 19 December 2012, vol 555, col 534f GC.   [216] Defamation Act 2013, sub-s 4(4).
[217] Cf KY Low (2014) 130 LQR 24.
[218] See, to like effect, A Mullis and A Scott (2014) 77 MLR 87, 89–91.

media merely report allegations made by others in the course of some dispute of public interest and do not adopt those allegations.[219] According to *Roberts v Gable*,[220] the significance was as follows:

> If upon a proper construction of the thrust of the article the defamatory material is attributed to another and is not being put forward as true, then a responsible journalist would not need to take steps to verify its accuracy. He is absolved from that responsibility because he is simply reporting in a neutral fashion the fact that it has been said without adopting the truth.[221]

The Supreme Court adopted the reportage doctrine. In *Flood v Times Newspapers Ltd*, Lord Phillips did not dispute the idea that the doctrine does not require verification of the *accuracy* of the allegation, but stated that it does require that 'proper steps' be taken to verify that the allegation *was made*.[222] His Lordship held that the doctrine encompasses cases where the media report 'the fact that the police are investigating the conduct of an individual, or that he has been arrested, or that he has been charged with an offence'.[223]

Statute The reportage doctrine has been put on a statutory footing. Defamation Act 2013, sub-section 4(3) provides:

> If the statement complained of was, or formed part of, an accurate and impartial account of a dispute to which the claimant was a party, the court must in determining whether it was reasonable for the defendant to believe that publishing the statement was in the public interest disregard any omission of the defendant to take steps to verify the truth of the imputation conveyed by it.

The placement of this provision within section 4 indicates the relationship of the main defence to the new statutory exposition of the reportage doctrine. The wording of the provision indicates also the continued relevance of the *Reynolds* factors, excluding any attempt to verify the truth of allegations made.

Section 8 Honest opinion

(A) Modern defence

Defamation Act 2013, section 3 creates a defence of 'honest opinion'. This replaces the former common law defence of 'fair comment', which arose with respect to comments about the claimant or the claimant's conduct in connection with matters of public interest. Fair comment encompassed reasonable remarks upon true or privileged statements of fact. The comments were required to constitute an honestly held opinion, meaning that the defendant did not believe the statements to be untrue and, therefore, was not

---

[219] *Al-Fagih v HH Saudi Research and Marketing (UK) Ltd* [2001] EWCA Civ 1634.
[220] [2008] QB 502.   [221] [2008] QB 502, at [61].   [222] [2012] 2 AC 273, at [77].
[223] [2012] 2 AC 273, at [35].

actuated by malice.[224] The Government noted perceived problems with the honest comment defence, such as its 'complexity', technical nature, and the resultant uncertainty that arose in its application.[225]

Elements The new statutory defence represents a significant departure from the prior law, no longer requiring proof that the opinion be in the public interest.[226] Section 3 provides that the defence is available when three conditions are met: the statement complained of was a statement of opinion; it indicated 'whether in general or specific terms the basis of the opinion'; and 'an honest person could have held the opinion' by reference to specified matters. The defence 'is defeated if the claimant shows that the defendant did not hold the opinion'. Each of these matters will be considered in turn.

Rationale Before doing so, a word should be said about the purpose of this defence. Its origin lies in protection of criticism of literary works and works of art. Eventually, the defence came to encompass comment upon other matters of public interest.[227] A wide ambit of speech in the form of comment or opinion is permissible, in part, because it 'can be recognised by readers as viewpoints with which they can choose to agree or disagree'. '[P]rovided that the inferential nature of the assertion is clear and the facts on which the opinion is based made available, the possibility of reasonable readers being misled' is greatly reduced. In this sense, there is a strong contrast to assertions of fact, about which readers typically are not 'invited to demur'.[228]

(B) Statement of opinion

Under Defamation Act 2013, section 3 the first requirement of the defence is that the defendant must prove that 'the statement complained of was a statement of opinion'.[229] The intention is that the phrase 'opinion' should cover inferences from facts, although the whole question is to be examined from the point of view of the 'ordinary person'.[230] The Court of Appeal has adopted a wide approach to what comprises opinion, which encompasses inferences from facts. This was evident in *British Chiropractic Association v Singh*,[231] which concerned a letter published in the *Guardian* newspaper's 'Comment and debate' section stating that 'there was not a jot of evidence' for claims made by a professional association about the efficacy of chiropractic treatment. Lord Judge CJ

---

[224] *Reynolds v Times Newspapers Ltd* [2001] 2 AC 127, at 193.

[225] Ministry of Justice, *Draft Defamation Bill Consultation Paper* (Cm 8020, 2011), 18 and 20.

[226] Apart from this change, the new provision is designed to simplify and clarify the existing law: Explanatory Notes to the Defamation Act 2013, at [19]. Relevant case law would constitute 'a helpful but not binding guide to interpreting' the provision: ibid [27]. Nevertheless, caution must be applied in using the pre-existing case law.

[227] *Joseph v Spiller* [2011] 1 AC 852, at [33]; P Mitchell, *The Making of the Modern Law of Defamation* (2005), ch 8.   [228] A Mullis and A Scott (2014) 77 MLR 87, 91–2.

[229] Defamation Act 2013, sub-s 3(2).   [230] Explanatory Notes to the Defamation Act 2013, at [21].

[231] [2011] 1 WLR 133.

acknowledged that the subject matter was an area of epidemiology in which 'the relationship of primary fact to secondary fact, and of both to permissible inference, is heavily and legitimately contested'.[232] His Lordship went on to say that the phrase 'not a jot of evidence', taken in the context of a debate about the efficacy of chiropractic treatment, meant 'that there is no worthwhile or reliable evidence for it. That is as much a value judgment as a contrary viewpoint would be.'[233] The court was not to assume the position of 'an Orwellian ministry of truth'.

(C) Basis of opinion

The second requirement of the defence is that the defendant must prove that 'the statement complained of indicated, whether in general or specific terms, the basis of the opinion'.[234] This requirement is said to reflect the law as established in *Joseph v Spiller*.[235] In that case, Lord Phillips explained the reason for such a requirement as follows:

> The [opinion] must . . . identify at least in general terms what it is that has led the commentator to [form] the [opinion], so that the reader can understand what [it] is about and the commentator can, if challenged, explain by giving particulars of the subject matter of his [opinion] why he expressed the views that he did.[236]

Another reason for the requirement is that, in the absence of a factual basis for an opinion, the reader will be compelled to speculate, if not simply assume, that adequate grounds exist for it.[237] Although there have been judicial observations to the effect that the statement of facts accompanying an opinion must be such as to allow readers to make their own assessment of it,[238] this requirement was denied in *Joseph v Spiller* as being unrealistic.[239] What is required under the legislation is reference at least in 'general' terms. This is a reflection of case law holding that, where the facts are relatively widely known, a general rather than specific reference to them is sufficient.[240]

Illustrations The operation of the rule might be illustrated by a couple of examples. If the defendant were to say that 'X is a disgrace', the hearer would no doubt believe that they were based on unstated facts. The defendant could not plead honest opinion in respect of those words alone. If, however, he had added 'he has deserted his wife and family', the original words might well be regarded as an opinion about the stated facts.[241] And it has been held that a defendant who implied that a play was adulterous could not rely on the common law defence where the court found as a fact that adultery was not dealt with in the play.[242]

---

[232] [2011] 1 WLR 133, at [18].   [233] [2011] 1 WLR 133, at [26].
[234] Defamation Act 2013, sub-s 3(3).   [235] [2011] 1 AC 852.   [236] [2011] 1 AC 852, at [104].
[237] *Hunt v Star Newspaper Co Ltd* [1908] 2 KB 309, at 319.
[238] Eg, *Tse Wai Chun v Cheng* [2001] EMLR 777, at [19]; *Hunt v Star Newspaper Co Ltd* [1908] 2 KB 309, at 319.   [239] [2011] 1 AC 852, at [98]–[99] and [103].
[240] *Joseph v Spiller* [2011] 1 AC 852, at [96] and [102]–[103]; *Kemsley v Foot* [1952] AC 345.
[241] See *Cooper v Lawson* (1838) 8 Ad & El 746.   [242] *Merivale v Carson* (1887) 20 QBD 275.

(D) Honest person could have held opinion

The third requirement of the defence is that the defendant must prove that 'an honest person could have held the opinion'. This is established by reference to either 'any fact which existed at the time the statement complained of was published' or 'anything asserted to be a fact in a privileged statement published before the statement complained of'.[243]

Facts As to the first basis for proving that an honest person could have held the opinion, the requirement is that the defendant prove the existence of any relevant fact that could substantiate the opinion. Obviously, if the facts relied upon are not proved to be true, the defendant will not be able to invoke the defence simply by proving that his opinion was honestly held. Moreover, it is necessary that any facts relied upon and proved to be true are a sufficient basis for the opinion. 'If the fact was not a sufficient basis for the opinion, an honest person would not have been able to hold it.'[244] It appears that there need be no correlation between the facts that the defendant actually relied upon in forming his opinion and those which eventually are used at trial to satisfy the objective test. The result is to 'enable a defendant who has published an opinion on the basis of wholly false facts to succeed in the defence at trial if he or she is able to discover some other fact of which he or she was previously ignorant . . . on which an honest person could have based the comment'.[245]

In *Merivale v Carson*, Lord Esher made certain observations that remain relevant under the new statutory test. He observed that '[e]very latitude must be given to opinion and to prejudice' before application of the test and that '[m]ere exaggeration, or even gross exaggeration' would not be decisive against the defendant. 'However wrong the opinion expressed may be in point of truth, or however prejudiced the writer, it may still be within the prescribed limit.'[246] The court's task is to assess whether the opinion in question fell within reasonable bounds, given that it is not possible (in most cases) to determine the actual convictions with which an opinion was uttered at the time of utterance.

Privileged statements As to the second basis for proving that an honest person could have held the opinion, this concerns 'anything asserted to be a fact in a privileged statement published before the statement complained of'.[247] Defamation Act 2013, sub-section 3(7) provides a list of statements that are to be regarded as 'privileged statements'. These are statements with respect to which the person responsible for publication (not necessarily the defendant), would have available to him at least one of the following defences if an action for defamation were brought in response to it: a defence under Defamation Act 2013, section 4 (publication on a matter of public interest); a defence under Defamation Act 2013, section 6 (peer-reviewed statement in a scientific or academic journal); a defence under Defamation Act 1996, section 14 (reports of court proceedings protected by absolute privilege); or a defence under Defamation Act 1996,

---

[243] Defamation Act 2013, sub-s 3(4).   [244] Explanatory Notes to the Defamation Act 2013, at [23].
[245] See A Mullis and A Scott (2014) 77 MLR 87, at 94.   [246] (1887) 20 QBD 275, at 280–1.
[247] Defamation Act 2013, sub-s 3(4)(b).

section 15 (other reports protected by qualified privilege). The effect is to create a consistent approach to actionability in defamation, by providing that the defendant is not liable in circumstances where other statements which can be relied upon to ground an opinion would be protected by one of the stated defences. However, the use in subsection 3(4)(b) of the word 'before' precludes the use of privileged statements published contemporaneously with impugned opinions. This appears to be a case of legislative oversight and there have been calls for statutory amendment.[248]

(E) When defence defeated

Under Defamation Act 2013, sub-section 3(5) the 'defence is defeated if the claimant shows that the defendant did not hold the opinion'. The defence will not be defeated if the defendant's reason for making that statement is associated with the pursuit of his own private ends, so long as he holds the impugned opinion.[249] According to the Explanatory Notes, the defence will fail 'if the claimant was actuated by malice'.[250] No doubt, this is correct where 'malice' is interpreted to mean lack of belief. However, malice in the sense of 'intention to injure' would appear to be irrelevant to the issue. Thus, where the defendant held the impugned opinion, it would not matter that he had 'abused his right' to hold the opinion and made the statement with the intention to injure.[251]

Three-party cases The provision does not apply in circumstances indicated by subsection 3(6), these being where:

> the statement complained of was published by the defendant but made by another person ('the author'); and in such a case the defence is defeated if the claimant shows that the defendant knew or ought to have known that the author did not hold the opinion.

An example is provided by the Explanatory Notes, which hypothesise a case in which 'an action is brought against a newspaper editor in respect of a comment piece', rather than against the writer. In such a case, the defence would be defeated 'if the defendant knew or ought to have known that the author did not hold the opinion'.[252]

Section 9 Apology

The offer or the making of an apology is not a defence at common law, although it may be given in evidence in mitigation of damages. Under statute, however, it is a defence.

> In an action for a libel contained in any public newspaper or other periodical publication, it shall be competent to the defendant to plead that such libel was inserted in such

---

[248] See A Mullis and A Scott (2014) 77 MLR 87, at 93–4.

[249] Eg, *Grobbelaar v News Group Newspapers Ltd* [2001] 2 All ER 437 (revd on other grounds [2003] EMLR 1).   [250] Explanatory Notes to the Defamation Act 2013, at [25].

[251] Compare this to the common law: *Thomas v Bradbury, Agnew & Co Ltd* [1906] 2 KB 627. On the other hand, if the statement is made as part of a conspiracy, an action might lie in that tort, so long as damage *beyond* mere damage to reputation can be shown.   [252] Explanatory Notes to the Defamation Act 2013, at [26].

> newspaper or other periodical publication without actual malice, and without gross negligence, and that before the commencement of the action, or at the earliest opportunity afterwards, he inserted in such newspaper or other periodical publication a full apology for the said libel, or, if the newspaper or periodical publication . . . should be ordinarily published at intervals exceeding one week, had offered to publish the said apology in any newspaper or periodical publication to be selected by the [claimant] in such action.[253]

Two things ought to be noted about this provision: first, every such defence must be accompanied by a payment of money into court by way of amends;[254] second, the issues of malice, gross negligence, and the adequacy of the apology are to be decided separately by the trier of fact. Defamation Act 2013, section 12 might also be relevant in this regard (considered earlier).

Section 10 Remedies

(A) Powers of court

The Defamation Act 2013 provides courts with specific powers in relation to defamatory statements. Under section 12, the court has the power to order the defendant to publish a summary of its judgment. And, under section 13, the court has power to make orders with respect (essentially) to persons not before it who have been involved in the publication of defamatory matter. The court has the power to order removal of a statement from a website or the cessation of the distribution, sale, or exhibition of the defamatory matter.

(B) Damages

General principles The main function of the tort of defamation is to vindicate the claimant, to compensate him for his loss of reputation (the extent to which he is held in less esteem and respect, and suffers loss of goodwill and association),[255] and to deter future defamation.[256] Although judgment in favour of the claimant will serve to vindicate his reputation, an award of damages frequently is required to compensate for the full effect of the wrong done.[257] The principles ordinarily applicable to damages at large apply.[258] Compensation may be given for insult or injury to feelings.[259] Persistence in an unsubstantiated plea of truth will lead to a higher award. Occasionally the claimant's loss of reputation will cause him a knock-on financial loss—for example, loss of business. That loss is recoverable as special damage and is awarded in addition to general damages so long as the loss can be shown with sufficient precision.[260] Bodies that trade for profit are entitled

---

[253] Libel Act 1843, s 2.   [254] Libel Act 1845, s 2.

[255] See *Dingle v Associated Newspapers Ltd* [1961] 2 QB 162. A view exists that compensation includes vindication: *Sloutsker v Romanova* [2015] EMLR 27, at [77].

[256] *Secretary of State for the Environment etc* [2009] 1 WLR 2780; *Sloutsker v Romanova* [2015] EMLR 27, at [96].   [257] *Cairns v Modi* [2013] 1 WLR 1015, at [31]; *Sloutsker v Romanova* [2015] EMLR 27, at [80].

[258] See ch 26.   [259] *Goslin v Corry* (1844) 7 Man & G 342; *Ley v Hamilton* (1935) 153 LT 384, at 386.

[260] See, eg, *Collins Stewart Ltd v Financial Times Ltd* [2005] EMLR 5.

to compensation for 'serious financial loss'[261] and, as mentioned in chapter 20, this will be for proven losses in sales and other revenue streams. In addition to these heads, damages may be aggravated by such matters as the mode, circumstances, and extent[262] of publication as well as the conduct of the defendant from publication to verdict.[263]

Slander In the case of ordinary slanders (but not the two exceptional cases of imputations of crime and of professional incompetence), actual damage must be proved. It is doubtful whether any damages other than those for actual damage are recoverable for such slanders.[264] If this is correct, the rules in relation to aggravated and exemplary damages do not apply.

Mitigation and reduction Evidence of the claimant's bad reputation will be a ground for mitigating the level of damages, since a reputation already largely lost is necessarily of less value. The defendant's belief in the truth of his statements,[265] their fairness,[266] and any provocation by the claimant[267] may all serve to mitigate the damages awarded. Where the defendant is unable to prove the substantial truth of an impugned statement, he may be able to rely nonetheless on the facts proved to reduce the damages.[268] Indeed, in an exceptional case, he may do so to reduce the damages almost to vanishing point.[269]

Exemplary damages Exemplary damages may be awarded where the defendant calculated that the money to be made out of his wrongdoing probably would exceed compensation payable for the defamation, and where he defamed the claimant either knowing his conduct to be illegal or reckless as to its illegality.[270] Where several claimants are libelled, the amount of exemplary damages may take into account the fact that the defendant has libelled more than one person; but the total should not exceed that representing a proper sum by way of punishment of the defendant.[271]

Having said as much, the courts' ability to award exemplary damages against media defendants is subject to provisions in the Crime and Courts Act 2013. The provisions are concerned with persons who publish news-related material in the course of a business, which is written by different authors and subject to editorial control.[272] The

---

[261] Defamation Act 2013, sub-s 1(b).

[262] The courts will take into account the ability of libels to spread far and wide via social networking and other internet sites: *Cairns v Modi* [2013] 1 WLR 1015, at [27].

[263] *Praed v Graham* (1889) 24 QBD 53. For restrictions on the award of aggravated damages against news media, see Crime and Courts Act 2013, ss 39 and 41–2.

[264] There is an *obiter dictum* of Williams J in *Brown v Smith* (1853) 13 CB 596 to the effect that no other damages are available.

[265] *Bryce v Rusden* (1886) 2 TLR 435; *Forsdike v Stone* (1868) LR 3 CP 607 (bona fide mistake of identity).

[266] *Smith v Scott* (1847) 2 Car & Kir 580; *East v Chapman* (1827) Mood & M 46.

[267] *Moore v Oastler* (1836) 1 Mood & R 451n.

[268] See, eg, *Burstein v Times Newspapers Ltd* [2001] 1 WLR 579. Note, however, that to introduce such evidence, it must be so clearly relevant to the subject matter of the libel or C's character as to produce an obvious risk of the jury assessing damages on a false basis: *Turner v News Group Newspapers* [2006] EWCA Civ 540.

[269] *Pamplin v Express Newspapers Ltd (No 2)* [1988] 1 All ER 282.

[270] *Cassell & Co Ltd v Broome* [1972] AC 1027.

[271] *Riches v News Group Newspapers Ltd* [1986] QB 256.   [272] Crime and Courts Act 2013, s 41.

starting point is that exemplary damages may not be awarded against such defendants where regulated by a recognised regulator, although this is subject to narrow exceptions.[273] Where the defendant is not regulated, or else an exception applies, so that a court has power to award exemplary damages, the court must be satisfied that a claim for exemplary damages has been made, 'the defendant's conduct has shown a deliberate or reckless disregard of an outrageous nature for the claimant's rights', that the conduct in question ought to be punished, and that there is no other adequate remedy.[274] The legislation provides various considerations to be taken into account in determining whether an award of exemplary damages is appropriate.[275] The amount awarded must not be more than the minimum required to punish the defendant and must be proportionate to the seriousness of the conduct.[276]

Control over awards At one time, it was feared that damages awards were becoming excessive. The turning point came in *Sutcliffe v Pressdram Ltd*,[277] where the Court of Appeal set aside an award warning that, in assessing any element of aggravated damages, misconduct by the defendant is relevant only insofar as it increases the injury to the claimant. Moreover, it was held in *John v MGN Ltd*[278] that damages should be calculated after considering the levels of damages awards made in personal injuries cases (while recognising that no direct analogy can be drawn because of the different nature of the 'injury' involved).

Evidence The rules governing evidence of reputation are complex. The governing principle is that general evidence alone is permitted (and then, only after prior notice and particulars have been given). Evidence of specific facts in order to demonstrate the disposition of the claimant is not currently admissible.[279] The court is concerned with the esteem in which the claimant is in fact held—with his established reputation.[280] It is not concerned with his actual character, or with the reputation that he may deserve. Thus, where, on a privileged occasion, a newspaper published extracts from a parliamentary report, and then embellished this report with details not found in the report, it could not reduce its damages by asserting that the claimant's reputation was already tarnished by the privileged publication of the parliamentary report.[281] Where the defendant has persisted in a plea of truth, it is the claimant's reputation at the time of the trial which counts in assessing damage to reputation.[282]

(C) Injunctions

Claimants in defamation actions often seek interlocutory injunctions as soon as they have served the claim so as to prevent further publication. The courts, concerned not

---

[273] Crime and Courts Act 2013, s 34.   [274] Crime and Courts Act 2013, s 34.
[275] Crime and Courts Act 2013, s 35.   [276] Crime and Courts Act 2013, s 36.
[277] [1991] 1 QB 153.   [278] [1997] QB 586.
[279] *Scott v Sampson* (1882) 8 QBD 491; *Turner v News Group Newspapers Ltd* [2006] EWCA Civ 540.
[280] *Plato Films Ltd v Speidel* [1961] AC 1090.   [281] *Associated Newspapers Ltd v Dingle* [1964] AC 371.
[282] *Cornwell v Myskow* [1987] 2 All ER 504.

to interfere unduly with media freedom, normally do not grant such injunctions when the case is contested and the claimant is unable to show that a defence of truth, honest opinion, public interest, or privilege is likely to fail at the eventual trial.[283] The Human Rights Act 1998, sub-section 12(3), is relevant in this context, for it provides that no injunctive relief may be granted to restrain a publication 'unless the court is satisfied that the applicant is likely to establish [at trial] that publication should not be allowed'. In *Cream Holdings v Banerjee*,[284] the House of Lords watered down a prior decision in which it had been stressed that sub-section 12(3) had been inserted into the 1998 Act in order to protect freedom of expression.[285] Their Lordships stated that, for the purposes of sub-section 12(3), 'likely' meant merely 'more probably than not'. Finally, according to *British Data Management plc v Boxer Commercial Removals plc*,[286] if publication of a libel is threatened but has not yet occurred, a *quia timet* injunction may be awarded if the claimant is able to set out with reasonable certainty the gist of the libel.[287] And the courts will readily grant injunctions to successful claimants if further publication of the offending statement is likely.[288]

Conclusions

It is a defence to defamation that the claimant has consented to the publication of an allegedly defamatory statement concerning him. In addition, several other defences exist that represent an attempt to balance the competing interests of freedom of speech and reputation. We have seen, for example, that it is a defence to defamation: that the statement of the defendant is of a factual nature and that the facts are proved to be true or substantially true; that, under qualified privilege, there is a common interest in publication and the statement is not made with 'malice'; the statement was on a matter of public interest and that the defendant reasonably believed that its publication was in the public interest; and the statement was in the nature of opinion, that it indicated the factual basis upon which it was made, and that it could have been held by an honest person by reference to either facts existing at the time or certain privileged statements published before the opinion.

Problem question

Donny Donaldson is a candidate for a local election running on the Bizarre Raving Loony Party ticket. He makes a statement in the local council chamber accusing a fellow

---

[283] *Bonnard v Perryman* [1891] 2 Ch 269. For illustrations see *Crest Homes Ltd v Ascott* [1980] FSR 396; *Harakas v Baltic Mercantile and Shipping Exchange Ltd* [1982] 2 All ER 701.

[284] [2004] 3 WLR 918.

[285] *Greene v Associated Newspapers Ltd* [2005] 3 WLR 281.   [286] [1996] 3 All ER 707.

[287] Note that C need not prove verbatim the wording of the threatened libel.

[288] *Monson v Tussauds Ltd* [1894] 1 QB 671.

councilor (Jodril Jeremiah) of 'squandering ratepayers' money on coffee and donuts at charity events rather than sending the money to the poor in little green envelopes'. This is reported in the *Local Gazette*, the reporter (Lilly Lamour) adding the comment that 'Mr Jeremiah has probably enjoyed a few too many donuts in his time. Who knows when he last saw his toes?' Mr Jeremiah leads a band of party members outside the offices of the *Local Gazette* chanting 'Stop the Abuse of Local Pollies. Jail Lilly Lamour for her crimes!' Lilly responds in a television interview by saying that 'Mr Jeremiah is the one who has committed the abuses. I know of several of his ex-colleagues who have had to seek the protection of the women's refuge.'

Advise the protagonists of any defences available to these defamatory statements.

 Visit **http://www.oup.com/uk/street15e/** for answer guidance.

Further reading

DESCHEEMAEKER, 'Veritas non est Defamatio?' Truth as a Defence in the Law of Defamation' (2011) 31 *Legal Studies* 1

MULLIS AND SCOTT, 'Tilting at Windmills: The Defamation Act 2013' (2014) 77 *Modern Law Review* 87

SHARLAND AND LOVELAND, 'The Defamation Act 1996 and Political Libels' [1997] *Public Law* 113

WILLIAMS, 'Defaming Politicians: The Not So Common Law' (2000) 63 *Modern Law Review* 748

YOUNG, 'Fact, Opinion and the Human Rights Act 1998' (2000) 20 *Oxford Journal of Legal Studies* 89

PART VII
Privacy

22

Privacy actions in tort

KEY ISSUES

(1) Origins of actions
Privacy actions in tort law have their origins in the equitable wrong of breach of confidence. Yet the tort actions have developed in several ways that represent significant departures from their equitable origins. Actions in tort law do not require proof of any obligation of confidentiality. Nor are they governed by the traditional maxims of equity. In this way, privacy actions in tort law have fully seceded from their equitable foundations.

(2) Human rights considerations
An important backdrop to the operation of the privacy actions in tort is the European Convention on Human Rights. The case law reveals a strong influence being exerted by both the Article 8 right to respect for privacy and the (often conflicting) Article 10 right to freedom of expression

(3) Gist of the tort actions
An established action in tort lies where X unjustifiably discloses to others private information concerning Y. The key elements of the tort are that (1) there should be a reasonable expectation of that information that it should be kept private; and (2) the disclosure of that information is unjustified. In addition to this action, there is a nascent action in tort for unwarranted intrusions into the private lives of others.

(4) Defences
Beyond the role played by public interest in judging whether a disclosure was justified, two defences of potential significance are (1) consent to the disclosure or intrusion; and (2) the fact that private information (barring photographic information, which is treated differently) is already in the public domain.

Section 1 Introduction

Privacy Privacy might be conceptualised as freedom from unwanted oversight.[1] Securing privacy permits rest, self-reflection, learning, the protection of dignity, the enjoyment of intimacy with others, and/or facilitates all kinds of interactions between persons. It does not necessarily entail living in a state of solitude, because persons in

---

[1] R Wacks, *Privacy and Media Freedom* (2013), 21 (referring to 'unwanted gape').

close relationships will have a legitimate desire for privacy, as will those who deal at arm's length in business and other settings. In order to obtain a state of privacy, frequently individuals will create 'barriers' to oversight through various means, including physical, behavioural, and cultural barriers.[2] Privacy is infringed when what a person does or says is, without consent, communicated to others so that they may see, hear, or read about these things.[3]

Challenges to privacy Modern life presents many challenges to individual privacy. These arise from a number of sources including the density of urban living, the development of surveillance and other technologies, the interests of the State in security and crime control, and the insatiable hunger of the media for news, information, and photographic imagery. Tort law is incapable of addressing the full width of privacy concerns (in part because of disagreement about the extent to which privacy should be respected),[4] but it does have a part to play. In determining the proper ambit of tortious protection, courts inevitably need to contend with the countervailing factors of truth and freedom of speech.

Background to tort Whereas the wrongful invasion of privacy has been recognised for some time as the basis for an action in tort in the United States[5] and New Zealand,[6] privacy actions in tort have appeared more recently in English law. These actions have a complicated history, which has seen them branch off[7] from the equitable action for breach of confidence (which remains focused upon the source of information rather than its content)[8] and has been informed by the incorporation of relevant provisions of the European Convention on Human Rights into English law through the Human Rights Act 1998. The birth of the main action for misuse of private information can be located in the House of Lords' decision in *Campbell v MGN Ltd*,[9] which provided a remedy for publication of photos of a model leaving a meeting of Narcotics Anonymous. Each year that passes provides further confirmation that a new tort has been established. However, the case law obfuscates this development to some extent because of its continued extensive reference to the European Convention. The Convention has no necessary implication for the common law of tort, so long as the fundamental rights and freedoms embodied within it are protected somewhere in English law. In the circumstances, it appears that English tort law can now stand on its own feet in offering protection for misuse of private information and related actions. Before discussing the tort actions in detail, the wider context of protection for privacy is examined, starting with the European Convention.

---

[2] K Hughes (2012) 75 MLR 806, esp. 810 and 812.   [3] S Todd (2015) 27 SAcLJ 731, 731.

[4] See R Wacks, *Privacy and Media Freedom* (2013), 8 and 240 (advocating a narrow approach so that legal rules can be applied with a degree of certainty).

[5] Second Restatement of Torts at §§ 652A–652I (1977).   [6] *Hosking v Runting* [2004] NZCA 34.

[7] *Vidal-Hall v Google, Inc* [2015] 3 WLR 409, at [21] (separate and distinct causes of action, misuse of private information being a tort) and [43] (the misuse tort has no equitable characteristics).

[8] R Wacks, *Privacy and Media Freedom* (2013), 79–80.   [9] [2004] 2 AC 457.

European Convention   Article 8 of the European Convention imposes the obligation on all public authorities (including the police, immigration authorities, etc) to respect private life.[10] Given that the courts are public authorities for these purposes, coupled with the fact that they are required to develop the common law consistently with the rights embodied in the Convention,[11] it seems apparent that the Convention enjoys a measure of 'horizontal effect'. One basis for this contention is the fact that the European Court of Human Rights has intimated that Article 8 does more than merely impose a negative obligation on the state and public bodies *not to interfere with* citizens' privacy. It also 'may involve the adoption of [positive] measures designed to secure respect for private life even in the sphere of the relations of individuals between themselves'.[12] As mentioned earlier, Article 8 has informed the development of the tort of misuse of private information in English law, there being extensive reference to it in the case law.

Extant actions   But even beyond the application of the Convention, there are several extant torts that provide some, albeit incidental, protection to our interest in privacy. For example, the law of private nuisance is helpful inasmuch as it confers a cause of action in relation to substantial and unreasonable interferences with the use or enjoyment of land. Equally, the tort of trespass to land offers protection against physical intrusions; while the law of defamation seeks to guard our reputations against the publication of harmful untruths. Most significantly, however—at least in common law terms—has been the rapid evolution of the protection of privacy out of the longstanding equitable obligation to respect confidences. Indeed, as one judge explained:

> In the great majority of situations where the protection of privacy was justified, an action for breach of confidence would provide the necessary protection … . A duty of confidence would arise whenever the party subject to the duty was in a situation where he either knew or ought to [have] know[n] that the other party could reasonably expect his privacy to be protected. The range of situations in which protection can be provided is therefore extensive.[13]

Thus, at the turn of the Millennium, the prevailing view was that any general protection of privacy was 'grounded … in the *equitable doctrine* of breach of confidence'.[14] Indeed, it took another half a decade before a senior judge was prepared to accept that a new *tort* based on the misuse of private information had emerged.

Privacy tort Cognisant of Commonwealth authority,[15] in *Campbell v MGN*[16] Lord Nicholls noted that the relevant cause of action had 'shaken off the limiting constraint of the need

---

[10]   The European Court of Human Rights' conception of private life under the article is expansive. See, eg, *Axel Springer AG v Germany* [2012] EMLR 15, at [83].

[11]   Human Rights Act 1998, ss 2 and 6.

[12]   *Von Hannover v Germany* (2005) 40 EHRR 1, at [57]. On the other hand, the Convention right could not be construed so as to impose on newspapers a duty to inform people in advance when the newspaper editors propose to publish information which concerns them: *Mosley v UK* [2011] ECHR 774.

[13]   *A v B plc (a company)* [2002] EMLR 371, at 382.

[14]   *Douglas v Hello! Ltd (No 1)* [2001] QB 967, at 1001 (emphasis added).

[15]   *Hosking v Runting* [2004] NZCA 34. In that case, the New Zealand Court of Appeal identified two heads of liability: one, in equity, protecting confidentiality; the other, in tort, protecting wrongful publicity about private lives.   [16]   [2004] 2 AC 457.

for an initial confidential relationship' before suggesting that '*the tort* is better encapsulated now as a misuse of private information'.[17] Although his Lordship was the only member of the House of Lords to describe the action in terms of a tort, there are now such profound differences between the action for misuse of private information and the action for breach of confidence that it was correct for him to have seen the action in this way.[18] We can take it, then, that a new tort—albeit one falling short of the general protection of privacy—was recognised in *Campbell v MGN*, the facts of which case were as follows:

C, a famous model, claimed damages from D, a newspaper group, in respect of an alleged breach of confidence and an infringement of her privacy rights under the Human Rights Act 1998. D had published (1) stories about C attending Narcotics Anonymous; (2) details of her treatment for drug addiction; and (3) a photograph of her at a place where Narcotics Anonymous held meetings. C was prepared to concede that the *Daily Mirror* was entitled to publish the fact that she was a drug addict and that she was in need of treatment, but she alleged that publication of the details of her treatment together with the photograph were a step too far and that this amounted to a wrongful publication by the newspaper of private information.

Recognising fully the need to balance the newspaper group's right to freedom of expression against Ms Campbell's right to respect for privacy, the House of Lords held by a bare majority that publication of Ms Campbell's treatment details along with the photograph suggesting her attendance at a Narcotics Anonymous meeting was indeed a step too far. These details were more than what was necessary to put the record straight (bearing in mind that Ms Campbell had lied in public previously, denying her drug addiction). That being so, her claim not to have private information concerning her misused in this way succeeded. However, the most remarkable feature of the case was the way in which the action was viewed: namely, as an action based on the misuse of private information. The subsequent case law has endorsed this understanding of the common law.[19]

Section 2 Elements of the actions

(A) General observations

In the immediate wake of the *Campbell* case, it seemed to have been confirmed that the misuse of private information of a *personal* kind could ground an action for damages. Subsequently, the House of Lords had occasion to consider whether commercially exploitable private information—in the form of photographs taken at a celebrity wedding—would attract the same protection.[20] In *Douglas v Hello! Ltd (No 3)*, their

---

[17] [2004] 2 AC 457, at [14] (emphasis added).

[18] Apart from the absence of any need to impart the information in circumstances attracting confidentiality, another salient difference is the absence of any need to apply the traditional equitable maxims.

[19] See, eg, *JIH v NGM Ltd* [2011] EMLR 9, at [55]; *Thornton v TMG Ltd* [2010] EWHC 1414, at [36]; *Murray v Express Newspapers* [2008] 3 WLR 1360, at [27].

[20] [2008] 1 AC 1. This approach is consistent with the way in which the argument proceeded in *Vestergaard Frandsen A/S v Bestnet Europe Ltd* [2013] 1 WLR 1556.

Lordships held that such commercially valuable private information, at least in the hands of a publisher, was to be regarded as falling within the existing law on breach of confidence.[21] That being so, commercially exploitable information must be distinguished from purely private information with no intrinsic commercial value. Lord Hoffmann put it this way: '[t]he information in this case was capable of being protected, not because it concerned the ... private life [of Michael Douglas and Catherine Zeta-Jones], but simply because it was information of commercial value over which the Douglases had sufficient control to enable them to impose an obligation of confidence'.[22]

To some extent, the decision in this case might be seen as a retrograde one in that it stymies the development of the new tort of misuse of private information. It represents a significant departure from the orthodox approach to the equitable obligation to maintain a confidence in that it involved 'information' acquired by the publisher from a third party, rather than information provided by the Douglases in confidence. Nonetheless, the fact remains that the case was dealt with on the basis of the equitable action, and for this reason it must be seen as running parallel to the new tort where information of intrinsic commercial value is concerned.

(B) Private information and 'reasonable expectation'

(1) General principles

Private nature Not all personal information attracts the protection of the privacy tort. This is because, as *Campbell v MGN Ltd* insists, the claimant must be able to show also that she held a reasonable expectation that the information in question would be kept private.[23] As the main tort action in privacy is limited to the misuse of private information, misuse of public information cannot ground an action.[24] But this simple statement does not tell the full story. First, we need to bear in mind the principle according to which something should *not* be construed as being common knowledge just because all the relevant component parts of a particular piece of information are in the public domain already. Thus, just because the public could find something out by putting A and B together in order to get C (when A and B are already common knowledge), this does not mean that C cannot be regarded as protected information. If a member of the public has to go through the process of putting A and B together in order to possess the precise information constituting C, then C may well be regarded as private information.[25] Second, the courts appear to have become willing to protect private information by way of injunction in appropriate cases, despite the availability of protected information on the internet; that is to the extent that protection is possible still in order to avoid the *further* harm that would come from publication in hard copy form—such as in the newspapers.[26]

---

[21] [2008] 1 AC 1, at [113]–[119].   [22] [2008] 1 AC 1, at [124].

[23] *Campbell v MGN* [2004] 2 AC 457, at [21] and [85], and [134].

[24] *BBC v Harper Collins Publishers Ltd* [2011] EMLR 6.

[25] *Saltman Engineering Co v Campbell Engineering Co* (1948) 65 RPC 203.

[26] *PJS v News Group Newspapers Ltd* [2016] AC 1081 (case of intrusion with the potential for a 'media storm').

Reasonable expectation The issue is: what factors will be taken to generate the requisite 'reasonable expectation' of privacy? The courts have held the test to be an objective one, to be looked at from the point of view of the person whose privacy is at stake. The court will look at all of the circumstances in a broad way. Factors that are relevant to this issue include:[27] the attributes of the claimant, including her age;[28] the nature of the activity in which the claimant was engaged; the place at which the activity was happening—taking into account that expectations of privacy arise sometimes even when the person is in a public place such as a café or swimming pool;[29] the nature and purpose of the use of information in question; the purposes for which the information came into the hands of the publisher; and the effect of publication on the claimant, which might involve consideration not simply of what was subjectively experienced, but of the wider impact upon her.[30] The courts will be more assiduous to protect private information concerning children.[31] The fact of minority creates a strong presumption that information about the claimant will be kept private. However, in determining the extent of protection offered (including whether an injunction should be granted to prevent publicity), the court has little choice but to take into account relevant actions of the parents which have compromised the child's reasonable expectation of privacy.[32]

Scope of principle In determining to what extent a reasonable expectation of privacy arises, the courts acknowledge that privacy has several layers and that they are more likely to protect deeper layers without necessarily protecting more superficial layers. Thus, in one case it was observed that there might be a pertinent difference between publicising 'the bare fact of a relationship', such as an extramarital affair, and publicising 'information as to the contents or details of that relationship'.[33] This takes account of the fact that the public might be seen to have an interest in the general point about the relationship, which could, for example, impact upon a politician's fitness for office or a sportsman's integrity in advertising a product.

(2) Examples of information protected by the tort

There is no set type of information in respect of which the claimant can assert a reasonable expectation of privacy. But the following two kinds of information are among the more prevalent types:

(a) Information about health and medical conditions

In just the same way that disclosures of medical information have been taken to be capable of grounding an action in equity based on breach of confidence, the *Campbell*

---

[27] *In re JR38* [2015] 3 WLR 155, at [88]; *Weller v Associated Newspapers Ltd* [2016] 1 WLR 1541; *Murray v Express Newspapers plc* [2009] Ch 481, at [35]–[36].

[28] *Weller v Associated Newspapers Ltd* [2016] 1 WLR 1541, at [31].

[29] *Weller v Associated Newspapers Ltd* [2016] 1 WLR 1541, at [61].

[30] *Weller v Associated Newspapers Ltd* [2016] 1 WLR 1541, at [36].

[31] *AAA v Associated Newspapers Ltd* [2013] EWCA Civ 554, at [10]–[11]; *K v News Group Newspapers* [2011] 1 WLR 1827, at [19].

[32] *AAA v Associated Newspapers Ltd* [2013] EWCA Civ 554, at [33]–[34].

[33] *Hutcheson v News Group Newspapers Ltd* [2012] EMLR 2, at [26]. See also *Browne v Associated Newspapers Ltd* [2008] QB 103, at [57] ff.

case[34] indicates that such information can form the basis for an action under the new tort of misuse of private information. However, there would appear to be an important distinction between the two actions in this context. The tort only permits claims by those to whom the information relates personally. By contrast, it would appear possible for, say, a hospital which compiles and holds patients' medical records to invoke the equitable action since it, too, has a vested interest in their confidentiality being maintained.[35]

(b) Sexual information

Unauthorised disclosure of private details concerning one's sexual relationships (or even sexuality)[36] can result in commission of the tort. As Lord Mance stated in *PJS v News Group Newspapers Ltd*, 'the starting point is [] that there is not, without more, any public interest in a legal sense in the disclosure or publication of purely private sexual encounters, even though they involve adultery or more than one person at a time'.[37] However, such information might not always give rise to a reasonable expectation of privacy. If, for example, the claimant were a public figure whose honesty could be seen to turn on the disclosure of such factual information, there might be a case for disclosing so much of the otherwise private information as is necessary in the public interest to confirm or refute the allegations about that person's honesty. So, as Lord Woolf CJ put it in one case: 'where a public figure chooses to make untrue pronouncements about his or her life, the press will normally be entitled to put the record straight'.[38] If the sexual conduct of the claimant is criminal in nature, this too would apparently justify disclosure.[39]

(C) Unjustified disclosures

General An important limit on the availability of this misuse tort made clear in the *Campbell* case is that disclosure, in order to be actionable, must have been unjustified. Determination of what amounts to an 'unjustified disclosure' involves examining the whole context in which disclosure is made and balancing two competing human rights—viz, the right to respect for our private lives and the right to freedom of expression—neither of which is absolute.

European Convention The balancing exercise to be undertaken as between the imperatives of Articles 8 and 10 of the European Convention is to be undertaken in a structured way. According to Lord Mance in *PJS v News Group Newspapers Ltd*, the authorities have established the following rules:[40] first, the presumption is that neither

---

[34] See also *Z v Finland* (1997) 25 EHRR 371.
[35] See *Ashworth Security Hospital v MGN* [2001] FSR 559.
[36] See, eg, *Dudgeon v UK* (1981) 4 EHRR 149.   [37] [2016] AC 1081, at [32].
[38] *A v B* [2003] QB 195, at [43]. This does not mean, however, that public figures have *no* right to privacy. If their honesty is not in question, there is no reason why matters completely unrelated to their public lives should not attract protection: *X v Persons Unknown* [2007] EMLR 10.
[39] *LNS v Persons Unknown* [2010] EWHC 119.
[40] [2016] AC 1081, at [20].

Article is to be preferred over the other; second, where their values are in conflict, it is necessary for the court to study with 'an intense focus' the 'comparative importance of the rights being claimed in the individual case'; third, 'the justifications for interfering with or restricting each right must be taken into account'. Finally, any restriction on the exercise of free speech must be proportionate with the nature of the interests at stake.

Public interest In *Campbell v MGN Ltd*, Baroness Hale identified that there were different classes of speech, each of which warranted different levels of protection. While she saw political free speech as central to a democratic society, she indicated that mere gossip serving no political, educational, or artistic purpose would be more difficult to justify (even though it might help to sell certain publications) if it were to impact negatively on another's privacy interest.[41] Equally, she envisaged a general freedom to discuss the private lives of 'public figures, especially those in elective office' since this otherwise private information might well be 'relevant to their participation in public life'.[42] In essence, what her Ladyship was describing was a 'public interest' justification for the disclosure of otherwise private information. Subsequent cases demonstrate the importance of this matter in the context of the misuse of private information.[43] Thus, in order to justify disclosure, the information must of its very nature be of a kind that ought to be disclosed.[44] So, for example, the expression of legitimate doubt about the safety of criminal convictions might well be taken to be a matter of public interest:

> In *Lion Laboratories Ltd v Evans*,[45] Cs sought to prevent publication of internal memoranda leaked by employees to the press. The memoranda cast doubt on the reliability of the intoximeter manufactured by Cs and used by the police to test alcohol levels in drivers. The Court of Appeal refused to grant an injunction. The public interest in the reliability of the product which could, if unreliable, result in unfair prosecutions outweighed any private rights of Cs. Disclosure of this information to the proper authorities was therefore justified.

On the other hand, the release of private information that satisfies the mere prurient interest of members of the public will not qualify as being in the public interest. Thus, as Eady J has put it: 'it is not for the state or for the media to expose sexual conduct which does not involve any significant breach of the criminal law'.[46]

Other factors Other factors have been identified which might be examined in undertaking the balancing exercise between the interests protected by each of Articles 8 and

---

[41] *Campbell v MGN* [2004] 2 AC 457, at [148]. See also *K v News Group Newspapers* [2011] 1 WLR 1827, at [21].

[42] *Campbell v MGN* [2004] 2 AC 457, at [148]. Others in respect of whom there is apparently an equivalent public interest include clergymen, headmasters, and senior civil servants (*McKennit v Ash* [2008] QB 73) as well as high-profile bankers at a time of banking crisis (*Goodwin v NGN Ltd* [2011] EWHC 1437).

[43] See, eg, *Goodwin v NGN Ltd* [2011] EWHC 1437; *JIH v NGN Ltd* [2011] EMLR 15; *Mosley v NGN Ltd* [2008] EMLR 20.

[44] *Cambridge Nutrition Ltd v BBC* [1990] 3 All ER 523.   [45] [1985] QB 526.

[46] *Mosley v NGN Ltd* [2008] EMLR 20, at [127]. See also *PJS v News Group Newspapers Ltd* [2016] AC 1081, at [21], [24], and [32].

10 of the European Convention. These were identified in *Weller v Associated Newspapers Ltd* as being:[47]

> (i) how well known is the person concerned and what is the subject of the report; (ii) the prior conduct of the person concerned; (iii) the content, form and consequences of the publication and (iv) the circumstances in which the [misuse occurred].

(D) Intrusions into private life

The protection of private information is just one example of the ways in which tort law has the potential to protect privacy interests. Absent any general tort protecting privacy, the courts are extending the reach of the action in tort in a measured way. In the latest development, the Supreme Court has confirmed the existence of another privacy action in tort law for *intrusions* into private life. In *PJS v News Group Newspapers Ltd*,[48] the court approved prior judicial holdings and academic commentary to the effect that: tort law is concerned with protecting privacy from intrusions, even where no private information is at stake; the focus is upon preventing intrusions which would cause substantial distress or embarrassment; this tort action is suitable to protection from publication of photographic imagery of a sexual nature. However, it appears that the tort will cover a variety of things including incursions into personal space, personal activities (such as undressing and showering), and personal affairs (such as bank account details).[49] The advantage of the new privacy action in tort is that 'it concentrates on the local and concrete harm to the claimant at a particular time',[50] especially insofar as it has an emotional or sensory impact.[51]

Although cases involving compromising and embarrassing photographs formerly were to be analysed under the main action for misuse of private information, following the *PJS* case these will tend now to fall within the tort action for privacy based on intrusion. Compromising or embarrassing photographs are a special concern for tort law given that, as Baroness Hale put it in *Campbell v MGN Ltd*, '[a] picture is "worth a thousand words" because it adds to the impact of what the words convey'.[52] Thus, while it is one thing to report in words that X is a drug addict, it is another thing to publish a photograph of X in all her drug-addicted misery. It was for this reason that the Court of Appeal in *Douglas v Hello! Ltd* pointed out that, insofar 'as a photograph does more than convey information and intrudes on privacy by enabling the viewer to focus on intimate personal detail, there will be a fresh intrusion of privacy when each additional viewer sees the photograph'.[53] That being so, although there was an agreement with *OK! Magazine* that various authorised photographs could be published, this did 'not, however, provide a defence to a claim … [based on] the publication of unauthorised

---

[47] [2016] 1 WLR 1541, at [73].

[48] [2016] AC 1081, at [29] and [32]; citing *CTB v News Group Newspapers Ltd* [2011] EWHC 1326 (QB); *Goodwin v News Group Newspapers Ltd* [2011] EMLR 27; and Warby et al (eds), *Tugendhat and Christie's The Law of Privacy and the Media* (2nd edn, 2011).

[49] S Todd (2015) 27 SAcLJ 731, 752–6.   [50] OM Butler (2016) 75 CLJ 452, 455.

[51] S Todd (2015) 27 SAcLJ 731, 735.   [52] [2004] 2 AC 457, at [155].

[53] *Douglas v Hello! Ltd* (No 6) [2006] QB 125, at [105].

photographs'.[54] Furthermore, the fact that pictures are taken in a public place does not necessarily undermine their intrusiveness if published. If their taking and publication were unauthorised, and particularly if the photographs were taken covertly, an action is potentially available.[55]

Section 3 Defences and remedies

Defences It has been established already that a disclosure of private information in the public interest provides a justification for that disclosure. But, in terms of defences, we must note that it will be a defence to show that the disclosure was made with the prior consent/authorisation of the claimant.[56]

Remedies in general As regards remedies, both injunctions[57] (prior to disclosure) and compensatory damages[58] (after disclosure) will be available. Also, where X has obtained possession of certain private personal information concerning Y it will be possible to obtain an order for the return of the confidential documents.[59]

Injunctions If there has been disclosure of private information, it is a question of fact and degree as to whether substantial privacy remains. One distinction is that between 'information which is made available to a person's circle of friends or work colleagues and information which is widely published in a newspaper'.[60] However, in *PJS v News Group Newspapers Ltd*,[61] the Supreme Court was prepared to uphold an injunction despite significant online publication of private information in order to prevent further harm being done. In determining whether or not to issue (or uphold) an interim injunction against publication by the media, the court must consider Human Rights Act 1998, section 12, which contains certain safeguards for freedom of expression. Thus, sub-section (3) provides that no relief 'is to be granted so as to restrain publication before trial unless the court is satisfied that the applicant is likely to establish that publication should not be allowed'. Under sub-section (4) the court is required to have particular regard to the importance of the Convention right to freedom of expression and, where the proceedings relate to material which appears to be journalistic, literary,

---

[54] *Douglas v Hello! Ltd* (No 6) [2006] QB 125, at [107].

[55] *Campbell v MGN* [2004] 2 AC 457, at [134]. See also *Peck v UK* [2003] EMLR 15, where an attempted suicide was captured on CCTV and the European Court of Human Rights held that it was a breach of Art 8 of the European Convention to disclose that footage to newspapers and broadcasters.

[56] *Weller v Associated Newspapers Ltd* [2016] 1 WLR 1541, at [35]. For further statutory defences, see Investigatory Powers Act 2016.

[57] Guidelines on the issue of interim non-disclosure orders are available: Practice Guidance (Interim Non-disclosure Orders) [2012] 1 WLR 1003. These emphasise that interim injunctive relief will be granted in exceptional cases only.

[58] Eg, *Gulati v MGN Ltd* [2017] QB 149 (damages for loss of control following misuse of information and for mental distress).

[59] See, eg, *Tchenguiz v Immerman* [2011] 2 WLR 592.

[60] *Browne v Associated Newspapers Ltd* [2008] QB 103, at [61].   [61] [2016] AC 1081.

or artistic material to (1) the extent to which (i) the material has, or is about to, become available to the public or (ii) it is, or would be, in the public interest for the material to be published; and to (2) any relevant privacy code.

Exemplary damages Although there has been a question whether exemplary damages are available for this tort,[62] it is hard to see why such damages should not be available where the disclosure of information has made the defendant a profit that exceeds the compensatory sum payable to the claimant.[63] In any case, the award of both aggravated and exemplary damages in privacy actions against relevant media defendants for the publication of news-related material is now subject to Crime and Courts Act 2013, sections 34–42 (considered in chapter 21).

Conclusions

There is no general right to privacy in English law. Rather, the courts have (over the last 20 years or so) been developing narrow bases upon which an action based on breaches of interests in privacy might be brought. In this chapter, we have seen that there are two such tort causes of action at the moment—both of which are still developing. One relates to the misuse of private information and the other relates to intrusions upon the claimant's private life. Given the increasing array of electronic and other threats to privacy, one can expect this to be an area of tort with growing importance.

Problem question

At the Wallingsworth School, the principal Joyce Jayce gave a speech about the importance of morality and marital fidelity. Two students from the school, Adi and Bobbi, suspect that Joyce might not practice what she preaches. One night they sneak on to Joyce's property. Through the venetian blinds, they are able to see that Joyce is engaged in a sexual liaison with the two deputy principals from the school. Bobbi takes a photo of this tryst with her iPhone. The next morning, Adi and Bobbi wave a placard at the school gates which reads: 'Principal Joyce and Deputy Principals in Love Tryst. Our School's Morality Revealed'. Joyce denies any wrongdoing. The local press take an interest in this story and the next morning there is a headline in the *Wallingsworth Sentinel* 'Love Tryst at Local School Revealed', along with a picture of the love-making scene.

Advise Joyce about any actions that she might have for breaches of the right to privacy.

 Visit **http://www.oup.com/uk/street15e/** for answer guidance.

---

[62] *Mosley v NGN Ltd* [2008] EMLR 20.
[63] Such a case would seem to fall neatly within the second category of case for which exemplary damages might be sought according to *Rookes v Barnard* [1964] AC 1129. For details, see ch 26.

Further reading

GILIKER, 'A Common Law Tort of Privacy? The Challenges of Developing a Human Rights Tort' (2015) 27 *Singapore Academy of Law Journal* 761

HUGHES, 'A Behavioural Understanding of Privacy and its Implications for Privacy Law' (2012) 75 *Modern Law Review* 806

KENYON AND RICHARDSON (eds), *New Dimensions in Privacy Law: International and Comparative Perspectives* (2006)

McDONALD, 'Privacy Claims: Transformation, Fault, and the Public Interest Defence' in Dyson et al, *Defences in Tort* (2015), ch 15

MOREHAM, 'Beyond Information: Physical Privacy in English Law' (2014) 73 *Cambridge Law Journal* 350

MOREHAM, 'Unpacking the Reasonable Expectation of Privacy Test' (2018) 134 *Law Quarterly Review* (forthcoming)

PHILLIPSON, 'Transforming Breach of Confidence? Towards a Common Law Right of Privacy under the Human Rights Act' (2003) 66 *Modern Law Review* 726

PHILLIPSON, 'Privacy: the Development of Breach of Confidence—The Clearest Case of Horizontal Effect?' in D Hoffman (ed), *The Impact of the UK Human Rights Act on Private Law* (2011), ch 7

RICHARDSON, *The Right to Privacy: Origins and Influence of a Nineteenth-Century Idea* (2017)

WACKS, *Privacy and Media Freedom* (2013)

PART VIII
Misuse of process and public powers

23

Misuse of process and public powers

KEY ISSUES

(1) Three main torts
In this chapter, three principal causes of action are considered: malicious prosecution, abuse of process, and misfeasance in a public office. Malicious prosecution arises where the defendant is responsible for a legal claim brought against the claimant without reasonable cause, this claim being determined in the claimant's favour in circumstances where the defendant was actuated by malice in prosecuting the claim and where the claimant has suffered damage as a result. Abuse of process arises where the defendant has commenced legal proceedings for a wrongful predominant purpose. Unlike the case with malicious prosecution, there is no need for the claimant to prove want of reasonable and probable cause or that the proceedings were terminated in his favour. Also by contrast to malicious prosecution, damage to fame, person, or property need not be proved. *Any* special damage suffices.

Misfeasance in a public office arises where egregious and improper administrative action, which the relevant officer knows to be unlawful, causes loss to an individual.

(2) Common issues
In each of the three torts a balance must be struck between the protection of individuals' interests and rights, on the one hand, and the efficient conduct of public administration and the administration of justice, on the other. To help ensure that a proper balance is struck, the need to show malice becomes an important touchstone of liability in the first and third causes of action.

(3) Immunity
This chapter explains relevant aspects of the law on the immunity of witnesses for what is said in court and in preparation for giving evidence in court. Neither malicious prosecution nor misfeasance in public office is defeated by this immunity.

Section 1 Introduction

The motive with which an act is done generally does not make that act tortious. As we shall see in this chapter, there are certain limited exceptions to that general rule. The essence of the wrongful conduct in the following group of torts is the misuse of rights conferred on individuals for the public good. It is the abuse of those rights for private benefit or other improper ends that gives rise to tortious liability.

Section 2 Malicious prosecution

Origins and purpose Malicious prosecution protects the interest that persons have in freedom from unjustifiable litigation. It arises where the defendant is responsible for a legal claim brought against the claimant without reasonable cause, this claim being determined in the claimant's favour in circumstances where the defendant was actuated by malice in prosecuting the claim and where the claimant has suffered damage as a result.[1] The origins of the tort lie at a point in English legal history when most *criminal* prosecutions were brought privately (although enforcement of the criminal law by private parties was itself of benefit to the state). The problem was that the 'fact that the state's coercive powers were invoked by a private individual, who controlled both the initiation and conduct of the proceedings, gave rise to frequent abuse . . .'.[2] The object of the tort is to remedy such abuse.[3] Today there are few private prosecutions[4] so that some question has been raised about the importance of this tort in its application to criminal proceedings. However, the tort lives on because it has been extended to cover the malicious commencement of *civil* proceedings.[5]

(A) Elements of the tort

(1) Institution of wrongful proceedings

Actively instrumental The defendant to a claim of malicious prosecution must have been 'actively instrumental' in instigating the proceedings which are complained about.[6] In *Martin v Watson*,[7] the House of Lords confirmed the ancient rule that, if X merely gives information to a magistrate[8] or a police officer,[9] upon which the magistrate or police officer *independently* decides to launch a prosecution, that does not render X a prosecutor for the purposes of this tort. The decision to prosecute rests with the public officials who determine that legal proceedings against the claimant should go ahead.[10]

---

[1] *Willers v Joyce* [2016] 3 WLR 477, at [5].
[2] *Crawford Adjusters v Sagicor General Insurance (Cayman) Ltd* [2013] 3 WLR 927, at [136].
[3] *Martin v Watson* [1994] 2 All ER 606; *Gregory v Portsmouth CC* [2000] 1 AC 419.
[4] *Willers v Joyce* [2016] 3 WLR 477, at [131].
[5] *Willers v Joyce* [2016] 3 WLR 477; *Crawford Adjusters v Sagicor General Insurance (Cayman) Ltd* [2013] 3 WLR 927.   [6] *Danby v Beardsley* (1880) 43 LT 603, at 604.
[7] [1996] AC 74.   [8] *Cohen v Morgan* (1825) 6 Dow & Ry KB 8.
[9] *Danby v Beardsley* (1880) 43 LT 603. Nor will supplying information to police which is used to ground an arrest engage liability for false imprisonment: *Davidson v CC of North Wales* [1994] 2 All ER 597.
[10] This is in direct contrast to circumstances where D initiates a private prosecution. However, note that there might be cases where a public prosecution is brought, but on the facts of the case D effectively has required that the prosecution go ahead, formally accepting responsibility for the initiation of the relevant proceedings: see, eg, *Mohamed Amin v Jogendra Kumar Bannerjee* [1947] AC 322.

However, where one police officer is in truth and substance the originator of a prosecution which is brought by another then that first officer will be responsible for 'having set the law in motion against the' claimant.[11]

The deliberate provision of false information *might* need to be treated differently where the complainant is the sole person who has knowledge of the facts pertaining to the alleged offence. In *Martin v Watson*,[12] the defendant had a history of ill-feeling towards the claimant. She set out deliberately to deceive police officers by making an entirely false allegation that the claimant had exposed himself to her on several occasions. The House of Lords held her liable for malicious prosecution because the facts relating to the alleged offences were known only to her, removing any possibility that the police had exercised independent judgement in bringing the prosecution. It was appropriate to treat the defendant as having procured the subsequent prosecution.

Following the Supreme Court decision in *Willers v Joyce*[13] (discussed in section 3), courts might have to devise analogous rules about who in truth and substance is to be regarded as the originator of wrongfully brought *civil* proceedings.

Relevant proceedings The tort of malicious prosecution lies where the claimant has been subjected to a criminal prosecution as a consequence of which he lost, or risked losing, his liberty and/or his reputation and/or the cost of defending the charge.[14] Traditionally, actions have been available also for certain civil proceedings which have the potential to result in grave prejudice at, or close to, the outset of proceedings,[15] including maliciously procuring a warrant of arrest[16] and maliciously procuring a search warrant[17] (although the latter actions typically fail[18] because the damage to the claimant ensues not from the warrant being granted, but from its execution through entry into his premises, or the seizure of property).

In *Crawford Adjusters v Sagicor General Insurance (Cayman) Ltd*,[19] the Privy Council held that actions would lie with respect to the wrongful institution of civil proceedings for fraudulent misrepresentation (deceit) and conspiracy. This was in circumstances where the senior vice-president of the claimant company tipped off the media as to a wrongful allegation, resulting in 'massive damage' to the defendant's reputation and 'to the willingness of third parties to employ him'. In upholding the defendant's counter-claim in malicious prosecution, Lord Wilson stated that:

> Substantial damage to the reputation of [a claimant] can be caused by false allegations being made in civil proceedings long before it is restored, even if full restoration is then possible, by his vindication at trial.[20]

---

[11] *Comr of Police v Copeland* [2014] EWCA Civ 1014, at [26] (quoting *Martin v Watson* [1996] 1 AC 74, at 80) and [27]. [12] [1996] AC 74.

[13] [2016] 3 WLR 477.

[14] *Manley v MPC* [2006] EWCA Civ 879.

[15] So described, without the adjective, in *Crawford Adjusters v Sagicor General Insurance (Cayman) Ltd* [2013] 3 WLR 927, at [67]. Eight exceptional cases are set out. [16] *Roy v Prior* [1971] AC 470.

[17] *Gibbs v Rea* [1998] AC 786.

[18] See *Gibbs v Rea* [1998] AC 786, at 797; *Reynolds v MPC* [1985] QB 881. [19] [2014] AC 366.

[20] [2014] AC 366, at [61].

This point was affirmed by the other Law Lords in the majority, Lord Kerr believing that the instant case was a 'graphic example of the inadequacy of alternative torts'.[21] The view of the majority, expressed by Lord Wilson, was that there was a need for 'the law to be true to the reasons for its very existence', which is that 'wrongs should be remedied'.[22] This sentiment informed the subsequent decision of a specially constituted UK Supreme Court in *Willers v Joyce*[23] to extend the tort of malicious prosecution so that it applies to the malicious commencement of civil proceedings more generally. Lord Clarke stated that there is:[24]

> no sensible basis for accepting that the tort of malicious prosecution of a crime exists in English law, whereas the tort of malicious prosecution of a civil action does not. Not only are the ingredients the same, but it seems to me that, if a claimant is entitled to recover damages against a person who maliciously prosecutes him for an alleged crime, a claimant should also be entitled to recover damages against a person who maliciously brings civil proceedings against him. The latter class of case can easily cause a claimant very considerable losses. They will often be considerably greater than in a case of malicious prosecution of criminal proceedings.

Although there is some strength in the underlying arguments, Lord Mance, dissenting in the *Willers* case, warned that 'the recognition of a general tort in respect of civil proceedings' will carry the 'law into unchartered waters, inviting fresh litigation about prior litigation, the soundness of its basis, its motivation and its consequences'.[25] Time will tell whether this is so.

(2) Termination in favour of the claimant

In order to sue for malicious prosecution, the proceedings upon which the claim is based must have terminated in the claimant's favour.[26] Even though the claimant has been convicted of a lesser offence,[27] or has had his conviction quashed on appeal,[28] or has been acquitted on a technicality (for example, a defect in the indictment),[29] this requirement is satisfied. The same *might* be true where the claimant has escaped prosecution for offence X but the facts alleged in seeking to secure a prosecution for that offence are passed on by the police to a local authority in order that it may obtain an anti-social behaviour order against the claimant.[30] However, if the conviction of the claimant stands, there is no possibility of obtaining a remedy in this tort.[31] Finally, the claimant appears to satisfy the test of successful termination if he proves that the

---

[21] [2014] AC 366, at [118].   [22] [2014] AC 366, at [73].   [23] [2016] 3 WLR 477.

[24] *Willers v Joyce* [2016] 3 WLR 477, at [86]. There is a logical flaw in the reasoning in the second sentence of this quote, given that there never was an established rule that actions could be brought with respect to failed civil claims until determined in this very case—let alone a parallel or separate tort.

[25] *Willers v Joyce* [2016] 3 WLR 477, at [132].

[26] This requirement is not imposed where, eg, an arrest or search warrant is procured. But it was considered applicable in an action based on an attempt to construct a tort of malicious refusal of bail: *Gizzonio v CC of Derbyshire* (1998) *The Times*, 29 April.   [27] *Boaler v Holder* (1887) 51 JP 277.

[28] *Reynolds v Kennedy* (1748) 1 Wils 232.   [29] *Wicks v Fentham* (1791) 4 Term Rep 247.

[30] *Daar v CC of Merseyside* [2005] EWCA Civ 1774.

[31] *Basébé v Matthews* (1867) LR 2 CP 684. Nor can C sue if he is merely bound over to keep the peace: *Everett v Ribbands* [1952] 2 QB 198.

defendant has discontinued the proceedings[32] (but he cannot sue while the proceedings are still pending).[33] Rules of an equivalent nature will be applicable to the wrongful commencement of civil claims.

(3) Absence of reasonable and probable cause

Malicious prosecution is treated with some caution by the courts, fearful of discouraging the enforcement of the law against suspected offenders and anxious to protect the interest in bringing litigation to a close.[34] This judicial attitude is reflected in the development of the requirement that there must be an absence of reasonable and probable cause on the part of the prosecutor. Thus, the claimant has the difficult task of proving a negative—a burden which he does not discharge merely by proving malice on the part of the defendant.[35] Furthermore, the court will not order the defendant to give particulars of the grounds on which he prosecuted.[36] The House of Lords has approved the following definition of reasonable and probable cause:

> an honest belief in the guilt of the accused based upon a full conviction, founded upon reasonable grounds, of the existence of a state of circumstances, which, assuming them to be true, would reasonably lead any ordinary prudent and cautious man, placed in the position of the accuser, to the conclusion that the person charged was probably guilty of the crime imputed.[37]

Since then it has been held, further, that, in order for the claimant to succeed on the issue of reasonable and probable cause, he must satisfy either the subjective test or the objective test of lack of (reasonable) belief[38]—as follows:

Subjective test The first alternative is that the defendant did not believe that the claimant probably was guilty of the offence or in breach of relevant civil obligations. Evidence should be given by the claimant of facts which would permit the inference that the defendant did not believe in the claimant's guilt[39] or breach of relevant civil obligations. It is not enough merely to supply evidence of reasons for non-belief. (Indeed, according to the Canadian courts, it is quite possible for a public prosecutor to have serious personal doubts about the claimant's guilt yet still have reasonable and probable cause to institute a charge against him if the evidence is strong but not entirely watertight.[40]) If such evidence is relied on, there must be evidence also that those reasons were operative in fact.

Objective test The second alternative is that a person of ordinary prudence and caution would not conclude, in the light of the facts in which he honestly believed, that the claimant probably was guilty of an offence or in breach of a civil obligation. It is impossible to enumerate all the factors relevant to deciding whether there was reasonable and probable cause.

---

[32] *Gilding v Eyre* (1861) 10 CBNS 592, at 604 (*obiter*).   [33] *Watkins v Lee* (1839) 5 M & W 270.

[34] See, eg, *Martin v Watson* [1994] 2 All ER 606 (revd [1996] AC 74).

[35] *Johnstone v Sutton* (1786) 1 Term Rep 510.   [36] *Stapley v Annetts* [1969] 3 All ER 1541.

[37] *Hicks v Faulkner* (1881) 8 QBD 167, at 171 (affd (1882) 46 LT 130); *Herniman v Smith* [1938] AC 305.

[38] *Glinski v McIver* [1962] AC 726; *Reynolds v MPC* [1985] QB 881.

[39] See, eg, *Clifford v CC of Hertfordshire* [2011] EWHC 815 (where an expert had advised the prosecutor in terms creating doubt about the soundness of a prosecution).   [40] *Miazga v Kvello* [2009] 3 SCR 339.

However, important points would be that the defendant acted in good faith on the advice of counsel[41] (although this would not be conclusive),[42] or on the advice of the police,[43] where the defendant, however honest his act, had taken reasonable care to inform himself of the facts,[44] and regardless of whether the defendant's mistake was one of fact or law.[45]

(4) Malice: improper purpose

The claimant must prove malice on the part of the defendant.[46] In this context, he must show 'any motive other than that of simply instituting a prosecution for the purpose of bringing a person to justice'[47] or proving a breach of civil obligations. The question is *not* whether the defendant is inspired by hatred or angry,[48] but whether the defendant has a purpose other than bringing an offender to justice or proving a breach of civil obligations. In other words—that the claimant's commencement of action does not constitute a bona fide use of the court's processes.[49] There is malice, for instance, if the defendant uses the commencement of proceedings as a means of blackmail or any other form of coercion. Moreover, there was evidence of malice where a defendant landlord made a charge in order to evict the claimant tenant from his house,[50] and where a defendant accused the claimant of exposing himself to her as part of a long-running vendetta between neighbours.[51] Where the motives of the defendant are mixed, the claimant will fail unless he establishes that the *dominant* purpose is something other than the vindication of the law.[52] However, it is crucial to note that a claimant who proves malice, but fails to prove want of reasonable and probable cause, still fails.[53] Therefore, should a tenant establish that his landlord has instituted proceedings against him for stealing the landlord's fixtures with the object of determining his tenancy, the tenant's action in this tort will not succeed if he fails to prove absence of reasonable cause.[54]

(5) Damage

Malicious prosecution is an action on the case meaning that damage must be proved in order to found an action.[55] In *Savile v Roberts*, Sir John Holt CJ stated that there are three kinds of damage for which the tort permitted a remedy:

> The damage to a man's fame, as if the matter whereof he is accused be scandalous . . .
>   [Damage] such as is done to the person, as where a man is put in danger to lose his life, limb or liberty, which has always allowed a good foundation of such an action . . .

---

[41] *Ravenga v Mackintosh* (1824) 2 B & C 693. Cf *Bradshaw v Waterlow & Sons Ltd* [1915] 3 KB 527.

[42] *Abbott v Refuge Assurance Co Ltd* [1962] 1 QB 432; *Howarth v Chief Constable of Gwent* [2011] EWHC 2836, at [20].   [43] *Malz v Rosen* [1966] 2 All ER 10.

[44] *Abrath v NE Rly Co* (1833) 11 QBD 440, at 451.

[45] *Philips v Naylor* (1859) 4 H & N 565. In *Riches v DPP* [1973] 2 All ER 935, it was held that allegations of malice and want of reasonable cause in an action against the DPP stood no chance of success when the committing magistrate, the trial judge, and the jury all shared the same view of the evidence held by the DPP.

[46] *Wershof v MPC* [1978] 3 All ER 540; *Brown v Hawkes* [1891] 2 QB 725.

[47] *Stevens v Midland Counties Rly Co* (1854) 10 Exch 352.

[48] *Brown v Hawkes* [1891] 2 QB 718, at 722.   [49] *Willers v Joyce* [2016] 3 WLR 477, at [55].

[50] *Turner v Ambler* (1847) 10 QB 252.   [51] *Martin v Watson* [1995] 3 All ER 559.

[52] *Abbott v Refuge Assurance Co Ltd* [1962] 1 QB 432.   [53] *Silcott v MPC* (1996) 8 Admin LR 633.

[54] *Turner v Ambler* (1847) 10 QB 252.   [55] *Savile v Roberts* (1698) 3 Salk 16; 91 ER 664.

> [D]amage to a man's property, as where he is forced to expend his money in necessary charges, to acquit himself of the crime of which he is accused.[56]

As regards reputation, damages are permitted 'irrespective of how an individual subjectively reacts' to a prosecution and whether the claimant is high-ranking or homeless.[57] In *Crawford Adjusters v Sagicor General Insurance (Cayman) Ltd,*[58] the availability of an action in circumstances of mere financial loss was affirmed. Although Lord Wilson stated that damages for such loss are available where the financial loss 'was foreseeable', with respect, this is not the ordinary principle in cases of malicious wrongdoing. Liability extends to all loss caused by the defendant's wrongdoing.

(B) The Crown Prosecution Service

The Crown Prosecution Service (CPS) and its officers enjoy no general immunity in tort, in particular against claims for malicious prosecution or misfeasance in a public office.[59] However, the CPS owes no *general*[60] duty of care in relation to the conduct of prosecutions either. The Court of Appeal has held that such liability in negligence might have an 'inhibiting effect on the discharge by the CPS of its central function of prosecuting crime'.[61] Furthermore, the courts will be vigilant to ensure that any action in malicious prosecution brought against the CPS is not in reality a disguised claim for negligence. Incompetence is not to be equated with (or taken to be evidence of) malice.[62]

(C) Defences

No questions on defences call for special comment other than that of whether it is a defence to establish that the claimant was guilty of the offence for which he was prosecuted. Obviously, in the rare case where a defendant had no reasonable cause and was malicious, and the proceedings terminated in the claimant's favour, and yet, at the trial for malicious prosecution the defendant is able to establish the guilt of the claimant, the claimant would recover very small damages at best. Indeed, there is some authority for the view that in such a case the action fails altogether.[63]

(D) Usefulness of tort

The function of malicious prosecution comes very close to that of defamation. However, malicious prosecution might arise for loss of personal liberty without damage to reputation, or for mere financial loss. There is a significant distinction also between malicious

---

[56] (1698) 1 Lr Raym 374, at [378]. See also *Manley v MPC* [2006] EWCA Civ 879.
[57] *Calix v A-G of Trinidad and Tobago* [2013] 1 WLR 3283, at [10] and [12].   [58] [2014] AC 366, at [77].
[59] *Elguzouli-Daf v MPC* [1995] QB 335.
[60] But where prosecutors undertook to provide information to magistrates, a duty of care was owed to C: *Welsh v CC of Merseyside Police* [1993] 1 All ER 692.   [61] *Elguzouli-Daf v MPC* [1995] QB 335.
[62] *Thacker v Crown Prosecution Service* (1997) *Times*, 29 December.
[63] *Heslop v Chapman* (1853) 23 LJQB 49, at 52. Cf *Shrosbery v Osmaston* (1877) 37 LT 792, at 794.

prosecution and the tort of false imprisonment. In false imprisonment, the initial act is wrongful in itself: for example, where an arrest is made without proper adherence to the procedural requirements. By contrast, malicious prosecution presupposes that the proper procedural formalities have been carried out, and is concerned with the *purposes* for which they were used. Where the defendant gives information to the police about a suspected breach of a court order and the police make an arrest but no prosecution follows, no action in malicious prosecution lies because of the absence of court proceedings.[64]

Section 3   Abuse of process

For the purposes of this tort, the leading case is *Grainger v Hill*:[65]

> D was liable when he had C arrested, ostensibly for non-payment of a debt, but in fact in order illegally to compel him to surrender the register of a vessel, without which C could not put to sea.

The case established that, in this tort, the claimant need not prove want of reasonable and probable cause; nor need the proceedings have terminated in his favour.[66] The claimant must show simply that the predominant purpose of the other party in using the legal process has been other than that for which it was designed.[67] Winfield and Jolowicz note that the tort cannot be viewed as 'the same thing as a general tort of malicious issue or use of civil proceedings'. Proceedings must be used in order to gain an 'illegitimate advantage' and overt acts must be present to this effect.[68] It is this requirement that keeps the bounds of this tort in check. Thus, a defendant who issued by mistake a plaint note for a debt which had been paid already was held not liable.[69] By contrast to malicious prosecution, however, damage to fame, person, or property need not be proved. *Any* special damage suffices.[70] As with malicious prosecution, where the defendant gives information to the police about a suspected breach of a court order and the police make an arrest but no prosecution follows, there is no action in abuse of process because of the absence of court proceedings.[71] The appropriate action (if any) would be in false imprisonment for wrongful arrest.

---

[64] *Crawford v Jenkins* [2016] QB 231, at [56]–[57].

[65] (1838) 4 Bing NC 212; *Gibbs v Pike and Wells* (1842) 9 M & W 351; *Speed Seal Products Ltd v Paddington* [1986] 1 All ER 91.

[66] See also *Crawford Adjusters v Sagicor General Insurance (Cayman) Ltd* [2014] AC 366, at [62]; *Speed Seal Products Ltd v Paddington* [1986] 1 All ER 91.

[67] *Crawford Adjusters v Sagicor General Insurance (Cayman) Ltd* [2014] AC 366, at [65]; *Metall und Rohstoff AG v Donaldson Lufkin & Jenrette Inc* [1989] 3 All ER 14, at 50; *Clissold v Cratchley* [1910] 2 KB 244.

[68] WVH Rogers, *Winfield and Jolowicz on Tort* (18th edn, 2010), 939–40.

[69] *Corbett v Burge, Warren and Ridgley Ltd* (1932) 48 TLR 626.

[70] For instance, if a suit in deceit was instituted for the purpose of damaging C's credit. In *Smith v East Elloe RDC* [1956] AC 736, their Lordships held there to be jurisdiction to hear a claim that a clerk to a council knowingly and in bad faith wrongfully procured a compulsory purchase order to be made and confirmed by a minister, even though a statute precluded the courts from challenging the validity of the order itself on grounds of bad faith.   [71] *Crawford v Jenkins* [2016] QB 231, at [56]–[57].

Section 4 Misfeasance in a public office

General A successful application for judicial review of administrative action which results in an administrative process being quashed as unlawful or invalid does not create any liability of itself for loss or damage suffered by the applicant.[72] However, the tort of misfeasance in a public office[73] might offer a remedy for the gross misuse of administrative powers.[74] Where an individual suffers loss consequent upon egregious, improper administrative action, which the relevant officer knows to be unlawful, that loss is recoverable in tort.[75] The underlying rationale is that public power is conferred to be exercised only for the public good, and not for improper purposes.[76] Notwithstanding the fact that the tort allows the courts the opportunity to signal their disapproval of such abuses of public power, it is not actionable per se, and no damages will be available unless special damage is proved. In one case, then, the action failed because the claimant-prisoner failed to show consequential loss resulting from the non-privileged opening of his letters by prison officers.[77] On the other hand, where material damage is proved, such as loss of liberty,[78] the courts might be minded to signal their disapproval in strident terms and exemplary damages may be awarded.[79]

Two bases for action In *Three Rivers District Council v Bank of England (No 3)*,[80] the House of Lords laid down the test for liability in the tort of misfeasance in a public office. Liability arises in two ways. The first, malice-based action, is made out where, in bad faith, a defendant abuses his powers (or neglects his duties) as a public officer specifically intending to injure the claimant and the claimant suffers material harm.[81] By contrast, the second form of the tort exists where, in bad faith, the defendant acts knowingly beyond his powers (or inconsistently with his duties) and knows that in so acting he is likely to injure the claimant (or a class of people to which the claimant belongs), and the claimant suffers material harm.

The second version of the tort—to which reckless indifference is an integral part—was considered in more detail in two subsequent cases. In *Southwark LBC v Dennett*,[82] May LJ emphasised this need for recklessness in the defendant's actions. He held that subjective recklessness is required, and not mere reckless indifference (should there be a difference between these two things). In *Akenzua v Secretary of State for the Home*

---

[72] *Dunlop v Woollahra MC* [1982] AC 158.   [73] See J Murphy (2011) 31 OJLS 51.

[74] *Jones v Swansea CC* [1990] 3 All ER 737.

[75] *David v Abdul Cader* [1963] 3 All ER 579; *Davis v Bromley Corpn* [1908] 1 KB 170.

[76] *Three Rivers DC v Bank of England (No 3)* [2000] 2 WLR 1220; *Jones v Swansea CC* [1990] 1 WLR 54.

[77] *Watkins v Secretary of State for the Home Department* [2006] 2 WLR 807 (misfeasance established, but no harm shown). Cf *Ashby v White* (1703) 2 Ld Raym 938.

[78] See, eg, *Karagozlu v MPC* [2007] 1 WLR 1881.

[79] *Watkins v Secretary of State for the Home Department* [2006] 2 WLR 807; *Kuddus v CC of Leicestershire Constabulary* [2002] 2 AC 122.   [80] [2000] 2 WLR 1220.

[81] Arguably, on this version of the tort, if the public officer believes that his abuse of power ultimately is in the public interest, there is no bad faith present (and thus no liability).

[82] [2008] LGR 94, at [13]. See also *McCreaner v Ministry of Justice* [2015] 1 WLR 354, at [56].

Department,[83] the Court of Appeal had to consider whether the class of individuals to which the claimant belonged must be a particular, identifiable class of persons:

> X had been released from custody by the defendant in order to serve as a police informant. X later murdered a woman whose personal representatives subsequently brought an action for misfeasance in a public office based on the fact that a man who had a history of violence and violent proclivities had been released recklessly from custody.

Notwithstanding the way in which the test for the tort had been expressed in the *Three Rivers* case, the Court of Appeal held that there was no need to identify a particular class of persons. As Sedley LJ explained, the reference in *Three Rivers* to knowledge of a class of persons to which the claimant belonged was 'not a freestanding requirement of [this] tort'. The requirement is instead 'derived from the antecedent proposition that the intent or recklessness must relate . . . to the kind of harm suffered'.[84] In other words, demonstrating knowledge of a class was not an end in itself, it is simply *a* means of showing that there are persons whose interests the defendant intended to affect or was recklessly indifferent towards.

In either of its two forms, it is clear that misfeasance in a public office may be used to obtain a remedy where ordinary negligence principles would be of no help because of a lack of foreseeability and/or proximity for the purposes of establishing a duty of care.[85]

Public office   By definition, the tort can be committed only by those in a public office. The question is how widely the term 'public office' is to be interpreted. *Roncarelli v Duplessis*[86] provides a good example of the tort being applied to a politician. The *Three Rivers* case shows its applicability to an institution such as the Bank of England. An action for misfeasance in a public office might lie also against a government department,[87] a local authority,[88] or potentially even a judge.[89]

Vicarious liability   At one time, in order to relieve an employer of vicarious liability for an employee's tortious conduct, the unlawful conduct had to be beyond the authorised duties of the employee. Thus, it was extremely difficult to characterise acts of misfeasance in a public office as ones that would support a finding of vicarious liability.[90] Nowadays, however, the broader-based, 'close connection' test for vicarious liability promulgated in *Lister v Hesley Hall Ltd*[91] is likely to make the imposition of vicarious liability easier. After all, that test has been used to catch the most flagrant acts of battery and sexual abuse.

---

[83]   [2003] 1 WLR 741.   [84]   [2003] 1 WLR 741, at [19].

[85]   See further E Chamberlain (2010) 88 Can Bar Rev 579.

[86]   (1959) 16 DLR (2d) 689: C lost his liquor licence after D, Premier of Quebec, ordered the Quebec Licensing Commission to revoke the licence. D acted against C as part of his campaign against Jehovah's Witnesses. C recovered damages for this malicious abuse of the licensing process.

[87]   *Racz v Home Office* [1994] 2 WLR 23.

[88]   *Jones v Swansea CC* [1990] 3 All ER 737 (where the action lies against a local council, C must show that the majority of those supporting the relevant resolution did so with intent to harm him).

[89]   *Rawlinson v Rice* [1998] 1 NZLR 454; *Cannon v Tahche* [2002] VR 317.

[90]   See, eg, *Racz v Home Office* [1994] 2 WLR 23.   [91]   [2002] 1 AC 215.

Section 5 Immunities

Principle It is an old principle of the common law that persons are not civilly liable for evidence given in court.[92] The immunity extends to various acts preparatory to court proceedings. It promotes both the ability to speak freely in the course of proceedings and the avoidance of a multiplicity of actions when the initial action is determined in favour of the defendant.[93]

Types of claim An immunity prevents actions in defamation regarding the giving of false information to the police where this is used to ground a prosecution[94] and regarding words uttered as a witness in court.[95] An immunity prevents actions for conspiracy against police who conspire to defame the claimant at a criminal trial.[96] A claim in respect of imprisonment caused by the defendant giving false evidence on oath at the claimant's trial is barred:[97] perjury is a crime, not a tort. An immunity operates also to prevent an action in negligence for deficiencies in a report prepared by a health authority-employed psychiatrist, pursuant to an investigation for child abuse, which leads to child protection proceedings.[98]

Extent Where witness immunity exists, it extends beyond the actual presentation of evidence to cover also the preparation of evidence that will (or would) be given in court. But it does not attach to 'things that would not form part of the evidence in a judicial enquiry'.[99] Moreover, a distinction must be drawn between evidence that a witness gives (or has stated he would give) in court, and evidence that has been fabricated (such as a fabricated interview). The House of Lords has made clear that an immunity does not extend to the latter.[100]

Non–application There is no immunity for either malicious prosecution[101] or misfeasance in public office.[102] Similarly, there is no immunity in cases of malicious arrest.[103] These actions involve inherently serious allegations, including the presence of malice (or bad faith) and demonstrate a disregard for civic obligations. In more recent times, it has been held that witness immunity does not extend to protect expert witnesses who provide services for reward and owe obligations of care under the contract against proceedings by their clients in the tort of negligence.[104]

---

[92] *Roy v Prior* [1971] AC 470.   [93] *Singh v Reading BC* [2013] 1 WLR 3052, at [23].
[94] *Westcott v Westcott* [2009] 2 WLR 838.   [95] See ch 22.   [96] *Marrinan v Vibart* [1963] 1 QB 528.
[97] *Hargreaves v Bretherton* [1959] 1 QB 45, approved *obiter* in *Roy v Prior* [1971] AC 470, at 477. In *Evans v London Hospital Medical College* [1981] 1 All ER 715, it was held that this immunity extends to statements made before the issue of a writ or the institution of a prosecution. But note *Palmer v Durnford Ford (a firm)* [1992] QB 483 restricting immunities of expert witnesses.   [98] *X v Bedfordshire CC* [1995] 2 AC 633, at 755.
[99] *Singh v Reading BC* [2013] 1 WLR 3052, at [66].
[100] *Darker v CC of West Midlands Police* [2001] 1 AC 435.
[101] *Jones v Kaney* [2011] 2 AC 398, at [82]; *Taylor v Director of Serious Fraud Office* [1999] 2 AC 77, at 215 and 219.   [102] *Jones v Kaney* [2011] 2 AC 398, at [82]; *Martin v Watson* [1996] AC 74, at 88–9.
[103] *Roy v Prior* [1971] AC 470.   [104] *Jones v Kaney* [2011] 2 AC 398.

Conclusions

In this chapter, we have considered three principal causes of action: malicious prosecution, abuse of process, and misfeasance in a public office. These are torts with respect to which a balance must be struck between the protection of individuals' interests and rights, on the one hand, and the efficient conduct of public administration and the administration of justice, on the other. To help ensure that a proper balance is struck, the need to show malice becomes an important touchstone of liability in the first and third causes of action. The chapter has explained, also, relevant aspects of the law on the immunity of witnesses for what is said in court and in preparation for giving evidence in court. Neither malicious prosecution nor misfeasance in public office is defeated by this immunity.

Problem question

Giovanni is a government officer working for Revenue Protection. He has been given a tip-off by Mary-Lou, who used to be Zane's girlfriend, that Zane does not pay all of his taxes. Giovanni organises visits by Revenue Protection officers (who do not reveal their real employment) to Zane's business and they make several orders for goods. In each case, Zane declares his income and pays the appropriate taxes. Despite this, Giovanni brings a prosecution for failure to pay taxes against Zane based on Mary-Lou's oral evidence. The prosecution against Zane fails.

Advise Zane as to any action that he might have for misuse of process or public powers.

 Visit **http://www.oup.com/uk/street15e/** for answer guidance.

Further reading

MURPHY, 'Misfeasance in a Public Office: A Tort Law Misfit' (2011) 31 *Oxford Journal of Legal Studies* 51

WELLS, 'The Abuse of Process' (1985) 102 *Law Quarterly Review* 9

PART IX
Parties and remedies

24

Vicarious liability

KEY ISSUES

(1) General

Vicarious liability entails one legal person being made jointly liable for a tort committed by another. In most cases, the person made liable is the employer and it foots the bill for compensation. There are two general requirements in proving vicarious liability (aside from the commission of the tort). The first is a relationship requirement and the second is a connection requirement.

(2) Relationship requirement

Traditionally, the relationship requirement has been satisfied by proof of a relationship of employer and employee as between the person to be made liable and the wrongdoer. However, the courts now permit the recognition (supposedly in exceptional cases) of liability where the person to be made liable and the wrongdoer are in a relationship 'akin to employment'.

(3) Connection requirement

The connection requirement is satisfied where either: the commission of the tort fell within the wrongdoer's authority to act; or some other sufficient connection existed between acts arising pursuant to the relationship and the commission of the tort.

(4) Strict liability doctrine

Given that these are the elements, it will be appreciated that vicarious liability is a doctrine of strict liability. This is to say that the vicariously liable person is liable regardless of fault on her part. The court does not inquire into the existence of fault in that person.

(5) Liability for independent contractors

Liability might arise in a number of ways for the failures of independent contractors, including, *inter alia*, cases in which the 'employer' was either personally negligent or else owed the claimant a non-delegable duty. Although both of these alternatives are forms of personal liability, they differ insofar as non-delegable duties arise in restricted circumstances and involve strict liability—while neither of these are features of the tort of negligence.

Section 1 Introduction

Vicarious liability entails one legal person being made jointly liable for the tort committed by another. In *most* cases, the person made liable is the employer and it foots the bill for compensation. In the circumstances, vicarious liability can operate in the perverse way of protecting the actual wrongdoer from the financial consequences of her actions.[1] The actual wrongdoer is likely to be subject to disciplinary or other proceedings meted out by the vicariously liable entity (usually an organisation) rather than by a court.[2] Given the perverse effects of vicarious liability upon ordinary notions of tortious responsibility,[3] this is a doctrine that both the courts and the commentators have found difficult to explain beyond the fact that it provides a pragmatic means of obtaining compensation for loss.

There are two broad requirements for proving vicarious liability (aside from the commission of a tort). The first is a relationship requirement and the second is a connection requirement. Traditionally, the relationship requirement has been satisfied by proof of a relationship of employer and employee as between the person to be made liable and the wrongdoer. However, courts now permit the recognition (perhaps still in exceptional cases only) of liability where the person to be made liable and the wrongdoer are in a relationship 'akin to employment'. The connection requirement is satisfied where either: the commission of the tort fell within the wrongdoer's authority to act; or some other sufficient connection existed between acts arising pursuant to the relationship and commission of the tort. There is a real sense in which the first alternative falls within the ambit of the second—although the first alternative is a surer way to establish liability than the second. Given that these are the elements, we see that vicarious liability is a doctrine of strict liability. The court does not inquire into the existence of fault in the vicariously liable person.[4]

In what follows, we consider the relationship and connection requirements of vicarious liability. However, it must be understood that this is a doctrine of tort law which has both expanded significantly in its reach, and appears still to be in a process of change. There are indications that vicarious liability might be developing into two separate but related doctrines—one dealing with employment relationships, and the other dealing with organisational responsibility for wrongdoing. However, it is too soon to structure a work on tort law to reflect this potential development because the Supreme Court in *Cox v Ministry of Justice* has insisted that the employment relationship remains at the heart of the doctrine.[5] But the potential for such development ought to be kept in mind.

This chapter examines also some exceptional cases in which one person might be made personally liable for torts committed by other persons—these cases involving the non-delegable duty.

---

[1] P Morgan (2012) 71 CLJ 615, at 625. See also P Giliker, *Vicarious Liability in Tort: A Comparative Perspective* (2010), 30–3 (on practice regarding employers' indemnity and insurers' subrogation rights).

[2] P Giliker, *Vicarious Liability in Tort: A Comparative Perspective* (2010), 41.

[3] P Giliker, *Vicarious Liability in Tort: A Comparative Perspective* (2010), 1.

[4] *Armes v Nottinghamshire CC* [2017] UKSC 60, at [91]; *Bernard v A-G of Jamaica* [2004] UKPC 47, at [21]; *Weddall v Barchester Healthcare Ltd* [2012] EWCA Civ 25, at [63].   [5] [2016] AC 660, at [15].

Section 2 Employees and independent contractors

The basic distinction We begin by considering the relationship requirement, which requires familiarity with the rules relating to employment. The law divides workers (to use a neutral term) into two groups:

(1) Those employed to perform services in connection with the affairs of the employer, who are engaged on a *contract of service*. Such persons are 'employees'.

(2) Those who do work for another, but who are not controlled by that other in the performance of the work. Normally, such work will be carried out in pursuance of a *contract for services*. Such persons are 'independent contractors'.

If an employee commits a tort in the course of her employment, or in doing something that has a sufficiently close connection to her employment, her employer will be vicariously liable for the tort regardless of whether she herself committed a tort.[6] If the person who commits the tort is not an employee or akin to an employee, then the 'employer' cannot be held liable unless she herself has (1) acted in a way so as to be treated as a joint tortfeasor; or (2) breached a non-delegable duty owed to the claimant.[7]

Factors to consider Given the importance of the distinction between employees and independent contractors, we need to consider what factors are indicative of a relationship of employment. In *E v English Province of Our Lady of Charity*, Ward LJ provided a neat summary of the main considerations:

> [A]n employee is one who is paid a wage or salary to work under some, if only slight, control of his employer in his employer's business for his employer's business. The independent contractor works in and for his own business at his risk of profit or loss.[8]

In this statement, important features include both the issue of control and that of risk-for-reward (or investment in the enterprise). We shall consider both of these features, as well as the issue of the intention of the parties.

(A) Control

Traditional conception Traditionally, courts marked the distinction between an employee and an independent contractor by use of the control test.[9] According to this test, a person is an employee where the employer 'retains the control of the actual performance' of the work.[10] This was a more meaningful test in bygone years when England and Wales were predominantly agricultural and industrial nations in which work was done largely by labourers or crafts-persons under the direction of employers who had

---

[6] *Bartonshill Coal Co v McGuire* (1858) 3 Macq 300, at 306.

[7] *Bull v Devon Area HA* [1993] 4 Med LR 117.   [8] [2013] QB 722, at [70].

[9] 'The final test . . . lies in the nature and degree of detailed control over the person alleged to be a servant': *Performing Right Society Ltd v Mitchell and Booker (Palais de Danse) Ltd* [1924] 1 KB 762, at 767.

[10] *Honeywill and Stein Ltd v Larkin Bros (London's Commercial Photographers) Ltd* [1934] 1 KB 191, at 196.

the same, or even greater, technical skill than them. Ordinarily, it would be enough to say that the employer could tell the worker not merely what task was to be performed, but how it should be performed as well. If the employer could do both of these things, the person engaged was regarded as an employee. Conversely, where a supposed employer lacked the power to direct what the worker was to do, the absence of relevant control would be fatal to the suggestion that she was an employee.[11]

Changed circumstances   Working patterns have changed so much that it is difficult to slot employment relationships into the traditional analytical framework of control.[12] For example, many employees work at home these days, or possess technical skills which are not possessed by their employers. In consequence, the control test does not prove adequate by itself on every occasion.[13] In addition a court might hold someone to be an employee for policy reasons even though aspects of her work suggest more that she is an independent contractor. In *Lane v Shire Roofing Co (Oxford) Ltd*,[14] for example, the Court of Appeal drew attention to the policy reasons that exist within the field of health and safety at work to decide a borderline case in favour of classifying the worker as an employee.

Application of control test   Notwithstanding its limitations, the control test remains helpful in some instances, and in deciding whether enough 'control' is exercised over another to make her an employee one must take into account several factors, no single one of which is conclusive. The criteria include the extent to which the employer can control the details of the work, whether the method of payment is on a time or a job basis,[15] whose tools, equipment, and premises are to be used,[16] the skill called for in the work, the freedom of selection of labour by the employer, and the power to dismiss. In addition to these kinds of factor, courts examine whether a person 'is employed as part of the business, and her work is done as an integral part of the business',[17] although it might be more accurate to substitute the word 'organisation' for the word 'business', given that there is no need for the employment to be profit-making (as many cases in recent times demonstrate).

Dual employment   In *Viasystems (Tyneside) Ltd v Thermal Transfer (Northern) Ltd*,[18] the Court of Appeal had to consider whether a fitter's mate supplied on a labour-only basis by A to B could trigger the vicarious liability of A or B. It was found that both A *and* B had sufficient control of the mate to prevent his negligence. May LJ

---

[11]   *Various Claimants v Catholic Child Welfare Society* [2013] 2 AC 1, at [36].

[12]   *Cox v Ministry of Justice* [2016] AC 660, at [29].

[13]   *Short v J & W Henderson Ltd* (1946) 62 TLR 427, at 429. The inadequacy of this test was noted in *Cassidy v Ministry of Health* [1951] 2 KB 343, at 352.   [14]   [1995] IRLR 493.

[15]   Employees generally are paid by the hour, whereas independent contractors are paid for the complete job.

[16]   *Quarman v Burnett* (1840) 6 M & W 499.

[17]   *Stevenson, Jordan & Harrison Ltd v MacDonald and Evans* [1952] 1 TLR 101, at 111. In *Bank Voor Handel en Scheepvaart NV v Slatford* [1953] 1 QB 248, at 295, Denning LJ said: 'It depends on whether the person is part and parcel of the organisation' (revd on other grounds [1954] AC 584).   [18]   [2006] 2 WLR 428.

analysed the issue by focusing upon the relevant negligent act and then asking whose responsibility it was to prevent it.[19] The route taken by Rix LJ was different. In his view, the critical issue was whether the worker 'is so much a part of the work, business or organisation of both employers that it is just to make both employers answer for his negligence'.[20] Importantly, both members of this two-judge Court of Appeal recognised that there was never a formal contract of employment between B and the careless mate! They were content to deem him to be the employee of both A and B and to impose liability jointly and equally between them.[21] In the subsequent decision of the Supreme Court in *Various Claimants v Catholic Child Welfare Society,* Rix LJ's integration test was preferred to May LJ's control test, Lord Phillips stating that the latter was too stringent.[22]

(B) Personal investment in the enterprise

Another approach to determining who is an employee is to ask: 'Is the worker in business on h[er] own account?'[23] In answering this question the court will look at who owns the tools used, who paid for the materials, and whether the worker stands to make anything from a profit to a loss on completion of the enterprise. Thus, where a building worker simply is paid, and neither hires her own help nor provides her own equipment, and has no say in the control of the site, her position will be that of an employee rather than an independent contractor.[24] However, there is another sense in which the phrase 'personal investment in the enterprise' can be used, which might be pertinent to the question in hand. If the person engaged need not personally invest her own endeavour into the enterprise, but has the option of delegating the task to some other person, this is likely to be indicative of a contract for services rather than a contract of service.[25]

(C) Intention of the parties

The intention of the parties, recorded in the terms of their agreement, provides an indicator of whether there is a contract of service or a contract for services[26]—especially in borderline cases. However, the parties' express intentions are not conclusive of the matter. Thus, in one case where the parties agreed that the worker should be treated as self-employed for reasons of tax and national insurance payments, the court held there to be a contract of employment nonetheless.[27]

---

[19] [2006] 2 WLR 428, at [16].   [20] [2006] 2 WLR 428, at [79].

[21] Since vicarious liability does not require fault to be shown on the part of the employer, it followed that liability ordinarily would be split evenly between the two employers (assuming equal control): [2006] 2 WLR 428, at [52] and [85].   [22] *Various Claimants v Catholic Child Welfare Society* [2013] 2 AC 1, at [45].

[23] *Lee Tin Sang v Chung Chi-Keung* [1990] 2 AC 374; *Lane v Shire Roofing Co (Oxford) Ltd* [1995] IRLR 493.

[24] *Montreal v Montreal Locomotive Works* [1947] 1 DLR 161.

[25] *MacFarlane v Glasgow CC* [2001] IRLR 7.

[26] *Johnson v Coventry Churchill International Ltd* [1992] 3 All ER 14.

[27] *Young & Woods Ltd v West* [1980] IRLR 201. See also *Ferguson v Dawson Partners (Contractors) Ltd* [1976] 1 WLR 1213.

(D) Some particular cases examined

In the majority of cases, there is no difficulty in determining the status of a given worker. Agricultural and factory workers, office clerical staff, and the like are classified ordinarily as employees; whereas garage proprietors, house builders, and dry-cleaners are independent contractors. Similarly, a chauffeur is an employee, but a taxi driver is not. However, borderline or hybrid cases arise from time to time. Sales representatives, for example, might fall into either category, depending on the circumstances.[28] We turn now to consider a number of case studies in greater depth.

(1) Agency workers

Those who work ad hoc on temporary contracts acquired through an employment agency may be treated, on occasion, as employees of the agency for the purposes of each separate engagement.[29] Whether the general arrangement—that is, the worker being registered on the agency's books—could amount to a contract of employment would appear to turn on the question whether there is a mutuality of obligation between the worker and agency (that is, a duty to provide work on the part of the agency and a duty to accept it on the part of the worker).[30] In turn, this question can be answered not merely by reference to the documentary evidence associated with the engagement,[31] but by reference also to what was actually said and done at the time of the engagement.[32] If the agency has no day-to-day control over the tasks performed by the worker, this tends to indicate that she is not an employee of the agency.[33]

(2) Hospital staff

At one time, the courts were quite vexed by the issue of which members of hospital staff are employees. This issue exposed the problems of the 'control' test. How could lay members of a hospital board be said to 'control' a highly skilled neurosurgeon? After much uncertainty, it is now settled that house surgeons,[34] radiographers,[35] nurses, and assistant medical officers[36] in the full-time service of hospitals are employees.[37] Part-time anaesthetists have been held to be employees also on the basis that they are

---

[28] Or the holder of a university research fellowship who is required also to act as a part-time demonstrator.

[29] *McMeechan v Secretary of State for Employment* [1997] IRLR 353. Cf *Montgomery v Johnson Underwood Ltd* [2001] IRLR 269 (the worker was not an employee because, unlike in *McMeechan*, there was no review or grievance procedure between the agency and the worker that could be taken to be indicative of the formality of their relationship).

[30] In *Carmichael v National Power plc* [1999] 1 WLR 2042, Lord Irvine said (at 2047) that a contract of employment required an 'irreducible minimum of mutual obligations'. See also *Clark v Oxfordshire HA* [1998] IRLR 125; *Dacas v Brook Street Bureau (UK) Ltd* [2004] IRLR 358.

[31] For instance, the fact that the agency only pays the worker according to time sheets supplied by the employer (suggesting that the worker is not an employee of the agency): *Montgomery v Johnson Underwood* [2001] IRLR 269.

[32] *Franks v Reuters Ltd* [2003] EWCA 417.   [33] *Dacas v Brook Street Bureau (UK) Ltd* [2004] IRLR 358.

[34] *Collins v Hertfordshire CC* [1947] KB 598; *Cassidy v Ministry of Health* [1951] 2 KB 343.

[35] *Gold v Essex CC* [1942] 2 KB 293.   [36] *Cassidy v Ministry of Health* [1951] 2 KB 343.

[37] So, too, are educational psychologists and teachers engaged by a local education authority (*Phelps v Hillingdon LBC* [2001] 2 AC 619), as are education officers performing the statutory functions of such authorities (*Carty v London Borough of Croydon* [2005] EWCA Civ 19).

members of the hospital organisation.[38] Surgeons and consultants working under the National Health Service, even though engaged part-time only, will be employees for the same reason. They all operate as part and parcel of the NHS enterprise. It is only when the surgeon or consultant treats the patient under a private contract between them alone that the hospital is not answerable for her torts.

(3) Borrowed employees

Often it is difficult to decide whose employee a person is when she is lent by her employer to another. The leading decision here is *Mersey Docks and Harbour Board v Coggins and Griffiths (Liverpool) Ltd*:[39]

> The Board owned many mobile cranes, each operated by skilled drivers who were engaged and paid by it. In the ordinary course of its business, the Board hired out a crane to the respondents, a stevedoring company, for use in unloading a ship. The power to dismiss the driver remained with the board even though the contract provided that he was to be the servant of the hirers. While loading the cargo, the driver was under the immediate control of the hirers in the sense that the hirers could tell him which boxes to load and where to place them, but they could not tell him how to manipulate the controls of the crane. A third party was injured by negligent handling of the crane by the driver.

The House of Lords was called upon to decide whose servant he was at the time of the accident. It held that the Board was solely liable. There is a very strong presumption[40] that someone remains the employee of the general or permanent employer although another employer borrows her services. Where cranes or vehicles are let out on hire with a driver, the owner is responsible for her employee's negligence unless she specifically divested herself of all possession and control.[41] But if the system of work that is used is unsafe, then, according to *Morris v Breaveglen Ltd*,[42] the general employer is liable for she has a non-delegable duty to ensure the provision and operation of a safe system of work. (On the other hand, it should not be forgotten that where *both* the general employer and the employer to whom the employee has been loaned have control over the employee, both employers can be held vicariously liable in respect of the employee's torts.)[43]

(4) Police officers

Under the Police Act 1996, section 88, the chief officer of police for any police area is vicariously liable for those torts committed by constables exercising or purporting to exercise their functions.[44] And vicarious liability can be imposed even where the tort in question is committed by an off-duty officer who makes it clear that she is a police officer.[45]

---

[38] *Roe v Minister of Health* [1954] 2 QB 66.   [39] [1947] AC 1.

[40] For an example where the company 'borrowing' employees did become vicariously liable, even though there was no formal contract of employment between the temporary employer and the employee, see *Hawley v Luminar Leisure* [2006] EWCA Civ 30.

[41] And the original employer will, of course, be primarily liable if she hires out an incompetent driver: *McConkey v Amec plc* (1990) 27 Con LR 88.

[42] [1993] PIQR P294.   [43] *Viasystems (Tyneside) Ltd v Thermal Transfer (Northern) Ltd* [2006] 2 WLR 428.

[44] See, eg, *Rowlands v CC Merseyside* [2007] 1 WLR 1065.   [45] *Weir v Bettison* [2003] EWCA Civ 111.

Section 3 Relationships akin to employment

New alternative As mentioned, the relationship requirement might now be satisfied in circumstances where the person to be made liable is not the wrongdoer's employer. This development has occurred, in part, in order to ensure that the law on responsibility for the acts of others keeps pace with changing work and other relevant relationships.[46] The leading case is *Various Claimants v Catholic Child Welfare Society* ('*CCWS*'):[47]

> Actions were brought for acts of proven or alleged sexual abuse committed by brother teachers who had occupied various roles at a residential institution for boys. The case involved the Institute of Brothers, which was an unincorporated international association of brothers with organisational responsibility for Catholic education conducted in England and elsewhere. The Institute placed brothers in schools teaching a Catholic syllabus, including the residential institution in question. The brothers were employed by school managers (CCWS), who did not contest their own vicarious liability but sought contribution from the Institute.

The Supreme Court held that '[w]here the defendant and the tortfeasor are not bound by a contract of employment, but their relationship has the same incidents, that relationship can properly give rise to vicarious liability where it is "akin to that between an employer and an employee"'.[48] Lord Phillips found the following features to be significant in establishing that the relationship between the Institute and the brothers was akin to employment:

> i) The Institute was subdivided into a hierarchical structure and conducted its activities as if it were a corporate body
>
> ii) The teaching activity of the brothers was undertaken because the Provincial [an officer of the Institute] directed the brothers to undertake it . . .
>
> iii) The teaching activity undertaken by the brothers was in furtherance of the objective, or mission, of the Institute
>
> iv) The manner in which the brother teachers were obliged to conduct themselves was dictated by the Institute's rules.[49]

Lord Phillips recognised that there were differences from the typical employment relationship in that there was neither a contract nor a payment for service, but his Lordship did not believe these matters to be 'material'.[50] The Court went on to find that a close connection had existed 'between the relationship between the brothers and the Institute and the employment of the brothers as teachers in the school'.[51]

---

[46] *Cox v Ministry of Justice* [2016] AC 660, at [29].

[47] [2013] 2 AC 1. The 'akin to' test was developed earlier in 2012 in *E v English Province of Our Lady of Charity* [2013] QB 722 and relied upon by the Supreme Court.

[48] *Various Claimants v Catholic Child Welfare Society* [2013] 2 AC 1, at [47].

[49] *Various Claimants v Catholic Child Welfare Society* [2013] 2 AC 1, at [56].

[50] *Various Claimants v Catholic Child Welfare Society* [2013] 2 AC 1, at [57]–[58].

[51] *Various Claimants v Catholic Child Welfare Society* [2013] 2 AC 1, at [91].

In *Cox v Ministry of Justice*, the Supreme Court distilled what it thought to be at the heart of the reasoning in the *CCWS* case. Lord Reed stated that there were three important factors: (1) a tort which was committed as a result of an activity having been undertaken by the tortfeasor on behalf of the defendant; (2) that activity having been a part of the defendant's business activity—although the 'business' need be neither commercial nor profit-making; and (3) the fact that the defendant, by employing the tortfeasor to carry on the activity, created the risk of a tort being committed by the tortfeasor.[52]

Further applications The *CCWS* case gives rise to a number of questions about what other relationships might be found to be 'akin to employment'. Indeed, it raises the issue whether employment will continue as the paradigm case of vicarious liability or whether there will be movement away from this type of thinking.[53] There are signs that the courts are willing to extend the bounds of vicarious liability to relationships well beyond employment, recent examples of extended vicarious liability involving the liability of the Ministry of Justice for the negligence of a prisoner taking part in rehabilitative work,[54] the liability of a council for acts of sexual abuse against children committed by foster carers that the council had trained and monitored,[55] and the liability of a bishop for sexual abuse committed by a priest.[56] In *Armes v Nottinghamshire County Council*, Lord Hughes (in a dissenting judgment) thought that the true question in vicarious liability cases has become one of whether 'the tortfeasor is acting as an integral part of the defendant's enterprise'—which need not be commercial or profit-making.[57] This reflects the fact that one strain of the doctrine apparently is being re-orientated towards organisational liability for wrongdoing. Indeed, given this development, it has been speculated that the *CCWS* case will open the way to suits against professional regulatory bodies in episodes of 'regulatory failure',[58] against parent companies for the torts of their subsidiaries,[59] and against franchisors for the torts of franchisees.[60]

Section 4 Liability in respect of employees

(A) Introduction

The second requirement of vicarious liability is a 'connection' requirement. An employer is liable whenever her employee commits a tort in the course of her employment or in circumstances sufficiently closely connected to her employment. (The same rule applies

---

[52] [2016] AC 660, at [22] and [30].

[53] See, eg, J O'Sullivan (2012) 71 CLJ 485, 487. *Woodland v Essex CC* [2014] AC 537, at [3], suggests that the employee-independent contractor distinction remains fundamental, but this is not inconsistent in itself with greater liability on the basis of other relationships.   [54] *Cox v Ministry of Justice* [2016] AC 660.

[55] *Armes v Nottinghamshire CC* [2017] UKSC 60.

[56] *E v English Province of Our Lady of Charity* [2013] QB 722.   [57] [2016] UKSC 60, at [76].

[58] S Deakin, A Johnston, and B Markesinis, *Markesinis and Deakin's Tort Law* (7th edn, 2013), 565.

[59] See M Petrin (2013) 76 MLR 603, 612–13.

[60] P Morgan (2013) 129 LQR 139, 143 (also suggesting that local authorities might become vicariously liable for the torts of foster carers, as to which see P Morgan (2012) 20 TLJ 110).

to those in a relationship akin to employment. For ease of treatment, we will subsume them into the following discussion.) All the elements of the particular tort[61] must generally occur within, or in close connection with, the employer–employee relationship. Thus, the employer will be answerable if the tort was committed before the employment relationship ceased to exist, even if the harm occurred after that date.[62]

Where a duty of care imposed on the employer has been breached, but the claimant cannot prove which of her employees is responsible for the breach, the employer is liable nonetheless.[63] Accordingly, in *Roe v Minister of Health* the Court of Appeal held (*obiter*) that, where a claimant established negligence on the part of one or more of several employees of the defendant hospital authority, the defendant authority would be vicariously liable although the claimant could not prove which of those employees committed the negligent act.[64] Further, the *ratio decidendi* of *Cassidy v Ministry of Health* is that, where the claimant has been injured as a result of some operation in the control of one or more employees of a hospital authority (and she cannot identify the particular employee who was in control), and in all other respects the requirements of the *res ipsa loquitur* rule in respect of the act are satisfied, the hospital authority is vicariously liable unless it ousts the operation of that rule.[65]

(B) In the course of the employee's employment

At one time, vicarious liability could only be imposed when the wrongdoing employee acted 'in the course of his employment'.[66] While a rival test has emerged since then, based on acts closely connected to the employee's contract of employment, it is still true that any tortious act committed within the course of an employee's employment suffices for the purposes of vicarious liability. That being so, the *legal* question of when an act falls within a 'course of employment' remains of some importance (although it is less significant nowadays).[67]

(1) The course of employment: general principles

At one time, it was accepted that the crucial distinction was that between an employee's wrongful mode of doing authorised work (for which the employer would be liable) and her performance of some unauthorised act (for which the employer would not be liable).[68] Such a simplistic distinction was never entirely satisfactory,[69] for some cases

---

[61] A procedural bar against suing the servant will not prevent the master from being vicariously liable: *Staveley Iron and Chemicals Co Ltd v Jones* [1956] 1 All ER 403; *Broom v Morgan* [1953] 1 QB 597.

[62] *Briess v Woolley* [1954] AC 333.

[63] *Grant v Australian Knitting Mills Ltd* [1936] AC 85; *Olley v Marlborough Court Ltd* [1949] 1 KB 532 (a guest left the bedroom key at the hotel office; upon the key being taken and the bedroom being burgled, the onus was cast on the hotel to prove that they and their staff had taken reasonable care of the key).

[64] [1954] 2 QB 66.   [65] [1951] 2 KB 343.

[66] Even though the act is outside the scope of employment the employer still can be liable for breach of her own duty to provide a safe system of work: see, eg, *Hudson v Ridge Manufacturing Co Ltd* [1957] 2 QB 348.

[67] Just this question was raised in *HSBC Bank plc v 5th Avenue Partners Ltd* [2009] EWCA Civ 296, in which case it was said (at [56]) that the question of whether an act was done in the course of employment was a mixed one of fact and law.

[68] *Goh Choon Seng v Lee Kim Soo* [1925] AC 550.   [69] See P Cane (2000) 116 LQR 21.

involving deliberate misconduct fitted awkwardly into the 'unauthorised mode' (as opposed to 'unauthorised act') category. Of course it is uncontentious to regard negligence in the performance of a job as a wrongful mode of doing an authorised act; but an employee's deliberate, heinous acts are more difficult to classify in such terms. That said, on occasion the cases have regarded such egregious (even criminal) conduct in terms of wrongful modes of performing authorised acts. An example is provided by *Century Insurance Co Ltd v Northern Ireland Road Transport Board*:[70]

> The driver of a petrol lorry, while transferring petrol from the lorry to an underground tank at a petrol station, struck a match in order to light a cigarette and then threw it, still alight, on the ground. An explosion and a fire ensued.

His employers were held liable for the damage caused: he had acted in the course of carrying out his task of delivering petrol. It was an unauthorised way of doing what he was employed to do.

In recent years, there has been a rash of cases the Commonwealth over in which the employee committed various crimes of violence and sexual abuse which have forced the courts to abandon their somewhat artificial endeavours to squeeze these cases of deliberate wrongdoing into the 'unauthorised mode' category.[71] They have preferred to deal with such cases according to the 'close connection test' that will be examined shortly. For now, however, it is useful to provide some general guidance on how the courts determine what does and does not come within the concept of authorised acts.

(2) Authorised conduct within limits of time and space

Normally, an employee's acts are within the scope of her employment only during her authorised period of work. However, she will be treated as being within the scope of her employment during a period which is not unreasonably disconnected from the authorised period. Thus, someone paid to work until 6pm who stays on for a few extra minutes in order to finish a job will be within the scope of her employment.[72] But an employee who comes into her employer's premises without permission during her holiday is not within the scope of her job.[73]

By extension from the foregoing, employees travelling to and from their places of work ordinarily are not regarded as being within the course of their employment. However, there are instances where travel is so closely connected with a person's work that this principle cannot apply. In *Smith v Stages*,[74] for example, an employee had been working away from his home and his usual workplace. He was involved in a road accident driving home in his own car so that he could resume work at his usual place of employment the next day. He was paid for the day he needed to drive back as a normal working day.

---

[70] [1942] AC 509.

[71] See, eg, *Mattis v Pollock* [2003] 1 WLR 2158; *NSW v Lepore* [2003] HCA 4; *Bazley v Curry* [1999] 2 SCR 534; *Jacobi v Griffiths* (1999) 174 DLR (4th) 71; *Lister v Hesley Hall Ltd* [2002] 1 AC 215.

[72] See, eg, *Ruddiman & Co v Smith* (1889) 60 LT 708.

[73] *Compton v McClure* [1975] ICR 378.

[74] [1989] AC 928. See also: *Vandyke v Fender* [1970] 2 QB 292; *Elleanor v Cavendish Woodhouse Ltd and Comerford* [1973] 1 Lloyd's Rep 313.

The House of Lords held that he remained within the course of his employment. His journey from A to B was part and parcel of his job, and, in effect, his employers directed that he make the journey.[75]

Of course, there are many jobs where travel itself is the essence of the employment. The work of sales representatives is an obvious example. But what if such an employee makes a detour from her set pattern of work for her own purposes, say, to visit a friend or to do some shopping? On occasion, the courts have been called upon to decide whether such detours fall within the scope of employment. The classic ruling is that of Parke B in *Joel v Morison*:

> If he was going out of his way, against his master's implied commands when driving on his master's business, he will make his master liable; but if he was going on a frolic of his own, without being at all on his master's business, the master will not be liable.[76]

Whether the detour by the employee is a 'frolic of his own' is a matter of fact and degree.[77]

(3) Express prohibitions

Often an employer expressly forbids certain acts. But it does not follow from this that an act done in defiance of the prohibition is outside the scope of employment. If that were so, the employer would have only to issue specific orders not to be negligent in order to escape liability for her employee's negligence. The House of Lords has laid down the rule as follows:

> [T]here are prohibitions which limit the sphere of employment, and prohibitions which only deal with conduct within the sphere of employment. A transgression of a prohibition of the latter class leaves the sphere of employment where it was, and consequently will not prevent recovery of compensation. A transgression of the former class carries with it the result that the man has gone outside the sphere.[78]

A few illustrative examples are helpful. In *Canadian Pacific Rly Co v Lockhart*,[79] the defendants prohibited their staff from driving uninsured cars on the company's business. In breach of this instruction, S drove an uninsured car negligently, while engaged on the company's business, and injured the claimant. The defendants were held liable, the Judicial Committee holding that:

> it was not the acting as driver that was prohibited, but the non-insurance of the motor car, if used as a means incidental to the execution of the work which he was employed to do. It follows that the prohibition merely limited the way in which, or by means of which, the servant was to execute the work which he was employed to do, and that breach of the prohibition did not exclude the liability of the master to third parties.[80]

---

[75] In similar vein see *Ministry of Defence v Radclyffe* [2009] EWCA Civ 635.

[76] (1834) 6 C & P 501, at 503.

[77] Compare *Whatman v Pearson* (1868) LR 3 CP 422 and *Storey v Ashton* (1869) LR 4 QB 476.

[78] *Plumb v Cobden Flour Mills Co Ltd* [1914] AC 62, at 67 (a workers' compensation case, but the principles are the same).

[79] [1942] AC 591.   [80] [1942] AC 591, at 601.

Likewise, a garage hand employed to move vehicles in a garage, but forbidden to drive them, was acting in the course of his employment when he drove a van out of the garage on to the highway (in order to make room in the garage for another vehicle), and collided on the highway with the claimant's van.[81] These cases can be contrasted to *Rand v Craig*.[82] There, the defendant employed his servants to carry rubbish from X to Y. Instead they deposited some of this rubbish on the claimant's land. The defendant was held not vicariously liable for this trespass because the employees were employed, not to carry rubbish generally, but only to carry it from X to Y. Therefore, the act was of a kind that the defendant was impliedly forbidden to do.

If a driver gives a lift to a third party in breach of her employer's instructions and tortiously injures that passenger through careless driving, the courts approach the question of the employer's liability as follows. The issue does not turn on the fact that the passenger is a trespasser.[83] Instead, the employer will be held not liable if her prohibition has marked the limits of the scope of employment, so that giving the lift was outside that scope. On the other hand, if the prohibition affects only the mode in which the employee is to perform her duties, the employer can be vicariously liable. Two cases show the distinction.[84] In *Twine v Bean's Express Ltd*,[85] the employer had a contract to employ his vans on Post Office business. Contrary to his express instruction his driver gave a lift to a third party. It was held that giving the lift was outside the scope of employment. Operating what was in effect a 'free taxi service' was not the job the driver was employed to do. But contrast this case with that of *Rose v Plenty*:[86]

> A milkman employed a 13-year-old boy to deliver and collect milk bottles on his milk round contrary to his employer's order that children were not to be used in this way. The driver negligently injured the boy.

The employer was held vicariously liable because the prohibition affected only the manner in which the milkman was to perform his duties of delivering milk and did not limit the scope of those duties. He was delivering milk, and the boy he had recruited to assist him was part of that enterprise.

(C) Close connection between the wrongful act and the employee's work

Frequently, employees act in ways with respect to which they have no express authority, but which are calculated nevertheless to further some proper objective of their employer. Unless the method of accomplishing this objective is so outrageous that no employer reasonably could be taken to have contemplated such an act as being within the scope of

---

[81] *LCC v Cattermoles (Garages) Ltd* [1953] 2 All ER 582. [82] [1919] 1 Ch 1.

[83] *Young v Box & Co* [1951] 1 TLR 798; *Rose v Plenty* [1976] 1 All ER 97.

[84] Though note that the distinction can sometimes appear illusory. In *Gravil v Carroll* [2008] ICR 1222 a specific prohibition against assaulting opposition players did not, apparently, mean a rugby player was acting beyond the scope of his employment when he punched an opponent *after the match*.

[85] (1946) 175 LT 131.

[86] [1976] 1 All ER 97. As to the principles applicable when a prohibition is statutory, see *Alford v National Coal Board* [1952] 1 All ER 754.

employment, the employer will be liable for torts thus committed, as the following cases show. *Poland v John Parr & Sons* is the leading case:[87]

> H, an employee of Ds, while going home to dinner, reasonably believed that a boy was stealing sugar from a bag on a passing lorry of his employers. He struck the boy, who fell and, in consequence, had to have a leg amputated. Although H's act in defence of his employer's property was tortious, it was not sufficiently excessive to be outside the scope of his employment.

Holding that 'a servant has an implied authority upon an emergency to endeavour to protect his employer's property if he sees it in danger or has reasonable ground for thinking that he sees it in danger',[88] the Court of Appeal found the defendants liable. However, Atkin LJ did point out that:

> where the servant does more than the emergency requires, the excess may be so great as to take the act out of the class. For example, if H had fired a shot at the boy, the act might have been in the interest of his employers, but that is not the test.[89]

Now consider *Warren v Henlys Ltd:*[90]

> A garage attendant employed by Ds accused C, in violent language, of leaving the garage without paying for his petrol. After paying, C called the police and said that he would report the attendant to his employers. On hearing this, the attendant assaulted C.

It was held that there was no evidence that 'this assault . . . was so connected with the acts which the servant was expressly or impliedly authorised to do as to be a mode of doing those acts'.[91]

An example of conduct unconnected with the employer's work is seen in *Makanjuola v Metropolitan Police Commissioner*.[92] A police officer extracted sexual favours from the claimant in return for a promise not to report her to the immigration authorities. It was held that his act was entirely for his own purposes and not an act his employer authorised. Of course, were the officer's proclivities known to senior officers, it might have been possible to argue that there was a breach of a primary duty of care to the public; but those proclivities were not known. Finally, where the acts of prison officers are in broad furtherance of the interests of the Home Office, the Home Office remains liable even though the officers' acts amount to misfeasance in a public office.[93]

(1) Battery, etc

Employer's interests Evidence that the employee's conduct was a criminal or otherwise wilful wrongdoing will not necessarily negate the possibility of imposing vicarious liability.[94] For example, an employer might be liable in respect of acts of

---

[87] [1927] 1 KB 236.   [88] [1927] 1 KB 236, at 240.   [89] [1927] 1 KB 236, at 245.
[90] [1948] 2 All ER 935. In *Keppel Bus Co Ltd v Sa'ad bin Ahmad* [1974] 2 All ER 700, a bus conductor struck a passenger after a quarrel. Although the conductor's duties extended to keeping order, his employer was not vicariously liable because there was no evidence of disorder.
[91] [1948] 2 All ER 935, at 938.   [92] [1992] 3 All ER 617.   [93] *Racz v Home Office* [1994] 2 AC 45.
[94] *Lloyd v Grace, Smith & Co* [1912] AC 716; *Mohamud v Wm Morrison Supermarkets plc* [2016] AC 677.

harassment[95] or where an over-enthusiastic defence of her interests results in battery, which is in the circumstances a crime as well as a tort.[96] Similarly, in *Vasey v Surrey Free Inns*,[97] an employer was held liable in respect of battery upon the claimant committed by two door attendants in his employ. Crucially, the door attendants' acts were in response to the claimant having caused damage to the employer's premises by kicking them. As such, the door attendants' actions were construed as being in furtherance of the employer's interests.[98]

Outside employer's interests There might be cases where the wrongful conduct is in no sense in the employers' interests, but where they are sufficiently connected[99] to 'the field of activities assigned to the employee' so that the employers may be held vicariously liable for that conduct nonetheless.[100] Dishonest or criminal acts are per se no bar to the imposition of vicarious liability.[101] In *Mohamud v Wm Morrison Supermarkets plc*,[102] a service station mini-mart employee dismissed a customer's request to print out a document and then followed him out into the forecourt where he punched the man. The employer was liable given that the attack took place on the employer's premises and during work hours.[103]

Further guidance can be obtained by the contrasting results in two sets of scenarios. The theft of the mink stole in *Morris v C W Martin & Sons Ltd*[104] by the man entrusted with the job of cleaning it has been viewed by the House of Lords as being a case in which the employee used an unlawful mode of doing his job.[105] However, the theft of the stole by a cook in the canteen at the firm's factory would be an act unrelated to his employment. Accordingly, the employer would not be held vicariously liable (which is not to say that she would escape personal liability for employing persons known to be dishonest, thus placing her in breach of a non-delegable duty to care properly for the fur).

Another set of contrasting scenarios arose in two joined cases involving employees who reacted violently to employer requests. In *Wallbank v Wallbank Fox Designs Ltd*, the employer was liable for a battery committed in circumstances where the employee had been asked to load metal furniture frames into an oven and reacted to this immediately and spontaneously, whereas, in *Weddall v Barchester Healthcare Ltd*, there was

---

[95] See, eg, *Iqbal v Dean Manson Solicitors* [2011] EWCA Civ 123, at [63].

[96] *Poland v Parr* [1927] 1 KB 236.   [97] [1996] PIQR P373.

[98] See also *Mattis v Pollock* [2003] 1 WLR 2158 (door attendant committed an assault hundreds of metres from the nightclub at which the trouble had started and vicarious liability was imposed); *Weir v Bettison* [2003] EWCA Civ 111 (a chief constable was held vicariously liable for an assault committed by an off-duty police officer who assaulted a would-be thief after indicating that he was a police officer and that he proposed to take the culprit to a police station).   [99] *Lister v Hesley Hall Ltd* [2002] 1 AC 215.

[100] *Mohamud v Wm Morrison Supermarkets plc* [2016] AC 677.

[101] *Port Swettenham Authority v TW Wu & Co* [1979] AC 580; *Mohamud v Wm Morrison Supermarkets plc* [2016] AC 677.   [102] [2016] AC 677.

[103] This means that *Graham v Commercial Bodyworks Ltd* [2015] ICR 665 (work prank gone wrong) probably would be decided differently now.   [104] [1966] 1 QB 716.

[105] *Lister v Hesley Hall Ltd* [2002] 1 AC 215. This interpretation is questionable since two members of the Court of Appeal seem to have viewed the case as turning primarily upon the non-delegable duty arising out of the bailment of the fur. It is notable that Lord Nicholls deliberately left this case to one side when considering the close connection test in *Dubai Aluminium Co Ltd v Salaam* [2003] 2 AC 366, at [27]–[28].

no liability for battery where the employee had been rung at home to see whether he wanted to work a nightshift, and, being drunk, had mis-interpreted his supervisor's words and rode into the workplace with the purpose of inflicting serious harm.[106] In the former case, the Court of Appeal held that the 'risk of an over-robust reaction to an instruction is a risk created by the employment'. In the latter case, the request was held to be no more than a 'pretext for an act of violence unconnected with work'.[107]

Mere opportunity insufficient It has long been held that the employer cannot be held *vicariously liable* simply for supplying the mere opportunity for the employee to commit a crime. Instead, the criminal act must be much more closely connected with the contract of employment. The leading case is *Lister v Hesley Hall Ltd*:[108]

> A warden living in a boarding house attached to a school owned and managed by Ds had systematically sexually abused for about three years Cs, who were boys at the school with emotional and behavioural difficulties. Ds had no knowledge of the abuse. Cs claimed damages against Ds for the personal injuries they suffered, arguing, inter alia, that Ds were vicariously liable for the torts committed by the warden.

The House of Lords held Ds vicariously liable, emphasising the close contact he had had with the pupils by virtue of his job and the inherent risks his job carried with it. At the heart of their Lordships' decision was the fact that there was a sufficiently close connection between the work that the warden had been employed to do and the acts of abuse that he had committed for those acts to justify the defendants' vicarious liability.[109] As Lord Clyde put it:

> The opportunity to be at the premises would not in itself constitute a sufficient connection between his wrongful actings and his employment. In addition to the opportunity which access gave him, his position as warden and the close contact with the boys which that work involved created a sufficient connection between the acts of abuse which he committed and the work which he had been employed to do.[110]

Inherent risk What seems to lie at the heart of the *Lister* case is not that the job provided the mere circumstances in which the tort took place but that the tort constituted a particular risk which was inextricably linked to the employer's type of business.[111] As Lord Clyde explained, the employer is to be held liable where 'the risk is one which experience shows is inherent in the nature of the business'.[112] Certainly, there was an inherent risk

---

[106] [2012] EWCA Civ 25.   [107] [2012] EWCA Civ 25, at [45] and [54].   [108] [2002] 1 AC 215.
[109] In similar vein, see: *Maga v Birmingham Roman Catholic Archdiocese Trustees* [2010] 1 WLR 1441; *Brink's Global Services v Igrox Ltd* [2010] EWCA Civ 1207.   [110] [2002] 1 AC 215, at [50].
[111] In *Gravil v Carroll* [2008] ICR 1222, the Court of Appeal preferred to ask whether the occurrence in question was an 'ordinary incident' of a rugby match before holding a rugby club liable for a post-match punch thrown by one of its players at an opposition player. See also *Maga v Birmingham RC Archdiocese Trustees* [2010] 1 WLR 1441.
[112] [2002] 1 AC 215, at [65]. It might be argued that the focus on the nature of the employer's business tends to blur the distinction between the employer's primary and vicarious liability (see *Balfon Trustees Ltd v Peterson* [2001] IRLR 758, at [28]). But the decision in *Lister* is assuredly based on the latter.

of sexual abuse of children in *Lister*, as there was in *Armes v Nottinghamshire County Council*, which concerned the placement by a council of children with foster carers.[113]

Scope of rule A moment's reflection reveals that child abuse, by whatever means, could never be viewed as a mere unauthorised mode of performing an authorised act. But the 'close connection test' adopted in *Lister*, which stresses the intimate connection between the employee's tort and the nature of her employment, readily embraces such cases[114]—with the result that it appears harder to insist upon the idea that employers are not liable in circumstances where they have supplied the mere opportunity for employees to commit torts.

(2) Fraud

Statement of rule An employee's fraud might also result in vicarious liability. *Lloyd v Grace, Smith & Co*[115] is the leading case:

> In an action to recover title deeds by C (who was a client of D, a firm of solicitors), the material point was whether the firm was liable for the act of its managing clerk, who, when C consulted him about selling her property and realising a mortgage, fraudulently induced her to sign documents transferring those properties to him. The managing clerk was employed, among other things, to carry out conveyancing transactions. Although the firm derived no benefit from these frauds, perpetrated by its employee for his own purposes, it was held liable for his acts.

In such cases, according to *Lloyd*, the usual question that must be posed appears to be whether the employee was acting with either the actual or ostensible authority of the employer.[116] And, so long as such authority exists, it does not matter that the defrauded party had reasonable grounds for suspicion about what was going on: the court will not require such parties to make enquiries about the legitimacy of a transaction.[117]

Ostensible authority Cases of actual authority are unlikely to be very problematic. But cases of ostensible authority do prove tricky. In this respect, it will be important to advert to the fact that the employee appeared to be acting in a manner that would benefit the employer rather than the employee personally. But if the act is intended only to benefit the employee, and the fraud is not intimately bound up with the employee's employment,[118] vicarious liability ought not to be imposed. (This does not mean, however, that the employer could not potentially be held liable in some cases on the alternative basis of breach of a non-delegable duty.)[119]

---

[113] [2017] UKSC 60, esp. at [61].

[114] In similar vein, see *Bazley v Curry* (1999) 174 DLR (4th) 45; *Jacobi v Griffiths* (1999) 174 DLR (4th) 71.

[115] [1912] AC 716.

[116] [1912] AC 716, at 725. This approach has since been endorsed in *Stone and Rolls Ltd v Moore Stephens* [2009] 3 WLR 455.   [117] *Quinn v CC Automotive Group Ltd* [2011] 2 All ER (Comm) 584.

[118] In *JJ Coughlan v Ruparelia* [2003] EWCA Civ 1057, the Court of Appeal stressed the importance of considering whether the transaction in question, 'viewed fairly and properly', was the kind of transaction that forms part of the ordinary business of a solicitor.

[119] Certainly, there were those in the High Court of Australia who preferred to see *Lloyd* as a case of non-delegable duty: see *New South Wales v Lepore* [2003] HCA 4, at [110] and [235].

In *Dubai Aluminium Co Ltd v Salaam*,[120] all the fraudulent acts necessary to make the employee personally liable took place within (or in close connection with) his course of employment and vicarious liability could be imposed. By contrast, in *Crédit Lyonnais Bank Nederland NV v Export Credits Guarantee Department*,[121] part of the fraud was committed by the employee and part of it by a third party. The House of Lords therefore refused to combine the two sets of acts so as to make the employer vicariously liable for the combined acts of the two fraudsters. Crucially, not all the relevant acts occurred within the course of the employee's employment.

Section 5 Statutory duty and vicarious liability

For a time it was unclear whether an employer could be held vicariously liable for an employee's breach of a statutory duty imposed directly on the employee but not the employer. The matter was resolved in *Majrowski v Guy's and St Thomas' NHS Trust*, which held that an employer can be so liable. Lord Nicholls said:

> Unless the statute expressly or impliedly indicates otherwise, the principle of vicarious liability is applicable where an employee commits a breach of a statutory obligation sounding in damages while acting in the course of his employment.[122]

So far as the Crown is concerned there is specific statutory provision setting out its position: the rather obscurely worded Crown Proceedings Act 1947, sub-section 2(3), has the effect of making the Crown liable for breaches of statutory duty by its employees.

Section 6 Agency

General We have seen that a person who does work for another might be either an employee or an independent contractor. But such a person *might* simultaneously be an agent. This is because the category of 'agent' partially overlaps with the categories of both 'employee' and 'independent contractor'. And while agency is of importance primarily within the law of contract, it is not without significance in this context.

Misrepresentation The tort of deceit provides an example of where tort law *is* concerned with the existence of agency arrangements. Where a principal provides authority to another person to negotiate a contract on her behalf, she might be liable for the fraud of her 'agent'. So, for example, if an estate agent, in the course of negotiating the sale of her principal's house, knowingly makes untrue statements about that house to a

---

[120] [2003] 1 Lloyd's Rep 65.   [121] [2000] 1 AC 486.
[122] [2007] 1 AC 224, at [17]. See also *Iqbal v Dean Manson Solicitors* [2011] IRLR 428 (vicarious liability for acts prohibited by the Protection from Harassment Act 1997).

third party who acts on them to her detriment, the principal will be liable in deceit. And yet the estate agent is not the principal's employee. This liability exists only where the principal can be said to have held out the estate agent as someone authorised to make such representations in the course of making the contract.[123] This provides a valuable clue to the key issue here—such misrepresentations, though capable of giving rise to tortious liability, are so intimately associated with, and inseparable from, the contractual relation to which end the agency is directed that they assume the quality of contract, where agency is important per se.[124]

The concept of agency is applicable also to merely negligent statements made by an estate agent.[125] But it is an essential prerequisite of liability of the principal that the agent acted within the scope of the authority which the principal's acts led the claimant to believe the agent enjoyed. Where the agent is an employee of the principal, the agent cannot act beyond the scope of her authority yet still remain within the general course of her employment.[126]

Vehicle owners The other area which demands special attention is the liability of a vehicle owner when the vehicle is driven by someone else. Of course, the owner is liable if her employee drives it negligently in the course of her employment. The courts have not stopped there, however, and the House of Lords in *Morgans v Launchbury*[127] affirmed that if the vehicle is driven by the owner's agent, and she is driving it for the owner's purposes, the owner will be liable. The facts in *Morgans v Launchbury* were as follows:

> D owned the car. With her permission, her husband took it on a pub-crawl. When he was too drunk to drive, he asked his drinking companion to drive. D was held not liable for the damage caused by the companion's negligent driving.

The House of Lords held that the driver was not the agent of the owner, and that a car owner is liable only if the driver is her employee acting in the course of her employment or is her authorised agent driving for, and on behalf of, the owner. The House rejected the argument that it was so desirable to find someone liable who was covered by compulsory third-party insurance, that it should hold the owner liable for anyone who drove with her permission.[128]

---

[123] Cf *Uxbridge Permanent Benefit Building Society v Pickard* [1939] 2 KB 248, at 254–5. For further endorsement of the 'holding out' principle, see *Lloyd v Grace, Smith & Co* [1912] AC 716; but for criticism of the way in which this case has been interpreted, see J Murphy, 'Juridical Foundations of Common Law Non-Delegable Duties' in JW Neyers et al (eds), *Emerging Issues in Tort Law* (2007), ch 14.

[124] Notably, then, the close-connection test for vicarious liability cannot be used in relation to agents: *M v Hendron* [2007] CSIH 27.

[125] *Kooragang Investments Pty Ltd v Richardson & Wrench Ltd* [1982] AC 462. In that case, therefore, the principal was held not liable for the agent's negligent statement because the agent was not authorised to make the valuations which formed the subject of the negligent statements.

[126] *Armagas Ltd v Mundogas SA, The Ocean Frost* [1986] AC 717.   [127] [1973] AC 127.

[128] In *Norwood v Navan* [1981] RTR 457, a husband was held not liable for the negligence of his wife when driving his car for family shopping.

Section 7 Liability in respect of an independent contractor

Normally, an 'employer' is not liable merely because an independent contractor commits a tort while undertaking work for her. Certain exceptions exist in relation to various torts of 'strict liability'. Thus, there may be liability on the part of an 'employer' in private nuisance,[129] under the rule in *Rylands v Fletcher*[130] and in respect of a breach of statutory duty.[131] But leaving these examples to one side, it is clear that an employer generally will be liable only in connection with torts committed by independent contractors in one of three ways.

(A) Authorizing, procuring, and ratifying torts

General In many circumstances the law will attribute to a person the conduct of another being, whether human or animal, if she has instigated that conduct. She who instigates or procures another to commit a tort is deemed to have committed the tort herself.[132] It matters not whether that other was an employee, an independent contractor, or an agent (human or otherwise). In *Ellis v Sheffield Gas Consumers Co*[133] the facts were as follows:

> Having no legal power to do so, Ds' gas undertaking employed an independent contractor to dig up a part of a street. C fell over a heap of earth and stones made by the contractor in the course of digging, and Ds were held liable on the ground that they had authorised this nuisance.

It is not always easy to decide whether the defendant can be said to have authorised the tortious act. Where a lessee was empowered to erect certain structures, but the lease reserved to the lessor the right to approve the plans for such structures (which right the lessor is not reported to have exercised), this was not enough to make the lessor answerable for the lessee's negligence in the course of building the structure.[134] On the other hand, although a taxi driver is not an employee, if her client orders her to drive fast or to take other risks, she is jointly responsible for any ensuing tort.[135]

Ratification If a person commits a tort while purporting to act on behalf of another, but in fact does so without her authority, and that other later ratifies the act which amounted to a tort, she becomes answerable for the tort in the same way as if she had given authority prior to its commission. However, to be liable on this basis, the principal must know at the time of ratification[136] of the doing of an act which constitutes a

---

[129] See, eg, *Matania v National Provincial Bank Ltd* [1936] 2 All ER 633; *Alcock v Wraith* (1991) 58 BLR 20.
[130] (1868) LR 3 HL 330.   [131] *Hosking v De Havilland Aircraft Co Ltd* [1949] 1 All ER 540.
[132] And even if that other has a defence, the principal still may be liable: *Barker v Braham* (1773) 3 Wils 368 (D authorised a sheriff to arrest C on an illegal warrant; although the sheriff was protected from liability by reason of acting under the warrant, D was still liable in false imprisonment).   [133] (1853) 2 E & B 767.
[134] *Hurlstone v London Electric Rly Co* (1914) 30 TLR 398.
[135] Cf *M'Laughlin v Pryor* (1842) 4 Man & G 48. Mere failure to object or other acquiescence would not be enough.   [136] *Freeman v Rosher* (1849) 13 QB 780.

tort. But she needn't know that the act was tortious. Thus, if she ratifies the purchase of goods which the vendor had no right to sell, she is liable in conversion still, even though she is unaware that the sale was unlawful.[137]

(B) Personal negligence on the part of the employer

There might be such an element of personal negligence on the part of the employer as to make her liable for the acts of her independent contractor, and this might be so even though the duty of care owed by the employer in a particular case is not so extensive as to make the employer liable merely because her independent contractor has been negligent. For example, the employer is liable where she carelessly appoints an incompetent contractor. Equally, where the risk of harm is foreseeable in the absence of precautions, a failure by the employer to provide in the contract for those precautions is actionable negligence.[138] *Robinson v Beaconsfield RDC*[139] furnishes another example of personal negligence on the part of the employer:

> Ds employed contractors to clean out cesspools in their district. No arrangements were made for the removal of the deposits of sewage upon their removal from the cesspools by the contractors. The contractors deposited sewage on C's land. Ds were held liable for their failure to take proper precautions to dispose of the sewage.

It probably follows from the decision in *Robinson* that it would be negligence to fail to undertake a proper inspection after a job has been completed. Pursuant to the Occupiers' Liability Act 1957, proper discharge of the common duty of care where contractors have been engaged involves making such inspections after the work has been completed.[140]

(C) Breach of a non-delegable duty

General In some cases, a duty-ower's obligation has been so widely drawn that it is not discharged by properly instructing and supervising a competent contractor to perform work on her behalf. There is a positive, non-delegable duty to 'see that care is taken'. Such obligations arise in cases in which the duty-ower has protective custody over a vulnerable person, custody being delegated to another,[141] in analogous cases involving vulnerable persons, and in cases involving the occupation of adjoining land. In addition, employers have long been recognised to owe to their employees obligations which are described as 'non-delegable' relating to the provision of competent staff, the provision of a safe place of work with proper plant and equipment, and the general management or system of work (including supervision). However, there is considerable confusion in the law on these obligations, which makes it difficult to discuss them in a systematic way. Reference is made later to selected aspects of the employers'

---

[137] *Hilbery v Hatton* (1864) 2 H & C 822.   [138] Cf *Hughes v Percival* (1883) 8 App Cas 443.
[139] [1911] 2 Ch 188.   [140] Occupiers' Liability Act 1957, s 2(4)(b).
[141] *Woodland v Essex CC* [2014] AC 537, at [12] and [23].

non-delegable duties only.[142] Although there has been debate about the matter, it will be submitted that the breach of a non-delegable duty results in strict liability on the part of the duty-ower.[143]

Two kinds of case In *Woodland v Essex County Council*,[144] the Supreme Court identified two broad kinds of case in which non-delegable duties are said to arise:

> The first is a large, varied and anomalous class of case[] in which the defendant employs an independent contractor to perform some function which is either inherently hazardous or liable to become so in the course of his work … . Their justification, if there is one, should probably be found in a special public policy for operations involving exceptional danger to the public …
>
> The second category of non-delegable duty … comprises cases where the common law imposes a duty upon the defendant which has three critical characteristics. First, it arises not from the negligent character of the act itself but because of an antecedent relationship between the defendant and the claimant. Second, the duty is a positive or affirmative duty to protect a particular class of persons from a particular class of risk[], and not simply a duty to refrain from acting in a way that foreseeably causes injury. Third, the duty is by virtue of that relationship personal to the defendant. The work required to perform such a duty may well be delegable, and usually is. But the duty itself remains the defendant's.

The duty-ower's obligation might originate in either statute or the common law.[145]

Hazardous activities The first category of non-delegable duty identified by the Supreme Court in the *Woodland* case involves hazardous activities. Where, for example, the duty-ower is carrying out operations on or near a highway, and those operations (performed by independent contractors) pose serious risks of harm to highway users, she will be amenable to liability for breach of a non-delegable duty. Consider *Holliday v National Telephone Co*:[146]

> In laying telephone wires along a street, Ds engaged an independent contractor to solder the tubes in which these wires were carried. In negligently using a benzolene lamp, the contractor injured a passer-by. Ds were held liable.

Other circumstances in which a non-delegable duty has been held to arise include: where one carries out structural operations that threaten damage to neighbouring

---

[142] See, for greater detail, eg, H Collins, K Ewing, and A McColgan, *Labour Law* (2012); S Deakin and GS Morris, *Labour Law* (6th edn, 2012).

[143] See now *Armes v Nottinghamshire County Council* [2017] UKSC 60, at [31] and [45]. Note that the law in this area is poorly theorised. For attempts to explain it, compare J Murphy, 'Juridical Foundations of Common Law Non-Delegable Duties' in JW Neyers et al (eds), *Emerging Issues in Tort Law* (2007), ch 14 and id (2007) 30 UNSWLJ 86 with C Witting (2006) 29 UNSWLJ 38.

[144] [2014] AC 537, at [6]–[7].

[145] *Armes v Nottinghamshire County Council* [2017] UKSC 60, at [38].

[146] [1899] 2 QB 392. In *Pickard v Smith* (1861) 10 CBNS 470, the same principle was applied to hold a railway refreshment room proprietor liable to a passenger who fell down a hole which the employee of D's independent contractor negligently left on the platform.

premises;[147] where re-roofing takes place on a row of terraced houses featuring well-known difficulties with the 'joins';[148] and where open fires on bush land are lighted.[149] Despite the established nature of this category of case, in the *Woodland* case Lord Sumption expressed doubt about its cogency. His Lordship stated that many of the relevant decisions are 'founded on arbitrary distinctions between ordinary and extraordinary hazards which may be ripe for re-examination'.[150]

Relationship-based duties The second class of non-delegable duty identified by the Supreme Court in the *Woodland* case features antecedent relationships between the duty-owner and the claimant. Lord Sumption stated that, in these cases, 'the defendant is assuming a liability analogous to that assumed by a person who contracts to do work carefully'. The point of the analogy with contract is that the 'contracting party will normally be taken to contract that the work will be done carefully by whomever he may get to do it'.[151]

A patient who is accepted for treatment in an NHS hospital will be able to rely upon a non-delegable duty in order to sue the NHS authorities that stand behind those engaged to provide the patient's actual specialist treatment. The rationale is that hospital authorities have an obligation to provide proper treatment at all stages, and this cannot be cast off simply by entrusting it to competent staff. Such a non-delegable duty formed the basis of Denning LJ's judgment in *Cassidy v Ministry of Health*,[152] holding that a hospital authority that ran a casualty department had an obligation to provide proper medical and nursing care for all those who presented themselves complaining of illness or injury.[153]

A direct, non-delegable duty to patients has several consequences in today's health service. With the increasing use of agency staff, the hospital might be able to escape vicarious liability by arguing that the patient is unable to prove that a person for whose work the hospital is responsible was at fault. But if the hospital owes its patients a personal, non-delegable duty of care, such an escape route is blocked. Even if negligent treatment is provided by an independent contractor, the hospital will be liable.[154]

A second established category of relationship-based non-delegable duty involves the obligation of the school for the physical safety of its pupils.[155] In *Woodland v Essex County Council*,[156] the Supreme Court accepted this category of non-delegable duty and held that it extended to encompass swimming lessons held outside school grounds and conducted by an unincorporated business. In general, liability arises 'for the negligence of independent contractors only if and so far as the latter are performing functions which the school has assumed for itself a duty to perform, generally in school hours and on school premises (or at other times or places where the school may carry out its

---

[147] *Hughes v Percival* (1883) 8 App Cas 443 (party wall negligently cut into while contractor was rebuilding part of adjoining premises); *Alcock v Wraith* (1991) 58 BLR 20. Dubitante *Woodland v Essex CC* [2014] AC 537, at [9]–[11].   [148] *Alcock v Wraith* (1991) 58 BLR 20.

[149] *Black v Christchurch Finance Co* [1894] AC 48. And see *Balfour v Barty-King* [1957] 1 QB 496 (owner liable for a fire when an independent contractor plumber used a blowlamp in a loft to thaw D's frozen pipes).

[150] [2014] AC 537, at [6].   [151] [2014] AC 537, at [7].

[152] [1951] 2 KB 343, at 362–3. This approach was approved in *Woodland v Essex CC* [2014] AC 537, at [15]–[16].   [153] *Barnett v Chelsea and Kensington Hospital Management Committee* [1969] 1 QB 428.

[154] See, eg, *M v Calderdale and Kirklees HA* [1998] Lloyd's Rep Med 157.

[155] *Commonwealth v Introvigne* (1982) 150 CLR 258.   [156] [2014] AC 537.

educational functions)'.[157] Liability does not arise where independent contractors default in their obligations in the provision of extra-curricular activities outside school hours.[158]

The Employer's Liability (Defective Equipment) Act 1969 must be noted at this juncture also. It applies when, for the purposes of her business, an employer provides equipment (which includes any plant and machinery, vehicle, aircraft, and clothing) for her employee and the employee suffers personal injury in the course of her employment in consequence of a defect in that equipment. The injury is then deemed also to be attributable to the negligence of the employer if the defect is attributable wholly or partly to the negligence, or other tort, of an independent contractor or other third party.[159]

The Act leaves unchanged the common law duty of the employer to provide and ensure the operation of a safe system of work in respects other than the provision of equipment.[160] And this duty is an onerous one as *McDermid v Nash Dredging and Reclamation Co Ltd*[161] illustrates:

> C was employed as a deck hand by Ds. He was instructed to go and work on another tug owned by a different company within the same group as Ds. As a result of the negligence of that tug master, who was not an employee of Ds, C suffered severe injuries. Ds were held liable for failing to provide and ensure the operation of a safe system of work.

It was no excuse that they did not have any control over the operation of the system in question. The non-delegable duty in respect of the safety of their employee was not discharged by delegating that duty to the master of the tug. The duty was one not just to devise, but also to *ensure the operation of,* a safe system of work.[162]

Collateral negligence A non-delegable duty-ower will not be liable for the 'collateral negligence' of their contractors. In *Padbury v Holiday and Greenwood Ltd*,[163] A employed B to fit casement windows into certain premises. B's employee negligently placed a tool on the window sill on which he was working. The wind blew the casement open and the tool was knocked off the sill on to a passer-by. Holding the employer not liable, Fletcher Moulton LJ said:

> [B]efore a superior employer could be held liable for the negligent act of a servant of a sub-contractor it must be shown that the work which the sub-contractor was employed to do was work the nature of which, and not merely the performance of which, cast on the superior employer the duty of taking precautions.[164]

If a hospital owes a non-delegable duty to patients in respect of their treatment, it does not follow that the hospital is liable when an agency doctor negligently backs her car

---

[157] [2014] AC 537, at [25].   [158] [2014] AC 537, at [25].

[159] See also Use of Work Equipment Regulations 1998, SI 1998/2306, reg 4, considered in *Hide v Steeplechase Co (Cheltenham) Ltd* [2014] 1 All ER 405.

[160] Note the obligation to insure under the Employers' Liability (Compulsory Insurance) Act 1969.

[161] [1987] AC 906. See also *Davie v New Merton Board Mills Ltd* [1959] AC 604, at 646.

[162] For the argument that this case more closely resembles vicarious liability than non-delegable duty, see E McKendrick (1990) 53 MLR 770.   [163] (1912) 28 TLR 494.

[164] (1912) 28 TLR 494, at 495. Cf *Hardaker v Idle DC* [1896] 1 QB 335, at 342; *Thompson v Anglo-Saxon Petroleum Co Ltd* [1955] 2 Lloyd's Rep 363.

into yours when driving from one part of the hospital to another. That act is not within the hospital's non-delegable duty to patients.

In short, the duty-ower is liable for those risks of harm created by the work itself which the employer is having done. 'Collateral' means collateral to the risk which marks the limit of the duty-ower's legal obligations. If the duty-ower is to be liable, the danger must be inherent in the work; it is not enough that the contractor chooses a negligent way of performing it where the normal manner of performance would create no reasonably foreseeable peril to the claimant.

The scope of the rule There is little doubt that non-delegable duty has been under-theorised and misunderstood. One question that arises concerns its relationship to the tort of negligence. It has been said that the non-delegable duty arises in circumstances of a heightened standard of care and that the standard might be so high as to entail strict liability.[165] Although it is not easy to refute such an idea by reference to the cases, it is submitted that the following points reveal the error in this thinking: (1) The liability of the duty-ower is strict[166] not because it is very onerous in nature, but because the court *does not enquire* into whether the duty-ower has taken care where it is breached. Strict liability is liability *regardless* of fault. (2) The duty-ower's strict liability is to be distinguished from the liability of any person who does work on her behalf, the latter type of liability typically turning on the presence of negligence which makes the worker personally liable. (3) Often the circumstances in which a non-delegable duty is imposed are such that a heightened standard of care is called for.[167] This higher standard of care is required from *whoever does the work*—whether it be the duty-ower or a delegate. Where the duty-ower fails to do the job properly, there is no need to invoke a non-delegable duty—she is liable simply for a failure to reach the (heightened) standard of negligence. The strictness of the duty-ower's liability only becomes apparent where the fault lies in the way that her delegate does the work. (4) One must keep apart the two different forms of personal liability in the duty-ower—strict liability for breach of a non-delegable duty and personal negligence based on breach of a heightened standard of care.

Section 8 Justifications for vicarious and heightened standards of liability

Various justifications for the imposition of vicarious liability have been offered over the years. One rather pragmatic justification is that the employer normally will have much deeper pockets than the primary tortfeasor. For this reason, a claimant usually will be able to target a defendant worth suing (though this cannot be guaranteed).[168]

---

[165] J Murphy, 'Juridical Foundations of Common Law Non-Delegable Duties' in JW Neyers et al (eds), *Emerging Issues in Tort Law* (2007), ch 14 and id (2007) 30 UNSWLJ 86.

[166] *Armes v Nottinghamshire County Council* [2017] UKSC 60, at [31] and [45]; *Leichhardt MC v Montgomery* (2007) 230 CLR 22. [167] *Armes v Nottinghamshire County Council* [2017] UKSC 60, at [31].

[168] See, eg, *Merrett v Babb* [2001] 3 WLR 1 (the employer in this case had ceased to trade when the action was brought). Note, too, that where the employer is sued, she might seek an indemnity from the employee under the Civil Liability (Contribution) Act 1978.

The employer's pockets are 'deep' insofar as she is insured (or self-insured)[169] for such events and/or because often she will be in a position to pass on the cost of such insurance to the public in the form of increased prices for her product. A second justification is that, because the employer stands to make a profit from her employee working for her, it is only right that she should bear the risk of potential liability arising from the work done.[170] However, neither of these explanations fits with the increasing prevalence of charities and other non-profit organisations having to defend vicarious liability cases. In recent times, for example in *Mohamud v Wm Morrison Supermarkets plc*, the Supreme Court has fallen back upon an explanation of vicarious liability that is concerned with the employer 'putting into motion' the activities of the wrongdoer, it taking the risk that torts will be committed, and the importance of achieving justice for injured claimants.[171] This is a very broad justification for liability, which parallels the increasing width of the doctrine's reach. But such a broad explanation threatens to sever the results in vicarious liability cases from any sense of legal principle.

The view of vicarious liability favoured by the present author takes account of the fact that practically all defendants are organisations,[172] rather than individuals. An organisation is a legally recognised group of persons, which embodies a 'chain of command' and a formal decision-making structure. Legally recognised organisations include government departments, statutory authorities, companies and more sophisticated partnerships, and unincorporated associations. Organisations are amenable to deterrence in ways that individuals typically are not because they are characterised by formalised decision-making processes that permit assessment of risks, planning of activities to relevant standards of conduct, integrating mechanisms which ensure conformity to plans, and the taking of precautions. So, whereas deterrence is a strong explanation for the vicarious liability of institutions, it would not be so strong an explanation for the vicarious liability of individuals. Although Morgan has made the argument that one company might be vicariously liable for the torts committed by its subsidiary's employees,[173] the present author has argued that this is unlikely to arise because the law of limited liability protects the parent company from liability for its subsidiary's debts.[174]

Conclusions

This chapter has considered ways in which one person might be made legally responsible for a tort committed by another person. The main way in which such liability arises is through the doctrine of vicarious liability. Although the doctrine has applied

---

[169] *Various Claimants v Catholic Child Welfare Society* [2013] 2 AC 1, at [34]; *Weddall v Barchester Healthcare Ltd* [2012] EWCA Civ 25, at [63].

[170] *Weddall v Barchester Healthcare Ltd* [2012] EWCA Civ 25, at [63]. For an account of these and other putative justifications for vicarious liability see JW Neyers (2005) Alberta LR 287.

[171] [2016] AC 677, at [40] (citing *Bazley v Curry* (1999) 174 DLR (4th) 45, at [31]) and [45].

[172] Noted in *Various Claimants v Catholic Child Welfare Society* [2013] 2 AC 1, at [34].

[173] P Morgan (2015) 31 PN 276.

[174] C Witting, *Liability of Corporate Groups and Networks* (2018), ch 12.

for several centuries mainly in cases involving employees and their vicariously liable employers, the UK Supreme Court has expanded its reach in recent times so that it now covers certain (not fully specified) relationships 'akin to employment'. The doctrine appears to be moving in the direction of a more general organisation-type responsibility. In addition to the relationship requirement, vicarious liability requires also that there be a sufficient connection between the tort which has been committed and the relationship. While torts committed in the course of employment represent the central case, this is not the limit of vicarious liability.

Problem question

Susan runs a dog-walking business. She asks her life partner, Nellie, to walk dogs for her every now and then. Susan does not pay Nellie for this because they live together. But Susan does sometimes allow Nellie to use the company BMW as a 'thank-you' for walking the dogs (which Nellie hates to do). One afternoon, while on a walk, Nellie is negligent and one of the dogs bites a person, Roger, on the bike track. The dog also bites a school child, Jenna, who has just stepped outside the Happy Days School gate in order to go home at the end of the day.

Advise on the liabilities of Susan and the School for torts committed by Nellie.

 Visit **http://www.oup.com/uk/street15e/** for answer guidance.

Further reading

GILIKER, *Vicarious Liability in Tort: A Comparative Perspective* (2010)

MORGAN, 'Recasting Vicarious Liability' (2012) 71 *Cambridge Law Journal* 615

MORGAN, 'Vicarious Liability for Group Companies: The Final Frontier for Vicarious Liability?' (2015) 31 *Professional Negligence* 276

MORGAN, 'Vicarious Liability for Independent Contractors?' (2015) 31 *Professional Negligence* 235

MURPHY, 'Juridical Foundations of Common Law Non-Delegable Duties' in Neyers et al (eds), *Emerging Issues in Tort Law* (2007), ch 14

NEYERS, 'A Theory of Vicarious Liability' (2005) 43 *Alberta Law Review* 287

PRASSL, 'The Notion of the Employer' (2013) 129 *Law Quarterly Review* 380

PRASSL, *The Concept of the Employer* (2016)

STEVENS, 'Non-Delegable Duties and Vicarious Liability' in Neyers et al (eds), *Emerging Issues in Tort Law* (2007), ch 13

WITTING, 'Breach of the Non-Delegable Duty: Defending Limited Strict Liability in Tort' (2006) 29 *University of New South Wales Law Journal* 38

25

Capacity and parties

KEY ISSUES

(1) Capacity

A preliminary issue that might arise in a tort action concerns 'capacity'. This refers to the status of legal persons and their ability to sue or be sued in tort. Very young children cannot be held responsible in law for the consequences of actions that might otherwise be tortious. However, the law is more accepting of the responsibility of mentally disordered persons, especially where they have some understanding of the nature and quality of their acts.

(2) Concurrent tortfeasors

The claimant's injury might be the result of the torts of more than one person. In such a case, the claimant can sue all of the responsible persons. However, the law does not require this; it allows the claimant to sue for the full amount one only of the concurrent tortfeasors whose acts combine to cause the *same damage*. This reduces financial and other burdens upon the claimant in obtaining redress.

(3) Several tortfeasors causing different damage

Alternatively, the claimant's injuries might be the result of the independent acts of more than one person causing *separate items of damage*. In such a case, the liability of each tortfeasor is several; each is liable only for the damage that he causes.

(4) Contribution

Statute allows any person successfully sued in tort to seek contribution from other joint or concurrent tortfeasors (under (2) in this list, but not (3)). This might be done in the course of the original action commenced by the claimant, or in separate proceedings between tortfeasors. The law will apportion liability between these parties according to the extent of their responsibility.

Section 1 The Crown

(A) Vicarious liability

Rule Under the Crown Proceedings Act 1947, sub-section 2(1)(a), 'the Crown shall be subject to all those liabilities in tort to which, if it were a private person of full age and capacity, it would be subject in respect of torts committed by its servants or agents'.

Despite the generality of this statement of the Crown's vicarious liability, an employee *normally* must be directly or indirectly appointed by the Crown and paid wholly out of the Consolidated Fund or other specified national funds for this vicarious liability to be triggered.[1] The Crown is not vicariously liable for the torts of police officers,[2] or for the torts of borrowed employees.

Crown Although the term 'Crown' is not defined, the Crown Proceedings Act 1947 does not apply to employees of those bodies that are not deemed to be agents of the Crown. Many public bodies fall outside the Act.[3] In such cases, the ordinary law affecting public bodies and public officers will apply. Thus, it is important to be able to determine which public bodies are agents of the Crown. Relevant considerations include the nature of the functions undertaken and the extent to which the body in question is under ministerial control.[4]

(B) Non-vicarious liability

Rule The Crown Proceedings Act 1947, sub-sections 2(1)(b) and (c) make the Crown liable for any breach of those duties owed at common law to employees, agents, or independent contractors by an employer, and for any breach of the duties attaching at common law to the ownership, occupation, possession, or control of property.

Gap in coverage Sub-section 2(1) does not seem sufficiently wide to encompass all the cases in which an employer is liable otherwise than vicariously. While employers frequently are answerable for the acts of independent contractors—not because the independent contractor has committed a tort in the course of his work, but because the duty is a personal one imposed on the employer—the provision would not seem wide enough to cover breaches of non-delegable duty of this sort.[5]

Further liability The Crown is liable in tort to the same extent as private persons for breaches of statutory duty that have been imposed on it, provided the duty is imposed also on persons other than the Crown and its officers.[6] If the duty is imposed not on the Crown but directly on its employees, and an employee commits a tort while purporting to perform those statutory functions, 'the liabilities of the Crown in respect of the tort shall be such as they would have been if those functions had been conferred or imposed

---

[1] Crown Proceedings Act 1947, sub-s 2(6). The exception is that no such liability can be imposed in respect of the infringement of intellectual property rights except in accordance with s 3.

[2] For the liability of a chief constable to pay damages out of public funds to those harmed by a policeman's torts, see the Police Act 1996, s 88 and *Weir v Bettison* [2003] EWCA Civ 111.

[3] *Tamlin v Hannaford* [1950] 1 KB 18.

[4] *Bank voor Handel en Scheepvaart NV v Administrator of Hungarian Property* [1954] AC 584.

[5] Cf *Egerton v Home Office* [1978] Crim LR 494 (a duty was owed to a sexual offender in prison to keep a protective watch to guard against his being attacked by fellow prisoners).

[6] Crown Proceedings Act 1947, sub-s 2(2). The Occupiers' Liability Act 1957, s 6 provides that that Act shall bind the Crown and that the common duty of care imposed by it shall apply as a statutory duty for the purpose of the Crown Proceedings Act 1947.

solely by virtue of instructions lawfully given by the Crown'.[7] The Crown has the same liability also as other employers under the Employer's Liability (Defective Equipment) Act 1969.

(C) Exceptions

(1) Judicial errors

The Crown Proceedings Act 1947, sub-section 2(5) provides that the Crown shall not be liable 'in respect of anything done or omitted to be done by any person while discharging or purporting to discharge any responsibilities of a judicial nature vested in him, or any responsibilities which he has in connection with the execution of the judicial process'.[8]

(2) Armed forces

In *Mulcahy v Ministry of Defence*,[9] the Court of Appeal established that service personnel do not owe their fellows a duty of care in war-like conditions.[10] Although the existence of this 'immunity' was upheld in *Smith v Ministry of Defence*,[11] the Supreme Court held that it needs to be delimited carefully so as not to extend too far beyond the battlefield. Lord Hope stated:

> At the stage when [personnel] are being trained, whether pre-deployment or in theatre, or decisions are being made about the fitting of equipment to tanks or other fighting vehicles, there is time to think things through, to plan and to exercise judgment. These activities are sufficiently far removed from the pressures and risks of active operations against the enemy for it not to be unreasonable to expect a duty of care to be exercised, so long as the standard of care that it imposed has regard to the nature of these activities and to their circumstances.[12]

Section 2 Companies

Separate personality A company is a separate legal entity, able to enter into contracts, to own property, and to sue and be sued in its own name. It has a liability that is separate from that of its shareholders. Indeed, the ordinary rule is that the shareholders are not liable for the debts of the company in which they invest, except to the extent of any unpaid amounts on the shares that they hold.[13]

---

[7] Crown Proceedings Act 1947, sub-s 2(3). Presumably, this rule applies also where the duty in question is not imposed on persons other than employees of the Crown.

[8] See *Welsh v CC of Merseyside Police* [1993] 1 All ER 692. Under the Courts Act 2003, sub-s 31(1), immunity is granted to a justice of the peace only in respect of acts or omissions 'in the execution of his duty as a justice of the peace' and then only so far as those acts or omissions fall 'within his jurisdiction'.

[9] [1996] QB 732.

[10] This decision must now be read in the light of: *Barrett v Enfield LBC* [2001] 2 AC 550; *Phelps v Hillingdon LBC* [2000] 3 WLR 776.   [11] *Smith v Ministry of Defence* [2014] AC 52.

[12] *Smith v Ministry of Defence* [2014] AC 52, at [95]. See also [99]–[100] (discussing appropriate standard of care. Note that the minority argued persuasively that Lord Hope's caveats about the standard of care would not be sufficiently effective).   [13] Insolvency Act 1986, sub-s 74(2)(d).

Vicarious liability The company's liabilities might arise in several different ways. A company will be *vicariously liable* for the acts and omissions of its employees arising in the course of its business, where these cause loss to outsiders. This kind of liability is exactly the same as that which applies with respect to an employer who is a natural person. Vicarious liability is discussed in chapter 24.

Primary liability of company The more complex issue concerns the *primary* liability of the company, and the further liability of its directors, officers, and employees when a tort is committed. Let us consider first when the company is primarily liable. Directors are said to act *as the company*, thereby creating liability in the company, when they make decisions as the directing mind and will of the company.[14] They act in this way when making decisions at board meetings or on delegation of decision-making power from the board. The range of persons who could qualify as the directing mind and will of the company was extended by the House of Lords in *Director General of Fair Trading v Pioneer Concrete (UK) Ltd & Another (Re Supply of Ready Mixed Concrete (No 2))*,[15] which held that the court could examine the specific individuals who exercised management and control over the activity constituting the wrong. Given the way that decision-making power within the company may be delegated to particular individuals who are not necessarily board members, the directing mind and will might be found in any delegate holding the decision-making power of the board[16] or who is otherwise deemed to embody the company for the purposes of statute or legal policy.[17] In these cases, the wrongs of the individuals become the wrongs of the company.[18]

Directors and officers Where recourse to the company would not be viable, outsiders who have suffered a wrong at the hands of an individual director or officer may look to him for redress. The general principle is that individuals are liable for their own torts. 'Whether the principal is a company or a natural person, someone acting on his behalf may incur personal liability in tort . . .'.[19] But there must be some act or omission of the director or officer that amounts to a tort. A director will be personally liable for his own statements constituting deceit.[20] However, courts are reluctant to impose personal liability upon individual officers of a company for negligent misstatements made while

---

[14] *Lennard's Carrying Co Ltd v Asiatic Petroleum Co Ltd* [1915] AC 705; *Tesco Supermarkets Ltd v Nattrass* [1972] AC 153.

[15] [1995] 1 AC 456. See also *Meridian Global Funds Management Asia Ltd v Securities Commission* [1995] 2 AC 500.

[16] See *Tesco Supermarkets Ltd v Nattrass* [1972] AC 153, at 171.

[17] *Meridian Global Funds Management Asia Ltd v Securities Commission* [1995] 2 AC 500.

[18] *Bilta (UK) Ltd (in liq) v Nazir (No 2)* [2015] 2 WLR 1168. This liability base has been applied in criminal, regulatory, and civil proceedings: CA Png, *Corporate Liability: A Study in the Principles of Attribution* (2001), 19. Note, however, that the *Bilta* case decided that whether or not a director's fraud would be attributed to a company depends upon whether the company itself is seeking recompense from the fraudulent directors (no attribution) or third-party victims are seeking recompense from the company (attribution).

[19] *Williams v Natural Life Health Foods Ltd* [1998] 1 WLR 829, at 835. See also *Wah Tat Bank Ltd v Chan Cheng Kum* [1975] AC 507, at 514–15.

[20] *Standard Chartered Bank v Pakistan National Shipping Corp (No 2)* [2003] 1 AC 959. See also *Stone & Rolls Ltd v Moore Stephens* [2009] 1 AC 1391, at [132]–[136].

acting for the company. In such cases, it has been held that the claimant must establish the type of proximity that gives rise to an 'assumption of responsibility'.[21] Further, a claim for conversion against a company alleged to have been dealing with the claimant's goods in a manner inconsistent with its rights is not, prima facie, good as against a de facto director. The fact that the de facto director effectively ran the company and could issue directions to its staff does not create a personal liability in him, when the documents are in the possession of the company and not in him.[22]

Corporate groups In some cases, the question arises as to the liability of one company within a group of companies for the acts or omissions of another company in the group—usually the liability of the parent company for its subsidiary's torts. Ordinarily, the courts will respect the separateness of each entity. They will not 'lift the corporate veil' in order to fix liability in a company other than that which interacted with the claimant.[23] However, there might be cases of *evasion* of a prior obligation in which courts would be prepared to disregard the strictness of rules of separate legal personality and to extend liability from a subsidiary company to a parent company.[24] Further, in *Chandler v Cape plc*,[25] the Court of Appeal held that a parent company had owed *a duty of care* in negligence to employees of a subsidiary company (since dissolved), who contracted asbestosis during their employment with the subsidiary. This was on the basis of the proximity that arose between the parties, evidenced by parent company control over and decision-making for the subsidiary, especially with respect to matters of health and safety.

Section 3 Mentally disordered persons

When liable If a mentally disordered person has that state of mind which is required for liability in battery, his insanity is no defence.[26] The case most directly in point is *Morriss v Marsden*:[27]

> D violently attacked C, a complete stranger, while he was standing in the entrance hall of a hotel, and D was sued for battery. The defence raised was insanity. Stable J found that D was not in a condition of automatism or trance at the time of the attack on C, but that his mind directed the blows which he struck. He found also that at the material time D was a certifiable lunatic who knew the nature and quality of his acts but, because of his lunacy, did not know that what he was doing was wrong. The defence of insanity was held to be inapplicable.

---

[21] *Williams v Natural Life Health Foods Ltd* [1998] 1 WLR 829. For criticism, see C Witting (2013) 24 KLJ 343. [22] *Thunder Air Ltd v Hilmarsson* [2008] EWHC 355 (Ch).

[23] *Prest v Petrodel Resources Ltd* [2013] 2 AC 415; *Adams v Cape Industries plc* [1990] Ch 433.

[24] *Prest v Petrodel Resources Ltd* [2013] 2 AC 415. [25] [2012] 1 WLR 3111.

[26] This is so even if the defendant's insanity causes him to be under a delusion about the surrounding circumstances. The critical thing is that he possessed the state of mind required by the tort in relation to the act done: *Buckley and Toronto Transportation Commission v Smith Transport Ltd* [1946] 4 DLR 721.

[27] [1952] 1 All ER 925.

All that is required in battery is that the defendant must intend to strike the blow at the claimant. In *Morriss*, Stable J found that the defendant did so intend, and so the defendant was liable. At a more general level, the case supports the proposition that, in tort (as distinct from criminal law), a defendant who intentionally invades the claimant's protected interest will not be excused simply because he was unaware that the invasion was a wrongful act. According to the Court of Appeal in *Dunnage v Randall*, the same general rule applies in negligence. A mentally disordered person owes others in physical proximity to him a duty of care to act in a way which meets the objective external standard of action set by the law.[28]

When not liable In *Morriss v Marsden*, Stable J went on to say that:

> if a person in a condition of complete automatism inflicted grievous injury, that would not be actionable. In the same way, if a sleepwalker inadvertently, without intention or without carelessness, broke a valuable vase, that would not be actionable.[29]

The logic of this dictum means that a defence will lie in respect of all torts, including negligence[30] and those of 'strict' liability, in which the defendant's conduct was, because of his mental disorder, involuntary. As Vos LJ stated in the negligence case of *Dunnage v Randall*:

> People with physical and mental health problems should not properly be regarded as analogous to children, even if some commonly and inappropriately speak of adults with mental health problems as having a 'mental age of five'.
>
> [O]nly defendants whose attack or medical incapacity has the effect of entirely eliminating any fault or responsibility for injury can be excused . . .
>
> It is only if the defendant can properly be said to have done nothing himself to cause injury that he escapes liability.[31]

Under these parameters there will be a defence even if the conduct was intended by the defendant but the tort in question—for example, conspiracy—requires an improper purpose or malice.[32]

Section 4 Children

(A) Liability

A person is a child until he attains the age of 18 years.[33] Childhood as such is not a defence: but like all other defendants, a child is not liable for a specific tort if he lacked the required capacity for legal responsibility. Should a one-year-old infant pick up a letter defamatory of X, written by his father, and throw it through the window, whereupon

---

[28] *Dunnage v Randall* [2016] QB 639, considered earlier in ch 6.
[29] [1952] 1 All ER 925, at 927. [30] *Dunnage v Randall* [2016] QB 639.
[31] *Dunnage v Randall* [2016] QB 639, at [130]–[133]. [32] *Dunnage v Randall* [2016] QB 639, at [155].
[33] Family Law Reform Act 1969, sub-s 1(1).

Y picks it up and reads it, X will have no cause of action for libel against the infant. On the other hand, a 15-year-old youth who pushes a man into a swimming pool can be held liable in negligence and trespass.[34]

(1) Where the act of the child is also a breach of contract

With certain exceptions, a child is not liable for breach of contract.[35] Therefore, where the act of the child is merely an improper performance of one of the acts contemplated by such a contract, it will not be open to the person aggrieved to sue him in tort so as to evade the contractual immunity. But if the act complained of, though performed upon the occasion of a contract, is independent of it, the claimant can sue in tort. Thus, a child who had possession of goods under a hire-purchase agreement and who wrongfully disposed of them to a third party was liable to the true owner for the independent tort of detinue which he committed by wrongfully disposing of them.[36]

(2) Liability of the parent

Although a claimant might have no cause of action against the child, sometimes he can recover from the child's parent. The parent might be vicariously liable—for example, if the child is acting as his parent's chauffeur and drives the car negligently. Similarly, the parent will be liable if he instigates the son's commission of a tort, or if he has been negligent personally.[37] But the parent is not necessarily liable merely because his son has thrown a stone through his neighbour's window. Unless the parent ordered him to do so, or unless his negligent supervision caused the act complained of, he will not be liable.[38]

(B) Capacity to sue

Although normally he must sue by his next friend, a child is in the same position as any other claimant when suing in tort. A child can sue either parent and might wish to do so when the parent has an insurance policy (usually comprehensive household insurance) which covers the particular liability.[39] But the Court of Appeal has warned against the danger of too readily imposing liability for the 'rough and tumble of family life'.[40] And it is well established that a parent (or someone with quasi-parental responsibility) can lawfully exercise reasonable chastisement in respect of the child.[41]

---

[34] *Williams v Humphrey* (1975) *Times*, 20 February. For comment on inconsistencies in the law about childhood responsibility, see B Lyons (2010) 30 LS 257.

[35] See Minors' Contracts Act 1987.   [36] *Ballett v Mingay* [1943] KB 281.

[37] *Donaldson v McNiven* [1952] 2 All ER 691; *Newton v Edgerley* [1959] 3 All ER 337. The duty of school authorities is to take the care also that a reasonable parent would take: see, eg, *Ricketts v Erith BC* [1943] 2 All ER 629; *Rich v LCC* [1953] 2 All ER 376.

[38] The position in continental Europe is surveyed in P Giliker, *Vicarious Liability in Tort: A Comparative Perspective* (2010), ch 7.

[39] See, eg, *Ash v Lady Ash* (1696) Comb 357; *Young v Rankin* 1934 SC 499.

[40] *Surtees v Kingston-upon-Thames BC* [1991] 2 FLR 559.

[41] See, eg, *R v H* [2001] 2 FLR 431 (allegation of assault by father of his son).

Section 5 Joint torts

(A) Categories

There are three broad categories of case in which one person might suffer damage as the result of torts committed by two or more defendants: joint tortfeasors, several concurrent tortfeasors causing the same damage, and several tortfeasors causing different damage.[42]

(1) Joint tortfeasors

The category of joint tortfeasors[43] includes those in the following paragraphs:[44]

Vicarious liability Where the employer is vicariously liable for the tort of the employee, they are joint tortfeasors.

Procuring tort Where one person procures or prompts another to commit a tort, they are joint tortfeasors.[45] An example might arise where the managing director of a company orders an employee to do acts which constitute a tort. But a person who merely facilitated (rather than procured) a tort would not be a joint tortfeasor.[46]

Concerted action Where two or more persons with a joint purpose take 'concerted action to a common end'[47] and one of them commits a tort they are joint tortfeasors. The boundaries of this principle were the subject of sustained attention in *Fish & Fish Ltd v Sea Shepherd UK*.[48] According to the Supreme Court, liability arises where three elements are satisfied. First, D2 must act to assist D1 in the commission of acts amounting to a tort. D2's act must be substantial (more than merely facilitative) in nature.[49] Second, there must be a 'common design' as between D1 and D2 consisting in agreement of some kind (whether explicit or not) that they should work towards a common end.[50] Third, the primary wrongdoer must commit the tort regarding which D2's acts of assistance at least must be a contributing cause.[51] The most difficult aspect of this definition concerns the common design element. In the *Sea Shepherd* case, there were

---

[42] For full discussion, see *Clerk and Lindsell on Torts* (20th edn, 2010), ch 4.

[43] H Carty (1999) 19 LS 489.

[44] Cf *The Koursk* [1924] P 140, at 155.

[45] J Dietrich and P Ridge, *Accessories in Private Law* (2015), 115–16.

[46] *PLG Research Ltd v Ardon International Ltd* [1993] FSR 197.

[47] *The Koursk* [1924] P 140, at 152. Directors might be joint tortfeasors with a limited company where they directed or procured the tortious act or informed the company for the express purpose of doing a wrongful act: *Rainham Chemical Works Ltd v Belvedere Fish Guano Co* [1921] 2 AC 465, at 476; or if, after formation, the company adopted a deliberate policy of wrongdoing: *Oertli (T) A-G v E J Bowman (London) Ltd* [1956] RPC 282, at 292.

[48] [2015] AC 1229.

[49] [2015] AC 1229, at [21], [23], [37], [49], [57], and [58]. See also PW Lee (2015) 27 SAcLJ 853, 861.

[50] [2015] AC 1229, at [23], [37], and [55]. See also *Unilever plc v Gillette (UK) Ltd* [1989] RPC 583, 609; J Dietrich and P Ridge, *Accessories in Private Law* (2015), 117.

[51] PS Davies, *Accessory Liability* (2015), 12–13; J Dietrich and P Ridge, *Accessories in Private Law* (2015), 38.

various statements about what would suffice. Lord Sumption held that there must be a shared *intention* to commit the acts which prove to be tortious,[52] while both Lords Toulson and Neuberger would have accepted knowledge in D2 of D1's intention to commit a tort[53] (which is more consistent with the general law in this area).[54] Following on from this decision, the Court of Appeal in *Glaxo Wellcome UK Ltd v Sandoz Group*[55] accepted that four companies in a group each had the common intention and design of selling a certain product with a chosen design and get-up so as to create confusion about the origins of the product, thereby committing the tort of passing off (considered in chapter 14). This was in circumstances where each had a role to play in the development, testing, marketing, and sale of the allegedly infringing product. In so holding, Sir Timothy Lloyd stated that 'if the common design is shared between several parties to a combination, it matters not that some relevant acts are done only by one or some parties and other relevant acts are done by others'.[56] But there would be no joint tort in a case where one company merely sold to another company in the same group an infringing product.[57]

'Once a party has acted in concert with others in pursuit of a common design with knowledge of its general objects, such party is liable for what occurs in pursuit of those general objects "even though as to some of the incidents [the defendant might] not have anticipated that they would happen".'[58]

(2) Several concurrent tortfeasors causing the same damage

Two categories Several, or separate, or independent tortfeasors are of two kinds: those whose tortious acts combine to produce the same damage and those whose acts cause different damage to the same claimant.

Same damage It is convenient to call the first group several concurrent tortfeasors and they alone are illustrated in this section, which is concerned with acts that do not fit into any of the four subcategories of joint tortfeasors previously listed but which result in the infliction of the same damage to the claimant. In *Drinkwater v Kimber*,[59] a passenger in a motor car was injured in a collision between that car and another. Morris LJ said that the two drivers, both of whom were negligent, 'were separate tortfeasors whose concurrent acts caused injury to the female claimant'. Again, there was concurrent liability in *Thompson v LCC*,[60] where the claimant's house was damaged when its foundations subsided due to negligent excavation by D1 and a water company, D2, negligently allowing water to escape from its main. Finally, the facts in *The Koursk* illustrate a case in which there was only one unit of damage that was impossible to divide between the various tortfeasors:[61]

---

[52] [2015] AC 1229, at [44]. See PW Lee (2015) 27 SAcLJ 853, 862–4.

[53] [2015] AC 1229, at [27] and [60] respectively.

[54] J Dietrich and P Ridge, *Accessories in Private Law* (2015), 4, 12–13, 29, 43–60, 93–4, 116–17, and 127–30.

[55] [2017] EWCA Civ 227.   [56] [2017] EWCA Civ 227, at [31].

[57] [2017] EWCA Civ 227, at [32].

[58] J Dietrich and P Ridge, *Accessories in Private Law* (2015), 133, citing *Schumann v Abbott and Davis* [1961] SASR 149, at 155.

[59] [1952] 2 QB 281, at 292. See also *Fitzgerald v Lane* [1989] AC 328.

[60] [1899] 1 QB 840.   [61] [1924] P 140.

> *The Koursk*, while sailing in convoy, negligently changed course so that it bore down on the *Clan Chisholm*, which was careless in failing to reverse its engines in order to avoid a collision. Immediately after the impact, the *Clan Chisholm* collided with the *Itria*. Having recovered damages against the *Clan Chisholm* for an amount less than the loss suffered (because of a special statutory provision), the *Itria* sued *The Koursk*.

The Koursk and *Clan Chisholm* were held to be several tortfeasors causing the same damage.

(3) Several tortfeasors causing different damage

General Where two or more persons not acting in concert cause different lots of damage to the same claimant they are treated differently in law from either joint or several concurrent tortfeasors. In the straightforward kind of case, the two defendants inflict quite separate lots of damage on the claimant. For example, the first defendant gouges out the claimant's eye and the second defendant fractures his skull, whereupon the first defendant is answerable only for the damage resulting from the loss of the eye and the second defendant solely for the damage attributable to the fracture of the skull.

Borderline cases While the distinction between this category and several concurrent tortfeasors is clear in theory, there are cases in which it is difficult to decide whether there was an indivisible unit of damage, or whether the harm was capable of apportionment among the several defendants. The courts appear to have taken a sensible attitude in such cases, avoiding, if possible, saddling any one defendant with responsibility for more harm than he has caused. Accordingly, they display a marked preparedness to declare harm to be divisible.[62] Thus, in the common kinds of case of harm caused by the independent acts of various defendants—for example, pollution of rivers, or nuisance by smell or noise— the courts will not hold each defendant liable for the entire damage. They will endeavour to ascertain the respective contributions to the harm made by each defendant, and, failing that, they will generally apportion the loss equally between them.[63]

Asbestos exposure A difficult type of case concerns a claimant who has contracted mesothelioma in consequence of wrongful exposure to asbestos dust on the part of a number of former employers. In *Barker v Corus UK Ltd*,[64] it was held that, where more than one employer had been in breach of a duty (and might therefore have been responsible for the claimant's mesothelioma), liability should be apportioned among

---

[62] See, eg, *Royal Brompton Hospital NHS Trust v Hammond (No 3)* [2002] 1 WLR 1397; *Niru Battery Manufacturing Co v Milestone Trading Ltd (No 2)* [2003] 2 All ER (Comm) 365.

[63] *Bank View Mills Ltd v Nelson Corpn* [1942] 2 All ER 477, esp. at 483 (revd [1943] KB 337); *Pride of Derby and Derbyshire Angling Assocn Ltd v British Celanese Ltd* [1953] 1 All ER 179. See also *Dingle v Associated Newspapers Ltd* [1961] 1 All ER 897, at 916. The point was not discussed in the HL: [1964] AC 371. Sometimes the cumulative effect of the actions of D1 and D2 is greater than the sum of their respective contributions—this does not deter the courts from making them liable proportionately for the amount of harm which each would have caused in any event.

[64] [2006] 2 WLR 1027.

the various former employers according to their respective contributions to the risk of contracting the disease (gauged according to the length and intensity of exposure to asbestos dust).[65] While this indicated a clear desire to treat each employer as a several tortfeasor,[66] it is not clear why the different periods of risk were viewed as different damage, or even damage at all (given that risk generally is not treated as actionable loss in negligence law).[67] This difficulty and others besides[68] prompted the government to introduce legislation designed to reverse the decision in *Barker*, and to put in its place some form of statutory basis for claims by mesothelioma victims. This occurred in the shape of the Compensation Act 2006 (discussed in chapter 5). In *Sienkiewicz v Greif (UK) Ltd*, Lord Phillips P explained that the principle to be applied was as follows:

> When a victim contracts mesothelioma each person who has, in breach of duty, been responsible for exposing the victim to a significant quantity of asbestos dust and thus creating a 'material increase in risk' of the victim contracting the disease will be held jointly and severally liable for causing the disease.[69]

But the Act applies only to cases of mesothelioma, creating disparities in the treatment of other forms of physical injury.[70] The resultant liability regime has been the subject of criticism in the Supreme Court. Thus, in *Sienkiewicz*, Lord Phillips commented that the 2006 Act coupled with the test for causation in *Fairchild v Glenhaven Funeral Services Ltd*[71] 'has draconian consequences for an employer who has been responsible for only a small proportion of the overall exposure of a claimant to asbestos dust, or his insurers . . . '.[72]

(B) Distinguishing between joint tortfeasors, several concurrent tortfeasors, and other tortfeasors

There are four points of note that can be made in relation to the distinctions that exist between the various categories of multiple tortfeasors.

Extent of responsibility Concurrent tortfeasors, whether joint or several, are each answerable in full for the whole damage caused to the claimant. Several non-concurrent tortfeasors are answerable merely for that damage which each has caused. It is often of prime importance to decide, therefore, whether the defendants were acting in concert. Suppose that A and B are engaged on a hunting expedition and both of them simultaneously fire across a highway at game beyond the highway. If a shot injures a highway user, but it is not known which of A or B fired it, they are joint tortfeasors acting in concert, enabling the claimant to recover full damages from either.[73] However, if they are several

---

[65] [2006] 2 WLR 1027, at [48] and [109].   [66] [2006] 2 WLR 1027, at [62].

[67] This point was made in the speeches of both Lord Rodger and Baroness Hale.

[68] The most prominent other problem was identified by Lord Rodger: namely, that he could see no 'logical or otherwise compelling connection between the *Fairchild* exception and the introduction of several liability': [2006] 2 WLR 1027, at [87].

[69] [2011] 2 AC 229, at [1].   [70] [2011] 2 AC 229, at [176].   [71] [2003] 1 AC 32.

[72] [2011] 2 AC 229, at [58].   [73] *Arneil v Paterson* [1931] AC 560.

tortfeasors they have not brought about the same damage (for only one has caused damage) and the success of the action depends on proof of the commission of a tort by the one who is sued.[74] Questions of divisible harm do not arise where the defendants are joint tortfeasors because each joint tortfeasor is liable in full for all the harm sustained by the claimant.

Satisfaction Satisfaction[75] by any concurrent tortfeasor discharges the liability of all the others, whereas satisfaction by a several non-concurrent one does not.[76]

Joinder The courts are less willing to exercise their discretion under the Civil Procedure Rules to allow joinder of the defendants where the defendants concerned are not concurrent tortfeasors.

Contribution There is in general a right to contribution in the case of concurrent tortfeasors, but not in respect of other tortfeasors.

(C) Contribution

(1) Scope

The Civil Liability (Contribution) Act 1978, sub-section 1(1) provides that 'any person liable in respect of any damage suffered by another person may recover contribution from any other person liable in respect of the same damage (whether jointly with him or otherwise)'. At one time, the courts gave a wide interpretation to the meaning of the phrase 'same damage'.[77] However, the House of Lords overruled this broad approach in *Royal Brompton Hospital NHS Trust v Hammond (No 3)*.[78]

> A firm of architects had negligently issued extension certificates to contractors in respect of certain construction work commissioned by a developer. The building work was delayed and the developer sued the architects for negligence. The architects were unable to claim contribution from the contractors who actually carried out the delayed construction. The contractors were responsible for delayed construction per se, whereas the architects (by issuing the extension certificates) had caused the developer to lose the opportunity to sue the contractors for liquidated damages in respect of that delay. The question was whether the loss of opportunity to sue for liquidated damages was to be regarded as the same damage as the delay, per se.

---

[74] Cf *Cook v Lewis* [1952] 1 DLR 1.

[75] But note that a mere accord—ie, an agreement by C to accept some consideration in substitution for his strict legal remedy—with a several concurrent tortfeasor does not necessarily have this effect: everything turns on the interpretation of the accord: *Jameson v Central Electricity Generating Board* [2000] 1 AC 455; *Heaton v AXA Equity & Law Life Assurance Society plc* [2002] 2 AC 329.

[76] And see *Bryanston Finance Ltd v de Vries* [1975] QB 703. For the effect of C's accepting payment into court by D1 on his right to sue those others jointly liable, see *Townsend v Stone Toms & Partners* [1981] 2 All ER 690.

[77] See *Friends' Provident Life Office v Hillier Parker May and Rowden* [1997] QB 85.

[78] [2002] 1 WLR 1397.

Their Lordships insisted that the words 'liable in respect of the same damage' were to receive their ordinary and natural meaning and held that the loss of opportunity to sue for liquidated damage was not the same damage as the delayed construction.

(2) Who may claim contribution?

Under the Civil Liability (Contribution) Act 1978, a person who is liable is entitled to claim contribution from anyone else who is liable.[79] This applies even if an out-of-court settlement is reached. Thus, if a defendant can show that, assuming that the factual basis of the claim against him could be established, he would have been liable, he may claim contribution from anyone else who would have been liable with him.[80] If the defendant has settled because he was doubtful about his liability in law (even though the facts were established), he can obtain contribution only if he can prove that he was legally answerable, however bona fide and reasonable his decision to settle the claim. Furthermore, if he were liable at the time he made, was ordered to make, or agreed to make the payment, he is entitled to recover contribution even though he has since ceased to be liable either because of the expiry of a limitation period or otherwise.[81] And the right to claim contribution passes on the defendant's death to his personal representatives, whether or not his liability had, before his death, been established or admitted.[82]

(3) Those from whom contribution may be claimed

Contribution is recoverable from anyone who is liable for the same damage,[83] and on the authority of *K v P*[84] it is clear that the defence of *ex turpi causa* cannot be raised in order to defeat a claim for contribution.[85] If one party was originally liable but then ceased to be liable since the time the damage occurred—perhaps because the claimant waived his claim against that person—he would remain liable to make contribution to the other tortfeasor if that second tortfeasor were to be sued.[86] By contrast, where a settlement is reached with tortfeasor X but a later action is pursued against tortfeasor Y, the question of whether X (who settled) may be required to contribute to the damages later paid by Y will turn on the construction of the settlement agreement. *Jameson v Central Electricity Generating Board*[87] is the leading case:

---

[79] Civil Liability (Contribution) Act 1978, sub-s 1(1). Contribution may still be claimed from D2 where D1 made a payment in kind (ie, free remedial work): *Baker & Davies plc v Leslie Wilks* [2005] 3 All ER 603.

[80] Civil Liability (Contribution) Act 1978, sub-s 1(4); *Arab Monetary Fund v Hashim (No 8)* (1993) *Times*, 17 June.

[81] Civil Liability (Contribution) Act 1978, sub-s 1(2).

[82] *Ronex Properties Ltd v John Laing Construction Ltd* [1983] QB 398.

[83] Civil Liability (Contribution) Act 1978, sub-s 1(1). The potential contributory might want to be joined in the original claimant's action as a defendant: see, thus, *Davies v DTI* [2007] 1 WLR 3232.

[84] [1993] Ch 140.

[85] On the other hand, those factors relevant to raising the defence are factors of which the court may take note also in fixing the level of contribution (which can be 0%).

[86] Civil Liability (Contribution) Act 1978, s 1(3).

[87] [2000] 1 AC 455. For a similar 'constructionist' approach, see *Co-operative Retail Services Ltd v Taylor Young Partnership Ltd* [2002] 1 WLR 1419. But note that a properly interested third party may later invite the court to re-examine the meaning of any such agreement: *AB v British Coal Corp* [2004] EWHC 1372.

> Jameson was exposed to asbestos at work due to the fault of both his employer, X, and the CEGB where the exposure occurred. Jameson agreed a 'full and final settlement' with X. When Jameson died, his executors made an additional claim for loss of dependency under the Fatal Accidents Act 1976 from CEGB. It was held that this action could not be brought because of the finality of the wording of the settlement between X and Jameson. That being the case, there was no prospect of CEGB paying the additional sum, and then seeking a contribution to this sum from X.

If, on its proper construction, the settlement between X and Jameson had not ruled out a subsequent action brought by his executors against CEGB, then, in principle, X could have been required to contribute.[88] More commonly, the period of limitation for the claimant suing that defendant might have expired (the limitation period being two years after the right to contribution arose).[89] However, so long as contribution is sought before the expiry of the limitation period the contribution will be payable.[90]

(4) Amount of contribution recoverable

Rules By the Civil Liability (Contribution) Act 1978, sub-section 2(1):

> in any proceedings for contribution under section 1 above the amount of the contribution recoverable from any person shall be such as may be found by the court to be just and equitable having regard to the extent of that person's responsibility for the damage in question.

Sub-section 2(2) of the same Act provides that:

> The court shall have power in any such proceedings to exempt any person from liability to make contribution, or to direct that the contribution to be recovered from any person shall amount to a complete indemnity.

Factors Both the moral blameworthiness and the extent to which the act is directly connected to the damage caused are material in making this apportionment.[91] This view that moral blame is not the only criterion is supported by the cases which have authorised apportionment between a defendant liable for negligence at common law and one who was not negligent but who was in breach of a strict statutory duty.[92] On the other hand, moral blame alone will suffice where there is no causative potency on the part of one of the defendants.[93] Less controversially, where two employers are both

---

[88] See, eg, *Logan v Uttlesford DC and Hammond* [1986] NLJ Rep 541.

[89] The relevant date is the date of judgment or, where the case has been settled out of court, the date of the agreement to pay a final sum: Limitation Act 1980, sub-ss 10(3) and (4): *Jellett v Brooke* [2017] 1 WLR 1177. The period may be extended where the person seeking contribution is under a disability or is the victim of fraud, concealment, or mistake: Limitation Act 1980, sub-s 10(5).

[90] Civil Liability (Contribution) Act 1978, sub-s 1(3). The sub-section has a proviso that he is not liable if, on the expiry of the period of limitation or prescription, the right on which the claim against him was based was extinguished. But because most tort actions are not extinguished by limitation—conversion is the important exception—this proviso is of very limited importance in tort.

[91] *Miraflores (Owners) v George Livanos (Owners)* [1967] 1 AC 826, at 845; *Brown v Thompson* [1968] 2 All ER 708, at 709; *Cavanagh v London Passenger Transport Executive* (1956) *Times*, 23 October.

[92] Eg, *Jerred v Roddam Dent & Son Ltd* [1948] 2 All ER 104; *Dooley v Cammell Laird & Co Ltd* [1951] 1 Lloyd's Rep 271.

[93] *Brian Warwicker Partnership plc v HOK International Ltd* [2006] PNLR 5.

vicariously liable for the tort of a shared employee, it has been held to follow from the fact that there is no requirement of fault on the part of the employers held vicariously liable that their liability should be shared equally.[94]

Liability limits If there is a limit on the amount for which a defendant could be liable to the claimant, by reason of an agreement between the claimant and the defendant, or if the amount would have been reduced by reason of the Law Reform (Contributory Negligence) Act 1945,[95] then the maximum amount of contribution is that amount so limited or reduced.[96]

Indemnity The statute contemplates tortfeasors being entitled to a complete indemnity in some circumstances. For example, where a person who knows that he is not entitled to sell goods authorises an auctioneer to sell them and he does this immediately having been held liable in conversion, the auctioneer is entitled to an indemnity from his principal.[97] Most important is the relationship between employer and employee. In *Lister v Romford Ice and Cold Storage Co Ltd* the facts were as follows:[98]

> D, employed by C, took his father with him as mate. In reversing his lorry, D injured his father who, in an action against C, recovered damages in respect of D's negligent act. C brought an action against D claiming an indemnity in respect of the amount of the judgment and costs awarded against it.

The House of Lords held that the claimant was entitled to recover from the defendant for breach of the defendant's contractual obligation of care to his employer.[99] It follows that an employer who has been made vicariously liable for the tort of his employee can claim an indemnity from the employee. It was recognised before this decision that when the employer himself was at fault also he would not obtain a complete indemnity but must suffer a reduction in respect of his own fault.[100] But these cases were based on the

---

[94] *Viasystems (Tyneside) Ltd v Thermal Transfer (Northern) Ltd* [2006] 2 WLR 428.

[95] Suppose that C was injured by defective goods which he bought, but that C was also contributorily negligent. As contributory negligence is not a defence to actions for breach of strict contractual duties (*Barclays Bank plc v Fairclough Building Ltd* [1995] QB 214), the retailer will be liable in full to C, but his claim for contribution against the negligent manufacturer will be reduced to the extent to which a claim by C against the manufacturer would have been scaled down on account of C's contributory negligence.

[96] Civil Liability (Contribution) Act 1978, sub-s 2(3). The reduction to represent the degree of C's contributory negligence must be made before assessing the respective contributions of the tortfeasors: *Fitzgerald v Lane* [1989] AC 328.

[97] *Adamson v Jarvis* (1827) 4 Bing 66. For an illustration of a statutory right of indemnity, see the Civil Aviation Act 1982, sub-s 76(3).

[98] [1957] AC 555 (distinguished in *Harvey v R G O'Dell Ltd* [1958] 2 QB 78, at 106). And see *Vandyke v Fender* [1970] 2 QB 292, at 303.

[99] The Report of the Inter-Departmental Committee (1959) set up by the Ministry of Labour and National Service concluded that the decision raised no practical problem and that no legislative change was called for at that time. Moreover, in *Morris v Ford Motor Co Ltd* [1973] QB 792, it was held that the agreement in that case, being in an industrial setting so that subrogation against employees was unrealistic, contained an implied term excluding subrogation against them.

[100] Eg, *Jones v Manchester Corpn* [1952] 2 QB 852. Where the employer's liability is purely vicarious, involving no personal fault, he will obtain a 100% contribution from the negligent employee under the Civil Liability (Contribution) Act 1978, as in *Harvey v R G O'Dell Ltd* [1958] 2 QB 78.

Law Reform (Married Women and Tortfeasors) Act 1935, section 6.[101] What remains to be decided is whether, and if so on what principles, a reduction can be made in a claim by the employer based on a breach by the employee of his contract of employment.[102]

Conclusions

This chapter has considered issues concerned with the capacity of certain parties and principles of joint tort liability. The term 'capacity' refers to the status of legal persons and their ability to sue or be sued in tort. We examined the ways in which both government and companies become liable in tort. We saw also that very young children cannot be held responsible in law for the consequences of actions that might otherwise be tortious. However, the law is more accepting of the responsibility of mentally disordered persons, especially where they have some minimal understanding of the nature and quality of their acts.

The issue of joint torts is important because the claimant's injury might be the result of the torts of more than one person. In such a case, the claimant can sue all of the responsible parties. However, the law does not require this where more than one person is responsible for causing the *same damage*; it allows the claimant to sue for the full amount one only of the responsible persons. Statute then allows any person successfully sued to seek contribution from other responsible persons. Liability is apportioned between these parties according to the extent of their responsibility for the damage. Alternatively, the claimant's injuries might be the result of the independent acts of more than one person causing *separate items of damage*. In such a case, the liability of each tortfeasor is several; each is liable only for the damage that he causes.

Problem question

Yolanda is the director of a small company called Seville Financial Advice Ltd, which provides advice to retirees about investments that they should make in order to ensure that their savings will last through their retirement years. Yolanda failed to take care in putting together some of the advice documents—with the result that retirees became short of funds. Angelo had filled in the relevant forms online and never met Yolanda— although Yolanda did send her 13-year-old son around to deliver the advice documents personally to Angelo because Angelo had been in a hurry. Barbara spoke to Yolanda on the phone and Yolanda promised that 'my company and I will provide you with bespoke solutions to cater for your retirement needs and we guarantee that you will not need to

---

[101] *Lister v Romford Ice and Cold Storage Co Ltd* [1957] AC 555 left open the question whether an indemnity under the Act could also have been given.

[102] How far the Law Reform (Contributory Negligence) Act 1945 applies to a suit in contract is obviously pertinent. But see *Barclays Bank plc v Fairclough Building Ltd* [1995] QB 214 ruling out its applicability in relation to strict contractual duties.

worry'. After Barbara paid the fee (in an envelope addressed to 'Yolanda—private and confidential') the two women met by coincidence at a café and had a quick coffee and a chat.

Advise Angelo and Barbara as to who might be liable to them in negligence.

 Visit **http://www.oup.com/uk/street15e/** for answer guidance.

Further reading

BARKER AND STEELE, 'Drifting Towards Proportionate Liability: Ethics and Pragmatics' (2015) 74 *Cambridge Law Journal* 49

DAVIES, *Accessory Liability* (2015)

DAVIES, 'Accessory Liability for Assisting Torts' (2011) 70 *Cambridge Law Journal* 353

DIETRICH, 'Accessorial Liability in the Law of Torts' (2011) 31 *Legal Studies* 231

DIETRICH and RIDGE, *Accessory Liability in Private Law* (2015)

FERRAN, 'Corporate Attribution and the Directing Mind and Will' (2011) 127 *Law Quarterly Review* 239

LEE, 'Accessory Liability in Tort and Equity' (2015) 27 *Singapore Academy of Law Journal* 853

MARTIN-CASALS, *Children in Tort Law Part 1: Children as Tortfeasors* (2006)

OLIPHANT (ed), *Aggregation and Divisibility of Damage* (2009)

WATTS, 'Principals' Tortious Liability for Agents Negligent Statements: Is 'Authority' Necessary?' (2012) 128 *Law Quarterly Review* 260

WITTING, 'The Small Company: Directors' Status and Liability in Negligence' (2013) 24 *King's Law Journal* 343

26

Remedies

KEY ISSUES

(1) Limits to recovery

Both the rules on limitation of actions regarding causes of action commenced late, and the rules on mitigation by the claimant of her damages, can serve to exclude or limit the recovery of damages.

(2) Types of damages

Although most damages awards in English tort law are intended to compensate the claimant for the loss she has suffered, occasionally other forms of award are made, including: (1) nominal damages (where a right has been infringed without the claimant suffering tangible loss); (2) aggravated damages (where, beyond the mere infringement of a free-standing actionable right—in respect of which ordinary damages will be available—the defendant has affronted the claimant's human dignity); (3) exemplary damages (where, exceptionally, tort law recognises the suitability of adding a punitive element to the basic compensatory award); and (4) contemptuous damages (where the court forms a dim view of the bare legal claim that the claimant advances).

(3) Personal injury damages available to living claimants

The damages available to living claimants can be subdivided into two broad classes. The first involves damages for pecuniary losses (such as loss of earnings and costs of medical and nursing care). The second involves damages for non-pecuniary losses (such as pain and suffering). Often, computing the exact amount of the claimant's pecuniary loss is impossible (because no one can be sure how long the claimant would have remained fit and well, or how long the claimant would have remained in her current job, had the defendant's tort never been committed). Equally, placing an exact amount on such subjective matters as pain and suffering is impossible.

(4) Damages available after the tort victim has died

Damages that are awarded after the tort victim has died break down into two broad types. The first consists of 'survival actions', which are grounded in the Law Reform (Miscellaneous Provisions) Act 1934. With very few exceptions, the statute allows the victim's estate to pursue a tort claim that vested in the victim prior to her death. The second kind of claim that can be made post-death is one that treats the victim's death as the basis of the claim. In such cases, the deceased's dependants bring the action (for loss of support) under the Fatal Accidents Act 1976.

(5) Injunctions

A second form of remedy—often sought in connection with the torts of private nuisance and passing off—is an injunction. Various types of injunction can be sought depending on whether harm is ongoing or merely threatened, and on whether the defendant has to take positive steps to do something she is under a duty to do (as opposed to discontinuing the doing of something she is not lawfully entitled to do). In cases where some harm has been occasioned already and more is threatened, an injunction might be sought alongside damages. It is wrong therefore to see injunctions as simply an alternative to damages.

Section 1 Limitation of actions

(A) Introduction

Origins At common law there was no time limit restricting the right to sue. However, from 1540 limitation periods were introduced after the expiry of which an action in tort becomes time barred.[1] The victim of an alleged tort must serve her writ within a specified number of years or forfeit her remedy.

Rationale Limitation periods are necessary because, without them, potential defendants would face years of uncertainty not knowing whether or not they will be sued. A fair trial becomes increasingly difficult as witnesses' memories fade and, in some cases, witnesses leave the country or die.[2]

Potential injustice Of course, very short and rigid time limits could result in injustice to the claimant. She might not discover for some years that she has been the victim of a tort. Common examples include persons contracting industrial diseases and the losses suffered by the owners of negligently constructed buildings. Taking first damage to the body from working conditions: this is likely to be stealthy and progressive with definitive symptoms of disease not manifesting themselves until years after the disease was established.[3] Similarly, when a building is erected on defective foundations, cracks might begin to ruin the fabric of the building years before they become apparent.[4] It would scarcely be fair to deny the worker suffering from disease or the unfortunate homeowner a remedy simply because a rigid limitation period had expired before they could have realised that they might have a right to compensation.

---

[1] *AB v Ministry of Defence* [2013] 1 AC 78, at [6].

[2] See *AB v Ministry of Defence* [2013] 1 AC 78, at [6].

[3] See, eg, *Cartledge v E Jopling & Sons Ltd* [1963] AC 758 (pneumoconiosis from inhaling dust); *Thompson v Smiths Shiprepairers (North Shields) Ltd* [1984] QB 405 (industrial deafness).

[4] See, eg, *Murphy v Brentwood DC* [1991] 1 AC 398.

Statute The law on limitation is now contained mainly in the Limitation Act 1980 (as amended by the Latent Damage Act 1986).[5] In the case of actions for negligence, nuisance, or breach of duty—whether the duty exists by virtue of contract, statute,[6] or otherwise—when the damages claimed by the claimant consist of, or include, damages in respect of personal injuries to the claimant or any other person, the period of limitation is three years.[7] The term 'breach of duty' has been held to encompass intentional trespasses.[8] The term 'personal injuries' includes any disease and any impairment of a person's physical or mental condition.[9] However, it does not involve theft of body products.[10]

In cases of actions for negligence other than for personal injuries or death, the Latent Damage Act 1986[11] introduced a primary limitation period of six years (with provision in special circumstances for a further period of three years to run from the 'starting date' set by that Act). In either case, there is a final 'long-stop' of 15 years from the date of the act or omission constituting the negligence.[12]

An action for libel or slander ordinarily must be brought within one year, but there is a discretion to extend this time period.[13] Where the claimant sues in respect of a defective product under the Consumer Protection Act 1987, normally she must bring the action within three years of suffering the relevant damage, or within three years of acquiring the necessary knowledge of the facts to be able to sue if that date be later.[14] No action can be brought under the Consumer Protection Act 1987 more than ten years after the product was first put into circulation.[15] Yet the claimant might have an action in negligence still after that date where, even by then, she has not discovered her injury or damage or other relevant facts regarding her right of action in negligence. The limitation period for other tort actions remains six years.[16]

(B) When does a cause of action accrue?

General A cause of action accrues and the limitation period begins to run at that moment in time when a potential claimant is entitled to succeed in that action against the defendant. There must be in existence such a claimant and defendant. For example, if a tort is committed against the estate of a deceased person, and if her goods are taken away, the cause of action does not accrue until an executor or administrator is appointed.[17] On the other hand, a claimant whose car has been stolen by a thief whom she does

---

[5] For recommendations in favour of a streamlined, unitary approach to the limitation of actions in this context, see Law Commission, *Limitation of Actions* (No 270, 2001).

[6] A breach of a duty embodied in EU law that causes C to suffer the infringement of a right created by EU law will be treated in the same way as the breach of a domestic statutory duty: *R v Secretary of State for Transport, ex p Factortame Ltd (No 7)* [2001] 1 WLR 942.

[7] Limitation Act 1980, sub-s 11(1).   [8] *A v Hoare* [2008] 1 AC 844.

[9] Limitation Act 1980, sub-s 38(1).   [10] *Yearworth v North Bristol NHS Trust* [2010] QB 1.

[11] By inserting a new s 14A into the Limitation Act 1980.

[12] Limitation Act 1980, s 14B.   [13] Limitation Act 1980, s 4A.

[14] Consumer Protection Act 1987, sub-s 5(5) and Sch I.

[15] Consumer Protection Act 1987, sub-s 5(5) and Sch I.   [16] Limitation Act 1980, s 2.

[17] *Murray v East India Co* (1821) 5 B & Ald 204; *Pratt v Swaine* (1828) 8 B & C 285.

not know and cannot trace has a cause of action against that thief from the time of the theft.[18] When a cause of action lies without proof of damage, time always runs from the date of the wrongful act. Similarly, in libel, the limitation period runs from the date of publication even if the appropriate defendant cannot be identified at that stage.[19]

Negligence By contrast, in negligence the cause of action accrues only when damage is suffered. In fact, this is the case in all torts where damage is essential to the cause of action. But ascertaining exactly when damage occurs might be difficult. The crucial date is the date of the damage, not its discoverability.[20] So when a negligently constructed security gate is the reason for a burglary's commission, time runs from the date of the burglary, not the time of the negligent construction of the gate.[21] Where the relevant negligence consists of negligent advice, the question arises whether the damage founding the cause of action is suffered when the claimant relies on that advice,[22] or when the subsequent financial loss is suffered. *Nykredit Mortgage Bank plc v Edwards Erdman Group Ltd (No 2)*[23] supports the latter approach. As Lord Nicholls explained, a purchaser's cause of action accrues at the time of the purchase for '[sh]e suffers damage by parting with h[er] money and receiving in exchange property worth less than the price [s]he paid'.[24]

The injustice to a claimant who otherwise would lose her right to a remedy before she could know of its existence explains why special provision is now made in the tort of negligence for all forms of latent damage, with separate rules for personal injuries and other forms of damage.

(C) Special rules for personal injuries

Background The impetus for reform of the limitation rules concerning personal injuries came from cases relating to industrial disease. For example, where the claimant contracts pneumoconiosis from inhaling dust, her cause of action in negligence arises even though she is unaware of the onset of the disease. In *Cartledge v E Jopling & Sons Ltd*,[25] the House of Lords held that time started to run at common law as soon as the damage was suffered. Therefore, in this case time started to run once material scarring of the lung tissue had occurred, even though an X-ray examination would *not* have revealed it.

Statute The Limitation Act 1980[26] seeks to avoid the injustice that would arise where a cause of action for personal injuries would become time barred at common law before the claimant knew of it. Under the Act, the three-year limitation period begins to run either from the date of the accrual of the cause of action (that is, the date of the damage) or from the date of the claimant's knowledge of that damage, whichever is the later. The

---

[18] *RB Policies at Lloyd's v Butler* [1950] 1 KB 76.   [19] *Edwards v Golding* [2007] EWCA Civ 416.
[20] *Pirelli General Cable Works Ltd v Oscar Faber & Partners* [1983] 2 AC 1. Cf *Invercargill CC v Hamlin* [1996] 1 All ER 756 (doubting *Pirelli*).   [21] *Dove v Banhams Patent Locks Ltd* [1983] 2 All ER 833.
[22] *Forster v Outred & Co* [1982] 2 All ER 753.   [23] [1997] 1 WLR 1627.
[24] [1997] 1 WLR 1627.   [25] [1963] AC 758.   [26] Limitation Act 1980, s 11.

limitation period ends only three years after the date of the claimant's knowledge of the cause of action if that date is after three years from the accrual of the cause of action. If the claimant dies before the expiration of the period, the period as regards the cause of action surviving for the benefit of the estate of the deceased, by virtue of the Law Reform (Miscellaneous Provisions) Act 1934, section 1 is three years from the date of death or the date of knowledge of the personal representative.[27]

Knowledge When time runs from the date of a person's knowledge in a personal injuries case, under Limitation Act 1980, sub-section 14(1) the relevant date is the date on which she first had knowledge: (1) that her injury was significant; (2) that it was attributable in whole or in part to the alleged wrongful act or omission; (3) the identity of the defendant;[28] (4) and the identity of a third person (and any additional facts supporting the bringing of an action against the defendant) where that third person was guilty of the act or omission on which the claimant's case depends.

The case law upon these factors can be reduced to the following rules:[29] (1) The knowledge required to satisfy sub-section 14(1)(b) is a broad knowledge of the essence of the causally relevant act or omission to which the injury is attributable.[30] (2) In this context, the word 'attributable' means 'capable of being attributed to', in the sense of being a real possibility of a causal link.[31] (3) A claimant has the requisite knowledge when she knows enough to make it reasonable to begin to investigate whether she has a case against the defendant. She will have such knowledge if she so firmly believes that her condition is capable of being attributed to an act or omission which, in broad terms, she can identify such that she embarks on the preliminaries to litigation, for example, by going to a solicitor to seek advice about making a claim, submitting a claim to the defendant, and/ or beginning to collect evidence.[32] (4) On the other hand, the claimant will not have the requisite knowledge if her understanding of the defendant's act is so vague that she cannot be expected to know what she should investigate; or if her state of mind is such that she thinks her condition is capable of being attributed to the act or omission alleged to constitute negligence, but she is not sure about this, and would need to check with an expert before she properly could be said to know that it was. (5) While taking legal advice does not prove of itself that the claimant has a belief of sufficient confidence, the actual commencement of proceedings is taken to be proof of the requisite knowledge.[33]

Sub-section 14(1) provides that knowledge that any acts or omissions did, or did not, as a matter of law, involve negligence, nuisance, or breach of duty is irrelevant.[34] In effect

---

[27] Limitation Act 1980, sub-ss 11(5), (6). For the corresponding application of these provisions to claims under the Fatal Accidents Act 1976, see sub-s 12(1) and s 33.

[28] C might have been knocked down by a hit-and-run driver, or D's firm might be a member of a group of interlocking companies: *Simpson v Norwest Holst Southern Ltd* [1980] 2 All ER 471.

[29] See esp. *AB v Ministry of Defence* [2013] 1 AC 78; *Spargo v North Essex District HA* [1997] PIQR P235.

[30] *Nash v Eli Lilly & Co* [1993] 1 WLR 782.

[31] *Haward v Fawcetts* [2006] 1 WLR 683, at [10]–[11]; *AB v Ministry of Defence* [2013] 1 AC 78, at [35] and [79].

[32] *AB v Ministry of Defence* [2013] 1 AC 78, at [12] and [83]; *Halford v Brookes* [1991] 1 WLR 428.

[33] *AB v Ministry of Defence* [2013] 1 AC 78, at [3], [12], [54]–[55], and [67].

[34] But where C's action relies on D's omission, 'knowledge' cannot exist until C knows that something else could and should have been done: *Forbes v Wandsworth HA* [1997] QB 402.

the claimant is deemed to know the legal significance of facts.[35] Furthermore, as regards knowledge of facts, it is not just the claimant's *actual* knowledge that is relevant. Sub-section 14(3) makes the following provision for constructive knowledge of the facts:

> For the purposes of this section, a person's knowledge includes knowledge which he might reasonably have been expected to acquire:
>
> (a) from facts observable or ascertainable by him; or
>
> (b) from facts ascertainable by him with the help of medical or other appropriate expert advice which it is reasonable for him to seek; but a person shall not be fixed under this subsection with knowledge of a fact ascertainable only with the help of expert advice so long as he has taken all reasonable steps to obtain (and, where appropriate, act on) that advice.

This sub-section encourages a claimant to seek expert advice expeditiously.[36] If she fails to do so and remains ignorant in consequence, the burden lies with the defendant to show that it was unreasonable for the claimant not to seek advice taking account of purely objective criteria, but excluding subjective factors such as the intellect and character of the particular claimant.[37] Once one has ascertained what the claimant actually knew and thereafter added to that such knowledge as can be imputed under sub-section 14(3),[38] the test of whether the claimant ought to have instituted proceedings at an earlier date becomes an objective one.[39]

If the claimant does consult an expert, she is not prejudiced if the expert fails to find, or inform her of, the ascertainable facts.[40] Furthermore, since the sub-section only applies to knowledge of a 'fact', it follows that a claimant who delays suing because she has received erroneous legal advice will find that time runs against her if she has not issued a writ.[41]

Extension of time   In exceptional cases, the victim of personal injuries who fails to start her action in time might be able to proceed still with the permission of the court. By sub-section 33(1) of the 1980 Act, the court may allow an action to proceed notwithstanding the expiry of limitation periods. The court has a discretion to extend the statutory time limits if it considers it equitable to do so having regard to the degree to which the ordinary limitation rules prejudice the claimant and the degree to which any exercise of the power would prejudice the defendant. It may have particular significance in cases where the claimant is now an adult but whose claim centres on child abuse suffered many years previously.[42] Whatever the factual basis, the court must have regard

---

[35] See *Brooks v J & P Coates (UK) Ltd* [1984] 1 All ER 702.
[36] See, eg, *B v Ministry of Defence* [2010] 117 BMLR 101 (point not considered on appeal: [2013] 1 AC 78).
[37] *Adams v Bracknell Forest BC* [2005] 1 AC 76.
[38] This knowledge is a deemed subjective knowledge: *AB v Ministry of Defence* [2013] 1 AC 78, at [9].
[39] *A v Hoare* [2008] 1 AC 844, at [34]–[35].   [40] *Marston v British Railways Board* [1976] ICR 124.
[41] *Leadbitter v Hodge Finance Ltd* [1982] 2 All ER 167.
[42] For guidance on the use of the s 33 discretion in such cases, see *AB v Nugent Care Society* [2010] PIQR P3; *XA v YA* [2011] PIQR P1.

to all the circumstances,[43] including the following (listed in sub-section 33(3)): (a) the length of, and the reasons for, the delay on the part of the claimant;[44] (b) the effect of the delay on the cogency of the evidence in the case; (c) the conduct of the defendant after the cause of action arose, including her response to the claimant's request for information; (d) the duration of any disability of the claimant arising after the cause of action;[45] (e) the extent to which the claimant acted promptly and reasonably once she knew of the facts which afforded her a cause of action; and (f) the steps taken by the claimant to obtain medical, legal, or other expert advice and the nature of any such advice received.[46] A very wide discretion is given to the court, which is not limited to these factors.[47] For example, the fact that the defendant is insured is a relevant consideration,[48] as is the fact that the case might involve putting the defendant to greater expense in defending the action than the action is worth.[49] However, there is one restriction. Where the claimant has commenced proceedings and then discontinued them, the discretion will be exercised in her favour in the most exceptional case only.[50]

(D) Latent damage in non-personal injuries cases

Pirelli case The special provision made by the Limitation Act 1980, section 11 to assist claimants who lacked the necessary knowledge to start an action was restricted to actions for personal injuries. Yet the problems limitation periods pose for the victim of a latent defect can be just as acute in relation to damage to property. A series of Court of Appeal decisions sought to establish that the cause of action in such cases accrued only when the defect was discoverable.[51] But in *Pirelli General Cable Works Ltd v Oscar Faber & Partners*[52] the House of Lords overruled those decisions as being inconsistent with *Cartledge v E Jopling & Sons Ltd*[53] The facts in *Pirelli* highlight the problems of latent damage:

> In 1969, Cs engaged Ds to advise them in relation to building a new chimney. Ds' design was negligently produced. Cracks occurred in the chimney and it had to be replaced. Cs first discovered the cracks in 1977 but they first arose in 1970. Cs served their writ in 1978 contending that the (six-year) limitation period did not begin to run until 1977 when they first reasonably could have discovered the defect.

---

[43] Here the court cannot simply consider the effects of not exercising the discretion on just C or D: *KR v Bryn Alyn Community (Holdings) Ltd* [2003] 1 FCR 385. Further, the courts are slow to find the balance of prejudice in favour of C in the absence of cogent medical evidence showing a serious effect on C's health: *Robinson v St Helen's MBC* [2002] EWCA Civ 1099.

[44] Here the delay means the delay after the expiry of the normal time limit: *McDonnell v Walker* [2010] PIQR P5.

[45] See, eg, *Barrow v Consignia plc* [2003] EWCA Civ 249.

[46] But note that C is not necessarily to be associated with her dilatory (or otherwise negligent) legal advisers: *Das v Ganju* [1999] Lloyd's Rep Med 198.

[47] See, eg, *Firman v Ellis* [1978] QB 886; *Steeds v Peverel Management Services Ltd* [2001] EWCA Civ 419.

[48] *Kelly v Bastible* (1996) 36 BMLR 51.   [49] *Nash v Eli Lilly & Co* [1993] 4 All ER 383.

[50] *Walkley v Precision Forgings Ltd* [1979] 2 All ER 548.

[51] See *Sparham-Souter v Town and Country Developments (Essex) Ltd* [1976] QB 858.

[52] [1983] 2 AC 1.   [53] [1963] AC 758.

The House of Lords held that the cause of action accrued in 1970 when the damage first occurred so the claim was time barred. Indeed, it is a general principle in latent damage cases that time begins to run from the date on which damage actually did occur. That said, pinning down the date on which damage *actually* occurred can involve some nice distinctions. So, in one case where A misadvised B so that B entered into a commercially inadvisable insurance arrangement, the critical date was held to be that on which B entered into the arrangement rather than the subsequent date on which an insured party made a claim on the basis of the policy.[54] The financial loss suffered was contingent on entering into a misconceived arrangement, and actually entering into the arrangement was treated as 'the damage which the claimants . . . suffered'.[55]

Two further acute difficulties for claimants emerged from the decision in *Pirelli*. In an *obiter dictum*,[56] Lord Fraser suggested that, where a defect was so gross that the building was 'doomed from the start',[57] time would begin to run even earlier: from the completion of the building. The result of such a doctrine—that is, that the worse the negligence, the more favourable the limitation period would be to the defendant—did not find favour in later decisions.[58] The second difficulty arising from the case in relation to latent defects affected 'subsequent owners' of buildings. In *Pirelli* it was said that time did not start to run again in favour of the subsequent owner once she acquired the property.[59] But subsequent owners' problems were more acute than being entitled only to the tag end of their predecessors' limitation period. The essence of the claim in such a case is financial loss associated with the diminished value of the property that the subsequent owner has acquired. According to the House of Lords in *Murphy v Brentwood District Council*,[60] such claims generally are inadmissible; yet their Lordships managed also to approve *Pirelli* on the basis that it was said to fall within the principle enunciated in *Hedley Byrne v Heller*.[61] As a consequence, there has been continuing confusion.[62]

Statutory reform The Law Reform Committee reported on problems concerning latent damage to property in 1984.[63] Their proposals largely were incorporated into the Latent Damage Act 1986, which applies not solely to latent damage to property but also to all negligence actions other than claims in respect of personal injury or death. The Act took effect by inserting sections 14A and 14B into the Limitation Act 1980. The limitation period in actions to which they apply now are either six years from the date on which the cause of action accrued or three years from the 'starting date' when the claimant had the necessary knowledge of the facts to bring an action.

---

[54] *Axa Insurance Ltd v Akther & Darby* [2010] 1 WLR 1662.
[55] *Axa Insurance Ltd v Akther & Darby* [2010] 1 WLR 1662, at [82]. In similar vein, see *Pegasus Management Holdings SCA v Ernst & Young* [2010] 3 All ER 297. Cf *Law Society v Sephton & Co* [2006] 2 AC 543 (C's loss was contingent, but C was not misled into entering into an inadvisable arrangement).
[56] [1983] 2 AC 1, at 16.　　[57] See *Dove v Banhams Patent Locks Ltd* [1983] 2 All ER 833.
[58] See, eg, *Ketteman v Hansel Properties Ltd* [1987] AC 189.　　[59] [1983] 2 AC 1, at 18.
[60] [1990] 2 All ER 908.　　[61] [1990] 2 All ER 908, at 919.
[62] See E McKendrick (1991) 11 LS 326.
[63] Law Reform Committee, *Twenty-fourth Report: Latent Damage* (Cmnd 9390).

'Knowledge' in this context is defined in sub-sections 14A(6)–(8) in terms virtually identical to those used to define 'knowledge' in the original section 14 for the purpose of extending the three-year period to bring an action in respect of personal injuries.[64] Section 14B of the 1980 Act imposes a 'long-stop' of 15 years from the date of the act or omission constituting the alleged negligence. Once 15 years have elapsed, no action can be brought, even though the claimant might not have discovered the relevant damage. This is because section 14B contains no provision similar to section 33 of the 1980 Act, which, as we have seen, gives a judge the discretion to override this final limitation period.[65]

The Latent Damage Act 1986 represents a worthy attempt at compromise between the rights of claimants and defendants, but it leaves some key questions unanswered. First, sections 14A and 14B apply to actions for negligence. But are they applicable also to actions for nuisance or breach of statutory duty where the essence of the wrong complained of is also often the absence of reasonable care?[66] Second, no clear definition of damage is provided.

Successive owners   The Latent Damage Act 1986, section 3 addresses the rights of successive owners of property. It provides that, where a cause of action has accrued to A while she has an interest in that property, 'then provided B acquires the property' after the date on which the original cause of action accrued,

> but before the material facts about the damage have become known to any person who, at the time when he first had knowledge of the facts, has any interest in the property; a fresh cause of action in respect of that negligence shall accrue to that other person on the date on which he acquires his interest in the property.

The limitation period as against the new owner is either six years from when her cause of action accrued (that is, her acquisition of the property) or three years from when she acquired knowledge of the relevant facts (subject once again to the 15-year 'long-stop' in section 14B of the Limitation Act 1980).

Three further points must be raised about the Latent Damage Act 1986, section 3. First, section 3 is difficult to reconcile with *Murphy v Brentwood District Council*, which generally denies the existence of any duty of care in such cases.[67] Second, although drafted with defective buildings in mind, the section applies to all property including goods. Finally, the new cause of action for the subsequent property owner arises only where her predecessor did not have actual or constructive knowledge of the relevant defect.

[64]   See, eg, *Spencer-Ward v Humberts* [1995] 06 EG 148. In assessing C's knowledge, account will be taken of misleading advice provided by 'experts' in the past that now prevents C from knowing that an actionable case exists: *Oakes v Hopcroft* [2000] Lloyd's Rep Med 294.

[65]   But see the Latent Damage Act 1986, s 2 regarding fraud, concealment, or mistake.

[66]   For a 'yes' answer, see R James (1994) 45 NILQ 301.

[67]   *Murphy* does not deny a duty of care where the defective property poses a threat of damage to other property, nor does it do so where the property damage is of the kind often referred to as 'complex structure' damage. These would appear to be the only two exceptions to the seeming redundancy of s 3 in this context.

(E) Continuing wrongs

Where the defendant's act is a continuing wrong—for example, if she erects a building on the claimant's land and there is a continuing trespass—so long as it endures, a cause of action will lie, provided it is based on the continuance of that wrong during the six years (or three years in the case of personal injuries) immediately preceding the action.[68]

(F) Effect of disability of the claimant

If, on the date when any right of action accrued, the person to whom it accrued was a minor or a person of unsound mind,[69] the action can be brought at any time before the expiration of six years (or three years in the case of personal injuries) from the date when the person ceased to be under that disability, or died, whichever event first occurred.[70]

(G) Postponement of limitation periods in cases of fraud or concealment

Where the action is based on the fraud of the defendant or her agent, or of any person through whom she claims (or that person's agent), or where any fact relevant to the right of action deliberately is concealed by any such person, the period shall not begin to run until the claimant has, or with reasonable diligence could have, discovered the fraud or concealment.[71] Once a cause of action has arisen, subsequent concealment of facts relevant to the claimant's action will postpone the running of the limitation period.[72]

A tort is 'based upon fraud' only where fraud is a necessary allegation in order to constitute the cause of action.[73] (Presumably, deceit is the only tort based upon fraud in this sense.) Deliberate commission of a breach of duty in circumstances in which it is unlikely to be discovered for some time amounts to deliberate concealment of the facts involved in that breach of duty.[74] Despite the ambiguity of the language used in the provision ('deliberate conduct' does not necessarily imply deliberate harm), the House of Lords has made it clear that moral wrongdoing on the part of the defendant is an essential ingredient.[75] 'Fraud' in the Act is to be interpreted very widely.[76] It appears to signify simply 'conscious wrongdoing'.[77]

---

[68] *Hardy v Ryle* (1829) 9 B & C 603; *Earl of Harrington v Derby Corpn* [1905] 1 Ch 205.

[69] By the Limitation Act 1980, sub-s 38(3) 'a person is of unsound mind if he is a person who, by reason of mental disorder within the meaning of the Mental Health Act 1983 is incapable of managing and administering his property and affairs'.

[70] Limitation Act 1980, ss 28(1) and 28A.   [71] Limitation Act 1980, sub-s 32(1).

[72] *Sheldon v RHM Outhwaite (Underwriting Agencies) Ltd* [1996] AC 102.

[73] *Beaman v ARTS Ltd* [1949] 1 KB 550 (conversion was held not to be an action based on fraud).

[74] Limitation Act, sub-s 32(2).

[75] *Cave v Robinson Jarvis & Rolf* [2003] 1 AC 384: the moral wrongdoing on the part of D must exist *either* in respect of the act that constitutes the breach of a duty *or* in connection with the concealment of a duty that was breached without any malice.

[76] *Beaman v ARTS* [1949] 1 KB 550.   [77] *Beaman v ARTS* [1949] 1 KB 550, at 572.

Section 2 Mitigation of loss

Two rules We now assume that the claimant can bring a cause of action within time or that she benefits from a judicial extension of time. Another limit on her ability to recover is to be found in the principle that the claimant is obliged to 'mitigate her loss'. That expression covers two separate rules in the law of torts.

Claimant conduct First, evidence may be given of circumstances which justify a lesser award of damages.[78] For example, a defamation award might be reduced where the claimant provoked the defendant.[79]

Self-induced damage Second, the law does not allow a claimant to recover to the extent to which she has brought the loss upon herself[80] or was negligent after the commission of a tort against her so as to suffer further damage. *The Flying Fish*[81] illustrates the point:

> C's ship was damaged by the negligence of those in charge of D's vessel. C's captain showed want of nautical skill in that he refused aid after the collision. In consequence of this negligent refusal, the ship was destroyed. C was able to recover the damage caused by the collision but not that additional damage accruing when the ship was destroyed by the negligence of the captain.

In short, after damage has occurred and an action in tort is vested in the claimant she has an obligation to take care to mitigate her loss.

Burden of proof The burden of showing an unreasonable failure to mitigate lies with the defendant. Thus, where a claimant refuses treatment that could have lessened the consequences of her injury, the onus is on the defendant to show that the refusal was unreasonable.[82] Even if the claimant shows that the refusal of treatment is presently reasonable, a discount might be made if there is a chance both (1) that the claimant will accept the treatment in the longer term; *and* (2) that the treatment might succeed.[83]

Non-blameworthy conduct Where the claimant does take reasonable steps to minimise the consequences of the defendant's tort, she can recover for harm sustained by her in consequence of her action[84] or expenses incurred[85] regardless of whether her total loss would have been less had she not acted at all. Thus, if a claimant takes a new job because, by virtue of her injury she no longer can do the old one and the new job proves to be beyond her, there can be no reduction in the tortfeasor's liability based on the loss of that second job.[86]

---

[78] *Peruvian Guano Co Ltd v Dreyfus Bros & Co* [1892] AC 166, at 174; *Drane v Evangelou* [1978] 2 All ER 437.
[79] *Moore v Oastler* (1836) 1 Mood & R 451n.
[80] See, eg, *Dodd Properties Ltd v Canterbury CC* [1980] 1 All ER 928.
[81] (1865) 2 Moo PCCNS 77.   [82] *Geest plc v Lansiquot* [2002] UKPC 48, at [14].
[83] *Thomas v Bath District HA* [1995] PIQR Q19.   [84] *The Oropesa* [1943] P 32.
[85] *Kirkham v Boughey* [1958] 2 QB 338.   [86] *Morris v Richards* [2003] EWCA Civ 232.

Section 3 Introduction to damages

(A) Damages

A successful claim in tort typically yields a sum by way of damages. In *Knauer v Ministry of Justice*, the Supreme Court repeated the time-honoured statement that the aim of an award of damages in tort is designed, so far as money can do it, 'to place the person who has been harmed by the wrongful acts of another in the position in which he or she would have been had the harm not been done'.[87] Beneath this apparently simple statement lie a complex series of rules. In this section, general rules on the award of damages are examined, as are rules of damages as they apply to cases of personal injuries. The first point to note is that there are several different kinds of damages that a court has the power to award.

(1) Nominal

Some interests, for example freedom of movement, one's bodily integrity, and the possession of one's property are considered to be so important that any violation of them is a tort. The damages are said to be at large in such cases. This means that, although the interest protected might not have a precise cash value, the court is free, on proof of the commission of the tort, to award substantial damages.[88] By contrast, nominal damages will be awarded where the court decides in the light of all the facts that no damage has been sustained.[89] The function of nominal damages simply is to mark the vindication of a right that is actionable per se. Damages of this kind can be awarded, therefore, without the claimant having had to suffer any tangible damage. For example, in *R (on the application of WL (Congo)) v Secretary of State for the Home Department* technically there was a false imprisonment, but the appellants would have been detained in any event had the authorities acted in accordance with an existing policy as opposed to the unpublished one they actually followed. Nominal damages were awarded.[90] Again, in *Grobbelaar v News Group Newspapers Ltd*,[91] a professional footballer had been libelled insofar as he had been accused of actually fixing football matches. He had not technically *fixed* the result of the matches, thus the statement was untrue and libellous. However, he had accepted money in exchange for his attempts to throw the games, and was awarded a mere £1 in nominal damages.

Nominal damages nowadays are given *only* in respect of torts actionable per se[92] and must not be confused with small sums intended to compensate in cases of limited actual damage. This is to assume that courts will entertain such claims in the first place. There are signs that courts are no longer prepared to permit the bringing of actions which are designed simply to 'prove a point'.[93] These might be struck out and even found actions for

---

[87] [2016] AC 908, at [1]. But note the exception to this proposition that inheres in Fatal Accidents Act 1976, ss 3 and 4, remarked upon in *Cox v Ergo Versicherung* [2014] AC 1379, at [10].

[88] Eg, £5 damages was awarded in *Ashby v White* (1703) 2 Ld Raym 938 (right to vote); £50 in *Nicholls v Ely Beet Sugar Factory Ltd* [1936] Ch 343 (interference with a fishery).

[89] *The Mediana* [1900] AC 113, at 116; *Neville v London Express Newspaper Ltd* [1919] AC 368, at 392.

[90] [2011] 2 WLR 671.   [91] [2002] 1 WLR 3024.

[92] Cf *Embrey v Owen* (1851) 6 Exch 353, at 368.

[93] *White v Withers LLP* [2010] 1 FLR 859, at [62] (Ward LJ) and [72] (Sedley LJ, stating that the 'claim for a shilling in damages in order to prove a point and obtain an award of costs is history') (case of tort to goods).

abuse of process. This is a somewhat disturbing development, given the historical role of the courts in developing standards of interaction between persons and the fundamental importance that attaches to the ability of individuals to assert and defend their rights and interests.

(2) Contemptuous damages

These are derisory damages marking the court's low opinion of the claimant's claim or its disapproval of her conduct.[94] They differ from nominal damages in that they may be awarded in respect of any tort, not merely those actionable per se. Moreover, the award of contemptuous damages only might be material in deciding whether to allow costs to the claimant.

(3) General and special compensatory damages

Compensatory damages are of two broad kinds. General damages are awarded for losses that the law presumes to have resulted from the defendant's tort; special damages are awarded for losses that will not be presumed, such as the costs of medical treatment incurred prior to the hearing in a personal injury case.[95] To avoid injustice to the defendant, the claimant must give notice in her pleadings of, and substantiate any claim for, 'special damages'.[96]

While compensatory damages might have the *effect* of vindicating the claimant's rights, including the right to bodily integrity or right to choose whether to accept medical treatment after being informed properly of risk, there are not separate heads of damages relating to these things.[97] A full treatment of compensation for personal injury is given later in this section.

(4) Aggravated damages

Affront to dignity The general object of an award of damages in tort normally is to compensate the claimant for what she has lost or suffered as a consequence of the tort. Nonetheless, an award of damages sometimes may take into account the motives and conduct of the defendant where they combine to cause the claimant to suffer an affront to her dignity. Such damages are called 'aggravated damages' and they are available often where arrogant or high-handed conduct on the part of the defendant causes outrage or anger in the sentient, adult claimant.[98] However, in theory they should be no less available to the infantile or mentally incapacitated who are incapable of forming such feelings of outrage or anger. In short, affront to human dignity is not contingent on sentience.[99] Aggravated damages are not available to companies because of their inability subjectively to experience hurt to feelings.[100]

---

[94] See, eg, *Reynolds v Times Newspapers Ltd* [1998] 3 WLR 862 (C obtained damages of just 1p).

[95] In *R v Secretary of State for the Home Dept, ex p Greenfield* [2005] 1 WLR 673, at [11]–[12], Lord Bingham equated special damages with pecuniary loss; general damages with non-pecuniary loss.

[96] See, eg, *Domsalla v Barr* [1969] 1 WLR 630.

[97] See *R (Lumba) v Secretary of State for the Home Dept* [2012] 1 AC 245 and *Shaw v Kovac* [2017] EWCA Civ 1028, respectively.

[98] In *Horsford v Bird* [2006] UKPC 3, at [14], Lord Scott spoke of 'high-handed, insulting or oppressive conduct'.   [99] See J Murphy (2010) 69 CLJ 353.

[100] *Eaton Mansions (Westminster) Ltd v Stinger Compania de Inversion SA* [2014] HLR 4.

Compensatory Most scholars consider aggravated damages to be a form of compensation (although views vary on just what it is that they compensate). There is support in the case law for the view that they are compensatory. For example, Sir Thomas Bingham MR once said that the aggravated damages in defamation cases are not an exception to the idea that damages in tort serve a compensatory (as opposed to punitive) function 'since injury to the [claimant's] feelings and self-esteem is an important part of the damage for which compensation is awarded'.[101] But there is support also for the idea that they serve a punitive function (in that the courts will often seem to be attending to the deliberate, arrogant conduct of the defendant).[102] Yet, even in such cases, it appears incorrect to regard aggravated damages as a form of punishment. It is simply by highlighting conduct of this kind that we can see beyond the tangible injury to the claimant and identify, further, an infringement of her dignity. So, for example, even though the level of physical injury may be the same in both cases, there is a very real difference between having one's toes trodden on by mistake, and having them stamped upon deliberately. The affront that accompanies the stamping is what aggravated damages address.

Availability The range of torts for which aggravated damages can be awarded is broad. It includes trespass to the person[103] and to land,[104] defamation,[105] other torts based on deliberate falsehoods,[106] and private nuisance.[107] In *AB v South West Water Services Ltd*,[108] the Court of Appeal decided that they should not be available for actions in negligence. However, before aggravated damages can be ruled out for this tort, it must be remembered that negligence liability ultimately turns on a failure to meet the standard of care of the reasonable person. Deliberate conduct falling short of this standard can be relied upon in a negligence action. That being so, it is hard to disagree with Lord Neuberger's comment that: 'I cannot see why such damages should not logically be recoverable in some categories of negligence.'[109]

(5) Exemplary damages

Availability In *Kuddus v Chief Constable of Leicestershire*,[110] the House of Lords held that exemplary damages can be obtained in connection with virtually any tort.[111] These damages turn upon conduct that outrages the court and are awarded to punish and deter. Tort law can be shown to possess a deterrent function in certain circumstances. Organisations and those with managerial control might be prompted into taking extra

---

[101] *AB v SW Water Services Ltd* [1993] QB 507, at 532.

[102] See, eg, *KD v CC of Hampshire* [2005] EWHC 2550.

[103] See, eg, *Thompson v MPC* [1998] QB 498.   [104] *Drane v Evangelou* [1978] 1 WLR 455.

[105] *Sutcliffe v Pressdram Ltd* [1991] 1 QB 153.

[106] *Khodaparast v Shad* [2000] 1 All ER 545 (malicious falsehood); *Archer v Brown* [1985] QB 401 (deceit).

[107] *Thompson v Hill* (1870) LR 5 CP 564.

[108] [1993] 1 All ER 609, at 629. See also *Kralj v McGrath* [1986] 1 All ER 54.

[109] *Ashley v CC of Sussex* [2008] 1 AC 962, at [102].

[110] [2002] 2 AC 122.

[111] The doubt that exists relates to the availability of exemplary damages for breach of statutory duty where the statute in question *does not* specifically authorise such an award: see *Kuddus v CC of Leicestershire* [2002] 2 AC 122, at [45]. Cf *Design Progression Ltd v Thurloe Properties Ltd* [2005] 1 WLR 1 for such an award for breach of the Landlord and Tenant Act 1998, sub-s 1(3).

steps to prevent employees behaving in ways that might generate such awards.[112] And professional and trade associations can play a similar function with respect to their members. Having said as much, in *Rookes v Barnard*,[113] Lord Devlin limited exemplary damages awards to three categories of case:

(a) Where the claimant has been the victim of oppressive, arbitrary, or unconstitutional action by servants of government

The phrase 'oppressive, arbitrary, or unconstitutional' is to be understood *disjunctively*, so that it is enough if impugned action was merely oppressive, or arbitrary, or unconstitutional. That being so, if unlawful conduct by a police officer can be proved, it is not necessary to show that it was arbitrary and oppressive as well.[114] 'Servants of government' encompass central and local government officers and also include police officers[115] and prison officers guilty of misfeasance in a public office[116] or false imprisonment.[117]

(b) Where the defendant's conduct has been calculated by her to make a profit for herself which might exceed the compensation payable to the claimant

Within this category fall those such as publishers, as in *Cassell & Co Ltd v Broome*,[118] who calculate that a libel might help sell so many copies of a publication that they will profit despite having to pay compensatory damages to the victim.[119] The idea is that they should learn that 'tort does not pay'.[120] In this context, 'carelessness alone, however extreme, is not enough' unless the inference can be drawn 'that the publisher had no honest belief in the truth of what he published'.[121] But the category is not limited to cases of defamation; it can be invoked, for example, where conspirators falsely imprison immigrants and force them to work as prostitutes,[122] or where landlords commit torts against tenants by driving them out of their property in order to profit by letting it to someone else at a higher rent.[123]

(c) Where authorised by statute

There are very few examples of this category in which the statute expressly permits the claimant to sue for exemplary damages.[124]

(d) Three further considerations

As well as establishing that the tort in question falls into one of the three categories outlined in *Rookes v Barnard*, it seems that three further requirements must obtain. First,

---

[112] See, eg, *Rowlands v CC of Merseyside* [2007] 1 WLR 1065, at [47].
[113] [1964] AC 1129.   [114] *Holden v CC of Lancashire* [1987] QB 380.
[115] *Casssell & Co Ltd v Broome* [1972] AC 1027; *Thompson v MPC* [1998] QB 498.
[116] *Racz v Home Office* [1994] 2 WLR 23.
[117] *Muuse v Secretary of State for the Home Department* [2010] EWCA Civ 453.
[118] [1972] AC 1027.
[119] Judging whether there is a likely profit is to be construed widely. Potential damages awards are included, as are benefits in kind that can be recovered by C: *Borders (UK) Ltd v MPC* [2005] EWCA Civ 197.
[120] Note the limits of this argument in *AB v SW Water Services Ltd* [1993] 1 All ER 609.
[121] *John v MGN Ltd* [1996] 2 All ER 35, at 57.   [122] *AT v Gavril Dulghieru* [2009] EWHC 225.
[123] *Drane v Evangelou* [1978] 2 All ER 437.
[124] See, eg, the Reserve and Auxiliary Forces (Protection of Civil Interests) Act 1951, sub-s 3(2).

the claimant must be able to show that she herself was the victim of the tort.[125] Relatives invested with a cause of action upon the victim's death do not possess the right to sue for exemplary damages.[126] Second, exemplary damages must be necessary to effect proper punishment of the defendant. If the defendant has been prosecuted for the equivalent crime, normally no award of exemplary damages will be made[127] (although the fact that the defendant has been fined will not be determinative in every case[128]). Finally, a bare majority in *A v Bottrill*[129] held that the court will consider whether the defendant's behaviour rose to the level of outrageous conduct warranting condemnation.

(B) Damages for living claimants

The function and the anomalies of tort law are well illustrated when we consider the general rules governing the compensation of personal injuries. The victim's financial future might well turn on whether she can establish that her injuries are someone else's 'fault'; essentially, that a tort was committed. Should she succeed, she and her family will receive a level of compensation which will help to meet her material needs and will far exceed the total of social welfare benefits available to an equally severely injured person unable to prove 'fault'[130] on the part of another. This gives rise to the potential for unfairness in the treatment of persons who suffer from essentially the same sorts of injuries, one group receiving adequate means for treatment and recovery and another group being left to the public health system and their own (invariably limited) resources. While the debate on compensating personal injuries via tort law has raged for decades, there seems little to no prospect of the tort system being overhauled in England and Wales.

Role of speculation Historically, damages have been granted on a once-and-for-all basis[131] which inevitably—because of the role played by speculation—leads to imperfections in the compensatory awards made. Indeed, the process of assessing lump-sum damages often consists of little more than judicial guesstimates: 'How long will the claimant actually live?'; 'Will she develop epilepsy in five years' time?' A claimant whose medical prognosis is judged overly pessimistically will gain a bonus, while the converse is true also. In short, individual justice gets sacrificed in the interests of finality and predictability. Unsurprisingly, such imperfections have attracted much criticism.[132] That

---

[125] *Rookes v Barnard* [1964] AC 1129, at 1227–8.

[126] Specific provision to this effect exists in the Law Reform (Miscellaneous Provisions) Act 1934, sub-s 1(2)(a)(*i*).

[127] See, eg, *Archer v Brown* [1985] QB 401 (no exemplary damages where D imprisoned for offence).

[128] *Devenish Nutrition Ltd v Sanofi-Aventis SA* [2007] EWHC 2394 (appeal on other grounds dismissed: [2009] Ch 390).

[129] [2002] 3 WLR 1406.

[130] For critique of the 'fault' principle, see P Cane, *Atiyah's Accidents Compensation and the Law* (8th edn, 2013).

[131] One exception is where a provisional award is made enabling C to re-apply for further damages if a risk of further damage (eg, epilepsy) materialises: see Supreme Court Act 1981, s 32A.

[132] See, eg, *Wright v British Rlys Board* [1983] 2 AC 773, at 776–8.

being the case, a system of periodic payments that can be adjusted over time to meet the claimant's needs generally is regarded as a more effective and just compensation mechanism in cases of severe injury.[133] While lump-sum awards can and will be made in respect of run-of-the-mill injuries, it is possible also to obtain a periodical payment order in respect of severely injured claimants (which can be made on a reviewable basis in certain circumstances).[134]

Periodical payments Periodical payments were first put on a statutory footing in 2005.[135] Yet unlike the voluntary structured settlements that they replaced, these orders can be imposed on the parties even if they are opposed to such an arrangement. (That said, a court will be unlikely to act contrary to the wishes of *both* parties.)[136] Drawing up the necessary initial schedule can be a complex matter (involving such matters as indexing),[137] and it is for this reason that periodical payments orders were made reviewable in certain circumstances so that modifications can be effected in the future, typically in light of a serious deterioration in the claimant's condition.[138] But reviewability is by no means the norm.

Two components Whether paid in the form of a lump sum or in the form of periodical payments, compensatory damages in tort have two main components: (1) pecuniary losses—primarily those resulting from loss of earnings or earning capacity (they include also the costs of medical and hospital expenses); (2) non-pecuniary loss—that is, pain and suffering and loss of amenity.[139] Let us examine each in turn.

(1) Pecuniary losses

(a) Loss of earnings

Prior to trial A number of years are likely to elapse between the infliction of the relevant injuries and the trial. Loss of earnings suffered up to the date of trial is part of the claimant's 'special damages' and must be pleaded specifically.[140] In making such pleas, all claims for loss of earnings (including business profits[141] and perquisites[142]) are to be calculated in a way that is consistent with deductions that would have been made by way of tax,[143] National Insurance, and other relevant items.

---

[133] But for criticism, see R Lewis, 'Appearance and Reality in Reforming Periodical Payments of Tort Damages in the UK' in JW Neyers et al (eds), *Emerging Issues in Tort Law* (2007), ch 19.

[134] See the Damages Act 1996, ss 2–2B.   [135] Damages Act 1996.

[136] *Thompstone v Tameside and Glossop NHS Trust* [2008] 1 WLR 2207.

[137] See, eg, *Thompstone v Tameside and Glossop NHS Trust* [2008] 1 WLR 2207.

[138] But note that, controversially, no facility for review is made in respect of the escalating costs of health care provision that may well rise at a rate in excess of inflation. See R Lewis, 'Appearance and Reality in Reforming Periodical Payments of Tort Damages in the UK' in JW Neyers et al (eds), *Emerging Issues in Tort Law* (2007), ch 19.

[139] For a detailed account of the composition of non-pecuniary loss see Law Com, *Damages for Personal Injury: Non-Pecuniary Loss* (No 257, 1999).

[140] *Ilkiw v Samuels* [1963] 2 All ER 879.   [141] *Kent v British Rlys Board* [1995] PIQR Q42.

[142] *Clay v Pooler* [1982] 3 All ER 570.

[143] *British Transport Commission v Gourley* [1956] AC 185.

Future earnings Loss of future earnings is recoverable also, though often this is a matter of some speculation[144] since the court must estimate the claimant's future employment prospects,[145] her future incapacity,[146] and the number of working years of which she has been deprived.[147] The traditional method is to arrive at a multiplicand (an estimate of the claimant's average net annual loss) and to multiply this by a multiplier (the number of working years lost by the claimant). Actuarial tables may be used in making these calculations.[148]

Multiplicand The courts will compensate loss of earning capacity[149] as readily as an actual loss of earnings. So a person who is a stay-at-home parent at the time of her injuries will be compensated for any loss of earning capacity running from the time when she would have been likely to return to remunerated work.[150] Young people who have not started earning will receive compensation for the damage to, or destruction of, their employment prospects. The older the child and the more evidence there is of her prospects of remunerated work, the larger the award will be.[151] With a very young child, the highly speculative nature of assessing her loss of earning capacity will not disentitle her from such an award, but it might mean a relatively small amount is received under this head. In *Croke v Wiseman*,[152] for example, a 21-month-old boy was permanently incapacitated in a medical accident. He was seven at the date of the trial and likely to survive until he was 40. To compensate him for his loss of earnings, a multiplicand of £5,000 and a multiplier of five years were adopted.

Multiplier The starting point for arriving at the multiplier is the number of remaining years in the claimant's working life.[153] The court must adjust this for contingencies such as future unemployment and sickness. In practice, the experience of the court has resulted in a multiplier which, for example, in the case of a 30-year-old, ordinarily would be about 17, reducing, in the case of a man of about 40, to about 12.[154]

Lost years An issue arises concerning use of the multiplier where the medical evidence suggests that the claimant will die early as a result of her injuries. Should she be able to recover compensation for her 'lost years' when, but for the fatal injury, she would have

---

[144] *Collett v Smith* [2009] EWCA Civ 583 (18-year-old professional footballer with uncertain prospects).

[145] In the tricky case of professional sportspersons, see *Collett v Smith* [2009] EWCA Civ 583.

[146] But note that this estimate is now subject to variation if the award takes the form of a reviewable periodic payment: Damages Act 1996, s 2B.

[147] This paragraph is based on *Taylor v O'Connor* [1971] AC 115 and *Cookson v Knowles* [1979] AC 556. See also *Herring v Ministry of Defence* [2003] EWCA Civ 528.

[148] Government Actuary's Dept, *Actuarial Tables for use in Personal Injury and Fatal Accident Cases* (7th edn, 2011) ('*Ogden Tables*'), use of an earlier edition of which was approved in *Wells v Wells* [1998] 3 All ER 481.

[149] *Smith v Manchester Corpn* (1974) 17 KIR 1; *Dhaliwal v Personal Representatives of Hunt* [1995] PIQR Q56.

[150] *Daly v General Steam Navigation Co Ltd, The Dragon* [1980] 3 All ER 696.

[151] See *Housecroft v Burnett* [1986] 1 All ER 332 (£56,000 for loss of earning capacity awarded to an intelligent 16-year-old girl).

[152] [1981] 3 All ER 852.

[153] If there is great uncertainty associated with the calculation, a lump sum will be granted based on the court's best estimate of C's loss: *Chase International Express Ltd v McRae* [2003] EWCA Civ 505.

[154] See *Pritchard v JH Cobden Ltd* [1988] Fam 22.

lived longer? Loss of income in the 'lost years' is recoverable,[155] subject to a deduction for living expenses which will no longer be incurred.[156]

For claimants injured in the middle of their working lives, when they have families and dependants, such income clearly should be recoverable. It is needed to ensure that, even after the claimant's premature death, her family does not suffer and that the claimant herself can enjoy relative peace of mind in what remains of her life. The Damages Act 1996, section 3 provides for this, allowing dependants to claim for those losses not compensated by the original award of damages.

In *Croke v Wiseman*,[157] considered earlier, no separate award was made in respect of loss of earnings in the 'lost years'. This seems to be standard practice in the case of young people, the courts treating the calculation of lost years as too speculative and preferring to make small adjustments to the multiplier.[158]

Discount rate The basic loss calculated by the court is reduced when the claimant receives a capital sum, which she is expected to invest in interest-bearing securities. In *Wells v Wells*,[159] it was held that there is an expectation that the prudent claimant will take advantage of index-linked government securities which yield a low but safe average net return. The relatively low return associated with such securities is reflected in a higher initial lump sum than would have been made previously. The award is calculated on the basis that the claimant will spend the income and part of the capital annually so that the capital will be exhausted at the age the court has assessed to be the appropriate age having regard to all the contingencies. In a *Consultation Paper*, the Ministry of Justice explained the operation of the discount rate using the following example:

> If one assumes that a claimant will require future care at an average annual cost of £10,000 on a life expectancy of 20 years, then, disregarding changes in the value of money, if the court were to award £200,000 the plaintiff would be over-compensated. This is because the £10,000 needed to purchase care in the twentieth year should have been earning interest for 19 years from when the payment is made. The amount by which the sum of £200,000 must be discounted is determined by the return that is expected from the investments it is assumed that the claimant will make. Thus, if one assumes a net return of 5 per cent, the sum payable would be £130,900, whilst at a net return of 3 per cent, the figure would be £153,200.[160]

The discount rate is now set by the Lord Chancellor at the rate of return on 'low-risk' investments,[161] this being factored into the actuarial tables so that the parties need not make extensive calculations of their own.[162]

---

[155] *Pickett v British Rail Engineering Ltd* [1980] AC 136.

[156] Including a pro rata sum for her consumption of housing, electricity costs, etc: *Harris v Empress Motors Ltd* [1983] 3 All ER 561.   [157] [1981] 3 All ER 852.

[158] See *Housecroft v Burnett* [1986] 1 All ER 332.   [159] [1998] 3 All ER 481.

[160] Ministry of Justice, *Damages Act 1996: The Discount Rate—How should it be set?* (CP12/2012), at [7].

[161] Pursuant to the Damages (Personal Injury) Order 2001 (SI 2001/2301). See Rt Hon D Liddington, 'Personal Injury Discount Rate' (Letter to HC Justice Select Committee, 7 September 2017), available at: http://www.parliament.uk/documents/commons-committees/Justice/correspondence/Personal-injury-discount-rate-Lidington-BN-personal-injury-discount-rate.pdf. If any party to the proceedings can show that a different rate is more appropriate in the particular case, the court may use that rate: Damages Act 1996, s 1(2).

[162] Ministry of Justice, *Damages Act 1996: The Discount Rate—How should it be set?* (CP12/2012), at [8].

(b) Medical, nursing, and hospital expenses

General A claimant is entitled to recover as special damages those medical, nursing, and hospital expenses incurred reasonably up to the date of trial.[163] Her predicted future expenses will then be estimated and awarded as general damages.[164] Where the claimant has received private health care or plans to arrange future treatment privately, the possibility that the claimant could have avoided these expenses by using the facilities of the NHS is to be disregarded.[165] Yet, if it is clear that private medical care will not be used, the court will refuse to entertain any claim that the claimant makes in respect of any such care she *might have elected* to use.[166] In other respects, the expenditure must be reasonable in relation to both the claimant's condition and the amount paid. If she has to live in a special institution or in special accommodation, the additional expense is recoverable.[167] She cannot claim the capital cost of acquiring special accommodation since she continues to own that accommodation.[168] But she can claim the additional annual cost over her lifetime of requiring special accommodation and the capital cost of any alterations or conversions needed to meet her disability that do not enhance the value of the property.[169] Any saving to the claimant attributable to her maintenance at public expense in a hospital, nursing home, or other institution is set off against any loss of earnings.[170]

Nursing care The claimant is able to claim her nursing expenses. If the court finds, however, that at some future time she will be unable to obtain all the private nursing services required, and will have to enter an NHS hospital, an appropriate deduction from future nursing expenses will be made.[171] On the other hand, where relatives or friends shoulder the burden of caring for the claimant, the claimant's right to compensation to pay for such services normally is unaffected.[172] She is entitled to receive a sum to recompense, for example, her spouse, parent, or friend.[173] That the carer has given up gainful employment must be taken into account and generally her loss should be made good, although the total cost of care should not exceed current commercial rates for

---

[163] Even hospice care is covered: *Drake v Foster Wheeler Ltd* [2011] 1 All ER 63.

[164] The courts will take expert evidence on such matters. But where conflicting medical evidence is presented, the judge will be entitled to form her own view of what care is likely to be needed: *Huntley v Simmons* [2010] Med LR 83.

[165] Law Reform (Personal Injuries) Act 1948, sub-s 2(4). If C does make use of the NHS she cannot recover what she would have had to pay if she had had private treatment: *Lim Poh Choo v Camden and Islington Area HA* [1980] AC 174.   [166] *Woodrup v Nicol* [1993] PIQR Q 14.

[167] *Shearman v Folland* [1950] 2 KB 43; *George v Pinnock* [1973] 1 All ER 926.

[168] *Cunningham v Harrison* [1973] QB 942.   [169] *Roberts v Johnstone* [1989] QB 878.

[170] Administration of Justice Act 1982, s 5.   [171] *Cunningham v Harrison* [1973] QB 942.

[172] *Hunt v Severs* [1994] 2 AC 350; *Donnelly v Joyce* [1974] QB 454 (mother gave up job to care for six-year-old C); *Cunningham v Harrison* [1973] QB 942 (a wife gave up her job to nurse her husband); *Roberts v Johnstone* [1989] QB 878 (care provided by adoptive mother). But note the important distinction between caring services and business services: *Hardwick v Hudson* [1999] 1 WLR 1770.

[173] In *Croke v Wiseman* [1981] 3 All ER 852, C had a life expectancy of 33 years, throughout which he would need continuous nursing by professional nurses and his parents. In awarding £119,000 for the future cost of nursing care the court took account of the mother losing her teacher's pension rights, valued at £7,000, on giving up her post.

professional nursing care.[174] Recompense is available even though the relative is simply caring for the claimant voluntarily, out of love.[175] The monetary value of gratuitous care formerly provided by the claimant for another member of the family must not be over-looked. So, for example, if X is injured by virtue of Y's tort, X may claim the value of the care she used to provide gratuitously for her disabled brother Z.[176] If a spouse provides gratuitous assistance in running the injured partner's business, no award will be made in relation to the value of these essentially commercial services.[177]

(c) Additional pecuniary losses and expenses

Recoverable losses Other losses and expenses that flow from the claimant's injuries gen-erally will be recoverable. These include such things as additional costs of coping with a life of disability,[178] expenses of removal to a specially adapted dwelling,[179] a specially built car,[180] etc. Similarly, the costs of obtaining assistance with housework will be recover-able, as will losses resulting from no longer being able to pursue a profitable hobby.[181]

No double recovery Where a claimant was permanently incapacitated and, in add-ition to loss of earnings, there was a 'cost of care' claim, the House of Lords in *Lim Poh Choo v Camden and Islington AHA* sought to avoid any duplication of damages as fol-lows:[182] a full award for loss of earnings was made in the usual way with no deduction for living expenses except in respect of the 'lost years'. In calculating the award for cost of care, however, a deduction was made for the living expenses the claimant would have incurred in any event had she not been injured.

(d) Deduction for benefits received

General The pecuniary losses and expenses resulting from injury might be offset by benefits received whether from social security, insurance provision, or charity.

Social security The Social Security (Recovery of Benefits) Act 1997 provides protec-tion for damages awards made in respect of pain, suffering, and loss of amenity against the recoupment of social security benefits. Taken together, section 8 of, and Schedule 2 to, the Act permit recoupment only as against compensation for loss of earnings, the cost of care, and loss of mobility. The scheme affects the defendant in the following way. As regards those damages that represent the amount payable in respect of pain,

---

[174] *Housecroft v Burnett* [1986] 1 All ER 332. Where, however, the carer's net loss of earnings is a lesser amount than the commercial rate for caring, the amount will be confined to the carer's net loss: *Fitzgerald v Ford* [1996] PIQR Q72.

[175] But here, it has been suggested that the amount should be equal to 75% of the commercial rate for help: *Fairhurst v St Helens and Knowsley HA* [1995] PIQR Q1.

[176] *Lowe v Guise* [2002] QB 1369.   [177] *Hardwick v Hudson* [1999] PIQR Q202.

[178] In *Kroeker v Jansen* (1995) 123 DLR (4th) 652 an award was made to a woman 'disabled from some of her housework beyond the level that her husband ought reasonably to do for her'.

[179] *Moriarty v McCarthy* [1978] 2 All ER 213 (paraplegic moving to a bungalow).

[180] *Housecroft v Burnett* [1986] 1 All ER 332.

[181] The award was made regardless of whether it was actually used to obtain domestic help: *Daly v General Steam Navigation Co Ltd, The Dragon* [1980] 3 All ER 696.   [182] [1980] AC 174.

suffering, and loss of amenity, the defendant is liable directly to the claimant. As regards the amount now paid to the claimant by way of state benefits in respect of loss of earnings, etc, the defendant is liable to the Secretary of State. The principle is simple: the state shall not bear the pecuniary cost of the defendant's tort, while the claimant should not be compensated twice over.

Other benefits Social security benefits are not the only collateral benefits that may result from the claimant's injury and consequent disability. Generally, charitable payments made to the claimant will not be deducted[183] nor will *ex gratia* payments made by employers.[184] Proceeds of personal insurance policies provided for by the claimant or her family will not be deducted.[185] But where the claimant receives sick pay as part of her contract of employment, she must account for those monies[186] (unless the contract provides that sick pay must be refunded in the event of a successful tort claim).[187]

In *Parry v Cleaver*[188] the House of Lords held that an occupational disability pension was not deductible regardless of whether it was contributory or discretionary. The test, their Lordships held, was twofold: was the money received of the same nature as what was lost; and, if not, was it a benefit intended still to be paid even if the claimant were to be reimbursed from another source? In the light of this test, statutory sick pay payable by the employer under the Social Security and Housing Benefits Act 1982 was held to be deductible.[189] It was seen as essentially the same as a contractual entitlement to sick pay. In *Smoker v London Fire and Civil Defence Authority*,[190] the House of Lords affirmed *Parry v Cleaver*. Thus, a contributory disability pension remains non-deductible even if provided and partly paid for by the employer.[191]

(2) Non-pecuniary losses

(a) Pain and suffering

The claimant is entitled to compensation for the pain and suffering, both actual and prospective, caused by the initial injury or subsequent surgical operations.[192] If her expectation of life has been reduced by her injuries, an award of damages for pain and suffering shall take account of any suffering caused or likely to be caused to her by awareness that her expectation of life has been shortened.[193] But neither a permanently unconscious claimant,[194] nor one who experiences anxiety at having developed

---

[183]   *Redpath v Belfast and County Down Rly* [1947] NI 167 (approved in *Parry v Cleaver* [1970] AC 1).

[184]   *Cunningham v Harrison* [1973] QB 942. Cf *Hussain v New Taplow Paper Mills Ltd* [1987] 1 All ER 417 (where D was the employer).

[185]   *Bradburn v Great Western Rly Co* (1874) LR 10 Exch 1 (approved in *Parry v Cleaver* [1970] AC 1).

[186]   *Turner v Ministry of Defence* (1969) 113 Sol Jo 585.

[187]   *Browning v War Office* [1963] 1 QB 750.

[188]   [1970] AC 1; followed in *Longden v British Coal Corpn* [1998] AC 653.

[189]   *Palfrey v Greater London Council* [1985] ICR 437.   [190]   [1991] 2 AC 502.

[191]   See also *McCamley v Cammell Laird Shipbuilders Ltd* [1990] 1 All ER 854.

[192]   *H West & Son Ltd v Shephard* [1964] AC 326; *Cutler v Vauxhall Motors Ltd* [1971] 1 QB 418.

[193]   Administration of Justice Act 1982, sub-s 1(1)(b). This Act abolished damages for loss of expectation of life as such, and as a separate head of damage.   [194]   *Wise v Kaye* [1962] 1 QB 638.

symptomless (and per se harmless) pleural plaques because of exposure to asbestos,[195] has a claim for pain and suffering.

(b) Loss of amenities

Compensation is recoverable for loss of faculty. Even though the accident has rendered the claimant a 'human vegetable' so that she is unaware of her injuries, she is entitled to claim for any loss of bodily function.[196] Damages cannot be refused simply because the claimant will be unable to use the damages in view of the severity of her injuries.[197] The court will take into account disfigurement,[198] deprivation of sexual pleasures,[199] loss of a holiday,[200] as well as more obvious losses, such as inability to play games or to walk. In short, damages under this head may take account of a wide range of subjective factors.

(c) Assessing the quantum

General Non-pecuniary damages differ from pecuniary damages in that there is no suggestion of a scientific method of deciding what sum should be awarded. Damages for loss of amenity and pain and suffering traditionally have been awarded as an aggregate lump sum. This sum represents an amount that society deems fair; and in this regard there has evolved a set of conventional principles which provide a provisional guide to the comparative severity of different forms of injury. This guide uses a system of brackets of damages into which particular types of injury fall. In other words, loss generally[201] is compensated according to a tariff—for example, a sum between £A and £B for the loss of an arm, between £X and £Y for the loss of an eye, etc. However, the particular circumstances of the claimant, including her age and any unusual deprivation which she suffers, are taken into account.

Levels of injury When considering the exact amount to award within the appropriate bracket, extreme physical pain, or the impairment of speech or hearing ought to justify an award above the average; whereas a lack of awareness of one's disability might justify an award at the lower end of the range.

(d) Provisional awards

Sometimes, the courts are called upon to award future damages where the claimant's medical prognosis is imprecise. For example, the injury might have created a risk of epilepsy developing later in life. The courts used to estimate the percentage chance of such a condition developing and award an equivalent proportion of damages for the results of that condition. Consequently, claimants were over compensated if the risk did not materialise and under compensated if it did. The Administration of Justice Act 1982 provided an alternative. Where as a result of the tort there is a chance that the claimant

---

[195] *Rothwell v Chemical & Insulating Co Ltd* [2008] AC 281.
[196] *H West & Son Ltd v Shephard* [1964] AC 326; *Lim Poh Choo v Camden and Islington AHA* [1980] AC 174.
[197] *H West & Son Ltd v Shephard* [1964] AC 326.   [198] *Oakley v Walker* (1977) 121 Sol Jo 619.
[199] *Cook v JL Kier & Co Ltd* [1970] 2 All ER 513.   [200] *Ichard v Frangoulis* [1977] 2 All ER 461.
[201] The courts may depart from the standard tariff where the circumstances require it. See, eg, *Griffiths v Williams* (1995) *Times*, 24 November.

will develop some serious disease or suffer some serious deterioration in her physical or mental condition at some time in the future, the court will assess damages on the assumption that the development or deterioration will not occur, but award further damages at a future date if it does so occur, upon an application made by the claimant.[202]

The rules on provisional damages have given rise to problems of application in the past so that, where the facility exists, courts might now much prefer to make use of reviewable periodical payments (considered earlier).

(e) Interest

The courts have the power to award interest on all or any part of an award of damages and should do so on awards for personal injuries or death unless there are 'special reasons' not to do so.[203] The general rule is that interest on pre-trial pecuniary loss will be payable at half the average rate on short-term investment accounts for that period.[204] Normally, no deduction of interest is made to take account of social security benefits received by the claimant.[205] Interest payable on non-pecuniary loss will be low.[206]

(3) Effect of dishonesty

Under the Criminal Justice and Courts Act 2015, section 57, where, in proceedings on a claim for damages in respect of personal injury (the 'primary claim'), the court finds that the claimant is entitled to damages in respect of the claim, but that the claimant has been fundamentally dishonest in relation to the primary claim or a related claim, the court must dismiss the primary claim, unless it is satisfied that the claimant would suffer substantial injustice if the claim were dismissed. But the court's order dismissing the claim must record the amount of damages that the court would have awarded to the claimant in respect of the primary claim but for its dismissal.

(C) Damage or destruction of goods

Frequently, claimants in personal injury actions have a claim for damage to goods such as their cars. Where the car or other goods are destroyed, damages comprise the cost of buying a replacement, together with compensation for loss of use pending replacement, with a deduction for the salvage value of the destroyed goods.[207] Where there is damage to goods, the damages represent the diminution in value, normally based on the cost of repair.[208] Damages are given also for loss of use, even though the goods were non-profit-

---

[202] The 1982 Act merely provided for rules to be made under it that grant this jurisdiction. See now Supreme Court Act 1981, sub-ss 32A(1) and (2); RSC Ord 37, rr 8–10.

[203] Supreme Court Act, s 34A.   [204] *Jefford v Gee* [1970] 2 QB 130.

[205] *Wisely v John Fulton (Plumbers) Ltd* [2000] 2 All ER 545. But where the benefits exceed the damages due to be paid, such a deduction may be made: *Griffiths v British Coal Corpn* [2001] 1 WLR 1493.

[206] *Lawrence v CC of Staffordshire* [2000] PIQR Q349; *Wright v British Rlys Board* [1983] 2 AC 773. The reasons are: (1) damages should take into account inflation up to the time of judgment; and (2) damages for non-pecuniary loss are often difficult to quantify until C's condition has stabilised.

[207] *Moore v DER Ltd* [1971] 3 All ER 517; *Thatcher v Littlejohn* [1978] RTR 369.

[208] *Dodd Properties (Kent) Ltd v Canterbury CC* [1980] 1 All ER 928.

earning and not replaced during repair.[209] If a substitute has been hired, the cost can be claimed provided the goods hired and the price paid are reasonable.[210]

Section 4 Death

Two issues arise when death ensues from a tort. First, the deceased's estate might wish to proceed with the cause of action which the deceased herself would have had if she had not died. Second, others—especially relatives—might claim that they have suffered a loss in consequence of the death. Two statutes need to be examined in this regard: the Law Reform (Miscellaneous Provisions) Act 1934 (dealing with the survival of actions) and the Fatal Accidents Act 1976 (dealing with death itself giving rise to a cause of action).

(A) Survival of actions

General The Law Reform (Miscellaneous Provisions) Act 1934 provides that, on the death of any person, all causes of action vested in her survive for the benefit of her estate subject to three significant exceptions.[211] The first exception is that actions for defamation do not survive. Second, the right of a person to claim under the Fatal Accidents Act 1976, section 1A for bereavement does not survive for the benefit of her estate.[212] Third, exemplary damages do not survive in the hands of the deceased's estate.[213] The reason why these actions die with the initial victim is that they are regarded as claims personal to the deceased; although why this should be true of exemplary (as opposed to aggravated) damages is hard to fathom.

Damages Where the death of the deceased has been caused by an act or omission giving rise to a cause of action, the 1934 Act enables her estate to bring proceedings in tort against the defendant.[214] Her estate can claim damages according to the usual principles for the period between when the cause of action arose and the death. Thus, damages can be awarded for the pain, suffering,[215] and loss of amenity[216] for that period during which the deceased actually suffered such deprivations. Damages can be awarded also for lost earnings[217] and medical expenses incurred up to the time of death,[218] including

---

[209] *The Mediana* [1900] AC 113; *HL Motor Works (Willesden) Ltd v Alwahbi* [1977] RTR 276.

[210] *HL Motor Works (Willesden) Ltd v Alwahbi* [1977] RTR 276 (reasonable to hire a Rolls-Royce until C's Rolls-Royce was repaired).   [211] Sub-section 1(1).

[212] Administration of Justice Act 1982, sub-s 4(1). It does, however, extend to a registered same-sex civil partner.   [213] Administration of Justice Act 1982, sub-s 4(2).

[214] For the limitation periods within which these proceedings must be brought, see the Limitation Act 1980, sub-ss 11(5)–(7).

[215] *Andrews v Freeborough* [1967] 1 QB 1 (£2,000 awarded to the estate of a child aged eight who remained unconscious for a year between the accident and death); *Murray v Shuter* [1976] QB 972 (£11,000 awarded to the estate of a man aged 36 in respect of loss of amenity during the four years he survived the accident in a coma).

[216] *Rose v Ford* [1937] AC 826 (£2 awarded for loss of leg amputated two days before death).

[217] *Murray v Shuter* [1976] QB 927.   [218] *Rose v Ford* [1937] AC 826.

palliative care in a hospice.[219] The damages awarded to the deceased's estate 'shall be calculated without reference to any loss or gain to h[er] estate consequent on h[er] death'.[220] Thus, if the deceased loses an annuity to which she was entitled, or if insurance monies become payable upon her death, these losses and gains are disregarded in computing damages under the 1934 Act. The rights conferred by the 1934 Act are in addition to any rights conferred by the Fatal Accidents Act 1976,[221] and the amount of damages is unaffected by any damages under the later legislation.

Lost years No damages can be awarded to the estate in respect of loss of income in the deceased's 'lost years'.[222] The potential overlap between claims by dependants under the Fatal Accidents Act for loss of dependency and an estate's claims for lost income from the 'lost years' is thus avoided.[223]

(B) Death as a cause of action

(1) Introduction

Origins Historically at common law no action in tort could be brought by third parties who suffered loss through the killing of another.[224] But fatal accidents became so frequent with the development of railways that in 1846 Parliament had to pass the Fatal Accidents Act, which made considerable inroads into the common law rule. The modern principles are now embodied in the Fatal Accidents Act 1976.[225]

Rule The Fatal Accidents Act 1976, sub-section 1(1) provides:

> If death is caused by any wrongful act, neglect or default which is such as would (if death had not ensued) have entitled the person injured to maintain an action and recover damages in respect thereof, the person who would have been liable if death had not ensued shall be liable to an action for damages, notwithstanding the death of the person injured.

The cause of action thereby created allows for awards of damages under three heads of loss as they accrue to the dependants:[226] loss of support, bereavement, and funeral expenses.

---

[219] *Drake v Foster Wheeler Ltd* [2011] 1 All ER 63.

[220] Law Reform (Miscellaneous Provisions) Act 1934, sub-s 1(2). For application see *Harland and Wolff plc v McIntyre* [2006] EWCA Civ 287.

[221] Law Reform (Miscellaneous Provisions) Act 1934, sub-s 1(5); *Yelland v Powell Duffryn Associated Collieries Ltd (No 2)* [1941] 1 KB 519.

[222] Law Reform (Miscellaneous Provisions) Act 1934, sub-s 1(2)(a).

[223] See *Gammell v Wilson* [1982] AC 27.

[224] *Baker v Bolton* (1808) 1 Camp 493; *Admiralty Comrs v SS Amerika* [1917] AC 38; *Cox v Ergo Versicherung* [2014] AC 1379, at [6]. See P Handford (2013) 129 LQR 420.

[225] See also related provisions in the Mesothelioma Act 2014 (dependants' claims for compensation for death from diffuse mesothelioma) and the Pneumoconiosis etc (Workers' Compensation) Act 1979 (dependants' claims for compensation for death arising from pneumoconiosis).

[226] Sums awarded do not form part of the estate of the deceased because the losses are those of the dependants: *Brownlie v Four Seasons Holdings Inc* [2016] 1 WLR 1814, at [86].

(2) Who can sue?

The action is brought in the name of the executor or administrator[227] of the deceased, and lies in respect of loss of support for the benefit of the following persons:[228] a spouse or former spouse;[229] registered and former registered same-sex civil partners;[230] children, grandchildren, fathers, mothers, step-parents, grandparents, brothers, sisters, uncles, aunts, and their issue; adopted and illegitimate dependants; stepchildren of the several categories.[231] If there is no executor or administrator, or if she fails to bring the action within six months after the death of the deceased, any dependant can bring it.[232] The Administration of Justice Act 1982 responded to social changes by including for the first time any person who was living with the deceased in the same household for at least two years before that date, and was living during the whole of that period as the deceased's spouse.[233]

(3) Nature of the act complained of

Cause of action It must be proved that the act caused the death.[234] Thereafter, it must be shown that there was a 'wrongful act, neglect or default' by the defendant. Presumably, these words embrace any tort.[235] Consequently, if the defendant's act was never actionable because she would have had a defence to any action brought by the deceased in her lifetime, no action will lie.[236] Where the deceased died partly as the result of her own fault and partly as the result of the fault of any other person, damages are reduced to a proportionate extent[237] in the same way that they are under the Law Reform (Contributory Negligence) Act 1945. If a dependant's contributory negligence is a cause of the deceased's death, that dependant's damages are reduced but the awards to other dependants are unaffected.[238]

---

[227] Fatal Accidents Act 1976, sub-s 2(1).   [228] Fatal Accidents Act 1976, sub-ss 1(2)–(5).

[229] By the Fatal Accidents Act 1976, sub-s 1(4), a former spouse includes a person whose marriage has been annulled or declared void as well as a divorced person. This provision applies even if the surviving former spouse has remarried: *Shepherd v Post Office* (1995) *Times*, 15 June. An equivalent definition is made in respect of a 'former civil partner': sub-s 1(4A).

[230] Fatal Accidents Act 1976, sub-ss 1(4)–(5) as amended by s 83 of the Civil Partnership Act 2004.

[231] Fatal Accidents Act 1976, sub-s 1(5)(a): 'any relationship by affinity shall be treated as a relationship by consanguinity, any relationship of the half-blood as a relationship of the whole blood, and the stepchild of any person as his child'. D must be given particulars of the dependants for whom a claim is made and of the nature of this claim: sub-s 2(4).

[232] Fatal Accidents Act 1976, sub-s 2(2).

[233] Fatal Accidents Act 1976, sub-s 1(3)(b), upheld as compatible with the European Convention on Human Rights: *Swift v Secretary of State for Justice* [2013] 3 WLR 1151.

[234] In *Pigney v Pointer's Transport Services Ltd* [1957] 2 All ER 807, the deceased committed suicide while in a depressive state induced by D's negligent act; the death was held to have been caused by that act, so that an action under the Fatal Accidents Act 1976 was successful.

[235] And a negligent breach of contract: *Grein v Imperial Airways Ltd* [1937] 1 KB 50.

[236] *Murphy v Culhane* [1977] QB 94 (if the deceased had failed because of the defence of *ex turpi causa* no action would lie under the Act).   [237] Fatal Accidents Act 1976, s 5.

[238] *Dodds v Dodds* [1978] QB 543. The negligent dependant might be required to make a contribution (under the Civil Liability (Contribution) Act 1978) towards the damages which D has to pay for the benefit of the dependants.

Limitation At the time of her death, the deceased must have been in a position to sue the defendant had she not died because of the wrongful act. If the limitation period expired between the injury and her death, the Limitation Act 1980 stipulates that no Fatal Accidents Act claim arises.[239] Ordinarily,[240] this means that if more than three years have elapsed between the injury and death, the claim will be time barred.[241] The Limitation Act 1980 provides also that, if the deceased had settled her own claim,[242] no action lies under the Fatal Accidents Act,[243] but an action still lies (and without any limit on the damages) if the claimant merely had agreed beforehand that no more than, say, £1,000 damages should be recoverable in the event of her being the victim of this tort.[244]

(4) Specific limitations on claims under the 1976 Act

Loss of support There are certain important limitations on the ability to sue. Let us begin with the action for loss of support. Any claim by a dependant lies only upon proof of pecuniary loss (that is, financial support that she would have received).[245] There must be a loss of 'prospective pecuniary advantage' and a 'speculative possibility' of pecuniary gain is not enough.[246] A parent could recover when her 16-year-old daughter died, having almost completed her unpaid dressmaking apprenticeship.[247] But the parent of a three-year-old child has no cause of action.[248] It is not essential that the dependant should have a legal right to that aid[249]—the loss of services gratuitously rendered is enough.[250] However, a distinction must be made between a pecuniary benefit to the dependant that would have accrued qua business relationship (as opposed to qua family relationship). If the loss is a business loss, no action is permitted under the Act. Thus, a father could not sue in respect of the loss of business contracts occasioned by the death of his son, who worked for the father's firm.[251]

Bereavement There are limits too on the availability of damages for bereavement.[252] This claim can be brought only for the benefit of (1) the surviving 'life partner' of the deceased (that is the deceased's wife, husband, or civil partner);[253] or (2) the relevant parent or parents of any unmarried children.[254] The bereavement action does not

---

[239] Limitation Act 1980, sub-s 12(1).
[240] The three-year period can be extended if the deceased did not have 'relevant knowledge' of her cause of action.   [241] Limitation Act 1980, sub-s 11(1).
[242] *Pickett v British Rail Engineering Ltd* [1980] AC 136, at 146–7 and 152.
[243] Limitation Act 1980, sub-s 12(1).   [244] *Nunan v Southern Rly Co* [1924] 1 KB 223.
[245] *Duckworth v Johnson* (1859) 4 H & N 653.
[246] *Davies v Taylor* [1974] AC 207: wife deserted husband five weeks before his death; shortly before his death he instructed a solicitor to begin divorce proceedings. The deserting wife had no claim as she failed to show a reasonable expectation of pecuniary benefit.
[247] *Taff Vale Rly Co v Jenkins* [1913] AC 1.   [248] *Barnett v Cohen* [1921] 2 KB 461.
[249] *Stimpson v Wood & Son* (1888) 57 LJQB 484 (the mere fact that a wife by her adultery had lost her legal right to maintenance did not bar her claim).   [250] *Berry v Humm & Co* [1915] 1 KB 627.
[251] *Sykes v NE Rly Co* (1875) 44 LJCP 191. See also *Behrens v Bertram Mills Circus Ltd* [1957] 2 QB 1 and *Malyon v Plummer* [1964] 1 QB 330.
[252] Fatal Accidents Act 1976, sub-s 1A(1).   [253] Fatal Accidents Act 1976, sub-s 1A(2)(a).
[254] Both parents may claim if she was legitimate; only the mother if she was illegitimate: sub-s 1A(2)(b).

extend to former spouses, former civil partners, or a heterosexual cohabitant who had been living with the deceased as spouse.

Illegal enterprise For public policy reasons, where the pecuniary loss is attributable to an illegal enterprise in which the deceased was engaged, no action will lie under the 1976 Act. Thus, in *Hunter v Butler*[255] it was held that no claim lay where the deceased had been earning wages while fraudulently claiming social security benefits. The court was concerned not to allow monies illegally gained to form the basis of a claim for dependency.

(5) Period of limitation

The action under the 1976 Act must be brought within three years from either the date of the death, or the date on which the claimant had (actual or constructive) knowledge of the death, whichever is the later.[256] Where there are several potential claimants, the limitation period runs separately against each. Where the dependant's limitation period has expired before an action was brought, the court has a discretionary power to extend the period.[257]

(6) Assessment of damages

Prior to trial In *Cookson v Knowles*,[258] the House of Lords held that, as a general rule, damages up to the date of trial are to be assessed separately from those after that date. For the first part, the loss of dependency will be multiplied by the actual period between the accident and the trial. Interest on that sum will then be awarded at half the short-term investment rate current during that period.

Future loss In *Davies v Powell Duffryn Associated Collieries Ltd*, Lord Wright explained the traditional method of measuring the damages:

> The starting point is the amount of wages which the deceased was earning, the ascertainment of which to some extent may depend on the regularity of his employment. Then there is an estimate of how much was required or expended for his own personal and living expenses. The balance will give a datum or basic figure which will generally be turned into a lump sum … . That sum, however, has to be taxed down by having due regard to uncertainties.[259]

The House elaborated upon this in *Taylor v O'Connor*.[260] The damages to a widow must make available to her to spend each year a sum free of tax equal to the amount of the dependency—an award sufficient to buy an annuity of that amount is not enough

---

[255] [1996] RTR 396. See also *Burns v Edman* [1970] 2 QB 541: no claim could be made by a widow who knew that her support came from the proceeds of her husband's crimes.

[256] Limitation Act 1980, sub-s 12(2).   [257] Limitation Act 1980, s 33.

[258] [1979] AC 556; *Corbett v Barking, Havering and Brentwood HA* [1991] 2 QB 408 (but the multiplier should be adjusted to take account of known facts).

[259] [1942] AC 601, at 617.   [260] [1971] AC 115.

because part of the annuity will be taxable. Naturally, similar principles are applicable to other dependants.

Multiplicand In *Cookson v Knowles*,[261] the House of Lords stated that the court will arrive at the amount of dependency (the multiplicand), in part, by estimating the probable rate of earnings of the deceased at the date of the trial. This will have to take into account what the deceased had been earning and any inflation between the death and the date of trial. The court will take account of other events occurring between the death and the trial that would have been expected to impact upon future earnings.[262] These might include such things as tax rates having been reduced.[263]

The multiplicand must take account of factors relating to the dependants themselves, such as the period over which dependency would be expected to last. This might include most (if not all) of the life of a spouse,[264] but a shorter duration in the lives of children. But no account can be taken of the fact that the dependant is of independent means.[265] So, if a professional woman loses her husband who is also a professional, it is no answer to say that she could support herself and her children. Hypothetical events which, but for the deceased's death, would have increased the dependant's dependency will not be taken into account. So, the claimant widow's greater prospective loss had she given up work to have a family, as she would have so desired, was disregarded in *Malone v Rowan*.[266] Further, in assessing damages payable to a widow in respect of the death of her husband, the court must not take into account the widow's remarriage or her prospects of remarriage.[267] However, such prospects might affect awards to her children.[268]

Although persons living together as man and wife, though not married, are treated as 'dependants' (subject to conditions),[269] the court has to take into account the fact that the dependant had no enforceable right to financial support by the deceased as a result of their living together when assessing damages.[270]

Multiplier In *Knauer v Ministry of Justice*,[271] the Supreme Court held that the multiplier must be calculated from the date of trial and should be such that the capital sum awarded together with the income earned by its investment will be exhausted by the end of the period intended to be covered.[272] In so doing, the court is now able to use the Ogden tables on fatal accident calculation in order to work out life expectancies and

---

[261] [1979] AC 556; *Corbett v Barking, Havering and Brentwood HA* [1991] 2 QB 408 (but the multiplier should be adjusted to take account of known facts).

[262] *Corbett v Barking, Havering and Brentwood HA* [1991] 2 QB 408.

[263] *Daniels v Jones* [1961] 3 All ER 24.

[264] If spouse B's own life expectancy is reduced on account of the negligence of the defendant responsible for spouse A's death, the shortfall in B's dependency claim under the Fatal Accidents Act 1976 can be recouped in a personal action in negligence: *Haxton v Philips Electronics UK Ltd* [2014] 1 WLR 2721.

[265] *Shiels v Cruikshank* [1953] 1 All ER 874.   [266] [1984] 3 All ER 402.

[267] Fatal Accidents Act 1976, sub-s 3(3).   [268] *Thompson v Price* [1973] QB 838.

[269] If an unmarried father is killed, even if the mother of his children has no claim, their children recover the loss of all the benefits which their father had provided for them, including such benefits given to the mother for the children's advantage—eg, the cost of her air fares for a family holiday: *K v JMP Co Ltd* [1976] QB 85.

[270] Fatal Accidents Act 1976, sub-s 3(4).   [271] [2016] AC 908.

[272] [2016] AC 908, at [6] and [27].

discounts thereon. Normal principle supposes that the dependants will spend a part of the capital annually as well as the whole of the income they receive from so much of the capital as remains.[273]

Deductions In assessing future earnings, probable deductions for income tax[274] and National Insurance are to be made. Benefits that have accrued or will, or might, accrue to any person from her estate or otherwise (such as insurance pay-outs and gratuities) as a result of the death are disregarded.[275]

Discount rate As with claims by living claimants (considered earlier), the basic loss calculated by the court is reduced when the claimant receives a capital sum, which she is expected to invest in interest-bearing securities.

Proportionate awards Damages other than damages for bereavement are set at an amount proportionate to the injury each dependant suffers.[276] The actual pecuniary loss resulting to each dependant from the death is ascertained[277] and the question of division is dealt with later.[278] Where an award is made to a widow and her children it has been suggested that the proportion awarded to the children should represent their genuine dependency.[279] The court should not simply award the bulk of the money to the widow on the assumption that she will provide for her children.[280] Among other things, the children need protection against the risk of their mother dying and the money passing into the hands of a step-parent.

Other pecuniary losses Courts have recognised that the death of a parent gives rise to other pecuniary losses over and above any loss of earned income. A series of cases have considered how damages should be assessed where a mother is tortiously killed. It might be that, at the time of her death, she was not working outside her home, or was doing so on a part-time basis only. The widower and children are entitled to compensation based on the reasonable cost to them of replacing the mother's services in the home.[281] The starting point for that assessment where the children are under school age[282] will be the cost of hiring a child-minder/housekeeper.[283] Allowance will be made for the fact

---

[273] *Young v Percival* [1974] 3 All ER 677. See also *Taylor v O'Connor* [1971] AC 115.

[274] *Bishop v Cunard White Star Co Ltd* [1950] P 240, at 250.   [275] Fatal Accidents Act 1976, s 4.

[276] Fatal Accidents Act 1976, sub-s 3(1). For the meaning of this provision see *Jameson v Central Electricity Generating Board* [2000] 1 AC 455.

[277] *Davies v Powell Duffryn Associated Collieries Ltd* [1942] AC 601, at 612. A dependant's damages are not reduced because her mother was contributorily negligent: *Dodds v Dodds* [1978] QB 543.

[278] *Dietz v Lennig Chemicals Ltd* [1969] 1 AC 170, at 183. The court is to direct how the award is to be divided: Fatal Accidents Act 1976, sub-s 3(2).

[279] *Benson v Biggs Wall & Co Ltd* [1982] 3 All ER 300.

[280] *Clay v Pooler* [1982] 3 All ER 570 (the children merely received pocket money).

[281] *Hay v Hughes* [1975] QB 790; *Corbett v Barking, Havering and Brentwood HA* [1991] 2 QB 408.

[282] The court in *Spittle v Bunney* [1988] 3 All ER 1031 assumed a diminishing need for 'motherly services' once a child is settled at school.

[283] Based on the net rather than the gross wage payable: *Spittle v Bunney* [1988] 3 All ER 1031.

that mothers do not work fixed hours and do not limit themselves to cooking, cleaning, and routine tasks. They provide more general care and moral guidance and those wider 'motherly services'[284] should be reflected in the award of damages. Where the father[285] or other relative[286] then gives up work to take over these duties, and in the light of the children's needs that is a reasonable course of action, compensation can be based on his (or their) loss of earnings rather than the cost of a child-minder.

The above assumes the existence of a family where the mother stays at home providing 100% of the child care and the father earns 100% of the family income. That is seldom the case these days. So there must be a reduction made for loss of 'motherly services' where the mother did not provide full-time care.[287] In *Hayden v Hayden*,[288] it was held that if the father undertook most of the mother's responsibilities after her death, there was no loss to the child in this respect. Yet *Hayden v Hayden* must be contrasted with *Stanley v Saddique*,[289] where the child's parents were not married. On the death of the mother, the father undertook full responsibility for his son and soon remarried. The evidence suggested that the stepmother was likely to make a much better parent than the deceased mother. The defendants argued that the benefit conferred by the acquisition of a stepmother more than cancelled out the loss of the original mother's services. But the court held that the Fatal Accidents Act 1976, section 4 prevented any such 'benefit' being taken into account.[290] *Stanley v Saddique* was followed, but with a critical qualification added, in *H v S*.[291] There it was said that the principle enunciated in *Hunt v Severs*[292] should be applied to such cases so that the amount representing the value of the lost gratuitous services should be held on trust for the benefit of the new voluntary carer (in this case, the father, who had not previously provided care for the claimant children).

Bereavement The sum to be awarded as damages for bereavement is £12,980.[293] Where both parents claim this sum, it is divided equally between them.[294]

Funeral expenses If the dependants have incurred funeral expenses in respect of the deceased, damages may be awarded in respect of those expenses.[295]

Section 5 Injunctions

(A) As a remedy per se or in addition to damages

Sometimes a remedy in damages might be inappropriate or insufficient to vindicate the claimant's rights. Where there is a risk that a tort will be repeated, the claimant might want an order to prohibit that repetition: an injunction.

---

[284] *Regan v Williamson* [1976] 2 All ER 241.   [285] *Mehmet v Perry* [1977] 2 All ER 529.
[286] *Cresswell v Eaton* [1991] 1 All ER 484 (aunt gave up job as a traffic warden).
[287] *Cresswell v Eaton* [1991] 1 All ER 484.   [288] [1992] 4 All ER 681.
[289] [1992] QB 1.
[290] On the broad meaning of 'benefit' in this context see also *O'Loughlin v Cape Distribution Ltd* [2001] EWCA Civ 178 (business flair of the deceased a benefit for the purposes of s 4).
[291] [2003] QB 965.   [292] See *Dimond v Lovell* [2002] 1 AC 384.
[293] Fatal Accidents Act 1976, sub-s 1A(3).   [294] Fatal Accidents Act 1976, sub-s 1A(4).
[295] Fatal Accidents Act 1976, sub-s 3(5).

Two kinds There are two broad kinds of injunction: prohibitory and mandatory. A prohibitory injunction may be issued against someone who has committed a trespass or a nuisance, for example, so that she will be restrained from repeating the tort in the future. By contrast, a mandatory injunction requires the defendant to undertake a positive act to put an end to a state of affairs amounting to an actionable interference with some proprietary interest on the part of the claimant, whether or not that interference is causing actual damage.[296] For example, a mandatory injunction may require her to pull down a wall which interferes with the claimant's right to light.

Interim injunctions Where an injunction is granted before the trial of an action pending fuller investigation into the case that will take place at the trial and in order to prevent the commission or continuance of an act alleged to be tortious, it is called an interim injunction.[297] Such an injunction is applied for commonly in respect of alleged economic torts where the claimant contends that the state of affairs resulting from the defendant's act is so serious that the defendant ought not to be allowed to continue it pending the hearing. At one level, the granting of an interim injunction might seem to be a pre-judgment of the case because it is a remedy granted to a claimant who has yet to prove that she has had her legal right infringed by the defendant. This begs the question whether in justice such injunctions should ever be granted.[298] So far as the courts are concerned, the matter is clear: there is no offence caused in considering the respective strength of both parties' cases and, if the claimant has a strong prima facie case, in granting such an order.[299] However, where an interim injunction effectively would ruin the defendant's livelihood, the courts will be slow to grant it without a hearing.[300]

Breach of confidence A further restriction on the availability of interim injunctions operates in relation to breach of confidence and is to be found in the Human Rights Act 1998, sub-section 12(3). This provides that no such injunction should be granted if it is likely to restrict freedom of expression *unless* the court is satisfied that the applicant is likely to establish that the publication in question should not be permitted. Of course, everything turns on what is meant by 'likely'. In *Cream Holdings Ltd v Banerjee*,[301] the House of Lords held that the term is susceptible to more or less restrictive interpretations depending on the circumstances of the case, including the severity of the consequences associated with publication. By itself, this is a fairly unhelpful thing to say. But three observations can be made to help clarify matters. First, the Court of Appeal held in *Greene v Associated Newspapers Ltd*[302] that the common law on defamation has not been changed by sub-section 12(3). Second, and by contrast, it was held in the *Cream Holdings* case that sub-section 12(3) might be especially relevant in cases of breach of confidence; for while one's reputation can be restored for the purposes of defamation

---

[296] See, eg, *Jones v Llanrwst UDC* [1911] 1 Ch 393. [297] See C Gray (1981) 40 CLJ 307.

[298] For the argument that injunctions should be available before any form of measurable harm has occurred, and outside an interference with a proprietary interest, see J Murphy (2007) 27 OJLS 509.

[299] *Browne v Associated Newspapers Ltd* [2008] QB 103, at [42].

[300] *Series 5 Software Ltd v Clarke* [1996] 1 All ER 853. [301] [2005] 1 AC 253.

[302] [2005] 1 All ER 30.

law, confidentiality once breached is lost for good. Third, Lord Nicholls suggested in the *Cream Holdings* case that, in a non-exceptional case, the crucial word, 'likely', should be understood to mean 'more likely than not'.

Search orders Two important forms of interim injunction are the search order and the freezing injunction. A search order is a mandatory injunction (formerly known as an *Anton Piller* order) that requires the defendant to allow the claimant entry to premises to search for property infringing the claimant's rights, or documents relevant to her claim. In actions for breach of intellectual property rights, such orders are crucial to ensure the defendant cannot destroy incriminating documents prior to the trial of the action.

Freezing injunctions By contrast, a freezing injunction prohibits the defendant from moving her assets abroad or from disposing of assets within the jurisdiction.[303] In this way, the claimant ensures that if she obtains judgment against the defendant there will be property in the jurisdiction against which to enforce that judgment. Both search orders and freezing injunctions are draconian measures[304] and claimants will be required not only to justify their claims for such orders but also to give undertakings to return property seized and compensate the defendants should their suit ultimately fail.

Other injunctions A perpetual injunction is a final order issued after the hearing of the action. A *quia timet* injunction may be issued to restrain a tort which has not yet been committed but commission of which is threatened, so long as substantial damage appears imminent.[305]

Jurisdiction The jurisdiction of the High Court[306] to grant injunctions is often said to be discretionary; but this is not strictly a fair description.[307] An interim injunction may be granted even though the claimant has not made out a prima facie case provided there is a 'serious question' to address and the court decides on the balance of convenience that such an order is warranted.[308] The courts exercise sparingly their 'discretion' to grant mandatory injunctions and will refuse unless very serious damage otherwise would occur.[309] A prohibitory injunction will be granted to a claimant on proof that her proprietary rights are wrongfully being interfered with unless special circumstances exist.[310]

---

[303] *Mareva Cia Naviera SA v International Bulkcarriers SA* [1975] 2 Lloyd's Rep 509.

[304] See *Columbia Pictures Industries Inc v Robinson* [1987] Ch 38.

[305] *Lemos v Kennedy Leigh Development Co Ltd* (1961) 105 Sol Jo 178.

[306] Supreme Court Act 1981, sub-s 37(1).

[307] See S Waddams, *Dimensions of Private Law—Categories and Concepts in Anglo-American Legal Reasoning* (2003), 180.

[308] *American Cyanamid Co v Ethicon Ltd* [1975] AC 396. See also *Garden Cottage Foods Ltd v Milk Marketing Board* [1982] QB 1114. Public policy considerations also figure: *Dep't of Social Security v Butler* [1995] 1 WLR 1528.

[309] *Redland Bricks Ltd v Morris* [1970] AC 652 lays down the rules governing the exercise of this 'discretion'.

[310] *Pride of Derby and Derbyshire Angling Association Ltd v British Celanese Ltd* [1953] Ch 149.

Public interest Sometimes the public interest in not restraining the activity in question will be a relevant consideration.[311] But even so, the courts will be reluctant to leave the victim of a serious interference with a mere remedy in damages.[312] The most the courts seem willing to do (almost as a matter of course) in order to mitigate the consequences of their granting injunctions is suspend the coming into force of the injunction for a short period[313] or impose time restrictions on it.[314]

(B) Injunctions where an action in tort does not lie

Occasionally the courts have granted injunctions to protect title to property, even where no tort is established.[315] But this is an exceptional use. The normal rule is that a final injunction will not be granted unless the relevant elements of an extant tort have been shown to be present. The rationale underpinning this general approach is that it is wrong to restrain another from engaging in some form of lawful conduct in this way and that it is wrong similarly to compel another to act in a particular way when that other has not transgressed any law. But as regards the title to property exception *Gee v Pritchard*[316] is instructive. The claimant obtained an injunction to prevent the defendant from disclosing confidential and private material contained in letters (which had been returned to the claimant, but of which the defendant had kept copies) written by the claimant to the defendant. According to the court, an injunction would serve to protect the claimant's right of property in the letters.

Conclusions

This chapter began with consideration of certain limits on recovery of damages in tort cases. It considered rules on limitation of actions, which prevent the bringing of actions beyond relevant time limits unless a court extends the time available in which to bring those actions, as well as rules on mitigation of damages which prevent awards that the claimant reasonably could have avoided. The chapter then went on to consider the general rules governing the award of damages, especially as they arise in cases of personal injury and death. The damages available to living claimants for personal injuries can be subdivided into two broad classes. The first involves damages for pecuniary losses (such as loss of earnings and costs of medical and nursing care). The second involves damages

---

[311] See, eg, *Miller v Jackson* [1977] QB 966, at 981 and 988; *Dennis v Ministry of Defence* [2003] EWHC 793.

[312] *Shelfer v City of London Electric Lighting Co* [1895] 1 Ch 287. See also *Kennaway v Thompson* [1981] QB 88.

[313] In *Woollerton & Wilson Ltd v Richard Costain Ltd* [1970] 1 All ER 483, Ds (building contractors) operated a crane in Cs' air space. The court suspended the injunction until Ds completed the building because Cs had refused reasonable compensation and the air space had become valuable only because of Ds' activities. Cf *John Trenberth Ltd v National Westminster Bank Ltd* (1979) 253 EG 151 (holding *Woollerton* to be wrongly decided).

[314] Eg, *Dunton v Dover DC* (1977) 76 LGR 87.

[315] See *Loudon v Ryder (No 2)* [1953] Ch 423; *Springhead Spinning Co v Riley* (1868) LR 6 Eq 551. The possibility of an injunction, even though no tort has been committed, is doubly important when it is noted that the Supreme Court Act 1981, s 50 enables the court to grant damages in addition to, or in substitution for, an injunction. See *Marcic v Thames Water Utilities Ltd (No 2)* [2002] QB 1003. [316] (1818) 2 Swan 402.

for non-pecuniary losses (such as pain and suffering). Damages that are awarded after the tort victim has died also fall into two broad classes. The first consists of 'survival actions', which are grounded in the Law Reform (Miscellaneous Provisions) Act 1934. With very few exceptions, the statute allows the victim's estate to pursue a tort claim that vested in the victim prior to her death. The second kind of claim is one that treats the victim's death as the basis of the claim. In such cases, the deceased's dependants bring the action (for loss of support) under the Fatal Accidents Act 1976. The chapter concluded by observing the existence of another type of remedy in the injunction. Various types of injunction can be sought depending on whether harm is ongoing or merely threatened, and on whether the defendant has to take positive steps to do something she is under a duty to do. In cases where some harm has been occasioned already and more is threatened, an injunction might be sought alongside damages.

Problem question

Go through as many of the prior problem questions in this book as you wish and advise further on what sorts of remedies would be awarded by the court in resolution of those problems.

Further reading

BEEVER, 'The Structure of Aggravated and Exemplary Damages' (2003) 23 *Oxford Journal of Legal Studies* 87

CANE, *Atiyah's Accidents Compensation and the Law* (8th edn, 2013)

GILEAD, GREEN, AND KOCH (eds), *Proportional Liability: Analytical and Comparative Perspectives* (2013)

HANDFORD, 'Lord Campbell and the Fatal Accidents Act' (2013) 129 *Law Quarterly Review* 420

HARDER, *Measuring Damages in the Law of Obligations: The Search for Harmonised Principles* (2010)

LAW COMMISSION, *Limitation of Actions* (2001)

LEWIS, *Deducting Benefits from Damages for Personal Injury* (2000)

LEWIS, 'Appearance and Reality in Reforming Periodical Payments of Tort Damages in the UK' in Neyers et al (eds), *Emerging Issues in Tort Law* (2007), ch 19

MURPHY, 'Rethinking Injunctions in Tort Law' (2007) 27 *Oxford Journal of Legal Studies* 509

MURPHY, 'The Nature and Domain of Aggravated Damages' (2010) 69 *Cambridge Law Journal* 353

ROGERS (ed), *Damages for Non-Pecuniary Loss in a Comparative Perspective* (2001)

Appendix 1
Additional Chapter

An additional chapter to accompany this text can be found at the following location: http://www.oup.com/uk/street15e/

Liability in tort for damage caused by animals can be placed into five distinct categories, each to be considered in the online chapter.

The first category consists of common law liability. Over the years, the courts have held that a range of familiar torts—including negligence, battery, nuisance, and public nuisance—can all be committed through the instrumentality of animals. For these purposes, it does not matter whether the animal is of a kind that is commonly tamed or domesticated.

The second, third, fourth, and fifth categories of liability for animals to be considered all derive from the Animals Act 1971 and relate, in turn, to liability for dangerous animals, liability for non-dangerous species, liability for straying livestock, and liability for loss of livestock caused by dogs.

In the second category, the 1971 Act creates a somewhat complex rule of strict liability for damage caused by dangerous animals. The Act provides its own definition of what constitutes a dangerous species. This definition turns upon the pivotal issues of whether it is a species that is not commonly domesticated in the British Isles and whether a full-grown animal of that species has either a propensity to cause harm or a propensity to cause severe harm in the event (which need not be independently likely) that it does cause harm.

In the third category, the 1971 Act also provides a complex liability rule in relation to animals that do not belong to a dangerous species. Critical to such liability is knowledge on the part of the animal's keeper (which term is defined by the Act) of the unusual characteristics in the particular animal or those that are not normally found in animals of the same species except at particular times or in particular circumstances.

In the fourth category, the 1971 Act instantiates rules applicable to straying 'livestock'. The term livestock receives specific definition under the Act.

In the final category, the Act sets specific limits on the circumstances in which liability will be incurred for injury to livestock caused by dogs.

Index

Page references preceded by 'W' relate to the additional chapter 'Animals', which can be found in the online resources.